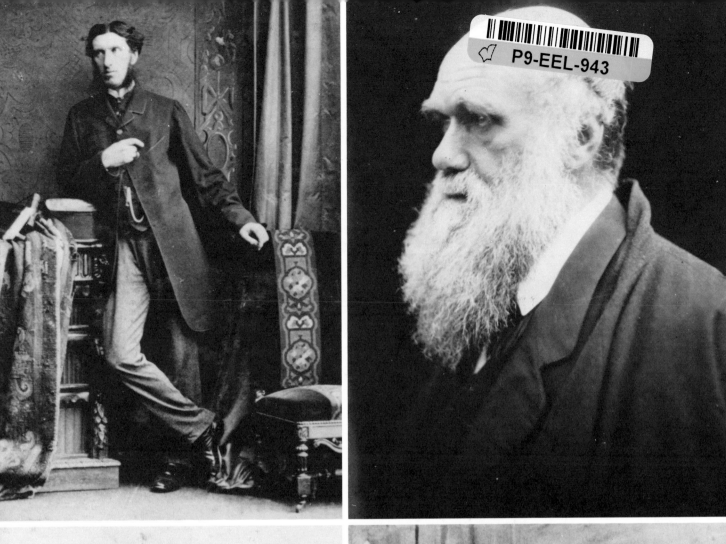

6870

Victorian Prose Writers After 1867

Dictionary of Literary Biography

Victorian Prose Writers After 1867

6870

Edited by
William B. Thesing
University of South Carolina

A Bruccoli Clark Layman Book
Gale Research Company • Book Tower • Detroit, Michigan 48226

Manufactured by Edwards Brothers, Inc.
Ann Arbor, Michigan
Printed in the United States of America

Library of Congress Cataloging-in-Publication Data

Victorian prose writers after 1867.

(Dictionary of literary biography; v. 57)
"A Bruccoli Clark Layman book."
Includes index.
1. English prose literature—19th century—History and criticism. 2. English prose literature—19th century—Bio-bibliography. 3. Authors, English—19th century—Biography—Dictionaries. I. Thesing, William B. II. Series.
PR781.V52 1987 828'.808'09 87-336
ISBN 0-8103-1735-4

For Patrick Brantlinger and Donald Gray

and for students and teachers of Victorian studies

Contents

Contents

Plan of the Series

. . . Almost the most prodigious asset of a country, and perhaps its most precious possession, is its native literary product—when that product is fine and noble and enduring.

Mark Twain*

The advisory board, the editors, and the publisher of the *Dictionary of Literary Biography* are joined in endorsing Mark Twain's declaration. The literature of a nation provides an inexhaustible resource of permanent worth. It is our expectation that this endeavor will make literature and its creators better understood and more accessible to students and the literate public, while satisfying the standards of teachers and scholars.

To meet these requirements, *literary biography* has been construed in terms of the author's achievement. The most important thing about a writer is his writing. Accordingly, the entries in *DLB* are career biographies, tracing the development of the author's canon and the evolution of his reputation.

The publication plan for *DLB* resulted from two years of preparation. The project was proposed to Bruccoli Clark by Frederick G. Ruffner, president of the Gale Research Company, in November 1975. After specimen entries were prepared and typeset, an advisory board was formed to refine the entry format and develop the series rationale. In meetings held during 1976, the publisher, series editors, and advisory board approved the scheme for a comprehensive biographical dictionary of persons who contributed to North American literature. Editorial work on the first volume began in January 1977, and it was published in 1978.

In order to make *DLB* more than a reference tool and to compile volumes that individually have claim to status as literary history, it was decided to organize volumes by topic or period or genre. Each of these freestanding volumes provides a biographical-bibliographical guide and overview for a particular area of literature. We are convinced that this organization—as opposed to a single alphabet method—constitutes a valuable innovation in the presentation of reference material. The volume plan necessarily requires many decisions for the placement and treatment of authors who might properly be included in two or three volumes. In some instances a major figure will be included in separate volumes, but with different entries emphasizing the aspect of his career appropriate to each volume. Ernest Hemingway, for example, is represented in *American Writers in Paris, 1920-1939* by an entry focusing on his expatriate apprenticeship; he is also in *American Novelists, 1910-1945* with an entry surveying his entire career. Each volume includes a cumulative index of subject authors and articles. The final *DLB* volume will be a comprehensive index to the entire series.

With volume ten in 1982 it was decided to enlarge the scope of *DLB*. By the end of 1986 twenty-one volumes treating British literature had been published, and volumes for Commonwealth and Modern European literature were in progress. The series has been further augmented by the *DLB Yearbooks* (since 1981) which update published entries and add new entries to keep the *DLB* current with contemporary activity. There have also been occasional *DLB Documentary Series* volumes which provide biographical and critical background source materials for figures whose work is judged to have particular interest for students. One of these companion volumes is entirely devoted to Tennessee Williams.

The purpose of *DLB* is not only to provide reliable information in a convenient format but also to place the figures in the larger perspective of literary history and to offer appraisals of their accomplishments by qualified scholars.

We define literature as the *intellectual commerce of a nation:* not merely as belles lettres but as that ample and complex process by which ideas are generated, shaped, and transmitted. *DLB* entries are not limited to "creative writers" but extend to other figures who in this time and in this way influenced the mind of a people. Thus the series encompasses historians, journalists, publishers, and screenwriters. By this means readers of *DLB* may be aided to perceive literature not as cult scripture in the keeping of cultural high priests but as at the center of a nation's life.

DLB includes the major writers appropriate to each volume and those standing in the ranks immediately behind them. Scholarly and critical counsel has been sought in deciding which minor figures to include and how full their entries should be. Wherever possible, useful references are made to figures who do not warrant separate entries.

Each *DLB* volume has a volume editor responsible for planning the volume, selecting the figures for inclusion, and assigning the entries. Volume editors are also responsible for preparing, where appropriate, appendices surveying the major periodicals and literary and intellectual movements for their volumes, as well as lists of further readings. Work on the series as a whole is coordinated at the Bruccoli Clark Layman editorial center in Columbia, South Carolina, where the editorial staff is responsible for the accuracy of the published volumes.

One feature that distinguishes *DLB* is the illustration policy—its concern with the iconography of literature. Just as an author is influenced by his surroundings, so is the reader's understanding of the author enhanced by a knowledge of his environment. Therefore *DLB* volumes include not only drawings, paintings, and photographs of authors, often depicting them at various stages in their careers, but also illustrations of their families and places where they lived. Title pages are regularly reproduced in facsimile along with dust jackets for modern authors. The dust jackets are a special feature of *DLB* because they often document better than anything else the way in which an author's

work was launched in its own time. Specimens of the writers' manuscripts are included when feasible.

A supplement to *DLB*—tentatively titled *A Guide, Chronology, and Glossary for American Literature*—will outline the history of literature in North America and trace the influences that shaped it. This volume will provide a framework for the study of American literature by means of chronological tables, literary affiliation charts, glossarial entries, and concise surveys of the major movements. It has been planned to stand on its own as a vade mecum, providing a ready-reference guide to the study of American literature as well as a companion to the *DLB* volumes for American literature.

Samuel Johnson rightly decreed that "The chief glory of every people arises from its authors." The purpose of the *Dictionary of Literary Biography* is to compile literary history in the surest way available to us—by accurate and comprehensive treatment of the lives and work of those who contributed to it.

The *DLB* Advisory Board

*From an unpublished section of Mark Twain's autobiography, copyright © by the Mark Twain Company.

Foreword

DLB 57: Victorian Prose Writers After 1867 is the sequel to *DLB 55: Victorian Prose Writers Before 1867* and a complement to *DLB* volumes 18, 21, 32, and 35 on Victorian novelists and poets. In the present work the emphasis is on writings of nonfiction prose, a genre broadly defined to include letters, journals, diaries, sermons, speeches, reviews, biographies, autobiographies, and travel writings, as well as historical, philosophical, political, critical, and scientific books and essays. The writers treated in this volume worked within the historical context bounded by the years from 1867 to 1901. By 1901 many royal subjects had begun to view themselves as the "late Victorians" and to feel that a new era was dawning with the new century. Many of the figures covered in this volume outlived the Queen, who died in 1901. With only a few exceptions, however, they had published most of their important works before her successor, Edward VII, ascended the throne.

As Richard D. Altick puts it in *Victorian People and Ideas* (1973): "From the seventies onward, . . . a strong tide set in against the confident orthodoxies of the mid-Victorian period. Economic and social individualism was retreating before a mild, tentative, but, in comparison with what had gone before, revolutionary expansion of the powers of the state; the moral aesthetic was turned inside out by art for art's sake; the evasiveness of conventional fiction was challenged by realists like Hardy, Moore, and Gissing; Tennyson, though still the age's most popular poet, suffered a marked decline in critical esteem. Oscar Wilde discovered that the easiest way to celebrity was to posture and speak *pour épater le bourgeoisie*. . . . Thus the panoply of dogma and dicta which had nourished the conventional Victorian mind had come under attack long before the Queen died."

Between 1867 and 1901 cherished notions of British individualism indeed met new challenges from the growing dominance of government. In 1870 Forster's Education Act was passed, and in 1880 elementary education became compulsory. According to Altick in *The English Common Reader: A Social History of the Mass Reading Public, 1800-1900* (1957), the 1870 legislation marked the climax of agitation for a national school system: "The Forster Act is usually spoken of as a great landmark in the history of the reading public, because, by establishing governmental responsibility for education wherever voluntary effort was insufficient, it made schooling easier to obtain (and less easy to avoid) than ever before in England's history." In remote rural areas and in newly industrialized urban centers, state-sponsored education was much needed. To a prose writer such as Matthew Arnold, however, who spent thirty-five years working as a school inspector, some of these new developments were mixed blessings. Nevertheless, Arnold believed that the State could assist in improving the quality of humanistic education in England. Other writers voiced differing concerns: T. H. Huxley called for expanded study of science in the schools, and William Morris emphasized the need to cultivate authentic arts and crafts.

There were also heated, and sometimes violent, debates concerning the issue of worldwide "expansion of the powers of the state" (to use Altick's words again) during the last three decades of the nineteenth century. In 1876 Victoria was proclaimed Empress of India; in 1887 enthusiastic imperialist sentiment was clearly in the air during the celebrations of the Queen's Golden Jubilee. And yet throughout this entire period violence erupted frequently as sympathizers for the cause of Irish nationalism pressed their demands. Socialist demonstrations and dock strikes occupied the attention of Londoners in 1887 and in 1889. The very foundations of the British Empire seemed in danger of giving way as the Boer War dragged on in South Africa from 1899 to 1902. William Ewart Gladstone and other politicians introduced home rule bills to help settle the Irish controversy; among social critics, E. B. Tylor advocated new ways of viewing third-world cultures; and William Morris, anticipating later writings by J. A. Hobson, argued that industrial capitalism was shaping public opinion and leading England down the self-destructive path of militarization and imperialism. Despite these political controversies, travel writing continued to flourish in the later years of the Victorian period as Charles M. Doughty described life in Arabia, Anthony Trollope chronicled visits to North America, Australia, and elsewhere, and Robert Louis Stevenson reported on adventures in the South Seas.

But writers such as Stevenson also expressed concerns regarding the challenges to cultural stability and orthodox religious belief that were posed by Charles Darwin and other Victorian scientists. Stevenson feared that Victorian science was thrusting the human intellect into "zones of speculation, where there is not habitable city for the mind of man." Many writers shared Stevenson's apprehension over Darwin's new scientific theories, especially when the implications for humankind were elaborated in detail in Darwin's *The Descent of Man* (1871). Reactions to Darwin's ideas were legion, ranging from the intensely bitter retorts of Samuel Butler to the poignant and personal account of the conflict between science and religion recorded in Edmund Gosse's *Father and Son* (1907).

Of the thirty figures covered in *Victorian Prose Writers After 1867*, five are of major importance and receive extended treatment: Matthew Arnold, Charles Darwin, William Morris, Walter Pater, and Oscar Wilde. Both the quality of their prose and the nature and extent of their influence on their contemporaries and on posterity have been considered in selecting them as the subjects of master entries.

To explore the critical ideas about prose current in the nineteenth century and to provide some sampling of Victorian prose writing, Patrick Scott has compiled an appendix entitled "Victorians on Rhetoric and Prose Style." He has brought together for the first time material from several different strands of Victorian criticism. From the early- and mid-Victorian years, the appendix includes Romantic-influenced, or "vitalist," discussions of prose by Thomas Carlyle and George Henry Lewes, some rather conservative stylistic evaluation by contemporary periodical critics, such as Cockburn Thomson and William Forsyth, and the more theoretical analyses of such rhetoricians as Richard Whately and Alexander Bain. Herbert Spencer's "The Philosophy of Style" (1854), republished in its entirety, raises issues that are still central to modern debates over the readability and evaluation of prose. From the late-Victorian period, the appendix includes, along with essays by such well-known commentators as Walter Pater and Oscar Wilde, Robert Louis Stevenson's technical analysis of prose

rhythm, John Addington Symonds's suggestive comments on the psychology of prose style, and Frederic Harrison's practical advice to aspirant prose writers. Among the topics debated are the changing audience and new publishing opportunities for prose writers and the differences that political commitment, gender, or national culture may make in one's prose style. While the selections do show a general trend toward increasing emphasis on the formal and aesthetic qualities of prose writing, what is perhaps most notable is how widespread, and how acute, was Victorian discussion of formal questions and of the relationship between form and content, well before the beginning of the aesthetic movement. Much of the material included here, especially the pieces by Whately and Bain on Victorian rhetorical theory, is not widely known to students; very little of it is available in the standard literary anthologies; and many of the periodical items are difficult to obtain outside of specialist collections or major research libraries. This appendix provides a fresh and expanded context for interpreting the Victorian art of prose.

Also included at the end of this volume is a selected bibliography that focuses on the most important studies of the social, cultural, historical, intellectual, rhetorical, artistic, and literary dimensions of Victorian nonfiction prose.

The contributors of the essays to this volume deserve special gratitude for their efficient and conscientious efforts. Geographically, they are located in diverse places, from California to New York, in Canada, and in England. Many of the contributors made valuable suggestions for illustrating their essays. Jerold J. Savory was especially helpful with the photographic reproduction of several *Vanity Fair* prints. Roger Mortimer, curator of Rare Books and Manuscripts at the Thomas Cooper Library, University of South Carolina, and William Cagle, director of the Lilly Library, Indiana University, were most helpful in locating items of interest in their respective collections. Jane and Amy Thesing also deserve special appreciation for enduring the eccentricities of an editor at work during the many long months of this project.

—William B. Thesing

Acknowledgments

This book was produced by Bruccoli Clark Layman, Inc. Karen L. Rood is senior editor for the *Dictionary of Literary Biography* series. Margaret A. Van Antwerp was the in-house editor.

Art supervisor is Pamela Haynes. Copyediting supervisor is Patricia Coate. Production coordinator is Kimberly Casey. Typesetting supervisor is Laura Ingram. Lucia Tarbox is editorial assistant. The production staff includes Rowena Betts, David R. Bowdler, Mary S. Dye, Charles Egleston, Kathleen M. Flanagan, Joyce Fowler, Karen Fritz, Judith K. Ingle, Judith E. McCray, Janet Phelps, Joan Price, and Joycelyn R. Smith. Jean W. Ross is permissions editor. Joseph Caldwell, photography editor, and Joseph Matthew Bruccoli did photographic copy work for the volume.

Walter W. Ross and Rhonda Marshall did the library research with the assistance of the staff at the Thomas Cooper Library of the University of South Carolina: Lynn Barron, Daniel Boice, Connie Crider, Kathy Eckman, Michael Freeman, Gary Geer, David L. Haggard, Jens Holley, Marcia Martin, Dana Rabon, Jean Rhyne, Jan Squire, Ellen Tillett, and Virginia Weathers.

Victorian Prose Writers
After 1867

Dictionary of Literary Biography

Matthew Arnold

Suzanne O. Edwards
The Citadel

See also the Arnold entry in *DLB 32, Victorian Poets Before 1850.*

BIRTH: Laleham-on-Thames, England, 24 December 1822, to Thomas and Mary Penrose Arnold.

EDUCATION: Second class degree, Oxford University, 1844.

MARRIAGE: 10 June 1851 to Frances Lucy Wightman; children: Thomas, William Trevenen, Richard Penrose, Lucy Charlotte, Eleanor Mary, Basil Francis.

DEATH: Liverpool, England, 15 April 1888.

BOOKS: *Alaric at Rome: A Prize Poem* (Rugby: Combe & Crossley, 1840);
Cromwell: A Prize Poem (Oxford: Vincent, 1843);
The Strayed Reveller and Other Poems, as A. (London: Fellowes, 1849);
Empedocles on Etna and Other Poems, as A. (London: Fellowes, 1852); republished as *Empedocles on Etna: A Dramatic Poem* (Portland, Maine: Mosher, 1900);
Poems: A New Edition (London: Longman, Brown, Green & Longmans, 1853);
Poems: Second Series (London: Longman, Brown, Green & Longmans, 1855);
Merope: A Tragedy (London: Longman, Brown, Green, Longman & Roberts, 1858);
England and the Italian Question (London: Longman, Green, Longman & Roberts, 1859); edited by Merle M. Bevington (Durham, N.C.: Duke University Press, 1953);
The Popular Education of France, with Notices of That of Holland and Switzerland (London:

Matthew Arnold, photographed by Camille Silvy in 1861 (National Portrait Gallery)

Longman, Green, Longman & Roberts, 1861);
On Translating Homer: Three Lectures Given at Oxford (London: Longman, Green, Longman & Roberts, 1861);

On Translating Homer: Last Words: A Lecture Given at Oxford (London: Longman, Green, Longman & Roberts, 1862);

Heinrich Heine (Philadelphia: Leypoldt/New York: Christern, 1863);

A French Eton; or, Middle Class Education and the State (London & Cambridge: Macmillan, 1864);

Essays in Criticism (London & Cambridge: Macmillan, 1865; Boston: Ticknor & Fields, 1865);

On the Study of Celtic Literature (London: Smith, Elder, 1867); with *On Translating Homer* (New York: Macmillan, 1883);

New Poems (London: Macmillan, 1867; Boston: Ticknor & Fields, 1867);

Schools and Universities on the Continent (London: Macmillan, 1868); republished in part as *Higher Schools and Universities in Germany* (London: Macmillan, 1874);

Culture and Anarchy: An Essay in Political and Social Criticism (London: Smith, Elder, 1869); with *Friendship's Garland* (New York: Macmillan, 1883);

St. Paul and Protestantism; with an Introduction on Puritanism and the Church of England (London: Smith, Elder, 1870; New York: Macmillan, 1883);

Friendship's Garland: Being the Conversations, Letters and Opinions of the Late Arminius, Baron von Thunder-ten-Tronckh; Collected and Edited with a Dedicatory Letter to Adolescens Leo, Esq., of "The Daily Telegraph" (London: Smith, Elder, 1871); with *Culture and Anarchy* (New York: Macmillan, 1883);

Literature and Dogma: An Essay towards a Better Apprehension of the Bible (London: Smith, Elder, 1873; New York: Macmillan, 1873);

God and the Bible: A Review of Objections to "Literature and Dogma" (London: Smith, Elder, 1875; Boston: Osgood, 1876);

Last Essays on Church and Religion (London: Smith, Elder, 1877; New York: Macmillan, 1877);

Mixed Essays (London: Smith, Elder, 1879; New York: Macmillan, 1879);

Irish Essays, and Others (London: Smith, Elder, 1882);

Discourses in America (New York & London: Macmillan, 1885);

Education Department: Special Report on Certain Points Connected with Elementary Education in Germany, Switzerland, and France (London: Eyre & Spottiswoode, 1886);

General Grant: An Estimate (Boston: Cupples, Up-ham, 1887); republished as *General Grant. With a Rejoinder by Mark Twain*, edited by J. Y. Simon (Carbondale: Southern Illinois University Press, 1966);

Essays in Criticism: Second Series (London & New York: Macmillan, 1888);

Civilization in the United States: First and Last Impressions of America (Boston: Cupples & Hurd, 1888);

Reports on Elementary Schools 1852-1882, edited by Sir Francis Sandford (London & New York: Macmillan, 1889);

On Home Rule for Ireland: Two Letters to "The Times" (London: Privately printed, 1891);

Matthew Arnold's Notebooks (London: Smith, Elder, 1902); republished as *The Note-Books of Matthew Arnold*, edited by Howard Foster Lowry, Karl Young, and Waldo Hilary Dunn (London & New York: Oxford University Press, 1952);

Arnold as Dramatic Critic, edited by C. K. Shorter (London: Privately printed, 1903); republished as *Letters of an Old Playgoer*, edited by Brander Matthews (New York: Columbia University Press, 1919);

Essays in Criticism: Third Series, edited by Edward J. O'Brien (Boston: Ball, 1910);

Thoughts on Education Chosen From the Writings of Matthew Arnold, edited by L. Huxley (London: Smith, Elder, 1912; New York: Macmillan, 1912);

Five Uncollected Essays of Matthew Arnold, edited by Kenneth Allott (Liverpool: University Press of Liverpool, 1953);

Essays, Letters, and Reviews by Matthew Arnold, edited by Fraser Neiman (Cambridge, Mass.: Harvard University Press, 1960.

Collections: *The Works of Matthew Arnold*, edited by G. W. E. Russell, 15 volumes (London: Macmillan, 1903-1904);

The Poetical Works of Matthew Arnold, edited by C. B. Tinker and H. F. Lowry (London & New York: Oxford University Press, 1950);

Complete Prose Works, edited by R. H. Super, 11 volumes (Ann Arbor: University of Michigan Press, 1960-1977);

The Poems of Matthew Arnold, edited by Kenneth Allott (London: Longmans, 1965);

Culture and the State, edited by P. Nash (New York: Teachers College Press, 1965).

OTHER: *A Bible-Reading for Schools: The Great Prophecy of Israel's Restoration (Isaiah, Chapters 40-66) Arranged and Edited for Young Learners,* edited by Arnold (London: Macmillan, 1872); revised and enlarged as *Isaiah XL-LXVI; with the Shorter Prophecies Allied to It, Arranged and Edited with Notes* (London: Macmillan, 1875);

The Six Chief Lives from Johnson's "Lives of the Poets," with Macaulay's "Life of Johnson," edited by Arnold (London: Macmillan, 1878);

The Hundred Greatest Men: Portraits of the One Hundred Greatest Men of History, introduction by Arnold (London: Low, Marston, Searle & Rivington, 1879);

Poems of Wordsworth, edited by Arnold (London: Macmillan, 1879);

Letters, Speeches and Tracts on Irish Affairs by Edmund Burke, edited by Arnold (London: Macmillan, 1881);

Poetry of Byron, edited by Arnold (London: Macmillan, 1881);

Isaiah of Jerusalem in the Authorised English Version, with an Introduction, Corrections and Notes, edited by Arnold (London: Macmillan, 1883);

"Charles Augustin Sainte-Beuve," in *Encyclopaedia Britannica*, ninth edition (London: Black, 1886), IX: 162-165;

"Schools," in *The Reign of Queen Victoria*, edited by T. H. Ward (London: Smith, Elder, 1887), II: 238-279.

A master of both poetry and prose, Matthew Arnold remains significant today for the same reasons that the Victorian Age as a whole retains significance. The Victorians—Arnold chief among them—struggled with issues that confront us well over a century later: social injustice, unequal educational opportunity, religious doubt, the uncertain role of the arts in the modern world, the restlessness and confusion of modern man. But Arnold's opinions on these issues differed from those of many of his countrymen. Surrounded by champions of British superiority, Arnold nonetheless refused to be satisfied with the accomplishments of nineteenth-century Englishmen. According to biographer Park Honan, when Arnold was only six months old, he seemed to his impatient father "backward and rather bad-tempered" because he would not lie still in his crib. For the rest of his life, Arnold's critics complained about his refusal to lie still—his unwillingness to be content with the signal achievements of the British.

Arnold's comments on society, religion, and aesthetics remain pertinent primarily because of the critical approach he advocated—an open-minded, receptive, intelligent appraisal of the issues—more so than because of specific conclusions he drew or suggestions he proposed. It is this critical method far more than his views on individual controversies that makes Arnold's work enduring. In his essay "Spinoza and the Bible" (collected in *Essays in Criticism*, 1865), Arnold accounts for the genius of men such as Spinoza, Hegel, and Plato and at the same time offers a fitting description of his own genius: "What a remarkable philosopher really does for human thought, is to throw into circulation a certain number of new and striking ideas and expressions, and to stimulate with them the thought and imagination of his century or of after-times." Arnold's own notions of "culture" and "the critical spirit"; of "sweetness and light"; of society divided into "Barbarians, Philistines, and Populace"; of the Christian God as a presence that can be known only as "The Eternal, not ourselves, that makes for righteousness" profoundly influenced his own times and continue to influence ours.

Matthew Arnold, the eldest son of Thomas and Mary Penrose Arnold, was born Christmas Eve 1822 at Laleham-on-Thames in Middlesex. Less than twenty miles west of London, Laleham was a pleasant pastoral spot. There, where his father kept a small school, Arnold spent the first six years of his life. In 1828 Thomas Arnold was appointed headmaster of Rugby School, and the Arnolds moved to the midlands to establish a new home in Warwickshire. Immediately the new headmaster began instituting revolutionary changes. A strict man, Dr. Arnold demanded adherence to a rigid code of morality, establishing for himself the goal of forming Christian gentlemen. His reforms spread into other areas of Rugby life as well. He broadened the traditional classical curriculum to include a more serious study of mathematics and modern languages. Concerned about the low morale of overburdened, underpaid teachers—a concern his son would later share—Thomas Arnold increased teachers' salaries, making it possible for them to relinquish their curacies and to become more committed to the school and to their pupils. And he set himself as a model for the masters as well as for the boys. He not only earned a reputation as a brilliant teacher of history and religion, but he also involved himself in the lives of his students—swimming with them, playing games

Fox How, Ambleside, the Arnold family retreat in the Lake District

with them, welcoming them into his home. Dr. Arnold's stellar pupil, and one of the most frequent visitors to the Arnold home, was Arthur Hugh Clough, who was later to become a poet and Matthew Arnold's closest friend.

Young Arnold himself proved to be a rather poor pupil, however. In 1830 he was sent back to school in Laleham. Eager to be allowed to return home, Arnold applied himself to his studies and showed sufficient improvement to be permitted to come back two years later to instruction under private tutors at his parents' home. In 1836 Matthew and his brother Tom enrolled at Winchester, but Matthew spent only one year there and entered Rugby in 1837. Still a less than devoted scholar, Matthew nevertheless received literary recognition as early as 1840 by winning the Rugby Poetry prize for *Alaric at Rome*. Otherwise, as Park Honan points out, the young Arnold "lived in the grandest juvenile defi-

ance of the fact that he was an Arnold." This defiance manifested itself in his appearance and in his behavior. At age fourteen, he bought and wore a monocle. On one occasion, having been reprimanded by his father for misbehavior in class, he amused his peers by making faces behind Dr. Arnold's back.

The hours Arnold spent in the classroom were offset by many pleasant holidays in the Lake District. In 1831 Dr. Arnold took his family to the north of England and on to Scotland for a vacation. While touring the Lake District, the Arnolds became acquainted with Wordsworth and Southey. They returned to the lakes for Christmas and again the following summer. The Arnolds became so fond of the spot and of the Wordsworths that they built a holiday house at Fox How in Ambleside, only a short walk from the Wordsworths' home at Rydal Mount. They stayed there for the first time in the summer of

1834. Thereafter, Fox How was a favorite family retreat, becoming home to Mrs. Arnold after the death of her husband; and years later, Matthew Arnold brought his own children there. Much of the imagery in his landscape poetry was inspired by the spot.

Arnold's poetic landscapes also are indebted to the region around Oxford where, to everyone's surprise, including his own, Arnold won one of two classical Open Balliol Scholarships in 1840. Even at Oxford his carefree attitude persisted. Fishing occupied many of the hours he was supposed to be devoting to his books. He swam nude by the riverbank, enjoyed drinking, lapsed in his regular attendance at chapel, and adopted the airs of the dandy—donning extravagant waistcoats and assuming an affected manner. He delighted in lighthearted pranks. On one occasion, reports Trilling, a friend named Hawker with whom he was traveling claimed that Arnold "pleasantly induced a belief into the passengers of the coach that I was a poor mad gentleman, and that he was my keeper."

The years at Oxford were marked by sober events as well. Arnold's father died suddenly of a heart attack on 12 June 1842, at the age of forty-seven. In the years that followed Arnold came to see himself as perpetuating many of his father's views on education, social welfare, and religion. In "Rugby Chapel," written over twenty years after the death of Thomas Arnold, Arnold shows his high regard for his father, remembering him as a son of God, as one of the "helpers and friends of mankind," as a leader worth following:

> . . . at your voice,
> Panic, despair, flee away.
> Ye move through the ranks, recall
> The stragglers, refresh the outworn,
> Praise, re-inspire the brave!
> Order, courage, return.

Arnold came to see his own mission as one of re-inspiring mankind, and he considered it an inherited mission. He wrote to his mother in 1869, "I think of the main part of what I have done, and am doing, as work which he [Thomas Arnold] would have approved and seen to be indispensable.

In the years immediately following his father's death, Arnold grew closer to Arthur Clough who felt the loss of Dr. Arnold almost as intensely as Matthew himself. Clough and Arnold shared much more than their grief, however.

Both were promising, but ultimately disappointing, students at Oxford; both felt strongly attached to Oxford, especially to the countryside surrounding the university; both were restless, unsettled young men. Most significantly, both were poets. They criticized one another's work and discussed their developing theories of art.

Despite the sobering effect of his father's death, Arnold continued to shirk his schoolwork. Unprepared for final examinations, he earned only second-class honors in 1844. Yet in 1845 he won a fellowship at Oriel College, Oxford, and spent the next two years reading widely in classical and German philosophy and literature and traveling in Europe as often as he could. At the age of twenty-four, he gave up his residency at Oxford. He took a temporary post as assistant master at Rugby for one term before accepting a position in London as private secretary to Lord Lansdowne, the lord president of the Privy Council.

While holding this position, Arnold wrote some of his finest poems and published them, signed with the initial *A.*, in two separate volumes: *The Strayed Reveller and Other Poems* (1849) and *Empedocles on Etna and Other Poems* (1852). The poems express in verse many of the ideas and opinions that Arnold expressed in his letters to Clough. These letters, collected in 1932 by H. F. Lowry, offer valuable insight into Arnold's thought as it developed from 1845 to 1861, the year of Clough's death. One of the dominant themes of both the letters and the poems is that of the intellectual and spiritual voice Arnold believed to be characteristic of nineteenth-century life. In September 1849 Arnold wrote, "My dearest Clough these are damned times—everything is against one—the height to which knowledge is come, the spread of luxury, our physical enervation, the absence of great *natures*, the unavoidable contact with millions of small ones, newspapers, cities, light profligate friends, moral desperadoes like Carlyle, our own selves, and the sickening consciousness of our difficulties. . . ." For Arnold, "this strange disease of modern life," as he called it in "The Scholar-Gipsy," led to disorientation, aimlessness, purposelessness. Looking about him, he witnessed the weakening of traditional areas of authority, namely the dwindling power of the upper classes and the diminishing authority of the Church. Man had no firm base to cling to, nothing to believe in, nothing to be sustained by. Instead, Arnold writes in "Stanzas from the Grand Chartreuse," he finds himself

"Wandering between two worlds, one dead,/The other powerless to be born."

Among Arnold's early poems are those love poems about a woman called Marguerite that he grouped under the heading "Switzerland." Although Arnold maintained throughout his life that Marguerite was imaginary, Park Honan has presented convincing, though not universally accepted, evidence that the poems were inspired by a real woman, Mary Claude, who lived near Fox How, and with whom Arnold fell in love in 1848. In the autumn of 1848 and again in 1849, Arnold traveled in the Swiss Alps and used this setting in the Marguerite poems. Mary Claude apparently did not encourage Arnold's affections, and the romance seems to have ended in 1849. Arnold used the Marguerite poems to explore the effects of modern life on love. In "To Marguerite–Continued," he concludes that the individual is essentially isolated: "in the sea of life enisled. . . . We mortal millions live *alone*. Surely, in the past, there was a sense of community; all men must once have been "Parts of a single continent!" But now each man is an island separated from every other man by "The unplumb'd, salt, estranging sea." Even love lacks the power to unite human beings.

The theme of man's alienation is echoed in later poems as well. In "Rugby Chapel," Arnold asks,

> What is the course of the life
> Of mortal men on the earth?–
> Most men eddy about
> Here and there—eat and drink,
> Chatter and love and hate,
> Gather and squander, are raised
> Aloft, are hurl'd in the dust,
> Striving blindly, achieving
> Nothing; and then they die–
> Perish;–and no one asks
> Who or what they have been.

And in "Dover Beach" the movement of the ocean calls to mind "the turbid ebb and flow/Of human misery" and "bring[s]/The eternal note of sadness in." The speaker longs for a refuge since the world "Hath really neither joy, nor love, nor light,/Nor certitude, nor peace, nor help for pain." Arnold's expressed longing for a retreat is not limited to "Dover Beach." For example, he envies the immortal Scholar-Gipsy wandering the hillsides around Oxford who "hast not felt the lapse of hours," who is "Free from the sick fatigue, the languid doubt" inherent in the modern condition. Arnold himself felt acutely the oppression of mortality. At age thirty he wrote to Clough, "How life rushes away, and youth. One has dawdled and scrupled and fiddle faddled–and it is all over."

In spite of such somber poetic reflections Arnold's demeanor remained persistently cavalier to the dismay and irritation of his family and friends. When Charlotte Brontë met him in 1850, her first impression was typical. She found him "striking and prepossessing; . . . [he] displeases from seeming foppery. I own it caused me at first to regard him with regretful surprise. . . . I was told however, that 'Mr. Arnold improved upon acquaintance.' So it was: ere long a real modesty appeared under his assumed conceit, and some genuine intellectual aspirations, as well as high educational acquirements, displaced superficial affectations." Even without such testimonies of Arnold's attributes, his poems and letters indicate that he was thinking deeply about the problems of the age and about the role of literature in helping man to cope with those problems.

Arnold's letters to Clough reveal his theory of poetry, particularly his notion of the purpose of poetry. As E. D. H. Johnson points out in *The Alien Vision of Victorian Poetry* (1952), Arnold tried "to reaffirm the traditional sovereignty of poetry as a civilizing agent." In a letter of 28 October 1852, he contended that "modern poetry can only subsist by its *contents:* by becoming a complete magister vitae as the poetry of the ancients did: by including, as theirs did, religion with poetry, instead of existing as poetry only, and leaving religious wants to be supplied by the Christian religion, as a power existing independent of the poetical." Arnold believed that great art, functioning as a civilizing agent to enrich the intellectual and spiritual life of man, had universal application. But his views did not coincide with those of his contemporaries who felt that art should have immediate, practical application to everyday experience.

The critics of Arnold's first two volumes of poems charged that his poetry did not consistently deal with contemporary life. Poems such as *Empedocles on Etna*, *Tristram and Iseult*, and "Mycerinus" (the last in *The Strayed Reveller*) seemed to them irrelevant for modern readers. Charles Kingsley's comments, published in 1849 in *Fraser's* magazine, are representative: "The man who cannot . . . sing the present age, and transfigure it into melody, or who cannot, in writing of past ages, draw from them some eternal lesson about this one, has no right to be versifying at all. Let him read, think, and keep to prose, till he has mastered the secret of the nineteenth century." Another complaint voiced by the critics and echoed by Arnold's sister Jane was that his poems expressed dissatisfaction with the age but offered no practical cures for its ills.

Arnold's third volume of verse–the first to bear his full name–appeared in 1853. It included such poems as "Sohrab and Rustum," one of Arnold's personal favorites, and "The Scholar-Gipsy," but it was the preface to the volume rather than the poems it contained that received the most attention. The "1853 Preface" served as both an introduction to the collection and as an answer to the critics of his earlier volumes.

Insisting "not only that it [poetry] shall interest, but also that it shall inspirit and rejoice the reader," Arnold explains in the preface that he has chosen to exclude *Empedocles on Etna* from the 1853 collection because the poem neither inspirits nor rejoices. He has rejected it, not because of readers' objections to the classical subject, but rather because the poem deals with a situation that is, ironically, an especially modern one. For the situation of Empedocles, he maintains, is one "in which a continuous state of mental distress is prolonged, unrelieved by incident, hope, or resistance; in which there is everything to be endured, nothing to be done;" in other words, in Arnold's view, a decidedly nineteenth-century dilemma. This for Arnold is the poem's flaw. In saying so, Arnold is not condemning tragedy in literature. He acknowledges that tragedy can produce high pleasure, but *Empedocles on Etna* is not tragedy; it is pathos. In this respect, then, Arnold agrees with his critics. A poem should not just expose problems or express discontent. Evaluating his own work he wrote to Clough in December 1852, "As for my poems they have weight, I think, but little or no charm." He contends in another letter that people need literature that will "*animate* and *ennoble* them...." He withdrew *Empedocles on Etna* because he believed it failed to do so.

But Arnold vehemently disagrees with critical objections to his use of classical subjects, pointing out that the past supplies subjects that touch "elementary feelings ... which are independent of time." Arnold defends classical subjects because of their universal relevance. In his edition of Arnold's letters to Clough, Lowry says of Arnold that "The deepest passion of his life

was for what is permanent in the human mind and the human heart," and he found this in classical literature. To Arnold, a topic's contemporaneity did not ensure its worth. The important point for the poet to keep in mind was that he should choose a significant subject, whether drawn from the past or the present, for "action" rather than "expression" is the most important part of a poem. In his own *Empedocles on Etna*, there is no action, another sense in which it is "modern." According to Arnold's preface, modern poetry suffers from its emphasis on expression or self-revelation. As Alba Warren explains in *English Poetic Theory* (1950), although he did not make it very plain in the "1853 Preface," "great poetry for Arnold is not lyric, subjective, personal; it is above all objective and impersonal...." In its subordination of expression to action, in its emphasis on the epic and the dramatic, Arnold concludes in his preface, classical Greek poetry is especially praiseworthy. The aspiring nineteenth-century poet, Arnold asserts, can learn much from classical writers.

Although the preface did not quiet his critics who persisted in echoing their former complaints, Arnold reserved more elaborate development of his position for a lecture he delivered in the autumn of 1857. At the age of thirty-four, he was elected to the poetry chair at Oxford University, a five-year appointment which required him to deliver several lectures each year. Traditionally, the lectures had been read in Latin, but Arnold decided to present his in English. He used the occasion of his inaugural lecture on 14 November 1857 to return to his views about the worth of classical literature and to introduce several other themes which reappear in his later work.

In this first lecture, entitled "On the Modern Element in Literature" and eventually published in *Macmillan's* magazine (February 1869), Arnold advocates a liberal education that features wide-ranging knowledge and the use of the comparative method to build knowledge and to shape understanding. For Arnold, poetry is the "highest literature," and he is confident that comparison among literatures will show that classical Greek poetry is the highest poetry. It is superior to other literatures because it is "adequate," by which Arnold means that it "represents the highly developed human nature" of a great age. Arnold believes that "adequacy" is rare because the great writer must be linked with a great epoch for great literature to be produced. In Arnold's opinion, the literature of Pindar, Aeschylus, Aristophanes, and Sophocles matches the greatness of the era in which they lived. Other great ages, such as the period of the supremacy of Rome, failed to produce great poets who were in sympathy with their age. The Elizabethan age was also inferior to classical Greece because the genius of Shakespeare and Milton was not matched by a great age; instead, they lived in a time characterized by a lack of religious toleration and by a lack of the critical spirit. As Arnold explains, the climate of the nineteenth century is similarly unconducive to the development of an "adequate" literature. The view he had expressed in an 1849 letter to Clough remains essentially unchanged in 1857: "how deeply *unpoetical* the

age and all one's surroundings are. Not unprofound, not ungrand, not unmoving:—but *unpoetical*." Because of "the enduring interest of Greek literature" founded on its "instructive fulness of experience," it has special relevance for modern man. Classical literature, Arnold argues, can provide the "intellectual deliverance" that modern man needs.

Arnold's next major prose work, *On Translating Homer*, was a series of three lectures given at Oxford in November and December 1860 and January 1861. In these essays, published together soon after the third was delivered, he evaluates selected translations of Homer, noting the strengths and weaknesses of each in an attempt to establish the characteristics of a well-written trans-

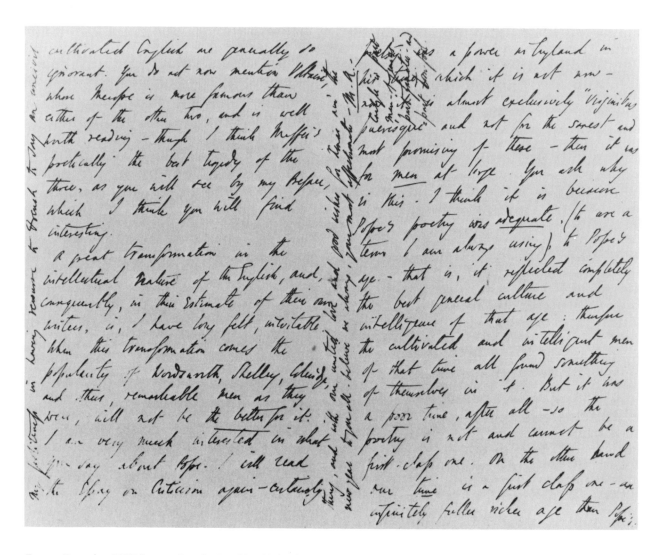

From a December 1857 letter written by Arnold to his brother Thomas (pp. 2-3, by permission of the Trustees of The Pierpont Morgan Library). Arnold's discussion of Pope's poetry as "adequate, (to use a term I am always using), to Pope's age" echoes views he had expressed the month before in the first lecture he delivered as Professor of Poetry at Oxford.

lation. He criticizes translators who have insisted on imposing "modern sentiment" on the material and is equally impatient with those who have become embroiled in background issues such as establishing the true identity of Homer. He insists that many translators have erred because they do not understand that the true purpose of translation is "to reproduce on the intelligent scholar ... the general effect of Homer." To achieve that end the translator must retain not only the content or "matter" of the original but also must capture its style or "manner." Arnold warns that style is frequently sacrificed, both by those who translate too literally and by those who embellish the original with quaint, pseudoarchaic language in an attempt to make the translation seem authentic. He proposes that the translator of Homer adopt the characteristics of Homer's poetry: simple but noble diction, plain thought, natural rhythm, and rapid movement. These are the traits inherent in "the grand style" of Homer.

In order to clarify his suggestions Arnold criticizes illustrative passages from a number of translations, using, as Robert H. Super points out in his notes to Arnold's *Complete Prose Works* (1960-1977), the touchstone method of judging poetry that he advocated twenty years later in "The Study of Poetry." These illustrations are central to Arnold's argument in the lectures, for he contends that one must develop a taste for or sensitivity to "the grand style." While the grand style is not strictly definable, it is clearly recognizable to the cultivated reader. He trusts that the reader will note the absence of the grand style from the passages he has condemned and will observe its presence in his own brief model translations.

In these three lectures Arnold drew on his own interest in classical literature, but he also capitalized on widespread contemporary interest in Homeric translation. Most of Arnold's negative remarks focus on a new rendering of Homer, the 1856 translation of the *Iliad* by Francis Newman—a translation marked by contorted diction and meter, and consequently lacking in the "grand style." Newman replied to Arnold's evaluation of his work in a lengthy pamphlet entitled *Homeric Translation in Theory and Practice, A Reply to Matthew Arnold,* published in 1861. Others echoed Newman's long-winded complaints about the faulty meter of Arnold's own translations and about the very premises of his essays, in particular his assertion about the purpose of translation.

For instance, Fitzjames Stephen, in an unsigned appraisal for the *Saturday Review,* agreed with Newman that it was impossible for a translation to produce the same effect as the original "simply because it is not the same thing as the original." Arnold was also criticized, even by members of his own family, for his dogmatic tone. Responding to such a charge from his sister Jane, who had accused him of "becoming as dogmatic as Ruskin," Arnold told her, "the difference was that Ruskin was 'dogmatic and *wrong.*' ..." On another occasion his reaction was more serious. Writing to Jane in 1861, he reminded her that in his position as lecturer he had to speak with authority, but agreed that use of a "dogmatic" tone would be self-defeating. As Kathleen Tillotson has pointed out in the 1956 article "Arnold and Carlyle," Arnold learned to present himself in future essays and speeches as "regrettably expert."

Arnold's tone was demonstrably modified in his very next lecture. Characteristically, Arnold was not satisfied with leaving his critics unanswered. He replied, primarily to Newman, in *On Translating Homer: Last Words,* a fourth Oxford lecture delivered 30 November 1861 and published the following year. Dismayed that he had so seriously offended Newman, he insisted that his respect for Newman as a scholar was genuine but pointed out that scholarship was not the issue. The issue was Newman's failure to produce a simple but noble "poetic" translation of Homer. He reiterated the major argument of his earlier lectures, dwelling on the characteristics of the grand style. Arnold explained that "the grand style arises in poetry, *when a noble nature, poetically gifted, treats with simplicity or with severity a serious subject.*" He then applied this description not only to translations of poetry but also to poetry itself by examining a wide range of English poets from Chaucer to Keats, from Milton to Wordsworth. Just as in the "1853 Preface," Arnold argued in these essays for the importance of the "whole," for the importance of harmony throughout a work.

Finding the time to write and deliver poetry lectures presented a challenge to Arnold since along with the duties demanded by his honorary title at Oxford were more pressing duties to his family and his job. In 1851 Arnold's appointment as an inspector of schools had provided him sufficient financial security to enable him to marry Frances Lucy Wightman. The marriage was a happy one. Flu, as she was called, frequently accompanied Arnold in his travels and was supportive of his work. According to Arnold, she proved to be "a very good judge of all prose" and criticized his essays and lectures. She provided a liberalizing influence as well, encouraging him to read modern novels and to attend art exhibits and operas. The Arnolds had six children to whom Arnold was a devoted, indulgent father.

During the thirty-five years Arnold spent as a school inspector, he repeatedly complained of his duties: the oppressively long hours, the exhausting travel, and the tiresome bureaucratic system. He spent his days questioning countless schoolchildren and writing endless reports on drainage, ventilation, equipment, teacher performance, and student achievement. Honan reports that in 1855, a "typical" year, Arnold examined 290 schools, 368 pupil-teachers, 97 certified teachers, and 20,000 students. It is little wonder that he claimed to be "worked to death." The depressing conditions he witnessed in the schools affected him deeply. He sympathized not only with ragged, care-worn children but with over-worked teachers as well. In 1854 he claimed, "No one feels more than I do how laborious is [the teachers'] work. . . . men of weak health and purely studious habits, who betake themselves to this profession, as affording the means to continue their favourite pursuits: not knowing, alas, that for all but men of the most singular and exceptional vigour and energy, there are no pursuits more irreconcilable than those of the student and of the schoolmaster."

Still, despite the negative aspects of his job, as Honan points out, Arnold's work exposed him to aspects of English and European life of which he probably would have otherwise remained ignorant, and thus enhanced his credibility as a social commentator: he earned respect as a social critic because he traveled throughout the country and to Europe and daily mingled with people of all levels, especially those of the middle class. The advantages of his job were not clear to Arnold, however. Fatigue and discouragement often overshadowed commitment and enthusiasm. He responded with dismay when people tried to relate his work in education to that of his father. In an 1856 letter to his brother William, Arnold confessed that when he was compared to his father he was tempted to reply: "My good friends, this is a matter for which my father certainly had a specialité, but for which I have none whatever. . . . I on the contrary half cannot

half will not throw myself into it, and feel the weight of it doubly in consequence. I am inclined to think it would have been the same with any active line of life on which I had found myself engaged—even with politics—so I am glad my sphere is a humble one and must try more and more to do something worth doing in my own way, since I cannot bring myself to do more than a halting sort of half-work in other people's way." Arnold's dedication to the improvement of education in England was more clearly indicated by his publications than by his perfunctory performance of routine duties.

On several occasions, Arnold escaped the drudgery of his ordinary assignments to travel in Europe where he studied foreign educational systems. The first such study took place in 1859 when Arnold was asked by the Education Commission to visit France, French Switzerland, and Holland to examine the elementary schools in those countries. He spent six months, from March through August of 1859, traveling about Europe, observing schools, and consulting with foreign officials. His report, *The Popular Education of France, with Notices of That of Holland and Switzerland,* published in 1861, records his observations and evaluations and his recommendations to England.

The introduction, entitled "Democracy" and later included in *Mixed Essays* (1879), presents Arnold's view that the national government should assume responsibility for educating its citizens. He anticipates middle-class fears of government repression of individual freedom but argues that in England the democratic system is strongly rooted, leaving no danger of loss of liberty if the State assumes control of certain public interests. According to Arnold, the State is the best agent for raising the quality of education. He repeats Edmund Burke's definition of the State as *the nation in its collective and corporate character.*" The State, because of its authority and resources, can distribute "broad collective benefits" to society at large.

Moreover, the very growth of democracy prompts Arnold to advocate a broad-based, state-supported educational program. Middle- and lower-class people were gaining more and more power of self-government; therefore, Arnold reasons, England must "make timely preparation" for the spread of democracy. This can best be accomplished by adequately educating the middle and lower classes. Upper-class schools were already excellent; it was the schools for the middle and lower classes that needed improvement. Arnold argues that our greatest fear should be of "the multitude being in power, with no adequate ideal to elevate or guide" it. He reminds his reader that "It is a very great thing to be able to think as you like; but, after all, an important question remains: *what* you think." Arnold once again praises ancient Athens, for it was in that society, he says, that people of all classes had "culture." It was in that society that the world witnessed "the middle and lower classes in the highest development of their humanity. . . ." By improving the education of the middle and lower classes, Arnold hoped to see a similar spread of culture in nineteenth-century England.

In the chapters following this important introduction, Arnold offers a detailed explanation of the French educational system and brief overviews of education in French Switzerland and Holland. Arnold finds much to be admired in the French system. While the French have not made elementary education compulsory, they have made it available to all. And while Arnold notes weaknesses in the system and concedes that all do not take advantage of educational opportunities, he finds that "the mental temper" of the French people has shown improvement. He longs for such improvement among the English.

Arnold continues his argument in "A French Eton," which appeared in three installments in *Macmillan's* magazine in September 1863, February 1864, and May 1864. He considered this "one of his most important works to date" and rightly so, for it is in this work that Arnold presents his views on education most concisely and forcefully. He focuses on secondary education, proposing the establishment throughout England of a network of "Royal Schools" (similar to such schools in France) to be distinguished by low fees, regular inspections, and government support. Arnold again voices concern about the existence of a powerful, but inadequately educated, un-"cultured," "self-satisfied" middle class and argues that a school system such as the one he describes would do much to urge "progress toward man's best perfection."

Parliamentary debates over government funding of education motivated Arnold to pick up his pen on other occasions in the early 1860s. Political discussion centered on the Revised Code, proposed by Robert Lowe, the vice-president of the Committee of Council on Education. The Revised Code outlined a plan for appropriating money to schools based on quantifiable "results" achieved by teachers in the classroom. Arnold was appalled by the utilitarian emphasis of the proposal. In "The Twice-Revised Code," an anonymous article that appeared in *Fraser's* magazine (1862), he expresses dismay that emphasis is to be placed on reading, writing, and arithmetic to the exclusion of other subjects. Arnold does not deny that many children, especially poor children, are inadequately trained in these subjects but contends that a reductive approach will not ensure better training. He is convinced children need the civilizing influence of a broader, more liberal curriculum. Arnold suggests reorganization of and reduction of the number of school inspectors to cut expenses.

Arnold's belief that all children should receive a liberal education surfaces in other ways too. In May 1872, for instance, he edited a version of chapters forty through sixty-six of Isaiah. Entitled *A Bible-Reading for Schools*, it was widely used as a textbook for children. In 1883 he produced *Isaiah of Jerusalem*, an accompanying version of the first thirty-nine chapters. Arnold believed that schoolchildren ought to study the Bible because, he says, it "is for the child in an elementary school almost his only contact with poetry and philosophy. . . ."

Arnold was sent abroad for seven months in 1865 by the Middle Class School Commission to study middle-class secondary education in France, Italy, Germany, and Switzerland. His report was completed late in 1867 and published in March 1868 under the title *Schools and Universities on the Continent*. Arnold had been among those considered for the position of secretary of the commission. All along he had claimed to have no interest in the position and so was not disappointed when the office went to someone else, but he was distressed that most of those named to the committee were opposed to state control of education. In a 1 December 1865 letter to his mother he confided, "I wish it was a better and more open-minded Commission. But this, like all else which happens, more and more turns me away from the thought of any attempt at direct practical and political action, and makes me fix all my care upon a spiritual action, to tell upon people's minds, which after all is the great thing, hard as it is to make oneself fully believe it so." Arnold used publications such as *Schools and Universities on the Continent* to try to affect people's minds by transforming their attitudes.

In his report Arnold argues for universal

educational opportunity. His view of the purpose of education is similar to his view of the purpose of art. He is much more concerned with enrichment and culture than with practicality and relevance. He recognizes that "The aim and office of instruction, say many people, is to make a man a good citizen, or a good Christian, or a gentleman; or it is to fit him to get on in the world, or it is to enable him to do his duty in that state of life to which he is called." But Arnold states emphatically, "It is none of these; . . . its prime direct aim is to enable a man *to know himself and the world.*"

Arnold recommends that the English adopt the trend in foreign schools of mandating the same subjects for all children in elementary school, after which each child may choose between humanistic or natural science curricula, depending on his aims and interests. At the elementary level, the child's education should be a comparative one. In order "to know himself and the world," a child should study other cultures, thereby gaining insight into his own. Convinced of the humanizing effects of literary study in particular, Arnold proposes the study of Greek literature and art since the Greeks excelled in these areas and since their works speak to all people in all ages; the study of "the mother tongue and its literature"; and the study of the literature of modern foreign languages.

Arnold points out that while the English rave about the high quality of their schools, the schools in Germany, Holland, and Switzerland are clearly superior. Still arguing for a better education for the middle classes, Arnold points again to the stagnation caused by complacency. He claims that the countries he has visited all "have a civil organisation which has been framed with forethought and design to meet the wants of modern society; while our civil organisation in England still remains what time and chance have made it." Because more and more the middle class is actually running industry, commerce, and government, it is especially important that it be well prepared to do so. In an effort to demonstrate the practical advantages of improved education, Arnold's *Schools and Universities on the Continent* draws attention to the dangers of inadequate education. Many professionals in England—engineers, chemists, doctors, teachers, and magistrates—lack proper training and certification. In other countries this is not the case. In France, for instance, those who dispense drugs and those who build bridges must be licensed to

do so; but licensing is not required in England. Teachers in France are certified for competency in certain areas, but in England teachers receive a general certification for all subjects. All of society, Arnold maintains, would benefit from the more competent professionals educated by an improved school system.

In order to administer a sound middle-class educational program, an education minister and a Council of Education should be appointed. Those who serve should be experts on education, not political favorites. Local boards would handle regional concerns. Arnold boldly claims that all schools should come under public supervision including such hallowed institutions as Rugby, Winchester, and Harrow.

Arnold was asked to make a third journey to the Continent to study elementary education at the end of 1885. He completed his travels in March of 1886 and two months later submitted his comments, published in 1886 as *Education Department: Special Report on Certain Points Connected with Elementary Education in Germany, Switzerland, and France.* In 1888 the report was republished for the public by the Education Reform League, an organization which championed universal education. For this edition, Arnold added a one-page preface in which he summarized his long-standing concerns about popular education, namely that the "existing popular school is far too little formative and humanizing, and that much in it, which its administrators point to as valuable *results,* is in truth mere machinery," and that one of the subjects that ought to be taught in elementary schools is religion because it *is* "a formative influence, an element of culture of the very highest value, and [therefore is] more indispensable in the popular school than in any other."

Throughout the 1860s, Arnold composed less and less poetry. Though he continued to write poems for the remainder of his life, his career as a poet had essentially ended by the close of the decade. His career as a prosodist, however, was just beginning. In his prose works Arnold pursued many of the same ideas he had introduced in his poems, most notably, man's need for spiritual and intellectual fulfillment in a materialistic, provincial society. Already in his Oxford lectures and in his education reports, Arnold had suggested one solution to man's problems—a liberal education. A liberal education would help man develop his critical faculties and would enrich him culturally. As an essayist, Arnold continued to address the subject of intellectual and spiritual growth.

Arnold won fame with his first collection of essays, *Essays in Criticism*, compiled from lectures and reviews written in 1863 and 1864 and published in 1865. The essays cover a wide range of topics as their individual titles indicate: "Maurice de Guérin," "Eugenie de Guérin," "Heinrich Heine," "Marcus Aurelius," "Spinoza and the Bible," "Joubert," "Pagan and Medieval Religious Sentiment," "The Literary Influence of Academies," and "The Function of Criticism at the Present Time." Despite the seeming diversity of the collection, in a 1956 article in *PMLA*, Robert Donovan has demonstrated the unity of *Essays in Criticism*. As Donovan explains, all the essays are about French writers or are inspired by Arnold's exposure to French literature and culture; all have as a common theme British insularity and complacency; all use the comparative method of argumentation; and all attempt to prove the value of studying literature. In short, Donovan notes, Arnold's major goal was "to introduce the British Philistine to a new realm of Continental ideas."

Arnold was moved to write "Maurice de Guérin" when a collection of the French writer's works appeared in print in 1860. Guérin had died in 1839 at the age of twenty-eight, having published nothing. George Sand was responsible for bringing his work before the public, and it was through her that Arnold first read the little-known Frenchman. In his essay, Arnold not only praises Guérin's writing but also takes the opportunity to express some of his ideas about literature, more specifically, his theory of poetry. He tells us that "the grand power of poetry is its interpretative power; by which I mean, not a power of drawing out in black and white an explanation of the mystery of the universe, but the power of so dealing with things as to awaken in us a wonderfully full, new, and intimate sense of them, and of our relations with them." Guérin succeeded in this in his prose but not in his verse, for Guérin used the alexandrine, which in Arnold's view was not an adequate "vehicle" for the highest poetry. He would have been better served by hexameters or by blank verse. Guérin's prose, however, is exceptional. It is marked by qualities that are usually assigned to poetry: "a truly interpretative faculty; the most profound and delicate sense of the life of Nature, and the most exquisite felicity in finding expressions to render that sense." Arnold elaborates on the interpretative power of

literature, saying it is expressed through both the "*natural magic*" of literature and its "*moral profundity*." Only a few writers, such as Shakespeare and Aeschylus, have mastered both. Most great authors master one or the other. Guérin, for instance, excelled in conveying "natural magic" and for this reason deserves to be read.

Arnold continues his attempt to cultivate appreciation of continental writers among provincial English readers in the essay "Heinrich Heine." For Arnold, the great German poet Heine truly possessed the critical spirit. Heine cherished the French spirit of enlightenment and waged "a life and death battle with Philistinism," the narrowness he saw typified in the British. Arnold acknowledges that Heine's assessment of the British was the true one and tries to explain how the British developed in this way. In the Elizabethan age, claims Arnold, England was open to new ideas but Puritanism crushed them. The English romantics failed to reinstitute the critical spirit. Coleridge turned to opium; Wordsworth grew introspective; Keats and Scott failed to "apply modern ideas to life." The German romantic Heine, however, was able to accomplish what the English romantics could not. "The wit and ardent modern spirit of France Heine joined to the culture, the sentiment, the thought of Germany." This achievement, despite his personal faults, made him a man of genius.

In his essays Arnold sees not only individual authors but also institutions as potentially upholding the critical spirit. "The Literary Influence of Academies" is devoted to praise of the French Academy, which was established to improve French language and literature. The English, he declares, would do well to establish an institution that would uphold standards of taste and help to offset the "materialism, commercialism, [and] vulgarization" of nineteenth-century life. The English, whose "chief spiritual characteristics" are "energy and honesty," in Arnold's view, can learn much from the French who are noted for their "openness of mind and flexibility of intelligence." Arnold argues that the "retarding" provincialism of English literature would profit by the influence of a "centre of correct information, correct judgment, [and] correct taste...." Though he recognizes that the English are unlikely ever to form an academy like the one in France, English writers, he concludes, should keep in mind such an institution's noble aims.

All of the *Essays on Criticism* essentially deal with the importance of liberal learning, wide read-

"Sweetness and Light," Frederick Waddy's caricature of Arnold published in Once a Week, *12 October 1873 (Collection of Jerold J. Savory)*

ing, and the development of the critical spirit. But the essay best known for its advocacy of these intellectual habits is "The Function of Criticism at the Present Time," which was originally delivered as a lecture at Oxford in October 1864. Arnold presents in this essay a memorable defense of the critical method. Opening with a reference to Wordsworth's disdain for literary criticism, Arnold agrees that "a false or malicious criticism had better never have been written." Admittedly, "the critical faculty is lower than the inventive," yet criticism does have merit; it too may be creative. Its most important function, however, is to create a climate suitable for the production of great art. Arnold repeats the claim he made in earlier lectures, most notably in "On the Modern Element in Literature," that great art depends on great ideas. Artistic genius "does not principally show itself in discovering new ideas." Instead, it works with ideas that are already "current." Arnold contends that "for the

creation of a master-work of literature two powers must concur, the power of the man and the power of the moment, and the man is not enough without the moment. . . ." The critical power can create an atmosphere in which art can flourish. In Arnold's words, it can "make the best ideas prevail," for criticism "obeys an instinct prompting it to try to know the best that is known and thought in the world. . . ." It is "disinterested," allowing "a free play of the mind on all subjects. . . ." Only by such wide exposure, only by objectivity, can it arrive at the best ideas.

Criticism is not immediately concerned with the practical. It is concerned with the life of the spirit and the mind. Arnold believed that his own age lacked great ideas. It was too complacent, too self-congratulatory to seek anything higher. Arnold quotes two of his contemporaries for illustration–Sir Charles Adderley declaring the English are "superior to all the world" and John Arthur Roebuck who is prompted by the Englishman's right "to say what he likes" to exclaim, "I pray that our unrivalled happiness may last." How can it be, wonders Arnold, that this same England– the nation of unrivalled happiness, the nation superior to the rest of the world–is the same nation in which a wretched girl, identified in the newspapers only by her surname, Wragg, strangles her illegitimate child? Criticism can show man the world as it truly exists. The critical spirit can turn man from self-satisfaction to a pursuit of excellence. The aim of criticism, Arnold explains, "is to keep man from a self-satisfaction which is retarding and vulgarising, to lead him towards perfection, by making his mind dwell upon what is excellent in itself, and the absolute beauty and fitness of things."

Arnold develops this view even more fully in his 1869 book *Culture and Anarchy*. As he indicates throughout his works, both poetry and prose, Arnold saw nineteenth-century England as a nation of mechanism and materialism, a nation in which men were content so long as they had the freedom to do as they pleased, in short, a nation marked by intellectual and spiritual anarchy. From Arnold's perspective, the Englishman was more prone to do than to think, and he was losing sight of the fact that action is of little value unless it is preceded by critical thinking. Arnold believed the solution involved the fostering of culture.

Arnold's second term as poetry chair at Oxford University expired in the summer of 1867, and he decided to use culture as the subject of his final address, a lecture he titled "Culture and Its Enemies." Delivered in June, the talk was published the next month as an essay in the *Cornhill Magazine* and aroused widespread critical disapproval.

In the essay, later included in *Culture and Anarchy*, Arnold continues to wage war against complacency. England, he insists, must not rest satisfied with her accomplishments but must continue to develop, and the method of culture–by which Arnold meant the method of liberal learning and objective, critical thought–can help her to do so. For culture signifies to Arnold the process of "getting to know, on all the matters which most concern us, the best which has been thought and said in the world; and through this knowledge, turning a stream of fresh and free thought upon our stock notions and habits. . . ."

Arnold attempts to show that culture and religion are similar forces, though culture is more comprehensive, having as its concern the development of all aspects of man's being whereas religion is concerned only with the development of man's spiritual aspect. But the aim of culture, says Arnold, is the same as the aim of religion: "human perfection." And perfection is something one moves *toward*. "Not a having and a resting, but a growing and a becoming, is the character of perfection as culture conceives it; and here, too, it coincides with religion." Culture is a combination of "sweetness," or beauty, and "light," or intelligence, and it strives "To make reason and the will of God prevail."

Arnold's views met with considerable scorn. His readers claimed that he was an elitist, a snob, and they labeled his scheme inadequately developed and impractical. Henry Sidgwick, reviewing "Culture and Its Enemies" for *Macmillan's* magazine, found the essay "over-ambitious, because it treats of the most profound and difficult problems of individual and social life with an airy dogmatism that ignores their depth and difficulty." And in a delightfully witty piece for the *Fortnightly Review*, which Arnold good-naturedly claimed made him laugh until he cried, Frederic Harrison asked, "And now, then, how do you get it [culture]? It is very good to tell me how beautiful this is; but if a physician tells me only what a beautiful thing health is, how happy and strong it makes those who possess it, and omits to tell me how I can gain health, or says only, Be healthy, desire, seek after health, I call him no physician, but a quack." If ever culture could be obtained, some still perceived it as worthless.

Many asked what good it was. Sidgwick voiced the opinion of many when he pointed out that Arnold's criticism of action seemed to stem from the fact that the program he advocated, that of culture, was incapable of any action at all. "Culture," Sidgwick maintained, "is always hinting at a convenient season, that rarely seems to arrive."

Arnold responded to his critics in a series of five essays published in the *Cornhill Magazine* in 1868. The series, entitled, "Anarchy and Authority," was collected along with "Culture and Its Enemies" to form *Culture and Anarchy*. In the essay series Arnold continues his championship of culture by stressing the present need for it. He criticizes England for having "a very strong belief in freedom, and a very weak belief in right reason. . . ." To justify his claim, he points out that while an Englishman cherishes his right to do as he likes, it never occurs to him that anyone other than an Englishman, and only a middle- or upper-class Englishman at that, ought to be able to do as he likes. Culture demonstrates such inconsistencies and shows that freedom without right reason leads to anarchy. One significant benefit of culture, therefore, would be that people would come "to like what right reason ordains, and to follow her authority. . . ."

To answer questions such as that posed by Frederic Harrison, Arnold suggests that culture is acquired through education, just as he had suggested in his education reports. Culture, he says, is "an endeavour to come at reason and the will of God by means of reading, observing, and thinking. . . ." Literature is one of the principal agents of culture. Arnold firmly believed in the power of literature to enrich and even to transform human life. He wrote in one version of the preface to *Culture and Anarchy*, "one must, I think, be struck more and more, the longer one lives, to find out how much, in our present society, a man's life of each day depends for its solidity and value on whether he reads during that day, and, far more still, on what he reads during it."

In discussing the three principal social classes in "Anarchy and Authority," Arnold finds each one too self-satisfied, too deficient in light, to be the standard bearer of culture. The Philistines, or members of the middle class, are more interested in the "machinery of business, chapels, tea-meetings, and addresses" from fellow Philistines than in the pursuit of sweetness and light. The barbarians, or aristocrats, are also unsuitable for they have always belonged to "an exterior culture" which "consisted principally in outward gifts and graces, in looks, manners, accomplishments, prowess," and are, consequently, lacking in light. The populace, or members of the working class, are as yet "raw and half-developed." Since none of the three social classes is a model of human perfection, the individual is left to pursue "right reason" and, thereby, to cultivate his own "best self."

In an effort to understand why true culture is so alien to modern man, Arnold examines the two major tendencies of human development: Hebraism and Hellenism, or energy and intelligence. "The uppermost idea with Hellenism," explains Arnold, "is to see things as they really are; the uppermost idea with Hebraism is conduct and obedience." Although Hellenism is "full of what we call sweetness and light," both are *contributions* to human development"; neither is sufficient alone. The two must be balanced within a society and within the individual. But in Victorian England, the balance did not exist. Therefore, "the real *unum necessarium* for us is to come to our best at all points."

Arnold contradicts those who have sneered that culture has no practical purpose. Having stated earlier that the motivating force behind culture is "the noble aspiration to leave the world better and happier than we found it," Arnold generalizes about how this will be accomplished. He applies the method of culture to current controversies about the disestablishment of the Irish Church, the real estate inheritance laws, the concept of free trade, and the legalization of marriage to one's deceased wife's sister to show that the critical approach espoused by culture will enable men to see things as they really are and to make wise decisions. Therefore, he declares, culture is practical because it endorses "a frame of mind out of which the schemes of really fruitful reforms may with time grow." Arnold is not troubled by the slow pursuit of perfection. In fact to him it is natural that the achievement of progress will take time. He quotes Goethe's precept "to act is easy, to think is hard." Arnold is able to look to the future with hope, to a time when "man's two great natural forces, Hebraism and Hellenism, will no longer be dissociated and rival, but will be a joint force of right thinking and strong doing to carry him on towards perfection."

In addition to his espousal of literature and education as agents of culture, Arnold also cham-

pioned religion as a profound cultural force. He wrote four great religious books: *St. Paul and Protestantism* (1870), *Literature and Dogma* (1873), *God and the Bible* (1875), and *Last Essays on Church and Religion* (1877). Arnold had two major purposes in these books: first, to save the Church from the dissolution threatened by scientific inquiry, and second, to demonstrate the need for a unified, national Church.

Originally published in the *Cornhill Magazine* as a series of three essays in October and November 1869 and February 1870, *St. Paul and Protestantism* was written, in Arnold's words, "to rescue St. Paul and the Bible from the perversions of them by mistaken men." In the first essay Arnold explains that he is principally concerned with Nonconformist religions such as Calvinist and Methodist that have distorted the teachings of St. Paul by claiming that their doctrines were founded on his writings. Arnold contends that a "critical" reading of St. Paul shows that "What in St. Paul is secondary and subordinate, Puritanism has made primary and essential. . . ." He refers to the Calvinist doctrine of election and to the Methodist doctrine of salvation through faith to demonstrate that the denominations are alike in emphasizing "what God does, with disregard to what man does." Paul, on the other hand, focused on man's righteousness. Furthermore, the Nonconformists drew erroneous conclusions because they ignored the poetic, or metaphorical, quality of biblical language. Often Paul spoke figuratively or rhetorically, yet his words were interpreted literally by those eager to justify "preconceived theories."

In the second essay Arnold develops more fully his argument that St. Paul stressed conduct, not doctrine. The Puritans saw Christ as having sacrificed himself to appease a God angered by man's disobedience, thereby winning man's salvation. But St. Paul saw Christ as a model for others to follow in their daily lives. Arnold insists that Pauline theology was not founded on Puritan beliefs about "*calling, justification, sanctification*" but instead on "*dying with Christ, resurrection from the dead,* [and] *growing into Christ.*" Paul believed in both physical and spiritual resurrection, but his emphasis was on the spiritual. According to Arnold, by death, Paul meant spiritual death, or "living in sin." The individual must imitate Christ and say "no" to sin, thereby effecting his own "resurrection to *righteousness*" in this life rather than assuming salvation will be his in a life to come.

Arnold presents his concern for religious unity in the third essay. The fragmentation of the Christian Church distressed Arnold as it had his father. Arnold hoped that if he adequately demonstrated the weak foundation of Puritan denominations he could help to effect a return of the Nonconformists to the Church of England. The essay states Arnold's belief that the Church has to meet the changing needs of the people it serves. The nineteenth-century Church itself, he argues, has to change. Because the doctrine of the Church of England has remained open, whereas that of the dissenting churches has been narrow and restrictive, he concludes that the Anglican Church "is more serviceable than Puritanism to religious progress. . . ." Arnold reminds his readers that "the Church exists, not for the sake of opinions, but for the sake of moral practice, and a united endeavour after this is stronger than a broken one." In other words, a unified Church is more conducive to "collective growth."

A fourth essay entitled "Modern Dissent" was written to serve as the preface for the publication of *St. Paul and Protestantism* in book form in April 1870. In it Arnold answers the criticisms already voiced by the readers of the serial version of the work. Attacked for his presumption in presenting his views as the "right" ones, Arnold says that his ideas are neither new nor his alone. Asserting that his interpretation of St. Paul is a reflection of the "Zeit-Geist," he insists that: "it is in the air, and many have long been anticipating it. . . ." In addition he points out that, unlike the Puritans who claim to possess truth, *the* Gospel, he admits that his "conception" of St. Paul's writings is an evolving one that tends toward truth, but does not pretend to be conclusive. Arnold maintains that he is disinterested; his "greatest care is neither for the Church nor for Puritanism, but for human perfection."

Still, as Ruth apRoberts shows in *Arnold and God*, Arnold is guilty of "overingenuity." His argument is not so disinterested as he claims. He often glosses over biblical passages inconsistent with his position. For Arnold, the Bible was literature and must be read as such. What he offers in *St. Paul and Protestantism* is, according to apRoberts, "a literary analysis of Scripture." Predictably, this approach elicited objections from many readers. As R. H. Super points out, *St. Paul and Protestantism* is a direct development of the arguments presented in *Culture and Anarchy*. Arnold's contemporaries certainly recognized it as such and adopted the phrases made famous by that

earlier work in their responses to this most recent one. An anonymous reviewer for the July 1870 issue of the *British Quarterly Review* wrote that "in Mr. Arnold's culture, perhaps in his nature, the Hellenic element is too exclusive; the Hebraic has scarcely any place. In all that he writes, the purely intellectual predominates over the emotional and spiritual. . . . Thus theology is to him merely a system of ethical ideas, and the Church merely a machinery for their culture–a national organization for the comprehension and good order of citizens of all varieties of theological belief." In his book *Culture and Religion* (1870), J. C. Shairp, a contemporary of Arnold's, argued that "They who seek religion for culture-sake are aesthetic, not religious. . . ." The same charge was later echoed by T. S. Eliot in *The Use of Poetry and The Use of Criticism* (1933), who found that Arnold had confused "poetry and morals in the attempt to find a substitute for religious faith."

Convinced of the merits of his argument, however, Arnold persisted in defending his case. Of *Literature and Dogma*, his second major work on religion, and by far the best known, Arnold said, "I think it, of all my books in prose, the one most important (if I may say so) and most capable of being useful." Following his earlier practice, *Literature and Dogma* appeared first in the *Cornhill Magazine* in serial installments and was later published as a book. The public must have agreed with Arnold's assessment of the importance of his work. Attesting to its popularity, Mudie's library bought copies for circulation; a less expensive, abridged "popular" edition was printed in 1883; and by 1924 sales of all editions had reached 21,000 copies.

In Arnold's words, "The object of *Literature and Dogma* is to re-assure those who feel attachment to Christianity, to the Bible, but who recognise the growing discredit befalling miracles and the supernatural" due to the influence of science. Arnold sets out to discover, using the method of culture, the "real experimental basis" of the Bible rather than operating from a "basis of unverifiable assumptions." Only culture can supply a valid interpretation of the Bible. In order to be a wise interpreter of the Bible, one must be widely read. According to Arnold, if one knows only the Bible, he does not really know even that. He concedes that applying a critical approach to biblical interpretation is very difficult because we have come to view the Bible "as a sort of talisman given down to us out of

Heaven." This inherited assumption makes it even more essential to apply the disinterested critical approach of culture. For, says Arnold, "To understand that the language of the Bible is fluid, passing, and literary, not rigid, fixed, and scientific, is the first step towards a right understanding of the Bible." In Arnold's opinion, as summarized by Basil Willey in *Nineteenth-Century Studies* (1949), it is a "false approach to the Bible which seeks to extract dogma from poetry."

Arnold reminds the readers of *Literature and Dogma* that the Bible is literature, and that biblical terms are literary terms. Even a term such as *God* cannot justifiably be used as if it were a scientific designation with a precise definition. Theologians have aimed at precision by defining God as "the great first cause, the moral and intelligent governor of the universe," when, in fact, such a definition cannot be verified. Instead, Arnold proposes to describe God "scientifically" as "the *not ourselves* which makes for righteousness," as *"the stream of tendency by which all things seek to fulfil the law of their being. . . ."* He admits that these definitions are inadequate, but, in his view, they express all that can be known for certain. While he doubted man's ability to describe satisfactorily the true nature of God, Arnold did not doubt God's existence. He maintains that God's existence is proven—not by the existence of the physical world or by other such tangible evidence—but by man's conscience, which is the guide to God's law. "The idea of *God*, as it is given us in the Bible, rests, we say, not on a metaphysical conception of the necessity of certain deductions from our ideas of cause, existence, identity, and the like; but on a moral perception of a rule of conduct not of our own making, into which we are born, and which exists whether we will or no; of awe at its grandeur and necessity, and of gratitude at its beneficence." All experience proves that God exists. There is something in man that urges him to fulfill the law of his being and that makes him happy when he does so. God is made manifest when man resists the temptation to give in to "the blind momentary impulses" of his weak nature and is subsequently "thrilled with gratitude, devotion, and awe, at the sense of joy and peace, not of his own making, which followed the exercise of this self-control. . . ."

The object of religion is conduct, and conduct, Arnold argues in *Literature and Dogma*, is three-fourths of life. Religion should become "personal," should make us care deeply about conduct. For Arnold, "the true meaning of reli-

gion is thus, not simply *morality*, but *morality touched by emotion*." This was the message of Jesus Christ. Arnold believed that religion had been weakened by the addition of *aberglaube*, or "extra-belief," to what is provable. These extra beliefs in events such as the resurrection of Christ or the virgin birth undermine religious truth and, for some, become more important than morality, which is the essence of religion.

Arnold asserts that extra belief in and of itself is not harmful and can even be beneficial if it helps one improve his conduct, but eventually the realization will come that there is no proof to support extra belief, and Arnold fears "then the whole certainty of religion seems discredited, and the basis of conduct gone." This is the danger inherent in overemphasizing what cannot be substantiated. Ultimately, religious doubt and uncertainty cannot be avoided. For Arnold, it is "the Time-Spirit which is sapping the proof from miracles,–it is the 'Zeit-Geist' itself." Explaining that the nineteenth century is a questioning age, a scientific age, Arnold concludes that there is no proof of the supernatural events the Bible records. Jesus' miracles were recorded by others; those who reported his actions were merely men, and therefore, fallible. Since most church dogma is founded on an acceptance of the miraculous, many traditional tenets of Christianity have been weakened. But Arnold tells his readers that this is only because the Church has drifted so far from the original aims of Christ. "Jesus never troubled himself with what are called Church matters at all. . . ." He dealt with experience, not with theory. Moreover, according to Arnold, there is practically no dogma in the Bible itself. The religious doctrine that it does contain can be summarized by two pronouncements: in the Old Testament, "Obey God!" and in the New Testament, "Follow Jesus!" Arnold asks, "Walking on the water, multiplying loaves, raising corpses, a heavenly judge appearing with trumpets in the clouds while we are yet alive,–what is this compared to the real experience offered as witness to us by Christianity? It is like the difference between the grandeur of an extravaganza and the grandeur of the sea or the sky." Arnold closes, "The more we trace the real law of Christianity's action the grander it will seem."

It was to be expected that *Literature and Dogma* would stir even more controversy than had *St. Paul and Protestantism*. Understandably, many of Arnold's critics were clergymen. John Tulloch, a clergyman reviewing the 1873 volume for *Blackwood's* magazine, was not alone in accusing Arnold of dabbling in "amateur theology." It is true that Arnold was not a theologian, but he did know the Bible. As apRoberts points out in *Arnold and God*, the notebooks Arnold kept from 1852 to 1888 record his reading lists and are filled with quotations from the Bible, in fact with more quotations from the Bible than from any other source. And Arnold had thought long and deeply about his views. Nevertheless, he was stirred to even wider reading and more extensive research in preparation for writing *God and the Bible* since he conceived it as "a review of objections" to *Literature and Dogma*.

In *God and the Bible* Arnold renews his commitment to making the Bible accessible. "All disquisitions about the Bible seem to us to be faulty and even ridiculous which have for their result that the Bible is less felt, followed, and enjoyed after them than it was before them." Arnold's sole aim is to help the reader "*to enjoy the Bible and to turn it to his benefit.*"

In the first three chapters–"The God of Miracles," "The God of Metaphysics," and "The God of Experience"–Arnold justifies the definition of God which he offered in *Literature and Dogma*. He repeats his claims that his definition of God as "*The Eternal, not ourselves, that makes for righteousness*" is verifiable and that a verifiable definition of God is essential for reading the Bible, a book in which "God is everything." In response to criticism of his refusal to profess belief in a personal God, in other words, a God "who thinks and loves," Arnold says he is unable to affirm or deny this notion of God and, thus, is more comfortable with a verifiable definition.

In three subsequent chapters, "The Bible Canon," "The Fourth Gospel from Without," and "The Fourth Gospel from Within," Arnold discusses current controversy about the biblical canon and the Gospel of John. The resolution of these controversies is "unessential" for enjoyment and appreciation of the Bible, but because some Bible readers ascribe undue importance to such questions, Arnold feels a disinterested appraisal is in order. His critical examination reveals that the positions taken by both popular religion and higher German criticism on these controversies are devoid of light. Both are extremist. Puritans ask no questions and without hesitation accept the Bible as truth while the higher German critics ask too many questions and mislead their followers by presuming that all questions can be answered. In Arnold's view, although there is not

H. Weigall's portrait of Arnold that hangs in the Athenaeum (reproduced by courtesy of the Athenaeum, London)

enough evidence to ascertain whether the Bible is literally true or false, the absence of certainty should not force one into either blind acceptance or debilitating doubt. "We should do Christians generally a great injustice," Arnold writes, "if we thought that the entire force of their Christianity lay in the fascination and subjugation of their spirits by the miracles which they suppose Jesus to have worked, or by the materialistic promises of heaven which they suppose him to have offered. Far more does the vital force of their Christianity lie in the boundless confidence, consolation, and attachment, which the whole being and discourse of Jesus inspire." Arnold describes his effort in his religious works as "an attempt conservative, and an attempt religious." He assures the reader that he has written "to convince the lover of religion that by following habits of intellectual seriousness he need not, so far as religion is concerned, lose anything."

The year 1877 saw publication of Arnold's *Last Essays on Church and Religion*, a collection of four essays, two of which had originally appeared in the *Contemporary* and two of which had first been published in *Macmillan's* magazine. Arnold was sincere in labeling these papers his "last" words on the subject. At the end of one of the essays, "The Church of England," he explains that he had originally pursued the topic of religion because he had witnessed the damaging effects of dogma and dissent on national religion. "However," he continues, "as one grows old, one feels that it is not one's business to go on for ever expostulating with other people upon their waste of life, but to make progress in grace and peace oneself." Of the four essays in the volume "The Church of England" and "A Psychological Parallel" are the most important.

In "The Church of England," presented as a lecture before an audience of clergymen at Sion College in 1876, Arnold seeks to explain how it is possible for him to condemn Christian doctrine and yet be an Anglican. His support for the Church derives from his view of it as "a great national society for the promotion of what is commonly called *goodness* . . . through the means of the Christian religion and of the Bible." Promoting goodness is the true "object of the Church" and the true "business of the clergy." The basis of religion and the mission of the Church are the improvement of conduct, not the promulgation of doctrine. Just as in *God and the Bible,* Arnold insists that men cannot do without Christianity, but "they cannot do with it as it is."

Arnold points out that many working-class people are turning from the Anglican Church because it has failed to support social reform. Clergymen have supplied physical aid to the oppressed but have not shown "a positive sympathy with popular ideals." Instead, the Church is perceived as "an appendage to the Barbarians . . . favouring immobility, preaching submission, and reserving transformation in general for the other side of the grave." Such a position not only alienates the masses from the Church, but also alienates the Church itself from the true ideals of the active Christian faith as presented in the Bible. "The Church of England" ends with the reassurance that the Anglican Church "by opening itself to the glow of the old and true ideal of the Christian Gospel, by fidelity to reason, by placing the stress of its religion on goodness, by cultivating grace and peace . . . will inspire attachment . . ." and will endure.

"A Psychological Parallel," is, according to apRoberts, "a comprehensive reprise" of Arnold's religious works, for in this essay Arnold contends

that whether one accepts or denies the supernatural in religion, he can still be a Christian and a supporter of the Church. Arnold first explores the possibility that a man like St. Paul may believe in the miraculous and still not be "an imbecile or credulous enthusiast." Arnold compares the belief of St. Paul in "the bodily resurrection of Jesus," to the belief of Sir Matthew Hale, the eminent seventeenth-century judge, in the existence of witches. These "parallel" cases demonstrate that a man may be psychologically influenced by the intellectual atmosphere of the times in which he lives, in other words, by the Zeit-Geist. Consequently, he "may have his mind thoroughly governed, on certain subjects, by a foregone conclusion as to what is likely and credible." Just as it was commonplace in the seventeenth century to believe in witchcraft, it was commonplace in St. Paul's day to believe in such events as the physical resurrection of the body after death. Arnold explains, "That a man shares an error of the minds around him and of the times in which he lives, proves nothing against his being a man of veracity, judgment, and mental power."

Arnold considers next the possibility that a man may not believe the miraculous and still support the Church. He points out that though the Zeit-Geist of the nineteenth century has caused many Victorians to doubt the literal truth of Church teachings, this uncertainty should not prevent their belonging to the Church. They must remember that the Church is first and foremost "a national Christian society for the promotion of goodness," and they should support it as such. Arnold asserts that the Church's emphasis on dogma should be relaxed. He goes so far as to argue that clergymen should not be required to subscribe to the Thirty-nine Articles, for he suspects there are many who cannot profess acceptance of all thirty-nine statements who would nevertheless be committed ministers to the true message of Christianity. Yet Arnold contends that the Book of Common Prayer should be retained because for the masses of Englishmen, "It has created sentiments deeper than we can see or measure. Our feeling does not connect itself with *any* language about righteousness and religion, but with *that* language." In that sense, the prayer book is like the Bible. And Arnold advocates using it as one would use the Bible—accepting the literal truth of part and reading the rest as the poetic "approximations to a profound truth." Arnold concludes, "It is a great error to think that whatever is thus perceived to be poetry ceases to be available in religion. The noblest races are those which know how to make the most serious use of poetry."

Having abandoned the subject of religion after completing his *Last Essays*, Arnold focused his writing during the last ten to twelve years of his life on social and literary topics, offering more elaborate or definitive statements of his views on matters that had long held great interest for him. For instance, R. H. Super has said of "A French Critic on Milton" from *Mixed Essays* (1879), "As an essay on critical method, it stands in much the same relation to Arnold's later critical essays as 'The Function of Criticism' [does] to the earlier." Just as "The Function of Criticism" instructs man in the application of the critical approach to all aspects of life, "A French Critic on Milton" instructs the reader in the application of the critical approach to the evaluation of literature. Arnold sets about explaining the critical method by comparing several critics of Milton. He dismisses Macaulay's "Essay on Milton" as popular "rhetoric," as nothing more than a "panegyric" on Milton and the Puritans. He discards Addison's criticism of Milton as a compilation of conventional platitudes. He also finds Samuel Johnson unsatisfactory as a critic of Milton. Though he avoids the rhetoric and conventionality of Macaulay and Addison, Johnson is not "sufficiently disinterested" or "sufficiently receptive" to judge fairly. However, in Arnold's view there has been an admirable judge of Milton—the French critic Edmond Scherer, who is "Well-informed, intelligent, disinterested, open-minded, [and] sympathetic." Scherer noted the weaknesses of Milton as a man and as an artist. His views were not influenced by Milton's avowed religious convictions or by the religious subjects of his poems. Especially satisfying to Arnold is Scherer's recognition of Milton's "true distinction as a poet"—the greatness of his style. Arnold is convinced that this is the conclusion to which a sensitive yet impartial criticism necessarily leads.

Many of Arnold's other late essays also deal with literature, and more specifically, with sound criticism of literature. The best known of his later collections is *Essays in Criticism, Second Series*, which Arnold began discussing with his publisher in January 1888, but which was not actually printed until November 1888, seven months after Arnold's death. The volume includes nine essays: "The Study of Poetry," "Wordsworth," "Thomas Gray," "John Keats," "Byron," "Amiel,"

"Count Leo Tolstoi," "Shelley," and "Milton." One of the most important, "The Study of Poetry," first appeared in 1880 as the introduction to *The English Poets*, an anthology edited by T. Humphry Ward. R. H. Super reminds that the essay was intended "to give some guidance to a middle-class public not sophisticated in the reading of poetry...." In an opening explanation of the value of literature, Arnold makes grand claims for poetry, saying "we have to turn to poetry to interpret life for us, to console us, to sustain us." In other words, poetry meets the same human needs as religion. Of course, only the best poetry accomplishes so much: "poetry, to be capable of fulfilling such high destinies, must be poetry of a high order of excellence." But "the best poetry will be found to have a power of forming, sustaining, and delighting us, as nothing else can."

Because poetry has so much to offer, Arnold continues, the reader must have some way to recognize the finest poetry. Neither a purely historical nor a purely personal critical method will serve since each is too biased. Arnold proposes instead a comparative method by which the reader will always have in mind "lines and expressions of the great masters" that he may apply "as a touchstone to other poetry" to help him detect "the presence or absence of high poetic quality, and also the degree of this quality." Arnold maintains that the greatness of poetry is revealed in both substance and style. The substance of great poetry may be recognized by its "truth and seriousness" and the style of great poetry by its "superiority of diction and movement." Beyond these general assertions, Arnold refuses to define, arguing that concrete examples of exceptional poetry will be more helpful than abstract theory or lists of characteristics. He offers a critical overview of the history of English poetry sprinkled with illustrative lines and passages to demonstrate the touchstone method. Arnold begins with Chaucer, whose poetry he deems superior in substance and style, or, to be more exact, in the rich view of human life it presents and in the "divine liquidness of diction" and "divine fluidity of movement" of its manner. These traits make Chaucer "the father of our splendid English poetry"; nevertheless, he does not attain the level of "one of the great classics." Though his poetry has truth, it lacks "high seriousness."

Acknowledging that both Shakespeare and Milton unquestionably belong "to the class of the very best," Arnold moves on to consider the merits of more controversial poets–those of the eighteenth century. In Arnold's estimation, Dryden and Pope are masters of prose rather than verse, for the characteristics of their style, "regularity, uniformity, precision, [and] balance," produce classic prose, not classic poetry. In a separate essay, "Thomas Gray," Arnold maintains that "The difference between genuine poetry and the poetry of Dryden, Pope, and all their school, is briefly this: their poetry is conceived and composed in their wits, genuine poetry is conceived and composed in the soul." "The Study of Poetry" concludes with a discussion of the works of Robert Burns and Thomas Gray. In Arnold's opinion, Burns fails to achieve greatness for much the same reasons Chaucer fails. Like Chaucer, Burns depicts the largeness of life, but he too lacks high seriousness. Gray, on the other hand, is a classic–the only eighteenth-century English classic, Arnold thinks. Arnold credits him with achieving such eminence because he gave himself up to a study of the Greeks, absorbing the qualities of exceptional poetry from them.

"The Study of Poetry" no more remained unchallenged than had any of Arnold's other works. Many, including contemporary critics, have disagreed with Arnold's choice of touchstone passages, and many have taken offense at Arnold's pronouncements about the merits of individual authors. Despite such objections, the essay remains an important piece of criticism historically and an important guide to Arnold's own tastes.

The other essays from the second series of *Essays in Criticism* that are especially noteworthy are those about the romantic poets. While Arnold was fully aware of the limitations of purely personal criticism, his assessments of writers did involve some personal commentary. Such subjective evaluations surface in his essays on the romantics. Coleridge is referred to as a genius "wrecked in a mist of opium," and Shelley is described as a "beautiful and ineffectual angel, beating in the void his luminous wings in vain." In fact, Shelley more than the others troubled Arnold. When Edward Dowden's two-volume biography of the poet was published in 1886, Arnold found the poet's life so scandalous that he claimed the biography should never have been written. Arnold's objections were not restricted to questions of perceived immorality though; he also faulted authors for what he thought to be unattractive character traits. Keats, for example, Arnold

considered effusive. He seemed a "sensuous man of a badly bred and badly trained sort" who virtually allowed himself to die young, "having produced too little and being as yet too immature" to achieve greatness. Despite his aversion to some of their personal qualities, Arnold tried to examine writers' works objectively. Thus, although he considers Keats an immature poet, Arnold commends Keats's celebration of beauty and judges him Shakespeare's equal in the creation of "natural magic" in his poems.

The two romantics Arnold holds in highest esteem are Byron and Wordsworth, both of whom had failed to receive the serious appreciation Arnold thought they deserved. For some reason, Arnold was able to gloss over Byron's sins though he could not overlook Shelley's. He praises Byron at length for his stand on social injustice. In regard to Byron's poems, he shows special fondness for the shorter pieces and for select sections from the longer works, claiming he "has a wonderful power of vividly conceiving a single incident, a single situation. . . ." Arnold likewise asserts that Wordsworth's best poems are his shorter ones. He considers "Michael" and "The Highland Reaper" poems which afford "a criticism of life," far superior to "philosophical" poems such as *The Excursion* and *The Prelude*. Arnold declares, "Wordsworth's poetry is great because of the extraordinary power with which Wordsworth feels the joy offered to us in nature, the joy offered to us in the simple primary affections and duties; and because of the extraordinary power with which, in case after case, he shows us this joy, and renders it so as to make us share it." For these reasons, Arnold ranks Wordsworth only after Shakespeare, Molière, Milton, and Goethe in his list of the premier poets of "the last two or three centuries."

Of the other pieces Arnold wrote on literature in the last decade of his life, the major one was an essay entitled "Literature and Science." In the autumn of 1880 Thomas Henry Huxley, noted proponent of science and a friend of Arnold's, had presented a lecture in Birmingham on the necessity for scientific knowledge. That address was subsequently published in Huxley's *Science and Culture, and Other Essays* (1881). In it he argues against Arnold's notion that the agent of true culture is humanistic education. Huxley claims, "for the purpose of attaining real culture, an exclusively scientific education is at least as effectual as an exclusively literary education."

"Literature and Science" was Arnold's reply,

given as a lecture at Cambridge in June 1882 and published two months later in the *Nineteenth-Century*. In 1883 Arnold delivered the lecture twenty-nine times to eager audiences in the United States. Arnold is quick to clarify at the beginning of his remarks that in his lifelong insistence on a broad, liberal, classical education and in his advocacy of knowing the best that has been thought and said, he has not meant to suggest that science should be ignored. As Fred A. Dudley points out in a 1942 *PMLA* article, Arnold thought training in science would teach people perception and open-mindedness, qualities he valued highly. Therefore, education should include the study of both science and belles lettres in Arnold's opinion. Still, in the lecture, he disagrees with Huxley that science was just as valuable in transmitting culture as literature. The study of science, argues Arnold, satisfies only one of the demands of human nature–the need for knowledge. And knowledge in isolation does not fill the needs of the human spirit. According to Arnold, unless knowledge is "put for us into relation with our sense for conduct, our sense for beauty, and touched with emotion by being so put," it will become "to the majority of mankind, after a certain while, unsatisfying, wearying." Literature, both classical and modern, provides the requisite synthesis of knowledge to conduct and beauty. It has "a fortifying, and elevating, and quickening, and suggestive power, capable of wonderfully helping us to relate the results of modern science to our need for conduct, our need for beauty." In that respect, the humanities are not "mainly decorative." Therefore, while men should know both science and literature, Arnold concludes that if one has to choose between the two, he had best choose literature. He acknowledges that the value of studying the classics and belles lettres in general is presently being questioned, yet he predicts, "they will not lose their place. What will happen will rather be that there will be crowded into education other matters besides, far too many; there will be, perhaps, a period of unsettlement and confusion and false tendency; but letters will not in the end lose their leading place. If they lose it for a time, they will get it back again. We will be brought back to them by our wants and aspirations."

In addition to literature, Arnold's later works often treat social topics. In his preface to *Mixed Essays* (1879), Arnold explains that while the essays treat a wide range of subjects they are unified by their concern with the broader subject of civilization. Literature is one aspect of civilization, but only one. Arnold maintains that although literature is "a powerful agency for benefiting the world and for civilising it, . . . literature is a part of civilisation; it is not the whole." Repeating ideas first presented in his lecture "Equality" (February 1878), he defines civilization as "the humanisation of man in society," accomplished primarily by the human need for expansion which manifests itself in the love of liberty and the love of equality. Beyond this, civilization must satisfy man's need for conduct, for intellect and knowledge, for beauty, and for manners. Arnold's social essays examine the success of both England and the United States in fulfilling these needs.

"The Future of Liberalism" (collected in *Irish Essays, and Others*, 1882) provides an elaboration of Arnold's assessment of civilization in Victorian England. Ever critical of the middle class, Arnold asserts that the greatest threat to the future of the Liberal party is its base in Philistinism, for, says Arnold, the Liberals "lean especially upon the opinion of one great class,–the middle class,–with virtues of its own, indeed, but at the same time full of narrowness, full of prejudices; with a defective type of religion, a narrow range of intellect and knowledge, a stunted sense of beauty, a low standard of manners; and averse, moreover, to whatever may disturb it in its vulgarity." In other words, the middle class is virtually uncivilized and will remain so until forced to confront its imperfections. Even with its Philistine foundation, the Liberal party in fostering love of liberty has a more promising future than the Conservatives, who are primarily concerned with keeping order. In order to retain power and influence, the Liberals must not rest satisfied; they must recognize man's continual need for expansion and must work diligently to alleviate the social and political inequality which has resulted in "an upper class materialised, a middle class vulgarised, a lower class brutalised."

Because Arnold perceives Americans to be merely "English people on the other side of the Atlantic," he attributes to American society many of the same weaknesses he notes in British society. American civilization is the topic of "A Word About America," published in the *Nineteenth-Century* (1882). In this essay Arnold observes that a significant difference between England and the United States is that democracy is more advanced in the United States, leaving fewer citizens members of the barbarian and populace classes. Assuming then that the Philistines comprise "the great bulk of the nation," Arnold suggests for America the same civilizing agents he has repeatedly recommended for the British–improved schools and improved arts.

At the time Arnold wrote "A Word About America," he had never visited the United States, but a year later, in 1883, having received an invitation from the Pittsburgh iron magnate Andrew Carnegie, Arnold, accompanied by his wife and daughter Lucy, sailed to America. The six months spent there were hectic ones, for Arnold was engaged in an extensive and demanding lecture tour in the course of which he met William Dean Howells, Oliver Wendell Holmes, John Greenleaf Whittier, and Mark Twain. Arnold's daughter Lucy also made new acquaintances, including that of Frederick Whitridge whom she married a year later. His daughter's move to New York motivated Arnold to make another trip to the United States just after he retired from school inspecting in May 1886.

Thus Arnold had paid two extended visits to America when he lectured on "Life in America" in January 1888. His remarks, published in April in the *Nineteenth-Century* under the title "Civilisation in the United States," reflect little change in the position he had outlined six years earlier. Arnold argues that while Americans have established a laudable democratic social system and have proven successful in commerce and industry, they have not cultivated beauty. Arnold cites the inferiority of American architecture, painting, and literature as evidence. Even American place names such as Briggsville, Higginsville, and Jacksonville indicate to him an inadequate national regard for the beautiful. He contends, "The Americans have produced plenty of men strong, shrewd, upright, able, effective; [but] very few who are highly distinguished." This situation is hardly surprising since the democratic system with its "glorification of 'the average man'" makes distinction rare. Arnold is convinced of the value of heritage and established culture and says that Americans apparently desire it since "all Americans of cultivation and wealth visit Europe more and more constantly." Arnold summarizes: "The human problem, then, is as yet solved in the United States most imperfectly; a great void exists in the civilisation over there: a want of what is elevated and beautiful, of what is interesting."

"Civilisation in the United States" was the last essay by Matthew Arnold to be published in his lifetime. He died suddenly of a heart attack on 15 April 1888. John Holloway's remarks on Arnold's style and rhetorical technique in his 1953 book *The Victorian Sage* provide a fitting summary of Arnold's prose. Holloway points out that Arnold "had no rigid doctrines to argue for, only attitudes." He argued for the cultivation of "certain habits and a certain temper of mind." Arnold, quite naturally, set himself as a model. It was essential that he present himself as the kind of person he most admired–"intelligent, modest, and urbane." As Holloway observes, in Arnold's prose, it is "his handling of problems" that is more important than his solutions to them. One of Arnold's contemporaries, John Burroughs, writing two months after Arnold's death, claimed that Matthew Arnold deserved to be read extensively, for only then could he be fully appreciated. In the prose "His effect is cumulative; he hits a good many times in the same place, and his work as a whole makes a deeper impression than any single essay of his would seem to warrant." The modern reader will still find much to savor in the prose of Matthew Arnold.

Letters:

Letters of Matthew Arnold, 1848-1888, edited by G. W. E. Russell, 2 volumes (London: Macmillan, 1895);

Unpublished Letters of Matthew Arnold, edited by Arnold Whitridge (New Haven: Yale University Press, 1923);

The Letters of Matthew Arnold to Arthur Hugh Clough, edited by H. F. Lowry (London & New York: Oxford University Press, 1932);

Matthew Arnold's Letters: A Descriptive Checklist, edited by A. K. Davis, Jr. (Charlottesville: University Press of Virginia, 1968).

Bibliographies:

Thomas B. Smart, *Bibliography of Matthew Arnold* (London: Davy, 1892);

Theodore G. Ehrsam, Robert H. Deily, and Robert M. Smith, eds., *Bibliographies of Twelve Victorian Authors* (New York: Wilson, 1936);

Vincent L. Tollers, ed., *A Bibliography of Matthew Arnold, 1932-1970* (University Park: Pennsylvania State University Press, 1974).

Biographies:

George Saintsbury, *Matthew Arnold* (New York: Dodd, Mead, 1899);

Lionel Trilling, *Matthew Arnold* (New York: Meridian Books, 1939);

E. K. Chambers, *Matthew Arnold: A Study* (Oxford: Clarendon Press, 1947);

A. L. Rowse, *Matthew Arnold: Poet and Prophet* (London: Thames & Hudson, 1976);

Park Honan, *Matthew Arnold, A Life* (New York: McGraw-Hill, 1981).

References:

Warren D. Anderson, *Matthew Arnold and the Classical Tradition* (Ann Arbor: University of Michigan Press, 1965);

Ruth apRoberts, *Arnold and God* (Berkeley: University of California Press, 1983);

Josephine Barry, "Goethe and Arnold's 1853 Preface," *Comparative Literature*, 32 (Spring 1980): 151-167;

E. K. Brown, *Matthew Arnold: A Study in Conflict* (Toronto & Chicago: University of Chicago Press, 1948);

William Buckler, ed., *Matthew Arnold's Books: Towards a Publishing Diary* (Geneva: Droz Press, 1958);

Buckler, *Matthew Arnold's Prose: Three Essays in Literary Enlargement* (New York: A.M.S. Press, 1983);

Buckler, "Studies in Three Arnold Problems," *PMLA*, 73 (1958): 260-269;

Vincent Buckley, *Poetry and Morality: Studies on the Criticism of Matthew Arnold, T. S. Eliot, and F. R. Leavis* (London: Chatto & Windus, 1959);

Douglas Bush, *Matthew Arnold: A Survey of His Poetry and Prose* (New York: Macmillan, 1971);

Joseph Carroll, *The Cultural Theory of Matthew Arnold* (Berkeley: University of California Press, 1982);

W. F. Connell, *The Educational Thought and Influence of Matthew Arnold* (London: Routledge & Kegan Paul, 1950);

Sidney Coulling, *Matthew Arnold and His Critics: A Study of Arnold's Controversies* (Athens: Ohio University Press, 1974);

A. Dwight Culler, *The Imaginative Reason: The Poetry of Matthew Arnold* (New Haven: Yale University Press, 1966);

Carl Dawson and John Pfordresher, eds., *Matthew Arnold: Prose Writings* (London: Routledge & Kegan Paul, 1979);

David J. DeLaura, *Hebrew and Hellene in Victorian England* (Austin: University of Texas Press, 1969);

DeLaura, "Matthew Arnold," in *Victorian Prose: A Guide to Research*, edited by DeLaura (New York: Modern Language Association, 1973), pp. 249-320;

Robert Donovan, "The Method of Arnold's *Essays in Criticism*," *PMLA*, 71 (December 1956): 922-931;

Fred A. Dudley, "Matthew Arnold and Science," *PMLA*, 57 (March 1942): 275-294;

T. S. Eliot, "Matthew Arnold," in his *The Use of Poetry and the Use of Criticism* (London: Faber & Faber, 1933), pp. 103-120;

Frederic E. Faverty, "Matthew Arnold," in *The Victorian Poets: A Guide to Research*, edited by Faverty (Cambridge: Harvard University Press, 1968), pp. 164-226;

Faverty, *Matthew Arnold the Ethnologist* (Evanston: Northwestern University Press, 1951);

"The Function of Matthew Arnold at the Present Time," a series of essays by Eugene Goodheart, George Levine, Morris Dickstein, and Stuart M. Tave published as part of a special issue of *Critical Inquiry*, 9 (March 1983);

Leon Gottfried, *Matthew Arnold and the Romantics* (London: Routledge & Kegan Paul, 1963);

W. B. Guthrie, ed., *Matthew Arnold's Diaries: The Unpublished Items* (Ann Arbor: University of Michigan Press, 1959);

John Holloway, "Matthew Arnold," in his *The Victorian Sage* (London: Macmillan, 1953), pp. 202-243;

E. D. H. Johnson, *The Alien Vision of Victorian Poetry: Sources of the Poetic Imagination in Tennyson, Browning, and Arnold* (Princeton: Princeton University Press, 1952);

James C. Livingston, *Matthew Arnold and Christianity: His Religious Prose Writings* (Columbia: University of South Carolina Press, 1986);

William A. Madden, *A Study of the Aesthetic Temperament in Victorian England* (Bloomington: Indiana University Press, 1967);

Patrick J. McCarthy, *Matthew Arnold and the Three Classes* (New York: Columbia University Press, 1964);

J. Hillis Miller, "Matthew Arnold," in his *The Disappearance of God* (Cambridge: Harvard University Press, 1963), pp. 212-269;

Fraser Neiman, *Matthew Arnold* (New York: Twayne, 1968);

William Robbins, *The Ethical Idealism of Matthew Arnold: A Study of the Nature and Sources of His Moral and Religious Ideas* (Toronto: University of Toronto Press, 1959);

Alan Roper, *Arnold's Poetic Landscapes* (Baltimore:

Johns Hopkins University Press, 1969);

James Simpson, *Matthew Arnold and Goethe* (London: Modern Humanities Research Association, 1979);

G. Robert Stange, *Matthew Arnold: The Poet as Humanist* (Princeton: Princeton University Press, 1967);

Robert H. Super, *The Time-Spirit of Matthew Arnold* (Ann Arbor: University of Michigan Press, 1970);

Kathleen Tillotson, "Arnold and Carlyle," *Proceedings of the British Academy*, 42 (1956): 133-153;

C. B. Tinker and H. F. Lowry, *The Poetry of Matthew Arnold: A Commentary* (London & New York: Oxford University Press, 1940);

Basil Willey, *Nineteenth-Century Studies: Coleridge to Matthew Arnold* (London: Chatto & Windus, 1949);

Raymond Williams, *Culture and Society, 1780-1950* (New York: Columbia University Press, 1958).

Papers:

Major collections of Arnold's papers are at the Beinecke Library, Yale University, and at the University of Virginia. Yale has notebooks, diaries, commonplace books, literary manuscripts, and over 200 letters. The Arthur Kyle Davis Papers at Virginia include mainly letters.

Charles Bradlaugh

(26 September 1833-30 January 1891)

Sandy Feinstein
Southwestern College

SELECTED BOOKS: *A Few Words on the Christians' Creed,* as Iconoclast (London: Privately printed, 1850);

The Bible, What It Is, as Iconoclast (London, 1857);

Has Man a Soul?, as Iconoclast (London, 1859);

Who Was Jesus Christ?, as Iconoclast (London, 1859; New York: Butts, 1890?);

New Life of Abraham, as Iconoclast (London, 1860; New York: Butts, 189?);

New Life of Jacob, as Iconoclast (London, 1861; New York: Butts, 188?);

A Few Words About the Devil, as Iconoclast (London, 1861; New York: Butts, 1874);

Jesus, Shelley, and Malthus: An Essay on the Population Question, as Iconoclast (London, 1861);

Were Adam and Eve our First Parents?, as Iconoclast (London: Privately printed, 1861);

Poverty: Its Effect on the Political Condition of the People, as Iconoclast (London, 1863);

A Plea for Atheism, as Iconoclast (London, 1864; New York: Butts, 188?);

Labour's Prayer, as Iconoclast (London, 1865);

Why Do Men Starve?, as Iconoclast (London: Privately printed, 1865);

George, Prince of Wales, with Recent Contrasts and Coincidences (London: Privately printed, 1870);

The Land, the People and the Coming Struggle (London, 1871; revised, 1882);

The Impeachment of the House of Brunswick (London, 1872; revised, London: Austin, 1873; Boston: Gill, 1875);

The Autobiography of C. Bradlaugh. A Page of His Life (London, 1873);

Taxation: How It Originated, How It is Spent, and Who Bears It (London, 1878);

Hints to Emigrants to the United States of America (London: Freethought Publishing, 1879);

Perpetual Pensions (London: Freethought Publishing, 1880);

The True Story of My Parliamentary Struggle (London: Freethought Publishing, 1882);

Genesis: Its Authorship and Authenticity (London: Freethought Publishing, 1882);

Debate Between H. M. Hyndman and Charles Bradlaugh. Will Socialism Benefit the English People? (London: Privately printed, 1884);

Northampton and the House of Commons. Correspondence Between Charles Bradlaugh, M.P., and the Right Hon. Sir Stafford Northcote, M.P.

(London: Privately printed, 1884);

John Churchill, Duke of Marlborough, 'The Mob', 'the Scum', and 'the Dregs' (London: Freethought Publishing, 1884);

England's Balance Sheet (London: Freethought Publishing, 1884);

The Atheistic Platform VIII. Some Objections to Socialism (London, 1884);

How Are We to Abolish the Lords? (London: Freethought Publishing, 1884; revised, 1890);

The Radical Programme (London, 1885);

Capital and Labour (London: Freethought Publishing, 1886);

Appeal to the Electors. Mr. Gladstone or Lord Salisbury: Which? (London: Freethought Publishing, 1886);

The Atheistic Platform IV. England's Balance Sheet for 1886 (London: Freethought Publishing, 1886);

A Letter to the Right Hon. Lord Randolph S. Churchill, M.P., Chancellor of the Exchequer (London, 1886);

Compulsory Cultivation of Land; What it Means, and Why it Ought to be Enforced (London: Freethought Publishing, 1887);

Socialism: Its Fallacies and Dangers (London: Freethought Publishing, 1887);

Notes on the Christian Evidences (London: Freethought Publishing, 1887);

The Channel Tunnel: Ought the Democracy to Oppose or Support It? (London: Bonner, 1887);

Socialism: For and Against, by Bradlaugh and Annie Besant (London: Freethought Publishing, 1887);

Employers' Liability Bill. Letter to Thomas Burt, M.P. (London, 1888);

Northampton's Voice on the Royal Grants (London: Bonner, 1889);

Parliament and the Poor: What the Legislature Can Do; What it Ought to Do (London, 1889);

The Rules, Customs and Procedures of the House of Commons (London: Sonnenschein, 1889);

The Eight Hours' Movement (London, 1889);

Speeches by Charles Bradlaugh (London: Freethought Publishing, 1890);

Labour and Law (London: Forder, 1891).

OTHER: *Half-Hours with the Freethinkers,* edited by Bradlaugh as Iconoclast and John Watts, first series (London: Watts, 1856-1857); second series (London: Watts, 1865).

Charles Bradlaugh's importance in the Victorian Age is as a man of radical ideas and actions,

Charles Bradlaugh, 1890 (photograph by Elliott & Fry)

not as a belletrist. According to his obituary in the *Yorkshire Evening Post,* "His place in the history of the nineteenth century will be very distinct, more distinct, perhaps, than that of any single figure to be met with in its annals." Bradlaugh's most recent biographer, David Tribe, succinctly summarizes the reason for Bradlaugh's profound historical impact: Bradlaugh "laid the foundation of lasting political and social change. He deserves at least a portion of the credit for obtaining the rubber-stamp House of Lords and monarchy, the freedom of speech and publication, the planned families, the television satire, even the 'permissive society'; . . . not only did he make myriads of silent converts and marginally stir the great apathetic masses, he forced the opposition to rethink their basic positions and rephrase their apologetics."

Bradlaugh expressed his influential views in scores of periodical articles and pamphlets. Many of these were pseudonymously published; many were privately printed and are exceedingly rare or not extant today, so that compilation of an exhaustive bibliography of Bradlaugh's published works is virtually impossible.

Charles Bradlaugh, the eldest son of Charles and Elizabeth Trimby Bradlaugh, was born 26 September 1833 in Bacchus Walk, Hoxton. He was almost entirely self-educated, his formal education having been completed by age eleven at a boys' school in Coalharbor Street, Hackney Road. By age twelve he was working, first as an errand boy in the solicitor's office where his father was employed, then as a wharf clerk and cashier to a firm of coal merchants. These two early occupations influenced his later career: he became a great amateur lawyer, successfully arguing the bulk of his many cases; he represented the concerns of miners and actively supported their efforts to unionize.

Bradlaugh's first political action was unintended, but one that had a crucial effect on his writing, his politics, and his activism. In 1848, when Bradlaugh was a fifteen-year-old Sunday school teacher, his parish priest, the Reverend John Graham Packer, asked his star pupil to prepare for the bishop's attendance by studying the four Gospels and the Thirty-nine Articles of the Church of England. After closely studying these religious documents, Bradlaugh was dismayed to find contradictions between the two texts. When he voiced his concern in a letter, his query was denounced as atheistic, and he was suspended for three months from his Sunday school office.

This adolescent experience marked the beginning of Bradlaugh's active and controversial political life. He soon found himself drawn to Bonner's Field to listen to Chartists and Freethinkers. Listening led to participation, participation to leadership; by age seventeen, he began to lead debates, first in the cause of Christianity, later in the cause of teetotaling and atheism. Bradlaugh prepared for these debates by reading widely and carefully; he came armed with facts and references. Hungry for knowledge, he taught himself French, Hebrew, Greek, and Arabic. At his death, he was found to have accumulated over 6,000 books.

Bradlaugh's first publication, however, suggested his personal experience more than his extensive reading. His first pamphlet, *A Few Words on the Christians' Creed,* was written in 1850 and dedicated to the Reverend Packer, the priest who had castigated him for questioning the sacred texts of the faith. In this pamphlet Bradlaugh compares God to "bigoted parsons of the

day," an apparent reference to Packer; he also argues the absurdity of the orthodox Trinity and of the Incarnation. Although a crude and unsophisticated work, it did excite a response in the *British Banner:* the lead article, written by a Dr. Campbell, denounced Bradlaugh's leaflet.

Without money and friends, expelled from his family as a result of Packer's interference, Bradlaugh enlisted in the Seventh Dragoon Guards, where he remained until October 1853. His corps was stationed in Ireland, and while he was there he concerned himself with the miseries of the Irish people, especially the inequities of the landlords and the question of home rule. During this time he did not write any pamphlets, though he frequently lectured on teetotaling while in Dublin.

After his family purchased his discharge from the military, he returned to England, again obtaining employment with a solicitor. To protect his employer from censure, he published under the pseudonym Iconoclast until 1868, the end of the period of his strongest antitheological works and the beginning of his efforts to enter Parliament. In 1855 Bradlaugh began his unsuccessful

Bradlaugh in the 1860s when he wrote under the pseudonym Iconoclast

marriage to Susannah Lamb Hooper, with whom he eventually had three children. The youngest, Charles, died of scarlet fever soon after the Bradlaughs separated, Susannah moving back to her father's Sussex home in 1870. Although the Bradlaughs' marriage seemed promising at first—Susannah Hooper's father was a strong supporter of Bradlaugh, a freethinker, and an ex-Chartist—Susannah became an alcoholic and lived more extravagantly than her husband could afford. When she died in 1877, the couple's two daughters, Hypatia and Alice, moved in with their father in London and remained devoted to him for the rest of his life.

In 1856, the year after his marriage, with a group of others Bradlaugh began a series of papers entitled *Half-Hours with the Freethinkers*. He also wrote a commentary on the Pentateuch, which he revised for publication in 1857 under the title *The Bible, What It Is*. Writing for the *National Reformer* in 1863 Bradlaugh described his intention in these and other antitheological works: "I have attacked the Bible; but never the letter alone; the Church, but never have I confined myself to a mere assault on its practices. I have deemed that I attacked theology best in asserting most the fulness of humanity. I have regarded iconoclasticism as a means, not as an end. The work is weary, but the end is well." At least one critic, though, has questioned that view; for Walter L. Arnstein, in his 1965 book *The Bradlaugh Case*, Bradlaugh's "forte lay in oratory and to a lesser degree in popular pamphleteering."

Bradlaugh was actively concerned with social and political as well as theological issues. He lectured in support of Garibaldi; he went to Italy in part to help the patriots, to Spain to express sympathy for the struggle to establish a republic; he took the French side in the Prussian conflict and received honors from France for his efforts; he defended the right of assembly in the streets and in the courts. To disseminate these and other ideas, in 1861 he founded the *National Reformer*, described by his daughter and biographer, Hypatia Bradlaugh Bonner, as "not merely a weekly journal, ... but my father's voice, my father's sword, my father's shield."

One of Bradlaugh's works in which the political and antitheological meet is *Jesus, Shelley, and Malthus: An Essay on the Population Question* (1861). In this early pamphlet, Bradlaugh explains why he must assail Jesus: "The Gospel doctrines are claimed as the central point upon which all morality must rest and the circle within which all teach-

ing must be limited." He sees Jesus as representing "thought fettered"; Shelley as representing free thought, "learning but not yet learned ... honest, but sometimes erring"; Malthus as representing "the special application of educated thought to the relief of the human family from at least some of the many evils under which its members suffer." This work also introduces a key issue for Bradlaugh, that of birth control, a subject he returns to in two 1865 pamphlets, *Why Do Men Starve?* and *Labour's Prayer*. He argues for teaching birth control and political economy as a way to raise the masses from the poverty that he believes Christianity seeks to justify. In the 1865 essays, and in *Poverty: Its Effect on the Political Condition of the People*, first published in the *National Reformer* in 1863, he quotes John Stuart Mill to support his argument that political economy and self-education must be encouraged to awaken the poor and alleviate their misery.

Mill returned Bradlaugh's admiration by supporting his first, unsuccessful attempt in 1868 to enter Parliament as the member from Northampton. He also commended his efforts against censorship, specifically his challenge to the law requiring sureties against "blasphemous or seditious libel." Bradlaugh's protest took the form of releasing an issue of the *National Reformer* with the inscription "printed in Defiance of Her Majesty's Government." When he was taken to court for disregarding the law and failing to yield the required sureties, he argued his own case and won. He was less lucky in his election efforts; he lost the vote again in 1874.

Another incident in which he defended the right of a free press occurred in 1877 when Bradlaugh and his coeditor Annie Besant republished *Fruits of Philosophy* by the American author and physician Charles Knowlton. This work openly discusses birth control, a subject so shocking at the time that the controversy attending Bradlaugh's and Besant's republication of Knowlton's work reached its height in one of the most significant trials of Victorian English history. While he and Mrs. Besant were exonerated from "any corrupt motive," the book was found to be "technically an obscene publication." The trial naturally drew more attention to the work than it would have received without such publicity.

Before and after the publication of Knowlton's book, Bradlaugh was no stranger to the courts. In 1855 Bradlaugh began a history of litigation and argument that was not to end until his death. In 1855 he argued at Westminster for the right to assemble in Hyde Park; in 1859 he defended himself successfully against a charge of disturbing the peace and breaking into a hall that he had contracted to use for a meeting; he argued numerous free speech cases. The two most important cases in which he was involved anticipate his later problems in parliamentary politics. In 1868 he argued against the sureties required of newspapers for the purpose of preventing blasphemous or seditious libel. In successfully rebutting such a charge aimed at silencing him, he struck an important blow for freedom of the press. In another case, in which Bradlaugh was a plaintiff in the Court of Common Pleas, the evidence he presented provoked an objection on the grounds that he was an atheist, whose sworn oath could have no credibility. Bradlaugh's victory in this case resulted in the Evidence Amendment Act (1869) and the Evidence Further Amendment Act (1870), which, in Bradlaugh's words, "gave Free-

thinkers the right to enter the witness box."

The controversy surrounding the publication of Knowlton's *Fruits of Philosophy* and of Bradlaugh's own bold pamphlets followed him into election politics. His opponents cast doubt on his honesty, morality, and loyalty, based on his controversial publications. The Liberal and Radical working-class electorate of Northampton, however, finally elected Bradlaugh in 1880. Once elected, Bradlaugh requested the right to affirm his allegiance rather than take the oath–a right he had won in the courts. This issue marked the beginning of an important parliamentary struggle, perhaps the most important in Bradlaugh's political and personal life. A committee of inquiry was formed and decided against his right to affirm; as a result, he planned to take the oath, but he made the mistake of publicly announcing–in a printed letter–that certain words in the oath were meaningless to him, though the oath itself would be binding. The speaker, however, denied him this course of

AUGUST 3RD 1881   MARCH 14TH 1888

Cartoon from St. Stephen's Review, *24 March 1888, depicting Bradlaugh's struggle to obtain passage of the Oaths Bill, which held that any person who refused to take an oath because of his atheism or his religious beliefs "shall be permitted to make his solemn affirmation instead of taking an oath in all places and for all purposes where an oath is or shall be required by law. . . ."*

action, too. The six-year struggle over his right to take his parliamentary seat became a central issue in his life and in England's courts and newspapers. Bradlaugh was eventually seated after numerous court cases, debates, parliamentary votes, reelections, and the involvement of the most important political figures of the time, including William Gladstone, Lord Randolph Churchill, John Morley, Cardinal John Henry Newman, and Queen Victoria. In the first Parliament of 1886 the new speaker of the house administered the oath and refused to allow any protest. Two years later Bradlaugh won passage of an affirmation bill, assuring that there would never be a replay of the debacle that frustrated him and his opponents.

During the fight, though, various of his publications resurfaced and were used to denigrate his character. Not only were his antitheological and birth-control publications used against him but his most important political pamphlets were also cited, misquoted, and regularly referred to out of context. The pamphlet most often cited by his critics was *The Impeachment of the House of Brunswick*, serialized in the *National Reformer* in 1871, published in pamphlet form in 1872 and in a revised edition in 1873. In this work Bradlaugh attacks the rights and prerogatives, the actions and behavior of the House of Brunswick, including Queen Victoria, her consort, and her children. Although in general Bradlaugh is a humorless writer, his satiric streak emerges in exclamatory refrains of "Honest family, these Brunswick" or "And this is the Brunswick family to which the English nation are required to be blindly loyal." This history devotes separate chapters to each monarch and carefully charts the monarchs' demands for funds, then the use, misuse, and abuse of these funds. Bradlaugh is fastidious about documenting expenditures, repeated requests for funds, adulterous relationships, alcoholic binges, and gambling forays; he also describes actions of the crown against civil liberties.

In his pamphlets Bradlaugh usually quoted figures, documented sources, and countered his critics with facts; in short, he was a careful researcher. And while he was not an elegant writer, he was a creditable one. He plods methodically from expenditure to expenditure, incident to incident, law to law, and point to point. It is easy to see why his opponents had such difficulty refuting his arguments and often chose personal attack rather than intelligent rebuttal.

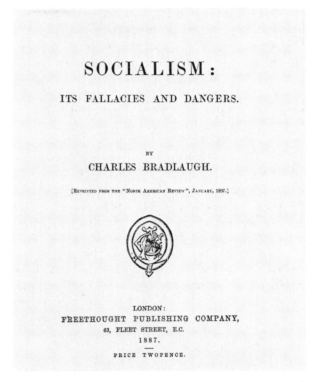

SOCIALISM:

ITS FALLACIES AND DANGERS.

BY

CHARLES BRADLAUGH.

[REPRINTED FROM THE "NORTH AMERICAN REVIEW", JANUARY, 1887.]

LONDON:
FREETHOUGHT PUBLISHING COMPANY,
63, FLEET STREET, E.C.
1887.

PRICE TWOPENCE.

Title page for the pamphlet in which Bradlaugh argued against Socialist advocacy of violent revolution

Attacks stemmed from his criticism of the royal family almost as often as they did from his endorsement of atheism and proposed social reforms such as birth control. Throughout his career he tried to weaken the royal power by challenging the House of Lords and the authority of the monarch. In *George, Prince of Wales, with Recent Contrasts and Coincidences*, published in 1870, well before his parliamentary imbroglio, he exposes the profligacy of the Prince of Wales by comparing him to his predecessor, the equally profligate son of George III. While fighting for his seat in Parliament in 1884, he published *How Are We to Abolish the Lords?* In this work, he recognizes the impossibility of dissolving the House of Lords, but he argues for at least diluting its power. He desires to convert the House of Lords "into a good senate" but worries that the only way to abolish the lords is by violent revolution, which he adamantly opposes.

Bradlaugh wrote his least controversial work, *Hints to Emigrants to the United States of America*, in 1879, before the frustration and fatigue of his parliamentary struggle. This work was written partly from correspondence and partly from experience; he had twice lectured in America to allay the ever-mounting debts and expenses accrued from almost constant litigation. In *Hints to Emigrants*, though Bradlaugh's scope is limited, he describes various American cities in detail. The work is divided into chapters focusing on cities in the eastern and midwestern states. He considers employment possibilities, wages, benefits, even the weather, and compares the state of employment in America to that in England. His touch is lighter than usual, perhaps because he was impressed by so many features of American life, including the charter of the University of Michigan promising free education "to all persons of either sex," the various kinds of housing available, and the harshness of winter.

Although Bradlaugh wrote primarily for radical causes and was in the vanguard on those issues, he rejected socialism vociferously. His later pamphlets are largely concerned with the new Socialist political party. These are not his strongest essays, for they too often nitpick, disregarding the spirit and intention of the new radicalism. His most famous argument against socialism is the 1884 debate with H. M. Hyndman, *Will Socialism Benefit the English People?*, which gave Socialist ideas an important early forum. Bradlaugh's main quarrel with socialism was its advocacy of violent revolution, which he considers in *Socialism: Its Fallacies and Dangers* (1887). His conservative views on socialism gained him new respect from the popular press. As Bernard Shaw pointed out in *The Quintessence of Ibsenism* (1891), "Bradlaugh had been the subject of many sorts of newspaper notices in his time. Thirty years ago, when the middle classes supposed him to be a revolutionist, the string of qualities which the press hung upon him were all evil ones, great stress being laid on the fact that as he was an Atheist, it would be an insult to God to admit him to Parliament. When it became apparent that he was an anti-socialist force in politics, he, without any recantation of his atheism, at once had the string of evil qualities exchanged for a rosary of good ones; but it is hardly necessary to add that neither the old badge or the new could ever give any inquirer the least clue to the sort of man he actually was. . . ."

On 13 January 1891 Bradlaugh suffered a cardiac asthma attack. He had constant medical attention and even, ironically, prayers. Throughout his short career in Parliament, Bradlaugh had worked to expunge the original resolution of 23 June 1880 declaring him ineligible to take the oath or affirm. While Bradlaugh lay in a coma, the motion passed at Gladstone's urging. At 6:30 A.M. on 30 January, Bradlaugh died of chronic renal disease and uremia. On 3 February 5,000 mourners gathered for the funeral at Brookwood Cemetery where, at Bradlaugh's request, not a word was spoken.

Until the end of his life, Bradlaugh's detractors were many; either he was too radical or not radical enough. On the one hand, Karl Marx dismissed him as the "huge self-idolator." On the other, Matthew Arnold saw him as "evidently capable, if he had his head given him, of running us all into great dangers and confusion." While Arnold and Marx attacked Bradlaugh's political action, Sir Henry Tyler condemned his writing as "cheap and pernicious literature" distributed "among the mass of people"; he "had poisoned and was poisoning the souls of millions of his fellow creatures." The 1920 edition of Oliver Elton's *A Survey of English Literature 1830-1880* explains that Bradlaugh was considered "an aggressive radical, atheist, and outlaw" with many "negative opinions." More recent criticism, too, has dealt almost exclusively with his colorful reputation and life rather than with his work.

Nevertheless, Bradlaugh's work is clearly important. The ideas for which he fought then are at the foundation of Western society today: equality for women, birth control, republicanism, land reform, labor reform, compulsory education, home rule, alleviation of poverty. Though his ideas have been appropriated, he probably never will be widely read, for his prose is serviceable and serious, little more. But as a dynamic personality who worked through the system to achieve his goals he is not likely to be forgotten.

Biographies:

Adolphe S. Headingly, *The Biography of Charles Bradlaugh* (London: Freethought Publishing, 1883);

Charles R. Mackay, *Life of Charles Bradlaugh, M.P.* (London: Gunn, 1888);

Hypatia Bradlaugh Bonner and John M. Robertson, *Charles Bradlaugh: A Record of his Life and Work*, 2 volumes (London: Unwin, 1898);

J. M. Robertson, *Life-Stories of Famous Men: Charles Bradlaugh* (London: Watts, 1920);

David Tribe, *President Charles Bradlaugh, M.P.* (London: Elek, 1971).

References:

Walter L. Arnstein, *The Bradlaugh Case: A Study in Late Victorian Opinion and Politics* (Oxford:

Clarendon Press, 1965);

Champion of Liberty: Charles Bradlaugh (Centenary Volume) (London: Watts, 1933);

S. Chandrasekhar, *"A Dirty Filthy Book": The Writings of Charles Knowlton and Annie Besant on Reproductive Physiology and Birth Control and an account of the Bradlaugh-Besant Trial* (Berke-ley: University of California Press, 1981);

Janet E. Courtney, *Freethinkers of the Nineteenth Century* (London: Chapman & Hall, 1920);

Preface to *A Selection of the Political . . . A Selection of the Political Pamphlets of Charles Bradlaugh,* edited by John Saville (New York: Augustus M. Kelley, 1970).

Samuel Butler

(4 December 1835-18 June 1902)

Hans-Peter Breuer
University of Delaware

See also the Butler entry in *DLB 18, Victorian Novelists After 1885.*

BOOKS: *A First Year in Canterbury Settlement* (London: Longmans, Green, 1863; New York: Dutton, 1915);

The Evidence for the Resurrection of Jesus Christ, as Given by the Four Evangelists, Critically Examined, anonymous (London: Williams & Norgate, 1865);

Erewhon; or, Over the Range, anonymous (London: Trübner, 1872; revised, 1872; republished under Butler's name, 1873; revised again, London: Richards, 1901; New York: Dutton, 1910);

The Fair Haven: A Work in Defence of the Miraculous Element in Our Lord's Ministry upon Earth, both as against Rationalistic Impugners and Certain Orthodox Defenders, by the Late J. P. Owen, Edited by W. B. Owen, with a Memoir of the Author, anonymous (London: Trübner, 1873; New York: Kennerly, 1913);

Life and Habit: An Essay after a Completer View of Evolution (London: Trübner, 1877; New York: Dutton, 1910);

Evolution, Old and New: or the Theories of Buffon, Dr. Erasmus Darwin, and Lamarck, as Compared with That of Mr. Charles Darwin (London: Hardwicke & Bogue, 1879; Salem, Mass.: Cassino, 1879; revised, London: Bogue, 1882; revised again, London: Fifield, 1911; New York: Dutton, 1914);

Unconscious Memory: A Comparison between the The-

Samuel Butler, self-portrait at age twenty-nine (courtesy of the Chapin Library, Williams College, Williamstown, Massachusetts)

ory of Dr. Ewald Hering, Professor of Physiology at Prague, and the Philosophy of the Unconscious of Dr. Edward von Hartmann; with Translations from these Authors (London: Bogue, 1880; New York: Dutton, 1910);

Alps and Sanctuaries of Piedmont and the Canton Ticino (London: Bogue, 1881; enlarged, London: Fifield, 1913; New York: Dutton, 1913);

Selections from Previous Works, with Remarks on Mr. G. J. Romanes' "Mental Evolution in Animals," and a Psalm of Montreal (London: Trübner, 1884);

Gavottes, Minuets, Fugues, and Other Short Pieces for the Piano, by Butler and Henry Festing Jones (London: Novello, Ewer, 1885);

Luck or Cunning as the Main Means of Organic Modification? An Attempt to Throw Additional Light upon the Late Mr. Charles Darwin's Theory of Natural Selection (London: Fifield, 1886);

Ex Voto: An Account of the Sacro Monte or New Jerusalem at Varallo-Sesia, with Some Notice of Tabachetti's Remaining Work at the Sanctuary of Crea (London: Trübner, 1888; revised and enlarged, 1889; London & New York: Longmans, Green, 1890);

Narcissus: A Dramatic Cantata in Vocal Score, With a Separate Accompaniment for the Piano-forte, by Butler and Jones (London: Weekes, 1888);

A Lecture on the Humour of Homer, January 30th 1892; Reprinted with a Preface and Additional Matter from the "Eagle" (Cambridge: Metcalfe, 1892);

On the Trapanese Origin of the "Odyssey" (Cambridge: Metcalfe, 1893);

The Life and Letters of Dr. Samuel Butler, Headmaster of Shrewsbury School 1798-1836, and Afterwards Bishop of Lichfield, 2 volumes (London: Murray, 1896; New York: Dutton, 1924);

The Authoress of the "Odyssey," Where and When She Wrote, Who She Was, the Use She Made of the "Iliad," and How the Poem Grew under Her Hands (London & New York: Longmans, Green, 1897; New York: Dutton, 1922);

Shakespeare's Sonnets Reconsidered, and in Part Rearranged; with Introductory Chapters, Notes, and a Reprint of the Original 1609 Edition (London & New York: Longmans, Green, 1899);

Erewhon Revisited Twenty Years Later, both by the Original Discoverer of the Country and by His Son (London: Richards, 1901; New York: Dutton, 1910);

The Way of All Flesh, edited by R. A. Streatfeild (London: Richards, 1903; New York: Dutton, 1910);

Essays on Life, Art, and Science, edited by Streatfeild (London: Richards, 1904);

Seven Sonnets and a Psalm of Montreal (Cambridge: Privately printed, 1904);

Ulysses: A Dramatic Oratorio in Vocal Score with Accompaniment for the Pianoforte, by Butler and Jones (London: Weekes, 1904; Chicago: Summy, 1904);

God the Known and God the Unknown, edited by Streatfeild (London: Fifield, 1909; New Haven: Yale University Press, 1917);

The Note-Books of Samuel Butler: Selections, edited by Jones (London: Fifield, 1912; New York: Kennerly, 1913);

Butleriana, edited by A. T. Bartholomew (London: Nonesuch, 1932);

Further Extracts from the Note-Books of Samuel Butler, edited by Bartholomew (London: Cape, 1934);

Samuel Butler's Notebooks: Selections, edited by Geoffrey Keynes and Brian Hill (London: Cape, 1951; New York: Dutton, 1951);

The Note-Books of Samuel Butler, Volume I (1874-1883), edited by Hans-Peter Breuer (Lanham, Md.: University Press of America, 1984).

Collection: The Shrewsbury Edition of the Works of Samuel Butler, edited by Henry Festing Jones and A. T. Bartholomew, 20 volumes (London: Cape/New York: Dutton, 1923-1926).

TRANSLATIONS: The Iliad of Homer, Rendered into English Prose for the Use of Those Who Cannot Read the Original (London & New York: Longmans, Green, 1898; New York: Dutton, 1921);

The Odyssey, Rendered into English Prose for the Use of Those Who Cannot Read the Original (London & New York: Longmans, Green, 1900; New York: Dutton, 1922).

PERIODICAL PUBLICATIONS: "On English Composition," as Cellarius, Eagle (St. John's College, Cambridge), 1, no. 1 (1858): 41-44;

"Our Tour," Eagle, 1, no. 5 (1859): 211-233;

"Our Emigrant," as Cellarius, Eagle, 2, no. 8 (1860): 101-113; 2, no. 9 (1860): 149-169; 3, no. 12 (1861): 18-36;

"Darwin on the Origin of Species: A Dialogue," Press (Christchurch, New Zealand), 20 December 1862;

"Darwin among the Machines," as Cellarius, Press, 13 June 1863; revised as "The Mechanical Creation," Reasoner (London), 1 July 1865;

"The English Cricketeers," *Press*, 15 February 1864;

"Lucubratio Ebria," *Press*, 29 July 1865;

"Precaution in Free Thought," *Reasoner*, 1 August 1865;

"Dedomenici da Rossa," *Drawing-Room Gazette* (London), 30 September 1871;

"Instead of an Article on the Dudley Exhibition," *Drawing-Room Gazette*, 11 November 1871;

"The Performance of 'Jephtha' at Exeter Hall," *Drawing-Room Gazette*, 25 November 1871;

"Performance of *Israel in Egypt* at Exeter Hall," *Drawing-Room Gazette*, 2 December 1871;

"Handel's *Deborah* and Bach's *Passion*," *Drawing-Room Gazette*, 2 March 1872;

"Free-thinking and Plain-Speaking," *Examiner* (London), 20 December 1873;

"A Clergyman's Doubts," *Examiner*, 15 February-14 June 1879;

"The Sub-division of the Organic World into Animal and Vegetable," *Science and Art* (May 1887): 21-24; (June 1887): 42-44;

"Quis Desiderio. . .?," *Universal Review* (July 1888): 411-424;

"A Sculptor and a Shrine," *Universal Review* (November 1888): 317-339;

"The Aunt, the Nieces, and the Dog," *Universal Review* (May 1889): 126-137;

"A Medieval Girl School," *Universal Review* (December 1889): 551-566;

"The Deadlock in Darwinism," *Universal Review* (April 1890): 523-540; (May 1890): 65-78; (June 1890): 238-252;

"Art in the Valley of Saas," *Universal Review* (November 1890): 411-424;

"Ramblings in Cheapside," *Universal Review* (December 1890): 513-523;

"The Humour of Homer," *Eagle*, 17, no. 97 (1892): 158-193;

"On the Trapanese Origin of the Odyssey," *Eagle*, 17, no. 99 (1892): 353-365;

"A Translation Attempted in Consequence of a Challenge," *Eagle*, 18, no. 103 (1894): 131;

"Not on Sad Stygian Shore," *Athenaeum*, no. 3871 (4 January 1902): 18;

"A Parody of a Simeonite Tract," in "Samuel Butler and the Simeonites," by A. T. Bartholomew, *Cambridge Magazine*, 2 (March 1913): 377-378.

Samuel Butler's reputation today rests almost entirely on his three fictional works–the posthumously published novel *The Way of All Flesh* (1903), together with the philosophical tales *Erewhon* (1872) and *Erewhon Revisited* (1901). Though he composed a few poems, a brief portrait of the fictional author of his 1873 work *The Fair Haven*, and two oratorio libretti (in collaboration with his friend Henry Festing Jones), he was not essentially what today is called a creative writer, a creator of fictions. Almost seventeen of the twenty volumes comprising the Shrewsbury Edition of his collected works fall into the category of nonfiction prose; and in these works Butler reveals himself as polemicist on religious and scientific issues, as philosopher, moralist, logician, classical scholar, art historian, editor, and translator.

He was in fact a didactic writer with a strong urge to engage in controversy and criticism. He preferred to be identified in the British Museum catalogue as "philosophic writer" and justly so, for even in his fiction he was concerned as much with hammering out his views as with developing character and episode. From the moment of its appearance *The Way of All Flesh* was regarded as an intellectual autobiography (this fact would be confirmed by Henry Festing Jones's voluminous biography published in 1919), and commentators have treated it as a compendium of Butler's most characteristic and influential convictions ever since. What remains most alive in the prose works are not so much the theories and arguments as the occasional moral observations, the witticisms, paradoxes, and self-indulgent musings of the sort that are scattered throughout *The Way of All Flesh*–nuggets that came to be called "Butlerisms":

> Dog-fanciers tell us that performing dogs never carry their tails; such dogs have eaten of the tree of knowledge, and are convinced of sin accordingly–they know that they know things, in respect of which, therefore, they are no longer under grace, but under the law, and they have yet so much grace left as to be ashamed. So with the human clever dog; he may speak with the tongues of men and angels, but so long as he knows that he knows, his tail will droop. . . . We must all feel that a rich young nobleman with a taste for science and principles is rarely a pleasant object. . . . Principles are like logic, which never yet made a good reasoner of a bad one, but might still be occasionally useful if they did not invariably contradict each other whenever there is any temptation to appeal to them. They are like fire, good servants but bad masters.

The passage presents a characteristic Butlerian paradox, said half in fun and more than half in earnest; it comes in the midst of a serious Lamarckian (and essentially anti-Darwinian) interpretation of the effects in the evolution of species of the inheritance of acquired characteristics; but its charm and significance are quite independent of the validity of Butler's theoretical position.

Butler's prose writings have sunk into virtual oblivion, although almost all of them were republished several times after his death in 1902 from pernicious anemia. In his lifetime he was forced to pay for the publication of his books with the exception of *Erewhon Revisited* (his last) because, save for *Erewhon*, they did not sell. He was, he claimed, an Ishmaelite among his generation of writers for having had the presumption to attack respected opinions in religious, artistic, and scientific matters, especially those of Darwin and his defenders. Indeed, of late-Victorian thinkers Butler was the most independent of the reigning intellectual fashions. He shrank instinctively from influential circles after enjoying the brief lionhood *Erewhon* earned him, consoling himself with the hope that he would be vindicated posthumously. Butler could remain complacent about popular and critical approval, for, despite financial hardships from which only his father's death in 1886 freed him, he managed to lead the life of a bachelor recluse free from the necessity of following a profession. But this very privilege permitted him to let intellectual curiosity lead him where it would, and it led him to out-of-the-way subjects of little general appeal then as now. His contribution to the Darwinian controversy, for example, did gain him the discipleship of Bernard Shaw, who retailored Butler's neo-Lamarckism into his own "Life Force" philosophy; nevertheless, Butler's books on evolution and other longer prose works, except insofar as they serve as commentary on the outlook presented in his still-popular fiction, have remained of interest only to scholars and specialists.

Butler stood apart because his sensibility was shaped by the outlook of the eighteenth century. Though a freethinker, he found the positivism of his day as dogmatic as that of evangelical orthodoxy. His rationalism was Laodicean, informed by the prevailing epicureanism of the time before Queen Victoria. His anti-Darwinist researches led him to eighteenth-century naturalists and philosophical divines such as Bishop Joseph Butler, author of the influential *The Analogy of Religion, Natural and Revealed* (1736); and his loyalties belonged to writers who shared his hardheaded common sense and pragmatism, writers like Defoe, Samuel Johnson, Jane Austen, the poet Samuel Butler, author of *Hudibras* (1663, 1664, 1678), and Jonathan Swift. *Erewhon,* in fact, owed much to *Gulliver's Travels* (1726) and *Robinson Crusoe* (1719, 1720). Butler was drawn to Benjamin Disraeli's witty sophistication and to Gilbert and Sullivan's operas, but the sentimentalism and high moral tone of his well-known contemporaries—George Eliot, Charles Dickens, and Tennyson—repelled him. To his favorite George Frideric Handel he paid his deepest respects by composing pieces entirely in the Handelian manner, for in the music after Handel's death Butler found nothing but decline into murky harmonic bombast. Butler's literary voice, too, stood apart from the fashionable florid ornateness of his day, for his style, remarkable for its terse, virile plainness, was influenced by that of earlier models, by John Bunyan's and Defoe's straightforward Anglo-Saxon English. In the most significant of his college essays, "On English Composition," Butler had already argued for deliberate artlessness without "accessories," for an economic, spontaneous simplicity achieved by forgetting oneself and concentrating on the matter at hand. Not surprisingly, Butler's most characteristic form of expression was the anecdote or epigrammatic observation in the manner of Francis Bacon and Samuel Johnson. He was, finally, by temperament, a satirist in an age when satire was at low ebb. The brief essays, skits, and poems he wrote while a student at St. John's College, Cambridge, already reveal a strong sense of irony, intellectual pugnacity, and the knack for mimicking other writers' voices. He was disposed to be suspicious of all straining after the sublime, of all that was highly touted, and he enjoyed flinging the plain man's scorn at it. Even in his most earnestly argued later writings he could not resist erupting occasionally into ironic playfulness or savage sarcasm.

He was not, however, a born writer; no demon drove him. He was gifted with a penetrating analytic intelligence able to range over many subjects; but as a young man he was not at first directed by any strongly felt urge save the ambition to make a mark. Butler, the son of Canon Thomas Butler and Fanny Worsley Butler, was born 4 December 1835 at Langar, near Birmingham. He grew up, one of four children, in the rectory home of his father, who was the vicar of

Langar-cum-Bramston in Nottinghamshire. Like his father, and before him his grandfather, Dr. Samuel Butler, headmaster of Shrewsbury and afterwards bishop of Lichfield, he was intended for the Church. In due course, again like father and grandfather, he entered St. John's College, Cambridge; in 1858, having placed twelfth in the first class of the Classical Tripos, he went up to London as lay assistant to the curate of St. James's Piccadilly. While there he experienced his first religious doubts, and when subsequently he declined to be ordained, a bitter quarrel ensued between father and son over a suitable alternative profession. Butler's wish to become a painter was unacceptable to Canon Butler. At last it was settled that the young Butler should immigrate to Canterbury Province, New Zealand, a settlement recently opened under Church of England sponsorship, to make his way as sheep farmer. When in the autumn of 1859 he set sail for the colony, he embarked on a journey which at once removed him from England and from the world represented by his father. For their bitter quarrel had crystallized in Butler the desire to reject the outlook he had implicitly trusted but which had directed him to what he now regarded as an untenable position. His first act of rebellion was to read, on the voyage out, Edward Gibbon's *History of the Decline and Fall of the Roman Empire* (1776-1788), a work which encouraged his satiric disposition and his progress toward freethinking pantheism.

This rebellion determined the form and manner in which he would eventually present himself to the reading public. His religious doubts grew until, in the third year on his New Zealand station, the whole of Christianity loomed as a fraud imposed by the deliberate conspiracy of the clergy. Later in 1874 when he returned to Charles Darwin's *On the Origin of Species* (1859), which he had read with enthusiasm soon after his arrival in the colony, he discovered that its argument was erected on shaky foundations and (so it seemed) similarly defended by not entirely disinterested cliques. The disappointment of his trust in both instances hardened his skepticism of all authoritative verdicts. Consequently virtually everything he wrote from 1872 on was informed by an urge to set the record straight, to expose the fraudulence of established opinions, and reveal the plain truth. The Swiftian energy and clear-headed (though literal-minded) rationalism with which Butler directed his campaigns were the chief reasons for his posthumous reputation as the great debunker of his age.

While in New Zealand, Butler had sufficient leisure to devote himself to the concerns that would dominate his life and writings: religion and evolution. His study of *On the Origin of Species*, a summary in the form of a dialogue of Darwin's theory, was published in the *Press* (Christchurch), 20 December 1862, with the title "Darwin on the Origin of Species: A Dialogue." Its clarity and succinctness was such that Darwin, when it came to his attention, wished to have it republished in England. The dialogue indicates that Butler had grasped in *On the Origin of Species* those implications subversive to an evangelical interpretation of Christian dispensation, of man's Fall and his Redemption. In fact, in the collision between the theological tradition of his father and the new positivism represented by Darwin, Butler eventually found the subject that roused his combative intellect and launched him on his writing career. For the present, however, he, not yet certain of his ground, was content to keep Christianity and Darwin balanced against each other: his Darwinist speaker in the dialogue concludes that the two dispensations are only apparently irreconcilable.

The dialogue was followed by one of his most brilliant intellectual tours de force, "Darwin among the Machines" (the Christchurch *Press*, 13 June 1863), a witty application of Darwin's theory to the realm of machines. Butler rewrote it upon his return to England as "The Mechanical Creation" (*Reasoner* [London], 1 July 1865) and expanded it in the chapters in *Erewhon* entitled "The Book of the Machines." The thesis is that machines are an incipient form of life developing through the agency of man who performs the function that natural selection performs in the realm of organic evolution. The original essay ends with a prophecy redolent with implications for the modern age: "day by day we are becoming subservient to them [machines]; more men are daily bound down as slaves to tend them, more men are daily devoting the energies of their whole lives to the development of mechanical life; . . . that the time will come when the machines will hold the real supremacy over the world and its inhabitants is what no person of a truly philosophic mind can for a moment question." In a companion piece, "Lucubratio Ebria," published after his return to London in the Christchurch *Press* (29 July 1865), Butler decided to look at machines more conventionally: assuming that man is a tool-wielding creature, it follows (by analogy) that all machines are purposive extensions of his limbs, and with these extra-corporeal limbs he was changing his environment and thus directing his evolutionary development. This view too was worked into *Erewhon.*

Both exercises were suggested by William Paley's *Natural Theology* (1802), a work Darwin knew thoroughly. Paley argued for design in nature by illustrating the analogy between human contrivances and limbs: if, for example, the watch, or the telescope, is evidence for design, then so too must be the eagle's eye, and this in turn implies the great Designer, God. In his essays Butler clearly if playfully tried to account for obvious design without recourse to this traditional solution and by so doing actually isolated the chief objection to the Darwinian theory: namely, that organic design, the adaptation of form to function, could not be explained simply as the outcome of random processes without a guiding principle. If machines were indeed extensions of limbs, then limbs themselves were aids and extensions of human purpose. Butler's logical experiments clearly suggested a bold story, but he was as yet too diffident to tell it.

These considerations of evolutionary questions were counterpointed by his close study of the evidences for the Christian faith, begun, very likely, during the months prior to his emigration. Gibbon's ironic mockery of the New Testament no doubt spurred the rebellious Butler to this task. He concentrated on the Resurrection accounts, and the discrepancies between those of Matthew and John provided him with grounds for doubting the historical accuracy of the four Gospels and for abandoning his faith altogether. He did not put his findings before the public until he was back in London, when he paid for the publication of the anonymous pamphlet *The Evidence for the Resurrection of Jesus Christ, as Given by the Four Evangelists, Critically Examined* (1865).

Though aware of the unorthodox and critical attitude to biblical texts in the 1860 *Essays and Reviews* (which included pieces by Benjamin Jowett and others) and acquainted with Bishop William Colenso's studies of the Pentateuch (1862-1879), Butler had little, if any, firsthand knowledge at the time of German biblical criticism. His arguments constitute chiefly a reply to Dean Henry Alford's commentary in his *Greek Testament* (1849-1861), in which the claims of the Tübingen school of higher criticism and of other biblical scholars are confronted. Unlike many contemporary evangelicals, Dean Alford held to no theory of verbal inspiration and did not find the

Mr. Heatherley's Holiday, *painting by Butler exhibited at the Royal Academy in 1874 (courtesy of The Tate Gallery, London). The subject of the painting is Thomas Heatherley of London, with whom Butler studied art beginning in the 1860s.*

Resurrection accounts troublesome to his faith since he relied on the cumulative effect of all evidence; nor did he see reason to set aside the accounts of miracles. Butler, however, adopted Gibbon's central axiom, that the supernatural elements in the Gospels were to be explained as "secondary" causes—strictly natural occurrences which to uneducated minds of the time seemed miraculous. When the "mythological" layer thus created by primitive enthusiasts had been stripped away from the Resurrection accounts, one could establish with certainty only, so Butler claimed, the empty tomb and Christ's reappearance on the third day. There was no evidence for his death on the cross. The plain facts were to be found in John, for Butler the only true eyewitness to the crucifixion; and by comparing his account with those of Luke, Mark, and Matthew (the most detailed), Butler detected a progressive filling in and dogmatizing of events after the crucifixion and before Christ's reappearance, an elaboration, he insisted, bound to occur over a thirty-to-forty-year period of oral transmission by followers kindled by "the power and beauty of Christ's own character." Butler did not impugn the Evangelists' sincerity as did the German Bruno Bauer; he also dismissed David Strauss's claim in *Das Leben Jesu* (1835) that the post-Resurrection appearances were hallucinations of Christ's grief-stricken followers. He admits the Evangelists were honest men, restricted by their limited knowledge, and by their intense hopes easily subject to autosuggestion. But with characteristic analytic relentlessness Butler reduced the question of Christ's death to a matter of how deep the Roman soldier's lance penetrated the Savior's side and suggested simply that it was far more probable that Joseph of Arimathea, who could not afford to reveal his actions, rescued Christ from the tomb and nursed him back to health.

Despite this justification of his apostasy, Butler shrank from radical rationalism. This unwillingness to make an absolute stand on either side of a moral issue was, in fact, one of Butler's most characteristic traits. In an essay, "Precaution in Free Thought," published in the *Reasoner* shortly after the pamphlet appeared (1 August 1865), he warned against the presumption of freethinkers who tumbled from one narrow dogmatic position into another. Once the miraculous element of Christianity is set aside, he declared, "we find little remaining which is not common to all those great schools of practice which have led historic ages." In his notes he later (in 1874) reiterated this position and said that he wished merely not to be snubbed and bullied for rejecting the supernatural: "As regards Christianity I should hope and think I am more Christian than not."

Having had his say in his essays and pamphlet, Butler virtually stopped writing. In the summer of 1864 he had sold his New Zealand station; he returned to London and set up in modest quarters in Clifford's Inn, where he would live, a bachelor, for the rest of his life. For a number of years he tried to realize his delayed ambition by studying at several art schools (chiefly at Heatherley's in Newman Street); he succeeded in having a few of his paintings exhibited at the Royal Academy. But by the spring of 1870 he had to admit that as a painter success would not be his. He was persuaded to work up his New Zealand articles with the result that in 1872 *Erewhon* was published anonymously. A trenchant satire, the work is full of ideas to which he would return again, including the Darwinian deductions that nature's moral standards were good health

and good luck (as well as a goodly balance of cash in hand) and that disease was a crime in her court but conventional immorality a mere curable misdemeanor.

Its unexpected success launched him on his writing career. Almost immediately he took up his Resurrection theory and elaborated it into an unsparing attack on the sentimental Broad Church apologetics called into play when the orthodox confronted arguments of biblical higher criticism. *The Fair Haven* (1873) falls into two parts, a fictional biography of the supposed writer John Pickard Owen, written by his brother, and a treatise that purports to be Owen's, supposedly refuting the Tübingen critics with a high-minded though entirely subjective defense. The biography first traces Owen's upbringing by his evangelical mother, then his rejection of faith–which provides Butler's alter-ego with the opportunity for scoring sharp points against Christ's teachings–and finally his confident attempts at reconciling his recovered faith with the position of rationalists, an effort so arduous it plunges Owen into mental debility and death. The treatise reflects this three-part format. First Owen scornfully undermines Strauss's hallucination theory; having thus won the reader's confidence, he fully concedes (as Butler had in his pamphlet) the case against the historicity of the Resurrection accounts and finally insists on the insignificance of Scriptural discrepancies; indeed, their function, he assures the reader, is both to ensure that Christ's teachings are rendered sufficiently imprecise and hence broad and universal, as well as to encourage an elevated Christ ideal that can stand up to the scrutiny of rationalist skeptics. After all, do not "all ideals gain by vagueness"? Hence contradictions and discrepancies in the Gospels, rather than stumbling blocks, are appointed to be the very means by which all men can come to the Christ ideal.

The reader was, in the context of each middle section, to see the sophistry of such face-saving. Yet, as the 1865 free-thought essay indicates, Christianity as ethical ideal expressed in part Butler's own religious position. He was to reassert this in the essay "A Medieval Girl School" (*Universal Review*, 1889) and again in *Erewhon Revisited* (1901). It is not surprising that some critics, Catholic ones too, were taken in and read the satire as a genuine defense of faith. Butler was only too happy to reveal their foolishness for falling for "Owen's" sentimental gush when he identified himself as author in a second edition rushed into print in the fall of 1873. But his critics had now been warned. Butler was a paradoxist; one could not be certain he was pulling his reader's leg. Such a reputation doubtlessly harmed him by making it more difficult for him to get the serious consideration he earnestly desired from the opinion-makers in literary circles.

Erewhon had been a bitter pill for Butler's father; he told his son it had in fact killed his mother, who died in April 1873. Butler vented his fury at this rejection by identifying himself as the author of the fifth edition of *Erewhon* (published in late spring 1873) and by commencing the fierce attack on his family, his upbringing, and all who had self-righteously hoodwinked him, that was to become the autobiographical novel *The Way of All Flesh*. He worked on it intermittently, completing it in 1884 in a much mellower mood. His chief preoccupations during the intervening years were questions raised by evolution, and his answers to them influenced his novel inevitably.

Sometime after 1875 Butler realized that once the genetic continuity between parent and offspring was admitted, he could show that the guiding principle of evolution was located in the purposive efforts of the organisms themselves, passed on from generation to generation by means of heritable unconscious memories. An organism's unconscious memory was a receptacle of the effect of individual efforts, and over countless repetitions such efforts and the resultant habits became heritable as unconscious memories or instincts. All organic development, in other words, was necessarily teleological even in the absence of final causes. This essentially Lamarckian theory Butler believed explained the origin of variations and provided the biological principle which gave accumulated variations a purposive direction. Quite simply, all creatures shaped themselves much as men shaped, improved, and refined machinery, which, by analogy, were also heritable receptacles of countless purposive attempts to solve problems.

This theory Butler developed with wit and grace in *Life and Habit* (1877) as an adjunct to Darwin's theory: it could account (logically at least), he claimed, for such baffling phenomena as reversion to feral characteristics (displacement of recently acquired memories by older, more ingrained ones) and the sterility of hybrids (the chaotic clash of strongly divergent memories). The theory also provided him with terms with which he redefined the religious concepts he had inher-

ited and which could serve as the point of departure for his general observations. So, for example, the knowable personal God was the original incarnation, the primordial personality from which all life had sprung and proliferated. God's unseen Kingdom was the inherited storehouse of past memories, those perennial values which are far surer guides than consciously acquired knowledge; and immortality was the absorption into the greater life of this "panzoistic God" immanent in the very atoms (for there could be no hard line drawn between the organic and inorganic). In short, with this naturalistic outlook, Butler had secularized finally his original faith. He outlined his new, essentially pantheistic faith in three articles which appeared in the London *Examiner* under the title "God the Known and God the Unknown" in 1879. With some alterations, the essays were brought together and published posthumously in book form in 1909.

In his next work, *Evolution, Old and New* (1879; revised, 1882), he sharpened his criticism of Darwin. By now he believed he had fully grasped the inadequacy of the theory of natural selection, which was not (as once he had believed) synonymous with the theory of evolution. The new book was a scholarly review and explication of the work of Darwin's predecessors, Dr. Erasmus Darwin, Buffon, and Lamarck, filled with extensive quotations from their principal works, designed to show that they each had constructed a complete theory of descent with modification almost entirely harmonious with Butler's own *Life and Habit* theory, and superior (except in detail) to Darwin's. These writers had succeeded in identifying, as Butler put it, "principles which shall give a definite purpose and direction to the variations whose accumulation results in specific, and ultimately generic differences." For this accomplishment Butler wished to praise them; he hoped also to show that, though Darwin had cavalierly waved them aside, he had nonetheless learned much more from them than he was prepared to admit in the preface to *On the Origin of Species*.

Butler's rehabilitation of older naturalists was quickly followed by *Unconscious Memory* (1880), a work inspired by an acrimonious disagreement between himself and Darwin. By now he was eager to justify his hardened anti-Darwinian stance, and he allowed himself the presumption of attacking Darwin's integrity and honesty. He recounts how he was led from regarding machines as extracorporeal limbs to discovering the absurdity of claiming that a random force such as natural selection could account for organic design. He further dismisses Eduard von Hartmann, who, in his *Philosophy of the Unconscious* (1869), had advanced the vitalistic theory (apparently inspired by Arthur Schopenhauer) that all organic evolution was presided over by an unconscious, blind, yet purposive force (*Urwillen*) independent of the individuality of organisms. Finally (perhaps so as not to imitate Darwin's ingratitude to his predecessors), Butler pays tribute to Prof. Ewald Hering of Prague by translating Hering's 1870 lecture "On Memory as a Universal Function of Organized Matter," which had anticipated the *Life and Habit* theory.

That Butler's mounting distrust of Darwin and of the dogmatism of his supporters mellowed his antiecclesiastical animus and fueled his desire for some sort of rapprochement with the Church is made plain by his essay "Rome and Pantheism," which he appended to the revised edition of *Evolution, Old and New*. In the Roman Church he sees a unifier, he writes; if only the Church could find a way to dissolve quietly its supernatural doctrines into a broad pantheism, he for one would rejoice: then she would represent the unifying faith of the future. Scattered remarks in subsequent works and his notebooks make clear how his dislike of doctrinaire scientists (already expressed in *Life and Habit*) led him to understand the Church both as the visible expression of the fundamental paradoxes underlying human existence and as the representative of a far more trustworthy, perennial ideal than the new positivism could offer. Contemporary free thought was simply too self-conscious: "The higher rules of life transcend the sphere of language. They cannot be gotten by speech, neither shall logic be paid the price thereof. They lie in the power of the Lord and in the departing from evil without knowing in words what the fear of the Lord is, nor yet the Lord, nor evil. There is nothing for it but a very humble hope that from the great unknown source our daily insight and daily strength may be given with our daily bread. And what is faith but Christianity, whether one believes" in the Resurrection or not?

Butler returned to the vexed question of natural selection in *Luck or Cunning as the Main Means of Organic Modification?* (1886). His satiric ire was now roused by a recent, fulsome biography of Darwin by Grant Allen, the popularizer of science who had laughed at Butler's *Life and*

Habit theory. In *Luck or Cunning?* Butler gives vent to his suspicions of Darwin most openly and unguardedly, and it is consequently the most significant of his four books on evolution. The "mindless theory of Charles Darwinian natural selection" is again assailed as illogical: for the Darwinists denied design in nature on the baseless ground that in the early kettle days no one had "foreseen so great a future development" as the railway, forgetting "that piece-meal *solvitur ambulando* design is more omni-present, all-seeing, all-searching, and hence more truly in the strict sense design, than any speculative leap of fancy, however bold or even at times successful." He brashly denies Darwin's originality: he had been no lone and "solitary" thinker, since Lamarck, Dr. Erasmus Darwin, and Robert Chambers's *Vestiges of the Natural History of Creation* (1844) had preceded and influenced him. Furthermore, Darwin possessed "average intellectual powers," his argument in *On the Origin of Species* was muddled, his intentions duplicitous. The many changes in the six editions of *On the Origin of Species* (to which Darwin never called attention) indicate that he had come to recognize the importance of the effects of use and disuse; yet he was eager to maintain from first to last that only the aggregation of fortuitous variations acted upon by natural selection was the main cause of evolutionary change and speciation. Butler continues by illustrating how close Darwinists, such as George Romanes in *Mental Evolution in Animals* (1883), came to endorsing the *Life and Habit* theory, while at the same time attacking anyone who did so in plain hearing. Romanes obviously wished to ride on Darwin's coattails.

The philosophic meditations on luck and chance are, however, the meat of the work: there Butler carries the logic of his position furthest and invests the whole of nature with intelligence. He does not deny luck's great dominion, but an organism's cunning is stronger "as regards the acquisition of property" which is but an extension of personality. The arbitrary divisions between organic and inorganic, between mind and matter, all contradictory categories, in fact, are untenable: "everything is both alive and dead at one and the same time." Butler's friend Alfred Tyler, recently deceased, had already shown experimentally that plants have intelligence. Soon enough the border between plant and nonplant would have to go. Consequently, "What is the stomach but a living sack . . . wherein we keep our means of subsistence?" Indeed, "What is the purse but a

The essence of language consisting in the closeness of association rather than in the symbol chosen.

It does not matter whether the symbols chosen be made with voice or gesture, or written character.

The essence is that any symbol shd be unvaryingly connected however arbitrarily; with the same idea.

If the symbols are few &c. the language is elementary

If the symbols are many &c. we have a highly developed language.

It is not easy to see how a rude language can be denied to the lower animals

And all things that live must be allowed to have ideas. about their own business.

We have only few & vague ideas about things that do not concern us.

Notes for Butler's "lecture on the genesis of feeling," given at the City of London College, 15 December 1887 (MA 3166, by permission of the Trustees of The Pierpont Morgan Library)

kind of abridged extra-corporeal stomach wherein we keep the money" which, by purchase, is converted into food? Everywhere mind assimilates or is assimilated. Consequently, in a monistic world such as this, one must have both random change and deliberate design. There is no logical escape: "the texture of the world is a warp and woof of contradiction in terms; of continuity in discontinuity, and discontinuity in continuity; of unity in diversity, and diversity in unity."

After 1880 Butler began to leave evolution behind and turn to new subjects. First to follow *Unconscious Memory* was *Alps and Sanctuaries of Piedmont and the Canton Ticino* (1881), a leisurely travel guide suffused by Butler's most congenial humor, richly illustrated with drawings by himself, H. F. Jones, and Butler's artist friend Charles Gogin, and with quotations from Handel's music. Here he pays tribute to the charm of places in the Canton Ticino and Italian Piedmont he had visited regularly during his annual holidays since 1865 and to the simple inhabitants of the region whom he held in warm affection. In the wayside chapels and sanctuaries he had found virtually unknown and mostly anonymous votive paintings and sculpture whose naiveté appealed to his love of sincere simplicity. In an essay included in the volume ("On the Decline of Italian Art") he condemns the academic training of artists in favor of the older apprentice system of learning by doing, for the former, Butler notes, destroys originality and leads to insincerity of expression. Significantly, Butler begins his guidebook by praising Handel and Shakespeare because their art was not ruled by the *gnostic* spirit–erudite, self-conscious, eager to impress–but by the spirit of *agape*–the kindly, sincere wish to please the audience, the very spirit that Butler found in northern Italian votive art. Because of its spirit Butler considered this art superior to the "high-falutin'" work of Michelangelo and Raphael.

He devoted a scholarly study, *Ex Voto: An Account of the Sacro Monte or New Jerusalem at Varallo-Sesia* (1888), to the most remarkable examples of this art in the numerous chapels on the Sacro Monte at Varallo. He traces this shrine's history from its foundation late in the fifteenth century by the Milanese Franciscan monk Bernardino Caimi (who was desirous of building "a copy of the most important sites in the Holy Land") and describes the works of Gaudenzio Ferrari, Giovanni D'Enrico, and the virtually unknown Giovanni Tabachetti (or Tabaguet) found in the chapels. The last sculptor Butler considered a genius, and he was able to discover his true identity as the Flemish Jean de Wespin (circa 1568-1615), one of three sculptor brothers from Dinant, Belgium. Butler's scholarship is now dated; but he undertook this project chiefly to justify his bold (and eccentric) claim that this art was in fact superior to anything of its kind, superior certainly to the art of Michelangelo, Raphael, and da Vinci. "Everything," he concedes, about votive paintings, "does go so dreadfully wrong in them, and yet we know it will all be set so perfectly right again directly, and that nobody will be really hurt. Besides, they are so naive, and free from 'high-falutin'; they give themselves no airs, are not review-puffed, and the people who paint them do not call one another geniuses. They are business-like, direct, and sensible. . . ." Tabachetti's creations in the Journey to Calvary Chapel represent "the most outstanding work that has ever been achieved in sculpture," while Ferrari's Crucifixion Chapel is "perhaps the most daringly ambitious attempt made in the history of art." Who can doubt the spirit of self-sacrifice manifested in this devotional art? And, Butler asks, is not a noble end lovelier and does it not bring "more peace at the last than one of self-seeking and self-indulgence?" Given this artistic unselfconsciousness, he finds it not difficult to predict that the spirit of Christianity certainly will remain, while the arrogant letter of science will not be truer. "I would as soon have a winking madonna or a forged decretal, as the doubtful experiments or garbled articles which the high priests of modern science are applauded with one voice for trying to palm off upon their devotees."

In 1888, the year *Ex Voto* was published, Butler's sisters presented him with the papers of his grandfather, Dr. Samuel Butler, the headmaster of Shrewsbury (1798-1836) and bishop of Lichfield (to his death in 1839). Contrary to what might be expected from his disparagement of education and educators in the two *Erewhon* books and in the novel *The Way of All Flesh*, Butler developed great esteem for his ancestor. The labor of editing these papers, occupying him intermittently for the next seven years, culminated in *The Life and Letters of Dr. Samuel Butler* (1896), a two-volume annotated selection of Dr. Butler's correspondence intended to illuminate the subject's personality as well as public school and church affairs during the early nineteenth century. Butler lets the letters speak for themselves, yet even so his polemical purpose is apparent. Major credit for the reform of the rough public schools of the early nineteenth century had been given to Dr. Thomas Arnold, headmaster of Rugby from 1828 to 1841. Butler suggests that this reputation is undeserved: Arnold's record, in fact, cannot match that of Dr. Butler, who, starting with but three or four pupils, expanded his school to a pupil population of 300, initiated scholarly competitions and examinations, and so improved the teaching of the classics that the two great universities had to change examination rules to prevent Shrewsbury boys from defeating the resident alumni.

Butler discovered much to admire in his grandfather's personality and outlook. Dr. Butler disliked the gloom of evangelical Methodism and sectarian self-righteousness; unlike Dr. Arnold, he possessed a robust sense of enjoyment, and he disliked the morbid "sentimentality" of his time. He was a tolerant, practical divine with a manly common sense, firm but kind, eager to promote his boys' interests, restrained in the common practice of flogging. Though he revered the classics, he objected to teaching them by gerund-grinding and accent-counting. In 1822 he had criticized (in an anonymous pamphlet) the university curriculum for promoting speculative knowledge by an excessive emphasis on mathematics: the "practical clown," Dr. Butler observed, is after all superior to the "speculative academic"—a sentiment not unlike those his grandson later expressed. Butler's admiration for Dr. Butler softened the bitter memories of his former school and of its headmaster, Dr. Benjamin Kennedy, Dr. Butler's successor whom he had ruthlessly satirized as Dr. Skinner in *The Way of All Flesh*. In fact Butler concludes the work on his grandfather by confessing that Dr. Kennedy "treated me with great forebearance—far more than I deserved." Under him he learned the Shrewsbury virtues: "Sincerity, downrightness, hatred of sham, love of work, and a strong sense of duty. What little of these noble qualities I dare pretend to, I owe hardly more to my parents than to the school at which they placed me, nor do I believe Shrewsbury would have possessed them in the measure in which they certainly existed among my own schoolfellows but for the deep impress of Dr. Butler's masculine and sagacious character."

After completing *Alps and Sanctuaries of Piedmont and the Canton Ticino*, Butler had begun to dabble in composition in collaboration with his friend Henry Festing Jones. Their first joint publications were a few short piano pieces in the Handelian manner (*Gavottes, Minuets, Fugues, and Other Short Pieces for the Piano*, 1885) and a secular oratorio, or "Dramatic Cantata" (*Narcissus*, 1888), about shepherds who gamble on the London Stock Exchange. Writing the libretto for the latter work revived Butler's interest in the Homeric epics (a second oratorio, *Ulysses*, begun by Butler and Jones in the 1890s, would not be published until 1904) and in the knotty question of their authorship, a subject that would occupy him for the next ten years and more. His dissatisfaction with existing English translations made him decide to prepare his own of both the *Iliad* and the *Odyssey*. Using colloquial prose, or (as he called it) "Tottenham Court Road English," the first was published in 1898, the second in 1900. By achieving deliberately unpoetical but terse Anglo-Saxon translations, he was cocking his snoot at the fashionable ornateness and archaisms of the well-known translations by Samuel Henry Butcher, Andrew Lang, and others. Butler took on the entire establishment of Greek scholarship when he produced *The Authoress of the "Odyssey"* (1897), in which he boldly asserted that the *Odyssey* was not Homeric but composed by a young Sicilian woman who disguised herself as Princess Nausicaa in book six, and furthermore, that Ulysses' voyages resolved "themselves into a voyage from Troy" and thence "round Sicily, beginning with Trapani and ending with the same place." It is a work of inspired and undervalued criticism.

Butler's treatment of the epic's geography is not essential to his criticism, though a few scholars have accepted his conclusions: Ithaca and Scheria, Butler claims, for example, are one city based on Trapani; the Ionian islands must refer to the four islands off Trapani's coast; and the Phaeacians are the Phocaeans, the Greek-speaking inhabitants of Sicily. Butler's reading of the epic, however, is essential and bristles with delightful insights. To justify his approach in unmasking the "real" author, he asserts that what most stirs us in art, literature, or music "is the communion with the still living mind of the man or woman to whom we owe it, and the conviction that that mind is as we would have our own to be. All else is mere clothes and grammar." The epic, Butler holds, is an extension of the author's personality, and he detects the hand of a headstrong, unmarried woman, disdainful of men's clumsy ways. Women dominate the poem and initiate all action, hardly a situation that a male writer would allow, and the men are stick figures in comparison to the fully realized portraits of the female characters. There is also a preponderance of detail relating to a woman's world, and to Butler it is obvious that the authoress is jealous of women's honor. She seems intent on removing from Penelope the slightest suspicion of flirtatiousness by having her remain, despite what her tolerating and entertaining suitors for ten years might suggest to readers, the long-suffering faithful spouse whom the wandering Ulysses eagerly longs to rejoin. After all, Butler points out, she could have locked the door once the suitors had left had she so desired; to send messages to them was hardly the way to be rid of them; besides, "Did she ever try snubbing?" And though the authoress knew Ulysses was in no hurry to return, she was not "going to admit anything so derogatory to the sanctity of married life, or at any rate to the power which a wife has over a husband."

Such observations do place the poem in a new light, even if Butler's method is suspect. For he interprets some details literally, while others, which do not suit his purpose, he chalks up to poetic license. He obviously deflects onto his "authoress" his bachelor suspicions of Victorian families, of the paterfamilias especially, as he had done in creating the fiercely independent Aunt Alethea in *The Way of All Flesh.* Even so, he was alive to many implications and subtleties which the epic's academic critics had missed entirely by treating it as an archaeological artifact.

The personalist interpretation of a text Butler used again in dealing with Shakespeare's sonnets, but *Shakespeare's Sonnets Reconsidered* (1899) lacks the light touch of *The Authoress of the "Odyssey."* It is an angry work: Butler unceremoniously dismisses the arguments of Southamptonites and Pembrokites concerning the identity of a "Mr. W. H.," to whom the 1609 printing of the sonnets was dedicated. The sonnets, he insists, were all addressed to a young, callous man, one William Hughes (later to become a naval cook), to whom Shakespeare in the greenness of youth had been attracted. By Butler's account, Hughes betrayed their friendship by luring Shakespeare to a pederastic rendezvous only to ambush him in flagrante delicto. Butler rearranged the sequence of the sonnets to argue that sonnet thirty-four reflects this deplorable episode, and the others mirror the steadily cooling relationship. Some of the "dark lady" sonnets, Butler claims, were written for Mr. W. H. to give to the lady, his paramour, as his own; others of this group deal with the two men again shortly before their final separation. The evidence suggests that Butler may

have read Shakespeare's sonnets as an expression of his own misfortune. In December of 1897 one Charles Paine Pauli died, a lifelong friend, so Butler had thought, with whom he had returned from New Zealand and whom he had supported with an annual allowance, thinking that Pauli was in need. Now Butler discovered that Pauli had been all along a successful barrister who had not so much as mentioned Butler's name in his will. The pain of discovering such deception on one side and his own gullibility on the other must have turned Butler's mind to the sonnets: he now thought he understood the story of devotion and disillusion to which they seemed to bear witness.

During the last decade of his life Butler began editing his "remains"–his correspondence and the notebooks he had been keeping since 1874 which would fill several volumes. Like the novel, *The Note-books* were introduced to a posthumous readership when Butler's biographer Henry Festing Jones published a selection from them in 1912. The edition added considerably to Butler's steadily growing renown, and it is consequently a peculiarity of Butler's literary reputation that it rests heavily on works published after his death. Butler used his notebooks to record stray thoughts which he often developed in his books or essays, and they contain therefore his most characteristic observations in the attractive epigrammatic form of which he was a master: "If virtue had everything her own way she would be as insufferable as dominant factions generally are. It is the function of vice to keep virtue within reasonable bounds."

This is one of Butler's many "counsels of imperfection." In such notes the reader perceives the kindly charm and slightly wicked humor hidden beneath the facade of the pugnacious philosopher with beetling brow; he meets the man who in his fight with the great had become a *vates sacer* to the ordinary folk and of the beauty of simplicity. As an old man he once accompanied a young Desmond MacCarthy to the dining-room table in a Swiss hotel to protect him from his father's wrath for being late for dinner. And he recorded, with some delight, a conversation with Mr. Garnett, the distinguished (yet freethinking) superintendent of the British Museum Reading Room: when asked by him about his next cantata, Butler replied that "we should try a sacred subject. He [Mr. Garnett] looked very proper and asked what one we had in view. I said demurely that we were thinking of the woman taken in adultery." Butler could not enter the world of his successful contemporaries, but, as the thousands of notes suggest, this aloofness gave him the freedom to laugh irreverently at them and what they represented and to formulate the wisdom underlying his tendency to be contrary, to give expression to the little uncomfortable realities propriety tends to disguise or ignore: "I really do not see much use in exalting the humble and meek; they do not remain humble and meek long when they are exalted."

Equally attractive, though virtually ignored, are a handful of essays (some of them–such as "How to Make the Best of Life" and "Thought and Language"–lectures first published posthumously) in which his plain man's wit parades in a most delightful dress. In "Quis Desiderio . . .?" (1888), for example, he confesses how much he is indebted to *Lives of Eminent Christians,* which has served as the perfect sloping desk necessary for his writing while he worked in the British Museum Reading Room: the essay is a remarkable send-up of the pompous self-importance often reflected in prominent writers' discussions of their craft. In "Ramblings in Cheapside" (1890)–once regularly anthologized–Butler imagines encounters with reincarnations of the great figures of history in the humblest of present-day stations and dress: "Dante is, or was a year or two ago, a waiter at Brissago on the Lago Maggiore, only he is better-tempered-looking, and has a more intellectual expression. He gave me his ideas upon beauty: 'Tutto ch'e vero e bello,' he exclaimed, with all his old self-confidence. I am not afraid of Dante. I know people by their friends, and he went about with Virgil, so I said with some severity to Dante, 'No, Dante, il naso della Signora Robinson e vero, ma non e bello'; and he admitted I was right." Such stray musings owe their charm to Butler's love of bringing the exalted and revered within the compass of the everyday world, of forcing them to surrender their self-conscious poses and kiss the earth; for him only in earthbound simplicity was there genuineness.

The best of his notes, together with the essays, form the most durable fund of Butler's eccentric wisdom–a tolerant, unpretentious, but literal-minded pragmatism grounded in the belief that man's sense of pleasure and convenience is the most reliable guide in moral and aesthetic dilemmas; or, put another way, common sense, as manifested in the most kindly and comely people, is the most solid standard for making judgments mankind has as yet found: "The good swell is

Butler at home, Clifford's Inn, Fleet Street, London (photograph by Alfred Emery Cathie)

the creature towards which all nature has been groaning and travailing until now. He is an ideal. He shows what may be done in the way of good breeding, health, looks, temper and fortune. He realises men's dreams of themselves at any rate vicariously; he preaches the gospel of grace." In Butler's view, self-interest and selfishness were not at all what anti-utilitarian Victorians had made of them; indeed the world had always been ruled by such tendencies. One should, therefore, try to make "the self-interest of cads a little more coincident with that of decent people." Post-Victorians who were turning their backs on the high seriousness and moral fervor of the recent Victorian past were ready to appreciate Butler's sort of disrespectful attitude and give hearing to one of the period's black sheep. Consequently Butler exerted a traceable influence on writers coming into their own during the first three decades of the twentieth century, especially in his role of rebel against the authority of school, home, and the church.

His outlook, based as it is on the value of money and property, and his common-sense philosophy are today seen as rather Victorian and bourgeois. Severe criticisms of his smugness multiplied from the late 1930s onward, and they have qualified the originally high estimate he once enjoyed. At the height of his fame Butler was regarded as an important figure, a brilliant and unjustly neglected debunker of his age. Bernard Shaw, in his preface to *Major Barbara* (1907), called him "the greatest English writer of the latter half of the XIX century," for Shaw saw in him the earliest and most brilliant exponent of the anti-Darwinian spirit gathering strength at the turn of the century, and the courageous prophet of Mammon, and the enlightened morality of good health. His fiercest detractor, Malcolm Muggeridge, acknowledged in a 1934 article, "Butler Re-Read," that his own generation was sprung from Butler's loins and that *The Way of All Flesh* remained terrifying because it portrayed so vividly "the very procreation of this our age." Today Butler no longer commands so central a position in the world of literature. Though critical interest continues to attend *Erewhon* and *The Way of All Flesh*, Butler's other works are considered minor, partly because much of what he attacked has vanished and partly because his subjects are specialized and remote. His art criticism is a footnote to Italian minor art; his excursion into higher criticism echoes the conclusions of his contemporaries' secular humanism. As an eccentric late Victorian who anticipated modern attitudes, he remains important; as scientific polemicist he exposed weaknesses in Darwin's historic *On the Origin of Species* (though this aspect of his work is rarely acknowledged); but it is as social critic and satirist, above all, that he still has much to say to delight and instruct the modern reader.

Letters:

Samuel Butler and E. M. A. Savage, Letters 1871-1885, edited by Geoffrey Keynes and Brian Hill (London: Cape, 1935);

The Family Letters of Samuel Butler (1841-1886), edited by Arnold Silver (Stanford, Cal.: Stanford University Press, 1962);

The Correspondence of Samuel Butler with His Sister May, edited by Daniel F. Howard (Berkeley: University of California Press, 1962).

Bibliographies:

Henry Festing Jones and A. T. Bartholomew, *The Samuel Butler Collection at Saint John's College Cambridge* (Cambridge: Heffer, 1921);

A. J. Hoppé, *A Bibliography of the Writings of Samuel Butler* (London: Bookman, 1925);

Carroll A. Wilson, *Catalogue of the Collection of Samuel Butler (of Erewhon) in the Chapin Library Williams College* (Portland, Maine: Southworth-Anthoensen, 1945);

Stanley B. Harkness, *The Career of Samuel Butler (1835-1902) A Bibliography* (New York: Burt Franklin, 1955);

Wayne G. Hammond, "Samuel Butler: A Checklist of Works and Criticism," 3 parts, *Butler Newsletter*, 3 (Summer 1980): 13-24; 3 (December 1980): 51-66; 4 (June 1981): 6-20.

Biographies:

Henry Festing Jones, *Samuel Butler: Author of 'Erewhon' (1835-1902), a Memoir*, 2 volumes (London: Macmillan, 1919);

P. N. Furbank, *Samuel Butler (1835-1902)* (Cambridge: Cambridge University Press, 1948);

Philip Henderson, *Samuel Butler* (London: Cohen & West, 1953);

Lee E. Holt, *Samuel Butler* (New York: Twayne, 1964).

References:

Willem G. Bekker, *An Historical and Critical Review of Samuel Butler's Literary Works* (Rotterdam: Nijgh & Van Ditmar's, 1925);

Gilbert Cannan, *Samuel Butler: A Critical Study* (London: Secker, 1915);

G. D. H. Cole, *Samuel Butler and The Way of All Flesh* (London: Home & Van Thal, 1948);

Benjamin Farrington, *Samuel Butler and the Odyssey* (London: Cape, 1929);

Joseph Fort, *Samuel Butler, l'écrivain: Étude d'un style* (Bordeaux: J. Bière, 1935);

R. S. Garnett, *Samuel Butler and His Family Relations* (London & Toronto: Dent/New York: Dutton, 1926);

John F. Harris, *Samuel Butler, Author of "Erewhon": The Man and His Work* (London: Richards, 1916);

Thomas L. Jeffers, *Samuel Butler Revalued* (University Park: Pennsylvania State University, 1981);

C. E. M. Joad, *Samuel Butler* (London: Parsons, 1924; Boston: Small, Maynard, 1925);

Paul Meissner, *Samuel Butler der Jüngere* (Leipzig: Tauchnitz, 1931);

Malcolm Muggeridge, *The Earnest Atheist: A Study of Samuel Butler* (London: Eyre & Spottiswoode, 1936);

Ralph Norrman, *Samuel Butler and the Meaning of Chiasmus* (Basingstoke, Hampshire: Macmillan, 1986);

Gerold Pestalozzi, *Samuel Butler der Jüngere, Versuch einer Darstellung seiner Gedankenwelt* (Zurich: Universität Zürich, 1914);

Robert F. Rattray, *A Chronicle and an Introduction: Samuel Butler* (London: Duckworth, 1935);

Clara G. Stillman, *Samuel Butler: A Mid-Victorian Modern* (New York: Viking, 1932; London: Secker, 1932);

Rudolf Stoff, *Die Philosophie des Organischen bei Samuel Butler* (Vienna: Phaedon Verlag, 1929).

Papers:

The largest collection of Butler's papers is housed at the St. John's College Library, Cambridge. The Carroll A. Wilson Collection at the Chapin Library, Williams College, has many first editions and the original manuscript of the notebooks. Butler's correspondence is at the British Library.

Charles Darwin

Charles Blinderman
Clark University

BIRTH: Shrewsbury, Shropshire, 12 February 1809, to Robert Waring and Susannah Wedgwood Darwin.

EDUCATION: Edinburgh University, 1825-1827; Cambridge University, B.A., 1831.

AWARDS AND HONORS: Fellow of the Royal Society, 1839; Royal Society Medal, 1853; D.Med. & Chirurg, Breslau, 1862; Copley Medal, 1864; D.Med. & Chirurg, Bonn, 1868; Hon. M.D., Leyden, 1875; LL.D., Cambridge, 1877; Daly Medal, Royal College of Physicians, 1879.

MARRIAGE: 29 January 1839 to Emma Wedgwood; children: William Erasmus, Anne Elizabeth, Mary Eleanor, Henrietta Emma, George Howard, Elizabeth, Francis, Leonard, Horace, and Charles Waring.

DEATH: Down, Kent, 19 April 1882.

BOOKS: *Letters on Geology* (Cambridge: Privately printed, 1835);

Journal and Remarks, 1832-1836, volume three of *Narrative of the Surveying Voyages of His Majesty's Ships Adventure and Beagle,* edited by Robert Fitzroy (London: Colburn, 1839); also published as *Journal of Researches into the Geology and Natural History of the Various Countries Visited by H.M.S. Beagle, under the Command of Capt. Fitzroy, R.N., from 1832 to 1836* (1 volume, London: Colburn, 1839; 2 volumes, New York: Harper, 1846);

The Structure and Distribution of Coral Reefs. Being the First Part of the Geology of the Voyage of the Beagle (London: Smith, Elder, 1842; New York: Appleton, 1896);

Geological Observations on the Volcanic Islands, visited during the Voyage of H.M.S. Beagle, Together with Some Brief Notices on the Geology of Australia and the Cape of Good Hope; Being the Second Part of the Geology of the Voyage of the Beagle, under the Command of Capt. Fitzroy . . . During the Years 1832 to 1836 (London: Smith, Elder, 1844); republished with *Geological Observations on South America,* 1846 (New York: Appleton, 1896);

Geological Observations on South America. Being the Third Part of the Geology of the Voyage of the Beagle (London: Smith, Elder, 1846); republished with *Geological Observations on the Volcanic Islands,* 1844 (New York: Appleton, 1896);

Geology (London: Clownes, 1849);

A Monograph on the Fossil Lepadidae; *or, Pedunculated* Cirripedes *of Great Britain* (London: Paleontographical Society, 1851);

A Monograph on the Sub-class Cirripedia, *with Figures of All Species,* 2 volumes (London: Ray So-

Charles Darwin in 1869, photographed by Julia Margaret Cameron (National Portrait Gallery)

ciety, 1851, 1854);

A Monograph on the Fossil Balandidoe *and* Verrucidoe *of Great Britain* (London: Paleontographical Society, 1854);

On the Origin of Species by means of Natural Selection, or the Preservation of Favoured Races in the Struggle for Life (London: Murray, 1859; New York: Appleton, 1860; six revisions, London: Murray, 1860-1876);

On the Various Contrivances by which British and Foreign Orchids are Fertilised by Insects, and On the Good Effects of Intercrossing (London: Murray, 1862; New York: Appleton, 1877);

The Variation of Animals and Plants under Domestication, 2 volumes (London: Murray, 1868; New York: Orange Judd, 1868);

The Descent of Man, and Selection in Relation to Sex, 2 volumes (London: Murray, 1871; New York: Appleton, 1871);

The Expression of the Emotions in Man and Animals (London: Murray, 1872; New York: Appleton, 1873);

On the Movements and Habits of Climbing Plants (London: Murray, 1875; New York: Appleton, 1876);

Insectivorous Plants (London: Murray, 1875; New York: Appleton, 1875);

The Effects of Cross and Self Fertilisation in the Vegetable Kingdom (London: Murray, 1876; New York: Appleton, 1877);

The Different Forms of Flowers on Plants of the Same Species (London: Murray, 1877; New York: Appleton, 1877);

The Power of Movement in Plants, by Darwin with the assistance of Francis Darwin (London: Murray, 1880; New York: Appleton, 1881);

The Formation of Vegetable Mould, through the Action of Worms, with Observations on Their Habits (London: Murray, 1881; New York: Appleton, 1882);

The Foundations of The Origin of the Species: Two Essays Written in 1842 and 1844, edited by Francis Darwin (Cambridge: University Press, 1909);

The Autobiography of Charles Darwin, edited by Francis Darwin (London: Watts, 1929; New York: Appleton, 1929); revised as *The Autobiography of Charles Darwin 1809-1882. With Original Omissions Restored,* edited by Nora Barlow (Cambridge: University Press, 1933).

OTHER: *The Zoology of the Voyage of H.M.S. Beagle, under the Command of Captain Fitzroy, R.N., during the Years 1832 to 1836,* edited, with introductions, by Darwin, 5 parts (London: Smith, Elder, 1840-1843).

Erasmus Darwin (1731-1802), the grandfather of Charles Darwin, achieved fame as a physician and notoriety as a popularizer of evolutionary biology in such poems as "The Botanic Garden," "Zoonomia," "The Loves of the Plants," and "The Temple of Nature." Both of Erasmus's sons were physicians. Charles Darwin's father, Robert, desired that his sons would continue the family tradition, but that was not to be. As Charles Darwin himself said, when he was sixty-seven years old, "I was born a naturalist."

His experiences at school from childhood to undergraduate adulthood confirm that self-analysis. Born in Shrewsbury, Shropshire, on 12 February 1809, he began his formal education when he was eight and a half years old, at Mr. Case's day school. Here he showed a precocious interest in gardening and in collecting pebbles, minerals, newts, birds' eggs, and beetles. He aspired then to know something of every pebble in front of the hall door. From 1818-1825 he attended Dr. Butler's boarding school, where he showed an equally strong lack of interest in the classical scholarship focused on by the educational system. The child dutifully learned his forty or fifty lines of Homer or Virgil daily and then promptly forgot them. The adult wrote harshly of Dr. Butler's: "The school as a means of education to me was simply a blank." He was, as he recalled, looked down upon as merely an "ordinary boy," a bit slow. His father shared that opinion of the schoolmasters and once angrily said to him, "You care for nothing but shooting, dogs, and rat-catching, and you will be a disgrace to yourself and all your family." Darwin always thought this opinion unjust.

Educational experiences after Dr. Butler's school did little to contradict Robert Darwin's unflattering opinion of his son's intellectual talent. In October 1825 Darwin was sent to Edinburgh University to commence the medical studies that his grandfather, uncle, and father had undertaken. Except for some lectures in chemistry, the instruction at Edinburgh was, for Darwin, no better than that to which he had been subjected earlier: his required work ranged from "intolerably" and "incredibly" dull lectures on geology to "disgusting" investigations of human anatomy. He did manage to visit some patients, poor people, consulting with his father on how to diagnose symptoms and effect whatever cure was possible. He was haunted for years by the memory of a surgical operation in those days before chloroform and once raced out of the surgical theater. He enjoyed shooting birds much more than attending lectures. There was little auspicious in his record at Edinburgh, and it seemed highly unlikely that Charles Darwin would ever become a physician.

His father, recognizing this unhappy truth, removed him from Edinburgh and, in 1828, sent him to Cambridge University, where he would study to become a clergyman. That Robert Darwin chose this career for his son is surprising, since Robert, like his own father, Erasmus, was unorthodox. Charles himself, finding nothing unpleasant in the prospect of becoming an Anglican clergyman, subscribed without protest to declaring his faith in the Thirty-nine Articles of the Anglican Church. In his autobiography, which ranks with those of John Henry Newman and John Stuart Mill as among the most important of the Victorian period, Darwin wrote, "I did not then in the least doubt the strict and literal truth of every word in the Bible. I soon persuaded myself that our Creed must be fully accepted. It never struck me how illogical it was to say that I believed in what I could not understand and what is in fact unintelligible." Considering the circumstance that orthodox clergymen attacked him fiercely throughout his life, he described his once having studied for the clergy as "ludicrous."

The three years he stayed at Cambridge University, 1828 to 1831, were, in his estimation, a waste of time. He was slow at mathematics, rarely attended the lectures in the classics (he had entirely forgotten whatever he had learned at Dr. Butler's school), and began to hang around with a set of friends who preferred singing, drinking, and playing cards to studying. What gave him even greater pleasure than this dissipation was collecting beetles. "I will give a proof of my zeal: one day on tearing off some old bark, I saw two rare beetles and seized one in each hand; then I saw a third and new kind, which I could not bear to lose, so that I popped the one which I held in my right hand into my mouth. Alas it ejected some intensely acrid fluid, which burnt my tongue so that I was forced to spit the beetle out, which was lost, as well as the third one." However, specimens of beetles that he collected were represented in a book, *Illustrations of British Entomology* (1828-1835), and Darwin was delighted to see a specimen ascribed to him: "captured by C. Darwin, Esq." In later years, a water beetle, *Colymbetes Darwinii;* a giant tortoise, *Testudo Darwinii;* an orchid, *Bonatea Darwinii;* and more than a hundred other animals and plants would be named after him—as well as sea channels and bays and sounds, mountains, towns, a volcano, a real college—Darwin College of Cambridge—and a fictional one—Darwin College in the 1937 Marx Brothers movie, *A Day at the Races.*

At Cambridge, professors Adam Sedgwick and John Henslow discovered in the undergraduate student an aptitude for scientific pursuits. On walking tours, Darwin would observe and study rocks and stratification with the geologist Sedgwick, and on excursions he would botanize with Professor Henslow, with whom he became close friends. To Henslow, Darwin read aloud passages from German naturalist Alexander von Humboldt's *Personal Narrative of Travels to the Equinoctial Regions of the New Continent,* a work which inspired in the young undergraduate "a burning zeal to add even the most humble contribution to the noble structure of Natural Science." The opportunity to make that contribution came in the form of an invitation transmitted from Capt. Robert Fitzroy to Professor Henslow.

Great Britain developed in the nineteenth century as one of the most active European colonizing countries. In order to conduct international trade and military affairs, it was necessary to have authentic records of oceanic currents, depths, harbors, and so forth. This work was undertaken on ships that sailed the world. One of these ships, H.M.S. *Beagle*, a brig of 235 tons (of the type nicknamed "coffins" because of vulnerability to storms) manned by Capt. Robert Fitzroy, was about to sail for Tierra del Fuego, at the southern tip of South America, and from there proceed to the South Seas and the Indian archipelago. Captain Fitzroy requested that Professor Henslow recommend a young man to be a companion on this voyage. On 24 August 1831 Henslow wrote to Darwin, inviting him to take Fitzroy's offer.

Darwin was eager to do so, but his father objected for several reasons, including his belief that such a "wild scheme" would be an impediment to a clerical career. As a result of support from Darwin's uncle Josiah Wedgwood, Robert Darwin relented, and when, on 27 December 1831, H.M.S. *Beagle* sailed from Devonport, C. Darwin, Esq., was aboard as companion to Captain Fitzroy.

The voyage of the *Beagle* was a critical episode in Darwin's life and, considering the impact his ideas had upon science, literature, philosophy, religion, and economics, important for the world. Although Darwin was taken on as companion, he indulged his interests in naturalism, surveying geological formations, collecting and identifying birds and insects and other animals, and investigating fossils. His independent investigations of these things suggested that natural theology was an invalid explanation for the history of the earth and its organisms.

Natural theology was a complex of ideas that dated back almost 2,000 years before Darwin accompanied Fitzroy on the *Beagle*. The complex was called "natural theology" because its fundamental principle was that a harmony existed between the book of revelations, that is, the Bible, and the book of nature, that is, everything from microscopic organisms to mountains to the starry heavens. According to natural theology, the earth was only 6,000 years old (the exact date of its birth had been calculated as 23 October 4,004 B.C., at 9 A.M.), its major changes had come about mostly through catastrophes (such as a universal flood), and God had created each species by it-

Capt. Robert Fitzroy of the H.M.S. Beagle *(courtesy of the Director of Greenwich Hospital and the Admiral President, Royal Naval College, Greenwich). Although Darwin's father disapproved his son's "wild scheme," Darwin sailed aboard the* Beagle *as a naturalist and companion to Fitzroy on 27 December 1831.*

self, designing each living being's structure for optimum adaptation to its environment. William Paley's *Natural Theology* (1802), one of the most famous of the hundreds of books on this theme, much impressed the young Cambridge undergraduate.

What Darwin discovered in South America could not easily be reconciled with natural theology, which was as much part of the scientific outlook of the day as it was of the religious. For example, in South America Darwin found the remains of mollusks on top of the Andes. He surmised that the Andes had not jutted from the earth in a fierce catastrophe, but had risen slowly, carrying the mollusks in that inexorable and gradual ascent. But for this 4,000-mile mountain range, peaking at 22,835 feet, to rise from the bottom of the sea must have taken much more than 6,000 years. Such a speculation was supported by a book Darwin took with him on the voyage, the first volume of the first edition of Charles Lyell's

Principles of Geology (1830-1833). Lyell proposed that the earth was older than 6,000 years, that it had developed gradually, and that phenomena that can be observed in the present (rivers cutting into their channels, expanding, meandering, depositing silt into deltas, wind erosion, upheaval of land masses, denudation) are uniform with what happened in the past. This uniformitarianism contradicted some of the assumptions of natural theology.

If God had created each species of animals as a separate entity, then, Darwin wondered, why was there a close similarity between the extinct *Megatherium* (a giant sloth) he dug out of the rocks and the smaller sloth he could observe hanging upside down from branches? He also found it hard to understand on the basis of natural theology why there were so many species of finches, all apparently related, yet each differing in some small measure, such as form or function of beak, from all the others. He began to hypothesize that perhaps the extant sloth had developed somehow from the extinct giant sloth whose bones he had unearthed and sent to Prof. Richard Owen in England, and that perhaps all the species of finches had developed from a single species. But he could not, at that time, figure out how such development–transmutation, as it was called then, or evolution, as the process came to be called–could have taken place. A few other people, particularly French naturalists, had tried to solve the same puzzle. One of these, John-Baptiste Lamarck (1744-1829), had proposed that evolution occurred because living things wanted to improve; they designed the change they wanted and then passed it on to their offspring in a progressive scheme.

That the voyage gave Darwin the training necessary to the profession of naturalist is clear. It can also be seen as the apprenticeship for Darwin as a writer. Captain Fitzroy thought that some parts of Darwin's journal were worth publishing. Darwin's sisters adored their brother's letters. Professor Henslow was so impressed by the letters he received that he had them privately printed in 1835 and distributed under the title *Letters on Geology*. Upon reading the letters to Henslow, Professor Sedgwick predicted that the former young divinity student would "take a place amongst the leading scientific men."

In the fall of 1836 the *Beagle* returned to England, and in December Darwin found lodgings at Cambridge, where he proceeded to revise his journal notes for publication and work on an ac-

count of Chilean geology for Charles Lyell. Four months later he moved to London, where he remained for two years, preparing geological and biological papers, seeing Charles Lyell often, taking excursions to study British geology, and, for relaxation, reading the poetry of Wordsworth and Coleridge. In July of 1836 he began the first of many notebooks on the question of how species originated, a subject which kept him well occupied, despite other projects, for twenty years. The year 1836 also saw the publication of the Bridgewater Treatises. Sponsored by the Earl of Bridgewater, these books discussed "the Power, Wisdom, and Goodness of God as Manifested in the Creation" and were dedicated to the proposition that biblical and scientific theories harmonized. Among the more important contributors to this series of eight texts were the philosopher of science William Whewell; the geologist William Buckland; and the physiologist Charles Bell. The title of Bell's contribution illustrates the ambition of the Bridgewater project: *The Hand, Its Mechanism and Vital Endowments, as Evidencing Design.*

Issues of a more personal kind than the fixity of species occupied his thoughts while he was living alone at Great Marlboro Street in London. "My God," he reflected in a personal note, "it is intolerable to think of spending one's whole life like a neuter bee working, working, and nothing after all.–No, no won't do.–Imagine living all one's days solitarily in smoky, dirty London house–Only picture to yourself a nice soft wife on a sofa, with good fire and books and music perhaps–compare this vision with the dingy reality of Gt. Marlboro St. Marry, marry, marry, Q.E.D." On 29 January 1839 Darwin married his cousin Emma Wedgwood, with whom he eventually had ten children, eight of whom survived. Later in the year he was elected Fellow of the Royal Society.

On 14 September 1842 Emma and Charles Darwin moved to Down, a village in Kent, where Darwin lived for the remaining forty years of his life, going into society less and less frequently, but often taking vacations for hydrotherapeutic treatments to cure various ailments, the most important gastric and cardiac. He was doubly fortunate to have a wife for comfort and amusement, since he was losing his interest in anything other than science.

In his autobiography he specified the beginning of his disaffection with poetry, painting, and music as having occurred around 1840, the time of his marriage and move to Kent. "Up to the age of thirty, or beyond it, poetry of many kinds, such as the works of Milton, Gray, Byron, Wordsworth, Coleridge and Shelley, gave me great pleasure, and even as a schoolboy I took intense delight in Shakespeare especially in the historical plays. I have also said that formerly Pictures gave me considerable, and music very great delight. But now [1876] for many years I cannot endure to read a line of poetry: I have tried lately to read Shakespeare and found it so intolerably dull that it nauseated me." But he developed an abiding taste for novels, those "not of a very high order." He liked the ones that ended happily. "A novel, according to my taste, does not come into the first class, unless it contains some person whom one can thoroughly love, and if it be a pretty woman all the better." He would rest in the afternoons, lying on his sofa, while Emma read these romantic sagas to him. "My mind," he went on in his autobiography, "seems to have become a kind of machine for grinding general laws out of large collections of facts."

As a scientist, Darwin investigated geological and biological phenomena and studied research relevant to such investigations. Like most functioning scientists then and now, he wrote about his discoveries, and he invented theories to explain them. His books and articles, sequentially published from 1839 onward, indicate that he was competent at writing along the spectrum from literature addressed to professional peers to popular works addressed to a wider audience. It must also be noted that he excelled at a kind of writing often overlooked–epistolary literature. He wrote thousands of letters, and from these emerges a personality most often tranquil, modest, disciplined, and good-natured, sometimes passionate, even teasing and humorous, and here and there melancholic.

To read his letters and private journals is to admire the man himself. But Darwin's fame rests on his extensive output of articles and books. His first publications were reports on geological subjects investigated during the *Beagle* survey–volcanic islands, elevation and denudation of mountains, the development of coral reefs, atolls, and lagoons. He also wrote papers on zoological subjects–*Sagitta*, terrestrial *Planaria*, fossil *Lepadidae*. In 1839 his first full-length book appeared simultaneously as *Journal and Remarks, 1832-1836*, volume three of the *Narrative of the Surveying Voyages of His Majesty's Ships Adventure and Beagle*, edited by Captain Fitzroy, and as an independent work, *Journal of Researches into the Geology and Natural History of the Various Countries Visited by H.M.S. Beagle*. The *Journal of Researches* attracted a large audience: it went into four English editions and was published in the United States. In the nineteenth century it was translated into (sequentially) German, French, Dutch, Italian, Russian, Swedish, Danish, Hungarian, and Japanese; and in the twentieth century into Chinese, Czech, Latvian, Greek, Portuguese, Finnish, Armenian, Ukrainian, Bulgarian, Romanian, Slovene, Korean, Flemish, Lithuanian, Hebrew, Hindi, and Turkish.

The *Journal of Researches* well typifies the kind of literature that Darwin himself relished, exemplified by Humboldt's *Personal Narrative*–travel literature, revelation of exotic lands, their fauna and flora and cultures. His style is immediate and personal, as is appropriate to a journal. For example, on 29 February 1832, at Bahia, he noted his exuberant response to a Brazilian forest: "The day has passed delightfully. Delight itself, however, is a weak term to express the feelings of a naturalist who, for the first time, has wandered by himself in a Brazilian forest. The elegance of the grasses, the novelty of the parasitical plants, the beauty of the flowers, the glossy green of the foliage, but above all the general luxuriance of the vegetation, filled me with admiration."

Writing of this kind, a style immediate, personal, full of value terms, is accessible not only to a professional audience but to a popular one as well; Darwin lets us see what he sees and provides dramatic interpretation with a literary flair comparable to Herman Melville's. *The Structure and Distribution of Coral Reefs* (1842) is the second of Darwin's full-length works based on the *Beagle* voyage. Characterized by fewer personal references and rarely indulging in revealing the effect of natural phenomena upon the author, it represents a point on the spectrum of scientific writing closer to the terminus of specialized scientific prose. In the course of its almost three hundred pages, this book endeavored to convince fellow geologists that Darwin's theory was superior to its contenders attempting to explain the structure, growth, and distribution of coral reefs.

"I found, just within the outer margin, the great mounds of Porites and Millepora, with their summits lately killed, and their sides subsequently thickened by the growth of the coral: a layer, also, of Nullipora had already coated the dead surface. As the external slope of the reef is the same round the whole of this and many other atolls, the angle of inclination must result from an adaptation between the growing powers

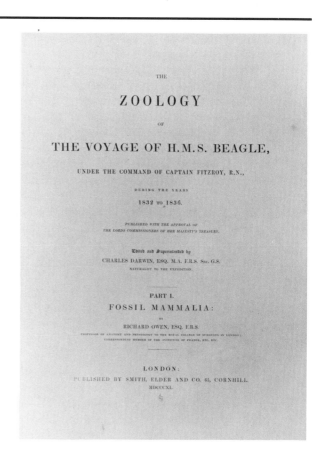

Left: advertisement for Darwin's first full-length work based on his journals from the Beagle *voyage; right: title page from the five-part survey supervised by Darwin in the late 1830s and early 1840s (Thomas Cooper Library, University of South Carolina)*

of the coral and the force of the breakers, and their action on the loose sediment. The reef, therefore, could not increase outwards without a nearly equal addition to every part of the slope, so that the original inclination might be preserved, and this would require a large amount of sediment, all derived from the wear of corals and shells, to be added to the lower part."

This is not the stuff of science popularization: the coral animals mentioned and the theories are unfamiliar; the passage has to be read slowly; and, in justice to Darwin, it should be read in context, for ninety-nine pages of explanation precede this description.

For eight years, from 1846 to 1854, Darwin focused on the study of a particular animal, the barnacle. Work on these crustaceans was tedious but gave him training in anatomy and taxonomy, which well supplemented the training he had already undergone in geology and zoology. As he had designed a new theory that replaced older ones in explaining the growth of coral reefs, so in the eight years he devoted to barnacles, he designed a new system of classification. The follow-

ing passage from one of his 1851 monographs finds a location further along the spectrum; it would be comprehensible only to those already familiar with the barnacle's anatomical structures and processes, the scientists to whom it is addressed: "The umbones (and primordial valves when distinguishable) are seated at the rostral angles; during growth the basal margin is not added to, and the occludent margin only to small extent; hence the main growth of the valve is at the upper end, and along the carina-tergal margin. In *L. fascicularis*, however, the basal reflexed margin is slightly added to beneath the umbo."

His letters of these years discuss the challenge of reorganizing the nomenclature of barnacles and the problems he had then and would continue to have with ill health. Several answers have been given to the question of why Darwin was chronically ill—that it was a result of the seasickness he had suffered during the *Beagle* voyage; that the black bug which bit him in Argentina (an event noted in his journal, 25 March 1835) had infected him with Chagas' disease; that he suffered from excessive eye strain, arsenic poisoning, an allergy to pigeons, inherited depression; or that it was psychosomatic, caused by his wife's opposition to the theory he was working out, by a fear of what others would say, or by a lingering feeling of fulfilling his father's prognosis that he would come to no good; or that he was a hypochondriac. Whatever the reason—this mystery has not been solved—he could work only a few hours a day. In those few hours, he accomplished, however, a good deal. The letters also discuss a variety of other subjects, such as submarine coal and *Vestiges of the Natural History of Creation*.

This book, published anonymously in 1844, is important in itself, for it presented for the first time in English literature a full scheme of evolution, from the coalescence of the planet earth to the introduction of primitive single-celled organisms and subsequent development of more complex multicelled organisms, sponges, worms, fishes, reptiles, mammals, to the origination and dispersion of human beings. It was a best-seller—more than 140,000 copies during its career of eleven editions. *Vestiges of the Natural History of Creation* is also important in its influence upon the novel and poetry. Although the author (Robert Chambers) expressed his belief that God had initiated the process, the evolutionary scheme worked out agitated people who found it contradictory to the Bible. One such person, the politician and novelist Benjamin Disraeli, satirized Chambers's volume in his novel *Tancred* (1847). In *In Memoriam* (1850), the poet Alfred Tennyson relied upon *Vestiges of the Natural History of Creation* (as well as upon Lyell's *Principles of Geology*) for scientific data dramatizing his own difficulties in reconciling the death of his friend Arthur Henry Hallam, the extinction of animals, the presence in human beings of the ape and tiger, the recklessness of nature, with the conviction that the universe had been intelligently planned for the achievement of a good purpose. Robert Browning alluded to evolution in "Cleon" (1855). People were writing about evolution in biological and popular literature before Darwin undertook his work.

A curious specimen of this time is a book by Philip Gosse. As a naturalist, with particular expertise in ornithology and ichthyology, and lay theologian, Gosse had a foot in both camps and was determined to reconcile disputes between evolutionary theory and biblical descriptions in an effort to restore the harmony of natural theology. His fancy was that fossils hinting at a very old earth were not really the remains of extinct animals: God had designed and planted these fossils to give the earth a coherent history which it actually had not undergone, just as He had given Adam a navel though Adam had no mother—hence the title of the book, *Omphalos* (1857). But straddling both camps led to awkwardness, and no one paid much attention to Gosse's work.

While working on his books on the *Beagle* voyage and on several other interests, such as barnacle nomenclature, Darwin accumulated data. The essential question was to discover what natural process could account for the descent of plants and animals from earlier species. In July of 1837, he opened his first notebook on "Transmutation of Species." In that notebook he wrote, "If we choose to let conjecture run wild, then animals, our fellow brethren in pain, disease, death, suffering, and famine—our slaves in the most laborious works, our companions in our amusements—they may partake of (?) our origin in one common ancestor—we may all be melted together."

In 1838 he read a book by the Reverend Thomas Malthus. *An Essay on the Principle of Population,* first published in 1798, proposed that human population grows faster than does the food supply available to it. An equilibrium is reached as famine, war, and disease reduce the population. Darwin recognized, as others have, that plants and animals tend to produce more offspring than can make livings in their environments. We have then, as the first premise, population pressure. The second premise is that members of any species vary, these variations occurring (somehow) spontaneously; thus an individual pigeon might be different from its sibling fledglings by having a fantail. If the variation is useful to the animal in enabling it to be a better predator, or to escape from predators more efficiently than its siblings, or to be more attractive to a mate, it will not only help insure the individual's survival, but it will also (somehow) be inherited and thus contribute to the survival of the offspring. Over a long period of time many such variations will gradually accumulate, and eventually a new species will arise.

This hypothesis of natural selection is analogous to the principle of artificial selection, whereby a pigeon fancier, for example, will pay special attention to that fantail pigeon in order to breed a new variety. In the natural order of things, a variety will transmute or evolve into a species. Natural selection is not synonymous with evolution; it is one among other explanations of how evolution took or takes place.

"I was so anxious to avoid prejudice," Darwin recollected in his autobiography, "that I determined not for some time to write even the briefest sketch of it. In June 1842 I first allowed myself the satisfaction of writing a very brief abstract of my theory in pencil in 35 pages; and this was enlarged during the summer of 1844 into one of 230 pages. . . ." There was reason for Darwin's reluctance to challenge prejudice: the French naturalist Buffon had been forced to recant because his ideas went counter to natural theology; the English physician William Lawrence had been charged with blasphemy; *Vestiges of the Natural History of Creation* had been published anonymously because Robert Chambers did not want to have his business enterprise (a publishing firm) injured; and Emma Darwin did not care for her husband's wild scheme. Perhaps Darwin felt that he was not yet prepared for his audience or that his audience was not prepared for him. He wrote to a close friend, the botanist Joseph Hooker, "I am almost convinced . . . that species are not (it is like confessing murder) immutable."

It might have been like confessing murder–of religious dogma–but Darwin was so convinced of the high and urgent importance of his hypothesis that he wrote to his wife, 5 July 1844: "I have just finished my sketch of my species theory. If, as I believe, my theory in time be accepted even by one competent judge, it will be a considerable step in science." This statement is followed by a will which specifies £400 as an endowment for continuing the work in case of Darwin's death. Darwin was, then, most eager in 1844 to see his theory of natural selection published. There is no certain answer as to why he waited fourteen years to do so.

In the early 1850s Darwin's barnacle monographs were published, and later in the decade he produced papers on fossils, volcanic rocks, icebergs, seeds, and bees. The provocation for the publication of his most momentous work may be traced to 1855 and to the speculations of Alfred Russel Wallace (1823-1913). While Darwin was working on barnacles, Wallace, in South America, was collecting butterflies and cogitating on their geographical distribution, adaptation, and the possibility that the various kinds he observed and studied had descended, with modifications, from ancestral species; in short, he was moving very much along the lines of Darwin's hypothesis, even to the point of having discovered the clue to natural selection in Malthus. In 1852 he read

a short paper by Herbert Spencer, "The Development Hypothesis," which in supporting the theory of evolution confirmed Wallace's suspicions. This essay by Spencer also used the word *evolution* as we do today and coined the phrase *survival of the fittest.*

In Sarawak, Borneo, housebound because it was the wet season, Wallace, reflecting upon the problem of how species arise, wrote an article entitled "On the Law That Has Regulated the Introduction of New Species" (1855). Given Spencer's "The Development Hypothesis" (1851), Wallace's paper, and other attempts to define evolution, it might be expected that Darwin would be a little apprehensive, or "vexed," as he put it, about the possibility of being scooped. On 3 May 1856 he wrote to Charles Lyell, wondering what he would do "if any one were to publish my doctrines before me." Lyell urged him to publish. But he hesitated: could he write a short paper? would anyone publish such a hypothesis? "It yet strikes me as quite unphilosophical," he wrote to Joseph Hooker on 11 May justifying his procrastination, "to publish results without the full details which have led to such results."

On 5 September 1857 he sent a long letter to the American naturalist Asa Gray, in which, apologizing for sharing with Gray so outrageous a hypothesis and requesting that Gray not mention it to anyone, he provided a clear and thorough outline of natural selection. "Without some reflection," he concluded, "it will appear all rubbish; perhaps it will appear so after reflection." Darwin still took no steps to negotiate publication of his manuscript, "Natural Selection." Nine months after the letter to Gray, in June of 1858, he received from Wallace the latter's latest paper, "On the Tendency of Varieties to Depart Indefinitely from the Original Type." "I never saw a more striking coincidence," he complained to Lyell on 18 June; "if Wallace had my MS. sketch written out in 1844, he could not have made a better short abstract! Even his terms now stand as heads of my chapters." He concluded, with a degree of sadness and frustration one can well imagine, "So all my Originality, whatever it may amount to, will be smashed. . . ." Darwin was worried that he had been scooped by Wallace, that people might accuse him of having plagiarized from Wallace, that his concern about originality was itself shameful.

Lyell and Hooker suggested a compromise, and on 1 July 1858, the hypothesis of natural selection was given to the world in the form of two papers–Wallace's essay and Darwin's letters to Asa Gray–presented to the Linnean Society of London. Hooker said that the audience was intensely interested, but that there was no discussion because the subject was too novel and too ominous. Darwin worked on his manuscript, an abstract of his voluminous notes. The publisher John Murray was interested. In a postscript to a letter to Lyell (28 March 1859), Darwin, still worried about subverting Christianity, asked: "Would you advise me to tell Murray that my book is not more *un*-orthodox than the subject makes inevitable. That I do not discuss the origin of man. That I do not bring in any discussion about Genesis, &c., &c., and only give facts, and such conclusions from them as seem to me fair." On 24 November 1859 John Murray published *On the Origin of Species by means of Natural Selection, or the Preservation of Favoured Races in the Struggle for Life.*

"God knows what the public will think," Darwin exclaimed on the eve of publication. The public thought the book worth having–booksellers bought up the first edition of 1,250 copies on the first day of publication. There were many reviews–Darwin himself collected 256 before he gave up–and they ran the gamut from the offensively hostile to the mildly skeptical to the very favorable. One credible survey estimates that of 74 reviews, roughly a quarter (17) were neutral, another quarter (19) favorable, and half (38) unfavorable. Professor Sedgwick wrote to Darwin (24 December 1859) that he had found parts of *On the Origin of Species* so funny that he laughed until his sides were almost sore; but the book gave him "more pain than pleasure," for there was much in it "utterly false and grievously mischievous." *On the Origin of Species* seemed to deny the operative agency of a deity. (Fifteen reviews, including those by Sedgwick and Richard Owen, are found in David L. Hull's *Darwin and His Critics*, 1973; the basic study of contemporary reception in Britain is Alvar Ellegård's *Darwin and the General Reader*, 1958; surveys and bibliographies on reception not only in Britain but also in other European countries, in the United States, Mexico, and the Islamic world are included in *The Comparative Reception of Darwinism*, edited by Thomas F. Glick, 1974.)

At the other extreme from Sedgwick was a review that appeared in the *Times* of London. While maintaining that Darwin's theory had not been fully proven, this review complimented Darwin for having designed the best explanation of how evolution proceeds. Darwin was amazed to find the *Times* coming out in support of his heterodox ideas. "It will do grand service," he wrote to Joseph Hooker. "If you should happen to be *acquainted* with the author," Darwin wrote to T. H. Huxley, "for Heaven-sake tell me who he is?" Huxley was himself the author of this review. Darwin had met Huxley, who was ten years younger, in 1855, but he had not shared his ideas about evolution. As an anatomist and paleontologist Huxley had the requisite scientific training to write authoritatively of the issues Darwin developed; as a writer of exceptional power and a man of exceptional passion, he was poised to emerge as Darwin's strongest defender. After reading *On the Origin of Species* he advised Darwin not to be disgusted by the considerable amount of abuse and misrepresentation which would be in store. And he solaced Darwin by reminding him that some of the group of friends were combative. And then: "I am sharpening up my claws and beak in readiness."

A second edition of *On the Origin of Species* was published in January of 1860 (3,000 copies), and in May a first edition was published in the United States (2,500 copies). Although it did not have a huge sale–36,000 in the nineteenth century, less than *Vestiges of the Natural History of Creation*–it assumed its place as one of the most important books of all time.

Huxley's claws and beak came into use at a meeting of the British Association for the Advancement of Science, held in late June of 1860 at Oxford University. The audience at this conference was looking forward to an anticipated attack by Samuel Wilberforce, bishop of Oxford, on Darwin's book. Bishop Wilberforce had the reputation of being an excellent orator. Huxley had not expected to attend the Saturday-morning session at which the bishop would indulge in his attack but was accosted by Robert Chambers (whom Huxley did not know was the author of *Vestiges of the Natural History of Creation*). Chambers taunted Huxley with deserting the cause, and Huxley said he would go and have his part of the fun. Several speakers offered their opinions of *On the Origin of Species*. Capt. Robert Fitzroy, who had inadvertently given Darwin the opportunity to research evolution on the *Beagle* voyage, held up a large copy of the Bible and shouted, "The book! the book!" Bishop Wilberforce, discourteously named by his opponents "Soapy Sam," attacked *On the Origin of Species* as unscientific, for, among other reasons, ignoring the fact that no one had ever seen evolution take place; and as un-

From one of Darwin's many letters to his Cambridge mentor John Henslow. In this letter, written in November 1839, Darwin suggests that Henslow write on plant life in the Galapagos and Tierra del Fuego (The Dannie and Hettie Heinemann Collection, by permission of the Trustees of The Pierpont Morgan Library).

tion from you on the general character of the Flora of T. del. Fuego. & especially of the alpine Flora.

The one point of land, which projects so far into temperate countries ought to be characterized by very peculiar forms in relation to the northern hemisphere. — Robert Brown has a very large & I believe perfect collection from Tierra del Fuego, which I daresay he would allow you to undertake, if you chose, as it has been in his possession about nine years. — I do not believe anyone has published any general account of the Flora of Patagonia, — such as my collection is. — it gives I am sure a very fair notion of the Flora — & the climate being so peculiar, I cannot say anything more remarkable than the contrast of it the Flora with the of Tierra del Fuego, although countries so near to each other. — Do think of these points. — I have written to D Colebatch — sent him my printed questions — Don't forget to bear in mind, as you said you would for me, to notice any facts either hostile or corroboratory of my view of the plants occasionally

Christian for positing a universe without the guiding supervision of God, and therefore threatening such basic Christian credenda as the existence of Adam, the redemptive mission of Jesus, and the immortality of the human soul. Toward the conclusion of his attack, the bishop turned to Professor Huxley and jokingly asked him whether he had descended from an ape on his grandfather's or his grandmother's side.

Huxley, thus unexpectedly invited to respond, rose and replied that he would prefer to descend from an ape than from a man like Bishop Wilberforce. This attack by a scientist on a clergyman, particularly on a clergyman as elevated as the bishop of Oxford, caused a sensation. A lady fainted. Darwin wrote to Huxley afterward, "I honour your pluck; I would as soon have died as tried to answer the Bishop in such an assembly. . . ." The incident at Oxford served to show the world that scientists would not passively tolerate ecclesiastical criticism of evolutionary theory.

In 1861 Darwin revised *On the Origin of Species* for its third edition (which appeared in April 1861). The work had already been translated into German; it would be translated into most other European and many non-European languages. While revising the *Origin of Species*, Darwin worked on other books: in 1862 appeared his *On the Various Contrivances by which British and Foreign Orchids are Fertilised by Insects, and On the Good Effects of Intercrossing*, and in 1868 *The Variation of Animals and Plants Under Domestication* was published.

The clergyman Charles Kingsley wrote to a friend of his: "The state of the scientific mind is most curious; Darwin is conquering everywhere, and rushing in like a flood, by the mere force of truth and fact." *On the Origin of Species* did conquer almost everywhere; as the years passed, more and more scientists came to discard older notions and accept Darwin's new interpretations. But it is critical to understand that Darwin's major book tried to achieve two distinct objectives: to prove that evolution, or "change of species by descent," occurred and still occurs; and to prove that the hypothesis of natural selection explains how evolution works. In writing to Asa Gray (11 May 1863) that "Natural Selection seems to me utterly unimportant, compared to the question of Creation *or* Modification," Darwin himself opted for the priority of the first of these objectives. The opinions of Darwin's three closest friends illustrate the range of acceptance of his views. Charles Lyell was for a long time un-

convinced that natural selection explained evolution, and though he converted (as late as 1868) to Darwin's theory in general, he was always uneasy about its application to the human species (the co-discoverer of natural selection, Alfred Wallace, rejected that application). T. H. Huxley, while finding Darwin's hypothesis of natural selection the best explanation available, never fully subscribed to it, though he did fully subscribe to the theory of evolution. Of the three, Joseph Hooker was the most partisan colleague. This spread of opinion among evolutionists continues today.

On the Origin of Species did not conquer by the mere force of truth and fact. It does seem plausible that Darwin's book achieved a steadfast fame greater than that of its more sensational and often erroneous predecessor, *Vestiges of the Natural History of Creation*, because it is replete with facts amenable to verification. Theory aside, *On the Origin of Species* remains a competent instructor in natural history. It also seems plausible that in stressing the role of competition, Darwin's volume fit in well with an economic system that also emphasized the importance of competition and thus complemented the culture's bias. But one might add to these reasons that *On the Origin of Species* conquered because it was written in a style that still intrigues readers: it is specialized scientific literature that, significantly, employs the techniques of popular literature. That the facts are scientific, or subject to empirical verification, is indisputable. But whether the theories are is another question, answered by claims that natural selection is in itself the most valid explanation of evolution, that it requires constant updating and modification, or that it is as fictional as the Genesis account or the *Omphalos* version of creation.

On the Origin of Species is popular because it is personal. In one letter Darwin told his friend Joseph Hooker a "good joke." A reviewer pointed out that "in the first four paragraphs of the introduction, the words 'I,' 'me,' 'my,' occur forty-three times! I was dimly conscious of the accursed fact. He says it can be explained phrenologically, which I suppose civilly means, that I am the most egotistically self-sufficient man alive; perhaps so." And he added in a postscript: "Do not spread this pleasing joke; it is rather too biting." Scientific literature tends to shy away from the involvement of the author in its effort to give the facts in themselves rather than in their effect upon the scientist. But Darwin throughout *On the Origin of Species* alludes to that effect, and is comfortable with phrases such

Portrait by George Richmond of Darwin's wife, Emma Wedg-wood Darwin (courtesy of Down House and The Royal College of Surgeons of England)

as "I think it highly probable," "I am doubtfully inclined to belief," "I must believe," "I can, indeed, hardly doubt." Bishop Wilberforce was well aware of this aspect of style, and discounted the scientific merit of Darwin's book partially because of its personal touch.

Another feature of popular literature in *On the Origin of Species* is simplicity of language, avoidance of technical terminology. Darwin commented on this aspect of his approach to writing: "I never study style; all that I do is try to get the subject as clear as I can in my own head, and express it in the commonest language which occurs to me. But I generally have to think a good deal before the simplest arrangement and words occur to me." The following passage, part of a discussion on the tendency of living things to overproduce, is an example of clear and simple prose: "The elephant is reckoned to be the slowest breeder of all known animals, and I have taken some pains to estimate its probable minimum rate of natural increase: it will be under the mark to assume that it breeds when thirty years old, and goes on breeding to ninety years old, bringing forth three pair of young in this interval; if this be so, at the end of the fifth century there would be alive fifteen million elephants, descended from the first pair."

Unlike scientific prose, the prose of *On the Origin of Species* is anecdotal. Darwin enjoyed telling, and readers enjoyed reading, stories about animals, especially about the odd behavior of animals or of their collectors (for instance, Darwin's popping a beetle into his mouth). One example of many such tales in *On the Origin of Species* concerns the relationship between clover and cats. Bumble bees fertilize red clover. Therefore, if the number of bees were diminished in a region, the clover would decline. Field mice account for the destruction of bees (by destroying their nests and combs). The number of field mice is dependent on the number of cats that destroy the mice. "Hence it is quite credible that the presence of a feline animal in large numbers in a district might determine, through the intervention first of mice and then of bees, the frequency of certain flowers in that district!" The late American cartoonist Walt Kelly was inspired to carry this one step further: clover–bees–mice–cats–and spinsters who keep cats.

Darwin is imaginative in the employment of figures of speech–personifications, metaphors, similes. The phrase *natural selection* is a personification, troublesome because it connotes a nature that can, like a human breeder, choose for survival what it likes. In a letter to a friend, Darwin said, apropos of the phrase's causing trouble, that if he had it to do over again, he would use the term *natural preservation*. He did come to employ Herbert Spencer's phrase *survival of the fittest* as a more neutral designation than "natural selection." The vocabulary of *On the Origin of Species* is rich in such words and phrases as *war, famine, dearth, the great and complex battle of life*. The view of nature that these terms suggest was commonplace then (and remains familiar today). Darwin's own grandfather had written that the first law of organic nature is "Eat or be eaten"; nature is "one great slaughter-house, one universal scene of rapacity and injustice." Tennyson had caught this view in the image "Nature red in tooth and claw."

Romantic optimism, that nature is benign, receives refutation in passages such as this: "We behold the face of nature bright with gladness, we often see superabundance of food; we do not see, or we forget, that the birds which are idly singing round us mostly live on insects or seeds, and are thus constantly destroying life; or we forget how largely these songsters, or their eggs, or their nestlings, are destroyed by birds and beasts of prey. . . ." Darwin sometimes saw nature as devilish and could not shake off horrors such as the incubation of the ichneumon fly—the female lays her eggs in bodies of living caterpillars, and the young eat their hosts. "What a book a devil's chaplain might write," he exclaimed to Joseph Hooker, "on the clumsy, wasteful, blundering, low, and horribly cruel works of nature!"

Yet the world of nature has its beauties and Darwin waxes poetical in describing them: "the plumed seed which is wafted by the gentlest breeze." There is an epic quality to the struggle, even for ants which, like little pirates, return from their marauding "burthened with booty." *On the Origin of Species* has been compared not only to epic literature, but to scriptural as well. Darwin is not reluctant to express his own ethical and aesthetic opinions about the incidents he describes, and he is often carried aloft by enthusiasm on what it all signifies—ultimate victory rather than despondent defeat, a happy ending.

The noted aspects of his style come together in the powerful concluding paragraph to the first edition of *On the Origin of Species:* "It is interesting to contemplate an entangled bank, clothed with plants of many kinds, with birds singing on the bushes, with various insects flitting about, and with worms crawling through the damp earth, and to reflect that these elaborately constructed forms, so different from each other, and dependent on each other in so complex a manner, have all been produced by laws acting around us. . . . Thus, from the war of nature, from famine and death, the most exalted object which we are capable of conceiving, namely, the production of the higher animals, directly follows. There is grandeur in this view of life, with its several powers, having been Originally breathed into a few forms or into one; and that, whilst this planet has gone cycling on according to the fixed law of gravity, from so simple a beginning endless forms most beautiful and most wonderful, have been, and are being, evolved." The perspective here is cosmic, reaching up from crawling worms to the spin of the planet around the sun, and it is infused with that chronic sense of appreciation of nature's rich and curious wonders that Darwin, as a literary figure of high talent, seduces readers into sharing.

For the second edition of *On the Origin of Species* Darwin inserted the phrase "by the Creator," so that the final line begins, "There is grandeur in this view of life, with its several powers, having been Originally breathed by the Creator into a few forms or into one. . . ." This alteration may

Darwin with his oldest child, William (courtesy of Down House and The Royal College of Surgeons of England)

suggest that Darwin was an evolutionary theist like Robert Chambers, Charles Kingsley, Charles Lyell, and many others then and now; or that he was attempting to placate opponents; or that by "the Creator" he simply meant natural laws.

Except for a warning that "Much light will be thrown on man and his history," Darwin did not mention human evolution in *On the Origin of Species.* Readers, were, however, more interested in that possibility than in the evolution of marine iguanas. Despite Darwin's not dwelling on this most dangerous subject, the implication that evolution applies to men as well as to lizards rattled Bishop Wilberforce's sabers as he cut *On the Origin of Species* at the Oxford meeting. Charles Lyell could not agree that human beings evolved without divine supervision—he refused, in his words, to go the "whole orang." A poem by Philip Egerton, published anonymously in an 1861 issue of *Punch,* begins:

> Am I satyr or Man?
> Pray tell me who can,
> And settle my place in the scale,
> A man in ape's shape,

An anthropoid ape,
Or a monkey deprived of its tail?

The Vestiges taught
That all came from naught,
By "development," so-called, "progressive;"
That insects and worms
Assume higher forms
By modification excessive.

Then Darwin set forth,
In a book of much worth,
The importance of "Nature's selection;"
How the struggle for life
Is a laudable strife,
And results in "specific distinction."

This poem also refers to geological finds showing that tool-making human beings lived at the same time as prehistoric animals and to a controversy between Huxley and Owen. Before the publication of *On the Origin of Species*, Huxley had been provoked by the anti-Darwinian Richard Owen to investigate the human being's relation to other primates. Huxley disagreed with Owen's contention that certain cerebral structures possessed by human beings accounted for their humanness, the lack of these structures for an ape's apishness. Huxley investigated, found these structures in the brains of apes, and monkeys as well, lectured on the subject, and, in 1863, published the first comprehensive account of human evolution: *Evidence as to Man's Place in Nature*. This includes reference to Neanderthal man, the only prehistoric humanoid fossil known at that time. The book was popular and sold well. "Hurray," wrote Darwin upon receiving it, "the Monkey Book has come."

Evidence as to Man's Place in Nature ignited a good deal of hostility. In an abusive article in the *Athenaeum* an anonymous commentator concluded that as Charles Lyell tried to remove human beings back in time, so Huxley aimed at degrading human beings, parading as he does the "gibbering, grovelling apes" who are supposed to be our ancestors. Where then "is our pride of ancestry, our heraldic pomp, our vaunted nobility of descent?"

The argument between professors Owen and Huxley on the presence or absence of those cerebral structures appeared in poems and in a squib entitled "A report of a sad case recently tried before the Lord Mayor, Owen *versus* Huxley" (published in *Punch*); in the pages of a best-selling children's book, Charles Kingsley's *The*

Water-Babies (1863); and in Edward Jenkins's *Lord Bantam* (1872).

Darwin was not altogether satisfied with Huxley's *Man's Place in Nature*, nor with Charles Lyell's *The Geological Evidences of the Antiquity of Man*, another book of 1863 on the subject of human evolution, and proceeded to collate his notes for his own contribution. *The Descent of Man, and Selection in Relation to Sex* (1871), a work on evolution second only to *On the Origin of Species* in impact, also is a combination of scientific and popular writing. It has the stylistic characteristics already noted for its predecessor, some of which are worth further exemplification. *The Descent of Man* is even more anecdotal than Darwin's earlier book. In passages showing human similarities to other primates, Darwin goes beyond comparative anatomy into comparative behavior—we learn of monkeys who will "smoke tobacco with pleasure," of baboons getting drunk on strong beer and suffering hangovers, of people who can move their outer ears and even their scalps—one paterfamilias "could, when a youth, pitch several heavy books from his head by the movement of his scalp alone; and he won wages by performing this feat."

The first part of *The Descent of Man* presents evidence of the development of human beings from some lower form. The second part expands on Darwin's hypothesis, also treated in *On the Origin of Species*, of sexual selection. This hypothesis rivals that of natural selection as an explanation of evolutionary development, accounting for horns, ornamentation, physique, color, and so on. Darwin constantly returned to Lyellian gradualism. Just as organs, bones, and other physical materials evolve from lower forms, so do such qualities as mother love, courage, cooperation, even conscience.

He describes such qualities in other animals, personifying animal behavior as he personified nature itself. "Several years ago a keeper at the Zoological Gardens showed me some deep and scarcely healed wounds on the nape of his own neck, inflicted on him, whilst kneeling on the floor, by a fierce baboon. The little American monkey, who was a warm friend of the keeper, lived in the same large compartment, and was dreadfully afraid of the great baboon. Nevertheless, as soon as he saw his friend in peril, he rushed to the rescue, and by screams and bites so distracted the baboon that the man was able to escape, after, as the surgeon thought, running great risk of his life." Darwin approved more of this "heroic little monkey" than he did of the Tierra del Fuego denizens that he observed during the *Beagle* voyage.

In his anthropological musings, Darwin contemplated reasons for the development of human races. He suggested that races developed for aesthetic reasons. For example, in Africa (which he selected as the site for the Origin of humankind), one group of ancestral males preferred dark skin and flattened noses in their females, and so the black race emerged. In Europe, ancestral females preferred men with beards, and so those men endowed with hair on their chins were selected, bred with these women, and passed their hirsuteness on to their male offspring. Sexual selection also accounts for the innate physical and mental differences between men and women. Our ancestral fathers were rivals for the women and, to be successful both in terms of living and loving, had to be strong and aggressive; our ancestral mothers, to attract these men and to take competent care of the babies, had to be beautiful, affectionate, unselfish. This is why men are stronger than women and women better looking than men. Or, to put it in Darwin's statement, "Man is more courageous, pugnacious and energetic than woman, and has a more inventive genius."

In *The Descent of Man,* Darwin offers ethical as well as aesthetic perspectives. On the one hand, he concedes (as his cousin Francis Galton, inventor of eugenics, maintained) that allowing the innately weak and feeble to reproduce will eventually weaken the human species, such allowance being contrary to the progressive improvement brought about by unfettered competition for survival. "We civilised men ... do our utmost to check the process of elimination; we build asylums for the imbecile, the maimed, and the sick; we institute poor-laws; and our medical men exert their utmost skill to save the life of everyone to the last moment. There is reason to believe that vaccination has preserved thousands, who from a weak constitution would formerly have succumbed to small-pox. Thus the weak members of civilised societies propagate their kind. No one who has attended to the breeding of domestic animals will doubt that this must be highly injurious to the race of man." On the other hand, two sentences later, he rejects this eugenical recommendation: "Nor could we check our sympathy, even at the urging of hard reason, without deterioration in the noblest part of our nature." Elsewhere in *The Descent of Man,* he cites

Caricature of Darwin by Sanbourne, published in Punch, *11 December 1875 (Collection of Jerold J. Savory)*

the golden rule, to do unto others as you would have them do unto you, as "the foundation of morality."

Other homilies appear in these pages as well: the "highest possible stage in moral culture is when we recognise that we ought to control our thoughts, and 'not even in inmost thought to think again the sins that made the past so pleasant to us,'" a statement which incidentally shows that Darwin, like his wife, read Tennyson.

The Descent of Man, though it clearly developed the thesis that human beings descended from and are akin to apelike animals, engendered less hostility than did *On the Origin of Species.* The critic for the *Quarterly Review,* continuing the cry that Darwinism was against both philosophy and religion, nevertheless regarded as an open question the proposition that "Man is a glorified ape." The *Non-Conformist* reviewer experienced no difficulty in reconciling Darwin with scripture—even if human beings were structurally similar to apes, they still had the breath of divine life in them. The writer for the *Spectator* discovered that Darwin had given "a far more wonderful vindication of theism than Paley's *Natural Theology.*"

Darwin is known today primarily as a zoologist, the author of *On the Origin of Species*. He also authored travel books, wrote letters assiduously, and produced an important autobiography. The picture of his activities as writer would not be complete if mention of his botanical works were omitted. In these works, he investigates contrivances–the cunning structures by which orchids invite insects to enter them and conduct fertilization, the ways by which plants move and climb, the variations achieved by plants and animals under domestication. On 30 November 1864 the Royal Society gave Darwin its Copley Medal, less for his *On the Origin of Species* than for his 1862 book on orchid fertilization. *The Variation of Animals and Plants under Domestication* (1868) is of interest for its hypothesis of pangenesis–a Lamarckian explanation of heredity, arguing that particles developed in an adult's body will be passed on to the germplasm. Thus, if a man were to develop his biceps, his male child would be born with a better potential for muscular development than would male children lacking an athletic father. Like the hypothesis of natural selection and like Darwin's account of racial and gender distinctions, pangenesis may well be thought of as fiction.

His botanical books averaged a sale of 2,200 copies each. That they were addressed mostly to a professional audience is indicated by this passage from his 1875 work *Insectivorous Plants*, which in its quantitative approach to the topic (digestive action), its unfamiliar terms, and its avoidance of reference to the author or to his aesthetic or ethical sensibilities, typifies specialized scientific prose: "One part of chondrin jelly was dissolved in 218 parts boiling water, and half-minim drops were given to four leaves; so that each received about 1/480 of a grain (.135 mg.) of the jelly; and, of course, much less of dry chondrin. This acted most powerfully, for after only 3 hrs. 30m. all four leaves were strongly inflected. Three of them began to re-expand after 24 hours., and in 48 hrs. were completely open; but the fourth had only partially re-expanded." The central thesis of the botanical books is the evolution of structure and function from primitive to more advanced forms.

The thesis of Darwin's 1872 book, *The Expression of the Emotions in Man and Animals*, again has to do with evolution, this time the evolution of instinct, of aesthetic taste, of blushing, of emotional response. In the notebooks he filled after the return of the *Beagle*, Darwin speculated on many subjects other than those for which he is known

today. He was inquisitive about the ways in which physical conditions bring about mental states. Is the mind independent of the body?, he asked, and answered: "Experience shows the problem of the mind cannot be solved by attacking the citadel itself.–the mind is function of body." In *On the Origin of Species*, in *The Descent of Man*, and in *The Expression of the Emotions in Man and Animals*, Darwin returned to psychology. *The Expression of the Emotions* opens up the last decade of his life. In its immediacy, infusion or intrusion of author, commonness of language, and narrating of stories, it is more like the popular passages of *On the Origin of Species* or *The Descent of Man* than like the scientific prose of his botanical works.

It remains a valuable guide to understanding body language. Scratching one's head (a sign, incidentally, of vulgarity) indicates perplexity; shutting one's eyes or turning away one's face indicates vehement rejection of a proposition, while one who nods his head or opens his eyes widely is ready to accept the proposition. Someone trying to remember something will raise his eyebrows. Darwin traces expressions of contempt, anger, astonishment, fear, love, disgust, defiance, constantly relating human behavior to that of other animals. Rabbits communicate by stomping loudly on the ground, porcupines rattle their quills, storks clatter beaks, dogs rub against masters, and babies clutch mothers. In *The Expression of the Emotions*, Darwin quotes dozens of travelers and other authorities, one of whom described a melancholic scene: "When overpowered and made fast, his grief was most affecting; his violence sunk to utter prostration, and he lay on the ground, uttering choking cries, with tears trickling down his cheeks." This is a description not of a human being, but of an Indian elephant.

Darwin's last book published in his lifetime was *The Formation of Vegetable Mould, through the Action of Worms, with Observations on Their Habits* (1881). "My heart & soul," he wrote while preparing for this book, "care for worms & nothing else in the world just at present." This volume measures transportation of soil (calculated at eighteen tons/acre/year) and suggests that worms have a glimmer of intelligence. Over 10,000 copies of the book were sold by 1888.

On 19 April 1882, in the seventy-fourth year of his life, Charles Darwin died. His coffin was borne into Westminster Abbey by ten pallbearers, among them T. H. Huxley, Joseph Hooker, and Alfred Russel Wallace, and inhumed close to the grave of Sir Isaac Newton.

Portrait of Darwin by John Collier (National Portrait Gallery)

Darwin's contributions to literature are important in their own right as well as for the influence they have had on subsequent works of nonfiction, fiction, poetry, and drama. Before turning to examples of Darwin's influence, some discussions of the concept of Darwinism will be useful. Like Christianity or Marxism, Darwinism has been variously defined, and the definitions do not always agree with one another. Darwinism, as it has come to be understood, is more than, and, in fact, sometimes is opposed to, the ideas of Charles Darwin. In the field of biology, Darwinism is synonymous with the concept of natural selection and, at times, with that of evolution. For anthropologists, to "believe" in Darwinism is to affirm the descriptions of human development from earlier animals, in a sequence retrogressing from primate through protoprimate mammal to mammalian reptile and so on. In philosophy, Darwinism connotes materialism. The notion of Darwinism was enlarged, particularly by T. H. Huxley, to include such propositions as animate beings are protoplasmic machines; mind is an epiphenomenon of a physical organ, the brain; everything in the universe is explicable in terms of matter, *spirit* being a word without any exis-

tent referent. In the area of religion, Darwinism is associated with humanism and the idea expressed by Huxley and others (not Darwin himself) that the Bible is not a scientific text and that some of its history is myth. The Social Darwinism of the economists, more Herbert Spencer's creation than it is Darwin's, relies on the analogy that as competition among plants and animals in the natural world leads to the survival of the fittest and thus to an improvement of the species, so competition among human beings in the social world will lead to progress. Reform Darwinism is the opposite of Social Darwinism, stressing (as in the works of Prince Kropotkin) cooperative behavior among animals as a model for cooperative behavior among human beings or (as described by Huxley) critical dissimilarities between conflict in the natural world and the need for cooperation in society.

In literature an orangutan had appeared as a character back in 1817, in Thomas Love Peacock's *Melincourt*, but after Huxley's, Lyell's, and Darwin's works on human evolution, the ape or the ape-man, the missing link, became something of a standard emblem for animal instincts within civilized human beings of the male sex. The most famous example is Dr. Jekyll's apish alter ego in Robert Louis Stevenson's *Strange Case of Dr. Jekyll and Mr. Hyde*. Mr. Hyde is like a troglodyte, scampering around the laboratory, hairy, brutish, given solely to the satisfaction of appetite. A less well-known and considerably funnier novel is W. H. Mallock's satire, *The New Paul and Virginia*. (For a full tracing of Darwin's influence upon the novel from 1860 to 1910, see Leo J. Henkin's *Darwinism in the English Novel*, 1940.) Jules Verne, H. G. Wells, and Arthur Conan Doyle were stimulated by the possibilities of the missing link as a character for fiction, as was the dramatist Eugene O'Neill in his play *The Hairy Ape*. Regression to a more primitive form within us also appears in Frank Norris's *McTeague*, Aldous Huxley's *After Many a Summer,* and William Golding's *Lord of the Flies*. In modern popular culture, the influence of Darwinian ideas on humankind's descent from and kinship to the ape and missing link can be discerned in innumerable movies, and traces are evident in werewolf and vampire movies and television shows.

Among the many other literary works that are noteworthy for their adoption, adaption, or refutation of Darwinism(s) are poems by Alfred Tennyson ("The Dawn," "The Making of Man," "Despair," "By an Evolutionist"); Robert Browning ("Prince Hohenstiel-Schwangau," "Fifine at the Fair," "Parleying with Bernard de Mandeville"); A. C. Swinburne ("Hertha," "Songs before Sunrise," "Genesis"); George Meredith ("Ode to the Spirit of Earth in Autumn," "The Woods of Westermain," "The World's Advance," "Lucifer in Starlight"); Matthew Arnold ("Dover Beach"); and Thomas Hardy ("Before Life and After," "God's Funeral," "Nature's Questioning," "The Darkling Thrush"). The playwright of the late nineteenth and early twentieth century most influenced by Darwinism (or by anti-Darwinism) in his view of evolution was Bernard Shaw (*Man and Superman* and *Back to Methuselah*), who relied for his view of evolution upon Samuel Butler, a critic of the randomness of natural selection.

The English author perhaps most influenced by Darwinism was Thomas Hardy. Like his poems, his novels, notably *Tess of the D'Urbervilles*, treat Darwinian issues such as the struggle for survival, the determining influence of heredity, the conflict between animal desires and social ritual, agnosticism, and the idea of a universe ungoverned by a loving God. Darwin's influence is also evident in Mrs. Humphry Ward's best-seller *Robert Elsmere* and in William Hale White's *The Autobiography of Mark Rutherford*. H. G. Wells, in *The Time Machine*, *The Island of Dr. Moreau*, and *Men Like Gods*, similarly treats Darwinian themes.

Darwinism made its impact on American literature in the late nineteenth and early twentieth centuries largely as a result of the adaptability of Social Darwinism, or Spencerism, to American society, then undergoing insistent growth in industry and banking.

American naturalist writers were influenced by Darwin, Huxley, Spencer (especially–in the half-century after 1860, over 370,000 copies of Spencer's books were sold in the United States), and, in various eclectic assortments, by the French naturalist-novelist Émile Zola and the German philosophers Friedrich Nietzsche and Arthur Schopenhauer. Jack London (*Martin Eden*, *The Call of the Wild*, *The Sea Wolf*, *The Human Drift*), Theodore Dreiser (*Jennie Gerhardt*, *An American Tragedy*, *The American Financier*), and Upton Sinclair (*The Jungle*) developed decidedly Darwinian ideas; Sinclair Lewis (*Main Street*, *Dodsworth*, *Elmer Gantry*, *Arrowsmith*), John Dos Passos (*Manhattan Transfer*, *U.S.A.*), and John Steinbeck (*Grapes of Wrath*, *Cannery Row*) followed suit.

In his autobiography Darwin wrote, "Nothing is more remarkable than the spread of skepticism or rationalism during the latter half of my life." He had himself been foremost in achieving freedom of thought on the subject of evolution, and his influence on posterity has been inestimable.

Letters:
The Life and Letters of Charles Darwin, including An Autobiographical Chapter, edited by Francis Darwin, 3 volumes (London: Murray, 1887);
More Letters of Charles Darwin. A Record of His Work in Hitherto Unpublished Letters, edited by Frances Darwin and A. C Seward, 2 volumes (London: Murray, 1903);
Emma Darwin, Wife of Charles Darwin. A Century of Family Letters, edited by Henrietta E. Litchfield, 2 volumes (London: Murray, 1915);
James Marchant, *Alfred Russel Wallace: Letters and Reminiscences*, 2 volumes (London: Cassell, 1916);
Darwin and Henslow: The Growth of an Idea; Letters, 1831-1860, edited by Nora Barlow (London: Murray, for the Bentham-Moxon Trust, 1967);
The Correspondence of Charles Darwin, 1821-1836, edited by Frederick Burkhardt and Sydney Smith, 2 volumes to date: volume 1, 1821-1836; volume 2, 1837-1843 (Cambridge: Cambridge University Press, 1985, 1986).

Bibliography:
R. B. Freeman, *The Works of Charles Darwin: An Annotated Bibliographical Handlist*, second edition (Folkstone: Dawson, 1978).

Biographies:
William Irvine, *Apes, Angels and Victorians: A Joint Biography of Darwin and Huxley* (London: Weidenfeld & Nicolson, 1955);
Gavin de Beer, *Charles Darwin; Evolution by Natural Selection* (London & New York: Nelson, 1963); republished as *Charles Darwin: A Scientific Biography* (Garden City: Doubleday, 1964);
Peter J. Vorzimmer, *Charles Darwin: The Years of Controversy* (Philadelphia: Temple University Press, 1970);
Peter Brent, *Charles Darwin* (New York: Harper & Row, 1981);
Ronald W. Clark, *The Survival of Charles Darwin* (New York: Random House, 1984).

References:

Philip Appleman, ed., *Darwin* (New York: Norton, 1970);

Gillian Beer, *Darwin's Plots: Evolutionary Narrative in Darwin, George Eliot and Nineteenth-Century Fiction* (London: Routledge & Kegan Paul, 1983);

Charles S. Blinderman, "The Great Bone Case," *Perspectives in Biology and Medicine*, 14 (Spring 1971): 370-393;

Blinderman, "Vampurella: Darwin and Count Dracula," *Massachusetts Review*, 21 (Summer 1980): 411-428;

A. Dwight Culler, "The Darwinian Revolution and Literary Form," in *The Art of Victorian Prose*, edited by George Levine and William Madden (New York: Oxford University Press, 1968);

Sydney Eisen and Bernard V. Lightman, *Victorian Science and Religion: A Bibliography with Emphasis on Evolution, Belief, and Unbelief, Comprised of Works Published from c.1900-1975* (Hamden, Conn.: Archon Books, 1984);

Alvar Ellegård, *Darwin and the General Reader* (Göteburg: University of Göteburg, 1958);

R. B. Freeman, *Charles Darwin. A Companion* (London: Dawson, 1978);

Barry G. Gale, "Darwin and the Concept of a Struggle for Existence. A Study in the Extrascientific Origins of Scientific Ideas," *Isis*, 63 (1972): 321-344;

Walker Gibson, "Behind the Veil: A Distinction between Poetic and Scientific Language in Tennyson, Lyell, and Darwin," *Victorian Studies*, 2 (1958-1959): 60-68;

Thomas F. Glick, ed., *The Comparative Reception of Darwinism* (Austin: University of Texas Press, 1974);

Howard E. Gruber, *Darwin on Man: A Psychological Study of Scientific Creativity* (London: Wildewood, 1974);

Leo J. Henkin, *Darwinism in the English Novel 1860-1910* (New York: Corporate Press, 1940);

Richard Hofstadter, *Social Darwinism in American Thought* (Philadelphia: University of Pennsylvania Press, 1944);

David L. Hull, *Darwin and His Critics* (Cambridge: Harvard University Press, 1973);

Stanley E. Hyman, "The 'Origin' as Scripture," *Virginia Quarterly Review*, 35 (Autumn 1959): 540-552;

William Irvine, "The Influence of Darwin on Literature," *Proceedings of the American Philosophical Society*, 103, no. 5 (1959): 616-628;

David Kohn, ed., *The Darwinian Heritage* (Princeton: Princeton University Press, 1985);

Benjamin Lease, "Two Sides to a Tortoise: Darwin and Melville in the Pacific," *Person*, 49 (1968): 531-539;

George Levine, "Darwin Among the Critics," *Victorian Studies*, 30 (Winter 1987): 253-260;

Gordon Mills, "The Influence of Darwinism on the Style of Certain American Writers," in *The Impact of Darwinian Thought on American Life and Culture* (Austin: University of Texas Press, 1959);

D. R. Oldroyd, *Darwinian Impacts* (Milton Keynes: Open University Press, 1980);

William J. Scheick, "Epic Traces in Darwin's *Origin of Species*," *South Atlantic Quarterly*, 72 (Spring 1973): 270-279;

C. N. Stavrou, "Darwinism in American Drama," in *The Impact of Darwinian Thought on American Life and Culture* (Austin: University of Texas Press, 1959);

Lionel Stevenson, *Darwin among the Poets* (Chicago: University of Chicago Press, 1932);

Stevenson, "Darwin and the Novel," *Nineteenth Century Fiction*, 15 (June 1960): 29-38.

Papers:

Darwin notebooks, letters, and other memorabilia are located at Down House, in Kent, under the authority of the Royal College of Surgeons, and at University Library, Cambridge.

Charles M. Doughty

(19 August 1843-20 January 1926)

Joan Corwin

See also the Doughty entry in *DLB 19, British Poets, 1880-1914.*

SELECTED BOOKS: *On the Jöstedal-Brae Glaciers in Norway* (London: Stanford, 1866);
Documents épigraphiques recueillis dans le nord de l'Arabie (Paris: Imprimerie Nationale, 1884);
Travels in Arabia Deserta, 2 volumes (Cambridge: Cambridge University Press, 1888; London: Cape/Boston: Warner, 1921); abridged by Edward Garnett as *Wanderings in Arabia,* 2 volumes (London: Duckworth, 1908; New York: Scribners, 1908);
Under Arms (London: Constable, 1900);
The Dawn in Britain, 6 volumes (London: Duckworth, 1906);
Adam Cast Forth (Sacred Drama in Five Songs) (London: Duckworth, 1908);
The Cliffs (A Drama of the Time, in Five Parts) (London: Duckworth, 1909);
The Clouds (London: Duckworth, 1912);
The Titans (Subdued to the Service of Man) (London: Duckworth, 1916);
Mansoul; or, The Riddle of the World (London: Selwyn & Blount, 1920; revised, London: Cape, 1923);
Hogarth's "Arabia" (London: Chiswick, 1922).

Charles M. Doughty, circa 1880

Charles M. Doughty's *Travels in Arabia Deserta* (1888) is an enduring contribution to the vast body of English travel literature. Doughty was one of the first Europeans to penetrate the interior of Arabia, and *Travels in Arabia Deserta,* his masterpiece, is both a memorable adventure story and an important scientific document. T. E. Lawrence called it "the first and indispensable work upon the Arabs of the desert." Its accuracy was such that it was used as a military textbook for Britain's campaign against the Turks in World War I. More important, in *Travels in Arabia Deserta* Doughty worked at forging a new prose style in an attempt to revitalize what he saw as corrupt Victorian English.

As Doughty said, "The book is not milk for babes": it is long, digressive, and detailed; many readers have found its style impenetrable and idiosyncratic. Yet, by drawing from Spenser, Chaucer, the Bible, and on the Arabic language, he developed a style that, although formal, is concrete and vital. The combination of Doughty's vivid language and accurate observation led Wilfrid Scawen Blunt to hail Doughty's work as "certainly the best prose written in the last two centuries."

Charles Montagu Doughty was born on 19 August 1843, the second son of the Reverend Charles Montagu Doughty of Theberton Hall, Suffolk. The infant Doughty was so weak that his father had him baptized almost immediately, but it was Doughty's mother, Frederica (daughter of the Honorable Frederick Hotham and grand-daughter of Beaumont, the second Baron Hotham), who died only a few days after the child's birth. When Doughty was six, his father died. Lifelong poor health and the early loss of both parents may have contributed to Doughty's reticence. But he was a mixture of equal parts of shyness and stubborn courage. Descended from gentry on both sides, he inherited from his father's clerical family a studious conservatism and from his mother's naval kinsmen a thirst for adventure.

Placed in the care of a maternal uncle, Frederick Goodwin Doughty of Martlesham Hall, Doughty was sent away to school in preparation for a naval career. A slight speech impediment, however, prevented his passing the navy's medical examination in 1856, and, thus disappointed in his first cherished ambition, Doughty turned his attention to another early interest, geology. A serious study of Suffolk chalk led to his report to the British Association, at their 1862 meeting in Cambridge, on flint implements in Hoxne.

Doughty brought his interest in geology to Gonville and Caius College, Cambridge, in 1861. Although a fellow student later recalled him as "shy, nervous and very polite," he already showed evidence of a strong will. Caius regulations on attendance at lectures and chapel were strict, and the Caius attitude toward that "new-fangled" field of natural science was disapproving. So Doughty moved in 1863 to the more liberal Downing College, which offered a natural science tripos, or examination. A journey in the same year to Norway to research glaciation interrupted his reading for the examination. His findings were published as a pamphlet, *On the Jöstedal-Brae Glaciers in Norway* (1866). He received a second-class in the tripos in 1865 and graduated the next year.

Doughty's approach to research, which added fieldwork to traditional scholarship, may have reflected the latest advances in scientific method, but Doughty himself can hardly be considered a revolutionary. He was absorbed by the past, and even his project to revitalize Victorian English involved by and large the retrieval of obsolete and archaic words. Doughty's family history, too, was strongly conservative: his forebears included prelates, ambassadors, admirals, a bishop, a judge, and a colonial governor. Not surprisingly, then, Doughty was intensely patriotic and considered all of his activities in light of their con-

tribution to the honor of England. Denied a naval career, he looked for another way to serve his country. As early as 1865, when he was still at Cambridge, he conceived the idea of the patriotic poem "wherein Roman, Celtic, and German *Origines* are treated of" that became his epic *The Dawn in Britain* (1906). Not only was the poem a celebration of national and racial origins; it was also Doughty's intention that the work restore English to the purity and strength it had possessed during what he considered its golden age–from the Middle Ages to the Renaissance–as represented by the works of Chaucer and Spenser. This mission to reform decadent modern English, particularly through his poetry, became Doughty's all-consuming ambition for the rest of his life. It lay behind his travels and studies; and his uncompromising devotion to this goal was at least partly responsible for his lifelong poverty and his withdrawal from the social and literary life of his contemporaries.

Doughty spent the period from 1865 to 1870 engaged in extensive independent reading, primarily in early English literature, in London and at Oxford's Bodleian Library, in preparation for writing his patriotic poem, which, in its manuscript form, was entitled "The Utmost Isle." An impressive list of the readings he ordered at the Bodleian appears at the end of D. G. Hogarth's 1928 biography, *The Life of Charles M. Doughty*. These five years also served as another kind of apprenticeship. Sometime during this course of study Doughty's family fortune was decimated by depreciation of investments, and he was now obliged to follow the kind of solitary, self-contained, and ascetic life he had always preferred. The experience of these years inured him to loneliness and hardship, thus serving as good training for his travels abroad, especially the taxing Arabian adventure. In 1870 his researches in history and language, combined with poor health and lack of money, took him abroad to Holland, where he gained, as he put it, a "philological feeling in English." There followed a four-year period as a "world-wanderer," a traveling student, says Hogarth, of "now linguistics, now geology, now archaeology, now geography, now ethnology, now history." His route ran south through France, Italy, Sicily, Spain (via North Africa, where he had his first experience of caravaning), and Greece. From there, in 1874, he suddenly turned to the "Bible-lands": Syria, Lebanon, Palestine and Egypt.

After a three-month journey on camelback

through the Sinai Peninsula, Doughty arrived at Maan and Petra (now in Jordan), where he learned of the monument inscriptions at Medain Salih and Hejr. Although he received no encouragement from the British and Turkish authorities at Damascus and no funds from either the British Association or the Royal Geographical Society, he resolved to investigate the inscriptions, then unknown and unrecorded by Europeans, and to take the opportunity to study the Bedouins, whose biblical life-style, Doughty thought, would put him in touch with England's pre-Christian racial heritage. Outfitted with medicines and a lymph for vaccination, he hoped to pass for a doctor and earn sustenance from the Arabs who came to him for treatment, a plan that collapsed when the lymph proved ineffective. He spent a year in Damascus learning Arabic. Then, "clothed as a Syrian of simple fortune," he accompanied a group of Persians who rode to join the annual pilgrim caravan which passed through Medain Salih on its way from Damascus to Mecca. They overtook the caravan on 12 November 1876.

The next twenty-one months of Doughty's life provided the material for the *Travels in Arabia Deserta*. Although Doughty adopted the desert costume and called himself Khalil ("friend"), he never pretended to believe in Islam: "the sun made me an Arab, but never warped me to Orientalism." On his person he carried his notebooks and scientific instruments (an aneroid barometer, a thermometer, and a pocket sextant), and his medicines and books made his saddlebags bulge deceptively. Actually, he traveled with almost no provision and in increasingly poor health, depending entirely on Arab generosity, trusting himself, as he writes in *Travels in Arabia Deserta,* to "an unlettered and reputed lawless tribesfolk." This strategy was made doubly hazardous by his refusal to masquerade as a Moslem. While he would have preferred to pass unnoticed as he recorded the spectacle around him, he refused to dissemble, but behaved in accordance with that devotion to truth which made him uncompromising in matters of diction and detail. In spite of the almost constant hunger and fear he suffered Doughty was able to gather a tremendous amount of scientific information on northwest Arabia. Some of his geographical and geological findings constitute true discoveries. But his greatest scientific contribution was anthropological. He made accessible to the Victorian reader an acute and detailed record of nomad life.

One can divide *Travels in Arabia Deserta* into five sections. The first concerns the journey with the pilgrim caravan to Medain Salih. From this section Doughty's description of the annual hajj endures as a vivid record of an event made obsolete in 1909 by the opening of the Hejaz railway. Doughty's primary concern during the march is to make himself as inconspicuous as possible among the Persian pilgrims who bring up the rear of the procession. In spite of his efforts to evade notice, he cannot restrain himself from objecting to the brutal punishment of an Arab thief; nor can he keep his camel in check when she balks and breaks her lead under the eyes of the caravan pasha.

Doughty escapes challenge, however, until he reaches the *kella*, or well tower, at Medain Salih, which he uses as a base for his excursions to explore the Nabataean monuments. The second part of the book deals with his residence at the *kella* and his treatment by the tower keeper Mohammed Aly, whose unstable temper erupts frequently and violently. Mohammed Aly deals the ultimate Arab insult to Doughty when, in a fit of anger, he pulls the Christian by the beard.

The third section describes Doughty's residence among the Fukara and Moahib Bedouin tribes. Though elsewhere in the narrative he claims to have passed only one good day in Arabia, here he admits that "lying to rest amidst wild basalt stones under the clear stars, in a land of enemies, I have found more refreshment than upon beds and pillows in our close chambers." For the most part Doughty was respected by the Bedouins; he was even called upon to intervene in the comic marital disagreements of the Fukara chief Zeyd and his impetuous young wife Hirfa.

The next section chronicles Doughty's visits among the fanatically religious town Arabs. At Hayil, he meets the dynast Ibn Rashid, whose bloody rise to power has made him a tragic figure of immense proportion, an Eastern Macbeth. The visit to Kheybar represents a low point in Doughty's fortunes. This legendary city proves to be a sinkhole of disease and superstition, a filthy, depressing place where "all is horror." There the traveler is imprisoned by the sadistic commandant Abdullah, who awaits the decision of the pasha of Medina concerning Doughty's fate. By the time he is released at the pasha's command, Doughty has spent two and a half months under almost constant threat of death. But even in such desperate circumstances, he attracts a defender; it is at Kheybar that he makes his greatest friend

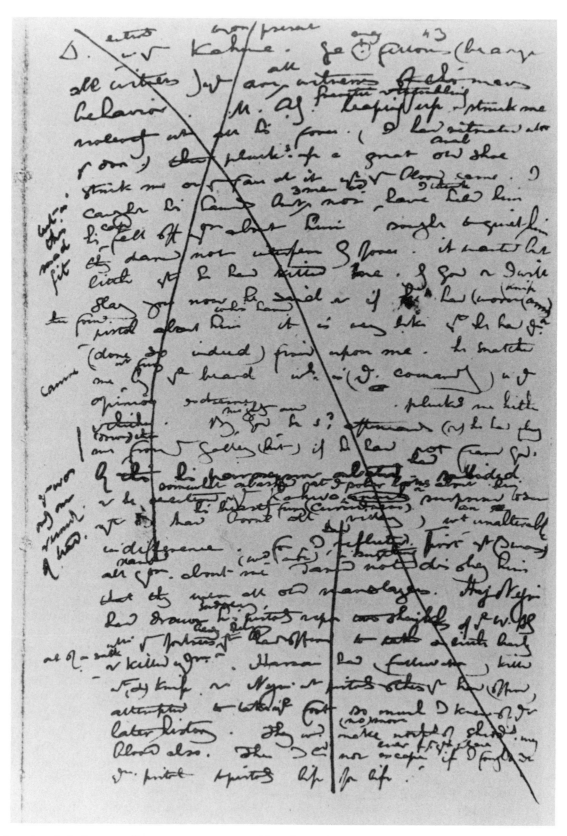

Page from Doughty's diary recording an angry encounter with Mohammed Aly, the keeper of the kella, *or well tower, at Medain Salih (D. G. Hogarth,* The Life of Charles M. Doughty, *1928). Doughty's residence at the* kella *is the subject of the second section of* Travels in Arabia Deserta.

in Arabia, Mohammed en Nejumy.

The climax of *Travels in Arabia Deserta* occurs as an exhausted and dispirited Doughty attempts to quit Arabia. En route to the coastal town of Jiddah, he encounters the mad dervish Salem, whose homicidal nature is just barely curbed by Maabub, a servant of the sherif of Mecca. Maabub warns Salem not to harm Doughty until he can be brought before the Meccan prince, who is quartered at Tayif. The episode vibrates with tension, as Doughty's life is repeatedly threatened by Salem. But the traveler's passiveness and feigned indifference finally disarm his attacker: "Dreadest thou not to die!"—"I have not so lived, Moslêm, that I fear to die." To Salem's chagrin, the sherif receives Doughty with grace and generosity and sees that his guest is bathed, fed, and clothed in fresh robes. The prince even provides an escort for the final peaceful ride to Jiddah. Having arrived safely, Doughty is welcomed by the British consul as the long adventure comes to an ironic close for one who began his journey without the support of the British authorities.

As the story progresses, Doughty, in the guise of Khalil, suffers increasing want and persecution. His treatment at the hands of the townspeople dramatizes the contrast between these fanatic Moslems and the desert nomads. Most of Doughty's troubles arise from his refusal to foreswear Christianity, which not only earns him the hatred of pious Moslems but also makes it possible for every villain who covets Doughty's saddlebags to attack him with impunity simply by invoking the name of Allah. At almost every stage of his journey, he is abused and threatened; the effect is cumulative, a continuously building sense of insecurity. Throughout, the traveler patiently submits to abuse, never resorting to the pistol he carries. It is this combination of resolve and pacifism that makes Doughty's Khalil a memorable figure.

It is the character of his persona Khalil that holds together Doughty's amorphous account. *Travels in Arabia Deserta* does not concern a single quest, but an odyssey of discovery. Although Doughty's initial motivation for his travels had been the monument inscriptions of Medain Salih and Hejr, he soon became equally fascinated with the desert and the people, particularly the Bedouins, who inhabited this most uncongenial of landscapes. As a result the story line meanders as Doughty faithfully records every step of his progress among the nomads and the townspeo-

ple. He often retraces his path and often makes short digressive side trips within larger moves from point to point. Similarly, his thoughts digress, sometimes making associative leaps even beyond the scope of the narrative. For instance, the Arabian *harras,* or lava fields, remind him of the eruption of Vesuvius, which he had witnessed in 1872, and his description of the event is valuable for both its poetry and its precision. In addition, because Doughty refused to select or subordinate details, *Travels in Arabia Deserta* appears to be indiscriminately glutted with information. What remains constant throughout the account is Khalil's steadfastness in the face of persecution, a reflection of the same personal integrity which motivated Doughty to transfer to Downing on behalf of his interest in geology and which characterized his efforts to reform the English language.

Critical praise for *Travels in Arabia Deserta* has traditionally focused on three strengths: the appropriateness of its style, its vividness and sincerity, and its inclusiveness. The language is well suited to Doughty's description of the "extreme desolation" of the "dead land." Doughty's artistry is apparent in his oft-quoted description of the desert, where "the sun, entering as a tyrant upon the waste landscape, darts upon us a torment of firey beams" and "the ears tingle with a flickering shrillness, a subtle crepitation it seems, in the glassiness of this sun-stricken nature." By fitting sound to sense in this way, Doughty was exercising a personal linguistic philosophy that had as its goal absolute precision in choosing words. During a period of study in the Bodleian Library, he worked relentlessly on a system of "Word Notes" that amounted to a personal dictionary of words whose meanings he considered concentrated and exact. Combining this rich exactness of diction with a fanatic devotion to fact, Doughty created in *Travels in Arabia Deserta* an impression of truth and immediacy. In the preface to the third edition, he likened his book to a "mirror, wherein is set forth faithfully some parcel of the soil of Arabia." Its accuracy, he felt, could withstand the scrutiny even of an Arab, who "smiting his thigh, should bear witness and cry '*Ay Wellah,* the sooth indeed!'"

Because of his devotion to truth Doughty refused to sacrifice events and details to the coherence of the narrative. This lack of selectivity had resulted in his taking only a second class in his examinations at Cambridge in 1865. The examining don later explained, "If you asked him for a collar he upset his whole wardrobe at your feet."

But the completeness of *Travels in Arabia Deserta* has usually been seen as a virtue. "Here you have all the desert," commended T. E. Lawrence, adding that Doughty included nothing simply for effect: there is no gratuitous exoticism, "no sentiment, nothing merely picturesque."

Many critics have commented on the peculiar detachment of Doughty's bitter narrator from his persona Khalil. Doughty warns the reader to consider his book "the seeing of an hungry man and the telling of a most weary man." But the gentle and stoic hero Khalil is a sympathetic figure who has been described as a distillation of Doughty's best qualities. In his 1981 book *Charles Doughty* Stephen Tabachnick sees him as "an idealized Everyman version of Doughty's personality.

The first sentence of *Travels in Arabia Deserta* raises the important question "What moved thee, or how couldst thou take such journeys into the fanatic Arabia?" Doughty's motives are revealed in his letters, in the text of *Travels in Arabia Deserta,* and in the various prefaces he wrote for the first, second, and third editions of the work. Most problematic is the motive that kept Doughty in Arabia at the mercy of fanatic believers. Another famous Arabian adventurer, Richard F. Burton, saw Doughty's submission to persecution as ignoble and his refusal to profess a belief in Islam as narrow-minded and imprudent. But Doughty's passivity and stubbornness were elements of an uncompromising ideal of Christian tolerance, what Hogarth describes as a "heart-felt piety and deep reverence for any *credo* based on Reason." Although Doughty admired much in the Arabs, he objected to what he saw as Islam's bloodthirsty fanaticism. His divided response is best illustrated by his famous description of the Semites as "like to a man sitting in a cloaca to the eyes, and whose brows touch heaven."

The rest of his motives are antiquarian: his interest in the origins of the earth, of humanity, and of language. His most obvious aim was scientific, "to add something to the common fund of Western knowledge." He was "as much Geologist as Nasrâny" (or Christian), as he wrote to Hogarth. But he was also as much anthropologist as geologist. As Doughty's "Story of the Earth," *Travels in Arabia Deserta* is concerned not only with the planet's "ancient rocks" but also with "Her manifold living creatures," among them "the human generations."

Doughty's interest in the Bible lands was more racial than religious. In moving from West to East, he was tracing civilization backward to its source. His interest in the origins of humanity generally, and of the British people in particular, inspired most of his writing. In Arabia, among the Bedouins, he was able to relive "that desert life, which was followed by their ancestors, in the Biblical tents of Kedar."

For Doughty, tracing the origins of humanity meant also tracing the origins of human speech. He felt that the English language had become increasingly decadent since the work of Spenser and Chaucer. His years at the Bodleian had been a philological journey backward to school himself in early English. In Arabia he hoped to find, in humanity's geographical "prehistoric Nest," traces of an even older, pure speech. According to Walt Taylor's 1939 work *Doughty's English,* in the Arabian wilderness Doughty found his ideal language, concrete and emotionally charged. The influence of Arabic words, rhythms, and irony combined with Doughty's admiration for Chaucer's *Canterbury Tales,* Spenser's *Faerie Queene,* and the King James Bible to produce a style, writes Thomas Assad in his *Three Victorian Travellers* (1964), that cannot be dated. Doughty recuperated from his Arabian experiences in India, returning to England by November 1878 to negotiate for the publication of his records found at Medain Salih. They were published under the auspices of the Parisian Académie des Inscriptions as *Documents épigraphiques recueillis dans le nord de L'Arabie* (1884).

In 1879 Doughty contacted the secretary of the Royal Geographical Society to request an interview concerning the Arabian discoveries. The interview never took place and Doughty did not renew contact with the apparently indifferent society until 1883, when he read a paper in his archaic diction at their November meeting. The first real test of Doughty's resolve concerning his linguistic mission came with the printing of this report in the society's proceedings. In a clash with Assistant Secretary H. W. Bates over revision of the language, Doughty insisted, "as an English Scholar I will never submit to have my language of the best times turned into the misery of today—that were unworthy of me." Pray let no word be altered," he warned, "or else I retire and must disown it altogether as not my work." In this early instance of unfavorable reaction to his developing style Doughty did acquiesce. After the next such encounter with editors, however, he described himself in a letter to his future wife as "self-willed, headstrong and fierce with opponents."

From 1881 to 1884, living for the most part in Italy, Doughty wrote a draft of *Travels in Arabia Deserta* which he submitted for publishers' consideration. Within one year, it was refused by three publishers, who found the style almost unintelligible. In all, Doughty spent four years revising the manuscript. Finally the University Press at Cambridge reluctantly accepted the work. Both parties became frustrated over the question of who was to have the last word on the revisions. Doughty prevailed, and *Travels in Arabia Deserta* was published in 1888.

In general reviewers applauded the stuff and condemned the style, although the critics for the London *Times* and the *Spectator* were wholly enthusiastic, and Doughty did receive fan letters from two men of distinguished qualifications, the Arabist Wilfrid Scawen Blunt and the poet Robert Bridges. Nevertheless, though there was always some demand for the book, the readership was small. When Doughty bought the copyright for £50 in 1906, Cambridge University Press was left with a net loss of just under £400. *Travels in Arabia Deserta* did eventually achieve some measure of popularity thanks to the appearance in 1908 of an abridged edition entitled *Wanderings in Arabia*, edited by Edward Garnett, and the republication in 1921 of the unexcised version with an introduction by the famed soldier-scholar T. E. Lawrence. The publication of the excerpts in 1908 created a tremendous demand for the original. *"For years,"* wrote Doughty, "hardly any copies . . . were sold. Now Friends tell me . . . they cannot be bought." The 500 reissue copies sold immediately at nine guineas apiece. From the start *Travels in Arabia Deserta* enjoyed a literary following. In addition to Robert Bridges, the Pre-Raphaelites Edward Burne-Jones and William Morris admired the book. Ironically the nineteenth-century poet with whom Doughty is often compared, Gerard Manley Hopkins, refused to read *Travels in Arabia Deserta* because he thought the archaisms an affectation.

Twentieth-century critics recognize the magnitude of Doughty's literary achievement. Excellent extended analyses of *Travels in Arabia Deserta* appear in books by Barker Fairley, Anne Treneer, and, most recently, Stephen Tabachnick. In addition, Lawrence's introduction to the 1921 edition, Norman Douglas's chapter in his *Experiments*, and John Middleton Murry's chapter in his *Countries of the Mind* provide useful appraisals of Doughty's prose masterpiece. More specifically, Walt Taylor's Society for Pure English

Doughty, circa 1922

tract on Doughty examines the influence of Arabic on the book's style. Richard Bevis, Ronald Storrs, and Stephen Tabachnick have written articles that deal with the question of motive. Jonathan Bishop's article considers Khalil's passive heroism. Ruth Robbins's analysis of the "Word Notes" offers important insights into Doughty's thought. Thomas Assad discusses Doughty's cultural response to Arabia. Finally, Annette McCormick's study of Hebrew parallelism in *Travels in Arabia Deserta* should be consulted as an aid in approaching Doughty's difficult sentence structure.

Doughty saw himself primarily as a poet and considered his Arabian experience as "a not wholly welcome life-day's interruption" in this vocation. After the publication of *Travels in Arabia Deserta* he devoted the rest of his life almost exclusively to his poetry, which is marked by a strong religious patriotic conservatism.

While wintering in Italy in 1886, Doughty met his future wife, Caroline Amelia McMurdo, daughter of Gen. Sir Montagu McMurdo. They were married in October; their two daughters,

Dorothy and Freda, were born in 1892 and 1894. After the publication of *Travels in Arabia Deserta* Doughty and his wife traveled in the Levant, returning to Italy where they spent the next nine winters. They passed their summers first in Switzerland and then in Henwick in Newbury. In 1898 the family settled year-round in England, spending significant periods of time at Tunbridge Wells, Eastbourne, and finally, Merriecroft, Sissinghurst, where Doughty enjoyed a reclusive country life until his death in 1926.

The Doughty family was dogged by poverty. Friends helped, particularly T. E. Lawrence, who arranged the sale of Doughty's manuscript "The Utmost Isle" as a gift to the Library of the British Museum, and Sydney Cockerell, who engineered the sale of the manuscript notes for *Travels in Arabia Deserta* on behalf of the Fitzwilliam Museum at Cambridge. Lawrence was also responsible for securing Doughty a £150 annual Civil List pension in 1922. In 1923 Doughty's financial troubles were solved by the inheritance of a £2,000 annuity.

Official recognition of Doughty's scientific and literary contributions came in his last twenty years: Oxford University made him an honorary doctor of letters in 1908, and Cambridge conferred a degree *honoris causa* in 1920. In 1912 he was awarded the Royal Geographical Society's Founders Gold Medal, and in 1922 he was elected an honorary fellow of the British Academy.

Doughty died on 20 January 1926 and was cremated at Golders Green. The funeral, which took place in the pouring rain, was attended by only Doughty's family and a very few friends. Among the latter, however, was the ever-faithful T. E. Lawrence.

In his lifetime Doughty's approach to his mission of reforming the English language was the same as his approach to Arabia. Both involved the exercise of his tremendous reserves of honesty, patience, and endurance: "The traveller must be himself, in men's eyes, a man worthy to live under the bent of God's heaven, and were it without a religion: he is such who has a clean human heart and long-suffering under his bare shirt; it is enough, and though the way be full of harms, he may travel to the ends of the world."

Biography:

D. G. Hogarth, *The Life of Charles M. Doughty* (Oxford: Oxford University Press, 1928).

References:

Thomas J. Assad, *Three Victorian Travellers: Burton, Blunt, Doughty* (London: Routledge, 1964);

Richard Bevis, "Spiritual Geology: C. M. Doughty and the Land of the Arabs," *Victorian Studies*, 16 (December 1972): 163-181;

Jonathan Bishop, "The Heroic Ideal in Doughty's *Arabia Deserta*," *Modern Language Quarterly*, 21 (March 1960): 59-68;

Richard Francis Burton, "Mr. Doughty's Travels in Arabia," *Academy*, 34 (28 July 1888): 47-48;

Norman Douglas, *Experiments* (London: Chapman & Hall, 1925), pp. 3-25;

Barker Fairley, *Charles M. Doughty: A Critical Study* (London: Cape, 1927);

T. E. Lawrence, Introduction to Doughty's *Travels in Arabia Deserta* (London: Cape, 1921);

Annette M. McCormick, "Hebrew Parallelism in Doughty's *Travels in Arabia Deserta*," in *Studies in Comparative Literature, Humanities Series*, 11, edited by Waldo F. McNeir (Baton Rouge: Louisiana State University Press, 1962), pp. 29-46;

John Middleton Murry, *Countries of the Mind: Essays in Literary Criticism*, first series, revised edition (London: Oxford University Press, 1931), pp. 104-114;

Ruth Robbins, "The Word Notes of C. M. Doughty," *Agenda*, 18 (Summer 1980): 78-98;

Ronald Storrs, "The Spell of Arabia: Charles Doughty and T. E. Lawrence," *Listener*, 38 (25 December 1947): 1093-1094;

Stephen E. Tabachnick, "Adam Cast Forth: The First Sentence of Doughty's *Arabia Deserta*," *Pre-Raphaelite Review*, 1 (May 1978): 49-63;

Tabachnick, *Charles Doughty* (Boston: Twayne, 1981);

Walt Taylor, *Doughty's English* (Oxford: Clarendon Press, 1939);

Anne Treneer, *Charles M. Doughty: A Study of his Prose and Verse* (London: Cape, 1935).

Papers:

Doughty's notes for *Travels in Arabia Deserta* are at the Fitzwilliam Museum, Cambridge; "Word Notes" are at the library of Gonville and Caius College, Cambridge; and the manuscript for "The Utmost Isle," an early version of *The Dawn in Britain*, is at the British Library.

James Anthony Froude

(23 April 1818-20 October 1894)

William J. Gracie, Jr.
Miami University

See also the Froude entry in *DLB 18, Victorian Novelists After 1885.*

BOOKS: *Shadows of the Clouds,* as Zeta (London: Ollivier, 1847);

A Sermon Preached at St. Mary's Church, on the Death of the Rev. George May Coleridge (Torquay: Croyden, 1847);

The Nemesis of Faith; or, The History of Markham Sutherland (London: Chapman, 1849; Chicago: Belfords, Clarke, 1879);

The Book of Job (London: Chapman, 1854);

History of England, 12 volumes: volumes 1-10 published as *History of England from the Fall of Wolsey to the Death of Elizabeth* (volumes 1-6, London: Parker, 1856-1860; volumes 7-8, London: Longmans, Green, Longmans, Roberts & Green, 1864; volumes 9-10, London: Longmans, Green, 1866); volumes 11-12 published as *History of England from the Fall of Wolsey to the Defeat of the Spanish Armada* (London: Longmans, Green, 1870); U.S. edition, 12 volumes, with titles as above (New York: Scribners, 1865-1870);

Short Studies on Great Subjects, 4 volumes (London: Longmans, Green, 1867-1883; New York: Scribners, 1871-1883);

Inaugural Address Delivered to the University of St. Andrews, March 19, 1869 (London: Longmans, Green, 1869);

The Cat's Pilgrimage (Edinburgh: Edmonston & Douglas, 1870; New Haven, Conn.: East Rock Press, 1949);

Calvinism: An Address Delivered at St. Andrews, March 17, 1871 (London: Longmans, Green, 1871; New York: Scribners, 1871);

The English in Ireland in the Eighteenth Century, 3 volumes (London: Longmans, Green, 1872-1874; New York: Scribner, Armstrong, 1873-1874);

The Life and Times of Thomas Becket (New York: Scribner, Armstrong, 1878);

Caesar: A Sketch (London: Longmans, Green,

1879; New York: Scribners, 1879);

Bunyan (London: Macmillan, 1880; New York: Harper, 1880);

Two Lectures on South Africa Delivered Before the Philosophical Institute, Edinburgh, Jan. 6 & 9, 1880 (London: Longmans, Green, 1880);

Thomas Carlyle, A History of the First Forty Years of His Life, 1785-1835, 2 volumes (London: Longmans, 1882; New York: Harper, 1882);

Luther: A Short Biography (London: Longmans, Green, 1883; New York: Scribners, 1884);

Thomas Carlyle, A History of His Life in London, 1834-1881, 2 volumes (London: Longmans,

Green, 1884; New York: Harper, 1884);

Oceana; or, England and Her Colonies (London: Longmans, Green, 1886; New York: Scribners, 1886);

The Knights Templars (New York: Alden, 1886);

The English in the West Indies; or, The Bow of Ulysses (London: Longmans, Green, 1888; New York: Scribners, 1888);

Liberty and Property: An Address (London: Liberty and Property Defence League, 1888);

The Two Chiefs of Dunboy; or, An Irish Romance of the Last Century (London: Longmans, Green, 1889; New York: Munro, 1889);

Lord Beaconsfield (London: Low, Marston, Searle & Rivington, 1890; New York: Harper, 1890);

The Divorce of Catherine of Aragon: Being a Supplement to The History of England (London: Longmans, Green, 1891; New York: Scribners, 1891);

The Spanish Story of the Armada and Other Essays (London: Longmans, Green, 1892; New York: Scribners, 1892);

Life and Letters of Erasmus (London: Longmans, Green, 1894; New York: Scribners, 1894);

English Seamen in the Sixteenth Century (London: Longmans, Green, 1895; New York: Scribners, 1895);

Lectures on the Council of Trent (London: Longmans, Green, 1896; New York: Scribners, 1896);

My Relations with Carlyle (London: Longmans, Green, 1903; New York: Scribners, 1903).

OTHER: "A Legend of St. Neot," in *Hermit Saints*, volume 3 of *Lives of the English Saints* (London: Toovey, 1844);

"Suggestions on the Best Means of Teaching English History," in *Oxford Essays* (London: Parker, 1855);

Reminiscences by Thomas Carlyle, edited by Froude (2 volumes, London: Longmans, Green, 1881; 1 volume, New York: Scribners, 1881);

Letters and Memorials of Jane Welsh Carlyle, prepared for publication by Thomas Carlyle, edited by Froude (3 volumes, London: Longmans, Green, 1883; 2 volumes, New York: Scribners, 1883).

PERIODICAL PUBLICATIONS: "Arnold's Poems," *Westminster Review*, 61 (January 1854): 146-159;

"Lord Campbell as a Writer of History," *Westminster Review*, 61 (April 1854): 446-479;

"Lord Macaulay," *Fraser's Magazine*, 93 (June 1876): 675-694;

"A Few Words on Mr. Freeman," *Nineteenth Century*, 5 (April 1879): 618-637;

"A Sibylline Leaf," *Blackwood's Magazine*, 133 (April 1883): 573-592;

"A Leaf from the Real Life of Byron," *Nineteenth Century*, 14 (August 1883): 228-242.

On 1 May 1937, the editors of the *Times Literary Supplement* used the occasion of the centenary of Victoria's accession and the coronation of her great-grandson George VI to celebrate "some of the literary accomplishments of the hundred years." James Anthony Froude, the Victorian novelist, historian, biographer, editor, and man of letters was one of several writers considered important enough to merit review. Although the reviewer introduced his subject in a backhanded way—Froude's rival William Stubbs had "wisdom," his incessant critic Edward A. Freeman had "scholarship"—the *TLS* writer concluded that Froude had so powerful a narrative style that few, if any, of his contemporaries could surpass him: "pages and sentences [of his prose] set forth power and endurance and suffering in eternal vibration, or hang in the air like chiming bells." It would be difficult to quarrel with such praise—even Froude's detractors agreed that his prose was unusually distinctive for its dramatic flair and for its frequent eloquence—but Froude's importance should not be limited solely to an appreciation of his style. That importance can be summarized in two ways. First, the literary accomplishment is impressive in its variety and originality: *The Nemesis of Faith* (1849) stands as an important mid-Victorian novel of religious doubt; the *History of England* (1856-1870) remains an example of vigorous narrative writing combined with original research; and the life of Thomas Carlyle (1882, 1884) is certainly one of the finest examples of English literary biography. Second, Froude himself remains a man of considerable interest. Although sometimes perceived only as the disciple of Carlyle, Froude's life has been more fairly summed up by Basil Willey in *More Nineteenth Century Studies* (1956). To Willey, Froude's life represents that point where the "crosscurrents" of religious faith and honest doubt "meet and divide."

James Anthony Froude was born on 23 April 1818 in Dartington, Devonshire, only fifteen miles from the sea he would use as the background for essays as early as "England's Forgotten Worthies," written in 1852, and *English Seamen in the Sixteenth Century*, published posthumously in 1895. His father, Robert Hurrell Froude, was rector of Denbury and Dartington and, from 1820 to his death in 1859, Archdeacon of Totnes; his mother, Margaret Spedding Froude, was a relative of James Spedding (see Tennyson's "To J. S.") and had given birth to seven children before James Anthony Froude was born on St. George's Day in 1818. Before Froude's third birthday, Mrs. Froude succumbed to tuberculosis, leaving the young boy in the care of a suddenly melancholy and austere father, a severe aunt, and a sadistic older brother. Of the eight Froude children, only three–William, James Anthony, and Margaret–escaped the disease that claimed their mother, but to anyone noting the young Froude's physical condition in the early 1820s, his chances for survival must have seemed slight. He had been christened at home because his parents feared he would not live long enough to be taken to church, and his early years were unusually full of terrors: his aunt, having decided he needed "bracing," took the three-year-old Froude from his bed and plunged him into an icy stream; Hurrell Froude, having concluded that his brother "wanted manliness," held the child by the heels as he stirred the bottom of a muddy pond with his head. But Froude himself, in the autobiographical fragment left in the care of his daughter Margaret and published virtually intact in Waldo Hilary Dunn's *James Anthony Froude: A Biography* (1961-1963), recalled his delighted discovery of the world of Grimm and the *Arabian Nights*. A brooding, melancholy father; a zealously religious older brother; a world of imaginative literature: all had profound influence on Froude's life and work.

Froude's formal education began in 1827 at Buckfastleigh School, just five miles from Dartington, and was, on the whole, a good experience: he learned Greek, discovered Homer, and had twice read the *Iliad* and *Odyssey* before he was eleven. His stay at Westminster School, which he entered as a king's scholar in 1830, was altogether different–so grim that as late as the early 1890s Froude described the place as a "den of wild animals" where no learning could take place. Painful as the memories were, they had at least a positive effect in giving Froude some of the more horrible examples of public-school corporal punishments that he used in his first novel, *Shadows of the Clouds* (1847). Archdeacon Froude, concluding that his youngest son's sluggish study habits,

rather than Westminster itself, had made the youth a poor educational risk, removed Froude from Westminster in 1833. Froude spent the next two years of improving health discovering Sharon Turner's *History of the Anglo-Saxons from the Earliest Period to the Norman Conquest* (1799-1805)–which he read voraciously–as well as Gibbon, Shakespeare, Spenser, and Byron. "History and poetry," he reported in the autobiographical fragment, "came to interest me for themselves, and I was thrown into the surprise of an awakening mind."

His awakening mind was surely stimulated by the atmosphere of the Oxford Froude joined in 1835. Entering Oriel College only a few months after the death of his brother Hurrell, Froude was made vividly aware of the Oxford (or Tractarian) movement, in part because he was the younger brother of Hurrell, one of the leading Tractarians, and in part because his rooms were immediately above John Henry Newman's. But, at least at first, Froude kept himself aloof from the Tractarians, and rather than join their attempts to steer the established church away from its more Latitudinarian and Erastian tendencies, he rediscovered his early love of Greek literature and, years later, wrote in the autobiographical fragment that "Herodotus was as charming as the *Arabian Nights* had been." Also while at Oxford, Froude met Harriet Bush, the sister of Froude's fellow undergraduate James Bush. Froude and Harriet Bush soon made plans for marriage, but their engagement was broken off when Harriet's father assessed Froude's impecunious prospects.

If Froude had intended to remain untouched by the Tractarian cause it was impossible to do so, but whatever Tractarian sympathies he may have felt disappeared after his stay as a tutor with an Irish evangelical family in 1841 and by his discovery of the work of Carlyle: the Irish family in its simple, unaffected piety showed him a side of Protestantism unrecognized by the Tractarians, and Carlyle showed him an entirely new way of relating past to present and truth to life. The dramatic words of the autobiographical fragment–Carlyle's books, says Froude, "passed like a flash of lightning," his teaching "transform[ed] the entire scheme of my thought and displace[d] the beliefs in which I had been bred"–give testimony of an excited young mind suddenly illuminated by the grand ideas of three distinctive, even radical interpretations of history, *The French Revolution* (1837), *On Heroes, Hero-*

Worship & The Heroic in History (1841), and *Past and Present* (1843).

Froude drew heavily, albeit in different ways, on memories of his earliest years and education in three works published in the 1840s: "A Legend of St. Neot," an unsigned biography published in 1844; *Shadows of the Clouds*, published under the pseudonym Zeta in 1847; and *The Nemesis of Faith*, published under his own name in 1849. Froude's first work was misquoted and misunderstood, his second was almost suppressed by an angry Archdeacon Froude's attempt to buy in order to destroy every copy in print, and his third was publicly burned: a sometimes confusing and nearly always controversial literary career had begun.

"A Legend of St. Neot" represented Froude's contribution to Newman's series *Lives of the English Saints*. But in his biography of a scarcely known hermit saint associated with Glastonbury and Cornwall, Froude worked almost immediately at cross purposes with the scheme of Newman's project. Froude portrayed St. Neot's life as one in which the supernatural played an insignificant role, and, moreover, he was determined to treat that life as legend. He makes his point clear enough on the second page of the biography: "[these] lives are not so much strict biographies, as myths, edifying stories compiled from tradition, and designed not so much to relate facts, as to produce a religious impression on the mind of the hearer." An increasingly skeptical Froude completed his life, or "legend," and withdrew from further participation in the series. Albert Frederic Pollard probably exaggerates when he claims in the *Dictionary of National Biography* that Froude's "faith was unequal to the strain put upon it by the miraculous stories he read" in connection with the series, and Herbert Paul, in *The Life of Froude* (1905), certainly misquotes his subject when he refers to the final line from "A Legend of St. Neot" as evidence of disbelief. The sentence—"This is all, and perhaps rather more than all, that is known of the life of the blessed St. Neot"—does not appear in Froude's text, but its presumed existence has been accepted by several critics.

In two novels written in quick succession in the late 1840s Froude turned away from the lives of saints in order to face a life far closer in time and space: his own. Both *Shadows of the Clouds* and *The Nemesis of Faith* are autobiographical novels—the first more transparently so than the second—and both focus on religious travails so

characteristic of the early Victorian period. Neither novel can be fairly said to rival the achievements of Froude's contemporaries–Thackeray's *Vanity Fair*, for example. Both *Shadows of the Clouds* and *The Nemesis of Faith* display, however, what Kathleen Tillotson, in *Novels of the Eighteen-Forties* (1954), has called the "revolutionary idealism" of the decade and both show Froude's imaginative if not wholly successful attempts to confront religious and sexual uncertainties.

Shadows of the Clouds consists of two juxtaposed stories: "The Spirit's Trials" deals with religious upheaval, courtship, and premature death; "The Lieutenant's Daughter" treats seduction, prostitution, and suicide. "The Spirit's Trials" tells a fairly simple story in a rather awkward way. Edward Fowler, the youngest of eight children, is bullied in school and terrorized at home. He survives these ordeals only to confront another when he falls in love with Emma Hardinge, the young daughter of a rural clergyman. Their love leads to engagement, but the engagement is broken off by Emma's father when Fowler's undergraduate debts are discovered. So autobiographical is this story that, at least until its ninth and final chapter, the correspondence between Froude and Fowler is almost exact: Fowler is Froude, the Canon Fowler is Archdeacon Froude, Emma Hardinge is Harriet Bush. There is, however, no evidence that Froude cherished his love for Harriet Bush until his own death, as Fowler cherishes Emma Hardinge. The final chapter includes a lengthy deathbed scene in which Emma ministers to Fowler, whose religious convictions remain as uncertain as ever. The uncertainties are reflected in a number of ways: Fowler predicts the end of Anglo-Catholicism, endorses Newman, embraces Carlyle, rejects bibliolatry. It is a curious, and for all its organizational difficulties, compelling narrative of a young mind tossed about by the various currents of mid-century faith and doubt.

Froude's second story, "The Lieutenant's Daughter," is so unusual in its organization (the narrative proceeds backward) and its language is so graphic that it may be said to treat an old, old story in a vividly new way. Catherine Gray, daughter of Lt. and Mrs. Gray of Exmouth, is seduced under promise of marriage by Henry Carpenter–and then abandoned by Henry when his parents threaten disinheritance. Cast aside and, to say the least, disillusioned, Catherine becomes a prostitute and, eventually, commits suicide. Because Froude begins his story with the suicide and then proceeds to trace those events which led to Catherine's unhappy end, his story joins the work of many Victorians who sought to expose social abuses and inequality—in this case, the exploitation of women. Less obvious but more interesting in its effect, the backward-moving narrative creates some unusual ironies, sharpest in the high-minded, even Shelleyan declarations of Henry's love which, when read with the knowledge of his victim's suicide, are not only ironic but also cynical. Whether Froude's father was offended more by the content of *Shadows of the Clouds* or by its language (in the brothel: "Lord William offers two hundred pounds . . . if it's fresh") cannot, now, be known. What is known is that the archdeacon attempted to suppress the book by buying every available copy. To more recent critics the work is a valuable, if flawed, contribution to the literature of social protest. To A. O. J. Cockshut in *Men and Women: A Study of Love in the Novel, 1740-1940* (1977), Froude's early stories are complementary in their bleak pessimism: "It is as if Froude had said to the public from behind his mask of anonymity, 'I will show you how hollow [are] your sexual conventions, how unjust, how hypocritical, and unfitted to human nature; and I will show you at the same time that the alternatives are, if anything, worse.'"

The Nemesis of Faith was Froude's first signed work as well as the recipient of his harshest review: the book was publicly burned at Exeter College, Oxford, upon its publication in 1849. At first glance, the novel seems similar to "The Spirit's Trials" of *Shadows of the Clouds* in its treatment of protagonist Markham Sutherland's childhood faith, but the novel moves far more rapidly than its predecessor to its central problem—whether Sutherland should take orders. Sutherland accepts a living and takes orders (Froude had taken deacon's orders in 1845), but he remains uneasy in his faith: the unease comes from some of the same doubts described in *Shadows of the Clouds*. A clergyman so consumed by doubt—and so honest about those doubts—will surely face difficulties, and Sutherland does. He offers the following candid judgment on the Bible: "Oh, what are we doing but making a very idol of the Bible, treating it as if we supposed that to read out of it and in it had mechanical virtue, like spells and charms—that it worked not as thought upon thought, but by some juggling process of talismanic materialism."

An even more forthright declaration on bibliolatry leads to his resignation of his living and, re-

calling the ordeal of Edward Fowler in *Shadows of the Clouds*, another trial of another clergyman's spirit. The trial makes up the second and third sections of the book—the second amounting to the lengthy "Confessions of a Skeptic" interlude in which Sutherland/Froude declares his belief in Christ and his disbelief in the church based on Christ's teaching, the third and final section describing a near-adulterous relationship between Sutherland and Helen Leonard.

Helen and Sutherland come to know each other during the protracted absences of Helen's husband and come close to fleeing to Italy—and away from Helen's husband. The thought of leaving her child makes Helen reluctant to consummate her relationship with Sutherland by running off with him, but this obstacle is soon removed when the child falls into Lake Como, becomes chilled, and dies after a brief illness. The lovers interpret the child's death differently: Helen admits her sin but attributes it to a loveless marriage; Sutherland sees the child's death as God's judgment on his immorality and, consequently, he leaves Helen. The young woman enters a convent and dies there "unreconciled with the church." Sutherland's end is more problematical. Coming close to suicide—an act prevented by an English clergyman recently converted to Rome (apparently Newman)—Sutherland suddenly reaffirms his faith. But in one crushing final paragraph, Froude turns his narrative upside down by concluding that Sutherland's faith "had been reared upon the clouds of sudden violent feeling, and no air castle was ever of more unabiding growth." The novel comes full circle: everything changes but doubt itself.

Just before the publication of *The Nemesis of Faith*, Froude wrote to Charles Kingsley and reviewed his novel succinctly: "There is something in the thing, I know, for I cut a hole in my heart and wrote with the blood." Though subjected to a public burning and described by Carlyle as a spiritual "bellyache" and by Monckton Milnes as a "bomb" thrown into the midst of the church, Froude's novel was soon discussed less passionately. In the May 1849 number of *Fraser's Magazine*, John Malcolm Ludlow found that he could not recommend the book for general perusal, but he nevertheless praised Froude for his prose style and for his "quite invaluable record of the fiery struggles and temptations through which the youth of this nineteenth century has to force its way in religious matters."

It is precisely that "invaluable record" that

critics have discussed in the hundred and some years since Ludlow's review. Basil Willey has treated the novel as a first draft for Froude's later essay (1881) on the Tractarian Movement, "The Oxford Counter-Reformation" (collected in *Short Studies*, volume 4, 1883). As such, Willey sees the novel as divided against itself–part of Froude is with Newman, part is with an idealized, even romanticized childhood faith. And Willey, like many other critics, finds the notion of nemesis ambiguously treated in the novel. Ludlow thought that nemesis was "faith's revenge on those who stray from her," but Willey argues, in an interpretation which is probably truer to Froude's sense of nemesis, that retribution comes to one for having believed the wrong things. In other words, Sutherland/Froude's faith begins to deteriorate when he discovers that his faith "had been partly fabulous." Froude's biographer Waldo Hilary Dunn says fairly that it has long ceased to be the fashion to treat *The Nemesis of Faith* "as if it were but a farrago of namby-pamby sentimentalism," for its record of its author's pain is vivid and convincing–especially in its contradictions and divisions. An interesting example of the novel's continuing attraction may be seen in Owen Chadwick's differing responses to Froude and to his novel. As recently as 1965, in a review of Dunn's biography, Chadwick described Froude's life as "memory complicated, anti-father, soul perplexed, judgment unbalanced"; in volume one of his *The Victorian Church* (1966) Chadwick found in the central character of *The Nemesis of Faith* a moving human being: "The only character [in the novel] that matters is not a puppet for the pulpit but a tangled living person with real hopes and fears."

The year 1849 was one of the most eventful in Froude's consistently eventful life, for in that year he published his *The Nemesis of Faith*, met Thomas Carlyle, and married for the first time. Of these three events, the most important was Froude's meeting Carlyle; in fact, no other relationship in a life crowded with close friendships would have so lasting an impact on the reputation of both men than the one which began in June 1849. Arthur Hugh Clough had encouraged Carlyle to meet with Froude, but it was James Spedding who introduced the two men in Carlyle's Chelsea home in mid 1849. Froude, at that time, was thirty-one, Carlyle was fifty-four. Froude's initial characterization of Carlyle's writings as a "flash of lightning" was recalled when he described his first face-to-face encounter with

Carlyle: Carlyle's eyes "were then of deep violet, with fire burning at the bottom of them, which flashed out at the least excitement." That description, written more than thirty years later in his multivolume biography of Carlyle (1882, 1884) testifies to the lasting impact made by the older man upon the younger; the relationship that developed between them was, for Froude, so close that it became one of discipleship. Throughout the 1850s Froude corresponded with Carlyle and, in his visits to London, would usually meet with Carlyle and his wife Jane Welsh. But after Froude's move to London in 1860, following the death of his wife, the friendship between the two men deepened considerably. Carlyle himself called on Froude in 1860 and asked him to become his riding companion. Although Froude declined, he reciprocated Carlyle's gesture in a far more important way–by meeting and talking with Carlyle at least two or three times a week for the next twenty-one years. The relationship was not entirely one-sided; for example, Froude helped sustain Carlyle's spirits in the weeks immediately following Jane Welsh Carlyle's sudden death on 21 April 1866. But that the relationship was principally one of master and disciple is clear from Froude's own words in his life of Carlyle: "Then and always I looked, and have looked, to him as my master. In a long personal intimacy of over thirty years, I learnt to reverence the man as profoundly as I honoured the teacher. . . ."

A few months before his first meeting with Carlyle, Froude accepted Charles Kingsley's offer of a safe harbor in which to ride out the storm of criticism swirling about *The Nemesis of Faith*, and joined his old friend at Ilfracombe, north Devon. It was there he met Charlotte Grenfell, the sister of Kingsley's wife Francis and the model for Argemone Lavington in Kingsley's *Yeast* (1851). Despite Charlotte Grenfell's deepening interest in Roman Catholicism and her tentative plans to become a nun, the two young people were attracted to one another and, sometime in the spring of 1849, became engaged. Ironically recalling the Reverend Bush's opposition to Froude's engagement to Harriet Bush, the Grenfells strongly objected to a match between their aristocratic daughter and the virtually penniless, uncomfortably controversial Anthony Froude. The couple nevertheless secured the Grenfells' half-hearted blessings and were married on 3 October 1849. They moved almost immediately to Manchester, where Froude tutored the daughters of the wealthy Manchester solicitor and Unitarian

Samuel Dunkinfield Darbisher until mid 1850. Quickly tiring of Manchester, the Froudes moved to a remote cottage called Plas Gwynant in north Wales so that Froude could devote his energies to writing. Before her early death in 1860, Charlotte would give birth to two daughters and one son (Georgina Margaret, Rose Mary, and Pascal Grenfell).

As dramatic as the burning of *The Nemesis of Faith* had been, it had at least the salutary effect of forcing a career change on Froude. The burning led to his resignation, under pressure, as a fellow of Exeter and his removal from Oxford, but it also led him to the profession which would occupy his mature years: the writing of history. Froude was in fact prevented by law from resigning his deacon's orders (prohibitions eventually ended with passage of the Clergy Difficulties Act in 1872), but he was not forced to surrender his pen. A stream of book reviews, articles, and even fables began to flow from that pen, reaching the pages of the *Westminster Review, Fraser's Magazine, Eclectic Review,* and the *Fortnightly Review* (most of his magazine articles were collected in the four volumes of *Short Studies on Great Subjects,* 1867-1883). Though the range of interests reflected in Froude's periodical writings is impressive enough, the recurrence of particular topics shows the direction his future research would take: the lives of the saints, the dissolution of the monasteries, the philosophy of Calvinism. Two of those early articles are especially noteworthy. In "England's Forgotten Worthies" (1852) and "The Science of History" (1864), both collected in *Short Studies,* volume 1 (1867), Froude underlines his preoccupation with history as essentially the history of great men–an idea clearly influenced by Carlyle–and his often vividly supported notion that historical writing should be "dramatic," even "poetic." His remarks in "The Science of History" on Shakespeare reveal an interest in the dramatic–and correlative lack of interest in the

Plas Gwynant in North Wales, where Froude and his wife Charlotte moved in the summer of 1850 so that he could devote his energy to writing

analytic—which would color his own writings and invite both praise and blame: " 'Macbeth,' were it literally true, would be perfect history; and so far as the historian can approach to that kind of model, so far as he can let his story tell itself in the deeds and words of those who act it out, so far is he most successful."

A lifelong interest in sixteenth-century English history—particularly the struggles of the English Reformation—produced Froude's historical masterpiece, the twelve-volume *History of England*, published at regular intervals from 1856 to 1870. As popular with the public as it was unpopular with academicians, the *History* was based on a considerable body of original research. In October 1853 Froude moved from the relative isolation of Plas Gwynant to Babbicombe, near Torquay, in order to have easier access to manuscript repositories in London and at Hatfield House, Hatfield, Hertfordshire (which held the papers of William Cecil, Lord Burghley). He mined the archives of Rolls House (now the Public Record Office) as well as the British Museum; he was able to gain permission to study unpublished manuscripts in the Chapter House of Westminster Abbey; and he was the first English historian to gain free access to the Spanish National Archives at Simancas. His Simancas research proved especially fruitful as his study of diplomatic exchanges between the Spanish ambassadors to London and the Spanish government in Madrid provided much new material which was published for the first time in the concluding volumes of the *History of England*. Readers should keep in mind when reviewing the generally hostile critical reception of the *History* that nine-tenths of Froude's authorities were in manuscript, that he worked with five languages, and that the Simancas holdings alone filled nine hundred volumes.

Froude saw his role in the *History of England* as that of advocate and revisionist. He viewed the English Reformation as a revolt of the laity against the clergy, a struggle between a united king and parliament against an alien, despotic pope and church of Rome. In taking such a view he sought to justify the more absolutist policies and practices of Henry VIII as actions made necessary by the mortal struggle of England against Rome. He justified the dissolution of the monasteries as simply a part of the struggle for freedom from foreign domination; he approved the execution of Thomas More because More was, after all, a Catholic first and an Englishman sec-

ond. Such views were strong and were strongly expressed in a variety of ways throughout the twelve volumes of historical narrative beginning with the fall of Wolsey—the first blow for freedom from an alien power—and concluding with the defeat of the Spanish Armada.

Dunn does not exaggerate when he characterizes the 1860s as "one of the happiest and most successful" periods of Froude's life. In 1861 he married Henrietta Elizabeth Warre; before the end of the decade he became the father of two more children (Ashley Anthony and Mary Caroline). In November 1860 he became editor of *Fraser's Magazine* and remained its sole editor for the next fourteen years, stepping down in 1874 after the death of his second wife and at the behest of Carlyle, who wanted William Allingham to succeed as editor. Before the close of the 1860s Froude added four more volumes to the initial six of his *History* and saw his reputation as historian and man of letters steadily increase. One example of that recognition was his election in 1868 as Lord Rector of St. Andrews University (his opponent had been the formidable Benjamin Disraeli). Six years later Froude's fame was acknowledged in another way when he was asked by Lord Carnarvon, colonial secretary in Disraeli's second ministry, to travel to South Africa and report on the desirability and feasibility of federation for the several states of Cape Town, the Orange Free State, the Transvaal, and Natal.

Froude's *History of England* was immensely successful with the public—his early biographer Herbert Paul claims that in 1856 Froude's name "was in all mouths"—but its critical reception was an entirely different matter. The earliest reviewers of the *History of England* were largely negative—and no wonder. Froude's Erastian position was anathema to High Churchmen, and his apologetic stance on Henry VIII was repugnant to liberals. Perhaps the most remarkable review was one written by Froude's brother-in-law Charles Kingsley in the January 1864 number of *Macmillan's Magazine*. In that review, of volumes seven and eight of the *History*, Kingsley managed to praise Froude and to insult Newman—a feat which impelled Newman to write his *Apologia pro Vita Sua* (1864). What is noteworthy in the majority of the reviews is their transparent partisanship: the critic for *Blackwood's Magazine* defended Mary Stuart against Froude's negative portrait, the writer for the *Westminster Review* regretted Froude's defense of "Tudor despotism" and reproved him for his "moral insensibility," but a clerical reviewer in the *Fortnightly* was enthusiastically receptive to Froude's stated theme in the *History of England*: "Through Christ came charity and mercy. From theology came strife and hatred." But by far the most persistent of Froude's contemporary critics was Edward Freeman, a fellow historian, a High Churchman, and a remarkably zealous opponent. His charges of inaccuracy, distortion, and even bad faith were thrown against Froude in a series of *Saturday Review* articles published from 1864 to 1892. Though Froude's offer to the editor of the *Review* to allow an independent panel of historians to examine the same manuscripts he had read and translated went unaccepted, there is, nevertheless, no question that he was occasionally inaccurate, nor can there be much doubt that he was a poor copyreader. But Freeman's charges were influential and probably inspired the unhappily succinct comment on Froude's "constitutional inaccuracy" made by Leslie Stephen in *Studies of a Biographer* (1902).

Twentieth-century critics have rarely concerned themselves with Freeman's charges, but Froude's status as a historian of the first rank has been much debated. One obvious problem in any estimate of Froude's value is his self-declared antipathy to what he called the "science" of history and his preference for what may be called the "literary." To what extent, in other words, is the literary historian of lasting value? Another problem has been Froude's vigorously Protestant interpretation of historical events. In the early twentieth century historians themselves were divided in their assessment of Froude's scholarship. Albert Frederic Pollard claimed in *Thomas Cranmer*, published in 1904, that there was "inadequate justification for the systematic detraction of Froude's *History*" and passed over Froude's Protestant bias with a brief comment: "He held strong views, and he made some mistakes; but his mistakes were no greater than those of other historians, and there are not half a dozen histories in the English language which have been based on so exhaustive a survey of original materials." In *History and Historians in the Nineteenth Century* (1913), G. P. Gooch was less sanguine when he described Froude's mind as one lacking "serenity and insight into differing modes of thought"–faults attributed, not surprisingly, to the historian's championing of Protestantism against Catholicism. By 1942 in *A History of Historical Writing*, James Westfall Thompson seemed to balance Froude's obvious bias against his astonishing research and to as-

"He created Henry VIII., exploded Mary Stuart, and demolished Elizabeth," caricature of Froude by Adriano Cecioni published in Vanity Fair, *27 January 1872 (Collection of Jerold J. Savory)*

sess the *History of England* as a largely "moral" work written by a man firmly convinced that "the yoke of Rome would have meant a dimming of the light of freedom and civilization." In 1961 L. M. Angus-Butterworth placed Froude in the gallery of British writers he described in *Ten Master Historians* and praised the *History of England* not only for its dramatic narrative but for its "proportion." What remains to be said is that most critics– historians as well as men of letters so temperamentally different as Leslie Stephen, Frederic Harrison (in *Tennyson, Ruskin, Mill and Other Literary Estimates*, 1899), and Lytton Strachey (in *Portraits in Miniature*, 1931)–unite in their praise of Froude's grandly dramatic, sweeping style. For all his insensitivity to suffering and his never-concealed bias, the so-called set pieces–the execution scenes of Cranmer, More, and Mary Stuart, and the destruction of the Armada–are hugely successful narratives.

The stage for Froude's *History of England* was immense, its leading actors heroic in stature: fitting complements for a society as heroic as the one Froude envisioned in England's sixteenth century. But in the biography which culminated his career and engendered yet another controversy, the drama is more akin to tragedy, its leading actor a tragically flawed man. Froude's biography of Carlyle–*Thomas Carlyle, A History of the First Forty Years of His Life, 1785-1835* (1882) and *Thomas Carlyle, A History of His Life in London, 1834-1881* (1884)–was commissioned by Carlyle himself. Carlyle left letters in Froude's care (at one point Froude estimated that he had 10,000 of them); he intended Froude to edit the *Reminiscences* of his early life, which Froude published shortly after Carlyle's death in 1881, and he named Froude his literary executor. To what extent Froude either honored or betrayed the trust placed in him by Carlyle has been debated from the first appearance of the biography almost to the present time; Froude's admirers have consistently defended him for doing little more than Carlyle had asked that he do, while his detractors have seen in Froude an example of what Oscar Wilde had in mind when he claimed that "every great man has his disciples and it is always Judas who writes the biography."

The great strength of Froude's life of Carlyle rests in its author's long and close relationship with its major character–or, one should say, two major characters, since the role of Jane Welsh Carlyle, the great man's wife, plays an exceedingly important part in the biography. Froude's intimacy with Carlyle gave him a vantage point on his subject comparable perhaps only to Boswell's on Johnson, and it is hardly surprising that these two great English literary biographers are often compared. In his preface to his 1979 abridged edition of Froude's biography, John Clubbe compares Froude with Boswell by describing Froude's depiction of his hero as a figure, like Boswell's Johnson, "vigorously reacting to an age he found increasingly alien. Like the heroes of old to which he is compared, he drew strength from his combat with its corrupting influence. His tragic nature set him both apart from and against his times." That a tragic character could also be petty, irascible, self-centered, and

Froude in the 1890s (photograph by Walery of London)

even violent was hardly a contradiction to Froude, and in his lengthy delineation of Carlyle's character he sought to portray the man's considerable strengths and manifold weaknesses. In so doing Froude felt he was following Carlyle's own belief that an idealizing biography gives the reader a "ghost" rather than the man himself: "If [Carlyle] was to be known at all, he chose to be known as he was, with his angularities, his sharp speeches, his special peculiarities, meritorious or unmeritorious, precisely as they had actually been."

Critical reaction to Froude's biography has produced a fascinating if not always edifying subgenre of its own–early critics reacting, for the most part, with horror, later critics fulfilling Froude's expectation, recorded in his diary, that "By and bye the world will thank me, but not in my own lifetime." The biography's early critics felt that Froude had in fact told too much about Carlyle's marriage, and such criticism was not confined to the reviews. Tennyson, for example, probably had Froude in mind when he wrote in "The Dead Prophet" (1885) that "his friends had stript him bare,/And rolled his nakedness everywhere/ That all the crowds might stare." Although Froude had prominent defenders–John Ruskin, Edward FitzGerald, Sir John Skelton–the lasting value of the biography has been recognized more in the twentieth century than it was in the nineteenth. Herbert Paul claimed in 1905 that Carlyle's fame owed "almost as much" to Froude's life of him as to his own writings, and in studies of English biography, Froude's life had been consistently praised–by Waldo Hilary Dunn in 1916 (*English Biography*), by Harold Nicolson in 1927 (*The Development of English Biography*), by Edgar Johnson in 1937 (*One Mighty Torrent*), and by Richard Altick in 1965 (*Lives and Letters*). More recent critics have paid particular attention to Froude's portraits of the Carlyles. For example, A. O. J. Cockshut argued in *Truth to Life* (1974) that the biography proceeds "dialectically"–that Froude "will never allow the greatness or the littleness of Carlyle to hold exclusive attention for long. He sees them as inseparable." In an essay in his 1976 volume *Carlyle and His Contemporaries*, John Clubbe discussed Froude's use of the Greek chorus in his biography as well as the influence of the stories of Oedipus and of Iphigenia on his interpretation of the Carlyles' life together; and in Clubbe's preface to his abridged edition of Froude's life he underlined the importance to the biographer of Carlyle's tragic character: "Believing that the Carlyles' life together was one of unutterable sadness, he wrote a history of it that is at its deepest level a tragedy and that moves us by its tragic power."

Though *The Nemesis of Faith*, the *History of England*, and the life of Carlyle must loom large in any discussion of Froude, Froude produced several other works which have bearing on his contribution to Victorian letters. An astonishingly prolific writer, he continued to move from fiction, to history, to travel writing, and to biography throughout the later years of writing the *History of England* and working on the Carlyle books (the life, the *Reminiscences*, and his edition of Jane Welsh Carlyle's *Letters and Memorials*). He produced from 1872 to 1874 his three-volume study *The English in Ireland in the Eighteenth Century*, and although this work has its admirers (Dunn in particular), it is disfigured by biases even stronger than those evident in the *History of England*. To his credit, Froude scarcely mitigates England's mistreatment of the Irish, but he suggests too often that the Irish were unfit for self-government. Similar remarks made while on a lecture tour in the

United States in 1872 led to threats against his life and a premature end to Froude's only visit to this country. His two books on the Empire–*Oceana; or, England and Her Colonies* and *The English in the West Indies*, published in 1886 and 1888–present a corrective to Froude's later pessimism. If one juxtaposes the *History of England* with the life of Carlyle one sees the general tendency–the epic has given way to the tragic. Carlyle became for Froude, in Cockshut's words, a "deposed king" in a dark time. But *Oceana* in particular expresses hope of renewal for England in the close confederation of her Anglo-Saxon colonies and dominions; in Australia, New Zealand, and Canada–not, conspicuously, in Ireland–will a stronger and more moral British Empire find its destiny. Froude's interest in fiction produced the late novel *The Two Chiefs of Dunboy; or, An Irish Romance of the Last Century* (1889); it is a didactic and, for Froude, unevenly written book which too often characterizes the Irish as a savage, even treacherous people. In this final phase of his life his interest in biography remained as strong as ever, even if his lives of Thomas Becket (1878), Caesar (1879), John Bunyan (1880), Martin Luther (1883), and Lord Beaconsfield (Benjamin Disraeli) (1890) hardly rival the achievement of his work on Carlyle.

Froude became Regius Professor of Modern History at Oxford in 1892, succeeding, in a consummate irony, his longtime opponent Freeman. Although able to complete only two academic years of lectures, he nevertheless contributed three more books to an already impressive canon. In his lectures on Erasmus, the Council of Trent, and English seamen of the sixteenth century–all published in book form from 1894 to 1896–he returned to earlier themes. In his first lecture on the Council of Trent, for example, he declared that "the Reformation was the hinge on which all modern history turned," and in his lively reenactments of the voyages of English seamen, he introduced a new generation of students to England's forgotten worthies. He outlived the Trinity term in 1894 by only a few months, dying of cancer on 20 October. He was buried on a hill in Salcombe, Devonshire, in sight of a sea as wide and glimmering as a body of literary works written with energy and passion over the course of fifty years.

Letters:

John Skelton, *The Table-Talk of Shirley: Reminiscences of and Letters from Froude, Thackeray,*

Disraeli, Browning, Rossetti, Kingsley, Baynes, Huxley, Tyndall and Others (Edinburgh & London: Blackwood, 1895);

Raymond M. Bennett, ed., "Letters of James Anthony Froude," *Journal of Rutgers University Library*, 11 (December 1947): 1-15; 12 (June 1949): 38-53; 25 (December 1961): 10-23; 26 (December 1962): 14-22;

Helen Gill Viljoen, ed., *The Froude-Ruskin Friendship as Represented Through Letters* (New York: Pageant, 1966).

Bibliography:

Robert Goetzman, *James Anthony Froude: A Bibliography of Studies* (New York: Garland, 1977).

Biographies:

Herbert Paul, *The Life of Froude* (London: Pitman, 1905);

Waldo Hilary Dunn, *James Anthony Froude: A Biography*, 2 volumes (Oxford: Clarendon Press, 1961-1963).

References:

Richard D. Altick, *Lives and Letters: A History of Literary Biography in England and America* (New York: Knopf, 1965);

L. M. Angus-Butterworth, *Ten Master Historians* (Aberdeen: Aberdeen University Press, 1961);

Kingsbury Badger, "The Ordeal of Anthony Froude, Protestant Historian," *Modern Language Quarterly*, 13 (March 1952): 41-55;

Owen Chadwick, *The Victorian Church*, 2 volumes (London: Black, 1966-1970);

John Clubbe, "Grecian Destiny: Froude's Portraits of the Carlyles," in *Carlyle and His Contemporaries*, edited by Clubbe (Durham: Duke University Press, 1976), pp. 317-353;

Clubbe, Preface to *Froude's Life of Carlyle*, edited by Clubbe (Columbus: Ohio State University Press, 1979);

A. O. J. Cockshut, *Men and Women: A Study of Love and the Novel, 1740-1940* (London: Collins, 1977);

Cockshut, *Truth to Life: The Art of Biography in the Nineteenth Century* (London: Collins, 1974);

Waldo Hilary Dunn, *Froude and Carlyle: A Study of the Froude-Carlyle Controversy* (London: Longmans, Green, 1930);

K. J. Fielding, "Froude and Carlyle: Some New Considerations," in *Carlyle Past and Present: A Collection of New Essays*, edited by Fielding and Roger L. Tarr (London: Vision, 1976),

pp. 239-269;

Andrew Fish, "The Reputation of James Anthony Froude," *Pacific Historical Review*, 1 (1932): 179-192;

G. P. Gooch, *History and Historians in the Nineteenth Century* (London: Longmans, Green, 1913), pp. 301-316;

William J. Gracie, Jr., "Faith of Our Fathers: The Autobiographical Novels of James Anthony Froude," *Victorians Institute Journal*, 10 (1981-1982): 27-43;

Phyllis Grosskurth, "James Anthony Froude as Historical Novelist," *University of Toronto Quarterly*, 40 (Spring 1971): 266-275;

Frederic Harrison, *Tennyson, Ruskin, Mill and Other Literary Estimates* (London & New York: Macmillan, 1899);

Gertrude Himmelfarb, "James Anthony Froude: A Forgotten Worthy," in her *Victorian Minds* (New York: Harper & Row, 1970);

Rosemary Jann, *The Art and Science of Victorian History* (Columbus: Ohio State University Press, 1985), pp. 105-140;

Harry Wells McGraw, "Two Novelists of Despair: James Anthony Froude and William Hale White," *Southern Quarterly Review*, 13 (October 1974): 21-51;

Howard Murphy, "The Ethical Revolt Against Christian Orthodoxy in Early Victorian England," *American Historical Review*, 60 (July 1955): 800-817;

Albert Frederic Pollard, *Thomas Cranmer* (New York: Putnam's, 1904), pp. 679-687;

Edward Sharples, Jr., "Carlyle and His Readers: The Froude Controversy Once Again," Ph.D. dissertation, University of Rochester, 1964;

Leslie Stephen, *Studies of a Biographer*, 4 volumes (New York: Putnam's, 1902);

Lytton Strachey, "Froude," in his *Portraits in Miniature* (New York: Harcourt, Brace, 1931), pp. 191-202;

James Westfall Thompson, *A History of Historical Writing*, 2 volumes (New York: Macmillan, 1942);

Kathleen Tillotson, *Novels of the Eighteen-Forties* (Oxford: Clarendon Press, 1954);

Basil Willey, *More Nineteenth Century Studies: A Group of Honest Doubters* (New York: Columbia University Press, 1956);

Robert Lee Wolff, *Gains and Losses: Novels of Faith and Doubt in Victorian England* (New York: Garland, 1977).

Papers:

In the United States, unpublished correspondence, manuscripts by Froude, and miscellaneous materials are at the Beinecke Rare Book and Manuscript Library, Yale University; Perkins Library, Duke University; the Huntington Library, San Marino, California; the University of Illinois Library at Urbana-Champaign; and the Harry Ransom Humanities Research Center, University of Texas at Austin. In Great Britain, important collections of Froude's unpublished correspondence may be found at the Bodleian Library, Oxford; the British Library, London; the Lambeth Palace Library, London; the University of Edinburgh Library; and the Tennyson Research Centre, City Library, Lincoln.

William Ewart Gladstone
(19 December 1809-19 May 1898)

Robert O'Kell
University of Manitoba

SELECTED BOOKS: *Speech . . . in the House of Commons, on Monday, June 3, 1833, on Colonial Slavery* (London: Proprietors of the *Mirror of Parliament*, 1833);

Speech delivered in the House of Commons on the motion of Sir George Strickland for the Abolition of the Negro Apprenticeship, March 30, 1838 (London: Hatchard, 1838);

The State in Its Relations with the Church (London: Murray, 1838; revised and enlarged, 2 volumes, 1841);

Church Principles Considered in their Results (London: Murray, 1840);

Substance of a Speech on the Motion of Lord John Russell for a Committee of the Whole House, with a view to the Removal of the Remaining Jewish Disabilities; Delivered in the House of Commons on Thursday, December 16, 1847 (London: Murray, 1848);

Remarks on the Royal Supremacy as It Is Defined by Reason, History, and the Constitution. A Letter to the Lord Bishop of London (London: Murray, 1850; revised, 1877);

Speech on the Commission of Inquiry into the State of the Universities of Oxford and Cambridge, Delivered on Thursday, July 18, 1850 (Oxford: Parker, 1850);

The Ecclesiastical Titles Assumption Bill. Speech . . . in the House of Commons, on the 25th of March 1851, on the Motion that the Bill be now read a second time (London: Bradley, 1851);

A Letter to the Earl of Aberdeen, on the State Prosecutions of the Neapolitan Government (London: Murray, 1851; New York, 1851);

A Second Letter to the Earl of Aberdeen, on the State Prosecutions of the Neapolitan Government (London: Murray, 1851);

Studies on Homer and the Homeric Age, 3 volumes (Oxford: Oxford University Press, 1858);

The Financial Statements of 1853, 1860-1863, to Which are Added a Speech on Tax-bills, 1861, and on Charities, 1863 (London: Murray, 1863; enlarged to include "Financial Statement of 1864," 1864);

Speech . . . on the Bill for the Extension of the Suffrage in Towns, May 11, 1864 (London: Murray, 1864);

Address on the Place of Ancient Greece in the Providential Order of the World; Delivered before the University of Edinburgh, on the Third of November, 1865 (London: Murray, 1865);

Speeches on Parliamentary Reform in 1866 (London: Murray, 1866);

"Ecce Homo" (London: Strahan, 1868);

A Chapter of Autobiography (London: Murray, 1868);

Juventus Mundi: The Gods and Men of the Heroic Age (London: Macmillan, 1869; Boston: Little, Brown, 1869);

Marriage With a Deceased Wife's Sister; Speech . . . in the House of Commons, July 21st, 1869, in support of Mr. Thomas Chambers' Marriage Bill (London: Seeleys, 1870);

The Vatican Decrees in Their Bearing on Civil Allegiance: A Political Expostulation (London: Murray, 1874); republished with *The Replies of Archbishop Manning and Lord Acton* (New York: Appleton, 1874);

The Church of England and Ritualism; Reprinted from the Contemporary Review and Revised (London: Strahan, 1875);

Vaticanism: An Answer to Reproofs and Replies (Lon-

This photograph of Gladstone was taken by J. E. Mayall in August 1861 (Victoria and Albert Museum)

don: Murray, 1875; New York: Harper, 1875);

Rome and the Newest Fashions in Religion, Three Tracts; The Vatican Decrees; Vaticanism; Speeches of the Pope (London: Murray, 1875; New York: Harper, 1875);

Bulgarian Horrors and the Question of the East (London: Murray, 1876; New York: Lovell, Adam, Wesson, 1876);

Homeric Synchronism: An Enquiry into the Time and Place of Homer (London: Macmillan, 1876; New York: Harper, 1876);

Lessons in Massacre; or, The Conduct of the Turkish Government in and about Bulgaria since May 1876. Chiefly from the Papers Presented by Command (London: Murray, 1877);

The Death of the Prince Consort: An Address delivered at Manchester, 23 April 1862, before the Association of Lancashire and Cheshire Mechanics' Institutes (London, 1879);

Gleanings of Past Years, 1843-78, 7 volumes (London: Murray, 1879; New York: Scribners, 1879);

Political Speeches in Scotland, November and December 1879; . . . with an Appendix, containing the Rectorial Address in Glasgow, and Other Nonpolitical Speeches (London: Ridgway, 1879);

Midlothian Addresses (Edinburgh: Midlothian Liberal Association, 1880); republished as *The Midlothian Campaign: Political Speeches Delivered in November and December 1879, and March and April 1880* (Edinburgh: Elliot, 1880);

Home Rule Manifesto. Address . . . to the Electors of Midlothian, May 1st, 1886 (London: National Press Agency, 1886);

The Irish Question. I History of an Idea. II Lessons of the Election (London: Murray, 1886; New York: Scribners, 1886);

Speeches on the Irish Question in 1886; with an Appendix Containing the Full Text of the Government of Ireland and the Sale and Purchase of Land Bills of 1886 (Edinburgh: Elliot, 1886);

The Impregnable Rock of Holy Scripture (London: Isbister, 1890; Philadelphia: Wattles, 1891; revised, London: Isbister, 1892);

Landmarks of Homeric Study; Together with an Essay on the Points of Contact Between the Assyrian Tablets and the Homeric Text (London & New York: Macmillan, 1890);

Archaic Greece and the East: An Address Delivered before the Ninth International Congress of Orientalists (London: Luzac, 1892);

Female Suffrage. A Letter to Samuel Smith, M.P. (London: Murray, 1892);

The Speeches and Public Addresses of the Right Hon. W. E. Gladstone, M.P., With Notes and Introductions, edited by A. W. Hutton and H. J. Cohen, 2 volumes (London: Methuen, 1892);

Later Gleanings: A New Series of Gleanings of Past Years, Theological and Ecclesiastical (London: Murray, 1897; New York: Scribners, 1897);

Gladstone's Speeches (London: Methuen, 1916);

The Gladstone Diaries, edited by M. R. D. Foot and H. C. G. Matthew, 8 volumes to date (Oxford: Clarendon Press, 1968-   );

The Prime Ministers' Papers: W. E. Gladstone, edited by John Brooke and Mary Sorensen, 4 volumes (London: H.M.S.O., 1971-1981).

OTHER: *A Manual of Prayers from the Liturgy, Ar-*

ranged for Family Use, compiled by Gladstone (London: Murray, 1845);

Translations, poems in several languages, with translations by Gladstone and George William, Lord Lyttleton (London: Quaritch, 1861);

Heinrich Schliemann, *Mycenae: A Narrative of Researches and Discoveries at Mycenae and Tiryns*, preface by Gladstone (London: Murray, 1878);

The Odes of Horace, translated by Gladstone (London: Murray, 1894; New York: Scribners, 1894);

The Psalter, with a Concordance and other Auxiliary Matter, edited with commentary by Gladstone (London: Murray, 1895);

The Works of Joseph Butler, edited by Gladstone, 2 volumes (Oxford: Clarendon Press, 1896; New York: Macmillan, 1896);

Studies Subsidiary to the Works of Bishop Butler, edited by Gladstone (Oxford: Clarendon Press, 1896; New York: Macmillan, 1896).

PERIODICAL PUBLICATIONS: "The Course of Commercial Policy at Home and Abroad," *Foreign and Colonial Quarterly Review*, 1 (January 1843): 222-273;

"From Oxford to Rome," *Quarterly Review*, 81 (June 1847): 131-166;

"Clergy Relief Bill," *Quarterly Review*, 86 (December 1849): 40-78;

"The Declining Efficiency of Parliament," *Quarterly Review*, 99 (September 1856): 521-570;

"Homer and His Successors in Epic Poetry," *Quarterly Review*, 101 (January 1857): 80-122;

"Prospects Political and Financial," *Quarterly Review*, 101 (January 1857): 243-284;

"The New Parliament and Its Work," *Quarterly Review*, 101 (April 1857): 541-584;

"Homeric Characters in and out of Homer," *Quarterly Review*, 102 (July 1857): 204-251;

"The Bill for Divorce," *Quarterly Review*, 102 (July 1857): 251-288;

"France and the Late Ministry," *Quarterly Review*, 103 (April 1858): 526-574;

"The Past and Present Administrations," *Quarterly Review*, 104 (October 1858): 515-560;

"Foreign Affairs–War in Italy," *Quarterly Review*, 105 (April 1859): 527-564;

"Tennyson's Poems–*Idylls of the King*," *Quarterly Review*, 106 (October 1859): 454-485;

"The Shield of Achilles," *Contemporary Review*, 23 (February 1874): 329-336;

"The Reply of Achilles to the Envoys of Agamem-non," *Contemporary Review*, 23 (May 1874): 841-848;

"Homer's Place in History," *Contemporary Review*, 24 (June 1874): 1-22;

"A Contribution towards Determining the Place of Homer in History and in Egyptian Chronology," *Contemporary Review*, 24 (July 1874): 175-200;

"The Life and Speeches of the Prince Consort–Court of Queen Victoria," as Etonensis, *Contemporary Review*, 26 (June 1875): 1-24;

"The Courses of Religious Thought," *Contemporary Review*, 28 (June 1876): 1-26;

"The Life and Letters of Lord Macaulay," *Quarterly Review*, 142 (July 1876): 1-50;

"The Hellenic Factor in the Eastern Problem," *Contemporary Review*, 29 (December 1876): 1-27;

"On the Influence of Authority in Matters of Opinion," *Nineteenth Century*, 1 (March 1877): 2-22;

"Aggression on Egypt and Freedom in the East," *Nineteenth Century*, 2 (August 1877): 149-166;

"The Paths of Honour and of Shame," *Nineteenth Century*, 3 (March 1878): 591-604;

"A Modern Symposium: Is the Popular Judgment in Politics More Just than That of the Higher Orders?," by Gladstone and others, *Nineteenth Century*, 4 (July 1878): 174-192;

"England's Mission," *Nineteenth Century*, 4 (September 1878): 560-584;

"The Sixteenth Century Arraigned before the Nineteenth: A Study on the Reformation," *Contemporary Review*, 33 (October 1878): 425-457;

"The Country and the Government," *Nineteenth Century*, 6 (August 1879): 201-227;

"Russia and England," *Nineteenth Century*, 7 (March 1880): 538-556;

"The Conservative Collapse; Considered in a Letter from a Liberal to an Old Conservative," as Index, *Fortnightly Review*, new series 27 (1 May 1880): 607-624;

" 'Locksley Hall' and the Jubilee," *Nineteenth Century*, 21 (January 1887): 1-18;

"Notes and Queries on the Irish Demand," *Nineteenth Century*, 21 (February 1887): 165-190;

"The History of 1852-1860, and Greville's Latest Journals," *English Historical Review*, 2 (April 1887): 281-302;

"*Robert Elsmere* and the Battle of Belief," *Nineteenth Century*, 23 (May 1888): 766-788;

"Mr. Forster and Ireland," *Nineteenth Century*, 24 (September 1888): 451-464;

"Daniel O'Connell," *Nineteenth Century,* 25 (January 1889): 149-168;

" 'Divorce'—A Novel," review of *Faithful and Unfaithful,* by Margaret Lee, *Nineteenth Century,* 25 (February 1889): 213-215;

"The Melbourne Government: Its Acts and Persons," *Nineteenth Century,* 27 (January 1890): 38-55;

"On Books and the Housing of Them," *Nineteenth Century,* 27 (March 1890): 384-396;

"On the Ancient Beliefs in a Future State," *Nineteenth Century,* 30 (October 1891): 658-676;

"The Olympian Religion," 4 parts, *North American Review,* 154 (February 1892): 231-241; 154 (March 1892): 365-376; 154 (April 1892): 489-502; 154 (May 1892): 613-625;

"Did Dante Study in Oxford?," *Nineteenth Century,* 31 (June 1892): 1032-1042;

"Vindication of Home Rule. A Reply to the Duke of Argyll," *North American Review,* 155 (October 1892): 385-394;

"The Place of Heresy and Schism in the Modern Christian Church," *Nineteenth Century,* 36 (August 1894): 157-174;

"True and False Conceptions of the Atonement," *Nineteenth Century,* 36 (September 1894): 317-331;

"Sheridan," *Nineteenth Century,* 39 (June 1896): 1037-1042;

"A Note on 'Was Pitt a Prophet?' by A.V. Dicey," *Contemporary Review,* 70 (September 1896): 314-315;

"Arthur Henry Hallam," *Youth's Companion,* 1 (6 January 1898): 1-3.

William Ewart Gladstone's enduring fame arises from his long and distinguished career in politics. He was prime minister four times (1868-1874; 1880-1885; 1886; and 1892-1894), and he, more than any other person, was responsible for the shaping of the late-Victorian Liberal party. But, although his public presence in the Victorian culture was primarily political in a direct sense, Gladstone was also an influential figure as a writer on an impressively wide range of topics.

Gladstone, fifth eldest of six siblings (four brothers and two sisters), was the son of John Gladstone, a wealthy Liverpool merchant, and his second wife, Anne Robertson Gladstone. The elder Gladstone had considerable ambitions for his son who was educated at Eton and Christ Church, Oxford, culminating an academic career of rare promise with Firsts in *Literae Humaniores* and Mathematics in 1831. While at Oxford Gladstone dis-

played, in equal proportions, an aptitude for classical studies, a love of disputation, and a commitment to religious and moral obligations, all of which were to be powerful influences on his character for the rest of his life. Under the guidance of his elder sister, Anne, Gladstone had his family's evangelical Anglicanism broadened and deepened to the point where he seriously contemplated a career in the Church. Dissuaded from this path by his father, he first entered the House of Commons in 1832 under the patronage of the Tory Duke of Newcastle. Two years later, at the age of twenty-five, he was appointed a junior Lord of the Treasury at the outset of Sir Robert Peel's abortive Conservative government of 1834-1835. Only a month later Gladstone became under secretary of the War and Colonial Office when that position fell unexpectedly vacant. Although his tenure there was extremely brief, he made a sharp and profound impression upon Peel and the other leaders of the party, thus ensuring his promotion when the Conservatives next resumed office.

On 25 July 1839 Gladstone married Catherine Glynne, the sister of Sir Stephen Glynne, ninth and last baronet of Hawarden Castle, Flintshire. Gladstone and his wife took up residence in London in 1840 and over the next fourteen years had eight children: William (1840), Agnes (1842), Stephen (1844), Catherine (Jessy) (1845), Mary (1847), Helen (1849), Henry (Harry) (1852), and Herbert (1854). All but Jessy, who died at the age of four, survived to adulthood. When the Glynne family's estates became financially entangled, Gladstone took over the responsibility and management of them, and in 1855 Sir Stephen Glynne, having no direct heir, settled the Hawarden property upon the Gladstones' eldest son, William. Thus, in effect, Hawarden Castle became the Gladstones' estate.

When the Conservatives resumed office in 1841 Peel appointed Gladstone vice-president of the Board of Trade, where he quickly mastered the details of an extensive reform of the tariff system. In 1843 he succeeded to the presidency of the Board of Trade and a place in Peel's cabinet. In early 1845 he resigned from the cabinet so that he could in good conscience privately support the Maynooth Bill for endowing the Catholic seminary in Dublin, a measure that he felt was inconsistent with his previously published opinions on the question of Church-State relations. But at the end of the year he returned to office as colonial secretary, a position he held for the duration of Peel's government, which soon tumbled down in the aftermath of the Corn Law debates. Gladstone's almost instinctive aversion to the flamboyant Benjamin Disraeli was at this time fanned into open hostility by the latter's witty and savage attacks on Peel in the sessions of 1845 and 1846. For Gladstone, Peel came to represent everything noble in politics, Disraeli everything immoral. In the early 1850s this animosity was deepened by his jealousy and revulsion when Disraeli became chancellor of the Exchequer in Lord Derby's government of 1852, just as Gladstone was beginning to recognize that financial policy could become the chief moral issue in government administration. His ensuing attack on Disraeli's second budget was a masterpiece of both technical competence and rhetorical fancy that did much to establish the melodramatic quality of their subsequent conflicts, both in their own views and in the minds of the public.

When Gladstone assumed the office of chancellor himself in Lord Aberdeen's coalition government in 1853, he began the task of embodying his own sense of fiscal responsibility in further reforms of the tax structure and in as much restraint with government estimates as the costs of the Crimean War permitted. There appeared to be some possibility in 1858 that Gladstone might join Lord Derby's Conservative ministry and he was reelected for Oxford University ostensibly as a Conservative. Instead, he became chancellor of the Exchequer again in Palmerston's government from 1859 to 1865, much to the chagrin of both his friends and enemies in Parliament who found his participation in a Whig administration somewhat anomalous. It was, however, in these years that Gladstone succeeded, despite the reluctance of his cabinet colleagues, in building the financial and political basis of his Liberalism with such measures as the commercial treaty with France, the repeal of the paper duty, and the establishment of the Post Office Savings Bank. At the same time his views on foreign affairs, much the opposite of Palmerston's, were developing the outline of his later conflicts with Disraeli. In the Palmerston years Gladstone came to see Europe as a family of nations, each with its own integrity and sovereignty. And he was morally opposed to any and all interventionist escapades and gratuitous military maneuvering on England's part.

The election of 1865, in which Gladstone was defeated at Oxford but returned for South Lancashire, best symbolizes his transition to Liberalism. By then it was clear to almost everyone, including the queen who was beginning to wish otherwise, that Gladstone was the heir to the Whig legacy and would be the central figure, and leader in the Commons, of any administration opposed by the Conservatives. He had already given intimation in 1864 that he understood that parliamentary politics in the future would depend on the party leaders' ability to shape public opinion on major issues, and that in keeping with this new basis, more reforms in governing institutions and establishments were inevitable. In any event Gladstone did not become prime minister and form his first ministry until December 1868, after Disraeli had thwarted the Liberal initiative and passed the more extensive 1867 Reform Bill, ensuring his own succession to Lord Derby as Conservative prime minister.

The defeat of Disraeli's short-lived administration came as a result of Gladstone's resolutions in the House of Commons on the disestablishment of the Irish Church, and, not surprisingly, Gladstone's sense of having a mission to pacify Ireland was the focus of his first ministry. The bill for the disestablishment of the Irish Church passed the House of Lords on July 1869, but the struggle with the peers over it reinforced his belief in the primacy of the will of the Commons on matters of popular or electoral mandate. Despite the ensuing Irish Land Act in 1870 which redefined tenants' rights and provided compensation for eviction, Ireland remained unpacified and turbulent, largely ungovernable within the conceptions of justice for the Irish then current in England. Gladstone's first ministry was, however, notably successful in introducing important domestic reforms in matters of education, labor relations, army administration, licensing of spirits, and election procedures.

When the Conservatives won the election of 1874, Gladstone found himself with no taste for leading a factious opposition, and so he resigned his position as leader of the Liberals in the House of Commons. He retired to his estate at Hawarden where he devoted considerable time to a vigorous pamphlet crusade over the Vatican decrees of 1870 proclaiming papal infallibility, and seemed, even to his friends, to have renounced any future in politics in favor of somewhat cranky theological disputation. It was the Bulgarian atrocities and Disraeli's Turkophile bias in the whole matter of the Eastern question (precipitated by the revolts against Turkish rule in the Balkan states and the subsequent interven-

Page from Gladstone's journal (reproduced from The Gladstone Diaries, *volume 1, edited by M. R. D. Foot, Oxford University Press, 1968). The first extant entry in the journal that Gladstone kept until his eighty-seventh birthday is dated July 1825 and, like the one above, was written while he was a student at Eton College. The journal is now at the Lambeth Palace Library.*

tion of the major European powers) that brought Gladstone out of his retirement in the summer of 1876. The situation had all the ingredients of Gladstone's most intense concerns. He wanted to avoid England's entanglement in another moral and financial morass like that of the Crimea; he wanted to come to the protection of Christian people being savagely suppressed by the immoral Turks; he wanted to restrain Disraeli's political adventuring in the name of power and patriotism; and he wanted to be at the forefront of a public debate that was rapidly dividing the whole country and which might ultimately lead to a constitutional crisis precipitated by the partisanship of the queen. In 1879 Gladstone decided to resume his leadership of the Liberal party and to campaign for the Midlothian seat, a Tory stronghold near Edinburgh. The tremendous impact of this campaign can be judged from his speeches, which are now available in a modern edition entitled *Midlothian Speeches, 1879*, prepared by M. R. D. Foot and published jointly by Leicester University Press and Humanities Press (1971). With the Liberal sweep in the election of 1880, he returned as prime minister to form his second ministry, composed, oddly, mostly of old-style Whigs.

The important domestic issues of the next few years had to do with the growing desperation of the Irish situation; the violence resulting from tenants' evictions, the growing power of Irish nationalist leader Charles Stewart Parnell, and the rise of parliamentary obstructionism. The Liberals' attempts to ameliorate coercion with significant land reform was, in effect, too little too late to alter the essentially revolutionary nature of the campaign for Irish home rule. Similarly, in foreign affairs Gladstone's fragile cabinet found the effects of their policies limited and distorted by the actions of others beyond their control. Gladstone's hopes for reason and restraint were partially, if temporarily, fulfilled in the settlement of the Transvaal conflict, granting domestic autonomy to the Boer state, but the occupation of Egypt and the disaster of Gen. Charles Gordon's fatal expedition to the Sudan with the consequent annihilation of the garrison at Khartoum in early 1885 showed how little they could accomplish and how unpopular they could be with the voters. From the perspective of later years, Gladstone's greatest success in his second ministry was the franchise act of 1884, which, together with a redistribution scheme, extended the electorate from three to five million by enfranchising ag-

ricultural workers in the counties and thus ending Whig and Tory control of rural seats. The franchise act was a major step toward electoral equality and universal suffrage. Very significantly, too, it extended the franchise to Ireland as well, thereby making inevitable a crisis over home rule.

Gladstone's private conversion to home rule took place in the summer of 1885—when the Conservatives were in power—but for some months he kept it a secret. When the disclosure finally came in December, it led him to a newly elected majority with Parnell and the Irish members as allies. But his discretion in attempting to support the previous Conservative initiative looked like deceit to many of his uninformed colleagues. Thus, Gladstone's third ministry began with both the Whigs and Radicals thoroughly estranged, and the defeat of his home rule bill was ensured, ninety-three Liberals voting in the majority when it came to a vote on 8 June 1886. In the ensuing election Lord Salisbury and the Conservatives, supported by seventy-eight dissenting Liberals and Unionists, returned to office with no immediate prospect of being able to solve the Irish dilemma.

When Gladstone resumed the prime minister's office in August 1892, four months before his eighty-third birthday, he did so largely from a sense that it was his duty to try once more to settle Ireland. Two years earlier he had been quite hopeful that, if there were again a Liberal majority, Parnell could soon lead the Irish to accept a home rule bill granting domestic autonomy but reserving Irish representation and the supremacy of Westminster for imperial matters. Such a plan was, however, disrupted by the scandal of the O'Shea divorce in which Parnell was named correspondent, despite the fact that Kitty O'Shea's husband had tacitly condoned their relationship. Parnell's subsequent collapse from the stress of public persecution left Gladstone's hope forlorn and both the Liberal and Irish parties badly split. Nevertheless, Gladstone prepared a second home rule bill granting autonomy in all matters except defense, customs, trade, and foreign relations. It was adopted by the Commons after eighty-five sittings in debate, Gladstone personally directing its passage against strong opposition. As expected, the House of Lords then vetoed the measure by an overwhelming majority, thus killing it for the time being. Without support in cabinet for a fight with the Lords on the issue of constitutional powers, and also in a minority over defense estimates, Gladstone decided to resign for the last

*Gladstone with his wife, Catherine Glynne Gladstone, circa
1870 (Picture Post Library)*

time, which he did on 3 March 1894, sixty-one
years after first being elected to the House of Commons. The politics he left behind was essentially
that of a modern democratic society very different from the world of privileged power that he
had entered as a young man. And that difference was to a considerable extent of his own
making.

To see the outline of his parliamentary career is not, however, to appreciate fully the impact Gladstone had on the culture at large. He
was among the most indefatigable of writers, and
his prose was a persuasive force, not just in political debates, but also in the shaping of public opinion on topics such as contemporary literature, classical studies, history, and religion. Although he
produced some book-length studies and anthologies, the vast majority of Gladstone's writings
first appeared as pamphlets or essays in the periodical press. Of works in this last category alone
he wrote over 150 pieces, often lengthy, the majority of which appeared in the most prestigious
and influential quarterly or monthly reviews.

These essays, perhaps more than any other evidence available, reveal Gladstone's enormous intellectual capacity and tremendous range of interests. And they show most clearly in what ways
Gladstone was an extraordinary and singular figure within his culture and in what ways he was a
typical middle-class Victorian.

Gladstone's first book was *The State in Its Relations with the Church* (1838). Reflecting his high Anglican, Tory view of society as an organic whole,
it argues that the providential design of history
can best be made manifest in a religious establishment. The central analogue of the State, Gladstone argues, is the family, and accordingly the actions of the State, general or specific, are governed by the same moral law which determines
the responsibilities of individual members of a
family. It is Gladstone's view that, like the family,
the State is a divine ordinance and, as such, is morally bound to pursue the ends of the Church by establishing peace, order, and the temporal wellbeing of man. The further stage of the argument, that a distinct form of national religion
best serves the approximation of an ideal state,
Gladstone rests upon historical evidence and pragmatic considerations. Only through a unity of belief and consistency of practice, he argues, can
the government, in the persons of its ministers,
make moral choices that rest upon the truth or
the nearest approximation to it. In short, pluralism debilitates the moral character of the State.

Much of the discussion in *The State in Its Relations with the Church* is implicitly an exploration of
the limits and powers of conscience for individuals pursuing political careers. As such, the work
clearly embodies to some degree an abstract justification of Gladstone's decision to accept and pursue his ambitions through a career in politics
rather than in the Church. But the work is also interesting because it is reactionary insofar as the urgency and energy of its argument are derived
from the sense of a necessary institution being
abandoned or betrayed by a society intent on defining itself in material terms. Indeed, what *The
State in Its Relations with the Church* demonstrates
above all else is the profound conservatism of the
young Gladstone's views about society and the
strength of his concern for moral and ethical values in politics. As he himself soon saw, however,
the defense of the established Church in such
terms raised virtually insoluble problems about
the toleration or exclusion of minorities and the
validity of the Irish Church. Thus, it is ironic but
not surprising that these issues would be the

major ones in Gladstone's later conversion to Liberalism.

Church Principles Considered in their Results (1840) is, in effect, a companion work to *The State in Its Relations with the Church*, but one that recognizes that the claims for a religious establishment would be more safely based on historical and pragmatic grounds than upon first principles. The complex discussion of the Church of England's theological doctrines and the lengthy account of its historical positions through time were unsuited to a wide readership, and the book had little impact beyond ecclesiastical circles. Most of Gladstone's political friends thought that he was likely to ruin his career with the publication of such works.

Gladstone contributed two essays on Homer to the *Quarterly Review* in 1857. They are preliminary discussions of Homer's characterizations and his realism, topics treated more fully in Gladstone's book *Studies on Homer and the Homeric Age*, published the following year. In "Homer and His Successors in Epic Poetry" (*Quarterly Review*, January 1857), he offers a direct comparison with Virgil and Milton, much to Homer's glory in being more ethical than Virgil and more believable than Milton. "Homeric Characters in and out of Homer" (*Quarterly Review*, July 1857) is mostly concerned with the distortions of Homer's characters in the works of later authors. *Studies on Homer and the Homeric Age* (1858) is not a work of lasting influence. Its value lies rather in its embodiment of Gladstone's vision of the classical world, a vision again deeply colored with moral issues. Homer's supremacy among epic poets is for Gladstone a function of his fidelity and vividness in presenting a mirror of man in a pre-Christian world. But what most absorbs Gladstone in his assessment of Homeric characters, especially the gods, are the relations that exist between sexuality and religion, and to some extent what could be termed the politics of the *Iliad* and the *Odyssey*. He insists that Homer's delineations of character are a priceless inheritance of all civilized men, but he is careful to show "the real chastity of Homer's mind" by noticing how authorial reverence and sympathy are withheld from deities who represent "an animal instinct in its state of gross excess." Likewise, he explicitly denies that much "interest can attach to . . . the shameful parts of the Greek mythology," and claims rather that "the real point of interest is to learn whether there was a time when man, even though he had lost the clear view of the guiding hand from above,

yet revolted against, or had not become familiar with, the deification of vicious passion." In finding a note of such a time in Homer, Gladstone is necessarily much concerned in this book, as he would be in later ones, with the authenticity and chronology of the Homeric texts. In 1869 Gladstone's popular condensation of his Homeric studies was published as *Juventus Mundi: The Gods and Men of the Heroic Age*. His investigations of the historical context of Homer's epics continued in *Homeric Synchronism: An Enquiry into the Time and Place of Homer* (1876) and *Landmarks of Homeric Study* (1890), both of which show considerable familiarity with the scholarly literature. Gladstone also wrote the preface to the English edition of Heinrich Schliemann's *Mycenae: A Narrative of Researches and Discoveries at Mycenae and Tiryns* (1878).

Gladstone's most important statement about the significance of classical studies for him and for Victorian culture was, however, a lecture he delivered 3 November 1865 at the University of Edinburgh. The *Address on the Place of Ancient Greece in the Providential Order of the World* is really a defense of the classical curriculum (but especially the Homeric epics) used in middle- and upper-class public schools and the universities in the face of the evangelical Christian attack on it as an instrument of privilege, lacking in utility, propriety, and truth. Interestingly, Gladstone's lecture, published in 1865 as a pamphlet, anticipates many of the specific points of Matthew Arnold's *Culture and Anarchy* (1869), though the scope of the latter is much greater and the emphasis ultimately much different. There is the same objection to the narrowness and inadequacy of Puritan or nonconformist conceptions of virtue and to their exclusion of all but the Gospels as a guide to life. There is a similar contrast of the Mosaic and Hellenic cultures and the same interest in the perfection of man in both social and spiritual terms. Indeed, Gladstone's admiration for the Greeks' "remarkable fulness, largeness, subtlety, elevation, and precision in their conception of human nature," and for the unity of poetry and religion embodied in their mythology, leads him to much the same perspective on Greek culture that Arnold reaches when he describes the Greeks' attempt at human perfection as "premature," needing a fuller development of "the moral and religious fibre in humanity" in order to succeed. Gladstone in his terms argues that Hellenic mythology, with its idea of the "near association of human existence in soul and body with the Divine," was a secular, primitive "counterpart to the

Gospel" and, as such, a preparation for a later, Christian stage in the providential design of history leading to man's perfection. Although his argument is put into explicitly religious terms, even to the extent that Apollo is seen as serving the same functions as the Son of God, Gladstone is really arguing for the same balance or harmony of aesthetic and moral energies the lack of which Arnold laments. Confident in his faith and his conviction that his own race is "the crown and flower of the visible creation," Gladstone argues for the legitimate, free use of every human faculty, and he endorses the study of human history and experience ("the Divine Government over the whole world at every period of its existence" as the true *preparatio evangelica*, the best earthly preparation for the eternal life). From such an assertion it is clear that Gladstone's interest in classical studies was genuinely complementary to his political career. So, not surprisingly, whenever the exigencies of office subsided, he turned to writing further essays on Greek culture; the most notable appeared in the *Contemporary Review* in the 1870s and in the *Nineteenth Century* and the *North American Review* in the 1890s.

Like his writings on classical subjects, Gladstone's essays on domestic political concerns range over his whole career. And again they show the centrality of his ethical and moral commitments. For example, in "The Course of Commercial Policy at Home and Abroad" (*Foreign and Colonial Quarterly Review*, January 1843), which is essentially a defense of Peel's gradualist, free-trade policy, Gladstone avows that England's providentially assigned commercial primacy is the "proper consequence of her possessing, in a superior degree, the elements of industrial greatness; . . . not merely its physical elements, such as geographical position, mineral wealth, abundant capital, but its moral elements, resolution, energy, skill, perseverance, and good faith." The most significant essays on domestic issues, however, are the ones he wrote for the *Quarterly Review* in the late 1850s, for this was the critical period when Gladstone found that, with the Peelites dissolved, and despite tempting offers from Derby and Disraeli, there was no future for him in the Conservative party. The alternative, however, was to join Palmerston's Whiggish administrations, which, with his scruples, Gladstone found difficult. It is therefore natural that these articles reflect both Gladstone's political frustrations and his growing sense of vocation as the defender and propagator of Peelite financial orthodoxy.

The essays in the *Quarterly Review* were unsigned, which seems to have given Gladstone freedom from the probity that office or ambition usually imposed. Gladstone's published attacks on Palmerston and his administrations are frequently intemperate, and occasionally the indignant rhetoric approaches the flamboyance of Disraeli or the extravagance of Carlyle. The most intense concern is, as usual, reserved for religious issues with political dimensions. In "The Declining Efficiency of Parliament" (*Quarterly Review*, September 1856), for example, there is a lengthy attack on the papacy and its policy of "direction" in family matters. In part this assault is Gladstone's reaction to the conversions to Catholicism of John Henry Newman, Henry Manning, and other Tractarians within the Oxford Movement, and also to the Papal Aggression of 1851 establishing a Catholic hierarchy in England. But his real concern is the constitutional one, that such direction in political matters would compromise the integrity of Roman Catholics who might be asked to serve as cabinet ministers. Similarly, in "The New Parliament and Its Work" (*Quarterly Review*, April 1857) Gladstone expresses anger about Palmerston's ecclesiastical appointments, accusing him of using political influence rather than merit or the needs of the Church as the criterion in the recent choice of four prelates, some of whom, he says, do not even "come up to the standard of intellectual mediocrity."

Perhaps more typical of Gladstone's writing is the essay "The Bill for Divorce" (*Quarterly Review*, July 1857), which combines his abilities at theological disputation, meticulous scholarship, and political polemic. In this piece Gladstone employs "the adamantine laws of grammar" to show that the texts of the New Testament insist on the indissolubility of marriage except by death and that the biblical concepts of separation for cause do not permit remarriage. The essay also contains a happy comparison with the Homeric epics where, among the Greeks, he finds, there is "no trace of polygamy" and adultery is condemned. Finally Gladstone provides a detailed summary of divorce from the practice of the early Christian Church to the parliamentary bills of Victorian England. It is interesting to note that, as he was in the classical essays, Milton is, for Gladstone, a villain comparable to "the wildest libertine" or "the veriest Mormon." And the reader must be thankful that England "was found proof against the seduction of the pestilent ideas" in the poet's essay *Doctrine and Discipline of Divorce*. For all the emo-

"CRITICS."

(WHO HAVE *NOT EXACTLY* "FAILED IN LITERATURE AND ART.")—*See Mr. D.'s New Work.*

Mr. G-d-s-t-ne. "HM!—FLIPPANT!"   Mr. D-s-r-li. "HA!—PROSY!"

Gladstone and Benjamin Disraeli reviewing each other's books. Cartoon by Sir John Tenniel published in Punch, *14 May 1870.*

tional rhetoric, however, Gladstone clearly sees and understands the implications of the proposed change in legislation–the secularization of a religious sacrament, the ultimate extension of grounds for divorce to mere incompatibility, and the dissolution of the patriarchal family as a bulwark of social stability. And he also perceives the discrimination against women in the proposed bill.

But in charting Gladstone's responses to women's issues over the course of his career, the consistent conservatism of his thinking on social topics becomes clear. In his speech on the question of legalizing marriage with a deceased wife's sister, delivered in 1869 and published in pamphlet form the following year, he maintains that he wants "to do no more than obviate the ruinous consequences of the present state of the law." And in 1892, in *Female Suffrage. A Letter to Samuel Smith, M.P.*, he opposes the current bill chiefly because it would force upon large numbers of reluctant women "a fundamental change in their whole social function . . . [and] Providential calling." It would, he argues, launch them

into "the whirlpool of public life," giving them the right to sit in Parliament and, inevitably, to hold office. It is not the fear that women will encroach on the power of men that disturbs him. Nor does he fail to see the obvious inequalities of their status. Rather his motive is expressed as the typically Victorian desire to protect woman's "delicacy, . . . purity, . . . refinement, . . . and elevation of her own nature." What he wants to avoid is the threat to the "sacred . . . precinct of the family." Thus, while for twenty years Gladstone had acknowledged "a presumptive case for some change in the law," in 1892 it is his "disposition . . . to take no step in advance until . . . convinced of its safety."

Gladstone's readiness to engage in moral controversy can also be clearly seen in his writings on foreign affairs, a topic which, even more than that of financial policy, seemed to provide him with antithetical arguments. His occasional pamphlets and speeches often begin with sorrowful reluctance, but the style and tone of these pieces quickly reveal his enormous moral energy and the fulfillment he obviously experienced in being committed to a righteous cause. For example, when Gladstone returned from Italy in the spring of 1851, he had a private correspondence published as *A Letter to the Earl of Aberdeen, on the State Prosecutions of the Neapolitan Government.* In the letter he asked Aberdeen to use the influence of the British government to mitigate the horrors of the political repression he had witnessed in Naples. Lord Aberdeen was sympathetic, but this nevertheless seemed to be a paradoxical request for the very sort of intervention Gladstone had previously deplored. Describing the suppression of political dissidence in Naples as an "outrage upon religion, upon civilisation, upon humanity, and upon decency," Gladstone seemed unaware that the pace of diplomacy could not hope to match his sense of urgency. The intensity and complexity of his feelings are evident in the language he uses to describe the prosecutions as "an awful profanation of public religion, . . . a prostitution of judicial office" and the "negation of God erected into a system of Government." Much the same moral intensity shapes his other essays on foreign affairs, the best example of which is the *Bulgarian Horrors and the Question of the East*, published in pamphlet form in 1876. Forty thousand copies of this pamphlet were sold in three days, and such popularity suggests that in it Gladstone spoke for the strongest feelings of his readers. Most of the essay is a controlled condemnation of the government's slowness to respond officially to the Turkish atrocities in Bulgaria, and of Disraeli's reluctance, once the facts were known, to condemn the Turks in unequivocal moral terms. But the appalling revelations in the press, of Christian women and children being tortured, raped, and murdered, excited Victorian sensibilities to an unprecedented degree. And Gladstone's final rage expressed his own and his countrymen's frustrations and fears. He refers in one passage to "the elaborate and refined cruelty–the only refinement of which Turkey boasts!–the utter disregard of sex and age–the abominable and bestial lust–and the entire and violent lawlessness which still stalks over the land." Later he protests that Turkey must never be allowed to revive "these fell Satanic orgies" or be granted immunity for her "unbounded savagery, her unbridled and bestial lust."

In a very real sense the Turkish atrocities, which propelled him back into the leadership of the Liberal party, confirmed what Gladstone already thought. His hatred of the Turks on moral grounds was of long standing, going back at least to the years of the Crimean War. And while attacking Palmerston in the 1858 *Quarterly Review* piece "The Past and Present Administrations," he had tellingly mocked the idea that a "Turk in a frock coat and trowsers was in effect a Christian." Moreover, in his classical essays he several times insists that, from Homer's day to the present, the line between monogamy and polygamy, between marital purity and sexual license, could be drawn at "the Bosphorus and the Dardanelles," as he put it in his address published in 1892 under the title *Archaic Greece and the East*. In the 1870s the real issue for Gladstone was the moral imperative of avoiding another war like the Crimean, a conflict that he believed was without just cause. Such a war, he argues in "The Paths of Honour and of Shame" (*Nineteenth Century*, March 1878), would be "contemptible in the eyes of reason, . . . ruinous in policy, . . . a crime in the sight of a man, and a sin of deep dye in the sight of God."

Most of Gladstone's prose on the Irish question was written in the 1880s in the form of speeches in the House of Commons or pamphlets related to election campaigns. It is important, however, to see these pieces in the light of *A Chapter of Autobiography* (1868) in which Gladstone attempts to explain his change of heart about the disestablishment of the Irish Church. What needed to be explained then was how the Tory author of *The State in Its Relations with the*

Church came at the time of the Maynooth debate in 1845 to believe that a foolish defense of the Irish ecclesiastical establishment would do the Church more harm than good, but that an act of disestablishment must await its most propitious moment. In the 1880s in his writings on the Irish question Gladstone uses precisely the same argument to defend his conversion to home rule. The basis of his new policy is his recognition that the previous one of amelioration and coercion has not worked and that the British Parliament can no longer be expected to establish honorable and friendly relations with the Irish people, given their desire to legislate their own affairs. But the strongest principle of his new policy is, as he writes in *The Irish Question* (1886), that it must endorse only action which is "within the limits of safety and prudence" and which will "obviate all danger to the unity and security of the Empire." Gladstone's sense of mission is, thus, clearly conservatively Liberal. And sustained by a biblical epigram ("When the fruit is brought forth, immediately he putteth in the sickle, because the harvest is come"), he argues that the moment of ripeness for home rule has arrived. Consequently, he affirms in his *Home Rule Manifesto* (1886), the government must act promptly and expeditiously to take advantage of the moderation of thought and language that currently prevails in Irish counsels and thus ensure that the inevitable granting of autonomy also makes "every arrangement for preservation of the Imperial prerogative . . . complete and absolute." In his pamphlets on the Irish question Gladstone employs his best rhetorical self, arguing in considered and rational tones, not only for his own consistency and uniformity of principle, but also for justice considered, as he put in his manifesto, in a "wise and conciliatory spirit."

Gladstone's essays and pamphlets on religious matters display how deeply his Christian faith permeated every aspect of his life. They show as well that, like most Victorians, he paradoxically felt both optimistic about the efficacy of the faith for individuals and pessimistic about the power of sinister forces at play in society. In 1868 his extended commentary on J. R. Seeley's anonymously published *Ecce Homo: A Survey of the Life and Work of Jesus Christ* (1865) appeared, first in three installments in *Good Words* and then in book form. Because of its language and affinity to secular biography, Seeley's volume was creating much offense in pious circles. Gladstone, however, defends the book's style and method, arguing that in preparing for the revelation of

Christ's divinity in purely human terms they are similar to the style and method of the Gospels themselves. He uses the opportunity provided by the controversy over *Ecce Homo* to make his favorite comparison of the ancient Greek and Christian religions, claiming here, as he does in several essays on Homer, that the anthropomorphism of Greek mythology, or humanizing of its gods, is "the very idea which the Gospel was to revive." The Christian religion, he writes, is a "restoration," a recovery of order from the anarchy and corruption which had befallen the old mythology by the time of Tiberius Caesar. Gladstone's chief point is, however, the Liberal one, that *Ecce Homo* is a timely book for Victorians in their crisis of faith, because it displays a "vitality, an earnestness, an eloquence, a power, all . . . derived from the deep and overflowing life of the wondrous Figure which it contemplates and sets forth."

The other side of Gladstone's religious feelings and ideas is shown in *The Vatican Decrees in Their Bearing on Civil Allegiance: A Political Expostulation* (1874). The Vatican Council of 1869-1870, with its doctrines of papal infallibility and papal authority, came as a confirmation to Gladstone of all that he, and many other Victorians, had long suspected about the temporal ambitions of the Vatican. In the 1850s his attacks, in several *Quarterly Review* articles, on the policy of priestly "direction" reflected a concern that it might compromise the loyalty of Catholic British citizens. In 1874, free at last of the constraints of public office which had prevented him from speaking earlier, Gladstone gives full vent to fears about the constitutional effects of the Vatican decrees. He sees them as nothing less than "the moral murder . . . of stifling conscience and conviction," and he claims that they represent a betrayal of the assurances given to the British government by Catholic bishops at the time of the emancipation movement in the 1820s. Those assurances, in Gladstone's words, had been that "the fangs of Mediaeval Popedom had been drawn, and its claws torn away." Now, in his conspiratorial theory of ultramontane politics, Gladstone fears that the papacy, moved by veiled prophets of "wild ambition . . . behind the throne" who wish to enslave the State, will seize whatever opportunities present themselves for manipulating English politics. But in charging that the Latin Church "has refurbished and paraded anew, every rusty tool which she was fondly thought to have disused," Gladstone sees himself as defending the civil rights of his Roman Catholic "fellow-country-men," just as he has "labored to maintain and extend" those rights for the past "thirty years." In effect, he sees the Vatican decrees as the darkest possible perversion of the ideal relation between State and Church which would secure their common welfare by reasoned assent, not simple obedience. His "expostulation" drew quick, but polite, responses in the London *Times* from Archbishop Manning and Lord Acton, who pointed out that the loyalty of English Catholics was limited only by "conscience and the law of God," qualifications that extended to every Christian.

"The Courses of Religious Thought" (*Contemporary Review*, June 1876) is a more balanced and thoughtful expression of Gladstone's religious views. Maintaining that Christianity is "the great, the imperial thought, tradition, and society of this earth," he surveys both its various forms and the current theistic and skeptical philosophies. He repeats, but in measured language, the essence of the earlier charges against the papal monarchy, but he is satisfied to itemize eight weaknesses of the system: its hostility to mental freedom, its incompatibility with the thought and movement of modern civilization, its pretensions against the State, its infringement of parental and conjugal rights, its jealousy of the free use of Holy Scripture, its alienation of the educated mind, its detrimental effect on the morality of the states where it prevails, and its tendency to sap veracity in the individual mind. In contrast, although he acknowledges its unfortunate isolation, Gladstone endorses the "Historical School" of Christianity, which finds its current visible form in High Church Anglicanism embodying respect for "history and mental freedom" and moderate views of ecclesiastical power. He is also sympathetic to Protestant Evangelicalism because it adheres to "nearly all the great affirmations of the Creeds" and "harmonizes with the movement of modern civilization . . . in uniting the human soul to Christ." The problem with this form of the Christian religion, he believes, lies in its naiveté and weakness of thought, and its consequent vulnerability to modern biblical criticism.

In the second section of the essay, Gladstone also accepts the sincerity and moral probity of those who cannot subscribe to Christian doctrine or practice but who follow a theistic or skeptical moral system of belief or thought. His reservation about such a course, however, is that it is only suitable to the lives of an intellectual elite and would likely have disastrous consequences if extended to the populace at large. In conclusion, he does not attempt a detailed account of such courses as Atheism, Materialism, Agnosticism, or Positivism because he feels that such a discussion would inevitably involve consideration of "the causes which have recently brought about, and which are still stimulating, a great movement of disintegration in the religious domain." This pessimistic note is apparently reinforced by his final sentence in which he acknowledges that "this multitudinous array of dislocated and . . . conflicting force . . . may wear in some eyes the appearance of an attempt to describe the field, and the eve, of the Battle of Armageddon."

It is important to recognize the conditional qualification in such a statement, for the strength of Gladstone's faith, however embattled, is more accurately reflected in the title of the 1890 collection of essays from *Good Words*, *The Impregnable Rock of Holy Scripture*. These pieces are an attempt to reconcile, for the ordinary Christian, the findings of modern geology, astronomy, and biblical scholarship with the material of the Pentateuch. Through the same steps of close textual analysis and inferential logic that characterize most of his historical, Homeric, and theological studies, Gladstone here proves for his reader that modern science corroborates the belief in the superhuman agency of the Creation and the histori-

cal validity of the Mosaic legislation. This "testimony of an old man" seems consciously framed to contradict the "champions of negation," exemplified by T. H. Huxley who, whatever his secular qualifications, is easily shown to be a "superficial reader" of the Gospels. What the scholarship of these essays demonstrates most clearly is that Gladstone's faith was sustained by the full engagement of his formidable intellect. Nevertheless, one suspects that, as for most Victorians, his real antagonist of faith was not evolutionary science, but complacent materialism.

Throughout the years of his busy public career Gladstone undertook numerous reviews of books of historical or literary importance. These reviews appeared in over a dozen different periodicals, ranging from the most prestigious to the obscure, and from the most conservative to the radical. Like his other writings they testify to the enormous scope of his curiosity, although, as Gladstone's diaries show, they represent a very small fraction of his avocational reading. Some of the essentially biographical pieces are among the most pleasant of Gladstone's essays for the modern reader, perhaps because disengagement from the subject in time frees him from the earnestness of urgent commitment. There is, for example, a warm and generous reassessment of Irish statesman Daniel O'Connell in the *Nineteenth Century*

One of the People–Gladstone in an Omnibus, *1885 painting by John Morgan (by permission of Lizbeth Schiff)*

(January 1889) and a fair, but perhaps for the queen too judicious, reflection on the life of the prince consort which appeared in the *Contemporary Review* (June 1875 with the signature "Etonensis"). But if Gladstone had some doubts about Prince Albert's religious sympathies and also about whether any man's reputation could sustain the claims of superiority inherent in the Hyde Park memorial to Albert, he had a genuine admiration for the prince's moral restraint and self-sacrificing nature and for his "lavish expenditure of brain power" for the common good. Interestingly it is the same "expenditure of brain power" and "sustained exertion" for which Gladstone praises Macaulay in his review of George Otto Trevelyan's *Life and Letters of Lord Macaulay* in the *Quarterly Review* (July 1876). Significantly, too, in the case of all three men, O'Connell, the prince, and Macaulay, he praises in similar terms the warmth and depth of their domestic affections, suggesting that such feelings were essential to their efficacy in public life. Such a view is not just a Victorian cliché, but an expression of deep

conviction and experience drawn from his own life. In that regard, it is perhaps worth noting that Gladstone's real bitterness with Disraeli came after Mrs. Disraeli's death, and that while she lived, Gladstone would often drop by Grosvenor Gate on the way home, after acrimonious debate in the Commons, to show that the hostility was not personal.

A brief perusal of any volume of *The Gladstone Diaries* (eight volumes have been published since 1968) will prove that Gladstone's appetite for books was voracious. Apart from his consuming interest in works of political, religious, or classical reference, he was also fond of contemporary poetry and fiction, and he read both regularly. His favorite novelist was Scott; his most esteemed modern poet was Tennyson. Gladstone's few reviews of novels are not sophisticated in critical terms, but they are not necessarily wrong in their judgments. They tend to focus on the plausibility of character or action judged by didactic criteria imposed by his own views on social morality or religious faith. Most typical is the lengthy discussion

Gladstone in old age (Radio Times Hulton Picture Library)

of Mrs. Humphry Ward's *Robert Elsmere* in the *Nineteenth Century* (May 1888), which finds Gladstone at odds with the author's aim of rescuing the ethical practice of Christianity from the grip of its preternatural and dogmatic elements. He is quite correct in seeing the structure, characterizations, and plot of the novel as flawed by their dependence on oversimplified ideational conflict between reason and emotion. But ultimately the essay is more a defense of his own views than an analysis of why the book had the impact it did on many less intellectual readers.

Not at all surprisingly, given his education and later classical studies, Gladstone was more attuned to the aesthetics of poetry than to those of fiction. His essay on Tennyson's poetry in the *Quarterly Review* (October 1859) expresses his sensitivity to the poet's mastery of language, meter, and metaphor, and eloquently praises the poet's dramatic powers. But this appreciation of technique is still only complementary to Gladstone's satisfaction with Tennyson's themes. Accordingly, he recommends the *Poems* (1842) because they reveal a grasp of "the classical idea," because they are "specimens of deep metaphysical insight," or because they are full of "ethical and social wisdom." Similarly, he is enthusiastic about *The Princess* (1847) because of "the force, purity, and nobleness of the main streams of thought, which are clothed in language full of all Mr. Tennyson's excellences." And much the same response is given to *In Memoriam* (1850), a poem which evokes Gladstone's strong personal sympathies because Arthur Henry Hallam, to whom the work is dedicated, was Gladstone's best friend at Eton, just as he was Tennyson's at Cambridge.

But when Tennyson explores conceptions of character or ideas alien to Gladstone's own, as he does in *Maud* (1855), Gladstone finds only "obscurity," "sound and fury," overpassing "all the bounds of moderation and good sense," and ultimately "the grosser folly" of seeming to advocate war. With the *Idylls of the King* (1859), however, Gladstone again feels "those profound moral harmonies" which enliven his aesthetic response, so that he sees not only the individual beauties of each line, but also the unity and epic grandeur of the whole.

Gladstone's response to the *Idylls of the King* is, in fact, a miniature tapestry of his whole life and character. There is every reason why the student of Homer would appreciate the elements of passion, power, and faith in the Arthurian legend. But Gladstone's response to Tennyson's re-

working of it reveals in a limited context what the classical, political, religious, and historical essays and the books reveal in a larger one: that the fabric of Gladstone's brilliant political career was continously woven from the threads of religious faith, sexual morality, and commitment to social stability. And even such a brief survey of his writings demonstrates that none of them is a mere curiosity or anomaly, and that they all illuminate one another and the full life of one of the nineteenth century's most remarkable politicians.

The Grand Old Man of Liberal politics (as Gladstone had become affectionately known to his admirers) spent the years of his retirement for the most part at Hawarden, where he continued his avocational interests in theology, classical studies, history, and literature. He was, however, in increasingly frail health, suffering from deteriorating eyesight and severe neuralgia. To ameliorate the effects of the latter he and his wife spent much of the winter months of his last three years in the south of France. Gladstone died peacefully at Hawarden amid the family on 19 May 1898. But his death was mourned by millions of citizens for whom his life had become a symbol of political courage and private integrity. He had declined the queen's traditional offer of a peerage at the time of his last resignation as prime minister, but upon his death he was accorded the honor of a state funeral and burial in Westminster Abbey.

Letters:

Correspondence on Church and Religion by William Ewart Gladstone, edited by D. C. Lathbury, 2 volumes (London: Murray, 1910; New York: Macmillan, 1910);

Gladstone and Palmerston: Being the Correspondence of Lord Palmerston with Mr. Gladstone, 1851-1865, edited by Philip Guedalla (London: Gollancz, 1928);

The Queen and Mr. Gladstone: A Selection from Their Correspondence, edited by Guedalla, 2 volumes (London: Hodder & Stoughton, 1933; Garden City: Doubleday, Doran, 1934);

Gladstone to his Wife, edited by A. Tilney Bassett (London: Methuen, 1936);

The Political Correspondence of Mr. Gladstone and Lord Granville, 1868-1876, edited by Agatha Ramm, 2 volumes (London: Historical Society of Great Britain, 1952);

The Gladstone-Gordon Correspondence, 1851-1896; Selections from the private correspondence of a British Prime Minister and a colonial governor, edited by Paul Knaplund (Philadelphia: American Philosophical Society, 1961);

The Political Correspondence of Mr. Gladstone and Lord Granville, 1876-1886, edited by Ramm, 2 volumes (Oxford: Clarendon Press, 1962).

Bibliographies:

The Wellesley Index to Victorian Periodicals, edited by Walter Houghton, 3 volumes (Toronto: University of Toronto Press, 1966-1979; London: Routledge & Kegan Paul, 1966-1979);

A Bibliography of Gladstone Publications at St. Deiniol's Library, compiled by Patricia Long (Hawarden: St. Deiniol's Library, 1977);

A Bibliography of Material Relating to W. E. Gladstone at St. Deiniol's Library, compiled by Caroline J. Dobson (Hawarden: St. Deiniol's Library, 1981).

Biographies:

John Morley, *The Life of William Ewart Gladstone*, 3 volumes (London: Macmillan, 1903; New York: Macmillan, 1903);

Philip Magnus, *Gladstone: A Biography* (London: Murray, 1954);

Sydney Checkland, *The Gladstone's: A Family Biography, 1764-1851* (Cambridge: Cambridge University Press, 1971);

E. J. Feuchtwanger, *Gladstone* (London: Lane, 1975);

Richard Shannon, *Gladstone*, vol. 1, 1809-1865 (London: Hamilton, 1982);

H. C. G. Matthew, *Gladstone, 1809-1874* (New York: Oxford University Press, 1987).

References:

Michael K. Barker, *Gladstone and Radicalism: The Reconstruction of Liberal Policy in Britain, 1885-1894* (Hassocks: Harvester, 1975);

Perry Butler, *Gladstone: Church, State, and Tractarianism; A Study of His Religious Ideas and Attitudes, 1809-1859* (Oxford: Clarendon Press, 1982);

Owen Chadwick, "Young Gladstone and Italy," *Journal of Ecclesiastical History*, 30 (April 1979): 243-259;

C. Eldridge, *England's Mission: The Imperial Idea in the Age of Gladstone and Disraeli, 1868-1880* (Chapel Hill: University of North Carolina Press, 1973);

D. A. Hamer, "Gladstone: The Making of a Political Myth," *Victorian Studies*, 22 (Autumn 1978): 29-50;

J. L. Hammond, *Gladstone and the Irish Nation* (London: Longmans, 1938; New York: Longmans, 1938);

Hammond and M. R. D. Foot, *Gladstone and Liberalism* (London: English Universities Press, 1952);

Peter J. Jagger, ed., *Gladstone, Politics and Religion: A Collection of Founder's Day Lectures Delivered at St. Deiniol's Library, Hawarden, 1967-1983* (London: Macmillan, 1985);

Bruce Kinzer, ed., *The Gladstonian Turn of Mind: Essays Presented to J. B. Conacher* (Toronto, Buffalo & London: University of Toronto Press, 1985);

Paul Knaplund, *Gladstone and Britain's Imperial Policy* (London: Allen & Unwin, 1927);

Hugh Lloyd-Jones, "Gladstone on Homer," *Times Literary Supplement*, 3 January 1975, pp. 15-17;

Peter Marsh, "The Primate and the Prime Minister: Archbishop Tait, Gladstone, and the National Church," *Victorian Studies*, 9 (December 1965): 113-140;

H. C. G. Matthew, "Disraeli, Gladstone, and the Politics of Mid-Victorian Budgets," *Historical Journal*, 22 (September 1979): 615-643;

Matthew, "Gladstone, Vaticanism, and the Question of the East," in *Religious Motivation: Biographical and Sociological Problems for the Church Historian*, edited by D. Baker (Oxford: Blackwell, 1978), pp. 417-442;

Agatha Ramm, "Gladstone's Religion," *Historical Journal*, 28 (June 1985): 327-340;

Deryck Schreuder, "Gladstone and the Conscience of the State," in *The Conscience of the Victorian State*, edited by Peter Marsh (Hassocks, U.K.: Harvester, 1979), pp. 73-134;

Richard Shannon, *Gladstone and the Bulgarian Agitation, 1876* (London: Nelson, 1963);

A. R. Vidler, *The Orb and the Cross: A Normative Study in the Relation of Church and State with References to Gladstone's Early Writings* (London: Society for Promoting Christian Knowledge, 1945);

G. M. Young, *Mr. Gladstone* (Oxford: Clarendon Press, 1944).

Papers:

There are collections of Gladstone's papers at the British Library, London, and at St. Deiniol's Library, Hawarden.

Edmund Gosse

(21 September 1849-16 May 1928)

Philip Dodd
University of Leicester

BOOKS: *Madrigals, Songs and Sonnets,* by Gosse and J. A. Blaikie (London: Longmans, Green, 1870);

On Viol and Flute (London: King, 1873; New York: Holt, 1883; enlarged, London: Kegan Paul, Trench, Trübner, 1890);

The Ethical Condition of the Early Scandinavian Peoples (London: Hardwicke, 1875);

King Erik (London: Chatto & Windus, 1875);

The Unknown Lover: A Drama for Private Acting, With An Essay on the Chamber Drama in England (London: Chatto & Windus, 1878);

Studies in the Literature of Northern Europe (London: Kegan Paul, 1879); revised and enlarged as *Northern Studies* (London: Scott, 1890);

New Poems (London: Kegan Paul, 1879);

Memoir of Samuel Rowlands (N.p.: Privately printed, 1879);

Résumé of a Pamphlet on the Industry and Trade of Germany during the first year of the new Protective Policy (London: H.M.S.O., 1881);

Memoir of Thomas Lodge (N.p.: Privately printed, 1882);

Gray (London: Macmillan, 1882; New York: Harper, 1882);

Seventeenth-Century Studies: A Contribution to the History of English Poetry (London: Kegan Paul, Trench, 1883; New York: Dodd, Mead, 1897);

Cecil Lawson: A Memoir (London: Fine Art Society, 1883);

A Critical Essay on the Life and Works of George Tinworth (London: Fine Art Society, 1883);

An Epistle to Dr. Oliver Wendell Holmes on his Seventy-fifth Birthday, August 29, 1884 (London: Privately printed, 1884);

Six Lectures Written to be Delivered before the Lowell Institute in December, 1884 (London: Privately printed, 1884);

The Masque of Painters; as Performed by the Royal Institute of Painters in Water Colours, May 19, 1885 (London: Privately printed, 1885);

From Shakespeare to Pope: An Inquiry into the Causes and Phenomena of the Rise of Classical Poetry in

courtesy of Jennifer Gosse

Edmund Gosse

England (Cambridge: University Press, 1885; New York: Dodd, Mead, 1885);

Firdausi in Exile and Other Poems (London: Kegan Paul, Trench, 1885);

Raleigh (London: Longmans, Green, 1886; New York: Appleton, 1886);

A Letter to the Editor of the "Athenaeum" (London: Privately printed, 1886);

Life of William Congreve (London: Scott/New York: Whittaker, 1888; revised and enlarged, London: Heinemann, 1924; New York: Scribners, 1924);

A History of Eighteenth-Century Literature (1660-1780) (London & New York: Macmillan, 1889);

Robert Browning: Personalia (London: Unwin, 1890; Boston & New York: Houghton Mifflin, 1890);

The Life of Philip Henry Gosse, F.R.S. (London: Kegan Paul, Trench, Trübner, 1890); republished as *The Naturalist of the Sea-shore* (London: Heinemann, 1896);

Gossip in a Library (London: Heinemann, 1891; New York: Lovell, 1891);

Poetry (Philadelphia: Lippincott, 1891);

Shelley in 1892: Centenary Address at Horsham, August 11, 1892 (London: Privately printed, 1892);

The Secret of Narcisse: A Romance (London: Heinemann, 1892; New York: Tait, 1892);

Wolcott Balestier: A Portrait Sketch (Westminster: Privately printed, 1892);

Questions at Issue (London: Heinemann, 1893; New York: Appleton, 1893);

The Rose of Omar. Inscription for the Rose-Tree Brought by Mr W. Simpson from Omar's Tomb at Naishapur, and Planted To-day on the Grave of Edward Fitzgerald, at Boulge, 1893 (N.p.: Privately printed, 1893);

In Russet & Silver (London: Heinemann, 1894; Chicago: Stone & Kimball, 1894);

The Jacobean Poets (London: Murray, 1894; New York: Scribners, 1894);

Critical Kit-Kats (London: Heinemann, 1896; New York: Dodd, Mead, 1896);

A Short History of Modern English Literature (London: Heinemann, 1897; New York: Appleton, 1897; revised and enlarged, London: Heinemann, 1924);

Henry Fielding: An Essay (Westminster: Constable/ New York: Scribners, 1898);

The Life and Letters of John Donne, Dean of St Paul's, 2 volumes (New York: Dodd, Mead/London: Heinemann, 1899);

The Character of Queen Victoria (New York: Scott, 1901);

English Literature: Edmund Spenser (Philadelphia: Lippincott, 1901);

English Literature. Elizabethan and Jacobean (Philadelphia: Lippincott, 1901);

Hypolympia; or, The Gods in the Island: An Ironic Fantasy (London: Heinemann, 1901; New York: Dodd, Mead/London: Heinemann, 1901);

The Challenge of the Brontës (London: Privately printed, 1903);

English Literature: An Illustrated Record, 4 volumes: volume 2 by Gosse and Richard Garnett, volumes 3 and 4 by Gosse (London: Heinemann, 1903; New York: Macmillan, 1903);

Jeremy Taylor (London: Macmillan, 1904; New York: Macmillan/London: Macmillan, 1904);

French Profiles (London: Heinemann, 1905; New York: Dodd, Mead, 1905);

Coventry Patmore (London: Hodder & Stoughton, 1905; New York: Scribners, 1905);

Sir Thomas Browne (New York & London: Macmillan, 1905);

Ibsen (London: Hodder & Stoughton, 1907); republished as *Henrik Ibsen* (New York: Scribners, 1908);

Father and Son: A Study of Two Temperaments, anonymous (London: Heinemann, 1907); republished as *Father and Son: Biographical Recollections* (New York: Scribners, 1907);

Introduction to A History of the Library of the House of Lords (London: Privately printed, 1908);

Biographical Notes on the Writings of Robert Louis Stevenson (London: Privately printed, 1908);

The Autumn Garden (London: Heinemann, 1909);

Swinburne: Personal Recollections (London: Privately printed, 1909);

The Collected Poems of Edmund Gosse (London: Heinemann, 1911);

Two Visits to Denmark, 1872, 1874 (London: Smith, Elder, 1911; New York: Dutton, 1912);

The Life of Swinburne, with a Letter on Swinburne at Eton by Lord Redesdale (London: Privately printed, 1912);

Portraits and Sketches (London: Heinemann, 1912; New York: Scribners, 1912);

Lady Dorothy Nevill: An Open Letter (London: Privately printed, 1913);

The Future of English Poetry (Oxford: Printed for the University by H. Hart, 1913);

Two Pioneers of Romanticism: Joseph and Thomas Warton (London: Published by Oxford University Press for the British Academy, 1915);

Inter Arma: Being Essays Written in Time of War (London: Heinemann, 1916; New York: Scribners, 1916);

Reims Revisited (N.p.: Privately printed, 1916);

Lord Cromer as a Man of Letters (London: Privately printed, 1917);

The Life of Algernon Charles Swinburne (London: Macmillan, 1917; New York: Macmillan, 1917);

The Novels of Benjamin Disraeli (London: Privately printed, 1918);

France et Angleterre: L'Avenir de leurs relations

intellectuelles (London: Hayman, Christy & Lilly, 1918);

Three French Moralists, and the Gallantry of France (London: Heinemann, 1918; New York: Scribners, 1918);

Some Literary Aspects of France in the War (London: Privately printed, 1919);

The First Draft of Swinburne's "Anactoria" (London: Privately printed, 1919);

Some Diversions of a Man of Letters (London: Heinemann, 1919; New York: Scribners, 1919);

A Catalogue of the Works of Algernon Charles Swinburne in the Library of Mr Edmund Gosse (London: Privately printed, 1919);

Malherbe and the Classical Reaction in the Seventeenth Century (Oxford: Clarendon Press, 1920);

Books on the Table (London: Heinemann, 1921; New York: Scribners, 1921);

Aspects and Impressions (London: Heinemann, 1922; New York: Scribners, 1922);

The Continuity of Literature (Oxford: Oxford University Press, 1922);

More Books on the Table (London: Heinemann, 1923; New York: Scribners, 1923);

Silhouettes (London: Heinemann, 1925; New York: Scribners, 1925);

Tallemant des Réaux; or, The Art of Miniature Biography: The Zaharoff lecturer (Oxford: Clarendon Press, 1925);

Swinburne: An Essay First Written in 1875 and Now First Printed (Edinburgh: Privately printed, 1925);

Poems (London: Benn, 1926);

Leaves and Fruit (London: Heinemann, 1927; New York: Scribners, 1927);

Selected Essays, 2 volumes (London: Heinemann, 1928);

An Address to the Fountain Club, 1923 (Steyning: Privately printed, 1931);

America: The Diary of a Visit, Winter 1884-1885, edited by Robert L. Peters and David G. Halliburton (Lafayette: English Literature in Transition, Purdue University, 1966);

A Norwegian Ghost Story, edited by W. M. Parker (St. Peter Port, Guernsey: Toucan Press, 1967);

Thomas Hardy, O.M., edited by Ronald Knight (Bulphan, Upminster: Knight & Knight, 1968);

Sir Henry Doulton: The Man of Business as a Man of Imagination, edited by Desmond Eyles (London: Hutchinson, 1970);

The Unequal Yoke (1886): A Novel (Delmar, N.Y.: Scholars' Facsimiles and Reprints, 1975).

Edmund Gosse's present reputation, at least outside the scholarly community, rests on his autobiography, *Father and Son* (1907). This was not always so. In 1931, three years after Gosse's death, T. S. Eliot reviewed Evan Charteris's *The Life and Letters of Sir Edmund Gosse* in the *Criterion*, claiming that "The place that Sir Edmund Gosse filled in the literary and social life of London is one that no one can ever fill again, because it is, so to speak, an office that has been abolished." Despite his tone, T. S. Eliot was paying tribute to Gosse's pivotal position in so many areas of English literary life during the preceding forty years. The range of Gosse's writings is impressive. An inventory of his principal nonfiction writings would include a substantial body of literary criticism and history and a number of important biographies as well as a major autobiography. He also produced volumes of poetry, novels, a drama, editions of the works of poets, and many translations, including renderings of Ibsen, whose name Gosse first introduced to the British reading public.

If T. S. Eliot was correct in his judgment that Gosse, the critic, was the last "man-of-letters," it may be as reasonable to claim that Gosse stands at the head of another tradition: that of modern biography. In fact, Gosse's admiration for Lytton Strachey may be a sign that he saw in the younger man's biographical practice confirmation of his own. Gosse was not only the biographer of others but also, in *Father and Son*, the autobiographer of his early life. Given this fact, it seems appropriate to rehearse in some detail those early years. Edmund William Gosse was born in September 1849 to Philip Henry Gosse, a self-taught naturalist and author of numerous books, and Emily Bowes Gosse, the author of *Abraham and His Children* (1855), a book on education, and numerous best-selling religious tracts. Gosse's parents were introduced to each other at a meeting in Hackney, London, of the Plymouth Brethren, a radical nonconformist sect, to which both belonged and whose organizing principles shaped Edmund Gosse's childhood and adolescence. *Father and Son* describes Gosse's early years, including the death of his mother when he was seven years old. Ann Thwaite's recent biography, *Edmund Gosse: A Literary Landscape, 1849-1928* (1984), makes it clear that Gosse, in *Father and Son*, exaggerates his isolation from other children during those years, his confinement in a London home, and the extent of his companionship of his mother during her treatment for cancer. For instance, he did have friends of his own age and did spend at least as much time by the sea as in London. Gosse's representation of his childhood owes as much to such fictional Victorian representations of children as Paul in Dickens's *Dombey and Son* (a title which that of Gosse's autobiography echoes) as it does to his own life.

Soon after his wife's death Philip Gosse turned his back on London and moved with his son in 1857 to a new house, Sandhurst, at St. Marychurch, near Torquay. The same year saw the publication of Philip Gosse's *Omphalos: An Attempt to Untie the Geological Knot,* a religious answer to evolutionism that suggested, among other things, that God had put fossils into the rocks in order to tempt geologists into infidelity. Philip Gosse's angry and pained response to the adverse reviews led him to a self-imposed isolation and to clinging even more firmly to his religion and to his only child. One wonders if Edmund Gosse's later renowned gregariousness was not a reaction against the principled loneliness of his father. After attending a number of schools, Edmund Gosse gained his first job at the age of seventeen, in part through the influence of his father's friend Charles Kingsley. He became junior assistant or transcriber at the British Museum on 22 January 1867. It is important to record that the severe nonconformist life Gosse led in his early years did not leave him the philistine Matthew Arnold claimed such nonconformity produced. He noted on his application to the British Museum, according to Ann Thwaite, that he spoke German, wrote French, and read Greek, Latin, and Italian, had a "rudimentary acquaintance with Danish and Hebrew" and "a somewhat extensive knowledge of English Literature, English History, Geography, Euclid and Arithmetic."

In his early years in London, Gosse was without apparent strain an example of that divided self which haunts late-nineteenth-century fiction from Gosse's friend Robert Louis Stevenson's *Strange Case of Dr. Jekyll and Mr. Hyde* (1886) to Oscar Wilde's *Picture of Dorian Gray* (1891). He was superintendent of a Sunday school and remained under the tutelage of his father for longer than *Father and Son* would have one believe, and yet during the same period was the intimate of the "pagan" A. C. Swinburne and numbered among his friends the Pre-Raphaelites. The incongruity of his life is caught in the fact that publication of his first volume of "Pre-

The young Gosse with his father, naturalist and author Philip Henry Gosse (courtesy of Jennifer Gosse). Their relationship was the basis of Gosse's best-known work, Father and Son, *published in 1907.*

Raphaelite" poetry, *Madrigals, Songs and Sonnets* (1870), a joint effort with John Blaikie, was paid for by Philip Gosse, who demanded and got certain changes of text.

Like so much Victorian nonfiction prose, from Thomas Carlyle to Walter Pater, Gosse's early essays were published in periodicals. His earliest sustained prose writings were devoted to Scandinavian subjects; in 1872, in such periodicals as the *Spectator* and the *Fortnightly Review,* he had four articles published on Henrik Ibsen, at that time an unknown and untranslated Norwegian poet and dramatist. Thirty-five years later, in *Father and Son,* Gosse would dramatize the extent of his father's religious demands on him with the phrase "Everything or Nothing," a quotation from Ibsen's *Brand.*

In 1875 Gosse married Ellen Epps, an intellectually ambitious woman who wanted to be a painter. The Gosses had one son and two daughters, the youngest of whom, Sylvia, became a well-known painter whose work is still found in public collections. In the year of his marriage, Gosse changed jobs, joining the Board of Trade as translator. Four years later he produced his first major prose work, *Studies in the Literature of Northern Europe* (1879), which included essays on the literature and life of Norway, Sweden, Denmark, Germany, and Holland. A revised and enlarged version was published as *Northern Studies* (1890). Gosse had visited Norway in 1871 and Denmark and Norway the following year, when he met such literary figures as Hans Christian Andersen, the poet Frederick Paludan Müller, and the novelist Björnstjerne Björnson. In general terms, Gosse's book contributed to the British concern with Scandinavian culture which stretches onward from Carlyle's *On Heroes, Hero-Worship & the Heroic in History* (1841) to William Morris's *Icelandic Journals* (unpublished until 1969) and still finds institutional expression in Anglo-Saxon studies within universities. What distinguishes Gosse's book is its address, at least in part, to contemporary Scandinavian works–not only Ibsen's but also, for example, Björnson's. Gosse later edited an English edition of the latter's novels. *Studies in the Literature of Northern Europe* was favorably received even if not all of the reviewers acknowledged Ibsen to be the important writer Gosse claimed. Certainly the most perspicacious judgment on the book came from Robert Louis Stevenson, who noted in a letter to Gosse that "Your personal notes of those you saw struck me as perhaps most sharp and 'best-held.' See as many people as you can and make a book of them before you die. That will be a living book, upon my word." Stevenson saw that Gosse's particular skill as a writer was primarily biographical. Titles Gosse gave to later volumes of criticism also suggest his stance as a portrait painter: *French Profiles* (1905) and *Portraits and Sketches* (1912).

Gosse's next major project was *Gray* (1882), a biography of the eighteenth-century poet Thomas Gray for the English Men of Letters series. Almost all of Gosse's biographies were either contributions to series or other commissioned works. For instance, his biography *Raleigh* (1886) was written for the English Worthies series and the *Life of William Congreve* (1888) for the Great Writers series. *Gray* moves through the poet's life, absorbing discussion of the poetry and referring it to the biography. An interesting survey of Gray's reputation in the eighteenth and nineteenth centuries completes the work. It would be rash indeed to recommend Gosse's biography to someone who wished to have an accurate account of Gray's life. Ann Thwaite in her bi-

ography of Gosse catalogues some of its errors. According to Thwaite, the scholar Leonard Whibley reportedly went so far as to claim that "every sentence in it was incorrect, inadequate, or misleading." The inaccuracies range from the wholly unwarranted assertion that Gray never took exercise to Gosse's statement that Rousseau had invited Gray to meet him. What Gosse's biography does best is describe the melancholia which afflicted the poet and identify its presence in the work. *Gray* was praised by literary figures as various as Leslie Stephen and Thomas Hardy.

As evidence of the range of Gosse's interests, one should note that the year after the appearance of *Gray* he produced *Seventeenth-Century Studies: A Contribution to the History of English Poetry* (1883), a volume of ten essays republished from *Cornhill Magazine*, on such authors as Richard Crashaw, Abraham Cowley, Robert Herrick, Thomas Lodge, Thomas Otway, and John Webster. During the years that these two books were published, in addition to fulfilling his duties with the Board of Trade, Gosse contributed pieces to various publications, including the *Encyclopaedia Britannica*, for which he wrote mostly on Scandinavian subjects, and the *Dictionary of National Biography*, which was edited by his friend Leslie Stephen.

Gray and *Seventeenth-Century Studies*, both of which enhanced Gosse's reputation, were published at a time when his literary friendships were growing in number and importance. In the early 1880s he formed friendships, always an important feature of his life, with such diverse figures as Thomas Hardy, William Dean Howells, and Coventry Patmore. Two endeavors in 1884 propelled Gosse further into the literary limelight. He undertook a lecture tour in the United States and was appointed Clark lecturer at Cambridge. The substance of his next major prose work, *From Shakespeare to Pope: An Inquiry into the Causes and Phenomena of the Rise of Classical Poetry in England* (1885), was the lectures he gave in Cambridge and in various places in the United States. Gosse's book aims to offer a number of critical essays which explain individual works in terms of large historical shifts and trace Romantic and Classical traditions in English poetry. However, it gained notoriety beyond its very modest merits as a consequence of the 1886 attack upon it by John Churton Collins in the *Quarterly Review*. In what was a famous essay, "English Literature at the Universities," Collins sought to expose Gosse's inaccuracy and ignorance, concluding that *From Shakespeare to Pope* "illustrates comprehensively the manner in which English literature should not be taught." Collins took Gosse to task for carelessness with dates, discussion of works he clearly had not read, and making untrustworthy generalizations about literary periods, which rested on no serious evidence.

Gosse's next two major projects were biographies: *Raleigh* (1886), the life of the Elizabethan adventurer, which is distinguished by its attention in the last five chapters to Raleigh's prose; and *Life of William Congreve* (1888), the first full-length biography of the dramatist, which contains a critical discussion of his plays. A revised and enlarged edition of the volume on Congreve was published in 1924. With *A History of Eighteenth-Century Literature (1660-1780)*, which was published in 1889, Gosse established himself, despite Churton Collins's best endeavors, as a scholar, particularly of eighteenth-century literature. Authors discussed include Dryden, Pope, Swift, Fielding, and Johnson. As usual, Gosse is most thoughtful about the prose, especially the novels. In the context of late-nineteenth-century censorship of such writers as Ibsen, Zola, and George Moore, Gosse's recommendation of Fielding's *Tom Jones*, often condemned as an immoral book, seems the act of a moderately brave man. *A History of Eighteenth-Century Literature* never went out of

print in Gosse's lifetime and was a considerable commercial success.

The year before publication of the history, Philip Gosse died, after a long decline. Soon afterward Gosse began work on what was to become a biography of his father, *The Life of Philip Henry Gosse, F.R.S.* (1890); it was republished in 1896 as *The Naturalist of the Sea-shore*. The son certainly felt that he had written a new kind of "naturalist" biography, in which the stance of the biographer was, as Gosse states in the preface, that of a scientific observer: "My only endeavour has been to present my father as he was, and in so doing I have felt sure of his own approval. He utterly despised that species of modern biography which depicts what was a human being as though transformed into the tinted wax of a hairdresser's block. He used to speak with strong contempt of 'goody-goody lives of good men.' "

Despite Gosse's claim, the biography does have the apparatus of the Victorian "Life and Letters" volumes. It is dense with Philip Gosse's own writings, especially his diary, and moves at a leisurely pace through the life, detailing his zoological studies and the conflict within him of science and religion. Part of the interest of *The Life of Philip Henry Gosse, F.R.S.* is that two of its contemporary readers, John Addington Symonds and

Gosse with his wife and daughters. Left to right: Sylvia, Tessa, and Ellen Epps Gosse.

George Moore, saw in that memorial volume the germ of an autobiography. As Symonds put it in a letter to Gosse: "I wish there were more of *you* in your Father's *Life*. You could write a fascinating autobiography if you chose; and I hope you will do this." Thus, by Stevenson, who had commented earlier on *Studies in the Literature of Northern Europe*, Moore and Symonds, Gosse was pressed to acknowledge that his talent was for the personal, for the (auto)biographical.

It is not clear why he was so reluctant to write the book he was pressed to produce. Perhaps his responsibilities distracted him. Certainly they were numerous. In the early 1890s he was, for instance, still involved in translating and promoting Ibsen. He also accepted more public responsibilities and became involved in working for the Royal Literary Fund and the Royal Society of Literature and the Society for Authors. As Ann Thwaite records, his "seniority" and influence meant that he "was already beginning to take on the role of a sort of elder statesman"; he "mixed a great deal with younger men–particularly with Arthur Symons, Yeats, Maurice Baring, Arthur Benson, . . . and Aubrey Beardsley." In 1892 he produced a novel, *The Secret of Narcisse: A Romance*, and in 1894 he contributed to what became, as a consequence of Beardsley's contribution, an infamous publication, the *Yellow Book*. Four volumes of criticism and a literary history also appeared about this time: in 1891, *Gossip in a Library*, which comprises twenty-six essays, many of which discuss literary taste and reputation; in 1893, *Questions at Issue*, a collection of reviews on topics which range from French Symbolism to the question of whether the United States had produced a truly American poet; in 1894, *The Jacobean Poets*, a University Extension manual containing essays on poetry from 1607 to 1625; in 1896, *Critical Kit-Kats*, which offers portraits and accounts of figures such as Pater, Christina Rossetti, and Walt Whitman; and in 1897, *A Short History of Modern English Literature*, an evolutionary account of literature from Chaucer to the 1890s. What these volumes demonstrate is not only Gosse's energy but also his engagement with an extraordinary range of literature.

His next major project was the two-volume biography *The Life and Letters of John Donne, Dean of St Paul's* (1899), perhaps Gosse's best claim to scholarly fame. After one has made the usual (and inevitable) observation that Gosse is inaccurate, particularly with regard to the letters, and that he too easily decodes the life from the poems, it is important to note that the biography was a major contribution to the reassessment of Donne and has been acknowledged as such. It was on the whole favorably reviewed, from the *Athenaeum* to the *Times* and the *Academy*. The *Spectator*, however, judged parts of it adversely, particularly the use of early poems as biographical material, and in the United States it was savaged in the *Nation* as a tissue of confusions.

Within four years of the Donne biography, Gosse produced in cooperation with Richard Garnett a four-volume project, *English Literature: An Illustrated Record* (1903). Garnett was responsible for the first volume, the second was a collaborative effort, and Gosse was the sole author of volumes three and four. Despite the work's scale, its modest historical and critical acumen leads one to the conclusion that after the life of Donne, Gosse's major achievements were all in the field of biography.

The year after the appearance of the *English Literature* volumes, which were republished in 1906, Gosse was offered the librarianship of the House of Lords, a post without any serious responsibilities, which was given as an acknowledgment of his services to literature. It is worth remembering that Gosse's extensive body of writing prior to 1904 had been produced during the years he worked at the Board of Trade.

As if to celebrate his release from daily toil, Gosse turned out four biographies as well as *Father and Son* from 1904 to 1907. *Jeremy Taylor* (1904), in the English Men of Letters series, examines the life and writings, including the prose, of the seventeenth-century Anglican clergyman. Unlike his biography of his father and the Donne biography, both of which were dense with historical documentation, *Jeremy Taylor* is a much more impressionistic work. It uses Taylor's life and, to work through an argument central to Gosse's own concerns, the relationship between religion and art. One might reasonably claim that Jeremy Taylor in its themes is an early rehearsal for *Father and Son*. *Sir Thomas Browne*, another of Gosse's contributions to the English Men of Letters series, and *Coventry Patmore,* in the Literary Lives series, were both published in 1905. In his biography of Browne, the seventeenth-century physician, Gosse weaves together his comments on Browne's ideas and writing in such works as *Religio Medici* into a narrative of the life. In its concentration on the relationship between religion and science, it looks back to Gosse's biography of his father and forward to *Father and Son*. The biog-

Thomas Hardy and Edmund Gosse, Max Gate, Dorchester, June 1927

raphy of Coventry Patmore, who was an important friend of Gosse in his early years in London, weaves together life and writings in Gosse's usual way. What is distinctive about *Coventry Patmore* is its explicit discussion of the importance of what Gosse calls "the sexual instinct" and its power to disrupt "civilised life," a formulation which reminds one that Gosse's biographies were written at the same time as Freud's case studies. With a slight respite Gosse produced two works two years later, in 1907: *Ibsen* and *Father and Son: A Study of Two Temperaments. Ibsen* is an extensive account of a writer with whom, as advocate, translator, and critic, Gosse had been involved for thirty years. Although it discusses the major plays, its real focus is on Ibsen's general antagonism toward European social and cultural life.

Gosse's judgment in that book on Ibsen's *Rosmersholm*—"It dissects the decrepitude of ancient formulas, it surveys the ruin of ancient faiths"—might well stand as a description of one of the impulses behind *Father and Son*, which was published anonymously. Concentrating on the first seventeen years of his life, Gosse dramatizes his upbringing within the Brethren faith and his gradual rebellion against and final rejection of that faith. If Gosse identifies the struggle within

his father as that between religion and science, he identifies the clash between his own natural impulses (including the aesthetic and the sexual) and his religious belief as that which characterized his own early life: "In my hot and silly brain, Jesus and Pan held sway together, as in a wayside chapel discordantly and impishly consecrated to Pagan and to Christian rites.

Unlike such Victorian autobiographies as Harriet Martineau's (1877) or Herbert Spencer's (1904), *Father and Son* does not incorporate documents into the autobiography or draw its formal properties from the essay form. Its innovativeness as autobiography is threefold. First, it stands at the head of a long line of twentieth-century English autobiographies and autobiographical novels (James Joyce's *Portrait of the Artist as a Young Man*, D. H. Lawrence's *Sons and Lovers*) which dramatize the rejection of settled beliefs and communities by the protagonist. Unlike Victorian autobiographies, which end with vocation, the reconciliation of socialization and self-development, *Father and Son* closes with the rejection of vocation. Second, the analysis in *Father and Son*, which focuses as much on adolescence as on childhood, recognizes the importance of sexuality and sexual drives in development. And third, Gosse brings autobiography into a close relationship with fiction; in his preface, like a naturalist novelist, he promises "a slice of life." *Father and Son* was an immediate success in Britain and in the United States and was translated into French in 1912. Its early reputation as a masterpiece has been maintained, and it figures in most critical accounts of autobiography.

Although Gosse produced an impressive list of books after the burst of activity from 1904 to 1907, it may fairly be said that, with one or two exceptions, they do not count among his major works. What distinguishes the last twenty-five years of his life is the breadth of his literary activities, of which his books were only a part. In late 1906 he was wooed by Lord Northcliffe to edit a *Daily Mail* literary supplement, the brief history of which Ann Thwaite records in her biography. In 1910 he was one of those who helped ensure that William Butler Yeats was offered a Civil List pension. In the same year he helped found An Academic Committee of English Letters which he hoped would be to literature what the British Academy was to scholarship. More generally, he was an influential adviser to Herbert Asquith's Liberal government on matters as diverse as the new Cambridge English chair, the Lord Chamberlain, and on who ought to be appointed in 1913 as the poet laureate. These were simply some of his activities which Ann Thwaite's biography records in absorbing detail. He was awarded the C.B. (Companion of the Order of Bath) in 1912. His written work during the period 1907-1912 ranged from a privately printed volume entitled *Biographical Notes on the Writings of Robert Louis Stevenson* (1908) to his *Collected Poems* (1911) and *Portraits and Sketches* (1912), a book of essays on figures such as André Gide, Andrew Lang, A. C. Swinburne, and Alfred Tennyson. The most interesting work of these years is *Two Visits to Denmark, 1872, 1874* (1911). In that book, Gosse contributes to the important contemporary debates about nationalism. As he puts it in his preface, the theme of *Two Visits to Denmark* is the "function and value of the small nations in the civilisation of the world." It was very favorably reviewed.

In 1914, the year of the outbreak of World War I, Gosse was sixty-five and was asked to retire as librarian to the House of Lords. Reluctantly he did so. He retired from nothing else, supporting young writers such as Siegfried Sassoon and at the same time completing a long-overdue task, *The Life of Algernon Charles Swinburne* (1917).

Gosse had first written about the poet for Georg Brandes's magazine *Der Nittende Aarhundrede* in 1875; the essay, entitled simply *Swinburne*, was separately published in English in a limited edition in 1925. In 1909 Gosse had a *Fortnightly Review* piece on the poet separately printed as *Swinburne: Personal Recollections*, and in 1912 he published his *Dictionary of National Biography* entry as the main text of his *The Life of Swinburne, with a Letter on Swinburne at Eton by Lord Redesdale*. The 1917 biography by Gosse, the early advocate of the "pagan" Swinburne, was attacked for its evasiveness. Certainly Gosse excluded accounts of the poet's sexual habits and of his drunkenness. Despite (or because of) its propriety, it sold extremely well. Part of the disappointment of *The Life of Algernon Charles Swinburne* may be due to Gosse's retreat into the kind of biography he had written of his father—overburdened by evidence and documentation. Given his friendship with the poet and his firsthand knowledge of the literary culture in which Swinburne wrote, Gosse kept himself out of the biography more than he might have.

Three French Moralists, and the Gallantry of France (1918) traces the *gloire* which inspired the French soldiers in World War I to the work of La Rochefoucauld, La Bruyère, and Vauvenaragues. In 1920 Gosse was given an honorary degree at Cambridge, in 1921 at Strasbourg, and in 1925 at the Sorbonne. In the same year he received the degree in Paris, he was knighted. His most consistent work during the last ten years of his life was for the *Sunday Times*, for which he began to write in 1919. He continued writing for the *Sunday Times* until 1928, when he underwent a prostate operation from which he did not recover. He died on 16 May 1928.

"I have not the peculiar gift which the teacher needs. Let me say quite clearly that I have always been an artist and never a tutor." These are Gosse's words in the preface to his *Selected Essays* (1928). They alert us to what we should value in Gosse and suggest that the attempts of some to establish him as a literary critic in the tradition of Matthew Arnold have been misplaced. Undoubtedly Gosse will and should remain an honored figure in the history of criticism in the sense that he first drew attention to writers as diverse as Stevenson, Swinburne, and Ibsen, even if he did not adequately understand their importance, as later critics, with the benefit of hindsight, would. Gosse's talent was for those still-undervalued arts—biography and autobiogra-

Sylvia Gosse's portrait of her father in old age (courtesy of Jennifer Gosse)

phy. With *Father and Son* he shifted the formal model for autobiography from the essay to the realist novel. With *Jeremy Taylor* he closed the door on biography as a positivist historical practice, the dominant Victorian mode, and inaugurated the modern practice of biography as an explicit dialogue between author and subject, institutionalizing the biographer's subjectivity within the biography. Gosse the critic is dead. Long live Gosse the biographer.

Letters:

The Correspondence of André Gide and Edmund Gosse, 1904-1928, edited by Linette F. Brugmans (London: Owen, 1959);

Sir Edmund Gosse's Correspondence with Scandinavian Writers, edited by Elias Bredsdorff (Copenhagen: Glydenal, 1960);

Transatlantic Dialogue: Selected American Correspondence of Edmund Gosse, edited by Paul F. Mattheisen and Michael Millgate (Austin & London: University of Texas Press, 1965).

Bibliographies:

A Catalogue of the Gosse Correspondence in the Brotherton Collection (Leeds: University of Leeds Library Publications, 1950);

James D. Woolf, "Sir Edmund Gosse: An Annotated Bibliography of Writing About Him," *English Literature in Transition (1880-1920),* 11, no. 3 (1968): 126-172;

"Edmund Gosse," in *English Prose and Criticism, 1900-1950,* edited by Christopher C. Brown and William B. Thesing (Detroit: Gale Research, 1983), pp. 179-198.

Biographies:

Evan Charteris, *The Life and Letters of Sir Edmund Gosse* (London: Heinemann, 1931);

Ann Thwaite, *Edmund Gosse: A Literary Landscape, 1849-1928* (London: Secker & Warburg, 1984).

References:

R. Victoria Arana, "Sir Edmund Gosse's *Father and Son:* Autobiography as Comedy," *Genre,* 10 (Spring 1977): 63-76;

Joseph O. Baylen, "Edmund Gosse, William Archer, and Ibsen in Victorian Britain," *Ten-*

nessee Studies in Literature, 20 (1975): 124-137;

Max Beerbohm, "A Recollection by Edm*nd G*osse," in his *A Christmas Garland* (London: Heinemann, 1912), pp. 135-146;

Elias Bredsdorff, Introduction to *Sir Edmund Gosse's Correspondence with Scandinavian Writers* (Copenhagen: Glydendal, 1960), pp. 1-23;

Jerome Hamilton Buckley, *Season of Youth: The Bildungsroman from Dickens to Golding* (Cambridge: Harvard University Press, 1974), pp. 25, 116-119, 302;

Charles Burkhart, "George Moore and *Father and Son,*" *Nineteenth-Century Fiction,* 15 (June 1960): 71-77;

John Churton Collins, "English Literature at the Universities," *Quarterly Review,* 163 (October 1886): 289-329;

Philip Dodd, "The Nature of Edmund Gosse's *Father and Son,*" *English Literature in Transition (1880-1920),* 22, no. 4 (1979): 270-280;

William J. Gracie, Jr., "Truth of Form in Edmund Gosse's *Father and Son,*" *Journal of Narrative Technique,* 4 (September 1974): 176-187;

Howard Helsinger, "Credence and Credibility: The Concern for Honesty in Victorian Autobiography," in *Approaches to Victorian Autobiography,* edited by George P. Landow (Athens: Ohio University Press, 1979), pp. 56-63;

James Hepburn, Introduction to Gosse's *Father and Son: A Study of Two Temperaments* (London: Oxford University Press, 1974), pp. xi-xvii;

William Irvine, Introduction to Gosse's *Father and Son* (Boston: Houghton Mifflin, 1965), pp. v-xlii;

Leslie Marchand, "The Symington Collection," *Journal of the Rutgers University Library,* 12 (1948): 1-15;

George Moore, *Avowals* (London: Heinemann, 1919), pp. 1-96;

E. Pearlman, "Father and Mother in *Father and Son,*" *Victorian Newsletter,* no. 55 (Spring 1979): 19-23;

Linda H. Peterson, "Gosse's *Father and Son:* The Evolution of Scientific Apology," in her *Victorian Autobiography: The Tradition of Self-Interpretation* (New Haven & London: Yale University Press, 1986), pp. 156-191;

Roger J. Porter, "Edmund Gosse's *Father and Son:* Between Form and Flexibility," *Journal of Narrative Technique,* 5 (September 1975):

174-195;

James K. Robinson, "A Neglected Phase of the Aesthetic Movement: English Parnassianism," *PMLA,* 67 (September 1953): 733-754;

Fredric R. Ross, "Philip Gosse's *Omphalos,* Edmund Gosse's *Father and Son,* and Darwin's Theory of Natural Selection," *ISIS,* 68 (March 1977): 85-96;

Ruth Z. Temple, "Sir Edmund Gosse," in her *The Critic's Alchemy* (New York: Twayne, 1953), pp. 185-228;

Douglas Wertheimer, "The Identification of Some Characters and Incidents in Gosse's *Father and Son,*" *Notes and Queries,* new series 23 (January 1976): 4-11;

Howard R. Wolf, "British Fathers and Sons, 1773-1913: From Filial Submissiveness to Creativity," *Psychoanalytical Review,* 52 (Summer 1965): 53-70;

James D. Woolf, "The Benevolent Christ in Gosse's *Father and Son,*" *Prose Studies,* 3 (September 1980): 160-175;

Woolf, " 'In the Seventh Heaven of Delight': The Aesthetic Sense in Gosse's *Father and Son,*" in *Interspace and the Inward Sphere: Essays on Romantic and Victorian Self,* edited by Norman A. Anderson and Margene E. Weiss (Macomb: Western Illinois University Press, 1978), pp. 134-144;

Woolf, *Sir Edmund Gosse* (New York: Twayne, 1972);

Virginia Woolf, "The Art of Biography," in her *The Death of the Moth and Other Essays* (London: Hogarth Press, 1942), pp. 119-126;

Clement H. Wyke, "Edmund Gosse as Biographer and Critic of Donne: His Fallible Role in the Poet's Rediscovery," *Texas Studies in Literature and Language,* 17 (Winter 1976): 805-819.

Papers:

An important collection of Gosse's letters and other manuscript material is in the Brotherton Collection, University of Leeds (see *A Catalogue of the Gosse Correspondence in the Brotherton Collection,* 1950). There is some Gosse material in the Symington Collection at the Alexander Library, Rutgers University. Other collections are at the Cambridge University Library and the British Library.

Frederic Harrison
(18 October 1831-13 January 1923)

Harry R. Sullivan
University of South Carolina

SELECTED BOOKS: *The Meaning of History* (London: Trübner, 1862);

Order and Progress (London: Longmans, Green, 1875);

The Present and the Future: A Positivist Address (London: Reeves & Turner, 1880);

The Choice of Books and Other Literary Pieces (London: Macmillan, 1886; New York: Harper, 1886);

Oliver Cromwell (London & New York: Macmillan, 1888);

Annals of an Old Manor House, Sutton Place, Guilford (London & New York: Macmillan, 1893);

The Meaning of History, and Other Historical Pieces (New York & London: Macmillan, 1894);

Studies in Early Victorian Literature (London & New York: Arnold, 1895);

William the Silent (London: Macmillan/New York: Macmillan, 1897);

Tennyson, Ruskin, Mill and Other Literary Estimates (London & New York: Macmillan, 1899);

Byzantine History in the Early Middle Ages. The Rede Lecture Delivered in the Senate House, Cambridge, June 12, 1900 (London: Macmillan/New York: Macmillan, 1900);

George Washington and Other American Addresses (London: Macmillan/New York: Macmillan, 1901);

John Ruskin (New York: Macmillan/London: Macmillan, 1902);

Theophano: The Crusade of the Tenth Century: A Romantic Monograph (London: Chapman & Hall, 1904; New York & London: Harper, 1904);

Chatham (New York: Macmillan/London: Macmillan, 1905);

Memories and Thoughts: Men—Books—Cities—Art (New York: Macmillan/London: Macmillan, 1906);

Nicephorus—A Tragedy of New Rome (London: Chapman & Hall, 1906);

The Creed of a Layman: Apologia pro Fide Mea (New York: Macmillan/London: Macmillan, 1907);

photograph by Barraud

The Philosophy of Common Sense (London: Macmillan, 1907; New York: Macmillan, 1907);

My Alpine Jubilee, 1851-1907 (London: Smith, Elder, 1908);

Realities and Ideals: Social, Political, Literary and Artistic (London: Macmillan, 1908; New York: Macmillan, 1908);

National and Social Problems (London: Macmillan, 1908; New York: Macmillan, 1908);

Autobiographic Memoirs, 2 volumes (London: Macmillan, 1911);

Among My Books (London: Macmillan, 1912; New York: Ober, 1912);

*The Positive Evolution of Religion: Its Moral and So-
cial Reaction* (London: Heinemann, 1913;
New York: Putnam's, 1913);

*The German Peril: Forecasts, 1864-1914; Realities
1915; Hopes 191-* (London: Unwin, 1915);

On Society (London: Macmillan, 1918);

Obiter Scripta, 1918 (London: Chapman & Hall,
1919);

On Jurisprudence and the Conflict of Laws (Oxford:
Clarendon Press, 1919);

Novissima Verba: Last Words, 1920 (London:
Unwin, 1921; New York: Holt, 1921);

De Senectute: More Last Words (London: Unwin,
1923).

OTHER: Auguste Comte, *Social Statics*, volume 2
of *System of Positive Polity*, translated by Harrison (London: Longmans, Green, 1875);

*The New Calendar of Great Men: Biographies of the
558 Worthies of All Ages and Nations in the Positivist Calendar of Auguste Comte*, edited, with
contributions, by Harrison (London & New
York: Macmillan, 1892);

L. Lévy Bruhl, *The Philosophy of Auguste Comte*,
translated by Kathleen de Beaumont-Klein,
introduction by Harrison (London: Sonnenschein, 1903);

*Carlyle and the London Library. Account of its Founda-
tion: Together with Unpublished Letters of Thomas Carlyle to W. D. Christie*, edited by Harrison (London: Chapman & Hall, 1907);

"John Ruskin," in *Encyclopaedia Britannica*, eleventh edition, 28 volumes (Cambridge: University Press, 1911), XXIII: 858-861;

"Positivism: Its Position, Aims, and Ideals," in
Great Religions of the World (New York & London: Harper, 1912).

Frederic Harrison, well known in his own
time for his vital part in the leading controversies
of the Victorian Age in England, has become in
the twentieth century little more than a name encountered here and there in the records of the
lives of his outstanding contemporaries. Few Englishmen in the nineteenth century had a more important role in furthering the cause of the working man and in the legitimization of trade unions—
possibly his most solid achievement. But as the
leading English Positivist, he championed various
political, religious, scientific, and literary ideas
that were bursting on the English intellectual
scene during the latter half of the nineteenth century. In the forefront of innumerable and varied
controversies, there was Frederic Harrison, hold-

ing his own with, and highly respected by, the leading figures of the age. In the wake of the cata-
clysm of the French Revolution and during the
rapid rise of modern science in the nineteenth century, he thought a reintegration of society had at
last become possible. This vision of a new world,
he was convinced, was best perceived in the Positivism of the Frenchman Auguste Comte, a philosophy that found its leading English exponent in
Harrison. In his 1933 book *Adventures of Ideas*, Alfred North Whitehead called this philosophy and
Jeremy Bentham's Utilitarianism the two greatest
intellectual movements of the nineteenth century. It is perhaps not too much to say that in
the life of no other Victorian can one find the development of the complex issues of the age more
fully revealed than in the career of Harrison.

Born in London on 18 October 1831, Harrison was named after his father, but the final *k* of
his first name was omitted to distinguish him
from his succcessful father, who had been
trained as an architect but who became a prosperous stockbroker. His mother, Jane Brice Harrison, was the daughter of Belfast merchants.
Harrison's first memories are of Muswell Hill, a
rural spot outside London to which the family
moved. It was during this idyllic early life in
these rustic surroundings that his parents in
1837 took him to the coronation of Queen Victoria in the immense city. The sheer pageantry of
the event enabled him to forget his first surprise
that a mere girl would succeed the king. This occasion, when Harrison was five, was his first exciting encounter with the outside world.

After the Harrisons moved to Oxford
Square, Hyde Park, in 1840, Frederic Harrison
first enrolled in day school for two years and
then attended King's College School until 1849.
Never having experienced life at a public school,
such as Eton or Harrow, he matriculated at
Wadham College, Oxford, in the politically momentous year of 1849, when throughout Europe
revolutionary changes were taking place that
would seriously affect the rest of his life. At
Wadham he met Richard Congreve, a scholar
who, Harrison thought, taught in the best tradition of Dr. Thomas Arnold and who would later
become a leading Positivist in England. It was at
Wadham that he began to question his early High-
Church training. He later decided not to take orders, slowly evolving from his early rather orthodox proclivities to a liberal interpretation of Christianity and then to a scientific Positivism, under
the influence of Congreve and several close

friends at Wadham.

During his years at Oxford, Harrison made three lifelong friends, forming a small group nicknamed by their detractors "Mumbo-Jumbo"–Edward Spencer Beesly, later professor of history at University College, London; John Henry Bridges, later M.D.; and George Earlam Thorley, later warden of Wadham College. Under their influence, Harrison clearly began to waver in his Christian beliefs, actually leaning more and more toward the ideas of the activists Richard Cobden and John Bright. "Mumbo-Jumbo" would provide the nucleus for the future Positivist Society, of which Harrison would become president and prime mover.

In 1855, two years after earning his B.A. degree, Harrison left Oxford and made the most momentous trip of his life–a visit to Auguste Comte in Paris, several years before the latter's death. Although he would later get to know many important public figures in England, France, and Italy, he thought that he had never met so impressive an individual as M. Comte; the only time the two men ever met, this visit was perhaps the supreme experience of Harrison's life.

In 1855 Harrison also commenced the study of law at Lincoln's Inn, now that he had given up an intended career in the church. But he had no relish for making a living in this way. Soon he was reading Comte, John Stuart Mill, Thomas Carlyle, and John Ruskin, and he was teaching at the Working Men's College with such notable men as Frederick Denison Maurice, Charles Kingsley, Thomas Hughes, and Ford Madox Brown. It was here that, in opposition to the rather different ideas of the college president Maurice, he drew up a plan to systemize the study of history, a sequential approach that he would adhere to his life long. All the time that he was supposed to be studying law, he was promoting with fellow young radicals various radical schemes, such as eliminating religious tests at the university. Often he would meet in his own chambers with such men as Benjamin Jowett, James Bryce, and John Bright–towering figures in the intellectual and political life of Victorian England–to draw up radical plans of action.

In the 1850s Harrison was full of enthusiasm for Italian independence, studying Italian (especially Dante) with one of Mazzini's colleagues in exile. As a result, he became interested in the struggles of other nations also striving for liberation from oppressors. Francis William Newman (John Henry Newman's brother) and Harrison encouraged others to write letters to newspapers in support of the Italian cause; their efforts might have helped form the foreign policies of the ministries of Palmerston and Russell in the early 1860s. Also Harrison took a trip entirely on his own to Italy, from where, without accepting any pay, he mailed dispatches to leading London periodicals.

He continued to be politically active in the 1860s as well. In 1866, for example, Harrison joined the Jamaica Committee, directed by John Stuart Mill, to oppose Gov. John Eyre for having used martial law to suppress Negro riots in the colony. In this vitally important trial, not unlike the memorable affair of Warren Hastings, eighteenth-century governor-general of British India, Thomas Carlyle headed the committee for the defense of Governor Eyre. Nearly all the leading literary figures of Victorian England were on either one side or the other. It was Harrison who drew up the procedures that would henceforth be used in the field of English martial law, procedures that would be revived by the South African Committee in 1901.

In the late 1860s, according to Beatrice and Sidney Webb in their *History of Trade-Unionism* (1894), Harrison worked out the principles upon which all future labor legislation during the century would rest. Between 1863 and 1875 Harrison contributed nearly seventy-five articles to several radical periodicals, many of them devoted to various legal and political problems revolving around labor law. In the mid 1860s Harrison began to be publicly identified as a Positivist. In 1865 he was offered the editorship of the radical journals the *Beehive* and the *Commonwealth*, but he declined both. However, he did accept membership (in the place of a representative from the unions) on the Royal Commission on Trade Unions, in which capacity, with his well-known legal expertise, he contributed crucial help to the cause of labor.

It was during this general period of his life that he was admitted to many influential Victorian clubs and societies, including the Reform Club, the Cobden Club (as a close friend of Cobden and Bright), and the prestigious Alpine Club (as fellow enthusiast with Leslie Stephen). In 1869 he became a life member of the London Library, helping to produce the new subject index that became a landmark in the history of English bibliography. In 1871 he was proposed as a member of the Cosmopolitan Club, where he associated with leading men from all areas of British

10. March.

Elm Hill. 1903
Hawkhurst.

Dear Mrs Ward, There cannot be a doubt that your book is a brilliant success, and will hold the public both here & abroad. I enjoy it more than anything you have ever done, & I am sure it will prove to be the most popular of all. The scheme is admirably original, new, interesting, & yet quite natural. The adaptation of Mad'le de l'Espinasse is complete and right in every way, historically & ethically. I hardly like to say more about the book, for I am so truly distrustful of my own judgment as to anything like modern fiction, & I am so little familiar with such art at all — I rarely open a romance, & when I do, I hardly know what I think of it. So I feel it almost an impertinence to pass an opinion. I trust my wife. She has been in bed for ten days, suffering acutely from facial neuralgia — but in the intervals of spasms of pain, she has read & re-read Lady Rose three times & keeps the book at her bed side, or I should have been able to read it sooner myself. We are familiar with Mad'le de l'Espinasse's letters & story.

But your Julie is a new creation of your own and quite twentieth Century. You used to be rather hard on us poor men; but now you have given us some men who are neither sentimental, selfish, nor priggish. The drawing of a Becky Sharp in a woman of fine nature & warm heart, in spite of an irregular life, is peculiarly interesting, & certainly one of the happiest conceptions in modern fiction. I think too you gain immensely by dispensing with any 'purpose' or 'movement' or 'philosophy' and giving yourself up to paint the later Victorian world of Mayfair. What a rotten, self-sufficient world it is! It is a delightful idea to make it all revolve round two Dukes. In fact the whole world consists of ducal families, familiars, parasites, dependants, & domestics. The very butlers feel themselves to be dukes in the servants hall. To have been at Eton, to dine with a cabinet minister, to stay at big house parties seems to them culture and real nobility. How indelibly snobbish at heart is Mayfair after all! Julie del'Espinasse was irregular, but she was not a snob. Our maddening ministers, and pompous dukes today are snobs to the tips of their fingers & dullards too. We have sworn off all such places & the peace of the country does us all the good in the world morally & physically. Do you go on to Rome? I shall attend the Historical Congress there from 2nd to 9th of April & return by Assisi & Perugia. I was so sorry that we could not see you when we ran up to town in January. I greatly value your kindness in sending me your latest — and your best work. Yours sincerely Frederic Harrison.

Letter from Harrison to Mrs. Humphry Ward, praising Ward's 1903 novel Lady Rose's Daughter *(by permission of Reginald F. P. Harrison, courtesy of the Colbeck Collection, Special Collections Division, Library, University of British Columbia, Vancouver, B.C.)*

life. But the most interesting organization to which Harrison belonged was the Metaphysical Society, where the great issues of the age were debated by leading personages. Here he crossed swords with all and sundry on all manner of subjects, including those of profoundest philosophical import. In the 1870s John Morley, one of his dearest friends, proposed Harrison for both the Political Economy Club and the prestigious Athenaeum.

But of even far greater importance than his moving in these social circles was Harrison's marriage to his first cousin Ethel in 1870 when he was nearly forty and she twenty. For the forty-six years of their completely compatible life together, Ethel was his counselor. In his 1927 biography, their son Austin (there were four sons and one daughter) wrote that few couples ever surpassed his parents in the sheer romance of living: "Today such a marriage would be styled Victorian, old-fashioned, yet man and woman can reach no higher."

Austin Harrison recalls that in personal habits, his father functioned like a clock. He arose very early, and after breakfast he retired to his room and worked until luncheon, after which time he generally took a walk. If meals were not served promptly, he would shout and remonstrate. In the evenings he read. He disliked small talk and held the Victorian conviction that the head of the family should always command respect. He was an indefatigable worker. Austin Harrison's volume is full of testimony to his father's unfailing vigor and hale-and-hearty spirits. Despite the obvious lack of acceptance of Positivism, even during its most popular period in the late nineteenth century, throughout Harrison's long life his loyalty to it never failed. Seldom has optimistic faith been more severely tried and tested.

Austin Harrison further emphasizes that his father had a firm and fixed opinion on everything and also an opinion on every opinion as well. He contrasted his father with his father's friend Henry James, who "thanked Heaven that he had no opinions." Harrison was in absolute contrast with Henry James, "the master of the indefinite," who enchanted the "nymphs of Mayfair." Unlike James, he never had a "rapt circle" of admirers. However, he was capable of overwhelming enthusiasms, but he despised flattery and toadyism. Nothing was more alien to him than merely being idle, nor could he understand Austin's once complaining of being exhausted.

Whenever not otherwise occupied, the peppery Harrison was always reading.

It is quite impossible to understand the theories of Harrison without also having a familiarity with those of Auguste Comte, the father of Positivism. As Comte explains in his *Cours de philosophie positive* (1830-1842), humanity has developed through two earlier states, the theological and the metaphysical, and is now entering the third and final one, the positive. The first two states depend on a belief in the Absolute, whereas the third, the positive, is grounded in the conviction that all truth must be relative. In other words, human thought passes from the ancient phase to the modern. With the rapid rise of modern science in the nineteenth century, man is learning to think in terms of only that which is demonstrable and to abandon fruitless attempts to fathom the unknowable. Rather than a theological God, Comte proposes a veneration of humanity—past, present, and future. Believing all supernatural matters to be beyond human ken, the Positivist thinks man is better off dealing with what he knows rather than with something that he has not the slightest inkling of.

Harrison agrees fundamentally with Comte on all basic Positivist theories. And, unlike John Stuart Mill and others who were sympathetic to Comte's ideas only up to the point of the so-called Religion of Humanity, Harrison believed that the Religion of Humanity would appeal to all man's concerns, all his inner drives, for this secular religion would become an integral part of man's daily life. Harrison did not attack any known religion, believing that supernatural religions served as necessary stages in man's development toward the culmination of his religious feelings in the ultimate secular Religion of Humanity when man attains the third, or positive, stage of his development. It is important to note that Harrison never conceived of himself as either an agnostic or an atheist.

In 1859 Harrison contributed to the *Westminster Review* an article entitled "Neo-Christianity," an analysis of *Essays and Reviews*, which was a symposium by seven liberal churchmen in an attempt to harmonize the traditional doctrines of the church with the tide of modern intellectual theories in the nineteenth century. It was Harrison's article that proved to be a bombshell, stirring controversy over the acute dilemma of orthodox Christianity in the middle part of the century. Harrison thought that rather than pour new wine into old bottles, the Reviewers, as they were called, should have recommended a root-and-branch solution. What he really implied was that these reviewers should adopt something not unlike the new Religion of Humanity, thus supporting a religion which modern man could find tenable, unshackled from the undemonstrable theology of yesteryear. Neo-Christianity, a term Harrison invents in this article, was too tenuous, holding on to too much that modern man could not sincerely believe. The only solution, obviously, was the Religion of Humanity, a secular approach which would meet all modern man's needs—affective, intellectual, and spiritual. This alternative, Harrison implies, is the only genuine solution. But, in fact, Harrison's so-called Neo-Christianity would actually in time come more and more to be the religion of the educated classes in Great Britain.

For an 1876 issue of the *Contemporary Review*, Harrison wrote a "Socratic dialogue" in reply to an article by Mark Pattison (one of the seven reviewers) which had attacked the Religion of Humanity. In this work, set amid the "studious groves" around Magdalen College in springtime, Sophistes (a don who admires Mark Pattison) is discussing the Religion of Humanity with Phaedrus (a London barrister, who is obviously Harrison himself). They are comparing Harrison's religion with Pattison's Neo-Christianity. If one were to select several pieces of Harrison's for an anthology of Victorian prose, he would do no better than to choose dialogues of this sort that are sprinkled throughout the pages of Harrison's copious writings. The pointed, telling, devastating irony of the dialogues is handled in a way that few, if any, Victorian prose masters can surpass.

T. H. Huxley was another important Victorian prose writer and a figure who was embroiled in as many scientific and religious controversies as Harrison. In "On the Physical Basis of Life" (*Fortnightly Review*, 1868) Huxley charged that Positivism is "Catholicism minus Christianity"; Harrison retorted that it is rather "Catholicism plus science." For his model of a system by which to order human life, Comte found the best one in the medieval Church, but without what he considered its theological superstitions and fanaticism. Positivism has nine sacraments which pertain to the various stages in a man's life, even one—Incorporation—seven years after his death when the individual is absorbed sacramentally into the unity of humanity for all time to come. Instead of a Calendar of Saints, Positivism has a calendar of the great men of humanity's history—heroes in poetry, public affairs, and science, who have contributed significantly to the development of humanity.

Neither Comte nor Harrison believed in personal immortality, rather subscribing to what they termed "subjective immortality," by which we bequeath the sum total of our contributions to humanity; it has nothing to do with our selfish preoccupation with saving our own souls. They would agree with T. H. Huxley who thought that man's faculties of mind, feeling, and will are all part and parcel of his physical organism. Harrison feared that the Christian heaven condemns man to an eternity of apathy, without objects, relationships, or growth—"an absolute nothingness, a nirvana of impotence."

Austin Harrison divides his father's life into two halves, separated by his marriage. In the first, he is a man of action in the various causes related to the contemporary world. In the second, he becomes devoted to his religion as a teacher of Positivism, reaching serenity as a Humanist, for to him Positivism is the consummation of Humanism. He now focuses increasingly on his literary work, spending the rest of his life writing and organizing numerous works for publication.

When some enthusiastic admirer maintained that he had read all Harrison's books, the author replied, "That is impossible; I couldn't read all of them myself." Harrison was indeed prolific. During the first years of the *Fortnightly Review*, the journal was often viewed as the house organ of the Positivists, with Harrison writing nearly half of the articles on Positivism. In *Autobiographic Memoirs*, published in 1911, he lists in a bibliography his articles in principal journals which had not been reprinted in his books, and the number is legion.

Harrison's first book, *The Meaning of History*, comprising two lectures, was published in 1862 and later expanded and retitled *The Meaning of History, and Other Historical Pieces* (1894). The book, which in its expanded version became one of Harrison's major works, reveals history as the handmaiden of social philosophy. History tells the unending story of the development of the social organism, of which all of mankind are so many cells. The best way to understand the Positivist theory of filiation, Harrison suggests, is to conceive of society growing as do the branches from the trunk of the tree. After taking the reader through the various stages of world history, Harrison contends that society has reached its final stage of industrial existence and that at this stage the guidance of mankind has passed from the priests to the scientists, philosophers, and poets.

The French Revolution was the great earthquake which destroyed the now-antiquated feudal and religious systems of the past, thus preparing the ground for a new world. Dating it from 1789, Comte developed a new calendar made up of thirteen equal months, with one extra day each year called Year Day. Each day was dedicated to the memory of a Positivist "saint," that is, to a great man who aided significantly in the development of humanity through the ages, whether he be scientist, political leader, poet, or some other kind of creative genius. In Harrison's view one's reading should be confined as practicably as possible to authors on Comte's quite extensive list of creative geniuses.

In addition to the Law of Three States (theological, metaphysical, and positive), Comte also proposed his Classification of the Sciences, which shows how the basic theoretical sciences reach the positive stage in man's comprehension; but in order to have a philosophy of the sciences, Comte introduced a subjective social science for which he invented the name *sociology*. Through the aid of this social science, for the first time man has access to a philosophy of the sciences which will give a coherent sense of human development through history.

In *Order and Progress* (1875), Harrison, as a subscriber to the theory of dualism rather than to that of monism, follows Comte in his theory of the two complementary sides of reality: the static and the dynamic. In the static view we can see the unity of the sciences in terms of their classification. In the dynamic view, we can see the development of the Law of the Three States in human understanding up to the stage of sociology. It is very important, Harrison notes, that man should not bother about those matters quite beyond his ability to know. It was not until the nineteenth century that the sciences developed sufficiently for man to reach the positive stage.

In 1875 Harrison translated Comte's *Social Statics*, the second volume of his *System of Positive Polity*. In 1880 Harrison split with his old friend Congreve, and the following year he aided in organizing the Positivist Society at London's Newton Hall (appropriately named after Sir Isaac Newton). He became president of the society and later, in 1893, editor of the new *Positivist Review*, to which he contributed copiously. At Newton Hall there were lectures on the arts, the sciences,

history, and contemporary political affairs. Everything, as the founders envisioned it, was to be free and there would be no compulsion of any kind. Harrison led expeditions of members to many of the historical and literary shrines about England, places dear to the memory of Humanity's saints.

For the Positivist, the home is the center of man's social life. It is there that he assimilates the virtues that should carry over into the general polity—love, responsibility, serving others, unselfishness, and veneration. Like the old polytheistic religions antedating Christianity, Positivism venerates the public virtues again, not merely the narrow private ones. Harrison believes that when the French Revolution proclaimed that men are free and equal, mankind passed a central turning point of history. The people now became the most important consideration of a social polity.

Oppugning the greed and the heartless competition of capitalism and the loss of freedom and the reliance on repression of communism, Positivism addresses itself to the whole range of the problems of human nature, teaching man to understand and to practice altruism. One can see that this injunction is the "belling of the cat" for Positivism, equivalent to the problem of sin for Christian theology. If only some philosophy could succeed in eradicating *amour-propre*, or human self-love! In essence, Positivism purports to be a kind of moral socialism.

The ultimate purpose of Positivism was to achieve its vision of a new social order founded on man's developed altruism (a word invented by Comte). Without the vices of either capitalism or communism, it would so order society, under the guidance of the Religion of Humanity, that man would realize the full utilization of his capacities under the moral guidance of a Positivist priesthood but without coercion and with no supernatural sanction. The reader will find discussion of these crucial problems in Harrison's essays of this general period, collected in *Order and Progress* and such other works as *The Creed of a Layman* (1907), *The Philosophy of Common Sense* (1907), *Realities and Ideals* (1908), *National and Social Problems* (1908), *The Positive Evolution of Religion* (1913), and *On Society* (1918).

In 1893 Harrison's *Annals of an Old Manor House* was published. The old manor house, built in the early sixteenth century, was Sutton Place, the family's country home. During Harrison's stays there, he grew curious about the history of the old mansion and set about to study its past

Sutton Place, the Harrison family estate described in Frederic Harrison's Annals of an Old Manor House *(by permission of Reginald F. P. Harrison)*

and its successive architectural embellishments. His researches carried him all the way back to the eleventh-century Domesday book, and his own volume is an example of history in depth, concentrating on the rich and colorful past of one old manor house and thereby unearthing many layers of English history, especially from the days of Henry VIII to Harrison's own day.

Harrison also loved to study the biographies of great men as Carlyle had done, and he produced a study of Oliver Cromwell in 1888, one of William the Silent in 1897, one of George Washington in 1901, one of John Ruskin in 1902, and one of Chatham in 1905. As a Positivist he was, of course, deeply interested in the history of great men who were the saints of Positivism.

Harrison was also interested in the lives of figures from the past. His fascination with the role Byzantium had played in the history of the world prompted him to write a romance as well as a drama on the exciting events of the tenth century. In 1904 he produced *Theophano*; two years later *Nicephorus*, his play based on the same material, was published. Together they tell the richly

colored story of Theophano (modeled on the historical Empress Irene, circa 750-803) and her relations with General (later Emperor) Nicephorus (based on a historical figure of the same name) during the period of the earliest crusades against the False Prophet, several centuries before the West launched its own crusades. Though not very successful, these literary works make informative and exciting reading, conveying a picture of an age even historians know far too little about.

Not least of Harrison's enthusiasms was his avid love of mountain climbing, which became a cult among such Victorians as his friend Leslie Stephen. In 1908 his book, *My Alpine Jubilee, 1851-1907*, was published, comprising letters he had written to his wife, Ethel, from the Alps and several periodical articles he had written on the general subject of mountain climbing. The enthusiastic tone of this work, dedicated to the memory of Stephen, may be caught in a few lines to Ethel: "I live again–I have breathed once more the air of the 'iced mountain top'–my heart expands at the sight of my beloved Alps. After fifty-six years the mountain fever throbs in my old veins. Bunyan's Pilgrim did not hail the vision of the Delectable Hills with more joy and consolation."

Despite his interests in Byzantium and mountain landscapes, Harrison devoted most of his energies to intellectual controversies of his own era. It was the Religion of Humanity that caused many English sympathizers to part company with Comte and to abandon Positivism. Mill charged Comte with an unhealthy passion for regulation, for stifling investigation by imposing an artificial unity based on an inflexible system. Harrison, in two lectures (later appearing in *On Society*) at Newton Hall in 1893, replied in his usual convincing way, believing that if he could answer Mill, he would simultaneously refute all the other critics, who simply repeated Mill's objections. Harrison's point was that Mill agreed with Comte far more than he disagreed. T. H. Huxley, another friend, lampooned the Religion of Humanity, and, again, Harrison replied in his cogent way, attempting to show that the great scientist Huxley was really a Positivist without knowing that he was. Harrison also conducted debates with other such friends as John Ruskin and Herbert Spencer, and with Matthew Arnold on no less a subject than Arnold's concept of Culture. Reading the arguments on both sides, it is evident that Harrison did not come out second best in any of these controversies.

Harrison compiled many of his published essays on literature in *The Choice of Books and Other Literary Pieces* (1886), *Studies in Early Victorian Literature* (1895), *Tennyson, Ruskin, Mill and Other Literary Estimates* (1899), *Novissima Verba* (1921), and *De Senectute: More Last Words* (1923). He always preferred the classics, believing that the modern world had little to add to the settled literary forms that had been established by the Ancients. Deeply imbued with Victorian moral convictions, Harrison is nonetheless a perceptive critic of literature. Although they are never obtrusive, the Positivist criteria are always present in his criticism. History has determined works of the first and second class, and the others are not important.

The Comtian heroes of humanity may be literary figures as well as scientists, religious leaders, philosophers, and men of public affairs, for the three great creations of humanity are philosophy, poetry, and polity. Feeling, the highest principle of existence, as expressed in supreme art, is united with thought and action to make up the three basic ingredients of humanity. And poetry, the most spontaneous, the most comprehensive,

Harrison in Alpine garb, photographed in 1907 by his daughter Olive Harrison (by permission of Reginald F. P. Harrison)

and the noblest of the arts, idealizes most and imitates least. Following Comte, in *The Choice of Books and Other Literary Pieces*, Harrison declares that the choice of books is basically the choice of education (the basis of Positivist culture and society), of the formation of moral and intellectual ideals: The great masterpieces of literature "are the master instruments of a solid education." But being well read is no guarantee that one has had a genuine education any more than lip service in church is a guarantee of religion. Books must become part of the very tissue of humanity, living in men and women throughout their entire existence. Reprehending the endless flow of books in the nineteenth century, Harrison avers, "Greece gave us the model and eternal type of written language, not only in epic, tragic, and comic poetry, but in imaginative prose and in pure lyric."

For Harrison, ancient literature ended with Alfred the Great, a new Charlemagne, who was superior to Alexander and Julius Caesar in natural grace and beauty of soul, "the only perfect man of action in the annals of mankind." Just as Homer was the father of ancient poetry, so

Dante was the father of modern European literature. Although Shakespeare was the greatest poetic genius of literature, the Greeks were the greatest tragedians, especially Aeschylus. Writing in the seventeenth century, Bunyan and Milton, in their respective ways, were inimitable. And the literature of the eighteenth century, Harrison contends, has been cruelly maligned, for it was a century with some of England's greatest writers and also the age in which most of the main musical forms were developed and in which Bach, Handel, Haydn, Mozart, Gluck, and the early Beethoven were prominent. The achievements of Western music in this age rivaled that of the medieval Gothic cathedrals.

Harrison appraises many of the men whom he knew intimately in the nineteenth century. Distributing praise and blame impartially, he concedes, however, that he is too close to his own age to give entirely valid judgments that only time can render. But, as always, his opinions are tempered by measured fairness and common sense.

When Harrison gave the Rede lecture in 1900 at Cambridge, the American ambassador heard him and invited him, the first Englishman ever to be accorded this honor, to deliver the annual Washington's birthday address at the Union Club in Chicago in 1901. While in America, Harrison met many notables from President Theodore Roosevelt on down; as he wrote Ethel, who was too ill to make the trip, he was treated like Dickens, Herbert Spencer, and the Prince of Wales all rolled into one.

American audiences most of all wanted to hear him tell of his experiences with the celebrities he had known over the past half century. He lectured at some of the outstanding universities in the East and also conversed with such diverse Americans as Mark Twain, Charles Eliot Norton, and J. P. Morgan, to mention a few. Small wonder that he was fairly overcome by the warm hospitality Americans showed him wherever he went.

In 1911 he produced his two-volume *Autobiographic Memoirs*, a fragmentary account of his life and writings to 1910. Earlier, in 1906, his *Memories and Thoughts: Men–Books–Cities–Art* had appeared, including published accounts of people and places he had known throughout his life. The roster of notables he was closely associated with reads like a catalogue of Europe's foremost men. In England he intimately associated with such people as Thomas Carlyle, John Ruskin, John Stuart Mill, John Bright, Francis William

and John Henry Newman, Henry Edward Manning, George Henry Lewes and George Eliot, Anthony Trollope, Alfred Tennyson, Robert Browning–the list goes on and on.

Harrison had lived in London throughout most of his life, mainly in Westbourne Terrace, Paddington. However, in 1902 he moved to Hawkhurst, Kent, and then in 1912 to Bath, where he resided in the Royal Crescent, a block of architecturally impressive buildings. He was an inveterate traveler who had visited France, Italy, Switzerland, the Near East, and America. His keen interest in architecture, city planning, and the history of specific places (he had served on the first London County Council) lasted his life long. Among the honors he received near the end of his life were the presidency of the Far Eastern Association, succeeding James (later Lord) Bryce, and the vice-presidency of the Royal Historical Society and the London Library. He also received honorary degrees from the universities of Oxford, Cambridge, and Aberdeen.

He vehemently detested smoking and had a strong distaste for the blood sports that English gentlemen have passionately loved. His son Austin attests to his characteristic Victorian proclivities, especially the stern sense of moral rectitude that figured prominently in his literary judgments as well as in the conduct of his personal life. He had no regard for making money, ever willing to contribute his services, the only remuneration being his personal sense of satisfaction. The Positivist mottoes "Live for others" and "Live openly" consistently regulated his personal life and conduct.

As Walter E. Houghton in *The Victorian Frame of Mind, 1830-1870* (1957) writes, " 'The reconstruction of society on a scientific basis' became an assumption of the time." Faith in science became ecstatic. As Christopher Kent wonders in his *Brains and Numbers: Elitism, Comtism, and Democracy in Mid-Victorian England* (1978), what might Comte have achieved practically had he had a Frederick Engels (as did Karl Marx) "to improve his communications with the outside world–a Frederic Harrison perhaps"? In *European Positivism in the Nineteenth Century* (1963), W. M. Simon, noting the small membership of the English Positivist Society, thinks its considerable prestige was due primarily to such gifted leaders as John Stuart Mill (favorable to Comte for a while) and to such influential supporters as George Henry Lewes and George Eliot, Harriet Martineau (an early sympathizer whose translation of Comte affected the young Harrison considerably), and to Harrison himself and his many friends, such as Richard Congreve, Edward Spencer Beesly, and Dr. John Henry Bridges. Also, the eminent opponents of College Positivism, such as Mill (later), Herbert Spencer, Huxley, Ruskin, and Matthew Arnold, to name a few, ironically lent intellectual prestige to the movement. Christopher Kent quotes the *Spectator* as classing Harrison with Froude, Arnold, and Carlyle–"always read, and never followed."

It is, perhaps, one of the surprising paradoxes of the Victorian era that Harrison remained throughout his long career, even in the early 1920s, totally devoted and committed to the doctrines of Auguste Comte–never blindly or slavishly, but nevertheless faithfully–although it had long been evident that the movement had not taken hold. Ironically Harrison was a man of hard common sense, and nearly all his writings are models of clarity and cogency. As the venerable turn-of-the-century English critic George Saintsbury (who knew Harrison during the latter's last decade) writes in a 1923 *Fortnightly Review* piece, there was very little in literature that Harrison did not attempt with his "vigorous and correct style" and "his very considerable experience." Saintsbury continues that he "never saw anything of his that was not worth reading, however little I might agree with the sentiments and opinions expressed." And further: "I hardly know anything sounder than the first three sections of *The Choice of Books*...." Harrison was healthy, vigorous, and indefatigable during his adult life. Morton Luce, in a 1923 article in *Nineteenth Century and After*, asserts that Harrison wrote more articles and pamphlets than anyone else in his generation. He terms Harrison "an unofficial Prose Laureate of half a century. He is nearly the last of those great souls who were the glory of our Victorian literature."

While Harrison, the quintessential Victorian, was reading the proofs of his forthcoming *De Senectute*–appropriately concerned with old age–he died peacefully at the age of ninety-one, and his ashes were mingled with those of his beloved wife, Ethel, and placed in an urn that rests in the chapel of Wadham College, Oxford. Doubtless, he would be satisfied to merge with the perpetual flow of the tide of humanity into the future, confident that the moral and spiritual energies of the individual live more intensely after his corporeal life on this earth has ceased. For Harrison, one lives so long as humanity does. He believed that the results of a parent's efforts may become apparent long before the individual has reached the grave. What can life mean in some other world without those very relative conditions and relationships that give it moral meaning? For Harrison, subjective immortality is sufficient.

References:

Austin Harrison, *Frederic Harrison* (New York & London: Putnam's, 1927);

Harry R. Sullivan, *Frederic Harrison* (Boston: Twayne, 1983);

Martha S. Vogeler, *Frederic Harrison: The Vocation of a Positivist* (Oxford: Clarendon Press, 1984).

Papers:

Harrison's papers are at the British Library (Positivist Papers), the British Library of Political and Economic Science at the London School of Economics, the libraries of Cornell, Harvard, Yale, and the University of Texas at Austin, as well as at the Huntington Library, the Library of Congress, and the Musée d'Auguste Comte, Paris.

Gerard Manley Hopkins

(28 July 1844-8 June 1889)

John Ferns
McMaster University

See also the Hopkins entry in *DLB 35, Victorian Poets After 1850.*

BOOKS: *Poems of Gerard Manley Hopkins,* edited by Robert Bridges (London: Milford, 1918); enlarged, edited by Bridges and Charles Williams (London: Oxford University Press, 1930); enlarged again, edited by W. H. Gardner (London & New York: Oxford University Press, 1948); revised, edited by Gardner (London & New York: Oxford University Press, 1956); enlarged again, edited by Gardner and N. H. MacKenzie (London & New York: Oxford University Press, 1967); corrected, edited by Gardner and MacKenzie (London & New York: Oxford University Press, 1970);

The Notebooks and Papers of Gerard Manley Hopkins, edited by Humphry House (London & New York: Oxford University Press, 1937); enlarged as *The Journals and Papers of Gerard Manley Hopkins,* edited by House and Graham Storey (London & New York: Oxford University Press, 1959);

The Sermons and Devotional Writings of Gerard Manley Hopkins, edited by Christopher Devlin (London & New York: Oxford University Press, 1959).

While Gerard Manley Hopkins's importance as a Victorian poet is well established, his significance as a Victorian prose writer is not as fully recognized. This is, perhaps, because his prose did not appear in single works, like John Ruskin's *Modern Painters,* Matthew Arnold's *Culture and Anarchy,* or Walter Pater's *Studies in the History of the Renaissance,* published in his lifetime but is found in such varied forms as essays, notes, sermons, and letters which were not collected and published until well after his death. Nevertheless, Hopkins is demonstrably one of the great writers of Victorian prose just as he is one of the era's great poets. He deserves consideration alongside such

Gerard Manley Hopkins, 1863 photograph by Hills & Saunders (Photography Collection, Harry Ransom Humanities Research Center, University of Texas at Austin)

acknowledged masters of Victorian prose as Arnold, Ruskin, Thomas Carlyle, and John Stuart Mill. As a literary critic, for example, Hopkins is surely the most important and perceptive critic of English poetry between Arnold and T. S. Eliot and an important link in the critical tradition they represent. His achievement in prose is intimately related to his achievement in poetry. In fact, the two achievements are really one; in his prose as well as in his poetry there is the same "strain of address" (as Hopkins called it), the same enthusiasm, feeling, love, inspiration, and sincerity–a unity of purpose confirmed in his Catholic faith and reaching back from Aquinas to Aristotle through Christ, whom Hopkins regarded as the best judge of literary ventures as well as of human lives.

Hopkins was born at Stratford, Essex, on 28 July 1844 to Manley and Kate Smith Hopkins. He was the eldest of their eight children who survived childhood. Manley Hopkins was a prosperous marine insurance adjuster and a minor poet. Gerard attended Highgate Grammar School (1854-1862) where he became an excellent student of Greek and Latin. He won an Exhibition scholarship to Balliol College, Oxford, in 1863.

In July 1866 Hopkins decided to become a Roman Catholic. He was received into the Catholic church by John Henry Newman in October 1866. In 1867 he graduated with a double-first class degree in classics. The following year he decided to enter the Society of Jesus, and as a consequence of this decision he burned his early poetry, inadvertently overlooking some working drafts. His nine years of Jesuit training took place at various Jesuit houses throughout Britain, in particular Roehampton, Stonyhurst, and St. Beuno's. In 1877 Hopkins was ordained a priest and during the next seven years carried out pastoral duties that included preaching and teaching in London, Oxford, Bedford Leigh, Liverpool, Glasgow, and Stonyhurst. The poverty and distressing social conditions that he witnessed in these industrial towns caused him to express deep concern in his letters to Robert Bridges and others.

He was appointed professor of Greek at Royal University College, Dublin, in 1884, a position he held until his early death from typhoid fever on 8 June 1889. The poetry which he began to write again late in 1875 and which he shared only with his family and a few friends, such as Robert Bridges, Richard Watson Dixon, and Coventry Patmore, was eventually published in an edition prepared by Bridges in 1918, nearly thirty years after Hopkins's death. The earliest extant letters, diary entries, and notebooks date from his later school days and earliest undergraduate years at Oxford University. The volume *The Notebooks and Papers of Gerard Manley Hopkins* (1937), edited by Humphry House in the 1930s and enlarged with the help of Graham Storey as *The Journals and Papers of Gerard Manley Hopkins* (1959) in the 1950s, contains, as well as early dia-

ries and journals, undergraduate essays on a range of subjects. Besides book lists, the volume includes etymological notes and Lenten self-admonitions. Its focal point is an extended journal mainly of nature observations but also of spiritual experiences that Hopkins kept from 1866 to 1875.

The chief influence on the technique of Hopkins's detailed nature observations was likely the art critic John Ruskin, who in volume one of his *Modern Painters* (1843) advised that "Every landscape painter should know the specific characters of every object he has to represent, rock, flower, or cloud." Together with this was the classical-Arnoldian wish which Hopkins shared to represent the object "as in itself it really is." These notes, then, written during an extended period of self-elected poetic silence become, at times, almost prose poems in their impassioned contemplation of nature–for example, bluebells, described by Hopkins in May 1871: "This day and May 11 the bluebells in the little wood between the College and the highroad and in one of the Hurst Green cloughs. In the little wood/opposite the light/they stood in blackish spreads or sheddings like the spots on a snake. The heads are then like thongs and solemn in grain and grape-colour. But in the clough/through the light/they come in falls of sky-colour washing the brows and slacks of the ground with vein-blue, thickening at the double, vertical themselves and the young grass and brake fern combed vertical, but the brake stuck the upright of all this with light winged transomes. It was a lovely sight.–"

This dense and detailed prose–which it took the greater selectivity of the beautiful sonnets of six years later, such as "Pied Beauty" and "Hurrahing in Harvest," to turn into poetry–is a prose that hardly knows what prose is. It is prose that lacks the discipline of writing for an audience, other than oneself. Much later, Hopkins was to complain to his friend and fellow poet Coventry Patmore about Patmore's and John Henry Newman's prose. The comments that follow he would no doubt have been willing to apply to his own early prose. To Patmore in October 1887 he wrote a passage that gives a good sense of what Hopkins thought successful prose should be: "It is that when I read yr. prose and when I read Newman's and some other modern writers' the same impression is borne in on me: no matter how beautiful the thought, nor, taken singly, with what happiness expressed, you do not know what *writing prose* is. At bottom what you do and what

Cardinal Newman does is to think aloud, to think with pen to paper. In this process there are certain advantages; they may outweigh those of a perfect technic; but at any rate they exclude that; they exclude the belonging technic, the belonging rhetoric the own proper eloquence of written prose. Each thought is told off singly and there follows a pause and this breaks the continuity, the *contentio*, the strain of address, which writing should usually have."

Hopkins goes on to argue that the beauty and eloquence of good prose cannot come wholly from the thought expressed. He offers Edmund Burke as an example of a prose writer who colorlessly transmitted his thought in prose. However, because Burke was an orator his writing emerged from an oratorical tradition and thus possessed the "strain of address" that Hopkins believed necessary to successful prose. John Henry Newman, Hopkins believes, does not follow the common tradition of English prose. He seems, Hopkins suggests, to write from the assumption that Edward Gibbon was the last master of traditional English prose as well as from the point of view that, since Gibbon cannot be emulated, it is best to "begin all over again from the language of conversation, of common life." Hopkins, then, tells Patmore that he (Patmore) writes prose from a conviction that the style of prose must be different from the style of poetry. But, Hopkins argues, prose style must be a "positive thing and not the absence of verse forms; . . . pointedly expressed thoughts are single hits and give no continuity of style." In Hopkins's view, good prose must always possess "continuity of style" and "strain of address." What Hopkins had discovered between 1871, when he wrote the bluebell passage, and 1887 was that to make his prose successful he needed to write with an audience in mind. Perhaps the bluebell passage shows "strain of address" and "continuity of style" but it does not possess them to the degree that the letter to Patmore does. Nevertheless, the journal of 1866-1875 does contain examples of moving prose when, for instance, Hopkins expresses the simple certainty of his religious belief. If Augustan prose lost the ability to express religion, Hopkins marvelously recovers that capacity for Victorian prose in the following passage from his journal for 8 October 1874, which possesses both "strain of address" and "continuity of style" even though Hopkins continues, here, to serve as his own audience. He had visited St. Winefred's well at Holywell with his Jesuit colleague Barraud, and there is a significant

movement in the passage from natural observation to something approaching religious rapture: "Bright and beautiful day. Crests of snow could be seen on the mountains. Barraud and I walked over to Holywell and bathed at the well and returned very joyously. The sight of the water in the well as clear as glass, greenish like beryl or aquamarine, trembling at the surface with the force of the springs, and shaping out the five foils of the well quite drew and held my eyes to it. Within a month or six weeks from this (I think Fr di Pietro said) a young man from Liverpool, Arthur Kent (?), was cured of rupture in the water. The strong unfailing flow of the water and the chain of cures from year to year all these centuries took hold of my mind with wonder at the bounty of God in one of His saints, the sensible thing so naturally and gracefully uttering the spiritual reason of its being (which is all in true keeping with the story of St. Winefred's death and recovery) and the spring in place leading back the thoughts by its spring in time to its spring in eternity: even now the stress and buoyance and abundance of water is before my eyes."

The passage begins, like many of his earlier nature observations, in notes rather than with continuous prose: "Bright and beautiful day. Crests of snow could be seen on the mountains." The images are more sharply differentiated than are those in the bluebell passage, but essentially Hopkins uses the same method of recording observation. What distinguishes this passage from the earlier one and leads to increasing "strain of address" and "continuity of style" is the consideration of the miraculous cure. Hopkins's reflection, then, deepens and, as he would in the poetry he was shortly to recommence writing, he moves from a sense of the natural to a perception of the divine. "The Windhover" and "Hurrahing in Harvest" provide analogies from the poetry to what is happening here. The prose style in the journal passage is affected and changes from the fragmentariness of the nature observation of "Bright and beautiful day" to the continuity of the long, concluding, perfectly clear and moving sentence. What impresses is the wonder of Hopkins's simple faith, the realization that despite the fact that he lived in an age of doubt he believed in miracles. As F. R. Leavis observed in the second annual Hopkins Lecture, published by the Hopkins Society in 1971, "Hopkins, in a wholly unpejorative sense, was simple. There is nothing equivocal in his verse, and in the letters we see the simplicity as that of a man of high intelli-

I think you wd. find in the history
of art that licences and eccentricities are to found fully as often
in beginners as in those who have
established themselves and can afford
them; those in Milton, Turner,
and Beethoven are at the end,
those in Shakspere, Keats, Millais,
and Tennyson at the beginning.
I did send that piece first to Macmillan's wh. is always having
things of Miss Rossetti. Part of
it was written two years and a
half ago and though that does
not sound much one changes
very fast at my age and I shd.
write better now, I hope.
    Believe me yr. affectionate friend,
    Gerard M. Hopkins.
    I am going to Birmingham to the
Oratory tomorrow for the last week.
    Jan. 16, 1867. — Oak Hill,
Hampstead.
    I want to make some slight
corrections in Barnfloor and Wine-
press wh. I have not time to do now,
and I want you to get the book

From a January 1867 letter written by Hopkins to his Oxford friend Edward William Urquhart (Verlyn Klinkenborg, Herbert Cahoon, and Charles Ryskamp, British Literary Manuscripts, Series II, From 1800 to 1914, *1981). The year after Hopkins wrote this letter defending the "licences and eccentricities" evident in his early verse, he decided to enter the Society of Jesus and ceased writing poetry for seven years.*

gence, fine human perception, irresistible charm and complete integrity."

Once Hopkins was ordained a priest at St. Beuno's Seminary, North Wales, in the fall of 1877, he had to assume priestly duties, one of which was preaching. His preaching, in London, Oxford, and eventually in Bedford Leigh and Liverpool, as well as the poetry he had recommenced writing in 1875, helped to extend the flexibility and range of his developing prose style. We should note, in this connection, that the sprung rhythm which he introduced into his poetry was, in his own words, "the nearest to the rhythm of prose, that is the native and natural rhythm of speech, the least forced, the most rhetorical and emphatic of all possible rhythms, combining, as it seems to me, opposite and, one wd. have thought, incompatible excellences, markedness of rhythm–that is rhythm's self–and naturalness of expression." For surely in recovering the alliterative rhythms of medieval verse in such poems as *The Wreck of the Deutschland* (1876), Hopkins was also recovering the rhythms of early English prose, with its two-beat phrases held together by stress patterns within and between phrases, its dependence on rhythm more than syntax to determine meaning, and its stringing together of main clauses connected by *and* and *but*. Just as Hopkins's poetry was influenced by Old and Middle English alliterative verse, his prose was influenced by early English prose. Understanding Hopkins's relationship to medieval prose and verse traditions helps to lead us to the heart of Hopkins's literary achievement. He brought poetry closer to the rhythm of prose. What he failed to achieve in prose as a preacher, he succeeded in presenting as a poet in such works as *The Wreck of the Deutschland*. But as his poetry and prose matured they came together in such a manner that in his later years Hopkins expressed similar thoughts in similar ways in both his meditation notes and in his sonnets of desolation.

The Sermons and Devotional Writings of Gerard Manley Hopkins, unpublished until 1959, contains both his less successful sermons and his deeply moving meditations. Though Hopkins was not thought by his Jesuit superiors or, apparently, by his audience to be a successful preacher, his sermons were clearly very carefully prepared. They demonstrate all the expected oratorical features such as repetition and accumulation, and Hopkins obviously took great care in his sermons to suit his matter to the capacity of his hearers. His

painstaking preparation is perhaps clearest in his sermons delivered to his largely working-class parishioners at Bedford Leigh in Lancashire. The following passage from a sermon delivered on 23 November 1879 shows that by that date Hopkins was completely aware of the importance of "strain of address" and "continuity of style." His sermon oratory is also carefully shaped, though it is not Hopkins's best prose. He is speaking of Christ: "I leave it to you, brethren, then to picture him, in whom the fulness of the godhead dwelt bodily, in his bearing how majestic, how strong and yet how lovely and lissome in his limbs, in his look how earnest, grave but kind. In his Passion all this strength was spent, this lissomness crippled, this beauty wrecked, this majesty beaten down. But now it is more than all restored, and for myself I make no secret I look forward with eager desire to seeing the matchless beauty of Christ's body in the heavenly light. . . ."

Despite his sensitive handling of repetition and accumulation here, Hopkins would not be remembered as a prose writer for prose like this. Its alliteration is a little too self-conscious and the passage exudes, in places, an air of almost Pre-Raphaelite or decadent loveliness.

It is in the three published volumes of his letters–to Robert Bridges, to his former schoolmaster Richard Watson Dixon, and to others, including his parents and his Oxford friend Alexander Baillie–that Hopkins's claim to importance as a writer of Victorian prose lies. And the claim must be made in this way: Hopkins's prose is of interest because it is important literary criticism which also illuminates the creative practice of a major English poet. The letters, moreover, reveal a sense of the discovery and lively development of fresh thought.

One important aspect of Hopkins's contribution to literary criticism in the letters is his striking out against Tennyson's Parnassian style in the hope of restoring a language of inspiration to English poetry. Hopkins's essential critique of Tennyson occurs in an early letter to his friend Baillie, written in September 1864 when Hopkins was twenty years old. He announces somewhat melodramatically to his friend, "Do you know, a horrible thing has happened to me. I have begun to *doubt* Tennyson." The reason for doubt is that Tennyson writes too much "Parnassian," which Hopkins differentiates from the language of inspiration in the following way: "I think then the language of verse may be divided into three kinds. The first and highest is poetry proper, the language of inspiration. The word inspiration need cause no difficulty. I mean by it a mood of great, abnormal in fact, mental acuteness, either energetic or receptive, according as the thoughts which arise in it seem generated by a stress and action of the brain, or to strike into it unasked. . . . the poetry of inspiration can only be written in this mood of mind, even if it only last a minute, by poets themselves."

Hopkins's best prose is inspired writing as is his best poetry. The sense of intense concentration on the object that Hopkins himself speaks of as *contentio* or "strain of address" is perceptible in Hopkins's prose especially when he feels the force of divine inspiration, as he does in the 1874 journal account of the visit to Holywell and as he does in a later letter to Dixon discussing Wordsworth's Immortality Ode. Parnassian, in contrast to the language of inspiration, is the "second kind" of poetic language that Hopkins argues can "only be spoken by poets but it is not in the highest sense poetry. . . . It is spoken *on and from the level* of a poet's mind, not, as in the other case, when inspiration which is the gift of genius, raises him above himself." He goes on to offer an analysis of a passage from *Enoch Arden* to establish his point that Tennyson palls because he writes too much Parnassian. Hopkins's own return in his poetry from the mellifluous, Latinate diction of Tennyson to a more Germanic, Anglo-Saxon diction in the writing of *The Wreck of the Deutschland* involves an important shift in the language of English poetry which is also reflected in Hopkins's prose. When Hopkins counters Bridges's dislike of Dryden in a letter of November 1887, he describes Dryden's language in a way that characterizes his own poetry and prose, "he is the most masculine of our poets; his style and his rhythms lay the strongest stress of all our literature on the naked thew and sinew of the English language, the praise that with certain qualification one would give in Greek to Demosthenes, to be the greatest master of bare Greek. . . ."

Hopkins was remarkably faithful, throughout his life as a critic, to his early judgment of Tennyson. He simply came to believe more and more fully that inspiration, whether in poetry or prose, came from God. A later judgment of Tennyson, in a letter to Dixon written in February or March 1879, shows the continuity in Hopkins's critical thought and is, as well, a representative example of his mature critical prose. The following passage shows a comprehensive grasp of Tennyson's canon to 1879 and a maturity of critical judgment: "You call Tennyson 'a great outsider'; you mean, I think, to the soul of poetry. I feel what you mean, though it grieves me to hear him depreciated, as of late year has often been done. Come what may he will be one of our greatest poets. To me his poetry appears 'chryselephantine'; always of precious mental material and each verse a work of art, no botchy places, not only so but no half wrought or low-toned ones, no drab, no brown-holland; but the form, though fine, not the perfect artist's form, not equal to the material."

Hopkins goes on to argue that Tennyson is at his best when inspired by personal feeling as in *In Memoriam* which Hopkins considers a divine work. Also, he admires Tennyson the pure rhymer and simple imaginer of "The Lady of Shalott," "Sir Galahad," "The Dream of Fair Women," and "The Palace of Art." However, Hopkins thinks that the want of perfect form in Tennyson's imagination comes out in his longer works—*Idylls of the King*, for example, which Hopkins considers "unreal in motive and incorrect. He shd. have called them *Charades from the Middle Ages*. . . ." Galahad, in one of the later *Idylls*, Hopkins considers "a fantastic charade-playing trumpery Galahad, merely playing the fool over Christian heroism." Although Hopkins finds the individual scenes from the *Idylls* triumphs of language and "of bright picturesque," the overall effect is that of a charade and not as dramatically convincing as the plays on Drury Lane. Tennyson's opinions are neither original nor independent in Hopkins's view and often sink into vulgarity. "Locksley Hall," *Maud, Aylmer's Field*, and *The Princess* are "ungentlemanly rows," though Tennyson, Hopkins notes, lacks the real rakishness and rascality of Goethe or Burns. For Hopkins, Tennyson is at his worst in such rhetorical pieces as "The Lord of Burleigh" and "Lady Clare Vere de Vere." He concludes, however, by reaffirming his admiration for Tennyson—"a glorious poet and all he does is chryselephantine."

Hopkins's assessment of Tennyson is typical of his critical prose in that it is both generous and critical, his language is colloquial ("no botchy places . . . no drab, no brown-holland"), and he provides a criticism of Tennyson that the common reader can grasp. Even the dubious criticism of *Maud* and *The Princess* as "ungentlemanly rows" gains point when we understand that Hopkins was making a moral rather than a merely social judgment. Hopkins thought that the perfect gentleman was Christ. In an 1879 letter to Bridges he makes a further comment on Tenny-

Hopkins in 1888, when he was professor of Greek at Royal University College, Dublin

son and an account of truly gentlemanly qualities he believes that the best poetry should possess: "Tennyson: his gift of utterance is truly golden, but go further home and you come to thoughts commonplace and wanting in nobility (it seems hard to say it but I think you know what I mean)." Then, speaking of Bridges's poetry he observes, "Since I must not flatter or exaggerate I do not claim that you have such a volume of imagery as Tennyson, Swinburne, or Morris, though the feeling for beauty you have seems to me pure and exquisite; but in point of character, of sincerity or earnestness, of manliness, of tenderness, of humour, melancholy, human feeling" are those of true gentlemanliness that, for Hopkins, characterize the best literature.

Another excellent example of Hopkins's critical prose is found in his letter of 23 October 1886 to Dixon when he defends Wordsworth's 1807 Immortality Ode against Dixon's indifference to the poem. In the latter part of the letter, Hopkins speaks of Wordsworth and Plato: "human nature in these men saw something, got a shock; wavers in opinion, looking back, whether there was anything in it or no; but is in

a tremble ever since. Now what Wordsworthians mean is, what would seem to be the growing mind of the English speaking world and may perhaps come to be that of the world at large/is that in Wordsworth when he wrote that ode human nature got another of those shocks, and the tremble from it is spreading. This opinion I do strongly share; I am, ever since I knew the ode, in that tremble. You know what happened to crazy Blake, himself a most poetically electrical subject both active and passive, at his first hearing: when the reader came to 'The pansy at my feet' he fell into a hysterical excitement. Now commonsense forbid we should take on like these unstrung hysterical creatures: still it was proof of the power of the shock."

Hopkins continues by arguing that the ode is better than anything else by Wordsworth. Wordsworth was an imperfect artist capable of deep insight in some instances and little in others, but the subject matter of the ode is "of the highest, his insight was at its very deepest, and hence to my mind the extreme value of the poem." Wordsworth's poetic execution, in Hopkins's view, rises to the occasion of his subject. His rhymes are "musically interlaced," his rhythms successful. Wordsworth's diction throughout the ode Hopkins considers "charged and steeped in beauty and yearning." Hopkins's oratorical and rhetorical style in the letter and the strain of his address reach their height in his final comment: "For my part I shd. think St. George and St. Thomas Canterbury wore roses in heaven for England's sake on the day that ode, not without their intercession, was penned. . . ." Again we have the sense of an enthusiastic critical intelligence, alive in its admiration of Wordsworth's ode. As in his criticism of Tennyson, Hopkins shows the acute critic's capacity to go directly to the heart of his subject. Whereas Tennyson is suspect in his inability to sustain inspiration, Wordsworth provides an inspired insight into the nature of immortality. Such significant perceptions, written from moral conviction and expressed with point, place Hopkins in the English critical tradition that includes Johnson, Coleridge, Wordsworth, Arnold, and culminates in the literary criticism of T. S. Eliot and F. R. Leavis. In both the passages on Tennyson and Wordsworth, Hopkins's moral and religious convictions, his "strain of address," and his capacity to sustain an argument or perception, his "continuity of style," are evident as they are, too, throughout his nature, sermon, and meditation writing. In addition to the commentaries on Tennyson and Wordsworth, Hopkins, in his letters, offers equally perceptive critical discussions of Milton, Browning, Barnes, and others. We see throughout the letters the delicacy, the fineness of Hopkins's sensibility, the warmth of his friendship, and the strength of his moral intelligence.

Two further aspects of Hopkins's prose deserve to be considered. His seriousness is frequently leavened by a sense of humor which helps to give freshness and vitality to his writing. His April 1871 letter describing to his sister Kate his response to a smallpox vaccination is spontaneous and amusing: "We were all vaccinated the other day. The next day a young Portuguese came up to me and said 'Oh misther 'Opkins, do *you* feel the cows in *yewer* arm?' I told him I felt the horns coming through. I do I am sure. I cannot remember now whether one ought to say the calf of the arm or the calf of the leg. My shoulder is like a shoulder of beef. I dare not speak above a whisper for fear of bellowing—there now, I am going to say I am obliged to speak low for fear of lowing. I dream at night that I have only two of my legs in bed. I think there is a split coming in both my slippers. Yesterday I could not think why it was that I would wander about a wet grass-plot: I see now. I chew my pen a great deal. The long and short of it is that my left forequarter is swollen and painful (I meant to have written arm but I could not)." In a letter to Bridges of 2 August 1871 his awareness of prose style is revealed in amusing parodies of Carlyle, written in imitation of Carlyle's "most ineffacious-strenuous heaven-protestations, caterwaul, and Cassandra-wailings." Writing to Bridges from Ireland in August 1884, he records an amusing incident: "I must tell you a humourous touch of Irish Malvolio or Bully Bottom, so distinctively Irish that I cannot rank it: it amuses me in bed. A Tipperary lad, one of our people, lately from his noviceship, was at the wicket and another bowling to him. He thought there was no one within hearing, but from behind the wicket he was overheard after a good stroke to cry out 'Arrah, sweet myself!'" And in the same year, in a letter to his sister, he produces a marvelous parodic transcription of Irish speech: "And now, Miss Hopkins darlin yell chartably exkees me writin more in the rale Irish be raison I was never rared to ut and thats why I do be slow with my pinmanship, bad luck to ut (saving your respects), and for ivery word I delineate I disremember two, and thats how ut is with me."

For Hopkins, however, the other side of this humor is the sense of melancholy present in the early letters and ever increasing through the last five years of his life, which he spent as professor of Greek at what is now University College, Dublin. The following paragraph from his retreat notes written at St. Stanilaus' College, Beaumont, on 1 January 1889 is surely the seed for one of his last sonnets of desolation, "Thou Art Indeed Just Lord": "I was continuing this train of thought this evening when I began to enter on that course of loathing and hopelessness which I have so often felt before, which made me fear madness and led me to give up the practice of meditation except, as now, in retreat and here it is again. I could therefore do no more than repeat *Justus es, Domine, et rectum judicium tuum* and the like, and then being tired I nodded and woke with a start. What is my wretched life? Five wasted years almost have passed in Ireland. I am ashamed of the little I have done, of my waste of time, although my helplessness and weakness is such that I could scarcely do otherwise. And yet the Wise Man warns us against excusing ourselves in that fashion. I cannot then be excused; but what is life without aim, without spur, without help? All my undertakings miscarry: I am like a straining eunuch. I wish then for death: yet if I died now I should die imperfect, no master of myself, and that is the worst failure of all. O my God, look down on me." In this disturbing passage one perceives the anguish that animates Hopkins's need to write. His final auditor is God.

Hopkins's prose underwent considerable and rapid development during his short career. From brief nature observations he moved to religious meditations on the divine origins of nature. After his ordination, he turned his developing awareness of the possibilities of prose to the writing of sermons. Throughout his life he was a lively and, when his religious duties allowed, prolific letter writer. His letters, with their moral intelligence, critical estimates of English poetry, and sensitivity to the dynamism and to the spiritual and physical poverty of his times, establish him as an important writer of Victorian prose. As a literary critic he has been unduly neglected, though it is perhaps not surprising that Hopkins's prose has been slower to gain acceptance than his poetry. It did not begin to be published until nearly twenty years after the first collection of his poetry appeared. However, the prose has been used by most critics of Hopkins's poetry because in expressing the drama of his inner life it provides the best introduction we have to that poetry. W. H. Gardner, in his two-volume *Gerard Manley Hopkins (1844-1889)* (1944, 1949), and F. R. Leavis, in *The Common Pursuit* (1952), are two critics who have realized the importance of Hopkins's prose particularly in relation to his poetry. Nevertheless, full-length studies of Hopkins as a Victorian prose writer and literary critic remain to be written.

Letters:

The Letters of Gerard Manley Hopkins to Robert Bridges, edited by Claude Colleer Abbott (London: Oxford University Press, 1935; revised and enlarged, 1955);

The Correspondence of Gerard Manley Hopkins and Richard Watson Dixon, edited by Abbott (London: Oxford University Press, 1935; revised and enlarged, 1955);

Further Letters of Gerard Manley Hopkins, edited by Abbott (London: Oxford University Press, 1938; revised and enlarged, 1956).

Bibliography:

Tom Dunne, *Gerard Manley Hopkins, A Comprehensive Bibliography* (Oxford: Clarendon Press, 1969).

Biographies:

G. F. Lahey, *Gerard Manley Hopkins* (London: Oxford University Press, 1930);

Eleanor Ruggles, *Gerard Manley Hopkins: A Life* (New York: Norton, 1944);

Alfred Thomas, *Hopkins the Jesuit: The Years of Training* (London: Oxford University Press, 1969);

Paddy Kitchen, *Gerard Manley Hopkins* (New York: Atheneum, 1979).

References:

Bernard Bergonzi, *Gerard Manley Hopkins* (New York: Macmillan, 1977);

Dolph Anthony Bischoff, "Gerard Manley Hopkins as Literary Critic," Ph.D. dissertation, Yale University, 1952;

Jerome Bump, *Gerard Manley Hopkins* (Boston: G. K. Hall, 1982);

Donald Davie, "Hopkins as a Decadent Critic," in his *Purity of Diction in English Verse* (London: Chatto & Windus, 1952), pp. 163-182;

John Ferns, "Hopkins's Revolt Against Parnassian: The Poet As Critic," in *Vital Candle: Victorian and Modern Bearings in Gerard Manley Hopkins*, edited by John S. North and Mi-

chael D. Moore (Waterloo, Ontario: University of Waterloo Press, 1984), pp. 113-123;

W. H. Gardner, *Gerard Manley Hopkins (1844-1889): A Study of Poetic Idiosyncrasy in Relation to Poetic Tradition*, 2 volumes (London: Secker & Warburg, 1944, 1949);

Alan Heuser, *The Shaping Vision of Gerard Manley Hopkins* (London: Oxford University Press, 1958);

Wendell Stacy Johnson, *Gerard Manley Hopkins, the Poet as Victorian* (Ithaca: Cornell University Press, 1968);

F. R. Leavis, "The Letters of Gerard Manley Hopkins," in his *The Common Pursuit* (London: Chatto & Windus, 1952), pp. 59-72;

Norman MacKenzie, *A Reader's Guide to Gerard Manley Hopkins* (Ithaca: Cornell University Press, 1981);

Paul L. Mariani, *A Commentary on the Complete Poems of Gerard Manley Hopkins* (Ithaca: Cornell University Press, 1970);

J. Hillis Miller, "Gerard Manley Hopkins," in his *The Disappearance of God: Five Nineteenth-Century Writers* (Cambridge: Harvard University Press, 1963);

Myron Ochshorn, "Hopkins The Critic," *Yale Review*, 54 (March 1965): 346-367;

John Pick, *Gerard Manley Hopkins: Priest and Poet* (London: Oxford University Press, 1942);

W. W. Robson, *Hopkins and Literary Criticism: Fifth Annual Hopkins Lecture* (London: Hopkins Society, 1974);

Patricia Lyn Skarda, "The Music of His Mind: Gerard Manley Hopkins As Literary Critic and Theorist," Ph.D. dissertation, University of Texas at Austin, 1973;

Alison G. Sulloway, *Gerard Manley Hopkins and the Victorian Temper* (London: Routledge, 1972);

M. G. Lloyd Thomas, "Hopkins As Critic," *Essays and Studies*, 32 (1946): 61-73;

R. K. R. Thornton, ed., *All My Eyes See: The Visual World of Gerard Manley Hopkins* (Sunderland: Coelfrith Press, 1975);

Anne Treneer, "The Criticism of G. M. Hopkins," in *The Penguin New Writing, 40*, edited by John Lehmann (Harmondsworth: Penguin, 1950), pp. 98-115.

Papers:

The most extensive collections of Hopkins's papers are at the Bodleian Library and at Campion Hall, Oxford, and at the Harry Ransom Humanities Research Center, University of Texas at Austin.

Richard Holt Hutton

(2 June 1826-9 September 1897)

Monika Brown

Pembroke State University

BOOKS: *The Incarnation and Principles of Evidence. With a Letter to the Writer by the Reverend F. D. Maurice*, Tracts for Priests and People, no. 16 (London & Cambridge: Macmillan, 1862);

The Relative Value of Studies and Accomplishments in the Education of Women: A Lecture (London: Emily Faithfull, 1862);

Studies in Parliament: A Series of Sketches of Leading Politicians, Reprinted from the "Pall Mall Gazette" (London: Longmans, Green, Reader & Dyer, 1866);

Essays Theological and Literary, 2 volumes (London: Strahan, 1871; revised and enlarged, London: Daldy, Isbister, 1877);

Essays in Literary Criticism (Philadelphia: Coates, 1876);

Holiday Rambles in Ordinary Places, by a Wife with Her Husband Republished from the "Spectator," anonymous, by Hutton only (London: Daldy, Isbister, 1877);

Sir Walter Scott (London: Macmillan, 1878; New York: Harper, 1878);

Essays on Some of the Modern Guides of English Thought in Matters of Faith (London & New York: Macmillan, 1887);

Cardinal Newman (London: Methuen, 1890; Boston & New York: Houghton, Mifflin, 1890; revised and enlarged, London: Methuen, 1892; Boston: Houghton, Mifflin, 1894);

Criticisms on Contemporary Thought and Thinkers, Selected from the "Spectator," 2 volumes (London & New York: Macmillan, 1894);

Aspects of Religious and Scientific Thought, Selected from the "Spectator," edited by Elizabeth M. Roscoe (London & New York: Macmillan, 1899);

Brief Literary Criticisms, Selected from the "Spectator," edited by Roscoe (London & New York: Macmillan, 1906).

OTHER: *Poems and Essays by the Late William Caldwell Roscoe*, edited, with a memoir, by Hutton, 2 volumes (London: Chapman &

photograph by Frederick Hollyer

Hall, 1860);

"The Political Character of the Working Class," in *Essays on Reform* (London: Macmillan, 1867), pp. 27-44;

Literary Studies, by the Late Walter Bagehot, edited,

with a memoir, by Hutton, 2 volumes (London: Longmans, Green, 1879; London & New York: Longmans, Green, 1891);
Economic Studies, by the Late Walter Bagehot, edited by Hutton (London: Longmans, Green, 1880; London & New York: Longmans, Green, 1888);
Biographical Studies, by the Late Walter Bagehot, edited by Hutton (London: Longmans, Green, 1881; London & New York: Longmans, Green, 1895).

Richard Holt Hutton, who spoke to two generations of English readers with a calm, authoritative voice in the liberal London weekly the *Spectator,* was a philosophically educated mid-Victorian man of letters who committed his voluminous writings to two related intellectual objectives. The first, influential in his own day, was to shape religious beliefs by rational arguments for and against various doctrines and antireligious positions; the second, of greater interest to modern readers, was to interpret and evaluate a few major nineteenth-century writers according to his moral, spiritual, intellectual, and aesthetic standards. Hutton's two central themes dominate his short *Spectator* articles, many of which were later collected in books. The same concerns are more fully treated in two popular biographies, *Sir Walter Scott* (1878) and *Cardinal Newman* (1890), and in longer periodical essays, the best of them republished in the two-volume *Essays Theological and Literary* (1871) and in *Essays on Some of the Modern Guides of English Thought in Matters of Faith* (1887).

If Hutton's influence on his age and his significance today derive in part from his choice of themes, he is also important for certain qualities of mind rarely found together in a single mid-Victorian writer: an intellectual independence that kept him from accepting any creed or position uncritically, a fair-mindedness toward the ideas and goals of those who disagreed with him, a devotion to careful logical analysis, and a deep, if guarded, emotional involvement with his subjects. As a literary critic, he is also noteworthy not only as an appreciator of intellectual depths and subtleties often overlooked by others but also as a close reader of poetry, for meaning and aesthetic effect. His main defects are related to his strengths: his impartiality deterred him from making judgments about relative merit, and his analytical precision could lead to long, wordy, and overly complex sentences. These two tendencies earned him a reputation for dullness among

H. Brooke's wood engraving of the owner and political editor of the London weekly the Spectator. *Townsend hired Hutton in 1861.*

some readers, most notably Virginia Woolf, who mentioned Hutton in *The Common Reader* (1925). But if Hutton's writings have rarely inspired either enthusiasm or controversy, he enjoyed almost unrivaled respect and influence among his British contemporaries, and modern scholars of his work, aided by Robert H. Tener's comprehensive bibliographies (*Victorian Periodicals Newsletter,* 1972-1973), have come to appreciate his insights into nineteenth-century literature and religious thought.

Richard Holt Hutton was born in Leeds on 2 June 1826. His mother was Susannah Holt Hutton; his father, Joseph Hutton, the son of a Unitarian minister in Dublin, followed in his own father's footsteps, taking over a London parish when Richard, his third son, was about ten. Closed out of the most prestigious universities by his religious background, Richard Hutton attended University College in London, where he and the future economist and political writer Walter Bagehot began their lifelong personal and intellectual friendship. After receiving a B.A. in 1845, with awards in both mathematics and philosophy, Hutton studied philosophy in Germany, where he left a lasting impression on the famed historian Theodor Mommsen. Hutton next studied for the Unitarian ministry with James Martineau in Manchester, but he was never called to a parish. In 1851 he married Anne Mary Roscoe and became, at twenty-five, editor of the Unitarian weekly *Inquirer,* to which both he and Bagehot contributed. Hutton left the paper two years later and went to the West Indies for his health; within a year his young wife was dead of yellow fever. Back in England, his religious faith shaken, Hutton studied law, taught mathematics at Bedford College, London, and wrote for the Unitarian *Prospective Review.* In 1855 he and Bagehot became founding editors and contributors of the *National Review,* a Unitarian monthly financed by Lady Byron. Three years later Hutton married Eliza Roscoe, his first wife's cousin, and took on, until 1860, an additional editorial position with the *Economist.* The death of his brother-in-law prompted Hutton to prepare for publication *Poems and Essays by the Late William Caldwell Roscoe* (1860).

Some of Hutton's most important work can be found in periodical articles he wrote from 1847 to the early 1860s. So unbiased was the young Unitarian that when his best early writings were collected in *Essays Theological and Literary* (1871), they received their most favorable notice from the Roman Catholic *Dublin Review,* which praised Hutton's "spirit of deep earnestness" and "very rare power of according perfect appreciation even when he is without sympathy." In critical methods, as in attitude, the two volumes exhibited what would become Hutton's distinguishing qualities. The theological essays reflected the period's religious controversies and Hutton's own drift toward the Anglicanism of his friend Frederick Denison Maurice. In analyzing various current isms–atheism, "popular pantheism," Higher Criticism, Roman Catholicism, and High Church Anglicanism, among others–Hutton impartially presented attractive features but emphasized flaws in reasoning and in interpretation of human morality and spirituality. Atheism, for instance, Hutton considered incompatible with man's intuitive recognition of spirituality, moral obligations, and moral freedom. Only the Christianity of Maurice, because, in Hutton's words, it recognized "the sacramental power of common every-day duty" and suggested that we can know God "in a true scientific sense," was a suitable modern faith. By identifying a spiritual dimension to all human actions, Maurice's doctrine, as Hutton

understood it, "endeared the Church of England to many of us who find much in her to which we cannot assent." That even a modern Christianity requires rationally admitting that Jesus was indeed God made flesh, Hutton admitted in an 1862 essay on the Incarnation which implied that he was leaning toward such belief, abandoning Unitarianism.

Hutton's *National Review* articles on major literary figures, extended by short reviews of newer works by the same authors, form the core of the literary volume of the 1871 collection of his writings. "The delineation of human nature, as a whole, is the highest aim of literature," Hutton declared in the preface to his 1860 edition of Roscoe's work; therefore he wrote about authors, mostly poets, who treated great questions, and he identified in the life and works of each, often through effective use of comparisons and contrasts with other great writers, a unique understanding of modern man's moral and spiritual condition. Yet unlike many of his contemporaries he recognized that poetry also deserves aesthetic evaluation. His critical approach is already evident in an 1856 essay that theological writer Henry Drummond would later call "the best critical piece . . . written in this century," a review of *The Life and Works of Goethe* (1855) by George Henry Lewes. To Hutton, Goethe's power over readers derives from his "presence of mind [i.e., intellectual detachment] in combination with a keen knowledge of men," qualities in which he is rivaled only by Shakespeare. Hutton recognized that Goethe's verse, even in translation, shows lyric power and vivid realism, but he found fault with Goethe's fictional and dramatic characters who, reflecting their creator's own behavior, lack true moral sense. Of Goethe's vision of the condition of modern man, Hutton perceptively declared: "He knew all the symptoms of disease, a few alleviations, no remedies."

In the writings of Wordsworth, Shelley, Browning, Clough, George Eliot, and Hawthorne, Hutton similarly analyzed manifestations of intellect, emotion, insight into human experience, spirituality, moral vision, and stylistic effects. He admired in Wordsworth the capacity for forging "spiritual meditation" from a fusion of intellect and intense feeling; in Shelley he found a dominant emotion, "intellectual desire." Among the first in England to appreciate Browning's poetry, especially for its intellectual depth, and Hawthorne's fiction, for its moral analysis of abnormal but believable personalities, Hutton was particularly perceptive on the novels of George Eliot. In an essay he later included in a collection entitled *Essays on Some of the Modern Guides of English Thought in Matters of Faith* (1887), he demonstrated that from *Adam Bede* (1859) on, Eliot, by blending "very deep speculative power" and exceptional "realistic imagination," had transformed realistic characterization, especially in her "analysis of psychological problems" and insight into human motivation. His understanding of her work enabled him even to recognize, as the author herself acknowledged, "chief elements of my intention" in her historical novel *Romola* (1863), the most ambitious and least appreciated of her early writings. If Hutton's insights often sound familiar to the modern critic, this is partly because they were so exceptional in his own day.

Before the 1871 *Essays Theological and Literary* appeared, Hutton had embarked on his most important professional assignment, one which would take him away from the sustained critical writing at which he excelled. In 1861 Meredith Townsend, new owner and political editor of the London liberal weekly the *Spectator*, interviewed the young man from the *National Review* for the position of literary editor. Only after Hutton had left the room did Townsend decide, on an impulse, to hire him. Thus, at thirty-five, the serious-minded journalist gained access to what he would use effectively for the remaining thirty-six years of his life, an influential organ for his literary judgments and especially for his religious, scientific, and moral concerns. Besides contributing over 3,500 short pieces to the paper, Hutton as editor shaped the tone of many others. One man who wrote for the *Spectator* remembered him as "essentially chivalrous, truthful, and sympathetic," but also as a "headmaster" who exercised an "iron hand" in selecting articles. Though Hutton and Townsend were bold enough to print A. C. Swinburne's 1862 review of Charles Baudelaire's controversial *Les Fleurs du Mal*, and even to side with the North and against most of England during the American Civil War, their paper grew in prestige and circulation. Publisher Alexander Macmillan in 1865 called the *Spectator* "the ablest and most influential of the weeklies." Critic Edward Dowden subscribed because of its "over-ruling intellectual conscience" and its "understanding heart in politics, which one can feel apart from its opinions."

While at the *Spectator*, Hutton worked on until 1864 at the *National Review*, published longer articles in various journals, and produced

lectures and pamphlets. In some writings of the 1860s and after he explored new subjects, ranging from the unsuitability of the British university curriculum to the average woman to the pleasures of travel. As writer of lead articles for the *Spectator*, Hutton also became interested in politics. In his most valuable work on this topic, *Studies in Parliament* (1866), he applied his liberal opinions and moral and intellectual criteria to analyzing with more partiality than usual the personalities and actions of well-known leaders of his day. Admired by political novelist Anthony Trollope, these essays on figures like William Gladstone and Benjamin Disraeli were later cited more for their style than for depth of insight. At the time of the Second Reform Bill, Hutton produced an essay entitled "The Political Character of the Working Class" (1867), and he continued to write leads on current issues into the 1890s.

For Hutton's main concerns–literary criticism and theological and ethical judgments–his early *Spectator* years, up to the mid 1870s, were a middle period, during which he extended earlier subjects and approaches. His literary articles in the *Spectator* and elsewhere, some incorporated into the second, revised and enlarged edition of his *Essays Theological and Literary* (1877), followed the careers of two early favorites, Browning and George Eliot, and of two new interests, Tennyson and Arnold. Hutton admired Tennyson's poetry not only for its spiritual and intellectual depth, especially in characterization, but also for its realistic details and poetic "beauty, grace, and harmony of effect." And he could appreciate the poetry of Arnold, even as he deplored the poet's profound skepticism, because Arnold, in Hutton's words, captures vividly the "spiritual unrest" of his age, expresses a Wordsworthian faith in the healing powers of nature, and writes with great "beauty and force." As literary editor Hutton could have contributed to the *Spectator* reviews of other major authors of his time, but he remained loyal to a few writers, mostly poets, who shared his deep concern for the spiritual as well as the moral condition of modern man.

In his theological articles of this middle period Hutton still defended his own beliefs mainly by criticizing other creeds. Two of the three new theological pieces in the second edition of his collected essays revealed his deepening commitment to an Anglicanism that valued both reason and spirituality. One, a "Preface" dated 1876, summarizes twenty years' observations about Christianity: "Romanism" insists on an impossible notion of "infallible" human authority, High Church Anglicanism gives ritual priority over moral guidance, and the Higher Criticism of Renan is too eager to discredit miracles. To those who questioned Christian acceptance of miracles, Hutton responded: "there is quite as much superstition in disbelieving what there is good reason to believe." For him, especially in the other new article in the collection, "Christian Evidences," empirical evidence exists for many miracles, even for Christ's divinity.

Hutton in the last two decades of his life became a living legend, a stern, heavily bearded sage occupying the cramped *Spectator* quarters. His writings, influenced by changes in the literature and the intellectual climate of the later nineteenth century, followed some fresh directions. Because he found little of interest in new literature, Hutton wrote criticism, less successfully than before, about authors of the two previous generations. His *Sir Walter Scott* (1878), in John Morley's English Men of Letters series, was an abridgment of John Gibson Lockhart's *Memoirs of the Life of Sir Walter Scott* (1837-1838), to which Hutton added moral analysis of Scott's financial crises and critical chapters on poetry and the Waverly novels. Though this would become Hutton's most often republished book, his criticism of the British writer he ranked second to Shakespeare disappointed even contemporaries; his comments on Scott's romanticism, characters, and picturesque description could not compare with his observations about writers in whom he found deep moral and spiritual vision. Hutton's later literary reviews in the *Spectator*, usually reactions to comments by other critics, were remarkable only on occasion, as when he explained how Wordsworth differed from true mystics or how Dickens, for all his realistic detail, created only "ideal" characters. Though some of these articles were republished after his death in *Brief Literary Criticisms* (1906), Hutton's best criticism of these later years appeared in works whose purpose was more theological and moral than literary.

If the twenty years after 1875 were from Hutton's perspective as unremarkable in theology as in literature, they were a peak period for a kind of writing with profound implications for religious faith: popular accounts of scientific discoveries about evolution and human physiology. Hutton, along with the poet Tennyson and the scientist Thomas Henry Huxley, belonged to the Metaphysical Society, founded in 1869 to discuss such implications. He also served on a commis-

sion that helped restrict the use of vivisection in experiments. It is not surprising, then, that as of 1874 the *Spectator* rarely criticized Christian creeds. Instead, in articles that later appeared in Hutton's *Criticisms on Contemporary Thought and Thinkers* (1894) and in the posthumous *Aspects of Religious and Scientific Thought* (1899), Hutton analyzed arguments against the existence of God, by atheists and agnostics, as well as proposals for alternative "religions," non-Christian creeds, and ethical systems ranging from Auguste Comte's Positivism to W. K. Clifford's "cosmic emotion." Hutton responded with several recurring arguments: reason and scientific knowledge, which can promote skepticism, may instead strengthen religious faith; science alone cannot explain why laws govern the natural world or why "miracles" sometimes occur; science cannot account for "consciousness, or memory, or will," or moral behavior, and thus cannot suggest reliable ethical standards; and admiration for scientific laws will never satisfy man's spiritual longings. Hutton thus made an indirect case for a rational Christian faith, one that accepts scientific findings while also offering answers and guidance in areas closed to science. If the fair-minded Hutton often made too good a case for antireligious positions, his analyses of their fallacies and limitations helped sustain many readers in religious faith.

Though new scientific theories and research, in areas ranging from evolution to ant-colony behavior, only strengthened Hutton's belief in divine purpose, he could offer few alternatives to the scientific understanding of human nature. Citing a decline in "religious genius," he turned in the 1880s to studies of five older literary moralists. Reverting to the sympathetic critical approach of his early writings on literature, Hutton produced some of his best longer articles, the core of *Essays on Some of the Modern Guides of English Thought in Matters of Faith* (1887). For three of his "guides," he built upon earlier judgments. Mostly passing over purely literary qualities, he focused on Matthew Arnold's noble doubts and high ideals, on Frederick Denison Maurice's sanctification of religious action, and on George Eliot's insight into human motivation and regrettable religious skepticism. Of Eliot, he declared that Christian faith could have made her "one of the most effective intellects the world has ever seen," replacing the melancholy of her vision with "vivacity" and her doubts with "certainty and grandeur." Another guide, the recently deceased Carlyle, was perceptively criticized by Hutton for the "destructive" emphasis in his historical vision but admired for understanding mass social movements and creating characters symbolic of "an Infinite Mind at Work behind the Universe."

The other "modern guide" soon became the subject of Hutton's most ambitious work, the intellectual biography *Cardinal Newman* (1890), the first volume of the English Leaders of Religion series, edited by A. M. M. Stedman. Supplementing Newman's *Apologia pro Vita Sua* (1864), Hutton traced the churchman's early spiritual quest within the Anglican faith and only briefly summarized his Roman Catholic writings. Although Hutton had little sympathy with a creed that elevated dogma over human reason, he recognized that Newman's spiritual and intellectual temperament allowed him to find in Catholicism a peace which had evaded him when he wrote as a Tractarian attempting to reform the Church of England. Hutton highlighted two traits that English readers could admire: nobility of character, shown in a life exceptional "in unity of meaning and constancy of purpose," and literary genius, displayed especially in Newman's moving treatments of conversion, in the historical novel *Callista* (1856), and of Christian dying in the poem *The Dream of Gerontius* (1865). When *Cardinal Newman* appeared after a spate of one-sided responses to Newman's death in 1890, some reviewers hoped it would be "widely read," for Hutton illuminated Newman's intellect and spirituality while showing that his doctrines could provide only limited guidance to average people.

By 1890 Hutton had begun withdrawing from his duties at the *Spectator*. He died in 1897, a few months after his wife. Of his funeral, the *Academy* reported: "Round his grave were grouped Anglicans, Roman Catholics, Unitarians, in about equal numbers and in equal grief." It was a fitting tribute to a man whose religious writings had helped intelligent readers reconcile science and faith and had taught devout Anglicans to respect their notorious apostate Newman. The modern reader can find in these works an unbiased and perceptive survey, spanning fifty years, of Victorian intellectual dilemmas and controversies, as well as interesting material on still-unresolved theological issues. Hutton's formerly less-appreciated essays on major literary figures deserve a modern edition and further reading and study. Though the author of a 1986 book on Hutton's criticism, Malcolm Woodfield, goes so far as to elevate his writings above those of Mat-

thew Arnold, it is perhaps most valuable to look at Hutton as a precursor of the modern "specialist" critic, and of the critical movement associated with F. R. Leavis. In an age when most reviewers felt competent, week after week, to take on whatever new works came their way, Hutton preferred, as he explained in an 1876 preface to an American collection of his *Essays in Literary Criticism*, "soaking [himself] thoroughly with a few great writers," mostly nineteenth-century poets and moralists, with whom he felt spiritual and intellectual kinship. For these writers Richard Holt Hutton became the rare sensitive reader who understood and appreciated their efforts to give imaginative form to what he called, echoing Wordsworth, "the burden of the mystery" of a world becoming ever more and, at the same time, ever less intelligible to its inhabitants.

Bibliographies:
Robert H. Tener, "The Writings of Richard Holt Hutton: A Check-List of Identifications," *Victorian Periodicals Newsletter*, no. 17 (September 1972): i-xvi, 1-183;

Tener, "R. H. Hutton: Some Attributions," *Victorian Periodicals Newsletter*, no. 20 (June 1973): 14-31.

Biography:
Alfred John Church, "Richard Holt Hutton," in his *Memories of Men and Books* (London: Smith, Elder, 1908), pp. 202-220.

References:
Alan W. Brown, *The Metaphysical Society: Victorian Minds in Crisis, 1869-1880* (New York: Columbia University Press, 1947), pp. 318-336;

Robert A. Colby, " 'How It Strikes a Contemporary': The 'Spectator' as Critic," *Nineteenth-Century Fiction*, 11 (December 1956): 182-206;

Patrick J. Creevy, "Richard Holt Hutton on Matthew Arnold," *Victorian Poetry*, 16 (Spring-Summer 1978): 134-146;

John Gross, *The Rise and Fall of the Man of Letters* (London: Weidenfeld & Nicolson, 1969), pp. 81-83;

[John Hogben], *Richard Holt Hutton of "The Spectator": A Monograph* (Edinburgh: Oliver & Boyd, 1899);

Gaylord C. LeRoy, "Richard Holt Hutton," *PMLA*, 56 (September 1941): 809-840;

Harold Orel, *Victorian Literary Critics* (London: Macmillan, 1984), pp. 58-89;

Robert H. Tener, "The Importance of Being Hutton," *Dalhousie Review*, 44 (Winter 1964-1965): 418-427;

Tener, "R. H. Hutton's Editorial Career": "I. The *Inquirer*," *Victorian Periodicals Newsletter*, new series 7 (June 1974): 3-9; "II. The *Prospective* and *National* Reviews," *Victorian Periodicals Newsletter*, new series 7 (December 1974): 6-12; "III. The *Economist* and the *Spectator*," *Victorian Periodicals Newsletter*, new series 8 (March 1975): 6-16;

William Beach Thomas, *The Story of the Spectator, 1828-1928* (London: Methuen, 1928), pp. 55-80;

Wilfrid Ward, "Three Notable Editors: Delane, Hutton, Knowles," in his *Ten Personal Studies* (London: Longmans, Green, 1908), pp. 48-77;

Julia Wedgwood, "Richard Holt Hutton," *Contemporary Review*, 72 (October 1897): 457-469;

Malcolm Woodfield, *R. H. Hutton, Critic and Theologian: The Writings of R. H. Hutton on Newman, Arnold, Tennyson, Wordsworth, and George Eliot* (London: Oxford University, Clarendon Press, 1986).

Papers:
The London offices of the *Spectator* have Hutton's seven volumes of "Records of Articles" published in that periodical; these cover 1874-1877 and 1880-1895. None of Hutton's manuscripts survived a 1927 fire. A few letters remain in the papers of James Martineau (Manchester College), T. H. Huxley (Imperial College of Science and Technology, University of London), John Ludlow and James Fitzjames Stephen (Cambridge University Library), and William Gladstone (British Library), among others.

T. H. Huxley
(4 May 1825-29 June 1895)

Jerold J. Savory
Columbia College

SELECTED BOOKS: *On the Educational Value of the Natural History Sciences* (London: Van Voorst, 1854);

The Oceanic Hydrozoa: *A Description of the* Calycophoridae *and* Psysophoridae *Observed During the Voyage of H.M.S. "Rattlesnake," in the Years 1846-1850* (London: Printed for the Ray Society, 1859);

Evidence as to Man's Place in Nature (London & Edinburgh: Williams & Norgate, 1863; New York: Appleton, 1863);

Lectures on the Elements of Comparative Anatomy (London: Churchill, 1864);

Lessons in Elementary Physiology (London: Macmillan, 1866; London & New York: Macmillan, 1871);

Lay Sermons, Addresses and Reviews (London: Macmillan, 1870; New York: Appleton, 1870);

A Manual of the Anatomy of Vertebrated Animals (London: Churchill, 1871; New York: Appleton, 1872);

Critiques and Addresses (London: Macmillan, 1873; New York: Appleton, 1873);

A Course of Practical Instruction in Elementary Biology, by Huxley with the assistance of H. N. Martin (London: Macmillan, 1875);

The Evidence of the Miracle of Resurrection (London: Printed for the Metaphysical Society, 1876);

American Addresses, with a Lecture in the Study of Biology (London: Macmillan, 1877; New York: Appleton, 1877);

A Manual of the Anatomy of Invertebrated Animals (London: Churchill, 1877; New York: Appleton, 1878);

Physiography: An Introduction to the Study of Nature (London: Macmillan, 1877; New York: Appleton, 1882);

Hume (London: Macmillan, 1878);

Introductory [science primer] (London: Macmillan, 1880; New York: Appleton, 1882);

Science and Culture, and Other Essays (London: Macmillan, 1881; New York: Appleton, 1882);

An Introduction to the Study of Zoology, Illustrated by the Crayfish (New York: Appleton, 1884);

T. H. Huxley in 1857 (photograph by Maull and Polyblank)

The Advance of Science in the Last Half-Century (New York: Appleton, 1887);

Social Diseases and Worse Remedies (London: Macmillan, 1891);

Essays on Some Controverted Questions (London & New York: Macmillan, 1892; New York: Appleton, 1892);

Evolution and Ethics (London & New York: Macmillan, 1893);

Collected Essays, 9 volumes (London: Macmillan, 1893-1894; New York: Appleton, 1894);

The Scientific Memoirs of T. H. Huxley, 5 volumes, edited by Michael Foster and E. Ray Lankester (London: Macmillan/New York: Appleton, 1898-1903);

T. H. Huxley's Diary of the Voyage of H.M.S. Rattlesnake, edited by Julian Huxley (London: Chatto & Windus, 1935; Garden City: Doubleday, Doran, 1936).

OTHER: "On the Theory of the Vertebrate Skull," in *Proceedings of the Royal Society of London,* 9 (1859): 381-487;

"Autobiography," in *From Handel to Hallé: Biographical Sketches with Autobiographies of Professor Huxley and Professor Herkomer,* edited by Louis Engel (London: Sonnenschein, 1890).

"I will leave my mark somewhere, and it shall be clear and distinct," wrote Thomas Henry Huxley to his sister in 1850, shortly after the twenty-five-year-old scientist had returned from four years of travels as assistant surgeon on H.M.S. *Rattlesnake* in its mission of surveying the passage between the Great Barrier Reef and the Australian coast. A few years later, following the 1859 appearance of Charles Darwin's *On the Origin of Species,* Huxley's "mark" was made in his self-designated role as "Darwin's Bulldog," the foremost advocate of Darwinian evolution.

Tenacious and articulate, Huxley became the Victorian era's clear and distinct voice in the most fiercely debated issue of his generation. But his role as Darwin's spokesman should not eclipse his own contributions as a leading Victorian scientist, educator, and essayist with remarkable literary gifts for combining rationalism and imagination. In fact, so clearly and forcefully did Huxley make his mark as a man of letters that many twentieth-century critics see him more in this capacity than in his role as a scientist. Some have noted the poetic qualities of his prose style, comparing some of his rhetorical methods to those of his contemporary Matthew Arnold.

By the time of the popular emergence of Darwinism in the 1860s, Huxley had already established his reputation as a scientist. He was born at Ealing, Middlesex, near London, on 4 May 1825, the seventh child of George Huxley, a rural schoolmaster from whom he inherited artistic ability, "a hot temper, and that amount of tenacity of purpose which unfriendly observers sometimes call obstinacy," and Rachel Withers Huxley, whom he credits in his 1890 "Autobiography" for giving him his physical appearance and his quick-witted mental ability. Recalling a childhood game of "preaching to my mother's maids in the kitchen" to imitate the parish vicar, he also notes that his name, Thomas, appropriately linked him with the biblical doubter, the "Apostle with whom I have always felt most sympathy." Huxley's early education was primarily at home through independent reading, and by age sixteen, when he began medical studies under a Dr. Chandler at Rotherhithe, he had mastered German, French, and Italian and had read Charles Lyell's *Principles of Geology* (1830-1833), William Hamilton on logic, and much of Thomas Carlyle, whose influence upon him was considerable.

After further studies with his physician

brother-in-law J. G. Scott and as a free scholar at Charing Cross Hospital, Huxley received top honors in chemistry, anatomy, and physiology and took his medical degree from the University of London in 1845, having published his first article–the identification of a structure in the human hair membrane, still known as Huxley's layer. On 3 December 1846 he set sail on H.M.S. *Rattlesnake*. In spite of inadequate books and tools to aid him, his travels allowed extensive research on marine animals. Huxley filled his notebooks with scientific data, and in Sydney he fell in love with an Australian, Miss Henrietta Heathorn, to whom he became engaged. By the time of their 1855 marriage, Huxley had become a Fellow of the Royal Society (5 June 1851), had fought despondency over his mother's death by occupying himself with his research, and had established his reputation as a formidable scientific investigator through regular contributions to the *Westminster Review* on contemporary science.

In 1854, when he was appointed lecturer in natural history at the Royal School of Mines, and in 1855, when he became naturalist to the geological survey investigating the English coast, Huxley's substantial salaries were supplemented by his writing of commissioned articles and textbooks on anatomy. Financially established for his marriage to Henrietta Heathorn, he continued his writing and lecturing. In 1862 he delivered a series of lectures on Darwin's theories to an audience of workingmen at the Royal School of Mines. The lectures were taken down in shorthand notes by an observer who identified himself as Mr. Hardwicke, published them as *On Our Knowledge of the Causes of the Phenomena of Organic Nature* (1862), and received both publisher's and author's profits. They were so popular that Huxley included them in the second volume of his *Collected Essays*, leaving them unedited from Mr. Hardwicke's published notes.

In 1859, following the birth of his first son and after recovering from illness which took him to Switzerland where his studies of glaciers led to further honors and publications, Huxley finally saw the publication of *The Oceanic* Hydrozoa, a description of his observations during the *Rattlesnake* voyage of earlier years. In that same year, in the *Proceedings of the Royal Society*, he published his 1858 Croonian Lecture, "On the Theory of the Vertebrate Skull," and was appointed secretary of the Geological Society. However, far more significant in terms of his long-term reputation were his 1859 and 1860 reviews of Darwin's *On the Origin of Species* in the London *Times* and *Westminster Review*. Darwin's book stated convictions toward which Huxley himself had been leaning, and it soon became a significant influence upon his career as a lecturer and writer.

Now launched into the turbulent waters of nineteenth-century controversy over Darwin's theory of evolution and its immediate implications for theology and education, as well as for science, Huxley embarked upon a wave that would carry him, as he put it, into the midst of "a gigantic movement greater than that which preceded and produced the Reformation." Even as early as 1856 he wrote out a plan for his life that proved strangely prophetic when he declared that he must ground himself in various branches of science in order to "seize the opportunities as they come, at the risk of the reputation for desultoriness. In 1860 I may fairly look forward to fifteen or twenty 'Meisterjahre,' and with the comprehensive views my training will have given me, I think it will be possible in that time to give a new and healthier direction to all Biological Science. To smite all humbugs, however big; to give a nobler tone to science; to set an example of abstinence from petty personal controversies, and of toleration for everything but lying; to be indifferent as to whether the work is recognized as mine or not, so long as it is done–are these my aims? 1860 will show."

Eighteen sixty and the following decades did, in fact, show his abilities as a preacher of the gospel of evolution with a credo based upon a view toward traditional religious belief that Huxley called "agnostic"–a term coined by him to describe his position against holders of orthodox faith, including such challengers as Bishop Wilberforce and Prime Minister Gladstone. With John Henry Newman, who had been a pupil of his father at Ealing, Huxley shared a skepticism that cleared the way for truth in spite of consequences. However opposite these two may have been in spirit, their methods and goals were remarkably alike. Both were solidly ethical in their quests for human dignity and happiness; both maintained strong personal, intellectual integrity in the presence of indignant opponents; and both were fluent defenders of their respective faiths, Huxley's based upon his conviction "that a deep sense of religion was compatible with the entire absence of theology."

In 1863 Huxley drew upon his increasing skill and popularity as a lecturer to working men on scientific discoveries and produced his first full-

An Encounter with the Natives of Redscar Bay, *drawing by Huxley included in John Macgillivray's* Narrative of the Voyage of H.M.S. Rattlesnake *(1854). From 1846 to 1850 Huxley served as assistant surgeon aboard the* Rattlesnake *on its mission to survey the passage between Australia and the Great Barrier Reef.*

length book, *Evidence as to Man's Place in Nature*, a pioneering work combining comparative anatomy, embryology, and palaeontology to demonstrate man's kinship with lower animals, especially apes. An extension of Darwin's ideas written in remarkably simple layman's language, *Evidence as to Man's Place in Nature* gave birth to the modern science of anthropology and increased in popularity because of the sensation created when, in 1861, London crowds saw their first gorillas. Huxley's point, however, was not to degrade man through demonstrating his animality; rather, it was to laud his remarkable development from such low origins, using his capacity for articulate speech to control instincts for moral and cultural achievements as a civilized being.

Evidence as to Man's Place in Nature was, in many ways, a culmination of the various interests that had claimed Huxley's attention from the time of his return from the *Rattlesnake* voyage, and it served as a fitting prologue to the themes and qualities of style that would characterize his

"mark" in the decades that followed. In addition to making a substantial contribution to science, it was also a vehicle for his mission as the prophetic voice of Darwinism; a work demonstrating his artistry as a writer using his language with dramatic simplicity; a challenging "lay sermon" on the unity of nature beneath its bewildering diversity and complexity; an educator's plea for recognition of the place of science in man's cultural advancement, and a rigorous statement of one who routinely tested his insights and ideas in the intellectually exciting atmosphere of lecture halls and public platforms before putting them into print.

In the decade following the publication of *Evidence as to Man's Place in Nature*, Huxley's increasing popularity as a lecturer, educator, and public advocate for the emerging new science led to his winning numerous offices and honors and to the writing of several essays that continue to keep his name among those of Newman, Mill, and Arnold in Victorian literary anthologies. One of his most significant achievements in 1864 was his helping to organize with eight fellow scientists, including

John Tyndall, Joseph Hooker, and Herbert Spencer, a dinner group known as the X Club. For nearly thirty years the group of nine gathered before each meeting of the Royal Society to discuss and plan the politics for the advancement of English science. Known as the "inner cabinet of science," they virtually shaped the direction of scientific affairs in mid-Victorian England and insured continuing contact among eminent researchers and educators.

Huxley's strong impact upon English education and his effective leadership among his fellow scientists were recognized throughout his career. His most recent biographer, Cyril Bibby, summarizes highlights of his honors and offices. "His honorary degrees included a D.C.L. from Oxford, LL.D.s from Cambridge and Edinburgh and Dublin, a Ph.D. from Breslau and M.D.s from Bologna and Erlangen and Würzburg. He became Croonian Lecturer at the Royal Society, Fullerian Lecturer at the Royal Institution and Hunterian Professor at the Royal College of Surgeons. Over many years he was Examiner in Physiology and in Comparative Anatomy to the University of London; he turned down invitations to a Professorship at Edinburgh and to both a Chair and a Mastership at Oxford; he rejected a most flattering and lucrative offer from Harvard. At various stages of his career he was Governor of Eton, of University College in London, of Owens College in Manchester; he became Crown Senator of the University of London and Rector of Aberdeen; he was an Elector to the Cambridge Chairs of Anatomy, Physiology, and Zoology and Comparative Anatomy."

In addition to his salaried appointments as inspector of salmon fisheries and as dean of the Royal College of Science, Huxley was also a fellow of the Royal Society, the Linnean Society, the Zoological Society, and the Royal College of Surgeons, as well as an honorary member or fellow of a dozen or more other scientific societies of the period. At various times he was president of the Royal Society, the office that he himself ranked as his highest honor, of the Geological Society, the Palaeontographical Society, the Ethnological Society, and the British Association. He was elected to London's first school board and served as a trustee of the British Museum, received the distinguished Copley and Darwin medals, and started a science column in the *Saturday Review* which gave rise to two influential journals, the *Natural History Review* and *Nature*.

In the midst of rapidly increasing professional responsibilities, including ongoing research and writing of textbooks, he prepared and gave three lectures in 1868 in which he related new scientific theories to conduct and culture in the modern world. These were his much-quoted "On a Piece of Chalk," "On the Physical Basis of Life," and "A Liberal Education and Where to Find It," the selections most frequently representing him in twentieth-century literary anthologies. "On a Piece of Chalk," addressed to the working men of Norwich, demonstrates Huxley's skill in communicating scientific theories to laymen by beginning with the local and familiar and moving inductively into the more remote vistas of geological discovery. As on other occasions he used such objects and substances as lobsters, mud, coal, and yeast as dramatic symbols to draw listeners into what James G. Paradis, in his 1978 book, calls the "Huxley Theater," so in this instance he begins with a piece of lecturer's chalk from the English chalk beds beneath their city to capture the attention of the men of Norwich. He explains how these beds have been formed by the skeletons of marine creatures, thus becoming the sea-bottom depository for geological fossil evidence of a vast drama of biological evolution that features primeval sea monsters and other creatures slowly evolving from them to inhabit sea and land. "A great chapter of the history of the world is written in the chalk," says Huxley, and "the chalk is vastly older than Adam himself." Stopping short of applying the evolutionary thesis to man, he concludes with crocodiles. "Either each species of crocodile has been specially created, or it has arisen out of some pre-existing form by the operation of natural causes. Choose your hypothesis; I have chosen mine." However, he adds, "If one species has come into existence by the operation of natural causes, it seems folly to deny that all may have arisen in the same way." The lecture was published in an 1868 issue of *Macmillan's Magazine*.

If Huxley's audiences were fascinated by his piece of chalk, they were electrified by his bold assertion that all life, from the amoeba to man, shares a common single substance–protoplasm. His lecture "On the Physical Basis of Life," given before an Edinburgh audience at the heart of Scotch Presbyterianism, flatly rejects all theories of vitalism and spontaneity by declaring that all life forces are determined by chemical ones; a combination of elements produces protoplasm, the physical basis for life, and the mind itself is but "the result of molecular forces." Although he leaves the door open to ethical responsibility by declaring that apparent natural law is only a probability and that matter is unknown, subject to the skeptic's questioning, the press immediately accused Huxley of advocating a gross materialism. When the lecture was published as an article in an 1868 number of the *Fortnightly Review,* the editor John Morley said that few periodical articles in the past generation had "excited so profound a sensation as Huxley's memorable paper." Huxley himself said that the essay "was intended to contain a plain and untechnical statement of one of the great tendencies of modern biological thought, accompanied by a protest, from the philosophical side, against what is commonly called Materialism." Although he denied being a materialist and said that he used materialistic terminology only as a tool to express scientific ideas, Huxley faced criticism with an almost evangelical zeal to proclaim his gospel of science in writings that followed. "On the Physical Basis of Life" brought into focus his scientific philosophy, his agnostic method, and his passion for promoting science in the educational reform movement of his day.

A third lecture in 1868, "A Liberal Education and Where to Find It," was Huxley's inaugural address as principal of South London Working Men's College. It appeared later in *Macmillan's Magazine* and was republished in the Boston weekly *Every Saturday,* thus bringing the Huxley message to American readers. In this lecture he takes on the whole English educational system from primary schools through universities, charging that fashionable training in Latin and classical literature is useless if it fails to prepare students for playing the "mighty game" of life, an idea he extends in a typically concrete and dramatic metaphor, in this case a chess game. "The chess-board is the world, the pieces are the phenomena of the universe, the rules of the game are what we call the laws of Nature. The player on the other side is hidden from us. We know that his play is always fair, just, and patient. But we also know, to our cost, that he never overlooks a mistake, or makes the smallest allowance for ignorance. To the man who plays well, the highest stakes are paid, with that sort of overflowing generosity with which the strong shows delight in strength. And one who plays ill is checkmated—without haste, but without remorse." Playing the game requires instruction in the laws of nature and the laws by which men govern themselves, which are best cultivated by a liberal education that develops the whole person with a body

disciplined by will as a strong and efficient "mechanism" and a mind stored with nature's truths as "a clear, cold logic engine." Although he insists upon including science in the curriculum, he adds the necessity of studying ethics and aesthetics to produce the whole person who is "in harmony with Nature."

In 1870 Huxley's *Lay Sermons, Addresses and Reviews* appeared. In addition to his three popular 1868 lectures, the book contains several essays on education, including a brief piece, "Emancipation–Black and White," devoted primarily to the "woman question" which was just beginning to be raised among writers of the time. Huxley, a devoted husband of a bright and capable woman and the affectionate father of several daughters, bluntly disapproves of sentimental "woman-worship" and of the super-woman image like that promoted by John Stuart Mill, who would make of woman an intellectual giant. In spite of doubting whether women need education much beyond childhood, he nonetheless boldly declares that their education is essential to progress, an advanced idea for his time. Educational issues, especially ones involving the place of science, comprise most of *Lay Sermons, Addresses and Reviews.* These essays, plus other, later ones collected in *Science and Education* (1893, volume three of *Collected Essays*), show the scope of his interests. Although his main aim, as he described it, was to bring Cinderella Science to her rightful throne in the educational kingdom, he by no means ignores the necessity for others in her royal family. To the students and fellow scientists at the opening of the new medical school at Owens College in Manchester, he argues for a breadth of study to ensure "that the position of the arts faculty in this institution will never by a hairsbreadth or shadow be diminished," and in an 1874 address at Aberdeen he strongly advocates "Professors of the Fine Arts in every University." He admonishes school boards to provide useful physical training and education in practical economics to slum children and argues that their instruction in science should go hand in hand with instruction in literature and the arts as "civilising influences."

Although Huxley frequently locked horns with the orthodox religious establishment and was known as the "bishop eater" for his provocative and challenging attacks on defenders of biblical literalism, he also supported the reading of the Bible, both for its literary merits and grandeur and for its ethical content. In this he was not far from his friend Matthew Arnold, in spite of their argument over the issue of humanistic education in England. "Science and Culture," an address that Huxley used as the title piece of his 1881 collection, asserts that a strictly scientific education is at least as liberal and certainly more useful than one devoted only to ancient literature in dead languages and stimulated Arnold's response in "Literature and Science" (*Nineteenth Century,* August 1882) with its plea for a more balanced view and its argument that man's instincts for conduct and beauty will always require humane letters. Huxley, in "On Science and Art in Education," an address given earlier in 1882 and published in *Nature* the following year, seems to have anticipated Arnold's criticism by conceding the need for literature and arts in education and life. In spite of the fundamental differences between these two friends, one with the instincts of the poet and the other with the instincts of a scientist and utilitarian, they shared a passion for educational reform, Arnold stressing the need for self-knowledge and Huxley declaring the need for knowledge of the world and nature. At any rate, their exchange, partly to clarify misunderstanding and emphases, led to a series of Victorian England's most articulate essays on education and, eventually, to a revolution in curriculum.

During the 1870s Huxley continued his writing on educational reform, his active participation in political controversies, his growing interest in philosophy, and his own research as a scientist. Throughout his career, he contributed substantially to facilitating the kind of scientific education he espoused through the publication of textbooks, such as his *Manual of the Anatomy of Vertebrated Animals* (published in 1871 and remaining the standard text for over twenty-five years), *A Course of Practical Instruction in Elementary Biology* (prepared with the assistance of H. N. Martin, 1875), and *A Manual of the Anatomy of Invertebrated Animals* and *Physiography: An Introduction to the Study of Nature* (both published in 1877). While these textbooks may be less interesting to literary scholars than his books on education, culture, and philosophy, they are models of expository prose for would-be writers of scientific and technical reports, especially in their demonstration of the art of definition, comparison and contrast, process analysis, and cause and effect. In addition to his textbook and scientific-report writing, Huxley gave courses and laboratory demonstrations to science teachers, served on many public boards, and became so well known to the public that demands upon his time

as a speaker and lecturer left him frequently exhausted for his personal research and family life, both of which he valued highly.

Two books during the 1870s deserve special note. The first, *American Addresses* (1877), includes his "Address on University Education," delivered at the 1876 opening of the Johns Hopkins University, and three lectures on evolution, delivered in New York City. In the first he advocates balancing instruction and research in order to prepare graduates for productive careers and for expanding verifiable knowledge. The evolution lectures comprise an excellent summary of his defense of the Darwinian hypothesis in which he draws upon sandstone geological formations in Connecticut and at Niagara Falls, much as he had done in his lecture "On a Piece of Chalk," to illustrate the evolutionary viewpoint against the creedal dogmatism of Bible literalists who support the Pentateuch's Genesis account. Loyalty to truth, he insists, must come before loyalty to creed.

The second book, *Hume* (1878), was prepared in less than two months at the request of John Morley for his English Men of Letters series. Although the biographical section is sketchy and superficial, the remainder on Hume's ideas is excellent. Hume's empiricism, religion, determinism, and ethics are treated clearly and concisely with wit and eloquence. As William Irvine has suggested in *Apes, Angels and Victorians* (1956), the book "not only makes Hume clearer than Hume, but improves and corrects him in many important particulars."

During the 1880s, while fighting recurring problems of ill health that had caused collapse in 1872, Huxley continued an expanding round of lectures, meetings, committees, scientific and public business, and travel that led his friend and fellow evolutionist Herbert Spencer to describe him as "continually taking two irons out of the fire and putting three in." Huxley had justified his active role in government in an 1871 address, "Administrative Nihilism," which attacked middle-class laissez-faire liberals, especially John Stuart Mill, by affirming the necessity for a certain amount of government regulation in promoting the welfare of all citizens. Even an established church has an important role, provided it eliminates theology and concentrates upon "an ideal of true, just, and pure living." Thus Huxley was a political activist for social and educational change, a ready debater on whatever causes he saw as worthy, from vivisection to home rule. Little wonder that his health suffered; even during

From an 1895 letter written by Huxley to his friend and fellow scientist Joseph Hooker, reporting that "The Dutchmen seem to have turned up something like 'the missing link' in Java" (Leonard Huxley, The Life and Letters of Thomas Henry Huxley, *1900*)

periods of recovery, he found that he could not "be comfortable without the stimulus" of work and controversy.

One strong stay and strength during periods of his most hectic activity and chronic health problems, and indeed throughout his life, was his family. "Love opened up to me a view of the sanctity of human nature, and impressed me with a deep sense of responsibility," he wrote to Charles Kingsley in a letter describing the major influences upon his life and philosophy. Henrietta Huxley remained a stabilizing presence not only as wife and mother but also as a keen reader-critic of her husband's work; and his constant flow of letters to her and to his children reveal a father who was clearly and lovingly present in their lives, even when he was away from home. The deaths of two of his seven children (Noel as a small boy in 1860, and Marion in 1887) deepened even more his affection for the remaining five. His eldest son, Leonard, provided two biographies of his father that reflect a son's strong love and admiration. Through Leonard and his wife, Matthew Arnold's niece Julia Arnold, Huxley became the grandfather of the twentieth-century novelist Aldous Huxley and of the biologist-social critic Julian Huxley, both of whom have written about their grandfather and perpetuated his memory.

Charles Darwin's death in 1882 and the death in that same year of the promising young scientist Francis Balfour were "heavy blows" to Huxley because these two represented to him "the best of the old and the best of the new." Although his spirits revived with his election as president of the Royal Society in 1883 and his receiving the D.C.L. from Oxford in 1884, continuing illness forced his retirement from all official appointments in 1885. However, an article by William Ewart Gladstone in the November number of *Nineteenth Century* stirred him back into action. Gladstone's assertion that the Genesis creation narrative is backed by scientific evidence received Huxley's immediate response in "The Interpreters of Genesis and the Interpreters of Nature," demonstrating Gladstone's scientific errors and declaring that the gulf between theology and science is too great to be bridged easily by semantically manipulating the facts. The debate continued and spurred Huxley's zeal for examining the theological assumptions of his time, a topic that occupied most of his later writing.

In "The Evolution of Theology," published in *Nineteenth Century* and later included in volume four of *Collected Essays*, he brings together his arguments against Gladstone with a style that continues to spark interest even though the subject of a dated religious controversy would suggest otherwise. Like H. L. Mencken, who saw Huxley as a master stylist of English prose, Huxley brought wit, sparkling illustrations, and debunking sarcasm to an otherwise sober discussion of issues. In this lengthy essay he traces Judaism's growth from primitive animism to advanced ethics in terms of responses to natural stimuli, an approach not unlike Matthew Arnold's in *God and the Bible* (1875). Also, like Arnold, he asserts that religion is debased by dogma and ritual and elevated by new discoveries and insights. In Arnold's case, these included the perspectives of literary higher criticism; in Huxley's case, they were the results of the scientific spirit that purges religion of dogmatism in favor of pure ethics. Science, Huxley declares, has no quarrel with "genuine religion" which provides the awe necessary to morality. He follows up this point in "Science and Morals," an 1886 *Fortnightly Review* piece in *Collected Essays*, volume nine, refusing to let science take the blame for modern wickedness; morality has no necessary connection with religious belief, demonstrated by the fact that even ages of great faith had their "scum and dregs."

In 1889 Huxley responded to a request from his friend Louis Engel to contribute to *From Handel to Hallé* (1890), a collection of biographical sketches, and provided a brief "Autobiography" which modestly recounts a distinguished career dedicated to the furthering of science, the "New Reformation." Just how successful this New Reformation had been in Huxley's opinion is doubtful, given the increasing pessimism in his later writing, a quality noted by several modern critics, including James G. Paradis (*T. H. Huxley: Man's Place in Nature*, 1978), who finds that Huxley's "philosophical outlook underwent a gradual transition from youthful Romanticism, influenced by writers like Carlyle and Goethe, toward increasing determinism at mid-career, to his final and startling fin de siècle declaration, almost on his deathbed, that man's hope lay in his revolt against nature." Similarly, Albert Ashforth (*Thomas Henry Huxley*, 1969) concludes that Huxley's early optimism vanished as he saw that scientific discoveries were not providing a basis for a "new morality" to replace the old one that they helped erode.

Huxley continued his cultural and theological criticism in *Social Diseases and Worse Remedies*

(1891) and *Essays on Some Controverted Questions* (1892), republished in 1893 in volume five of *Collected Essays, Science and Christian Tradition.* The 1893 volume is the best source for his series of essays on agnosticism. A prologue summarizes his view of the warfare of science and religion and declares that progress is achieved by the victory of naturalism over supernaturalism. Solar astronomy, embryology, and palaeontology have given unyielding facts of nature to support the great truth of evolution. The essays that follow are simply variations on this theme. His coined term *agnosticism* describes his philosophical position based upon the essence of science. Although he provides various definitions of the term, he argues that *agnostic* is not interchangeable with *infidel*, as Dr. Henry Wace had charged during Huxley's firey exchanges with Wace and W. C. Magee, bishop of Peterborough, in *Nineteenth Century.* Nor is it equated with *ignorance.* Charles Blinderman, in a 1957 article for *Scientific Monthly*, summarizes Huxley's idea of agnosticism well: "It was a confession of ignorance about things we do not, and perhaps cannot, know, things such as the essence of God or the immortal soul; but it was, on the other hand, a confession of faith about things we do know." And what we do know, according to Huxley, is "that there is order amidst the seeming confusion," a belief that Paradis finds more basic to the Huxlean vision than the idea of agnosticism with which Huxley has been identified. In his 1893 Romanes Lecture, published in *Evolution and Ethics* (volume nine of *Collected Essays*), Huxley contrasts the ceaseless cosmic process, the arena of change, suffering, and death, with the ethical process, the arena of social conscience which fosters a rational world of human cooperation and environmental improvement within a hostile and irrational universe. This position seems to move away considerably from his earlier one in *Evidence as to Man's Place in Nature* and has been a focal point for modern commentators on Huxley's development as a thinker and writer.

During 1893 and 1894 Huxley supervised the publication of his *Collected Essays,* preparing prefaces to each of the nine volumes. These prefaces deserve attention for their content and literary quality in that they provide summary reflections of the man upon his life and work, supplementing his brief "Autobiography," republished as the lead article in the first volume. In 1895, in the midst of what was to be his final crusade, this time for the reorganization of the University of London, the illness that had plagued him for many years finally conquered, and he died on 29 June 1895 at Eastbourne in the home to which he had retired a decade earlier. On 4 July he was buried at Finchley, without religious ceremony and next to his son, Noel, in a grave marked by an epitaph written by his wife:

> Be not afraid, ye waiting hearts that weep;
> For still He giveth His beloved sleep,
> And if an endless sleep He wills, so best.

A few years after his death, Michael Foster and E. Ray Lankester began editing his scientific memoirs, which were published in five volumes from 1898 to 1903. In 1900 his son Leonard combined letters and biographical commentary in his *Life and Letters of Thomas Henry Huxley.* His later intimate portrait of his father, *Thomas Henry Huxley: A Character Sketch* (1920; reprinted, 1969), provides a brief account of the man himself, especially his character, family ties, friendships, and table-talk humor. In 1935 Leonard's son Julian Huxley edited his grandfather's early diary which he kept during his *Rattlesnake* voyage. Other early biographies include *Thomas Henry Huxley* (1902) by Huxley's student and colleague Edward Clodd; J. R. Ainsworth Davis's study in the English Men of Science series (1907; reprinted, 1970); P. Chalmers Mitchell's *Huxley: A Sketch of His Life and Work* (1900); and Clarence Ayers's *Huxley* and Houston Peterson's *Huxley: Prophet of Science,* both appearing in 1932. Peterson's book is an interesting psychological interpretation of Huxley's aggressiveness as traced to a trauma from his first postmortem experience as a boy.

Later twentieth-century biographical studies, both books and essays, combine reviews of Huxley's life with commentaries on his writing, generally stressing the man as scientist, educator, philosopher, activist Darwinian, or literary stylist. John W. Bicknell provides a concise summary of Huxley's biographers and critics up to 1972 in his essay on Huxley in David J. DeLaura's *Victorian Prose: A Guide to Research* (1973), noting that "Huxley has suffered the fate of the accepted cultural hero by being oversimplified and, therefore, ignored, except by a few scholars." One of these is Cyril Bibby, whose well-documented books enable us to see Huxley's remarkable energy and vitality, his enormous contribution to the history of science, his literary genius, and, especially, his work as an educator. With strong concerns for both the ambitious middle-class and the working class and poor, Huxley, says Bibby, had a greater influence on the development of nineteenth-century university education than any other of his distinguished contemporaries, including John Henry Newman, Mark Pattison, and Benjamin Jowett. Another biographer-critic, William Irvine, stresses Huxley's educational contributions and provides enlightening scholarship on Huxley's relationship to Darwin and Darwinism. Irvine also adds to the growing appreciation for Huxley as a writer, as "a master of clear and compelling exposition, of cogent and resourceful argument, of satiric attack in controversy, of dramatic manoeuvre in propaganda."

Several studies, drawing on both published and unpublished material, provide fresh insights into Huxley's philosophy and the development of his ideas. Albert Ashforth's *Thomas Henry Huxley* (1969) shows Huxley's farsighted understanding of the impact of the new science upon traditional Western values concerning education, theology, philosophy, politics, morality, and art. Other critics have debated the inconsistencies and contradictions in Huxley's definitions of such terms as *agnosticism* and his shifting from an optimistic idealism to a darker "Calvinistic" pessimism and determinism. Loren Eiseley, in the introduction to a 1967 edition of Huxley's *On a Piece of Chalk*, was among the first to see "two faces" in Huxley—the sensitive, noble, sad young poet and the later polemic crusader. One of Huxley's most systematic and searching critics, Charles S. Blinderman, draws upon extensive work with many sources, including Warren R. Dawson's catalogue *The Huxley Papers* (1946), for several important articles beginning with an excellent 1957 biographical essay in *Scientific Monthly* which demonstrates Huxley's "catholicity of interests." His "T. H. Huxley: A Reevaluation of His Philosophy" (*Rationalist Annual*, 1966) paves the way for new approaches to Huxley's thought that move beyond earlier debates over whether his agnosticism was a cover for dogmatism or a term concealing real atheism and materialism. In Blinderman's view, Huxley's contradictions resulted not from masking but from genuine inner conflicts. There was a strain of idealism or nominalism in the midst of his materialism, foreshadowing Logical Positivism. Blinderman also discovers an intriguing connection between Darwinism and the Victorian Decadent movement in "Huxley, Pater, and Protoplasm" (*Journal of the History of Ideas*, 1982), in which he compares both the contents and ethical consequences of Darwinian materialism in Huxley's "On the

Huxley with his son Leonard and his grandson Julian (courtesy of Sir Julian Huxley)

Physical Basis of Life" and of Paterian aestheticism in Pater's "Conclusion" in *Studies in the History of the Renaissance* (1873) by examining the two essays in terms of their "articulation of the meaning of protoplasm."

Two books, Paradis's *T. H. Huxley: Man's Place in Nature* (1978) and Mario di Gregorio's *T. H. Huxley's Place in Natural Science* (1984), have special appeal to historians of science, but they also offer substantial discussions of Huxley's humanistic values, interdisciplinary ability, and intellectual development. Paradis, along with Bibby, gives an excellent discussion of the Huxley-Arnold controversy, documenting convincing evidence that renders impossible seeing the two in terms of simple opposition. Paradis also compares and contrasts Huxley and Carlyle in terms of their ideas of "Nature" and their concepts of the hero and antihero forged during a period when science was pointing to the interconnectedness of all existence and giving birth to "The New Victorian" in quest of "a great social and intellectual venture, a synthesis of knowledge" which attempted to comprehend "the enigma of the increasing intersections of cultural and natural history." Di Gregorio's book, while addressed primarily to science historians and scientists, will be helpful to literary scholars interested in the Darwin-Huxley relationship and to all seeking a substantial and up-to-date bibliography on Huxley and his critics.

Finally, one of the stimulating continuing debates concerns Huxley as a literary stylist, challenging William E. Buckler's view (in the introduction to his *Prose of the Victorian Period*, 1959) that while Huxley's style was richer in literary allusion and more lively than Mill's, both were really "journeymen" (howbeit of "a high order") as prose stylists. Earlier attempts by Huxley's grandson Aldous Huxley (*T. H. Huxley as a Man of Letters*, 1932, and "Thomas Henry Huxley as a Literary Man" in *The Olive Tree, and Other Essays*, 1936) note how Huxley used scientific and emotive statements to arouse aesthetic feelings and comments on several techniques, especially rhythm, iteration, and allusion, suggesting something of the poet in him. This idea has been picked up by several more recent critics, including Ashforth, Bibby, Blinderman, and J. H. Gardner. Gardner's "A Huxley Essay as 'Poem'" (*Victorian Studies*, 1970) is a provocative reading of "On the Physical Basis of Life" as poetry, rather than as rhetoric. The most penetrating analyses of Huxley's prose style, however, have been by Charles Blinderman, who demonstrates that Huxley used rhetoric effectively, even as he "fulminated" against it as "that pestilent cosmetic." In two 1962 essays, "T. H. Huxley's Theory of Aesthetics: Unity in Diversity" and "Semantic Aspects of T. H. Huxley's Literary Style," Blinderman draws upon Huxley's unpublished papers to show that his love of form shapes his method of exposition, which "was simply the method of anatomy." Huxley's papers reveal a theory of art that sees both scientists and artists as, in Coleridge's terms, "tamers of chaos." From his "taming" arsenal, Huxley skillfully uses rhetorical questions, hyphenated terms, rhythm, parallelism, antithesis, alliterative statement, hyperbole, personification, and eclectic allusions drawn from Eastern and Western literature, religion, art, music, history, and philosophy. Blinderman concludes that "the tension developed between his desire as a scientist to be exact and cold and his need as a polemical writer to be persuasive and at times hot, resulted in prose which has outlasted not only his scientific memoirs but also the literary remains of most of his contemporaries. It is Huxley's trial in achieving a balance between clarity and effectiveness that makes him a profitable study for the popularizer of science, the student of semantics, the lit-

erary man, anyone interested in the processes of communication."

As a pioneering scientist and educator, as an articulate interpreter of the intellectual forces that stirred his era and shaped the thinking of following generations, and as a Victorian prose writer increasingly recognized for his genuine artistry, Thomas Henry Huxley clearly has made his mark.

Letters:

Thomas Henry Huxley: List of His Correspondence with Miss Henrietta Anne Heathorn, Later Mrs. Huxley, 1847-54, edited by Jeanne Pingree (London: Imperial College of Science and Technology, 1969).

Bibliographies:

Warren R. Dawson, *The Huxley Papers: A Descriptive Catalogue of the Correspondence, Manuscripts and Miscellaneous Papers of the Rt. Hon. Thomas Henry Huxley* (London: Published for the Imperial College of Science and Technology by Macmillan, 1946);

Jeanne Pingree, *Thomas Henry Huxley: A List of His Scientific Notebooks, Drawings and Other Papers, Preserved in the College Library* (London: Imperial College of Science and Technology, 1968).

Biographies:

P. Chalmers Mitchell, *Huxley: A Sketch of His Life and Work* (New York & London: Putnam's, 1900);

Leonard Huxley, *The Life and Letters of Thomas Henry Huxley*, 2 volumes (London: Macmillan, 1900; New York: Appleton, 1900);

Edward Clodd, *Thomas Henry Huxley* (New York: Dodd, Mead, 1902);

J. R. Ainsworth Davis, *Thomas Henry Huxley* (New York: Dutton/London: Dent, 1907);

Leonard Huxley, *Thomas Henry Huxley: A Character Sketch* (London: Watts, 1920);

Clarence Ayers, *Huxley* (New York: Norton, 1932);

Houston Peterson, *Huxley: Prophet of Science* (New York & London: Longmans, Green, 1932);

William Irvine, *Apes, Angels and Victorians* (London: Weidenfeld & Nicolson, 1956);

Cyril Bibby, *T. H. Huxley: Scientist, Humanist and Educator* (London: Watts, 1959);

Irvine, *Thomas Henry Huxley* (New York & London: Longmans, Green, 1960);

Bibby, *Scientist Extraordinary: The Life and Scientific Writings of Thomas Henry Huxley, 1825-95*

(New York & Oxford: Pergamon, 1972).

References:

Albert Ashforth, *Thomas Henry Huxley* (New York: Twayne, 1969);

Cyril Bibby, ed., *The Essence of T. H. Huxley* (London: Macmillan/New York: St. Martin's, 1967);

Bibby, ed., *T. H. Huxley on Education: A Selection from His Writings* (Cambridge: University Press, 1971);

John W. Bicknell, "Thomas Henry Huxley," in *Victorian Prose: A Guide to Research,* edited by David J. DeLaura (New York: Modern Language Association, 1973);

Charles S. Blinderman, "Huxley, Pater, and Protoplasm," *Journal of the History of Ideas,* 43 (July-September 1982): 477-486;

Blinderman, "Semantic Aspects of T. H. Huxley's Literary Style," *Journal of Communication,* 12 (September 1962): 171-178;

Blinderman, "T. H. Huxley: A Re-evaluation of His Philosophy," *Rationalist Annual* (1966): 50-62;

Blinderman, "T. H. Huxley's Theory of Aesthetics: Unity in Diversity," *Journal of Aesthetics and Art Criticism,* 21 (Fall 1962): 49-55;

Blinderman, "Thomas Henry Huxley," *Scientific Monthly,* 84 (April 1957): 171-182;

Mario di Gregorio, *T. H. Huxley's Place in Natural Science* (New Haven & London: Yale University Press, 1984);

Loren Eiseley, Introduction to Huxley's *On a Piece of Chalk* (New York: Scribners, 1967);

Sydney Eisen, "Huxley and The Positivists," *Victorian Studies,* 7 (June 1964): 336-358;

J. H. Gardner, "A Huxley Essay as 'Poem,' " *Victorian Studies,* 14 (December 1970): 177-191;

Walter E. Houghton, "The Rhetoric of T. H. Huxley," *University of Toronto Quarterly,* 18 (January 1949): 159-175;

Aldous Huxley, *T. H. Huxley as a Man of Letters* (London: Macmillan, 1932);

Aldous Huxley, "Thomas Henry Huxley as a Literary Man," in his *The Olive Tree, and Other Essays* (London: Chatto & Windus, 1936);

Richard W. Noland, "T. H. Huxley on Culture," *Personalist,* 45 (January 1964): 94-111;

James G. Paradis, *T. H. Huxley: Man's Place in Nature* (Lincoln & London: University of Nebraska Press, 1978);

Oma Stanley, "T. H. Huxley's Treatment of Nature," *Journal of the History of Ideas,* 18 (January 1957): 120-127.

Papers:

The largest and most important collection of manuscript material (letters, essays, lectures, memoranda, and account books) is at the Haldane Library of the Imperial College of Science and Technology, University of London. A descriptive catalogue of this collection by Warren R. Dawson has been published as *The Huxley Papers* (1946), and Jeanne Pingree has prepared *Thomas Henry Huxley: A List of His Scientific Notebooks, Drawings and Other Papers* (1968).

Vernon Lee
(Violet Paget)
(14 October 1856-13 February 1935)

Debra Edelstein

BOOKS: *Studies of the Eighteenth Century in Italy* (London: Satchell, 1880; Chicago: McClurg, 1908);

Belcaro: Being Essays on Sundry Aesthetical Questions (London: Satchell, 1881);

Ottilie: An Eighteenth-Century Idyl (London: Unwin, 1883); republished with *The Prince of the Hundred Soups* (New York: Harper, 1886);

The Prince of the Hundred Soups: A Puppet-Show in Narrative (London: Unwin, 1883; New York: Lovell, 1886);

The Countess of Albany (London: Allen, 1884; Boston: Roberts Brothers, 1884);

Euphorion: Being Studies of the Antique and the Mediaeval in the Renaissance (2 volumes, London: Unwin, 1884; Boston: Roberts Brothers, 1884; revised, 1 volume, London: Unwin, 1885);

Miss Brown: A Novel (3 volumes, Edinburgh & London: Blackwood, 1884; 1 volume, New York: Harper, 1885);

A Phantom Lover: A Fantastic Story (Edinburgh: Blackwood, 1886; Boston: Roberts Brothers, 1886);

Baldwin: Being Dialogues on Views and Aspirations (London: Unwin, 1886; Boston: Roberts Brothers, 1886);

Juvenilia: Being a Second Series of Essays on Sundry Aesthetical Questions (2 volumes, London: Unwin, 1887; 1 volume, Boston: Roberts Brothers, 1887);

Hauntings: Fantastic Stories (London: Heinemann, 1890; New York: Lovell, 1890);

Vanitas. Polite Stories (London: Heinemann, 1892; New York: Lovell, Coryell, 1892; enlarged, London: Lane, Bodley Head/New York: Lane, 1911);

Althea: A Second Book of Dialogues on Aspirations and Duties (London: Osgood, McIlvaine, 1894);

Renaissance Fancies and Studies: A Sequel to "Euphorion" (London: Smith, Elder, 1895; New York: Putnam's/London: Smith, Elder,

1896);

Limbo and Other Essays (London: Richards, 1897; enlarged, London: Lane, Bodley Head/New York: Lane, 1908);

Genius Loci: Notes on Places (London: Richards, 1899; London: Lane, Bodley Head/New York: Lane, 1908);

The Child in the Vatican (Portland, Maine: Mosher, 1900);

Chapelmaster Kriesler: A Study of Musical Romanticists (Portland, Maine: Mosher, 1901);

In Umbria (Portland, Maine: Mosher, 1901);

Ariadne in Mantua: A Romance in Five Acts (Oxford: Blackwell, 1903; Portland, Maine: Mosher, 1906);

Penelope Brandling: A Tale of the Welsh Coast in the Eighteenth Century (London: Unwin, 1903);

Hortus Vitae: Essays on the Gardening of Life (London: Lane, Bodley Head/New York: Lane, 1903);

Pope Jacynth and Other Fantastic Tales (London: Richards, 1904; London: Lane, Bodley Head/New York: Lane, 1907);

The Enchanted Woods and Other Essays on the Genius of Places (London: Lane, Bodley Head/New York: Lane, 1905);

Sister Benvenuta and the Christ Child: An Eighteenth Century Legend (New York: Kennerley, 1905; London: Richards, 1906);

The Spirit of Rome: Leaves from a Diary (London: Lane, Bodley Head/New York: Lane, 1906);

The Sentimental Traveller: Notes on Places (London: Lane, Bodley Head/New York: Lane, 1908);

Gospels of Anarchy and Other Contemporary Studies (London & Leipzig: Unwin, 1908; New York: Brentano's/London: Unwin, 1909);

Laurus Nobilis: Chapters on Art and Life (London: Lane, Bodley Head/New York: Lane, 1909);

Beauty and Ugliness and Other Studies in Psychological Aesthetics, by Lee and Clementina Anstruther-Thomson (London: Lane, Bodley Head/New York: Lane, 1912);

Vital Lies: Studies of Some Varieties of Recent Obscurant-

Vernon Lee in academic dress. The portrait is by Lee's friend Mme. Berthe Noufflard (by permission of the Librarian, Library of Colby College, Waterville, Maine)

ism, 2 volumes (London: Lane, Bodley Head/
New York: Lane/Toronto: Bell & Cockburn,
1912);

The Beautiful: An Introduction to Psychological Aesthetics (Cambridge: Cambridge University Press,
1913; New York: Putnam's, 1913);

*The Tower of the Mirrors and Other Essays on the
Spirit of Places* (London: Lane, Bodley Head/
New York: Lane/Toronto: Bell & Cockburn,
1914);

Louis Norbert: A Two-Fold Romance (London: Lane,
Bodley Head/New York: Lane, 1914);

The Ballet of the Nations: A Present-day Morality (London: Chatto & Windus, 1915; New York:
Putnam's, 1915);

Peace with Honour: Controversial Notes on the Settlement (London: Union of Democratic Control, 1915);

Satan the Waster: A Philosophic War Trilogy (London: Lane, Bodley Head/New York: Lane,

1920);

*The Handling of Words and Other Studies in Literary
Psychology* (London: Lane, Bodley Head,
1923; New York: Dodd, Mead, 1923);

The Golden Keys and Other Essays on the Genius Loci
(London: Lane, Bodley Head, 1925; New
York: Dodd, Mead, 1925);

Proteus or the Future of Intelligence (London: Kegan
Paul, Trench, Trübner/New York: Dutton,
1925);

*The Poet's Eye. Notes on Some Differences between
Verse and Prose* (London: Leonard and Virginia Woolf at The Hogarth Press, 1926);

For Maurice: Five Unlikely Stories (London: Lane,
Bodley Head, 1927);

Music and its Lovers. An Empirical Study of Emotional and Imaginative Responses to Music (London: Allen & Unwin, 1932; New York:
Dutton, 1933).

OTHER: *Tuscan Fairy Tales, Taken Down from the
Mouths of the People*, edited anonymously by
Lee (London: Satchell, 1880);

Clementina Anstruther-Thomson, *Art and Man:
Essays and Fragments*, edited, with an introduction, by Lee (London: Lane, Bodley Head,
1924; New York: Dutton, 1924);

"J. S. S. In Memoriam," in *John Sargent*, by Evan
Charteris (London: Heinemann, 1927), pp.
233-255.

PERIODICAL PUBLICATIONS: "Les Aventures
d'une pièce de monnaie," *La Famille* (Lausanne), no. 10 (May 1870): 233-237; no. 12
(June 1870): 268-271; no. 14 (July 1870):
327-334;

"Vivisection: An Evolutionist to Evolutionists,"
Contemporary Review, 41 (May 1882): 788-811;

Review of *Florentine Painters of the Renaissance*, by
Bernard Berenson, *Mind*, new series 2
(1896): 270-272;

"Psychologie d'un écrivain sur l'art (observation
personnelle)," *Revue Philosophique*, 56 (September 1903): 225-254;

"Essais d'esthétique empirique: l'individu devant
l'oeuvre d'art," *Revue Philosophique*, 59
(January-February 1905): 43-60, 133-146.

"There is no doubt that Vernon Lee will be
read by her posterity," predicted Desmond
MacCarthy in 1931, "for her work is a rare combination of intellectual curiosity and imaginative sensibility." MacCarthy expressed the views of many
of Vernon Lee's contemporaries, who recognized

what Henry James called "her vigour and sweep of intellect" and who applauded her scholarly studies of eighteenth-century Italy and the Renaissance, her evocative sketches of places she loved, and her shrewd essays on stylistics and aesthetics. Like many authors of her era, she ventured into several genres: in addition to essays, she wrote historical and fantastic fiction, a play, a puppet show, and a hybrid work she called a "philosophic war trilogy." Yet the woman Walter Pater expected to stand "among the very few best critical writers of all time" receded into something of an intellectual curiosity after her death in 1935 and is today remembered primarily for her friendships with John Singer Sargent and Pater and for her feuds with Bernard Berenson and James.

It is an unjust fate for a writer dedicated from childhood to the intellectual life. Born Violet Paget at Château Saint-Léonard near Boulogne, Vernon Lee was reared to be another Mme de Staël and was, as a recent critic noted, "trained for art and literature as most girls of her generation were trained for marriage and domesticity." Under the direction of her mother, Matilda, and half brother, Eugene Lee-Hamilton, Paget endured what she called "educational tortures" inflicted by a series of governesses during her peripatetic childhood. Apparently for financial reasons, Henry Ferguson Paget moved his family every six months, mostly within Germany until 1866, when they began wintering in Italy. That first winter Paget met the Sargents, mother and son, who were to play an important role in her life. It was Mary Singer Sargent who persuaded the Pagets to winter in Rome the following year, and there the young girl had the epiphany that fired her imagination and changed her life.

In *Juvenilia* (1887) Vernon Lee recalled that at first she was "wild . . . to get away" from "that poor and ill-kept town" and was depressed by the antiquities and museums because "the galleries struck me as so many icy catacombs full of dead and petrified people." But the beauty of the Christmas ceremonies at St. Peter's wrought dramatic change: "From that moment . . . I was wild to be taken into those dark, damp little churches, resplendent with magic garlands and pyramids of lights, and full of the long, sweet, tearful, almost infantine notes of voices, whose strange sweetness seemed to cut into your soul, only to pour into the wound some mysterious narcotic balm. I was wild to be taken to those chilly galleries, where, while the icy water splashed in the

shells of the Tritons in the garden, the winter sunshine, white, cold, and brilliant, made the salt-like marble sparkle; and all those gods, all those goddesses, and nymphs, and heroes, all that nude and white and ice-cold world, seemed to seek me with their blank, white glance."

The child who had been locked in the schoolroom with Blair's *Rhetoric* and Buckle's *History of Civilization* and who with her family had moved all over Europe being "careful to see nothing on the way" found a new school for her imagination. With Mrs. Sargent as her guide, she explored the mysteries of the genius loci, the spirit of places, and developed the impressionistic appreciation of beauty that informs even her most cerebral writings.

The Roman winters enjoyed before the family finally settled in Florence in 1873 determined Paget's career. In 1868 she began her life as a writer by turning her interest in antique coins into a piece she called "Biographie d'une monnaie." When this history of a denarius made from a Macedonian helmet appeared as "Les Aventures d'une pièce de monnaie" in the Swiss publication *La Famille* in 1870, its author, cited only as Mlle V.P., was not yet fourteen. The work's chief interest is the way in which Paget uses the narrative frame to weave together lively portraits of the coin's owners and the history of Roman civilization from the time of Hadrian to her own day. A testament to her precocious erudition, this first publication is written in somewhat stilted French; with practice she would write more fluidly in French as well as in Italian, German, and English.

By 1870 Paget was also engaged in the research that would form the basis of her first book. She had been reading Charles Burney's *A General History of Music from the Earliest Ages to the Present Period* (1776-1789) and *Memoirs of the Life and Writings of the Abate Metastasio* (1796) and decided to write about the musical life of Italy in the eighteenth century. When she then discovered the Roman villa where the literary society Accademia degli Arcadi had met throughout that century, Paget found her cultural focus. Writing to a friend in 1873, she stated what would become her scholarly credo: "For any such work to be really interesting, its writer must not only have an unusual degree of knowledge on the precise subject of which he is treating, but also a large general view of all the subjects at all connected with it, for to hope to get at the real value of any particular branch of art seems to me preposterous without a more or less thorough acquaintance with aesthetics in general."

Equally preposterous, she came to feel, was a woman publishing such attempts at universal cultural history under her own name, for she was sure, as she wrote a friend in 1878, "that no one reads a woman's writing on art, history or aesthetics with anything but unmitigated contempt." Thus when her researches were published in *Fraser's Magazine* in 1878 and 1879, they were credited to Vernon Lee, the name Paget would use both professionally and personally for the rest of her life.

Those essays became the core of *Studies of the Eighteenth Century in Italy* (1880), the book that established Lee's reputation and gained her admis-

sion to the literary and artistic circles of London. Rather than mining the period for precursors of nineteenth-century social, political, and literary trends, Lee asked why Italian music and drama alone among European arts showed creative life in the eighteenth century. Answering that question entailed recreating the society in which the composers, singers, playwrights, and actors lived, and the book contains vivid descriptions of "drolly solemn pedants, dreaming of pastoral life and dinner-giving patrons," of "quaint little old-fashioned figures . . . fit for Hogarth or for Watteau." Lee renders cultural history through portraits of the people who lived it: she traces the fortunes of the Arcadian Academy through the intrigues and pettiness of its members, explains the

Inscription for Maurice Baring's copy of Lee's first book, Studies of the Eighteenth Century in Italy *(The Colbeck Collection, Special Collections Division, Library, University of British Columbia, Vancouver, B.C.)*

development of Italian music by reconstructing Burney's 1770 tour of Italy to gather material for his *History of Music*, and tells the history of Italian opera through the life of the poet and dramatist Metastasio. Three shorter pieces show how the decaying tradition of mask and pantomime received new life in Carlo Goldoni's realistic comedies and Count Carlo Gozzi's Venetian fairy comedies, in part because both these forms were responses to the everyday life of the lower classes. Lee's book dealt with much neglected material, and she received critical acclaim for treating with "conspicuous ability" what one reviewer called important if little-known themes. Although that same *Athenaeum* writer praised her style as "cultivated, neatly adjusted, and markedly clever," others voiced criticisms that would echo throughout her career. A writer for the *Spectator* accused her of "Carlylese," and a reviewer in the *Atlantic Monthly* attacked her prose as a "sort of riotous verbiage." Such comments did not hamper Lee's success, however, for *Studies of the Eighteenth Century in Italy* was adopted as a textbook in Italy, and a satisfied publisher issued another collection of her essays the following year.

In *Belcaro* (1881) Lee discusses her "art philosophy," which is "entirely unabstract, unsystematic, essentially personal" and directed toward trying to "enjoy in art what art really contains . . . by refraining from asking it to give what it cannot." She insists that what art contains is form, the appreciation of which must be distinguished from both the pleasure of personal associations and the intellectual meanings with which we invest it. In five essays on sculpture, literature, and music, Lee explores the relation between form and interpretation and criticizes those who substitute psychological, mystic, or poetic meanings for the simple enjoyment of configurations of sound or patterns of lines and colors. Three final essays address the moral implications of art, and Lee especially condemns John Ruskin for believing that "the whole system of the beautiful is a system of moral emotions, moral selections, and moral appreciation." In reality, she asserts, "Beauty is pure, complete, egotistic: it has no other value than its being beautiful." What appears to be an art-for-art's-sake stance, much influenced by Walter Pater, is at least partially youthful exuberance, for in only three years she would attack the aesthetes and their theories.

Her feverishly moral and personal attack came in *Miss Brown* (1884), a satiric novel that revealed an insensitivity and acerbity in Lee that had previously been harnessed by the intellectual force of her writing. Unleashed in a story that lambastes the sins, artifice, and malice of the artists of the "fleshy school," that lack of "delicacy" and "fineness," to use James's words, cost Lee her friends in the Pre-Raphaelite circle, cast a pall over her friendship with James, and overshadowed the publication of two other books that year, *The Countess of Albany* and *Euphorion*. The novel is essentially a Pygmalion tale in which the heroine finally recognizes the moral weakness and vanity of the poet and painter who has educated her and must choose between her desire for freedom and her Victorian duty to marry/save the opium-addicted man who "rescued" her from domestic service. Offended by a novel they felt slandered their lives and their art, the Morrises, Rossettis, Wards, and others cut Lee from their acquaintance. James, in his awkward position as the man to whom the novel was dedicated, had to modulate his criticism; but even he objected to her "savage" portrait, with its "too great an implication of sexual motives," and cautioned that "life is less criminal, less obnoxious, less objectionable, less crude, more *bon enfant*, more mixed and casual, and . . . more *pardonable*, than the unholy circle with which you have surrounded your heroine." The furor astonished Lee, who never imagined anyone would take the tale as a roman à clef and who thought she was writing a book to "moralise the world," not one that would be labeled "nasty." Her reaction shows both a lack of insight about her intended readers and an emotional obtuseness that would continue to mar her personal and professional relations.

It may also show, as Lee herself came to believe, that she was at that time "*obsessed* by the sense of the impurity of the world" and was perhaps "indulging a more depraved appetite for the loathesome, while I *fancy* that I am studying disease and probing wounds for the sake of diminishing both." In the introduction to *Euphorion* (1884), a collection of previously published essays on the Renaissance, she acknowledges the "imperious necessity which we sometimes feel to see again and examine . . . some horrible evil," and the book is permeated with the feverish language of revulsion. While exploring "the Renaissance's horrible anomaly of improvement and degradation," she focuses on the "moral gangrene" of the age, on the "carnival songs of ribald dirtiness," the "stories of filthy intrigue and lewd jest," and the "terrible and brilliant, the mysterious and shadowy crimes of lust and of blood." Her men and women "relish the profane and obscene fleshiness" of stage plays, read stories of the "ferocious heat of tragic lust," and indulge in the "grossest animalism," which results in the "lewd miracle" of childbirth. Written when Lee was in her late twenties, these essays on Elizabethan drama and medieval love, on the arts of poetry and portraiture, form, for all their scholarly merits, a diary of sexual crisis. The parasitic relationship between men and women in *Miss Brown* is a version of this struggle, as is the story of dreary and disillusioned love in *The Countess of Albany* (1884), a biography commissioned for the Eminent Women series. It is then perhaps no coincidence that at the time she wrote these essays, Lee became "passionately attached," to use her biographer's coy phrase, to a Mme Annie Meyer and entered the first of several obsessive, though by all accounts chaste, relationships with women.

Lee's impulse to "moralise the world" found less troubled expression in *Baldwin* (1886) and its sequel *Althea* (1894). Her growing concern for the place of the individual in society became more militant following trips to industrial areas during her annual visits to England. While her previous works in part addressed the moral responsibility of the artist, in these works Lee's primary focus is the moral duty of the financially and intellectually privileged. In her dialogues "The Responsibility of Unbelief" and "The Consolation of Belief" in *Baldwin*, she explains why she rejects the Christian concept of God and posits instead a sort of evolutionary humanism in which morality derives from the gradual development of responsible and thrifty relations between people. That morality, which she sums up with the term "honour," provides the basis for her argument against vivisection (which would remain a prominent issue in her work) in "Of Honour and Evolution" and for her criticism of the upper classes. Sounding themes that would reverberate in her writings for nearly fifty years, Lee condemns those who live in idle splendor: the history of the elite, she says, is a history of wasted capital—physical, intellectual, and moral. She argues that it is the duty of the privileged to eliminate the wastefulness at the base of all the struggles of mankind and to seek and propagate truth: namely, that only when "happiness is increased by sharing instead of diminished by robbing, can the world become large enough, and man sufficiently free."

Readers who resented being stormed in *Eu-*

Mary Robinson, Lee's traveling companion beginning about 1881 (by permission of the Librarian, Library of Colby College, Waterville, Maine). When Robinson announced her engagement to marry in 1887, Lee suffered a complete physical and emotional collapse.

phorion generally liked *Baldwin*, perhaps because the "prevailing sweetness and openness of its temper," in the words of an *Atlantic Monthly* reviewer, made its dogmatic aspects more palatable. In any case, the book helped heal the rift between Lee and her readers, many of whom noted a shift in her attitude toward the role of art in society. She announced that change in the introduction to her next book, *Juvenilia* (1887), where she dismisses the realm of art in which she has lived as "a phantom place of our fantastic building." She realizes that "there comes a time, to such of us as shall not remain eternally children, when, by the side of all questions artistic, there must arise other questions, less pleasant to contemplate, and less easy to solve." The essays in *Juvenilia* are suffused with that understanding. They are speculations on art prompted by reminiscences of times more innocent, and they reflect both her nostalgia and her sense that such moments of aesthetic pleasure are "unequally distributed" and divert the attention of the "small class . . . who need the least consoling in life" from the evils that await correction. The ethical tone of *Juvenilia* drew comment from Pater in his review in the *Pall Mall Gazette*, but his plea for her to abandon this "Puritanism" and resume her former style would be heeded only once–in *Renaissance Fancies and Studies* (1895), the sequel to *Euphorion* and her last volume of historical essays on art and literature.

Vernon Lee faced more than an intellectual turning point in 1887. That summer she broke with Mary Robinson, the woman who had been her traveling companion since her separation from Annie Meyer about 1881. When Robinson abruptly announced her engagement to James Darmsteter, a man who, by Lee's account, she "had then seen *thrice*, including the occasion upon which she asked him . . . to marry," Lee suffered a complete physical and emotional collapse. Fortunately she found herself in the care of a new friend, Clementina (Kit) Anstruther-Thomson–"the most wonderfully good, and gentle, and strong and simple of all created things . . . who talks slang like a schoolboy and cares in reality for nothing but pictures, and trees and grass, and Browning and Shelley, and what is right and wrong and why"–who followed her to Florence and nursed her back to health. It was the beginning of a ten-year relationship and collaboration that Lee credited with helping her pass from her juvenile interests to her mature studies in the "science of the Mind and the Mind's relations with Body."

While recovering her health and sorting out a new approach to art, Lee traveled extensively, expanded her circle of social and intellectual acquaintances, and returned to writing fiction. The supernatural tales in *Hauntings* (1890) were a critical success, but in *Vanitas* (1892), three modern morality tales, she proved that she had not matured in human relations as she had in aesthetic ones. With singular blindness, she reinvented her friendship with Henry James in the story "Lady Tal" and created a scandal that caused even more personal and professional damage than the flap over *Miss Brown*. It was widely known that Lee had sought James's help in the formation of *Miss Brown*, and the story of Lady Tal and Jervase Marion, who has all James's mannerisms and is "a kind of Henry James, of a lesser magnitude," was generally regarded as her febrile interpretation of the events of that time. Her portrayal of the Marion/James character as a cad who helps Lady Tal only to gather psychological evidence for his own novel offended everyone, as did Lady Tal's

tactless suggestion at the end of the story that the proper conclusion to his new novel would be a marriage between the thinly disguised principals. James, in a letter to his brother William, called her satire a form of "treachery" and "a particularly impudent and blackguardly thing to do to a friend." He simply ended their friendship without notice. William James did not suffer the affront in silence; he wrote Lee a letter that stung her to tears: "The portrait of my brother in the first story is clever enough, and I cannot call it exactly malicious. But the using of a friend as so much raw material for 'copy' implies on your part such a strangely *objective* way of taking human beings, and such a detachment from the sympathetic considerations which usually govern human intercourse, that you will not be surprised to learn that seeing the book has quite quenched my desire to pay you another visit." Her apologetic reply was graciously received by William, but Henry did not, as he wrote, "find her note at all convincing;–she is doubtless sorry to be disapproved of in high quarters, but her *procédé* was absolutely deliberate, and her humility, which is easy and inexpensive, after the fact, doesn't alter her absolutely impertinent nature. Basta!"

That "strangely *objective* way of taking human beings" was noted by others as well. Robert Browning, who remained friends with Lee until his death, praised her powers of observation in his poem "Inapprehensiveness" (collected in *Asolando*, 1889) but qualified the tribute by impugning her emotional insight. As those who cite the last lines of the poem as a paean fail to note, the concluding "Vernon Lee?" is a barbed question from an ignored suitor: a woman's rapt attention to the landscape blinds her to one whose "dormant passion" needs "but a look/To burst into immense life" and "wreak/Revenge on your inapprehensive stare." The situation mirrors the pattern of Lee's personal life: as her friend Ethel Smyth recalled, rather than acknowledging that she loved the women in her life "humanly and with passion . . . she refused to face the fact, or indulge in the most innocent demonstration of affection, preferring instead to create a fiction that to her these friends were merely *intellectual* necessities." So she bound them to her through "unbreakable cords to 'OUR WORK' "–but in the end there always "came a moment of violent disruption." Perhaps, as Smyth speculated, the "atmosphere of fantastic prodigy-worship" in which Lee was raised gave her "but slight chance of becoming a normal human being," with the result that "her life was cramped and her personal happiness rendered unattainable by the perpetual repression of human needs she had trained herself to ignore."

But few could ignore the fact that she was, as Henry James once wrote, "far-away the most able mind in Florence," and many were drawn to the "pyrotechnical charm" of her conversation, despite what Smyth called its "Mount Sinai touch." One who tried to get his demurrers into her brilliant monologues on art was Bernard Berenson, whom she described in 1893, in true mentor fashion, as "that little art critic who appears destined to become famous." Theirs was generally a friendly rivalry, enhanced rather than hurt by the almost simultaneous publication of her *Renaissance Fancies and Studies* (1895), a transitional work that hints at her new researches in psychological aesthetics, and his *Florentine Painters of the Renaissance* (1896), in which he introduces his notion of tactile values in art. Lee felt sufficiently versed in her new field to review Berenson's book for the philosophical journal *Mind*, recommending it with some condescension even though it "shows no traces of psychological training." Her own psychological training consisted of extensive reading in contemporary psychological literature, especially that published in Germany, and of elaborate experiments, with Kit Anstruther-Thomson as the medium, into physiological responses to works of art. The combination led her to formulate an aesthetics of empathy, which she published in her 1897 essay "Beauty and Ugliness" (subsequently republished as the title essay of her 1912 book). There she posits that "the aesthetic instinct, the imperious rejection of certain visual phenomena as ugly, and the passionate craving for certain others as beautiful," is "due to the dependence of one of the most constant and important intellectual activities, the perception of form, on two of the most constant and important of our bodily functions, respiration and equilibrium." It was a theory favorably received by all but Berenson, who accused her, and her "recording angel" Anstruther-Thomson, of stealing the idea from his conversations with them. The charge led to a lengthy and acrimonious correspondence that did not resolve the dispute, and the principals did not meet again for over twenty years.

While the experience soured Berenson's ambition to develop a psychology of art, Lee continued her research and produced several notable books on psychological aesthetics. Her 1912 collec-

tion *Beauty and Ugliness and Other Studies in Psychological Aesthetics*, which contains a more sophisticated theory of empathy, is credited with introducing the concept of *Einfühlung* (empathy) into English aesthetic discourse, and her subsequent primer *The Beautiful* (1913) remains a standard introduction to the topic. She expanded her application of psychological principles to literature and music and pioneered a form of subjective criticism in two of her last books. In *The Handling of Words and Other Studies in Literary Psychology* (1923), Lee calls writing "the craft of manipulating the contents of the Reader's mind," and she sees adjectives, adverbs, similies, and the rest as the "chief instruments by which the Writer can rearrange the thoughts and feelings of the Reader in such a way as to mirror his own." She proves her point through compelling stylistic analyses of passages from Stevenson, Hardy, Eliot, and others; and for both her insights and her method reviewers recommended the book as "invaluable" to every young writer. The more ambitious *Music and its Lovers* (1932) is, as its subtitle states, "an empirical study of emotional and imaginative responses to music." Questionnaires distributed over nearly twenty-five years provided Lee with the data for her observations about "listeners," who attend to "every detail of composition and performance," and "hearers," in whom music stimulates "memories, associations, suggestions, visual images and emotional states." Essentially a study of the psychology of music enjoyment, the book was praised for its comprehensive attempt to integrate the personal experience of beauty and its metaphysical implications.

Those studies were completed without the active participation of Anstruther-Thomson, who, wearied, in Peter Gunn's phrase, by her companion's "ceaseless cerebration," moved out of Lee's villa shortly after the feud with Berenson. Though they remained friends until Anstruther-Thomson's death in 1921, Lee was seriously depressed by what she felt as the loss of a life partner. Drained by the series of personal and professional crises, she sought solace in travel and in an old literary friend, the travel essay. From 1897 to 1925 she produced seven volumes of genius loci essays—*Limbo and Other Essays* (1897), *Genius Loci* (1899), *The Enchanted Woods and Other Essays on the Genius of Places* (1905), *The Spirit of Rome* (1906), *The Sentimental Traveller* (1908), *The Tower of the Mirrors and Other Essays on the Spirit of Places* (1914), and *The Golden Keys and Other Essays on the Genius Loci* (1925)—culled from her weekly contributions to the *Westminster Gazette*. Lee understood the Victorians' love of travel, and through her essays she invited them to recall old delights and to explore the texture and movement, lines and colors of enchanted places in Italy, Switzerland, Germany, and France. As a guide she was, in the words of one reviewer, "suave, imperturbably amiable, and thoroughly alive to whatever is picturesque or quaint or amusing"; and it was with these "buoyant, lucid" sketches "redolent of warm airs," in the words of another, that she found her widest public.

It was not the audience she desired, however, but she took advantage of the attention of the leisured classes to press home her aesthetic and social programs. The philosopher of *Baldwin* and *Althea* reemerges in lectures on the relationship between the cultivation of an aesthetic sense and the proper management of life in *Hortus Vitae* (1903), a collection of essays on such topics as "Reading Books," "Hearing Music," and "Receiving Letters," and in *Laurus Nobilis* (1909), a more serious and quite witty examination of the ways "art may . . . become the training-place of our soul." In *Laurus Nobilis* Lee asserts that the "higher harmonies" are beyond the reach of wasteful materialists, and she notes the correlation between the "development of the aesthetic faculties and the development of the altruistic instincts." Aesthetic enjoyment, she reminds us, is the "only kind of pleasure . . . which tends not to diminish by wastefulness and exclusive appropriation, but to increase by sympathy, the possible pleasures of other persons," and she urges her readers to forgo "expensive amusements requiring . . . a further sacrifice of all capacities for innocent, noble, and inexpensive interests, in the absorbing, sometimes stultifying, often debasing processes of making money."

While some critics found the mixed tone of these volumes bewildering, they did not mistake Lee's intentions in her three books on contemporary issues. The woman who began her career as an aesthete had turned moralist, and in *Gospels of Anarchy and Other Contemporary Studies* (1908), *Vital Lies* (1912), and *Satan the Waster* (1920), she assumed the role of Victorian sage. The first volume, a diffuse but readable book ostensibly assessing the contributions of such "anarchists" as Emerson, Nietzsche, Ruskin, and H. G. Wells, is actually an almanac of Lee's ideas on issues including duty, religion, nationalism, education, women's economic dependence, and utopian reform. It is a livelier but less ambitious book than

Vital Lies, in which Lee exposes the intellectual fraud of "obscurantism" as practiced by William James, Father George Tyrrell, Ernest Crawley, and Georges Sorel. She charges them, as her title drawn from Ibsen's *Wild Duck* indicates, with fabricating "vital lies," with applying "their logic to redefining truth in such a way as to include edifying and efficacious fallacy and falsehood." Neither work found the broad audience the author sought, no doubt because of her stylistic opacity, although *Vital Lies* did receive remarkably favorable press in the United States.

Where Lee made her mark as a social philosopher was with *Satan the Waster*, a pacifist manifesto that explores the devastating psychological effects of war. The core of the book is a satiric allegory, "The Ballet of the Nations," in which World War I is presented as a ballet staged by Death and Satan, with the Warring Nations as dancers and with personifications of the vices and virtues associated with patriotism as the orchestra. First published in book form for Christmas 1915, the ballet was hailed in the press and damned by the author's British friends, who were already incensed by her plea for American neutrality and by her opposition to Wells's call for the United States to cut off food to Germany as a way of ending the war. But when it was republished in 1920 as part of the "philosophic war trilogy" *Satan the Waster*, it found a more sympathetic audience, one that could, according to a *New Republic* reviewer, profit from it during the period of spiritual adjustment following the war. And when a writer for the *Times Literary Supplement* indicted the book as a failed satire and an unconvincing fable, no less a social critic than George Bernard Shaw rose to its defense. In a lengthy review in the *Nation*, he paid Lee the tribute that capped her career: "Vernon Lee, by sheer intellectual force, training, knowledge and character, kept her head when Europe was a mere lunatic asylum. . . . I take off my hat to the old guard of Victorian cosmopolitan intellectualism, and salute her as the noblest Briton of them all."

Shaw's praise was as much eulogy as tribute, for she was of the "old guard," and the war had erased both the physical and spiritual worlds in which she had lived. In the summer of 1917 she lamented that destruction in the essay that would later close her final volume of genius loci sketches, all written before the war: "The landscape of the soul . . . is devastated on all sides, scarce a stone remaining in place of whatsoever we had built for our shelter, pride and joy, edifices of common wisdom, beauty and common hopes, of all that is too rare and needful to be a single people's: all shattered, blasted, polluted, by the legion of devils, hoofed and snouted or slimily obscene, penned out of sight during the years of peace in subterranean places whose decorous bolted door War has set ajar or thunderously thrown open." With the violent passing of her era came a loss of faith in the perfectibility of man and in her role as a moral guide. So she lowered her public voice and turned her attention to more private publications. She pulled together the notes for *The Handling of Words and Other Studies in Literary Psychology*, made a final halfhearted appearance as an aesthetician in *The Poet's Eye* (1926), wrote *For Maurice* (1927), a farewell volume of short stories for her old friend Maurice Baring, and ended her quarter-century study with the 1932 publication of *Music and its Lovers*. There was nothing left to do: when she died in February 1935 she knew the public liked best the work she valued least and had discarded her serious writing as outmoded. But she held some hope of eventually finding a more appreciative audience that would rediscover her impressive contributions as an aesthetician, historian, and philosopher.

Letters:

Vernon Lee's Letters (London: Privately printed, 1937).

Bibliographies:

Phyllis F. Mannocchi, " 'Vernon Lee': A Reintroduction and Primary Bibliography," *English Literature in Transition 1880-1920*, 26, no. 4 (1983): 231-267;

Carl Markgraf, " 'Vernon Lee': A Commentary and Annotated Bibliography of Writings about Her," *English Literature in Transition 1880-1920*, 26, no. 4 (1983): 268-312.

Biography:

Peter Gunn, *Vernon Lee/Violet Paget, 1856-1935* (London: Oxford University Press, 1964).

References:

Van Wyck Brooks, "Notes on Vernon Lee," *Forum*, 45 (April 1911): 447-457;

Richard Cary, "Aldous Huxley, Vernon Lee and the *Genius Loci*," *Colby Library Quarterly* (June 1960): 128-140;

Cary, "Vernon Lee's Vignettes of Literary Acquaintances," *Colby Library Quarterly*, 9 (September 1970): 179-199;

Vineta Colby, "The Puritan Aesthete: Vernon Lee," in her *The Singular Anomaly, Women Novelists of the Nineteenth Century* (New York: New York University Press, 1970), pp. 235-304;

Burdett Gardner, "An Apology for Henry James's 'Tiger-Cat,' " *PMLA*, 68 (September 1953): 688-695;

Horace Gregory, "The Romantic Inventions of Vernon Lee," introduction to Lee's *The Snake Lady and Other Stories* (New York: Grove Press, 1954), pp. 1-24;

Richard Ormond, "John Singer Sargent and Vernon Lee," *Colby Library Quarterly*, 9 (September 1970): 154-178;

Ernest Samuels, *Bernard Berenson: The Making of a Connoisseur* (Cambridge: Harvard University Press, 1979), pp. 277-292;

Carl J. Weber, "Henry James and His Tiger-Cat," *PMLA*, 68 (September 1953): 672-687;

René Wellek, "Vernon Lee, Bernard Berenson and Aesthetics," in *Friendship's Garland: Essays Presented to Mario Praz on His 70th Birthday*, edited by V. Gabriel (Rome, 1966): II, pp. 233-251.

Papers:

The Vernon Lee Collection is at Colby College, Waterville, Maine.

W. H. Mallock

(7 February 1849-2 April 1923)

John Stasny

West Virginia University

See also the Mallock entry in *DLB 18, Victorian Novelists After 1885.*

BOOKS: *The Isthmus of Suez* (Oxford: Shrimpton, 1871);

Every Man His Own Poet; or, The Inspired Singer's Recipe Book (Oxford: Shrimpton, 1872; Boston: DeWolfe, Fiske, 1878);

The New Republic; or Culture, Faith, and Philosophy in an English Country House (2 volumes, London: Chatto & Windus, 1877-1879; 1 volume, New York: Scribner & Welford, 1878);

Lucretius (Philadelphia: Lippincott, 1878; Edinburgh & London: Blackwood, 1898);

The New Paul and Virginia; or, Positivism on an Island (London: Chatto & Windus, 1878-1879; New York: Scribner & Welford, 1878);

Is Life Worth Living? (London: Chatto & Windus, 1879; New York: Putnam's, 1879);

Poems (London: Chatto & Windus, 1880; Rochester, N.Y.: Fitch, 1880);

A Romance of the Nineteenth Century (2 volumes, London: Chatto & Windus, 1881; 1 volume, New York: Putnam's, 1881);

Social Equality: A Short Study in a Missing Science (London: Bentley, 1882; New York: Putnam's, 1882);

Atheism and the Value of Life: Five Studies in Contemporary Literature (London: Bentley, 1884);

Property and Progress; or, A Brief Enquiry into Contemporary Social Agitation in England (London: Murray, 1884; New York: Putnam's, 1884);

The Landlords and the National Income: A Chart Showing the Proportion Borne by the Rental of the Landlords to the Gross Income of the People (London: Allen, 1884);

The Old Order Changes: A Novel (3 volumes, London: Bentley, 1886-1887; 1 volume, New York: Putnam's, 1886);

In an Enchanted Island; or, A Winter Retreat in Cyprus (London: Bentley, 1889);

A Human Document: A Novel (3 volumes, London: Chapman & Hall, 1892; 1 volume, New

W. H. Mallock (photograph by Elliott & Fry)

York: Cassell, 1892);

Labour and the Popular Welfare (London: Black, 1893);

Verses (London: Hutchinson, 1893);

The Heart of Life: A Novel (3 volumes, London: Chapman & Hall, 1895; 1 volume, New York: Putnam's, 1895);

Studies of Contemporary Superstition (London: Ward & Downey, 1895);

Classes and Masses; or, Wealth, Wages, and Welfare in the United Kingdom: A Handbook of Social Facts for Political Thinkers and Speakers (London: Black, 1896);

*Aristocracy and Evolution: A Study of the Rights, the Or-
igin, and the Social Functions of the Wealthier
Classes* (London & New York: Macmillan,
1898);

The Individualist: A Novel (London: Chapman &
Hall, 1899);

*Doctrine and Doctrinal Disruption: Being an Examina-
tion of the Intellectual Position of the Church of
England* (London: Black, 1900);

Lucretius on Life and Death (London: Black, 1900);

*The Fiscal Dispute Made Easy; or, A Key to the Princi-
ples Involved in the Opposite Policies* (London:
Nash, 1903);

Religion as a Credible Doctrine (London: Chapman
& Hall, 1903; New York: Macmillan, 1903);

The Veil of the Temple; or, From Night to Twilight (London: Murray, 1904; New York: Putnam's,
1904);

The Reconstruction of Belief (London: Chapman &
Hall, 1905; New York: Harper, 1905);

A Critical Examination of Socialism (New York & London: Harper, 1907);

An Immortal Soul (London: Bell, 1908; New York:
Harper, 1908);

*The Nation as a Business Firm: An Attempt to Cut a
Path through Jungle* (London: Black, 1910);

*Social Reform as Related to Realities and Delusions:
An Examination of the Increase and Distribution
of Wealth from 1801 to 1910* (London: Murray, 1914; New York: Dutton, 1915);

The Limits of Pure Democracy (London: Chapman
& Hall, 1918; New York: Dutton, 1918);

Capital, War, and Wages: Three Questions in Outline
(London: Blackie, 1918);

Memoirs of Life and Literature (London: Chapman
& Hall, 1920; New York & London:
Harper, 1920).

William Hurrell Mallock is remembered primarily for *The New Republic* (1877-1879), the satirical novel which he began writing as an Oxford undergraduate and which won him accolades as a
brilliant wit, skilled parodist and caricaturist, and
incisive critic of the foibles and fallacies of some
of his famous contemporaries. When he followed
that triumph with his wonderfully wicked reductio ad absurdum of positivism in *The New Paul
and Virginia* (1878-1879), his career seemed safely
launched as a satirist, a successor to Thomas
Love Peacock or a Victorian reincarnation of
Diogenes, the cynic, or Democritus, the laughing
philosopher. Mallock subsequently published
seven more novels; more than a score of volumes
on a variety of religious, philosophical, sociologi-

cal, and critical subjects; three collections of poetry; and almost one hundred articles in periodicals. Whatever reputation he achieved during his
lifetime has not survived. Only three of his books
remain in print; the rest of his work is not readily available except in large research libraries.
"Nevertheless," as Albert V. Tucker wrote in a
1962 article on Mallock, "his work should not be
lightly dismissed. Though his mind was second-
rate in its lack of any real synthesis of thought
and feeling, Mallock should be classed somewhere below Carlyle, Ruskin, and Arnold."

Perhaps the reason for Mallock's failure to
achieve wider and more lasting fame lies in the exalted and exclusive circumstances of his birth and
life and in the fact that he began and remained
dramatically out of step in the modern "march of
mind." Mallock was born on the family estate
near Torquay in Devonshire, an estate with a
400-year tradition of landed aristocracy. He was
the eldest son of the Reverend William Mallock,
rector of Cheriton Bishop. His mother was Margaret Mallock, daughter of the Venerable Robert
Hurrell Froude and sister of Hurrell, William,
and James Anthony Froude, each of whom
gained fame in his respective realm. Mallock was
nurtured in an environment that, as he described
it in *Memoirs of Life and Literature* (1920), recognized two classes: "the men, women, and children who touched their hats and curtsied, and
the men, women, and children to whom these salu-
tations were made." His early private education
served only to confirm those prejudices. He went
to Oxford as something of a protégé of Benjamin Jowett, whom he grew to dislike for his liberalism and whom he later satirized in *The New Republic* under the guise of Dr. Jenkinson, the Broad
Church clergyman. It was at Oxford also that he
came to admire John Ruskin, who appears as the
sympathetic Mr. Herbert in *The New Republic* and
to whom Mallock dedicated his *Is Life Worth Living?* (1879).

After Oxford Mallock combined the typical
activities of the idle, wealthy bachelor-aristocrat
with that typical Victorian literary prolificacy that
leisure permitted. Mallock spent the "season" in
London; he dined in fashionable houses, engaging in sophisticated conversations such as those
that dominate his novels, attending luncheons,
garden parties, and balls. He regularly spent the
winter months on the Riviera; he loved Cannes
and once spent five months at Monte Carlo, playing inconclusively a new system at the gaming tables. In 1886 he spent an elegant winter in Cy-

prus, which yielded a travel book, *In an Enchanted Island* (1889). In 1890 he spent two months at a castle in Hungary as a guest of the prince and princess of Batthyany. There was, according to Amy Belle Adams in *The Novels of William Hurrell Mallock* (1934), "a delightful summer spent with Lord and Lady Amherst on the borders of Caithness" and a memorable yachting cruise among the Orkneys and the Outer Hebrides. Even when he visited the United States in 1906 he was able to find a society fashionable enough to provide a pleasant respite from the burdens of his lecture series on the errors and threats of socialism. Osbert Sitwell in *Laughter in the Next Room* (1948) gives a vivid picture of Mallock in 1919, an old man but still effective amid a milieu reminiscent of that described in *The New Republic* forty years earlier, organizing brilliantly as a "pillar of prejudice" the conversational attacks of his fellow houseguests against modern French art. Mallock, according to an anonymous commentator in *Century Magazine*, "speaks in his own way as a mouthpiece of the upper classes of Great Britain and Ireland." He was consistently conservative in every area of his thought. Perhaps it was that conservatism which made him hesitate to abandon the Anglicanism of his family traditions even though he was inclined toward Roman Catholicism. His sister, herself an ardent convert, called a Carmelite priest to administer conditionally the last rites of her church to her semiconscious brother, who died on 2 April 1923.

According to Hesketh Pearson and Hugh Kingsmill in *Talking of Dick Whittington* (1947), as a young man Mallock once visited Thomas Carlyle whose parting words to him were "Can ye hear me, Mr. Mallock? I didna enjoy your veesit, and I dinna want to see ye again." One can only speculate on the offense Carlyle took at Mallock that day. Did he seem–to use the familiar Carlylean phrase–too much a representative of the "idle game-preserving rich"? Too much of an exponent of the "dismal science"? Too skeptical of Carlyle's concept of the altruism of the hero as the source of the solution to society's ills? Mallock's later works reveal tendencies in each of those directions: *Property and Progress* (1884) defends the rights of inherited wealth and landed estates against the confiscatory recommendations of the American economist Henry George; a series of books, including *Labour and the Popular Welfare* (1893) and *A Critical Examination of Socialism* (1907), which offer refutations of Marxist

"Is life worth living?," drawing of Mallock published in Vanity Fair, *30 December 1882 (Collection of Jerold J. Savory)*

thought, rely heavily on classical economic thought from Adam Smith to David Ricardo; *Aristocracy and Evolution* (1898) rejects Herbert Spencer's evolutionary sociology with its denigration of "Great Men as the True Cause of Progress," but Mallock's "great inventor" who is "motivated solely by the passion of selfish 'greed' " is a Plugson of Undershot before his Carlylean conversion.

To discuss the important nonfiction works of Mallock without discussing *The New Republic* is like discussing Milton without attention to *Paradise Lost*. It is his masterpiece, a novel of ideas, but less a novel than are those of his model, Thomas Love Peacock. *The New Republic* has more narrative interest than Plato's *Republic* but less than Swift's *Gulliver's Travels*. It belongs, perhaps, to the genre Northrop Frye, in *Anatomy of Criticism* (1957), identifies as Menippean satire.

The New Republic offers a "*menu* for the conversation" of a group of men and women of various persuasions and interests who gather for a long weekend at the country house of Mallock's own persona, Otho Laurence. For example, under the thin disguise of Dr. Jenkinson and Mr. Storks, Benjamin Jowett, the liberal Broad Church clergyman, and T. H. Huxley, the agnostic evolutionary scientist, present and debate their ideas. Not only are the ideas of the Victorian nonfiction prose masters represented by the various characters, but the prose styles of especially Arnold, Pater, and Ruskin are brilliantly imitated or parodied. It is, for example, Walter Pater, thinly disguised by Mallock as Mr. Rose, whose famous comment in the "Conclusion" to *Studies in the History of the Renaissance* (1873) is paraphrased in Mallock's passage beginning "in the consciousness of exquisite living–in the making our own each highest thrill of joy that the moment offers us. . . ." That Dr. Jenkinson, the liberal, is something of the villain and that Mr. Herbert–John Ruskin in his characteristic conservatism–is the hero are representative of Mallock's own predilections. The dramatization of a wide spectrum of earnest Victorian thought and the imitation of recognizable prose styles have made *The New Republic* a pleasant book of background reading for the Victorian period.

Much of Mallock's nonfiction prose itself seems to belong to realms other than the literary although in the entire corpus can be found passages of exceptional rhetorical attractiveness worthy of comparison to the prose of his greater contemporaries. Two works, one early and one late, will serve to illustrate the range and feel of Mallock's nonfiction prose. The first is the very brief *Every Man His Own Poet; or, The Inspired Singer's Recipe Book* (1872), which was edited by Barry V. Qualls and republished in its entirety in the journal *Victorian Poetry* (Spring-Summer 1978). This book reveals Mallock in his youthful, witty, satirical mode. It provides a series of recipes for writing poetry, "a kind of palaestra of folly, a very short training in which will suffice to break down that stiffness and self-respect in the soul, which is so incompatible with modern poetry." There are directions for writing "an ordinary love poem," "a pathetic marine poem," "an epic poem like Mr. Tennyson," "an imitation of Mr. Browning," imitations of the Pre-Raphaelites, and of Morris, Byron, and Swinburne. One brief recipe, "How To Make An Ordinary Love Poem," will serve as an example: "Take two large and

tender hearts, which match one another perfectly. Arrange these close together, but preserve them from actual contact by placing between them some cruel barrier. Wound them both in several places, and insert through the openings thus made a fine stuffing of wild yearnings, hopeless tenderness, and a general admiration for stars. Then completely cover up one heart with a sufficient quantity of chill church-yard mould, which may be garnished according to taste with dank waving weeds or tender violets: and promptly break over it the other heart."

A Critical Examination of Socialism provoked a response from Bernard Shaw, *Socialism and Superior Brains* (1909), in which Shaw responded to Mallock's own tendency to resort to ad hominem argumentation, saying that "any Socialist over the age of six could knock Mr. Mallock into a cocked hat." In 1953, however, Mallock's book was cited in the *Times Literary Supplement* as among the "outstanding books of the half century, 1900-1950." The *Times* reviewer wrote that "as a logical exercise Mallock's book is almost impeccable" and concluded by noting Mallock's "extraordinary ability to see through formulas to fact, a quality so rare today as to give his book, nearly 50 years after its publication something of a power of prophecy." Mallock's book begins with an extended summary and refutation of the doctrine of Marx that all wealth is produced by labour. Mallock insists that "the undirected labour of the many is, in the modern world, impotent to produce anything." The leadership of men of ability and inventive genius is indispensable in an industrial economy, and recognizing that fact and providing motivation for such men is a difficulty for socialism given its egalitarian assumptions. Socialism would have to "eliminate the motive mainly operative among such men at present–namely that supplied by the possibility of exceptional economic gain. . . . Some motive of a different kind will have to be discovered by socialists which shall take the place of this." Socialists may rely on the hope that "the monopolists of business ability . . . will at once become amenable to the motives of the soldier, the artist, the philosopher, the inspired philanthropist, and the saint." However, such hopes, Mallock asserts, are "groundless and ludicrous." The Socialist scheme would "reorganize society on the basis of a moral conversion which is confined to the few only–which would exact from the able minority the maximum of effort and mortification, and secure the maximum of idleness and self-indulgence for the rest of the human race." Mallock's conclusion is that "Socialism may be worthless as a scheme, but it is not meaningless as a symptom. . . . It consists of a poisonous prescription founded on a false diagnosis. . . . Nations now grow rich through industry as they once grew rich through conquest . . . , and the only terms on which any modern nation can maintain its present productivity, or hope to increase it in the future, consist in the technical submission of the majority of men to the guidance of an exceptional minority." The working class, insists Mallock, is the beneficiary of remarkable progress. "It is a gift to the many from the few, or, at all events, it has its origin in the sustentation and the multiplication of their efforts, and would shrink in proportion as these efforts were impeded." Economic ills remain, but they can and will be alleviated by men of ability following "strictest business principles." The working class in the meantime need not live in "insanitary slums and alleys"; their lives would be improved "if much of the education, which now has no other effect than of generating impracticable ideas as to the abstract rights of man, were devoted to developing in men and women alike a greater mastery of the mere arts of household management."

Mallock spent his entire career in a conservative effort of resistance to what he considered misguided or ill-considered agitation for change. "The conservative," he wrote in *A Critical Examination of Socialism*, "differs from the Radical and the agitator, not because he sees less, but because he sees more." Throughout his entire career he levied harsh and often ad hominem criticism against would-be liberal reformers. His treatment of Henry George in *Property and Progress* is typical. "It has required greater skill on Mr. George's part to see his way into his errors," Mallock writes, "than it will require on ours to see the way out of them." Mallock is capable of vigorous, perhaps vicious, reductio ad absurdum. He reports that "Mr. George tells us . . . that the sight of all the poverty and distress in the world had led him to doubt in the possibility of a wise and benevolent God. But now . . . since he has found out how to remedy poverty, since he sees prospectively vice and misery dying away from earth, his faith in God, and in God's goodness, is coming back to him." Mallock's response is, "Does not Mr. George see, that, if the vice and misery that have so long existed in the world is any valid argument against the goodness of God, the argument would be strengthened, not destroyed, were this

evil suddenly to come to an end? As it is the Theist accepts its presence as a mystery, believing that there is some reason for it beyond his powers of comprehension; but, could it really be abolished by Mr. George's 'simple expedient,' he would at once ask why it was not abolished before? So far as regards the Deity, there is but one possible answer. He either did not wish to abolish it, or he did not know how to abolish it. Thus, in one case we should have to regard Mr. George as more benevolent than the Deity; or, in the other, the Deity as more stupid than Mr. George."

Mallock was not receptive to democratic urgings on behalf of the rights of the poor. "If there is anything sacred in the rights of the present wage-earners," he wrote in *Aristocracy and Evolution*, "there is something equally sacred in those of the greatest millionaires." In an article entitled "Fiction and Philanthropy," written in 1900 and published in the *Edinburgh Review*, he vividly expresses his view of the reality of the demands of liberal social reformers: "It is imaginable that the congenitally strong and the congenitally industrious might be persuaded to give to the congenitally stupid and the congenitally idle everything that they are too stupid and idle to make or to provide for themselves; but unless this remedy is to increase the evil it is designed to cure human nature must be altered not only by eradicating our selfishness, but by also eradicating a tendency in it which at present is universal, and which practically incapacitates a man from ever doing for himself anything which he can securely count on another man's doing for him." Such antiliberal sentiments as these go far to explain why Mallock no longer speaks, if he ever did, to a wide and popular audience. Mallock's nonfiction prose has fallen into oblivion and perhaps unfortunately, for, as Russell Kirk in *The Conservative Mind* (1953) observes, "If the conservative mind does indeed contrive to arrest the decay of Western civilization, Mallock will deserve great credit for being the author of a reasoned conservative apologetic."

References:

Amy Belle Adams, *The Novels of William Hurrell Mallock* (Orono, Maine: University Press, 1934);

Russell Kirk, *The Conservative Mind* (Chicago: Regnery, 1953), pp. 345-357;

John Lucas, "Conservatism and Revolution in the 1880s," in *Literature and Politics in the Nineteenth Century*, edited by Lucas (London: Me-then, 1971), pp. 173-219;

"W. H. Mallock: A Present-Day View," in "Thoughts and Second Thoughts Upon Some Outstanding Books of the Half Century, 1900-1950," *Times Literary Supplement*, special section, 28 August 1953, pp. xxix-xxx;

J. Max Patrick, Introduction to Mallock's *The New Republic* (Gainesville: University of Florida Press, 1950), pp. xi-xxxiv;

Hesketh Pearson and Hugh Kingsmill, *Talking of*

Dick Whittington (London: Eyre & Spottiswoode, 1947), pp. 204-207;

Osbert Sitwell, *Laughter in the Next Room* (Boston: Little, Brown, 1948), pp. 172-177;

Albert V. Tucker, "Mallock and Late Victorian Conservatism," *University of Toronto Quarterly*, 31 (January 1962): 223-241;

Raymond Williams, *Culture and Society 1780-1950* (London: Chatto & Windus, 1958), pp. 162-166.

George Meredith

(12 February 1828-18 May 1909)

Ronald J. Black
McKendree College

See also the Meredith entries in *DLB 18, Victorian Novelists After 1885,* and *DLB 35, Victorian Poets After 1850.*

BOOKS: *Poems* (London: Parker, 1851; New York: Scribners, 1898);

The Shaving of Shagpat: An Arabian Entertainment (London: Chapman & Hall, 1856; Boston: Roberts Brothers, 1887);

Farina: A Legend of Cologne (London: Smith, Elder, 1857);

The Ordeal of Richard Feverel: A History of Father and Son (3 volumes, London: Chapman & Hall, 1859; 1 volume, Boston: Roberts Brothers, 1887);

Evan Harrington; or, He Would Be a Gentleman (New York: Harper, 1860; 3 volumes, London: Bradbury & Evans, 1861);

Modern Love and Poems of the English Roadside, with Poems and Ballads (London: Chapman & Hall, 1862); edited by E. Cavazza (Portland, Maine: Mosher, 1891);

Emilia in England, 3 volumes (London: Chapman & Hall, 1864); republished as *Sandra Belloni* (London: Chapman & Hall, 1886; Boston: Roberts Brothers, 1887);

Rhoda Fleming: A Story (3 volumes, London: Tinsley, 1865; 1 volume, Boston: Roberts Brothers, 1886);

Vittoria, 3 volumes (London: Chapman & Hall, 1866; Boston: Roberts Brothers, 1888);

The Adventures of Harry Richmond (3 volumes, London: Smith, Elder, 1871; 1 volume, Boston: Roberts Brothers, 1887);

Beauchamp's Career (3 volumes, London: Chapman & Hall, 1876; 1 volume, Boston: Roberts Brothers, 1887);

The House on the Beach: A Realistic Tale (New York: Harper, 1877);

The Egoist: A Comedy in Narrative, 3 volumes (London: Kegan Paul, 1879; New York: Harper, 1879);

The Tragic Comedians: A Study in a Well-Known Story (2 volumes, London: Chapman & Hall, 1880; 1 volume, New York: Munro, 1881);

Poems and Lyrics of the Joy of Earth (London: Macmillan, 1883; Boston: Roberts Brothers, 1883);

Diana of the Crossways (3 volumes, London: Chapman & Hall, 1885; 1 volume, New York: Munro, 1885);

Ballads and Poems of Tragic Life (London: Macmillan, 1887; Boston: Roberts Brothers, 1887);

A Reading of Earth (London: Macmillan, 1888; Boston: Roberts Brothers, 1888);

Jump-to-Glory Jane (London: Privately printed, 1889; London: Sonnenschein, 1892);

The Case of General Ople and Lady Camper (New York: Lovell, 1890);

The Tale of Chloe: An Episode in the History of Beau Beamish (New York: Lovell, 1890);

One of Our Conquerors (3 volumes, London: Chapman & Hall, 1891; 1 volume, Boston: Rob-

George Meredith, circa 1862

erts Brothers, 1891);

Poems: The Empty Purse, with Odes to the Comic Spirit, to Youth in Memory and Verses (London: Macmillan, 1892; Boston: Roberts Brothers, 1892);

The Tale of Chloe; The House on the Beach; The Case of General Ople and Lady Camper (London: Ward, Lock & Bowdon, 1894);

Lord Ormont and His Aminta: A Novel (3 volumes, London: Chapman & Hall, 1894; 1 volume, New York: Scribners, 1894);

The Amazing Marriage, 2 volumes (London: Constable, 1895; New York: Scribners, 1895);

An Essay on Comedy and the Uses of the Comic Spirit (London: Constable, 1897; New York: Scribners, 1897);

Selected Poems (London: Constable, 1897; New York: Scribners, 1897);

The Nature Poems (London: Constable, 1898);

Odes in Contribution to the Song of French History (London: Constable, 1898; New York: Scribners, 1898);

The Story of Bhanavar the Beautiful (London: Constable, 1900);

A Reading of Life, with Other Poems (London: Constable, 1901; New York: Scribners, 1901);

Last Poems (London: Constable, 1909; New York: Scribners, 1909);

Chillianwallah (New York: Marion Press, 1909);

Love in the Valley, and Two Songs: Spring and Autumn (Chicago: Seymour, 1909);

Poems Written in Early Youth, Poems from "Modern Love," and Scattered Poems (London: Constable, 1909; New York: Scribners, 1909);

Celt and Saxon (London: Constable, 1910; New York: Scribners, 1910);

Up to Midnight (Boston: Luce, 1913).

Collection: *The Works of George Meredith*, De Luxe Edition, 39 volumes (London: Constable, 1896-1912); Library Edition, 18 volumes (London: Constable, 1897-1910); Boxhill Edition, 17 volumes (New York: Scribners, 1897-1919); Memorial Edition, 27 volumes (London: Constable, 1909-1911; New York: Scribners, 1909-1911).

OTHER: *The Cruise of the Alabama and the Sumter: From the Private Journals and Other Papers of Commander R. Semmes*, introductory and concluding chapters by Meredith (London: Saunders & Otley, 1864; New York: Carleton, 1864).

Although George Meredith's literary reputation has diminished somewhat since his death in 1909, he is still regarded as a major writer of the Victorian period. But besides producing fifteen novels, numerous pieces of short fiction, and several volumes of poetry, he also worked as a journalist during his career. He contributed articles on a wide range of subjects to some of the leading newspapers and journals of his time, and for a short period he served as the editor of the *Fortnightly Review* in addition to working as a manuscript reader and literary adviser for two publishing firms. Meredith's nonfiction prose writing also includes a famous essay on the nature of comedy.

Born in Portsmouth, England, on 12 February 1828, George Meredith was the only child of Augustus Meredith, a tailor, and Jane Macnamara Meredith, the daughter of a middle-class innkeeper. Meredith's mother died when he was five; and in 1838 Augustus went bankrupt, losing the tailoring business he had inherited from his father, Melchizedek Meredith. Augustus then moved to London where he married his housekeeper, with whom he had apparently been living for some time in Portsmouth. Meredith attended two boarding schools in England, and when he was fourteen his father sent him to the Moravian Brothers school at Neuwied on the Rhine, where he remained for two years. Because Meredith was extremely reluctant in his later years to discuss his youth, not much is known about the effect his childhood experiences had on him as an adult. According to his biographer Lionel Stevenson, late in his life he did mention that "I was a very timid and sensitive boy. I was frightened of everything; I could not endure to be left alone."

In 1846, just before Meredith turned eighteen, his father had him articled as a law clerk to Richard Charnock, a London solicitor. Having interests other than practicing or teaching law, Charnock provided him with practically no legal training, which did not disappoint Meredith, who had no desire to be a solicitor. While he was articled Meredith joined a coterie of young writers with whom Charnock associated, and it was at this time that he began his writing career. The group founded the *Monthly Observer,* contributed to the journal, and took turns editing it. During this period he met Mary Ellen Nicolls, an attractive widow and daughter of the novelist Thomas Love Peacock; she and Meredith were married in 1849. Eight years later their marriage began to collapse. In 1858 she left Meredith and their son, Arthur, and went to Italy with a young painter, Henry Wallis, with whom she had been having an affair for at least a year. Meredith refused to have any contact with his wife during the rest of her life and would not allow their son to visit her until shortly before her death.

From about 1858 to 1868 Meredith worked as a journalist for the *Ipswich Journal,* a Tory newspaper, writing at least one weekly editorial article and a column or two summarizing the news. In his editorials Meredith reflected the paper's staunchly Conservative views. Among his favorite targets were John Bright and other leaders of the Manchester School, whom he ridiculed in his articles for their support of franchise and parliamentary reform and their advocacy of a laissez-faire economic policy. Like many other members of the press at the time, Meredith sympathized with the South during the American Civil War. When John Bright gave a speech championing the Northern cause, Meredith told his readers: "We dub him Yankee and bid him good-bye." He was also contemptuous of Lincoln ("who cannot write grammar") and of the North in general.

Besides the *Ipswich Journal* Meredith wrote for such other Conservative papers as the *Morning Post* and the *Pall Mall Gazette.* His association with the Tory press, particularly the *Ipswich Journal,* has generated controversy among critics since Meredith was often an outspoken advocate of liberal and radical ideas which he expressed in some of his novels, letters, and comments to reporters. Some critics have argued that during the period he wrote for the *Journal* Meredith was a conservative and had no objection to the paper's political views; others have claimed that Meredith did not accept the *Journal*'s Conservative opinions or was at least latently hostile toward them and did the work merely out of economic necessity; and those taking a middle position between these two views have suggested that, while some of his editorials may have reflected his acceptance of the paper's sentiments, others he wrote did not accord with his true beliefs.

Although Meredith's political relationship with the Conservative press remains ambiguous, it is clear from his letters that he disliked journalism because it prevented him from devoting full

Meredith with his son Arthur, early 1860s

time to imaginative literature. In a letter written in 1868, he complained of being "tied to the pecuniary pen, and I am not a bright galley-slave." Nevertheless, Meredith had to turn to journalism to provide himself with a steady income, for his novels were not selling well and he had the expense of his son's education. His marriage to Marie Vulliamy in September 1864 and the subsequent birth of their two children, William Maxse and Marie Eveleen, added to Meredith's financial responsibilities, even though his wife possessed a small income. In January 1868 Meredith moved to Flint Cottage at the base of Box Hill near the town of Dorking. He was extremely fond of his new home, and the enjoyment he derived from climbing Box Hill at sunrise and taking long walks in the surrounding countryside helped ease the pressures of a demanding work schedule. He remained at Flint Cottage to the end of his life.

During the 1860s Meredith was interested in the political changes taking place in Europe, especially those occurring in Italy. In his novel *Vittoria* (1866), he compassionately portrays Italy's struggle for liberation from Austria during the revolution of 1848. When fighting again broke out between the two countries in 1866, Meredith was an ardent supporter of the Italian cause and eagerly accepted the assignment as a war correspondent offered to him by the *Morning Post*. Although he traveled with the Italian troops during some of their maneuvers, he witnessed little of the actual fighting and often had to rely on rumor and secondhand information in writing his reports. After the Italians were unable to defeat the Austrians in the major battle fought near the Po and Micino rivers on 24 July, Meredith's dispatches reflect his uncertainty that the Italians would be victorious, but they also express his unwavering faith in their courage and fighting prowess. In some of his dispatches he in fact romanticizes and exaggerates the Italians' bravery by portraying them as Homeric heroes. Meredith's dispatches began on 22 June and ended on 24 July, and in September he returned to England after the war had ended in a stalemate.

In addition to his other work as a journalist, Meredith submitted articles to the *Westminster Review*. Because he often wrote anonymously during his journalistic career and did not in later life document his work, the full extent of his contributions is not known. In a 1958 article in *Modern Language Review*, Gordon S. Haight has identified the literary reviews Meredith wrote for the Belles Lettres Art section of the *Westminster Review* in the April, July, and October 1857 and January 1858 issues. Even though the reviews provide some detailed analysis of the works, they are of interest primarily as examples of his early writing style rather than as expressions of a well-defined theory of literary criticism. Reviewing mostly second-rate novels and poems, Meredith skillfully uses his satirical wit to ridicule and reveal their artistic flaws. Occasionally he did review works by major novelists such as Melville's *The Confidence Man*, Trollope's *Barchester Towers*, and Flaubert's *Madame Bovary*, and his comments are generally favorable and often insightful. Gillian Beer, in a 1966 article in *Modern Language Review*, has verified Meredith's authorship for six essays contributed to the *Pall Mall Gazette* in 1868: "The Anecdotalist," "The Cynic of Society," "The Consummate Epicure," "A Working Frenchwoman," "The Third-class Carriage," and "English Country Inns." As these titles suggest, Meredith wrote on a variety of topics, and in the essays he often satirizes the customs and manners of English society. Using highly metaphorical language combined with an informal and urbane tone, Meredith creates an essay style that is, as Beer notes, "whimsical, ironic, learnedly allusive, using the mock-heroic as a cover for sentiment, the argument progressing through association rather than logic in an effect like that of conversation."

Meredith added to the income he was earning from journalism by working as a manuscript reader and literary adviser for Chapman and Hall from 1860 to 1895 and by serving as a reader to Mrs. Benjamin Wood, a wealthy and aging widow. During the years he worked for Chapman and Hall, Meredith rejected not only some books that later became best-sellers for other publishers but also early works by such authors as Thomas Hardy, George Gissing, and Bernard Shaw. A fairly common view, held especially by Meredith's first critics, is that his high literary standards prevented him at times from realizing the commercial value of the works he read. However, some evidence from Meredith's manuscript reports suggests that he did support the publication of some books written for popular taste that lacked high literary merit. Meredith's manuscript reports, the subject of Royal A. Gettmann's 1949 article in the *Journal of English and Germanic Philology*, also reveal that he was particularly concerned with a novelist's ability to develop an effective plot structure and to create dramatic scenes. While employed by Chapman and Hall, Meredith accepted a job as a reader from a rival publishing firm, Saunders and Otley, owned by Warren Adams. Shortly before Capt. Raphael Semmes and his Confederate warship the *Alabama* fought the U.S.S. *Kearsarge* in the waters outside Cherbourg harbor, Adams received the ship's log and the captain's journal which he hurriedly transformed into a book, *The Cruise of the Alabama and the Sumter* (1864). Meredith accepted the task of writing the first chapter and the last one, and in the latter he presents a vivid and stirring narration of the *Alabama*'s unsuccessful battle with the *Kearsarge*. But as his articles for the *Ipswich Journal* reveal, Meredith was unable to view the American Civil War objectively. In his sympathetic account of the *Alabama*'s plight and the superior valor of its defeated but undaunted crew members, Meredith once again became an apologist for the Southern cause.

Beginning in 1867 Meredith added to his already large number of journalistic duties by writing for the *Fortnightly Review*, a liberal periodical founded in 1865. He contributed articles, literary reviews, and poetry to the journal (which also published some of his novels in serial form) and served, in the absence of John Morley, as its editor from November 1867 to January 1868. Meredith was attracted by the democratic ideas expressed by the *Review* writers, and his involvement with the journal provided him with an intellectual climate that was compatible with his own radical views which were emerging at this time. One of the causes that Meredith enthusiastically supported for many years was home rule for Ireland. When Gladstone introduced a bill in Parliament for home rule in 1886, Meredith made his position on this issue known to his readers by writing an article entitled "Concession to the Celt" for the *Fortnightly Review*. In the article he points out the moral obligation of England, as a country dedicated to democratic principles, to grant freedom to Ireland and the political advantages to be gained by the English in doing so. Meredith became actively involved in politics for a short time, canvassing for his close friend Frederick Maxse in 1868 during Maxse's unsuccessful campaign for a seat in Parliament as a Radical. But Meredith was too much of an independent thinker to become a member of any party or to believe that any single ideology provided the answers to all the country's social and political problems.

Meredith's continuing interest in current news topics, both domestic and foreign, is evident in *Up to Midnight,* a series of dialogues he wrote for the weekly newspaper the *Graphic*. This journalistic project appeared in five issues of the paper from 21 December 1872 to 18 January 1873. Imitating the style of some of Thomas Love Peacock's fiction, Meredith creates a group of humorous characters who discuss and debate controversial news items and social problems during their stay in a country manor. The dialogues, which were collected in a single volume in 1913, cover a wide range of contemporary issues and events, such as polar expeditions, female suffrage, labor unrest and trade unionism, the Irish problem, England's imperialism in India, and political developments in Germany and France, including the death of Louis Napoleon III. But Meredith's attempt to create an entertaining and satirical commentary on these subjects is unsuccessful. Lacking adequate development, his characters remain uninteresting, one-dimensional figures who use stilted dialogue to express their various political opinions or emotional attitudes toward life. James S. Stone in a 1976 article in *English Studies in Canada* provides a contemporary historical background for many of the news items and issues discussed in the dialogues and presents a thorough analysis of Meredith's attempt to combine "journalistic commentary within an artistic structure." Stone argues that, although Meredith achieves some success in his treatment of foreign news topics, *Up to Midnight* "remains an artistic and journalistic failure overall."

One aspect of Meredith's literary work that has received considerable study is his use of comedy. Many of his novels contain comic elements which he uses to expose the moral imperfections in human nature. The importance that Meredith placed on comedy is also revealed in his well-known work of criticism, *An Essay on Comedy and the Uses of the Comic Spirit* (1897). The essay was originally presented as a lecture entitled "The Idea of Comedy and the Uses of the Comic Spirit" in February 1877 at the London Institution and was published in the *New Quarterly Magazine* in April of that year. The essay is generally regarded as a major contribution to the theory of comedy and as an important statement of Meredith's method as a comic writer. His novel *The Egoist* (1879) is the best illustration of the theory Meredith developed in the essay, and in the "Prelude" to that novel he briefly summarizes some of the ideas found in his critical study. Because the essay explores, in a somewhat digressive fashion, a wide range of issues related to the nature of comedy, a condensed summary of it can-

131

backward at the letter on her desk. She
had to answer the strangest of letters that
had ever come to her, & it was from her
dear Tony, the baldest intimation of the
weightiest pieces of intelligence which a
woman can communicate to her nearly
friend. The task of answering it was now
doubled. "I fear so. I fancy so," she said,
& she longed to cast eye over the letter
again, to see if there might possibly
be a loophole behind the lines.

"Then I must make my mind
up to it," said Redworth. "I think
I'll take a walk."

She smiled kindly. "It will be
our secret."

"I thank you with all my
heart, Lady Dunstane."

When she was alone she
took in the contents of the letter
at a hasty glimpse. It was of
one paragraph, & fired its shot

[left margin:] He was not a weaver of phrases in distress. His blunt reserve was eloquent of it to her, & she liked him the better; could have thanked him, too, for leaving her promptly.

From the manuscript for Meredith's novel Diana of the Crossways *(MA 781, p. 131, by permission of the Trustees of The Pierpont Morgan Library). By the time this novel was published, in 1885, Meredith no longer had to rely on his journalistic work for an income.*

not convey the full extent and complexity of the many ideas it encompasses. But there are five areas that are of particular importance in understanding Meredith's theory of comedy, and they are the characteristics unique to true comedy, the conditions necessary for it to exist, the purpose of comedy, the method it employs, and the effect it has on society.

Meredith devotes a large portion of *An Essay on Comedy and the Uses of the Comic Spirit* to a survey of comic writers and their works, and he takes as his examples English and Continental writers from the ancient to the modern period. One of his primary aims in presenting this survey is to show that although comedy is often used as a generic term for all literary forms that evoke laughter, it actually refers to a more limited type of expression and is distinct from satire and humor. In his assessment of English comic writers, which includes, among others, Henry Fielding, Oliver Goldsmith, and Jane Austen, he suggests that these authors excel primarily in writing satire and humor and that, therefore, true comedies are rare in English literature. For Meredith a crucial element that distinguishes satire and humor from comedy is the type of laughter produced. Whereas satire evokes derisive laughter by bitterly ridiculing its object, humor, he claims, generates cheerful and sympathetic laughter by treating its object with sentimentality. In contrast, comedy appeals to the intellect rather than the emotions and by doing so elicits "thoughtful laughter."

The writer whose works Meredith praises as best representing true comedy is Molière. He also argues that the area of human experience comedy explores is limited to the "operation of the social world upon" the characters. For comedy to exist and flourish he asserts that a civilized society of cultivated individuals is necessary to provide an appreciative audience. An additional prerequisite is that there be equality of the sexes in society. He takes his argument even further by saying that two criteria needed for a society to be civilized are that it produce comedies and allow freedom to women. (Women's liberation is an issue that Meredith strongly advocated in many of his literary works and in comments to reporters.) Equality of the sexes gains additional importance in his theory because comedy, he suggests, in a sense reaffirms that equality by showing men and women their "mutual likeness."

The purpose of comedy, Meredith explains, is to expose and correct folly which includes such human frailties as egotism, sentimentality, insin-

Meredith in old age (photograph by C. K. Shorter)

cerity, and hypocrisy. To accomplish these ends comedy employs the method of contrast; that is, it reveals the incongruity between a character's perception of himself and the way he actually is, between false actions and genuine behavior. Meredith uses the metaphor of the Comic Spirit to personify common sense, and it is the intellectual faculty that allows one to perceive the ironic contrasts. Also present in the essay is the idea that society is founded on common sense; otherwise the audience would not be "struck by the contrasts the Comic Spirit perceives." But common sense does not prevent the audience, Meredith claims, from deviating at times from reason and committing folly. In fact, the effect comedy has is to make members of the audience aware not only of the characters' foibles but of their own as well; and it is through the agency of thoughtful laughter that people achieve the self-knowledge needed for them to correct their behavior. Thus Meredith sees comedy as improving human conduct and ultimately as a means of furthering the advancement of society.

Although Meredith continued to write occasionally for newspapers and magazines until shortly before his death in 1909, most of his journalistic work was done during the 1860s and 1870s. By 1885 he had finally achieved success as a novelist and no longer had to rely on journalism for income. In assessing his prose works one finds in some of them the stylistic brilliance that characterizes his imaginative literature. But

Meredith's stature as a prose writer is not comparable with that of the great Victorian essayists such as Matthew Arnold and Thomas Carlyle. His prose works do, however, provide some understanding of the ideas and issues that concerned him and the values by which he judged, even though they do not reveal the full scope or complexity of his intellectual development. The prose work that remains Meredith's most important and the one that continues to stimulate critical discussion is *An Essay on Comedy and the Uses of the Comic Spirit.*

Letters:

The Letters of George Meredith, edited by C. L. Cline, 3 volumes (Oxford: Clarendon Press, 1970).

Bibliographies:

Michael Collie, *George Meredith: A Bibliography* (Toronto & Buffalo: University of Toronto Press, 1974);

John C. Olmsted, *George Meredith: An Annotated Bibliography of Criticism 1925-1975* (New York: Garland, 1978).

Biography:

Lionel Stevenson, *The Ordeal of George Meredith* (New York: Scribners, 1953).

References:

Joseph Warren Beach, *The Comic Spirit in George Meredith* (New York: Longmans, Green, 1911);

Gillian Beer, *Meredith: A Change of Masks: A Study of the Novels* (London: Athlone Press, 1970);

Beer, "Meredith's Contributions to the *Pall Mall Gazette*," *Modern Language Review*, 61 (July 1966): 395-400;

Edward V. Brewer, "The Influence of Jean Paul Richter on George Meredith's Conception of Comedy," *Journal of English and German Philology*, 29, no. 2 (1930): 243-256;

Frederick Dolman, "George Meredith as Journalist," *New Review*, 8 (March 1893): 342-348;

David E. Foster, "'The Pecuniary Pen': Meredith's Personal Dilemma," *English Language Notes*, 13 (March 1976): 184-190;

Royal A. Gettmann, "Meredith as Publisher's Reader," *Journal of English and Germanic Philology*, 48 (January 1949): 45-56;

Gordon S. Haight, "George Meredith and the *Westminster Review*," *Modern Language Review*, 53 (January 1958): 1-16;

Norman Kelvin, *A Troubled Eden: Nature and Society in the Works of George Meredith* (Stanford: Stanford University Press, 1961);

Joseph C. Landis, "George Meredith's Comedy," *Boston University Studies in English*, 2 (Spring 1956): 17-35;

E. Arthur Robinson, "Meredith's Literary Theory and Science: Realism vs the Comic Spirit," *PMLA*, 53 (September 1938): 857-868;

James S. Stone, "George Meredith's Neglected *Up to Midnight*," *English Studies in Canada*, 2 (Spring 1976): 61-82.

Papers:

The Altschul Collection at the Beinecke Rare Book and Manuscript Library, Yale University; the Berg Collection at the New York Public Library; and the Henry E. Huntington Library, San Marino, California, have collections of Meredith's papers.

George Moore

(24 February 1852-21 January 1933)

James Hipp, Barry Faulk, and Marc Demarest
University of South Carolina

See also the Moore entries in *DLB 10, Modern British Dramatists, 1910-1945*, and *DLB 18, Victorian Novelists After 1885*.

BOOKS: *Worldliness: A Comedy in Three Acts* (London?: Privately printed, *circa* 1874);

Flowers of Passion (London: Provost, 1878);

Martin Luther: A Tragedy in Five Acts (London: Remington, 1879);

Pagan Poems (London: Newman, 1881);

A Modern Lover (3 volumes, London: Tinsley, 1883; 1 volume, Chicago: Laird & Lee, 1890);

A Mummer's Wife (London: Vizetelly, 1885); republished as *An Actor's Wife* (Chicago: Laird & Lee, 1889);

Literature at Nurse, or Circulating Morals (London: Vizetelly, 1885);

A Drama in Muslin: A Realistic Novel (London: Vizetelly, 1886);

Parnell and His Island (London: Sonnenschein, Lowrey, 1887);

A Mere Accident (London: Vizetelly, 1887; New York: Brentano's, 1887);

Confessions of a Young Man (London: Sonnenschein, Lowrey, 1888; New York: Brentano's, 1888);

Spring Days: A Realistic Novel–A Prelude to Don Juan (London: Vizetelly, 1888); republished as *Shifting Love* (Chicago: Wilson, 1891);

Mike Fletcher: A Novel (London: Ward & Downey, 1889; New York: Minerva, 1889);

Impressions and Opinions (London: Nutt, 1891; New York: Brentano's, 1913);

Vain Fortune (London: Henry, 1891; New York: Collier, 1892);

Modern Painting (London: Scott, 1893; New York: Scribners, 1893);

The Strike at Arlingsford: A Play in Three Acts (London: Scott, 1893; New York: Scribners, 1893);

Esther Waters: A Novel (London: Scott, 1894; Chicago & New York: Stone, 1894);

The Royal Academy 1895 (London: New Budget, 1895);

George Moore, circa 1887

Celibates (London: Scott, 1895; New York: Macmillan, 1895);

Evelyn Innes (London: Unwin, 1898; New York: Appleton, 1898);

The Bending of the Bough: A Comedy in Five Acts (London: Unwin, 1900; Chicago & New York: Stone, 1900);

Sister Teresa (London: Unwin, 1901; Philadelphia: Lippincott, 1901);

An T-Úr-Gort (Dublin: Sealy, Bryers & Walker, 1902); republished in English as *The Untilled Field* (London: Unwin, 1903; Philadelphia:

181

Lippincott, 1903);

The Lake (London: Heinemann, 1905; New York: Appleton, 1906);

Memoirs of My Dead Life (London: Heinemann, 1906; New York: Appleton, 1907);

Reminiscences of the Impressionist Painters (Dublin: Maunsel, 1906);

The Apostle: A Drama in Three Acts (Dublin: Maunsel, 1911; Boston: Luce, 1911); revised as *The Apostle: A Drama in a Prelude and Three Acts* (London: Heinemann, 1923); revised again as *The Passing of the Essenes: A Drama in Three Acts* (London: Heinemann, 1930; New York: Macmillan, 1930);

Hail and Farewell: A Trilogy, 3 volumes (London: Heinemann, 1911-1914; New York: Appleton, 1911-1914);

Elizabeth Cooper: A Comedy in Three Acts (Dublin: Maunsel, 1913; Boston: Luce, 1913);

Esther Waters: A Play in Five Acts (London: Heinemann, 1913; Boston: Luce, 1913);

Muslin (London: Heinemann, 1915; New York: Brentano's, 1915);

The Brook Kerith: A Syrian Story (Edinburgh: Laurie, 1916; New York: Macmillan, 1916);

Lewis Seymour and Some Women (London: Heinemann, 1917; New York: Brentano's, 1917);

A Story-Teller's Holiday (London & New York: Cumann Sean-eolais na h-Eireann, 1918; revised, 2 volumes, London: Heinemann, 1928);

Avowals (London: Cumann Sean-eolais na h-Eireann, 1919; New York: Boni & Liveright, 1919);

The Coming of Gabrielle: A Comedy (London: Cumann Sean-eolais na h-Eireann, 1920; New York: Boni & Liveright, 1921);

Héliose and Abélard (2 volumes, London: Cumann Sean-eolais na h-Eireann, 1921; 1 volume, New York: Boni & Liveright, 1921);

In Single Strictness (London: Heinemann, 1922; New York: Boni & Liveright, 1922); republished as *Celibate Lives* (London: Heinemann, 1927; New York: Boni & Liveright, 1927);

Conversations in Ebury Street (London: Heinemann, 1924; New York: Boni & Liveright, 1924);

Peronnik the Fool (New York: Boni & Liveright, 1924; London: Heinemann, 1933);

Pure Poetry: An Anthology (London: Nonesuch, 1924; New York: Boni & Liveright, 1924);

Ulick and Soracha (London: Nonesuch, 1926; New York: Boni & Liveright, 1926);

The Making of an Immortal: A Play in One Act (New York: Bowling Green Press, 1927);

A Flood (New York: Harbor Press, 1930);

Aphrodite in Aulis (London: Heinemann, 1930; New York: Fountain Press, 1930);

The Talking Pine (Paris: Hours Press, 1931; Tempe, Ariz.: Hill, 1948);

A Communication to My Friends (London: Nonesuch, 1933).

Collections: *The Collected Works of George Moore*, Carra Edition, 21 volumes (New York: Boni & Liveright, 1922-1924);

Works of George Moore, Uniform Edition, 20 volumes (London: Heinemann, 1924-1933; New York: Brentano's, 1924-1933). ′

TRANSLATION: *The Pastoral Loves of Daphnis and Chloe: Done in English*, translated by Moore from the story by Longus and based on the 1559 French translation by Jacques Amyot (London: Heinemann, 1924).

George Moore's critical works occupy, as Helmut E. Gerber has noted, the crucial position between the essentially social and moral criticism of Matthew Arnold and John Ruskin, on the one hand, and the artistic elitism of T. S. Eliot and the strict formalism of John Crowe Ransom, on the other. His autobiographical writings offer subjective, but nonetheless intimate and incisive, views of the French Impressionist and Naturalist movements and of the Irish Renaissance. Yet Moore's nonfiction prose has been consistently ignored by critics and readers alike; the majority of his critical essays remain uncollected, and it is primarily as a protomodern novelist that Moore is known. This unfinished portrait of George Moore—one that would have dismayed him—is partially the result of the volume of Moore's work and partially due to the range and depth of his intellectual pursuits; he sought a grand synthesis of painting, literature, and social commentary—an achievement he envisioned but never attained. William Butler Yeats wrote of Moore: "I said once, 'You work so hard that, like the Lancelot of Tennyson, you will almost see the grail.' But now, his finished work before me, I am convinced that he was denied even that 'almost.' " Acknowledging this failure, perhaps we can also recognize Moore as the belletristic iconoclast that Ford Madox Ford, in *It was the Nightingale* (1933), described as "the most skillful man of letters of his day—the most skillful in the whole world," a precursor to and participant in the modernist revolution.

George Augustus Moore was born on 24 February 1852 to George Henry Moore of Moore Hall, County Mayo, Ireland, and Mary Blake Moore. As a boy, he received private tutoring, and, in 1861, was sent by his parents to Oscott, a Jesuit school. There, as he noted in *Confessions of a Young Man* (1888), "it pleased me to read 'Queen Mab' and 'Cain' amid the priests and ignorance of a hateful Roman Catholic college ... my poets saved me from intellectual savagery; for I was incapable at that time of learning anything." His father eventually removed him from Oscott at the school's suggestion. In 1868 George Henry Moore was elected to Parliament, and the family, including George, relocated to London. When, in 1870, George Henry Moore died while on business in Ireland, ownership of the family estates passed into Moore's hands, assuring him of a yearly income in excess of £500 upon reaching the age of majority and freeing him to pursue his wide-ranging interests: Kant, Spinoza, Mill, Dickens, Eliot, the theater, horseracing, and fashionable restaurants. In 1873 Moore left London for Paris to study painting at the Ecole des Beaux Arts.

By 1885, when his *Literature at Nurse, or Circulating Morals* was published, Moore had already written two novels and two plays and produced two volumes of mediocre poetry written in the spirit of Swinburne, Baudelaire, and the Decadents. He had studied painting in Paris, met Mallarmé, Zola, Manet, Monet, Degas, and Seurat, and returned to England in 1880 a self-confessed disciple of Naturalism. He had also become friendly with his cousin Edward Martyn, the Irish playwright. In short, the artistic concerns that were to dominate Moore's life–drama, the theory and practice of the novel, painting and Irish culture–were in evidence before Moore embarked on his career as a critic.

Responding to pressure from the Irish Land League, which was threatening to appropriate Moore's ancestral estate in County Mayo–his primary source of income–Moore returned to London from Paris in 1880 and began his career as a novelist. In 1884 Moore's novel of the previous year, *A Modern Lover*, was removed from the two major circulating libraries, Mudie's and Smith's, because of complaints that it was morally offensive. *Literature at Nurse, or Circulating Morals* (1885), is Moore's continuation and expansion of his article "A New Censorship of Literature," published in the *Pall Mall Gazette* (December 1884), as a response to this removal. A vitriolic attack

William Butler Yeats with Moore at Coole Park, the country home of Lady Gregory near Roxborough, East Galway, Ireland (by kind permission of Colin Smythe)

on the idea of the three-decker novel and de facto censorship of "morally degrading" literature by the circulating libraries, *Literature at Nurse* links the middlebrow Victorian taste for sentimental, romantic novels–a taste that engendered exclusion of other types of novels from the circulating libraries, and thereby from popular success–to what Moore saw as the historical inability of the English to produce a prose literature of lasting value. *Literature at Nurse, or Circulating Morals* also introduces a touchstone of Moore's criticism: the separation of literature and conventional morality, a separation he believed was necessary to eradicate a literature that pandered, as he put it, "to the intellectual sloth of to-day."

Confessions of a Young Man (1888), a fictionalized autobiography, treats Moore's time in Paris, where he had settled at the age of twenty-one, bringing with him his valet, "an original hatred of my native country, and a brutal loathing of the religion I was brought up in." At the outset of *Confessions of a Young Man*, Moore admits, "I came into the world apparently with a nature like a smooth sheet of wax, bearing no impress but capable of receiving any." The work recounts his early efforts to become a painter under the tutelage of a distant relative and fellow bohemian, Lewis Weldon Hawkins, Moore's immersion in the aesthetic coteries of Paris in the 1870s, and his encounters with Villiers de L'Isle-Adam, Octave Mirbeau, Mallarmé, Manet, and Monet. The work ends with a statement of Moore's disillusionment with his endeavors as an artist and his turn to literature: "I shivered; the cold air of morning blew in my face, I closed the window, and sitting at the table, haggard and overworn, I continued my novel."

In *Impressions and Opinions* (1891), Balzac replaces Zola at the apex of Moore's critical hierarchy. This volume, culled and revised from Moore's periodical essays, contains pieces on Verlaine, Laforgue, and Rimbaud that predate Arthur Symons's better-known *The Symbolist Movement in Literature* (1899). Although perceptive in its insights, *Impressions and Opinions* suffers from Moore's as yet uncertain habits of mind, habits which had notably evolved from their early Pateresque appreciative leanings to the modernist stylistics that characterize his mature criticism.

Moore's training as a painter and his decided deviance from the late-Victorian aesthetic orthodoxy are apparent in *Modern Painting* (1893). Another collection of revised periodical essays, *Modern Painting*, is noteworthy for an anti-

Ruskin revaluation of Whistler, a brilliant technical discussion of Seurat's pointillism, and essays on two quintessential Moore themes: the artistic failures of the nineteenth century and the innate evils of contemporary artistic education, which he felt destroyed all creativity and intellect in its emphasis on uniformity and outdated technical values. Together with *The Royal Academy 1895* (1895), *Modern Painting* shows Moore the Francophile privileging French art–particularly Impressionism–as the manifestation of a radically modern theory of art.

Disillusioned with England's overbearing colonialism in the Boer War and deeply interested in the Irish Renaissance, Moore moved from London to Dublin in 1901 and began work on *The Untilled Field*. This group of realistic short stories about Ireland was published in Gaelic in 1902, and in English in 1903. After his novel *The Lake* (1905), Moore produced *Memoirs of My Dead Life* (1906). Whereas *Confessions of a Young Man* centers on Moore's apprenticeship as a painter, *Memoirs of My Dead Life* expands on the elements of romance in Moore's early life experiences. Although beginning with essentially the same autobiographical material as *Confessions of a Young Man*, *Memoirs of My Dead Life* includes Moore's later exploits in London, framing all the material in an episodic, sketchlike format which reflects Moore's increasing interest in and greater control over the game of fictionalized autobiography.

Reminiscences of the Impressionist Painters (1906) alternates between an insider's discussion of the lives and relative merits of Manet, Monet, and Degas, and an extended explanation of Moore's now fully developed artistic credo. Moore believed that "[A]ll conventions, of politics, society, and creed, yes, and of art, too, must be cast into the melting-pot; he who would be an artist must melt down all things; he must discover new formulas, new molds, all the old values must be swept aside, and he must arrive at a new estimate. The artist should keep himself free from all creed, from all dogma, from all opinion." Together with *Memoirs of My Dead Life*, *Reminiscences of the Impressionist Painters* marks the culmination of Moore's aesthetic development; he did not deviate substantially from the stances implicit in these works during the remainder of his literary career.

Hail and Farewell: A Trilogy (1911-1914) evidences the innovative approach to autobiographical form stimulated by Moore's immersion in the Irish Renaissance, which brought his innate ten-

From the manuscript for Moore's Memoirs of My Dead Life *(MA 3421, by permission of the Trustees of The Pierpont Morgan Library). The portion of the manuscript from which this page is taken was not included in the published version of Moore's work, which appeared in 1906. By Moore's account, the material was stolen "by one of my secretaries and sold, I think, in America. . . ."*

dencies as a raconteur to the fore. *Hail and Fare-well* reflects Moore's mature approach to fictionalized autobiography, interweaving sketches of prominent literary figures, including AE (George Russell) and William Butler Yeats, and literary and social polemics, all rendered with deceptive ease and in a tone deeply indebted to Moore's newly revived sense of his Irish heritage. Far from hating the country of his birth, as he had as a young man, Moore now found in his image of Ireland a source of creative energy that was to sustain him for the remainder of his life, as the sage of Ebury Street.

In 1911 Moore, who never married, moved to 121 Ebury Street, London, and the following years saw the completion and publication of his finest nonfiction prose works: *Hail and Farewell*, *Avowals* (1919) and *Conversations in Ebury Street* (1924). The genius of *Avowals*, noteworthy for Moore's transcription of conversations with Edmund Gosse and others, rests primarily on Moore's explication of his highly selective and idiosyncratic reading of English literary history: "I cannot allow that there are any masterpieces in English prose narrative, for masterpieces are written only by first-rate minds, and I think you will agree with me that only the inferior or–shall we say?–the subaltern mind has attempted prose narrative in England." Moore surveys the history of English prose narrative from Defoe to Stevenson and, with the notable exceptions of Anne Brontë's *The Tenant of Wildfell Hall* (1848) and Walter Pa-

ter's *Marius the Epicurean* (1885), finds the English novel largely deficient in comparison with Continental narrative.

Conversations in Ebury Street is Moore's chef d'oeuvre; as a contemporary reviewer wrote in the London *Observer*, "There is no more beautiful prose now being written than that which Mr. Moore employs . . . . It moves as gently as the breathing of an infant. It is powerful and modest and limpid, and has a rare distinction of cadence. Poetry, nor the silver-snarling trumpets, need not be sought in it; but those who wish to learn how prose should be written will find no worthier master to-day than George Moore. This is classical writing." Continuing his critique of the English novel with *Conversations in Ebury Street*, Moore attacks the handling of life experience in Thomas Hardy and George Eliot, finding both constrained by a uniquely English triviality that substitutes inappropriate and unnecessary affectations for a rendering of the actual with a necessary depth of appropriate realistic detail. *Conversations in Ebury Street* also examines Shakespeare, Balzac, and several minor English painters. Moore passes judgment on the merits of each with a finality that, within the conversational format of the work, seems overly simplistic; yet the compelling power of Moore's personality renders each valuation strangely convincing.

Moore's final piece of nonfiction prose, *A Communication to My Friends* (1933), was originally intended as a general introduction to the Uni-

Moore, Edmund Gosse, and Haddon Chambers in 1919 at the home of London publisher William Heinemann

form Edition of his complete works but remained unfinished at his death, on 21 January 1933. *A Communication to My Friends* is at best an addendum to Moore's work, a series of informal notes on the writing and publication histories of his various works.

As Moore wrote in *Conversations in Ebury Street,* "the man who writes many books raises his tombstone." Moore's entombment in a seldom-visited corner of the canonical cemetery is as much the result of his apparently capricious critical stances and his prolific output as of a benign critical neglect of Moore and his pivotal position in the history of English letters. As Malcolm Brown noted in "The Craftsman as Critic," George Moore "was fundamentally an honest man, infinitely less limited than he might have been; and he sensed, even if he could not bring himself to say so directly . . . that too much sensitivity, as well as too little, may anaesthetize; that in the name of art one may either exalt or destroy art; that hatred of philistinism may transform a writer into a perfect likeness of the philistine, moving through the cultural heritage like a hooligan, like the philistine himself, finding the literary tradition only so much tiresome absurdity. . . . One need not condescend: for its purpose, Moore's critical manner could hardly be improved upon." But perhaps Ford Madox Ford described Moore's dilemma best: "I suppose it was his aloofness from life that made one always forget George Moore. . . . In an infinite number of reviews and *comptes rendus* of the literature of the world that I have read–and written–George Moore was almost invariably forgotten. That was due perhaps to the fact that he belonged to no school in England; perhaps to his want of personal geniality, perhaps to something more subtle." Whatever that "something more subtle" might be, it is clear that it has been a critical stumbling block to a fresh and balanced valuation of Moore's nonfiction prose.

Letters:
Letters from George Moore to Ed. Dujardin, 1886-1922, edited by John Eglinton (New York: Gaige, 1929);
George Moore: Letters to Lady Cunard, 1895-1933, edited by Rupert Hart-Davis (London: Hart-Davis, 1957);

George Moore in Transition: Letters to T. Fisher Unwin and Lena Milman, 1894-1910, edited by Helmut E. Gerber (Detroit: Wayne State University Press, 1968).

Bibliography:
Edwin Gilcher, *A Bibliography of George Moore* (De Kalb: Northern Illinois University Press, 1970).

Biography:
Joseph Hone, *The Life of George Moore* (London: Gollancz, 1936).

References:
Janet Egleson Dunleavy, ed., *George Moore in Perspective* (Gerrard's Cross: Colin Smythe, 1983);
Ford Madox Ford, *It Was the Nightingale* (Philadelphia & London: Lippincott, 1933);
Helmut E. Gerber, "George Moore: From Pure Poetry to Pure Criticism," *Journal of Aesthetics and Art Criticism,* 25 (Spring 1967): 281-291;
Douglas Hughes, ed., *The Man of Wax: Critical Essays on George Moore* (New York: New York University Press, 1971);
Graham Owens, ed., *George Moore's Mind and Art* (Edinburgh: Oliver & Boyd, 1968);
Ronald Schleifer, "George Moore's Turning Mind: Digression and Autobiographical Art in *Hail and Farewell,*" *Genre,* 12, no. 4 (1979): 473-503.

Papers:
Collections of Moore's papers can be found in the British Library, the National Library of Ireland, the Brotherton Library at the University of Leeds, the University of London Library, the Fitzwilliam Museum (Cambridge), the Bibliothèque Nationale (Paris), the University of Washington Library, the Academic Center Library (University of Texas at Austin), the Beinecke Rare Book and Manuscript Library (Yale), the Boston Public Library, the Houghton Library (Harvard), the Library of the State University of New York at Buffalo, Princeton University Library, and the New York Public Library.

John Morley

(24 December 1838-23 September 1923)

Philip L. Elliott
Furman University

BOOKS: *Modern Characteristics,* anonymous (London: Tinsley, 1865);

Studies in Conduct, anonymous (London: Chapman & Hall, 1867);

Edmund Burke: A Historical Study (London: Macmillan, 1867; New York: Knopf, 1924);

Critical Miscellanies, 4 series (volumes 1-2, Chapman & Hall, 1871, 1877; volume 1 republished, New York: Scribner & Welford, 1879; volumes 1-2 revised and republished with volume 3, London & New York: Macmillan, 1886; volume 4, London & New York: Macmillan, 1908); volume 4 also published as *Miscellanies Fourth Series* (London: Macmillan, 1908);

Voltaire (London: Chapman & Hall, 1872; revised, 1872; New York: Appleton, 1872);

Rousseau, 2 volumes (London: Chapman & Hall, 1873; New York: Scribner & Welford, 1878);

The Struggle for National Education (London: Chapman & Hall, 1873);

On Compromise (London: Chapman & Hall, 1874; London & New York: Macmillan, 1903);

Diderot and the Encyclopaedists (2 volumes, London: Chapman & Hall, 1878; 1 volume, New York: Scribner & Welford, 1878);

Burke (London: Macmillan, 1879; New York: Harper, 1879);

Life of Richard Cobden (2 volumes, London: Chapman & Hall, 1881; 1 volume, Boston: Roberts Brothers, 1881);

Ralph Waldo Emerson: An Essay (New York: Macmillan, 1884);

Walpole (London & New York: Macmillan, 1889);

Studies in Literature (London & New York: Macmillan, 1891);

Machiavelli: The Romanes Lectures Delivered in the Sheldonian Theatre, June 2, 1897 (London: Macmillan/New York: Macmillan, 1897);

Oliver Cromwell (London: Macmillan, 1900; New York: Century, 1900);

The Life of William Ewart Gladstone, 3 volumes (New York & London: Macmillan, 1903);

Literary Essays (London: Humphreys, 1906);

Speeches on Indian Affairs (Madras: Natesan, 1908; revised and enlarged, 1917);

Indian Speeches (London: Macmillan, 1909);

Science and Literature (Oxford: Privately printed, 1911);

Notes on Politics and History (London: Macmillan, 1913; New York: Macmillan, 1914);

Recollections, 2 volumes (London: Macmillan,

1917; New York: Macmillan, 1917);
Memorandum on Resignation, August 1914 (London: Macmillan, 1928; New York: Macmillan, 1928).
Collection: *The Works of Lord Morley* (15 volumes, London: Macmillan, 1921; revised, 12 volumes, London: Macmillan, 1923).

In the second half of the nineteenth century John Morley had a distinguished reputation as a man of letters, specifically as an editor and a biographer. In 1883 he became a member of Parliament and later served as secretary of state for Ireland and for India. The energy of his application to these endeavors was unfailing, and his level of achievement was high, though critics now consider him to have failed to achieve first rank either as a man of letters or as a politician. In his *Recollections* (1917), Morley devoted most of the two volumes to his political career, and contemporary scholarship has largely concentrated on his political role. Morley's other contributions, however, are worthy of note: his excellent work as editor of the *Fortnightly Review*, his studies in biography, and his literary criticism.

John Morley was born to Jonathan and Priscilla Donkin Morley at Blackburn, a center of the cotton-weaving industry. His father, a surgeon, was originally a Wesleyan who became a member of the Church of England after settling at Blackburn. Morley called his father a "born lover of books"; he had taught himself Latin and French and carried on his rounds pocket editions of Virgil, Racine, and Byron. He was a strict disciplinarian who encouraged his son's intellectual abilities by sending him to Hoole's Academy, University College School, and Cheltenham College, where he won an open scholarship to Lincoln College, Oxford. At Oxford, Morley lived in John Wesley's old rooms, which pleased his father since he intended his son for holy orders. The benefits of Oxford for Morley, however, were secular. One of the most important then and later was his friendship with John Cotter Morrison, the senior commoner, whose studies in French literature and biography paralleled Morley's later activities. While at Oxford, Morley read and came to know almost by heart John Stuart Mill's *On Liberty* (1859), a book which influenced him for the rest of his life; but at least as influential was his loss of religious faith, a loss which convinced him that he could not take holy orders. When he informed his father, the result was a bitter quarrel and a withdrawal of financial support. Morley

was forced to leave Oxford with only a pass degree.

As had Edmund Burke before him, he made his way to London and lived the precarious life of a free-lance journalist, often "scribbling with an empty paunch," as he later recalled. In 1863 John Cook, editor of the *Saturday Review*, placed him on retainer to write "middles" (miscellaneous articles appearing between editorials and reviews). Robert Cecil (later Lord Salisbury) and Leslie Stephen were also on the staff at this time. Morley's reserve is nicely illustrated by his account of sitting with Robert Cecil every Tuesday morning in the editorial anteroom "awaiting our commissions, but he too, had a talent for silence, and we exchanged no words, either now or on any future occasion, though, as it happened we often found something to say in public about each other's opinions and reasons in days to come." In 1863 Morley became acquainted with George Meredith, whose friendship and encouragement were most valuable. Morley's early admiration for John Stuart Mill became friendship when "New Ideas," one of his *Saturday Review* "middles," brought him to Mill's attention. As a frequent guest at Blackheath, Mill's home, Morley met George Grote, Herbert Spencer, and other friends of Mill. Other articles brought him the acquaintance of George Eliot and George Henry Lewes.

In "The Function of Criticism at the Present Time," a lecture delivered at Oxford in 1864, Matthew Arnold deplored criticism shaped by political and sectarian interests. In 1865 Anthony Trollope, John Cotter Morrison, and Frederick Chapman decided to found the *Fortnightly Review* (soon to become a monthly) as an imitation of the *Revue des Deux Mondes*, containing fiction, poetry, discussions of art, literature, and politics. The review was to belong to no party or sect, and contributions were to be signed, a very radical move in those days of anonymous journalism. George Henry Lewes was chosen as the first editor, and, when ill health forced his resignation in December 1866, Morley, largely through the influence of his old friend Morrison, became editor and began, according to John Gross in *The Rise and Fall of the Man of Letters* (1969), "as distinguished an editorial term of office as any in the nineteenth century."

Under Morley's leadership, the *Fortnightly* developed an unrivaled reputation as a magazine containing the advanced thought of the period. Morley had an outstanding group of contributors including T. H. Huxley, Herbert Spencer,

George Meredith, John Stuart Mill, Frederic Harrison, Anthony Trollope, Matthew Arnold, Leslie Stephen, Walter Pater, Joseph Chamberlain, Mark Pattison, Edmund Gosse, and George Saintsbury. A. C. Swinburne, William Morris, and Dante Gabriel Rossetti were among those contributing poetry. The major reason for Morley's success was his strong sense of mission. Like some other Victorians, he seemed to compensate for his loss of religious faith by an increased sense of duty. In his *Studies in Conduct* (1867) he very specifically expressed his antihedonism: "If the idea of self-denial is to be expunged from the list of things worthy of civilization, then society must inevitably fall to pieces. If men and women are to insist on drinking to the dregs the cup of every desire of their animal nature, without a thought of the effects which may flow from their gratification, then it is plain that most of the business of the world will come to a standstill." Morley was made of stern stuff; he saw clearly his duty to be a propagator of the truth dedicated to "the diffusion of rationalistic standards in things spiritual and temporal alike." He gained a small measure of fame by always spelling *God* with a small *g*, and anticlericalism was always the most obvious plank in the *Fortnightly*'s platform. Morley always got on well with individual clergymen but consistently attacked the priesthood and urged the disestablishment of the church. He gave special emphasis to science; one of the most outstanding and controversial essays published in the *Fortnightly Review* was T. H. Huxley's "On the Physical Basis of Life" (1869). Perhaps inevitably, the *Fortnightly* acquired a reputation as the voice of the English Positivists. Auguste Comte, the founder of the Religion of Humanity, was certainly an influence on Morley, although he never joined Comte's "new church." While he published articles by such fervid Comtean disciples as Frederic Harrison, Morley also published Huxley's comment that the Comtean philosophy was merely "Catholicism minus Christianity." Between 1867 and 1873, circulation of the *Fortnightly* rose from 1,400 to 2,500; Morley estimated that he had 30,000 readers.

Morley's writings for the *Fortnightly* fit loosely under four headings: biographical, theoretical, political, and literary. The biographical clearly predominates. Probably under the influence of Comte and Thomas Carlyle, Morley believed that the most important element in the study of human affairs was character. Movements and forces could best be understood through the lives of individuals. Although he specifically rejected Comte's hagiographic tendency to replace earlier religious saints with secular ones, he believed that "history becomes an instrument of moral training and acquires an aspect of practical moral significance." Burke and Carlyle had exposed the destructive side of the Enlightenment and French Revolution; Morley wanted to express both the destructive and constructive sides, to reconstruct these cultural experiences to meet nineteenth-century needs. Beginning with Maistre and proceeding to Voltaire, Rousseau, Diderot, Vanvenargues, Holbach, Turgot, and Condorcet, Morley wrote a series of studies on French thinkers and writers, ranging from short essays to full biographies. Most of these thinkers had attempted progress through enlightenment, sweeping away prejudice, superstition, and fanaticism, and shattering the tyranny of Church and State. Morley believed that the Church of England in the nineteenth century was still committed to the old positions and should be attacked in the same spirit in which Voltaire had attacked the institutional church of his day. Rousseau was valuable because he helped to keep alive "those instincts of holiness and brotherhood" which Morley hoped would replace the lost divinities. Morley found that much of the program of nineteenth-century liberalism had been anticipated by Diderot: "materialistic solutions in the science of man, humanitarian ends in legislation, active faith in the improvableness of institutions."

"Cut him open," George Meredith said of Morley, "and you will find a clergyman inside." Even though he had lost his belief in a supreme being, Morley retained a strong concept of duty and individual responsibility. He had believed for a time in some force in the universe which was producing improvement, but he later came to believe that progress was the result of individual effort. A good example of his individual effort is the energy he spent to reform the elementary-school system. The National Educational Act of 1870 had given to Anglican schools three-fourths of all money provided for instruction. Morley was able to show in a series of essays in the *Fortnightly* that one-fourth of the children emerged from church schools without the ability to read the Bible, write coherently, or do more than simple sums of arithmetic. The issue of church schools ultimately merged into the larger issue of disestablishment.

Character and incident were much more appealing to Morley than discussion of principles;

"The Fortnightly Review," caricature of Morley published in Vanity Fair, 30 November 1878, four years before Morley resigned his post as editor of the Fortnightly *(Collection of Jerold J. Savory)*

On Compromise, published in 1874, is his only full-scale treatment of ethical and social theory. The work is a central Victorian document in the tradition of Mill's *On Liberty* (which influenced it), and it epitomizes the spirit of the *Fortnightly Review*: "the diffusion and encouragement of rationalistic standards in things spiritual and temporal alike." The central questions of the book are to what extent respect for tradition, the opinions of others, and political considerations should be allowed to prevail over truth or to limit the search for truth, and to what extent compromise is justifiable in opinion, speech, and action. Only a fanatic would maintain that compromise is impossible, and Mor-

ley is certainly less rigid than one critic implied with his assertion that the only evidence of compromise in the work was the title. However, with "institutions that have outlived their time and interests and lost their justification," the rationalist must take the truth "courageously for his ensign and device, but neither force nor expect the whole world straightway to follow; . . . it is legitimate compromise to say, 'I do not expect you to execute this improvement, or to surrender that prejudice in my time. But at any rate it shall not be my fault if the improvement remains unknown or neglected. There shall be one man at least who has surrendered the prejudice, and who does not hide the fact.' "

Morley was a literary critic in the mode of Matthew Arnold, who, unlike twentieth-century critics with their close analyses of text or imagery, felt that the proper sphere of literary evaluation was the author's attitude toward experience and his sense of values. Morley was concerned with values and with the author's relationship to the currents of thought in his age: "we need synthetic criticism, which, after analysis has done its work, and disclosed to us the peculiar qualities of form, conception, and treatment, shall construct for us the poet's mental figure in its integrity and just coherence, and then finally, as the sum of its work, shall trace the relations of the poet's ideas, either direct or indirect, through the central currents of thought, to the visible tendencies of an existing age."

Unfortunately, Morley's best-known work of criticism, written early in his career, was a review of Swinburne's *Poems and Ballads* (1866), which did much to establish the popular negative estimate of Swinburne and which caused the poet's frightened publisher to withdraw the volume. Morley's unusually heated tone and exaggerated language suggest a prudish reaction to Swinburne's sensual detail, although Morley's ostensible complaint was that Swinburne counterfeited emotion: "never have such bountifulness of imagination, such mastery of the music of verse, been yoked with such thinness of contemplation and such poverty of genuinely impassioned thought." Despite the review, Morley and Swinburne remained friends, and Swinburne later contributed poems and reviews to the *Fortnightly*. Ultimately Morley was willing to accept the implications of the art-for-art's-sake movement as long as there was not a plethora of sensual detail. In 1873 he reviewed Pater's *Studies in the History of the Renaissance* and celebrated the humanistic direction of the movement. "Aesthetic spirits were no longer able to rest in a system associated with theology. . . . Mr. Pater says that love of art for art's sake has most of the true wisdom that makes life full. The fact that such a saying is possible in the mouth of an able and shrewd witted man of wide culture and knowledge, and that a serious writer should thus raise aesthetic interest to the throne lately filled by religion, only shows how void the old theologies have become."

Morley's best critical work was done in his essays on Macaulay, Byron, and Carlyle in which he is most concerned with the intellectual climate or shaping spirit of the age. In Byron's case, for example, he identifies this shaping spirit as revolutionary and sees it in his treatment of nature, in the antisocial tendencies of his characters, and in his protagonists set against "a society which was more concerned with the rights of property than with the spirit and dignity of man."

Alabaster prose is one term which has been used to describe Morley's style. Morley would probably prefer the qualifiers *sound* and *correct*. "As to literary form, I took too little thought, only seeking correctness, and that after all is the prime essential. The stylist provokes because he take endless trouble, is inexhaustible in strange devices of image and verbal collocation, invents ingenious standards of precision, takes nothing plain from heart and mind–only to bring upon his work that sense of insincerity and affectation." Morley's only irritating characteristic is an overuse of "as if." On the whole, his writing has the "regularity, uniformity, precision, balance" which Matthew Arnold felt were necessary for good prose, and while he lacks the charm and warmth of Arnold, he does have wit. He commented on the publication of Carlyle's works: "the edition will be complete in the course of another twelvemonth, and the whole of the golden Gospel of Silence will then be effectively compressed in thirty fine volumes."

Morley is at one with his age in using imagery of energy and machinery. He liked the image of the railway where machinery functioned in such a way as to require the engine to run on rails to one terminus whatever delays and disasters occurred. He presented his subjects in the context of a constant releasing of energy. He once wrote, "For the unreflecting portion of mankind the spectacle of energy on a large scale has always irresistible attractions; vigour becomes an end in itself and an object of admiration for its own sake." This expenditure of energy is an inter-esting contrast to Morley's own habits of composition. According to F. W. Hirst's *Early Life and Letters of John Morley* (1927), his table "was always clear and free from papers, which he kept in drawers," and he liked to write wearing "clean linen." Morley once wrote to a friend, "I wonder whether you agree with me in the proper garb for writing. Like Buffon, I insist on shaving and clean linen before sitting down to composition."

When Morley resigned his editorship in 1882, he took pride in the role of the *Fortnightly* and other reviews having "brought abstract discussion from the library down to the parlour, and from the serious student down to the man in the street, . . . controversies which had hitherto been confined to books and treatises were now to be admitted to popular periodicals, and the common man of the world would now listen and have an opinion of his own. . . . The clergy no longer have the pulpit to themselves, for the new reviews became more powerful pulpits, in which heretics were at least as welcome as orthodox."

Morley's resignation as editor in 1882 was the result of the gradual growth of his involvement in politics. At the end of 1867 he had made a visit to the United States, where he met Walt Whitman, Ralph Waldo Emerson, and Charles Sumner, but his strongest impression was of the Irish-Americans. Soon after his return to England, Morley was speaking publicly about the need to redress Irish grievances. In 1869 he stood as M.P. for Blackburn and was defeated. His marriage to Rose Mary Ayling took place in May 1870; the marriage produced no children. After 1875 the *Fortnightly* became the recognized organ for political radicalism supporting Irish home rule and opposing anti-imperialism and specifically attacking Sir Bartle Fere, governor of the Cape and high commissioner for the settlement of native affairs, for his actions in South Africa. In 1880 Morley lost again in a bid for Parliament, and in this year he assumed the editorship of the *Pall Mall Gazette*, changing the paper's orientation from conservatism to radicalism and from imperialism to Cobdenism. He continued to write many articles advocating Irish home rule. In 1883, the year after he resigned as editor of the *Fortnightly*, he was elected M.P. for Newcastle upon Tyne; in 1885 he became Gladstone's chief secretary for Ireland and helped write the first Home Rule bill.

Morley devoted a tremendous amount of energy to political matters in the years after 1883, but he did not abandon literature. After publishing his critical study of Edmund Burke in 1867, Morley also produced a biography of Burke for the English Men of Letters series. Morley had been a reader for Macmillan since the mid 1860s and in 1877 conceived this series, which was easily the most successful of the many sets of brief biographies that were beginning to appear. Morley was able to pay £100 per volume and was able to recruit many of the leading literary figures: Huxley wrote on Hume, Henry James on Hawthorne, Leslie Stephen on Swift, Pope, and Johnson, and Mark Pattison on Milton. In 1881 Morley produced his *Life of Richard Cobden* which had a much larger sale than any of his earlier books and made him widely known. In 1903 appeared *The Life of William Ewart Gladstone,* which became his best-selling publication: 30,000 copies in the first year and 100,000 more in the next decade. As a biographer Morley does not have a Boswell's interest in personal detail nor does he present weaknesses and failings in his subject (one reader complained that Morley presented Gladstone in continuous evening dress). Perhaps Morley's idealization of character stemmed from his own strong sense of order and decorum which led him to present Gladstone as he wished him to be. Certainly he was very alert to the educational potential of biography and wished to present his readers with ideal role models.

From 1905 to 1910 Morley served as secretary of state for India. In 1908 he was raised to the peerage as Viscount Morley of Blackburn and elected chancellor of Manchester University. In 1914 he resigned from Herbert Asquith's cabinet in protest against England's drift toward war. He produced his *Recollections* in 1917 and died in 1923, remaining to the end of his life an agnostic, a liberal, and an individual. One of his last comments in the *Recollections* provides an apt valediction: "if all is random, be not random thou."

In attempting to assess Morley's rank in the nineteenth century and his claim for continuing attention, one might regret his involvement in politics and feel with Thomas Hardy that this man who might have been the "Gibbon of his age" wasted energies in politics which would have been better spent in literature. Even so, his contri-

bution to literature is considerable. His studies of Voltaire, Rousseau, and Diderot are pioneering and just. *On Compromise,* while never attaining the status of Mill's *On Liberty,* is a valuable document for understanding Victorian concerns. However, Morley's greatest contribution is as a literary critic. His historical sense may not be exciting to those who prefer close textual analysis, but for readers who are interested in other ways to treat literature, Morley, with his concern for the writer's relationship with his age, offers a valuable model.

Biographies:

Saiyad Sadar Ali Khan, *The Life of Lord Morley* (London: Pitman, 1923);

F. W. Hirst, *Early Life and Letters of John Morley,* 2 volumes (London: Macmillan, 1927).

References:

Edward Alexander, *John Morley* (New York: Twayne, 1972);

Edwin M. Everett, *The Party of Humanity* (Chapel Hill: University of North Carolina Press, 1939);

John Gross, *The Rise and Fall of the Man of Letters* (London: Weidenfeld & Nicolson, 1969), pp. 99-112;

D. A. Hamer, *John Morley: Liberal Intellectual in Politics* (Oxford: Clarendon Press, 1968);

Frances W. Knickerbocker, *Free Minds: John Morley and His Friends* (Cambridge: Harvard University Press, 1943);

Warren Staebler, *The Liberal Mind of John Morley* (Princeton: Princeton University Press, 1943);

Basil Willey, "John Morley," in his *More Nineteenth Century Studies: A Group of Honest Doubters* (London: Chatto & Windus, 1956), pp. 248-301.

Papers:

Collections of papers and letters are at the India Office Library, Wadham College, Oxford; the London School of Economics; Imperial College; and the Library of Congress.

William Morris

Frederick Kirchhoff
Indiana University-Purdue University at Fort Wayne

See also the Morris entries in *DLB 18, Victorian Novelists After 1885,* and *DLB 35, Victorian Poets After 1850.*

BIRTH: Walthamstow, Essex, 24 March 1834, to William and Emma Shelton Morris.

EDUCATION: B.A., Exeter College, Oxford, 1856; M.A., 1875;

AWARDS AND HONORS: Honorary Fellowship, Exeter College, Oxford, 1882.

MARRIAGE: 26 April 1859 to Jane Burden; children: Jane Alice (Jenny) and Mary (May).

DEATH: Hammersmith, Middlesex, 3 October 1896.

BOOKS: *The Defence of Guenevere and Other Poems* (London: Bell & Daldy, 1858: Boston: Roberts Brothers, 1875);

The Life and Death of Jason: A Poem (London: Bell & Daldy, 1867; Boston: Roberts Brothers, 1867);

The Earthly Paradise: A Poem, 3 volumes (London: Ellis, 1868-1870; Boston: Roberts Brothers, 1868-1870);

Love Is Enough; or, The Freeing of Pharamond: A Morality (London: Ellis & White, 1873; Boston: Roberts Brothers, 1873);

The Story of Sigurd the Volsung and the Fall of the Niblungs (London: Ellis & White, 1876; Boston: Roberts Brothers, 1876);

Hopes and Fears for Art: Five Lectures Delivered in Birmingham, London, and Nottingham 1878-81 (London: Ellis & White, 1882; Boston: Roberts Brothers, 1882);

A Summary of the Principles of Socialism Written for the Democratic Federation, by Morris and H. M. Hyndman (London: Modern Press, 1884);

Textile Fabrics: A Lecture (London: Clowes, 1884);

Art and Socialism: A Lecture; and Watchman, What of

William Morris, late 1870s (William Morris Gallery)

the Night? The Aims and Ideals of the English Socialists of Today (London: Reeves, 1884);

Chants for Socialists: No. 1. The Day is Coming (London: Reeves, 1884);

The Voice of Toil, All for the Cause: Two Chants for Socialists (London: Justice Office, 1884);

The God of the Poor (London: Justice Office, 1884);

Chants for Socialists (London: Socialist League Office, 1885; New York: New Horizon Press, 1935);

The Manifesto of the Socialist League (London: Socialist League Office, 1885);

The Socialist League: Constitution and Rules Adopted at the General Conference (London: Socialist League Office, 1885);

Address to Trades' Unions (The Socialist Platform–No. 1) (London: Socialist League Office, 1885);

Useful Work v. Useless Toil (The Socialist Platform—No. 2) (London: Socialist League Office, 1885);

For Whom Shall We Vote? Addressed to the Working-Men Electors of Great Britain (London: Commonweal Office, 1885);

What Socialists Want (London: Hammersmith Branch of the Socialist League, 1885);

The Labour Question from the Socialist Standpoint (Claims of Labour Lectures—No. 5) (Edinburgh: Co-operative Printing, 1886);

A Short Account of the Commune of Paris (The Socialist Platform—No. 4) (London: Socialist League Office, 1886);

The Pilgrims of Hope: A Poem in Thirteen Parts (London: Buxton Forman, 1886; Portland, Maine: Mosher, 1901);

The Aims of Art (London: Commonweal Office, 1887);

The Tables Turned; or, Nupkins Awakened: A Socialist Interlude (London: Commonweal Office, 1887);

True and False Society (London: Socialist League Office, 1888);

Signs of Change: Seven Lectures Delivered on Various Occasions (London: Reeves & Turner, 1888; New York: Longmans, Green, 1896);

A Dream of John Ball and A King's Lesson (London: Reeves & Turner, 1888; East Aurora, N.Y.: Roycroft, 1898);

A Tale of the House of the Wolfings and All the Kindreds of the Mark (London: Reeves & Turner, 1889; Boston: Roberts Brothers, 1890);

The Roots of the Mountains: Wherein is Told Somewhat of the Lives of the Men of Burgdale, Their Friends, Their Neighbours, Their Foemen, and Their Fellows in Arms (London: Reeves & Turner, 1890; New York: Longmans, Green, 1896);

Monopoly; or, How Labour is Robbed (The Socialist Platform—No. 7) (London: Commonweal Office, 1890);

News from Nowhere: or, An Epoch of Rest: Being Some Chapters from a Utopian Romance (Boston: Roberts Brothers, 1890; London: Reeves & Turner, 1891);

Statement of Principles of the Hammersmith Socialist Society, anonymous (Hammersmith: Hammersmith Socialist Society, 1890);

The Story of the Glittering Plain Which Has Been Also Called the Land of Living Men or the Acre of the Undying (Hammersmith: Kelmscott Press, 1891; London: Reeves & Turner, 1891; Boston: Roberts Brothers, 1891);

Poems by the Way (Hammersmith: Kelmscott Press, 1891; London: Reeves & Turner, 1891; Boston: Roberts Brothers, 1892);

Address on the Collection of Paintings of the English Pre-Raphaelite School (Birmingham: Osborne, 1891);

Under an Elm-Tree: or, Thoughts in the Country-side (Aberdeen, Scotland: Leatham, 1891; Portland, Maine: Mosher, 1912);

Manifesto of English Socialists, anonymous, by Morris, H. M. Hyndman, and G. B. Shaw (London: Twentieth Century Press, 1893);

The Reward of Labour: A Dialogue (London: Hayman, Christy & Lilly, 1893);

Concerning Westminster Abbey, anonymous (London: Women's Printing Society, 1893);

Socialism: Its Growth and Outcome, by Morris and E. B. Bax (London: Sonnenschein, 1893; New York: Scribners, 1893);

Help for the Miners: The Deeper Meaning of the Struggle (London: Baines & Searsrook, 1893);

Gothic Architecture: A Lecture for the Arts and Crafts Exhibition Society (Hammersmith: Kelmscott Press, 1893);

The Wood beyond the World (Hammersmith: Kelmscott Press, 1894; London: Lawrence & Bullen, 1895; Boston: Roberts House, 1895);

The Why I Ams: Why I Am a Communist, with L. S. Bevington's Why I Am an Expropriationist (London: Liberty Press, 1894);

Child Christopher and Goldilind the Fair (2 volumes, Hammersmith: Kelmscott Press, 1895; 1 volume, Portland, Maine: Mosher, 1900);

Gossip about an Old House on the Upper Thames (Birmingham: Birmingham Guild of Handicraft, 1895; Flushing, N.Y.: Hill, 1901);

The Well at the World's End: A Tale (Hammersmith: Kelmscott Press, 1896; 2 volumes, London: Longmans, Green, 1896);

Of the External Coverings of Roofs, anonymous (London: Society for the Protection of Ancient Buildings, 1896);

How I Became a Socialist (London: Twentieth Century Press, 1896);

Some German Woodcuts of the Fifteenth Century, edited by S. C. Cockerell (Hammersmith: Kelmscott Press, 1897);

The Water of the Wondrous Isles (Hammersmith: Kelmscott Press, 1897; London: Longmans, Green, 1897);

The Sundering Flood (Hammersmith: Kelmscott Press, 1897; London: Longmans, Green, 1898);

A Note by William Morris on His Aims in Founding

the Kelmscott Press, Together with a Short Description of the Press by S. C. Cockerell and an Annotated List of the Books Printed Thereat (Hammersmith: Kelmscott Press, 1898);

Address Delivered at the Distribution of Prizes to Students of the Birmingham Municipal School of Art on 21 February 1894 (London: Longmans, Green, 1898);

Art and the Beauty of the Earth (London: Longmans, Green, 1899);

Some Hints on Pattern-Designing (London: Longmans, Green, 1899);

Architecture and History, and Westminster Abbey (London: Longmans, Green, 1900);

Art and Its Producers, and the Arts and Crafts of Today (London: Longmans, Green, 1901);

Architecture, Industry, and Wealth: Collected Papers (London: Longmans, Green, 1902);

Communism (Fabian Tract No. 113) (London: Fabian Society, 1903);

The Hollow Land and Other Contributions to the Oxford and Cambridge Magazine (London: Longmans, Green, 1903);

The Unpublished Lectures of William Morris, edited by Eugene D. LeMire (Detroit: Wayne State University Press, 1969);

Icelandic Journals of William Morris (Fontwell: Centaur Press, 1969; New York: Praeger, 1970);

A Book of Verse: A Facsimile of the Manuscript Written in 1870 (London: Scolar Press, 1980);

Socialist Diary, edited by Florence Boos (Iowa City: Windhover Press, 1981);

The Novel on Blue Paper, edited by Penelope Fitzgerald (London: Journeyman Press, 1982); *Dickens Studies Annual: Essays on Victorian Fiction,* volume 10, edited by Michael Timko, Fred Kaplan, and Edward Guiliano (New York: AMS Press, 1982), pp. 153-220;

The Ideal Book: Essays and Lectures on the Arts of the Book, edited by William S. Peterson (Berkeley & London: University of California Press, 1982);

The Juvenilia of William Morris, edited by Boos (New York: William Morris Society, 1983).

Collections: *The Collected Works of William Morris,* edited by May Morris, 24 volumes (London & New York: Longmans, Green, 1910-1915);

William Morris: Artist, Writer, Socialist, edited by Morris, 2 volumes (Oxford: Blackwell, 1936).

OTHER: "Mural Decoration," by Morris and J. H. Middleton, in *Encyclopaedia Britannica,* ninth edition, volume 17 (Edinburgh: Black, 1884; New York: Allen, 1888);

John Ruskin, *The Nature of Gothic: A Chapter of the Stones of Venice,* preface by Morris (London: Allen, 1892);

Thomas More, *Utopia,* foreword by Morris (Hammersmith: Kelmscott Press, 1893);

Robert Steele, ed., *Medieval Lore,* preface by Morris (London: Stock, 1893; Boston: Luce, 1907);

Arts and Crafts Exhibition Society, *Arts and Crafts Essays,* preface and three articles by Morris (London: Rivington, Percival, 1893; New York: Scribners, 1893).

TRANSLATIONS: *The Story of Grettir the Strong,* translated by Morris and Eiríkr Magnússon (London: Ellis, 1869; New York: Longmans, Green, 1901);

The Story of the Volsungs and the Niblungs, translated by Morris and Magnússon (London: Ellis, 1870; New York: Longmans, Green, 1901);

Three Northern Love Stories, and Other Tales, translated by Morris and Magnússon (London: Ellis & White, 1875; New York: Longmans, Green, 1901);

The Aeneids of Virgil Done Into English Verse (Boston: Roberts Brothers, 1875; London: Ellis & White, 1876);

The Odyssey of Homer Done Into English Verse, 2 volumes (London: Reeves & Turner, 1887);

The Saga Library, translated by Morris and Magnússon, 6 volumes (London: Quaritch, 1891-1905);

The Ordination of Knighthood, from William Caxton's translation of *The Order of Chivalry* (London: Reeves & Turner, 1892);

The Tale of King Florus and the Fair Jehane (Hammersmith: Kelmscott Press, 1893);

Of the Friendship of Amis and Amile, (Hammersmith: Kelmscott Press, 1894);

The Tale of the Emperor Coustans and of Over Sea (Hammersmith: Kelmscott Press, 1894);

The Tale of Beowulf, translated by Morris and A. J. Wyatt (Hammersmith: Kelmscott Press, 1895; London & New York: Longmans, Green, 1898);

The Story of Kormak, the Son of Ogmund, translated by Morris and Magnússon, edited by Grace Calder (London: William Morris Society, 1970).

Writing is only one element of William Morris's diverse achievement. He designed textiles, wallpapers, stained glass, rugs, tapestries, and embroidery; and he founded and managed a company to produce them. He was a leading influence on the Arts and Crafts movement in England and America and, through the work of his disciples, a major force in the reform of art education. He was a pioneer in the causes of historic preservation and environmentalism. His work as a typographer and printer produced some of the finest Victorian books and encouraged the revitalization of the art of printing. His activities as a revolutionary Socialist helped shape the direction of the British party system; the example of his commitment to socialism influenced the movement even when it took directions Morris himself had not envisioned.

William Morris earned his literary reputation as a narrative poet; in recent years, however, his most popular writing has been his earlier short poems and the lectures and prose romances he wrote during the last two decades of his life. His theoretical writings on the arts and crafts have exerted a profound influence on architecture and interior design in forms very different from Morris's own; and his writings on socialism, with their faith in a Communist society determined by human desire rather than political theory, remain a significant critique of twentieth-century Marxism.

Morris is a genuinely transitional figure. His life and work are grounded in a historical past they in many respects carry to its efflorescence, yet, at the same time, he reformulates the values of that past in ways that address themselves to the modern world. For this reason, as his biographer E. P. Thompson suggests, Morris should be seen neither as a man of the past nor as a man of the present, but as "a new kind of sensibility" unique in its "reassertion at a new level and in new forms of pre-capitalist values of community" and what Morris ironically termed "barbarism."

The juxtaposition of past and present can be traced to Morris's boyhood. His father was a bill broker who commuted daily to his London office from suburban Walthamstow, where William Morris, his eldest son, was born 24 March 1834. Although living only a few miles from the center of London, the Morris family had many of the features of a medieval household: brewing their own beer, baking their own bread, and observing the fourteenth-century customs of meals at high prime and Twelfth Night celebrations. Woodford Hall, where the family moved in 1840, was located on the edge of Epping Forest. Here Morris

and his brothers wandered on foot or rode their ponies, William on occasion wearing a toy suit of armor given him by his parents.

This world with its links to the past defined the values Morris sought to preserve. The extended family, sharing the common areas of a great house and its natural environs, became his ideal community. The forest setting of his romances is grounded in the forest of his childhood: his love of nature–of flowers and foliage–has its origins in the gardens of Elm House, where Morris was born, and Woodford Hall.

Yet a home like Woodford Hall was possible only because of his father's commercial position in the city. In an 1883 letter to fellow Socialist Andreas Scheu, Morris characterized his early life as "the ordinary bourgeois style of comfort" and reported having been brought up "in what I should call rich establishmentarian puritanism; a religion which even as a boy I never took to." His boyhood may have been idyllic, but there was something false in its circumstances. The traditionalism of Walthamstow was sustained, not by its roots in a traditional culture, but by the money that flowed from London–in large amounts after 1844, when his father's lucky investment in a copper mining company increased sharply in value. Past and present met in Woodford Hall but achieved no genuine synthesis.

As the eldest son in a family of nine, Morris enjoyed a special place in his parents' affections. His father seems to have exerted slight influence over him–unless the nervous temperament they shared was hereditary. In contrast his relationship with his mother was a crucial factor in his development. Morris was a sickly child, "kept alive" by his mother on calf's-foot jelly and beef-tea. When he grew stronger, however, her attention necessarily shifted to his six younger brothers and sisters, and the loss of his mother's undivided care was a profound emotional blow to the boy. Throughout his life he hungered for a love comparable to the sheltering care he had received in his first years, fearing, at the same time, that such love would be taken from him suddenly and without reason. Typically, Morris turned the anger he felt toward his mother in other directions. As a boy–and man–he was given to violent outbursts of temper, occasionally against human beings but more often against inanimate objects, venting his frustration at a world that could not be bent to his purposes.

To some extent, his two older sisters, Emma and Henrietta, compensated for Morris's loss of maternal attention. Emma was particularly close to him. Conditioned, however, to imagine himself deprived of love, Morris seems to have regarded her marriage in 1850 as a personal betrayal.

Although Morris was to become a man of remarkable strength and physical activity, his sickly childhood had encouraged him to take up reading at an early age. He had reportedly read all of Scott's Waverly novels by the age of seven. Throughout his life, in consequence, he approached events through the mediation of literary romance, and his most powerful experiences were associated with reading. As Morris's nineteenth-century biographer John W. Mackail reports, Emma recalled reading Clara Reeve's *The Old English Baron* with him "in the rabbit warren at Woodford, poring over the enthralling pages till both were wrought up to a state of mind that made them afraid to cross the park to reach home."

When Morris was nine years old, he was sent to a local preparatory school, first as a day scholar, later as a boarder. After his father's death in 1847 the family moved to a smaller residence, Water House, and Morris was sent to the recently founded Marlborough College, in Wiltshire, where he remained a student until Christmas 1851.

As a result of the school's disorganization, Morris was left much on his own. "As far as my school instruction went," he later wrote, "I think I may fairly say I learned next to nothing there, for indeed next to nothing was taught; but the place is in very beautiful country, thickly scattered over with prehistoric monuments, and I set myself eagerly to studying these and everything else that had any history in it, and so perhaps learned a good deal, especially as there was a good library at the school." His schoolfellows remembered him for his solitary walks, for his invention of endless stories "about knights and fairies," and for violent but short-lived bursts of temper. They also noted his need for constant activity, which often took the form of hours spent in netting, and for his habit of talking to himself. Clearly Morris was something of an anomaly among the other boys. Writing in 1874 to Philip Burne-Jones, then a student at Marlborough, he confessed to having led "a troublous life" his first two years at the school and went on to suggest something about his sense of isolation not only as an adolescent but also as a grown man: "Alas I did not fight enough in my time, from want of

hope let us say, not want of courage, or else I should have been more respected in my earlier days; in the few fights I had I was rather successful, for a little, and thin (yes) boy as I was: for the rest I had a hardish time of it, as chaps who have brains and feelings generally do at school, or say in all the world even, whose griefs are not much shared in by the hard and stupid: nor its joys either, happily, so that we may be well content to be alive and eager, and to bear pain sometimes rather than to grow like rotting cabbages and not to mind it."

One influence of Marlborough on Morris's intellectual development was its High Church flavor, which complemented his already well-developed love of romantic literature and the Middle Ages. This bias was strengthened by his year under the private tutelage of the Rev. F. B. Guy, when Morris returned to Walthamstow in 1852. Guy turned Morris into a decent classical scholar and introduced him to such works as Euripides' *Medea* that later influenced his own narrative poetry.

Morris passed his matriculation examination at Exeter College, Oxford, in June 1852 but, because the college was full, did not go into residence until the spring of 1853. Again, Morris's autobiographical letter to Scheu is revealing: "I took very ill to the studies of the place; but fell to vigorously on history and especially mediaeval history, all the more perhaps because at this time I fell under the influence of the High Church or Puseyite school; this latter phase however did not last me long, as it was corrected by the books of John Ruskin which were at the time a sort of revelation to me; I was also a good deal influenced by the works of Charles Kingsley, and got into my head therefrom some socio-political ideas which would have developed probably but for the attractions of art and poetry. While I was still an undergraduate, I discovered that I could write poetry, much to my own amazement; and about that time being very intimate with other young men of enthusiastic ideas, we got up a monthly paper which lasted (to my cost) for a year; it was called the *Oxford and Cambridge Magazine*, and was very *young* indeed." Most influential of Ruskin's books was *The Stones of Venice* (1851-1853), the final volume of which appeared the year Morris entered Oxford. Its chapter "On the Nature of Gothic" became a major factor in Morris's social thinking. "How deadly dull the world would have been twenty years ago but for Ruskin!" Morris wrote in 1894. "It was through him that I learned to give form to my discontent."

Foremost among the "young men of enthusiastic ideas" was Edward Burne-Jones, who was to become a lifelong friend and artistic collaborator. It was Burne-Jones who coined Morris's nickname "Topsy"–at times shortened to "Top"–after the wild-haired Topsy of *Uncle Tom's Cabin*; and through Burne-Jones Morris became friends with a Birmingham circle–Charles Faulkner, Richard Watson Dixon, and William Fulford. The group, later joined by Cormell Price, studied–of course–Ruskin, but also Tennyson and Carlyle; discovered the beauty of medieval architecture and Pre-Raphaelite painting; and fantasized themselves as a pseudomonastic "Brotherhood." Morris had been writing poetry for a good while, but with the encouragement of his Oxford friends, he began to take himself seriously as a writer and entered wholeheartedly in their project to publish a monthly magazine.

Morris's contributions to the *Oxford and Cambridge Magazine* (January-December 1856), which he at first edited and largely financed, having come into a £900-a-year income on his twenty-first birthday, included five poems, seven short romances, a contemporary love story, a review of Browning's *Men and Women*, a Ruskinesque description entitled "The Churches of North France," and a brief account of two engravings by the German artist Alfred Rethel. Romances such as "The Hollow Land" and "Svend and his Brethren" are the most successful of these pieces. The critical articles, because they are almost unique in his output, deserve attention.

Morris's account of Amiens Cathedral is the only completed essay in what was to have been a series of articles treating the churches he visited during his 1854 and 1855 summer walking tours of Belgium and Northern France. Because he was forced to rely on photographs to refresh his memory, the essay falls short of the precise architectural description Morris admired in Ruskin. However, Morris's naive enthusiasm defines his purpose as something more personal than Ruskin's quest for absolute values. Thinking of the medieval builders, he not only "can see through them very faintly, dimly, some little of the mediaeval times, else dead and gone from me for ever" but also professes to love "those same builders, still surely living, still real men and capable of receiving love, . . . no less than the great men, poets and painters and such like, who are on earth now; no less than my breathing friends." The cathedral, so perceived, is not an artifact of history, but an experience of timeless communion between past and present that foreshadows the dialectical conception of history in Morris's later writing.

With the exception of an 1870 review of Dante Gabriel Rossetti's *Poems*, Morris's early comments on Browning are his only published criticism of a contemporary writer. In placing Browning "high among the poets of all time, and I scarce know whether first, or second, in our own," Morris was disavowing his earlier admiration for Tennyson and declaring allegiance to the poet who was to influence strongly the poetry of his own first period. Significantly, the three poems "that strike [him] first"–"The Epistle of Karshish," "Cleon," and "Bishop Blougram's Apology"–treat questions of religious "belief and doubt" that had begun to disturb Morris. His remarks on Cleon, a figure with whom he has much in common, suggest the misgivings he may have come to have with the aesthetic elitism of his own Oxford circle: "Cleon, with his intense appreciation of beauty, is yet intensely selfish; he despises utterly the common herd; he would bring about, if he could, a most dreary aristocracy of intellect."

Morris is particularly interested in poems pertaining to art and to love. He is struck by the "intense, unmixed love; love for the sake of love" of Browning's love poems and demonstrates an unexpected sympathy for Andrea del Sarto's thankless passion for his unfaithful wife. Indeed, fulfillment seems less important to him than personal integrity in the face of loss. Fittingly, the poem he "love[s] the best of all in these volumes" is " 'Childe Roland to the Dark Tower Came,' " with its portrait of "a brave man doing his duty" in face of an uncertain outcome. In general the poems Morris singles out are the poems of disquietude and self-doubt that have continued to fascinate modern readers. More than a prescient critical judgment, however, Morris's emphasis is clearly a reflection of his own state of mind–in particular, of the inability to imagine himself a successful lover or artist that characterizes the fiction he contributed to the *Oxford and Cambridge Magazine*.

Morris had entered Oxford with the intention of becoming a clergyman. By 1855, however, he had determined to become an architect. Mackail writes that Morris's family regarded his decision with "disappointment and almost consternation"; nevertheless, having completed his final term at the university, Morris articled himself to

Jane Burden Morris, circa 1860 (Victoria and Albert Museum). She married Morris in April 1859.

the successful Gothic revivalist architect George Edmund Street, then working out of Oxford. Morris remained at Street's office less than a year—enough time to become close friends with Philip Webb, Street's senior clerk; to adopt Street's belief that architecture should encompass all elements of a building's design and decoration; and to discover that architecture, even so defined, was not to be his own profession.

Burne-Jones had left Oxford without a degree in 1855 to study art in London with Dante Gabriel Rossetti. Morris visited him regularly on weekends, and, when Street moved his office to London in August 1856, Morris came increasingly under the influence of Rossetti, who soon persuaded him to become a painter. As he wrote Cormell Price, "Rossetti says I ought to paint, he says I shall be able; now as he is a very great man, and speaks with authority and not as the scribes, I *must* try." Yet even in professing Rossetti's aestheticism, Morris remained vaguely

dissatisfied with a calling that had so little to do with the realities of the world: "I can't enter into politico-social subjects with any interest," he confessed to Price, "for on the whole I see that things are in a muddle, and I have no power or vocation to set them right in ever so little a degree. My work is the embodiment of dreams in one form or another."

With Burne-Jones he took lodgings at 17 Red Lion Square, furnishing them with massive, "intensely mediaeval" oak furniture of his own design. Here, amidst the chaos of bohemianism, Morris allowed his beard to grow and struggled to learn how to draw the human form. If his decision to become an architect had distressed his mother, his decision to become an artist was an even stronger blow. Yet, in estranging himself from his bourgeois family, he found new friends, including Ruskin, Rossetti, and other members of the Pre-Raphaelite circle, to take their place. Wherever Morris lived, he created a household.

In the summer of 1857 Morris and Burne-Jones joined Rossetti and a group of friends in painting Arthurian frescoes on the walls of the newly constructed Oxford Union. The experience of communal labor was much to Morris's taste. His painting—*How Sir Palomydes loved La Belle Iseult with exceeding great love out of measure, and how she loved not him again but Sir Tristram*—was the first begun and the first completed; Morris then went on to paint the roof with designs of animals and birds. However, neither Rossetti nor any of his co-workers understood the technique of mural painting, and their work, applied to an improperly prepared surface, deteriorated almost immediately.

It was in October 1857 that Morris met Jane Burden, the daughter of an Oxford stableman, whom Rossetti met at the theater and persuaded to sit as a model. Morris, who had adopted Rossetti's taste in women along with his general philosophy of life, found himself strongly attracted to her strange beauty, which he associated with the figures of Iseult and Guenevere.

In part to be near Jane Burden, Morris stayed on in Oxford, preparing for publication of his first collection of verse, *The Defence of Guenevere and Other Poems* (1858). This volume contains some of Morris's most original writing and, by dint of changing tastes, most of the poems for which he is known in the twentieth century. Like the best of Browning's dramatic monologues, the best of the poems in the collection—including the title poem itself—speak with a compelling realism that brings their medieval subject matter into stark immediacy. The book received a few favorable reviews and a few hostile ones largely attacking Morris for his association with Pre-Raphaelitism; however, it sold poorly, and it was not until Morris had established his reputation with later work that the volume became generally known.

By summer 1858 Morris was engaged to Jane Burden, and on 26 April 1859 they were married at Oxford. For Morris's family, his marriage to the daughter of a groom was the ultimate fall from respectability. Whether by choice or for lack of an invitation, neither his mother nor any of his brothers or sisters attended the wedding. The newlyweds spent a six-week honeymoon on the Continent and returned in June to begin a new phase of Morris's life.

Not long after his engagement Morris had commissioned Philip Webb to begin designs for a house. The site chosen was a piece of high ground ten miles south of London, near the village of Upton. Red House—so named because of its solid red brick construction—was at once Gothic and modern: a house that Morris could identify with the Middle Ages, the functionalism and simplicity of which nevertheless anticipates Modernist design.

Furnishing and decorating Red House was a problem Morris himself undertook to solve, typically enlisting the cooperation of his friends. As Mackail describes it: "Not a chair, or table, or bed; not a cloth or paper hanging for the walls; nor tiles to line fireplaces or passages; nor a curtain or a candlestick; nor jug to hold wine or a glass to drink out of, but had to be reinvented, one might almost say, to escape the flat ugliness of the current article. . . . Much of the furniture was specially designed by Webb and executed under his eye: the great oak dining-table, other tables, chairs, cupboards, massive copper candlesticks, fire-dogs, and table glass of extreme beauty." This experience led directly to the founding of the firm of Morris, Marshall, Faulkner and Company in 1861, "to undertake any species of decoration, mural or otherwise, from pictures, properly so called, down to the consideration of the smallest work susceptible of art beauty." In time, the firm produced stained glass, furniture, fabrics, wallpaper, tiles, embroidery, carpets, and tapestries, all of the highest quality. The styles of Morris and Company were not always innovative; however, the firm set a standard of production that was decisive in the history of British interior design.

Morris's two daughters, Jenny and May, were born at Red House, and his years there were the happiest time in his marriage. Morris enjoyed entertaining; his friends came down regularly from London for weekends or longer stays, and there was talk of adding a wing for Burne-Jones and his wife Georgiana. In 1865, however, Morris moved his family back to London, taking up residence above the workshop of the firm at 26 Queen Square. In part Morris made this transfer to be closer to his place of work, in part because the location and northern-lighted design of Red House had proved unhealthy. Whatever its justifications the move did not please his wife. No longer the mistress of an elegant suburban home, Jane Morris became increasingly estranged from her husband, increasingly given to poor health, increasingly involved with Rossetti, who began to imagine that it was he, not Morris, who had loved her at first sight.

The wares of the firm were beginning to become fashionable, but Morris's business earnings were as yet unable to compensate for the steadily decreasing income from his copper shares. Warrington Taylor, the firm's manager, repeatedly warned Morris that he was living beyond his means, but it was not until Taylor's death in 1870 that Morris learned how to discipline his expenditures.

During the summer of 1869, Morris took Jane to the spa at Bad-Ems in Hesse-Nassau. In the months following their return, her relationship with Rossetti apparently became a matter of public knowledge. Burne-Jones, meanwhile, had fallen desperately in love with Mary Zambaco, one of his models, and Morris found himself drawn into some kind of intimacy with Georgiana Burne-Jones, for whom he completed his first illuminated manuscript, *A Book of Verse*, in 1870.

It was during this difficult period that Morris returned to writing poetry. He had attempted "Scenes from the Fall of Troy" in the years following *The Defence of Guenevere* but found himself unequal to the task. Now, abandoning the dramatic monologue format, he began a series of extended narrative poems on traditional subjects, gathered under the title *The Earthly Paradise* and linked by the medieval device of a narrative frame. *The Life and Death of Jason*, originally intended as part of the series, outgrew the frame and was published separately in 1867. It was an immediate success; and with the publication of the four parts of *The Earthly Paradise* in the years 1868-1870, Morris found himself a major Victorian poet.

The *Sunday Times* reviewer called *The Life and Death of Jason* "one of the most remarkable poems of this or any other age"; writing in the *Nation*, the American scholar Charles Eliot Norton maintained that "no narrative poem comparable with this in scope of design or in power of execution has been produced in our generation." More widely reviewed, the successive volumes of *The Earthly Paradise* were praised for their effortless narration and for their precise descriptions of the natural world. The poems were easy to read, and so they appealed to a wide audience. Moreover, their non-Victorian subject matter was greeted as a welcome escape from mid-Victorian earnestness. (One of the few repeated objections to the work was its lack of Christian morality.)

The twenty-four tales and narrative frame of *The Earthly Paradise* for the most part reiterate the theme of a quest for happiness, often in romantic love, postponed or thwarted by the perversity of human nature. The poems have been criticized for slackness and diffusion; and Morris himself complained, "they are all too long and flabby—damn it!" However, the best of them are a remarkable achievement. Morris's versions of "The Story of Cupid and Psyche," "Pygmalion and the Image," "The Land East of the Sun and West of the Moon," "The Man Who Never Laughed Again," and "The Hill of Venus" are among the most compelling verse narratives of the Victorian period.

Although the narratives are equally balanced between classical and Germanic subjects, it is the latter that most strongly seized Morris's imagination. "The Lovers of Gudrun," the longest and perhaps the best of *The Earthly Paradise* tales, is a translation of the Icelandic Laxdale Saga. Morris had begun reading Icelandic soon after his first meeting with Eiríkr Magnússon in 1868; almost immediately they began publishing a series of translations from the sagas—*The Story of Gunnlaug the Wormtongue* (1869), *The Story of Grettir the Strong* (1869), *The Story of the Volsungs and the Niblungs* (1870), *Frithiof the Bold* (1871). The first and fourth of these translations, which originally appeared in serials, were published, along with additional material, as *Three Northern Love Stories, and Other Tales* (1875). And two decades later Morris and Magnússon returned to the task, with a series of Icelandic translations entitled *The Saga Library* (1891-1905), which Magnús-

Edward Burne-Jones with Morris, 1874, at Burne-Jones's home, The Grange, Fulham (Victoria and Albert Museum)

son continued in the years following Morris's death. Morris regarded this literature of the North as a national heritage, having a relationship to English culture comparable to the relationship of Homer to the Greeks. More personally, it offered an alternative to the self-reflective melancholy of his own *Earthly Paradise*—a gust of clear, cold air that would ultimately penetrate the closed space of introspection.

The first years of the 1870s were a period in which Morris struggled to rethink his life. Instead of a romantic youth, he found himself a heavyset man of middle years, strong enough to bash in a wall with his head—and often angry enough to do it. For reasons seemingly beyond his control, he was making a living, not as an artist, but as a kind of upper-class upholsterer. His dream of married life at Red House, with an ideally beautiful wife at the center of a circle of friends, had given away to living over a shop with a woman, if not fully in love with another man, then nevertheless no longer in love with him. And the circle of friends itself had disintegrated: the idealized Rossetti was now an enemy—

although Morris continued to treat him other-wise; Edward and Georgiana Burne-Jones, whom he had once imagined living with him as members of an extended family, were now as unhappily married as he and Jane. Morris's efforts to define his identity had reached a series of dead ends.

Among the signs of Morris's effort to rethink his life were his journeys to Iceland in 1871 and 1873. He kept a journal of his 1871 expedition, which he later transcribed and gave to Georgiana Burne-Jones. This journal, along with a fragmentary journal of the 1873 voyage, records his confrontation both with the harshness of the Icelandic landscape and with the place of the sagas in Icelandic culture. For Morris, the "grisly desolation" of the land, with its black volcanic mountains and icebound interior, was a lesson in the smallness of human pretensions. The backcountry trek by pony was itself challenging. The elementary need to survive in surroundings that made survival difficult placed the personal sorrows of his married life in a new perspective; the Icelanders themselves offered him a model of human endurance in the face of near overwhelming odds: "set aside the hope that the unseen sea gives you here, and the strange threatening change of the blue spiky mountains beyond the firth, and the rest seems emptiness and nothing else: a piece of turf under your feet, and the sky overhead, that's all; whatever solace your life is to have here must come out of yourself or those old stories, not over hopeful themselves."

Nor was this the only important step Morris took in 1871. A month before he set sail for Iceland, he had taken a joint lease with Rossetti on Kelmscott Manor, a gray stone Elizabethan country house near Lechlade on the upper Thames. Among Morris's motives in entering into the tenancy may have been providing his wife and Rossetti with a place in which they could be together; however, Morris quickly grew to love the "beautiful and strangely naif house" with deep affection and to identify himself with the "beautiful grey little hamlet called Kelmscott." Soon the presence of Rossetti, with his "ways so unsympathetic with the sweet simple old place," became an annoyance, but it was not until July 1874 that Rossetti gave up his share in the lease.

The need to redefine the self is the subject of the complex narrative poem *Love Is Enough; or, The Freeing of Pharamond*, published in 1873. Its hero, Pharamond, renounces his kingdom to search for a visionary woman; he finds her—in a distinctly Icelandic landscape—only to leave her to return to his kingdom, now in the hands of a usurper. The tale ends ambiguously, with Pharamond preparing to return to Azalais, but, for the time at least, without either love or power. Despite its links to *The Earthly Paradise, Love Is Enough* is a major step forward in Morris's development, to a point at which he is able to imagine himself freed of the unfulfilled desires that lay beneath the malaise of the earlier work. The personal significance of the story to Morris is suggested by the elaborate framing devices surrounding the fable of Pharamond's quest, and confirmed by May Morris, in her preface for *The Collected Works*: "No glimpse of the inner life of Morris was ever vouchsafed even to his closest friends–*secretum meum mihi*. It was a subject on which he never spoke save in *Love Is Enough*." The poem was generally well received by the critics but, as Morris himself realized, was too difficult to be a popular success.

During the same period Morris also tried his hand at writing a novel, in which the love triangle characteristic of many of his romances was restated in a realistic mode, but was discouraged from completing the project. The manuscript, published in 1982 as *The Novel on Blue Paper*, suggests yet another attempt to distance himself from the melancholy of *The Earthly Paradise*.

In October 1871 Rossetti had been the object of Robert Buchanan's pseudonymous attack, "The Fleshly School of Poetry." Similar attacks continued through the following winter and spring. Rossetti's paranoia intensified, and in June 1872 he attempted suicide with an overdose of chloral. After his recovery he continued to spend time with Jane Morris both at Kelmscott and elsewhere; however, the event may have subtly changed the balance of power between Morris and Rossetti, and encouraged Morris to force Rossetti's hand by threatening to give up his share of the Kelmscott Manor lease two years later.

At the end of 1872 Morris moved his family to "a *very* little house with pretty garden" on the main road between Turham Green and Hammersmith. Jane Morris, who described it as "a very good sort of house for one person to live in, or perhaps two," was evidently less than fully satisfied with Horrington House; nevertheless, it remained the family's London home for six years. Morris maintained a study and bedroom at Queen Square for his own use.

Despite his earnings from *The Earthly Paradise* and his other poetry, it was clear that the main source of his income would have to be the

"Rupes Topseia," drawing by Rossetti expressing his opposition to Morris's reorganization of Morris, Marshall, Faulkner and Company in 1875 (reproduced by courtesy of the Trustees of the British Museum). The original firm members are shown at top left; Jane Morris is at top right; Marx and Engels watch Morris's descent into hell.

firm. Of the original partners, Burne-Jones and Philip Webb had continued furnishing designs, for which they had been paid, but the others–Rossetti, Ford Madox Brown, Peter Paul Marshall, and Charles Faulkner–had contributed no capital and had long ceased to participate in any active sense. It was clearly Morris's business, and so he determined to assume sole proprietorship. Morris handled the affair with little tact, and Brown, with the support of Rossetti and Marshall, opposed him acrimoniously, demanding an equal share in the company's assets and ultimately settling on a thousand pounds each. (Rossetti, perversely, insisted on making a gift of his share to Jane Morris.)

Once the firm had been reincorporated under his sole ownership as Morris and Com-

pany, Morris entered into its work with renewed vigor. During the summer of 1875 he began a series of experiments with vegetable dyes, attempting to replace aniline dyes which he found unsatisfactory for quality textiles. As he wrote in his 1889 lecture, "Of Dyeing as an Art," "Any one wanting to produce dyed textiles with any artistic quality in them must entirely forgo the modern and commercial methods in favor of those which are at least as old as Pliny, who speaks of them as being old in his time." His correspondence with Thomas Wardle, owner of a Staffordshire dye works (and brother-in-law of George Wardle, who had succeeded Warrington Taylor as Morris's business manager), documents the intensity with which Morris entered into this effort. He studied early texts on dye making and visited Wardle's works in person, "even working in sabots and blouse in the dye-house myself . . . taking in dyeing at every pore."

For Morris, 1876 was a year of important changes. Jane Morris later in life told Wilfrid Scawen Blunt that she had ended her affair with Rossetti in 1875. Although she spent a fortnight with Rossetti at Bogner in March 1876, it would appear that their sexual relationship was over by the beginning of that year. Also at the beginning of 1876 Morris resigned his directorship of the mining company, an event he celebrated by sitting on the top hat he had been forced to wear to meetings of the board. In June of 1876 Morris's older daughter, Jenny, "a girl of fifteen, exceptionally bright, clever, and diligent, . . . already her father's chosen companion," was stricken with epilepsy. Her health never completely recovered, and she remained an invalid until her death in 1935. Morris, it has been argued, traced her illness to his own pathological anger and thus regarded himself as in some way responsible for it.

In addition, the year 1876 saw publication of the poem Morris considered his masterpiece. Writing to Charles Eliot Norton in 1869, he had characterized the Völsunga Saga, which he was then translating into prose, as "something which is above all art." "I had it in my head to write an epic of it," he had gone on to say, "but though I still hanker after it, I see clearly it would be foolish, for no verse could render the best parts of it, and it would only be a flatter and tamer version of a thing already existing." Despite these misgivings, Morris gave way to his hankering, and in 1876 produced *The Story of Sigurd the Volsung and the Fall of the Niblungs*, the work that effectively terminates his career as a narrative poet of traditional themes. Though hailed by critics as Morris's "greatest and most successful effort," "the crowning achievement of Mr. Morris' life," the work was not popular with the public because Morris's fidelity to his sources proved an obstacle to general readers.

It is not clear whether it was his failure to win a large audience with *The Story of Sigurd* or the press of new interests that led Morris to turn from poetry in the years that followed. Although he continued to be known as "The Author of *The Earthly Paradise*," he ceased to think of himself as primarily a poet and in 1877, despite the temptation, rejected the invitation to succeed Matthew Arnold as Oxford Professor of Poetry.

In respect to his future, the most important event of 1876 may have been Morris's entry into politics. Angered at the Turkish atrocities in Bulgaria and alarmed by the rumor that England was on the verge of supporting Turkey in her war with Russia, he wrote a letter to the *Daily News*, which was printed on 24 October. With high rhetoric, he appealed to the Liberal party and to the workingmen of England "to drop all other watch-words that this at least may be heard—No war on behalf of Turkey; no war on behalf of the thieves and murderers!" Morris may not have been attuned to the subtleties of foreign policy, but he recognized that behind Disraeli's effort to rouse support for the alliance lay the intention of exploiting Turkey economically. Joining the Liberal-Radical opposition to Disraeli, he was elected to the committee of the Eastern Question Association (EQA) and for the first time in his life encountered working-class politicians.

When war between Turkey and Russia broke out, the EQA distributed Morris's statement "Unjust War: To the Working-men of England" (1877). It is clear that he had begun to doubt the efficacy of Parliament—"the Tory Rump, that we fools, weary of peace, reason and justice, chose at the last election to 'represent' us"—and had begun to look to the working class as a source of political change. The government exerted pressure against the EQA, sending roughs to disrupt its meetings and spreading the rumor that, with the fall of Constantinople, Britain would lose its Indian Empire. Gladstone, who had originally supported the organization, backed down, as did nearly all other Liberal supporters of the neutrality movement. Only the Labor Representation League held firm.

In the end, the tide of jingoism prevailed,

and Disraeli's maneuverings gained Britain the island of Cyprus. Morris's response was anger and frustration; however, he had experienced the excitement of political activism. He knew what it was to speak before a large audience of supporters and to hold one's own against the threat of government violence. He had gained, moreover, a profound distrust of the political system.

His experience with the EQA was complemented by his experience as founding member of the Society for the Preservation of Ancient Buildings (SPAB)—or, as its opposition to removing the weathered surface of stonework led Morris to call it, "Anti-Scrape." As with the EQA, his involvement with the SPAB began with a letter to the editor. On 5 March 1877 he addressed the *Athenaeum*, protesting the "destruction" of Tewkesbury Minster by Sir Gilbert Scott, in the name of "restoration." Morris did not object to preserving an historic building from decay; however, he objected strenuously to replacing old work with new, real Gothic workmanship with nineteenth-century stone carving. Arguing that "our ancient buildings are not mere ecclesiastical toys, but sacred monuments of the nation's growth and hope," he proposed "an association for the purpose of watching over and protecting these relics, which, scanty as they are now become, are still wonderful treasures, all the more priceless in this age of the world, when the newly-invented study of living history is the chief joy of so many of our lives."

The Society for the Protection of Ancient Buildings was organized at a meeting later in the month, with Morris as secretary. He wrote the society's manifesto, which has continued to be republished in its annual report, and drew many of his friends, including Ruskin and Carlyle, into the cause. From the start, the SPAB had two classes of enemies, the architects who made their livings by restoration, and the clergymen who regarded churches as their personal property. Beginning with the society's formal protest over the removal of the seventeenth-century choir stalls at Canterbury Cathedral, Morris found himself engaged in one controversy after another. Nor was he merely concerned with preventing inappropriate restoration; in April 1878 he wrote the editor of the *Times* opposing the bishop of London's plans to destroy a number of Wren's City churches—buildings Morris disliked but recognized as irreplaceable in London's architectural history. "Surely," he declared, "an opulent city, the capital of the commercial world, can afford some small sacrifice to spare these beautiful buildings the little plots of ground upon which they stand. Is it absolutely necessary that every scrap of space in the City should be devoted to money-making. . . ?"

In time the work of the society extended beyond England, playing a major role in the effectual protest against the restoration of St. Mark's, Venice, in 1880. His experience in the organization taught Morris much about the conflict between private interests and public good. As his letter in behalf of Wren's churches suggests, he grew convinced that the enemy of "sacred memories"–of his sense of history as a living continuity with the past–was the capitalist system, with its subordination of all other values to those of the marketplace.

Although Morris had spoken at meetings of the society, his first formal public lecture, "The Lesser Arts," was delivered to the Trades Guild of Learning, London, 4 December 1877. He prepared diligently, writing the text with unusual care and practicing for delivery by reading *Robinson Crusoe* aloud to a group of friends. The lecture, like those that followed, is in fact a short essay; and, although Morris naturally became more fluent in the form as he became more practiced in it, the nearly one hundred lectures he wrote and delivered between 1877 and his death in 1896 are a notable achievement. As Bernard Shaw observed, Morris's having found time to write them in the midst of so much other activity, commercial, artistic and political, is difficult to imagine.

"The Lesser Arts" touches on several themes that Morris was to develop in subsequent lectures. He perceived the division between the "great arts" of sculpture, architecture, and painting and "that great body of [lesser] art, by means of which men have at all times more or less striven to beautify the familiar matters of everyday life," as a phenomenon unique to the past three centuries, and he argues that this division, which is based upon a deeper division in society itself, has led to the decay of both arts. Because the two purposes of decoration are "to give people pleasure in the things they must perforce *use*" and "to give people pleasure in the things they must perforce *make*," the absence of decoration on everyday objects reflects a society in which pleasure is largely absent from ordinary life. Even the wealthy, who fill their homes with "decoration (so-called)," have no real pleasure in their surroundings. In contrast, the high arts are

Portrait of Morris in 1880, by George Frederick Watts (National Portrait Gallery)

"mainly kept in the hands of a few highly cultivated men, who can go often to beautiful places, whose education enables them, in the contemplation of the past glories of the world, to shut out from their view the everyday squalors that the most of men move in." Faced with this elitism, Morris would be content to "sweep away all art for awhile," in hope that it be reborn in a new, more democratic form. But as yet he admits to "a sort of faith" that so radical a solution will prove unnecessary and that the growth of leisure will in time "bring forth decorative, noble, *popular* art."

"The Lesser Arts" adumbrates a society of the future founded on "simplicity of life, begetting simplicity of taste . . . simplicity everywhere, in the palace as well as in the cottage," but falters in its explanation of just how that society will be attained. Morris's personal experience working in the lesser arts had taught him their importance; ironically, however, he saw his own decorated work contributing little to the lives of ordinary people and being bought instead by the moneyed class he was coming to deplore. Even as Morris set about putting his own life in order, the tension between his desire for a better world and his own activities remained unresolved.

Morris's public life continued to evolve. He

had been appointed examiner at the School of Art, South Kensington, in 1876. In February 1878 he was invited to speak at the distribution of prizes at the Cambridge School of Art, and at about the same time was made president of the Birmingham Society of Arts for the current year.

Despite an attack of gout, in March 1878 Morris set about hunting for a new London residence. Jane Morris and the couple's two daughters were wintering in Italy, so the decision was very much his own. Morris was drawn to a three-storied, late-eighteenth-century house near the Thames in Hammersmith, and, after bringing Webb to inspect the structure, he took a lease on it in April. He now had two dwellings, connected by the Thames. To emphasize this bond, he renamed his London home Kelmscott House.

In April Morris joined his family in Italy, planning to take them on a tour of the northern Italian cities. Again, he suffered an attack of gout. He collapsed in a street at Genoa and had to be carried to his hotel room. By this point in his life, Morris's feelings about Italy were mixed. Wandering among the olive trees above the sea at Oneglia, he felt as if he "should be well contented to stay there always." Yet, writing to Georgiana Burne-Jones three weeks later, he confessed himself "quite out of sympathy" "with the later work of Southern Europe."

The Morrises took possession of Kelmscott House at midsummer, but it was not until late October, when redecoration was complete, that they moved into their new home. Morris had a tapestry loom built in his (separate) bedroom, where he practiced hand weaving, often in the early hours of the morning. He had begun the search for a larger space for the firm's manufactory that led to the establishment of the Merton Abbey Works in 1881. As a temporary measure, the coach house and stable at Kelmscott House were converted into a room for weaving rugs and carpets—which were given the trade name Hammersmith. (Later, the coach house became a meeting room for the Hammersmith Socialists.)

On 19 February 1879 Morris delivered his presidential address, "The Art of the People," before the Birmingham Society of Arts and the Birmingham School of Design. He reiterated many of the themes sounded in "The Lesser Arts," sharpening the rhetoric of his attacks on art for art's sake and plutocratic luxury. But he was less sure of himself in his historical predictions. Acknowledging "how obviously this age is one of transition from the old to the new," he found himself bewildered by the "strange confusion; . . . our ignorance and half-ignorance is like to make the exhausted rubbish of the old and the crude rubbish of the new." However, the language to describe historical change was not long to elude him. In February and April 1879, John Stuart Mill published his *Fortnightly Review* articles "Chapters on Socialism." Morris later described reading these articles, which set forth the general arguments for socialism "as far as they go, clearly and honestly," as an intellectual turning point in his life: his sense of a connection between the rise of capitalism and the decline of the lesser arts was vindicated, and his hitherto inchoate belief in the need for social change had now been grafted to a specific economic theory. In the years that followed, the idealistic socialism he learned from Mill would evolve, through his study of Marx and association with the principal figures of late-nineteenth-century British socialism, into a unique conception of a Communist future.

In the fall of 1879 Morris was elected treasurer of the National Liberal League, a small organization that attempted to promote workingmen candidates within the Liberal party. He joined in the league's support of Gladstone in the 1880 election, but it is clear from a political lecture he wrote in the first month of 1880 that he looked to goals far more radical than those of the Liberal party: "I think of a country where every man has work enough to do, and no one has too much: where no man has to work himself stupid in order to be just able to live: where on the contrary it will be easy for a man to live if he will but work, impossible if he will not (that is a necessary corollary): where every man's work would be pleasant to himself and helpful to his neighbour; and then his leisure from bread-earning (of which he ought to have plenty) would be thoughtful and rational."

In February 1880 Morris delivered a second Birmingham lecture, "Labour and Pleasure *versus* Labour and Sorrow," later retitled "The Beauty of Life." Once more he reiterated his belief in the necessity for "an *Art made by the people and for the people, a joy to the maker and the user*." Civilization, he argued, if it does not aim at "giving some share in the happiness and dignity of life to *all* the people that it has created . . . is simply an organized injustice, a mere instrument for oppression." Once more he reiterated his belief that "the greatest foe to art is luxury," now adding the counsel to begin the repudiation of luxury by casting out the clutter of the middle-class Victorian home: "if you want a golden rule that will fit everybody, this is it: *Have nothing in your houses that you do not know to be useful, or believe to be beautiful.*"

The early months of 1880 were a period of vague discontent because Morris sensed a need for change in his life, but was unsure of its direction. He contemplated giving up Kelmscott Manor, but instead, Kelmscott Manor took on greater significance as an image, not of the departed past, but of the continuity of the past within a historical process leading to a renewed future. In August 1880, with his family and a group of friends, Morris made a voyage up the Thames from London to Kelmscott, a trip which he was to repeat in later years and which he memorialized in the closing chapters of his utopian romance *News from Nowhere* (1890).

The following year, Morris moved the firm's works from their cramped quarters in Bloomsbury to Merton Abbey, on the banks of the river Wandle seven miles south of London. Here, amid large poplars and willows and an old-fashioned flower garden, Morris approximated the ideal working conditions he outlined in his 1884 essays "A Factory as It Might Be": "buildings . . . beautiful with their own beauty of simplicity as workshops"; "machines of the most ingenious and best approved kinds . . . used when necessary . . . to save human labour"; "no work which would turn men into mere machines." Morris allowed his workers flexible hours and a share in the company's profits, treating them as an extended family. He assigned responsibilities on the assumption that anyone could be trained to do any kind of work, and he assigned no work that he had not mastered himself. Yet, as much as he wrote about the individual worker's need to share in the creative process, he remained the chief artist, his employees simply carrying out–often laboriously–copies of his designs. Morris and Company remained a model of capitalist paternalism, rather than an experiment in Socialist production.

In a March 1881 speech before the London Institution entitled "The Prospects of Architecture in Civilization," Morris repeated his attack on the degrading ugliness of Victorian England and his call for a simple style of living. The only program for change he could suggest remained the renunciation of needless luxury; however, he recognized that this might not suffice and that there lurked a challenge he had yet to confront: "when we come to look the matter in the face, we cannot fail to see that even for us with all our strength it will be a hard matter to bring about that birth of the new art: for between us and that which is to be, if art is not to perish utterly, there is something alive and devouring; something as it were a river of fire that will put all that tries to swim across to a hard proof indeed, and scare from the plunge every soul that is not made fearless by desire of truth and insight of the happy days to come beyond."

The next year Morris collected this and four other lectures in the volume *Hopes and Fears for Art* (1882). The first period of his social activism was over. In April of the same year Rossetti, after a long period of physical decline, died, thus severing one of the few remaining threads that connected Morris with that time in the past when he denied the connection between art and social responsibility.

Morris was, in his own words, "on the look out for joining any body which seemed likely to push forward matters." And so, 13 January 1883, responding to the invitation of H. M. Hyndman, he joined the Democratic Federation (DF). Hyndman was a domineering ex-Tory who had converted to Marxism; under his leadership, the DF had held a series of conferences on "Stepping-stones" to socialism, which Morris attended, and in 1883 the federation began publishing Socialist pamphlets. Morris, once he had avowed his new political creed, adopted it with characteristic fervor. He began reading Marx's *Das Kapital* in Lêchatre's French translation, and entered into lengthy discussions with men such as Hyndman; the exiled German anarchist and designer Andreas Scheu, who contributed a significant internationalism to the movement; and the British Marxist theorist E. Belfort Bax. Their ideas became linked with his own; what Morris had hitherto seen as remediable class differences he now saw as a class struggle to be resolved only through destruction of the class system itself. As he wrote to C. E. Maurice in July, "I believe that the whole basis of Society, with its contrasts of rich and poor, is incurably vicious."

His March lecture "Art, Wealth, and Riches," delivered at the Manchester Royal Institution, was protested in the *Manchester Examiner.* The next month Morris gave the first of his purely political lectures as a Socialist, and in May he was elected to the Democratic Federation Executive. In November he delivered the lecture "Art and Democracy"–later retitled "Art under Plutocracy"–to the Russell Club, at University Col-

From a January 1885 letter written by Morris to fellow printer-bookbinder Thomas James Cobden-Sanderson, explaining the Socialist mission (MA 1753, by permission of the Trustees of The Pierpont Morgan Library)

lege, Oxford, in a session chaired, appropriately, by Ruskin. His long-standing distrust of aesthetic elitism, Morris restated as a notion of the common economic grounding of all human activities. Echoing Plato, he extended his definition of art to include not only the fine and lesser arts but "even the arrangement of the fields for tillage and pasture, the management of towns and of our highways of all kinds; in a word, . . . to the aspect of all the externals of our life" and argued that artists of all kinds were injured "by the system which insists on individualism and forbids cooperation." "All art, even the highest, is influenced by the conditions of labour of the mass of mankind, and . . . any pretentions which may be made for even the highest intellectual art to be independent of these general conditions are futile and vain." Specifically, it is the "superstition of commerce being an end in itself, of man as made for commerce, not commerce for man, of which art has sickened."

More shocking to his audience than these arguments was Morris's public admission that he was " 'one of the people called Socialists,' " and his peroration calling upon "those of you who agree with me to help us actively, with your time and your talents if you can, but if not, at least with your money, as you can." According to a report in the *Times*, "The Master of University then said to the effect that if he had announced this beforehand it was probable that the loan of the College-hall would have been refused." For this and subsequent lectures, Morris was assailed by the press not only for his political views, but also for presenting them in the guise of a discourse on art. As he wrote to Georgiana Burne-Jones, "I have been living in a sort of storm of newspaper brickbats, to some of which I had to reply: of course I don't mind a bit, nor even think the attack unfair."

For six years after he declared himself a Socialist, Morris devoted himself with enormous energy to the movement. His *Socialist Diary*, kept during the early months of 1887 (and edited for publication in 1981), suggests the hectic pace of this period. He was willing to speak anywhere in the country to any group that wanted to hear about socialism. The Democratic Federation pioneered in open-air propaganda and initiated the tradition of regular Sunday gatherings in Regent's Park and Hyde Park. In January 1884 the federation began publishing the weekly *Justice*. Morris regularly covered the journal's deficit and joined in selling it on the street.

The same month, before the Hampstead Liberal Club, he delivered his lecture "Useful Work v. Useless Toil" (published in 1885 as *The Socialist Platform–No. 2*). Morris was now confident that "the first step" in establishing "true Society" was the abolition of the nonproductive upper and middle classes. Already in this lecture, however, his unique contribution to Marxism is apparent. It will not suffice, he argues, that every man "reap the fruits of his labour" and "have due rest." "Nature will not be finally conquered til our work becomes a part of the pleasure of our lives." To a purely utilitarian socialism he adds the human need for taking pleasure in one's work.

From the start, Morris had recognized the contradiction in his position as a capitalist factory-owner and a Socialist advocating the overthrow of capitalism. His institution of profit sharing for his workers was an effort to resolve this contradiction, but he was forced to acknowledge that "no man is good enough to be any one's master without injuring himself . . . whatever he does for the servant." While "not a capitalist in the ordinary sense of the word," he was forced to "admit to his own conscience that he was one of a class that lives upon the labour of others." For this reason, he seriously contemplated the sale of his business. Morris himself might have been able to live on a reduced income, but he had a wife–with little sympathy for his new radicalism–and two daughters to support, and he was able to use his income to advantage in support of such activities as *Justice*. After a period of soul-searching, he determined to remain the owner of Morris and Company.

In the spring of 1884 Morris addressed a meeting of textile strikers in Lancashire. Returning to London, he took part in the first annual march to the grave of Karl Marx (who had died the preceding year). In June the Hammersmith Branch of the Democratic Federation was formed. In July Hyndman, having been forced from the presidency, nominated Morris to take his place. Morris declined, recognizing his lack of political qualifications–and attempting to distance himself from the conflict of Edward Aveling and Eleanor Marx with Hyndman. A month later, the organization changed its name to the Socialist Democratic Federation. Resentment over Hyndman's dictatorial tactics continued to grow, and in December Morris, with the majority of the Executive, resigned from the federation and founded an alternative organization, the Socialist League, with its own journal, *Commonweal*, which Morris

was to edit. Friedrich Engels, who never over-
came his initial impression of Morris as a neo-
phyte Marxist, characterized the leaders of those
who resigned (Aveling, Bax, and Morris) as "the
only honest men among the intellectuals—but
men as unpractical (two poets and one philosopher) as you could possibly find."

Although his experience was to teach him
"the frightful ignorance and want of impressibil-
ity of the average English workman," Morris at
this point seems to have believed that the crisis
of capitalism and rise of the proletariat were immi-
nent. He therefore joined the leadership of the Socialist League in espousing an ideological purity
that rejected parliamentary reform and any other
transitional measures. He thus isolated himself
not only from those friends and admirers who
were unwilling to follow him into socialism but
also from more moderate Socialists. (The Socialist Democratic Federation put up two candidates
for the 1885 parliamentary election; the Socialist
League countered with a pamphlet by Morris, *For
Whom Shall We Vote?*, urging workers not to cast bal-
lots.) Although he rejected their platform, it was
difficult for Morris to counter the anarchists who

in time came to dominate the Socialist League.

At the same time, the Socialist movement,
which had at first been treated as a joke, was beginning to be taken as a serious threat to the political system. In "Art Under Plutocracy," Morris
had called himself a representative of "reconstruc-
tive Socialism," in distinction to the "other people
who call themselves Socialists whose aim is not reconstruction, but destruction." Now, in May
1885, writing to Georgiana Burne-Jones, he contemplated the end of civilization: "how often it
consoles me to think of barbarism once more
flooding the world, and real feelings and passions, however rudimentary, taking the place of
our wretched hypocrisies." What Morris meant
by "barbarism" was not chaos. His earlier reading
of such historians as Edward A. Freeman had encouraged him to imagine the Germanic tribal organization underlying feudalism as a form of primitive communism. And feudalism itself he saw
from the positive perspective of Ruskin's "On the
Nature of Gothic," from *The Stones of Venice*. This
longing for "barbarism" may have linked Morris
in some ways to anarchist tendencies within the Socialist movement; however, as expressed in his

*The Hammersmith branch of the Socialist League. Morris's daughter Jenny is seated in the center of the front row; two seats to
her right is May Morris, her sister; Morris is in the second row, seventh from the right.*

later romances, it became the image of a renewed order, grounded in the simple life Morris found so appealing, historically explicable in terms of the Marxist notion he seems to have reached on his own that "The progress of life must be not on the straight line, but on the spiral."

Police persecution of the Socialists grew, often taking the form of harassment or arrest of public speakers. On 21 September 1885 Morris was present at the Thames Police Court for the trial of eight men arrested the previous day for speaking on the street. At the judge's sentence, the spectators, including Morris, cried "Shame," and the police began a general assault on them. Morris, defending himself, was arrested for disorderly conduct, accused by a policeman of having struck him on the chest and broken his helmet strap. He denied the charge and was dismissed, paying bail, as became his custom, for some of the working-class demonstrators.

On 8 February 1886 Socialist speeches in Trafalgar Square and Hyde Park precipitated a riot of the unemployed, with rumors of a march on the West End of London. Two weeks later a demonstration by the Socialist Democratic Federation was attacked by the police. The following July Morris was arrested for speaking on the street and fined a shilling. (The two working-class men arrested with him were fined twenty pounds; when they refused to pay, they were sentenced to two months in jail.)

Meanwhile Morris's other work continued. Although he could not devote himself to it with full energy, he kept a watchful eye on the firm, for which his daughter May, who had followed him into socialism, was now designing chintzes and wallpapers. In addition to his writing for *Commonweal*–which included his poem on the Paris Commune, *The Pilgrims of Hope* (serialized beginning in 1885, separately published the following year)–Morris was working on his English verse translation of *The Odyssey*, which appeared in 1887. In November 1886 his first Socialist romance, *A Dream of John Ball*, began in *Commonweal*, with separate publication following in 1888. And he continued to write lectures setting forth the goals and principles of socialism, talks now based on a fairly thorough understanding of Marxist economics. In "How We Live and How We Might Live" (1884) he established four "claims for decent life": "First, a healthy body; second, an active mind in sympathy with the past, the present, and the future; thirdly, occupation fit for a healthy body and an active mind; and

fourthly, a beautiful world to live in." In his elaboration of these claims, Morris seriously grapples with the problem of a Socialist future, addressing himself to such questions as the future of the family and the nature of education.

On 13 November 1887 ("Bloody Sunday"), Morris was present when police and soldiers brutally attacked radical demonstrators in Trafalgar Square. Well-dressed women in the surrounding houses and hotels clapped and cheered as the demonstrators were clubbed or ridden down by mounted police. Three men were killed and two hundred hospitalized. Morris confessed himself "astounded at the rapidity of the thing and the ease with which military organization got its victory. I could see that numbers were of no avail unless led by a band of men acting in concert and each knowing his part." A week later, Alfred Linnell was ridden down by the police in Northumberland Avenue. Morris wrote "A Death Song" for the benefit of his family, and was one of the pallbearers at the funeral, for which a great procession marched from Soho to Bow Cemetery.

Bloody Sunday was Morris's closest experience of political violence, and it influenced his account of revolution in *News from Nowhere*. Unlike Shaw, his companion in the march to Trafalgar Square, he was not encouraged by the experience to work within the political system. Rather, it taught him the need for strict military organization if any revolutionary force were to make a stand against the powers of the state, and therefore discouraged his belief that radical social change would take place in the near future.

The years 1888 and 1889 saw the gradual dissolution of the Socialist League. As more and more of its members rejected its antiparliamentarianism, the league became increasingly dominated by left-wing extremists. As progress in legislation and unionism was made on various fronts, the league's ideological purism seemed less and less relevant. Morris himself was attacked by the Fabians for espousing views that cast ridicule on socialism. However there could be no doubt about the honest passion with which he advanced his opinions. E. P. Thompson quotes Edward Carpenter's assessment of Morris's speech at the International Socialist Working-Men's Congress in Paris, July 1889, as "one of the most effective in the session."

In 1888 Morris saw publication of *Signs of Change*, a collection of his most important Socialist lectures. The following year he produced *A*

Tale of the House of the Wolfings and All the Kindreds of the Mark, a romance treating the confrontation of Germanic tribal society with Roman militarism. In 1890 a related work, *The Roots of the Mountains*, appeared, portraying a later stage of tribal society in conflict with invading Huns. In these re-creations of the past, he attempted to portray the elements of communal society he hoped would reappear under communism. They thus foreshadow the utopian romance *News from Nowhere*, which he published in installments of *Commonweal* in 1890.

News from Nowhere is at once the summation of Morris's Socialist philosophy and a deeply personal exploration of his own desires for a future society. It is also a farewell to the Socialist League, which in May had removed Morris from the editorship of *Commonweal*. In November, the Hammersmith Branch withdrew from the league, reconstituting itself as the Hammersmith Socialist Society. Its manifesto disavowed both parliamentarianism and anarchism; however, the society was open to anyone who wanted to join and cooperated with other Socialist organizations.

For the last six years of his life Morris continued various forms of activism, but on a much reduced scale. The failure of the Socialist League taught him to distrust his abilities, and, after a serious attack of gout in February 1891, his health was broken. There were, as always, new interests. No longer devoting all his superfluous funds to socialism, he began amassing a library of early books and illuminated manuscripts. In 1891 he published a collection of short poems, *Poems by the Way*, and began publishing *The Saga Library*. Two years earlier, he had given special attention to the typography and binding of *A Tale of the House of the Wolfings*. Typically, Morris soon realized that he could do it all better if he did it himself. In 1890 he founded the Kelmscott Press, which began printing the following January.

Throughout the 1880s Morris had been at least peripherally involved with the growing Arts and Crafts movement, the chief inspiration for which had been his own accomplishments as a designer and artisan. He had misgivings about any reform of the arts that was not grounded in political revolution; however, he could not refuse to second the work of self-avowed disciples such as W. R. Lethaby and Walter Crane. In 1888 he had been elected a member of the recently founded Art Workers' Guild; and in the same year he had participated in the first exhibition of the Arts and Crafts Exhibition Society. It was Emery Walk-

er's lecture on printing delivered at the 1888 exhibition—in particular, his concern with the importance of the total page—that spurred Morris's interest in the subject.

Totality was the keynote of the Kelmscott Press. Morris designed the type, ornamentation, and layout of the books, and chose their paper and binding materials with great care. He published his own works as well as a library of the writings that had meant most to him throughout his life. Altogether the Kelmscott Press printed fifty-three books, including an edition of Chaucer with woodcuts by Burne-Jones that is considered its masterpiece. Morris also wrote a series of prose romances for publication by the press: *The Story of the Glittering Plain Which Has Been Also Called the Land of Living Men or the Acre of the Undying* (1891), *The Wood beyond the World* (1894), *The Well at the World's End* (1896), *The Water of the Wondrous Isles* (1897), and *The Sundering Flood* (1897). The romances are deliberately escapist and, like the Kelmscott Press, represent Morris's recovered willingness to indulge himself in doing the things he liked best. They were not widely reviewed and were faulted by some critics for their archaic diction and syntax. However, some readers, including W. B. Yeats—who had attended the Socialist evenings at Hammersmith—admired their capacity to evoke an imaginary world, and twentieth-century psychological and genre criticism has come to recognize them as classic works of literary fantasy.

In 1892 Morris was considered a possible successor to Tennyson as poet laureate. He was pleased by Gladstone's support and found the idea of a Marxist courtier wryly amusing, but politely declined the offer. As a Socialist, Morris now worked toward unity of the movement and in 1893 had reached the position of hoping for the establishment of "a due Socialist party." In the same year, with Bax, he revised some earlier jointly written *Commonweal* materials into the book *Socialism: Its Growth and Outcome*. In the final years of his life, according to E. P. Thompson, "Morris stood *above* the movement—not in the sense of standing apart from it, but in the sense of comprising in his own person a point of unity above the divisions. . . . he was no longer so closely engaged in the day-to-day struggle of the movement. But this very disengagement meant that he could work for the unity he so much desired with better effect."

In December 1895 he made his last open-air speech, at the funeral of Sergius Stepniak; in

Frontispiece depicting Kelmscott Manor included in the 1892
Kelmscott Press edition of Morris's News
from Nowhere

January 1896 he gave his last talk in the Hammersmith clubroom, and days later, his last public address. His health deteriorated steadily during the months that followed–although he continued writing and designing. In July he traveled to Norway, hoping to benefit from the sea voyage, but the journey failed to raise his spirits and on his return in August it was clear that he did not have long to live. His friends did their best to cheer his final weeks, and Morris responded with heartfelt affection. He died quietly on 3 October and was buried three days later in Kelmscott churchyard.

While critical opinion of Morris's other writings has fluctuated radically since 1896, the lectures on art and socialism have steadily assumed greater importance and are now generally taken to be his most important literary work. In the years following his death, his two collections of lectures were supplemented by the volume *Architecture, Industry, and Wealth* (1902), edited by his literary executor, Sydney Cockerell; by volumes twenty-two and twenty-three of *The Collected*

Works (1910-1915), edited by May Morris; by the two volumes of *William Morris: Artist, Writer, Socialist* (1936), also edited by May Morris; and by Eugene D. LeMire's *The Unpublished Lectures of William Morris* (1969). In addition, the best of the lectures have been republished in a variety of other editions and, with *News from Nowhere* and a handful of poems from *The Defence of Guenevere*, comprise the bulk of the various selections from Morris published in the twentieth century.

Morris's lectures continue to be read, not only as classics of Victorian prose but also as crucial statements about the nature of design and the possibility of a humane socialism. If the Modernist architecture that evolved from Morris's belief in honest simplicity has reached a dead end, it may be because his belief in the need for a human scale in building was ignored. If the communism of the twentieth century has failed to live up to Marx's hopes for the future, it may be because it has ignored Morris's belief in the value of pleasure in ordinary life and paid inadequate heed to his distrust of the centralized state. For these reasons, his lectures on art and socialism–in fact, lectures on the same subject–remain provocative. Here, as nowhere else in his writing, Morris speaks with a clarity and vigor it is difficult to resist. "There is more life in the lectures, where one feels that the whole man is engaged in the writing," Raymond Williams wrote in 1958, "than in any of the prose and verse romances. . . . Morris is a fine political writer, in the broadest sense, and it is on that, finally, that his reputation will rest."

Letters:
The Letters of William Morris to His Family and Friends, edited by Philip Henderson (London & New York: Longmans, Green, 1950);
The Collected Letters of William Morris, edited by Norman Kelvin, volume 1, 1848-1880 (Princeton: Princeton University Press, 1984).

Bibliographies:
H. Buxton Forman, *The Books of William Morris Described, with Some Account of His Doings in Literature and in the Allied Crafts* (London: Hollings, 1897; Chicago: Way & Williams, 1897);
Temple Scott [J. H. Isaacs], *A Bibliography of the Works of William Morris* (London: Bell, 1897);
William E. Fredeman, "William Morris & His Circle: A Selective Bibliography of Publications," *Journal of the William Morris Society,* 1

(Summer 1964): 23-33; 2 (Spring 1966): 13-26;

Fredeman, *Pre-Raphaelitism: A Bibliocritical Study* (Cambridge: Harvard University Press, 1965);

David and Sheila Latham, "William Morris: An Annotated Bibliography," *Journal of the William Morris Society*, 5 (Summer 1983): 23-41;

John J. Walsdorf, *William Morris in Private Press and Limited Editions: A Descriptive Bibliography of Books by and about William Morris, 1891-1981* (Phoenix: Oryx Press, 1983);

K. L. Goodwin, *A Preliminary Handlist of Manuscripts and Documents of William Morris* (London: William Morris Society, 1984);

Gary L. Aho, *William Morris: A Reference Guide* (Boston: G. K. Hall, 1985).

Biographies:

John W. Mackail, *The Life of William Morris*, 2 volumes (London & New York: Longmans, Green, 1899);

E. P. Thompson, *William Morris: Romantic to Revolutionary* (London: Laurence & Wishart, 1955; New York: Monthly Review Press, 1955; revised, London: Merlin Press, 1977; New York: Pantheon, 1977);

Philip Henderson, *William Morris: His Life, Work and Friends* (London: Thames & Hudson, 1967; New York: McGraw-Hill, 1967);

Jack Lindsay, *William Morris: His Life and Work* (London: Constable, 1975).

References:

R. Page Arnot, *William Morris; The Man and the Myth, Including Letters of William Morris to J. L. Mahon and Dr. John Glasse* (London: Lawrence & Wishart, 1964);

Patrick Brantlinger, " 'News from Nowhere': Morris's Socialist Anti-Novel," *Victorian Studies*, 19 (September 1975): 35-49;

G. B. J. [Georgiana Burne-Jones], *Memorials of Edward Burne-Jones*, 2 volumes (London & New York: Macmillan, 1904);

Blue Calhoun, *The Pastoral Vision of William Morris* (Athens: University of Georgia Press, 1975);

Fiona Clark, *William Morris: Wallpapers and Chintzes*, revised edition (London: Academy, 1974);

G. D. H. Cole, *William Morris as a Socialist* (London: William Morris Society, 1960);

Gerald H. Crow, *William Morris, Designer*, special issue of *Studio* (Winter 1934);

Joseph R. Dunlap, *The Book That Never Was: Wil-*

liam Morris, Edward Burne-Jones and "The Earthly Paradise" (New York: Oriole Editions, 1971);

Peter Faulkner, *Against the Age: An Introduction to William Morris* (London & Boston: Allen & Unwin, 1980);

Faulkner, ed., *William Morris: The Critical Heritage* (London & Boston: Routledge & Kegan Paul, 1973);

Peter Floud, "The Inconsistencies of William Morris," *Listener*, 52 (14 October 1954): 615-617;

William E. Fredeman, ed., *Victorian Poetry: An Issue Dedicated to the Work of William Morris*, 13 (Fall-Winter 1975);

Bruce J. Glasier, *William Morris and the Early Days of the Socialist Movement* (London & New York: Longmans, Green, 1921);

John Goode, "William Morris and the Dream of Revolution," in *Literature and Politics in the Nineteenth Century*, edited by John Lucas (London: Metheun/New York: Barnes & Noble, 1971), pp. 221-280;

Graham Hough, "William Morris," in his *The Last Romantics* (London: Duckworth, 1948; New York: Barnes & Noble, 1971), pp. 83-133;

Frederick Kirchhoff, "Travel as Anti-Autobiography in William Morris' *Icelandic Journals*," in *Approaches to Victorian Autobiography*, edited by George Landow (Athens: Ohio University Press, 1979), pp. 292-310;

Kirchhoff, *William Morris* (Boston: Twayne, 1979);

Karl Litzenberg, "The Social Philosophy of William Morris and the Doom of the Gods," in *Essays and Studies in English and Comparative Literature*, University of Michigan Publications, 1 (1933): 183-203;

Paul Meier, *William Morris: The Marxist Dreamer*, translated by Frank Gubb, 2 volumes (Hassocks: Harvester Press, 1978; Atlantic Highlands, N.J.: Humanities Press, 1978);

A. L. Morton, "The Dream of William Morris," in his *The English Utopia* (London: Lawrence & Wishart, 1953), pp. 149-182;

Paul Needham, ed., *William Morris and the Art of the Book* (New York: Pierpont Morgan Library, 1976; London: Oxford University Press, 1976);

Linda Parry, *William Morris Textiles* (London: Weidenfeld & Nicolson, 1983; New York: Viking, 1983);

A. Charles Sewter, *The Stained Glass of William Morris and His Circle*, 2 volumes (New Haven & London: Yale University Press for the Paul Mellon Centre for Studies in British Art,

1975);

Carole Silver, *The Romance of William Morris* (Athens: Ohio University Press, 1982);

H. Halliday Sparling, *The Kelmscott Press and William Morris, Master-Craftsman* (London: Macmillan, 1924);

Peter Stansky, *Redesigning the World: William Morris, the 1880s and the Arts and Crafts* (Princeton: Princeton University Press, 1985);

Stansky, *William Morris* (Oxford & New York: Oxford University Press, 1983);

Paul Thompson, *The Work of William Morris* (London: Heinemann, 1967; New York: Viking, 1967);

Lionel Trilling, "Aggression and Utopia, A Note on William Morris's 'News from Nowhere,'" *Psychoanalytic Quarterly*, 42 (April 1973): 214-225;

Raymond Watkinson, *William Morris as Designer* (London: Studio Vista, 1967; New York: Reinhold, 1967);

Raymond Williams, *Culture and Society* (London: Chatto & Windus, 1958).

Papers:

The major collection of Morris's letters and manuscripts is held by the British Library, London. Other principal collections are at the Bodleian Library, Oxford; the Henry E. Huntington Library, San Marino, California; the Pierpont Morgan Library, New York; the Victoria and Albert Museum Library, London; the William Morris Gallery, Walthamstow; and the Sanford and Helen Berger Collection, Carmel, California.

Walter Pater

Hayden Ward
West Virginia University

BIRTH: London, 4 August 1839, to Richard Glode and Maria Pater.

EDUCATION: B.A., Queen's College, Oxford University, 1862.

DEATH: Oxford, 30 July 1894.

BOOKS: *Studies in the History of the Renaissance* (London: Macmillan, 1873); revised and republished as *The Renaissance: Studies in Art and Poetry* (London: Macmillan, 1877; New York: Macmillan, 1877; revised again, London & New York, 1888; revised again, London & New York, 1893);

Marius the Epicurean; His Sensations and Ideas (2 volumes, London: Macmillan, 1885; 1 volume, London & New York: Macmillan, 1885; revised, 2 volumes, London & New York: Macmillan, 1892);

Imaginary Portraits (London & New York: Macmillan, 1887; New York: Macmillan, 1899);

Appreciations, with an Essay on Style (London & New York: Macmillan, 1889);

Plato and Platonism: A Series of Lectures (London:

Walter Pater (photograph by Elliott & Fry)

Macmillan, 1893; London & New York: Macmillan, 1893);

An Imaginary Portrait (Oxford: Privately printed, 1894); republished as *The Child in the House: An Imaginary Portrait* (Boston: Copeland & Day, 1895);

Greek Studies: A Series of Essays (New York & London: Macmillan, 1895; London & New York: Macmillan, 1901);

Miscellaneous Studies: A Series of Essays (New York & London: Macmillan, 1895; London & New York: Macmillan, 1900);

Gaston de Latour: An Unfinished Romance (New York & London: Macmillan, 1896; London: Macmillan, 1902);

Essays from "The Guardian" (London: Privately printed, 1896; Portland, Maine: Mosher, 1897);

Uncollected Essays (Portland, Maine: Mosher, 1903);

Sketches and Reviews (New York: Boni & Liveright, 1919).

Collections: Edition DeLuxe, 9 volumes (London & New York: Macmillan, 1900-1901);

New Library Edition, 10 volumes (London: Macmillan, 1910).

Walter Pater is important to English literary history because he combines a commitment to the romantic theory that art is essentially an expression of personality with a sympathetic response to the scientific and historical studies of the Victorian period that suggest how complex and ambiguous "personality" is. Pater's writings explore the ways in which biology, psychology, history, religion, and myth shape the individual's understanding of his own times and help him to interpret the bearing of the past upon the present. In this linking of aesthetics to religion, history, and science, Pater bridges, more subtly than any other writer of the late Victorian period, the dominant Romanticism of his own century and the dominant Modernism of the twentieth.

Few of his personal papers or anecdotal reminiscences by his acquaintances exist to provide a clear, accurate, or full biography of Pater. As Ian Fletcher has remarked in his 1959 volume, *Walter Pater,* "We must seek the inner man in the books." However, some information about Pater's early life is known. Walter Horatio Pater was born 4 August 1839 in Shadwell, a district of East London, the younger son of Richard and Maria Pater. Dr. Pater was a surgeon whose practice seems to have consisted mostly in treating the many poor people living in the neighbor-

hood. He died when his second son was only four years old. After Dr. Pater's death, Pater's mother moved with her four children to the north London suburb of Enfield, near the home of her sister, Pater's favorite "Aunt Bessie." Pater's older brother William left home at fifteen, in 1851, and Pater lived with his mother and two younger sisters, Clara and Hester. One may suppose that the young Pater felt the absence of male companionship during the later years at Enfield and was rather isolated from his mother and sisters. Certainly, his young fictional heroes seem to be loners, seeking eagerly but tentatively for glamorous, authoritative, older male friends.

In 1853 the Pater family moved to Harbledown, near Canterbury, so that Pater could attend the King's School, attached to the famous cathedral. As a day student, Pater lived at home and does not seem to have entered fully into school life. He did form close friendships with two boys, Henry Dombrain and John Rainier McQueen. The three kept rather to themselves and were known in the school as "the Triumvirate" (Pater represents the situation fictionally in his late, uncompleted novel, *Gaston de Latour,* 1896). The boys shared the pleasure of rambling about the countryside and an intense interest in religious matters.

In 1858, the year he matriculated at Queen's College, Oxford, Pater traveled to Heidelberg, where Aunt Bessie, who had become guardian of the Pater children upon Maria Pater's death in 1854, had taken Pater's sisters to complete their education. In Heidelberg, Pater awoke to the richness of German culture, and, upon returning to Oxford, reportedly studied German so that he could read the works of George Wilhelm Friedrich Hegel, the great aesthetician and philosopher of history, whose ideas were greatly to influence him. Indeed, one of the reasons Pater was appointed a fellow at Brasenose College seems to have been his reputed expertise as a Hegel scholar. He also read other German Romantics–Schiller, Fichte, and Goethe most prominently–from whom he garnered ideas about the importance of aesthetic experience in the development of the ideal cultured man.

While at Queens, Pater developed other intellectual interests. He was tutored in Greek by Benjamin Jowett, who later became the translator of Plato and master of Balliol College. On his own, Pater read the work of Sainte-Beuve, Gautier, Baudelaire, and Flaubert, contemporary French writers with a less than respectable reputa-

The Pater family home at Harbledown, near Canterbury, where Pater lived while he was a day student at King's School in the 1850s

tion in staid Oxford. From them, Pater acquired a sense of the discipline and autonomy of "art for art's sake." This vague, confusing term meant to Pater that the value and pleasure of art in no way depended upon its intention or ability to inculcate morality. The aesthetic form was a good one in itself, regardless of whether or not it taught one how to live. In Flaubert, Pater found the sanction for his idea that the artist's only responsibility is to insure that his work is the perfect fulfillment of his artistic intention. In Baudelaire's book of poems *Les Fleurs du mal* (1857), Pater discovered that the attraction of art can lie in its delicate images of mingled beauty and decay, that the perception of evil and death can heighten the desire for the beautiful but transient things of the world.

So, by the time he graduated from Queen's with a second-class degree, in 1862, Pater had already acquired a considerable knowledge of the literatures of ancient Greece, eighteenth-century

Germany, and nineteenth-century France. With these credentials, he became a probationary fellow of Brasenose College in February 1864. In July he read to the Old Mortality, an essay society that he joined earlier in the year, a paper entitled "Diaphaneité" (the word, though Pater incorrectly placed the accent mark from the original French, means "the quality of being transparent"), which, although it was not published until after his death, is the earliest surviving piece of prose that Pater wrote. It prepares the reader to understand his other early essays, including those that went into his first book, *Studies in the History of the Renaissance* (1873).

In "Diaphaneité," Pater says that receptivity to a wide range of experience or impressions and a desire to express one's inner self fully and accurately in outward form are the leading qualities of the aesthetic personality. By implication, all truth depends on the relation of observer and experience. Self-expression is the record of that relation at one moment of its shifting existence.

In his first published essay, on Coleridge, in an 1866 issue of *Westminster Review*, Pater says that the transparency and expressiveness described in "Diaphaneité" are the attributes with which modern humanity must confront reality. Writing enthusiastically under the influence of evolutionary theory (Darwin's *On the Origin of Species* had appeared in 1859), Pater remarks that science reveals "types of life evanescing into each other by inexpressible refinements of change," not only by present physical change but also "by remote laws of inheritance, the vibration of long-past acts." As a consequence, modern humanity faces "a world of finely linked conditions, shifting intricately as we ourselves change." In this situation, Pater declares, morality can no longer be based on a presumed eternal and universal order of truths, on the belief in an "absolute spirit," which seeks "to arrest every object in an eternal formula." Rather, morality must be based on the "relative spirit": "The relative spirit, by its constant dwelling on the more fugitive conditions or circumstances of things, breaking through a thousand rough and brutal classifications, and giving elasticity to inflexible principles, begets an intellectual *finesse* of which the ethical result is a delicate and tender justice in the criticism of human life." For Pater, Coleridge represents the futile resistance of the idealist tradition to a new epistemology based upon the empirical analysis of the physical world. Modern science, in the relative spirit, will win out over traditional philosophy on this point. Pater approves.

Relativist as he is, he still finds a use for idealism. In a *Westminster Review* essay on William Morris (1868), part of which was reprinted as Pater's "Conclusion" in *Studies in the History of the Renaissance* (1873) and part as "Aesthetic Poetry" in *Appreciations, with an Essay on Style* (1889), he transmutes idealism into historicism. The study of the past corresponds to the recollection of important moments in the individual life; autobiography and historiography merge. One traces the influence on, or survival in, one historical age of the customs and art of earlier ages, just as one tries to understand the effect of past personal experience on one's present life. This tracing of historical survivals becomes, for the modern relativist, the equivalent of the recovery of lost perfect "forms" for the idealist. Morris's poetry is an example, because in its imitation of medieval poetry, it reveals the ancient "pagan sentiment" for beauty mingled with death that survives from Greek religion into the Christianity of the Middle Ages.

While his reading of Morris suggested to him the survival of Greek religious sentiment into the Middle Ages, Pater describes, in an important 1867 *Westminster Review* essay, the German aesthetician Johann Joachim Winckelmann (1717-1768) tracing the pagan or "Hellenic" sentiment back to its source, in his studies of the copies of Greek statues displayed at Rome, statues that express with perfect clarity the sentiment they embody. In Pater's view, by an intense empathy, Winckelmann simultaneously understands the diaphanous ideal of Greek art and works to attain it in his own writing: "This key to understanding of the Greek spirit, Winckelmann possessed in his own nature.... Penetrating into the antique world by his passion, his temperament, he enunciated no formal principles, always hard and one-sided. Minute and anxious as his culture was, he never became one-sidedly self-analytical. Occupied ever with himself and developing his genius, he was not content, as so often happens with such natures, that the atmosphere between him and other minds should be thick and clouded; he was ever jealously refining his meaning into a form, express, clear, objective." Again, to express one's own nature perfectly at the same time one uncovers the "secret" or "formulas" of a historical culture or art form is to live the diaphanous ideal, to live in what Pater calls "the spirit of art."

This judgment of Winckelmann reflects Pater's notion of his own work as a writer. What

Pater says of Winckelmann and his study of Greek art is most important as a historical analogue for the work of the scholar and artist in the nineteenth century. Not surprisingly, then, Pater concludes the essay by answering the question, "Can we bring that ideal into the gaudy, perplexed light of modern life?" He tells us that Goethe, whom Pater and many of his contemporaries (including Carlyle and Arnold) took to be the modern master spirit of self-culture, sought to impart "the blitheness and universality of the antique ideal" to art that would "contain the fullness of the experience of the modern world," as Winckelmann had done. Late in the essay on Winckelmann, Pater suggests that he and his contemporaries must continue Goethe's endeavor: modern art must "rearrange the details of modern life" so as to impart "the sense of freedom" to an age conscious of a new kind of necessity or determinism that comes from the experiments and theorizing of modern science, a biological and historical determinism that is like "a magic web woven through and through us ..., penetrating us with a network subtler than our subtlest nerves, yet bearing in it the central forces of the world."

To define that "network," and the "central forces" that it transmits, is the purpose of two of the most famous early essays that eventually went into *Studies in the History of the Renaissance*, or *The Renaissance*, as it came to be known by virtue of its 1877 retitling.

In the "Conclusion," Pater describes as a kind of equivalent of the ancient doctrine of "perpetual flux" the modern scientific idea of continuous physical change. Both the individual and the world he inhabits are always becoming and vanishing, each moment of life a "concurrence" of forces that meet only to part. In such a world, the individual has only "flickering" impressions of the world beyond himself, impressions that seem to disappear even before he can apprehend them: "Every one of those impressions is the impression of the individual in his isolation, each mind keeping as a solitary prisoner its own dream of a world. Analysis goes a step farther still, and assures us that those impressions of the individual mind to which, for each one of us, experience dwindles down, are in perpetual flight; that each of them is limited by time, and that as time is infinitely divisible, each of them is infinitely divisible also; all that is actual in it being a single moment, gone while we try to apprehend it, of which it may be more truly said that it has ceased to be than that it is.... It is with this movement, with the passage and dissolution of impressions, images, sensations, that analysis leaves off—that continual vanishing away, that strange, perpetual weaving and unweaving of ourselves."

Pater argues boldly in the "Conclusion" for the thesis which is latent in all his early work: that the observation and recording of sense impressions is more important than abstract thinking. The cool laser-light of perception he describes in "Diaphaneité" and the "blitheness" and "repose" of Greek art are replaced for the modern aesthetic sensibility by the need to "burn always with a hard, gemlike flame" in a diamond-heat of the senses: "Not to discriminate every moment some passionate attitude in those about us, and in the very brilliancy of their gifts some tragic dividing of forces on their ways is ... to sleep before evening. With this sense of the splendour of our experience and of its awful brevity, gathering all we are into one desperate effort to see and touch, we shall hardly have time to make theories about the things we see and touch."

In Pater's view, the observation not of ordinary life but of great works of art will give "the highest quality to your moments as they pass, and simply for those moments' sake." This is so because art imparts a beautiful, enduring order to experience that experience itself usually lacks.

Perhaps the numerous detractors of Pater, such as W. H. Mallock who ridiculed him as "Mr. Rose" in his satire *The New Republic* (1877-1879), were right to see in his narrowly focused prescription for the satisfying life an abnegation of social concern or responsibility, but they were wrong to see a call to immoral thrill-seeking. Indeed, as Pater's famous image of the burning gem suggests, this life of "eager observation" necessitates a dedication, a mental toughness, a polished craft in reporting the results that are quite alien to the sloppy sensualism he was accused of inspiring.

In the "Preface," Pater describes the critical method and view of Western history that underlie the other essays of *Studies in the History of the Renaissance*. Beauty, he holds, is not abstract but concrete, not universal but particular, not eternal but relative to the historical conditions under which it was produced and in which it is observed. One can understand the beautiful only in terms of the "formula" of particular works of art or of the lives of individual artists. Therefore, general aesthetic theories are useless. On this point, Pater disagrees not only with eighteenth-century aestheticians but with his contemporaries Ruskin and Arnold as well. In explaining the method of

the aesthetic critic in analyzing the "formula" of each of the great artists whose lives and works he will discuss, Pater employs that analogy with physical science that he had introduced in the earlier-written "Conclusion": "And the function of the aesthetic critic is to distinguish, to analyze, and separate from its adjuncts, the virtue by which a picture, a landscape, a fair personality in life or in a book, produces this special impression of beauty or pleasure, to indicate what the source of that impression is, and under what conditions it is experienced."

Also in the "Preface," Pater asserts that the Renaissance is not a historical period, separate from the Middle Ages, but rather a cultural impulse that originated within the Middle Ages themselves, a groundswell of assertion for individual physical and moral freedom that had its roots in France in the twelfth and thirteenth centuries, reached its zenith in fifteenth-century Italy and returned to France for its twilight in the sixteenth century.

The structure of *Studies in the History of the Renaissance* reflects this view. The first essay, "Two French Stories," treats the melding of the Hellenic "sweetness" with the "curious strength" of the Middle Ages. Pater observes that this sweetness and strength are to be seen in the "legend" of Eloise and Abelard, and that of Tannhäuser. He devotes most of the essay, however, to showing that these qualities are also exemplified by the less familiar story of Amis and Amile (like that of Palemon and Arcite in Chaucer's "Knight's Tale") and *Aucassin and Nicolette*, a prose tale of young lovers written in the thirteenth century. In the next six essays, Pater analyzes some of the writers and painters of the Italian Renaissance in whose work, he believes, the influence of ancient Greece transforms the cultural residue of the Middle Ages into a new humanism. Pico della Mirandola's effort to reconcile Platonic philosophy with Christianity is an early stage in this transformation, as are the pictures of Sandro Botticelli, which combine the visionary qualities of medieval painting with the definite, concrete forms Pater thinks characteristic of Greek art. Of the sculptor Luca della Robbia, Pater notes that he combines the "pure form" of the Greeks with a considerable individual expressiveness somewhat like that of Michelangelo, only less passionate. Indeed, in his essay on Michelangelo's poetry, Pater says that the sonnet form was a stringent discipline upon the artist's emotions. In essays on Leonardo da Vinci, Giorgione, and the French poet Joachim du Bellay, Pater further considers the way in which artistic form at once expresses and controls the personality of its creator. As the eighth essay, he includes the Winckelmann piece because that classical scholar, in the eighteenth century, is "the last fruit of the Renaissance."

The most important of the essays in *Studies in the History of the Renaissance* is on Leonardo da Vinci. For the details of Leonardo's life, Pater draws on Giorgio Vasari's sixteenth-century *Lives of the Most Eminent Painters, Sculptors, and Architects* and on the 1855 study of the Renaissance by the French historian Jules Michelet, whose theories of history were an important influence generally on Pater.

As Winckelmann is for Pater the great intuitive interpreter of the surfaces of Hellenic idealism, Leonardo da Vinci is the great interpreter of depths, a seeker of "the sources of spring beneath the earth or of expression beneath the human countenance." In his studies of nature, Leonardo embodies that element in the Renaissance that anticipates the modern spirit of scientific investigation. But the science of late-fifteenth-century Italy, writes Pater, was "all divination, clairvoyance, unsubjected to our modern formulas, seeking in an instant of vision to concentrate a thousand experiences." Pater invites the reader to regard Leonardo as a magician in his way of experimenting with new materials and concepts as an inventor or painter. Using a backwards, mirror handwriting to record his discoveries, sketching mysterious but wonderfully suggestive drawings and cartoons, he was ever in search, suggests Pater, of a way to free familiar subjects from traditional associations and to substitute striking and disturbing images in which corruption taints beauty.

In Pater's view Leonardo was more interested in "human personality" than in nature. "He became above all a painter of portraits," producing the disconcerting portrait of an androgynous Saint John the Baptist and the *Medusa*, with its head of snaky hair, which Pater had seen in the Uffizi Gallery in Florence during his 1865 trip to Italy. (The *Medusa* is no longer attributed to Leonardo.) There are da Vinci's chalk drawings of "clairvoyant" women, "through whom, as through delicate instruments, one becomes aware of the subtler forces of nature, and the modes of their action, . . . all those finer conditions wherein material things rise to that subtlety of operation which constitutes them spiritual. . . ."

Here are the "forces" at work in each individual life, of which Pater had written in the "Conclusion," symbolized in the experimental drawings of the fifteenth-century painter.

Inspired partially by an essay by A. C. Swinburne entitled "Notes on Designs of the Old Masters in Florence," published in the *Fortnightly Review* for July 1868, Pater describes the *Mona Lisa* (or *La Gioconda*, as it is sometimes called) as "Leonardo's masterpiece," the perfectly diaphanous form, with "a beauty wrought out from within upon the flesh," on which "all the thoughts and experience of the world" are expressed. As Pater interprets her, "Lady Lisa" becomes the "symbol of the modern idea" of the "fancy of a perpetual life, sweeping together ten thousand experiences." She suggests the "idea of humanity as wrought upon by, and summing up in itself, all modes of thought and life." In *Art and the Creative Unconscious* (1959) the German psychiatrist Erich Neumann writes of the *Mona Lisa* and of Pater's description of it that "with Mona Lisa's smile was born the soul of modern man."

In his evocation of the *Mona Lisa*, Pater gave to the English literary world of the 1890s a kind of inspiration that led William Butler Yeats to present that passage, arranged as free verse, as the opening poem of *The Oxford Book of Modern Verse, 1892-1935* (1936) and to comment in the introduction to the volume: "I recall Pater's description of the Mona Lisa; had the individual soul of da Vinci's sitter gone down with the pearl divers or trafficked for strange webs? or did Pater foreshadow a poetry, a philosophy, where the individual is nothing, the flux of *The Cantos* of Ezra Pound . . . human experience no longer shut into brief lives, cut off into this place and that place. . . ?"

As Pater stresses the modern, symbolic qualities in Leonardo's art, so, in other essays in *Studies in the History of the Renaissance*, he emphasizes characteristics or habits of his subjects that parallel attitudes or methods of nineteenth-century scientific or historical studies. For example, Botticelli's painterly sensibility "usurps the data before it as the exponent of ideas, moods, visions of its own." In the essay on Giorgione, Pater describes a "striving after otherness" (*Anders-streben*) by which each art achieves "a partial alienation of its own limitations, by which the arts are able . . . reciprocally to lend each other new forces." This idea is the aesthetic equivalent to the evolutionary impulse in the life sciences, to which Pater finds the relative spirit attuned. Finally, in writ-

Pater as a fellow at Brasenose College, Oxford, 1872. Drawing by Simeon Solomon (Fondazione Horne, Florence).

ing of the Neo-Platonic Humanism of Pico della Mirandola, Pater sees a prefiguration of the nineteenth-century predilection for discovering patterns in history. In Pico, he discerns an attitude more characteristic of nineteenth-century historicism, of the kind found in *Studies in the History of the Renaissance*, than it is of the writings of Pico himself: "Nothing which has ever interested living men and women can wholly lose its vitality— no language they have spoken, nor oracle beside which they have hushed their voices, no dream which has once been entertained by actual human minds."

In his biography of Pater, published in 1906, Arthur C. Benson emphasizes the liberating effect of the publication of *Studies in the History of the Renaissance* on 1 March 1873: "It gave Pater a definite place in the literary and artistic world. . . . The younger generation was thrilled with a sense of high artistic possibilities." But if youth was thrilled, maturity, at least within the Oxford establishment, was appalled. The Reverend John Wordsworth, grandnephew of the poet and,

like Pater, a fellow of Brasenose College, wrote to Pater about his book: "Could you indeed have known the dangers into which you were likely to lead minds weaker than your own, you would, I believe, have paused."

With characteristic reticence, Pater responded publicly to neither the criticism nor the praise. He was, at least, mindful enough of John Wordsworth's stricture to have deleted the offending "Conclusion" from the second edition of the book in 1877 and to have restored it to the third edition of 1888, with an explanatory note that, fifteen years later, echoes Wordsworth's phrasing: "This brief 'Conclusion' was omitted in the second edition of this book, as I conceived that it might possibly mislead some of the young men into whose hands it might fall." Indeed, *Studies in the History of the Renaissance* became a kind of cult book, treasured and even rapturously recited by at least two generations of Oxford undergraduates.

The Macmillan brothers, Pater's publishers for *Studies in the History of the Renaissance* as for the subsequent books, haggled with him over the form of the book as well as the number of copies to be printed. Both the first and second editions had printings of 1,250 copies, while the third had 1,500 and the fourth, in 1893, 2,000, suggesting the book's slightly growing reputation over a twenty-year period. American editions of 1,000 copies each were published in 1887 and 1890, as Pater's reputation blossomed modestly among a transatlantic audience. The pattern of producing several editions in approximately the same number of copies as those published editions of *Studies in the History of the Renaissance* was to be more or less the same for his later books. By modern standards, Pater was never a best-seller.

Pater soon developed a new literary form, derived from the method of his Renaissance essays, that was to characterize the most important work of the rest of his career, the fictionalized historical studies he called "imaginary portraits." His earliest portrait, "The Child in the House," was published in the August 1878 *Macmillan's Magazine*. Over fifteen years later limited editions of this work appeared in both England and the United States. On a slip of paper, among his unpublished, fragmentary writings now at Harvard University, Pater wrote: "Child in the House: voilà, the germinating, original, source, specimen of all my imaginative work."

"The Child in the House" is an autobiographical sketch to the extent that the states of mind

Pater attributes to his character, Florian Deleal, were frequently Pater's own: the susceptibility to intense impressions of beauty mixed with pain or tinged with mortality, a sacramentalist sense of the beautiful holiness of the rituals of human life, the eagerness for vision of the transcendental spiritual life in actual persons and places. The minutely recorded memory of these impressions is the core of the older Florian's religious attitude: "His way of conceiving religion came then to be in effect what it ever afterwards remained—a sacred history indeed, but still more a sacred ideal, a transcendent version or representation, under intenser and more expressive light and shade, of human life and its familiar or exceptional incidents. . . . A place adumbrated itself in his thoughts, wherein those sacred personalities, which are at once the reflex and the pattern of our nobler phases of life, housed themselves; and this region in his intellectual scheme all subsequent experience did but tend still further to realize and define. Some ideal, hieratic persons he would always need to occupy it and keep a warmth there." The "process of brainbuilding" which Florian recalls in his own life is the evolution of the mythic possibility in one's own experience, the discovery of multiple, symbolic meanings that connect the individual life to the collective life of humanity across the boundaries of space and time that define history.

A more personal version of Winckelmann's discovery of the diaphanous unity of form and religious sentiment in Greek art, and of the relevance of that ideal to his own development as man and writer, this "brainbuilding" is the underlying subject of Pater's major work, *Marius the Epicurean; His Sensations and Ideas* (1885).

The book was a long time in gestation. Pater began it in the spring of 1881, and in December 1882 he went to Rome to do background research. By July 1883 he could write to his friend Violet Paget, who wrote under the pseudonym Vernon Lee: "I have hopes of completing one half of my present chief work—an Imaginary Portrait of a peculiar type of mind in the time of Marcus Aurelius—by the end of this Vacation, and meant to have asked you to look at some of the MS. perhaps. I am wishing to get the whole completed, as I have visions of many smaller pieces of work the composition of which would be actually pleasanter to me. However, I regard this present matter as a sort of duty. For, you know, I think that there is a . . . sort of religious phase possible for the modern mind . . . , the conditions of

which phase it is the main object of my design to convey."

Pater's purpose was to define, in the story of a young man's search for a philosophy by which to live in second-century Rome, the kind of religious belief or state of mind that he considered possible for a thoughtful person in late Victorian England. Repeatedly in the novel, Pater makes explicit and implicit parallels between his fictional world and the circumstances of modern life. In both worlds, the condition of religion is fragmented into many competing sects or cults, and old liturgies and rituals survive, divorced from their traditional dogmatic significances. Many philosophies are available to supplant traditional religion.

In the first of the four parts into which he divides the novel, Pater exposes the impressionable Marius to two materialist philosophies, the Aesculapian cult of bodily health and the sensual literary aestheticism, or "Euphuism," practiced by Flavian, the friend Marius meets in Pisa, who comes to symbolize early in Marius's life the mingled beauty and corruption of the pagan world.

While at the temple of Aesculapius, Marius learns what Pater had taught some years earlier in the "Conclusion" to *Studies in the History of the Renaissance*: the need, throughout life, to cultivate "the capacity of the eye": "To keep the eye clear by a sort of exquisite personal alacrity and cleanliness, extending even to his dwelling place; to discriminate, ever more and more fastidiously, select form and colour in things from what was less select; to meditate much on beautiful visible objects, on objects more especially connected with the period of youth."

As an intended corrective to the perceived licentiousness of his description of diaphanous clarity in the "Conclusion," Pater emphasizes here, as elsewhere in *Marius*, the moral poise of his "epicurean" doctrine, a poise that Marius comes to see is lacking in his friend Flavian, in whose aestheticism there is not only an unhealthy sensualism but also an impulse to satire (Pater remarks that Flavian reads the legend of Cupid and Psyche, in which Marius innocently finds an idealized representation of love, as though he were reading the work of Jonathan Swift!). For Marius, the decorous restraint of his childhood religion is preserved in an unfailing conscience that keeps him from excess.

However, in Flavian's "Euphuism" (Pater recalls in the term the most extravagant of Elizabethan literary styles), Marius finds an intriguing sublimation of religious zeal and sexual energy into the perfection of language of full and exotic self-expression. Marius himself becomes for a period (like the youthful Pater) a poet, and then a kind of diarist, as he seeks always to match the word to the idea. At this point, for Marius, literary style is a variant of ritual, the organic form or medium seeking to discover a new and adequate content.

At eighteen, with Flavian recently dead from fever, Marius ponders his need to understand, not in some doctrinal way, but in his own terms, the meaning of his life in relation to the larger world: "Still with something of the old religious earnestness of his childhood, he set himself . . . to determine his bearings, as by compass, in the world of thought; to get that precise acquaintance with the creative intelligence itself, its structures and capacities, its relation to other parts of himself and to other things, without which certainly no poetry can be masterly. . . . An exact estimate of realities, as towards himself, he must have–a delicately measured gradation of certainty in things, from the distant, haunted surmise or imagination, to the actual feeling of sorrow in his heart. . . ."

Marius's youthful readings of Heraclitus, Epicurus, and Lucretius, each in some way based upon the view of life as continuously changing, incline him to skepticism, to a "despair of knowledge" of the external world for which he tends to compensate "with a delightful sense of escape in replacing the outer world of other people by an inward world as himself really cared to have it. . . ." This tension between a "vision" of a transcendent order and the impressions of the changeful material world is continual in the novel–indeed, it is one of the common elements in all of Pater's writings.

Under the influence of the "New Cyrenaicism," the sensationalist philosophy he learns from the teachings of Aristippus, Marius develops a more focused, if still tentative, sense of his purpose in life: "To understand the various forms of ancient art and thought, the various forms of actual human feeling . . . , to satisfy, with a kind of scrupulous equity, the claims of these concrete and actual objects on his sympathy, his intelligence, his senses . . . , and in turn become the interpreter of them to others: this had now defined itself for Marius as a very narrowly practical design: it determined his choice of vocation to live by."

As did Winckelmann, Marius comes to equate knowing the self in the present with knowing the past; one does not precede or cause the other. The two knowledges are one, simultaneous. When one has this double vision, he must become an "interpreter . . . to others." To this end, Marius goes to Rome, as did Winckelmann, but to study rhetoric instead of statues. However, beyond learning to see and speak, Marius must learn how to live. He must discover ethics in aesthetics. The central ethical conflict for Marius is embodied in two "hieratic persons" (to recall Florian Deleal's phrase): the handsome young soldier, Cornelius, who represents "some possible intellectual formula" that turns out to be early Christianity, and the emperor, Marcus Aurelius, for whom Marius works as a kind of secretary, whose famous *Meditations* are the most admired expression of Roman Stoicism.

In contradiction of his own Cyrenaic enthusiasm for the physical life before him, Marius perceives in the emperor's oration to his court, on the theme of the evanescence and insignificance of life, only a will to indifference: "Consider how quickly all things vanish away–their bodily structure into the general substance; the very memory of them into that great gulf and abysm of past thoughts. Ah! 'tis on a tiny space of earth thou art creeping through life–a pigmy soul, carrying a dead body to its grave." Marius believes his own sense of the value of life, contingent on his perception of its fragility and brevity, to be morally superior to the willed indifference of the emperor to the spectacle of suffering, both by humans and animals. The emperor's studied apathy, broken only when his own young son dies and the philosopher is overcome by the man, allows him to tolerate what to Marius is the deeply evil spectacle of the gladitorial games and their concomitant torture of animals. (Only later does Marius hear of the brutal torments of the Christian martyrs by previous emperors.) Marius thinks that "he, at least, the humble follower of the bodily eye, was aware of a crisis in life, in this brief, obscure existence, a fierce opposition of real good and real evil around him, the issues of which he must by no means compromise, or confuse; of the antagonisms of which the 'wise' Marcus Aurelius was unaware."

Marius rejects Aurelius's Stoicism because, as he understands it (not accurately, defenders of Aurelius would argue), he believes that this philosophy is based on the emperor's illusory belief in his own moral infallibility, an idea that Marius's own relativist skepticism contradicts. However, if he rejects the main teachings of the emperor, Marius does accept, in his own eclectic way, one preachment of Aurelius: " ' 'Tis in thy power to think as thou wilt.' " Here, Marius finds sanction for his own ruminations on "the will as vision," during a ride in the Sabine Hills outside Rome.

Drawing on the theory of material flux he had presented in the "Conclusion" of *Studies in the History of the Renaissance*, Pater has Marius reason, "after the analogy of the bodily life," that his own spirit might participate in "that great stream of spiritual energy" in such a way that the "material fabric of things" might be considered as "but an element in a world of thought," and, if that were so, the "prison-wall" of the material world might actually be penetrable, "actually dissolving all around him," under the power of his own intense apprehension. Marius comes to believe, more strongly than before, in the strength of diaphanous vision to perceive the ideal in the material, described by Pater as characterizing the career of Winckelmann. With a new "quiet hope, a quiet joy," in his new belief, Marius thinks, in Pater's words: "Must not all that remained of life be but a search for the equivalent of that ideal, among so-called actual things–a gathering together of every trace or token of it, which his actual experience might present?"

Marius finds this ideal realized in the actual when he is taken by his friend Cornelius to visit the primitive Christian church in the house of the Roman matron Cecilia. Here, in the intimate presence of the dead in their catacombs, and in the decorous but joyous ritual of an early morning Mass, Marius finds a religion that combines with his recollections of the "Religion of Numa" of his childhood a promise of resurrection, of eternal life, that seems to combine the human with the divine. But the emphasis in Marius's thoughts is on the human: "It was Christianity in its humanity, or even its humanism, in its generous hopes for man, its common sense, and alacrity of cheerful service, its sympathy with all creatures, its appreciation of beauty and daylight."

Marius finds in the second-century Christian Church not the asceticism that would take hold in later centuries, but the idea of culture, to which he has already given his assent. His witnessing of the Mass confirms his prior belief–Pater's own–that ritual is the element that links aesthetic philosophy to at least possible belief, especially when the ritual has been divorced from no longer credible dogma and is thereby opened up to new transcendent significance in the form of re-

vitalized myth. The dying gods of pagan myth give way to the dying and resurrection of Christ. The early Church that Marius observes, for which he feels such a strong affinity but to which he is never converted, is a model of that "religious phase" that Pater hoped would be possible for the modern mind, a form of faith more enduring than faith itself.

At the end of the novel, Pater has Marius and Cornelius taken prisoner by anti-Christian soldiers. Marius stays behind as the supposed Christian when Cornelius is released. Falling ill of fever, Marius is left behind by the soldiers, in the care of peasants, to await his death.

Not only has Marius not become a Christian convert, but he also seems at the end to back away from his evident attraction to Christianity and to revert to an earlier epicureanism, although it is now so elemental, so austere, so abstract, as to be unidentifiable with any doctrine, either that of Epicurus or of Aristippus: "Surely, the aim of a true philosophy must be, not in futile efforts toward the complete accommodation of man to the circumstances in which he chances to find himself, but in the maintenance of a kind of candid discontent, in the face of the very highest achievement; the unclouded and receptive soul quitting the world finally, with the same fresh wonder with which it had entered the world still unimpaired, and going on its blind way at last with the consciousness of some profound enigma in things, as but a pledge of something further to come."

Marius's closing thought is of the diaphanous sensibility described as though it were one of Plato's migrating souls, entering material form in life only to cast it off again in death, before going on to another form. Christianity, like the other philosophies and religions Marius encounters, is merely one more "aesthetic adventure." For reasons he does not explain, Pater denies his hero final faith, but leaves him a composed skepticism–a strange last reversal of the apparent direction of the entire novel.

However, the ending is ambiguous: although Marius remains unconverted at his death, the peasants who tend him do not know this and, from his circumstances, conclude that he is, in fact, a Christian. Just before he dies, they administer wafer and water, and Marius dies with the apparent sacrament if not the faith of the religion he has admired as his ideal-in-the-actual. One astute twentieth-century reader has pointed to the irony of Pater's ending, that it makes "a Christian saint out of a pagan skeptic."

That observation sets the tone for the critical reception of *Marius the Epicurean* in Pater's own time. Most of the reviewers found Pater's attention to historical detail, his inclusion of translations of classical authors–Apuleius, Lucian, and Aurelius–and his highly wrought though difficult style more worthy of praise than they did the "aesthetic" philosophy of the book. As the London *Times* reviewer put it, " 'Marius the Epicurean' may be briefly described as fine writing and hard reading."

Mrs. Humphry Ward's review in *Macmillan's Magazine* (May 1885) is analytical. She observes that the book is more about nineteenth-century England than about second-century Rome, and that it reveals an essentially "English characteristic": "As a nation we are not fond of direct 'confessions.' All our autobiographical literature, compared to the French or German, has a touch of dryness and reserve. It is in books like 'Sartor Resartus,' or 'The Nemesis of Faith,' 'Alton Locke,' or 'Marius,' rather than in the avowed specimens of self-revelation which the time has produced, that the future student of the nineteenth century will have to look for what is deepest, most intimate, and most real in its personal experience. In the case of those natures whose spiritual experience is richest and most original, there is with us, coupled with a natural tendency to expression, a natural tendency to disguise. We want to describe for others the spiritual things which have delighted or admonished ourselves, but we shrink from too great a realism of method. English feeling, at its best and subtlest, has always something elusive in it, something which resents a spectator, and only moves at ease when it has succeeded in interposing some light screen or some obvious mask between it and the public."

"Disguise," "screen," "mask": these terms suggest the oblique, distorting, symbolic modes of expressiveness that characterize modernist literature. Yeats later chose the term "mask" to define that antitype of the actual self through which the poet must, in one phase of his art, speak. In Pater's case, the concept of a disguise or mask for the presumably diaphanous sensibility takes the form mainly of myth as, unlike Marius, the heroes of his later imaginary portraits are seen as avatars of the dying god Dionysus. Pater uses the motif of the gods-in-exile, which he probably discovered in the German poet Heinrich Heine, as a mythic disguise in his later work, and this disguised transparency Mrs.

Sketch of Pater by Charles Holmes, a student at Brasenose College who later became director of London's National Gallery (by permission of Constable Publishers)

Ward's trenchant comment defines as it appears in *Marius the Epicurean*.

In order to work full-time on *Marius*, Pater had resigned his tutorial duties at Brasenose, although not his fellowship, in 1883. In 1885 he and his sisters moved to London, where he lived as a modest literary celebrity. The move coincided with his being rejected for the Slade Professorship in the fine arts that Ruskin had vacated; once again, Pater had been snubbed by official Oxford. In his house at 12 Earl's Terrace, London, Pater entertained what Violet Paget called a "fashionable Bohemian element," although Frank Harris was more struck by the "austere simplicity" of the Pater home: "The house might have belonged to a grocer." Another visitor thought that Pater himself looked like "a retired artillery officer in reduced circumstances"–an impression borne out by late photographs. In the summer of 1893, perhaps weary of fashionable life, Pater and his sisters moved back to Oxford, to a house at 64 St. Giles, near the famous Martyrs' Monument.

Pater's writing during the London years was diverse and extensive. In addition to revising his earlier essays, he produced seven "imaginary portraits," four of which appeared in a book of that title in 1887. These pieces are "A Prince of Court Painters," "Sebastian van Storck," "Duke Carl of Rosenmold," and "Denys l'Auxerrois."

"A Prince of Court Painters" presents the career of the French painter Jean Antoine Watteau (1684-1721), supposedly through selective entries in the diary of the older sister of Watteau's disciple Jean-Baptiste Pater, with whom Walter Pater and his sisters liked to claim a distant kinship. In Pater's sketch Watteau, a native of Valenciennes in northern France, goes to Paris to study art and soon develops a "new manner" of painting that becomes fashionable. Despite his success as a painter of the elegant amusements of the French court, Watteau is restless, contemptuous of the brilliant but superficial world he has idealized in his art. What he experienced in his childhood and youth, his "vision within," carries over into his mature period as a genius who is master of an alien world from which he wishes to escape. As the narrator writes: "He will overcome his early training; and these light things will possess for him always a kind of representative or borrowed worth, as characterizing that impossible or forbidden world which the mason's boy saw through the closed gateways of the enchanted garden. Those trifling and petty graces, the *insignia* to him of that noble world of aspiration and ideas, even now that he is aware, as I conceive, of their true littleness, bring back to him by the power of association, all the old magical exhilaration of his dream–his dream of a better world than the real one. There, is the formula, as I apprehend, of his success–of his extraordinary hold on things so alien from himself."

The Romantic impulse to recover, amid alien circumstances, the original dream of childhood or youth underlies the behavior of most of Pater's diaphanous heroes. It is the motive of Florian Deleal, of Marius, and even, as Pater treats him, of the historical Winckelmann. It is only in the later imaginary portraits that the emphasis falls more decisively on the alienation and less on the recovery.

Most somber, perhaps, is the case of Sebastian van Storck, the son of a wealthy Dutch burgomaster and the cynosure of that seventeenth-century world depicted by the genre-painters of the time, who seeks to escape altogether from the physical world into the realm of abstract theory. Taking refuge in his tower room, he comes to think of reality as the product of "his own lonely thinking power." The symbol of this absolute thought is the sea, which, in Holland, always threatens to overwhelm the life depicted by the painters. Sebastian's love of the sea is a death wish. However, he has some residual affection for life and is partially redeemed from his aberration when he rescues a small child from the onrushing waters of a seastorm, although he himself drowns.

In contrast to Watteau and Sebastian van Storck, Duke Carl of Rosenmold has an explicit mythic identity: he is an Apollo figure, seeking to bring "enlightenment" to his sleepy little duchy in the last years of the eighteenth century. Carl has a vision of his true mission, which is to prepare the way for the *Aufklärung*, or awakening, by developing the latent cultural powers of Germany: "Here, he began to see that it could be in no other way than by action of informing thought upon the vast material of which Germany was in possession: art, poetry, fiction, an entire imaginative world, following reasonably upon a deeper understanding of the past, of nature, of one's self–an understanding of all beside through the knowledge of one's self. To understand, would be the indispensable first step towards the enlargement of the great past, of one's little present, by criticism, by imagination."

Again, as with Winckelmann and Marius, to know oneself is to know history. This passage is perhaps the most cogent statement Pater ever made of the historical role of diaphanous man as "an interpreter . . . to others." Carl's labors, Pater notes, anticipate the work of the great German thinkers of the late eighteenth and early nineteenth centuries, when German culture was the richest in Europe, the source of the cultural enhancement of England itself. Especially in Goethe, greatest of German Romantics, Duke Carl's Apollonian role as culture-bringer is fulfilled.

As "Duke Carl of Rosenmold" depicts the Apollonian side of diaphanous man, "Denys l'Auxerrois" represents the vestigial presence of Dionysian worship in medieval Christianity. We do not see the "quaint legend" of Denys, Dionysus reborn, in the person of the likable but peculiar young artisan of thirteenth-century Auxerre, with special gifts for gardening, playing ball, and making music, at first hand, but rather through the fragmentary interpretation of a nineteenth-century antiquarian scholar, who pieces together the details of the legend from a fragment of stained glass (depicting Denys), an old set of tapestries that portray the legend, and certain antique priestly notes that he finds in the cathedral of Saint Étienne.

Throughout most of the portrait, Denys's Dionysian identity is handled rather playfully, but, eventually, as the mythic embodiment of irrational impulse, Denys symbolically has a maddening effect on the townspeople of Auxerre. They give themselves to drunken and violent revelry, and finally tear Denys himself to pieces in a savage ritual hunt, as the original god, or his human surrogate, was torn to pieces by ecstatic Greek worshippers, his remnants being scattered to ensure a fruitful harvest. Unlike his prototype, Denys is not resurrected with the spring planting; instead, his heart is buried by a frightened monk in a dark corner of the cathedral–symbolic of Denys's alien, pagan status in a Christian world.

Imaginary Portraits was Pater's favorite among his own books. However, the volume received a more muted critical reception than either *Studies in the History of the Renaissance* or *Marius the Epicurean*. Critics disagreed about which of the portraits was most impressive. Oscar Wilde favored "Sebastian van Storck," while George Woodberry, an American admirer of Pater, thought "A Prince of Court Painters" the "most highly finished" of the pieces. A third critic, Eleanor Catherine Price, judged *Imaginary Portraits* "the saddest book that Mr. Pater has yet written," and thought "Denys l'Auxerrois" "the most adorned with touches in Mr. Pater's own peculiar style." None of the critics was much impressed by "Duke Carl of Rosenmold," although one may think that, for Mrs. Ward's student of the nineteenth century, it is in many respects the most interesting of the four portraits.

Subsequently, three more of Pater's short imaginary portraits appeared in magazines: "Hippolytus Veiled" (*Macmillan's Magazine*, 1889), "Emerald Uthwart" (*New Review*, 1892), and "Apollo in Picardy" (*Harper's Magazine*, 1893). (Earlier, he had written a fragment, "An English Poet," that was not published until 1 April 1931 in the *Fortnightly Review*.)

"Hippolytus Veiled," based on a lost version of the *Hippolytus* of Euripides (circa 480–circa 406 B. C.), tells of the son of Theseus and Antiope, queen of the Amazons, who is raised in a remote village of ancient Greece when his father, prince of Athens, casts off Antiope and takes the sensuous Phaedra as his queen. Hippolytus grows into a chaste and devout youth, a worshipper of the stern nature goddess Artemis. When he goes to Athens, Phaedra, his stepmother, attempts to seduce him to the worship of Aphrodite, goddess of love. When Hippolytus refuses, Phaedra tells Theseus that he has seduced her, and the prince curses his son, who is eventually killed when Poseidon, god of the sea, causes Hippolytus's beloved chariot-horses to panic and drag him to death along the rough seashore stones.

Unlike Pater's earlier diaphanous heroes, Hippolytus is not so much an Apollonian symbol of light brought to illuminate the new age of cultural development as a symbol of forces and attitudes "veiled," virtually lost in the dark of history, brought to light by the penetrative light of the scholar's imagination. "Hippolytus" is Pater's most intimate and touching sketch of the remote past.

"Apollo in Picardy" is, in effect, a companion piece to "Denys l'Auxerrois" in which the mysterious god-in-exile comes among the monks of a rural monastery to shock them violently out of the torpor of abstract thought that Pater consistently regards as the besetting defect of medieval Christianity. Apparently without intent, the god kills a young novice of the monastic order, Hyacinth, as he had killed his mythic namesake. Like Hippolytus, Hyacinth is a symbol of Pater's idea that beautiful youth must die as a harbinger of, a sacrifice to, the irresistible forces of natural or historical change.

The third of these short portraits, "Emerald Uthwart," is especially interesting, for like the earliest, "The Child in the House," it is set in England and draws upon more elements of Pater's own life than the other portraits. In fact, the immediate inspiration for its composition was a nostalgic 1891 visit that Pater made to the King's School in Canterbury.

Emerald is the promising son of an otherwise decaying rural family of Sussex, raised in perfect natural freedom but sent to school to be disciplined into an English gentleman. Mythically, he is a Dionysus figure endowed with a genius for "submissiveness," being shaped by the Apollonian ascetic rigor of the school. Emerald becomes a synthesis of just those historical and personal attributes that appealed in the early 1890s, when

Rudyard Kipling was the literary rage. Indeed, Emerald seems, in historical retrospect, to be the type of that clear-eyed, idealistic youth that went off to die in World War I. However, Emerald and his friend James Stokes fight in the Napoleonic war, during which Stokes is executed for desertion and Emerald is sent in disgrace from the army. After wandering in France, he comes home, is forgiven his sin, and dies as a result of an old bullet wound close to the heart.

In this strange tale, Pater reflects the tensions between the individual's need for freedom and self-esteem and the inclination of national life to repress and subordinate those qualities for its own purposes. Pater stresses ironically the similarities and differences between the nurturing discipline of school and the mindless regimentation, conducive to restlessness and disobedience, of the army. Emerald, whose "submissiveness" makes him ideally suited to this discipline, also possesses a sensitivity and intelligence that make him resentful of and vulnerable to the destructive power of authority that is too repressive. He seems, somewhat like the hero of A. E. Housman's sequence of poems, *A Shropshire Lad* (1896), born to be a victim, one whose special aura is also the cause of his death. (*Billy Budd*, Herman Melville's posthumously published novella, also treats such a figure.) Pater's Emerald is the type of many successive youthful "dying gods" in English and American fiction.

On 15 November 1889 a collection of Pater's earlier periodical essays on English literature appeared under the title *Appreciations*. In the introductory essay, "Style," Pater asserts that imaginative prose presents not fact, but the writer's "sense of fact"; it makes "an appeal to the reader to catch the writer's spirit . . . , his peculiar intuition of a world, prospective, or discerned below the faulty conditions of the present, in either case changed somewhat from the actual world." Repeatedly, Pater brings his theory back to this key point of expressiveness: literary art is the representation of "fact as connected with soul, of a specific personality, in all its preferences, its volition and power."

Pater devotes much of "Style" to describing the way the diaphanous writer acquires the language necessary for this perfect expression of the inner vision. He must be eclectic, drawing not only on the language of metaphysics and the pictorial arts, but also, and especially, on the language of science, since science gives the most precise formulation of the actual conditions of life,

as the modern world knows it. Pater is the first critic wholeheartedly to assert the indispensable fusion of personal, intuitive insight with scientific method as the basis of criticism, of all literary art. The perfect style must balance "soul" with "mind." That is, the expression of personality must come in a logically cogent structure of thought attained by craftsmanship, a subject that Pater gives new emphasis in this late essay. Nowhere else does Pater speak so insistently of the necessity for intellectual effort to achieve moral significance in writing.

The other essays in *Appreciations*, written from 1874 to 1886, not surprisingly follow the method of criticism Pater defines in the "Preface" to *Studies in the History of the Renaissance*: they seek the unique "formula" of a writer through an analysis of his life and selected works. For example, Wordsworth exhibits the habit of Romantic poets of discovering "an intimate consciousness of the expression of natural things"; "He has a power . . . of realising, and conveying to the consciousness of the reader, abstract and elementary impressions–silence, darkness, absolute motionlessness: or, again, the whole complex sentiment of a particular place, the abstract expression of desolation in the long white road, of peacefulness in a particular folding of the hills. In the airy building of the brain, a special day or hour even, comes to have for him a sort of personal identity . . . , it has a presence in one's history, and acts there, as a separate power or accomplishment; and he has celebrated in many of his poems the 'efficacious spirit,' which, as he says, resides in these 'particular spots' of time." Above all, Wordsworth, as Pater interprets him, teaches that "being," rather than "doing," is "the principle of all the higher morality." Wordsworth shows that "to withdraw the thoughts for a little while from the mere machinery of life, to fix them, with appropriate emotions, on the spectacle of those great facts in man's existence which no machinery affects . . . is the aim of all culture."

Charles Lamb is a subject more amenable to Pater's ideas than is Wordsworth. Essentially a lover of old things, rather out of temper with his time, Lamb the antiquarian essayist possessed an "intellectual epicureanism" that enabled him, in *Specimens of English Dramatic Poets Contemporary with Shakespeare* (1808), to bring to modern attention the disregarded work of Elizabethan dramatists other than Shakespeare. (Although Pater does not mention the fact, Lamb and his sister, Mary, produced *Tales from Shakespeare*, 1807, a retelling of some of the plays that became a children's classic.) But Lamb's greatest triumph was to treat, in his *Essays of Elia* (1823, 1833), his own age from an antiquarian perspective; he shows how a later age will see his own: "But it is part of the privilege of the genuine humourist to anticipate this pensive mood with regard to the ways and things of his own day; to look upon the tricks in manner of the life about him with that same refined purged sort of vision, which will come naturally to those of a later generation. . . ."

This "purged sort of vision" is that of the diaphanous sensibility, which can express through itself the kind of selective or idealized apprehension of the living, contemporary world that is usually attainable only from works of art or the inert patterns of the past. In this respect, the "humor" of Lamb is like that of Walter Scott and Charles Dickens. Lamb's essays, in some ways, writes Pater, are a "mimicry" of the subjects and style of the seventeenth-century physician and writer, Sir Thomas Browne. Pater does not mention Lamb in his essay on Browne, published in May 1886 in *Macmillan's Magazine*, but what he says of the "humourist" in the Browne essay is consonant with his definition of the term in the essay on Lamb. To Pater, these writers, for all their differences of personal character and historical circumstance, share the qualities of the diaphanous sensibility: "It is, in truth, to the literary purpose of the humourist, in the old-fashioned sense of the term, that this method of writing—of the humourist to whom all the world is but a spectacle in which nothing is really alien from himself, who has hardly a sense of the distinction between great and little among things that are at all, and whose half-pitying, half-amused sympathy is called out especially by the seemingly small interests and traits of character in the things or the people around him."

More than Lamb's, however, Browne's humor is tinged with a kind of cheerful if morbid curiosity in the presence of death amid the activities of daily life: one of his most noteworthy works is a treatise on a set of burial urns from the days when Britain was under Roman occupation. Browne's curious studies and his physician's vocation make him, despite his many old-fashioned habits and beliefs, a kind of precursor, along with Francis Bacon, of the modern scientific investigator. Perhaps his best-known work is the *Religio Medici* ("A Doctor's Religion," 1643), and Pater points to the relevance of this work for a nineteenth-century audience beset by the appar-

ently hopeless conflict between scientific discovery and traditional religious belief: "He presents, in an age, the intellectual powers of which tend strongly to agnosticism, that class of minds to which the supernatural view of things is still credible."

Appreciations includes Pater's three essays on Shakespeare. The first of these, on *Love's Labour's Lost*, focuses on Shakespeare's comic treatment of the extravagant Euphuistic language popular with writers in the 1590s, the period of Shakespeare's own earliest works, such as *Romeo and Juliet*, the elaborate figurative language of which is much like that of the Euphuistic writers. The essay on *Measure for Measure* is Pater's most insightful on Shakespeare. Calling the play "the central expression of his moral judgment," Pater makes it into a parable of the moral necessity for critical understanding informed by love.

In "Shakespeare's English Kings" Pater makes the history plays a "humorous" expression of sympathy for the fallibility of mere mortals, only very occasionally asserting the divinity that hedges a king. Especially, Pater focuses on King Richard II, the self-styled lyric poet, whose capricious policies and infatuation with his ability to image his own prisoner's plight in clever language, cause his overthrow by the ruthless Bolingbroke. In possibly 1853, the young Pater had seen the eminent Victorian tragic actor Charles Kean in a production of *Richard II*, and, as he says in the essay, the memory stuck. In the poeticizing and self-pity of Richard, Pater finds the most apt example for his thesis that "Shakespeare's kings are not, nor are meant to be, great men." The view is one-sided (especially when one considers the full context of *Henry IV*, Parts 1 and 2, and *Henry V*) but supportable.

In the Pre-Raphaelite poet and painter Dante Gabriel Rossetti, Pater finds a Victorian embodiment of the diaphanous sensibility, clearly expressed in Rossetti's work. Both as a poet in his own right and as a translator of Dante's *Vita Nuova* and other works of medieval Italian poetry, Rossetti possessed the "gift of transparency in language," and Pater's description of the precise felicity of Rossetti's language anticipates what he will say, five years later, in "Style," about the disciplined eclecticism that fuses form and matter in good writing. Pater also finds in the poems of Rossetti that the "common things" of nature "are full of human or personal expression, full of sentiment," as in "The Woodspurge," in which Rossetti evokes something like the "pagan sentiment"

First page from the unfinished manuscript for "Tibalt the Albigense," one of several "imaginary portraits" begun by Pater in his late years (by permission of the Houghton Library, Harvard University) that Pater asserts is the basis of all religious feeling. With Rossetti, we seem to enter "some revival of the old mythopoeic age," as the modern artistic consciousness seeks in the vividly imaged past, as in its minutely realized impression of the present, some form to serve as the expressive symbol of itself.

The closing essay of *Appreciations*, "Postscript" (originally titled "Romanticism" when it was published in *Macmillan's Magazine*, November 1876), was written in 1876 and is an extended definition that has affinities with Pater's description of the Renaissance spirit in his earlier book of essays. Romanticism, with a restless curiosity that leads it to seek "a beauty born of unlikely elements," elements in which strangeness and wildness are more common than familiarity and order, is an assertion of freedom in many facets of life, as it throws off or adapts older aesthetic forms to new significance. It is the dominant historical impulse of the nineteenth century, which seeks in an eclectic way to realize its characteristic art: "our curious, complex, aspiring age still abounds in subjects for manipulation by the literary as well as by other forms of art. For the literary art, at all events, the problem just now is, to induce order upon the contorted, proportionless accumulation of our knowledge and experience, our science and history, our hopes and disillusion. . . . In literature as in other matters it is well to unite as many diverse elements as may be: that the individual writer or artist, certainly, is to be estimated by the number of graces he combines, and his power of interpenetrating them in a given work." That paradox, of inducing unitary, transparent order by an eclectic (that is, carefully selected but various) means, is at the heart of Pater's moral aesthetic. In many different forms, the principle of eclectic order is central to the aesthetics of modern art.

The critics especially liked the essays on Wordsworth and Lamb, although at least one critic, W. J. Courthope, writing for *Nineteenth Century* in April 1890, objected to Pater's assertion that Wordsworth teaches the supremacy of "being" over "doing" as the basis of the moral life. Courthope also felt that Pater's "sympathetic" method did not eliminate the necessary critical standards for a valid "objective" criticism. One critic, Mrs. Margaret Oliphant, who had earlier chastised Pater for his interpretation of Botticelli, took him to task again, in *Blackwood's Magazine* for January 1890, for what she believed to be his pedantry in "Style" in trying to force

French models, in the shape of Flaubert, on the forms of English prose. She also found his theory of eclectic vocabulary obscure.

The matter of Pater's own style was once again debated. John Addington Symonds, to some extent Pater's rival as an interpreter of the Renaissance, wrote in a letter of 19 January 1890, during a bout of influenza, "I tried Pater's 'Appreciations' to-day, and found myself wandering about among the precious sentences, just as though I had lost myself in a sugar-plantation—the worse for being sweet." On a more positive note, Arthur Symons, in the *Athenaeum* (14 December 1889), characterized Pater's style in *Appreciations*, in contrast to the style of *Studies in the History of the Renaissance*, as having "less sensuousness, a severer ordering and ornament, more of what he calls '*mind* in style'; more freedom also." William Watson, writing in the *Academy* (21 December 1889), believed that *Appreciations* would "consolidate its author's fame as one of the most catholic of living critics, and beyond rivalry the subtlest artist in contemporary English prose."

Pater's last book published in his lifetime was *Plato and Platonism*, worked up from lectures he delivered to undergraduates in 1891. "I have tried to treat the subject in as popular a manner as possible," he assured his editor in discussing this volume, which appeared on 10 February 1893.

In the first three chapters, Pater describes the early Greek philosophies from which Plato's philosophy developed. Specifically, the doctrine of Heraclitus, that all reality is perpetual motion, is opposed by the doctrine of Parmenides that all phenomena are ultimately, absolutely one, at perpetual rest. The opinions of Heraclitus and Parmenides are combined in the "doctrine of number" taught by the mysterious Pythagoras, wherein the relative motion of all things is in accord with mathematical ratios that reflect the harmony of the "music of the spheres."

Along the way, Pater establishes some corollary terms: the doctrine of motion reflects the diversity of the centrifugal Ionian culture of Athens, its many-sidedness, the impulse of all things to go their own way, the tendency of forces to fly off in all directions. The Parmenidean doctrine of the One at perpetual rest expresses the impulse of individual persons and things to cohere to a central authority or community, the centripetal impulse that Plato found expressed in the Dorian culture of Athens's great rival city, Sparta (or "Lacedaemon," as Pater usually calls it, referring to the region to the north of Athens where

Sparta was situated). These related oppositions–Heraclitean/Parmenidean, Ionian/Dorian, centrifugal/centripetal–are all ways of conceiving the opposition between the sensuous life and the ideal life. Plato's purpose was to define the way in which the changefulness of the physical world, and of Athenian society, could be brought into harmonious stability and hierarchical order of the quasi-ideal kind at Sparta.

Pater suggests that Plato stands, like Marius, as a kind of analogue for nineteenth-century thinkers, trying to balance the claims of evolutionary theory and historical relativism with the still precious but no longer wholly credible doctrines of Christian belief. The theory of ideas is almost a metaphor for traditional Christian theology, and Plato's commitment to the claims of the changeful physical world is a metaphor for the nineteenth-century intellectual's necessary allegiance to the "relative spirit" and to the many implications of the historical and scientific concept of "development."

Pater makes of Socrates, the great philosophical inspirer of Plato and the central figure in the Platonic Dialogues, a teacher who inculcates in his students the need for a self-questioning, skeptical examination of the conditions of actual experience and of the degree to which they conform to the ideal. The famed "Socratic method" of question-and-answer, the dialogue, not so much of the teacher and student but of the teacher's "mind with itself," as it explores such issues as the nature of Justice and the Good, becomes presumably a model for dialogues that the students may subsequently hold for themselves within their own minds. Socrates presents himself (whether he is as he says he is, is a moot point for Pater) as an inquirer after truth, not the dogmatic proponent of truths he already knows. He instills in Plato a belief in the reality of the ideal as it relates to the issue of how we are to live, and this belief makes Plato the adamant opponent of the Sophists, the Athenian school of philosophers and rhetoricians who teach that not the discovery of truth, but the ability to make other people believe that what one says is the truth, is the goal of education. The Sophists, priding themselves on the powers of argument they train in their pupils, are symptomatic of the dangerous centrifugality, of the excessive individualism, that Plato discerned in Athens–and, one may infer, that Pater discerned in late-nineteenth-century England.

Increasingly, Pater turns away from the radi-

cal, almost solipsistic individualism he had avowed in the "Conclusion" to *Studies in the History of the Renaissance*, toward an embrace of something like religious orthodoxy and, by implication, even state authoritarianism, as his account of Plato's effort to apply the Dorian spirit to the diffuse Ionian spirit of Athens suggests. In Lacedaemon, Pater finds "the very genius of conservatism" expressed. This Dorian culture, which Pater read about in the writings of the German scholar Karl Otfried Müller (1797-1840), has a social and educational structure that reminds Pater not only of "the novices at school in some Gothic cloister," but "of our own English schools" as well. His description of the ascetic training of Spartan youth blends Müller's scholarship with his own recently refreshed impressions of English public-school life, so evident in "Emerald Uthwart," which was written about the same time as the "Lacedaemon" chapter of *Plato and Platonism*.

In this Spartan education, as presumably in its modern English equivalent, the spiritual and the physical are treated as inseparable: the "outer form" of the body becomes expressive of the inner discipline of the students, who realize the ideal of humanity in the aesthetic exercises they perform–appropriately, simple, ritualistic dance set to a severe Dorian music that Pater compares to the Gregorian music of the medieval Christian Church. This Lacedaemonian dancing, says Pater, perfectly exemplifies the kind of "imitative" art that Plato believed contributed to the solidarity of the individual and the community. Ritual dance is an element in Sparta's "religion of sanity."

Perhaps because he was disturbed by the hedonistic interpretations his own earlier works had received in the popular press and among the undergraduates and academic authorities of Oxford, Pater wanted to present Plato as the source of an institutional tradition, blending the secular and the religious, that would assure the moral soundness of the individual life modeled in "the spirit of art." The final chapter of *Plato and Platonism*, "Plato's Aesthetics," attempts precisely that justification.

According to Pater, Plato is "the earliest critic of the fine arts. He anticipates the modern notion that art as such has no end but its own perfection–'art for art's sake.'" As Pater explains Plato's views on the matter in *The Republic*, the perfection of artistic technique in craft or performance is congruent with the individual's moral development, as he comes perfectly to fulfill his "function" in the communal life. "Platonic aesthetics," Pater writes, "are ever in close connection with Plato's ethics. It is life itself, action and character, he proposes to colour; to get something of the irrepressible conscience of art, that spirit of control, into the general course of life, above all into its energetic or impassioned acts."

Although *Plato and Platonism* was, on the whole, well received, individual reviewers found fault with some of Pater's points of interpretation. Richard Holt Hutton, editor of the *Spectator*, felt that Pater did not rightly represent the awesome, aloof reality of Plato's "ideas," not to be attributed to or controlled by gods or men. Plato's conception of the ideal was not that it was associated with, or embodied in, a "personality," but that it was abstract from the experiential world. Lewis Campbell, Scottish classicist, writing in the *Classical Review*, found Pater's representation of the mysticism of Plato "inadequate." Most critics praised, more warmly than they did Pater's analysis of Plato's own thought, his description of the pre-Socratic philosophies. But Pater's view of Plato as, at once, the philosopher of the "absolute" and the master spirit of skepticism was confirmed by the American classical scholar Paul Shorey of the University of Chicago, in a review for the *Dial* (1 April 1893).

After *Plato and Platonism*, Pater's reputation began to grow toward the considerable stature it would reach in the first decade of the twentieth century. However, he did not produce another book before his death the next year, only some short magazine pieces and several incomplete manuscripts, which were collected or published for the first time only posthumously, by his literary executor Charles Shadwell, who had the cooperation of Pater's sisters.

In 1895 Shadwell prepared for publication two volumes of Pater's essays, *Greek Studies* and *Miscellaneous Studies*. The first of these collections contains "A Study of Dionysus" and "Demeter and Persephone," both published originally in 1876, "Hippolytus Veiled," and several lesser essays on Greek sculpture, poetry, and coins. *Miscellaneous Studies*, as the title suggests, is a more scattered collection. "The Child in the House," "Emerald Uthwart," and "Apollo in Picardy" are included, as well as late essays on Raphael (published in *Fortnightly Review*, October 1892) and Pascal (unfinished at Pater's death and published posthumously in *Contemporary Review*, February 1895).

The most controversial posthumous publication was *Gaston de Latour* (1896), which Pater intended to be a historical novel similar in method to *Marius the Epicurean*. He had six chapters published in periodicals: the first five appeared in *Macmillan's Magazine* from June to October 1888; the seventh was printed in the *Fortnightly Review* of 1 August 1889. Pater abandoned *Gaston de Latour* in 1891, and the rest of the novel was left in manuscript at his death. Of these manuscripts, his literary executor Charles Shadwell found only that of chapter six suitable for publication in the book edition. However, the remaining six manuscript chapters have recently been edited for publication, and the novel may appear soon in a complete, if unrevised, form.

The characterization and plot of *Gaston de Latour*, set in turbulent sixteenth-century France, are even more attenuated than those in *Marius the Epicurean* and the *Imaginary Portraits*. The central figure is a young man from central France who is ordained in the Roman Catholic Church and is sent for training to the great cathedral at Chartres. He is given by a friend a copy of the poems of Pierre de Ronsard, which have the effect of opening his eyes to the beauty of the physical world, much as Marius's study of Cyrenaic philosophy affected him. When he is taken by the same friend who had given him Ronsard's poems to meet Ronsard himself Ronsard gives Gaston a letter of introduction to take to Montaigne.

As Pater presents him, Montaigne is the skeptical philosopher and the apologist for Renaissance Humanism, as against the ascetic practices of medieval religion. Montaigne is an early expositor, in Pater's view, of the modern relative spirit.

In describing Montaigne's "doctrinal egotism," Pater gives another clear statement of the skeptical attitude of belief in the sovereign power of the individual creative imagination, a central tenet of his work from the early "Conclusion" to his late lectures on Plato, in which he stresses discipline rather than expression of individual powers. Pater's interest in Montaigne apparently subsided once he had deeply engaged himself with the study of Plato. The truth of Montaigne is the old truth of the diaphanous sensibility: "Whatever truth there might be, must come for each of us from within, not from without. To that wonderful microcosm of the individual soul, of which, for each one, all other worlds are but elements,— to himself,—to what was apparent immediately to him . . . , he confidently dismissed the enquirer. His own egotism was but the pattern of the true intellectual life of every one."

Gaston, however, finds a more fully compelling philosophy in the discourse at Paris, "Shadows of Ideas," given by the Italian philosopher Giordano Bruno (1548?-1600), whose "lower pantheism" becomes, in Pater's terms, the recognizable forerunner of Romantic aesthetics: "The divine consciousness has the same relation to the production of things as the human intelligence to the production of true thoughts concerning them. Nay! those thoughts are themselves actually God in man: a loan to man also of His assisting spirit, who, in truth, is the Creator of things, in and by His contemplation of them. For Him, as for man in proportion as man thinks truly, thought and being are identical, and things existent only in so far as they are known." Man participates in the creative process by virtue of his thinking power. His awareness that God is animate in all things obligates him to be ever alert in discerning the minute particularity of the "details of life and character." Reading the passing spectacle of human life and of the natural world in Bruno's philosophy, one perceives "the full revelation, the story in detail, of that one universal mind, struggling, emerging ... in various orders of being,–the veritable history of God." History as the concrete evolution of the mind of God: Pater has made Bruno a precursor of the Hegelian philosophy in which Pater's own historical and aesthetic views are rooted.

When Walter Pater died at his Oxford home, on 30 July 1894, the tone of the obituaries and the various eulogistic statements was respectful but rather muted, like the reviews of his publications, as though the issue of his presumed bad influence on the "aesthetic" climate of the age had still to be skirted. The *Times* notice is representatively ambiguous: "As a teacher Mr. Pater has exercised considerable influence on modern Oxford. The picturesqueness and, to a certain extent, the mannerism of his writings possessed much fascination for youthful minds of a particular caste. That that influence was always wholesome we do not pretend to say. . . ."

Preaching a funeral sermon in Brasenose College Chapel in October 1894, Frederick William Bussell, Pater's closest friend in the last years who became vice-principal of the college two years after Pater's death, stressed the personal kindliness and good humor of Pater the man, qualities that, as Bussell observed, did not always come through in the writings. Further, Bussell gave a brief account of Pater's personal habits and routine day's work that must have reassured

Pater's grave, Holywell Cemetery, Oxford

doubters: "He never smoked; rarely took tonic or medicine of any kind; and has left an example which it would be well if every student could follow; spending his morning in writing or lecturing, some part of the afternoon in correcting the composition of noon, and, in the evening, closing his books entirely;–regarding it as folly to attempt to make up for idleness in the day by unseasonable labour at a time when reading men are best in bed."

Perhaps the two most substantial memorial essays from the 1890s are by Edmund Gosse and Lionel Johnson, the young poet and critic, member of the Rhymers' Club, a group to which Yeats belonged. (Yeats describes the influence of Pater on the group in the chapter of his 1938 *Autobiography* entitled "The Tragic Generation.") Most interesting in Gosse's biographical sketch (*Contemporary Review*, December 1894), written twelve years before Arthur C. Benson's brief "authorized" biography of 1906, is an account of Pater's method of composition: "It has been said, and repeated, that Pater composed his best sentences without any relation to a context, and wrote them down on little squares of paper, ready to stick them in at appropriate and effective places. This is nonsense; it is quite true that he used such squares of paper, but it was for a very different purpose. He read with a box of these squares beside him, jotting down on each, very roughly, anything in his author which struck his fancy, either giving an entire quotation, or indicating a reference, or noting a disposition. He did not begin, I think, any serious critical work without surrounding himself by dozens of these little loose notes." Gosse also quotes Pater's response to the proposals for toughening and regularizing the curriculum and the general discipline of undergraduate life at Oxford: " 'I do not know what your object is. At present the undergraduate is a child of nature: he grows up like a wild rose in a country land; you want to turn him into a turnip, rob him of all grace, and plant him out in rows.' "

Lionel Johnson, like Gosse, speaks of Pater in the Oxford context: "Emphatically the scholar and man of letters, there was in his life and work a perfect expression of that single-hearted devotion to fine literature, yet without a shadow of pedantry, which is ceasing to flourish in our ancient academic places. There is yet deeper sorrow, upon which I cannot touch, save to say that to younger men concerned with any of the arts, he was the most generous and gracious of helpful friends. In due time, they will be able to think, with nothing but a reverent affection, of the admired writer at last laid to rest under the towers and trees of his own Oxford."

This identification of Pater with Oxford was also the point of attack for those critics who, in the early years of the twentieth century, denigrated the favorable reputation that Pater enjoyed in the decade following his death. The American "New Humanists," Irving Babbitt and Paul Elmer More, teachers and allies of T. S. Eliot, who himself mounted after World War I the most sustained and influential attack on Pater's reputation, were contemptuous of Pater's critical approach and scholarly knowledge. In an article in *Publications of the Modern Language Association* in 1906, Babbitt condemned "impressionist" criticism of the kind Pater wrote, because it merely records the author's pleasurable response to a work of art, with no external criteria as a guide. In a 1911 review of the New Library Edi-

tion of Walter Pater for the *Nation*, More was even more sweeping: "The simple truth is that Pater was in no proper sense of the word a critic at all. History was only an extension of his own ego, and he saw himself whithersoever he turned his eyes." Beyond dismissing Pater himself, More depicted the enthusiasm he inspired as symptomatic of the isolated, devitalized condition of Oxford itself: "Paterism might without great injustice be defined as the quintessential spirit of Oxford, emptied of the wholesome intrusions of the world–its pride of isolation reduced to sterile self-absorption, its enchantment of beauty alembicated into a faint Epicureanism, its discipline of learning changed into voluptuous economy of sensations, its golden calm stagnated into languid elegance."

T. S. Eliot's attack on Pater culminated in his 1930 essay in the *Bookman*, "Arnold and Pater," the general theme of which is the failure of the Victorians to achieve any kind of coherent or credible religious belief in reaction to the challenges of modern scientific theory and philosophic thought: "The dissolution of thought in that age, the isolation of art, philosophy, religion, ethics, and literature, is interrupted by various chimerical attempts to effect imperfect syntheses. Religion became morals, religion became art, religion became science or philosophy; various blundering attempts were made at alliances between various branches of thought. Each half-prophet believed that he had the whole truth. . . ." Speaking of *Marius the Epicurean*, Eliot sniffs, "I do not believe that Pater, in this work, has influenced a single first-rate mind of a later generation." And *Studies in the History of the Renaissance* "propagated some confusion between life and art which is not wholly irresponsible for some untidy lives."

Along with a repudiation of things Victorian that generally characterized British and American culture between the end of World War I and the finish of World War II, the censure of Eliot, perhaps the most eminent poet and critic of the period, was enough to ensure that most of the Victorian titans would languish in obscurity or disrepute. Pater sank into total eclipse.

But, since the late 1940s, Pater has enjoyed a renewed critical interest and, for the first time, sustained discussion of the complexity of his work. This renewal began with Graham Hough's *The Last Romantics* (1949), which places Pater in a line of intellectual history that runs from Ruskin, through Dante Gabriel Rossetti and the other Pre-Raphaelites, to Yeats. The essay on Pater begins with a rejoinder to Eliot and goes on to suggest that, as much as Arnold and Pater reflect the philosophical preoccupations of the later Victorian age, Pater at least must be thought of as a precursor of literary modernism. Hough is not altogether enthusiastic about Pater, but because of Pater's "temperament" and complex version of "impressionism," his work is the matrix out of which the next great literary generation was to emerge.

In *Romantic Image* (1957), an important study of the evolution of modern symbolist poets from the work of their nineteenth-century forebearers, Frank Kermode quotes Hough on Pater: "His ideal is the kind of art where thought and its sensible embodiment are completely fused." A few pages later, Kermode connects Yeats explicitly to Pater: Yeats "is the poet in whose work Romantic isolation achieves its full quality as a theme for poetry, being no longer a pose, a complaint, or a programme; and his treatment of it is very closely related to his belief in what Pater called 'vision' and the French called Symbol."

In his 1959 monograph, *Walter Pater*, Ian Fletcher, like Kermode, echoes Hough in asserting that Pater's work represents "all the triumphs and failures of a temperament." Fletcher distinguishes Pater from Arnold, against the judgment of Eliot: "Again, Pater is always a scholar as Arnold quite strikingly was not. Furthermore, Pater is perhaps the first English critic of importance to have the historical sense very profoundly developed."

Other important studies in the 1960s contributed to a deeper understanding and a fuller appreciation of Pater's writings. Among these is U. C. Knoepflmacher's *Religious Humanism and the Victorian Novel* (1965), most useful because it enables the reader to compare the religious views of Pater with those of George Eliot and Samuel Butler. In 1967 Gerald C. Monsman, in *Pater's Portraits*, for the first time discussed in systematic detail the mythic patterns in Pater's fiction. David J. DeLaura's *Hebrew and Hellene in Victorian England* (1969) treats Newman, Arnold, and Pater in a way that gives specific density to the emerging critical consensus that Pater is a major writer, in the context of his own time as well as in the context of modern literature.

In 1970 *Letters of Walter Pater*, a scholarly edition by Lawrence Evans of most but not all of Pater's extant correspondence, was published. The letters do not generally shed much light on Pater's work except occasionally to establish the chro-

nology of composition or the climate of opinion in which Pater believed himself to be working. However, the edition is thoroughly annotated and provides much information about Pater's relations to other people.

Despite the dearth of materials noted early by Gosse and more recently by Fletcher, Michael Levey was able to write a short 1977 biography, *The Case of Walter Pater*, that clears away most of the factual and interpretative errors of Thomas Wright's 1907 *Life of Walter Pater*. In 1980 Donald L. Hill produced the first scholarly edition of Pater's work, *The Renaissance: Studies in Art and Poetry: The 1893 Text*, with thorough explanatory notes; the next year saw publication of Billie Andrew Inman's *Walter Pater's Reading, 1858-1873*, an annotated bibliography of Pater's borrowings from Oxford libraries that sheds much light on the sources of Pater's work. A second volume by Inman, covering Pater's reading from 1874 to 1877, is forthcoming.

In his 1977 introductory study of Pater for the Twayne series, Gerald C. Monsman discusses Pater's influence on later writers: among modern poets, Gerard Manley Hopkins (who was a student of Pater at Brasenose), Yeats, Wallace Stevens, Ezra Pound, T. S. Eliot (despite his subsequent disapproval of Pater), W. H. Auden. Among novelists, Pater's influence can be observed in the work of Henry James, Joseph Conrad, Virginia Woolf, James Joyce, D. H. Lawrence, and Marcel Proust–virtually a pantheon of literary Modernism.

Perhaps the most comprehensive assertion of Pater's role as the bridge between Romanticism and Modernism is that of Harold Bloom in "The Crystal Man," his introductory essay to the *Selected Writings of Walter Pater* (1974): "Though Pater compares oddly, perhaps not wholly adequately, with the great Victorian prose prophets, he did what Carlyle, Ruskin, Newman, Arnold could not do: he fathered the future. Himself wistful and elaborately reserved, renouncing even his own strength, he became the most widely diffused (even though more and more hidden) literary influence of the later nineteenth upon the twentieth century."

In ways that scholars have already examined and continue to explore, through textual studies, biographical research, and critical analysis, Pater's dual role as encapsulator of the past and father to the future is becoming more fully understood, as he emerges from the limited and often prejudicial interpretations of previous generations. His place as an extremely important if highly mannered and difficult writer in the body of nineteenth-century English literature seems, at last, well established.

Letters:
Letters of Walter Pater, edited by Lawrence Evans (Oxford: Oxford University Press, 1970).

Bibliographies:
Lawrence Evans, "Walter Pater," in *Victorian Prose: A Guide to Research*, edited by David J. DeLaura (New York: Modern Language Association, 1973);

Samuel Wright, *A Bibliography of the Writings of Walter H. Pater* (New York: Garland, 1975);

Franklin E. Court, *Walter Pater: An Annotated Bibliography of Writings About Him* (De Kalb: Northern Illinois University Press, 1980).

Biographies:
Arthur C. Benson, *Walter Pater* (London: Macmillan, 1906);

Thomas Wright, *The Life of Walter Pater*, 2 volumes (London: Everett, 1907);

Germain d'Hangest, *Walter Pater: l'homme et l'oeuvre*, 2 volumes (Paris: Didier, 1961);

Michael Levey, *The Case of Walter Pater* (London: Thames & Hudson, 1977).

References:
Philip Appleman, "Darwin, Pater, and a Crisis in Criticism," in *1859: Entering an Age of Crisis*, edited by Appleman, William A. Madden, and Michael Wolff (Bloomington: University of Indiana Press, 1959), pp. 81-85;

Harold Bloom, "The Crystal Man," Introduction to *Selected Writings of Walter Pater* (New York: New American Library, 1974);

Bloom, "The Place of Pater: *Marius the Epicurean*," in his *The Ringers in the Tower* (Chicago: University of Chicago Press, 1971);

Eugene Brzenk, "The Unique Fictional World of Walter Pater," *Nineteenth-Century Fiction*, 13 (December 1958): 217-226;

Jerome Hamilton Buckley, *The Triumph of Time: A Study of the Victorian Concepts of Time, History, Progress, and Decadence* (Cambridge: Harvard University Press, 1966);

Edmund Chandler, *Pater on Style: An Examination of the Essay on "Style" and the Textual History of "Marius the Epicurean"* (Copenhagen: Rosenkilde & Bagger, 1958);

Barbara Charlesworth, *Dark Passages: The Deca-dent Consciousness in Victorian Literature* (Madison: University of Wisconsin Press, 1965);

Ruth C. Child, *The Aesthetic of Walter Pater* (New York: Macmillan, 1940);

Kenneth Clark, Introduction to Pater's *The Renaissance* (New York: World, 1961; London: Collins, 1961);

John J. Conlon, *Walter Pater and the French Tradition* (London: Associated University Presses, 1982);

Richmond Crinkley, *Walter Pater: Humanist* (Lexington: University Press of Kentucky, 1970);

David J. DeLaura, *Hebrew and Hellene in Victorian England* (Austin: University of Texas Press, 1969);

David Anthony Downes, *Victorian Portraits: Hopkins and Pater* (New York: Bookman, 1965);

"Essays in *Marius*," *English Literature in Transition*, 27, nos.1-2 (1984): 5-155;

Albert J. Farmer, *Walter Pater as a Critic of English Literature* (Grenoble: Didier & Richard, 1931);

Ian Fletcher, *Walter Pater* (London: Longmans, Green, 1959);

John Smith Harrison, "Pater, Heine, and the Old Gods of Greece," *Publications of the Modern Language Association*, 39 (September 1924): 655-686;

Graham Hough, *The Last Romantics* (London: Duckworth, 1949), pp. 134-174;

Bernard F. Huppé, "Walter Pater on Plato's Aesthetics," *Modern Language Quarterly*, 9 (September 1948): 315-321;

Billie Andrew Inman, "The Organic Structure of *Marius the Epicurean*," *Philological Quarterly*, 41 (April 1962): 475-491;

Inman, *Walter Pater's Reading, 1858-1873* (New York: Garland, 1981);

Lionel Johnson, "Notes on Walter Pater," in *Post Liminium: Essays and Critical Papers by Lionel Johnson*, edited by Thomas Whittemore (London: Matthews, 1911);

Frank Kermode, *Romantic Image* (London: Routledge & Kegan Paul, 1957; New York: Macmillan, 1957);

U. C. Knoepflmacher, *Religious Humanism and the Victorian Novel* (Princeton: Princeton University Press, 1965);

R. T. Lenaghan, "Pattern in Walter Pater's Fiction," *Studies in Philology*, 58 (January 1961): 69-91;

John A. Lester, Jr., *Journey Through Despair, 1880-1914* (Princeton: Princeton University Press, 1968);

Gordon MacKenzie, *The Literary Character of Walter Pater* (Berkeley: University of California Press, 1967);

Perry Meisel, *The Absent Father: Virginia Woolf and Walter Pater* (New Haven: Yale University Press, 1980);

J. Hillis Miller, "Walter Pater: A Partial Portrait," *Daedalus*, 105 (Winter 1976): 97-113;

Gerald C. Monsman, "Pater Redivivus," in *The Victorian Experience: The Prose Writers*, edited by Richard A. Levine (Athens: Ohio University Press, 1982), pp. 203-239;

Monsman, *Pater's Portraits: Mythic Pattern in the Fiction of Walter Pater* (Baltimore: Johns Hopkins University Press, 1967);

Monsman, *Walter Pater* (Boston: Twayne, 1977);

Monsman, *Walter Pater's Art of Autobiography* (New Haven: Yale University Press, 1980);

Louise Rosenblatt, "The Genesis of Pater's *Marius the Epicurean*," *Comparative Literature*, 14 (Summer 1962): 242-260;

Nathan A. Scott, Jr., *The Poetics of Belief: Studies in Coleridge, Arnold, Pater, Santayana, and Heidegger* (Chapel Hill: University of North Carolina Press, 1985), pp. 62-89;

R. H. Seiler, ed., *Walter Pater: The Critical Heritage* (London: Routledge & Kegan Paul, 1980);

Derek Stanford, "Pater's Ideal Aesthetic Type," *Cambridge Journal*, 7 (May 1954): 488-494;

Jean Sudrann, "Victorian Compromise and Modern Revolution," *English Literary History*, 26 (September 1959): 425-444;

Ruth Z. Temple, "The Ivory Tower as Lighthouse," in *Edwardians and Late Victorians*, edited by Richard Ellmann (New York: Columbia University Press, 1960), pp. 28-49;

Paul Turner, "Pater and Apuleius," *Victorian Studies*, 3 (March 1960): 290-296;

Anthony Ward, *Walter Pater: The Idea in Nature* (London: Macgibbon & Kee, 1966);

René Wellek, "Walter Pater," in *A History of Modern Criticism, 1750-1950*, volume 3 (New Haven: Yale University Press, 1965), pp. 381-399;

Helen Hawthorne Young, *The Writings of Walter Pater: A Reflection of British Philosophical Opinion from 1860 to 1900* (Lancaster, Pa.: Bryn Mawr Press, 1933).

Papers:

Pater left few personal papers or manuscripts. However, the major collection of manuscripts is at Harvard University. Most of the material is from Pater's later years and much of it is unpublished. Included are several fragmentary "imaginary portraits" and drafts of several lectures. Harvard also has the manuscript of the 1880 version of the Coleridge essay. Manuscript for the published chapters of *Gaston de Latour* is in the Berg Collection at the New York Public Library, while Duke University has recently acquired the manuscript of the unpublished chapters. "Measure for Measure" is in the Folger Shakespeare Library, Washington, D.C., and "Diaphaneité" is at the King's School, Canterbury. The manuscript of the essay on Pascal, Pater's last, is at the Bodleian Library, Oxford.

George Saintsbury

(23 October 1845-28 January 1933)

Richard W. Oram
University of Toledo

SELECTED BOOKS: *Primer of French Literature*
(Oxford: Clarendon Press, 1880; New York:
Harper, 1881; revised and enlarged, Oxford: Clarendon Press, 1884, 1888, 1896,
1912);

Dryden (London: Macmillan, 1881; New York:
Harper, 1881);

A Short History of French Literature (Oxford: Clarendon Press, 1882; revised and enlarged, 1897);

Marlborough (London: Longmans, Green, 1885;
New York: Appleton, 1886);

A History of Elizabethan Literature (London & New
York: Macmillan, 1887);

Manchester (London: Longmans, Green, 1887);

Essays in English Literature: 1780-1860 (London:
Percival, 1890; New York: Scribners, 1891);

Essays on French Novelists (London: Percival, 1891;
New York: Scribners, 1891);

The Earl of Derby (London: Low, Marston, 1892;
New York: Harper, 1892);

Miscellaneous Essays (London: Percival, 1892; New
York: Scribners, 1892);

*Inaugural Address Delivered at Edinburgh on the 15th
October, 1895* (Edinburgh & London: Blackwood, 1895);

*Essays in English Literature: 1780-1860, Second Se-
ries* (London: Dent, 1895; New York: Scribners, 1895);

Corrected Impressions (London: Heinemann, 1895;
New York: Dodd, Mead, 1895);

*A History of Nineteenth Century Literature:
1780-1895* (New York & London: Macmillan, 1895);

The Flourishing of Romance and the Rise of Allegory
(Edinburgh & London: Blackwood, 1897;
New York: Scribners, 1897);

Sir Walter Scott (Edinburgh & London: Oliphant,
Anderson & Ferrier, 1897; New York: Scribners, 1897);

A Short History of English Literature (New York &
London: Macmillan, 1898);

Matthew Arnold (Edinburgh: Blackwood, 1899;
New York: Dodd, Mead, 1899);

A History of Criticism and Literary Taste in Europe

from the Earliest Texts to the Present Day, 3 volumes (Edinburgh & London: Blackwood,
1900-1904; New York: Dodd, Mead, 1900-
1904); parts revised and enlarged as *A
History of English Criticism; Being the English
Chapters of A History of Criticism and Literary
Taste in Europe, Revised, Adapted, and Supple-*

mented (Edinburgh & London: Blackwood, 1911; New York: Dodd, Mead, 1911);

The Earlier Renaissance (Edinburgh & London: Blackwood, 1901; New York: Scribners, 1901);

A History of English Prosody from the Twelfth Century to the Present Day, 3 volumes (London & New York: Macmillan, 1906-1910);

The Later Nineteenth Century (Edinburgh & London: Blackwood, 1907; New York: Scribners, 1907);

Historical Manual of English Prosody (London: Macmillan, 1910);

A History of English Prose Rhythm (London: Macmillan, 1912);

The English Novel (London: Dent/New York: Dutton, 1913);

A First Book of English Literature (London: Macmillan, 1914);

The Peace of the Augustans: A Survey of Eighteenth Century Literature as a Place of Rest and Refreshment (London: Bell, 1916);

A History of the French Novel (to the Close of the 19th Century), 2 volumes (London: Macmillan, 1917-1919);

Notes on a Cellar-Book (London: Macmillan, 1920; New York: Macmillan, 1933);

A Scrap Book (London: Macmillan, 1922);

A Second Scrap Book (London: Macmillan, 1923);

A Last Scrap Book (London: Macmillan, 1924);

A Consideration of Thackeray (London: Oxford University Press, 1931);

Prefaces and Essays, edited by Oliver Elton (London: Macmillan, 1933);

George Saintsbury: The Memorial Volume: A New Collection of His Essays and Papers, edited by John W. Oliver and Augustus Muir (London: Methuen, 1945); republished as *A Saintsbury Miscellany: Selections from His Essays and Scrap Books* (New York: Oxford University Press, 1947);

French Literature and Its Masters, edited by Huntington Cairns (New York: Knopf, 1946);

A Last Vintage, edited by Oliver, Muir, and Arthur Melville Clark (London: Methuen, 1950).

Collection: *The Collected Essays and Papers of George Saintsbury*, 4 volumes (London & Toronto: Dent/New York: Dutton, 1923-1924).

OTHER: John Dryden, *The Works of John Dryden*, edited by Sir Walter Scott; revised, corrected, and enlarged by Saintsbury, 18 volumes (London: Paterson, 1882-1893);

Specimens of French Literature from Villon to Hugo, selected and edited by Saintsbury (Oxford: Clarendon Press, 1883; revised, 1892);

Specimens of English Prose Style from Malory to Macaulay, selected and annotated by Saintsbury (London: Kegan Paul, 1885; London: Kegan Paul/Chicago: Jansen, McClurg, 1886);

Henry Fielding, *The Works of Henry Fielding*, edited by Saintsbury, 12 volumes (London: Dent, 1893-1899);

English Prose, edited by Sir Henry Craik; contains 37 introductions by Saintsbury, 5 volumes (London: Macmillan, 1893-1896);

Honoré de Balzac, *Comédie humaine*, edited by Saintsbury, 40 volumes (London: Dent, 1895-1900);

Minor Poets of the Caroline Period, edited by Saintsbury, 3 volumes (Oxford: Clarendon Press, 1905-1921);

The Cambridge History of English Literature, edited by Sir A. W. Ward and A. R. Waller; contains 20 chapters by Saintsbury, 14 volumes (Cambridge: Cambridge University Press, 1907-1921);

William Makepeace Thackeray, *The Oxford Thackeray*, edited by Saintsbury, 20 volumes (London: Oxford University Press, 1908).

George Saintsbury was one of the most influential literary critics, along with Leslie Stephen and Edmund Gosse, of the late Victorian era and early twentieth century. In terms of sheer quantity of writing, he surpassed most of his prolific contemporaries; during a sixty-year career as a journalist and academic critic, he produced hundreds of essays, reviews, and prefaces in addition to literary histories, anthologies, critical editions, and other books. No period of English literature was foreign to him, and his knowledge of French literature was nearly as thorough. Such prodigality and scope have made Saintsbury's work as a whole difficult to digest, accounting in part for the lack of attention paid to him. He also defies easy categorization as a critic because of his unwillingness to associate himself with particular schools of criticism or theories of literature. Yet Saintsbury's writings are fundamentally "all of a piece," to use a phrase he applied to Thackeray. Throughout his career, he held fast to a belief in the separability of form and subject matter, eschewing moral judgment in favor of fair-minded appraisal. His criticism invariably relied on comparisons of texts and authors, an approach suited to one who had perhaps read more of English literature than any critic of his day. Like other great English journalist-critics, he valued aesthetic theories less than his own well-educated literary palate.

George Edward Bateman Saintsbury, the second son of a middle-class family, was born in Southampton on 23 October 1845. His father, George Saintsbury, was superintendent of the docks. In 1850 Saintsbury, his wife (the former Elizabeth Wright), and family moved to Kensington, a western suburb of London. From the few reminiscences of his early years he has left us, we can gather that the young George Saintsbury's stay at King's College School in the Strand was pleasant enough. In 1863 he entered Merton College, Oxford, receiving a First in Moderations in 1865. Unexpectedly, he failed to get a First class in Greats (classical literature) the next year, perhaps because he held a few unorthodox opinions, but more likely because of his unwillingness to confine himself to the required readings. Despite this setback, which led to the rejection of his five applications for a fellowship, Saintsbury's memories of Oxford were fond. He was instructed by the lectures of Benjamin Jowett and inspired by E. B. Pusey, a leader of the Tractarian, or Oxford, Movement and still a potent influence at Oxford in the 1860s. Saintsbury and his circle were known as the "Merton popes" because of their High-Church persuasion; Saintsbury himself was jocularly referred to as "the Saint." He and his friends read widely in Carlyle and the modern French writers. One of his most treasured books from his Oxford days was a volume of Baudelaire's poetry a friend had brought back from Paris.

Lacking a fellowship and newly married to Emily Fenn King, Saintsbury left Oxford in 1868 to take a teaching post at Manchester Grammar School. After a brief stint as a writer for the *Manchester Guardian*, he moved on to become classical master at Elizabeth College on the island of Guernsey, near the French coast. During his six years there, Saintsbury haunted the local bookshops—in one of them he once caught a glimpse of the exiled Victor Hugo—and devoted long hours to reading French literature, especially fiction. By 1874, when he accepted the headmastership of the Elgin Educational Institute in Morayshire, Scotland, Saintsbury's decade of reading had given him a grounding in French literature unparalleled among his English contemporaries. It was natural that his first reviews for the *Academy* and the *Fortnightly Review* should concern French authors.

Saintsbury's career as a literary journalist began in earnest with the publication of a critical essay on Baudelaire in the *Fortnightly Review* for October 1875. This pioneering study appeared when the poet was still virtually unknown to English readers, despite A. C. Swinburne's efforts to champion his cause. The article sets out to make the reader "comprehend fully the aim and object of the work" by seeing it as a whole. Saintsbury dismisses the issue of Baudelaire's supposed immorality, arguing that it is necessary to separate one's reaction to the distasteful subject matter from the appreciation of Baudelaire's poetic technique. Thus "Baudelaire" is significant for its early exposition of Saintsbury's fundamental principle of the supremacy of form over content, though it is worth noting that he approvingly quotes a passage from Baudelaire on the dangers of an immoderate passion for pure form.

A small inheritance came to hand in 1876, freeing Saintsbury from teaching and permitting him to undertake a full-time journalistic career in London. John Morley, the editor of the *Fortnightly Review*, encouraged him to follow the success of his article on Baudelaire with a series of articles on French novelists. These essays, which began to appear in 1878 and were collected in 1891 as *Essays on French Novelists*, included some of the earliest criticism in English on Gustave Flaubert and Théophile Gautier. Saintsbury's growing reputation in this field led the editors of the ninth edition of the *Encyclopaedia Britannica* to commission over thirty articles on French authors and the general survey of French literature, reprinted in *French Literature and Its Masters* (1946). With the publication of the *Primer of French Literature* (1880), *A Short History of French Literature* (1882), and *Specimens of French Literature from Villon to Hugo* (1883), Saintsbury clearly established himself as the leading English exponent of French literature. *A Short History of French Literature* soon became a standard text, and eight editions appeared before 1918. Although the French critic Edmond Scherer complained about the book's factual errors, the work was generally well received on the Continent.

Rather than rely on secondary sources in his essays and histories concerning French literature, Saintsbury preferred to fall back on his two decades of personal acquaintance with it. The advantage of this approach is that familiar texts are presented freshly, without the imposition of received ideas. However, Saintsbury's self-reliance was also responsible for the imbalances and omissions noted by reviewers. Both *A Short History of French Literature* and the *Essays on French Novelists* avoid placing writers in their historical, social, or political contexts, for Saintsbury never regarded himself as a commentator on French culture as a whole.

Dryden, the first of Saintsbury's books on English literature, appeared in John Morley's English Men of Letters series in 1881. Saintsbury's lifelong enthusiasm for the author animates the slender volume. Its favorable reception led William Paterson, an Edinburgh publisher, to invite Saintsbury to revise Sir Walter Scott's 1808 edition of Dryden's works. Saintsbury completed his editorial labors within a few years, but the publication of the eighteen-volume set, which began in 1882, dragged on for a decade. In spite of the usefulness of the critical commentary, the enterprise was vitiated by Saintsbury's questionable choices of copy-texts. The precision we have come to expect of twentieth-century textual scholars was not characteristic of Saintsbury: when a quarto edition of a Dryden play cited in his edition was found to be nonexistent, he casually dismissed the ghost text as a mere "Boojum." Devotees of scholarly trivia he habitually viewed as quibblers or dryasdust pedants.

The income from his books and editions during the 1880s and early 1890s was supplementary to the living he derived from his literary journalism. Late in life, Saintsbury confessed with mingled pride and self-mockery that his contributions taken together would amount to over a hundred volumes "of the 'Every Gentleman's Library' type." As John Gross notes in his *Rise and Fall of the Man of Letters* (1969), Saintsbury belonged to an age which was not ashamed of literary mass production. He never saw himself as a hack and indeed felt free to turn down work which did not interest him. Saintsbury thrived on the less glamorous aspects of a working journalist's life—the constant reading of review copies, the need for production of a certain quantity of text on demand, the rush to beat deadlines, and even the insecurity of the trade, which he found immensely charming.

His work was published in *London*, edited by W. E. Henley, the *National Review*, the *Pall Mall Gazette* under Morley, and the *St. James Gazette*, to name only a few of the periodicals to which he contributed during the 1880s. Saintsbury was most closely associated with the *Saturday Review*. His good friend Andrew Lang was responsible for introducing him to the editors of this weekly in 1880. Lang and Saintsbury would frequently accompany each other on the long walk from the Fleet Street offices of the paper to their homes in Kensington. As a contributor and later as assistant editor in charge of literary reviewing, Saintsbury was complimented, as he later remarked in *Notes on a Cellar-Book*, for his ability to put on a variety of " 'jackets'; literary, political, historical, philosophical, culinary, and even theological, not to mention others." From his youth he was a Tory of the most conservative stripe, and his politics meshed well with the editorial position of the *Saturday Review*. Saintsbury was asked to take over the paper's assault on the Liberal party's Irish policies. He complied with satiric columns on William E. Gladstone and Parnellism. Saintsbury's usual intellectual independence kept him from becoming a mere partisan. On one occasion he was given an opportunity to print Richard Pigott's infamous forgeries of letters attributed to Irish Nationalist leader Charles Stewart Parnell but saw through the deception and refused to participate in the libel.

The bulk of Saintsbury's literary journalism was meant to be ephemeral and does not bear rereading. Exceptional in this regard are the essays on English authors published in *Macmillan's Magazine* from 1886 to 1895 and assembled in two series of *Essays in English Literature: 1780-1860* (1890, 1895). Often prompted by the appearance of a new biography or edition, these essays are among his best work in the genre. Saintsbury touches upon the highlights of each subject's career and engages him in what he terms a sort of "conversation by books." The *Essays in English Literature* are, above all, exercises in appreciation. Without neglecting the shortcomings of such minor figures as W. M. Praed or "Christopher North" (pseudonym of John Wilson), Saintsbury manages to present their work in the best possible light. Moreover he never allows his personal dislike for Sydney Smith's Whiggery or William Cobbett's radicalism to interfere with his delight in Smith's wit or Cobbett's fiery intensity.

Saintsbury, his wife, and two sons moved to Fulbourn in 1887 and later to Reading. He commuted to London from both locations. When not in Fleet Street, he read and wrote at the Savile Club. Saintsbury's friends and fellow clubmen during this period, in addition to Lang, were W. E. Henley, Austin Dobson, H. D. Traill, and W. P. Ker. He was also an acquaintance of Robert Louis Stevenson, one of the few contemporary fic-

A HISTORY

OF

ELIZABETHAN LITERATURE

BY

GEORGE SAINTSBURY

London

MACMILLAN AND CO.

AND NEW YORK

1887

Title page for Saintsbury's first history of English literature

tion writers he admired. Saintsbury's seemingly secure position on the staff of the *Saturday Review* suddenly evaporated in 1892, when he and many of his colleagues decided they could not work for the paper's new management. Although he was distressed to find himself, as he told Oliver Elton, temporarily "incomeless, disestablished, *and* disendowed," there were numerous invitations to supply prefaces and other editorial matter for books. Sir Henry Craik, for example, commissioned more than thirty introductions to writers represented in his five-volume *English Prose* (1893-1896).

Saintsbury's editorial labors and his 1887 *History of Elizabethan Literature* enhanced his reputation in academic circles. Despite serious competition from Henley and Sir Walter Raleigh, Saintsbury was appointed to the Regius Professorship of English at the University of Edinburgh in September 1895. Aware that some faculty objected to his journalistic origins, he silenced the mutter-

ings by bidding farewell to twenty years of reviewing. In the lecture hall, Saintsbury could be rambling, diffuse, opinionated, and occasionally sarcastic. Most students, however, responded favorably to his wit and absolute mastery of his subject. The Regius Professor lived first in Murrayfield House and later at 2 Eton Terrace, where the library was often the scene of lunchtime literary discussions with students. In the morning, Saintsbury would stride forth with bowler hat and umbrella, an imposing but approachable figure with a prominent nose and flowing beard. He delivered his lectures rapidly and in a high-pitched voice. Saintsbury's teaching method reflected the same emphasis on the refinement of the appreciative faculties found in his writings. "I do not wish to teach you how to write," he once remarked, in reference to his students. "I wish to teach you how to read, and to tell you what there is to read."

Having renounced reviewing, Saintsbury set about collecting earlier work and researching new literary histories. *Corrected Impressions*, published by Heinemann in 1895, brought together previously published essays on nineteenth-century writers; it was followed by *A History of Nineteenth Century Literature: 1780-1895* (1895). Saintsbury wryly recorded the observation of someone who found the title of the volume of essays absurd: "I don't believe he ever changed a first impression in his life!" Nonetheless, Saintsbury did insist on the importance of reevaluating one's judgments of literature in the light of subsequent reading. His tribute to Thackeray in *Corrected Impressions* is one of many pieces on a writer he greatly admired and frequently quoted. At first one is surprised by his laudatory essay on William Morris, but it is typical of Saintsbury to separate his personal contempt for Morris's socialism from his admiration for the poet's lyric gifts.

Before he arrived at Edinburgh, Saintsbury had planned *A Short History of English Literature* to complement his earlier history of French writing. The book required less than a year of work and was published in 1898. A novel feature of this short history is the incorporation of "interchapters," brief interpretative essays on the development of particular literary genres and themes. On its appearance the book was met by John Churton Collins's hostile notice in the *Saturday Review*. Collins listed Saintsbury's factual errors (most of them minor), claimed that the critic could not have personally consulted some tests, and concluded with an attack on his vulgarity. To his credit, Saintsbury silently corrected some of the errors in later editions but chose not to reply directly. Had he done so, he might well have touched off a pointless quarrel like that ignited by Collins's equally acerbic review of Edmund Gosse's *Short History of Modern English Literature*, published the preceding year. In any case, Saintsbury's history went on to enjoy popular and long-lasting acceptance as a standard, reliable guide.

The first of the major studies which firmly established Saintsbury's reputation as the leading academic critic of the early twentieth century was *A History of Criticism and Literary Taste in Europe from the Earliest Texts to the Present Day* (1900-1904). The adjectives "immense," "epic," and "monumental" have rightly been applied to the three-volume work, which was the first attempt to survey the entire field of European criticism in detail. Saintsbury's intention was to provide a universal "Atlas" of criticism, beginning with the ancient Greeks and concluding with Heinrich Heine, Matthew Arnold, Walter Pater, and other moderns. Some critics and epochs fare better than others. Longinus, for example, is given disproportionate emphasis because of Saintsbury's wholehearted endorsement of his doctrine of the sublime and the essentiality of the "poetic moment." Neoclassical theorists, proponents of scientific aesthetics, and the more philosophically inclined critics such as Hegel are less sympathetically treated.

The conclusion of *A History of Criticism* is worth examining in some detail for its exposition of Saintsbury's fundamental critical principles. Here he proposes a "new" criticism based solely on the criterion of how much pleasure a literary work produces in the reader. Before approaching the individual work the ideal critic will have undertaken a comprehensive course of reading, so that he can perceive his subject against the background of literary history as a whole. Universal reading allows the critic to compare works, and the process of comparison leads to the development of the critical faculties. In Saintsbury's view the critic must "divest himself of any idea of what a book *ought to be*, until he has seen what it is." Saintsbury concludes by arguing that appreciation–the ability to perceive and analyze the pleasure derived from reading–is the ultimate goal of criticism.

Because Saintsbury aims to provide a "simple and straightforward History of [criticism's] actual accomplishments" in isolation from its philosophical and historical contexts, the study has frequently provoked objections. The aesthetician

Benedetto Croce, among others, felt that Saintsbury was "barren of philosophy" and that his study lacked any theoretical basis. More recently, René Wellek has forgiven Saintsbury's unphilosophical turn of mind while attacking his whimsicality and the "poverty and haziness" of his analyses of particular genres and critics. Nevertheless, for over a half a century no student of the development of criticism could afford to ignore *A History of Criticism*. Though superseded in many respects, it still stands as a monument to Saintsbury's ability to master a vast subject.

Within two years after the appearance of the final volume of *A History of Criticism*, the first volume of the equally massive *History of English Prosody from the Twelfth Century to the Present Day* (1906-1910) was published. The wide-ranging coverage of his history of English verse forms remains unsurpassed. Analyses of hundreds of individual passages are rewarding, and the responsiveness of Saintsbury's ear to felicities of sound and meter have been much admired. This should not be surprising, for Saintsbury was fonder of poetry than of other genres. The history of prosody has been from the outset among the most controversial of his works, having been attacked by critics ranging from Amy Lowell to Karl Shapiro. Their objections arise from Saintsbury's rejection of both accent and stress as the foundations of English prosody and his failure to substitute a fully adequate theory of his own. For him, the foot (that is, a combination of long and short syllables) is the fundamental unit of prosody, but it is unclear whether the terms "long" and "short" refer to stress or to duration of vocalization. Characteristically, he raises this problem himself, only to dismiss it as irrelevant. *A History of English Prosody*, then, shows Saintsbury at his best as an anthologist of and commentator on poetry, while it reveals his deficiencies as a theorist.

A History of English Prose Rhythm (1912) was the last of the major critical studies to appear during the Edinburgh years, although the two-volume *History of the French Novel* (1917-1919) was begun at the end of this period. Saintsbury's attempt to discover how particular prose passages "work" on the reader was largely original. He returned to the notion of foot-scansion in his analyses of prose from Middle English writers to John Ruskin. These discussions were largely admired at the same time the work as a whole was faulted for its lack of system. As his friend and colleague Oliver Elton observed, it was "a history and a body of criticism rather than a theory."

Although his major works since 1900 had appeared at the rate of a volume every two years, Saintsbury also found the time to undertake several editorial projects, including the *Minor Poets of the Caroline Period* (1905-1921), which encouraged other critics to begin the reevaluation of secondary cavalier and metaphysical poets, and the highly regarded *Oxford Thackeray* (1908). He was also the major contributor to *The Cambridge History of English Literature* (1907-1921). When not writing, attending to his academic duties, or walking, Saintsbury could be found among his books. "Reading is to me like *mental breathing*," he once told a friend.

At the age of seventy, Saintsbury gave up his chair at Edinburgh in order to devote more time to his invalid wife. When he resigned in June 1915, he was among the most influential members of the faculty and had received honorary degrees from his own university (1919), as well as from Aberdeen (1898), Durham (1906), and Oxford (1912). His move to Southampton in late 1915 required a major sacrifice: both his extensive wine cellar and his fifteen-thousand-volume library were sold at auction. The last of the books written at Edinburgh, *The Peace of the Augustans: A Survey of Eighteenth Century Literature as a Place of Rest and Refreshment* (1916) is one of his most enjoyable critical works. This work is best regarded as a collection of highly personal and sometimes idiosyncratic appreciations, rather than a comprehensive history of the period. The misleading formula of "rest and refreshment" in the subtitle has led some scholars to charge that Saintsbury perceived Augustan literature as little more than light entertainment. A reading of the chapter on Swift, whose personal pessimism and allusive wit greatly resemble Saintsbury's, does not bear out this charge. Saintsbury is quite aware of what he terms—borrowing a phrase from Whitman—the "accepted hells beneath" in Swift's works. Yet he points out that the pessimism rarely disrupts the equipoise and sense of classical restraint. *The Peace of the Augustans* also demonstrates Saintsbury's deep affinities with Samuel Johnson, whose quiet stoicism embodies the Augustan ideal of "peace." Like Johnson and Swift, Saintsbury regards the world from a fundamentally Tory perspective. He perceives the Augustan virtue of self-restraint as an antidote to the excesses of twentieth-century literature and life.

Two passages from *The Peace of the Augustans* give a fair sample of Saintsbury's mature style:

> But Swift never wearies, for as Bossuet said of human passion generally, there is in this greatest master of one of its most terrible forms *quelque chose d'infini*, and the refreshment which he offers varies unceasingly from the lightest froth of pure nonsense, through beverages middle and stronger, to the most drastic restoratives—the very strychnine and capsicum of irony.

> Common sense salted and spirited with humour; inflexible principle combined with utmost charity; wide knowledge without pedantry (the notion of Johnson as a typical pedant probably still survives, but only in the poorest wits, unenriched with even the slightest knowledge); curiosity again tempered by a wholesome skepticism which applied to all things provable, while it respected things where proof is not in place . . . a courage mental, moral, and physical, utterly fearless of every person and everything but God and God's doomsman Death; other good things that could be catalogued almost to weariness,—all are to be found in Johnson, and most of them are, as has been said, specific for the opposite qualities so common in our day.

The style is typically polemical (but rarely ill-tempered in tone), humorous, hyperbolic, and energetic. The distinctiveness of Saintsbury's voice was apparent to his early readers; Oscar Wilde attacked him for lapses in syntax and usage, while others found the style convoluted or vulgar. From that day to the present, the adjective "conversational" has been applied to his writings. Even in his weightier histories, he seems to be engaging the reader in one of those wide-ranging literary chats for which he was celebrated at Edinburgh. In his attempt to load every rift with ore, Saintsbury often piles aside upon aside, parenthesis upon parenthesis, until his sentences are full to bursting with the weight of his immense learning. At times, the parenthetical material spills over into explanatory footnotes, of which he was a past master. Edmund Wilson found a reading of Saintsbury to be like an entertaining "gigantic after-dinner talk with an old gentleman" who is both enormously garrulous and singularly knowledgeable. The conversational parentheses in Saintsbury sometimes remind one of the authorial asides in two of his favorite novelists, Fielding and Thackeray, and it is significant that he found their intrusions highly commendable.

Saintsbury once wrote that "for those who hate jokes and literary allusions one can only pray, 'God help them!' " His style is extremely allusive, drawing upon his reading in both "high" and "low" literature. Many of his more recondite allusions are lost on the modern reader; indeed, they were often the despair of his contemporary audience. The numerous comparisons of literature to food and drink are indications of his hedonistic, impressionistic approach to the appreciation of literature. Saintsbury's humor, which is frequently self-mocking, relies heavily on the use of abstruse or archaic vocabulary ("estesian," "stramineous," "concionatory") and hyperbole. Like Shakespeare, he has been accused of a willingness to lose the world for the sake of a pun. Saintsbury's style is admittedly anathema to purists, but it has also been esteemed for its originality and verve.

After a brief stay in Southampton, the Saintsburys moved to Bath. During his retirement from teaching, Saintsbury led an ordered and productive existence. Until his wife died in 1924, he devoted many hours to her care. Saintsbury always rose early, spent much of the morning at the typewriter, and continued his incessant reading, despite increasingly poor eyesight. Freed from academic responsibilities, he returned to literary journalism with pleasure and contributed to periodicals on a regular basis during the 1920s. Relatively few modern authors, however, were to his taste. Although some writers of the younger generation condescendingly regarded him as a Victorian anachronism, his circle of admirers was considerable. In 1922 three hundred friends gathered to wish him well on his seventy-seventh birthday; Saintsbury replied with a touching speech, in which he remarked that he wished to be remembered as one who had lacked literary talent but had great appreciative faculties.

Notes on a Cellar-Book, a small volume published in 1920, went through four trade editions in his lifetime and brought him new readers who were unfamiliar with his criticism. Some of these well-wishers founded a Saintsbury Club to honor him. The cellar-book essays on wine and its enjoyment are worthy successors to the essays of William Hazlitt (J. B. Priestley and others have pointed to the "gusto" of both authors) and the food-related journalism of Thackeray, whose obiter dicta on wines are frequently quoted in Saintsbury's work. In the tradition of the familiar essay, Saintsbury digresses at will, combining remembrances of cellars past with autobiographical snippets, etymological and historical observations, and good-natured criticism of prohibitionists and teetotaling "pussyfoots."

Notes on a Cellar-Book was followed by three collections of essays of the early 1920s. *A Scrap Book* (1922), *A Second Scrap Book* (1923), and *A Last Scrap Book* (1924) are unabashedly desultory, ranging over topics as various as the names of race-horses, Trade Unionism, Oxford in the 1860s, and the significance of red hair. Since Saintsbury refused to write his memoirs and discouraged biographers, the reminiscential essays on his Oxford career, his days as a journalist, and his friends Andrew Lang and H. D. Traill are of considerable interest. Saintsbury used the scrapbooks to expound his early-Victorian brand of Toryism, founded on his belief in the value of "Inequality, Individualism, Heredity, Property, etc." Throughout his career, he took particular pride in opposing most changes in the English political and social systems since the Reform Bill of 1832.

In his last years, Saintsbury occasionally ventured out but preferred to remain in his dusty rooms in the Royal Crescent at Bath. His good friend Helen Waddell remembered him in his eighties as a still-impressive figure "with straggling grey hair and black skull-cap, gaunt as Merlin and islanded in a fast-encroaching sea of books." In this description we recognize the rabbinical-looking Saintsbury of the William Nicholson portrait at Merton College, Oxford. The last of his books published during his lifetime was *A Consideration of Thackeray* (1931), a collection of prefaces and other essays on his favorite English novelist. Saintsbury died at Bath on 28 January 1933 and was interred in a Southampton cemetery. Over the next fifteen years, friends and colleagues edited for publication several collections of his fugitive writings.

Saintsbury's reputation as an academic critic has declined steadily since his death. His impressionism, his lack of interest in the theory and philosophy of criticism, and his disdain for the historical and social contexts of literature have all contributed to that decline. In an age of academic specialization Saintsbury's very versatility, his mastery of so many different literary periods and genres are too easily misperceived as evidence of dilettantism. Yet his texts on the history of criticism, English prosody, and prose rhythm still command respect, and his anthologies are models of their kind. As a periodical essayist Saintsbury maintained a remarkably high standard despite the remarkable size of his output. The best of his literary articles (principally those gathered in *The Collected Essays and Papers of George Saintsbury,* 1923-1924) and familiar essays deserve to be better known. It comes as no surprise that the twentieth-century critics who have been kindest to Saintsbury–Edmund Wilson, H. L. Mencken, and J. B. Priestley–are professional literary journalists. They respond warmly to his omniverous literary appetites, his iconoclasm and dislike for pedantry, and above all to his contagious enthusiasm for what he considered the best things in life: reading, writing, and wine tasting.

Bibliographies:

W. M. Parker, "A Saintsbury Bibliography," in Saintsbury's *A Last Vintage,* edited by John W. Oliver, Augustus Muir, and Arthur Melville Clark (London: Methuen, 1950), pp. 244-255;

"George Saintsbury," in Christopher C. Brown and William B. Thesing, *English Prose and Criticism, 1900-1950: A Guide to Information Sources* (Detroit: Gale, 1983), pp. 387-397.

References:

Oliver Elton, "George Edward Bateman Saintsbury: 1845-1933," *Proceedings of the British Academy,* 19 (1933): 325-344;

John Gross, *The Rise and Fall of the Man of Letters* (London: Weidenfeld & Nicolson, 1969), pp. 139-149;

Walter Leuba, *George Saintsbury* (New York: Twayne, 1967);

Harold Orel, *Victorian Literary Critics* (London: Macmillan/New York: St. Martin's, 1984), pp. 151-176;

Stephen Potter, "King Saintsbury," in his *The Muse in Chains: A Study in Education* (London: Cape, 1937), pp. 126-139;

J. B. Priestley, "Mr. George Saintsbury," in his *Figures in Modern Literature* (London: Lane, 1928), pp. 170-195;

Dorothy Richardson, "Saintsbury and Art for Art's Sake in England," *PMLA,* 59 (March 1944): 243-260;

A. Blyth Webster, "A Biographical Memoir," in *A Saintsbury Miscellany,* edited by John W. Oliver and Augustus Muir (New York: Oxford University Press, 1947), pp. 27-73;

René Wellek, *A History of Modern Criticism,* volume 4, *The Later Nineteenth Century* (New Haven & London: Yale University Press, 1965), pp. 416-428;

Edmund Wilson, "George Saintsbury's Centenary" and "George Saintsbury: Gourmet and Glutton," in his *Classics and Commercials* (New York: Farrar, Straus, 1950), pp. 306-310, 366-371.

Papers:

Saintsbury's letters to Edmund Gosse are in the Brotherton Library, University of Leeds. Other collections of his correspondence are at Merton College, Oxford; the National Library of Scotland; and Queen's College, Belfast.

Bernard Shaw
(26 July 1856-2 November 1950)

John Greenfield
McKendree College

See also the Shaw entry in *DLB 10, Modern British Dramatists, 1900-1945.*

SELECTED BOOKS: *Cashel Byron's Profession* (London: Modern Press, 1886; unauthorized edition, New York: Munro, 1886; revised, London: Scott, 1889); revised again, including *The Admirable Bashville* (London: Richards, 1901; Chicago: Stone, 1901);

An Unsocial Socialist (London: Sonnenschein, Lowrey, 1887; unauthorized edition, New York: Brentano's, 1900; authorized edition, New York: Brentano's, 1908);

The Quintessence of Ibsenism (London: Scott, 1891; unauthorized edition, Boston: Tucker, 1891); revised and enlarged (London: Constable, 1913; New York: Brentano's, 1913);

Manifesto of English Socialists, anonymous, by Shaw, William Morris, and H. M. Hyndman (London: Twentieth Century Press, 1893);

Widowers' Houses (London: Henry, 1893);

Plays: Pleasant and Unpleasant, 2 volumes (London: Richards, 1898; Chicago: Stone, 1898);

The Perfect Wagnerite (London: Richards, 1898; Chicago & New York: Stone, 1899; revised, London: Richards, 1902; New York: Brentano's, 1909);

Love Among the Artists (unauthorized edition, Chicago & New York: Stone, 1900; authorized, revised edition, London: Constable, 1914);

Three Plays for Puritans: The Devil's Disciple, Caesar and Cleopatra, & Captain Brassbound's Conversion (London: Richards, 1901; Chicago & New York: Stone, 1901);

Man and Superman (Westminster: Constable, 1903; New York: Brentano's, 1904);

The Common Sense of Municipal Trading (Westminster: Constable, 1904; New York: Lane, 1911);

The Irrational Knot (New York: Brentano's, 1905; London: Constable, 1905);

Dramatic Opinions and Essays, 2 volumes (unauthorized edition, New York: Brentano's, 1906; authorized edition, 1907; London:

Bernard Shaw, 1886 (photograph by Frederick Hollyer)

Constable, 1907);

John Bull's Other Island and Major Barbara, also includes *How He Lied to Her Husband* (New York: Brentano's, 1907; London: Constable, 1907);

The Sanity of Art (London: New Press, 1908; New York: Tucker, 1908);

Press Cuttings (London: Constable, 1909; New York: Brentano's, 1913);

The Doctor's Dilemma, Getting Married, and the Shewing-Up of Blanco Posnet (London: Constable, 1911; New York: Brentano's, 1911);

Misalliance, The Dark Lady of Sonnets, and Fanny's First Play (London: Constable, 1914; New York: Brentano's, 1914);

Common Sense about the War (London: Statesman Publishing Company, 1914);

Heartbreak House, Great Catherine, and Playlets of the War (New York: Brentano's, 1919; London: Constable, 1919);

Back to Methuselah (New York: Brentano's, 1921; London: Constable, 1921);

Saint Joan (London: Constable, 1924; New York: Brentano's, 1924);

Table-Talk of G.B.S.: Conversations on Things in General between George Bernard Shaw and His Biographer, by Shaw (uncredited) and Archibald Henderson (New York & London: Harper, 1925; revised, London: Chapman & Hall, 1925);

Translations and Tomfooleries (London: Constable, 1926; New York: Brentano's, 1926);

The Intelligent Woman's Guide to Socialism and Capitalism (London: Constable, 1928; New York: Brentano's, 1928);

Immaturity (London: Constable, 1930);

The Apple Cart (London: Constable, 1930; New York: Brentano's, 1931);

Music in London, 1890-1894, 3 volumes (London: Constable, 1931; New York: Wise, 1931);

Our Theatres in the Nineties, 3 volumes (London: Constable, 1931; New York: Wise, 1931);

What I Really Wrote About the War (New York: Brentano's, 1932; London: Constable, 1932);

The Adventures of the Black Girl in Her Search for God (London: Constable, 1932; New York: Dodd, Mead, 1933);

Too True to be Good, Village Wooing & On the Rocks: Three Plays (London: Constable, 1934; New York: Dodd, Mead, 1934);

Short Stories, Scraps and Shavings (London: Constable, 1934; New York: Dodd, Mead, 1934);

The Simpleton, The Six, and The Millionairess (London: Constable, 1936); republished as *The Simpleton of the Unexpected Isles, The Six of Calais & The Millionairess* (New York: Dodd, Mead, 1936);

London Music in 1888-89. As Heard by Corno di Bassetto (Later Known As Bernard Shaw) (London: Constable, 1937; New York: Dodd, Mead, 1937);

Cymbaline Refinished (Edinburgh: Privately printed, 1937);

Geneva (London: Constable, 1939; enlarged, 1940); revised and republished in *Geneva, Cymbaline Refinished, & Good King Charles* (London: Constable, 1947; New York: Dodd, Mead, 1947);

In Good King Charles's Golden Days (London: Constable, 1939);

Everybody's Political What's What (London: Constable, 1944; New York: Dodd, Mead, 1944);

Sixteen Self Sketches (London: Constable, 1949; New York: Dodd, Mead, 1949);

Buoyant Billions (London: Constable, 1950);

Buoyant Billions, Farfetched Fables, & Shakes versus Shav (London: Constable, 1951; New York: Dodd, Mead, 1951);

An Unfinished Novel, edited by Stanley Weintraub (London: Constable/New York: Dodd, Mead, 1958);

Shaw on Theater, edited by E. J. West (New York: Hill & Wang, 1958; London: MacGibbon & Kee, 1958);

How to Become a Musical Critic, edited by Dan H. Laurence (London: Hart-Davis, 1960; New York: Hill & Wang, 1961);

Shaw on Shakespeare, edited by Edwin Wilson (New York: Dutton, 1961; London: Cassell, 1961);

Platform and Pulpit, edited by Laurence (New York: Hill & Wang, 1961; London: Hart-Davis, 1962);

The Matter with Ireland, edited by Laurence and David H. Greene (New York: Hill & Wang, 1962; London: Hart-Davis, 1962);

The Religious Speeches of Bernard Shaw, edited by Warren Sylvester Smith (University Park: Pennsylvania State University Press, 1963);

George Bernard Shaw on Language, edited by Abraham Tauber (New York: Philosophical Library, 1963; London: Owen, 1965);

The Rationalization of Russia, edited by Harry M. Geduld (Bloomington: Indiana University Press, 1964);

Shaw on Religion, edited by Smith (London: Constable, 1967; New York: Dodd, Mead, 1967);

Saint Joan: A Screenplay, edited by Bernard F. Dukore (Seattle & London: University of Washington Press, 1968);

Shaw: An Autobiography, 1856-1898, compiled and edited by Weintraub (New York: Weybright & Talley, 1969; London, Sydney & Toronto: Reinhardt, 1970);

Shaw: An Autobiography, 1898-1950. The Playwright Years, compiled and edited by Weintraub (New York: Weybright & Talley, 1970; London, Sydney & Toronto: Reinhardt, 1970);

Bernard Shaw: Passion Play: A Dramatic Fragment, edited by Jerald E. Bringle (Iowa City: University of Iowa at the Windhover Press, 1971);

Bernard Shaw: The Road to Equality: Ten Unpublished Lectures and Essays, 1884-1918, edited by Louis Crompton with the assistance of Hilayne Cavanaugh (Boston: Beacon Press, 1971);

Bernard Shaw's Nondramatic Literary Criticism, edited by Weintraub (Lincoln: University of Nebraska Press, 1972);

Bernard Shaw: Practical Politics, edited by Lloyd J. Hubenka (Lincoln & London: University of Nebraska Press, 1976);

Shaw and Ibsen: Bernard Shaw's The Quintessence of Ibsenism and Related Writings, edited by J. L. Wisenthal (Toronto, Buffalo & London: University of Toronto Press, 1979);

The Collected Screenplays of Bernard Shaw, edited by Dukore (London: Prior, 1980; Athens: University of Georgia Press, 1980);

Shaw's Music, edited by Laurence, 3 volumes (London: Reinhardt/Bodley Head, 1981; New York: Dodd, Mead, 1981);

Bernard Shaw: The Diaries 1885-1897, edited by Weintraub, 2 volumes (University Park & London: Pennsylvania State University Press, 1986).

Collections: Collected Edition of the Works of Bernard Shaw, volumes 1-30 (London: Constable, 1930-1932); republished as the *Ayot St. Lawrence Edition* (New York: Wise, 1930-1932); volumes 31-33 (London: Constable, 1934-1938);

Standard Edition, 37 volumes (London: Constable, 1947-1951);

The Bodley Head Bernard Shaw: Collected Plays with Their Prefaces, 7 volumes (London, Sydney & Toronto: Reinhardt/Bodley Head, 1970-1974); republished as *Collected Plays with Their Prefaces* (New York: Dodd, Mead, 1975).

OTHER: "The Basis of Socialism: Economic" and "The Transition to Social Democracy," in *Fabian Essays in Socialism*, edited by Shaw (London: Fabian Society, 1889); unauthorized edition, edited by H. G. Wilshire (New York: Humboldt, 1891).

Had Shaw died in the same year that Queen Victoria did (1901), he would not be known as one of the greatest playwrights in English since Shakespeare, but he would still be recognized as one of the major figures of the literary and intellectual scene in late Victorian England. Though some of the plays he wrote before the turn of the century may be counted as successful dramas, his major contributions to the intellectual and literary climate of the 1880s and 1890s were as a critic, a polemicist, and a personality. He was acquainted personally with many of the major writers and celebrities of the period, and had he not been so controversial–often outrageous and even antagonistic–he might have been presumed to have been consciously forging a career for himself as a man of letters. And in another way he was doing precisely that: by spending long hours in the British Museum reading and writing and by channeling his diverse talents, creative energies, and critical intelligence into art, music, politics, and literature, he became one of the leading men of letters between the 1890s and World War I.

Shaw's success could hardly have been predicted from his family background. Born George Bernard Shaw on 26 July 1856 at Upper Synge Street, Dublin, he was the third and youngest child and only son of George Carr and Lucinda Elizabeth Gurly Shaw. Shaw's parents had so little in common with one another that he seldom experienced the feeling of a unified, harmonious family. As a member of the Protestant ascendancy in Ireland, Shaw's father was a gentleman, but he was an unambitious, unsuccessful grain merchant, and as Shaw's mother discovered too late, he was prone to drink. Shaw's mother, in contrast, had pretensions to gentility and the ambition to be an operatic singer. Shaw himself was embarrassed by his father's drunkenness and poverty, but he was also cynical about his mother's snobbery and lack of affection. Shaw and his mother both felt the humiliation when financial straits forced him to attend the Central Model Boys' School, an institution whose students were mostly lower-middle-class Catholic children. At fifteen Shaw escaped the confinement of formal schooling altogether when his uncle secured him a job at the Townshend estate agents.

The education that would really matter to Shaw, however, continued in his voracious reading of the Bible, Shakespeare, Dickens, and Bunyan; he also discovered in himself a kinship with the rebellious spirit embodied in the writings of Blake, Byron, and most strongly, Shelley. Attending the theater to see French melodramas, cut versions of Shakespeare, and the plays of the Irish-born Dion Boucicault, and frequenting the National Gallery of Ireland, where he learned to idolize Michelangelo, were both great escapes that would also serve him well later in his career. The strongest and most immediate and pervasive influence on him at this time, however, was neither literature nor art but music. His mother made sure that the Shaw household never lacked for music; she and Shaw's two older sisters, Agnes and Lucy, all aspired to be professional singers, and Shaw himself sang and played the piano. In the preface to the 1937 collection of reviews entitled *London Music in 1888-89*, Shaw recalls, "I could sing and whistle from end to end leading works by Handel, Haydn, Mozart, Beethoven, Rossini, Bellini, Donizetti, and Verdi." From the time Shaw was ten years old, George John Vandeleur Lee, a notable Dublin music teacher, conductor, and voice trainer, set up the Shaws in his households, alternating between Torca Cottage on Dalkey Hill and One Hatch Street, where Lee gave his lessons. Lee in effect took the place of Shaw's diffident and dissolute father, both as a husband, at least emotionally, to Shaw's mother and as a father figure to the children. When in 1872 Lee decided to test his talents in London, Shaw's mother did not take too long to decide that she and her daughters would follow him. Shaw stayed with his father in Dublin until 1876; then at the age of twenty, he set out to London to join his mother and make his career.

The next eight years (1876-1884), judged by either the standards of financial independence or literary success, were lean ones, although they were important years in Shaw's development as a writer and thinker. He lived at his mother's with apparently little more status or welcome than a boarder until he married at the age of 42 in 1898. He practiced his skills as a music critic by ghostwriting reviews for Lee and wrote a youthful, semiautobiographical novel entitled *Immaturity* (written in 1879 but not published until the collected edition of 1930-1932). From one of his early culture heroes, Shelley, Shaw got the idea for vegetarianism, a practice he held to from the 1880s throughout his life. After a brief stint with the Edison Telephone Company of London (1879-1880), he tried to pursue his career as a novelist, writing four more unsuccessful novels. *The Irrational Knot* (written in 1880, serialized from 1885 to 1887, and published in book form in 1905) is, as Shaw says in its preface, "a morally original study of a marriage," which means in Shaw's terms a sharp, realistic analysis of the problems and tensions inherent in relationships between men and women. *Love Among the Artists* (written in 1881, serialized in 1887 and 1888, and published in book form in 1900) stems from Shaw's observations of the tensions between artistic (musical) and personal (love and marriage) concerns. Shaw's fourth novel, *Cashel Byron's Profes-*

sion (written in 1882, serialized in 1885 and 1886, and published in book form in 1886), has as its protagonist a prizefighter and stems from Shaw's own interest and participation in boxing. Finally, as its title suggests, *An Unsocial Socialist* (written in 1883, serialized in 1884, and published in book form in 1887) reflects Shaw's preoccupation with social issues and socialist ideas. But Shaw's career did not lie in the path of a novelist.

Shaw met stimulating people and heard and read about ideas in the 1880s that were to change his life. Beginning in 1880 with the Zetetical Society, a debating group, Shaw began to attend and join various intellectual, literary, and political organizations, including the Shelley Society, the Browning Society, and the New Shakespeare Society. In 1882 he heard the American economist and reformer Henry George speak on the land question, an experience that had the effect on Shaw of an almost immediate and passionate conversion to the religion of socialism. Shaw reflected upon his subsequent reading of Marx's *Das Kapital* in a French translation: "I was a coward until Marx made a Communist of me and gave me a faith: Marx made a man of me." Actually Shaw, under the influence of Philip Wicksteed and other economic theorists, came finally to reject the Marxian labor theory of value in favor of Stanley Jevons's utility theory of value. Shaw came to see Marx not as a scientific economist but, like himself, as a moralist and social critic.

Though Shaw had attended the meetings of various socialist groups and was acquainted with some of their leaders, such as Henry Hyndman of Democratic Federation and William Morris of the Socialist League, Shaw was drawn in 1884 to the little band of socialists that comprised the recently formed Fabian Society: Thomas Davidson, Havelock Ellis, Ramsay MacDonald (a future prime minister), Hubert Bland, his wife Edith Nesbit, Frank Podmore, and E. R. Pease. Shortly thereafter Shaw met Sidney Webb and persuaded him to join the society, along with Sydney Olivier, Graham Wallas, and the actress Annie Besant. Shaw and several other of the late joiners, joined still later by H. G. Wells and Beatrice Potter (who married Webb), soon came to dominate the Society, tirelessly writing pamphlets and essays and giving speeches to further the cause of socialism. Shaw edited the volume entitled *Fabian Essays in Socialism* (published in London in 1889), to which he also contributed two essays, "The Basis of Socialism: Economic" and "The Transition to

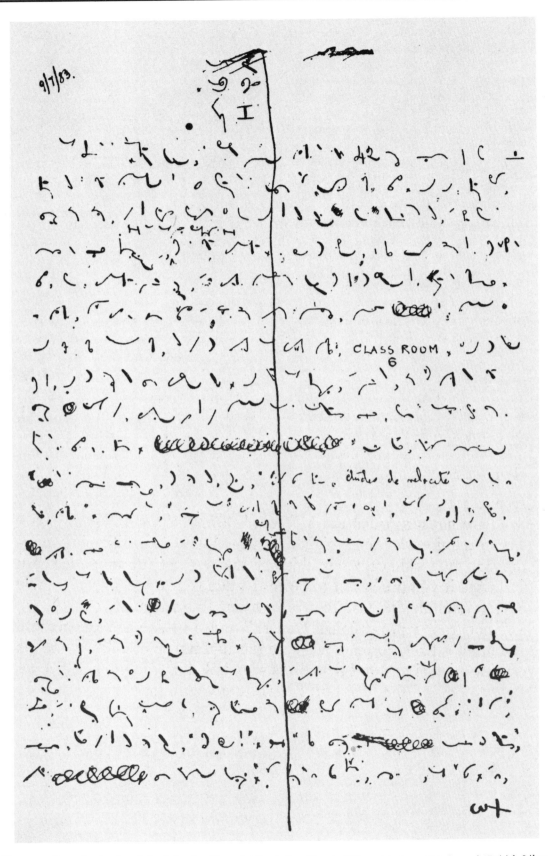

First page from the shorthand draft for An Unsocial Socialist, *Shaw's fifth and last completed novel (British Library)*

Social Democracy."

The title page of the Fabian Society's first tract explained the society's name, an ad hoc explanation by Frank Podmore: "For the right moment you must wait, as Fabius did most patiently, when warring against Hannibal, though many censured his delays; but when the time comes you must strike hard, as Fabius did, or your waiting will be in vain and fruitless." Witnessing the police violence against the crowd on "Bloody Sunday" (13 November 1887) in Trafalgar Square convinced Shaw and most of the Fabians that they should concentrate on gradually trying to reason others into acceptance of their stands on particular issues rather than trying to foment revolutionary action. In addition to their usual methods of giving speeches and writing pamphlets, the Fabians developed a strategy of "permeation," which entailed penetrating other organizations and indoctrinating persons of power with their ideas and programs. For example, Shaw, who was on the executive council of the Fabians from 1885 to 1911, and the Fabians helped to launch the Labour party in 1893 and helped candidates favorable to their views get elected to various offices. Shaw's concern in his Fabian essays with the immorality of capitalism, manifested by living off the labor of others, informs many of his other writings as well.

Amid all of this Fabian activity Shaw met another man who was to change his life: William Archer, who was drawn to Shaw when he first observed him at the British Museum reading *Das Kapital* and the score of Wagner's *Tristan und Isolde*, alternating between the two. Archer, who was both the drama critic and the reluctant art critic for the *World*, invited Shaw to accompany him to exhibitions, and Shaw gave him ideas for his reviews. When Archer tried to give him half the money he had received for the art reviews, and Shaw returned it, Archer responded by persuading his editor, Edmund Yates, to hire Shaw as the art critic. Shaw now had the opportunity to turn one of his boyhood interests into a living; thus, in 1885 he began what was to be off and on a lifetime career as a journalist and critic. Following John Ruskin and William Morris, Shaw championed the Pre-Raphaelite artists, such as Edward Burne-Jones and Holman Hunt, but he was also capable of admiring the less well established Impressionists, praising Degas, Monet, Manet, and Pissarro for, in his words, their "natural, observant, real style." He disliked the sentimentality and conventional themes that he saw in

Cover design by Walter Crane for the 1889 volume edited by Shaw. Two of Shaw's essays were included in the volume along with contributions by Sidney Webb, Annie Besant, William Clarke, Graham Wallas, and Hubert Bland.

much romantic art, but, in addition to recognizing photography as an art, he boldly praised the newest and most challenging painter on the scene–James McNeill Whistler–for his courage in being a rebel and a groundbreaker.

Shaw's reputation as a defender of the new spirit in art made him the choice of Benjamin Tucker, editor of the American journal *Liberty*, to refute Max Nordau's book *Degeneration*, which, in its English translation, had created a stir in the early 1890s. Nordau's pessimistic book asserts that "modern works of art are symptoms of disease in the artists," who in turn represent the decay of the human race. Nordau's attack on Shaw's culture heroes–Henrik Ibsen, Richard Wagner, Leo Tolstoy, John Ruskin, and the Pre-Raphaelites, including William Morris–succeeded in arousing Shaw's ire. The result was a reasoned but devastating attack upon Nordau's book. Shaw begins his review, "A Degenerate's View of Nordau" (1895, revised and published in 1908 as *The*

Sanity of Art), with a defense of Wagner, Ibsen, the Impressionists, and other artists on the grounds that their art is sane, healthy, and vital; then he launches into an attack on Nordau's book as contradictory, arbitrary, and self-pleading.

In 1888 Shaw and other Socialists had been hired to write for T. P. O'Connor's *Star*, but when O'Connor discovered how radical their articles were he was forced to fire most of them; however, Shaw persuaded O'Connor to keep him on as the music critic, thus giving him yet another opportunity to make use of earlier knowledge and experience, this time from the music that he had picked up from his mother and Lee. Saying that he "had to invent a fantastic personality with something like a foreign title," Shaw adopted the pseudonym Corno di Bassetto, Italian for bassett horn, and wrote weekly music reviews for the *Star* from 1888 to 1890 (collected as *London Music* in 1937), before becoming music critic for *World* from 1890 to 1894; the reviews he wrote for the latter (collected as *Music in London*, 1931), he signed with his initials, G. B. S.

Though many of Shaw's acquaintances were skeptical of his qualifications as a music critic, he proved himself more than equal to the task; as Shaw recalled in one of the pieces eventually collected in *Shaw's Music* (1981), "the alleged joke was that I knew nothing about it. The real joke was that I knew all about it." Shaw had very definite ideas about what it meant to be a critic; it required independence, forthrightness, high standards, and, above all, a willingness to express personal opinions strongly and clearly: "a criticism without personal feeling is not worth reading. It is the capacity for making good or bad art a personal matter that makes a man a critic. The artist who accounts for my disparagement by alleging personal animosity on my part is quite right: when people do less than their best, and do that less at once badly and self-complacently, I hate them, loathe them, detest them, long to tear them limb from limb and strew them in gobbets about the stage or platform. . . . In the same way, . . . when my critical mood is at its height, personal feeling is not the word: it is passion: the passion for artistic perfection—for the noblest beauty of sound, sight, and action—that rages in me."

Shaw was comfortable discussing all aspects of musical productions—the composers and their compositions, the orchestral sounds, the staging, the singers' voices, and the dramatic aspects of opera—and he demanded the best from all concerned with a production, from the composer to the singers. He divided music into two broad categories, absolute (instrumental, orchestral) and dramatic (operatic); Shaw was more interested in the latter but recognized that the highest music unifies both, the best example of which for Shaw was Mozart's *Don Giovanni*. Shaw applied three criteria to composers: feeling, upon which count Rossini failed miserably and Beethoven succeeded; thought, which Schubert lacked and Mozart exemplified; and inspiration, which Shaw defined as "poetic intentions adequately and characteristically expressed," exemplified by Wagner. Shaw viewed his music reviews as a way of reclaiming musical appreciation and understanding from the philistines and the snobs; accordingly, he took his appeal to the people, demanding, for example, a state-supported program that would make good music more accessible to the common people. Though some of his fellow critics jealously complained about his lack of technical knowledge and performers rankled under his withering criticism, Shaw was popular with his readers because his prose was not jargon-ridden but lively, witty, often humorous, and always clear. With characteristically Shavian confidence, he warned those who questioned his musical knowledge: "Don't be in a hurry to contradict G.B.S., as he never commits himself on a musical subject until he knows at least six times as much about it as you do." Shaw's music reviews (collected in three volumes as *Shaw's Music*, 1981) deserve to be read not only by Shavian scholars and musicologists but by anyone who enjoys reading excellent prose.

At the urging of Frank Harris, editor of the *Saturday Review*, Shaw left the *World* to become drama critic for Harris's magazine from January 1895 through May 1898. In the 151 weekly reviews that he wrote during these years (collected as *Our Theatres in the Nineties*, 1931), Shaw ranges over an array of topics, usually, however, focusing upon actual performances: the tradition, history, and influence of the theater (Shakespeare, Jonson, and Marlowe); the content and quality of the contemporary drama scene (Ibsen, Wilde, Pinero, and the French playwright Victorien Sardou); drama in performance (actresses and actors, many of whom Shaw knew personally: Ellen Terry, Sarah Bernhardt, Henry Irving, and Forbes-Robertson); production, stage management, and stage design. Shaw carried the same uncompromising high standards, as well as the same wit and humor, from his music criticism to his drama criticism. As with anything he undertook, Shaw viewed his mission as that of a reformer, arguing in an essay entitled "Church and Stage" that the theater is, or should be, the modern church. People must be able to go to the theater to see life portrayed realistically and to hear important ideas discussed. Thus Shaw had little patience with comedies, such as Oscar Wilde's *The Importance of Being Earnest* (1895), that only amused but failed to move him. He was even harsher with Arthur Wing Pinero's *The Second Mrs. Tanqueray* (1893) and *The Notorious Mrs. Ebbsmith* (1895), attacking them for their false morality, sensationalism, artificiality, and hackneyed conventionality.

Shaw believed that one of the biggest impediments to intelligent theater was the so-called well-made play, characterized by predictable characters, mechanical or formulaic plots, and the absence of ideas. For such plays Shaw coined the term "sardoodledom" in a review of Sardou's *Fedora*. But by far, Shaw's most controversial drama criticism was his disrespectful treatment of Shakespeare. Though Shaw had read Shakespeare since he was a boy and knew all of his plays inti-

mately, he believed that the "Bardolatry" that dominated the contemporary theatrical scene was an impediment to the progress of the theater and the introduction of new ideas. Thus he exaggerates his attack on Shakespeare to shock readers into seeing the bard as he really is, faults and all. For instance, contrasting Shakespeare and Bunyan, to the disadvantage of the former, in a review of a dramatization of *The Pilgrim's Progress*, Shaw observes, "Shakespear wrote for the theatre because, with extraordinary artistic powers, he understood nothing and believed nothing. Thirty-six big plays . . . and . . . not a single hero! Only one man in them all who believes in life, enjoys life, thinks life worth living . . . and that man– Falstaff !" Even so, Shaw was incensed when Shakespeare's plays were cut without understanding or misstaged or misacted, all faults with which he charged the actor-producer Henry Irving. Shaw's theater criticism aims at improving the theater by making it more responsive to social issues and new ideas.

The best hope of accomplishing such high goals for the theater, Shaw believed, lay in the chal-

Shaw with Charlotte Payne-Townshend, fellow member of the Fabian Society whom Shaw married in 1898

lenging dramas of the Norwegian playwright Henrik Ibsen. In his reviews of Ibsen's plays and most extensively in *The Quintessence of Ibsenism* (1891; revised and enlarged, 1913), which actually began as a lecture to the Fabian Society as part of a project on socialism and literature, Shaw defends the vital and realistic drama of Ibsen. He regards Ibsen as a reformer who like many reformers before him–Luther, Cromwell, Wollstonecraft, and Shelley–has been misunderstood and condemned. Shaw begins by reiterating the terms of Clement Scott's recent attack on *Ghosts* for its immorality, Shaw emphasizing that Ibsen, like Shelley, was criticized for being a pioneer who dared to say that the conventionally wrong, morally speaking, might be right. Shaw believed that Ibsen and Shelley were each the one of a thousand who dared to be realists, by which he meant both seeing things as they are and having the courage to be unconventional. Out of the same thousand Shaw avers that 750 would be philistines content with the status quo and 249 would be idealists who know there are problems but try to cover these problems with illusionary ideals and moral platitudes. Shaw observes that in the typical Ibsen play, such as *Brand*, the woman is unwomanly (that is, to her credit she is not like the faint hearted, weak Victorian stage heroine) and the villain is an Idealist (that is, he is determined "to do nothing wrong").

Shaw enters into the raging Ibsen controversy not only to defend him against pious, prudish, and misunderstanding critics but also to help the unprepared English theatergoers, used to a diet of sensational and predictable plots, understand and accept Ibsen's, and Shaw's, new kind of drama. In short, Ibsen breaks the rules and conventions of traditional drama. Besides changing the traditional roles of heroes and villains, realists and idealists, and men and women, Ibsen's plays trick the audience into a false judgment and then reveal it to be false. Though many of Shaw's contemporaries, as well as some later critics, have accused Shaw of trying to turn Ibsen into a Socialist, or of neglecting the poetry in his dramas, or in general of Shavianizing Ibsen, within the limits of what he proposes to do, Shaw succeeds in isolating and explaining the new elements in Ibsen's drama.

As he had with Ibsen, Shaw undertook to be the great defender and proponent of Richard Wagner in several of his music reviews and most fully in *The Perfect Wagnerite* (1898). Shaw believed he was particularly qualified to interpret the composer because, like Wagner, he had studied both music and revolutionary politics. Shaw's strategy is to render *The Niblung's Ring* (Shaw's anglicization of Wagner's title) comprehensible by interpreting it not as an opera about mythological beings but as a drama about contemporary life, in effect a modern social allegory about greed, love, masters, slaves, and rebellion. The class of dwarfs, represented by Alberic, illustrates how human nature is perverted toward greed–the hoarding instincts of capitalism–in the absence of love. Alfred Turco in *Shaw's Moral Vision* (1976) equates the other classes with the three divisions in *The Quintessence of Ibsenism:* the giants are the philistines, "patient, toiling, stupid, respectful, money-worshipping people"; the gods are the idealists, "intellectual, moral, talented people who devise and administer States and Churches" (Woton, Loki, and Fricka); and the heroes are the realists (Siegfried and Brynhild). Shaw avers that both Wagner and Shelley slightly miss the point in seeing love rather than the life force as the agent which will finally carry "human nature to higher and higher levels." Shaw concedes that the political allegory of *The Niblung's Ring* can only be carried to the point at which it dissolves in the pure power of music and concludes with a plea for presenting the opera in England as it has been performed at Das Festspielhaus, Wagner's theater at Bayreuth.

Beginning in the mid 1880s, Shaw wrote essays on general literary topics ("Fiction and Truth," "Romance and Real Sex," for example) as well as essays, reviews, and introductions to novelists (Samuel Butler, Wilkie Collins, Charles Dickens, George Moore, Arnold Bennett, and others) and poets (Shelley, Keats, Poe, and others). The essays, which appeared in such journals as the *Pall Mall Gazette*, were collected as *Bernard Shaw's Nondramatic Literary Criticism* in 1972. The year 1898 marked a turning point in Shaw's life and career. After amorous relationships with various women, including the actresses Jenny Patterson, Florence Farr, and Ellen Terry (the last only through correspondence), Shaw married Charlotte Payne-Townshend, a wealthy Irishwoman and fellow Fabian. In 1898 too, Shaw's first seven plays, collected in two volumes as *Plays: Pleasant and Unpleasant*, were published, and from that point on, though he continued to write essays about social and political issues for the Fabian Society, reviews and essays, and long prefaces for his own plays, he no longer had to earn his living from journalism and so channeled most of his energies into being a playwright. Shaw never stopped speaking his mind and thereby causing controversy. For example, the 1914 publication of *Common Sense About the War* as a special supplement to the *New Statesman* caused a public outcry from friends and enemies alike against Shaw for his audacity in questioning the government's policies in a time of crisis. After the devastation of the war was over, Shaw was forgiven and regarded as a prophet. In 1928 Shaw showed his continuing interest in controversial social questions in *The Intelligent Woman's Guide to Socialism and Capitalism*. In 1925 Shaw was awarded the Nobel Prize for Literature. On 26 July 1950, his ninety-fourth birthday, the Shaw Society of America was founded. Shaw died 2 November 1950 at Ayot St. Lawrence, "Shaw's Corner," where he and Charlotte had first taken up residence in 1905.

As a prose writer Shaw succeeded in creating the persona of G.B.S., ruthlessly honest, always clear, shockingly controversial, and undauntedly polemical. He was capable only of telling the truth as he saw it, incapable of telling people falsehoods that they wanted to hear. During his long, famous, and active life Shaw was acquainted either through correspondence or in person with many leading intellectual and literary figures and elicited books about himself as early as G. K. Chesterton's *George Bernard Shaw* (1909) and H. L. Mencken's *George Bernard Shaw: His Plays* (1905). From these first books onward, most criticism of Shaw has recognized the importance of the prose writings that stemmed from his work as a journalist and political activist in understanding Shaw as dramatist and man of letters. Thus Shaw's Victorian prose writings are essential for students of Shaw, invaluable for those interested in the social and literary milieu of the 1880s and 1890s, and rewarding to readers who appreciate clear, lively, witty prose.

Letters:

Letters from George Bernard Shaw to Miss Alma Murray (Mrs. Alfred Forman) (London: Privately printed, 1927);

Ellen Terry and Bernard Shaw: A Correspondence, edited by Christopher St. John (New York: Fountain Press/London: Constable, 1931);

More Letters from George Bernard Shaw to Miss Alma Murray (Mrs. Alfred Forman) (London: Privately printed, 1932);

Florence Farr, Bernard Shaw, W. B. Yeats, edited by Clifford Bax (Dublin: Cuala Press, 1941;

Shaw at his desk in the garden hut of his home at Ayot St. Lawrence

New York: Dodd, Mead, 1942; London: Home & Van Thal, 1946);

Bernard Shaw and Mrs. Patrick Campbell: Their Correspondence, edited by Alan Dent (London: Gollancz, 1952; New York: Knopf, 1952);

Advice to a Young Critic and Other Letters [to R. Golding Bright], edited by E. J. West (New York: Crown, 1955; London: Owen, 1956);

Bernard Shaw's Letters to Granville Barker, edited by C. B. Purdom (New York: Theatre Arts Books, 1957; London: Phoenix House, 1957);

To A Young Actress: The Letters of Bernard Shaw to Molly Tompkins, edited by Peter Tompkins (New York: Potter, 1960; London: Constable, 1961);

Collected Letters, edited by Dan H. Laurence, 3 volumes to date: 1874-1897 (New York: Dodd, Mead, 1965); 1898-1910 (New York: Dodd, Mead, 1972); 1911-1925 (New York: Viking, 1985);

Bernard Shaw and Alfred Douglas: A Correspondence, edited by Mary Hyde (New Haven & New York: Ticknor & Fields, 1982);

The Playwright and the Pirate. Bernard Shaw and Frank Harris, a Correspondence 1898-1930, edited by Stanley Weintraub (University Park: Pennsylvania State University Press, 1982);

Bernard Shaw: Agitations. Letters to the Press 1875-1950, edited by Dan H. Laurence and James Rambeau (New York: Ungar, 1985);

Bernard Shaw's Letters to Siegfried Trebitsch, edited by Samuel A. Weiss (Stanford: Stanford University Press, 1986).

Bibliographies:

Dan H. Laurence, *Bernard Shaw: A Bibliography*, 2 volumes (London: Oxford University Press, 1982);

Christopher C. Brown and William B. Thesing, "George Bernard Shaw," in *English Prose and Criticism, 1900-1950: A Guide to Information Sources* (Detroit: Gale Research, 1983), pp. 403-424;

J. P. Wearing, ed., *G. B. Shaw: An Annotated Bibliography of Writings about Him*, volume 1: 1871-1930 (De Kalb: Northern Illinois University Press, 1986);

Donald Haberman, ed., *G. B. Shaw: An Annotated Bibliography of Writings about Him*, volume 3 (De Kalb: Northern Illinois University Press, 1986).

Biographies:

Archibald Henderson, *George Bernard Shaw. His Life and Works* (London: Hurst & Blackett, 1911; Cincinnati: Steward & Kidd, 1911);

Frank Harris, *Bernard Shaw. An Unauthorized Biography Based on First-hand Information, with a Postscript by Mr. Shaw* (London: Gollancz, 1931; New York: Simon & Schuster, 1931);

Henderson, *Bernard Shaw, Playboy and Prophet* (New York: Appleton, 1932);

Hesketh Pearson, *Bernard Shaw. His Life and Personality* (London: Collins, 1942); republished as *Bernard Shaw: A Full-Length Portrait* (New York: Harper, 1942; revised, London: Methuen, 1951; New York: Atheneum, 1963);

R. F. Rattray, *Bernard Shaw. A Chronicle* (New York: Roy, 1951);

St. John Ervine, *Bernard Shaw. His Life, Work and Friends* (London: Constable, 1956; New York: Morrow, 1956);

Henderson, *George Bernard Shaw. Man of the Century* (New York: Appleton-Century, 1956);

Allan Chappelow, *Shaw the Villager and Human Being. A Biographical Symposium* (London: Skilton, 1961);

Margaret Shenfield, *Bernard Shaw: A Pictorial Biography* (New York: Viking, 1962);

Aubrey Williamson, *Bernard Shaw: Man and Writer* (New York: Crowell-Collier Press, 1963);

Stanley Weintraub, *Private Shaw and Public Shaw. A Dual Biography of Lawrence of Arabia and Bernard Shaw* (New York: Braziller, 1963; London: Cape, 1963);

B. C. Rosset, *Shaw of Dublin. The Formative Years* (University Park: Pennsylvania State University Press, 1964);

J. Percy Smith, *The Unrepentant Pilgrim. A Study of the Development of Bernard Shaw* (Boston: Houghton Mifflin, 1965);

John O'Donovan, *Shaw and the Charlatan Genius* (Dublin: Dolmen Press, 1965);

Allan Chappelow, *Shaw—"The Chucker-Out": A Biographical Exposition and Critique* (London: Allen & Unwin, 1969);

Nathaniel Harris, *The Shaws. The Family of Bernard Shaw* (London: Dent, 1977);

Margot Peters, *Bernard Shaw and the Actresses* (Garden City: Doubleday, 1980).

References:

Elsie B. Adams, *Bernard Shaw and the Aesthetes* (Columbus: Ohio State University Press, 1971);

George S. Barber, "Shaw's Contributions to Music Criticism," *PMLA*, 72 (December 1957): 1005-1017;

Alan P. Barr, "Diabolonian Pundit: G. B. S. as Critic," *Shaw Review*, 11 (January 1968): 11-23;

Barr, *Victorian Stage Pulpiteer: Bernard Shaw's Crusade* (Athens: University of Georgia Press, 1973);

Eric Bentley, *Bernard Shaw, 1856-1950* (New York: New Directions, 1957);

Gordon N. Bergquist, *The Pen and the Sword: War and Peace in the Prose and Plays of Bernard Shaw* (Salzburg: Institut fur Englishche Sprache und Literatur, 1977);

Charles A. Berst, ed., "Bernard Shaw Scholarship of the Past 25 Years, and Future Priorities: A Transcript of the 1975 MLA Conference of Scholars on Shaw," *Shaw Review*, 19 (May 1976): 56-72;

Berst, ed., *Shaw and Religion* (University Park: Pennsylvania State University Press, 1981);

William Blissett, "Bernard Shaw: Imperfect Wagnerite," *University of Texas Quarterly*, 27 (1958): 185-199;

Hans-Peter Breuer, "Form and Feeling: George

Bernard Shaw as Music Critic," *Journal of Irish Literature*, 11 (September 1982): 74-102;

Ian Britain, "Bernard Shaw, Ibsen, and the Ethics of English Socialism," *Victorian Studies*, 21 (Spring 1978): 381-401;

Britain, "A Transplanted Doll's House: Ibsenism, Feminism and Socialism in Late-Victorian and Edwardian England," in *Transformations in Modern European Drama*, edited by Ian Donaldson (Atlantic Highlands, N.J.: Humanities, 1983), pp. 14-54;

Ivor Brown, *Shaw in His Time* (London: Nelson, 1965);

D. R. Cherry, "The Fabianism of Shaw," *Queen's Quarterly*, 69 (Spring 1962): 83-93;

G. K. Chesterton, *George Bernard Shaw* (London & New York: Lane/Bodley Head, 1909);

John Clive, "The Versatile Signor di Bassetto: An Essay in Crime Prevention," *Daedalus*, 111 (Summer 1982): 51-63;

Fred D. Crawford, "Bernard Shaw's Theory of Literary Art," *Journal of General Education*, 34 (Spring 1982): 20-34;

Louis Crompton, Introduction to his *The Road to Equality: Ten Unpublished Lectures and Essays, 1884-1918* (Boston: Beacon Press, 1971);

Daniel Dervin, *Bernard Shaw: A Psychological Study* (Lewisburg, Pa.: Bucknell University Press, 1975);

Roland A. Duerksen, "Shelley and Shaw," in his *Shelleyan Ideas in Victorian Literature* (The Hague: Mouton, 1966): 166-197;

Bernard F. Dukore, *Bernard Shaw, Playwright: Aspects of Shavian Drama* (Columbia: University of Missouri Press, 1973);

Harold Fromm, *Bernard Shaw and the Theater in the Nineties: A Study of Shaw's Dramatic Criticism* (Lawrence: University of Kansas Press, 1967);

Arthur Ganz, *George Bernard Shaw* (New York: Grove Press, 1983);

John Gassner, "Bernard Shaw and the Making of the Modern Mind," *College English*, 23 (April 1962): 517-525;

Gassner, "Shaw as a Drama Critic," *Theatre Arts*, 35 (May 1951): 26-29, 91-95;

Gassner, "Shaw on Ibsen and the Drama of Ideas," in his *Ideas in the Drama: Selected Papers from the English Institute* (New York: Columbia University Press, 1964), pp. 71-100;

Gassner, "Shaw on Shakespeare," *Independent Shavian*, 2 (Fall 1963): 1, 3-5; 2 (Winter 1963-1964): 13, 15, 23-24;

Daniel Charles Gerould, "George Bernard Shaw's

Criticism of Ibsen," *Comparative Literature*, 15 (Spring 1963): 130-145;

A. M. Gibbs, *The Art and Mind of Shaw: Essays in Criticism* (New York: St. Martin's, 1983);

Charles I. Glicksberg, "The Criticism of Bernard Shaw," *South Atlantic Quarterly*, 50 (January 1951): 96-108;

Michael Goldberg, "The Dickens Debate: G. B. S. vs. G. K. C.," *Shaw Review*, 20 (September 1977): 135-147;

Norbert Greiner, "Shaw's Aesthetics and Socialist Realism," *Shaw Review*, 22 (January 1979): 33-45;

Nicholas Grene, *Bernard Shaw: A Critical View* (New York: St. Martin's, 1984);

Martha Hadsel, "The Uncommon-Common Metaphor in Shaw's Dramatic Criticism," *Shaw Review*, 23 (September 1980): 119-129;

Janice Henson, "Bernard Shaw's Contribution to the Wagner Controversy in England," *Shaw Review*, 1 (January 1961): 21-26;

Eldon C. Hill, *George Bernard Shaw* (Boston: Twayne, 1978);

Michael Holroyd, ed., *The Genius of Shaw: A Symposium* (New York: Holt, Rinehart & Winston, 1979);

James Hulse, "Shaw: Socialist Maverick," in his *Revolutionists in London: A Study of Five Unorthodox Socialists* (Oxford: Clarendon Press, 1970), pp. 111-137;

Paul A. Hummert, *Bernard Shaw's Marxian Romance* (Lincoln: University of Nebraska Press, 1973);

William Irvine, "G. B. Shaw's Musical Criticism," *Musical Quarterly*, 32 (July 1946): 319-332;

Irvine, "Shaw's Quintessence of Ibsenism," *South Atlantic Quarterly*, 46 (April 1947): 252-262;

Jack Kalmar, "Shaw on Art," *Modern Drama*, 2 (September 1959): 147-159;

R. J. Kaufman, ed., *G. B. Shaw: A Collection of Critical Essays* (Englewood Cliffs, N.J.: Prentice-Hall, 1965);

Julian B. Kaye, *Bernard Shaw and the Nineteenth-Century Tradition* (Norman: University of Oklahoma Press, 1958);

Carlyle King, "G.B.S. on Literature: The Author as Critic," *Queen's Quarterly*, 66 (Spring 1959): 135-145;

Louis Kronenberger, ed., *George Bernard Shaw: A Critical Survey* (Cleveland: World, 1953);

Dan H. Laurence, "Bernard Shaw and the *Pall Mall Gazette*: II," *Shaw Bulletin*, 1 (September 1954): 8-10;

Laurence, "Genesis of a Dramatic Critic," *Modern*

Drama, 2 (September 1959): 178-183;

Laurence, *Shaw: An Exhibit* (Austin: University of Texas, Humanities Research Center, 1977);

Jerry Lutz, *Pitchman's Melody, Shaw about "Shakespear"* (Lewisburg, Pa.: Bucknell University Press, 1974);

Keith May, *Ibsen and Shaw* (New York: St. Martin's, 1985);

Norman MacKenzie and Jeanne MacKenzie, *The Fabians* (New York: Simon & Schuster, 1977);

Frederick P. W. McDowell, "Victorian Shaw," *Victorian Newsletter*, no. 11 (September 1957): 16-19;

David Morse, "Shaw, the Victorian," *Encounter*, 22 (February 1964): 78-80;

Arthur H. Nethercot, "Bernard Shaw, Philosopher," *PMLA*, 69 (March 1954): 57-75;

Richard M. Ohmann, *Shaw: The Style and The Man* (Middleton, Conn.: Wesleyan University Press, 1962);

Barbara Peart, "Shelley and Shaw's Prose," *Shaw Review*, 15 (January 1972): 39-45;

Thomas Postlewait, "Bernard Shaw and Science: The Aesthetics of Causality," in *Victorian Science and Victorian Values: Literary Perspectives*, edited by James Paradis and Postlewait (New York: New York Academy of Sciences, 1981), pp. 319-358;

Norman Rosenblood, ed., *Shaw: Seven Critical Essays* (Toronto: University of Toronto Press, 1971);

Shaw Review (Pennsylvania State University Press), special issues: *Shaw/Shakespeare* (May 1971), *Shaw/Shelley* (January 1972), *Shaw and Science Fiction* (May 1973), *Shaw and Woman* (January 1974), *Shaw around the World* (January 1977), *Shaw and Dickens* (September 1977), and *Shaw and Myth* (May 1978);

M. Shenfield, "Shaw as a Music Critic," *Music and Letters*, 39 (October 1958): 378-384;

Albert H. Silverman, "Bernard Shaw's Shakespeare Criticism," *PMLA*, 72 (September 1957): 722-736;

J. Percy Smith, "G.B.S. on the Theater," *Tamarack Review*, 15 (1960): 73-86;

Smith, "Superman Versus Man: Bernard Shaw on Shakespeare," *Yale Review*, 42 (Autumn 1952): 67-82;

Smith, *The Unrepentant Pilgrim: A Study of the Development of Bernard Shaw* (Boston: Houghton Mifflin, 1965);

Warren S. Smith, *The Bishop of Everywhere* (University Park: Pennsylvania State Press, 1982);

Smith, *The London Heretics: 1870-1914* (London:

Constable, 1968);

E. E. Stokes, Jr., "Bernard Shaw and Economics," *Southwestern Social Science Quarterly*, 39 (December 1958): 242-248;

Stokes, "Shaw and William Morris," *Shaw Bulletin*, 1, no. 4 (Summer 1953): 16-19;

E. Strauss, *Bernard Shaw: Art and Socialism* (London: Gollancz, 1942);

Michael Timko, "Entente Cordiale: The Dramatic Criticism of Shaw and Wells," *Modern Drama*, 8 (May 1965): 39-46;

Alfred Turco, "Ibsen, Wagner, and Shaw's Changing View of 'Idealism,'" *Shaw Review*, 17 (May 1974): 78-85;

Turco, *Shaw's Moral Vision. The Self and Salvation* (Ithaca: Cornell University Press, 1976);

Turco, "Shaw's Pragmatist Ethic: A New Look at *The Quintessence of Ibsenism*," *Texas Studies in Literature and Language: A Journal of the Humanities*, 17 (Winter 1976): 855-879;

Barbara Bellow Watson, *A Shavian Guide to the Intelligent Woman* (New York: Norton, 1964);

Rodelle Weintraub, ed., *Fabian Feminist* (University Park: Pennsylvania State University Press, 1977);

Rodelle Weintraub and Stanley Weintraub, eds., *Shaw. The Annual of Bernard Shaw Studies*, continuing the *Shaw Review* (University Park: Pennsylvania State University Press, 1981-); special issues: *Shaw and Religion*, 1 (1981); *Shaw Plays in Performance*, 3 (1983); *Shaw Abroad*, 5 (1985); *The Neglected Plays*, 7 (1987);

Stanley Weintraub, "Bernard Shaw," in *Anglo-Irish Literature: A Review of Research*, edited by Richard J. Finneran (New York: Modern Language Association, 1976), pp. 167-215;

Weintraub, "Bernard Shaw," in *Recent Research on Anglo-Irish Writers—A Supplement to Anglo-Irish Literature: A Review of Research*, edited by Finneran (New York: Modern Language Association, 1983), pp. 67-84;

Weintraub, *The Unexpected Shaw: Biographical Approaches to Shaw and His Work* (New York: Ungar, 1982);

Robert F. Whitman, "Born Again: A Review of Recent Shaw Scholarship," *Texas Studies in Literature and Language: A Journal of the Humanities*, 20 (Spring 1978): 267-301;

Whitman, *Shaw and the Play of Ideas* (Ithaca: Cornell University Press, 1977);

Raymond Williams, "Shaw and Fabianism," in his *Culture and Society 1780-1950* (New York: Columbia University Press, 1958), pp. 179-185;

S. Winsten, ed., *G.B.S. 90: Aspects of Bernard*

Shaw's Life and Work (New York: Dodd, Mead, 1946);

J. L. Wisenthal, "Shaw and Ibsen," in his *Shaw and Ibsen: Bernard Shaw's The Quintessence of Ibsenism and Related Writings* (Toronto: University of Toronto Press, 1979), pp. 3-73.

Papers:

The major repositories of Shaw correspondence and manuscripts are the Shaw Archive at the British Library, London, and the Hanley Collection at the Harry Ransom Humanities Research Center, University of Texas at Austin. Other important collections are at the National Library of Ireland, the New York Public Library (Berg Collection), the University of North Carolina (Henderson Collection), Cornell University (Burgunder Collection), Bucknell University (Butler Collection), and the Houghton Library of Harvard University. The libraries of Boston University, Yale University, and Hofstra University have significant holdings as well.

Herbert Spencer
(27 April 1820-8 December 1903)

James G. Kennedy
Northern Illinois University

SELECTED BOOKS: *The Proper Sphere of Government* (London: Brittain, 1843);

Social Statics (London: Chapman, 1851; New York: Appleton, 1865; abridged, revised, and republished with *The Man 'versus' the State* (1884) (London: Williams & Norgate, 1892; New York: Appleton, 1892);

The Principles of Psychology (London: Longman, Brown, Green, Longmans, 1855; revised and enlarged, 2 volumes, London: Williams & Norgate, 1870, 1872; New York: Appleton, 1871, 1873);

Essays, Scientific, Political, and Speculative, first, second, and third series (3 volumes: volume 1, London: Longman, Brown, Green, Longmans & Roberts, 1858; volumes 2-3, London: Williams & Norgate, 1863, 1874; New York: Appleton, 1864, 1874); volumes 1-2 republished in part as *Illustrations of Universal Progress: A Series of Discussions* (New York: Appleton, 1864); revised and enlarged edition under original title, 3 volumes (London: Williams & Norgate, 1891; New York: Appleton, 1891);

First Principles (published in six parts, 1860-1862; 1 volume, London: Williams & Norgate, 1862); republished as *First Principles of a New System of Philosophy* (New York: Appleton, 1864);

Education: Intellectual, Moral, and Physical (London: Williams & Norgate, 1861; New York: Appleton, 1861);

The Principles of Biology, 2 volumes (London: Williams & Norgate, 1864, 1867; New York: Appleton, 1864, 1867; revised and enlarged, London: Williams & Norgate, 1898, 1899; New York: Appleton, 1898, 1900);

The Study of Sociology (London: King, 1873; New York: Appleton, 1874);

The Principles of Sociology, 3 volumes, 8 parts: volume 1, 3 parts (New York: Appleton, 1874-1875; London: Williams & Norgate, 1876; enlarged, London: Williams & Norgate, 1885; New York: Appleton, 1886); volume 2, part 4, published as *Ceremonial Institutions* (London: Williams & Norgate, 1879; New York: Appleton, 1880); volume 2, part 5, published as *Political Institutions* (London: Williams & Norgate, 1882; New York: Appleton, 1882); volume 3, part 6, published as *Ecclesiastical Institutions* (London: Williams & Norgate, 1885; New York: Appleton, 1886); volume 3, parts 6-8 (London: Williams & Norgate, 1896; New York: Appleton, 1896);

The Principles of Ethics, 2 volumes, 6 parts: volume 1, part 1, published as *The Data of Ethics* (London: Williams & Norgate, 1879; New York: Appleton, 1879); volume 2, part 4, published as *Justice* (London: Williams & Norgate, 1891; New York: Appleton, 1891); volume 1, parts 1, 2, and 3 (London: Williams & Norgate, 1892; New York: Appleton, 1892; volume 2, parts 4, 5, and 6 (London: Williams & Norgate, 1893; New York: Appleton, 1893);

The Man 'versus' the State (London & Edinburgh: Williams & Norgate, 1884; New York: Appleton, 1884);

The Factors of Organic Evolution (London: Williams & Norgate, 1887; New York: Appleton, 1887);

The Inadequacy of 'Natural Selection' (London: Williams & Norgate, 1893; New York: Appleton, 1893);

Various Fragments (London: Williams & Norgate, 1897; New York: Appleton, 1898; enlarged, London: Williams & Norgate, 1900; New York: Appleton, 1900);

Facts and Comments (London: Williams & Norgate, 1902; New York: Appleton, 1902);

An Autobiography, 2 volumes (London: Williams & Norgate, 1904; New York: Appleton, 1904).

OTHER: *Descriptive Sociology; or Groups of Sociological Facts*, parts 1-8, classified and arranged by Spencer, compiled and abstracted by David Duncan, Richard Schepping, and James Collier (London: Williams & Norgate, 1873-1881; New York: Appleton, 1873-1881).

In the 1860s and 1870s Herbert Spencer was the foremost living English philosopher. But he was so speculative that by 1880 in England his works rivaled those of Charles Darwin or John Stuart Mill only among libertarians and readers astonished by his ingenious scientism. His syntheses in a number of fields–political philosophy, education, metaphysics, biology, sociology, and ethics–were reductive, importing categories from biology into the human sciences. Since 1915 the post-Spencerian social sciences have separated from the natural sciences on the grounds that culture and its medium, language, are irreducible categories.

In the third quarter of his century, Spencer was a giant. To the century-old English ideology of uniform, self-acting laws of nature–Adam Smith's law of supply and demand, Thomas Malthus's law of population, and Jeremy Bentham's Utilitarian law of the natural identity of interests in society–he contributed a law of equals. He relied on a widely credited cause of biological variation, use inheritance, to assure slow progress, in both reason and moral sentiments, from the survival of the fittest in the struggle for existence in society. Even before Darwin decisively severed it from theology, he engaged in encyclopedic extensions of the biological principle of continuity (imperceptible gradations in all living things) backward from organisms to nebula and forward to mind and human society.

Yet Spencer fell into fatal errors. In his evolutionary version of the Great Chain of Being, his method was only deductive, aiming at a priori (self-evident) truths. His test of truth, invariability of belief, led him to conflate perception and conception and argue that the negation of the perception of force was inconceivable. Desirous of demonstrating both universal evolution and philosophical realism, he reduced everything, even mind, to "the Persistence of Force" (or "the persistence of some Cause which transcends our knowledge"). Aiming to show that a world without a Supreme First Cause (God) still showed universal and inevitable laws, he deduced a utopia free from all uncertainty. Use inheritance would inevitably bring about the complete congruity of a priori knowledge and the laws of nature. Then all would be just as it must be: all laws of nature would be invariable beliefs, and all would be right with the world. But at that time everything would prove everything: nothing could be a fact, for nothing would be falsifiable. It is understandable that by 1874 physicists James Clerk Maxwell and Peter Guthrie Tait insisted on precise definitions of "force" and rested belief on observation and experiment rather than on Spencer's promise of the evolution of intuitive perceptions.

Spencer was encouraged in both his assurance that the sciences were the knowledge most worth having and in his belief in self-evident and radical truths by his father, William George Spencer. Born in Derby on 27 April 1820 to Harriet Holmes Spencer, Herbert early became so painfully aware of his mother's subservience to his father, a martinet, that the son later gave it as a reason for his never marrying. A private schoolmaster, the elder Spencer was honorary secretary of the Derby Philosophical Society, founded by Erasmus Darwin in 1783 and famous in the field of English amateur science. He faithfully attended Quaker meeting Sunday mornings and practiced a fifteenth-century rebel custom, continued by the Quakers, of wearing a hat in the presence of authority. The father was a patient tutor and an always interested correspondent with his son, teaching him not to puzzle but to delight in his intuitions. The son undertook only one set of experiments in his life (on circulation of sap in plants) and mastered no field of any science, depending instead on questioning specialist friends. From his father's love of learned discussion, the son gathered that deduction best united facts. Later Thomas Henry Huxley quipped that Spencer's notion of a tragedy would be "the slaying of a beautiful deduction by an ugly fact."

In July 1833 William George Spencer took his thirteen-year-old son 130 miles to Hinton Charterhouse near Bath, where the elder Spencer's younger brother, the Reverend Thomas Spencer, a ninth wrangler at Cambridge University, was to tutor his nephew in mathematics and languages. After ten days, bitterly resenting his uncle's scholarly discipline, Herbert Spencer ran away and walked home to Derby within three days. He went back for three years' study, with summer vacations at home, and then worked as a civil engineer on a railway under one of his father's former pupils. He refused a promotion be-cause he had fallen under the spell of Uncle Thomas's politics. One of the few clergymen in the Church of England who cooperated with Dissenters, the uncle was the first chairman of the new workhouse at Bath, lectured on temperance, and agitated for the repeal of the Corn Laws and for universal male suffrage. During 1842 uncle and nephew worked through the Complete Suffrage Union with moral-force Chartist Henry Vincent. Agreeing with his uncle on individualism, Spencer wrote a series of letters for the *Nonconformist*, a militant Dissenting newspaper edited by his uncle's acquaintance Edward Miall. The letters became Spencer's first book, *The Proper Sphere of Government* (1843), in which he synthesized what he had learned secondhand from his uncle: William Paley's natural theology and Adam Smith's political economy. The message was that the Creator designed man to progress in a self-regulating economy that kept society in equilibrium. In a well-governed country, the legislature would restrict itself to the administration of justice and would not meddle in matters of health, education, poor relief, or religion, and as Thomas Spencer preached, poverty would be the result of misconduct. There was an additional sign that the nephew could not yet resist his uncle's influence. Having read of J. B. Lamarck's theories of transmutation of species in Charles Lyell's *Principles of Geology* in 1840, Spencer proposed both inheritance of a tendency to morality and his uncle's belief in the visitation of the sins of one generation on generations to come.

Thomas Spencer's connections eventually led Herbert Spencer to a job in London in 1848. Having been introduced by his uncle to a Liverpool merchant, the nephew so successfully introduced the man to liberal Whigs in Derby that they made the merchant their candidate and then their M.P. In return, Spencer received easy work as a copyreader for the *Economist*, the key financial weekly for the newly wealthy who believed in individualism. In London, Spencer lived across the street from John Chapman's publishing business and boardinghouse, where he met Mary Ann Evans after Chapman had published his *Social Statics* in 1851. (The future George Eliot professed her love for Spencer in July 1852, but, not returning her favor, he soon introduced her to George Henry Lewes.) At the *Economist*, one of the editors, Thomas Hodgskin, opened his library and mind to his young colleague. Spencer did not learn Hodgskin's critique of the exchange value of labor in classical economics but did adopt Hodgskin's individualism and his confidence in the uniformity of nature even in economic and social phenomena.

The result was *Social Statics*, an attack on Utilitarianism and an affirmation of the natural rights of individuals that verged on anarchism. Spencer rejected Bentham's empirical ethics because people could never know enough to calculate the consequences of their acts and because human nature was both indefinitely variable and improving, not uniform and simple (and mean) as Bentham had supposed. He held that Bentham had contradicted himself in denying natural rights while maintaining the greatest number's right to happiness. Instead Spencer proposed an absolute ethic for people to keep before them as they progressed toward perfection. He posited an innate moral sense (a premise of the Scottish common-sense philosophers), which guided people to the natural exercise of their faculties (Paley's definition of happiness). Since God willed that people be happy, He intended that people should be free to use their faculties. So people had an instinct (or intuitive perception) of their natural rights to exercise their capabilities.

They also had, as a reflex of this innate sense of personal rights, an innate sympathy for others (an idea adapted from Adam Smith), from which developed a sentiment of justice, or respect for others' rights.

Spencer's conclusion, then, about social relationships was that each person had freedom to do all his/her will, provided that he/she did not infringe (that is, directly block) the equal freedom of another. Since private land ownership infringed on the equal freedom of landless people to use the earth, people would eventually nationalize the land and lease it to the highest bidders. Also equal freedom dictated suffrage for workers and for all women and recognition of children's rights and of the right to ignore the State. Legislation for any purpose other than justice could only interfere with the slow movement toward a perfect society, where each individual would be a self-sufficient person who would both spontaneously fulfill his or her nature and incidentally perform social functions. Then society would be harmonious, government would be unnecessary, and complete civilization would result from complete individuality. Meanwhile, in the present transi-

Spencer's parents, Harriet and William George Spencer

tion between savage and social life, many generations of men and women would have to suffer the harsh discipline of labor, study, and postponement of gratification until human nature became perfectly adapted to social existence. Private charity might aid victims or those who helped themselves; but the improvident, the faithless, the weak, the unhealthy, and the imbecile members of society were "nature's failures," whom it would be wrong to aid.

Prior to publication Spencer had revised *Social Statics* twice according to a theory of effective English sentences that he had culled in 1843-1844 from rhetoricians' handbooks. In 1852 *Westminster Review* published "The Philosophy of Style," in which he displayed his time's view that written symbols should enable a simple correspondence of thoughts and feelings in both writer and reader. More interestingly, he proposed that forcible expression in English could be achieved by proliferating sentence beginnings. Encountering first a series of phrasal or clausal qualifications, an educated reader would gain speed in comprehension and apprehend the delayed base subject with most force. In recommending such left-branching sentences and *Paradise Lost* as a model, Spencer did not note that Milton had metrical stress to override the right-branching tendency of English syntax. The many introductory elements in Spencer's own sentences divert beginning stress from subjects and produce blandness. By practicing his theory, Spencer generated long sentences against the grain of the language and produced the illusion that an unflurried omniscience was letting facts speak for themselves.

As early as 1852, Spencer believed that he had a "sensation" in store for thoughtful readers; and when he began writing *The Principles of Psychology* in 1854, he felt it would be as important as "Newton's *Principia*." In 1853 he had published "The Universal Postulate" in Chapman's *Westminster Review*, and he based part one of his psychology on this essay. Following theists Sir William Hamilton and William Whewell, he proposed the inconceivability of its negation as the test of every truth and argued that absolute uniformities in thought corresponded to absolute uniformities in things. To Spencer's claim that no one could deny belief when a subject and a predicate invariably united in thought, John Stuart Mill replied that belief did not rule out conception of the converse. Mill's point was only a verbal quibble to Spencer, who saw the transition from perception

to conception as indefinite as that between instinct and perception. He extended to mental phenomena the principle of continuity in animal species that he had already affirmed in "The Development Hypothesis" (1851) and had read in Robert Chambers's anonymously published *Vestiges of the Natural History of Creation* (1844). The advance in intelligence in living things correlated with the minute stages of development in nervous organization. As from organism to organism nervous systems showed imperceptible gradations, so mind developed insensibly from the sense of touch, and then from the other senses, to reasoning. Spencer's psychology was original for directing students of mind to biology rather than introspection and for extending learning by association from the individual's experience to the experiences of the species. Through environmentally produced modifications in the nervous system that were handed down by a very long series of human and animal ancestors, the experience philosophy could explain all mental relations, including reflexes, instincts, and intuitions (for example, of space and time). All impetus came from external forces; the brain and the mind simply adjusted and modified each other in the process over time. Free will was an illusion to Spencer since he had no conception of people's resources in language for initiating and sharing choices.

The American positivist Chauncey Wright objected (in 1865) that both in *Social Statics* and in *The Principles of Psychology* Spencer had elevated hypotheses, which could be tested by experience, into absolute tests of experience. Just as Spencer's moral sense derived from observation and had only relative authority, so the authority of invariable beliefs depended wholly on experience, and their cause, uniformities in nature, was only probable. Few read the first edition of Spencer's work on psychology.

Spencer's health broke down when he was at the height of his evolutionary argument in 1855, and thereafter he had to limit his daily work. But from 1857 to 1859, he produced many long essays, including "Progress: Its Law and Cause," "Transcendental Physiology," and "The Nebular Hypothesis"; and "Moral Education," "Physical Education," and "What Knowledge is of Most Worth?" The first three, along with essays from 1854, appeared in his *Essays, Scientific, Political, and Speculative* (1858-1874); the second three, with "Intellectual Education" from 1854, in *Education: Intellectual, Moral, and Physical* (1861). In "Progress" he applied Karl von Baer's law of embryological development from the homogeneous to the heterogeneous to all manner of human and natural phenomena and attributed heterogeneity (or, progress) to an inevitable multiplication of effects from every cause. In the essay on physiology, he identified the instability of the homogeneous as the origin of evolution and integration as a secondary process in evolution. The essay on a nebular origin for the solar system enabled him to point to continuity in the heavens (diffused matter insensibly condensing into a system in equilibrium) as well as on earth, without appealing to the First Cause of natural theology. In both "Progress" and "What Knowledge is of Most Worth?" he singled out the "sincere man of science" as truly religious because he is aware of "the unknowable," of the impossibility of absolute knowledge about external or internal worlds.

T. H. Huxley, who had met him in 1852, recalled Spencer as the only person who had been a respectable, thorough evolutionist before 1858. From his *Essays, Scientific, Political, and Speculative* of that year, Spencer began to sketch a mechanics of "evolution," a word he thought free of the anthropomorphic associations of progress. He drew the ideas of correlation and conservation of physical forces from William R. Grove's syntheses *On the Correlation of Physical Forces* (1846) and added views of motion as rhythmical and along the line of least resistance. During the next two years, he found his explanation of universal evolution (that is, heterogeneity) in an ongoing redistribution of matter and motion and rested all physical processes on the mystery he called the Persistence of Force. In the spring of 1860, he sought subscriptions for ten volumes of "Synthetic Philosophy." Because of his admittedly limited knowledge in some areas, he never wrote three of the volumes: two on astronomic and geologic evolution and one on the sociology of language, science, and the fine arts. He wrote all the others, including double volumes on biology, psychology, and ethics and three volumes on sociology, and began at once writing a volume on metaphysics, *First Principles*. Before he had finished it, he produced *Education: Intellectual, Moral, and Physical*, drawing from his father's practice and works by Joseph Priestley and Claude Marcel. He emphasized science as the most practical study and the most effective discipline and counseled teachers to rely on sympathy not authority, to invent examples beyond the textbook to engage students, to trust to the natural consequences of their actions to punish students, and to balance study with physical exercise, including free play. Eventually all but one of the teacher-training colleges in England made *Education* required reading. In writing the longer second part of *First Principles*, Spencer followed his own advice (and perhaps his practice during three months of schoolteaching under his father in 1837) by introducing his "principles through the medium of examples."

Spencer's most influential book, *First Principles* (1862), aimed to reconcile science and religion and provide a *"completely-unified* knowledge" in a formula of evolution. Mark Francis, in his 1973 dissertation at Cambridge University, has placed the book as the culmination of "the new reformation," a radical movement in the 1850s for freedom of instinctive religious feelings, led by Leigh Hunt, James Martineau, and Francis W. Newman. Supporters, including John Tyndall, W. R. Greg, George Henry Lewes, John Chapman, George Eliot, and Sara Hennell, rallied around the weekly review the *Leader*, in which Spencer had published "The Development Hypothesis." They opposed natural theology and, like the Scottish common-sense philosophers, favored self-evident first principle, basing faith, for example, on an inborn sense of the Infinite. In part one of *First Principles*, Spencer turned upside down the arguments of Henry L. Mansel (*The Limits of Religious Thought Examined*, 1858) and Sir William Hamilton ("On the Philosophy of the Unconditioned," 1829). They had proposed that, given mutually contradictory inconceivables–Mansel, Absolute: First Cause: Infinite; Hamilton, Infinite: Absolute–the law of noncontradiction would require one of them to be true and so would imply existence beyond human conception. Their aim was to bid readers, then, to believe their religious feelings as something inconceivable. Spencer used their arguments not to point to faith but to affirm the necessity of something beyond thought. A scientist's religion would admit an unknowable reality underlying basic concepts: space, time, force, matter, consciousness. He had already taken this position in "Progress: Its Law and Cause" and in "The Nebular Hypothesis," in which he had hailed an "Unknown Power," "a First Cause . . . transcending the 'mechanical God of Paley,' " the esteemed theologian of design in nature. In *First Principles* Spencer pointed to the persistence (that is, the recurrence) in the mind of something surviving all changes in relation and attributed it to the Persistence of Force everywhere. So in part one of *First Principles*, his philosophy became assimilable to the perennial philosophy, especially Chinese Tao-ism (circa 300 B.C.), which speaks of the Unnamable as the origin of all things. His speculations were enthusiastically received by the New Reformationists and, as Ronald E. Martin shows in *American Literature and the Universe of Force* (1981), by idealists in the United States who wished a vague religiosity to accompany their faith in progress.

In part two, Spencer presented evolution as if it were a universal law. He actually sketched only a trend from homogeneity to heterogeneity, through concatenations of the effects of motion in matter, which led to segregation and integration of matter, disintegration of motion, equilibrium, and then dissolution. Of his examples, only facts from embryology were unquestionable; all the others were at best hypotheses—the conservation of force, for example—and often were only question-begging characterizations of social phenomena. (One tautology set the evolutionary limit of an individual as a perfect adjustment of mental force and all surrounding forces of the industrial society in an equilibrium of supply and demand.) Though aiming at the history of every object from inception to disintegration, Spencer began not with the origin of the universe but with the nebular theory of the solar system. He used correlations of forces, but, in spite of Tyndall's warning, he did not credit William Thomson's second law of thermodynamics. Though the amount of energy available for work was decreasing, Spencer supposed that the radiation of the stars would not be lost and would gradually return integrated matter to nebular form. Scientists—James Clerk Maxwell, Peter Tait, William James, Karl Pearson—objected to his vague use of the term *force*. Rather than precise measurements of space relations, a priori Persistence of Force was the basis of Spencer's concepts of matter and motion. Yet the apparent comprehensiveness and coherence of *First Principles* impressed many: T. H. Huxley, who read the proofs; John Fiske, Olive Schreiner, Hamlin Garland, Lafcadio Hearn, Theodore Dreiser, Arnold Bennett, Jack London. In appearing to bind the smallest things with the greatest, Spencer's definition of cosmic evolution seemed to be a natural law promising progressive harmony.

Meanwhile Charles Darwin had published *On the Origin of Species* in 1859. The year before he had seen Spencer's 1851 essay on development by "continual modifications due to change of circumstances" and admired it. In 1852 Spencer had also written on population pressure ("Theory of Population Deduced from the General Law of Animal Fertility"), identifying as "select" those survivors whose nervous systems developed in inverse relation to their fertility. By this law Spencer could find in population increase, contrary to Thomas Malthus, "the proximate cause of progress" which involved "enlargement of the nervous centre." Having made no special study of individual variation, Spencer's optimism in 1852 about the perfectibility of the human species was even stronger than his individualism. In contrast, when Darwin had read Malthus in September 1838, he had seen life as an individual struggle for existence in which advantageous differences between individuals led to survival of individuals and so gradually to the inception of new species. Spencer the evolutionist was taken unawares in 1859 by Darwin's argument from contemporary data of slow variation in living things to a universal gradual variation of organisms in time, through natural selection. In separate essays in 1857, 1858, and 1859, Spencer had been insisting that physical conditions, specifically, incident forces, were the cause of organic modifications and that use inheritance was "the *only* law [of 'gradual differentiation'] of which we have any evidence." (The essays were "Transcendental Physiology," "A Criticism on Professor Owen's Theory of the Vertebrate Skeleton," and "The Laws of Organic Form.") He never relinquished his view that the environment, and not individual variation, was the proximate cause of organic evolution. However, he gave room to Darwin's theory in the first edition of the two-volume *The Principles of Biology*, on which he worked for four years after finishing *First Principles*. Only after Darwin's death did he feel compelled to assert the primacy of his own law, the inheritance of acquired characteristics.

In volume one of his biology (1864), Spencer presented data and inductions, as he would do in the first volumes of his psychology (revised and enlarged), his sociology, and his ethics. He wished to explain by physical causes the contingency, the randomness of Darwinian evolution. An organism was a moving equilibrium of incident forces and physiological functions. In what has been called Spencer's Law (though it was anticipated by Rudolf Leuckart and Galileo), he correlated weight and volume with cubes of dimensions, and strength and surface with squares of dimensions. So increase in size meant less surface area for heat loss and for absorption of food.

Also weight of birds and growth in land animals were limited compared with the possibilities of whales, pike, and crocodiles, which were supported by the water they displaced. Although correspondence of internal and external was characteristic of life, Spencer saw that as an organism counteracted external changes, it became less like its environment. To account for use inheritance, he postulated that everywhere in the organism, physiological units of subcell size bore (by polarity) individual traits established by inheritance. Trusting to Persistence of Force, he argued that local adaptations to external forces would superimpose new traits on all units, no matter how distant, including those in the germ cells. But because units were already the result of innumerable ancestral adaptations, new individual functions would have infinitesimal effect, and even after continuing for generations, very little effect, on structure. So hereditary change would be glacially slow. What Darwin had called spontaneous variation could be explained by miscellaneous combinations of units. A fertilized egg might receive different numbers of units from each parent and each grandparent, and the embryo might receive incident forces that distributed parental and ancestral units still more unequally.

Spencer and Darwin shared some common grounds in biology. First, Spencer's elegant physiological units were only a version of the ancient idea of pangenesis, the collection in the germ cells of particles from the rest of the organism. Darwin produced his own version, calling the particles gemmules. Second, both did not clearly distinguish biological and social evolution. With different emphases, both promised that use inheritance and the struggle for existence brought about progress; both neglected innovation and transmission of traits in culture through language. Third, Spencer invented, and Darwin adopted, *survival of the fittest* as a clearer term than *natural selection*. But both neglected how the substitute term distracted attention from the survival of offspring to that of individuals and how the use of the superlative was not absolutely accurate: the *fit* had descendants. Fourth, Spencer elevated use inheritance from a subordinate role in Lamarck's theory of progressive biological change, to priority, as "direct equilibration," over natural selection ("indirect equilibration"), which at best only accelerated modification. Darwin at first refuted but later adopted use and disuse as causes of modification that were equal to natural selection. Neither saw illogicality in supposing

that a function arising in response to conditions in one life could recur without regard to conditions in a descendant's life.

For volume two of *The Principles of Biology* (1867), Spencer drew many of the figures, recorded microscopic observations of the circulation of sap, and was well pleased with the result. He deduced the differentiation of homologous parts from dissimilar incident forces acting over generations. So vertebral columns and layers of wood resulted from persistent transverse strains exerted by muscles on notochords and by winds on stems. As he recited his spell of the redistribution of matter as a result of motion, Spencer slipped into calling the Persistence of Force "the deepest knowable cause" of organic change and an "ultimate fact," whereas in *First Principles* he had described it as "the persistence of some Cause which transcends our knowledge and conception." Also in volume two, casting nutrition and reproduction as antithetical, he expanded to all organisms his view of 1852 that population pressure encouraged development. But in the revised and enlarged edition of volume two published in 1899, he foresaw 21,000-year climatic cycles and withdrew the perfectibility of the human species that he had forecast in 1867 and 1851. Although both Mill and Darwin said that all in all Spencer's biology was wonderfully clever, the latter remarked that only years of work could establish the scientific value of its speculations. T. H. Huxley and Joseph Hooker had read the proofs of both volumes for mistakes in zoological and botanical facts, but in the 1880s and 1890s Spencer was unaided when in several articles in the *Contemporary Review*, he challenged Darwin's arguments from correlated growth (or coadaptation) and August Weismann's from the specialization of germ cells.

In 1864 Mill had praised Spencer for affiliating mind and nerves: that is, for showing that mental and neural events could be viewed as counterparts, rather than opposites. The adjustments of internal, physiological environments to external environments implied the parallelism of psychological phenomena to physiological phenomena. Spencer developed this idea of psychological parallelism in detail in the second, revised and enlarged edition of *The Principles of Psychology* (1870, 1872). Sometimes he made it clear that he was paralleling discontinuous series of phenomena each of which had its own order. He acknowledged again and again that subjective relations did not obtain beyond consciousness and that one could know only feelings. But his evolutionary associationism impelled him to deduce development of not only the nervous system but also the mind, from causal relations between environment, nerves, and feelings. Going beyond David Hartley's suggestion that vibrations in the nerves paralleled association of ideas, he misleadingly called the unit of feeling a "nervous shock." So, arguing that our only conception of force was a perception of resistance, based on feelings of muscular tension, he asserted that feelings were mental forces transformable into physical forces capable of exercising nerves and muscles.

While dictating his biology and then revising his psychology, Spencer acquired several badges of success. In December 1864 Huxley included him in a new dinner club of a few leading agnostic men of science, the X Club, which convened before the monthly Royal Society meeting. In 1856 Spencer had been disappointed not to have been nominated for the Royal Society for his psychology, and he refused to be a candidate in 1874 and declined eighteen honors from overseas learned societies from 1876 to 1897. But he missed few gatherings of the X Club until it lapsed in the 1890s, even attending the meeting a week after his father's death in 1866. In 1862 he had met an American correspondent, advocate, and editor, Edward L. Youmans, who not only went on to lecture about the Synthetic Philosophy but also founded the *Popular Science Monthly* in 1872, to publish Spencer's essays. In 1866 Spencer received $7,000 in securities from American admirers when he announced that he could not afford to continue having his *Principles of Biology* published. In 1868, when he was elected to the Athenaeum Club, the resort in London of many male middle-class intellectuals, he found lifetime facilities for such conversation as his nerves would allow and for reading periodicals, playing billiards, dining, and napping. Finally, he began to pay the expenses of three assistants who, starting in 1867, 1870, and 1872, digested for him hundreds of books on primitive and civilized peoples. Using tables of Spencer's devising, the three scholars compiled extracts from travelers' reports and tabulated the historical characteristics of many societies in return for shares of the profits from eight volumes entitled *Descriptive Sociology* (1873-1881). In 1859 Spencer had declared that descriptions of institutions were "the only [practical] history"; but when the series did not sell, he covered his costs with his American friends' gift and with profits from *The Study of Sociology*

(1873). This collection of articles, his prolegomena to an account of the evolution of social groups, has been the most popular work of general sociology ever produced in England.

Perhaps the most memorable portion of this volume is Spencer's case (in chapter nine, "The Bias of Patriotism") against Matthew Arnold's charge (in 1864 in "The Function of Criticism at the Present Time") that England lacked a disinterested, speculative criticism of ideas. Marshaling British contributions to logic, mathematics, and the natural sciences, Spencer easily found Arnold guilty of "the bias of anti-patriotism." The poet, in his attack on Englishmen's liking for the practical, had not specified scientific ideas as among the best thoughts in the world. The leading idea of *The Study of Sociology* is that the individuals, or units, in a society, or aggregate, determine its nature. Preparation in biology, Spencer argued, would enable a sociologist to assume that acculturation proceeded only through inherited modifications and that the functions of social groups, both in the economy and the state, conformed, like functions of body organs and limbs, to the zoologist Henri Milne-Edwards's idea of a physiological division of labor. Preparation in psychology would enable the sociologist to see the motives of social change as individuals' feelings and thoughts and to look for the origins of those in prehistory. Women's feelings and ideas, for example, were socially conservative because among savages and ever since their reproductive role had lessened their mental capacities and led them to admire power more than freedom. Spencer's account of social change included no term—like network or class—to correlate individuals' feelings and social relations, apparently because his Radical upbringing left him unable to conceive of an elite as a force for social change. Nevertheless *The Study of Sociology* became the introductory text and Spencer the leading figure for this new field in the United States, where William Graham Sumner won faculty permission to use the book at Yale in 1881.

By 1876 Spencer had completed volume one of *The Principles of Sociology*, including accounts of the savage mind, the social organism, and domestic institutions. He had anticipated the second topic in *Social Statics* and in "The Social Organism" (1860). His aim was to show that society was a moving equilibrium of structures resulting from, and in turn changing, the functions of individuals (that is, what they do, not what they intend). To illustrate this concept, he asserted analogous mutual dependence of parts in animals and nations, without admitting that biology had not proven that organic systems were fully integrated. Neither had political economy shown that social structures were clearly separate in functions. He applied Spencer's Law: increase of mass brought increase of structure in organisms and societies. He deduced that as an organism grew in size by compounding groups of cells, so a tribe had a process of compounding to go through (during wars) before becoming a nation. He argued that as late-evolved organs might develop early in an embryo, so in recent societies institutions might soon appear though they had appeared late in older societies. The cause would be modifications in human nature, not conscious social imitation and planning. He elaborated parallels between organic and social systems because he was committed to continuity between animal and human aggregates. He paralleled animal digestive and vascular systems with a society's industrial base and transportation network and sympathetic and vasomotor nervous systems with industrial and financial regulating systems. As conflict with other organisms developed an animal's nervomotor coordinating system, so war was the sole initiator of both cooperation and centralized government among primitive people. Always an individualist, however, Spencer limited his organicism by locating consciousness only in persons and by refusing to idealize any state as the mind of its society.

Spencer's account of primitive people found them first living in isolation, unrestrainedly following their impulses: animal, sexual, and parental instincts and a childlike love of approbation. Postulating that the laws of thought were the same everywhere, Spencer deduced that savages, like civilized people, classified objects and relations by likeness and presupposed causality. Seeing changes around them, they supposed metamorphosis; seeing the living lose and regain animation, they imagined a spirit double that left and returned to a body. So they developed funeral rites, then worship of ancestral spirits, animal ancestors, totems, and deities. In this way, Spencer thought to discredit claims of innate ideas of deity; but by reducing religion to fear and worship of ancestors, he neglected feelings of awe and reports of magic later used by James Frazer (*The Golden Bough*, 1890). He also neglected the work of Edward B. Tylor, who had anticipated Spencer's ghost-theory. Part three, "Domestic Institutions," began with the commonplace nine-

Portrait of Spencer painted in 1872 by J. B. Burgess (National Portrait Gallery)

teenth-century views that primitive people were promiscuous and that matriliny was usual. Spencer deduced that from living as brutes people had evolved kinship groups and that marriage relations had universally shown evolution from simple to complex: polyandry to polygyny to monogamy. In fact, society had preceded kinship systems and marriage relations, which had evolved divergently within different societies, monogamy having often been early, and matriliny often absent.

Spencer's new idea in 1877, when he began *Ceremonial Institutions* (1879), was that earliest government consisted in ceremonies, but that preoccupation with badges of honor was now retrogressive in the present day. That year he turned from sociology to writing "a code of natural ethics" to show that his philosophy could be a guide to right living. The result, *The Data of Ethics*, part one of *The Principles of Ethics*, renewed his attack (from *Social Statics*) on the Utilitarians' calculation of pleasures but now explained moral intuitions by evolution rather than by God's will. Since he still held that mankind was changing for the better (but the Utilitarians did not), he insisted that people needed to keep in view fully evolved conduct (which he confusingly called Absolute Ethics) rather than expediency. The three highest moral emotions–the egoistic sentiment of liberty and the altruistic sentiments of self-restraint and generosity–would become moral intuitions in all people only when war ceased and population pressure lessened. Until then, people would be least wrong to seek to enhance life by subordinating simpler feelings to more complex ones and by identifying with others' complex satisfactions.

To his ethics, Spencer brought from his psychology his idea that the brain was a register of an infinite number of ancestral experiences. People could adjust to social life by trusting their preferences for physical pleasures; such desires would derive from organic benefits inherited from earlier life-preserving or life-enhancing experiences. Since many ancestral experiences, however, would have been antisocial (by Spencer's account of savages), people needed to distrust emotional preferences for immediate gratification and to favor feelings that aimed at remote pleasures. In this way they would accumulate experiences of justice, providence, and beneficence (participation in others' pleasures). Many generations' repetitions of such remote pleasures would establish, through inheritance, such organic effects that people would feel the highest sentiments and spontaneously act to increase agreeable feelings for themselves and others. In the short run, conscience would continue to coerce people, and sympathies for the improvident would be too painful and unwise to indulge. In the long run, people would become perfectly just and kind.

Spencer admitted that his account might seem valid only to an optimist, but fifteen years later he was hurt when Huxley rejected instincts as guides to conduct. Utilitarian Henry Sidgwick and intuitionist G. E. Moore both pointed out that Spencer may have explained the evolution of people's desire for pleasure, but he had not shown why people were right to value it. He needed to argue not only that remote pleasures work out for the best in the long run but also that no one should wish any other good now– general happiness or beauty, for example. It did not occur to Spencer to do this, because his psychology was determinist: very slow evolving feelings were prior to and stronger than reasoning; indeed, will was a surplus of feeling and only apparently free. In his ethics, sociology, and political writings, however, Spencer implied that searching one's feelings for those tending to increase life for self, offspring, and worthy others would make preference for those feelings self-evident.

In 1880 and 1881, as he was dictating *Political Institutions*, part five of *The Principles of Sociology*, Spencer became incensed with recent actions of the English State: regulative legislation at home and military interventions in Egypt. His lifelong distrust of government was reinforced by his findings that political organization had evolved from chieftainships into militant societies and only recently had begun to develop structures that could become industrial societies. In militant societies, such as Sparta, Incan Peru, czarist Russia, a despotic, hierarchical central administration compelled the cooperation of all individuals in its projects and honored patriotism, bravery, and faith. Industrial society, which Spencer hoped would organize in Britain, would have only government specialized for defense and negative regulation of individuals' aggressions or breaches of contract. The society would aim at free trade and world peace. Individuals would be free to cooperate or compete and would value each other's freedom and all peaceful occupations. Little interested in political history, Spencer was unaware that he was reworking a traditional contrast of civil and military societies. Still a Radical antagonist of rank and connections, he sharply contrasted two types of societies but neglected to show how the first could evolve into the second.

In the summer of 1881, Spencer initiated the Anti-Aggression League against English imperialism and felt he had spoken well against military adventurism at the first (and only) meeting of the league in June 1882. In the fall of 1882, he toured northeastern United States, a guest of Youmans and Andrew Carnegie, and spoke to an assemblage at Delmonico's, an audience of businessmen, lawyers, editors, clergy, scientists, and educators. Worn out by these exertions, he rested but soon decided to warn English Liberals that they were deserting individualism and becoming new Tories. The occasion was Tory leader Lord Salisbury's support for public housing, consistent with Disraeli's policy (from 1874 to 1880) of government intervention to solve social problems. Spencer's "The New Toryism" (one of four essays in *Contemporary Review*, 1884) overlooked the fact that since 1833 first the Whig and then the Liberal parties had included both interventionists (such as Edwin Chadwick) and individualists (such as John Bright). Even the latter group had favored some legislation for welfare. Indeed Spencer, in a second essay, "The Coming Slavery," recalled the example of his Uncle Thomas, who, by enforcing the New Poor Law of 1834 in his parish, had been the government's agent in reducing both pauperism and the rates (the tax paid for public aid). However, much more than Liberals who legislated for education or sanitation, Spencer abhorred the socialists (such as H. M. Hyndman and Henry George), whom he saw as not only interfering with people's accepting the consequences of their own conduct but also advocating retrogression to a militant society of slaves. Only the sufferings of free individuals could eventually induce cures for character defects. In two more essays, "The Sins of Legislators" and "The Great Political Superstition," Spencer admonished legislators to consider remote results, not calculate immediate effects. Only the laws of nature could remold the average national character; legislators should never tax or restrict "the better" (he meant the fittest) for the sake of the "idle and improvident." People's natural rights took precedence over legal rights bestowed by any state; minorities might not acknowledge majority rule when it infringed on such a natural right as the use of one's own property. In 1884 Spencer collected the four essays as *The Man 'versus' the State*.

In 1885 he returned to *The Principles of Sociology*, recording in *Ecclesiastical Institutions*, part six, that on the whole clerical agencies had been useful, especially in teaching postponement of gratification, a finding surprising from one whom Mill had found "as anti-clergymanish as possible." The next year Spencer's earnestness about social evolution led him to attack Darwin's emphases on correlated growth and natural selection and to elevate environmental forces and use inheritance as the major initiators of evolution in higher animals. As late as 1883, Spencer had declared Darwin's factors "a chief cause." But in *The Factors of Organic Evolution* (in *Nineteenth Century*, 1886, and published in book form the following year), he neglected one of his own first principles, the multiplication of effects, and argued that in Darwin's account an improbable number of unrelated variations had combined to produce the giraffe's neck. Citing Darwin's *Variation of Animals and Plants under Domestication* (1868), Spencer was intent on showing that natural selection was dependent upon natural forces having first caused modifications in structure. As he explained in his 1895 preface to *The Factors of Organic Evolution*, use inheritance produced all complex mental phenomena and molded people "far more rapidly and comprehensively" than natural

selection could do.

Spencer may have been gradually enfeebled by his nightly use of morphine, which he continued despite his father's death from an overdose. In any event, he became an invalid in 1886 and turned to dictating his autobiography, which he had begun in 1875, intending that it be published posthumously. When he had finished it in 1889 and still survived, he returned first to *The Principles of Ethics*, part four, *Justice* (1891). As it had been years earlier (in *The Proper Sphere of Government* and *Social Statics*), his topic was social justice among adult human individuals: the equal freedom of every person to use, without interference, life, land, private property, exchange, and free speech. An individual was entitled to his or her gains, provided he/she had not directly blocked or injured another. Now Spencer grounded justice not in God's will but in biology. Over innumerable generations, he argued, an early instinct of personal rights had evolved into an egotistic sentiment of liberty and finally into an a priori belief in equal freedom. Further advance in human life required that adults accept the consequences of their activities and natures. While it was just to treat the young according to need, adults had to live with inherited superiorities or inferiorities in body, mind, or circumstances. Government should function only as an umpire of equal freedom. As such, it should defend the poor against aggressions by the rich, restrict pollution of the air, and supervise new uses of land and water. Although he still acknowledged the justice of public ownership of the land, he saw no just way to achieve it, since he credited all land values (and land taxes paid) to landowners rather than to unpaid-for labor (Hodgskin) and population increase (Henry George).

In 1892 Spencer abridged and revised *Social Statics*, retracting his early support not only for public lands but also for workers' and woman suffrage, children's rights, and the right to ignore the State, as well as much on equal freedom, on the ground that his *Justice* was definitive. He introduced, however, the view that moral feeling in individuals was a force that could not be increased by government: the conservation of force was "as true in ethics as in physics." Although he was once again extending continuity from matter to mind until all tautologically was the Persistence of Force, his aim was to defend the phenomena of self-help and altruism, which at the same time he was explaining in the remaining parts of *The Principles of Ethics*. In 1893, in part five, "Negative Beneficence," he counseled mercy toward those suffering losses through circumstances that were not their fault. In part six, "Positive Beneficence," he advised that while government had nothing to do with personal outcomes freely incurred, persons should give relief to "the good poor." He encouraged sympathy not only toward the sick or unemployed who were provident but also toward those suffering from inferiorities in nature or upbringing. But justice overruled sympathy to the improvident. His determinism led Spencer to consider no other ground for an individual's desert of benefits above what competition brought except the potential in him or her for advance of life. He was aware of the long working day and the privations of the English people. But he saw no remedy and advised restraint of sympathy, unless it not only lessened another's pain but also contributed to the survival of the fittest and so hastened happiness for future generations.

Also in 1893 and 1894, under the general title "The Inadequacy of 'Natural Selection,'" Spencer wrote four essays for the *Contemporary Review* against August Weismann's theory that germ cells were unaffected by individual adaptations. Holding that "right beliefs, not only in Biology and Psychology, but also in Education, Ethics, and Politics" derived from the role of use inheritance in evolution, he argued that Weismann's theory was inconceivable. He could imagine his own physiological units, but he could not think how a germ cell could carry all the variables for a peacock's feather. Once again, he denied that correlated growth and natural selection were sufficient causes, although A. R. Wallace and Weismann had already falsified use inheritance with the evidence that unused organs never disappeared. Moreover, Weismann had found use and disuse an unnecessary hypothesis deduced from, rather than explaining, the facts of variation and so had emphasized geographical diversity rather than individual adaptation. Spencer's essays were published in book form in 1893, under the general title he had given them for the *Contemporary Review*.

In 1896 Spencer completed *The Principles of Sociology*, publishing parts seven and eight, on professional and industrial institutions, together with part six as volume three. In the division of labor, he described specialization as the line of least resistance for the individual and voluntary piecework as the highest form of combined labor, thereby revealing his own social place as a thinker working

alone at will with language. Never having worked cooperatively with others on a project, he underestimated to the end people's capabilities to cooperate with and for others and to generate options through communication in language. The least evolutionary part of his sociology, his account of industrial society did not describe how competition had already led to concentration of capital and monopolies in the marketplace. So he did not foresee the next consequences: rationalization of the workplace and bureaucratization of management. He ended his sociology as he had begun: with the caveat that not every society evolved; only all societies together met his definition of "increase of heterogeneity."

Spencer retraced the steps of his thinking in "The Filiation of Ideas" (1899), a piece first published in David Duncan's 1908 biography. Translations of his works had been available in Europe and Japan since the 1870s, and he was nominated for the Nobel Prize for Literature in 1902. Spencer's influence was most potent in the United States, where in the 1890s three Supreme Court justices avowed his political philosophy, recognized corporations as individuals, and rejected government interference in regulating hours of work, wage minimums, and child labor. In the United States more than 365,000 volumes of his works had sold in authorized editions by the end of 1903; perhaps as many more in Britain; and sixty translations in nine languages may have brought the total to a million sold. When he died on 8 December 1903, Spencer had made the fortune by philosophy that he had joked about to Youmans in 1872. He left an estate that by today's standards would be worth half a million dollars, sufficient to fund publication of *Descriptive Sociology* until 1934.

Though seen by some admirers as a second Newton, Spencer never trained himself to do precise scientific work. Instead he was a master of scientism, first naturalizing cosmological categories such as Force in speculations on scientific fields and then transferring such apparently scientific categories as incident forces to discussions of humanity and society. He also could arouse religious feelings when he transferred such a scientific term as *energy* to cosmology: though scientists achieved the largest conceptions, their thoughts were inadequate to the "Infinite and Eternal Energy" of the universe. Unfortunately, in tracing continuity across such diverse phenomena, he reduced variables to elementary mechanics and plunged his biology and psychology, as well as his metaphysics, into the tautology Persistence of Force. Because his sociology and ethics rested on his biology and psychology, his system has suffered a Humpty-Dumptian fate. Some points have been salvaged: Spencer's Law, the survival of the fittest, functionalism, and the law of equal freedom, which has fared best, especially among anarchists and libertarians.

Biographies:

[The Misses Baker], *Home Life with Herbert Spencer by Two*, edited by A. G. L. Rogers (Bristol: J. W. Arrowsmith, 1906);

David Duncan, *The Life and Letters of Herbert Spencer* (London: Methuen, 1908).

References:

Robert C. Bannister, *Social Darwinism: Science and Myth in Anglo-American Social Thought* (Philadelphia: Temple University Press, 1979), pp. 34-96;

Ernest Barker, *Political Thought in England from Spencer to the Present* (New York: Holt, 1915), pp. 84-132;

Edward Bristow, "The Liberty and Property Defense League and Individualism," *Historical Journal*, 18 (December 1975): 761-789;

J. W. Burrow, *Evolution and Society: A Study in Victorian Social Theory* (Cambridge: Cambridge University Press, 1966), pp. 179-227;

Joseph A. Buttigieg, "Individual Freedom in a Structured Universe: Spencer, Galsworthy, and *The Man of Property*," *Research Studies*, 48 (December 1980): 198-209;

Robert L. Carneiro, "Herbert Spencer as an Anthropologist," *Journal of Libertarian Studies*, 5 (Spring 1981): 153-210;

Carneiro, Introduction to *The Evolution of Society: Selections from Herbert Spencer's 'Principles of Sociology,'* edited by Carneiro (Chicago: University of Chicago Press, 1967), pp. ix-lvii;

Frederick B. Churchill, "The Weismann-Spencer Controversy over the Inheritance of Acquired Characters," in *Human Implications of Scientific Advance*, edited by E. G. Forbes (Edinburgh: Edinburgh University Press, 1975), pp. 451-468;

F. Howard Collins, *An Epitome of the Synthetic Philosophy* (London: Williams & Norgate, 1889);

George Bion Denton, "Early Psychological Theories of Herbert Spencer," *American Journal of Psychology*, 32 (January 1921): 5-15;

Denton, "Herbert Spencer and the Rhetoricians," *PMLA*, 34 (1919): 89-111;

Denton, "Origin and Development of Herbert Spencer's Principle of Economy," in *The Fred Newton Scott Anniversary Papers* (Chicago: University of Chicago Press, 1929), pp. 55-92;

Hugh S. Elliot, *Herbert Spencer* (New York: Holt, 1917);

Louis Bruce Fike, "Despotism, Liberty, and Retrogression: The Political Philosophy of Herbert Spencer," Ph.D. dissertation, Brown University, 1969;

Mark Francis, "Herbert Spencer and the Myth of Laissez-Faire," *Journal of the History of Ideas*, 39 (April-June 1978): 317-328;

Francis, "The Origins of the Spencerian Philosophy and the New Reformation," Ph.D. dissertation, Cambridge University, 1973;

H. G. Good, "The Sources of Spencer's *Education*," *Journal of Educational Research*, 13 (May 1926): 325-335;

Kate Gordon, "Spencer's Theory of Ethics in its Evolutionary Aspect," *Philosophical Review*, 11 (November 1902): 592-606;

Scott Gordon, "The London *Economist* and the High Tide of Laissez-Faire," *Journal of Political Economy*, 63 (December 1955): 461-488;

John N. Gray, "Spencer on the Ethics of Liberty and the Limits of State Interference," *History of Political Thought*, 3 (Winter 1982): 465-481;

T. S. Gray, "Herbert Spencer: Individualist or Organicist?," *Political Studies*, 33 (June 1985): 236-253;

Gray, "Herbert Spencer on Women: A Study in Personal and Political Disillusion," *International Journal of Women's Studies*, 7 (May/June 1984): 217-231;

Gray, "Herbert Spencer's Theory of Social Justice–Desert or Entitlement?," *History of Political Thought*, 2 (Spring 1981): 161-186;

John C. Greene, "Biology and Social Theory in the Nineteenth-Century: Auguste Comte and Herbert Spencer," in *Critical Problems in the History of Science*, edited by Marshall Clagett (Madison: University of Wisconsin Press, 1959), pp. 419-446;

Malcolm Guthrie, *On Mr. Spencer's Formula of Evolution* (London: Trübner, 1879);

Guthrie, *On Mr. Spencer's Unification of Knowledge* (London: Trübner, 1882);

Alan Hart, "The Synthetic Epistemology of Herbert Spencer," Ph.D. dissertation, University of Pennsylvania, 1965;

Richard P. Hiskes, "The Nature of Society and

the Organic Community: Spencer," in *Community Without Coercion* (Newark: University of Delaware Press, 1982), pp. 57-83;

Hiskes, "Spencer and the Liberal Idea of Community," *Review of Politics*, 45 (October 1983): 595-609;

Richard Hofstadter, *Social Darwinism in American Thought*, revised edition (Boston: Beacon, 1955), pp. 31-50;

T. H. Huxley, *'Evolution and Ethics' and Other Essays* (1894), volume 9 of *Collected Essays*, 9 volumes (New York: Olms, 1970), pp. 46-116;

James Iverach, "Herbert Spencer," *Critical Review of Theological and Philosophical Literature*, 14 (January and May 1904): 99-112, 195-209;

William James, "Herbert Spencer," *Atlantic Monthly*, 94 (July 1904): 99-108;

James, "Remarks on Spencer's Definition of Mind as Correspondence," *Journal of Speculative Philosophy*, 12 (January 1878): 1-22;

J. Vernon Jenson, "The X Club: Fraternity of Victorian Scientists," *British Journal for the History of Science*, 5 (June 1970): 63-72;

Greta Jones, *Social Darwinism and English Thought: The Interaction Between Biological and Social Theory* (Brighton: Harvester, 1980), pp. 56-62, 78-88;

James G. Kennedy, *Herbert Spencer* (Boston: Twayne, 1978);

Cargill Gilston Knott, *Life and Scientific Work of Peter Guthrie Tait* (Cambridge: Cambridge University Press, 1911), pp. 254, 279-288;

A. L. Kroeber, "The Superorganic," *American Anthropologist*, new series 19 (April-June 1917): 163-213;

Lillie B. Lamar, "Herbert Spencer and His Father," *University of Texas Studies in English*, 32 (1953): 59-66;

Roy M. MacLeod, "The X-Club: A Social Network of Science in Late-Victorian England," *Notes and Records of the Royal Society of London*, 24 (1970): 305-322;

Donald MacRae, Introduction to Spencer's *The Man 'versus' the State, with Four Essays on Politics and Society*, edited by MacRae (Harmondsworth & Baltimore: Penguin, 1969), pp. 7-54;

Ronald E. Martin, *American Literature and the Universe of Force* (Durham, N.C.: Duke University Press, 1981), pp. 6-95;

P. B. Medawar, "Herbert Spencer and the Law of General Evolution," in his *The Art of the Soluble* (London: Methuen, 1967), pp. 39-58;

William L. Miller, "Herbert Spencer's Theory of

Welfare and Public Policy," *History of Political Economy*, 4 (Spring 1972): 207-231;

John D. Molloy, "Spencer's Impact on American Conservatism, 1870-1912," Ph.D. dissertation, University of Cincinnati, 1959;

George Edward Moore, *Principia Ethica* (1903) (Cambridge: Cambridge University Press, 1959), pp. 48-58;

James R. Moore, *The Post-Darwinian Controversies: A Study of the Protestant Struggle to Come to Terms with Darwin in Great Britain and America, 1870-1900* (Cambridge: Cambridge University Press, 1979), pp. 161-173;

Robert Edward Moore, "Spencer's Naturalistic Theory of Ethics," Ph.D. dissertation, University of Pennsylvania, 1969;

Ellen Frankel Paul, "Herbert Spencer: The Historicist as a Failed Prophet," *Journal of the History of Ideas*, 44 (October-December 1983): 619-638;

Jeffrey Paul, "The Socialism of Herbert Spencer," *History of Political Thought*, 3 (Winter 1982): 499-514;

J. D. Y. Peel, *Herbert Spencer: The Evolution of a Sociologist* (New York: Basic Books, 1971);

Robert G. Perrin, "Herbert Spencer's Four Theories of Social Evolution," *American Journal of Sociology*, 81 (May 1976): 1339-1359;

David C. Rapoport, "Military and Civil Societies," *Political Studies*, 12 (June 1964): 178-201;

Jay Rumney, *Herbert Spencer's Sociology: A Study in the History of Social Theory* (London: Williams & Norgate, 1934);

Richard L. Schoenwald, "Town Guano and 'Social Statics,'" *Victorian Studies*, 11, Supplement (Summer 1968): 691-710;

Harold Issadore Sharlin, "Herbert Spencer and Scientism," *Annals of Science*, 33 (September 1976): 456-465;

Henry Sidgwick, *Lectures on the Ethics of T. H. Green, Mr. Herbert Spencer, and J. Martineau* (London: Macmillan, 1902), pp. 135-312;

Sidgwick, "Philosophy and Physical Science," *Academy*, 4 (1 April 1873): 131-134;

C. U. M. Smith, "Evolution and the Problem of Mind: Part 1, Herbert Spencer," *Journal of the History of Biology*, 15 (Spring 1982): 55-88;

Smith, "Herbert Spencer's Epigenetic Epistemology," *Studies in History and Philosophy of Science*, 14 (March 1983): 1-22;

George H. Smith, "Herbert Spencer's Theory of Causation," *Journal of Libertarian Studies*, 5 (Spring 1981): 113-152;

Hillel Steiner, "Land, Liberty and the Early Herbert Spencer," *History of Political Thought*, 3 (Winter 1982): 515-533;

Arthur J. Taylor, "The Originality of Herbert Spencer," *University of Texas Studies in English*, 34 (1956): 101-106;

J. Arthur Thomson, *Herbert Spencer* (London: Dent, 1906);

Edward B. Tylor, "Mr. Spencer's *Principles of Sociology*," *Mind*, 2 (April 1877): 141-156, 415-423;

Norman T. Walker, "The Sources of Herbert Spencer's Educational Ideas," *Journal of Educational Research*, 22 (November 1930): 299-308;

James Frazier Wall, "Social Darwinism and Constitutional Law with special reference to Lochner v. New York," *Annals of Science*, 33 (September 1976): 465-476;

A. R. Wallace, *Darwinism* (1889) (London: Macmillan, 1889), pp. 411-420;

James Ward, *Naturalism and Agnosticism*, 2 volumes (London: Black, 1903), I: 185-302;

August Weismann, "On Heredity," in *Essays upon Heredity and Kindred Biological Problems*, 2 volumes, edited by E. B. Poulton, translated by S. Schönland and A. E. Shipley (Oxford: Clarendon, 1891-1892), I: 67-106;

John White, "Andrew Carnegie and Herbert Spencer: A Special Relationship," *Journal of American Studies*, 13 (April 1979): 57-71;

David Wiltshire, *The Social and Political Thought of Herbert Spencer* (New York: Oxford University Press, 1978), pp. 168-191;

Chauncey Wright, "The Philosophy of Herbert Spencer," *North American Review*, 100 (April 1865): 423-475;

Wright, "A Physical Theory of the Universe," *North American Review*, 99 (July 1864): 1-33;

Robert M. Young, "Darwinism and the Division of Labour," *Listener*, 2264, 17 August 1972, pp. 202-205;

Young, "Darwin's Metaphor: Does Nature Se-

lect?," *Monist*, 55 (July 1971): 442-503;

Young, "The Impact of Darwin on Conventional Thought," in *The Victorian Crisis of Faith*, edited by Anthony Symondson (London: Society for the Propagation of Christian Knowledge, 1975), pp. 13-35;

Young, "Malthus and the Evolutionists: The Common Context of Biological and Social Theory," *Past and Present*, 43 (May 1969): 109-145;

Young, *Mind, Brain, and Adaptation in the Nineteenth Century: Cerebral Localization and Its Biological Context from Gall to Ferrier* (Oxford: Oxford University Press, 1970), pp. 150-196;

Young, "Natural Theology, Victorian Periodicals, and the Fragmentation of the Common Context," in *Darwin to Einstein: Historical Studies on Science and Belief*, edited by Colin Chant and John Fauvel (London: Longman, 1980), pp. 69-107;

Young, "The Naturalization of Value Systems in the Human Sciences," in *Problems in the Biological and Human Sciences*, edited by Michael Bartholomew, Bernard Norton, and Young (Milton Keynes: Open University Press, 1981), pp. 63-110. *

Papers:

The British Library has manuscripts of *Social Statics, The Principles of Psychology, First Principles, Essays, Scientific, Political, and Speculative, The Principles of Biology, The Study of Sociology, The Principles of Sociology,* and *The Data of Ethics*. According to research by Mark Francis, Spencer materials can be found at the University of London Library, the London School of Economics Library, the British Library of Political and Economic Science, and the Lyon Playfair Library, Imperial College of Science and Technology.

Leslie Stephen

(28 November 1832-22 February 1904)

John W. Bicknell
Drew University

BOOKS: *The Poll Degree from a Third Point of View* (London: Macmillan, 1863);

Sketches from Cambridge. By a Don (London & Cambridge: Macmillan, 1865);

The "Times" on the American War: A Historical Study (London: Ridgeway, 1865; New York: Abbatt, 1915);

The Playground of Europe (London: Longmans, Green, 1871; London & New York: Longmans, Green, 1894);

Essays on Freethinking and Plainspeaking (London: Longmans, Green, 1873; New York: Putnam's, 1877);

Hours in a Library, 3 series in 3 volumes (London: Smith, Elder, 1874-1879); first series republished (New York: Scribner, Armstrong, 1875); enlarged, 3 volumes (London: Smith, Elder, 1892; New York: Putnam's, 1894);

History of English Thought in the Eighteenth Century, 2 volumes (London: Smith, Elder, 1876; New York, Putnam's, 1876);

Samuel Johnson (London: Macmillan, 1878; New York: Harper, 1878);

Alexander Pope (London: Macmillan, 1880; New York: Harper, 1880);

Swift (London: Macmillan, 1882; New York: Harper, 1882);

The Science of Ethics (London: Smith, Elder, 1882; New York: Putnam's, 1882);

Life of Henry Fawcett (London: Smith, Elder, 1885; New York: Putnam's, 1886);

An Agnostic's Apology, and Other Essays (London: Smith, Elder, 1893; New York: Putnam's/ London: Smith, Elder, 1893);

The Life of Sir James Fitzjames Stephen (London: Smith, Elder, 1895; New York: Putnam's, 1895);

Social Rights and Duties, 2 volumes (London: Sonnenschein/New York: Macmillan, 1896);

Studies of a Biographer, 4 volumes (London: Duckworth, 1898-1902; New York: Putnam's/ London: Duckworth, 1898-1902);

The English Utilitarians, 3 volumes (London:

Leslie Stephen, 1902

Duckworth, 1900; New York: Putnam's/ London: Duckworth, 1900);

George Eliot (London: Macmillan, 1902; New York: Macmillan, 1902);

Robert Louis Stevenson: An Essay (New York & London: Putnam's, 1902);

English Literature and Society in the Eighteenth Century (London: Duckworth, 1904; New York & London: Putnam's, 1907);

Hobbes (New York & London: Macmillan, 1904);

Some Early Impressions (London: Leonard & Virginia Woolf at the Hogarth Press, 1924);

Men, Books, and Mountains, Essays by Leslie Stephen,

edited by S. O. A. Ullman (Minneapolis: University of Minnesota Press, 1956);

Sir Leslie Stephen's Mausoleum Book, edited by Alan Bell (London: Oxford University Press, 1977).

OTHER: Hermann von Alexander Berlepsch, *The Alps: or Sketches of Life and Nature in the Mountains*, translated by Stephen (London: Longmans, Green & Roberts, 1861);

"The Allelein-Horn," in *Vacation Tourists and Notes of Travel in 1860*, edited by Francis Galton, 3 volumes (London: Macmillan, 1861-1864), I: 264-281;

"The Ascent of the Schreckhorn" and "The Eiger Joch," in *Peaks, Passes and Glaciers*, second series, edited by E. S. Kennedy, 2 volumes (London: Longman, Green, Longman & Green, 1862), II: 3-14, 15-32;

"On the Choice of Representatives by Popular Constituencies," in *Essays on Reform* (London: Macmillan, 1867), pp. 85-125;

"The Writings of W. M. Thackeray," in *The Works of William Makepeace Thackeray*, 24 volumes (London: Smith, Elder, 1878-1879), XXIV: 315-378;

William Kingdon Clifford, *Lectures and Essays*, edited by Stephen and Frederick Pollock, 2 volumes (London: Macmillan, 1879; London & New York: Macmillan, 1886);

The Works of Henry Fielding, Esq., edited with a biographical essay by Stephen, 10 volumes (London: Smith, Elder, 1882);

"Richardson's Novels. Introduction," in *The Works of Samuel Richardson*, 12 volumes (London: Sotheran, 1883-1884), I: ix-lv;

The Dictionary of National Biography, 66 volumes, volumes 1-21 edited by Stephen; volumes 22-26 edited by Stephen and Sidney Lee; volumes 27-36 include contributions by Stephen (London: Smith, Elder, 1885-1901);

Margaret Veley, *A Marriage of Shadows, and Other Poems*, preface by Stephen (London: Smith, Elder, 1888; Philadelphia: Lippincott, 1889);

"James Dykes Campbell" (prefatory memoir), in *Samuel Taylor Coleridge*, by Campbell (London: Macmillan, 1896; New York: Macmillan, 1896);

Emile Legouis, *The Early Life of William Wordsworth, 1770-1798*, translated by J. W. Matthews, prefatory note by Stephen (London: Dent, 1897);

James Payn, *The Backwater of Life, or Essays of a Literary Veteran*, introduction by Stephen (London: Smith, Elder, 1899);

"Evolution and Religious Conceptions," in *The Nineteenth Century: A Review of Progress* (London & New York: Putnam's, 1901), pp. 370-383;

Letters of John Richard Green, edited by Stephen (London & New York: Macmillan, 1901).

PERIODICAL PUBLICATIONS: "The Political Situation in England," *North American Review*, 107 (October 1868): 543-567;

"The Comtist Utopia," *Fraser's Magazine*, 80 (July 1869): 1-21;

"Mr. Matthew Arnold and the Church of England," *Fraser's Magazine*, 82 (October 1870): 414-431;

"Mr. Maurice's Theology," *Fortnightly Review*, 21 (May 1874): 595-617;

"Mr. Ruskin's Recent Writings," *Fraser's Magazine*, 89 (June 1874): 688-701;

"Sidgwick's Methods of Ethics," *Fraser's Magazine*, 91 (March 1875): 306-325;

"Art and Morality," *Cornhill Magazine*, 32 (July 1875): 91-101;

"Genius and Vanity," *Cornhill Magazine*, 35 (June 1877): 670-684;

"An Attempted Philosophy of History," *Fortnightly Review*, 33 (May 1880): 672-695;

"Mr. Bradlaugh and His Opponents," *Fortnightly Review*, 34 (August 1880): 176-187;

"The Moral Element in Literature," *Cornhill Magazine*, 43 (January 1881): 34-50;

"Bishop Butler's Apologist," *Nineteenth Century*, 39 (January 1896): 106-122;

"The Will to Believe," *Agnostic Annual* (1898): 14-22.

Alpine climber and essayist, editor of the *Cornhill Magazine* and the *Dictionary of National Biography*, literary critic and historian, biographer, militant agnostic, historian of ideas, eminent pedestrian, Leslie Stephen has been called the next most important Victorian man of letters after Matthew Arnold. On whichever rung of the ladder of eminence one wishes to place him, there is no doubt that he ranks much higher than the attention paid him until recently by twentieth-century critics and scholars would indicate. In the last decade, however, he has been receiving more scrutiny, in part because he was the father of Virginia Woolf, but equally in recognition of his own intellectual power and literary skill. Noël Annan's *Leslie Stephen: The Godless Victorian* (1984), a much augmented version of his earlier study *Leslie Stephen: His Thought and Character in Relation to His Time* (1951), is illuminated by scholarly and critical work of the last three decades, as well as by Annan's matured judgment. It marks a turning point in Stephen studies; critics are now prepared to honor his mind and art. Readers note that the prose itself, while abjuring the cloud-capped towers of Ruskin and less engaging than Arnold's, is capable of considerable variety, from the sinewy, tough prose of philosophical, theological, or political argument, to the impassioned eloquence of "An Agnostic's Apology"; from the steel-engraving beauty of his Alpine essays to the relaxed amiability of "In Praise of Walking"; from the equable perspicacity of his literary criticism to the deadpan irony of "Did Shakespeare Write Bacon?" The irony emerges in private as well as in public; he told his wife once that he had just seen a friend who said he was feeling stupid and couldn't write; Stephen observed that he refrained from replying that that was better than feeling stupid and being able to write.

Stephen was born in London on 28 November 1832. From his parents he inherited an extreme sensitivity and a love of poetry, and he learned from those two descendants of the Clapham evangelicals the habit of hard work and the virtues of candor and integrity. His father, Sir James Stephen, undersecretary for the colonies, drew up the legislation for the abolition of slavery in the British Empire and was so fearful of sensuous pleasure that he once smoked a cigar and found it so delicious that he never smoked again. "A skinless man," he was subject to nervous breakdowns. Leslie's mother, Catharine Venn Stephen, was more gently strung, sturdy and good-humored, fond of literature. It is from her journals that we get a picture of the supersensitive young Leslie, who hated pictures of the Resurrection, would not ride a donkey on Sunday, and chanted poetry so much that it set his blood racing. A doctor prescribed vigorous exercise, humdrum subjects of study, and no poetry. Eton was the remedy chosen, a remedy that failed for reasons that may well include a severe flogging that Stephen remembered sixty years later. Turned over to tutors in 1848, he entered King's College, London, where he prepared himself for Cambridge.

Stephen entered Cambridge at eighteen and left it fourteen years later. Here he became the tough-bodied and tough-minded political and philosophical radical of his maturity. He discovered the pleasures of rowing in the Trinity Hall

boat and striding across the landscape at a pace few could match. Equally energetic were his orations at the Cambridge Union, where he supported the ballot, parliamentary reform, and the admission of dissenters to the universities. Taking his "First" in January 1854, he was offered a fellowship that required him to take orders as a clergyman. His sister and his cousin told him he lacked the required sense of clerical vocation, but he put their objections aside to please his father and to achieve independence. If he lacked clerical zeal, he had more than enough to be a college tutor. For ten years he lectured and tutored undergraduates of all abilities, coached the boat to more than one notable victory, and endeared himself to the undergraduates by his unconventionality and genuine interest in their welfare. To some of his contemporaries, in fact, Leslie Stephen did not seem to be much more than a rowing tough or an Alpine *Bergsteiger*, but it is clear from the notebooks he kept in the shorthand his mother taught all her children that he was reading the great books of the day and sufficient philosophy to be appointed examiner in moral sciences in 1862. Men who had watched Stephen shed garment after garment on the towpath until scandalously denuded were astounded at the news. They were no less astounded when in the same year he told the master he could no longer perform divine service and resigned his tutorship.

Between 1859, when he renewed his clerical vows, and the summer of 1862 he had been reading and discussing Mill's *A System of Logic* (1843) and *On Liberty* (1859), some German Higher Criticism, and Darwin's *On the Origin of Species* (1859). He had watched the behavior of the orthodox over the charges of heresy brought against the contributors to *Essays and Reviews* (1860), who had dared to endorse German Higher Criticism of the Scriptures and hence were dubbed "The Seven Against Christ." Like many others, Stephen decided that the Bible was not history and that a deity who would arbitrarily condemn millions of his creatures to everlasting damnation was not one he could worship. Giving up his faith cost him more anguish than he later would admit, and choosing to leave Cambridge could not have been easy; he was giving up a vocation for which he was admirably fitted and without any sure knowledge of what he could take up in its place. Reluctant to depart, he stayed on till 1864 when it became clear that he must break with a place where he had no real occupation. One suspects the decision was hastened by his visit to America in the summer of 1863 where he began lifelong friendships with James Russell Lowell and Oliver Wendell Holmes, Jr., and gathered ammunition for his stinging pamphlet *The "Times" on the American War* (1865), in which, angered by the biased reporting of the London *Times*, he exposed the writers' incompetence, inaccuracy, and prejudice.

His radical pen had been ignited. "I resolved to take to literature," he wrote in his journal and moved to London where he lived with his mother and sister and, in early 1865, began writing for the *Saturday Review* and the *Pall Mall Gazette*. In 1866 he began contributing a weekly report on things English to the New York *Nation*. In the same year he wrote his first essay for the *Cornhill Magazine*. Thus, in two years he had made a name for himself and was drawing a sufficient income to enable him to support a wife— Harriet Marian ("Minny") Thackeray, the novelist's daughter, whom he married on 19 June 1867. Soon he was writing for *Fraser's Magazine* on religious questions, university reform, and Auguste Comte, and in 1871 he made his debut in the radical *Fortnightly Review*. His maiden *Fortnightly* essay, a critique of Balzac, called forth enthusiastic comments from Mrs. George Grote (wife of the historian of Greece). Lady Stephen told her daughter-in-law that Mrs. Grote thought "Leslie's article on Balzac the most perfect specimen of consummate criticism she's ever read both for entering into the spirit of the author and for the style and 'her dear historian' ... thought the same." George Smith, publisher of the *Pall Mall Gazette* and the *Cornhill Magazine*, spotted Stephen's talents and, in 1871, snapped him up as editor of the *Cornhill*.

Meanwhile, he had been climbing Alps and writing about them in the *Alpine Journal* and elsewhere. Collected in the first edition of *The Playground of Europe* (1871), his Alpine essays were, and are, considered by many to be some of his best writing. Stephen's biographer, Frederic William Maitland, quotes two noted members of the Alpine Club, James Bryce and Douglas Freshfield, as judging that the Alpin essays became models for anyone choosing to write about mountain climbing. Stephen considered "Sunset on Mont Blanc" to be his best, but his second wife, Julia, preferred "A Bye-Day in the Alps"; others have delighted in "The Ascent of the Schreckhorn" and the poetic "Alps in Winter." As Maitland, Annan, and others have pointed out, the Alps were for Stephen not just a series

Minny and Leslie Stephen, 1867 (from Leslie Stephen's Photograph Album, in the Smith College Library Rare Book Room; reproduced with the permission of Professor and Mrs. Quentin Bell and Smith College). This photograph was probably taken while Stephen and his first wife were on their honeymoon in Switzerland.

of challenges; the vision from the top of a peak could stir in him the emotion he no longer derived from the Church, "the sense sublime / Of something far more deeply interfused," as Wordsworth put it in one of the many poems Stephen had by heart. Not that stirring of the sense sublime ever tempted him to return to the faith of his fathers, as can be seen from the piece included in Stephen's 1873 collection *Essays on Freethinking and Plainspeaking*, "A Bad Five Minutes in the Alps."

The radical in religion was also a Victorian radical in politics. Already in 1865 he had taken aim at the universities in a mild satire, *Sketches from Cambridge. By a Don*, as well as at the *Times*. Not only had he worked for the election of his Millite friend Henry Fawcett to a professorship at

Cambridge but he had also taken a vigorous role in Fawcett's campaign to be elected to Parliament from Brighton (1864) and in the following year joined John Stuart Mill's committee to prosecute Governor Edward John Eyre of Jamaica and supported, as well, Mill's campaign to enter Parliament. In 1866 the agitation for parliamentary reform, especially of the franchise, was swelling to a roar in the midlands and at Hyde Park; poverty in the East End of London was reaching dreadful proportions. Throughout this period of Stephen's life, which includes the Reform Bill of 1867, the Education Act of 1870, and ends with the defeat of Gladstone in 1874 and the death of Minny Stephen in November 1875, Stephen often wrote on political, religious, and ecclesiastical subjects. To *Essays on Reform* (1867), that "manifesto of young Liberalism," he contributed an essay reassuring his audience that opening the franchise to the working class would not result in a Parliament of factory hands, and in the next year wrote an account of the political situation for the *North American Review* (October 1868) in which he looked forward to "the beginning of a peaceful revolution in England, which will unsettle many of the firmest foundations of the established order of things." One of the foundations that Stephen and an articulate group of young academic radicals wished to demolish was the established church. To such men as John Morley and Stephen, the Anglican church was the praying section of the Tory party, "a mean serving maid of the rich," in Morley's words, and an opponent of social and scientific progress; whereas, as Stephen put it, "the atheists, infidels, and rationalists . . . have taught us to take a fresh interest in our poor fellow denizens of the world." Collected in *Essays on Freethinking and Plainspeaking* are the best of his challenges to the orthodox as well as pieces on such eighteenth-century figures as Shaftesbury, Mandeville, and Warburton. These are essays that Stephen worked on while he was preparing his masterpiece, *History of English Thought in the Eighteenth Century*, which finally emerged in 1876.

Why the eighteenth century, which Carlyle had declared bankrupt? For years Stephen had been contemplating a magnum opus. At first it was to be on political economy, later on America, then on political philosophy, but the preparatory studies took him into historical criticism and philosophy—Spinoza, Hegel, Comte, Strauss, and Renan, as Stephen's 1906 biographer, Maitland, tells us, and specifically into religious thought

and its history. Mark Pattison's essay on eighteenth-century religious thought published in the 1860 *Essays and Reviews* turned Stephen's attention directly to the Deists, whom he began to see as forerunners of Victorian rationalists, like himself, fighting the old battles over again, but now in the new context created by German historical criticism of the Bible and Darwinism. *History of English Thought in the Eighteenth Century*, then, is a notable document in the history of Victorian rationalism. Stephen not only reveals but also dissects the theological views which he believes are still all too current. One hero is David Hume, *le bon David;* another is Adam Smith, the lucid economist and moralist; still another, surprisingly enough, is Bishop Joseph Butler, who earns Stephen's praise because of his refusal to pretend that evil can be easily explained or explained away. The message for Stephen's own time was twofold: first, imitate Hume's "high merit of having unflinchingly enquired into the profoundest of all questions" and abhor the hypocrisy, "the sham beliefs, and the indolent scepticism" which "is the penalty . . . we have had to pay for our not daring to meet the doubts openly expressed by Hume, and by Hume alone"; second, recognize what Butler shows us, "that no vigorous creed can be reconciled with a tacit denial of the evils which disturb the world and perplex the intellect."

History of English Thought in the Eighteenth Century, however, is not just tract for the times. Its scope, its energetic and systematic setting forth of the principal ideas in theology, philosophy, political theory, and political economy, as well as their relations to each other, culminating in a final chapter, "Characteristics"—all this was an important landmark not only in the "Queen Anne Revival" but also in the practice and theory of intellectual history. Influenced in part by Auguste Comte's three-stage theory of history, acquainted with William Edward Hartpole Lecky's history of rationalism (1865) and Henry Thomas Buckle's history of English civilization (1857-1861), Stephen was well versed in nineteenth-century theories of history and theories of society. Both his studies of Darwin and his observation of events in his own lifetime convinced him that ideas sprang out of the social and political context, not vice versa, and that their fate was determined more by the relevance to the social situation than to their inherent logic or lack thereof. Here he broke with his predecessors, notably Mill and Comte, as well as with all philosophical idealists.

Stephen's contribution to intellectual history as a discipline as well as to the history of eighteenth-century thought is profound. Nothing comparable precedes *History of English Thought in the Eighteenth Century* or has succeeded it. Remaining a standard authority, it survives its errors and omissions because it is powerfully and vividly written. The intellectual passion that suffuses its pages and the imagery that dramatizes the conflict of ideas make it an account of a great debate conducted by a great debater.

While he was writing his history he was also an admired editor of the *Cornhill Magazine*. In the editorial chair first occupied by his late father-in-law, William Makepeace Thackeray, Stephen took on a magazine designed to publish fiction, poetry, essays, and articles, though not too weighty—no Schopenhauer, he told philosopher and psychologist James Sully, and nothing to shock the mind of a young lady. Under his direction and encouragement, the *Cornhill* published Thomas Hardy, Henry James, Grant Allen, James Sully, Margaret Oliphant, Anny Thackeray, John Addington Symonds, Robert Louis Stevenson, William Ernest Henley, Sidney Colvin, George Meredith, Edmund Gosse, Frances Power Cobbe, Eliza Lynn Linton, and W. E. Norris, among others. For several years the *Cornhill* maintained a reasonably high literary standard, one reason being that Stephen could attract and hold his contributors.

One author with whom he had close ties was Thomas Hardy, whose account of their relationship, as reported to Maitland, is one of the standard examples of author and editor dealing with a squeamish public. No doubt Stephen felt uncomfortable with the excessive prudery of his readers but the editor himself was squeamish and, like Matthew Arnold, felt that some French novelists paid too many tributes to "the Goddess of Lubricity." Hardy's account also registers his surprise at finding that the illustrator for the *Cornhill*'s 1874 serialization of *Far From the Madding Crowd* was a woman, Helen Paterson, whom he later called the best of his illustrators. Though by no means a feminist, Stephen, in his chivalrous way, encouraged women writers, among them Margaret Oliphant. Stevenson, Sully, and Gosse all testify to the help he gave them not only by accepting their work but by his severe tutelage. Norris in his essay on Stephen for the Jubilee issue of the *Cornhill* (January 1910) remarks that though kind, Stephen was not indulgent; "more than once he made me rewrite whole chapters," and adds, "he himself was at infinite trouble over the discharge of his duties."

For four years of his tenure at the *Cornhill* he was a secure, happy man. Marriage agreed with him; Minny was a delightful companion, at home, in the Alps, or on a second journey to America (1868). In 1870 a daughter, Laura, was born prematurely and had to be kept in cotton wool for three months. Then, in 1875, Minny Stephen became pregnant again; following medical advice, during the autumn she went to Switzerland and returned in apparently good health. On the night of 27 November, feeling uncomfortable, Minny retired early and chose to sleep with her maid so as not to disturb her husband. In the night she had what was called a convulsion (eclampsia of pregnancy, no doubt); she never recovered consciousness and died the next day, Stephen's birthday. He was devastated. His sister-in-law Anny Thackeray (later Ritchie), was devastated too; and there was Laura, five years old, retarded and difficult. The household at 8 Southwell Gardens was wrapped in gloom. Stephen and Anny Thackeray comforted each other, but they also got on each other's nerves. She clung to a belief in the hereafter and he dourly repelled any such, to him, illusory consolation. He resigned from all his clubs, became a virtual recluse, and struggled against collapse. He did what all the Stephens did when stressed—he worked. He finished *History of English Thought in the Eighteenth Century*, which came out in October 1876, and compiled his own index for the work. Between January 1876 and December 1877, he wrote fourteen essays for the *Cornhill* and four more for the *Fortnightly*.

He had made his reputation as a historian of ideas and also, even more than T. H. Huxley, as the leading spokesman for agnosticism; he was elected to the Athenaeum. But none of this seemed to matter. To Charles Eliot Norton he wrote on 5 March 1876, "My life was so happy a few months ago that it seemed to be that unhappiness was impossible. Now it is so unhappy that it seems like a dream; . . . the hideous mass of commonplace life thrusts itself between me and my old happiness, and further—what is an unfortunate peculiarity of mine—that unhappiness tries my temper. I am more fretful and irritable by disposition than you perhaps know and sometimes I bully my best friends shamefully. The problems of making sorrow ennobling instead of deteriorating is a terribly hard one." In late June he and Anny Thackeray moved to 11 Hyde Park South, close to Julia Duckworth, at Number 13, a widow

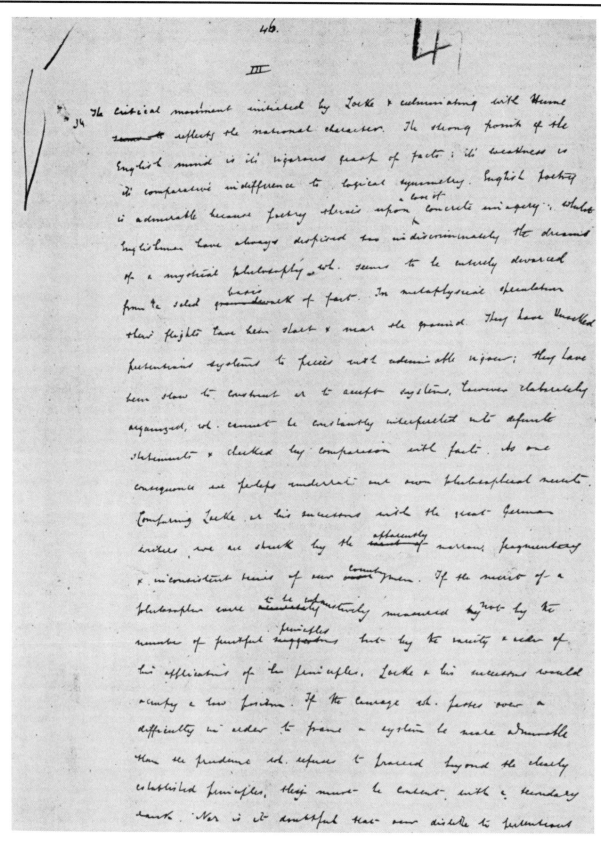

with three children, an old friend to Anny and Minny. She had been at 8 Southwell Gardens the night before Minny Stephen died.

Proximity made easier the progress from friendship and sympathy to affection and love. Early in 1878 Julia Duckworth gave Stephen her consent; on March 26 they were married, and soon Stephen and Laura moved into 13 Hyde Park Gate (later 22 Hyde Park Gate). In six years Julia and Leslie Stephen produced four children, two of whom, Vanessa and Virginia, became the high priestesses of Bloomsbury. The marriage came to have a fame all its own, memorialized by Stephen in his *Mausoleum Book* (1977), by Virginia Woolf in "Reminiscences" and "A Sketch of the Past" (included in *Moments of Being*, revised edition, 1985), and most notably in Mr. and Mrs. Ramsay of Woolf's *To the Lighthouse* (1927). Moreover, the marriage and the characters of Leslie and Julia Stephen as parents have been debated, with varying proportions of heat and light, by numerous Woolf scholars in search of explanations for the lives and art of both Virginia and Vanessa. Certainly it was a remarkable marriage. Both Leslie and Julia were people of intellect, passion, and distinctive, even difficult, character. Julia Stephen, in addition to running an extensive household, was the self-appointed nurse and comforter of her mother and anyone else in the family and beyond who needed medical care or advice about nursing; sometimes she spent weeks away from home on some mission of mercy, leaving the children with her husband and the servants. Leslie Stephen spent many hours at home working in his study. When Julia was away, he was often in the nursery, attempting to teach or just to amuse the children, reading to them or drawing marvelous animals and fantastic creatures for their delight. Then he would go off to the Alps with Gabriel Loppé and Melchior Anderreg or on some leg-stretching stroll from Winchester to Land's End to St. Ives. To these absences (both his and hers) we owe over four hundred letters from Leslie to Julia (regrettably none of hers to him seems to have survived). From these it is clear that he adored her to the point of reverence and was the most uxorious of men. It is clear from other sources that her devotion to this tall, red-bearded, blue-eyed intellectual matched his to her. She could handle his cantankerousness, soothe his ruffled and easily disturbed sensibilities, and see that the "author" could do his work.

Part of that work was the literary criticism that appeared in the *Cornhill* before he left it in 1882, the bulk of which was published in the three-volume *Hours in a Library* (1874, 1876, 1879), though some essays were added to the edition of 1892. Stephen never thought of himself as fundamentally a literary critic, yet, as Nöel Annan has said, Stephen did for the English novel what Arnold and others did for poetry. His preferred model was the French critic Sainte-Beuve, whose interest in linking author and work suited his own concerns. Likewise, increasingly he explored the relations among author, audience, and the social forces influencing both. He felt that criticism ought to be scientific, though what he meant was that the critic should stick to what could be said about a work by looking at it carefully and studying its bearings on the human condition; in short, "scientific" meant "inductive"; it meant being downright and specific rather than airy and gushing. Stephen's essays on Defoe, Balzac, Hawthorne, and Crabbe, to name only a few examples, illustrate his characteristic method and skill as a superb diagnostician of the special emotional effects produced by individual authors or their characters. One would not easily give up his observation that we cannot expect from Clarissa Harlowe any "of the outbreaks against the laws of society customary with George Sand's heroines. If she had changed places with Maggie Tulliver, she would have accepted the society of the *Mill on the Floss* with perfect contentment."

His great pleasure in reading was to find the author in the work, so it is no surprise that his critical essays, as well as his longer studies *Alexander Pope* (1880), *Samuel Johnson* (1878), and *Swift* (1882), are always part biography. Boswell's *Life of Samuel Johnson* was a favorite book; Walter Scott and Thackeray favorite novelists; and Wordsworth, about whom he wrote one of his best critical essays, a revered poet. He liked works that were "manly" and could show a feminine delicacy, but could bear neither the "effeminate" nor the "morbid." Scott and Fielding and Johnson were "manly" without being brutal; they could face facts and the brutalities of life without sentimentality or self-pity or priggishness or prurience. Coventry Patmore, he told Julia's mother, was "effeminate"; his poetry, "twaddle." He thought Tennyson's *Idylls of the King* bad. He had more difficulty with such ambiguous characters and writers as Horace Walpole and Laurence Sterne but in a curious way appreciated them, as Annan points out, in spite of his moral objections to their characters. Moreover, he disliked didacticism; though ethics and aesthetics were, in his view, intimately connected, he had learned from Coleridge that literature had to be criticized as literature: "the moral of a poem is not in this or that proposition tagged to it or deducible from it, moral or otherwise; but the total effect of the stimulus to the imagination and affections, or what Coleridge would call its dynamic effect." This statement may be taken as his mature position on the matter. Virginia Woolf recalled, too, how he would snort when his children preferred a novelist's ideal hero to "a far more lifelike villain." The consensus is, both from his contemporaries and his twentieth-century critics, that he was a useful, independent-minded, and readable literary critic.

Yet Stephen did not have a high opinion either of criticism in general or of his own in particular. He preferred to think that his line was philosophy. Moreover, like others in his era, he judged that his generation of rationalists had a more important task, namely, to demonstrate that morality could survive theology. To people like Stephen, John Morley, T. H. Huxley, or George Eliot the Dostoyevskian formula "If God did not exist everything becomes possible" was sheer nonsense. Surely there was a basis for ethics in reason or science! Clearly the primary moral quality was the courage to be honest and have "an unflinching respect for realities." So Stephen had written in his "Apology for Plainspeaking" (collected in *Essays on Freethinking and Plainspeaking*) in 1873. He addressed the problem specifically in his essay-review of Henry Sidgwick's *Methods of Ethics* (1874) in an 1875 issue of *Fraser's Magazine;* there, as well as in the chapter on moral philosophy in *History of English Thought in the Eighteenth Century,* he demonstrated the interest that led him to begin composing a treatise on ethics soon after Minny Stephen's death. Early in 1877 he sketched out his "Thoughts on Morals," which became *The Science of Ethics* (1882). Stephen thought it his best book, but neither his contemporaries nor posterity has agreed. Even Maitland, as affectionate a biographer as one would care to have, admitted that it lacked skillful exposition and quoted a friend as remarking that it was the only dull book Stephen ever wrote. "As ethics, it is worthless," Annan writes; it is, as others maintain as well, another example of the difficulty of trying to mount an ethical theory on the analogy between organism and society. Not a typical social Darwinist, Stephen nevertheless used the biological metaphor with all its pitfalls; he attempted to synthesize Comte and Darwin, and if he did not succeed in working this all out to satisfy such critics as Henry Sidgwick or G. E. Moore, his insistence that moral rules originated in the family, grew within a social context, and were adopted to make possible the health and survival of society was an idea that has received a good deal of attention over the last hundred years. Nor was his idea of human excellence contemptible. His 1880 *Fortnightly Review* essay on Spinoza concludes with an eloquent statement defining the ideal human being. Though too long to quote here, the passage contains one sentence revealing an essential element in Stephen: the duty of the ideal human being, he writes, "is to labour for the extension of truth, not to try to prop up mere dying error; and to promote the growth of a social order which has the chance of permanence in so far as it satisfies the legitimate aspirations of mankind."

The ideal human would also be a great walker, not only on Alpine slopes but across the fields, hills, and meadows of England, violating "No Trespassing" signs on principle and ignoring foul weather as much as possible. Late in 1879 the Sunday Tramps were organized, with long-gaited Stephen as leader and chief navigator. Every other Sunday the "Chief" would set the course, compass in hand, timetable in his head, few words on his lips unless the party dawdled; then his power of harangue brought even the most sluggish hastening to the nearest railway station. He could be a good companion, if often taciturn or sardonic in conversation. As Maitland remarked, Stephen sometimes "liked a companion who had nothing to say and said it at great length." In this way, apparently, he passed his walk about the big toe of England, as he called Land's End, in the spring of 1882 to reach St. Ives, Cornwall, where stood Talland House, to which he had purchased the lease the year before. Early in 1882 his third child was born, the daughter who was to immortalize the house and harbor of St. Ives as well as Godrevy Lighthouse forty-five years later. That was where the family spent their long summers, until the last in 1894. It was where they went fishing and the babies bathed naked at the beach. It was also where Stephen recharged his batteries, drained by the stress and worry of getting out volume after volume of *The Dictionary of National Biography,* of which he became editor in 1882.

The circulation of the *Cornhill* had dropped from over 20,000 in 1871 to 12,000 by 1882.

When George Smith, the publisher, told Stephen of the situation, they agreed that new blood might save the magazine; Stephen promptly resigned, somewhat depressed, despite Smith's assertion that the problem was "the goodness of the magazine and the bad taste of the public." In any case, Smith had a major project afoot, *The Dictionary of National Biography*, and wanted Stephen to be its first editor at a salary of £800. After some cogitation he took it on, for his publisher, for his family, and for the generations to come. Smith chose Stephen because he knew his man, and his man knew how to choose assistants and contributors. Together they performed a kind of miracle in getting out the promised four volumes a year until, some years after he had retired from the editorial chair, the sixty-third volume made its appointed appearance. The excellent subeditor he chose was Sidney Lee, born Solomon Lazarus Lee, a brilliant young Balliol B.A. with a passion for Elizabethan scholarship, calm when Stephen was tense, an efficient office manager. Stephen himself became the superb, concise biographer, who set the pattern early with his life of Joseph Addison, the standard model for all contributors. "No flowers, by request" was said by Canon Ainger to have been the motto; thus many "lives" had their adipose tissue removed by the editor, who came to believe that the art of writing consisted in making one word do the work of two. Untrained as a historical scholar, he soon caught the antiquarian fever and contributed 378 biographies, many of them written after he was no longer editor. Few have mastered the art of the purposive articulation of fact as well as he; in fact, the style is so lean and muscular that it is a shock to run into such straight-faced irony as his remark that George Eliot's Tito Melema was one of her "finest feminine characters" or the terse judgment that Robert Owen was "one of those intolerable bores who are the salt of the earth." The master of the black-and-white portrait could occasionally practice caricature.

The work came close to killing him. He worried. Haunted by the possibility of a volume being late or that too many errors would be found, he would wake at night "with the horrors." When Julia Stephen was away nursing her mother, he groaned to her of the "D.D."–damned dictionary–and as time went on the groans increased; on one occasion he told her that on his return from St. Ives he had shrunk from the task of reading proofs for a whole day. But in the first years he does not seem to have

known how to do anything but overwork. In 1883 he was offered a lectureship at Trinity College, Cambridge, and accepted the offer, giving a set of lectures during Lent of 1884. In November Henry Fawcett died and his widow asked Stephen if he would write the life of his old friend from Trinity Hall. He counted it a privilege to do so. To complete the task he had not only to set down his memories of their lives together at Cambridge–that was the easiest part–but also to get up a knowledge of the workings of the post office, which Fawcett had managed, and also of the Indian affairs, especially Indian finance, concerns to which Fawcett had devoted several years of his long parliamentary career. He finished before the end of 1885 and had the satisfaction of knowing that his *Life of Henry Fawcett*, published that year, went through five editions in short order. It is generally regarded as the most engaging of his book-length biographies and contains some of his more moving utterances, not only in reminiscences of his youth but also in recognition of Fawcett's zeal for the cause of the unfortunate or of minorities, for woman suffrage, or for simple justice to the population of India.

By the end of 1886 the strain began to tell. It was not only the work on the dictionary articles but also the stress of dealing with some of his contributors. One in particular, Alexander Grosart, plagiarized articles from the *Encyclopaedia Britannica* and other sources, invented bibliographies, and indulged in other nefarious practices. The result was that, as Stephen wrote to Charles Eliot Norton, "Our first volume has been delayed by this clerical scoundrel"; hence a doubling of efforts to get it out on time. Then there had been Professor Edward A. Freeman, who insisted that all the Anglo-Saxon names beginning with *A* or *e* should be spelled *AE* and resigned in a huff when the editor decided such orthography would be unbearable. Then there had been another delay with the first volume, caused by a shocking number of misprints. So the proofs were read again and Smith hired more rooms to give an increased staff more space. In January 1887 Stephen was sent to the Alps for a rest. He enjoyed himself hugely in Zermatt, relived his youth, all the while complaining to Julia that he could just as well be at home. Back at home, overwork and hypertension continued. By the fall of 1889 he had had two attacks of nervous exhaustion; he asked that Sidney Lee's name be put next to his on the volume due in March 1890. That winter he went to the Alps again and came back only to catch influenza (a recurring Stephen illness). The doctors said he must retire, and, at Julia Stephen's insistence, retire he did, directing that his name be removed from the title page of volume twenty-seven. His connection with the *DNB* did not cease, however; he continued to write biographies. Finally, in September 1899, he wrote his last "life," on Arthur Young. In May of the following year he attended, as he wrote in a letter to his sister-in-law, a "grand dinner with the Prince of Wales" at the Carlton Hotel. Stephen, who had been suffering from increasing deafness over a period of several years, was unable to hear the speeches; he was utterly bored and left as soon as he decently could. The dinner was only one of the many honors given the *DNB* and its editors. To many, even now, the dictionary is Leslie Stephen's most lasting contribution to scholarship.

The year 1891 was marked by the death of James Russell Lowell, a death that signaled the end of a long intimacy and revived memories of Stephen's first visit to America in 1863 and of the second, with Minny in 1868. Knowing that Lowell's end was near, Stephen crossed the ocean in June 1890 on the S.S. *Scythia* to see his old friend for the last time and to receive an LL.D. from Harvard. The letters he wrote to Julia during this journey are among his most interesting as he had the leisure on board to describe his fellow passengers. From the United States he wrote of people met, places seen, and other events–the Cambridge intelligentsia, the household of Charles Eliot Norton (his dearest friend in America), his visit to Beverly Farms to visit Oliver Wendell Holmes, Jr., and his wife, who, Stephen lamented, had grown excessively fat, and, of course, Lowell himself. Then, too, there was Stephen's first baseball game, Harvard versus Yale, and the Harvard commencement exercises and frolic.

From the end of his editorship to the end of his life he continued to write–essays, lectures, and books–and to read everything from French novels to Adolph von Harnack's *Lehrbuch der Dogmengeschichte*. He also compiled some of his older writings for republication. *An Agnostic's Apology, and Other Essays*, which appeared in 1893, includes pieces written by Stephen in the 1870s and 1880s. As he told Norton, he took some trouble to revise them "to make the detached articles into a kind of whole." To the younger generation, the book came as a breath of fresh air. Maitland called Stephen "one of our liberators"; Pro-

Stephen (right), circa 1870, with his Alpine guide Melchior Anderegg (from Leslie Stephen's Photograph Album, in the Smith College Library Rare Book Room; reproduced with the permission of Professor and Mrs. Quentin Bell and Smith College)

fessor Samuel Alexander of Manchester (1859-1938) told Harold Laski that when he was a young man at Oxford, "things like the *Agnostic's Apology* seemed like beacons of light in a world which the theologians seemed to possess lock, stock, and barrel"; and in her *Diary* (volume 3, 1980), Virginia Woolf records that in 1926 Francis Birrell told her that her father had dominated the twentieth century by pulling down the whole edifice and making it possible for Birrell to have a decent life, meaning that Stephen by his life had shown that morality could survive theology.

Not content to refurbish earlier works, he continued labor on the sequel to *History of English Thought in the Eighteenth Century*, first contemplated in the 1880s and actually begun in 1891. By the end of 1894 he had finished the first volume of *The English Utilitarians*, in which he traced historical background and set forth the life and thought of Jeremy Bentham. While plodding away at the Benthamites he wrote essays for the *National Review* and was elected president of the London Library, but what distracted him from the Utilitarians in this period was writing the life of his brother, James Fitzjames Stephen, who died, a broken man, in 1894. His sister-in-law Mary Stephen asked him to write it, and he could not refuse. It was no easy task. Difficult enough was getting acquainted with all the legal lore necessary to deal with his brother's voluminous works of law and codification; even more difficult was dealing with his feelings about Fitzjames whom he loved as a brother but whose opinions in politics and ethics he deplored. Then there were the complaints and needs of Mary Stephen, who did not want anything to discolor the idol. As usual, Stephen wrote at top speed, from November 1894 till the spring of 1895. Posterity has agreed that it is not up to the life of Fawcett, though the early chapters, which tell a good deal about the home life of the Stephens, have charmed and interested later students of Leslie Stephen's childhood.

In his 19 April 1895 letter Stephen told Norton it had been a terrible winter; he had been losing friends and acquaintances. The letter makes no mention of what he had seen in his wife's face a few days before. Writing to her on 16 April he says, "I am still rather haunted by your looks—you were so tired and weak; and I am afraid that you must have been shivering ever since I saw you." Influenza had taken its toll; her resistance gone, she succumbed to rheumatic fever that a "weakness of the heart," in Stephen's phrase, could not withstand. On the morning of 5 May her oldest son, George, called his stepfather down from the study. Julia Stephen was dying at the age of forty-nine. The blow, Stephen wrote, "shattered" his life. If the death of Minny had maimed his inner security, the death of Julia withdrew the one person who could both soothe and reassure him, soothe his horrors and fears (of financial disaster, for example), restore his fragile self-confidence, and check his "tantarums," as they were known in the family, and flashes of temper. He may well have feared for his sanity, for he knew from his father's and his own history that he was susceptible to breakdown; probably, as Virginia Hyman has argued in a 1980 article

in *Biography*, writing a memoir for his children (the *Mausoleum Book*) was an exercise in self-preservation. For two years his stepdaughter, Stella Duckworth, took over her mother's role; then, in April 1897, she married Jack Hills; again a prop was removed, and his mind trembled. Then, in July, to augment the litany of death, Stella died, an unborn child in her womb. Stephen's eldest daughter, Vanessa, took over the household at the age of eighteen and endured brutal explosions of rage on Wednesdays if the books did not balance or if expenses seemed too great. As before, "unhappiness tried [his] temper." A moment after the fireworks were over, Virginia, still trembling in anger, would be asked if she cared to take a walk. Thus in studies of Virginia Woolf we often hear about "the old wretch," her father. Based on her own descriptions, she was thoroughly ambivalent about him: she records the scholar father, and the social father, and the father who encouraged her to devour his library, engaged Clara Pater and Janet Case to teach her Greek and saw to it that Vanessa got the best artistic training available, while the sons, Thoby and, eventually, Adrian, went up to Cambridge.

All the while, in his study Stephen worked on. The Ethical Society of London asked for his addresses to their various groups and had them published in two volumes under the title *Social Rights and Duties* (1896). He did not think much of their value and later readers have tended to agree with him, but they find "Forgotten Benefactors" memorable and moving as it contains a deeply felt, implicit tribute to Julia Stephen and to the kind of life and affection he had shared with her. In 1898 his stepson Gerald created the publishing firm of Duckworth and Company. An early item on its list was Stephen's four-volume *Studies of a Biographer* (1898-1902), composed of what he characteristically called "twaddlings" from the *National Review*. The studies ranged from such general ones as "Biography" and "The Evolution of Editors" to those of recent scholarship or biographies of such older worthies as John Donne and John Byrom and included the superb essay "Wordsworth's Youth"; in addition to older writers, Stephen was able to portray with judicious wit and wisdom a number of his contemporaries, such as Trollope, Tennyson, Huxley, Benjamin Jowett, Walter Bagehot, and Matthew Arnold. Only one of the studies deals with religion, but as Noël Annan notes, the essay on Pascal is "the most interesting of all Stephen's religious essays."

Between the first and second pair of volumes in *Studies of a Biographer* finally appeared the three-volume *English Utilitarians* (1900), too long on the stocks, as Maitland put it, and, as Stephen himself admitted, marred by "logic-chopping." Far more than in *History of English Thought in the Eighteenth Century*, however, especially in the first volume, he succeeded in showing the close relationship between social conditions and the history of ideas; in short, in writing intellectual history as he had said it should be written a quarter of a century before. Complementing French historian Elie Halévy's *The Growth of Philosophical Radicalism* (1901-1904), Stephen is strong on the social background whereas Halévy is strong on the filiation of ideas. W. G. Pogson Smith's essay on both books in the *English Historical Review* (April 1902) presented a balanced comparison, praising Stephen as "the foremost living exponent in England of the historical method in the interpretation of the history of ideas." The fact is that the prose of *The English Utilitarians* is often vivid and Stephen's ability to image an idea remarkable, but he has a tendency to get bogged down in minutiae. In short, the later work lacks the passion of *History of English Thought in the Eighteenth Century*, especially in the volumes he wrote after Julia's death, and therefore, though able, cannot be judged a classic; it was not republished until 1950.

Meanwhile honors had been pouring in. Edinburgh, Harvard, and Cambridge had given him honorary degrees (1885, 1890, 1892). In 1892 he had succeeded Lord Tennyson as president of the London Library and three years later the Massachusetts Historical Society elected him to membership. In 1901 Oxford conferred an honorary doctorate, and the next year Stephen became one of the original members of the British Academy. More prized than these honors, however, were new friends. One was F. W. Maitland, the historian, who had married Stephen's niece and was to be his biographer. Another was Alice

Stephen with his second wife, Julia Duckworth Stephen, and children, Adrian (at Julia's right), Gerald Duckworth, Virginia, Thoby, and Vanessa Stephen, and George Duckworth (from Leslie Stephen's Photograph Album, in the Smith College Library Rare Book Room; reproduced with the permission of Professor and Mrs. Quentin Bell and Smith College)

Green, widow of the historian John Richard Green and herself a historian of some stature. She asked him to edit her husband's letters, which he did, coming to enjoy the task as he went. Another was Mrs. Humphry Ward who was, as Stephen told Norton, so kind to him that he would stop turning up his nose at her attempts "to preach Christianity and water" in her writings. He needed all the new friends he could get, for the old were dying fast; each passing he recorded at the end of the memoir he had written for the children, so that its final pages are a dismal necrology which inspired the children to call it the *Mausoleum Book*, a title adopted for the 1977 published version edited by Alan Bell. To Norton he confessed to times of depression but added that he kept tolerably cheerful and had not the slightest desire to commit suicide.

His vitality continued, even in his last significant works, *George Eliot* (1902), *Hobbes* (1904), and the little masterpiece *English Literature and Society in the Eighteenth Century* (1904). Inaugurating a second series of the English Men of Letters volumes, John Morley offered his old friend a choice of James Anthony Froude, Robert Browning, or George Eliot. He chose Eliot, whom he had known in the 1870s. Though he admired her early works inordinately and judged all but the concluding section of *The Mill on the Floss* to be superb fiction, he found *Felix Holt*, *Romola*, and *Daniel Deronda*, as well as *The Spanish Gypsy*, rather boring but not without great moments. In general, modern criticism has modified Stephen's view that the later work is inferior to the earlier, but it is notable that some of his perceptions still hold.

Hobbes he enjoyed writing, though regretting that there was so little biographical information; what he found made him think "Hobbes, qua man . . . delicious," but he was not able to finish the volume until September 1903 and did not live to see the book in print. The first interruption came from a request from Oxford in early 1902 that he give the Ford Lectures for 1903. The second was the discovery in April that he was suffering from cancer, though the surgery was not performed until December of that year. He set about writing the lectures at once but when he finished was too weak to read them and asked his nephew Herbert Fisher to take his place. While composing them came the final, official honor, the KCB–Knight Commander of the Bath–awarded at the time of Edward VII's coronation, primarily in recognition of his services to

the nation in editing the *Dictionary of National Biography*. Reluctant at first to accept, he yielded to family insistence; the king's equerry arrived on the appointed day in February 1903, "very polite and pleasant," as Stephen described him, to deliver the star of the Order of the Bath.

English Literature and Society in the Eighteenth Century (the Ford Lectures) is a remarkable distillation of a lifetime of absorption in the history, thought, and literature of his favorite century. Republished five times by 1947, this book, a short history of eighteenth-century culture, clearly set literary study in the direction defined by Stanley Hyman in *The Armed Vision* (1948) as being "the organized use of non-literary techniques and bodies of knowledge to obtain insights into literature." In 1951 it was regarded by Annan as introducing a new form of literary study, the sociological, and thus, Annan notes, the lectures are "prolegomena to a new branch of study." Many twentieth-century studies of the interrelation of literature and society, both Marxist and non-Marxist, are surely in Stephen's tradition. *English Literature and Society in the Eighteenth Century* was, however, more than a portent; it achieves in small compass a coordination of theory and practice Stephen had been unable to effect fully in his big books. Through a skillful use of imagery Stephen creates a texture and a structure to correspond with the fluid movements of history, thus giving the reader a vivid sense of the interaction of society, ideas, and literature. It is justly considered a minor classic.

Stephen's last days are recorded in detail in Maitland's *Life and Letters of Leslie Stephen*, in which are also included a few pages by his daughter Virginia, whose letters to Violet Dickinson along with Stephen's own to friends and acquaintances give a picture of his dignified courage and serenity in facing the death he knew was coming. He read voraciously to the end. Like Lear, the great rage had died within him, and he seemed to Virginia, if not to Vanessa, to be a lovable creature, who was ready to die on his own account but would like to have lived on to see what happened to the young. Old friends came to visit and letters poured in, especially after he became Sir Leslie. A few days before the end, Lord Haldane told him he was like Socrates, teaching them all how to die. "You will all of you make me vain," Stephen replied, smiling. Painlessly, he sank into a coma and died on the morning of 22 February 1904. Two days later the funeral was held at Golders Green, where he was cremated.

His ashes were buried at Highgate Cemetery.

Biography:

Frederic William Maitland, *The Life and Letters of Leslie Stephen* (London: Duckworth, 1906).

References:

Noël Annan, *Leslie Stephen: The Godless Victorian* (New York: Random House, 1984);

Jeffrey von Arx, *Progress and Pessimism: Religion, Politics, and History in Late Nineteenth-Century Britain* (Cambridge: Harvard University Press, 1985);

Quentin Bell, "The Mausoleum Book," *Review of English Literature,* 6 (January 1965): 9-18;

Merle M. Bevington, *The Saturday Review, 1855-1868* (New York: Columbia University Press, 1941);

John W. Bicknell, "Leslie Stephen as an Intellectual Historian," Ph.D. dissertation, Cornell University, 1950;

Bicknell, "Leslie Stephen's *English Thought in the Eighteenth Century*: A Tract for the Times," *Victorian Studies,* 6 (December 1962): 103-120;

Bicknell, "Mr. Ramsay was Young Once," in *Virginia Woolf and Bloomsbury: A Centenary Celebration,* edited by Jane Marcus (Bloomington: Indiana University Press, 1987);

Bicknell, "The Unbelievers," in *Victorian Prose: A Guide to Research,* edited by David J. DeLaura (New York: Modern Language Association, 1973);

Ronald William Clark, *The Victorian Mountaineers* (London: Batsford, 1953);

Charles Crawley, *Trinity Hall: The History of a Cambridge College, 1350-1975* (Cambridge: Cambridge University Press, 1976);

Edwin Everett, *The Party of Humanity: The Fortnightly Review and its Contributions, 1865-1874* (Chapel Hill: University of North Carolina Press, 1939);

Winifred Gérin, *Anne Thackeray Ritchie* (Oxford: Oxford University Press, 1981);

Kenneth Graham, *English Criticism of the Novel, 1875-1900* (London: Oxford University Press, 1965);

John Gross, *The Rise and Fall of the Man of Letters* (London: Weidenfeld & Nicolson, 1969);

Bruce Haley, *The Healthy Body and Victorian Culture* (Cambridge: Harvard University Press, 1978);

Katherine Hill, "Virginia Woolf and Leslie Stephen: History and Literary Revolution,"

PMLA, 96 (May 1981): 351-362;

Virginia Hyman, "Concealment and Disclosure in Sir Leslie Stephen's *Mausoleum Book,*" *Biography,* 3 (Spring 1980): 121-131;

Hyman, "Late Victorian and Early Modern: Continuities in Criticism of Leslie Stephen and Virginia Woolf," *English Literature in Transition,* 23, no. 3 (1980): 44-54;

Hyman, "Reflections in the Looking Glass: Leslie Stephen and Virginia Woolf," *Journal of Modern Literature,* 10 (July 1983): 197-216;

Q. D. Leavis, "Leslie Stephen: Cambridge Critic," in *A Selection from Scrutiny,* edited by F. R. Leavis (Cambridge: Cambridge University Press, 1968);

Jean Love, *Virginia Woolf: Sources of Madness and Art* (Berkeley: University of California Press, 1977);

Desmond MacCarthy, *Leslie Stephen* (Leslie Stephen Lecture) (Cambridge: Cambridge University Press, 1937);

Oscar Maurer, Jr., "Froude and *Fraser's Magazine 1860-1874,*" Studies in English by the Department of English, University of Texas, 28 (1949): 213-243;

Maurer, "Leslie Stephen and the *Cornhill Magazine,*" *University of Texas Studies in English,* 32 (1953): 67-95;

Maurer, "My Squeamish Public: Some Problems of Victorian Magazine Publishers and Editors," *University of Virginia Studies in Bibliography,* 12 (1959): 21-40;

Maurer, "Pope and the Victorians," *Studies in English by the Department of English, University of Texas,* 24 (1944): 211-238;

C. W. F. Noyce, *Scholar Mountaineers: Pioneers of Parnassus* (London: Dobson, 1950);

S. P. Rosenbaum, "An Educated Man's Daughter: Leslie Stephen, Virginia Woolf and the Bloomsbury Group," in *Virginia Woolf: New Critical Essays,* edited by Patricia Clements and Isobel Grundy (Totowa, N.J.: Barnes & Noble, 1983);

C. R. Sanders, "Sir Leslie Stephen, Coleridge, and Two Coleridgeans," *PMLA,* 55 (September 1940): 795-801;

John W. Robertson Scott, *The Story of the Pall Mall Gazette, of its First Editor Frederick Greenwood and of its founder George Murray Smith* (London & New York: Oxford University Press, 1950);

Barbara Ann Schmidt, "In the Shadow of Thackeray: Leslie Stephen as the Editor of the *Cornhill Magazine,*" in *Innovators and Preach-*

ers: *The Role of the Editor in Victorian England*, edited by Joel Wiener (Westport, Conn.: Greenwood Press, 1985), pp. 77-96;

Martin Stemerick, "From Stephen to Woolf: The Victorian Family and Modern Rebellion," Ph.D. dissertation, University of Texas at Austin, 1982;

John Timmerman, "Leslie Stephen as a Biographer," Ph.D. dissertation, Northwestern University, 1948;

Samuel J. Tindall, Jr., "Leslie Stephen as Editor of the *Cornhill Magazine*," Ph.D. dissertation, University of South Carolina, 1969;

J. D. Wilson, *Leslie Stephen and Matthew Arnold as Critics of Wordsworth* (Leslie Stephen Lecture) (Cambridge: Cambridge University Press, 1939);

Virginia Woolf, "Leslie Stephen, the Philosopher at Home," in her *The Captain's Deathbed and Other Essays* (New York: Harcourt, Brace, 1950);

Woolf, "Reminiscences" and "A Sketch of the Past," in her *Moments of Being*, edited by Jeanne Schulkind, revised edition (New York & London: Harcourt Brace Jovanovich, 1985);

David D. Zink, *Leslie Stephen* (New York: Twayne, 1972).

Papers:

The major depositories of Stephen letters are at the Houghton Library, Harvard University; the Perkins Library, Duke University; the Henry W. and Albert Berg Collection, New York Public Library; the National Library of Scotland; the Pierpont Morgan Library, New York; the Bodleian Library, Oxford; the Brotherton Library, University of Leeds; and the Macmillan Archives, British Library. Such manuscripts as are known to exist are scattered: the Perkins Library at Duke holds about forty manuscripts of articles Stephen wrote for the *Cornhill Magazine*; the Pierpont Morgan Library holds the manuscript for *History of English Thought in the Eighteenth Century*; the Berg Collection has the manuscript of *The Science of Ethics*; the British Library holds the bound manuscript of the *Mausoleum Book* (as well as Stephen's first draft), a "Calendar of Correspondence" made by Stephen, and a "Book of Extracts" from the letters written between Stephen and Julia Duckworth in the years preceding their marriage. Two of Stephen's surviving notebooks containing comments on his reading as well as the draft of a philosophical treatise (never finished or published) are held by the Rose Memorial Library, Drew University.

Robert Louis Stevenson

(13 November 1850-3 December 1894)

Richard A. Boyle

See also the Stevenson entry in *DLB 18, Victorian Novelists After 1885.*

BOOKS: *The Pentland Rising* (Edinburgh: Privately printed, 1866);

An Appeal to the Clergy (Edinburgh & London: Blackwood, 1875);

An Inland Voyage (London: Kegan Paul, 1878; Boston: Roberts Brothers, 1883);

Edinburgh: Picturesque Notes, with Etchings (London: Seeley, Jackson & Halliday, 1879; New York: Macmillan, 1889);

Travels with a Donkey in the Cévennes (London: Kegan Paul, 1879; Boston: Roberts Brothers, 1879);

Virginibus Puerisque and Other Papers (London: Kegan Paul, 1881; New York: Collier, 1881);

Familiar Studies of Men and Books (London: Chatto & Windus, 1882; New York: Dodd, Mead, 1887);

New Arabian Nights (2 volumes, London: Chatto & Windus, 1882; 1 volume, New York: Holt, 1882);

The Silverado Squatters (London: Chatto & Windus, 1883; New York: Munro, 1884);

Treasure Island (London: Cassell, 1883; Boston: Roberts Brothers, 1884);

A Child's Garden of Verses (London: Longmans, Green, 1885; New York: Scribners, 1885);

More New Arabian Nights: The Dynamiter, by Stevenson and Fanny Van de Grift Stevenson (London: Longmans, Green, 1885; New York: Holt, 1885);

Macaire (Edinburgh: Privately printed, 1885);

Prince Otto: A Romance (London: Chatto & Windus, 1885; Boston: Roberts Brothers, 1886);

Strange Case of Dr. Jekyll and Mr. Hyde (London: Longmans, Green, 1886; New York: Scribners, 1886);

Kidnapped (London: Cassell, 1886; New York: Scribners, 1886);

Some College Memories (Edinburgh: University Union Committee, 1886; New York: Mansfield & Wessels, 1899);

The Merry Men and Other Tales and Fables (London:

This photograph of Stevenson at age thirty-five was taken by his stepson Lloyd Osbourne

Chatto & Windus, 1887; New York: Scribners, 1887);

Underwoods (London: Chatto & Windus, 1887; New York: Scribners, 1887);

Memories and Portraits (London: Chatto & Windus, 1887; New York: Scribners, 1887);

Memoir of Fleeming Jenkin (London & New York: Longmans, Green, 1887);

The Misadventures of John Nicholson: A Christmas Story (New York: Lovell, 1887);

The Black Arrow: A Tale of the Two Roses (London: Cassell, 1888; New York: Scribners, 1888);

The Master of Ballantrae: A Winter's Tale (London: Cassell, 1889; New York: Scribners, 1889);

The Wrong Box, by Stevenson and Lloyd Osbourne (London: Longmans, Green, 1889;

New York: Scribners, 1889);

Ballads (London: Chatto & Windus, 1890; New York: Scribners, 1890);

Father Damien: An Open Letter to the Reverend Dr. Hyde of Honolulu (London: Chatto & Windus, 1890; Portland, Maine: Mosher, 1897);

Across the Plains, With Other Memories and Essays (London: Chatto & Windus, 1892; New York: Scribners, 1892);

A Footnote to History: Eight Years of Trouble in Samoa (London: Cassell, 1892; New York: Scribners, 1892);

Three Plays: Deacon Brodie, Beau Austin, Admiral Guinea, by Stevenson and W. E. Henley (London: Nutt, 1892; New York: Scribners, 1892);

The Wrecker, by Stevenson and Osbourne (London: Cassell, 1892; New York: Scribners, 1892);

Island Nights' Entertainments: Consisting of The Beach of Falesá, The Bottle Imp, The Isle of Voices (London: Cassell, 1893; New York: Scribners, 1893);

Catriona: A Sequel to Kidnapped (London: Cassell, 1893; New York: Scribners, 1893);

The Ebb-Tide: A Trio and a Quartette, by Stevenson and Osbourne (Chicago: Stone & Kimball, 1894; London: Heinemann, 1894);

The Body-Snatcher (New York: Merriam, 1895);

The Amateur Emigrant from the Clyde to Sandy Hook (Chicago: Stone & Kimball, 1895; New York: Scribners, 1899);

The Strange Case of Dr. Jekyll and Mr. Hyde, with Other Fables (London: Longmans, Green, 1896);

Weir of Hermiston: An Unfinished Romance (London: Chatto & Windus, 1896; New York: Scribners, 1896);

A Mountain Town in France: A Fragment (New York & London: Lane, 1896);

Songs of Travel and Other Verses (London: Chatto & Windus, 1896);

In the South Seas (New York: Scribners, 1896; London: Chatto & Windus, 1900);

St. Ives: Being the Adventures of a French Prisoner in England (New York: Scribners, 1897; London: Heinemann, 1898);

The Morality of the Profession of Letters (Gouverneur, N.Y.: Brothers of the Book, 1899);

A Stevenson Medley, edited by S. Colvin (London: Chatto & Windus, 1899);

Essays and Criticisms (Boston: Turner, 1903);

Prayers Written at Vailima, With an Introduction by Mrs. Stevenson (New York: Scribners, 1904; London: Chatto & Windus, 1905);

The Story of a Lie and Other Tales (Boston: Turner, 1904);

Essays of Travel (London: Chatto & Windus, 1905);

Essays in the Art of Writing (London: Chatto & Windus, 1905);

Essays, edited by W. L. Phelps (New York: Scribners, 1906);

Lay Morals and Other Papers (London: Chatto & Windus, 1911);

Records of a Family of Engineers (London: Chatto & Windus, 1916);

The Waif Woman (London: Chatto & Windus, 1916);

On the Choice of a Profession (London: Chatto & Windus, 1916);

Poems Hitherto Unpublished, edited by G. S. Hellman, 2 volumes (Boston: Bibliophile Society, 1916);

New Poems and Variant Readings (London: Chatto & Windus, 1918);

Robert Louis Stevenson: Hitherto Unpublished Prose Writings, edited by H. H. Harper (Boston: Bibliophile Society, 1921);

When the Devil Was Well, edited by William P. Trent (Boston: Bibliophile Society, 1921);

Confessions of a Unionist: An Unpublished Talk on Things Current, Written in 1888, edited by F. V. Livingston (Cambridge, Mass.: Privately printed, 1921);

The Best Thing in Edinburgh: An Address to the Speculative Society of Edinburgh in March 1873, edited by K. D. Osbourne (San Francisco: Howell, 1923);

Selected Essays, edited by H. G. Rawlinson (London: Oxford University Press, 1923);

Castaways of Soledad: A Manuscript by Stevenson Hitherto Unpublished, edited by Hellman (Buffalo: Privately printed, 1928);

Monmouth: A Tragedy, edited by C. Vale (New York: Rudge, 1928);

The Charity Bazaar: An Allegorical Dialogue (Westport, Conn.: Georgian Press, 1929);

The Essays of Robert Louis Stevenson, edited by M. Elwin (London: Macdonald, 1950);

Salute to RLS, edited by F. Holland (Edinburgh: Cousland, 1950);

Tales and Essays, edited by G. B. Stern (London: Falcon, 1950);

Silverado Journal, edited by John E. Jordan (San Francisco: Book Club of California, 1954);

From Scotland to Silverado, edited by James D. Hart (Cambridge: Harvard University Press, 1966);

The Amateur Emigrant with Some First Impressions of America, edited by Roger G. Swearingen, 2 volumes (Ashland, Oreg.: Osborne, 1976-1977);

A Newly Discovered Long Story "An Old Song" and a Previously Unpublished Short Story "Edifying Letters of the Rutherford Family," edited by Roger G. Swearingen (Hamden, Conn.: Archon Books, 1982; Paisley, Scotland: Wilfion, 1982);

Robert Louis Stevenson and "The Beach of Falesá": A Study in Victorian Publishing with the Original Text, edited by Barry Menikoff (Stanford: Stanford University Press, 1984).

Collections: *The Works of R. L. Stevenson,* Edinburgh Edition, 28 volumes, edited by Sidney Colvin (London: Chatto & Windus, 1894-1898);

The Works of Robert Louis Stevenson, Vailima Edition, 26 volumes, edited by Lloyd Osbourne and Fanny Van de Grift Stevenson (London: Heinemann, 1922-1923; New York: Scribners, 1922-1923);

The Works of Robert Louis Stevenson, Tusitala Edition, 35 volumes (London: Heinemann, 1924);

The Works of Robert Louis Stevenson, South Seas Edition, 32 volumes (New York: Scribners, 1925).

When one reads the nonfiction work of Robert Louis Stevenson along with the novels and short stories, a more complete portrait emerges of the author than that of the romantic vagabond one usually associates with his best-known fiction. The Stevenson of the nonfiction prose is a writer involved in the issues of his craft, his milieu, and his soul. Moreover, one can see the record of his maturation in critical essays, political tracts, biographies, and letters to family and friends. What Stevenson lacks, especially for the tastes of this age, is specificity and expertise: he has not the depth of such writers as John Ruskin, Walter Pater, or William Morris. But he was a shrewd observer of humankind, and his essays reveal his lively and perspicacious mind. Though he lacked originality, he created a rapport with the reader, who senses his enthusiastic embrace of life and art. If Stevenson at first wrote like one who only skimmed the surface of experience, by the end of his life he was passionately committed to his adopted land of Samoa, to his own history, and to the creation of his fiction.

Robert Louis Stevenson was born to Thomas and Margaret Isabella Balfour Stevenson in Edinburgh on 13 November 1850. From the beginning he was sickly. Through much of his childhood he was attended by his faithful nurse, Alison Cunningham, known as Cummy in the family circle. She told him morbid stories about the Covenanters (the Scots Presbyterian martyrs), read aloud to him Victorian penny-serial novels, Bible stories, and the Psalms, and drilled the catechism into him, all with his parents' approval. Thomas Stevenson was quite a storyteller himself, and his wife doted on their only child, sitting in admiration while her precocious son expounded on religious dogma. Stevenson inevitably reacted to the morbidity of his religious education and to the stiffness of his family's middle-class values, but that rebellion would come only after he entered Edinburgh University.

The juvenilia that survives from his childhood shows an observer who was already sensitive to religious issues and Scottish history. Not surprisingly, the boy who listened to Cummy's religious tales first tried his hand at retelling Bible stories: "A History of Moses" was followed by "The Book of Joseph." When Stevenson was sixteen his family published a pamphlet he had written entitled *The Pentland Rising,* a recounting of the murder of Nonconformist Scots Presbyterians who rebelled against their royalist persecutors.

In November 1867 Stevenson entered Edinburgh University, where he pursued his studies indifferently until 1872. Instead of concentrating on academic work, he busied himself in learning how to write, imitating the styles of William Hazlitt, Sir Thomas Browne, Daniel Defoe, Charles Lamb, and Michel de Montaigne. By the time he was twenty-one, he had contributed several papers to the short-lived *Edinburgh University Magazine,* the best of which was a fanciful bit of fluff entitled "The Philosophy of Umbrellas." Edinburgh University was a place for him to play the truant more than the student. His only consistent course of study seemed to have been of bohemia: Stevenson adopted a wide-brimmed hat, a cravat, and a boy's coat that earned him the nickname of Velvet Jacket, while he indulged a taste for haunting the byways of Old Town and becoming acquainted with its denizens.

The most significant work from his student days was "On a New Form of Intermittent Light for Lighthouses," a scientific piece that explained the economical combination of revolving mirrors and oil-burning lamps. He read it before the Royal Scottish Society of Arts on 27 March 1871 and received the society's Silver Medal. The paper, a result of his engineering studies, revealed his keen eye for technical detail. Only two weeks later, however, Stevenson took a long walk with his father and declined to follow the family profession of engineering; he meant to become a writer. Thomas Stevenson insisted that the young man study law, and his son stuck to the bargain long enough to receive, in 1875, a law degree he barely used.

It was not the first time that Stevenson disappointed his father. In January 1873 Thomas Stevenson discovered some papers that seemed to suggest that the young Stevenson was an atheist. Father and son had their worst falling out. In letters to his student chums, especially to Charles Baxter, Stevenson called himself a "damned curse" on his family. Though it is tempting to see his filial rebellion as a classic Victorian melodrama, father and son did reconcile. The episode is more important in having given the author one of the enduring themes of his fiction. It runs from "An Old Song," a short story published in an 1877 issue of the weekly *London*, to the masterly romance *Weir of Hermiston* (1896), left unfinished. It also threads through his nonfiction, in which it is tempered by a tone of reconciliation. For example, in "Crabbed Age and Youth," written in 1877, Stevenson seems to be looking for the common bond that father and son share.

In the decade after his university graduation, Stevenson steeped himself in life, finding an essential core of good humor in people and things. Something of the lightheartedness of this period survives in the humorous essays in *Virginibus Puerisque and Other Papers* (1881), published when the author was thirty-one years old. The essays in this collection had been originally published from 1876 to 1879 in the *Cornhill*, *Macmillan's*, and *London* magazines. The collection received little attention from the critics, but the brilliant whimsy and ironic tone in these pieces were well matched to their loose structures, modeled after Thomas Browne's and William Hazlitt's works, which Stevenson admired. He pretends to analyze marriage in "Virginibus Puerisque" and the relationship between old and young in "Crabbed Age and Youth"; he mounts a pseudophilosophical defense of sloth in "An Apology for Idlers" and humorously advocates the old method of illuminating cities in "A Plea for Gas Lamps." In "Child's Play," "El Dorado," and "Pan's Pipes," the author seems more entranced with the flight of his own rhetoric than he does with the topic at hand. There is a more serious

Decorative title page for Stevenson's 1878 account of his trip down the Oisé River in France (Thomas Cooper Library, University of South Carolina)

side to the collection as well: in "Aes Triplex" and "Ordered South" Stevenson deals with his physical frailty and the trips away from Scotland's rugged winters he had taken for his health. As a boy, Stevenson had been to the Continent several times, and he grew up to love purposeless, rambling tours across Europe.

In *An Inland Voyage* (1878), written from a journal he had kept of a trip down the French river Oise with his friend Walter Simpson, Stevenson glories in the slow pace of his vagabond life traveling through France. The young author expresses pleasure at having been suspected of being a Prussian spy by the French gendarmes and pride at having endured hunger, cold, and misery on a journey that, from Stevenson's account, sounds like one of the oddest and most aimless ever undertaken. The publication of *An Inland Voyage* was significant: it was his first full-length book and was reviewed kindly by the critics, though it did not enjoy as many printings as his next travelogue did.

Travels with a Donkey in the Cévennes (1879) has something of the same sense of aimlessness and introspection as *An Inland Voyage,* but it lacks the other's high spirits. Its more somber, melancholy tone is due to the fact that Stevenson had fallen in love, and the relationship was a difficult one. On a trip to a French artists' colony in July 1876 with his cousin Bob, Stevenson had met Fanny Van de Grift Osbourne, a married woman, an American, and ten years Stevenson's senior. She had been living in Paris and had come to the sleepy summer colony of Grez to recuperate after the death of her son. By the time she returned to America in 1878, Stevenson had fallen deeply in love with her; he undertook his walking tour through the mountains in France in part as a restorative to his emotional life.

In August 1879 Stevenson received a cablegram from Fanny Osbourne, who by that time had rejoined her husband in California. Details are vague, but there seems to have been some last attempt by Osbourne to break with Stevenson; the contents of the cable were never revealed by either to family or friends. With the impetuosity of one of his own fictional characters, Stevenson set off from Greenock, Scotland, on 7 August 1879 for America. On 18 August Stevenson landed, sick, nearly penniless, in New York. From there he took an overland train journey in miserable conditions to California, where he nearly died. After meeting with Fanny Osbourne in Monterey, and no doubt depressed at the uncertainty of her divorce, he went camping in the Santa Lucia mountains, where he lay sick for two nights until two frontiersmen found him and nursed him back to health. Still unwell, Stevenson moved to Monterey in December 1879 and thence to San Francisco, where he fluctuated between life and death, continually fighting off illness.

Stevenson characteristically turned the ocean-crossing and transcontinental journey into grist for the literary mill. "The Story of a Lie" and "The Amateur Emigrant" were two products of Stevenson's trip. The former, a short story, was published in the *New Quarterly Magazine* in 1879. In the latter, a travelogue, Stevenson noted the harsher side of life, especially for the immigrant passenger aboard ship sailing for America. Its grim tone distressed his friends and family. Certain passages were considered too graphic by

the publisher and by Stevenson's father: Thomas Stevenson bought all the copies of the already printed travelogue because he found it beneath his son's talent. Stevenson also produced a travelogue about the train journey, "Across the Plains," which was published as the title piece of his 1892 essay collection. The suppressed piece and "Across the Plains" were eventually published together in *The Amateur Emigrant from the Clyde to Sandy Hook* in 1895, the year after Stevenson's death.

When Stevenson left Scotland so abruptly he temporarily estranged his parents. They were also upset about his relationship with a married woman. However, hearing of their son's dire circumstances, they cabled him enough money to save him from poverty. Fanny Osbourne obtained her divorce from her husband, and she and Stevenson were married on 19 May 1880 in San Francisco. For their honeymoon they headed to Mount Saint Helena in Napa Valley, California–partly on the recommendation of friends concerned about Stevenson's frail health and partly because their meager finances afforded them no more than the rundown shack they were able to rent at Silverado, on the side of the mountain.

Stevenson also turned this experience into literature: he wrote *The Silverado Squatters* in 1880 from a journal he kept during the approximately two months they spent at the abandoned mine site. It is a pleasant description of their adventures and their domestic life and includes portraits of the people living around Saint Helena and Calistoga in the Napa Valley. The work was first serialized in the *Century Magazine* in 1883 and later that year was published as a book.

When both husband and wife were well enough for extended travel, they returned across the continent and set sail from New York, landing in Britain on 17 August 1880. Fanny Stevenson was soon accepted at the Stevenson family home on 17 Heriot Row. She became a favorite of Stevenson's father and a staunch ally of his mother, with whom she shared the duty of attending to Stevenson's health.

In the next seven years, 1880 to 1887, Stevenson did not flourish as far as his health was concerned, but his literary output was prodigious. Writing was one of the few activities he could do when he was confined to bed because of hemorrhaging lungs–"Bluidy Jack" he nicknamed the recurrent bleeding. But, despite illness, he wrote some of his most enduring fiction, notably *Treasure Island* (1883), *Kidnapped* (1886), *Strange Case of*

Robert Louis Stevenson and His Wife, *1885 painting by John Singer Sargent (Collection of Mrs. John Hay Whitney). In an October 1885 letter Stevenson described the painting as "excellent, but . . . too eccentric to be exhibited." Though he admired "that witty touch of Sargent's," he concluded that the painting "looks dam [sic] queer as a whole."*

Dr. Jekyll and Mr. Hyde (1886), and *The Black Arrow* (1888). He was also busy writing essays and collaborating on plays with W. E. Henley, the poet, essayist, and editor who championed Stevenson in London literary circles and who became the model for Long John Silver in *Treasure Island.* Although he settled well into domestic life with Fanny, Stevenson's letters revealed that he rejoiced in returning to his friends—to fellow artists such as Edmund Gosse and Henley, to Sidney Colvin, his longtime literary adviser, and to Charles Baxter, the confidant from his university days who remained his closest friend as well as financial adviser.

It was also a period of much traveling. His and Fanny's various temporary residences in England, Switzerland, and southern France had more to do with his probable tuberculosis (it was never diagnosed as such during his lifetime) than with his love for travel. It was at Braemar in Scotland that *Treasure Island* was begun, sparked by a map that Stevenson had drawn for the entertain-

ment of his twelve-year-old stepson Lloyd Osbourne. Stevenson had quickly imagined a pirate adventure story to accompany the drawing, and a friend arranged for it to be serialized in the boys' magazine *Young Folks,* where it appeared from October 1881 to January 1882. By the end of the 1880s, it had become one of the most popular and widely read books of the period. William Ewart Gladstone was supposed to have stayed awake all night to read it, and Stevenson, no supporter of Gladstone, snapped upon learning the news that the man would have done better "to attend to the imperial affairs of England." In the seven-year period from 1880 to 1887 Stevenson's output also included essays on the craft of fiction. In these, in which the reader might expect Stevenson to exhibit a more objective attitude than he had in the travelogues, the author's cultivated discursiveness and rambling rhetoric are not always successful.

Stevenson had a very uncomplicated view of art; he would have rewritten Horace to assert that it was better to entertain than to instruct. Consequently his critical essays on literature contain few sustained analyses of style or content. They are more entertaining to read for the narrator's tone than they are instructive about the fine points of writing. In " 'A Penny Plain and Twopence Coloured' " (1884), Stevenson recounts how the seeds of his craft were sown in childhood when he purchased Skelt's Juvenile Drama—a toy set of uncolored or crudely colored cardboard characters (hence the title of Stevenson's essay) who were the principal actors in a usually melodramatic adventure. Stevenson maintained that his art, his life, and his mode of creation were all in some part derivative of the highly exaggerated and romantic world that he had inherited from Skelt's toy.

The same love for the exaggerated world of romance and adventure informs the essays "A Gossip on Romance" (1882) and "A Gossip on a Novel of Dumas's" (1887). Again Stevenson maintains that the better end of reading and writing is entertainment, a claim that led some critics to accuse him of escapism. French realists, such as Émile Zola, had begun to explore the harsher sides of reality in their fiction. To some extent English realists, George Gissing, for example, and Americans, including William Dean Howells and Henry James, agreed in practice with the tenets of realism. But the bulk of Stevenson's literary criticism is explicitly in favor of the romance. He saw himself as the literary descendant of Sir Walter Scott. The best storytelling, he felt, had the ability to whisk readers away from themselves and their circumstances.

It was particularly the tendency in French realism to dwell on sordidness and ugliness that Stevenson rejected. In an 1877 essay, "François Villon: Student, Poet, and Housebreaker," he castigates the French medieval poet François Villon for lying about the poor: Villon had made them out to be as greedy, covetous, and deceitful as he, but he had not the courage to depict their nobility. Stevenson reiterated this theme, but with an eye on the nineteenth-century French realist Zola, in his essay "The Lantern-Bearers" (1888). In this piece he describes a childhood game wherein vacationing schoolboys belted tin bull's-eye lanterns to their waists, buttoned their topcoats over the lanterns, and met in some remote cove to reveal, at a password, the lit lanterns beneath their coats. Stevenson likens the average person to the boy who joyfully walks in the dark knowing he has a lantern "within" him. All people are

noble, although Zola (and realists like him) would dismiss them as dreary lumps of humanity, seeing only the topcoats of mundane dullness, completely missing the nobility that it is the artist's job to uncover.

Stevenson attempted to justify his attack upon realism on technical grounds. In both "A Note on Realism" (1883) and "A Humble Remonstrance" (1884), Stevenson analyzes different types of fiction. The 1883 essay maintains that realism differs from romance only according to the writer's choice of style. In "A Humble Remonstrance," Stevenson answers Henry James's claim in "The Art of Fiction" (1884) that the novel competes with life. Stevenson protests that no novel can ever hope to match life's complexity; it merely abstracts from life to produce a harmonious pattern of its own. Henry James essentially agreed: he had made the point earlier that reality was too immense to capture in art. At Bournemouth, where the Stevensons lived from 1884 to 1887, James came calling in the spring of 1885 and was mistaken for a tradesman. Gradually, however, the two men became close friends. James, in fact, was one of the few of her husband's associates whom Fanny Stevenson trusted. Watchful of her husband's health, she resented the friends who kept Stevenson up into the night.

Fanny Stevenson had never been content to remain on the outside of her husband's craft; she coupled her nursing with editorial duties and alienated some of her husband's friends in the process. Doubtless she had kept him alive from Silverado to Bournemouth, but barring some of his lively friends from seeing Stevenson caused some resentment. W. E. Henley had the worst falling out with Fanny Stevenson, partly because of his drinking and partly because he exhausted Stevenson by keeping him at work collaborating on plays that had little promise. The major crisis occurred after the Stevensons had settled at Saranac Lake, New York (the move was supposed to have been only a temporary leave-taking of Scotland), on 3 October 1887. Henley accused Fanny, in a letter marked confidential, of having stolen a story from Stevenson's cousin, ignoring or forgetting that Fanny had permission to rework the story.

Stevenson was crushed, although he eventually forgave Henley, who never admitted he had done anything wrong. What made the accusation harder to bear was that it came on the heels of Thomas Stevenson's death. The elder Stevenson had died after a long illness in May 1887, plunging his son into a deep depression. In the spring

Page from the original manuscript for In the South Seas, *Stevenson's essay collection based on his observations during three South Pacific cruises in 1888, 1889, and 1890 (American Art Association/Anderson Galleries, sale 4249, 8-9 April 1936)*

of that year Stevenson contemplated arranging his martyrdom in Ireland, intending to die at the hands of night riders, in the theory that his death—he was by now the well-known author of the *Strange Case of Dr. Jekyll and Mr. Hyde*—would draw attention to the injustices suffered there. Partly out of that bizarre wish came *Confessions of a Unionist* (1921), an explanation to Americans why Ireland should continue to be ruled by England. Written in January 1888, it was rejected by Stevenson's American publisher and never published during his lifetime.

In 1888 the main threads of Stevenson's art and life seemed to snap; he wrote the last of his literary essays for *Scribner's* magazine by May, and his serious quarrel with Henley had opened his eyes to betrayal. In a letter he wrote to Baxter in May 1888, he sounded as though he was gambling for new stakes. He informed his friend that he would take a South Seas cruise, one that he expected to heal him emotionally as well as physically: "I have found a yacht, and we are going the full pitch for seven months. If I cannot get my health back . . . 'tis madness; but of course, there is the hope, and I will play big."

The Stevenson party—including Stevenson, his wife, his stepson, and his mother—chartered the yacht *Casco* and sailed southwest from San Francisco to the Marquesas Islands, the Paumotus, and the Society Islands, and thence northward from Tahiti to the Hawaiian Islands by December of 1888. They camped awhile in Honolulu, giving Stevenson time to visit Molokai's leper settlement and to finish his novel *The Master of Ballantrae* (1889). In June 1889 they set out southwest from Honolulu for the Gilbert Islands aboard the schooner *Equator*. From there in December 1889 the Stevensons traveled to the island of Upolu in Samoa. By that time Stevenson realized that his health could never stand a return to Scotland, despite his friends' urgings and his own homesickness. Gosse and Colvin, in particular, urged him to return. Only James and Baxter seemed to react sympathetically to Stevenson's predicament: each time that he ventured far from the equator he fell sick. In October 1890 the Stevenson party returned to Samoa to settle, after a third cruise that took them to Australia, the Gilberts, the Marshalls, and some of the remoter islands in the South Seas.

Stevenson detailed his three cruises and adventures in the letters he wrote to his friends, exulting in his newfound health, relating incidents of life on the open sea, and capturing the flavor of life lived away from Western civilization. From 1889 to 1894 his attitude toward the islanders in his letters gradually changed from paternalism to sympathy for their troubles with Western imperialism. He studied South Seas politics to espouse plans that he believed would ensure harmony between the whites and the indigenous races of the South Pacific. The naiveté of his early letters is absent from his remarkable book of essays on the various island groups and their peoples—*In the South Seas*. Written from material he had collected on the three cruises, the book reveals a much shrewder observer of human nature and politics than the man who had written *Confessions of a Unionist*. He viewed the islanders as humans who were not without a valid culture of their own. They were not all cannibals, nor were they all noble savages. As for politics, he advocated self-rule for the islands, a view that did not always make him popular with contemporary travelers and settlers in the Pacific. But he was never predictable. While he was in Hawaii, for example, Stevenson felt himself drawn to the royalists—those who wanted the United States out of Hawaii. But he resisted becoming involved in their intrigues because he did not fully trust the royalists themselves.

In the South Seas had a checkered publishing history, not so much because of the radical nature of its political views, but because it was not so colorful as his former travelogues. Twenty-two copies for copyright purposes were printed in 1890 by the London firm Cassell; an enlarged text, bearing the Scribners imprint, was published in New York in 1896, and the first British edition, from Chatto and Windus, appeared in 1900. Although Stevenson was happy with his work, his friends back home thought he was wasting his talent on politics when he should have been writing fiction. The complicated publishing history of *In the South Seas* suggests that it may have been too serious for those who wanted Stevenson to remain the introspective traveler he had been when he was younger. The work, however, did find an admirer in Joseph Conrad, who highly approved of its form and its portrayal of life on the edge of civilization.

While Stevenson was in Hawaii, in June 1889 he visited the government's leper colony on Molokai. According to Fanny Stevenson, her husband had first gone to the island on a fact-finding mission, expecting to uncover the "truth" about Father Damien DeVeuster, the missionary to the lepers who had died only a month earlier.

Stevenson at Vailima, his Samoan estate, dictating to his stepdaughter and amanuensis Isobel Strong

His admiration was awakened by firsthand reports of the man's courage and resourcefulness which contradicted then-current rumors that the priest had contracted leprosy through intimacies with female patients. In Sydney, Australia, eight months later Stevenson read an attack in the religious press upon Damien by a Dr. Charles M. Hyde, a former missionary to Molokai, who maintained that these rumors were true. The letter by Hyde was circulated throughout the South Seas and the world. Stevenson was so provoked that he wrote his famous *Father Damien: An Open Letter to the Reverend Dr. Hyde of Honolulu* (1890) in a hotel lobby, in uncharacteristic haste.

His defense of Father Damien was curious. It did not deny Hyde's charges so much as it suggested that their publication was an indication of the meanness, cowardice, and jealousy of Hyde. Though defending Damien DeVeuster's character was a way for Stevenson to identify with the good work of the missionary priest, the defense involved some risk. Stevenson fully expected to be sued and financially ruined by Hyde–by a libel

suit he knew, as a lawyer, he had little chance of winning. Luckily for the Stevensons, Hyde contented himself with dismissing the author as a crank. The episode had a profound effect on Stevenson and his work on the South Seas. He continued to champion the oppressed even when it seemed to threaten his safety and security.

While he lived in the Pacific, Stevenson kept up his usual impressive literary output. From 1888 to 1894 the author finished *The Wrecker* (1892), a collaboration with Lloyd Osbourne; *Island Nights' Entertainments* (1893), containing "The Beach of Falesá," "The Bottle Imp," and "The Isle of Voices"; and *The Ebb-Tide* (1894), again a collaboration with his stepson. He also completed the sequel to *Kidnapped, Catriona,* published in 1893. At his death in December 1894 two novels lay unfinished–*St. Ives* (1897), a potboiler about a French prisoner who escapes from a Scottish jail to England, and *Weir of Hermiston* (1896), generally acknowledged to be a masterpiece although it is a fragment. In his last years he also worked industriously at his nonfiction.

With *In the South Seas* finished, he completed *A Footnote to History,* published in 1892. At his death *Records of a Family of Engineers* (1916) lay unfinished.

Stevenson had gathered material on Samoa for *In the South Seas* but later realized that he had enough for more than one book. The Samoan political situation in the late 1880s and early 1890s was complex. Historically the Samoans had chosen a king from among several tribal high chiefs. Because of friction over trade in the islands, Germany, England, and the United States had attempted but aborted a plan to divide the islands into protectorates. In 1888 the Germans banished Laupepa, one of three tribal chiefs in contention for kingship, the other two being Tamasese and Mataafa. After a short war between the other two chiefs (in which some Germans died) the three Western nations formed a tripartite consulate and established Laupepa as king of Samoa and Mataafa as vice-king. Arguing that Mataafa had, by rights and power, more claim to kingship than his rival, Stevenson advocated Mataafa's cause in *A Footnote to History* and continued writing letters to several British newspapers well into 1894, stirring up a hornet's nest of controversy for himself in Samoa. His book earned him the resentment of the Germans and threats of deportation from harassed British officials. When the Germans banished Mataafa to the Marshall Islands in 1893, Stevenson's agitation could do no more than secure the release of some of Mataafa's supporters who were jailed in Apia.

In *A Footnote to History* Stevenson advocated justice and compromise among the Samoan factions. He wanted to bring the affair before the public, to acquaint Westerners with the effects of imperialistic policies they tacitly supported. Though he apologized for the tempest-in-a-teapot nature of the rebellion, he believed *A Footnote to History* performed a service for the beleaguered country.

In the last two years of his life Stevenson's letters to his friends in Great Britain increasingly revealed his longing for Scotland and the frustration he felt at the thought of never seeing his homeland again. To S. R. Crockett he wrote, "I shall never see Auld Reekie. I shall never set my foot again upon the heather. Here I am until I die, and here will I be buried. The word is out and the doom written." It may have been this preoccupation with Scotland and its history that made *Weir of Hermiston* so powerful a tale. With its theme of filial rebellion, its evocation of Scotland's topography, language, and legends, it is a masterly fragment and the most Scottish of all his works. *Records of a Family of Engineers,* a biographical work that recounts his grandfather's engineering feats, reveals that Stevenson was trying to find a bridge back to his own family and finally coming to terms with his earlier rejection of the engineering profession. In *Records of a Family of Engineers* he depicts his grandfather as a scientist-artist, linking his own growing objectivity in his style of writing to the technical yet imaginative work of his forebears. Increasingly Stevenson's art embraced more of the everyday world and drew on his experiences in the South Seas for its strength. His South Seas work, both nonfiction and fiction, gradually grew more powerful than the earlier works for which he is, ironically, more famous. When he died of a stroke on 3 December 1894 in his house at Vailima, Samoa, he was at the height of his creative powers.

The Samoan faction that he had helped to free from jail assembled at his house to cut a path to the top of Mt. Vaea, where he was buried. He had been rich, famous, an adventurer, and a legend in his homeland; the report of his death created a small shock wave throughout the literary world. Almost immediately the Stevenson family began attempts to glorify the memory of Stevenson, and this action was to work against the writer's literary reputation. They dickered over who would best edit Stevenson's letters. Baxter and James steered clear of the unenviable task, which fell to Sidney Colvin. There also appeared memoirs by Stevenson's friends who did him the disservice of writing hagiography instead of biography. The inevitable reaction of the succeeding literary generation to this presentation of Stevenson as a demisaint was severe. The worst of it amounted to speculation about Edinburgh prostitutes whom the youthful Stevenson might have known and the exact amount of impropriety in Stevenson's relationship with Fanny before their marriage. From personal attacks on Stevenson, critics turned to style: he was accused of blind imitation, having nothing to say and saying it oddly, and of promoting a spineless escapism.

What Stevenson was left with was a literary reputation based solely on his romances—a reputation that solidly ignored his South Seas fiction, his essays, his travelogues about America and the Pacific, and the letters that revealed his enthusiasm for his craft and for the islanders of the South Pacific. Because of this failure to acknowledge his breadth as a writer, he is often remembered primarily as an author for children; his reputation as the author of *Treasure Island* has prevented many adults from reading any of his other works. But he may yet survive the injustice. G. K. Chesterton's 1927 book *Robert Louis Stevenson* restored a sense of balance to the examination of the author's life and letters. Recent studies have turned more attention to Stevenson's less-well-known works, attempting to integrate the various strata of his literary output. Consequently, Stevenson has risen in stature since the early 1900s. The centennial of his death may bring a scholarly reappraisal of Stevenson that will move him from the second rank of Victorian authors to the first.

Letters:

Sidney Colvin, ed., *The Letters of Robert Louis Stevenson to His Family and Friends*, 2 volumes (London: Methuen, 1899; New York: Scribners, 1899);

De Lancey Ferguson and Marshall Waingrow, eds., *R. L. S.: Stevenson's Letters to Charles Baxter* (New Haven: Yale University Press, 1956; London: Oxford University Press, 1956).

Bibliography:

W. F. Prideaux, *A Bibliography of the Works of Robert Louis Stevenson*, revised edition, edited and supplemented by Mrs. Luther S. Livingston (London: Hollings, 1918).

Biographies:

Graham Balfour, *The Life of Robert Louis Stevenson* (New York: Scribners, 1901);

Janet Adam Smith, *Robert Louis Stevenson* (London: Duckworth, 1947);

David Daiches, *Robert Louis Stevenson* (Norfolk, Conn.: New Directions, 1947);

J. C. Furnas, *Voyage to Windward: The Life of Robert Louis Stevenson* (New York: Sloane, 1951);

Jenni Calder, *RLS: A Life Study* (London: Hamilton, 1980).

References:

G. K. Chesterton, *Robert Louis Stevenson* (London: Hodder & Stoughton, 1927);

Edwin M. Eigner, *Robert Louis Stevenson and Romantic Tradition* (Princeton: Princeton University Press, 1966);

J. A. Hammerton, ed., *Stevensoniana* (Edinburgh: Grant, 1910);

Robert Kiely, *Robert Louis Stevenson and the Fiction of Adventure* (Cambridge: Harvard University Press, 1965);

Janet Adam Smith, ed., *Henry James and Robert Louis Stevenson: A Record of Friendship and Criticism* (London: Rupert Hart-Davis, 1948);

Roger G. Swearingen, *The Prose Writings of Robert Louis Stevenson: A Guide* (Hamden, Conn.: Archon, 1980).

Papers:

Collections of Stevenson's papers are at the Beinecke Rare Book and Manuscript Library, Yale University; the Pierpont Morgan Library, New York; the Henry E. Huntington Library, San Marino, California; the Widener Library, Harvard University; the Edinburgh Public Library; the Silverado Museum, Saint Helena, California; and the Monterey State Historical Monument Stevenson House, Monterey, California.

A. C. Swinburne

(5 April 1837-10 April 1909)

Donald Gray

Indiana University

See also the Swinburne entry in *DLB 35, Victorian Poets After 1850.*

SELECTED BOOKS: *The Queen-Mother. Rosamond. Two Plays* (London: Pickering, 1860; Boston: Ticknor & Fields, 1866);

Atalanta in Calydon (London: Moxon, 1865; Boston: Ticknor & Fields, 1866);

Chastelard (London: Moxon, 1865; New York: Hurd & Houghton/Boston: Dutton, 1866);

Poems and Ballads (London: Moxon, 1866; London: Hotten, 1866); republished as *Laus Veneris, and Other Poems and Ballads* (New York: Carleton/London: Moxon, 1866);

Notes on Poems and Reviews (London: Hotten, 1866);

A Song of Italy (London: Hotten, 1867; Boston: Ticknor & Fields, 1867);

An Appeal to England Against the Execution of the Condemned Fenians (Manchester, 1867);

William Blake: A Critical Essay (London: Hotten, 1868; New York: Dutton, 1906);

Notes on the Royal Academy Exhibition, 1868, by Swinburne and William Michael Rossetti (London: Hotten, 1868);

Songs before Sunrise (London: Ellis, 1871; Boston: Roberts Brothers, 1871);

Under the Microscope (London: White, 1872; Portland, Maine: Mosher, 1899);

Bothwell (London: Chatto & Windus, 1874);

George Chapman: A Critical Essay (London: Chatto & Windus, 1875);

Songs of Two Nations (London: Chatto & Windus, 1875);

Essays and Studies (London: Chatto & Windus, 1875);

Erechtheus: A Tragedy (London: Chatto & Windus, 1876);

Note of an English Republican on the Muscovite Crusade (London: Chatto & Windus, 1876);

A Note on Charlotte Brontë (London: Chatto & Windus, 1877);

Poems and Ballads, Second Series (London: Chatto & Windus, 1878; New York: Crowell, 1885?);

A Study of Shakespeare (London: Chatto &

A. C. Swinburne, 1869 (photograph by Elliott & Fry)

Windus, 1880; New York: Worthington, 1880);

Songs of the Springtides (London: Chatto & Windus, 1880; New York: Worthington, 1882?);

Studies in Song (London: Chatto & Windus, 1880; New York: Worthington, 1880);

Specimens of Modern Poets: The Heptalogia or The Seven Against Sense (London: Chatto & Windus, 1880);

Mary Stuart (London: Chatto & Windus, 1881; New York: Worthington, 1881);

Tristram of Lyonesse and Other Poems (London:

Chatto & Windus, 1882; Portland, Maine: Mosher, 1904);

A Century of Roundels (London: Chatto & Windus, 1883; New York: Worthington, 1883);

A Midsummer Holiday and Other Poems (London: Chatto & Windus, 1884);

Marino Faliero: A Tragedy (London: Chatto & Windus, 1885);

Miscellanies (London: Chatto & Windus, 1886; New York: Worthington, 1886);

A Study of Victor Hugo (London: Chatto & Windus, 1886);

Locrine: A Tragedy (London: Chatto & Windus, 1887; New York: Alden, 1887);

A Study of Ben Jonson (London: Chatto & Windus, 1889; New York: Worthington, 1889);

Poems and Ballads, Third Series (London: Chatto & Windus, 1889);

The Sisters: A Tragedy (London: Chatto & Windus, 1892; New York: United States Book Company, 1892);

Astrophel and Other Poems (London: Chatto & Windus, 1894);

Studies in Prose and Poetry (London: Chatto & Windus, 1894);

Robert Burns. A Poem (Edinburgh: Printed for the Members of the Burns Centenary Club, 1896);

The Tale of Balen (London: Chatto & Windus, 1896; New York: Scribners, 1896);

Rosamund, Queen of the Lombards: A Tragedy (London: Chatto & Windus, 1899; New York: Dodd, Mead, 1899);

Love's Cross-Currents: A Year's Letters (Portland, Maine: Mosher, 1901; London: Chatto & Windus, 1905);

Poems & Ballads, Second & Third Series (Portland, Maine: Mosher, 1902);

Percy Bysshe Shelley (Philadelphia: Lippincott, 1903);

A Channel Passage and Other Poems (London: Chatto & Windus, 1904);

The Poems of Algernon Charles Swinburne, 6 volumes (London: Chatto & Windus, 1904; New York & London: Harper, 1904);

The Tragedies of Algernon Charles Swinburne, 6 volumes (London: Chatto & Windus, 1905; New York: Harper, 1905);

The Duke of Gandia (London: Chatto & Windus, 1908; New York & London: Harper, 1908);

The Age of Shakespeare (New York & London: Harper, 1908; London: Chatto & Windus, 1908);

Three Plays of Shakespeare (London & New York: Harper, 1909);

The Marriage of Monna Lisa (London: Privately printed, 1909);

In the Twilight (London: Privately printed, 1909);

The Portrait (London: Privately printed, 1909);

The Chronicle of Queen Fredegond (London: Privately printed, 1909);

Of Liberty and Loyalty (London: Privately printed, 1909);

Ode to Mazzini (London: Privately printed, 1909);

Shakespeare (London: New York, Toronto & Melbourne: Henry Frowde, 1909);

The Ballade of Truthful Charles and Other Poems (London: Privately printed, 1910);

A Criminal Case (London: Privately printed, 1910);

The Ballade of Villon and Fat Madge (London: Privately printed, 1910);

The Cannibal Catechism (London: Privately printed, 1913);

Les Fleurs du Mal and Other Studies (London: Privately printed, 1913);

Charles Dickens (London: Chatto & Windus, 1913);

A Study of Victor Hugo's "Les Misérables" (London: Privately printed, 1914);

Pericles and Other Studies (London: Privately printed, 1914);

Thomas Nabbes: A Critical Monograph (London: Privately printed, 1914);

Christopher Marlowe in Relation to Greene, Peele and Lodge (London: Privately printed, 1914);

Lady Maisie's Bairn and Other Poems (London: Privately printed, 1915);

Félicien Cossu: A Burlesque (London: Privately printed, 1915);

Théophile (London: Privately printed, 1915);

Ernest Clouët (London: Privately printed, 1916);

A Vision of Bags (London: Privately printed, 1916);

The Death of Sir John Franklin (London: Privately printed, 1916);

Poems From "Villon" and Other Fragments (London: Privately printed, 1916);

Poetical Fragments (London: Privately printed, 1916);

Posthumous Poems, edited by Edmund Gosse and Thomas James Wise (London: Heinemann, 1917);

Rondeaux Parisiens (London: Privately printed, 1917);

The Italian Mother and Other Poems (London: Privately printed, 1918);

The Ride from Milan and Other Poems (London: Privately printed, 1918);

A Lay of Lilies and Other Poems (London: Privately printed, 1918);

Queen Yseult, A Poem in Six Cantos (London: Privately printed, 1918);

Lancelot, The Death of Rudel and Other Poems (London: Privately printed, 1918);

Undergraduate Sonnets (London: Privately printed, 1918);

The Character and Opinions of Dr. Johnson (London: Privately printed, 1918);

The Queen's Tragedy (London: Privately printed, 1919);

French Lyrics (London: Privately printed, 1919);

Contemporaries of Shakespeare (London: Heinemann, 1919);

Ballads of the English Border, edited by William A. MacInnes (London: Heinemann, 1925);

Lesbia Brandon, edited by Randolph Hughes (London: Falcon Press, 1952); republished in *The Novels of A. C. Swinburne* (New York: Farrar, Straus & Cudahy, 1962);

New Writings by Swinburne, edited by Cecil Y. Lang (Syracuse: Syracuse University Press, 1964).

Collection: *The Complete Works of Algernon Charles Swinburne*, edited by Edmund Gosse and Thomas James Wise, 20 volumes (London: Heinemann/New York: Wells, 1925-1927).

As he was in his own time, Algernon Charles Swinburne is now principally esteemed as a poet rather than as a writer of prose. But during the half century of his literary career Swinburne wrote and had published a great deal of prose on a variety of topics and in several forms: fiction, a few essays on painting and history, some pornographic sketches, letters to the press on politics and literature, and, most important, books and essays of literary criticism. Most of his writing about literature appeared in periodicals addressed to general readers who wanted to keep abreast of literature and literary study just as they wanted to know about ideas and events in politics, science, and other precincts of their culture. In one of his early critical essays Swinburne wrote, "The hardest work and the highest that can be done by a critic studious of the right is first to discern what is good, and then to discover how and in what way it is so." His service to readers was to tell them what was good in contemporary British and French writing, to reassess the work of the major British Romantic writers of the first part of the nineteenth century, to bring forward the claims of neglected or undervalued writers such as William Blake and Charlotte Brontë, and to help bring the dramatic literature of the English Renaissance to a prominent place in literary history.

Swinburne also suggested to his readers a way of responding to literature. Fundamental to his own taste and to the defenses of his poetry he mounted in the pamphlets *Notes on Poems and Reviews* (1866) and *Under the Microscope* (1872) is the idea that the pleasures of literature are primarily affective and aesthetic rather than intellectual and ethical. The style of his essays—his ornamented diction and elaborate metaphors, the obvious rhythms of his sentences, the high pitch of his attempts to communicate his own engagement with literature—was designed to provide a literary experience while describing one, to act as both model and agent in bringing readers into the intense and self-justifying satisfactions of literature. Swinburne's first biographer, Edmund Gosse, wrote that in the 1860s and 1870s when these essays first began to appear, "the sensation they caused was reverberant. By all young aestheticians of that and the next few years, the advent of the *Fortnightly Review* with a critical article by Swinburne in it was looked forward to as a great event."

Swinburne's prolixity and overdecorated prose are probably now a burden on his once-high reputation as a literary critic. Even during the latter half of his career, in the 1880s and 1890s when his prose became yet more mannered and he no longer wrote much about contemporary writers, his criticism began to seem fussily bookish. It is difficult now, although the claim has been made, to maintain that Swinburne is a major nineteenth-century British literary critic. It is difficult even to choose a single essay of his that without firm-minded editing can stand as seminal or summary in the way of some essays by other nineteenth-century poets—Ralph Waldo Emerson, for example, Matthew Arnold, or William Butler Yeats. But in his time Swinburne both articulated and furnished ideas about literature that became current among many mid- and late-Victorian readers and writers. Because he quite consciously wrote prose as a poet, deliberately displaying his ability to make literature as one of his warrants to stand in judgment of it, the themes, manner, poses, and voices of his prose sometimes provide an interesting gloss on his poetry.

Swinburne began writing prose for publication almost as soon as he went up to Oxford in 1856. He was born into landed families of some distinction and antiquity. His mother, Jane Hamilton Swinburne, was the daughter of the Earl of Ashburnham, whose family had held land in the south of England since before the Norman invasion. His father, Charles Henry Swinburne, a captain and later an admiral in the navy, was of a northern English family that in the seventeenth and eighteenth centuries had supported the Stuart kings and pretenders. Swinburne was educated by tutors until he entered Eton in 1849 and was tutored again at home before he entered Oxford. At Oxford he joined an undergraduate society that published collections of its members' papers. Some of Swinburne's contributions predicted the range and mix of his mature writing: a canto of a long poem on an Arthurian theme, a political essay Swinburne described as "A terrific onslaught on the French Empire and its Clerical supporters," and an essay on the plays of Christopher Marlowe and John Webster.

Swinburne's childhood and his time at Oxford contain other anticipations of his later character and conduct. He claimed, perhaps inaccurately, that like Goethe and Victor Hugo he was born "all but dead, and certainly not expected to live an hour." His appearance as a child and young man was odd–a large head framed in an aureole of red hair atop a slight, short body. From childhood he had a nervous habit of jerking his hands and feet when excited, and as a young man he acquired a skipping, dancing walk. His voice was high, sometimes shrill. Later he was to use it to bring admirers unconsciously to their knees when he declaimed his poetry. But at Oxford and after he was well known for his exuberant abuse of cabbies and college authorities and for such self-delighting tirades as his speech to the Oxford Union advocating tyrannicide.

He possessed unusual physical stamina and courage. His ambition as a boy was to become a cavalry officer. When in 1854 his parents refused his wish, he found, as he put it in a letter to Mary Leith, "a chance of testing my nerve in the face of death" by scaling a dangerous cliff near his home on the Isle of Wight. He was turned away by an overhang on his first try, surprised by a "heaving cloud" of sea gulls on his second ("at least, I really don't think the phrase exaggerates the density of their 'congregated wings' "), and then lost his footing near the top. "I swung in the air by my hands from a ledge on the cliff which just gave room for the fingers to cling and hold on. There was a projection of rock to the left at which I flung out my feet sideways and just reached it; this enabled me to get breath and

crawl at full speed (so to say) up the remaining bit of cliff. At the top I had not strength enough left to turn or stir; . . . I became unconscious–as suddenly and utterly and painlessly as I did many years afterwards when I was 'picked up at sea' by a Norman fishing boat upwards of three miles (they told me) off the coast of Etretât, and could just clutch hold of the oar they held out; but that is not in this story–which I hope is not too long for the reader." This proud, wry, self-consciously literary account of a defiant act of self-validation is characteristic. In the career he entered instead of the military Swinburne sought occasions in which he could display himself in courageous contests, now against powerful institutions and narrow prejudices. At the same time he found ways in which he could show that he too was enjoying the dash and vividness with which he was doing his quite serious work of turning experience into literature.

In 1859 Swinburne's neglect of his formal studies made it prudent for him to cease work at Oxford and live for a winter with a private tutor. When he returned in 1860 he put off the completion of his degree until he finally decided to leave without taking it, "not formally but informally expelled," as he wrote near the end of his life, comparing himself to Shelley and making his departure seem rather more dramatic than the drifting away that, in fact, it was. Given an allowance by his father, who in 1860 had also paid for the publication of two verse dramas Swinburne had written at Oxford, *The Queen-Mother* and *Rosamond*, Swinburne settled in London to his life's work in literature, the only occupation he ever practiced. He began to contribute to the *Spectator*, an important weekly journal of literature and politics–reviews of books by Victor Hugo and Charles Baudelaire, some of his own poems, and a defense of George Meredith's sonnet sequence "Modern Love," which had been attacked for its frank treatment of a broken marriage and an adulterous love affair. "There are pulpits enough for all preachers in prose," Swinburne contended; "the business of verse-writing is hardly to express convictions; and if some poetry, not without merit of its kind, has at times dealt in dogmatic morality, it is all the worse and all the weaker for that." In 1865 he produced a historical poetic drama, *Chastelard*, and his most important book so far, the dramatic poem *Atalanta in Calydon*.

Atalanta in Calydon, classic in structure and punctuated by eloquent lyric choruses, was favora-

Drawing of Swinburne attributed to Simeon Solomon (Fitzwilliam Museum, Cambridge)

bly reviewed. But when Swinburne's first collection of poems, *Poems and Ballads*, was published in 1866, he opened himself to attacks of the kind from which he had tried to defend Meredith. He had advertised what was coming in a review in the *Spectator* of Baudelaire's poetry: "he has chosen to dwell mainly upon sad and strange things—the weariness of pain and the bitterness of pleasure—the perverse happiness and wayward sorrows of exceptional people. It has the languid, lurid beauty of close and threatening weather—a heavy, heated temperature, with dangerous hothouse scents in it."

Swinburne's own explorations of fevered and painful states of sensual excitement and exhaustion in such poems as "Dolores" and "Faustine" and his treatment of the Tannhauser myth in "Laus Veneris" were reviewed as blasphemous, obscene, and, perhaps most wounding, puerile in their wish to shock. The response so unsettled the original publisher, the well-esteemed house of Moxon, that it withdrew the book from circulation. Swinburne and his friends, who had

been unsuccessful earlier in interesting other eminent publishers (Macmillan and John Murray) in the book, settled on John Camden Hotten, a publisher whose public and semiprivate lists included pirated works of American literature and some marginally pornographic works of erotica. Hotten republished *Poems and Ballads* in 1866. In his response to his critics in *Notes on Poems and Reviews* Swinburne insisted that his book was "dramatic, many-faced, multifarious; and no utterance of enjoyment or despair, belief or unbelief, can properly be assumed as the assertion of its author's personal feeling or faith." He regretted that work like his was judged by inappropriately delicate standards of decorum: "It would seem indeed as though to publish a book were equivalent to thrusting it with violence into the hands of every mother and nurse in the kingdom as fit and necessary food for female infancy." With some justice he argued that his poems "were assuredly written with no moral or immoral design; but the upshot seems to me moral rather than immoral, if it must needs be one or the other." Swinburne clearly enjoyed himself in his reply, happy both to exercise the gifts for verbal controversy he had practiced at Oxford and to promote himself as a glowing rebel against the pallid orthodoxies of mid-Victorian Britain.

In 1868 Swinburne produced *William Blake: A Critical Essay,* the first extensive study of the work of that then-neglected poet and artist. He liked Blake's heretical cast: "He was the very man for fire and faggot." He especially admired *The Marriage of Heaven and Hell,* "the greatest of all his books," because its dramatic play of contraries and its inversion of conventional values, somewhat in the manner of *Poems and Ballads,* created a profoundly unsettling humor "of that fierce, grave sort, whose cool insanity of manner is more horrible and more obscure to the Philistine than any sharp edge of burlesque or glitter of irony: it is huge, swift, inexplicable." Swinburne's reading of Blake's later prophetic books is tentative and superficial; "into these darker parts of the book," he wrote of *Jerusalem,* "we will not go too deep." But he understood the iconography of Blake's designs, and he set out forcefully two of the central tenets of Blake's system. The tyrannies of Church and State enforce fallen humanity's erroneous perceptions of the division between good and evil, sense and soul, Jehovah and Satan; and redemption lies in the overthrow of conventional authority and the return of human faculties to their original harmony.

Swinburne's statement of Blake's belief provided a text he himself was to elaborate a few years later in his poem "Hertha": "the very root or kernel of this creed is not the assumed humanity of God, but the achieved divinity of Man; not incarnation from without, but development from within; not a miraculous passage into flesh, but a natural growth into godhead."

Near the end of his life Swinburne remembered, with his usual exaggeration, that his book on Blake was received "with reviling and ridicule and such general contempt that almost all the copies were sold as 'remainders.'" In fact, the book did not receive much attention at all. But Swinburne had already begun the series of essays in the *Fortnightly Review* that won him an audience and a reputation as a literary critic like that he had already achieved as a poet of a new sensibility. In 1875 he collected these essays with some others in *Essays and Studies*, which went into a second edition in 1876 and three more editions in Swinburne's lifetime. In this collection, and especially in its four best essays–a preface to a selection of Byron's poetry (first published in 1865), long reviews of new books of poems by Matthew Arnold (1867) and Dante Gabriel Rossetti (1870), and a review (1872) of Victor Hugo's *L'Année terrible*, poems about the siege of Paris and the events of the Commune–Swinburne set out the fundamental themes of his literary criticism.

One sign of greatness for Swinburne was a resistance like Blake's to dominant cultural authority. An honorable example of a great poet's relation with such authority was Hugo's exile from the restored empire of Napolean III and his expulsion from Belgium in 1870 because of his republican sympathies. Ordinary people, Swinburne wrote, trim and temporize: "If Torquemada is in power you warm yourself at the stake." "But there must be somebody on the side of the stars! somebody to stand up for brotherhood, for mercy, for honour, for right, for freedom, and for the solemn splendour of absolute truth." He put Rossetti in the rank of writers just below Hugo who stand "in the vanguard of their time," "a light-bearer and leader of men." He was unsure of Byron's rank because of the deficiencies of his craft: "No poet of equal or inferior rank ever had so bad an ear." But like Hugo and Rossetti, Byron was abused by "every obscure and obscene thing that lurks for pay or prey among the fouler shallows and thickets of literature." In the years of his own rebelliousness Swinburne was ready to forgive much to a poet so at odds with

his time. "His glorious courage, his excellent contempt for things contemptible, and hatred of hateful men, . . . gave much of their own value to verse not otherwise or not always praiseworthy."

Another evidence of worth for Swinburne was the presence in writers he admired of a creed like Blake's, a membership in a kind of godless church of the sacred wonder of the material and human world. Swinburne recalled how, still a boy at school, he welcomed Arnold's "Empedocles on Etna" and its severe scrutiny of makeshift ways of belief in a world without warrants of divine order and presence. "We have had Christian sceptics, handcuffed fighters, tongue-tied orators, plume-plucked eagles; believers whose belief was a sentiment, and free-thinkers who saw nothing before Christ or beyond Judea. To get at the bare rock is a relief after acres of such quaking ground." He liked Arnold's "creed of self-sufficience, which sees for man no clearer or deeper duty than that of intellectual self-reliance, self-dependence, self-respect." He admired the grace of what he took to be a dignified materialism: "it is no reason or excuse for living basely instead of nobly, that we must live as the sons and not as the lords of nature." He thought that Rossetti's poems also bespoke a material creation still full of mystery and the possibility of joy. There too he found no "hybrid jargon" of "liberalised Christianism," none of "the semi-Christianity of [Tennyson's] 'In Memoriam' or the demi-semi-Christianity of 'Dipsychus' [by Arthur Hugh Clough], . . . no letch after Gods dead or unborn, such as vexes the weaker nerves of barren brains, and makes pathetic the vocal lips of sorrowing skepticism and 'doubt that deserves to believe.'"

Finally, however, Swinburne believed that ideas, however right-minded, were not enough to make a good poem or a great poet. The creed of a poem must be fused with and enacted in its craft. "No work of art has any worth of life in it that is not done on the absolute terms of art; that is not before all things and above all things a work of positive excellence as judged by the laws of the special art to whose laws it is amenable." Swinburne wrote of Arnold's elegiac poems that their "sweet sufficiency of music, so full and calm, buoys and bears up throughout the imperial vessel of thought"; "as with all poets of his rank, the technical beauty is at one with the spiritual." In Rossetti too there is "an ardent harmony, a heat of spiritual life" that creates a "sweet and sovereign unity of perfect spirit and sense, of

First page of the manuscript for Swinburne's memoir of his friendship with Dante Gabriel Rossetti, written soon after Rossetti's death in 1882 and printed for private circulation in 1910 (T. Earl Welby, A Study of Swinburne, *1926)*

fleshly form and intellectual fire." The explicit politics of Hugo's poems made Swinburne consider whether ideas in poetry might be so important, immediate, and practical in their effect that they won precedence over the poetry and were irreconcilable with it. He quoted one of his own dicta: "art for art's sake first, and then all things shall be added to her." If the laws of art are fulfilled, there is no reason that a poem with political or moral intentions cannot be as good as one without. "In a word, the doctrine of art for art is true in the positive sense, false in the negative; sound as an affirmation, unsound as a prohibition."

Swinburne was undoubtedly speaking for himself as well as for Hugo in this formulation. In 1871 he had collected in *Songs before Sunrise* some of his own poems carrying strong political and moral messages and purposes. He had been introduced to the Italian nationalist Guiseppe Mazzini in 1867. Mazzini tried to focus Swinburne's enthusiastic but footless hostility to kings, popes, and other oppressors (at Oxford he used to scream at the mention of the name of Napoleon III) by asking him to use his gifts to inspirit those fighting for Italian freedom. Swinburne had already begun *A Song of Italy,* which appeared in 1867, and in the late 1860s some of his poems sympathetic to Italian nationalism ("The Halt Before Rome," "Super Flumina Babylonis") appeared in magazines before they were collected in *Songs before Sunrise.* The freedoms imagined in this volume, however, are larger than the liberation of Italy. In "Hertha" and "The Hymn of Man" Swinburne describes a human evolution to godhead like that he had learned from Blake. In "To Walt Whitman in America" he honors the power of poetry to move readers to perceive and realize the essential joy of human and natural existence. "After all, in spite of jokes and perversities," he wrote in an 1866 letter, "it is nice to have something to love and to believe in as I do in Italy." The beliefs expressed in *Songs before Sunrise* give its poems an energy very different from the tonalities of enervation and painful frustration characteristic of *Poems and Ballads.*

Swinburne's personal life in the late 1860s and all through the 1870s, however, was disorderly and self-destructive. His friends worried about his drunkenness and his habit of launching into shrill, manic tirades; his outburst in a café when he read a review of *Poems and Ballads* so frightened the waiters that his companion urged him to shout in French. He became a member of a circle that read and wrote to one another about the pornographic books of Sade and other writers. He patronized a brothel that catered to his taste for being whipped, and he conducted an absurd and quite public affair with the actress Adah Isaacs Menken, who ended it admitting that "she hadn't been able to get him up to the scratch, and couldn't make him understand that biting's no use." He was often ill, sometimes injured when he fell or fainted, and periodically had to be rescued from London to recuperate at his family's home. Finally, during a serious illness in 1879, Theodore Watts (later Watts-Dunton), a lawyer and a writer, arranged for Swinburne to share a house with him in one of the still-suburban sections of London near Putney Heath.

For the rest of Swinburne's life Watts managed his domestic and professional affairs, even after Watts's marriage in 1905. Swinburne was content and grateful to "the best of friends." He withdrew into his library and his increasing deafness, following a sober routine of reading, writing, a daily walk on the heath, and a glass of beer. He regularly went on holiday to the sea and his mother's house, occasionally dined in London, and played the part of a grand eminence to visitors at rather stuffy luncheons and dinners. He was still excitable: about schoolboy whippings in an extraordinary exchange of letters late in his life with his cousin Mary (Gordon) Leith; about the babies he met on his walks and around whose prams he danced in pleasure; about the sea, swimming, and the glory of the British navy and empire. But he lived out his life almost entirely in his reading and writing. In the last thirty years of his life he produced eight volumes of poetry, six plays in verse, a long verse narrative on an Arthurian theme, a volume of poetic parodies (*Specimens of Modern Poets: The Heptalogia,* 1880), two collections of literary criticism (*Miscellanies,* 1886, and *Studies in Prose and Poetry,* 1894), and books on Shakespeare (1880), Hugo (1886), Ben Jonson (1889), and the dramatists of the English Renaissance (*The Age of Shakespeare,* 1908).

Swinburne's poetry after *Songs before Sunrise* is often diffuse and subdued. Although he gave much time to the composition of verse drama, most of his best poems are lyric. Their tone is often elegiac, autumnal, or retrospective, as in his summary of his career in "Thalassius" and his powerful examination of his gift and purpose as a poet in "On the Cliffs," which appeared in the same volume of poems published in 1880. When he recovered the energy of his earlier poetry, it was often in verse on events remembered from his youth and early manhood ("A Channel Passage," 1899, and "The Lake of Gaube," 1899). In his translations of Villon, in accomplished parodies of contemporary British poets for *Specimens of Modern Poets: The Heptalogia,* and in imitations of English ballads, his adoption of another voice also sometimes enabled him to resume some of his earlier dramatic playfulness, irreverence, and readiness to explore the dark excitements of frustrated and destructive motives and feelings.

The literary criticism of the latter half of Swinburne's career is also often less trenchant than his earlier prose. After the publication of *Essays and Studies* in 1875, Swinburne produced more than sixty essays in literary criticism. More than twenty are on Shakespeare and other Renaissance dramatists and poets. A few essays make up a desultory history of English poetry, and most of the rest were on Hugo and nineteenth-century British writers from Wordsworth, Walter Savage Landor, Charles Lamb, and Byron to Dickens, Charles Reade, Wilkie Collins, and Kenneth Grahame. Swinburne often surrendered to a tendency remarked by his mother and his best friend: "What you say," his mother wrote to Watts, "about his spoiling his writing by 'not knowing when to stop' is–so very true. I constantly de-

plore it!" Because in his later essays he often wrote to introduce readers to relatively unfamiliar writers or to rank writers according to the worth of their entire achievement, many of his essays, especially those on Renaissance drama, break down into annotated catalogues of the writers' canons. But he continued to write for periodicals central to the general intellectual culture of late-Victorian Britain–the *Fortnightly, Contemporary Review, Academy, Athenaeum, Quarterly Review.* Most of his books and collections of literary criticism went into second and third editions. A dozen or so essays published after *Essays and Studies* are especially worthy of note: a preface to George Chapman's writing (1875) and an article on him for the *Encyclopaedia Britannica* (1876), essays on John Webster (1886) and Cyril Tourneur (1887), the essays collected in *A Study of Ben Jonson* (1889), the monograph *A Note on Charlotte Brontë* (1877), "Wordsworth and Byron" (1884), "Tennyson and Musset" (1881), "Mr. Whistler's Lecture on Art" (1888), and some of the reviews collected in *A Study of Victor Hugo* (1886). In these essays Swinburne put forward his ideas about the nature and purpose of literature to a new generation who now received them not as weapons against the established order but as pro-

Unsigned caricature of Swinburne as Pan, published in the Christmas 1880 number of Truth *(Collection of Jerold J. Savory)*

nouncements from within it.

In his criticism Swinburne retained his taste for the broken, wicked, oddly original, and even perverse. He might have seen something of himself in the sensibility that made Chapman's gnarled and dark verse: "a profuse and turbid imagination, a fiery energy and restless ardour of moral passion and spiritual ambition, with a plentiful lack of taste and judgment, and a notable excess of those precious qualities of pride and self-reliance which are at once needful to support and liable to misguide an artist on his way of work." He liked the "salt" and "savour of venturesome and humorous resolution" of Webster's villains and the "dauntless versatility of daring, . . . invincible fertility of resource" of Jonson's. He digressed in his essay on Chapman to praise the harsh harmonies of Robert Browning's poetry. He admired Dickens's comedy (all his life Swinburne could do excellent imitations of the voice of *Martin Chuzzlewit*'s Sairey Gamp in his letters), and he placed the circumstantial realism of George Eliot's fiction much below the romances of the Brontës, with their extraordinary characters and singular constructions.

Increasingly, in the latter part of his career Swinburne insisted that art explicitly ennoble and harmonize the broken or exceptional experience it renders. From the beginning he had acknowledged the moral implications of poetry like Baudelaire's (and his own): "Like a medieval preacher, when he has drawn the heathen love, he puts sin on its right hand, and death on its left." In 1871, in a very good essay on the seventeenth-century dramatist John Ford, he surprised himself ("I trust that I shall not be liable to any charge of Puritan prudery") by condemning some of the matter of Ford's plays as "utterly indecent, unseemly and unfit for handling." In the 1880s and 1890s he sometimes sounded like the critics of *Poems and Ballads* in his attacks on Henrik Ibsen, Emile Zola, and other "French pornographers and coprologists." He also seemed to join his critics when he argued in "Mr. Whistler's Lecture on Art" that to give exclusive value to the formal qualities of art is to be isolated "in the fairyland of fans, in the paradise of pipkins, in the limbo of blue china, screens, pots, plates, jars, joss-houses, and all the fortuitous frippery of Fusi-yama." Or worse: Swinburne thought that the French lyric poet Alfred Musset, "a singer who cannot but sing," had slipped into reactionary politics because "in the flower of his working days" he had thought himself "too good to be

put to any nobler use: too poetic to be a patriot, too aesthetic to be a partisan, too artistic to serve an earthly country or suffer in a human cause, his only country being art." For Swinburne it was no longer sufficient to allow that art can sometimes admit politics and morality. "All sane men," Swinburne wrote in "Wordsworth and Byron," will concede "that a school of poetry divorced from any moral idea is a school of poetry divorced from life."

Swinburne still maintained that the essential condition for poetry is that it be poetic. "Wordsworth was wrong in thinking himself a poet because he was a teacher, whereas in fact he was a teacher because he was a poet." But sometimes he now wrote as if the test for poetry was itself moral, a largeness and magnanimity of comprehension in which the perception of evil summons up mercy, courage, or a righteous anger that harmonizes the discord. In an essay on *King Lear* (1902) he praised Shakespeare's conversion of darkness, storm, and "the superhuman inhumanity of an unimaginable crime" into a testimony of "what man may be, at the highest of his powers and the noblest of his nature." Similarly Hugo's dramatization of the repentance of Judas in *La Fin de Satan* became an "assurance of his faith that the victories of evil carry retribution within them" and that "the natural conscience" yearns for "righteousness in expiation, . . . the certitude of compensatory justice." "And yet he was at all points a poet," he wrote of Tourneur: "there is an accent of indomitable self-reliance, a note of persistence and resistance more deep than any note of triumph, in the very cry of his passionate and implacable dejection, which marks him as different in kind from the race of the great prosaic pessimists whose scorn and hatred of mankind found expression in the contemptuous and rancorous despondency of Swift or of Carlyle."

Fundamentally, however, for Swinburne late as well as early "the first indispensable quality of a singer is to sing." The presence of song cannot be explained. "There must be something in the mere progress and resonance of the words, some secret in the very motion and cadence of the lines, inexplicable by the most sympathetic acuteness of criticism." But the absence of song is unmistakable, at least to Swinburne, and decisive. He put Jonson in the second rank of poets because he lacked "fragrance" and "singing power." No longer tolerant of Byron's defective ear, he withdrew his high estimate of his poetry because "in all the composition of his composite nature there was neither a note of real music nor a gleam of real imagination." All he had ever really admired in Whitman, Swinburne wrote in 1887, were some attractive opinions about freedom and other matters that found "here and there a not inadequate expression in a style of rhetoric not always flatulent or inharmonious." He rested his argument for the superiority of Wordsworth to Byron on a handful of lines such as "The sleepless soul that perished in its pride": "All that Wordsworth could do–and the author of the *Excursion* could do much–to make us forget his genius is itself forgotten when such a line, such a phrase as this, revives in our memory the vibration of its music, the illumination of its truth."

Perhaps the most powerful word in Swinburne's criticism is *harmony*. He meant by it a union of matter and manner, a music like that of Wordsworth's that carries readers to a truth, an "innate and spiritual instinct of sweetness and fitness and exaltation which cannot but express itself in height and perfection of song." By harmony he also meant a moral or ethical vision that balances and resolves evil by mercy, terror by noble expiation or forgiveness. But harmony takes its name from song, and it is essentially the singing that matters. The measure of poetry was an achievement like that of Shelley, "the perfect singing-god; his thoughts, words, deeds, all sang together." In his literary criticism in the 1880s and 1890s Swinburne consistently argued that the lyric and its effects were central to the worth of all kinds of poetry, to the highest forms of drama, and even to the romantic prose fiction of the Brontës and others. Song and intense feeling were his definition not just of nineteenth-century Romantic poetry, and not just of poetry, but of literature itself.

None of Swinburne's other prose has the sustained interest of his literary criticism. He wrote occasionally for publication on politics. In 1867 he produced a pamphlet against the execution of some Irish nationalists and another in 1876 expressing his "English Republican" views on the proper British response to Turkish brutality and Russian expansionism in the Near East. His politics were always fitful and enthusiastic. After they helped him to the high achievement of *Songs before Sunrise* they gradually sputtered out in cranky letters to editors about the necessity of union between England and Ireland and a boyish patriotism that also infected his late literary criticism. (Despite the evidence of his own life, he was persuaded near its end that the English were

too honest and clean-hearted to foul themselves with indecent matter in literature.) Swinburne's talent for outrage made him a ready polemicist. His parodies of pedantic Shakespearian scholarship in "Report of the Proceedings of the First Anniversary Session of the Newest Shakespeare Society" (1876) and "Tennyson or Darwin?" (1888) are often funny. In both the jokes go on too long, and Swinburne's quarrel with scholars who neglected the poetry of Shakespeare's plays while they fussed about attributions of authorship and accurate texts also degenerated into a public exchange of epithets in which he was addressed as "Pigsbrooke" and he addressed his opponent, F. J. Furnival, as "Brothelsdyke." Swinburne's invective was more telling when it was part of essays whose other tactics and purposes checked his tendency to become hectic and finally tedious.

Swinburne read a good deal of fiction and wrote on it interestingly, especially in his essays on Charles Reade (1884) and Wilkie Collins (1889), in which he entertains the notion that the novel holds the place in nineteenth-century letters that writing for the stage held in the Renaissance. In the 1860s and 1870s he played around with some sketches about flagellation and a burlesque novel in French, "La Fille de policeman" (first published in 1964 in *New Writings by Swinburne*), about a sister of Victoria who lives as a prostitute. He also took his own fiction as seriously as his later comparison of it to dramatic writing suggests. One novel, *A Year's Letters*, appeared in the *Tatler* under the pseudonym Mrs. Horace Manners in 1877 and was republished in book form, under Swinburne's name, as *Love's Cross-Currents* in 1901. He worked in the 1860s and 1870s on another, *Lesbia Brandon*, first published from its uncompleted manuscript in 1952. He had little gift for narration in prose, a deficiency also apparent in the cluttered account of Mary, Queen of Scots he wrote for the *Encyclopaedia Britannica* (1883). The completed chapters of *Lesbia Brandon* are obsessive set-pieces in which Swinburne indulges fantasies about transvestism, lesbianism, and the pleasures of receiving pain. It is hard to see how they could be shaped and pushed forward to make a plot. He was wiser, or luckier, in his choice of an epistolary form for *Love's Cross-Currents*. In his criticism of fiction and drama he was greatly interested in character. In the letters of this novel he gave his characters distinctive voices and points of view that carry it through its clumsy exposition and quick turns of plot. One of the characters, Reginald Harewood, the author wrote late in his life, is "rather a coloured photograph of, Yours, A.C. Swinburne." To a degree so is the character of Lady Midhurst, a malicious, gossipy, interfering woman who moves the plot by watching, and helping, two sets of foolish lovers edge toward disaster before she sets them right in a cynical accommodation to the customs of marriage and property in affluent families. The counterpoint of the voices of *Love's Cross-Currents* is like that Swinburne claimed for *Poems and Ballads*. The novel is a comic version of the world of that volume and of some of his best poems; it is a world of exhaustion and disillusion, drained of the high promise and satisfactions of romantic love.

In his own letters Swinburne displays most of the interests and habits of his other prose. He was, as always, prolific. The six-volume edition of his letters completed in 1962 contains over 1,900 letters written by him, and biographers and literary scholars have since published additional correspondence. Swinburne's are letters of a life saturated with literature. They are full of opinions about writers and books, from the New Testament to the children's books of Mrs. Molesworth. He holds forth about his own writing, advises friends about theirs, discusses the accuracy of literary texts and dates with bibliographers and scholars, orders new and rare books, complains to Watts when magazines are a day late in being forwarded to him on holiday, imitates Dickens and Richardson, parodies Carlyle, and sustains for fifty years a steady murmur of astonishingly diverse literary quotation and allusion. In the 1860s and 1870s, when he was pressed for money and changing publishers, his letters say a great deal about the prices he received from editors for his essays and poems and from publishers for his books. Sometimes his arrangements with editors and writers also say something about how the worthies of the mid-Victorian literary establishment maintained themselves in it. For example, he persuaded the editor of the *Fortnightly* to let him review Rossetti's poems and then advised Rossetti about the selection and organization of the volume before he reviewed it.

Swinburne's character in his letters is often unattractive. The letters about whipping, Sade's works, and other pornography, as well as his ardent letters describing his meetings with Mazzini, are uncomfortable in their arrested juvenility. As in his essays he liked to see himself as a gentleman preyed upon by the vulgar vermin of Grub Street. That pose is also unattractive—in his habit,

The last photograph of Swinburne, by J. B. Poole

for example, of ordering his publishers around as if they were village tradesmen—and sometimes false. For Swinburne was himself as petty and vicious in his prosecution of literary feuds and dislikes as any of the writers he attacks as lice and toads in *Under the Microscope* and other essays. In effect, he tried to organize a professional boycott against one of his most persistent critics by refusing to write for any magazine that published Robert Buchanan's work, and he was fertile in his invention of coarse epithets ("Mrs. Bitcher Stew": Harriet Beecher Stowe; "Thomas Cloacina and his goody": Thomas and Jane Welsh Carlyle) for people who in some way affronted his idea of the dignity of letters.

Yet there is in Swinburne's letters a genuine dignity conferred by the deep feelings of his life in literature. In 1876, during a recuperation from his disorderly life in London, he wrote from his mother's house to the literary critic John Churton Collins to thank him for a complimentary letter about his poems. "Your letter gave me great pleasure and a sense of something, in the rather dull monotonous puppet-show of my life, which often strikes me as too barren of action or enjoyment to be much worth holding on to, better than nothingness—or at least seeming better for a minute. As I don't myself know any pleasure physical or spiritual (except what comes of the sea) comparable to that which comes of verse in its higher moods, I am certainly glad to know that I can give this to others as others again have to me." During this same passage in his life he wrote to Watts of his admiration for a lecture by the scientist John Tyndall on the relations between science and theology. "No mythology can make its believers feel less afraid or loth to be reabsorbed into the immeasurable harmony with but the change of a single individual note in a single bar of the tune, than does the faintest perception of the lowest chord touched in the whole system of things. Even my technical ignorance does not impair, I think, my power to see accurately and to seize firmly the first thread of the great clue, because my habit of mind is not (I hope) unscientific, though my work lies in the field of art instead of science; and when seen and seized even that first perception gives me an indescribable sense as of music and repose." Swinburne never lost his confidence that literature offers a harmony in which the pleasure of form carries in it an intuition of a beautifully ordered system of things. The purpose of his poetry at its most ambitious was to take readers to the limits of mortal and material existence and make them feel the power that lay within these bounds. The intentions of his literary criticism at its best were to take readers to literary texts that performed similar offices and to show them how to experience them.

Letters:

The Swinburne Letters, edited by Cecil Y. Lang, 6 volumes (New Haven: Yale University Press, 1959-1962).

Bibliographies:

Thomas James Wise, *A Bibliography of the Writings of Swinburne,* 2 volumes (London: Privately printed, 1919, 1920); revised as *A Bibliography of the Writings in Prose and Verse of Algernon Charles Swinburne,* volume 20 of *The Complete Works of Algernon Charles Swinburne* (London: Heinemann/New York: Wells, 1927);

William E. Fredeman, "Algernon Charles Swinburne," in his *Pre-Raphaelitism: A Bibliocritical Study* (Cambridge: Harvard University Press, 1965), pp. 216-220;

Clyde K. Hyder, "Algernon Charles Swinburne," in *The Victorian Poets,* revised edition, edited

by Frederic Faverty (Cambridge: Harvard University Press, 1968), pp. 227-250;

Jerome Buckley, "Algernon Charles Swinburne," in his *Victorian Poets and Prose Writers,* revised edition (Arlington Heights, Ill.: AHM, 1977), pp. 72-74;

Kirk H. Beetz, *Algernon Charles Swinburne: A Bibliography of Secondary Works, 1861-1980* (Metuchen, N.J. & London: Scarecrow Press, 1982).

Biographies:

Edmund Gosse, *The Life of Algernon Charles Swinburne* (London & New York: Macmillan, 1917); republished as volume 19 of *The Complete Works of Algernon Charles Swinburne* (London: Heinemann, 1927);

Harold Nicolson, *Swinburne* (London: Macmillan, 1926);

Georges Lafourcade, *La Jeunesse de Swinburne* (London: Oxford University Press, 1928);

Lafourcade, *Swinburne: A Literary Biography* (London: Bell, 1932);

Jean Overton Fuller, *Swinburne: A Critical Biography* (London: Chatto & Windus, 1968);

Mollie Panter-Downes, *At the Pines: Swinburne and Watts-Dunton in Putney* (London: Hamilton, 1971);

Philip Henderson, *Swinburne: Portrait of a Poet* (New York: Macmillan, 1974);

Donald Thomas, *Swinburne: The Poet in His World* (New York: Oxford University Press, 1979).

References:

John A. Cassidy, *Algernon C. Swinburne* (New York: Twayne, 1968);

Samuel C. Chew, *Swinburne* (Boston: Little, Brown, 1929);

T. E. Connolly, *Swinburne's Theory of Poetry* (Albany: State University of New York Press, 1964);

T. S. Eliot, "Swinburne as Critic," in his *The Sacred Wood* (London: Methuen, 1920), pp. 17-24;

Ian Fletcher, *Swinburne* (Essex: Published for the British Council by Longman, 1973);

Clyde K. Hyder, *Swinburne's Literary Career and Fame* (Durham: Duke University Press, 1933);

Hyder, ed., *Swinburne as Critic* (Boston: Routledge & Kegan Paul, 1972);

Hyder, ed., *Swinburne Replies* (Syracuse: Syracuse University Press, 1966);

Hyder, ed., *Swinburne: The Critical Heritage* (London: Routledge & Kegan Paul, 1970);

John O. Jordan, "Swinburne on Culver Cliff: The Origin of a Poetic Myth," *Biography*, 5 (Spring 1982): 143-160;

Cecil Y. Lang, "Swinburne's Lost Love," *PMLA*, 74 (March 1959): 123-130;

Robert Lougy, "Swinburne's *The Children of the Chapel*: A Historical Novel for Young Victorian Readers," *Clio*, 12 (Winter 1983): 123-128;

Jerome J. McGann, *Swinburne: An Experiment in Criticism* (Chicago: University of Chicago Press, 1972);

Kerry McSweeney, *Tennyson and Swinburne as Romantic Naturalists* (Toronto: University of Toronto Press, 1981);

Catherine W. Morley, "Swinburne as Art Critic," *Journal of Pre-Raphaelite Studies*, 1 (1981): 91-103;

Ross Murfin, *Swinburne, Hardy, and Lawrence and the Burden of Belief* (Chicago: University of Chicago Press, 1978);

William B. Ober, "Swinburne's Masochism," in his *Boswell's Clap and Other Essays* (Carbondale: Southern Illinois University Press, 1979), pp. 43-48;

Robert L. Peters, *The Crowns of Apollo: Swinburne's Principles of Literature and Art* (Detroit: Wayne State University Press, 1965);

Meredith B. Raymond, *Swinburne's Poetics* (The Hague: Mouton, 1971);

Eileen Souffrin, "Swinburne and *Les Misérables*," *Revue de Litterature Comparée*, 34 (1960): 578-585;

F. A. C. Wilson, "Swinburne's Dearest Cousin: The Character of Mary Gordon," *Literature and Psychology*, 19, no. 2 (1969): 89-99;

William Wilson, "Behind the Veil, Forbidden: Truth, Beauty, and Swinburne's Aesthetic Strain," *Victorian Poetry*, 22 (Winter 1984): 427-437;

Gillian Workman, "*La Soeur de la Reine* and Related 'Victorian Romances' by Swinburne," *Harvard Library Bulletin*, 21 (October 1973): 356-364.

Papers:

The major collection of Swinburne's manuscripts and letters is at the British Library. Other important collections of letters are at the Beinecke Rare Book and Manuscript Library, Yale University; Rutgers University Library; the National Library of Wales; and the Brotherton Library, Leeds University. Extensive collections of manuscripts are at the Harry Ransom Humanities Research Center, University of Texas at Austin; the New York Public Library; the Mayfield Library, Syracuse University; the Brotherton Library, Leeds University; the Huntington Library, San Marino, California; the Public Library of New South Wales; the Pierpont Morgan Library, New York; the Free Library of Philadelphia; Trinity College of Cambridge University; the Library of Congress; and the libraries of Rutgers, Harvard, Yale, Princeton, and the University of Michigan.

John Addington Symonds

(5 October 1840-19 April 1893)

David L. Chapman

BOOKS: *The Escorial. A Prize Poem, Recited in the Theatre, Oxford, June 20, 1860* (Oxford: Shrimpton, 1860);

The Renaissance. An Essay Read in the Theatre, Oxford, June 17, 1863 (Oxford: Hammans, 1863; New York: Dodd, Mead, 1898);

An Introduction to the Study of Dante (London: Smith, Elder, 1872; London: Black/New York: Macmillan, 1899);

The Renaissance of Modern Europe. A Review of the Scientific, Artistic, Rationalistic, Revolutionary Revival, dating from the 15th Century. Being a Lecture delivered before the Sunday Lecture Society, The 24th November, 1872 (London: Sunday Lecture Society, 1872);

Studies of the Greek Poets, 2 volumes (London: Smith, Elder, 1873, 1876; New York: Harper, 1880);

Sketches in Italy and Greece (London: Smith, Elder, 1874); republished in *Sketches and Studies in Southern Europe*, 2 volumes (New York: Harper, 1880);

Renaissance in Italy, 7 volumes (London: Smith, Elder, 1875-1886; New York: Holt, 1881-1887);

Callicrates, Bianca, Imelda, Passio Amoris Secunda, A Rhapsody, Liber Temporis Perditi (Bristol: Privately printed, *circa* 1875-1880);

Crocuses and Soldanellas (Bristol: Privately printed, *circa* 1875-1880);

Genius Amoris Amari Visio (Bristol: Privately printed, *circa* 1875-1880);

The Lotos Garland of Antinous [and *Diego*] (Bristol: Privately printed, *circa* 1875-1880);

Love and Death: A Symphony (Bristol: Privately printed, *circa* 1875-1880);

The Love Tale of Odatis and Prince Zariadres (Bristol: Privately printed, *circa* 1875-1880);

Old and New (Bristol: Privately printed, *circa* 1875-1880);

[*Pantarkes*] (Bristol: Privately printed, *circa* 1875-1880);

Rhaetica (Bristol: Privately printed, *circa* 1875-

by permission of the University Library, Bristol

1880);

Tales of Ancient Greece, No. 1 (Bristol: Privately printed, *circa* 1875-1880);

Tales of Ancient Greece, No. 2 (Bristol: Privately printed, *circa* 1875-1880);

Many Moods: A Volume of Verse (London: Smith, Elder, 1878);

Shelley (London: Macmillan, 1878; New York: Harper, 1878);

320

Sketches and Studies in Italy (London: Smith, Elder, 1879); republished in *Sketches and Studies in Southern Europe*, 2 volumes (New York: Harper, 1880);

New and Old: A Volume of Verse (London: Smith, Elder, 1880; Boston: Osgood, 1880);

Animi Figura (London: Smith, Elder, 1882);

Italian Byways (London: Smith, Elder, 1883; New York: Holt, 1883);

A Problem in Greek Ethics (N.p.: Privately printed, 1883);

Fragilia Labilia (N.p.: Privately printed, 1884; Portland, Maine: Mosher, 1902);

Wine, Women, and Song (London: Chatto & Windus, 1884; Portland, Maine: Mosher, 1899);

Shakespeare's Predecessors in the English Drama (London: Smith, Elder, 1884; London: Smith, Elder/New York: Scribners, 1900);

Vagabunduli Libellus (London: Kegan Paul, Trench, 1884);

Sir Philip Sidney (London: Macmillan, 1886; New York: Macmillan, 1886);

Ben Jonson (London: Longmans, Green, 1886; New York: Appleton, 1886);

Essays Speculative and Suggestive, 2 volumes (London: Chapman & Hall, 1890; New York: Scribners, 1894);

A Problem in Modern Ethics: Being an Enquiry into the Phenomenon of Sexual Inversion. Addressed Especially to Medical Psychologists and Jurists (N.p.: Privately printed, 1891?);

Our Life in the Swiss Highlands, by Symonds and Margaret Symonds (London & Edinburgh: Black, 1892);

The Life of Michelangelo Buonarroti. Based on Studies in the Archives of the Buonarroti Family at Florence, 2 volumes (London: Nimmo, 1893; London: Macmillan/New York: Scribners, 1900);

In the Key of Blue and Other Prose Essays (London: Mathews & Lane/New York: Macmillan, 1893);

Walt Whitman: A Study (London: Nimmo, 1893; London: Routledge/New York: Dutton, 1906?);

On the English Family of Symonds (Oxford: Privately printed, 1894);

Blank Verse (London: Nimmo, 1895; New York: Scribners, 1895);

Giovanni Boccaccio as Man and Author (London: Nimmo, 1895);

Das Konträre Geschlechtsgefühl, by Symonds and Havelock Ellis, edited by Dr. Hans Kurella (Leipzig: George H. Wingard's Verlag, 1896); English version revised as *Sexual Inversion*, by Symonds and Ellis (London: Wilson & Macmillan, 1897); republished, omitting appendices by Symonds and without Symonds's name on the title page (Philadelphia: Davis, 1901);

Last and First; Being Two Essays (New York: Brown, 1919);

Gabriel: A Poem, edited by Timothy D'Arch Smith and Robert L. Peters (London: deHartington, 1974);

Memoirs of John Addington Symonds, edited by Phyllis Grosskurth (London: Hutchinson, 1984; New York: Random House, 1984).

OTHER: John Addington Symonds, M.D., *Verses*, edited by Symonds, Jr. (Bristol: Privately printed, 1871);

The Sonnets of Michael Angelo Buonarroti and Tommaso Campanella, translated by Symonds (London: Smith, Elder, 1878; Portland, Maine: Mosher, 1895);

Wine, Women, and Song: Mediaeval Latin Students' Songs, translated by Symonds (London: Chatto & Windus, 1884; Portland, Maine: Mosher, 1899);

Christopher Marlowe, edited by Havelock Ellis, general introduction by Symonds (London: Vizetelly, 1887);

Thomas Heywood, edited by A. Wilson Verity, introduction by Symonds (London: Vizetelly, 1888);

Webster and Tourneur, introduction and notes by Symonds (London: Vizetelly, 1888);

The Life of Benvenuto Cellini, translated with an introduction by Symonds (London: Nimmo, 1888; New York: Scribner & Welford, 1888);

The Memoirs of Count Carlo Gozzi, translated with an introduction by Symonds (London: Nimmo, 1890).

As he lay dying in a Roman hotel room in April 1893, John Addington Symonds had good reason to be proud of his literary life. He had left behind a long and impressive list of works: translations, biographies, poetry, criticism, and a significant seven-volume history of the Renaissance in Italy. He had achieved a position of moderate fame in the world of Victorian letters. He should have rested easy.

However, in addition to being one of his era's finest historians and essayists, Symonds was homosexual and had produced several revolutionary works on the history and rights of inverts. He had also penned a candid autobiography, which, though it remained unpublished, made no bones about his temperament. Concerned that these writings would cause his family embarrassment and grief, a few hours before his death Symonds wrote a pathetic note to his wife, Catherine, assuring her that nothing would be published without her consent. "You see how the great question was supreme in his mind to the very last," Catherine Symonds wrote a few months after her husband's death. The Question–homosexuality–colored nearly every word Symonds committed to paper, and without understanding this aspect of his character, it is impossible to comprehend either the man or his work.

Homosexuality was but one of the significant forces in Symonds's life. Another important influence was his father, John Addington Symonds, Sr. By today's standards, the relationship between Symonds and his father seems to have been excessively close, but perhaps these suffocating family ties are understandable because of the strained circumstance of Symonds's birth and early childhood. At his birth in Bristol on 5 October 1840, John Addington Symonds was a puny and feeble child who survived seemingly against all odds. He had been preceded by three brothers and a sister who had died in infancy. A healthy daughter, Charlotte, was born in 1842. Symonds's mother, Harriet Sykes Symonds, died when her son was only four years old, leaving her physician husband a widower at thirty-seven. Dr. Symonds had a practice and a family to maintain, and he pursued both tasks with typically Victorian thoroughness. The elder Symonds was a remarkable man by any standards. He had achieved minor celebrity as physician and lecturer, and he also harbored a profound love of literature and scholarship that he took great pains to inculcate into his young son. The doctor was fond of holding literary soirées to which he invited many of the luminaries of the day. At one meeting, Symonds later recalled, he was privy to the witty conversation of Gladstone, Tennyson, Palgrave, and his father as they discussed Greek translations and moral values in art.

Being the offspring of an illustrious father was not easy for parent or child, and the strains of this relationship were apparent from an early date. As Symonds described it in his *Memoirs*, which were not published until 1984, he never seemed able to measure up to his father's expectation, despite constant efforts to please. Though

Symonds with his father, John Addington Symonds, Sr., and his sister, Charlotte (by permission of the University Library, Bristol)

Dr. Symonds loved his bright and impressionable son, he felt it necessary to present a facade of adamantine self-righteousness and scholarly correctness. Thus, precocious though he was, young Symonds was sharply aware of his intellectual inferiority to his father, and he strove by constant study to close the gap between them.

Thanks to his advanced learning, Symonds was ahead of his fellows when he was sent to Harrow in 1854 to begin his schooling. An earnest lad, raised in a rich and intense environment, Symonds believed himself morally and mentally superior to his classmates–an attitude that quickly gained him a reputation as a self-satisfied prig. Almost universally despised by the other students, Symonds was miserable, and he poured out his grief to his father in long letters filled with frustration and homesickness. Eventually, however, he settled into an uneasy truce with his classmates and even struck up a few feeble friendships.

Unfortunately, one of Symonds's friends confided that Harrow's headmaster, Dr. Charles Vaughan, had fondled him and written love letters. Symonds, shocked and outraged, eventually told his father of the incident. With the energy of an avenging fury, the elder Symonds hounded Vaughan until he resigned his post to live in obscurity with the threat of exposure and disgrace hanging over his head. The episode left an indelible mark on young Symonds, afflicting him with pangs of guilt and increasing his view of himself as a pariah; "I do not think," he wrote in his *Memoirs*, "I have ever quite recovered tone and equilibrium after the tension of those weeks."

After Harrow, Symonds went up to Oxford where he entered Balliol College in 1858. There he found the climate more congenial to his intellectual and aesthetic sensibilities, and he began to flourish as an undergraduate, attending lectures, writing essays, and engaging in the other pursuits of Oxford scholars. However, as Symonds reveals in his *Memoirs*, since his days in Harrow's sixth form, he had indulged in a succession of emotionally intense but chaste love affairs with likeminded youths. The situation eventually reached the point where he could no longer keep his mind on his studies without a massive effort of will: "I have ceased to care about the Schools," he wrote in his diary in 1861. "My ship has sailed into a magic sea with tempests of its own."

Though Symonds was unsettled emotionally, Oxford never became the bitter ordeal his public school days had been. There were pleasant moments, even triumphs. Symonds enjoyed a close relationship with Benjamin Jowett, the avuncular master of Balliol; he had a wide circle of friends; and he thrived on the highly charged intellectual atmosphere of college life. He was also beginning to dabble in poetry with some gratifying results. In 1860 he wrote a long instructive poem titled *The Escorial* which won him the Newdigate Prize. The poem, published at Oxford that year, was Symonds's first appearance in print.

Symonds found university life so pleasant that upon completion of his studies, he decided to apply for a fellowship. He found a position at Magdalen College in October 1862, but soon was beset by problems. Word leaked out about Symonds's sexual leanings and he was forced to defend himself publicly against charges of moral turpitude. Ironically, Symonds could not bring himself to consummate his homoerotic fantasies. In his *Memoirs* he explains the three reasons for his sexual reticence: first, he feared his father's reaction should he ever find out; second, his own ideals of purity forbade such conduct; and third, he worried that a similar fate to Vaughan's awaited him if he gave in to his instincts.

Under the strain of accusations, scandal, and his self-imposed chastity, Symonds's health broke. He began to display signs of nervousness along with weakened lungs that preceded consumption. At various times he suffered from headaches, temporary blindness, and painful genital inflammations. As a last resort, he consulted a specialist recommended by his father, a doctor who advised his patient either to take a mistress or get married as soon as possible. A year later, in 1864, Symonds wed Catherine North, daughter of the M.P. for Hastings. To have married with such sangfroid did not bode well for the relationship.

After a disastrous honeymoon, Symonds settled uneasily into the life of a family man. His health declined steadily, and though he was able finally to take up marital relations and to sire four children, his emotional suffering continued. Symonds began to put his mind to literary works. He started contributing articles on literature, history, and travel to such journals as *Saturday Review*, *Cornhill Magazine*, and *Fortnightly Review*. In 1869 he did a major part of the work in preparing *The Poems and Prose Remains of Arthur Hugh Clough*, edited by Clough's widow. In addition he continually wrote poetry–page after page of painfully labored verse on noble and antique subjects. Because of their largely homosexual subject matter they were privately printed in small, very limited editions and then discreetly distributed among the chosen few. Only a few of these "peccant pamphlets," as Symonds dubbed them, have survived–precious relics of the author's frustration and loneliness.

On 25 February 1871 Dr. John Addington Symonds died. Although his son was grief stricken, he must have also felt relief as he moved his young family into Clifton Hill House, the mansion where he had been raised. Encouraged by his new freedom and by the promising reception of his articles, Symonds embarked on his most ambitious projects to date. He had long been interested in the Italian Renaissance, and one of the key figures that fascinated him was the poet Dante. Accordingly, in 1872 his first major book, *An Introduction to the Study of Dante*,

Symonds and Catherine North on their wedding day, 10 November 1864 (by permission of the University Library, Bristol)

was published. It received mixed notices, but the publishers, Smith, Elder and Company, were sufficiently impressed to put out another collection of Symonds's essays on classical subjects, *Studies of the Greek Poets* (1873). This volume was more favorably reviewed by the critics; the author, in fact, got a note from the poet A. C. Swinburne, who pronounced the book "delightful." Pleased by the reactions of the critics and the public, Symonds gathered energy and information for another work—one which would ultimately eclipse everything else he produced.

Volume one of Symonds's *Renaissance in Italy*, which appeared in 1875, is perhaps the most vivid and colorful of the seven books that eventually formed the work. Entitled *The Age of Despots*, it reveals the author's often morbid fascination with the bizarre characters of a turbulent era: the Borgias, the Sforzas, the Medicis, and others.

If Symonds was trying to out-Browning Browning and the many he inspired, his intent was a noble one. In *Renaissance in Italy* he weaves a broad and varied tapestry of Italian life, culture, and politics in a bold attempt to produce a

complete history of civilization along the lines of the German *Kulturgeschichte*, designed to touch on nearly every aspect of the life of an era. As Symonds envisioned it, his history was to be a banquet of delights that included anecdotes, biographies, dates, artistic commentary, family sagas, and political observations. The plan was ambitious, and it is little wonder that it succeeds only occasionally. His work's principal strength is its sweeping scope and grand vision, but its main weakness is its often ill-defined format and want of direction. If Symonds's work lacks the clarity and passion of Walter Pater's *Studies in the History of the Renaissance* (1873) or if it fails to capture the essence of the era as does Jacob Burckhardt's *The Civilization of the Renaissance in Italy* (1860), it nevertheless offers ample rewards of its own. Symonds's *Renaissance in Italy* can be counted a success in its lively portrayal of individuals and in the author's superb sense of the visual which he uses to re-create Renaissance art masterpieces for his readers.

Volume two of *Renaissance in Italy*, published in 1877, covers the rebirth of interest in classical

Symonds with his third child, Margaret, in 1872 (by permission of the University Library, Bristol)

scholarship. Volume three, *The Fine Arts* (1877), concentrates principally on two major artists, Michelangelo and Benvenuto Cellini, the two figures who, for Symonds, best sum up the mores and sensibilities of the times. Two volumes on Italian literature followed in 1881, tracing the progress of humanism in the works of such figures as Dante, Boccaccio, Boiardo, Ariosto, and Aretino. The last two volumes of *Renaissance in Italy–The Catholic Reaction–*appeared in 1886. In these Symonds reverts to the discussion of such villainous deeds as the Spanish Inquisition, the machinations of the Jesuits, and the brutality of the Spanish hegemony over Europe.

It took Symonds almost ten years to bring his massive work to its conclusion. Like any writer, Symonds grew and changed during the decade, and his skill as a critic and historian improved markedly with experience. Though he pro-

duced many other books over the course of his career, this monumental history must always stand as Symonds's crowning achievement. The contemporary reaction to *Renaissance in Italy* was generally favorable. There were few Victorian literati who did not sample at least one or two of the ponderous volumes. Benjamin Disraeli perhaps spoke most clearly for the readers of his generation. He described Symonds as "a complete scholar," one who "has a grasp of his subject which, from the rich variety of its elements, can never be one of simplicity, and yet which from his complete hold, he keeps perspicuous."

In spite of the positive reviews, most informed readers were well aware of Symonds's shortcomings. His style was often uneven, he did not fully understand the scientific achievements of the time, and he tended to overemphasize the importance of art and literature. Even so, his appreciation of the painters and his firm understanding of the *Zeitgeist*, or spirit, of the era has never been surpassed.

Because of his love of the Renaissance, Symonds next turned his talents to related projects. In the past he had occupied himself with translations of Michelangelo's sonnets. Symonds now returned to them with renewed interest, and in 1878 he produced an edition that included the artist's poetry as well as sonnets by the Italian philosopher Tommaso Campanella. Perhaps inspired by Michelangelo's writing, Symonds began to have poetry of his own published. *Many Moods* appeared in 1878, *New and Old* in 1880, *Animi Figura* in 1882, and his final volume of poetry, *Vagabunduli Libellus*, in 1884. Precious and overly refined, these poetic works are not to modern tastes; nor were they to the liking of many of Symonds's contemporary reviewers.

Poor critical reaction to his verses, however, was hardly his greatest problem at the time. In 1877 while Symonds was riding on the downs near Clifton, a blood vessel in his lungs suddenly burst and the consequent hemorrhage left him on the verge of death for many weeks. Since another winter in England would obviously kill him, it was imperative that he find a more salubrious climate than the damp and cold atmosphere of Bristol. After considering moves to Egypt and Davos Platz in Switzerland, Symonds, with his wife and family, left for the Engadine region in the Swiss Alps.

Almost at once the cold, dry mountain air acted as a tonic to the ailing writer. His strength and will to live returned to him with a speed that surprised even the doctors. Remote and isolated, Davos Platz was to be Symonds's home for the rest of his life. Although he often bemoaned his life in lonely exile, Symonds grew to love the area and its sturdy, simple inhabitants. In 1880 the decision was made to sell Clifton Hill House and move to Davos permanently. One year later Symonds began construction of Am Hof, a large, gracious home on the outskirts of the Swiss village.

Remote though it might have been, Switzerland had one distinct advantage over England: it was closer to Italy and the palaces of culture. It was also closer to the Italian pleasure domes—a proximity of which Symonds took increasing advantage in his later years. After the birth of their fourth daughter in 1875, Symonds and his wife had agreed to cease sleeping together. It was an arrangement that seemed to please them both: Catherine had a marked aversion to sexual relations, and her husband was far happier in the embrace of others. Though they continued to live together, both partners remained solitary and unfulfilled in their marriage.

After five years of steady improvement Symonds's health returned to near normal in 1884. In that year he produced one of his most popular books, *Wine, Women, and Song*, a lusty collection of goliardic verse which he translated from the medieval Latin much in the tradition of the *Carmina Burana*, which had been published in Germany in 1847. Perhaps these vivacious and risqué songs put Symonds in the right mood to attack his next subject, a translation of Benvenuto Cellini's autobiography.

Vital, forceful, and colorful, Cellini was the exact opposite of the moody, brooding, introspective Symonds. Thus it is no surprise that when he began to translate the memoirs, Symonds found himself thoroughly caught up in the life of the famous goldsmith-sculptor. Symonds's translation of *The Life of Benvenuto Cellini* (1888) has proved one of his most enduring works, one of his few books that has remained constantly in print.

Because of the tremendous popularity of Symonds's version of the autobiography, the pub-

Symonds at Davos Platz, Switzerland, where he settled permanently in 1880

lisher, J. C. Nimmo, persuaded him to turn to the work of another vigorous Italian: the eighteenth-century Venetian dramatist Count Carlo Gozzi. Despite his highly interesting life, Gozzi never appealed to Symonds in the same way that Cellini did, and the translator soon became bored with the playwright's autobiography. In 1890 Symonds's translation—a bowdlerized version of the life—appeared, and *The Memoirs of Count Carlo Gozzi* —or "Useless Memoirs," in the author's phrase—is filled with literary anecdotes and the earthy remembrances of a minor Casanova. By the time it was published Symonds was hard at work on another project that had much more interest for him.

Late in 1890 Nimmo contacted Symonds with another project, one which consumed him with as much fervor as the autobiography of Cellini had. Nimmo offered Symonds 500 guineas to produce a biography of Michelangelo. Despite a recurrence of ill health, it was an offer Symonds could not refuse. Because one of the principal criticisms of Symonds's *Renaissance in Italy* was that he had not consulted enough primary sources, he traveled throughout Italy getting a firsthand look at the paintings, sculpture, and architecture of the master, but more important, he obtained permission from the Italian government to consult the previously closed Buonarroti Archives in Florence.

Plainly obsessed with his subject, Symonds worked at first nine hours a day, later even longer, taking brief respites for quick meals and a little rest. The artist consumed him with curiosity. One of Symonds's secret goals was to determine whether Michelangelo was homosexual, as he had long suspected. "I have wrestled with his 'psyche,'" he wrote in a letter to critic and fellow invert Edmund Gosse, adding that if the artist "had any sexual energy at all (which is doubtful), he was a U [an *Urning*, or homosexual]."

Symonds grew more interested in Michelangelo's personality than in his art, and thus only three of fifteen chapters of *The Life of Michelangelo Buonarroti* (1893) deal with critical commentary. Symonds's revolutionary discoveries in the previously unedited letters showed that the artist had an unusually intense affection for the Roman youth Tommaso Cavalieri. Symonds's tactful revelations were therefore the first to verify openly the artist's homosexual tendencies.

Contemporary critical reaction to Symonds's biography was generally good, though several reviewers were quick to point out that Symonds

was far more reliable when he dealt with the artist's literary output than with his other works. Herbert Horne, writing in the *Fortnightly Review* (January 1893), echoed that opinion when he wrote that Symonds's skill in dealing with the character and the poetry of Michelangelo is not always sustained when he approaches the sculpture, the painting, and the architecture. He described the book as "a delicate chain of arguments, based upon authoritative documents," a work "likely to retain a foremost place among the lives of Michelangelo."

As Symonds completed his biography, he was already involved in another important project. In July of 1891 Symonds received a note from the young Havelock Ellis, obliquely hinting that he would be interested in a collaboration with the older writer on the subject of homosexuality. Symonds had acquired an underground reputation as an authority on homosexuality, and he had worked with Ellis on several previous occasions, most importantly as the author of introductions for three volumes in the Mermaid series of Elizabethan dramatists (*Christopher Marlowe*, 1887; *Thomas Heywood*, 1888; and *Webster and Tourneur*, 1888) for which Ellis served as general editor.

The two men agreed to look into the subject with a scientific thoroughness that had hitherto been absent. Symonds had already written and privately printed two works on the subject, *A Problem in Greek Ethics*, which appeared in 1883, and its companion volume, *A Problem in Modern Ethics*, apparently published in 1891. Both works were printed in very small editions and distributed among sympathetic readers. The new collaborative effort by Ellis and Symonds was to be an open and widely distributed volume, available to all students of human behavior. *Sexual Inversion*, to be the first book in a series entitled Studies in the Psychology of Sex, incorporated sections from Symonds's earlier works as well as carefully collected case histories of representative inverts.

It should have been evident from the start that such a controversial subject would run into legal problems. Mr. and Mrs. Grundy were powerful figures to deal with in Victorian Britain, a fact with which the two writers seemed to be unconcerned. Since he had serious difficulties finding an English publisher, Ellis was forced finally to take the book to Germany. The first British edition did not appear until 1897, four years after Symonds's death. Declared obscene by the British courts in the year it first appeared, *Sexual Inversion* was subsequently published in America. In

to publish. I have nothing to relate except the evolution of a character somewhat strangely constituted in its moral and aesthetic qualities." Contrary to his pessimistic prediction, Symonds's document was eventually published one hundred years after his death. In the *Memoirs of John Addington Symonds* (1984) modern readers are afforded a glimpse of a rare individual's torment and eventual fulfillment. Symonds's candor and probity are truly exceptional. However, sex and self-revelation were not the only subjects that occupied Symonds's mind in these final years of his life.

In his encyclopedic look at the era, *The Eighteen-Nineties* (1913), Holbrook Jackson describes Symonds's collection of impressionistic studies, *In the Key of Blue and Other Prose Essays* (1893), as "a book so typical in some ways of the Nineties that it might well have been written by one of the younger generation." Physically, this volume is Symonds's most beautiful. Artist and designer Charles Ricketts created the stylized hyacinths and laurel leaves that twine and curve across the cream-colored binding. Of the essays the title work is probably the most successful of the collection. It is an impressionistic piece in prose and verse, attempting to convey the dreamy, liquid quality of the color blue as the author envisions it against several differently colored backgrounds. Significantly, the author uses the device of a handsome Venetian *facchino* dressed in his traditional blue blouse whom Symonds then "poses" in different attitudes and different locales. In its skillful blending of prose and poetry, its rich romantic imagery, and its slightly decadent subject matter, *In the Key of Blue* gave the younger generation of writers much to admire.

The 1893 collection provided Symonds with a renown that he well deserved. The book was followed by a study of one of his favorite writers, Walt Whitman. Symonds had long been one of the American poet's chief English supporters, and it is not difficult to see what his attraction was. Here was a writer of homosexual temperament who had the temerity to announce his inclinations to the world. Symonds had been mesmerized by Whitman's courage and poetic skill and, in 1871, had begun a correspondence with him that lasted for many years. It was Symonds who wrote the famous letter to the American inquiring indiscreetly about the older man's sex life. Whitman shot back an angry (and probably mendacious) letter claiming to have begotten six illegitimate children. Though disappointed by the poet's response, Symonds produced his commen-

Symonds in Venice (by permission of the University Library, Bristol)

all later editions, Symonds's name and most of his contributions had been expunged by his wife and her nervous advisers.

By 1893 it was baldly evident that Symonds was slowing down. The years of hard work, the strain of constant bad health, and the frequent travel had taken a serious toll. Only one aspect of his existence seemed to improve: his private life. Frustration and indecision left him as Symonds grew older. He had come to grips with his sexual nature at last. Inspired by Cellini and Gozzi, Symonds decided to write his autobiography. This was not to be a plodding literary life; rather, it would be a soul-baring psychological history, with no punches pulled regarding the author's sexual leanings. Symonds had no illusions about this time-consuming and arduous work. Writing the memoirs, he noted in a letter, "is a foolish thing to do, because I do not think they will ever be fit

tary titled simply *Walt Whitman: A Study*. It was published on 19 April 1893, but its author was not able to enjoy its success. Ironically, he died in Rome on the same day.

To the end of his life Symonds continued to respect heroic and powerful men; Whitman was the final figure in a long series that had begun with Symonds's father. Symonds never really had the self-confidence to trust his own emotions fully, and his writings suffered accordingly. "I may rave, but I shall never rend the heavens," he had once written in a fit of brutal self-evaluation. "I may sit and sing, but I shall never make earth listen." In many respects, the opinion is remarkably clear sighted. His works are not widely read, and it is his life that most fascinates modern readers. In his memoirs, letters, and Phyllis Grosskurth's fine biography, Symonds lives most vividly. Critic Arthur Symons perhaps caught his secret. "It was the life in him, the personality," he wrote, "that gave the man his real interest, his real fascination." Symonds had a life of both extraordinary torment and richness. It is only when his colorful inner life is revealed that Symonds can truly be understood as a man and a writer.

Letters:

The Letters and Papers of John Addington Symonds, edited by H. F. Brown (London: Murray, 1923);
The Letters of John Addington Symonds, edited by Her-

bert M. Schueller and Robert L. Peters, 3 volumes (Detroit: Wayne State University Press, 1967-1969).

Bibliography:

Percy L. Babington, *Bibliography of the Writings of John Addington Symonds* (London: Castle, 1925).

Biographies:

Horatio F. Brown, *John Addington Symonds: A Biography*, 2 volumes (London: Nimmo, 1895);
Van Wyck Brooks, *John Addington Symonds: A Biographical Study* (New York: Kennerley, 1914; London: Richards, 1914);
Phyllis Grosskurth, *John Addington Symonds* (London: Longmans, Green, 1964; New York: Holt, Rinehart & Winston, 1964).

References:

Katherine Furse, *Hearts and Pomegranates* (London: Davies, 1940);
Margaret Symonds, *Out of the Past* (London: Murray, 1925);
Arthur Symons, *Studies in Prose and Verse* (London: Dent, 1904), pp. 85-90.

Papers:

Some of Symonds's papers are at the University of Bristol; others are privately held.

Arthur Symons

(28 February 1865-22 January 1945)

Karl Beckson
Brooklyn College of the City University of New York

See also the Symons entry in *DLB 19, British Poets, 1880-1914.*

SELECTED BOOKS: *An Introduction to the Study of Browning* (London & New York: Cassell, 1886; revised and enlarged, 1887);

Days and Nights (London & New York: Macmillan, 1889);

Silhouettes (London: Elkin Mathews & John Lane, 1892; revised and enlarged, London: Smithers, 1896; Portland, Maine: Mosher, 1909);

London Nights (London: Smithers, 1895; London: Smithers/New York: Richmond, 1896; revised, London: Smithers, 1897);

Amoris Victima (London: Smithers, 1897; London: Smithers/New York: Richmond, 1897);

Studies in Two Literatures (London: Smithers, 1897);

Aubrey Beardsley (London: Unicorn Press, 1898; revised and enlarged, London: Dent, 1905);

The Symbolist Movement in Literature (London: Heinemann, 1900; revised, London: Constable, 1908; New York: Dutton, 1908; revised again and enlarged, New York: Dutton, 1919);

Images of Good and Evil (London: Heinemann, 1900);

Poems, 2 volumes (London: Heinemann, 1901; New York: John Lane, 1902);

Cities (London: Dent/New York: Pott, 1903);

Plays, Acting and Music (London: Duckworth, 1903; revised and enlarged, London: Constable, 1909; New York: Dutton, 1909);

Studies in Prose and Verse (London: Dent, 1904; London: Dent/New York: Dutton, 1904);

Spiritual Adventures (London: Constable, 1905; New York: Dutton, 1905);

A Book of Twenty Songs (London: Dent, 1905);

The Fool of the World & Other Poems (London: Heinemann, 1906; New York: John Lane, 1907);

Studies in Seven Arts (London: Constable, 1906; New York: Dutton, 1906);

Cities of Italy (London: Dent, 1907; New York: Dutton, 1907);

William Blake (London: Constable, 1907; New York: Dutton, 1907);

The Romantic Movement in English Poetry (London: Constable, 1909; New York: Dutton, 1909);

Knave of Hearts, 1894-1908 (London: Heinemann, 1913; New York: John Lane/London: Heinemann, 1913);

Figures of Several Centuries (London: Constable, 1916; New York: Dutton, 1916);

Tragedies (London: Heinemann, 1916; New York: John Lane, 1916);

Tristan and Iseult: A Play in Four Acts (London: Heinemann, 1917; New York: Brentano's, 1917);

Cities and Sea-Coasts and Islands (London: Collins, 1918; New York: Brentano's, 1919);

Colour Studies in Paris (London: Chapman & Hall, 1918; New York: Dutton, 1918);

The Toy Cart: A Play in Five Acts (Dublin & London: Maunsel, 1919);

Studies in the Elizabethan Drama (New York: Dutton, 1919; London: Heinemann, 1920);

Cesare Borgia, Iseult of Brittany, The Toy Cart (New York: Brentano's, 1920);

Charles Baudelaire (London: Elkin Mathews, 1920; New York: Dutton, 1920);

Lesbia and Other Poems (New York: Dutton, 1920);

Love's Cruelty (London: Secker, 1923; New York: Boni, 1924);

Dramatis Personae (Indianapolis: Bobbs-Merrill, 1923; London: Faber & Gwyer, 1925);

The Café Royal and Other Essays (London: Beaumont Press, 1923);

Studies on Modern Painters (New York: Rudge, 1925);

Parisian Nights: A Book of Essays (London: Beaumont Press, 1926);

Notes on Joseph Conrad, With Some Unpublished Letters (London: Myers, 1926);

Eleanora Duse (London: Elkin Mathews, 1926; New York: Duffield/London: Elkin Mathews & Marrot, 1927);

A Study of Thomas Hardy (London: Sawyer, 1928);

courtesy of Princeton University Library

Studies in Strange Souls (London: Sawyer, 1929);

Mes Souvenirs (Chapelle-Réanville, France: Hours Press, 1929);

From Toulouse-Lautrec to Rodin. With Some Personal Recollections (London: John Lane, 1929; New York: King, 1930);

Confessions: A Study in Pathology (New York: Cape & Smith, 1930);

A Study of Oscar Wilde (London: Sawyer, 1930);

Wanderings (London & Toronto: Dent, 1931);

Jezebel Mort and Other Poems (London: Heinemann, 1931);

A Study of Walter Pater (London: Sawyer, 1932);

Amoris Victimia [*sic*] (London: Privately printed, 1940);

The Memoirs of Arthur Symons: Life and Art in the

1890s, edited by Karl Beckson (University Park & London: Pennsylvania State University Press, 1977).

Collection: *The Collected Works of Arthur Symons*, 9 volumes (London: Secker, 1924).

OTHER: *Essays by Leigh Hunt,* edited by Symons (London: Walter Scott, 1887);

Philip Massinger, edited by Symons, 2 volumes (London: Vizetelly, 1887, 1889);

The Works of William Shakespeare, edited by Henry Irving and Frank A. Marshall (London: Blackie & Son, 1888-1890)—volumes 4-8 include introductions by Symons;

The Book of the Rhymers' Club (London: Mathews, 1892)—includes poems by Symons;

The Second Book of the Rhymers' Club (London: Mathews & John Lane/New York: Dodd, Mead, 1894)—includes poems by Symons;

Charles Baudelaire, *Les Fleurs du mal, Petits Poèmes en prose, Les Paradis artificiels*, translated by Symons (London: Casanova Society, 1925); republished as *Baudelaire: Prose and Poetry* (New York: Boni, 1926).

Of late-nineteenth-century writers of prose, such as Edmund Gosse, George Moore, and George Saintsbury, Arthur Symons has been acknowledged as a crucial figure in the development of Modernism, as the most important disciple of Walter Pater, and as a significant influence on such modernists as William Butler Yeats, James Joyce, Ezra Pound, and T. S. Eliot. He was the most important aesthetic critic who acquainted the British in the 1890s with literary Decadence and the Symbolist Movement (both having developed in France), and he edited the *Savoy*, the only truly avant-garde periodical in that decade. In short, Symons—a poet, short-story writer, translator, travel writer, playwright, editor, and critic—was the complete man of letters in the late-nineteenth and early-twentieth centuries until a severe mental breakdown halted his career for almost two years (1908-1910). Although he recovered slowly to resume his writing, he was permanently altered by an afflicted mind.

Such a literary figure, at the forefront of the artistic renaissance of the 1890s, emerged from an unlikely background and even more unlikely parents. Arthur William Symons (he dropped his middle name early in his career) was born in Milford Haven, Wales, on 28 February 1865, the only son of Rev. Mark Symons, a dour Wesleyan minister whose clerical duties required constant moves from parish to parish (usually every three years); Symons's birth in Wales (where his father was serving at the time) has produced the erroneous impression that he was Welsh. His mother, Lydia Pascoe Symons, was the daughter of a well-to-do farmer. Both of Symons's parents were descended from Cornish forebears, and Symons took pride in his own Celtic origins and in Cornwall.

Because of his father's constant moves, Symons later said that he "had never known what it was to have a home, as most children know it." This sense of rootlessness had a profound psychological effect on the young Symons, whose later bohemianism and restlessness were shaping factors in his development as a writer. By the age of nine, he had already written his first poem, "The Lord is Good," to be expected from a minister's son, but he soon discovered Byron (no doubt a discovery kept from his father), and he attempted imitations of his work. Soon he was familiar with the work of such poets as Swinburne, Tennyson, and Browning, who became an inspiration.

When in 1879 the Symonses moved to Bideford, in the West Country, Arthur was enrolled in the High Street Classical and Mathematical School, where he studied for three years. During these adolescent years he discovered the work of George Borrow, whose semi-autobiographical novel *Lavengro* (1851), describing his adventures among the gypsies, stimulated Symons to study Romany. Indeed, for the remainder of his life, he studied the lives of the gypsies and talked with them in their language whenever possible. In time he was convinced that he could no longer attend church and subscribe to his parents' faith. Though grieved, they respected his decision.

When the Browning Society was founded in the summer of 1881, Symons joined immediately: here was a vicarious connection with the literary world of London. As a result, he began corresponding with the cofounder, Frederick J. Furnivall. By June 1882 he had decided to leave school (he was now seventeen), for self-education in contemporary literature (not a subject taught there) was more instructive. He was now determined to embark upon a literary career.

In December he saw his first article in print—in the *Wesleyan-Methodist Magazine*—with the title "Robert Browning as a Religious Poet." In the essay Symons asserts that the "keynote" of Browning's system is that "God is love"—a view similar to the bardolotry at the Browning Society.

But Symons also insists that Browning is a "dramatic poet," an idea developed in a paper—"Is Browning Dramatic?"—which was read by Furnivall at a meeting of the society. Symons now focused not on the message but on the medium—that is, the manner in which Browning's dramatic monologues revealed "the drama of the interior, a tragedy or comedy of the soul" and the "subtlest secrets of the most abnormal consciousness" (in short, an epiphany revealed at a critical moment).

Impressed with the young Symons's paper, Furnivall asked him to write introductions to *Venus and Adonis* and other works by Shakespeare for the Shakespeare Quartos Facsimiles series that Furnivall was editing. The introductions reveal a talent on the part of this nineteen year old for combining biography, history, and criticism in a pleasing, striking style. As a result of his research, he began to study the works of Walter Pater, particularly his *Studies in the History of the Renaissance* (1873), a work that many perceived as an inspiration for the Aesthetic Movement, or, at the very least, a stimulus to those advocating a subjective approach to art and life. For Symons, Pater was not the extravagant advocate of a simple "art-for-art's-sake" doctrine but the proponent of an enriched aesthetic hedonism, yet with a "somewhat chill asceticism, a restraint sometimes almost painful," with "a refinement upon refinement, a choice and exotic exquisiteness, a subtle and *recherché* beauty." Symons began a two-year correspondence with Pater before they met.

Furnivall now asked Symons to write a "primer" on Browning. Here was an opportunity to establish himself as a critic, though he wished to be known principally as a poet. However, he proceeded with the study, which appeared as *An Introduction to the Study of Browning* in 1886 (Symons was only twenty-one). Pater was pleased with the book on one of his "best-loved writers"; George Meredith, to whom the book was dedicated, and Browning himself praised the work. The reviews were generally favorable, though the *Saturday Review* objected to Symons's assertion that Browning was "second to Shakespeare alone."

Noteworthy in the Browning study is Symons's comparison of Browning and Pater (two writers who formed the youthful Symons as poet and critic). Just as Browning revealed "the soul to itself" in a dramatic moment that flashed "the truth out by one blow," Pater urged his readers to be "present always at the focus where the greatest number of vital forces unite in their purest energy." The moment of crisis, then, in a Browning monologue, when character and situation reveal their essence, is, as Joyce was later to call it, an "epiphany" and, as Virginia Woolf called it, "a moment of Being."

The success of the book brought Symons more opportunities as a literary journalist in the leading periodicals, and in 1889 he saw the appearance of his first volume of poems, *Days and Nights* (dedicated to Pater), which contains poems too obviously influenced by Browning, though Symons reveals his capacity to write in a variety of forms. Besides the monologues, there are poems derived from his reading of the French Decadents and the early Tennyson, as in "Satiety" ("I cannot sin,/It wearies me") and "The Opium Smoker" ("I am engulfed, and drown deliciously"). Furnivall disliked the volume, but Pater praised it lavishly: "In this new poet, the rich poetic vintage of our time has run clear at last."

With the 1890s, a decade that would propel him to the center of the London literary world, Symons would establish an enduring reputation as one who helped shape fin-de-siècle literature and the beginnings of Modernism in Britain. In this decade, Symons, convinced that he had liberated himself from religious imperatives, pursued a bohemian existence without the restraints that he had been brought up to observe; with time, however, the divisions of flesh and spirit, the inability to maintain a cohesive sense of self, took their tragic toll.

In March 1890 Symons and Havelock Ellis went to Paris for three months. (Ellis, who had commissioned Symons to edit the plays of Philip Massinger for the Mermaid Series of Elizabethan Dramatists, met Symons in 1888 after nearly two years of correspondence and spent eight days in Paris with him in September 1889.) From their hotel on the Left Bank, they explored the cultural life of the city: its museums, its theaters, its literary cafés. They met Paul Verlaine (who was to exercise a profound influence on Symons), Stéphane Mallarmé (the "high priest" of the Symbolists), Dumas *fils*, Remy de Gourmont, and Joris-Karl Huysmans, whose novel *A Rebours* (*Against the Grain*) Symons later called "the breviary of the Decadence." By the end of June, after brief visits to Rouen and Dieppe, Symons returned, as he put it, "a wiser & gayer man." He had absorbed the literary currents associated with Decadence and Symbolism, terms that in France were used with little distinction.

In August he edited the *Academy* for three weeks while its regular editor was on holiday and took rooms in Hampstead with Ernest Rhys, the editor of the Camelot series who had commissioned Symons to edit Leigh Hunt's essays in 1887. Earlier in 1890, Rhys, William Butler Yeats, and others had been meeting to read their verse to one another; they agreed to call their group the "Rhymers' Club" (without officers or membership rules), and undoubtedly Rhys invited Symons to join them at their usual meeting place in the Cheshire Cheese off Fleet Street. The club published two anthologies in 1892 and 1894, to which Symons contributed several poems. Including such figures as Ernest Dowson, Lionel Johnson, Richard Le Gallienne, and John Davidson, the club was dominated by Irishmen and others loosely calling themselves Celts who wished to divorce themselves from the restrictive English literary tradition: some believed in an elitist art for art's sake but others were Socialists and activists. In short, it was a heterogenous group that espoused several conflicting causes.

In January 1891 Symons moved into rooms in Fountain Court, The Temple, where he lived for ten years. Havelock Ellis later rented two of his rooms but permitted Symons to sublet them whenever he was not in London. John Gray (poet, dandy, and later priest) and the Irish novelist and critic George Moore, among others, also lived in The Temple, and Symons's social life revolved about this setting of law students and barristers. In 1892 Symons (as Silhouette) became the regular reviewer of drama and music-hall entertainment in the *Star*, a popular newspaper, to which he brought an analytical intelligence that prompted Yeats to refer to him as a "scholar in music halls." Symons advertised his affairs with dancers with such ardor that some of his friends merely smiled with incredulity. Said the painter Will Rothenstein: "At The Crown Arthur Symons would give us ecstatic accounts of his latest acquaintance in the Corps de Ballet. . . . I used to say of him that he began every day with bad intentions, and broke them every night." George Moore recalled Symons as "a man of somewhat yellowish temperament, whom a wicked fairy had cast for a parson."

In his second volume of poems, *Silhouettes* (1892), Symons abandoned lengthy Browning-esque monologues and confined himself to short impressionistic lyrics obviously influenced by his reading of Verlaine and other French Decadents and Symbolists, particularly Baudelaire. "Maquillage"–a celebration of cosmetics, in which

Portrait of Rhoda Bowser Symons by J.-E. Blanche. Symons married the aspiring actress in January 1901.

artifice improves upon nature—and "Morbidezza" are two examples. In addition, poems celebrate the city and the dance (as in the notable "Javanese Dancers"), which, as Frank Kermode has written in his 1957 book, had become in the nineteenth century the "Romantic Image" of nondiscursive, autonomous art fusing form and content. The critical reception of *Silhouettes* was encouraging, a reviewer in the *Speaker*, for example, calling it "a very great advance" from *Days and Nights*.

In November 1893 (in the same month that Symons had acted as host to Verlaine, who gave a series of lectures in England) Symons's famous essay, "The Decadent Movement in Literature," appeared in *Harper's New Monthly Magazine*. Attempting to correct Richard Le Gallienne's mistaken notion of Decadence as an attempt "to limit beauty to form and colour, scornfully ignoring the higher sensibilities of heart and spirit," Symons contended that Decadence had "branches" or subdivisions: Symbolism and Impressionism. All sought "the very essence of truth" by flashing upon the sensibility "the finer sense of things un-

seen, the deeper meaning of things evident." Decadence—"an oversubtilizing refinement upon refinement, a spiritual and moral perversity"—had, as its intent: "To fix the last fine shade, the quintessence of things; to fix it fleetingly; to be a disembodied voice, and yet the voice of a human soul: that is the ideal of Decadence, and it is what Paul Verlaine has achieved."

Late in 1893 Symons became deeply involved with a ballet dancer named Lydia (he never gave her last name), the most devastating affair of his life, an obsession that would never leave him, despite the fact that by early 1896 it ended. This loss and the death of his mother—another Lydia—occurred simultaneously, thereby intensifying grief and guilt.

Symons's most Decadent volume of verse, *London Nights* (1895), was published by a former solicitor determined to establish his name by exploiting the new and daring. Symons referred to him as "my cynical publisher, Leonard Smithers, with his diabolical monocle." The poems depict sexual love with a new candor and include a series of poems about a woman named Bianca, who is clearly Lydia, seen as a femme fatale. In addition, poems on the city and the theater as manifestations of the poet's interior state are Symons's attempt to imitate the French Symbolists. But the volume also has Wordsworthian nature poems, surprising in such a book celebrating art and artifice. The most disturbing review came from the *Pall Mall Gazette* critic, who called Symons "a dirty-minded man."

In the spring of 1895 Oscar Wilde's arrest for homosexuality had resulted, unjustifiably, in the firing of Aubrey Beardsley as art editor of the *Yellow Book* (guilt by association: Beardsley had illustrated Wilde's *Salome* with daring pictures). Smithers asked Symons to edit a new magazine as the *Yellow Book*'s rival; seizing the opportunity, Symons recruited Beardsley as the principal illustrator of the *Savoy* (the title proposed by Beardsley), which attracted such contributors as Yeats, Verlaine, Conrad, Ellis, Shaw, Dowson, Max Beerbohm, and Hubert Crackanthorpe. Symons contributed poems and prose from its first number in January 1896, to its final number in December, when he wrote all of its contents and Beardsley provided all of the illustrations. In one of his well-known essays, "At the Alhambra: Impressions and Sensations," Symons's fascination with theatrical artifice, the dance, and the charm of "symbolic corruption" (evoked by make-up) established him, after Baudelaire, as the foremost writer celebrating the artificial as opposed to the natural. In the final number of the *Savoy*, Symons's translation of Mallarmé's Symbolist poem "Hérodiade" made a notable impression upon Yeats, who echoed it in his verse play *A Full Moon in March* (1935). The magazine failed financially when Smithers turned it from a quarterly into a monthly, but it was the most daring avant-garde periodical of its time, focusing upon Symbolist and Decadent writers, Nietzsche, the occult, and Beardsley's striking (expurgated, unfinished) novel *Under the Hill* with his droll illustrations.

In August 1896 Symons visited Ireland and the Aran Islands with Yeats (their friendship having deepened since the latter had rented two of Symons's rooms in The Temple from October 1895 to March 1896, their discussions on Symbolism proving invaluable to them both). At Edward Martyn's "mysterious castle" in Galway, Symons, anticipating Yeats's later imagery, climbed "the winding staircase in the tower," as he describes it in "A Causerie: From a Castle in Ireland" in the *Savoy*, October 1896. He concludes the causerie facetiously by expressing his urgent need to return to London, "for I have perceived the insidious danger of idealism ever since I came into these ascetic regions." Before he left, however, he wrote, among the "weedy rocks" of Rosses Point, a preface to the second, revised edition of *London Nights* (1897), in which he asserted, in opposition to his harshest critics, that art could never be the servant of morality, a Paterian view that he maintained throughout his career.

Early in 1897 Symons's *Amoris Victima* appeared, for the most part a series of poems on his lacerating love affair with Lydia. He had written the poems at the urging of Yeats, an attempt by him to move Symons in the direction of personal passion and "great issues" rather than the impersonal impressionistic verse he had been writing. Reviewing the volume, Yeats asserted that *Amoris Victima* "will set Mr. Symons' name much higher with the dozen or so of men and women to whom poetry is the first interest in life." And in "no accurate sense," Yeats stated, was Symons a "decadent."

In the same year Symons's first volume of miscellaneous essays appeared, *Studies in Two Literatures*, consisting of previously published material on English and French writers, such as Pater, William Morris, Christina Rossetti, Benjamin Constant, Gautier, Huysmans, and Maupassant, as well as introductions to *Measure for Measure, An-*

tony and Cleopatra, Winter's Tale, Macbeth, and *Twelfth Night* written for the volumes of the Henry Irving Shakespeare edition published from late 1888 to late 1890. Symons's dedicatory epistle to George Moore reveals their agreement on "first principles": that "a work of art has but one reason for existence, that it should be a work of art, a moment of the eternity of beauty." The reviewer for the *Athenaeum* pointed to the volume as the "ablest book" of the Paterian "school" of criticism, and Edmund Gosse recommended it to the *Academy* for its annual prize, but Symons failed to receive the award.

When Wilde was released in 1897 after two years of imprisonment, Symons told Smithers that he wished to help him in some way. His opportunity came when Smithers published *The Ballad of Reading Gaol* (1898). Reviewing it, Symons discerned in Wilde "a great spectacular intellect, to which, at last, pity and terror have come in their own person, and no longer as puppets in a play." Wilde, who had come to be contemptuous of Symons's voluminous journalism, was enormously pleased with the review: "it is admirably written," he told Smithers, "and most . . . artistic in its mode of approval. . . ." Revising his estimate of Symons, he told Vincent O'Sullivan that he had written to his solicitor to inquire about "shares in Symons Ltd. . . . I think one might risk some shares in Symons."

When Beardsley died in March 1898, in his twenty-sixth year, Symons wrote an obituary essay in praise of the artist, despite the fact that Beardsley had grown progressively cool toward him during their association on the *Savoy*. Though, as Symons told Gosse, it was his "first serious attempt at art criticism," the essay reveals a mastery of the "bewildering characteristics" of Beardsley's temperament and its relationship to his art; indeed, it remains one of the finest brief evaluations of Beardsley. Yeats, who declared it a "masterpiece," was no doubt moved by Symons's insight that Beardsley was "a profoundly spiritual artist" and that "abstract spiritual corruption" is revealed in "beautiful form; sin transfigured by beauty."

On one of his numerous Continental trips, this time in Spain, Symons had an extraordinary experience at the monastery on the mountain at Montserrat, believed to have been the site of the castle of the Holy Grail. In a travel essay published in 1898 (and included in *Cities and Sea-Coasts and Islands,* 1918), he described his communion with the "beauty of Montserrat . . . exquisite, heroic, sacred, ancient." He left after three days at the "moment of perfection," recalling the vision of the mountain, with its implications of spiritual ascent, that would "always rise for me, out of the plain of ordinary days . . . where I had perhaps seen the Holy Graal." This spiritual re-awakening is evoked by Symons's use of suggestive imagery as though of a Symbolist poem.

During this time Symons was preparing *The Symbolist Movement in Literature,* consisting of re-written reviews and articles previously published on such figures as Mallarmé, Verlaine, Rimbaud, Laforgue, Maeterlinck, and Villiers de l'Isle-Adam. Meanwhile, he was carrying on an intense courtship of a young woman (nine years younger than he) introduced to him by Ernest Rhys's sister. Rhoda Bowser, the daughter of a wealthy New-castle shipbuilder, had come to London to study music, but she also hoped to go on the stage. In a brief essay of early 1900, titled "The Choice," written expressly for her, Symons discusses the sincerity of Huysmans's conversion to Roman Catholicism and its effect on his art, but Symons's intent is the expression of a Paterian vision of life and art to justify himself to Rhoda: "A man who goes through a day without some fine emotion has wasted his day, whatever he has gained in it. . . . Art begins when a man wishes to immortalise the most vivid moment he has ever lived. Life has already, to one not an artist, become art in that moment. And the making of one's life into art is after all the first duty and privilege of every man."

When his friend Ernest Dowson died in February 1900, Symons wrote a lengthy appreciation for the *Fortnightly Review* (to appear in June), a piece which continued what has been called the Dowson legend, much disputed by some of Dowson's friends. This well-balanced essay incorporates material from a causerie that had appeared in the *Savoy* (August 1896) but without naming Dowson: "the face of a demoralised Keats" and other such passages suggesting a dissipated, even decadent Dowson, whose "favorite form of intoxication" was hashish and whose penchant for "strange, squalid haunts" in Dieppe harbor and dissipation in Brussels suggest the Romantic myth of the self-destructive artist (later exploited by Yeats in his memoir "The Tragic Generation," included in Yeats's 1938 autobiography).

In March 1900 *The Symbolist Movement in Literature*—Symons's most important work—was finally released. (Its delay was caused by Heinemann's unsuccessful attempt to secure an

Symons in 1915 (photograph by Elliott & Fry)

American publisher, and, like several of Symons's books, the date on the title page—1899 in this case—does not correspond to the actual date of publication.) In his dedicatory epistle to Yeats, Symons acknowledges his friend's genius as "the chief representative of that [Symbolist] movement in our country." Using the term "Mysticism," he speaks to Yeats: "you have seen me gradually finding my way, uncertainly but inevitably, in that direction which has always been to you your natural direction."

In Symons's view the Symbolist Movement is notable for its quest for a transcendental reality. Decadence, he states, had been a "mock-interlude" that "diverted the attention of the critics while something more serious was in preparation." But, as Anna Balakian has suggested in *The Symbolist Movement* (1967), the two terms were so "intertwined in the late nineteenth century in France that without the 'decadent' spirit [morbid preoccupation with death, futility, and nihilistic despair] there would be little to distinguish symbolism from Romanticism"; notably, withdrawal into dream worlds pervades Symbolist poetry. Of the Symbolist poets discussed by Symons, Mallarmé best exemplifies the essential elements of the movement: the artist as priest; the work of art as mystical embodiment, nondiscursive, vaguely allusive. "Remember his principle," Symons writes of Mallarmé; "that to name is to destroy, to suggest is to create." The poem becomes "visible music."

The critical reception of *The Symbolist Movement in Literature* was disappointingly mixed, a number of reviewers unwilling or unable to concede the originality of Symons's vision. Even Yeats found the book puzzling, "curiously vague in its philosophy . . . but there is a great deal of really very fine criticism," he told Lady Gregory. One problem that later critics have found is Symons's inconsistent view of the transcendental reality evoked by Symbolist writers, but in his 1969 book on Symons John M. Munro has suggested that the author "was not searching for a consistent philosophy" but for "intimations of spirituality." Ruth Z. Temple, while praising much of the book in *The Critic's Alchemy* (1953) (she calls the essays on Mallarmé, Verlaine, and Laforgue "distinguished"), regards Symons's "failure to distinguish the artist's delight in the visible world from the philosophical and literary doctrine of materialism" as an error, for the Symbolist Movement was a rejection of the latter. Finally–and most important–T. S. Eliot regarded Symons's work as a "revelation," a book that had "affected the course of my life." Such a tribute was recognition that other critics, such as Edmund Gosse and George Moore, who had also written about the French Symbolists, lacked Symons's imaginative vision.

On 16 January 1901 Symons moved out of The Temple, and on 19 January, in Newcastle, he married Rhoda Bowser, despite her repeated warnings to him of her extravagance. Symons continued reviewing for the *Star* as well as other periodicals, but difficulties in earning a living from journalism were persistent. The need to provide for himself and his wife created new tensions and–Yeats complained–a progressive withdrawal from friends. Still, after an extensive Continental tour, Symons was receptive to a young writer brought to him by Yeats in early December 1902: James Joyce, an admirer of *The Symbolist Movement in Literature* who sought Symons's help in having his own verse published. Symons eventually helped place Joyce's *Chamber Music* (1907) and reviewed it favorably.

In 1903 *Cities* appeared, Symons's previously published travel essays, and *Plays, Acting and Music*, a collection of such reviews as "An Apology for Puppets," "Nietzsche on Tragedy," "Sir Henry Irving," "Sarah Bernhardt," and "Music, Staging, and Some Acting"–all of which had appeared in the *Academy* and the *Star*. A recent critic, Katharine Worth, in *The Irish Drama of Europe from Yeats to Beckett* (1978), has insisted that Symons, "the most concrete of critics," was "a voice crying sixty years ahead of his time for a technique of total theatre which would put the arts of dance, mime, song, scene on an equal footing with words."

In October 1905 one of Symons's most important works was published–*Spiritual Adventures*, his only volume of short fiction, "imaginary portraits," as he called them, reminiscent of Pater's. "A Prelude to Life," the first of eight stories, is a fictionalized autobiographical portrait of the alienated artist as a narcissistic young man; indeed, in many respects it foreshadows Joyce's novel and may have been an influence. The other stories depict various states of psychological and aesthetic isolation (characters are driven by religious or artistic ideals), resulting, on occasion, in madness. Reviewers predictably focused upon the "aesthetic decadence" in the volume, the *Saturday Review* critic, for example, pointing out that Symons was "consumed by a sort of feverish curiosity." Later commentators have recognized its striking originality: Ezra Pound remarked that, as "culture," it is "worth all the freudian tosh in existence," and Frank Kermode has called it "an unjustly neglected book."

Following his usual practice, Symons collected articles published in periodicals for his *Studies in Seven Arts* (1906), containing incisive discussions of Whistler, Wagner, Rodin, Gordon Craig's stage designs, nineteenth-century painting, cathedrals, arts and crafts. The volume, in short, is a fearless venture into all the arts. "The World as Ballet," one of Symons's most eloquent and influential essays, sums up his vision of the dance as the "living symbol," nondiscursive and autonomous, fusing motion and image into a seamless unity. As Yeats was later to suggest in his poem "Among School Children" (1928): "How can we know the dancer from the dance?"

In 1907 Symons was at work on a study of William Blake. His most scholarly full-length work, it suggested Blake's affinity with the French Symbolists and refuted existing critical opinion (advanced, for example, by Yeats in a three-volume edition of Blake, which he coedited with Edwin J. Ellis) that Blake had attempted to create a coherent mythology. During this period he was also reviewing widely. He increasingly complained of his financial difficulties, which were intensified by the purchase and cost of repair of a seventeenth-century timbered cottage in Wittersham, Kent. In addition, he was deeply disappointed by his failure to make his mark as a dramatist. By the summer of 1908 he was in a disturbed state, but he was planning to spend the autumn with Rhoda in Italy.

On 26 September while in Venice, Symons suddenly left his wife and went to Bologna; she joined him there, where they spent, he reported, "an intolerable week" quarreling. She left for London; he went to Ferrara, where in a state of disorientation, he wandered through the countryside until interned by local police in what he called a "dungeon," bound hand and foot by fetters. In London Rhoda Symons prevailed upon the Italian ambassador to request a search for her husband; eventually, he was returned to London, where he was placed in a mental institution, then certified as insane. His psychosis intensified, but by the spring of 1909 he had a sudden remission; he remained in the institution until early 1910, but throughout most of that time, he was permitted to leave on one-day excursions with an attendant in the company of a friend, Agnes Tobin, an American translator of Petrarch. During this time, the painter Augustus John also provided much-appreciated friendship.

Symons's mental breakdown substantially destroyed a brilliant career, for as a poet and critic he was never the same again. His writings, particularly in criticism, reveal a sometimes subtle, sometimes gross incoherence and his critical discernment lacks the imaginative quality it once had. He resumed his career, however, within a few years, publishing many articles and books—indeed, more than twenty-five volumes (for the most part, republications of previously published reviews and articles). In his new poems there is limited artistic interest, though they have considerable biographical importance in revealing an afflicted mind obsessed with sexual perversity and sin. Much of his new critical writing focuses on literary interests before his breakdown, as though tragically fixed on a period that he could not escape. After his return to Kent and Island Cottage in April 1910, Rhoda Symons, aware that no

Symons at home, Island Cottage, Wittersham, Kent

cure was possible for her husband, embarked upon a moderately successful theatrical career that had many disappointments (roles were difficult to obtain), though she appeared in some dozen plays through the 1920s, but her increasing emotional instability and progressively bad health proved an additional burden to Symons.

Symons's life, divided between Wittersham and London, where the Symonses maintained a series of flats, provided some stimulus for his return to the literary world. In Kent he enjoyed the friendship of Conrad from 1910, and in London he continued his friendship with Augustus John. He lost the friendship of Yeats, however, who, pained by his certainty that Symons would never fully recover, believed that Rhoda's demands had been a major factor in the breakdown.

An indication of Symons's impaired judgment is obvious in his 1919 edition of *The Symbolist Movement in Literature*, to which he added previously published essays on Zola, Balzac, Flaubert, Cladel, Gautier, Baudelaire, Mérimée, and the Goncourt brothers–many of whom he had said in his original introduction were not Symbolists. This edition, states Richard Ellmann in the preface to a 1958 edition, "shows a curious indifference to the book's earlier rationale." Symons also omitted his dedicatory epistle to Yeats, perhaps in resentment over his former friend's seeming indifference.

In the 1920s Symons (sometimes with Rhoda) visited Paris several times, thanks to the financial assistance of the American lawyer and patron of the arts John Quinn, who purchased many of his manuscripts. In 1925 he dined with Joyce and Valery Larbaud, and he was invited to the salon of the American expatriate Natalie Barney. Clearly, his name still commanded attention.

In 1924 the publisher Martin Secker issued nine volumes of Symons's *Collected Works* out of a projected sixteen volumes, but sales were such that he decided not to continue, a major disappointment for Symons, who contemplated legal action. Symons's translation of Baudelaire's *Les Fleurs du mal* in 1925 prompted T. S. Eliot to declare that Symons had made Baudelaire "a poet of the nineties, a contemporary of Dowson and Wilde," implying that though Symons was "as great a translator as Mr. Symons can be," he had failed to sound the Baudelairean depths with respect to the Frenchman's despair at his sin.

Of Symons's postbreakdown books, perhaps the most remarkable is *Confessions: A Study in Pa-*

thology (1930), an account of his collapse in Italy and its aftermath. What is immediately apparent is its circumstantiality (its wandering away from the central point and returning periodically). Despite this element, the narration of the events in Italy is harrowing; indeed, the dungeon scenes recall the descriptive power of Poe, a writer whom Symons greatly admired. The cruelty that Symons endured and the incarcerations in Italy and England, with their attendant indignities suffered by such a renowned man of letters, are brilliantly described, and his bizarre delusions have, at times, comic elements of the absurd. In addition, the volume includes tributes to such friends as Agnes Tobin, Augustus John, and John Quinn (whom, nevertheless, he characterizes as "sinister" perhaps because Quinn finally called a halt to his generous purchases of Symons's manuscripts). *Confessions*, a major work in the literature of madness, is a plea for understanding and a celebration of Symons's "obstinate nature" and "strength of will" (his judgments) that enabled him to survive the "tragic crisis" of 1908-1909.

As Symons progressively lived a more secluded life in Wittersham, his visits to London–and especially to the Café Royal, the literary café popular among writers and artists in the 1890s, the last remaining link he had to his former existence–were now only sporadic excursions. John Betjeman, who once encountered him at the café, wrote:

I saw him in the Café Royal,
    Very old and very grand.
Modernistic shone the lamplight
    There in London's fairyland.

Betjeman noted that no one spoke to him.

In 1936 Rhoda Symons died of leukemia; Symons, left to the care of his housekeeper, Mrs. Bessie Seymour, lived out his life in subdued contentment. He made a new friend, the Russian-born sculptor Dora Gordine, whose exhibitions he reviewed twice. But he was still obsessed by his love affair with Lydia, the ballet dancer, and in 1940 he had privately printed a little pamphlet on the affair that he had written in the 1890s using the title and including some poems from his 1897 volume *Amoris Victima*.

During World War II, which he followed with interest, Mrs. Seymour moved him to her flat in London when invasion of the coast seemed possible. In 1944, when the threat subsided, she moved him back to the Wittersham cottage. That winter he fell ill, developed a fever, and died in the early morning of 22 January 1945 at the age of seventy-nine. He was buried in a Wittersham cemetery where Rhoda's ashes had been deposited. One gravestone marks the site.

After Symons's death (when obituaries noted the passing of an aesthete from an age long since past), his reputation and importance, largely ignored by the Modernism that flowered between the two world wars, were reassessed by Ruth Z. Temple's *The Critic's Alchemy*, which devoted five chapters to Symons, and by Frank Kermode's *Romantic Image* (1957), which regarded Symons as "crucial" to the development of the leading images associated with Modernism. Finally, John M. Munro's full-length critical study, *Arthur Symons* (1969), developed the point, suggested by previous critics, that Modernism cannot be regarded as separate from late-nineteenth-century literary developments that Symons helped to shape, that indeed they were continuous. Ezra Pound told Floyd Dell in 1911 that he found his "sanity" in such "gods" as Plato, Longinus, Dante, Spinoza, Pater, and Symons–an extraordinary tribute (and an ironic one), but the view of Symons as a major influence in his day warrants such ironies, for Modernism embraces and develops the paradoxes inherent in the Romantic spirit–that of a determined rejection of the past but, simultaneously, a retention of its continuity with the present.

Letters:

Karl Beckson and John M. Munro, "Letters from Arthur Symons to James Joyce, 1904-1932," *James Joyce Quarterly*, 4 (Winter 1967): 91-101;

Bruce Morris, "Arthur Symons's Letters to W. B. Yeats," in *Yeats Annual No. 5*, edited by Warwick Gould (London: Macmillan, 1987), pp. 46-61.

Bibliographies:

Carol Simpson Stern, "Arthur Symons: An Annotated Bibliography of Writings about Him," *English Literature in Transition*, 17, no. 2 (1974): 77-133;

Karl Beckson, Ian Fletcher, Lawrence W. Markert, and John Stokes, *Arthur Symons: A Bibliography* (New York: Garland, forthcoming).

Biography:

Roger Lhombreaud, *Arthur Symons: A Critical Biog-*

raphy (London: Unicorn Press, 1963);

Karl Beckson, *Arthur Symons: A Life* (Oxford: Clarendon Press/New York: Oxford University Press, forthcoming 1987).

References:

Anna Balakian, *The Symbolist Movement* (New York: Random House, 1967);

Karl Beckson, "The Critic and the Actress: The Troubled Lives of Arthur and Rhoda Symons," *Columbia Library Columns*, 33 (November 1983): 3-10;

Beckson, "Symons' 'A Prelude to Life,' Joyce's *A Portrait*, and the Religion of Art," *James Joyce Quarterly*, 15 (Spring 1978): 222-228;

Beckson and John M. Munro, "Symons, Browning, and the Development of the Modern Aesthetic," *Studies in English Literature*, 10 (Autumn 1970): 687-699;

Barbara Charlesworth, *Dark Passages: The Decadent Consciousness in Victorian Literature* (Madison: University of Wisconsin Press, 1965);

Patricia Clements, "Symons: The Great Problem," in her *Baudelaire and the English Tradition* (Princeton: Princeton University Press, 1985), pp. 184-217;

Richard Ellmann, "Discovering Symbolism," in his *Golden Codgers: Biographical Speculations* (New York & London: Oxford University Press, 1973);

Ellmann, "Introduction" to Symons's *The Symbolist Movement in Literature* (New York: Dutton, 1958);

Ian Fletcher, "Explorations and Recoveries–II: Symons, Yeats and the Demonic Dance," *London Magazine*, 7 (June 1960): 46-60;

Frank Kermode, "Poet and Dancer Before Diaghilev," *Partisan Review*, 28 (January-February 1961): 48-75;

Kermode, *Romantic Image* (London: Routledge & Kegan Paul, 1957);

Bruce Morris, "Elaborate Form: Symons, Yeats, and Mallarmé," in *Yeats: An Annual of Critical and Textual Studies*, edited by Richard Finneran (Ann Arbor: UMI Research Press, 1986), pp. 99-119;

John M. Munro, *Arthur Symons* (New York: Twayne, 1969);

Munro, "Arthur Symons and W. B. Yeats: The Quest for Compromise," *Dalhousie Review*, 45 (Summer 1965): 137-152;

Ruth Z. Temple, *The Critic's Alchemy: A Study of the Introduction of French Symbolism into England* (New York: Twayne, 1953);

R. K. R. Thornton, *The Decadent Dilemma* (London: Arnold, 1983);

Katherine Worth, *The Irish Drama of Europe from Yeats to Beckett* (Atlantic Highlands, N.J.: Humanities Press, 1978);

W. B. Yeats, "The Tragic Generation," in *The Autobiography of William Butler Yeats* (New York: Macmillan, 1938).

Papers:
The largest collection of Symons's letters and literary manuscripts is at Princeton University. Columbia University has more than 2,000 letters, consisting of Arthur and Rhoda Symons's exchanges. Less extensive holdings are at the British Library, the Bodleian Library (Oxford), the New York Public Library, and the libraries of Harvard University, Queen's University (Kingston, Ontario), University of Iowa, University of Arizona, Northwestern University, Yale University, and the University of Texas at Austin.

Anthony Trollope

(24 April 1815-6 December 1882)

Timothy J. Evans
Richard Bland College of the College of William and Mary

See also the Trollope entry in *DLB 21, Victorian Novelists Before 1885.*

BOOKS: *The Macdermots of Ballycloran* (3 volumes, London: Newby, 1847; 1 volume, Philadelphia: Peterson, 1871);

The Kellys and the O'Kellys; or, Landlords and Tenants: A Tale of Irish Life (3 volumes, London: Colburn, 1848; 1 volume, New York: Munro, 1882);

La Vendée: An Historical Romance, 3 volumes (London: Colburn, 1850);

The Warden (London: Longman, Brown, Green & Longmans, 1855; New York: Dick & Fitzgerald, 1862);

Barchester Towers (3 volumes, London: Longman, Brown, Green, Longmans & Roberts, 1857; 1 volume, New York: Dick & Fitzgerald, 1860);

The Three Clerks: A Novel (3 volumes, London: Bentley, 1858; 1 volume, New York: Harper, 1860);

Doctor Thorne: A Novel (3 volumes, London: Chapman & Hall, 1858; 1 volume, New York: Harper, 1858);

The Bertrams: A Novel (3 volumes, London: Chapman & Hall, 1859; 1 volume, New York: Harper, 1859);

The West Indies and the Spanish Main (London: Chapman & Hall, 1859; New York: Harper, 1860);

Castle Richmond: A Novel (3 volumes, London: Chapman & Hall, 1860; 1 volume, New York: Harper, 1860);

Framley Parsonage (3 volumes, London: Smith, Elder, 1861; 1 volume, New York: Harper, 1861);

Tales of All Countries, 2 volumes (London: Chapman & Hall, 1861-1863);

Orley Farm (20 monthly parts, London: Chapman & Hall, 1861-1862; 1 volume, New York: Harper, 1862);

The Struggles of Brown, Jones, and Robinson, by One of the Firm (New York: Harper, 1862; London: Smith, Elder, 1870);

North America (2 volumes, London: Chapman & Hall, 1862; unauthorized edition, 1 volume, New York: Harper, 1862; authorized edition, 2 volumes, New York: Lippincott, 1862);

Rachel Ray: A Novel (2 volumes, London: Chapman & Hall, 1863; 1 volume, New York: Harper, 1863);

The Small House at Allington (2 volumes, London: Smith, Elder, 1864; 1 volume, New York: Harper, 1864);

Can You Forgive Her? (20 monthly parts, London: Chapman & Hall, 1864-1865; 1 volume, New York: Harper, 1865);

Hunting Sketches (London: Chapman & Hall, 1865; Hartford, Conn.: Mitchell, 1929);

Miss Mackenzie (2 volumes, London: Chapman & Hall, 1865; 1 volume, New York: Harper, 1865);

The Belton Estate (3 volumes, London: Chapman

Morris L. Parrish Collection,
Princeton University Library

& Hall, 1866; pirated American edition, 1 volume, New York: Harper, 1866; authorized American edition, 1 volume, New York: Lippincott, 1866);

Travelling Sketches (London: Chapman & Hall, 1866);

Clergymen of the Church of England (London: Chapman & Hall, 1866);

The Claverings (New York: Harper, 1867; 2 volumes, London: Smith, Elder, 1867);

Nina Balatka: The Story of a Maiden of Prague, 2 volumes (Edinburgh & London: Blackwood, 1867; London & New York: Oxford University Press, 1951);

The Last Chronicle of Barset (32 weekly parts, London: Smith, Elder, 1867; 1 volume, New York: Harper, 1867);

Lotta Schmidt and Other Stories (London: Strahan, 1867; London & New York: Ward & Lock, 1883);

Linda Tressel (2 volumes, Edinburgh & London:

Blackwood, 1868; 1 volume, Boston: Littell & Gay, 1868);

He Knew He Was Right (32 weekly parts, London: Virtue, 1868-1869; 1 volume, New York: Harper, 1870);

Phineas Finn: The Irish Member (2 volumes, London: Virtue, 1869; 1 volume, New York: Harper, 1869);

Did He Steal It? A Comedy in Three Acts (London: Privately printed, 1869);

The Vicar of Bullhampton (11 monthly parts, London: Bradbury & Evans, 1869-1870; pirated American edition, 1 volume, New York: Harper, 1870; authorized American edition, 1 volume, New York: Lippincott, 1870);

An Editor's Tales (London: Strahan, 1870);

The Commentaries of Caesar (Edinburgh & London: Blackwood, 1870; Philadelphia: Lippincott, 1870);

Ralph the Heir (19 monthly parts, London: Hurst & Blackett, 1870-1871; 1 volume, New York: Harper, 1871);

Sir Harry Hotspur of Humblethwaite (London: Hurst & Blackett, 1871; New York: Harper, 1871);

The Golden Lion of Granpère (London: Tinsley, 1872; New York: Harper, 1872);

The Eustace Diamonds (New York: Harper, 1872; 3 volumes, London: Chapman & Hall, 1873);

Australia and New Zealand, 2 volumes (London: Chapman & Hall, 1873);

Lady Anna (2 volumes, London: Chapman & Hall, 1874; 1 volume, New York: Harper, 1874);

Phineas Redux (2 volumes, London: Chapman & Hall, 1874; 1 volume, New York: Harper, 1874);

Harry Heathcote of Gangoil: A Tale of Australian Bush Life (London: Low, Marston, Low & Searle, 1874; New York: Harper, 1874);

The Way We Live Now (20 monthly parts, London: Chapman & Hall, 1874-1875; 1 volume, New York: Harper, 1875);

The Prime Minister (8 monthly parts, London: Chapman & Hall, 1875-1876; 1 volume, New York: Harper, 1876);

The American Senator (3 volumes, London: Chapman & Hall, 1877; 1 volume, New York: Harper, 1877);

Christmas at Thompson Hall (New York: Harper, 1877; London: Low, 1885);

The Lady of Launay (New York: Harper, 1877);

Is He Popenjoy? A Novel (3 volumes, London: Chapman & Hall, 1878; 1 volume, New York:

Harper, 1878);

How the "Mastiffs" Went to Iceland (London: Virtue, 1878);

South Africa, 2 volumes (London: Chapman & Hall, 1878);

An Eye for an Eye (2 volumes, London: Chapman & Hall, 1879; 1 volume, New York: Harper, 1879);

John Caldigate (3 volumes, London: Chapman & Hall, 1879; 1 volume, New York: Harper, 1879);

Cousin Henry: A Novel (2 volumes, London: Chapman & Hall, 1879; 1 volume, New York: Munro, 1879);

Thackeray (London: Macmillan, 1879; New York: Harper, 1879);

The Duke's Children: A Novel (3 volumes, London: Chapman & Hall, 1880; 1 volume, New York: Munro, 1880);

The Life of Cicero, 2 volumes (London: Chapman & Hall, 1880; New York: Harper, 1880);

Dr. Wortle's School: A Novel (New York: Harper, 1880; 2 volumes, London: Chapman & Hall, 1881);

Ayala's Angel (3 volumes, London: Chapman & Hall, 1881; 1 volume, New York: Harper, 1881);

Why Frau Frohmann Raised Her Prices, and Other Stories (London: Isbister, 1882; New York: Harper, 1882);

The Fixed Period: A Novel (2 volumes, Edinburgh & London: Blackwood, 1882; 1 volume, New York: Harper, 1882);

Lord Palmerston (London: Isbister, 1882);

Marion Fay: A Novel (3 volumes, London: Chapman & Hall, 1882; 1 volume, New York: Harper, 1882);

Kept in the Dark: A Novel (2 volumes, London: Chatto & Windus, 1882; 1 volume, New York: Harper, 1882);

The Two Heroines of Plumplington (New York: Munro, 1882; London: Deutsch, 1953);

Not if I Know It (New York: Munro, 1883);

Mr. Scarborough's Family (3 volumes, London: Chatto & Windus, 1883; 1 volume, New York: Harper, 1883);

The Landleaguers (3 volumes, London: Chatto & Windus, 1883; 1 volume, New York: Munro, 1883);

An Autobiography (2 volumes, Edinburgh & London: Blackwood, 1883; 1 volume, New York: Harper, 1883);

Alice Dugdale and Other Stories (Leipzig: Tauchnitz, 1883);

La Mère Bauche and Other Stories (Leipzig: Tauchnitz, 1883; New York: Munro, 1884);

The Mistletoe Bough and Other Stories (Leipzig: Tauchnitz, 1883);

An Old Man's Love (2 volumes, Edinburgh & London: Blackwood, 1884; 1 volume, New York: Lovell, 1884);

The Noble Jilt: A Comedy, edited by Michael Sadleir (London: Constable, 1923);

London Tradesmen, edited by Sadleir (London: Mathews & Marrot, 1927; New York: Scribners, 1927);

Four Lectures, edited by M. L. Parrish (London: Constable, 1938);

The Tireless Traveler: Twenty Letters to the "Liverpool Mercury" 1875, edited by Bradford Allen Booth (Berkeley & Los Angeles: University of California Press, 1941);

Novels and Tales, edited by J. Hampden (London: Pilot Press, 1946);

The Parson's Daughter and Other Stories, edited by Hampden (London: Folio Society, 1949);

The Spotted Dog and Other Stories (London: Pan, 1950);

Mary Gresley and Other Stories, edited by Hampden (London: Folio Society, 1951);

The New Zealander, edited by N. John Hall (London: Oxford University Press, 1972);

Miscellaneous Essays and Reviews (New York: Arno, 1981);

Writings for Saint Paul's Magazine (New York: Arno, 1981).

Collections: *The Oxford Illustrated Trollope,* edited by Sadleir and F. Page, 15 volumes (Oxford: Oxford University Press, 1948-1954);

Selected Works of Anthony Trollope, edited by Hall, 62 volumes (New York: Arno, 1980).

OTHER: *British Sports and Pastimes,* edited with contributions by Trollope (London & New York: Virtue, 1868).

As Bradford Allen Booth points out in his introduction to *The Tireless Traveler,* "The casual reader, glancing over Trollope's bibliography, probably overlooks the twelve [*sic*] titles of biography, essays and travels, for the world has refused to accept Trollope's extravagant estimate of these books, and rightly chooses to remember him as a novelist." As a novelist Trollope was indeed prolific and successful. The Barsetshire novels alone comprise fourteen volumes; the Palliser novels, sixteen; and there are at least half a dozen other novels that Trollope enthusiasts believe to be "major" works. Of the nonfiction only *An Autobiography* continues to be widely read.

The works of nonfiction prose, though, are rewarding in their own right and often reveal explicitly aspects of Trollope's character that are only suggested in the novels. The extent of his nonfiction writing is typically Trollopian when one takes into account the bulk of his personal correspondence and the writing he produced in the performance of his duties at the post office. Trollope estimates in his autobiography that he wrote in his official capacity "some thousands of reports, —many of them necessarily very long...." Of the published works, most fall into one of three categories: travel, social commentary, and biography. His more miscellaneous works, such as the collection *Writings for Saint Paul's Magazine* (1981), have a broader range of topics and include criticism of literature, art, and music. Most of his miscellaneous essays, however, are concerned with politics, a subject that is also touched on in the works on travel, social criticism, and biography.

Trollope's nonfiction is also overshadowed on occasion by interest in his active personal and professional life. Born 24 April 1815 in Keppel Street, Russell Square, London, Trollope was the fourth child of Thomas Anthony Trollope, a failed barrister who, in an attempt to salvage his fortunes, also failed at farming. His mother, Frances Milton Trollope, eventually turned to writing to put the family on a more secure footing. To escape their creditors, in April 1834 the family moved to Bruges, Belgium, where Trollope's father, sister, and brother Henry died of consumption. Back in England, at the age of nineteen Trollope obtained a clerkship at the post office. By 1864 he had risen to the second highest office, one step short of the secretaryship. In 1844 he had married Rose Heseltine, with whom he subsequently had two sons, Henry Merivale and Frederick Anthony.

In addition to writing and working at the post office Trollope maintained an active interest in politics. His one attempt at elected office–a seat in Parliament representing Beverley for which he stood in the late 1860s–was unsuccessful. His victorious opponent was unseated for buying votes, but instead of awarding the seat to Trollope, Parliament disfranchised the borough. Politics, however, remained a frequent focus of Trollope's writing, both fiction and nonfiction.

His first book-length work of nonfiction, and also his first travel book, was *The West Indies and the Spanish Main* (1859), written soon after

The Bertrams (1859) and before he began *Castle Richmond* (1860). While Trollope's own evaluation of his travelogue as "the best book that has come from my pen" is probably overstated, the book is important for two reasons. It is well written and established at an early date for both Trollope and his readers that the writer could successfully produce a work that was not set in Barsetshire. It also set Trollope's technique for all of his subsequent travel writings. He wrote as he journeyed, producing his finished copy as soon as his trip had ended. His critics, particularly in areas that thought his treatment of their homelands less than flattering, attacked him for this practice. They suggested that writing under such conditions and then eschewing revision resulted in inaccurate reporting. Trollope, however, defended his method, insisting that "it is the best way of producing to the eye of the reader, and to his ear, that which the eye of the writer has seen and his ear heard."

Trollope's second venture into nonfiction prose has drawn the most critical attention of the travel books. *North America* (1862) was written, as its author readily admitted, in an attempt to soothe some of the enmity caused by his mother's "very popular, but, as I had thought, a somewhat unjust book," *Domestic Manners of the Americans* (1832). The son's book was written during his second visit to the United States and Canada and discusses prominently the American Civil War, which was at that time taking place. This study and *South Africa* (1878) were probably the least successful of Trollope's nonfiction attempts.

The most ambitious of the travel books is *Australia and New Zealand* (1873). Trollope and his wife spent eighteen months–from May 1871 to December 1872–on the journey described in this work, a trip undertaken primarily to visit their son Frederick, who was a shepherd in Australia. The book was successful and was republished the next year as four separate and independent volumes, *New Zealand, Victoria and Tasmania, New South Wales and Queensland,* and *South Australia and Western Australia.* Perhaps the most interesting aspect of the book is Trollope's obvious and continued fascination with politics, in spite of the debacle of his standing for the seat in Beverley in 1868. Each province in Australia and New Zealand is discussed, but the focal point of each section is Trollope's analysis of the provincial politics and governmental forms.

The final two works in which Trollope deals primarily with his travels are different from the

"A Novel Trick," cartoon published in the Observer of
South African Affairs *(Port Elizabeth), 13 September
1877, criticizing Trollope for the hasty visit to South Africa
that provided material for his 1878 travel book*

earlier travelogues. *The Tireless Traveler*, not published until 1941, is a collection of twenty letters
written to the *Liverpool Mercury* in 1875 during
Trollope's circumnavigation of the world. His letters describe Italy, the Suez Canal, Ceylon, Australia, Hawaii, San Francisco, and other points
that Trollope thought his readers would find interesting. Bradford Allen Booth, who edited the letters for their 1951 publication in book form,
does not claim much more for them than an interesting supplement for biographers interested in
what Trollope was doing in 1875. The letters, however, are brief and more readable than any of his
earlier travel books, and the approach Trollope
used can be said to anticipate that of the lighthearted *How the "Mastiffs" Went to Iceland* (1878),
a book Trollope never intended for general circulation. The description of this pleasure junket
sponsored by John Burns was privately printed
under the imprint of Virtue and Company and
was intended only for the participants. This vol-

ume reveals a side of Trollope that suggests he
had achieved the serenity, security, and social acceptance that he had been unable to find as a
young man. His mild flirtations with the young ladies on the excursion and his participation in pic-
nics and even water-battles on board ship present
a stark contrast to the gruff and assertive persona he generally presented to the public.

Trollope's earliest attempt at nonfiction was
a social commentary rather than a travelogue,
but an unfavorable review of the manuscript by
Longman's reader in 1855 convinced the writer
to abandon the project and begin instead
Barchester Towers (1857), the sequel to Trollope's
1855 novel, *The Warden*. The early social commentary was finally published in 1972 as *The New Zealander*. The book's attempt to provide an "outsider's" view of England perhaps tells readers more
about how Trollope viewed himself than it tells
about England. The focus of this work on politics and bureaucratic corruption would later be
presented in a much more subtle and effective
manner in the Palliser novels.

Most of Trollope's social commentary was
written during his editorships of the *Pall Mall Gazette* (1865-1866) and *St. Paul's Magazine*
(1867-1870). His contributions to these and other
journals covered a wide range of topics, but it
was primarily the social commentaries that he
wrote for these periodicals that were later published in book form. In this category are *Hunting
Sketches* (1865), *Travelling Sketches* (1866), *Clergymen of the Church of England* (1866), and *London
Tradesmen* (1927). Trollope's social commentary
written during the 1860s is rarely harsh and is typified by the observation that English tourists
travel to see the sights, whereas other Europeans
travel to meet people. He rarely, though, attempts to draw conclusions from his observations. His contributions to the *Pall Mall Gazette*
and *St. Paul's Magazine* are important primarily because he used them as proving grounds for ideas
and topics that he later expanded into books or
used as scenes in his novels. The numerous hunting scenes in Trollope's novels, for instance, were
first tried in his essays, and the hunting ladies in
the 1865 novel *Miss Mackenzie* first appeared in
Hunting Sketches. Occasionally the process is reversed, and material from the novels reappears
in the journal pieces: the questions about hunting parsons that Trollope raises in *The Small
House at Allington* (1864) are, for example, answered in *Hunting Sketches*.

The third main category of Trollope's nonfic-

TRAVELLING SKETCHES.

BY

ANTHONY TROLLOPE.

[REPRINTED FROM THE "PALL MALL GAZETTE."]

LONDON:
CHAPMAN AND HALL, 193, PICCADILLY.
1866.

Title page for Trollope's 1866 collection of social commentaries written while he was editor of the Pall Mall Gazette *(Thomas Cooper Library, University of South Carolina)*

tion is biography: a dozen or so obituaries of contemporary writers, two biographical studies of men of his age, and two books about men from his study of the classics. The first of these works was *The Commentaries of Caesar* (1870), which he produced at the request of publisher John Blackwood, to whom he gave the copyright as a present. The book, as Trollope noted in his autobiography, was "most faintly damned by most faint praise" by the majority of reviewers and received some scathing criticism because of its unscholarly approach. Dean Merivale, an old friend to whom Trollope sent a copy, thanked the author for his "comic Caesar," a reply that devastated Trollope. Nevertheless, the novelist concluded in his autobiography that "it is a good book" and noted that the light tone was typical of Blackwood's series, Ancient Classics for English Readers, for which it was commissioned.

What classicists objected to was Trollope's metaphorical style, a style that readers of his novels held in high regard. A single example illustrates Trollope's approach. Speaking of Caesar's early military campaigns, he writes, "The experience, however, which we have of great and encroaching empires tells us how probable it is that the protection of that which the strong already holds should lead to the grasping of more, till at last all has been grasped. It is thus that our own empire in India has grown. It was thus that the Spanish empire grew in America. It is thus that the empire of the United States is now growing. It was thus that Prussia, driven, as we all remember, by the necessity of self-preservation, took Nassau the other day, and Hanover and Holstein and Hesse. It was thus that the wolf claimed all the river, not being able to endure the encroaching lamb. The humane reader of history execrates, as he reads, the cruel, all-absorbing, ravenous wolf. But the philosophical reader perceives that in this way, and in no other, is civilization carried into distant lands. The wolf, though he be a ravenous wolf, brings with him energy and knowledge." Trollope carries the wolf/lamb metaphor throughout his presentation of Caesar. The book, in line with Blackwood's series, was obviously intended for a popular audience.

Two other political figures that received Trollope's attention were Cicero and Lord Palmerston. In *The Life of Cicero* (1880) Trollope presents the man he probably admired most among all classic writers. He attempts to justify the life of a man he felt had been misjudged by historians and insists that such writers as James Anthony Froude, who attacked Cicero as cowardly and unpatriotic, were missing the essential selflessness with which Cicero served Rome. Because Trollope himself often felt misunderstood and undervalued, particularly early in life, he no doubt sees much in Cicero with which he can identify. In fact, he tends to portray Cicero in terms of an Englishman's life: "What a man he would have been for London life! How he would have enjoyed his club. . . ."

Two years after publication of *The Life of Cicero*, Trollope finished *Lord Palmerston* (1882), one of his last writings before his fatal stroke. In this book Trollope examines an English politician who he believed was also misunderstood. The writer's desire is to chronicle the politician's commitment to "Catholic emancipation and the maintenance of English influence at home and abroad, and, above all things, the suppression of the

My Education. 1815 to 1834.

Chap I.

In writing these pages, which for the want of a better name I shall be fain to call the autobiography of so insignificant a person as myself, it will not be so much my intention to speak of the little details of my private life, as of what I, and perhaps others round me, have done in literature; of my failures and successes such as they have been, and their causes, and of the opening which a literary career offers to men & women for the earning of their bread. And yet the garrulity of old age, and the aptitude of a man's mind to recur to the passages of his own life, will I know tempt me to say something of myself; — nor without doing so should I know how to throw my matter into any recognised and intelligible form. That I, or any man, should tell everything of himself, I hold to be impossible. Who could endure to own the doing of a mean thing? Who is there that has done none? But this I protest; — that nothing that I say shall be untrue. I will set down naught in malice; nor will I give to myself, or others, honour which I do not believe to have been fairly won.

My boyhood was I think as unhappy as that of a young gentleman could well be, my misfortune arising from a mixture of poverty and gentle standing on the part of my father, and from an utter want on my own part of that juvenile manhood which enables some boys to hold up their heads even among the distresses which such a position is sure to produce.

I was born in 1815, in Keppel Street Russell Square, and while a baby was carried down to Harrow where

Page from the manuscript for Trollope's An Autobiography, *completed in 1876 but not published until 1883, the year after Trollope's death (British Library)*

slave trade." This study is the least fluent of his biographical excursions.

Trollope's only full-length biography of a literary figure was *Thackeray* (1879), in which he examines the author he thought to be the outstanding literary figure of the age. The book, an outgrowth of an obituary Trollope had written for the *Cornhill Magazine*, chronicles the career of "the man whom I regard as one of the most softhearted of human beings, sweet as Charity itself, who went about the world dropping pearls, doing good, and never willfully inflicting a wound." This biography, part of the English Men of Letters series, was successful among readers and reviewers and has been republished several times. It is an unabashed tribute to a writer Trollope sincerely admired.

Of other works of nonfiction by Trollope, the best known is *An Autobiography* (1883), one of six posthumous nonfiction works. The autobiography appalled one generation and appealed to the next for precisely the same reason. The novelist's open, honest explanation of writing as a practical occupation annoyed pretentious writers at the turn of the century. But Trollope's openness has resurrected his reputation to a level he, no doubt, would find surprising. Opinions about a writer's achievement often vary greatly as literary expectations change, but seldom has a single work created such divergent and strongly felt opinions in successive generations of readers and critics as *An Autobiography*.

Two critics who have been instrumental in restoring Trollope's reputation are Michael Sadleir, in *Trollope: A Commentary* (1927), and Bradford Allen Booth, in *Anthony Trollope: Aspects of His Life and Art* (1958), both of whom defended Trollope's view of the writer's profession expressed in *An Autobiography*.

Trollope's occasional nonfiction contributions to various journals would not secure his reputation by themselves. His more substantial works, such as the travelogues and *An Autobiography*, as well as his biographies of Cicero and Thackeray, are the primary examples of his nonfiction prose. Nevertheless, these articles and reviews remain of interest, and new collections continue to appear. *Miscellaneous Essays and Reviews* and *Writings for Saint Paul's Magazine*, two volumes published by Arno Press in 1981, suggest that there is always room on the shelves for more volumes by Anthony Trollope.

Letters:

Letters of Anthony Trollope, edited by Bradford Allen Booth (London: Oxford University Press, 1951);

The Letters of Anthony Trollope, edited by N. John Hall, 2 volumes (Stanford: Stanford University Press, 1983).

Bibliographies:

Mary Leslie Irwin, *Anthony Trollope: A Bibliography* (London: Pitman, 1926);

Michael Sadleir, *Trollope: A Bibliography* (London: Constable, 1928).

Biographies:

T. H. S. Escott, *Anthony Trollope: His Work, Associations, and Literary Originals* (London: Chapman & Hall, 1913);

Michael Sadleir, *Trollope: A Commentary* (London: Constable, 1927);

Lucy Poate Stebbins and Richard Poate Stebbins, *The Trollopes: The Chronicle of a Writing Family* (London: Secker & Warburg, 1947);

James Pope Hennessy, *Anthony Trollope* (Boston: Little, Brown, 1971);

C. P. Snow, *Trollope: His Life and Art* (London: Macmillan, 1975).

References:

Bradford Allen Booth, *Anthony Trollope: Aspects of His Life and Art* (Bloomington: Indiana University Press, 1958);

Booth, "Trollope and the 'Pall Mall,'" *Nineteenth Century Fiction*, 4 (June 1949): 51-69; 4 (September 1949): 137-158;

N. John Hall, ed., *The Trollope Critics* (London: Macmillan, 1981);

John Halperin, *Trollope Centenary Essays* (New York: St. Martin's, 1982);

Donald Smalley, ed., *Trollope: The Critical Heritage* (London: Routledge & Kegan Paul/New York: Barnes & Noble, 1969);

Robert H. Super, *Trollope in the Post Office* (Ann Arbor: University of Michigan Press, 1981).

Papers:

There are collections of Trollope's papers at the Bodleian Library, Oxford, and at the Beinecke Rare Book and Manuscript Library, Yale University.

Edward Burnett Tylor

(2 October 1832-2 January 1917)

Patrick Brantlinger
Indiana University

BOOKS: *Anahuac: or, Mexico and the Mexicans. Ancient and Modern* (London: Longman, Green, Longman & Roberts, 1861);

Researches into the Early History of Mankind and the Development of Civilization (London: Murray, 1865; revised, London: Murray, 1878; Boston: Estes & Lauriat, 1878);

Primitive Culture: Researches into the Development of Mythology, Philosophy, Religion, Art, and Custom, 2 volumes (London: Murray, 1871; Boston: Estes & Lauriat, 1874);

Anthropology: An Introduction to the Study of Man and Civilization (London: Macmillan, 1881; New York: Appleton, 1881).

PERIODICAL PUBLICATIONS: "The Religion of Savages," *Fortnightly Review*, 6 (15 August 1866): 71-86;

"Remarks on Language and Mythology as Departments of Biological Science," *Report of the British Association for the Advancement of Science* (1868): 120-121;

"Mr. Spencer's 'Principles of Sociology,'" *Mind*, 2 (April 1877): 141-156;

"On the Game of Patolli in Ancient Mexico and Its Probably Asiatic Origin," *Journal of the Royal Anthropological Institute of Great Britain and Ireland*, 8 (November 1878): 116-131;

"How the Problems of American Anthropology Present Themselves to an English Mind," *Transactions of the Anthropological Society of Washington*, 3 (1885): 81-95;

"On a Method of Investigating the Development of Institutions: Applied to Laws of Marriage and Descent," *Journal of the Royal Anthropological Institute of Great Britain and Ireland*, 18 (February 1889): 245-272;

"Stone Age Basis for Oriental Study," *Smithsonian Institution Annual Report* (1893): 701-708.

E. B. Tylor (photograph by Maull and Fox)

The writings of Edward Burnett Tylor, "founder of modern anthropology," are classics of Victorian social science and of "the warfare between science and religion." Even though much of its evolutionary framework was discarded by later anthropologists, Tylor's greatest work, *Primitive Culture* (1871), established many of the themes of the modern "human sciences," including folklore and comparative religion as well as anthropology, and influenced the work of Andrew Lang, James Frazer, and Franz Boas, among others.

The son of Harriet Skipper Tylor and Joseph Tylor, a prosperous Quaker industrialist who owned a brass foundry in London, Tylor was educated at Grove House, a private school run by the Society of Friends. Because of his family's Nonconformism, he was unable to attend Oxford or Cambridge, though years later he became the first professor of anthropology at Oxford. At sixteen he went to work in his father's business, but six years later he was diagnosed as consumptive and advised to travel. Tylor sailed to North America in 1855, spending a year in the southern United States and then visiting Cuba. Aboard an omnibus in Havana, he met another English traveler who used the familiar Quaker *thou;* thus began his friendship with Henry Christy, banker and amateur ethnologist, who invited Tylor to accompany him on a four-month tour of Mexico. Christy's ethnological interests and Tylor's own observations of Mexican life and customs sowed the seeds of Tylor's interest in anthropology and the "early history of mankind." In 1858 Tylor married; he and his wife, the former Anna Fox, produced no children. By 1862 Tylor had joined the Ethnological Society of London; more important, by the same date he had read Darwin's *On the Origin of Species* (1859). Until Christy's death in 1865, Tylor continued to help with the older man's ethnological researches, including work with the French archaeologist Edouard Lartet, excavator of Stone Age sites in the Dordogne Valley.

Tylor's first book, *Anahuac: or, Mexico and the Mexicans, Ancient and Modern* (1861), hovers between colorful travelogue and amateur anthropological study. Tylor's habits of careful observation and sympathetic response to strange mores are intermingled with an ethnocentricism which he was soon partially to shed. He sees the impoverished Indian communities of Mexico as steeped in savage superstitions, or, what is little better, in Roman Catholic mystification. The conclusion of *Anahuac* forecasts a future takeover of Mexico by the United States, which, Tylor implies, would bring Mexico into the orbit of progressive civilization. Interesting chiefly because of its relation to Tylor's later work, *Anahuac* deserves a distinct although minor place in the history of Victorian travel narratives.

Tylor's scientific bent shows up more clearly in his second book, *Researches into the Early History of Mankind and the Development of Civilization* (1865). Here several lines of scientific thought converge. By 1865 there was already a rich literature of archaeology, presenting increasingly complex versions of "prehistory" and early civilization. In an 1864 paper, fourteen years before the discovery of the cave paintings at Altamira in Spain, Lartet and Christy showed that peoples of the Old Stone Age had produced artworks of considerable skill. Tylor's second book appeared in the

Tylor's wife, Anna Fox Tylor

same year as John Lubbock's *Prehistoric Times,* in which Lubbock coined the terms *palaeolithic* and *neolithic.* The work of the archaeologists was buttressed by that of the geologists; Charles Lyell's three-volume *Principles of Geology,* which presented perhaps the most influential challenge to the biblical story of creation prior to Darwin's *On the Origin of Species,* appeared from 1830 to 1833 and went through many editions. Darwin's theory of biological evolution was preceded by much theorizing about the origin of races, species, life, and the cosmos which challenged religious orthodoxy. Historical criticism of the Bible–the so-called Higher Criticism–also provided new, rigorous ideas about religion and ancient history that could not be squared with orthodoxy. Given his liberal Quaker heritage, Tylor was more than tolerant of scientific rationalism; he was well-prepared to accept and defend the best of the new scientific theories about biological and social genesis.

Researches into the Early History of Mankind and the Development of Civilization begins with a question fundamental to all historical research:

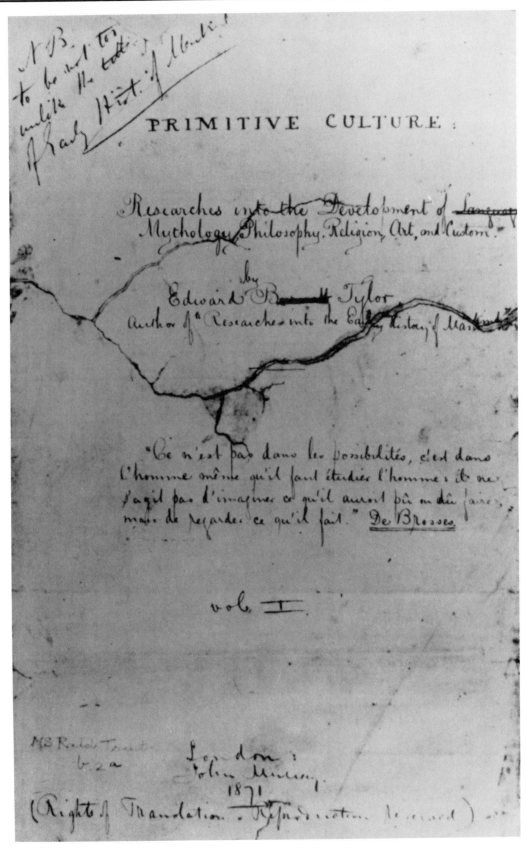

Title page from a late manuscript for Tylor's most important work (Bodleian Library, Oxford, MS. Rad. Trust b. 2a.)

"When similar arts, customs, beliefs, or legends are found in several distant regions, among peoples not known to be of the same stock, how is this similarity to be accounted for?" One possible explanation is independent invention; the other is cultural diffusion. Though both can be found at work in history, both also, in different ways, argue strongly for a universal pattern of human development. What Tylor found most striking in the ethnological record was the sameness of human response to similar conditions around the world. Basic tools such as the fire drill, the potter's wheel, and the bow and arrow occur everywhere at roughly equivalent stages of social development. So do less-material phenomena such as mythologies, kinship patterns, and marriage customs. In contrast to a number of earlier theorists, who postulated separate creations for the separate races (polygenism), Tylor presents a forceful case for the unity of human nature. The "uniform development of the lower civilization is," he declares, "a matter of great interest" for understanding later history.

Tylor's most important work, *Primitive Culture* (1871), argues even more forcefully for the unity of mankind. Although a cultural evolutionist who distinguishes "lower" from "higher" levels of social development, Tylor dismisses the racism endemic in Victorian social theory: "it appears both possible and desirable to eliminate considerations of hereditary varieties . . . and to treat mankind as homogeneous in nature, though placed in different grades of civilization." Variations of history and geography are of little more significance than those of race. "The ancient Swiss lake-dweller may be set beside the medieval Aztec, and the Ojibwa of North America beside the Zulu of South Africa. As Dr. Johnson contemptuously said when he had read about Patagonians and South Sea Islanders in Hawkesworth's Voyages 'one set of savages is like another.'" But it isn't just that groups of savages resemble one another; civilized peoples also resemble savages, as "higher" stages of culture continue to reflect "lower" ones. "When it comes to comparing barbarous hordes with civilized nations, the consideration thrusts itself upon our minds, how far item after item of the life of the lower races passes into analogous proceedings of the higher, in forms not too far changed . . . and sometimes hardly changed at all." Connecting modern "savage" societies with "civilized" ones by evolution, moreover, involves analogizing between modern "savages" and the "hypothetical primitive condi-

tion" of mankind. Past and present, primeval and modern, far and near, the alien and the familiar Tylor shows to be united by the bond of a common human nature.

Four years after Matthew Arnold's *Culture and Anarchy*, Tylor presented a nearly antithetical definition of culture that, with variations, has served anthropologists ever since. In the first paragraph of *Primitive Culture*, Tylor writes: "Culture or Civilization, taken in its wide ethnographic sense, is that complex whole which includes knowledge, belief, art, morals, law, custom, and any other capabilities acquired by man as a member of society." Culture for Tylor is inclusive and universal rather than exclusive and elitist, as it is for Arnold. It is the commonest stuff of everyday life in every society, including the most primitive, rather than the highest or best accessible only to an educated minority. As a cultural evolutionist, Tylor distinguishes three basic "grades" of social evolution: "savagery," characterized by hunting and gathering; "barbarism," characterized by nomadic herding and rudimentary agriculture; and "civilization," characterized by writing and city-building. These grades Tylor sometimes evaluates in moralistic lower-to-higher terms ("savages," for instance, are like "children" whose "moral standards are real enough, but . . . far looser and weaker than ours"). But from such judgments Tylor frequently passes to another, almost satiric perspective, according to which the survivals of savage traits in the midst of civilization–belief in ghosts, for example–suggest how childish modern peoples can be. A satiric note, too, is struck by the discovery of savages within civilization: "in our great cities, the so-called 'dangerous classes' are sunk in hideous misery and depravity. If we have to strike a balance between the Papuans of New Caledonia and the communities of European beggars and thieves, we may sadly acknowledge that we have in our midst something worse than savagery."

As a scientific rationalist influenced by Utilitarianism, in *Primitive Culture* Tylor expresses the belief that the course of social evolution has been mainly progressive. At the same time, like George Eliot, he has an acute awareness of the great complexity of social change, which is rarely straightforward. Published in the same year as the first parts of Eliot's *Middlemarch*, *Primitive Culture* is also characterized by complex organicist metaphors suggesting the "slow growth" and "decay" of social "flora and fauna." Tools, myths, and customs are the "species" whose "evolution" the ethnologist seeks to trace. Though progress or "growth" is the general direction of history, "civilization is a plant much oftener propagated than developed." Regression or "decay" is always possible, and in the transition from "savagery" to "civilization," the virtues of simplicity, independence, and closeness to nature may be lost.

Much of *Primitive Culture* is an examination not of savage or barbarian societies but of the survivals from earlier stages in the midst of later ones. Along with his "comparative method," Tylor's "doctrine of survivals" is one of his key contributions to anthropology. Survivals are "fragments of a dead lower culture embedded in a living higher one." Superstitions of all sorts are obvious examples, fragments from older religious doctrines which have otherwise died out. Survivals are cultural fossils which allow the ethnologist to analyze the various strata or stages of social change, even in the absence of written evidence. They are therefore of great theoretical and methodological value to the project of an evolutionary anthropology.

Because of its emphasis on mythic survivals or superstitions, *Primitive Culture* is in large part a study of the evolution and decay of religion. Tylor's patient accumulation of examples, similar to Darwin's amassing of facts, ultimately implies that religion itself is a survival or anachronism. "Animism is . . . the groundwork of the Philosophy of Religion, from that of savages up to that of civilized men." Of course the mere suggestion that religion evolves is subversive to orthodoxy, as the members of the Tractarian, or Oxford, Movement realized. Like the French positivist Auguste Comte, Tylor thinks of human reason as struggling out of the morass of primitive superstitions that he documents, through a stage of higher religious development marked especially by Christianity, toward scientific rationality. "Physics, Chemistry, Biology, have seized whole provinces of the ancient Animism" or religion, and Tylor sees this as progress. Anthropology for Tylor is a "reformer's science" aiming at the completion of the religious reformation begun in the sixteenth century. With "modern science and modern criticism as new factors in theological opinion," Tylor writes, he and many others "are eagerly pressing toward a new reformation," an idea which T. H. Huxley also expressed. In some lines that Tylor contributed to Andrew Lang's "Double Ballade of a Primitive Man," Tylor writes: "First epoch, the human began,/ Theologians all to expose,–/'Tis the *mission of*

primitive man." *Primitive Culture* is thus not only a pioneering anthropological classic but also an important contribution to the "warfare between science and religion" which characterizes Victorian intellectual history.

According to Leslie White, in the foreword to the abridged edition of 1960, Tylor's 1881 volume, *Anthropology: An Introduction to the Study of Man and Civilization*, "is still one of the best general introductions to the subject in the English language." Despite Tylor's stress on evolution, which modern anthropologists have largely discarded, his basic categories and lucid style make for an effective guide to the science which he did so much to establish. Among Tylor's numerous periodical essays, one which anthropologists refer to as seminal is "On a Method of Investigating the Development of Institutions," which shows how statistics can be applied to "laws of marriage and descent."

Much of Tylor's later career was devoted to teaching, organizing, consolidating anthropology as a field of scientific investigation. A measure of his unwritten contributions to the intellectual life of Victorian England can be gained by an enumeration of the posts he held and the honors he received. Tylor helped create an anthropology division in the British Association and was chosen its first president in 1884. At Oxford Tylor was appointed curator of the University Museum (1883), reader in anthropology (1884), and finally the first professor of anthropology (1896). He served as president of the Anthropological Society (starting in 1891), was selected honorary fellow of Balliol College (1903), and was knighted (1912). Although anthropology was the creation of many nineteenth-century investigators, there is good reason for calling it "Mr. Tylor's science." *The Golden Bough* by Tylor's disciple, Sir James Frazer, had a powerful influence on modern literature, but Tylor's *Primitive Culture* was more important in shaping the general contours of modern social and cultural theory.

Letters:

Letters from Edward B. Tylor and Alfred Russel Wallace to Edward Westermarck, edited by K. Rob V. Wikman (Turku, Finland: Åbo Akademi, 1940).

Bibliography:

Barbara W. Freire-Marreco, "A Bibliography of Edward Burnett Tylor from 1861 to 1907," in *Anthropological Essays Presented to Edward Burnett Tylor in Honour of His 75th Birthday,* edited by W. H. R. Rivers, R. R. Marett, and Northcote W. Thomas (Oxford: Clarendon Press, 1907), pp. 375-409.

References:

John W. Burrow, *Evolution and Society: A Study in Victorian Social Theory* (Cambridge: Cambridge University Press, 1966);

Margaret T. Hodgen, *The Doctrine of Survivals: A Chapter in the History of Scientific Method in the Study of Man* (London: Allenson, 1936);

Abram Kardiner and Edward Preble, *They Studied Man* (New York: Mentor, 1963);

Andrew Lang, "Edward Burnett Tylor," in *Anthropological Essays Presented to Edward Burnett Tylor in Honour of His 75th Birthday*, edited by W. H. R. Rivers, R. R. Marett, and Northcote W. Thomas (Oxford: Clarendon Press, 1907), pp. 1-15;

Joan Leopold, *Culture in Comparative and Evolutionary Perspective: E. B. Tylor and the Making of 'Primitive Culture'* (Berlin: Reimer, 1980);

Robert R. Marett, *Tylor* (London: Chapman & Hall, 1936; New York: Wiley, 1936);

T. K. Penniman, *A Hundred Years of Anthropology* (London: Duckworth, 1965);

George W. Stocking, *Race, Culture, and Evolution: Essays in the History of Anthropology* (New York: Free Press, 1968).

Oscar Wilde

Donald Lawler
East Carolina University

See also the Wilde entries in *DLB 10, Modern British Dramatists, 1900-1945, DLB 19, British Poets, 1880-1914,* and *DLB 34, British Novelists, 1890-1929: Traditionalists.*

BIRTH: Dublin, 16 October 1854, to Dr. William Robert Wills Wilde and Jane Francesca Elgee Wilde.

EDUCATION: Trinity College, Dublin, 1871-1874; B.A., Magdalen College, Oxford University, 1878.

MARRIAGE: 29 May 1884 to Constance Lloyd; children: Cyril, Vyvyan.

DEATH: Paris, 30 November 1900.

BOOKS: *Newdigate Prize Poem: Ravenna, Recited in the Theatre, Oxford 26 June 1878* (Oxford: Shrimpton, 1878);

Vera; or, The Nihilists: A Drama (London: Privately printed, 1880);

Poems (London: Bogue, 1881; Boston: Roberts Brothers, 1881);

The Duchess of Padua: A Tragedy of the XVI Century, Written in Paris in the XIX Century (New York: Privately printed, 1883);

The Happy Prince and Other Tales (London: Nutt, 1888; Boston: Roberts, 1888);

The Picture of Dorian Gray (London, New York & Melbourne: Ward, Lock, 1891);

Intentions (London: Osgood, McIlvaine, 1891; New York: Dodd, Mead, 1891);

Lord Arthur Savile's Crime & Other Stories (London: Osgood, McIlvaine, 1891; New York: Dodd, Mead, 1891);

A House of Pomegranates (London: Osgood, McIlvaine, 1891; New York: Dodd, Mead, 1892);

Salomé: Drame en un acte (Paris: Librairie de l'Art Indépendent/London: Mathews & Lane, Bodley Head, 1893); republished as *Salome: A Tragedy in One Act*, translated into English by Alfred Douglas (London: Mathews & Lane/Boston: Copeland & Day, 1894);

Lady Windermere's Fan: A Play about a Good Woman (London: Mathews & Lane, Bodley Head, 1893);

The Sphinx (London: Mathews & Lane, Bodley Head/Boston: Copeland & Day, 1894);

A Woman of No Importance (London: Lane, Bodley Head, 1894);

The Soul of Man [first published in the *Fortnightly Review* as "The Soul of Man Under Socialism"] (London: Privately printed, 1895); re-

published as *The Soul of Man Under Socialism*
(London: Arthur L. Humphreys, 1912);
The Ballad of Reading Gaol, as C.3.3. (London:
Smithers, 1898);
*The Importance of Being Earnest: A Trivial Comedy
for Serious People* (London: Smithers, 1899);
An Ideal Husband (London: Smithers, 1899);
The Portrait of Mr. W.H. (Portland, Maine:
Mosher, 1901); edited by Vyvyan Holland
(London: Methuen, 1958);
De Profundis (London: Methuen, 1905; New York
& London: Putnam's, 1905);
Impressions of America, edited by Stuart Mason (Sun-
derland, U.K.: Keystone Press, 1906);
The Suppressed Portion of "De Profundis" (New
York: Reynolds, 1913);
To M. B. J., edited by "Stuart Mason" (C. S.
Millard) (London: Privately printed, 1920);

For Love of the King: A Burmese Masque (London:
Methuen, 1923);
Essays of Oscar Wilde, edited by Hesketh Pearson
(London: Methuen, 1950);
Literary Criticism of Oscar Wilde, edited by Stanley
Weintraub (Lincoln: University of Nebraska
Press, 1968);
The Artist as Critic: Critical Writings of Oscar Wilde,
edited by Richard Ellmann (New York: Ran-
dom House, 1969).

Collections: *First Collected Edition of the Works of
Oscar Wilde*, edited by Robert Ross (volumes
1-11, 13-14, London: Methuen, 1908; Boston: Luce, 1910; volume 12, Paris: Carrington, 1908);
Second Collected Edition of the Works of Oscar Wilde,
edited by Ross (volumes 1-12, London: Methuen, 1909; volume 13, Paris: Carrington,
1910; volume 14, London: Lane, 1912);
Complete Works of Oscar Wilde, edited by Vyvyan
Holland (London: Collins, 1948).

PLAY PRODUCTIONS: *Vera; or, The Nihilists*,
New York, Union Square Theatre, 20 Au-
gust 1883;
Guido Ferranti: A Tragedy of the XVI Century, New
York, Broadway Theatre, 26 January 1891;
Lady Windermere's Fan, London, St. James's The-
atre, 20 February 1892;
A Woman of No Importance, London, Haymarket
Theatre, 19 April 1893;
An Ideal Husband, London, Haymarket Theatre, 3
January 1895;
The Importance of Being Earnest, London, St.
James's Theatre, 14 February 1895;
Salomé, Paris, Théâtre de l'Oeuvre, 11 February
1896; London, New Stage Club at Bijou, 10
May 1905;
A Florentine Tragedy, by Wilde with opening
scene by T. Sturge Moore, London, King's
Hall, 10 June 1906.

Oscar Wilde as man and artist is a study of ex-
tremes and contradictions. He approached life em-
pirically, as Walter Pater had taught him at Oxford, but the pupil determined to pursue sensation beyond art into life. Wilde insisted that the
two greatest arts were life and literature. His success in each is measured by the depth of his failures. He dominated his age by personality, yet following his release from prison, he went into exile
and assumed a new name. He who had sought
fame and success spent his last years as a dilettante of anonymity. Wilde was a man who knew

himself too well to believe in anything for very long; consequently, he believed in everything and died a convert to Roman Catholicism, concluding perhaps the longest deferred conversion since Augustine. In contrast to Augustine, however, the church congratulated itself very little over the declaration of Wilde. If we are to find Mr. Oscar Wilde, therefore, we should look for him not in a consistently maintained position but rather in phase along the trajectory between the modifying illusions of certainty and uncertainty, objective and subjective. He studied dandyism at Oxford during the interlude between Darwin and Freud, but Wilde began to see the poses of Victorianism as weak reflections of the life of art. And so he followed the logic of decadence to its self-destructive conclusion. In this as in many other things, Wilde was prematurely modern.

Born on 16 October 1854 in Dublin to a mother and father of distinguished accomplishments, Oscar Wilde was the second of three children. His older brother, William, preceded him in school and grew up to become a journalist. He died a year before Oscar. The third child, a younger sister, died in childhood. Wilde honored her memory with the poem "Requiescat," uncharacteristically objectivist, distinguished by unfeigned sentiment and admired by Yeats, who reprinted it in *A Book of Irish Verse* (1895). The character of his parents seems to have determined to an unusual degree the life and career of their genius son. Wilde at least thought so, and the question of influence, especially that of inherited characteristics and motives of behavior, became an important theme in his major prose and dramatic works, as it was, indeed, in the lives of his parents.

Sir William Wilde was a famous eye and ear surgeon, author of the standard text *Aural Surgery*, and for a time Surgeon Oculist in Ordinary to the Queen. His second-born was named after King Oscar of Sweden, one of his most famous patients. Sir William produced an exhaustive study of the 1851 Irish medical census, for which he was later knighted, and was author of more than twenty books on archaeology, natural history, ethnology, and Irish folklore. He was also a notorious womanizer, who left a trail of illegitimate offspring along the byways of his travels and excursions. His appetites eventually led to a scandalous libel trial brought by William Wilde against Miss Mary Josephine Travers, a quondam patient who alleged publicly that she had been violated by the doctor with the assistance of chloroform. William Wilde was forced to sue for libel, just as his son

later did against Queensberry with similar results. The senior Wilde lost the suit, and even though the jury's award to Miss Travers was one farthing, William Wilde had become déclassé in the Dublin social register. Oscar's mother tolerated her husband's indiscretions with a bohemian forbearance. She was in her own right a personage of note: Jane Francesca Elgee, known by her pen name, Speranza, was a poet, essayist, folklorist, advocate of women's rights, and revolutionary patriot. In 1848 her call for young men to take arms for liberty published in the *Nation* had the good fortune to be noticed by British authorities who banned the weekly and put its editor on trial for sedition. Jane Elgee became a national heroine. She married three years later and devoted herself thereafter to her children, to her salon, which became known throughout Europe, and to her folklore research and writing. It is ironic that following the death of William Wilde in 1876, Speranza was forced to apply for a pension from the crown, which she received after a suitable amount of crow had been ingested. Thereafter, she moved her salon to London, where it flourished in threadbare grandeur until her death in 1896.

Oscar Wilde, who spent much of his adult life practicing what he preached against in art, believed in the destiny implied in his own heritage. He felt himself intended from an early age to achieve greatness as a man of letters, but he was also determined to become celebrated or, if need be, notorious. Perhaps this ambition was a form of natural emulation, but it may have been also competitive. Like Wilde himself, his readers should find it difficult to ignore repeated patterns of behavior extending through two generations of Wildes. To a psychologically minded generation, these patterns look less like predestination and more like the foundations of psychic disorder. Wilde himself had no trouble accepting the evolutionary implications of inherited characteristics or theories of avatars, but he preferred the effect produced by the rather gothic mixture of the new and the old explanations–the difference, perhaps, between the artist and the scientist.

Wilde's schooling is worth more attention than that of most other writers of equal stature because of Wilde's notorious susceptibility to the influence of both ideas and personalities. Of his years, 1864-1871, at Portora Royal School, Enniskillen, Ulster, almost nothing is known, except that he won an entrance scholarship to Trinity College, Dublin, and seems to have enjoyed fishing, tennis, golf, and other outdoor pursuits rather in the line of conventional boyhood interests. While at Trinity, Wilde distinguished himself by winning prizes for classical scholarship, including the Berkeley Gold Medal for Greek and a foundation scholarship. His mentor at Trinity was Rev. John P. Mahaffy, professor of ancient history. It was Mahaffy who seems to have introduced Wilde to the worship of Greek culture, a passion he was to retain his entire life. Wilde spent part of the summer before entering Magdalen College, Oxford, on a classical scholarship, editing Mahaffy's *Social Life in Greece from Homer to Menander* (1874). Twenty years later as a reviewer, he was to comment rather unfavorably on two of his former mentor's later works. Following the trials that ruined Wilde in the 1890s, Mahaffy retaliated by declaring that Wilde was the greatest failure of his tutorship.

Wilde's years at Oxford were decisive in shaping his mind and establishing the direction of his future development. At Oxford, Wilde was influenced by the example as well as the thought of Matthew Arnold, to whom he later sent a volume of his own poems, and by the drama of John Henry Newman's conversion to Catholicism and his expression of both personality and belief. Wilde's own desire for conversion to Rome was thwarted by his father, a prohibition blamed by Wilde very late in life as denying him means of resisting the temptations of his nature.

The two schooling figures that were to exercise the most profound and lasting influence over Wilde were John Ruskin and Walter Pater, both of whom taught Wilde. Ruskin reinforced Wilde's passion for art and combined it with a Carlylian moral commitment to social justice. Although it is a far cry from Ruskin's *"Unto this Last"* (1862), and *The Storm-Cloud of the Nineteenth Century* (1884), Wilde's *The Soul of Man Under Socialism* (1895) is his final homage to Ruskin. If Ruskin inspired Wilde's early career at Oxford, it was Pater who produced the most profound and lasting effect, appealing to and defining Wilde's sense of modernism. Pater's contribution to Wilde's development as an artist cannot be restricted to a single work. It expresses itself rather obviously in Wilde's lectures on art given in America and England and more subtly in the prose poems, in some of the tales, and the essays of *Intentions* (1891).

During his Oxford career, the pattern of Wilde's future life began to take form. He continued to travel in the summer, going with Mahaffy both to Italy in 1875 and to Greece and Rome in 1877. Although he was or pretended to be a dilatory student, he won firsts in Mods in 1876 and Greats in 1878, the year he also won the Newdigate prize for *Ravenna*, a poem remembered solely for that fact. Meanwhile, Wilde gave up golf and hunting for dandyism and began to establish a reputation among undergraduates and dons as an aesthete. He graduated triumphantly in November 1878. It is little wonder then that he dreamed of an academic career, but his application for a full fellowship was denied and his essay "The Rise of Historical Criticism" failed to win the Chancellor's English Essay Prize at Oxford during the next term.

The essay is worth brief notice here for several reasons. Although it is an academic essay, steeped in the still operative influences of Ruskin and Pater and in Wilde's own interest in Greek literature and ideas, it forecasts the course of Wilde's development as the eventual critical successor to Arnold, from his early apprentice work as a disciple of Ruskin and Pater through his stormy friendship with James Abbott McNeill Whistler to eventual mastery in the later essays of *Intentions*, *The Portrait of Mr. W.H.*, *The Soul of Man Under Socialism*, and *De Profundis*. The essay identifies the Greek spirit with modernism, especially in the disposition of modern scientific and critical thinking. This rationalism, with its emphasis on iconoclasm and revolt against authority, is one defining motive of Wilde's later critical manner. A key feature of Wilde's argument in "The Rise of Historical Criticism" is the rejection of the supernatural and mystical as out of place in historical criticism and, by implication, for the modern historical spirit. Curiously, this incongruity became the very reason why the irrational, the supernatural, and the mystical are enshrined in much of Wilde's own prose fiction. The reader also finds an early record of Wilde's rejection of "the inculcation of moral lessons as an aim to be consciously pursued" in favor of the true motive of both art and history which is the creation of beauty.

The modern reader should not look for the distinctively witty, paradoxical style found in the later prose and in the social dramas. The one such example in the essay is closer, perhaps, to undergraduate wisecrackery (albeit of a superlative order) when Wilde writes in part three of "Teiresias, who may be termed the Max Müller of the Theban cycle." Wilde never mentioned Müller, one of his Oxford tutors, without ridicule, describing Müller's controversial theory concerning the origins of myth in erroneous etymology as "an epidemic among adjectives." Nevertheless, this early essay demonstrates that in the prose, the rational mode of Wilde's mind and personality is ascendant. The switching point, however, then and in the later work, is always art, in which the demonic was ever for Wilde the source of the inspiration, if not of the shaping power of art, which came from the artist's instinct for beauty and his skill in its execution.

In "The Rise of Historical Criticism," when it came to methodology, Pater's influence was strongest, a distinction he was soon to share with Whistler whenever Wilde was operating in his critical mode. When it came to ethical and social ideals, however, it was Ruskin who was the schooling eminence, especially in the stress Wilde occasionally gave economic and social forces in evolution. Observed strictly from the viewpoint of influence, it would seem that *The Portrait of Mr. W.H.* and *Intentions* belong to Pater, while *The Soul of Man Under Socialism* and *De Profundis* go to Ruskin. The truth is, however, that such a reductionism misses the very qualities in these works that make them Wilde's rather than simply extensions of Pater and Ruskin modulated to another key.

With the failure of Wilde's academic essay to win the chancellor's prize and the subsequent collapse of his scholarly pretensions, a sequence in which one cannot help suspecting a linkage, Wilde set about making of himself a public literary figure. During the following decade, Wilde progressed through a series of poses from poet to prophet in which he sought and found public recognition, if little approval. The motivation for this behavior was both complex and curious. We may suppose an established baseline appetite for public spectacle in his parental ancestry and his own conscious awareness of past lives acting through present forms, an idea he could have picked up from either parent and one that was reinforced by Pater. This idea appears so often in the prose, both fiction and nonfiction, as to amount to almost a signature. Although Wilde frequently ridiculed public approval of poetasters and bad art, he sought and luxuriated in public approval of his own work. Perhaps disappointment of early success was implicated in the increasingly dyspeptic view Wilde took of popular journalism as his career matured, or perhaps it was Wilde's own experience as reviewer and reviewee during the latter 1880s. In any case, while there were

times that he despaired of popular success, he always accepted it as his due when it came, despairing the more loudly when it was withheld. Yet together with this rather garden-variety authorial vanity, Wilde was incubating a philosophy of dandyism, inspired by Benjamin Disraeli and Whistler and encouraged by his French counterparts. Eccentricity in dress and manner complemented a campaign to storm the English-speaking literary world.

Wilde was everywhere to be seen in the late 1870s and early to mid 1880s. His poetry appeared regularly, even in *Punch*, which used it and the public Wilde as laughingstocks. The aesthetic attitudes, worship of intensity in both art and life, the artificial posturing of the poet on the town were burlesqued in the popular press. Wilde made himself into such a comic-opera figure that for the character Bunthorne in *Patience*, Gilbert and Sullivan's homage to aesthetic folly, the actor and director took Wilde for the model even though Gilbert had intended William Morris as the target. The degree to which Wilde had preempted the vanguard of Aestheticism is demonstrated by his lecture tour of American cities arranged by D'Oyly Carte. Wilde was to be the stalking horse for the touring opera company, creating sufficient notoriety to make *Patience* risible in the colonies. Wilde made the most of his opportunity, and his lectures were such a success that the tour was expanded several times to include American and Canadian cities outside the itinerary of the touring D'Oyly Carte Company. Wilde even arranged to have his first play, a melodrama titled *Vera; or, The Nihilists*, produced in New York City.

D'Oyly Carte's original contract with Wilde called for one lecture, "The English Renaissance of Art," to be given in a few major cities. With success, Wilde eventually added three more talks, including "The Practical Application of the Principles of the Aesthetic Theory to Exterior and Interior House Decoration, With Observations upon Dress and Personal Ornaments," referred to as "The House Beautiful," "Art and the Handicraftsman," and "The Irish Poets of '48." Wilde's tour success depended upon personal eccentricity and courage more than on a great public interest in his subjects. Crowds came to laugh at the famous aesthete as a curiosity, but Wilde won them over by proving that clowns may be philosophers. He was at his best when challenged to display both his ready wit and his theatrical instincts, which never failed him during his ten-month tour of

Wilde in 1883 after his American lecture tour (Mander and Mitchenson Theatre Collection)

phetic "The secret of life is in art."

The lecture on house decoration was more clearly intended for Wilde's American audience and serves as an elegant synthesis of the ideas of Ruskin and Morris, as does the lecture on "Art and the Handicraftsman," which is in its published version little more than a collection of notes edited by Robert Ross. Wilde's original contributions to the ideas in the lecture on decoration are that Whistler's Peacock Room was "the finest thing in color and art decoration which the world has known since Correggio" and that the only well-dressed men Wilde had encountered in the entire United States were the western miners. The house decoration piece ends on the Ruskinesque note that there is no better way to "learn to love Nature than to understand Art." By the time Wilde delivered his "Lecture to Art Students of the Royal Academy" in London (30 June 1883), his movement away from this position is clear in the argument that the artist should have nothing to do with the facts of the object, "but with its appearance only" and appearance is nothing more than "a matter of effect merely." Wilde follows this rejection of the Ruskin credo with a panegyric to "a man living amongst us who unites in himself all the qualities of the noblest art, whose work is a joy for all time, who is himself, a master of all time. That man is Mr. Whistler."

Whistler was to be the last and in some ways most important of the schooling figures to influence Wilde. The butterfly's famous 1878 lawsuit against Ruskin symbolized the competition between Ruskin's moral aesthetic and Whistler's philosophy of art, which substituted irony for ethical imperatives. It is true that Wilde's apprenticeship to Whistler was short-lived and that the two quarreled publicly by telegram and in the press on and off into 1890 with increasing acrimony. Wilde's last word came in a letter to the editor of *Truth* in response to Whistler's venomous attribution of habitual plagiarism: "as for borrowing Mr. Whistler's ideas about art, the only thoroughly original ideas I have ever heard him express have had reference to his own superiority as a painter over painters greater than himself." Whistler's final salvo was given when the Whistler-Wilde correspondence was given a prominent place in the former's *The Gentle Art of Making Enemies* (1890). Nevertheless, the Whistler phase had two lasting effects: it inspired Wilde to adopt the witty, paradoxical public mask of the artist among the philistines and as a corollary con-

the United States and Canada.

The lectures in both style and content help trace Wilde's development as a public man of letters and aesthetic impresario. "The English Renaissance of Art" is by far the most English and formal of the tour lectures. It is an apologia for the new generation of artists with whom Wilde identified himself, presumably the generation of A. C. Swinburne, William Morris, Dante Gabriel Rossetti, and their aesthetic successors. The ideal that inspired this aesthetic new wave was, according to Wilde, the union of Hellenism with "intensified individualism." He takes up positions that he was to defend again and again throughout his career, such as "a consciousness of the absolute difference between the world of art and the world of real fact." Art is justified by its perfection of form, not by its content: "Indeed one should never talk of a moral or an immoral poem—poems are either well written or badly written, that is all." The essay ends with a virtual paraphrase of Pater's "Conclusion" in *Studies in the History of the Renaissance* (1873) and Wilde's pro-

firmed Wilde in a more exclusive aestheticism antipathetic to nature. Wilde's success in America had confirmed something else as well–that Wilde was taken more seriously as an artist and achieved popular success by occupying a marginal position in society and, then, by force of personality, compelling an audience to accept both the philosophy and the artist, if only for an hour. Wilde, the self-proclaimed artist, had by virtue of his dandyism, so it seemed, succeeded through marginality and controversy.

Wilde's notoriety on both sides of the Atlantic had done more than genius itself to advance the sale of his *Poems*, which appeared in June 1881 in an English edition originally paid for by the poet, and then in an American edition in October. In less than a year *Poems* went through no less than five editions. It took ten more years for a sixth edition to appear. Events began to move more quickly following the American lecture tour. Wilde had begun his dramatic career in 1879 by writing *Vera; or, The Nihilists*, which was printed in an acting edition in September 1880 and finally produced in New York at the Union Square Theatre in August 1883, with Wilde back from England in attendance. It ran one week to mostly poor notices. While stumping New York

on his lecture tour, he had convinced Hamilton Griffon that he should write a five-act tragedy for Mary Anderson. In 1883 Wilde completed *The Duchess of Padua,* a play he later regretted as unartistic. It was first staged anonymously under the title *Guido Ferranti* at the Broadway Theatre, New York, in January 1891. Clearly, Wilde's debut as a playwright was not auspicious. Wilde, therefore turned his talents back to lecturing, devoting much of 1883-1884 to a tour of England and Scotland, delivering his "House Beautiful" talk and "Personal Impressions of America."

During late 1883, Wilde became engaged to Constance Lloyd and married her in a celebrated aesthetical wedding on 29 May 1884. The couple moved to Tite Street, where they lived in somewhat tight circumstances for several years on what Wilde earned writing reviews and Constance had from a small pension. Wilde wrote regularly for the *Pall Mall Gazette* and the *Dramatic Review* during the next three years. There is no doubt that Wilde found the regular discipline of reviewing new books, especially poetry, often tedious, even onerous. It is probably fair to say that the level of Wilde's reviewing seldom rises above that which is adequate to the occasion, but here and there we encounter sudden efflores-

The Private View at the Royal Academy, 1881 painting by William Powell Frith (by permission of C. J. R. Pope). According to William Gaunt in The Restless Century *(1972), one of Frith's aims in the painting was to satirize "what he described as 'the aesthetic craze.'" Wilde, in the foreground toward the right wearing a top hat and boutonniere, is set in contrast to the "no-nonsense man of letters," Anthony Trollope, at the far left in front.*

cences of Wilde's superior creative and critical gifts. Wilde's taste in writers, art, and music agrees with modern preferences in most cases, although he did find W. G. Watts "the most powerful of all our English artists" ("The Grosvenor Gallery, 1879"). In writing of W. G. Wills, a prolific writer of the time admired by Wilde, and of his new play *Olivia*, Wilde insists that the true artist is known by originality of treatment not of subject. "It is only the unimaginative who ever invents. The true artist is known by the use he makes of what he annexes, and he annexes everything." This is a nostrum we must apply to Wilde's own frequent borrowings if we are to see them for what they were, at least to Wilde–not mere plagiarism but most often unconcealed annexations, left to our recognition–in Wilde's terms, as "forms of literary acting."

There are further clues to Wilde's own practice and aesthetic philosophy. In the review "*Twelfth Night* at Oxford" (*Dramatic Review*, 20 February 1886), Wilde writes: "The manner of an artist is essentially individual, the method of an artist is absolutely universal. The first is personality which no one should copy. . . ." Later, in a review of George Sand's collected letters in the *Pall Mall Gazette* (6 March 1886), Wilde insists that "art without personality is impossible," a theme reiterated in the later criticism and one at the heart of Wilde's own critical practice, especially in such works as *The Portrait of Mr. W.H.*, the dialogues of *Intentions*, and *De Profundis*. Wilde gives another insight into his own methodology in the same review, "The Letters of a Great Woman," when he reveals his view that "art for art's sake is not meant to express the final cause of art but is merely a formula of creation." The junction of aestheticism as a formal cause and personality as an efficient cause is one of the two polarities of *The Picture of Dorian Gray* (1891), the other being the junction of absolute morality and magic. Taken all together, these themes are as prominent in Wilde's life as they were to become in his mature works.

Wilde's wit is legendary. Biographies of him are spiced with witty examples from his conversations, letters, and writings. Given Wilde's dandyism, with his emphasis on individuality, paradoxical wit, and aesthetic absolutism, it is no wonder that critics have been reluctant to take him seriously as either an aesthetic or moral philosopher. He was both; but the safest course is to make no distinction among such remarks as the following: "Most modern calendars mar the sweet simplicity of our lives by reminding us that each day that passes is the anniversary of some perfectly uninteresting event" ("A New Calendar," *Pall Mall Gazette*, 17 February 1887). "However, all work criticises itself" ("A Note on Some Modern Poets," *Woman's World*, December 1888). "One's real life is so often the life that one does not lead" ("L'Envoi," Wilde's introduction to Rennell Rodd's *Rose Leaf and Apple Leaf*, 1882). "I look forward to a reaction in favor of the cultural criminal" ("*Olivia* at the Lyceum," *Dramatic Review*, 30 May 1885). Each of these statements, most readers would agree, is a reasonably typical example of Wilde's aphoristic style and yet the focus of each aphorism differs and with it the value. Wilde moves us from popular custom to critical theory, thence to prophetic statements on the individual and social levels. It is an obvious mistake, therefore, to assume that because the style and tone are the same, the author is always working on surfaces of calendars or upon green carnations hoping to shock in order to get attention.

In 1884 the May issue of the *Nineteenth Century* included Wilde's essay "Shakespeare and Stage Costume" which argues the case for both accurate and appropriate costuming based on scientific, that is, archaeological evidence. Retitled "The Truth of Masks," it appeared later with many changes as one of the essays of *Intentions* and included a conclusion which dramatizes Wilde's intermediate development as an essayist, stylist, and thinker. The original essay on stage costume is an Oxford essay; its revised version, despite its earnestness of argument, deserves to stand alongside the others by virtue of its peroration if nothing else: "Not that I agree with everything that I have said in this essay. There is much with which I entirely disagree. The essay simply represents an artistic standpoint, and in aesthetic criticism attitude is everything. For in art there is no such thing as a universal truth. A Truth in art is that whose contradictory is also true. And just as it is only in art-criticism, and through it, that we can apprehend the Platonic theory of ideas, so it is only in art-criticism, and through it, that we can realise Hegel's system of contraries. The truths of metaphysics are the truths of masks." This meditation on the performance of the critical faculty in art is the theoretical foundation on which stands not only Wilde's mature criticism but also the later fiction and drama as well.

Wilde had four stories published in 1887 along with his ongoing review work. "The

Canterville Ghost" appeared in the *Court and Society Review* (in the February and March numbers). Thereafter, Wilde began to write reviews for that periodical, as well. "Lady Alroy" appeared in *Saunder's Irish Daily News* (May); Wilde later changed the title to "The Sphinx without a Secret" when it appeared in *Lord Arthur Savile's Crime & Other Stories* (1891). The title story of that volume appeared in the *Court and Society Review* in May, and "The Model Millionaire" appeared in the *World* in June.

In spring 1887 Wilde assumed editorship of the *Woman's World*, a position he held until fall of 1889. He began the project with more enthusiasm than one might suppose who did not know Wilde's mother and his early upbringing. Under his direction an indifferent publication titled *Lady's World* became the more modern *Woman's World*, which endeavored to print the best in literature, art, and fashion by, about, and for women. Wilde's dream of editing a publication which would become, as he put it in a letter, "the recognized organ for the expression of women's opinions on all subjects of literature, art, and modern life" depended more than he appreciated at first on both his involved direction and his contribution of a regular column of literary notes. By mid 1888, Wilde had given up the literary column and had become little more than a figurehead. Despite good reviews and a strong initial surge in subscriptions, *Woman's World* never met Wilde's expectations. Perhaps he grew weary of recruiting potential contributors. More likely, as his own literary affairs flourished, he became pressed for time. Then again, Wilde was the first to admit that he found it difficult to maintain a long-term commitment to any project. Whatever the case, his gradual disengagement from *Woman's World* signaled the approaching end of Wilde's role as a regular, anonymous periodical reviewer. He was preparing to step forward as an author, playwright, and celebrity rather than remain simply a man of letters.

In May 1888 *The Happy Prince and Other Tales* was published with illustrations by Walter Crane and Jacomb Hood. An exquisite collection of fairy tales intended to be read aloud to children by adults, the volume contains Wilde's most popular stories in this genre. Another popular collection of stories, *A House of Pomegranates* (1891), reveals movement away from the naive eschatology of the earlier tales toward a darker, more qualified moralism like that expressed in "The Fisherman and His Soul" and in the novel *The Picture*

of Dorian Gray (1891). Wilde's experimental development of the fairy tale may be taken as part of the pattern of personal innovation he was performing in fiction, criticism, and drama during the late 1880s and early 1890s.

During the early years of his marriage, Wilde had worked harder than he ever had, kept a relatively low public profile, and begun to reap the harvest of maturing and disciplined genius as the 1880s came to an end. The only continuing storm clouds from the earlier days when he affected knee britches, silk stockings, and sunflowers and worshiped Lillie Langtry in public were the occasional complaints of plagiarism from Whistler and newspaper tempests, such as the complaints of Herbert Vivian that Wilde had reneged on a promise to write a preface to Vivian's reminiscences. Vivian's revenge was to report private conversations without permission and to blame Wilde as a plagiarist in a patronizing manner. However, by the end of 1889, Wilde had provided his enemies plenty of ammunition with the publication that year of "The Portrait of Mr. W.H." in the July issue of *Blackwood's Edinburgh Magazine*.

The work represents in a practical sphere the gospel he preached in January with "The Decay of Lying" in the *Nineteenth Century*. It was in criticism at the time an original and unique work and has never been fully appreciated, not even by academic critics. It is both a work of fiction and criticism, each mode modifying and undercutting the other. If it were written today, it would be hailed as a work of critical deconstructionism. As it was, the dimension that caused the most comment was the implication, hardly original to Wilde, that Shakespeare had written his sonnets for a young man. By current standards, Wilde's handling of the theme was tasteful, discrete, and ambiguous. However, Wilde's enemies in the popular press, who knew something of his private shenanigans, were alarmed by Wilde's flirtation with disclosure, not so much of Shakespeare, but of an issue that many were in agonies of embarrassment to keep beneath public notice. Wilde was satisfied to have written a work that presented so many mixed signals to the reader as to create a sort of amazed perplexity. One did not know whether to take it as criticism, as fiction, parody, exposé, confession, or hoax. The theme is one of those paradoxes loved by Wilde which often form the core of his poems in prose. Faith is at issue, not religious or supernatural faith, but rather belief in a theory about the

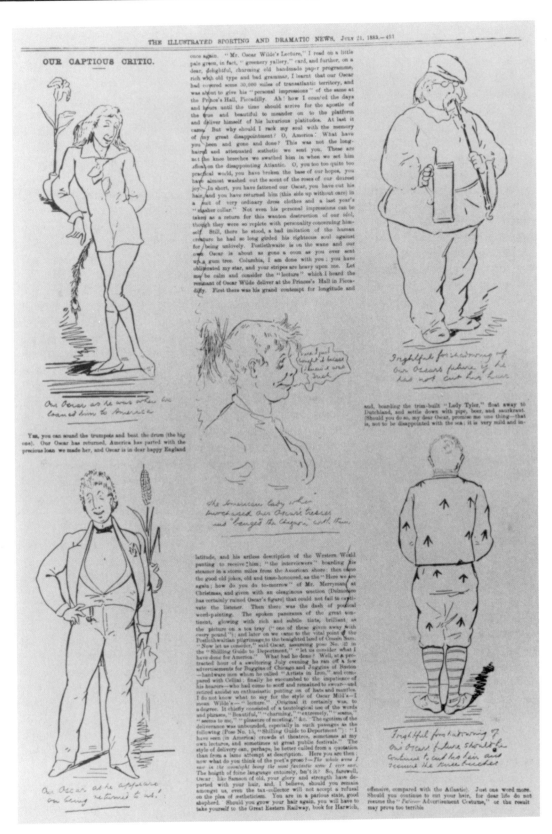

From a review of a July 1883 lecture Wilde delivered in London. According to Sheridan Morley in Oscar Wilde *(1975), the last car-*
toon on this page is "a chillingly (albeit accidentally) accurate forecast of the prison garb" Wilde would wear from 1895 to 1897.

person to whom the Shakespeare sonnets are dedicated. The theory is transparently fictitious, but it has the beauty of so thoroughly explaining everything in the sonnets that it seems an affront to reason itself that Willie Hughes, the boy actor in Shakespeare's company, never should have existed. Cyril Graham, a character out of Wilde's scrapbook of Oxford pinups, commits suicide for the sake of the theory. A painting of the fictitious Willie is forged to provide vulgar evidence. George Erskine, whose faith Cyril Graham tried to inspire, is finally convinced by the faith of the narrator, who loses his own faith upon Erskine's conversion.

In part, "The Portrait of Mr. W.H." burlesques a school of criticism and controversy about the sonnets that flourished especially in the 1870s and 1880s. Wilde avoids mere parody of the methods and arguments of every man of letters, from Frank Harris to Bernard Shaw, who had his theory about the sonnets. Instead, he challenges the heuristic foundations and practice of interpretive and historical criticism by demonstrating that criticism prefers the formal perfection of fiction to the disorder of data. "The Portrait of Mr. W.H." begins with faith and ends with forgery, showing that the former alone gives life to art, whereas a commonplace, rational demand for proof betrays faith into seeking impossible correlatives of itself.

The so-called Cleveland Street scandal involving the sons of wealthy and even titled families and telegraph-boy prostitutes made titillating reading for the public during the interlude between the appearance of "The Portrait of Mr. W.H." and *The Picture of Dorian Gray*, which debuted in the July 1890 number of *Lippincott's Monthly Magazine*. The scandal Wilde's novel created dominated the press during the summer; every day or week there appeared a fresh attack upon the alleged viciousness of the work, followed by witty defenses from Wilde. The furor lasted until Henry Morton Stanley's *In Darkest Africa* (1890) appeared in print to provide readers with a new topic of conversation. In defending *The Picture of Dorian Gray* against unspecified charges of indecency, Wilde clearly won the art-and-morality debate. Since Dorian's sins were not specified, Wilde took the philistine literalist side, claiming that those who found vice in the story had brought it themselves. Moreover, he fell back on familiar positions, arguing that art and morality were absolutely separate issues and that literature was to be judged on aesthetic not

moral grounds. And he confounded his critics with the admission that if the book had a serious fault, it was that the moral of the story was too obvious. He vowed to correct the flaw in a revision. The entire question of *The Picture of Dorian Gray* and censorship was to be reopened at the trials in 1895. Then also, Wilde took the high ground with the unwitting assistance of his adversaries and scored nearly every point.

The debate over the morality of *The Picture of Dorian Gray* has remained a red herring ever since. Wilde's critics were absolutely right in suspecting him of using the book as a Trojan horse to smuggle homosexuality into contemporary literature as a fit theme. Since they would not name the sin, Wilde simply called it theirs. Yet there was no overt homosexuality in the original version, only hints of indirect reference and implications of behavior. Above all, these traces are carried in the tone, which also exploited such an atmosphere of artistic and moral decadence that the novel has remained a byword for the English decadence ever since. Recent criticism agrees that Wilde was flirting with self-disclosure in writing the original version and withdrew from his advanced position in the revised version that appeared in book form the year following the *Lippincott's* publication. In fact, Wilde's supposed disclosure complex is complemented by an elaborate allegorical structure that runs from roman à clef to the moral allegory which almost all readers recognized.

There is no doubt that *The Picture of Dorian Gray* and some of the other stories seem uncannily prophetic of the fate that awaited Oscar Wilde. In 1886 Wilde met Robert Ross, who eventually became his literary executor. Biographers now accept Ross's account that he first led Wilde into homosexual practice and that Erskine of *The Portrait of Mr. W.H.* and Ernest, the respondent in the dialogue "The Critic as Artist," were reflections of Ross and the many evenings he and Wilde spent together in conversations over books and the arts. Shortly before writing *The Picture of Dorian Gray*, Wilde met Robert H. Sherard, the first of several incarnations of Wilde's ideal of male beauty. Sherard remained a staunch friend and defender of Wilde, disbelieving the charges against Wilde in the trials until Wilde himself told him the truth. Sherard lived to write biographical works in defense of his dead friend. Wilde also met John Gray, an aesthetic poet, later an intimate of André Rafflovich and, later still, a priest. Gray, who was another incarnation of Cyril Graham ("The Portrait of Mr. W.H.") and Dorian Gray, took to signing his name Dorian in his letters to Wilde.

It was after the appearance of the book version of *The Picture of Dorian Gray* in 1891 that Wilde met Lord Alfred Douglas at Oxford. He became the great romance of Wilde's life and led him to ruin and imprisonment. Bosie Douglas was the immature youngest son of the infamous Marquess of Queensberry, whom Douglas hated. He was the final incarnation of Dorian Gray in Wilde's life in every way, including temperament. Wilde's meetings with Sherard, Gray, and Douglas, when related to *The Picture of Dorian Gray* seem a set of "meaningful coincidences" of the kind Jung describes in relation to synchronistic events. If it seems that Wilde took *The Picture of Dorian Gray* as a guide for the years that followed, one must remember that such behavior is precisely what would be expected from an obsessive personality. When combined with Wilde's public role as a dandy and his aesthetic interest in magical thinking and self-dramatization, the potential of an aesthetic superstition leading to self-destruction simply became overwhelming.

In the meantime, the triumphs of 1891 were not yet complete. His two longest and best-known works of critical prose also appeared in that year. "The Soul of Man Under Socialism" came out in February in the *Fortnightly Review*. It was later privately printed under the title *The Soul of Man* in 1895. The essay has enjoyed a much greater appreciation in France, Germany, and especially in Russia than it has in either England or the United States. In it Wilde seems to return to questions of art and social justice. Though his masters here are clearly Ruskin and Morris, Wilde's version of socialism as the political extension of his philosophy of individualism is his own. To say that the socialism Wilde writes about is visionary understates the case profoundly. Socialism will "relieve us from that sordid necessity of living for others which, in the present condition of things, presses so hardly upon almost everybody." Since there is to be no poverty after socialism has reformed society, there will be no misery, private property, and no crime. Wilde's formula for eliminating crime is to eliminate its cause, punishment: "crime will be seen as a form of dementia to be cured by physician's care and kindness." Wilde's instinctive reading of the modern temper is remarkably insightful, even when he is writing a utopian prescription. The modern world, about whose critical and intel-

Wilde and Lord Alfred Douglas in 1893 (Sotheby's sale, 18 December 1985). Their relationship led to the trials that brought about Wilde's ruin.

lectual spirit Wilde wrote more frequently than is realized, "desires to get rid of pain and the suffering that pain entails. It trusts to Socialism and Science as its methods. What it aims at is an Individualism expressing itself through joy."

In May 1891 *Intentions* appeared, Wilde's final public statement on criticism, in effect closing an inquiry that had extended over a dozen years, beginning with "The Rise of Historical Criticism." The essays collected under the title were the much-revised "The Truth of Masks," "The Critic as Artist," "Pen, Pencil, and Poison," and "The Decay of Lying." Each of the essays had appeared previously. Wilde led off the volume with "The Decay of Lying" because he thought it his best: "Out of my dinner with Robbie came the first and best of all my dialogues," he once proclaimed in a letter. The essay is in the form of a Platonic dialogue, although Vivian does nearly all the talking and is clearly Wilde's mouthpiece. Cyril, his respondent, critics agree, is Robbie Ross presented as an Oxonian. Vivian reads to

Cyril his essay on the "new aesthetics," presented with an appealing, whimsical diffidence. The reader hears echoes of Wilde's table talk, so highly praised by friends and enemies as the most brilliant of its time. And how that discomforted Mr. Whistler!

"The Decay of Lying" begins innocently enough with Vivian's foppish and petulent complaint about nature's lumpy and crawling inadequacies, wittingly invoking Emerson as the authority for a whimsical approach to all things serious. The essay is another of Wilde's Trojan horses, for disguised in the witty tone and dandyish manner, Wilde attacks the referential foundations of Romanticism and both the art and the criticism that devolved from the privileged position of nature. Wilde embezzles the capital of realism, intending to leave the movement bankrupt in favor of what he names romance. Art is superior to nature and should not be judged by discredited standards of realism since its purpose is to say beautiful and untrue things. Furthermore, Vivian assures the distracted Cyril, life imitates art. It is nature which is crude and unfinished, like a dull-witted pupil, learning her best effects from artists but then tirelessly repeating them ad nauseam.

This is Wilde's parabolic analysis of that phase of Romanticism he wishes to retain, namely the privileged position of the imagination and the Coleridgean agenda that there is a distinctively human contribution to all sensation and knowledge. Wilde wishes to go even further. He directly refutes Renan, one of his earlier cultural heroes who preached that art expresses the temper of the times, "the moral and social conditions that surround it, under whose influence it is produced." Vivian insists rather that "art never expresses anything but itself." The corollaries of this principle read like the paradoxes of *Alice in Wonderland* or thought experiments in post-Einsteinian physics. Thus, "the nineteenth century as we know it is largely an invention of Balzac." Since the Middle Ages as they are represented in art are "simply a definite form of style," there is no reason at all why latter-day medievalists with "this same style should not be produced in the nineteenth century." Wilde's attack is on the notion of a preferred style identifiable as modernist, an idea which he rejects both in theory and practice. The idea that art can be defined in critical terms as a form of lying was a calculated effront to doyens and dowagers of received opinion. It is also another instance of the

author's playful invitation to enjoy the prospect of a self-contradictory proposition.

"Pen, Pencil, and Poison. A Study in Green" first appeared in Frank Harris's *Fortnightly Review* (January 1889). It is written in the form of an appreciation which takes up an extreme dandyish or aesthetic position. The title says it all, with its alliterative emphasis, implied synaesthesia, and its allusiveness to Whistlerian art and attitude. The essay, like the one before it, creates its own climate of skepticism and opposition. In contemporary critical idiom, it deconstructs itself; but it does so in cold blood, with *sang-froid*, so to speak. The essay proposes that the reader entertain an aesthetics of murder in the case of Thomas Griffiths Wainewright, Charles Lamb's friend, and a model of dandyish counterinsurgency, "dilettante of things delightful, but also a forger of no mean or ordinary capabilities, and as a subtle and secret poisoner almost without rival in this or any age." The argument is perverse and is so intended. Beyond the shock of its aberrant entertainment, the argument subtly involves the reader in the semblance of suspending moral judgment for its sake and thus collaborating in the outrage. The reader becomes, as it were, the unindicted coconspirator.

In addition to Wilde's half-sincere machinery of self-indictment (an extension of the symbolism of *The Picture of Dorian Gray*), the essay reinforces and to some extent advances already established critical beachheads. Art's first appeal is to taste, often referred to by Wilde under the code name "artistic temperament." Anticipating "The Decay of Lying," the writer charges that the arts must borrow from each other not from life in an "ugly and sensible age"; and foreshadowing *The Picture of Dorian Gray* and the experience of the author himself, the writer reflects in "Pen, Pencil, and Poison," "One can fancy an intense personality being created out of sin." The point is not whether the reader agrees that Wilde had chosen deliberately, even self-consciously, a life of sin for reasons of what may be termed experimental aesthetics. Wilde believed it and said so. The danger, not only of disclosure and ruin but the moral danger to his soul were what tempted him: "It's like feasting with panthers," he wrote in a famous phrase.

"The Critic as Artist" is another dialogue, only longer and more complex than "The Decay of Lying." It is Wilde's most ambitious work of criticism, and it places him both within the tradition of Arnold and Pater as their successor but at the same time it also places him beside that tradition, far more at home with post-structuralism than with new criticism or formalism. Reason seems against this assessment and yet in practice over the intervening years it has been so. Whereas both new criticism and formalism prize irony, they are less enthusiastic over an irony that undercuts the foundations of reasoned critical inquiry. Wilde is, in short, critically disreputable and subversive.

"The Critic as Artist" first appeared in two parts, over Wilde's objections, in the *Nineteenth Century* (July and September 1890) under the title "The True Function and Value of Criticism with Some Remarks on the Importance of Doing Nothing." As with "The Truth of Masks," the new title betokened considerable changes and revisions, although Wilde did not appear to have any uniform practice about revisions and titling. If he had, "The Portrait of Mr. W.H.," *The Picture of Dorian Gray*, and *The Soul of Man Under Socialism* would have been given entirely new titles to go along with their internal changes.

The manner and tone of "The Critic as Artist" has been called simply Wildean, and there is no objection to such a term as long as one bears in mind that Wilde identified himself with more than one self and one style in the prose and fiction. This dialogue is written in the voice of the dandy–the same voice heard from Vivian in "The Decay of Lying," from Lord Henry in *The Picture of Dorian Gray*, and from the parade of dandys in the plays beginning with Lord Darlington of *Lady Windermere's Fan* and ending with practically everyone in *The Importance of Being Earnest*.

In a way, "The Artist as Critic" is a synthesis of Wilde's major critical statements, almost as though he were summing up some of the themes of a life's work in criticism. If anything, it is more radical than the other essays. The playful wit and the reflexive irony seem to push the dialogue to the frontiers of the dramatic. In this essay Wilde collects things from his own earlier reviews and develops them more fully than before. Complementing the marginal aesthetic positions adopted in the other essays, is the Oriental philosophy of quietism that appears so aptly incongruous. Wilde returns also to the notion that life and literature are the "two supreme and highest arts." The dialogue treats criticism practically and from a variety of theoretic bases. The most radical is the claim that "criticism is really creative in the highest sense of the word. Criticism is, in fact, both creative and independent." That

is, while it may take art for its starting point, it is a new creation– "is in its way more creative than creation, as it has least reference to any standard external to itself, and is, in fact its own reason for existence."

But if Wilde declares criticism's independence from explication, he stresses its authenticity as "the only civilized form of autobiography." Wilde begins undermining the conventional idea of the intentions of literary criticism from the proposition that criticism is "impressive purely" and that it must as a consequence or corollary internalize everything. Wilde wishes to stress that criticism hinges absolutely on personality and its intensification by the critic. Relying partly on Baudelaire and French critics, Wilde argues in "The Critic as Artist" that the road to understanding others is through intenser individualism. The practical business of the literary critic is not so much interpretation as revealing the work of art in "some new relation to our age." Wilde was to write of himself later in *De Profundis* in similar terms as one "who stood in symbolic relations to the art and culture of my age"–not simply in what he said but rather by what he was. Although it was not an important purpose, Wilde does outline through Gilbert criteria for elite literature in the form of three questions: Does it stand in intellectual relation to the age? Does it bring a new element of pleasure? Does it suggest a fresh departure of thought, or passion, or beauty?

Wilde's assault upon the foundations of Romantic criticism next focuses on an unexpected target–the imagination. The critical spirit opposes imagination because the former is the "result of heredity. It is simply concentrated race experience." In order to realize one's own life and times, one must realize others and all the ages that have preceded the present. Wilde invokes the scientific principle of heredity to reveal "the absolute mechanism of all action, and so freeing us from the self-imposed and trammelling burden of moral responsibility. . . ." The sphere that remains is the subjective, and that is where the artist must expect to do his work.

Nevertheless, despite Gilbert's statement that all art is immoral and all thinking dangerous, Wilde has no intention of leaving the last word to paradox. The shade of Arnold and the schooling figure of Pater could not have permitted it. In the end, Wilde turned from the pleasures of scandalizing philistia to a celebration of the potential power of criticism, starting with an invocation of Arnold's insistence that criticism makes culture possible.

One of the intentions of "The Critic as Artist" lies in the reiteration of the Wildean doctrine of the separation of art and ethics by the emphasized familiar strategy of reversal. Wilde proposes that only through criticism shall humans "rise superior to race-prejudices," preparing readers for the claim that "Aesthetics are higher than ethics. They belong to a more spiritual sphere. . . . Even a colour-sense is more important in the development of the individual, than a sense of right and wrong." Indeed, in Wilde's view, this claim is absurdly true because the aim is to promote the full development of individualism. All restraint, especially that of traditional ethical teaching, therefore becomes impedimental.

This line of thought was to be more fully developed after the debacle of 1895. The intervening four years were the most successful, complex, and dangerous of his life. After the harvest of 1891 Wilde turned to drama once again with renewed confidence. Theatrical by nature, his table talk had already become legendary. He complained once in a letter that in his stories, his characters never do anything but sit around and chatter. He began with the Victorian invention of the mediated melodrama, an antecedent of contemporary situation comedy. The action plays on Wilde's favorite theme, disclosure, this time of the secret parentage of the worthy heroine and title character, Mrs. Windermere. It introduces as the instigator in this well-made play Mrs. Erlynne, a character at a dinner party in *The Picture of Dorian Gray*, whose past was enough like that of the once worshipful Lillie Langtry, that the Jersey Lily never forgave Wilde the resemblance. The play *Lady Windemere's Fan* was as vulgar a success as the author could have hoped, to the dismay of such would-be playwrights as Henry James. Since Wilde wrote it as a period piece, it has remained essentially undiminished in its broad appeal.

Wilde turned his hand next to the grounds of tragedy, but chose instead an epical inversion of the confrontation of Salome and John the Baptist. The play was written in French, something the popular press made merry of in its caricatures, and was to be performed in London by Sarah Bernhardt. Indeed, the play was in rehearsal when it was denied a license on the technicality of an old law designed to prohibit the performance of mystery plays in reformed England. Wilde threatened to forsake puritan England for the Continent unless the ban was lifted. It was not revoked in Wilde's lifetime and persisted well into the twentieth century. *Salomé* was performed in Paris and was a great success. The play was translated by Bosie Douglas into English with considerable assistance and some intervention by Wilde himself. It was published in London and Boston in 1894 with wonderfully poisonous illustrations by Aubrey Beardsley.

In the plays that followed Wilde seemed to be moving the well-made social comedy in the direction of Richard Sheridan or perhaps even William Congreve. Not since the latter had wit so dominated the stage. In 1893 *A Woman of No Importance* was produced in London. During the following year Wilde was at work on the two plays that closed out his brief rise to the pinnacle of the London theater: *An Ideal Husband* and the incomparable *The Importance of Being Earnest*. During this period Wilde's feasting with panthers became almost daily fare. His vices were more flagrantly practiced. His very appearance changed, at least as reflected in the eyes of those who described him at dinner or at the theater or those who, like Toulouse-Lautrec, sketched him. The interpretation was unanimous: Wilde seemed in an advancing stage of moral and physical degeneracy. Even his handwriting deteriorated, lending credence to speculation about a possible recurrence of syphilis. So it seems that *The Picture of Dorian Gray* comes to life in the jowls of its author's later self: life imitating and ratifying art. Wilde was haunted by the imagination of disaster and the magical belief that he was living out of control, unable to check his own momentum, waiting for some outside force or event to do it for him.

In 1893 he moved out of his house into a hotel. He visited Constance Wilde and the children and often took them on holidays with him, but increasingly his hidden life and the more public association with Bosie Douglas consumed his time and his interest. For the first time, Wilde had the means to live as a gentleman. Although his income was prodigious, his expenses rose to meet it. He supported Douglas and his vices as well as his own. The end of Wilde's season came at the moment of greatest fame and success following the triumphant opening of *The Importance of Being Earnest* at the St. James's Theatre in February 1895. *An Ideal Husband* had been staged the previous month.

At Wilde's club, the Marquess of Queensberry, Bosie Douglas's father, had left his card with the insulting declaration "for Oscar Wilde

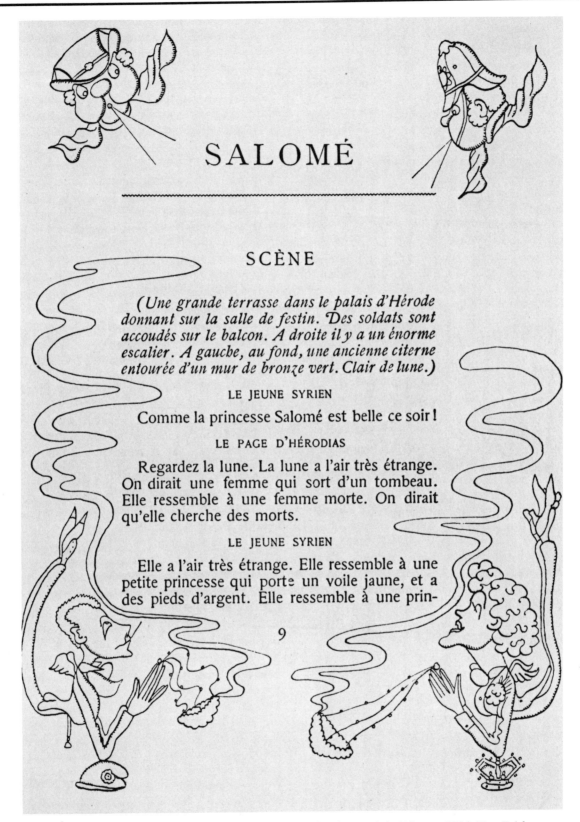

SALOMÉ

SCÈNE

(Une grande terrasse dans le palais d'Hérode donnant sur la salle de festin. Des soldats sont accoudés sur le balcon. A droite il y a un énorme escalier. A gauche, au fond, une ancienne citerne entourée d'un mur de bronze vert. Clair de lune.)

LE JEUNE SYRIEN

Comme la princesse Salomé est belle ce soir !

LE PAGE D'HÉRODIAS

Regardez la lune. La lune a l'air très étrange. On dirait une femme qui sort d'un tombeau. Elle ressemble à une femme morte. On dirait qu'elle cherche des morts.

LE JEUNE SYRIEN

Elle a l'air très étrange. Elle ressemble à une petite princesse qui porte un voile jaune, et a des pieds d'argent. Elle ressemble à une prin-

9

First page of the text in Max Beerbohm's copy of Wilde's play produced in Paris in February 1896 (Eva Reichmann, courtesy of Brigham Young University Library). Beerbohm's pen-and-ink embellishments depict John Bull and an English policeman trying to disperse smoke from the censers swung by Wilde (bottom right) and Lord Alfred Douglas, whose English translation of the play was published in 1894.

posing as Somdomite" [*sic*]. Wilde had been in Algiers with Bosie, meeting the local boys. Instead of ignoring the card as he could have done easily, Wilde instituted a suit for slander against the marquess at the enthusiastic prompting of Bosie. The case was heard on 5 April. Queensberry's defense was justification. The defense began with the strategy of citing Wilde's "Phrases and Philosophies for the Use of the Young," which appeared in an Oxford undergraduate magazine titled *Chameleon. The Picture of Dorian Gray* was also indicted as an example of a literary work calculated to promote vice and subvert virtue. Wilde was at his most eloquent in answering what was called the "literary part of the case," and he turned the court into a theater on the first day of the trial, scoring heavily on the defense attorney, Edward Carson. However, on the second day, the defense began to question Wilde on his relations with a series of young men whose names had been provided by Alfred Taylor, one of Wilde's procurers. Wilde was no longer able to hold his own under examination. The day ended with Carson promising to produce witnesses who would swear to Wilde's homosexual involvement with several notorious "renters," as they were called. At the beginning of the third day, Carson called Taylor to the stand and Wilde's attorney, Sir Edward Clarke, moved to end the trial before more damage was done. Accordingly, Queensberry was awarded a directed verdict of not guilty with costs to be paid by Wilde. The latter proved more ruinous, perhaps, than the former because when the costs could not be met, Wilde was sold up as a bankrupt and all his personal belongings and the contents of the Tite Street house were auctioned. Also lost were his manuscripts and his rights to his literary properties.

Following the Queensberry trial, Wilde went to the Cadogan hotel to await his fate, ignoring opportunities to "levant" to Europe provided by friends. Even the authorities expected him to leave England to avoid prosecution and waited until after the last boat train had left the station before producing a warrant. But Wilde stayed. He had promised his mother and brother he would stay and fight, even though he knew there was no chance of successful defense against the witnesses who could be brought against him. He did try to hire a new attorney to defend him, but he was told that it was too late for that. Thereafter, he seemed unable to take further action. He felt as though control of events had been taken from his hands. He remained in his room drinking hock and soda until the warrant was served. Two trials followed, the first ending in a hung jury. In the second trial, Wilde and Taylor were separately tried. Wilde was convicted and sentenced to two years at hard labor.

During confinement, he was permitted few books and little writing paper, and that for letters only. Consequently, the only writing he took with him from prison upon release was the long letter written to Bosie Douglas entitled "De Profundis." The letter had a history of its own after Wilde turned it over to Robert Ross, whom he had named literary executor, with instructions to copy it and send the original to Douglas. Later, Douglas was to claim he never received the letter and had read only the shortened version published by Ross in 1905 with all specific references to its addressee eliminated. Indeed, Douglas later sued for libel Arthur Ransome, an early critic, who had named Douglas the tormentor Wilde had referred to in the letter. Douglas lost the suit and went to prison for a short period in consequence. Once again, life imitated art to the extent that a certain poetic justice was served. The "De Profundis" letter was not published in its full, original version until the fifty-year seal placed upon it by Ross and the Courts was broken. It appears in *The Letters of Oscar Wilde* edited by Rupert Hart-Davis (1962).

As one would expect, the letters are livelier and more witty than those of his contemporaries and have taken their place among the great letters in the literature. "De Profundis" is the highlight of the collection, certainly, and it remains today an extraordinary documentation of the attempt of a writer to deal with the collapse of both his fortunes and expectations. He had lost everything, including his family and his reputation, and lived in solitary confinement, with the exception of exercise periods, for nearly two years. The letter to Douglas moves back and forth between complaints, apparently quite legitimate, over Douglas's deficiencies of character and what they had cost Wilde in both money and suffering, and his own attempt to transcend his condition through a new philosophy of aesthetics based on suffering. Wilde's habit of self-dramatization leads him to compare himself to Christ and to take Christ as the model for a new aesthetics. In "De Profundis" Wilde, for once, was being neither ironic nor insincere. His difficulty, he well knew, was to find a way through pain without resorting to bitterness and hatred.

One of the dominant threads running

through the "De Profundis" letter is the theme "Whatever is realized is right." Perhaps in the end that is the judgment literary history has passed upon "De Profundis," regarding it as a human document more than a literary one. Since it is both a letter and an apologia, it transcends private or public utterance, becoming both at the same time. Since the letter is all but unclassifiable, critics have regarded its mixed intentions with mixed tolerance and indifference. This much may be said: that Wilde wrote in both personal and public voices. The attempt at both a formal strategy of structural development and representation of themes from earlier essays is undercut to some degree by the personal complaints directed at Douglas. Wilde's newly espoused philosophy of suffering is intended to be the resolving and mediating force, but it is not sufficiently developed as an aesthetic principle to succeed completely. We must remind ourselves as well of the shift in tone and voice in the letter. Gone is the manner of the dandy, a pose no longer tenable in Wilde's new circumstances. Perhaps it was a role no longer possible to one who had lost very nearly all that could be lost and who had suffered two years of unremitting shame and pain. The newly chastened wit was perhaps not equal to the necessity of finding both a new identity and a new voice in which to write.

In *The Ballad of Reading Gaol* (1898) Wilde continued the experiment of "De Profundis," moving in the direction of finding a new style to suit the new subject matter that the circumstances of his life had forced upon him. Wilde, however, was no tragic poet, though *The Ballad of Reading Gaol*, written and published under the pseudonym C.3.3. after his release from prison, is an extraordinary poem, perhaps his best. Wilde wrote nothing more for publication after *The Ballad of Reading Gaol*, except for some letters on prison reform. His mute exile testified more eloquently than any apologia could have that the artist had died before the man.

To Wilde's everlasting credit, he took the role of martyr that society forced upon him with a dignified acceptance known only to great and generous natures. Nor did he excuse himself in his complaints to Bosie Douglas or plead innocence to friends who would have believed him if he but made the claim. Despite the attempt to achieve a higher level of awareness through philosophy and suffering, the aftermath of prison was, as Wilde foresaw, a sordid anticlimax. A man who had spent nearly twenty years posing as one

who posed, who saw life as a succession of moments and sensations to be experienced and enjoyed to the fullest, was ill-equipped to pursue the reformed life of the penitent. His hopes of being received into a Roman Catholic monastery upon release were disappointed when his application was rejected. He went instead to live in France under an assumed name, Sebastian Melmoth. In France took place the reunion and reconciliation with Bosie Douglas. The Douglas family contributed to Wilde's support, belatedly fulfilling its commitment of funding given before the first trial.

There was nothing but a symbolic reconciliation at the grave of Constance Wilde after her death in March 1898. Wilde was never to see either of his sons again. In 1899 his brother William died of the effects of alcoholism in London. Wilde's mother had passed away during her son's imprisonment. Wilde himself died in Paris of cerebral meningitis (an aftereffect of an ear injury sustained in prison) on 30 November 1900. Two days before, finding Wilde semicomatose, Robert Ross brought in a priest to administer the last rites of the Catholic Church, fulfilling his longstanding promise to Wilde that, in the end, the writer would be formally made a Catholic. Ross's promise was part of a bargain he had made with Wilde, who had wanted to convert after prison. Ross discouraged him from doing so at the time because Wilde could not promise to give up his private life as a practicing homosexual. Ross's part of the bargain was fulfilled when his friend was on his deathbed. Perhaps both men recognized this strategy as the only one guaranteed to preserve a conversion sincerely wished but perhaps despaired of being maintained. Shortly before the end, Wilde observed that he was dying as he had lived, beyond his means. He was buried in the Bagneux graveyard, but the body was later moved to Père Lachaise Cemetery, where it now rests beneath a controversial monument sculpted by Jacob Epstein.

Oscar Wilde's reputation probably has not changed as much over the years as some critics imagine, although there is no doubt that the temper of that reputation has been modified by time and that since World War II, his reputation as a writer has certainly risen. *The Importance of Being Earnest* is held to be a masterpiece, and most critics accept the designation of *The Picture of Dorian Gray* as a classic, however much they may regret perceived deficiencies. *Salome* is considered more problematic than either of these, even by critics prepared to claim for it the status of a master-piece of Decadence, in itself a severe qualification. The letters are also praised, being rated below only those of Byron or Keats. Beyond these areas of consensus, opinions differ much as they did a century ago, with many supporting claims that Wilde is indeed a major writer and influence and others dismissing him as a personality more than an author.

During the period from Wilde's death at age forty-six to World War II, criticism remained largely biographical and forensic. Alfred Douglas remained a figure of contradiction, at times leading the opposition to Wilde's reputation with scurrilous attacks and later recanting and repenting, pleading justification in an unconsciously grotesque parody of his father. Wilde's cause had its champions, led by the conscientious and hardworking Robert Ross, and in later years by Vyvyan Holland, Wilde's younger son. Serious criticism of Wilde as a writer practically begins with Edouard Roditi's *Oscar Wilde*, published by New Directions in 1947. Productive criticism since then has developed in three well-defined areas. Biography continues to be the chief attraction for critics. Biographical studies of Wilde surpass in number those of all other Victorians, with the major biographies promised by Hart-Davis and Richard Ellmann yet to come, and the *MLA Bibliography* records a steady stream of notes and minor biographies of Wilde. Biographical study has been stimulated by the annotated edition of Wilde's *Letters* prepared by Hart-Davis and by the critical and biographical studies of Ellmann and H. Montgomery Hyde. Hart-Davis's edition of *More Letters of Oscar Wilde* appeared in 1985. In the area of bibliography early work by Christopher Millard (whose pseudonymous bibliography appeared in 1914) has been supplemented, corrected, and brought forward by E. H. Mikhail, Ian Fletcher, and John Stokes. The third area to flourish in post-World War II criticism is academic study of Wilde, a development that probably would have amused and pleased him most.

If Wilde's reputation is to rise any higher than it has, it will be as the result of the work of those critics who are turning attention to the intellectual relation between the man and his works and the age. Edouard Roditi, Barbara Charlesworth, Epifanio San Juan, Christopher S. Nassaar, Rodney Shewan, and Richard Ellmann lead in this area. As critics approach the centennials of Wilde's major prose works, the inevitable revaluations may quicken appreciation of *Intentions*, which deserves higher esteem, and *The Soul of Man Under Socialism*, which is held in high regard in Europe. Many of the stories, particularly the fairy stories, are so well established as classics and hence outside the critical epicenter that they may continue to escape serious analysis. Perhaps Isobel Murray's edition of *The Complete Shorter Fiction of Oscar Wilde* (1979) is an omen that revaluation of the Wilde canon will extend to areas heretofore of little interest to critics.

Surely in an era of revisionism and deconstructionism, there are new and ostensibly sympathetic forces at work likely to enhance the status of Oscar Wilde, the man and his work, in the critical community. If that should happen, criticism will have finally caught up with both history and culture in rating Wilde a master.

Letters:

The Letters of Oscar Wilde, edited by Rupert Hart-Davis (New York: Harcourt, Brace & World, 1962);

More Letters of Oscar Wilde, edited by Hart-Davis (New York: Vanguard, 1985).

Bibliographies:

Stuart Mason [Christopher Millard], *Bibliography of Oscar Wilde* (London: Laurie, 1914);

Donald L. Lawler, "Oscar Wilde in the *New Cambridge Bibliography of English Literature*," *Papers of the Bibliographical Society of America*, 67 (1973): 172-188;

E. H. Mikhail, *Oscar Wilde: An Annotated Bibliography of Criticism* (Totowa, N.J.: Rowman & Littlefield, 1978);

Ian Fletcher and John Stokes, "Oscar Wilde," in *Recent Research on Anglo-Irish Writers*, edited by Richard Finneran (New York: Modern Language Association, 1983).

Biographies:

Robert H. Sherard, *The Life of Oscar Wilde* (New York: Kennerley, 1907);

Arthur Symons, *A Study of Oscar Wilde* (London: Sawyer, 1930);

Hesketh Pearson, *The Life of Oscar Wilde* (London: Methuen, 1946); republished as *Oscar Wilde: His Life and Wit* (New York: Harper, 1946);

Vyvyan Holland, *Son of Oscar Wilde* (New York: Dutton, 1954);

Lewis Broad, *The Friendships & Follies of Oscar Wilde* (New York: Crowell, 1955);

Rupert Croft-Cooke, *The Unrecorded Life of Oscar Wilde* (London & New York: Allen, 1972);

H. Montgomery Hyde, *Oscar Wilde: A Biography* (New York: Farrar, Straus & Giroux 1975).

References:

Karl Beckson, ed., *Oscar Wilde: The Critical Heritage* (New York: Barnes & Noble, 1970);

Joyce Bentley, *The Importance of Being Constance* (London: Hale, 1983);

Patrick Byrne, *The Wildes of Merrion Square* (London: Staples Press, 1953);

J. E. Chamberlin, *Ripe Was the Drowsy Hour: The Age of Oscar Wilde* (New York: Seabury, 1977);

Barbara Charlesworth, *Dark Passages: Decadent Consciousness in Victorian Literature* (Madison: University of Wisconsin Press, 1965);

Philip K. Cohen, *The Moral Vision of Oscar Wilde* (Rutherford, N.J.: Fairleigh Dickinson University Press, 1976);

Richard Ellmann, "The Critic as Artist as Wilde," in his *The Artist as Critic. Critical Writings of Oscar Wilde* (New York: Random, 1968);

Ellmann, ed., *Oscar Wilde: A Collection of Critical Essays* (Englewood Cliffs, N.J.: Prentice-Hall, 1969);

Regina Gagnier, *Idylls of the Marketplace: Oscar Wilde and the Victorian Public* (Stanford: Stanford University Press, 1986);

Richard Gilman, *Decadence* (New York: Farrar, Straus & Giroux, 1979);

H. Montgomery Hyde, ed., *The Trials of Oscar Wilde* (London: Hodge, 1948); republished as *The Three Trials of Oscar Wilde* (New York: University Books, 1956); enlarged as *Famous Trials*, seventh series: *Oscar Wilde* (Baltimore: Penguin, 1963);

Lloyd Lewis and Henry Justin Smith, *Oscar Wilde Discovers America [1882]* (New York: Harcourt, Brace, 1936);

Stuart Mason [Christopher Millard], ed., *Oscar Wilde: Art and Morality* (London: Jacobs, 1907);

E. H. Mikhail, *Oscar Wilde: Interviews and Recollections*, 2 volumes (London: Macmillan, 1979);

Christopher S. Nassaar, *Into the Demon Universe. A Literary Exploration of Oscar Wilde* (New Haven: Yale University Press, 1974);

Arthur Ransome, *Oscar Wilde. A Critical Study* (London: Secker, 1912);

Edouard Roditi, *Oscar Wilde* (Norfolk, Conn.: New Directions, 1947);

Epifanio San Juan, Jr., *The Art of Oscar Wilde* (Princeton: Princeton University Press, 1967);

Rodney Shewan, *Oscar Wilde: Art and Egoism* (New York: Barnes & Noble, 1977);

Terence de Vere White, *The Parents of Oscar Wilde: Sir William and Lady Wilde* (London: Hodder & Stoughton, 1967);

Frances Winwar, *Oscar Wilde and the Yellow Nineties* (New York: Harper, 1940).

Papers:

The largest collection of Wilde's papers is at the William Andrews Clark Memorial Library, University of California at Los Angeles. There are additional collections at the New York Public Library; the Pierpont Morgan Library; the Beinecke Library, Yale University; the British Library; the Harry Ransom Humanities Research Center, University of Texas at Austin; the Houghton Library, Harvard University; the University of Edinburgh Library; The Rosenbach Museum, Philadelphia; and Magdalen College, Oxford University.

Victorians on Rhetoric and Prose Style

Edited by Patrick Scott

Richard Whately

From *Elements of Rhetoric* (1828; revised, 1846)

The first major English treatise on prose composition in the nineteenth century was also the culmination of the long tradition of classical rhetoric. Indeed Whately's Elements of Rhetoric *gained its reputation by its polemic and clear-headed adaptation of Aristotelian rhetorical principles to the political and religious controversies of the early nineteenth century. Richard Whately (1787-1863) was a forceful and rather domineering Oxford don, fellow of Oriel College from 1811, principal of St. Alban's Hall (1825-1831), professor of political economy, and from 1831 to his death Archbishop of Dublin. His two textbooks,* Elements of Logic *(1826) and* Elements of Rhetoric *(1828), were designed to prepare Oxford students for future careers as preachers or as statesmen, but Whately's love of debate and his frequent drawing of examples from articles in the* Edinburgh *and* Quarterly *reviews make his analyses of much wider application in discussion of early Victorian controversial prose. The first extract, on the debating principle of "the burden of proof," grows out of a legalistic view of argument, but as Whately developed it, especially in the revised version given here (from the seventh edition, 1846), the concept took in also much greater awareness of the complex psychological factors involved in gaining consent to a controversial idea; Whately's ideas in this extract almost certainly influenced the later* An Essay in Aid of a Grammar of Assent *(1870), by his younger Oxford colleague John Henry Newman, who had collaborated with Whately in the development of his textbooks. The second extract deals with "perspicuity," or readability, in prose style, an issue that was to be discussed repeatedly throughout the century; Whately's discussion is notable for the attention it gives, not to abstract principles of "good style," but to rhetorical variables such as audience or the difficulty of the material being communicated. Whately's textbook was regularly reprinted in England in the 1830s and 1840s, and, partly because of its classical emphasis and religious orthodoxy, it also supplanted the older Scottish rhetorics in many American colleges in the middle decades of the century.—Ed.*

It is a point of great importance to decide in each case, at the outset, in your own mind, and clearly to point out to the hearer, as occasion may serve, on which side the *Presumption* lies, and to which belongs the [onus probandi] *Burden of Proof.* For though it may often be expedient to bring forward more proofs than can be fairly *demanded* of you, it is always desirable, when this is the case, that it should be *known,* and that the strength of the cause should be estimated accordingly.

According to the most correct use of this term, a "Presumption" in favour of any supposition, means, not (as has been sometimes erroneously imagined) a preponderance of probability in its favor, but, such a *pre-occupation* of the ground, as implies that it must stand good till some sufficient reason is adduced against it; in short, that the *Burden of proof* lies on the side of him who would dispute it.

Thus, it is a well-known principle of the Law, that every man (including a prisoner brought up for trial) is to be *presumed* innocent till his guilt is established. This does not, of course, mean that we are to *take for granted* he is innocent; for if that were the case, he would be entitled to immediate liberation: nor does it mean that it is antecedently *more likely than not* that he is innocent; or, that the majority of these brought to trial are so. It evidently means only that the "burden of proof" lies with the accusers;—that he is not to be called on to prove his innocence, or to be dealt with as a criminal till he has done so; but that they are to bring their charges against him, which if he can repel, he stands acquitted.

Thus again, there is a "presumption" in favour of the right of any individuals or bodies-corporate to the property of which they are in *actual possession.* This does not mean that they are, or are not, *likely* to be the rightful owners: but merely, that no man is to be disturbed in his possessions till some claim against him shall be established. He is not to be called on to prove his right; but the claimant, to disprove it; on whom consequently the "burden of proof " lies.

A moderate portion of common-sense will enable any one to perceive, and to show, on which side the Presumption lies, when once his attention is called to this question; though, for want of attention, it is often overlooked: and on

377

the determination of this question the whole character of a discussion will often very much depend. A body of troops may be perfectly adequate to the defence of a fortress against any attack that may be made on it; and yet, if ignorant of the advantage they possess, they sally forth into the open field to encounter the enemy, they may suffer a repulse. At any rate, even if strong enough to act on the offensive, they ought still to keep possession of their fortress. In like manner, if you have the "Presumption" on your side, and can but *refute* all the arguments brought against you, you have, for the present at least, gained a victory: but if you abandon this position, by suffering this Presumption to be forgotten, which is in fact *leaving out one of, perhaps, your strongest arguments,* you may appear to be making a feeble attack, instead of a triumphant defense.

Such an obvious case as one of those just stated, will serve to illustrate this principle. Let any one imagine a perfectly unsupported accusation of some offence to be brought against himself; and then let him imagine himself–instead of replying (as of course he would do) by a simple denial, and a defiance of his accuser to prove the charge,–setting himself to establish a negative,–taking on himself the burden of proving his own innocence, by collecting all the circumstances indicative of it that he can muster: and the result would be, in many cases, that this evidence would fall short of establishing a certainty, and might even have the effect of raising a suspicion against him;[1] he having in fact kept out of sight the important circumstance, that these probabilities in one scale, though of no great weight perhaps in themselves, are to be weighed against absolutely nothing in the other scale.

The following are a few of the cases in which it is important, though very easy, to point out where the Presumption lies.

There is a Presumption in favour of every *existing* institution. Many of these (we will suppose, the majority) may be susceptible of alteration for the better; but still the "Burden of proof" lies with him who proposes an alteration; simply, on the ground that since a change is not a good in itself, he who demands a change should show cause for it. No one is *called on* (though he may find it advisable) to defend an existing institution, till some argument is adduced against it; and that argument ought in fairness to prove, not merely an actual inconvenience, but the possibility of a change for the better.

Every book again, as well as person, ought

to be presumed harmless (and consequently the copy-right protected by our courts) till something is proved against it. It is a hardship to require a man to prove, either of his book, or of his private life, that there is no ground for any accusation; or else to be denied the protection of his Country. The Burden of proof, in each case, lies fairly on the accuser. I cannot but consider therefore as utterly unreasonable the decisions (which some years ago excited so much attention) to refuse the interference of the Court of Chancery in cases of piracy, whenever there was even any *doubt* whether the book pirated *might* not contain something of an immoral tendency.

There is a "Presumption" against any thing *paradoxical,* i.e. contrary to the prevailing opinion: it may be true; but the Burden of proof lies with him who maintains it; since men are not to be expected to abandon the prevailing belief till some reason is shown.

Hence it is, probably, that many are accustomed to apply "Paradox" as if it were a term of reproach, and implied absurdity or falsity. But correct use is in favour of the etymological sense. If a Paradox is unsupported, it can claim no attention; but if false, it should be censured on *that* ground; but not for being *new.* If true, it is the more important, for being a truth not generally admitted. "Interdum vulgus rectum videt; est ubi peccat" [Sometimes the people see what is right when they sin]. Yet one often hears a charge of "paradox and nonsense" brought forward, as if there were some close connection between the two. And indeed, in one sense this is the case; for to those who are too dull, or too prejudiced, to admit any notion at variance with those they have been used to entertain, *that* may appear nonsense, which to others is sound sense. Thus, "Christ crucified" was "to the Jews, a stumbling-block," (paradox,) "and to the Greeks, foolishness;" because the one "required a sign" of a different kind from any that appeared; and the others "sought after wisdom" in their schools of philosophy. . . .

A Presumption evidently admits of various degrees of strength, from the very faintest, up to a complete and confident acquiescence.

The person, Body, or book, in favour of whose decisions there is a certain Presumption, is said to have, so far, "Authority"; in the strict sense of the word.[2] And a recognition of this kind of Authority,–an *habitual* Presumption in favour of such a one's decisions or opinions–is usually called "Deference."

It will often happen that this deference is not recognized by either party. A man will perhaps disavow with scorn all deference for some person– a son or daughter perhaps, or an humble companion,–whom he treats, in manner, with familiar superiority; and the other party will as readily and sincerely renounce all pretension to Authority; and yet there may be that "habitual Presumption" in the mind of the one, in favour of the opinions, suggestions, &c. of the other, which we have called Deference. These parties however are not using the *words* in a different sense, but are unaware of the state of the *fact*. There is a Deference; but *unconscious*.

Those who are habitually wanting in Deference towards such as we think entitled to it, are usually called "arrogant"; the word being used as distinguished from *self-conceited, proud, vain,* and other kindred words. Such persons may be described as having an habitual and exclusive "self-deference."

Of course the persons and works which are looked up to as high authorities, or the contrary, will differ in each Age, Country, and Class of men. But most people are disposed,–measuring another by their own judgment,–to reckon *him* arrogant who disregards what *they* deem the best authorities. That man however may most fairly and strictly be so called who has no deference for those whom he *himself* thinks most highly of. And instances may be found of this character; *i.e.* of a man who shall hold in high estimation the ability and knowledge of certain persons–rating them perhaps above himself–whose most deliberate judgments, even on matters they are most conversant with, he will nevertheless utterly set at nought, in *each particular case* that arises, if they happen not to coincide with the idea that first strikes his mind.

For it is to be observed that *admiration, esteem,* and *concurrence in opinion,* are quite distinct from "Deference," and not necessarily accompanied by it. If any one makes what appears to us to be a very just remark, or if we acquiesce in what he proposes on account of the reasons he alleges,–this is not Deference. And if this has happened many times, and we thence form a high opinion of his ability, this again neither implies, nor even necessarily produces Deference; though in reason, such *ought* to be the result. But one may often find a person conversant with two others, A, and B, and estimating A without hesitation as the superior man of the two; and yet, in any case whatever that may arise, where A and B differ in their judgment, taking for granted at once that B is in the right.

Admiration, esteem, &c. are more the result of a judgment of the *understanding;* (though often of an erroneous;) "Deference" is apt to depend on *feelings;*–often, on whimsical and unaccountable feelings. It is often yielded to a vigorous *claim,*–to an authoritative and overbearing demeanour. With others, of an opposite character, a soothing, insinuating, flattering, and seemingly submissive demeanor will often gain great influence. They will yield to those who seem to yield to them; the others, to those who seem resolved to yield to no one. Those who seek to gain adherents to their School or Party by putting forth the claim of *antiquity* in favour of their tenets, are likely to be peculiarly successful among those of an arrogant disposition. A book or a Tradition of a thousand years old, appears to be rather a *thing* than a *person*; and will thence often be regarded with blind deference by those who are prone to treat their contemporaries with insolent contempt, but who "will not go to compare with an old man."[3] They will submit readily to the authority of men who flourished fifteen or sixteen centuries ago, and whom, if now living, they would not treat with decent respect. . . .

* * *

It is sufficiently evident (though the maxim is often practically disregarded) that the first requisite of Style not only in rhetorical, but in all compositions,[4] is Perspicuity; since, as Aristotle observes, language which is not intelligible, or not clearly and readily intelligible, fails, in the same proportion, of the purpose for which language is employed. And it is equally self-evident (though this truth is still more frequently overlooked) that Perspicuity is a *relative* quality, and consequently cannot properly be predicated of any work, without a tacit reference to the class of readers or hearers for whom it is designed.

Nor is it enough that the Style be such as they are *capable* of understanding, *if* they bestow their utmost attention: the degree and the kind of attention, which they have been *accustomed,* or are *likely* to bestow, will be among the circumstances that are to be taken into the account, and provided for. I say the *kind,* as well as the degree, of attention, because some hearers and readers will be found slow of apprehension indeed, but capable of taking in what is very copiously and gradually explained to them; while others, on the contrary, who are much quicker at catching the sense of what is expressed in a short compass, are incapable of *long* attention, and are not only wearied, but absolutely bewildered, by a diffuse Style.

When a numerous and very mixed audience is to be addressed, much skill will be required in adapting the Style, (both in this, and in other respects) and indeed the Arguments also, and the whole structure of the discourse, to the various minds which it is designed to impress; nor can the utmost art and diligence prove, after all, more than partially successful in such a case; especially when the diversities are so many and so great, as exist in the congregations to which most Sermons are addressed, and in the readers for whom popular works of an argumentative, instructive, and hortatory character, are intended. It is possible, however, to approach indefinitely to an object which cannot be completely attained; and to adopt such a Style, and likewise such a mode of reasoning, as shall be level to the comprehension of the greater part, at least, even of a promiscuous audience, without being distasteful to any.

It is obvious, and has often been remarked, that extreme conciseness is ill-suited to hearers or readers whose intellectual powers and cultivations are but small. The usual expedient, however, of employing a *prolix* Style by way of accommodation to such minds, is seldom successful. Most of those who could have comprehended the meaning, if more briefly expressed, and many of those who could not do so, are likely to be bewildered by tedious expansion; and being unable to maintain a steady attention to what is said, they forget part of what they have heard, before the whole is completed. Add to which, that the feebleness produced by excessive dilution, (if such an expression may be allowed,) will occasion the attention to languish; and what is perfectly attended to, however clear in itself, will usually be but imperfectly understood. Let not an author, therefore, satisfy himself by finding that he has expressed his meaning so that, *if* attended to, he cannot fail to be understood; he must consider also (as was before remarked) *what* attention is likely to be paid to it. If on the one hand much matter is expressed in very few words to an unreflecting audience, or if, on the other hand, there is a wearisome prolixity, the requisite attention may very probably *not* be bestowed.

It is remarked by Anatomists, that the nutritive quality is not the only requisite in food;—that a certain degree of *distention* of the stomach is re-quired, to enable it to act with its full powers;—and that it is for this reason hay or straw must be given to horses, as well as corn, in order to supply the necessary bulk. Something analogous to this takes place with respect to the generality of minds; which are incapable of thoroughly digesting and assimilating what is presented to them, however clearly, in a very small compass. Many a one is capable of deriving that instruction from a moderate sized volume, which he could not receive from a very small pamphlet, even more perspicuously written, and containing every thing that is to the purpose. It is necessary that the attention should be detained for a certain time on the subject: and persons of unphilosophical mind, though they can attend to what they read or hear, are unapt to dwell upon it in the way of subsequent meditation.

The best general rule for avoiding the disadvantages both of conciseness and of prolixity is to employ *Repetition:* to repeat, that is, the same sentiment and argument in many different forms of expression; each, in itself brief, but all, together, affording such an expansion of the sense to be conveyed, and so detaining the mind upon it, as the case may require. Cicero among the ancients, and Burke among the modern writers, afford, perhaps, the most abundant practical exemplifications of this rule. The latter sometimes shows a deficiency in correct taste, and lies open to Horace's censure of an author, *"Qui variare cupit rem prodigialiter unam"* [Who desires to vary a single topic excessively]: but it must be admitted that he seldom fails to make himself thoroughly understood, and does not often weary the attention, even when he offends the taste, of his readers.

Care must of course be taken that the repetition may not be too glaringly apparent; the variation must not consist in the mere use of other, synonymous, words; but what has been expressed in appropriate terms may be repeated in metaphorical; the antecedent and consequent of an argument, or the parts of an antithesis may be transposed; or several different points that have been enumerated, presented in a varied order, &c.

It is not necessary to dwell on that obvious rule laid down by Aristotle, to avoid uncommon, and, as they are vulgarly called, *hard* words, *i.e.* those which are such to the persons addressed; but it may be worth remarking, that to those who wish to be understood by the lower orders of the English,[5] one of the best principles of selection is to prefer terms of *Saxon* origin, which will generally be more familiar to them, than those derived from the Latin, (either directly, or through the medium of the French,) even when the latter are more in use among persons of education.[6] Our language being (with very trifling exceptions) made up of these elements, it is very easy for any one, though unacquainted with Saxon, to observe this precept, if he has but a knowledge of French or of Latin; and there is a remarkable scope for such a choice as I am speaking of, from the multitude of synonymes derived, respectively, from those two sources. The compilers of our Liturgy being anxious to reach the understandings of all classes, at a time when our language was in a less settled state than at present, availed themselves of this circumstance in employing many synonymous, or nearly synonymous, expressions, most of which are of the description just alluded to. Take, as an instance, the Exhortation:– "acknowledge" and "confess;"–"dissemble" and "cloke;"–"humble" and "lowly;"–"goodness" and "mercy;"–"assemble" and "meet together." And here it may be observed, that (as in this last instance) a word of French origin will very often not have a *single word* of Saxon derivation corresponding to it, but may find an exact equivalent in a *phrase* of two or more words; *e.g.* "constitute," "go to make up;"–"suffice," "be enough for;"–"substitute," "put in the stead," &c. &c.

It is worthy of notice, that a Style composed chiefly of the words of French origin, while it is less intelligible to the lowest classes, is characteristic of those who in cultivation of taste are below the highest. As in dress, furniture, deportment, &c., so also in language, the dread of vulgarity constantly besetting those who are half-conscious that they are in danger of it, drives them into the extreme of affected finery. So that the precept which has been given with a view to perspicuity, may, to a certain degree, be observed with an advantage in point of elegance also.

In adapting the Style to the comprehension of the illiterate,[7] a caution is to be observed against the ambiguity of the word *"Plain;"* which is opposed sometimes to *Obscurity,* and sometimes to *Ornament.* The vulgar require a perspicuous, but by no means a dry and *unadorned* style; on the contrary, they have a taste rather for the overflorid, tawdry, and bombastic: nor are the ornaments of style by any means necessarily inconsistent with perspicuity; indeed Metaphor, which is among the principal of them, is, in many cases, the clearest mode of expression that can be adopted; it being usually much easier for uncultivated minds to comprehend a similitude or analogy, than an abstract term. And hence the language of savages, as has often been remarked, is highly metaphorical; and such appears to have been the case with all languages in their earlier, and consequently ruder and more savage state.

---

1. Hence the French proverb, "Qui s'excuse, s'accuse" [who excuses himself, accuses himself].

2. See article "Authority," in Appendix to *Elements of Logic.*

3. Shakespeare, *Twelfth Night.*

4. In Poetry, perspicuity is indeed far from unimportant; but the most perfect degree of it is by no means so essential as in Prose works. See Part III. Chap. III. § 3.

5. This does not hold good in an equal degree in Ireland, where the language was introduced by the higher classes.

6. A remarkable instance of this is, that while the children of the higher classes almost always call their parents "Papa!" and "Mamma!" the children of the peasantry usually call them by the titles of "Father!" and "Mother!"

7. See *Elements of Logic,* "Fallacies," Chap. III. § 5. p. 146.

Reprinted from *Elements of Rhetoric,* seventh revised edition (London: Parker, 1846).

Thomas de Quincey
From "Rhetoric"[1] (1828; revised, 1859)

Thomas de Quincey (1785-1859), author of the Confessions of an English Opium-Eater *(1821), was one of the most prolific men of letters of the early nineteenth century, contributing essays on literature, history, and philosophy to the* London Magazine *and to* Blackwood's Edinburgh Magazine. *He had been an early admirer of the English romantic poets Wordsworth and Coleridge, and he became one of the major mediators of German thought to English readers. He derived from his romantic and German mentors a fundamental contrast between mechanical or rule-bound thought and organic, imaginative realization, and his essays on language and style see in imaginative freedom the basis of all successful literary composition. Although he had himself been educated at Oxford, and still claimed to follow some Aristotelian concepts, his essays were widely influential in the early Victorian period as making a counterpoise to more traditional, classically derived ideas of prose or rhetorical analysis. The first of the two essays excerpted here, "Rhetoric," appeared in the December 1828 issue of* Blackwood's Edinburgh Magazine *as a review of Richard Whately's classical* Elements of Rhetoric *(1828); de Quincey revised the essay for the collective* de Quincey *edition of his writings (volume 11, 1859). One of de Quincey's aims was to rescue the term* rhetoric *from being mere technique or decoration to its original, more philosophical concern with content, and his essay provides a useful polemic introduction to the romantic or "vitalist" emphasis on the organic nature of prose, as well as evidence of early-nineteenth-century reaction against eighteenth-century stylistic formality. The text here is de Quincey's revised essay.—Ed.*

No art cultivated by man has suffered more in the revolutions of taste and opinion than the art of Rhetoric. There was a time when, by an undue extension of this term, it designated the whole cycle of accomplishments which prepared a man for public affairs. From that height it has descended to a level with the arts of alchemy and astrology, as holding out promises which consist in a mixed degree of impostures wherever its pretensions happened to be weighty, and of trifles wherever they happened to be true. If we look into the prevailing theory of Rhetoric, under which it meets with so degrading an estimate, we shall find that it fluctuates between two different conceptions, according to one of which it is an art of ostentatious ornament, and according to the other an art of sophistry. A man is held to play the rhetorician when he treats a subject with more than usual gaiety of ornament, and, perhaps we may add, as an essential element in the idea, with *conscious* ornament. This is one view of Rhetoric; and under this what it accomplishes is not so much to persuade as to delight, not so much to win the assent as to stimulate the attention and captivate the taste. And even this purpose is attached to something separable and accidental in the *manner*. But the other idea of Rhetoric lays its foundation in something essential to the *matter*. This is that rhetoric of which Milton spoke as able "to dash maturest counsels and to make the worse appear the better reason." Now, it is clear that *argument* of some quality or other must be taken as the principle of this rhetoric; for those must be immature counsels indeed that could be dashed by mere embellishments of manner, or by artifices of diction and arrangement.

Here then we have in popular use two separate ideas of Rhetoric: one of which is occupied with the general end of the fine arts–that is to say, intellectual pleasure; the other applies itself more specifically to a definite purpose of utility, viz. fraud.

Such is the popular idea of Rhetoric; which wants both unity and precision. If we seek these formal teachers of Rhetoric, our embarrassment is not much relieved. All of them agree that Rhetoric may be defined *the art of persuasion*. But, if we inquire what *is* persuasion, we find them vague and indefinite or even contradictory. To waive a thousand of others, Dr. Whately, in the work before us, insists upon the *conviction* of the understanding as "an essential part of persuasion"; and, on the other hand, the author of the *Philosophy of Rhetoric* is equally satisfied that there is no persuasion without an appeal to the *passions*. Here are two views. We, for our parts, have a third which excludes both. Where conviction begins, the field of Rhetoric ends; that is our opinion: and, as to the passions, we contend that they

382

are not within the province of Rhetoric, but of Eloquence. . . .

    . . . The rhetorician's art in its glory and power has silently faded away before the stern tendencies of the age; and, if, by any peculiarity of taste or strong determination of the intellect, a rhetorician *en grande costume* were again to appear amongst us, it is certain that he would have no better welcome than a stare of surprise as a posture-maker or balancer, not more elevated in the general estimate, but far less amusing, than the acrobat, or funambulist, or equestrian gymnast. No; the age of Rhetoric, like that of Chivalry, has passed amongst forgotten things; and the rhetorician can have no more chance for returning than the rhapsodist of early Greece or the troubadour of romance. So multiplied are the modes of intellectual enjoyment in modern times that the choice is absolutely distracted; and in a boundless theatre of pleasures, to be had at little or no cost of intellectual activity, it would be marvellous indeed if any considerable audience could be found for an exhibition which presupposes a state of tense exertion on the part both of auditor and performer. To hang upon one's own thoughts as an object of conscious interest, to play with them, to watch and pursue them through a maze of inversions, evolutions, and harlequin changes, implies a condition of society either, like that in the monastic ages, forced to introvert its energies from mere defect of books (whence arose the scholastic metaphysics, admirable for its subtlety, but famishing the mind whilst it sharpened its edge in one exclusive direction); or, if it implies no absolute starvation of intellect, as in the case of the Roman rhetoric, which arose upon a considerable (though not very various) literature, it proclaims at least a quiescent state of the public mind, unoccupied with daily novelties, and at leisure from the agitations of eternal change.

    Growing out of the same condition of society, there is another cause at work which will for ever prevent the resurrection of rhetoric: viz. the necessities of public business, its vast extent, complexity, fulness of details, and consequent vulgarity, as compared with that of the ancients. . . .

    Under these malign aspects of the modern structure of society, a structure to which the whole world will be moulded as it becomes civilized, there can be no room for any revival of rhetoric in public speaking, and, from the same and other causes, acting upon the standard of public taste, quite as little room in written composition.

In spite, however, of the tendencies to this consummation, which have been long ripening, it is a fact that, next after Rome, England is the country in which rhetoric prospered most at a time when science was unborn as a popular interest, and the commercial activities of aftertimes were yet sleeping in their rudiments. This was in the period from the latter end of the sixteenth to the middle of the seventeenth century; and, though the English Rhetoric was less rigorously true to its own ideal than the Roman, and often modulated into a higher key of impassioned eloquence, yet unquestionably in some of its qualities it remains a monument of the very finest rhetorical powers. . . .

    In a single mechanical quality of good writing, that is in the structure of their sentences, the French rhetoricians, in common with French writers generally of that age, are superior to ours. This is what in common parlance is expressed (though inaccurately) by the word *style,* and is the subject of the third part of the work before us. Dr. Whately, however, somewhat disappoints us by his mode of treating it. He alleges, indeed, with some plausibility, that his subject bound him to consider style no further than as it was related to the purpose of persuasion. But, besides that it is impossible to treat it with effect in that mutilated section, even within the limits assumed we are not able to trace any outline of the law or system by which Dr. Whately has been governed in the choice of his topics. We find many very acute remarks delivered, but all in a desultory way, which leave the reader no means of judging how much of the ground has been surveyed and how much omitted. We regret also that he has not addressed himself more specifically to the question of English style,–a subject which has not yet received the comprehensive discussion which it merits. In the age of our great rhetoricians it is remarkable that the English language had never been made an object of conscious attention. No man seems to have reflected that there was a wrong and a right in the choice of words, in the choice of phrases, in the mechanism of sentences, or even in the grammar. Men wrote eloquently, because they wrote feelingly; they wrote idiomatically, because they wrote naturally and without affectation; but, if a false or acephalous structure of sentence, if a barbarous idiom or an exotic word happened to present itself, no writer of the seventeenth century seems to have had any such scrupulous sense of the dignity belonging to his own language as should make it a duty to reject it or worth his while to remodel a line.... We English even at this day have no learned grammar of our language; nay, we have allowed the blundering attempt in that department of an imbecile stranger (Lindley Murray) to supersede the learned (however imperfect) works of our own Wallis, Lowth, &c.; we have also no sufficient dictionary; and we have no work at all, sufficient or insufficient, on the phrases and idiomatic niceties of our language....

Hence an anomaly not found perhaps in any literature but ours,–that the most eminent English writers do not write their mother tongue without continual violations of propriety. With the single exception of William Wordsworth, who has paid an honourable attention to the purity and accuracy of his English, we believe that there is not one celebrated author of this day who has written two pages consecutively without some flagrant impropriety in the grammar (such as the eternal confusion of the preterite with the past participle, confusion of verbs transitive with intransitive, &c.), or some violation more or less of the vernacular idiom. If this last sort of blemish does not occur so frequently in modern books, the reason is that since Dr. Johnson's time the freshness of the idiomatic style has been too frequently abandoned for the lifeless mechanism of a style purely bookish and artificial....

1. Suggested as an excursive review by Whately's *Elements of Rhetoric*.

Reprinted from *Works*, volume 10, edited by David Masson (London: A. & C. Black, 1897).

Thomas de Quincey

From "Style" (1840; revised, 1859)

De Quincey's essay on style, first published in four parts in Blackwood's Edinburgh Magazine *in 1840-1841, is an attack on what he argues were the prevailing fallacies of early Victorian prose theorists—the attempt to assess content independent of style, and the overvaluing of Latin-derived symmetry in sentence structure. De Quincey develops his argument, however, into a wide-ranging assessment of the strengths and weaknesses of many different English prose styles, past and current, commenting on national styles in prose and their political origins, on the connections between oral speech patterns and written style, and on the stylistic consequences of the rise of newspaper journalism. The extracts given here all come from part one of the essay, originally in the July 1840 issue of* Blackwood's; *de Quincey revised the essay for the Collective Edition of his writings (Volume 11, 1859). The text here is de Quincey's revised essay.—Ed.*

. . . In no country upon earth, were it possible to carry such a maxim into practical effect, is it a more determining tendency of the national mind to value the *matter* of a book not only as paramount to the *manner,* but even as distinct from it, and as capable of a separate insulation. What first gave a shock to such a tendency must have been the unwilling and mysterious sense that in some cases the matter and the manner were so inextricably interwoven as not to admit of this coarse bisection. The one was embedded, entangled, and interfused through the other, in a way which bade defiance to such gross mechanical separations. But the tendency to view the two elements as in a separate relation still predominates, and, as a consequence, the tendency to undervalue the accomplishment of style. . . .

Generally and ultimately it is certain that our British disregard or inadequate appreciation of style, though a very lamentable fault, has had its origin in the manliness of the British character; in the sincerity and directness of the British taste; in the principle of "*esse quam videri,*" which might be taken as the key to much in our manner, much in the philosophy of our lives; and, finally, has had some part of its origin in that same love for the practical and the tangible which has so memorably governed the course of our higher speculations from Bacon to Newton. But, whatever may have been the origin of this most faulty habit, whatever mixed causes now support it, beyond all question it is that such a habit of disregard or of slight regard applied to all the arts of composition does exist in the most painful extent, and is detected by a practised eye in every page of almost every book that is published.

If you could look anywhere with a right to expect continual illustrations of what is good in the manifold qualities of style, it should reasonably be amongst our professional authors; but, as a body, they are distinguished by the most absolute carelessness in this respect. Whether in the choice of words and idioms, or in the construction of their sentences, it is not possible to conceive the principle of lazy indifference carried to a more revolting extremity. Proof lies before you, spread out upon every page, that no excess of awkwardness, or of inelegance, or of unrhythmical cadence, is so rated in the tariff of faults as to balance in the writer's estimate the trouble of remoulding a clause, of interpolating a phrase, or even of striking the pen through a superfluous word. In our own experience it has happened that we have known an author so laudably fastidious in this subtle art as to have recast one chapter of a series no less than seventeen times: so difficult was the ideal or model of excellence which he kept before his mind; so indefatigable was his labour for mounting to the level of that ideal. Whereas, on the other hand, with regard to a large majority of the writers now carrying forward the literature of the country from the last generation to the next, the evidence is perpetual not so much that they rest satisfied with their own random preconceptions of each clause or sentence as that they never trouble themselves to form any such preconceptions. Whatever words tumble out under the blindest accidents of the moment, those are the words retained; whatever sweep is impressed by chance upon the motion of a period, that is the arrangement ratified. To fancy that men thus determinately careless as to the grosser elements of style would pause to survey distant proportions, or to adjust any more delicate symmetries of good compositions, would be visionary. As to the links of connexion, the transitions, and the many other functions of logic in good writing, things are come to such a pass that what was held true of Rome in two separate ages by two great rhetoricians, and of Constantinople in an age long posterior, may now be affirmed of England: the idiom of our language, the mother tongue, survives only amongst our women and children; not, Heaven knows, amongst our women who write books–they are often painfully conspicuous for all that disfigures authorship–but amongst well-educated women not professionally given to literature. Cicero and Quintilian, each for his own generation, ascribed something of the same pre-eminence to the noble matrons of Rome; and more than one writer of the Lower Empire has recorded of Byzantium that in the nurseries of that city was found the last home for the purity of the ancient Greek. . . .

The pure racy idiom of colloquial or household English, we have insisted, must be looked for in the circles of well-educated women not too closely connected with books. It is certain that books, in any language, will tend to encourage a diction too remote from the style of spoken idiom; whilst the greater solemnity and the more ceremonial costume of regular literature must often demand such a non-idiomatic diction upon mere principles of good taste. But why is it that in our day literature has taken so determinate a swing towards this professional language of books as to justify some fears that the other extreme of the free colloquial idiom will perish as a living dialect? The apparent cause lies in a phenomenon of modern life which on other accounts also is entitled to anxious consideration. It is in newspapers that we must look for the main reading of this generation; and in newspapers, therefore, we must seek for the causes operating upon the style of the age. Seventy years ago this tendency in political journals to usurp upon the practice of books, and to mould the style of writers, was noticed by a most acute observer, himself one of the most brilliant writers in the class of satiric sketchers and personal historians that any nation has produced. Already before 1770 the late Lord Orford, then simply Horace Walpole, was in the habit of saying to any man who consulted him on the cultivation of style,–"Style is it that you want? Oh, go and look into the news-

papers for a style." This was said half contemptuously and half seriously. But the evil has now become overwhelming. One single number of a London morning paper,–which in half a century has expanded from the size of a dinner napkin to that of a breakfast tablecloth, from that to a carpet, and will soon be forced, by the expansions of public business, into something resembling the mainsail of a frigate,–already is equal in printed matter to a very large octavo volume. Every old woman in the nation now reads daily a vast miscellany in one volume royal octavo. The evil of this, as regards the quality of knowledge communicated, admits of no remedy. Public business, in its whole unwieldy compass, must always form the subject of these daily chronicles. Nor is there much room to expect any change in the style. The evil effect of this upon the style of the age may be reduced to two forms. Formerly the natural impulse of every man was spontaneously to use the language of life; the language of books was a secondary attainment, not made without effort. Now, on the contrary, the daily composers of newspapers have so long dealt in the professional idiom of books as to have brought it home to every reader in the nation who does not violently resist it by some domestic advantages. Time was, within our own remembrance, that, if you should have heard, in passing along the street, from any old apple-woman such a phrase as "I will *avail myself* of your kindness," forthwith you would have shied like a skittish horse; you would have run away in as much terror as any old Roman upon those occasions when *bos loquebatur*. At present you swallow such marvels as matters of course. The whole artificial dialect of books has come into play as the dialect of ordinary life. This is one form of the evil impressed upon our style by journalism: a dire monotony of bookish idiom has encrusted and stiffened all native freedom of expression, like some scaly leprosy or elephantiasis, barking and hide-binding the fine natural pulses of the elastic flesh. Another and almost a worse evil has established itself in the prevailing structure of sentences. Every man who has had any experience in writing knows how natural it is for hurry and fulness of matter to discharge itself by vast sentences, involving clause within clause ad infinitum; how difficult it is, and how much a work of art, to break up this huge fasciculus of cycle and epicycle into a graceful succession of sentences, long intermingled with short, each modifying the other, and arising musically by links of spontaneous connexion. Now, the plethoric form of period, this monster model of sentence, bloated with decomplex intercalations, and exactly repeating the form of syntax which distinguishes an act of Parliament, is the prevailing model in newspaper eloquence. Crude undigested masses of suggestion, furnishing rather raw materials for composition and jottings for the memory than any formal developments of the ideas, describe the quality of writing which *must* prevail in journalism: not from defect of talents,–which are at this day of that superior class which may be presumed from the superior importance of the function itself,–but from the necessities of hurry and of instant compliance with an instant emergency, granting no possibility for revision or opening for amended thought, which are evils attached to the flying velocities of public business. . . .

 . . . Pedantry, though it were unconscious pedantry, once steadily diffused through a nation as to the very moulds of its thinking, and the general tendencies of its expression, could not but stiffen the natural graces of composition, and weave fetters about the free movement of human thought. This would interfere as effectually with our power of enjoying much that is excellent in our past literature as it would with our future powers of producing. And such an agency has been too long at work amongst us not to have already accomplished some part of these separate evils. Amongst women of education, as we have argued above, standing aloof from literature, and less uniformly drawing their intellectual sustenance from newspapers, the deadening effects have been partially counteracted. Here and there, amongst individuals alive to the particular evils of the age, and watching the very set of the current, there may have been even a more systematic counteraction applied to the mischief. But the great evil in such cases is this, that we cannot see the extent of the changes wrought or being wrought, from having ourselves partaken in them. *Tempora mutantur*; and naturally, if we could review them with the neutral eye of a stranger, it would be impossible for us not to see the extent of those changes. But our eye is *not* neutral; we also have partaken in the changes; *nos et mutamur in illis*. And this fact disturbs the power of appreciating those changes. Every one of us would have felt, sixty years ago, that the general tone and colouring of a style was stiff, bookish, pedantic, which, from the habituation of our organs, we now feel to be natural and within the privilege of learned art. Direct objective qualities it is

always by comparison easy to measure; but the difficulty commences when we have to combine with this outer measurement of the object another corresponding measurement of the subjective or inner qualities by which we apply the measure; that is, when besides the objects projected to a distance from the spectator, we have to allow for variations or disturbances in the very eye which surveys them. The eye cannot see itself; we cannot project from ourselves, and contemplate as an object, our own contemplating faculty, or appreciate our own appreciating power. Biasses, therefore, or gradual warpings, that have occurred in our critical faculty as applied to style, we cannot allow for: and these biasses will unconsciously mask to our perceptions an amount of change in the quality of popular style such as we could not easily credit.

 Separately from this change for the worse in the drooping idiomatic freshness of our diction, which is a change that has been going on for a century, the other character defect of this age lies in the tumid and tumultuary structure of our sentences. The one change has partly grown out of the other. Ever since a more bookish air was impressed upon composition without much effort by the Latinized and artificial phraseology, by forms of expression consecrated to books, and by "long-tailed words in *osity* and *ation*," –either because writers felt that already, in this one act of preference shown to the artificial vocabulary, they had done enough to establish a differential character of regular composition, and on that consideration thought themselves entitled to neglect the combination of their words into sentences or periods; or because there is a real natural sympathy between the Latin phraseology and a Latin structure of sentence,–certain it is and remarkable that our popular style, in the common limited sense of arrangement applied to words or the syntax of sentences, has laboured with two faults that might have been thought incompatible: it has been artificial, by artifices peculiarly adapted to the powers of the Latin language, and yet at the very same time careless and disordinate. There is a strong idea expressed by the Latin words *inconditus, disorganized,* or rather *unorganized.* Now, in spite of its artificial bias, that is the very epithet which will best characterize our newspaper style. To be viewed as susceptible of organization, such periods must already be elaborate and artificial; to be viewed as not having received it, such periods must be hyperbolically careless. . . .

There are many other researches belonging to this subtlest of subjects, affecting both the logic and the ornaments of style. . . . But for instant practical use, though far less difficult for investigation, yet for that reason far more tangible and appreciable, would be all the suggestions proper to the other head. . . . Half a dozen rules for evading the most frequently recurring forms of awkwardness, of obscurity, of misproportion, and of double meaning, would do more to assist a writer in practice, laid under some necessity of hurry, than volumes of general disquisition. It makes us blush to add that even grammar is so little of a perfect attainment amongst us that, with two or three exceptions (one being Shakspere, whom some affect to consider as belonging to a semi-barbarous age), we have never seen the writer, through a circuit of prodigious reading, who has not sometimes violated the accidence or the syntax of English grammar.

Whatever becomes of our own possible speculations, we shall conclude with insisting on the growing necessity of style as a practical interest of daily life. Upon subjects of public concern, and in proportion to that concern, there will always be a suitable (and as letters extend a growing) competition. Other things being equal, or appearing to be equal, the determining principle for the public choice will lie in the style. Of a German book, otherwise entitled to respect, it was said–*er lässt sich nicht lesen*–it does not permit itself to be read, such and so repulsive was the style. Among ourselves this has long been true of newspapers. They do not suffer themselves to be read *in extenso;* and they are read short, with what injury to the mind we have noticed. The same style of reading, once largely practised, is applied universally. To this special evil an improvement of style would apply a special redress. The same improvement is otherwise clamorously called for by each man's interest of competition. Public luxury, which is gradually consulted by everything else, must at length be consulted in style. . . .

Reprinted from *Works,* volume 10, edited by David Masson (London: A. & C. Black, 1897).

Thomas Carlyle

From "The Hero as Man of Letters: Johnson, Rousseau, Burns" (1841)

Thomas Carlyle (1795-1881), as one of the outstanding critics, social analysts, and historians of the early Victorian period, was especially concerned with the changing role of the essayist and prose writer in the period. In his early essay "Signs of the Times" (1829) he had argued that new technology, and the new marketing methods, had changed the nature of literature: "Literature, too, has its Paternoster-Row mechanism, its Trade-dinners, its Editorial conclaves, and huge subterranean puffing bellows; so that books are not only printed, but, in great measure, written and sold, by machinery. . . . In no former era has Literature, the printed communication of Thought, been of such importance as it is now . . . the true Church of England, at this moment, lies in the Editors of its Newspapers." In his essay "Characteristics" (1831), he had extended these criticisms from ephemeral and periodical literature to the "upper" regions of imaginative literature also: "Spontaneous devotedness to the object, . . . what we call inspiration, has well-nigh ceased to appear in Literature . . . at the last Leipzig Fair [for book-sellers], there was advertised a Review of Reviews. By and by, it will be found that all Literature has become one boundless self-devouring Review." It was against this background of dissatisfaction with the contemporary scene that in 1840 Carlyle included "The Hero as Man of Letters" in his lecture series on the role of heroes in shaping human history; although the three men he discusses (Samuel Johnson, Jean-Jacques Rousseau, and Robert Burns) were all eighteenth-century writers, Carlyle's focus was clearly on what their stories could illustrate about the plight and opportunities for a heroic man of letters in the early Victorian period. The original lecture was delivered on 19 May 1840 and published in Carlyle's On Heroes, Hero-Worship and the Heroic in History. *The text reprinted here is from the Centenary Edition of Carlyle's works–Ed.*

Hero-Gods, Prophets, Poets, Priests are forms of Heroism that belong to the old ages, make their appearance in the remotest times; some of them have ceased to be possible long since, and cannot any more show themselves in this world. The Hero as *Man of Letters*, again, of which class we are to speak today, is altogether a product of these new ages; and so long as the won-drous art of *Writing*, or of Ready-writing which we call *Printing*, subsists, he may be expected to continue, as one of the main forms of Heroism for all future ages. He is, in various respects, a very singular phenomenon.

He is new, I say; he has hardly lasted above a century in the world yet. Never, till about a hundred years ago, was there seen any figure of a Great Soul living apart in that anomalous manner; endeavouring to speak-forth the inspiration that was in him by Printed Books, and find place and subsistence by what the world would please to give him for doing that. Much had been sold and bought, and left to make its own bargain in the marketplace; but the inspired wisdom of a Heroic Soul never till then, in that naked manner. He, with his copy-rights and copy-wrongs, in his squalid garret, in his rusty coat; ruling (for this is what he does), from his grave, after death, whole nations and generations who would, or would not, give him bread while living,–is a rather curious spectacle! Few shapes of Heroism can be more unexpected.

Alas, the Hero from of old has had to cramp himself into strange shapes: the world knows not well at any time what to do with him, so foreign is his aspect in the world! It seemed absurd to us, that men, in their rude admiration, should take some wise great Odin for a god, and worship him as such; some wise great Mahomet for one god-inspired, and religiously follow his Law for twelve centuries: but that a wise great Johnson, a Burns, a Rousseau, should be taken for some idle nondescript, extant in the world to amuse idleness, and have a few coins and applauses thrown him, that he might live thereby; *this* perhaps, as before hinted, will one day seem a still absurder phasis of things!–Meanwhile, since it is the spiritual always that determines the material, this same Man-of-Letters Hero must be regarded as our most important modern person. He, such as he may be, is the soul of all. What he teaches, the whole world will do and make. The world's manner of dealing with him is the most significant feature of the world's general position. Looking well at his life, we may get a glance, as deep as is readily possible for us, into the life of those singular centuries which have produced him, in which we ourselves live and work.

There are genuine Men of Letters, and not genuine; as in every kind there is a genuine and a spurious. If *Hero* be taken to mean genuine, then I say the Hero as Man of Letters will be found discharging a function for us which is ever honourable, ever the highest; and was once well known to be the highest. He is uttering-forth, in such a way as he has, the inspired soul of him; all that a man, in any case, can do. I say *inspired;* for what we call 'originality,' 'sincerity,' 'genius,' the heroic quality we have no good name for, signifies that. The Hero is he who lives in the inward sphere of things, in the True, Divine and Eternal, which exists always, unseen to most, under the Temporary, Trivial: his being is in that; he declares that abroad, by act or speech as it may be, in declaring himself abroad. His life, as we said before, is a piece of the everlasting heart of Nature herself: all men's life is,—but the weak many know not the fact, and are untrue to it, in most times; the strong few are strong, heroic, perennial because it cannot be hidden from them. The Man of Letters, like every Hero, is there to proclaim this in such sort as he can. Intrinsically it is the same function which the old generations named a man Prophet, Priest, Divinity for doing; which all manner of Heroes, by speech or by act, are sent into the world to do.

Fichte the German Philosopher delivered, some forty years ago at Erlangen, a highly remarkable Course of Lectures on this subject: *'Ueber das Wesen des Gelehrten,* On the Nature of the Literary Man.' Fichte, in conformity with the Transcendental Philosophy, of which he was a distinguished teacher, declares first: That all things which we see or work with in this Earth, especially we ourselves and all persons, are as a kind of vesture or sensuous Appearance: that under all there lies, as the essence of them, what he calls the 'Divine Idea of the World'; this is the Reality which 'lies at the bottom of all Appearance.' To the mass of men no such Divine Idea is recognisable in the world; they live merely, says Fichte, among the superficialities, practicalities, and shows of the world, not dreaming that there is anything divine under them. But the Man of Letters is sent hither specially that he may discern for himself, and make manifest to us, this same Divine Idea: in every new generation it will manifest itself in a new dialect; and he is there for the purpose of doing that. Such is Fichte's phraseology; with

which we need not quarrel. It is his way of naming what I here, by other words, am striving imperfectly to name; what there is at present no name for: The unspeakable Divine Significance, full of splendour, of wonder and terror, that lies in the being of every man, of every thing,—the Presence of the God who made every man and thing. Mahomet taught this in his dialect; Odin in his: it is the thing which all thinking hearts, in one dialect or another, are here to teach.

Fichte calls the Man of Letters, therefore, a Prophet, or as he prefers to phrase it, a Priest, continually unfolding the Godlike to men: Men of Letters are a perpetual Priesthood, from age to age, teaching all men that a God is still present in their life; that all 'Appearance,' whatsoever we see in the world, is but as a vesture for the 'Divine Idea of the World,' for 'that which lies at the bottom of Appearance.' In the true Literary Man there is thus ever, acknowledged or not by the world, a sacredness: he is the light of the world; the world's Priest;—guiding it, like a sacred Pillar of Fire, in its dark pilgrimage through the waste of Time. Fichte discriminates with sharp zeal the *true* Literary Man, what we here call the *Hero* as Man of Letters, from multitudes of false unheroic. Whoever lives not wholly in this Divine Idea, or living partially in it, struggles not, as for the one good, to live wholly in it,—he is, let him live where else he like, in what pomps and prosperities he like, no Literary Man; he is, says Fichte, a 'Bungler, *Stümper.*' Or at best, if he belong to the prosaic provinces, he may be a 'Hodman'; Fichte even calls him elsewhere a 'Nonentity,' and has in short no mercy for him, no wish that *he* should continue happy among us! This is Fichte's notion of the Man of Letters. It means, in its own form, precisely what we here mean.

In this point of view, I consider that, for the last hundred years, by far the notablest of all Literary Men is Fichte's countryman, Goethe. To that man too, in a strange way, there was given what we may call a life in the Divine Idea of the World; vision of the inward divine mystery: and strangely, out of his Books, the world rises imaged once more as godlike, the workmanship and temple of a God. Illuminated all, not in fierce impure fire-splendour as of Mahomet, but in mild celestial radiance;—really a Prophecy in these most unprophetic times; to my mind, by far the greatest, though one of the quietest, among all the great things that have come to pass in them. Our chosen specimen of the Hero as Literary Man would be this Goethe. And it were a very pleasant plan for me here to discourse of his heroism: for I consider him to be a true Hero; heroic in what he said and did, and perhaps still more in what he did not say and did not do; to me a noble spectacle: a great heroic ancient man, speaking and keeping silence as an ancient Hero, in the guise of a most modern, high-bred, high-cultivated Man of Letters! We have had no such spectacle; no man capable of affording such, for the last hundred-and-fifty years.

But at present, such is the general state of knowledge about Goethe, it were worse than useless to attempt speaking of him in this case. Speak as I might, Goethe, to the great majority of you, would remain problematic, vague; no impression but a false one could be realised. Him we must leave to future times. Johnson, Burns, Rousseau, three great figures from a prior time, from a far inferior state of circumstances, will suit us better here. Three men of the Eighteenth Century; the conditions of their life far more resemble what those of ours still are in England, than what Goethe's in Germany were. Alas, these men did not conquer like him; they fought bravely, and fell. They were not heroic bringers of the light, but heroic seekers of it. They lived under galling conditions; struggling as under mountains of impediment, and could not unfold themselves into clearness, or victorious interpretation of that 'Divine Idea.' It is rather the *Tombs* of three Literary Heroes that I have to show you. There are the monumental heaps, under which three spiritual giants lie buried. Very mournful, but also great and full of interest for us. We will linger by them for a while.

Complaint is often made, in these times, of what we call the disorganised condition of society: how ill many arranged forces of society fulfil their work; how many powerful forces are seen working in a wasteful, chaotic, altogether unarranged manner. It is too just a complaint, as we all know. But perhaps if we look at this of Books and the Writers of Books, we shall find here, as it were, the summary of all other disorganisation;—a sort of *heart*, from which, and to which, all other confusion circulates in the world! Considering what Book-writers do in the world, and what the world does with Book-writers, I should say, It is the most anomalous thing the world at present has to show.—We should get into a sea far beyond sounding, did we attempt to give account of this: but we must glance at it for the sake of our subject. The worst

element in the life of these three Literary Heroes was, that they found their business and position such a chaos. On the beaten road there is tolerable travelling; but it is sore work, and many have to perish, fashioning a path through the impassable!

Our pious Fathers, feeling well what importance lay in the speaking of man to men, founded churches, made endowments, regulations; everywhere in the civilised world there is a Pulpit, environed with all manner of complex dignified appurtenances and furtherances, that therefrom a man with the tongue may, to best advantage, address his fellow-men. They felt that this was the most important thing; that without this there was no good thing. It is a right pious work, that of theirs; beautiful to behold! But now with the art of Writing, with the art of Printing, a total change has come over that business. The Writer of a Book, is not he a Preacher preaching not to this parish or that, on this day or that, but to all men in all times and places? Surely it is of the last importance that *he* do his work right, whoever do it wrong;—that the *eye* report not falsely, for then all the other members are astray! Well; how he may do his work, whether he do it right or wrong, or do it at all, is a point which no man in the world has taken the pains to think of. To a certain shopkeeper, trying to get some money for his books, if lucky, he is of some importance; to no other man of any. Whence he came, whither he is bound, by what ways he arrived, by what he might be furthered on his course, no one asks. He is an accident in society. He wanders like a wild Ishmaelite, in a world of which he is as the spiritual light, either the guidance or the misguidance!

Certainly the Art of Writing is the most miraculous of all things man has devised. Odin's *Runes* were the first form of the work of a Hero; *Books*, written words, are still miraculous *Runes*, the latest form! In Books lies the *soul* of the whole Past Time; the articulate audible voice of the Past, when the body and material substance of it has altogether vanished like a dream. Mighty fleets and armies, harbours and arsenals, vast cities, high-domed, many-engined,—they are precious, great: but what do they become? Agamemnon, the many Agamemnons, Pericleses, and their Greece; all is gone now to some ruined fragments, dumb mournful wrecks and blocks: but the Books of Greece! There Greece, to every thinker, still very literally lives; can be called-up again into life. No magic *Rune* is stranger than a

Book. All that Mankind has done, thought, gained or been: it is lying as in magic preservation in the pages of Books. They are the chosen possession of men.

Do not Books still accomplish *miracles*, as *Runes* were fabled to do? They persuade men. Not the wretchedest circulating-library novel, which foolish girls thumb and con in remote villages, but will help to regulate the actual practical weddings and households of those foolish girls. So 'Celia' felt, so 'Clifford' acted: the foolish Theorem of Life, stamped into those young brains, comes out as a solid Practice one day. Consider whether any *Rune* in the wildest imagination of Mythologist ever did such wonders as, on the actual firm Earth, some Books have done! What built St. Paul's Cathedral? Look at the heart of the matter, it was that divine Hebrew BOOK,—the word partly of the man Moses, an outlaw tending his Midianitish herds, four thousand years ago, in the wildernesses of Sinai! It is the strangest of things, yet nothing is truer. With the art of Writing, of which Printing is a simple, an inevitable and comparatively insignificant corollary, the true reign of miracles for mankind commenced. It related, with a wondrous new contiguity and perpetual closeness, the Past and Distant with the Present in time and place; all times and all places with this our actual Here and Now. All things were altered for men; all modes of important work of men: teaching, preaching, governing, and all else.

To look at Teaching, for instance. Universities are a notable, respectable product of the modern ages. Their existence too is modified, to the very basis of it, by the existence of Books. Universities arose while there were yet no Books procurable; while a man, for a single Book, had to give an estate of land. That, in those circumstances, when a man had some knowledge to communicate, he should do it by gathering the learners round him, face to face, was a necessity for him. If you wanted to know what Abelard knew, you must go and listen to Abelard. Thousands, as many as thirty-thousand, went to hear Abelard and that metaphysical theology of his. And now for any other teacher who had something of his own to teach, there was a great convenience opened: so many thousands eager to learn were already assembled yonder; of all places the best place for him was that. For any third teacher it was better still; and grew ever the better, the more teachers there came. It only needed now that the King took notice of this new phenome-

non; combined or agglomerated various schools into one school; gave it edifices, privileges, encouragements, and named it *Universitas*, or School of all Sciences: the University of Paris, in its essential characters, was there. The model of all subsequent Universities; which down even to these days, for six centuries now, have gone on to found themselves. Such, I conceive, was the origin of Universities.

It is clear, however, that with this simple circumstance, facility of getting Books, the whole conditions of the business from top to bottom were changed. Once invent Printing, you metamorphosed all Universities, or superseded them! The Teacher needed not now to gather men personally round him, that he might *speak* to them what he knew: print it in a Book, and all learners far and wide, for a trifle, had it each at his own fireside, much more effectually to learn it!— Doubtless there is still peculiar virtue in Speech; even writers of Books may still, in some circumstances, find it convenient to speak also,—witness our present meeting here! There is, one would say, and must ever remain while man has a tongue, a distinct province for Speech as well as for Writing and Printing. In regard to all things this must remain; to Universities among others. But the limits of the two have nowhere yet been pointed out, ascertained; much less put in practice: the University which would completely take-in that great new fact, of the existence of Printed Books, and stand on a clear footing for the Nineteenth Century as the Paris one did for the Thirteenth, has not yet come into existence. If we think of it, all that a University, or final highest School can do for us, is still but what the first School began doing,—teach us to *read*. We learn to *read*, in various languages, in various sciences; we learn the alphabet and letters of all manner of Books. But the place where we go to get knowledge, even theoretic knowledge, is the Books themselves! It depends on what we read, after all manner of Professors have done their best for us. The true University of these days is a Collection of Books.

But to the Church itself, as I hinted already, all is changed, in its preaching, in its working, by the introduction of Books. The Church is the working recognised Union of our Priests or Prophets, of those who by wise teaching guide the souls of men. While there was no Writing, even while there was no Easy-writing or *Printing*, the preaching of the voice was the natural sole method of performing this. But now with Books!—

He that can write a true Book, to persuade England, is not he the Bishop and Archbishop, the Primate of England and of All England? I many a time say, the writers of Newspapers, Pamphlets, Poems, Books, these *are* the real working effective Church of a modern country. Nay not only our preaching, but even our worship, is not it too accomplished by means of Printed Books? The noble sentiment which a gifted soul has clothed for us in melodious words, which brings melody into our hearts,–is not this essentially, if we will understand it, of the nature of worship? There are many, in all countries, who, in this confused time, have no other method of worship. He who, in any way, shows us better than we knew before that a lily of the fields is beautiful, does he not show it us as an effluence of the Fountain of all Beauty; as the *handwriting*, made visible there, of the great Maker of the Universe? He has sung for us, made us sing with him, a little verse of a sacred Psalm. Essentially so. How much more he who sings, who says, or in any way brings home to our heart the noble doings, feelings, darings and endurances of a brother man! He has verily touched our hearts as with a live coal *from the altar*. Perhaps there is no worship more authentic.

Literature, so far as it is Literature, is an 'apocalypse of Nature,' a revealing of the 'open secret.' It may well enough be named, in Fichte's style, a 'continuous revelation' of the Godlike in the Terrestrial and Common. The Godlike does ever, in very truth, endure there; is brought out, now in this dialect, now in that, with various degrees of clearness: all true gifted Singers and Speakers are, consciously or unconsciously, doing so. The dark stormful indignation of a Byron, so wayward and perverse, may have touches of it; nay the withered mockery of a French sceptic,– his mockery of the False, a love and worship of the True. How much more the sphere-harmony of a Shakspeare, of a Goethe; the cathedral-music of a Milton! They are something too, those humble genuine lark-notes of a Burns,–skylark, starting from the humble furrow, far overhead into the blue depths, and singing to us so genuinely there! For all true singing is of the nature of worship; as indeed all true *working* may be said to be,–whereof such *singing* is but the record, and fit melodious representation, to us. Fragments of a real 'Church Liturgy' and 'Body of Homilies,' strangely disguised from the common eye, are to be found weltering in that huge froth-ocean of Printed Speech we loosely call Literature! Books are our Church too.

Or turning now to the Government of men. Witenagemote, old Parliament, was a great thing. The affairs of the nation were there deliberated and decided; what we were to *do* as a nation. But does not, though the name Parliament subsists, the parliamentary debate go on now, everywhere and at all times, in a far more comprehensive way, *out* of Parliament altogether? Burke said there were Three Estates in Parliament; but, in the Reporters' Gallery yonder, there sat a *Fourth Estate* more important far than they all. It is not a figure of speech, or a witty saying; it is a literal fact,–very momentous to us in these times. Literature is our Parliament too. Printing, which comes necessarily out of Writing, I say often, is equivalent to Democracy: invent Writing, Democracy is inevitable. Writing brings Printing; brings universal every-day extempore Printing, as we see at present. Whoever can speak, speaking now to the whole nation, becomes a power, a branch of government, with inalienable weight in law-making, in all acts of authority. It matters not what rank he has, what revenues or garnitures: the requisite thing is, that he have a tongue which others will listen to; this and nothing more is requisite. The nation is governed by all that has tongue in the nation: Democracy is virtually *there*. Add only, that whatsoever power exists will have itself, by and by, organised; working secretly under bandages, obscurations, obstructions, it will never rest till it get to work free, unencumbered, visible to all. Democracy virtually extant will insist on becoming palpably extant.–

On all sides, are we not driven to the conclusion that, of the things which man can do or make here below, by far the most momentous, wonderful and worthy are the things we call Books! Those poor bits of rag-paper with black ink on them;–from the Daily Newspaper to the sacred Hebrew BOOK, what have they not done, what are they not doing!–For indeed, whatever be the outward form of the thing (bits of paper, as we say, and black ink), is it not verily, at bottom, the highest act of man's faculty that produces a Book? It is the *Thought* of man; the true thaumaturgic virtue; by which man works all things whatsoever. All that he does, and brings to pass, is the vesture of a Thought. This London City, with all its houses, palaces, steam-engines, cathedrals, and huge immeasurable traffic and tumult, what is it but a Thought, but millions of Thoughts made into One;–a huge immeasurable Spirit of a THOUGHT, embodied in brick, in iron, smoke, dust, Palaces, Parliaments, Hackney Coaches, Katherine Docks, and the rest of it! Not a brick was made but some man had to *think* of the making of that brick.–The thing we called 'bits of paper with traces of black ink,' is the *purest* embodiment a Thought of man can have. No wonder it is, in all ways, the activest and noblest.

All this, of the importance and supreme importance of the Man of Letters in modern Society, and how the Press is to such a degree superseding the Pulpit, the Senate, the *Senatus Academicus* and much else, has been admitted for a good while; and recognised often enough, in late times, with a sort of sentimental triumph and wonderment. It seems to me, the Sentimental by and by will have to give place to the Practical. If Men of Letters *are* so incalculably influential, actually performing such work for us from age to age, and even from day to day, then I think we may conclude that Men of Letters will not always wander like unrecognised unregulated Ishmaelites among us! Whatsoever thing, as I said above, has virtual unnoticed power will cast-off its wrappages, bandages, and step-forth one day with palpably articulated, universally visible power. That one man wear the clothes, and take the wages, of a function which is done by quite another: there can be no profit in this; this is not right, it is wrong. And yet, alas, the *making* of it right,–what a business, for long times to come! Sure enough, this that we call Organisation of the Literary Guild is still a great way off, encumbered with all manner of complexities. If you asked me what were the best possible organisation for the Men of Letters in modern society; the arrangement of furtherance and regulation, grounded the most accurately on the actual facts of their position and of the world's position,–I should beg to say that the problem far exceeded my faculty! It is not one man's faculty; it is that of many successive men turned earnestly upon it, that will bring-out even an approximate solution. What the best arrangement were, none of us could say. But if you ask, Which is the worst? I answer: This which we now have, that Chaos should sit umpire in it; this is the worst. To the best, or any good one, there is yet a long way.

One remark I must not omit, That royal or parliamentary grants of money are by no means the chief thing wanted! To give our Men of Letters stipends, endowments and all furtherance of cash, will do little towards the business. On the whole, one is weary of hearing about the omnipotence of money. I will say rather that, for a genuine man, it is no evil to be poor; that there ought to be Literary Men poor,–to show whether they are genuine or not! Mendicant Orders, bodies of good men doomed to *beg*, were instituted in the Christian Church; a most natural and even necessary development of the spirit of Christianity. It was itself founded on Poverty, on Sorrow, Contradiction, Crucifixion, every species of worldly Distress and Degradation. We may say, that he who has not known those things, and learned from them the priceless lessons they have to teach, has missed a good opportunity of schooling. To beg, and go barefoot, in coarse woollen cloak with a rope round your loins, and be despised of all the world, was no beautiful business;–nor an honourable one in any eye, till the nobleness of those who did so had made it honoured of some!

Begging is not in our course at the present time: but for the rest of it, who will say that a Johnson is not perhaps the better for being poor? It is needful for him, at all rates, to know that outward profit, that success of any kind is *not* the goal he has to aim at. Pride, vanity, ill-conditioned egoism of all sorts, are bred in his heart, as in every heart; need, above all, to be cast-out of his heart,–to be, with whatever pangs, torn-out of it, cast-forth from it, as a thing worthless. Byron, born rich and noble, made-out even less than Burns, poor and plebeian. Who knows but, in that same 'best possible organisation' as yet far off, Poverty may still enter as an important element? What if our Men of Letters, Men setting-up to be Spiritual Heroes, were still *then*, as they now are, a kind of 'involuntary monastic order'; bound still to this same ugly Poverty,–till they had tried what was in it too, till they had learned to make it too do for them! Money, in truth, can do much, but it cannot do all. We must know the province of it, and confine it there; and even spurn it back, when it wishes to get farther.

Besides, were the money-furtherances, the proper season for them, the fit assigner of them, all settled,–how is the Burns to be recognised that merits these? He must pass through the ordeal, and prove himself. *This* ordeal; this wild welter of a chaos which is called Literary Life: this too is a kind of ordeal! There is clear truth in the idea that a struggle from the lower classes of society, towards the upper regions and rewards of society, must ever continue. Strong men are born there, who ought to stand elsewhere than there. The manifold, inextricably complex, universal struggle of these constitutes, and must constitute, what is called the progress of society. For Men of Letters, as for all other sorts of men.

How to regulate that struggle? There is the whole question. To leave it as it is, at the mercy of blind Chance; a whirl of distracted atoms, one cancelling the other; one of the thousand arriving saved, nine-hundred-and-ninety-nine lost by the way; your royal Johnson languishing inactive in garrets, or harnessed to the yoke of Printer Cave; your Burns dying broken-hearted as a Gauger; your Rousseau driven into mad exasperation, kindling French Revolutions by his paradoxes: this, as we said, is clearly enough the *worst* regulation. The *best*, alas, is far from us!

And yet there can be no doubt but it is coming; advancing on us, as yet hidden in the bosom of centuries: this is a prophecy one can risk. For so soon as men get to discern the importance of a thing, they do infallibly set about arranging it, facilitating, forwarding it; and rest not till, in some approximate degree, they have accomplished that. I say, of all Priesthoods, Aristocracies, Governing Classes at present extant in the world, there is no class comparable for importance to that Priesthood of the Writers of Books. This is a fact which he who runs may read,—and draw inferences from. 'Literature will take care of itself,' answered Mr Pitt, when applied-to for some help for Burns. 'Yes,' adds Mr Southey, 'it will take care of itself; *and of you too,* if you do not look to it!'

The result to individual Men of Letters is not the momentous one; they are but individuals, an infinitesimal fraction of the great body; they can struggle on, and live or else die, as they have been wont. But it deeply concerns the whole society, whether it will set its *light* on high places, to walk thereby; or trample it under foot, and scatter it in all ways of wild waste (not without conflagration), as heretofore! Light is the one thing wanted for the world. Put wisdom in the head of the world, the world will fight its battle victoriously, and be the best world man can make it. I call this anomaly of a disorganic Literary Class the heart of all other anomalies, at once product and parent; some good arrangement for that would be as the *punctum saliens* of a new vitality and just arrangement for all. Already, in some European countries, in France, in Prussia, one traces some beginnings of an arrangement for the Literary Class; indicating the gradual possibility of such. I believe that it is possible; that it will have to be possible.

By far the most interesting fact I hear about the Chinese is one on which we cannot arrive at clearness, but which excites endless curiosity even in the dim state: this namely, that they do attempt to make their Men of Letters their Governors! It would be rash to say, one understood how this was done, or with what degree of success it was done. All such things must be very *un*successful; yet a small degree of success is precious; the very attempt how precious! There does seem to be, all over China, a more or less active search everywhere to discover the men of talent that grow up in the young generation. Schools there are for every one: a foolish sort of training, yet still a sort. The youths who distinguish themselves in the lower school are promoted into favourable stations in the higher, that they may still more distinguish themselves,—forward and forward: it appears to be out of these that the Official Persons, and incipient Governors, are taken. These are they whom they *try* first, whether they can govern or not. And surely with the best hope: for they are the men that have already shown intellect. Try them: they have not governed or administered as yet; perhaps they cannot; but there is no doubt they *have* some Understanding,—without which no man can! Neither is Understanding a *tool,* as we are too apt to figure; 'it is a *hand* which can handle any tool.' Try these men: they are of all others the best worth trying.—Surely there is no kind of government, constitution, revolution, social apparatus or arrangement, that I know of in this world, so promising to one's scientific curiosity as this. The man of intellect at the top of affairs: this is the aim of all constitutions and revolutions, if they have any aim. For the man of true intellect, as I assert and believe always, is the noblehearted man withal, the true, just, humane and valiant man. Get *him* for governor, all is got; fail to get him, though you had Constitutions plentiful as blackberries, and a Parliament in every village, there is nothing yet got!—

These things look strange, truly; and are not such as we commonly speculate upon. But we are fallen into strange times; these things will require to be speculated upon; to be rendered practicable, to be in some way put in practice. These, and many others. On all hands of us, there is the announcement, audible enough, that the old Empire of Routine has ended; that to say a thing has long been, is no reason for its continuing to be. The things which have been are fallen into decay, are fallen into incompetence; large masses of mankind, in every society of our Europe, are no longer capable of living at all by the things which have been. When millions of men can no longer by their utmost exertion gain food for themselves, and 'the third man for thirty-six weeks each year is short of third-rate potatoes,' the things which have been must decidedly prepare to alter themselves!—I will now quit this of the organisation of Men of Letters.

Reprinted from *The Works of Thomas Carlyle*, Centenary Edition, edited by H. D. Traill (New York: Scribners, 1896-1901); volume 5: *On Heroes, Hero-Worship and the Heroic in History*.

Herbert Spencer
"The Philosophy of Style" (1852)

Herbert Spencer (1820-1903) is best known as a political and social philosopher, and as one of the founding fathers of both sociology and psychology. Central to nearly all his work are twin emphases on empirical observation as the basis of theory and on patterns of development or evolution in ideas and social arrangements as much as in biology. Much of this major work falls into the later Victorian period, but his early essay on the principles of prose style was originally presented as a scientific and "utilitarian" answer to the classical and romantic theories of Whately and de Quincey; it appeared in the October 1852 issue of the Westminster Review *and is reprinted here in its entirety. Spencer argues that English sentence structure had been steadily evolving toward easier comprehensibility over the previous centuries, and that good style could be based on analysis of the changes that had occurred. Spencer took no account of original and difficult early Victorian prose styles, such as that of Carlyle, which were in his terms historical throwbacks, but his theory became very influential among later Victorian teachers and theorists of prose (such as Alexander Bain), and he anticipated much twentieth-century discussion of prose readability and the psychology of language processing. —Ed.*

1. *Elements of Rhetoric.* By Richard Whately, D.D., Archbishop of Dublin. John W. Parker.

2. *Lectures on Rhetoric and Belles Lettres.* By Hugh Blair, D.D.

3. *The Philosophy of Rhetoric.* By George Campbell, D.D.

4. *Elements of Rhetoric.* By Lord Kaimes.

Commenting on the seeming incongruity between his father's argumentative powers and his ignorance of formal logic, Tristram Shandy says:— "It was a matter of just wonder with my worthy tutor, and two or three fellows of that learned society, that a man who knew not so much as the names of his tools, should be able to work after that fashion with them." Sterne's intended implication that a knowledge of the principles of reasoning neither makes, nor is essential to, a good reasoner, is doubtless true. Thus, too, is it with grammar. As Dr. Latham, condemning the usual school drill in Lindley Murray, rightly remarks:— "Gross vulgarity is a fault to be prevented; but the proper prevention is to be got from habit—not rules." Similarly there can be little question that good composition is far less dependent upon acquaintance with its laws than upon practice and natural aptitude. A clear head, a quick imagination, and a sensitive ear will go far towards making all rhetorical precepts needless. He who daily hears and reads well framed sentences, will naturally more or less tend to use similar ones. And where there exists any mental idiosyncrasy—where there is a deficient verbal memory, or but little perception of order, or a lack of constructive ingenuity—no amount of instruction will remedy the defect. Nevertheless, *some* practical result may be expected from a familiarity with the principles of style. The endeavor to conform to rules will tell, though slowly. And if in no other way, yet, as facilitating revision, a knowledge of the thing to be achieved—a clear idea of what constitutes a beauty, and what a blemish—cannot fail to be of service.

No general theory of expression seems yet to have been enunciated. The maxims contained in works on composition and rhetoric are presented in an unorganised form. Standing as isolated dogmas—as empirical generalizations, they are neither so clearly apprehended, nor so much respected as they would be were they deduced from some simple first principle. We are told that "brevity is the soul of wit." We hear styles condemned as verbose or involved. Blair says that every needless part of a sentence "interrupts the description and clogs the image"; and again, that "long sentences fatigue the reader's attention." It is remarked by Lord Kaimes, that "to give the utmost force to a period, it ought, if possible, to be closed with the word that makes the greatest figure." That parentheses should be avoided, and that Saxon words should be used in preference to those of Latin origin, are established precepts. But, however influential the truths thus dogmatically embodied, they would be much more influential if reduced to something like scientific ordination. In this, as in other cases, conviction will be greatly strengthened when we understand the *why*. And we may be sure that a perception of the general principle of which the rules of composition are partial expressions, will not only bring them home to us with greater force, but will discover to us other rules of like origin.

On seeking for some clue to the law underlying these current maxims, we may see shadowed forth in many of them, the importance of economizing the reader's or hearer's attention. To so present ideas that they may be apprehended with the least possible mental effort, is the desideratum towards which most of the rules above quoted point. When we condemn writing that is wordy, or confused, or intricate—when we praise this style as easy, and blame that as fatiguing, we consciously or unconsciously assume this desideratum as our standard of judgment. Regarding language as an apparatus of symbols for the conveyance of thought, we may say that, as in a mechanical apparatus, the more simple and the better arranged its parts, the greater will be the effect produced. In either case, whatever force is absorbed by the machine is deducted from the result. A reader or listener has at each moment a limited amount of mental power available. To recognize and interpret the symbols presented to him requires part of this power: to arrange and combine the images suggested requires a further part; and only that part which remains can be used for the realization of the thought conveyed. Hence the more time and attention it takes to receive and understand each sentence, the less time and attention can be given to the contained idea; and the less vividly will that idea be conceived. How truly language must be regarded as a hindrance to thought, though the necessary instrument of it, we shall clearly perceive on remembering the comparative force with which simple ideas are communicated by mimetic signs. To say "Leave the room," is less expressive than to point to the door. Placing a finger on the lips is more forcible than whispering, "Do not speak." A beck of the hand is better than "Come here." No phrase can convey the idea of surprise so vividly as opening the eyes and raising the eyebrows. A shrug of the shoulders would lose much by translation into words. Again, it may be remarked that when oral language is employed, the strongest effects are produced by interjections, which condense entire sentences into syllables. And in other cases, where custom allows us to express thoughts by single words, as in *Beware, Heigho, Fudge*, much force would be lost by expanding them into specific verbal propositions. Hence, carrying out the metaphor that language is the vehicle of thought, there seems reason to think that in all cases the friction and inertia of the vehicle deduct from its efficiency; and that in composition the chief if not the sole thing to be done, is to reduce this friction and inertia to the smallest possible amount. Let us then inquire whether economy of the recipient's attention is not the secret of effect, alike in the right choice and collocation of words, in the best arrangement of clauses in a sentence, in the proper order of its principal and subordinate propositions, in the judicious use of simile, metaphor, and other figures of speech, and even in the rhythmical sequence of syllables.

The superior forcibleness of Saxon English, or rather non-Latin English, first claims our attention. The several special reasons assignable for this may all be reduced to the general reason—economy. The most important of them is early association. A child's vocabulary is almost wholly Saxon. He says, *I have*, not, *I possess—I wish*, not *I desire;* he does not *reflect*, he *thinks;* he does not beg for *amusement*, but for *play;* he calls things *nice* or *nasty*, not *pleasant* or *disagreeable*. The synonymes which he learns in after years never becomes so closely, so organically connected with the ideas signified, as do these original words used in childhood; and hence the association remains less powerful. But in what does a powerful association between a word and an idea differ from a weak one? Simply in the greater ease and rapidity of the suggestive action. It can be in nothing else. Both of two words, if they be strictly synonymous, eventually call up the same image. The expression—it is *acid*, must in the end give rise to the same thought as—it is *sour:* but because the term *acid* was learnt later in life, and has not been so often followed by the thought symbolized, it does not so readily arouse that thought as the term *sour;* If we remember how slowly and with what labour the appropriate ideas follow unfamiliar words in another language, and how increasing familiarity with such words brings greater rapidity and ease of comprehension, until, from its having been a conscious effort to realize their meanings, their meanings ultimately come without any effort at all; and if we consider that the same process must have gone on with the words of our mother tongue from childhood upwards, we shall clearly see that the earliest learnt and oftenest used words, will, other things equal, call up images with less loss of time and energy than their later learnt synonymes.

The further superiority possessed by Saxon English in its comparative brevity obviously comes under the same generalization. If it be an advantage to express an idea in the smallest number of words, then will it be an advantage to express it in the smallest number of syllables. If circuitous phrases and needless expletives distract the attention and diminish the strength of the impression produced, then do surplus articulations do so. A certain effort, though commonly an inappreciable one, must be required to recognise every vowel and consonant. If, as we so commonly find, the mind soon becomes fatigued when we listen to an indistinct or far removed speaker, or when we read a badly written manuscript; and if, as we cannot doubt, the fatigue is a cumulative result of the attention required to catch successive syllables; it obviously follows that attention is in such cases absorbed by each syllable. And if this be true when the syllables are difficult of recognition, it will also be true, though in a less degree, when the recognition of them is easy. Hence, the shortness of Saxon words becomes a reason for their greater force, as involving a saving of the articulations to be received.

Again, that frequent cause of strength in Saxon and other primitive words—their imitative character, may be similarly resolved into the more general cause. Both those directly imitative, as *splash, bang, whiz, roar, &c.*, and those analogically imitative, as *rough, smooth, keen, blunt, thin, hard, crag, &c.*, by presenting to the perceptions symbols having direct resemblance to the things to be imagined, or some kinship to them, save part of the effort needed to call up the intended ideas, and leave more attention for the ideas themselves.

The economy of the recipient's mental energy into which we thus find the several causes of the strength of Saxon English resolvable, may equally be traced in the superiority of specific over generic words. That concrete terms produce more vivid impressions than abstract ones, and should, when possible, be used instead, is a current maxim of composition. As Dr. Campbell says, "The more general the terms are, the picture is the fainter; the more special they are, the brighter." We should avoid such a sentence as:

—In proportion as the manners, customs, and amusements of a nation are cruel and barbarous, the regulations of their penal code will be severe.

And in place of it we should write:
—In proportion as men delight in battles, tourneys, bull-fights, and combats of gladiators, will they punish by hanging, beheading, burning, and the rack.

This superiority of specific expressions is clearly due to a saving of the effort required to translate words into thoughts. As we do not think in generals but in particulars—as, whenever any class of things is referred to, we represent it to ourselves by calling to mind individual members of it—it follows that when an abstract word is used, the hearer or reader has to choose from among his stock of images, one or more, by which he may figure to himself the genus mentioned. In doing this, some delay must arise—some force be expended; and if, by employing a specific term, an appropriate image can be at once suggested, an economy is achieved, and a more vivid impression produced.

Turning now from the choice of words to their sequence, we shall find the same general principle hold good. We have, *à priori*, reason for believing that there is usually some one order of words in a sentence more effective than every other, and that this order is the one which presents the elements of the proposition in the succession in which they may be most readily put together. As in a narrative, the events should be stated in such sequence that the mind may not have to go backwards and forwards in order to rightly connect them; as in a group of sentences, the arrangement adopted should be such, that each of them may be understood as it comes, without waiting for subsequent ones; so in every sentence the sequence of words should be that which suggests the component parts of the thought conveyed, in the order most convenient for the building up of that thought. To duly enforce this truth, and to prepare the way for applications of it, we must briefly inquire into the mental process by which the meaning of a series of words is apprehended.

We cannot more simply do this than by considering the proper collocation of the substantive and adjective. Is it better to place the adjective before the substantive, or the substantive before the adjective? Ought we to say as with the French—*un cheval noir;* or to say as we do—a black horse? Probably, most persons of culture would decide that one is as good as the other. Alive to the bias produced by habit, they would ascribe to that the preference they feel for our own form of expression. They would suspect those educated in the use of the opposite form of having an equal preference for that. And thus they would conclude that neither of these instinctive judgments is of any worth. There is, however, a philosophical ground for deciding in favor of the English custom. If "a horse black" be the arrangement used, immediately on the utterance of the word "horse," there arises, or tends to arise, in the mind, a picture answering to that word; and as there has been nothing to indicate what *kind* of horse, any image of a horse suggests itself. Very likely, however, the image will be that of a brown horse; brown horses being equally or more familiar. The result is that when the word "black" is added, a check is given to the process of thought. Either the picture of a brown horse already present in the imagination has to be suppressed, and the picture of a black one summoned in its place; or else, if the picture of a brown horse be yet unformed, the tendency to form it has to be stopped. Whichever be the case, a certain amount of hindrance results. But if, on the other hand, "a black horse" be the expression used, no such mistake can be made. The word "black" indicating an abstract quality arouses no definite idea. It simply prepares the mind for conceiving some object of that colour; and the attention is kept suspended until that object is known. If, then, by the precedence of the adjective, the idea is conveyed without the possibility of error, whereas the precedence of the substantive is liable to produce a misconception, it follows that the one gives the mind less trouble than the other, and is therefore more forcible.

Possibly it will be objected that the adjective and substantive come so close together, that practically they may be considered as uttered at the same moment; and that on hearing the phrase, "a horse black," there is not time to imagine a wrongly coloured horse before the word "black" follows to prevent it. It must be owned that it is not easy to decide by introspection whether this be so or not. But there are facts collaterally implying that it is not. Our ability to anticipate the words yet unspoken is one of them. If the ideas of the hearer kept considerably behind the expressions of the speaker as the objection assumes, he could hardly foresee the end of a sentence by the time it was half delivered; yet this constantly happens. Were the supposition true, the mind, instead of anticipating, would be falling more and more in arrear. If the meanings of words are not realized as fast as the words are uttered, then the loss of time over each word must entail such an accumulation of delays as to leave a hearer entirely behind. But whether the force of these replies be, or be not admitted, it will scarcely be denied that the right formation of a picture will be facilitated by presenting its elements in the order in which they are wanted; and that, as in forming the image answering to–a red flower, the notion of redness is one of the components that must be used in the construction of the image, the mind, if put in possession of this notion before the specific image to be formed out of it is suggested, will more easily form it than if the order be reversed; even though it should do nothing until it has received both symbols.

What is here said respecting the succession of the adjective and substantive is obviously applicable, by change of terms, to the adverb and verb. And without further explanation, it will be at once perceived, that in the use of prepositions and other particles most languages spontaneously conform with more or less completeness to this law.

On applying a like analysis to the larger divisions of a sentence, we find not only that the same principle holds good, but that the advantage of respecting it becomes marked. In the arrangement of predicate and subject, for example, we are at once shown that as the predicate determines the aspect under which the subject is to be conceived it should be placed first; and the striking effect produced by so placing it becomes comprehensible. Take the often quoted contrast between–"Great is Diana of the Ephesians," and–Diana of the Ephesians is great. When the first arrangement is used the utterance of the word "great" arouses those vague associations of an impressive nature with which it has been habitually connected; the imagination is prepared to clothe with high attributes whatever follows; and when the words–"Diana of the Ephesians" are heard, all the appropriate imagery which can, on the instant, be summoned, is used in the formation of the picture: the mind being thus led directly, and without error, to the intended impression. When, on the contrary, the reverse order is followed, the idea–"Diana of the Ephesians," is conceived in any ordinary way, with no special reference to greatness; and when the words–"is great," are added, the conception has to be entirely remodelled–whence arises a manifest loss of mental energy, and a corresponding diminution of effect. The following verse from Coleridge's "Ancient Mariner," though somewhat irregular in structure, well illustrates the same truth.

"Alone, alone, all, all alone,
Alone on a wide wide sea!

And never a saint took pity on
My soul in agony."

Of course the principle equally applies when the predicate is a verb or a participle. And as effect is gained by placing first all words indicating the quality, conduct, or condition of the subject, it follows that the copula should have precedence. It is true, that the general habit of our language resists this arrangement of predicate, copula, and subject; but we may readily find instances of the additional force gained by conforming to it. Thus in the line from "Julius Cæsar"—

"Then *burst* this mighty heart:"

priority is given to a word embodying both predicate and copula. In a passage contained in "The Battle of Flodden Field," the like order is systematically employed with great effect.

"The Border slogan rent the sky!
A Home! a Gordon! was the cry;
Loud were the clanging blows;
Advanced,—forced back,—now low, now high,
    The pennon sunk and rose;
As *bends* the bark's mast in the gale
When *rent are* rigging, shrouds, and sail,
    It wavered 'mid the foes."

Pursuing the principle yet further, it is obvious that for producing the greatest effect, not only should the main divisions of a sentence observe this sequence, but the subdivisions of these should be similarly arranged. In nearly all cases, the predicate is accompanied by some limit or qualification called its complement; commonly, also, the circumstances of the subject, which form its complement have to be specified: and as these qualifications and circumstances must determine the mode in which the ideas they belong to shall be conceived, precedence should be given to them. Lord Kaimes notices the fact, that this order is preferable; though without giving the reason. He says,—"When a circumstance is placed at the beginning of the period, or near the beginning, the transition from it to the principal subject is agreeable: is like ascending or going upward." A sentence arranged in illustration of this may be desirable. Perhaps the following will serve.

—Whatever it may be in theory, it is clear in practice the French idea of liberty is—the right of every man to be master of the rest.

In this case were the first two clauses up to the word "practice" inclusive, which qualify the subject, to be placed at the end instead of the beginning, much of the force would be lost; as thus:

—The French idea of liberty is—the right of every man to be master of the rest; in practice at least, if not in theory.

The effect of giving priority to the complement of the predicate, as well as the predicate itself, is finely displayed in the opening of "Hyperion."

"*Deep in the shady sadness of a vale*
Far sunken from the healthy breath of morn
Far from the fiery noon and eve's one star
Sat grey-haired Saturn, quiet as a stone."

Here it will be observed, not only that the predicate "sat" precedes the subject "Saturn," and that the three lines in italics constituting the complement of the predicate, come before it, but that in the structure of that complement also, the same order is followed; each line being so arranged that the qualifying words are placed before the words suggesting concrete images.

The right succession of the principal and subordinate propositions in a sentence will manifestly be regulated by the same law. Regard for economy of the recipient's attention which, as we find, determines the best order for the subject, copula, predicate and their complements, dictates that the subordinate proposition shall precede the principal one when the sentence includes two. Containing, as the subordinate proposition does, some qualifying or explanatory idea, its priority must clearly prevent misconception of the principal one; and must therefore save the mental effort needed to correct such misconception. This will be clearly seen in the annexed example:

—Those who weekly go to church, and there have doled out to them a quantum of belief which they have not energy to work out for themselves, are simply spiritual paupers.

The subordinate proposition, or rather the two subordinate propositions, contained between the first and second commas in this sentence, almost wholly determine the meaning of the principal proposition with which it ends; and the effect would be destroyed were they placed last instead of first.

The general principle of right arrangement in sentences which we have traced in its application to the leading divisions of them, equally determines the normal order of their minor divisions. The several clauses of which the complements to the subject and predicate generally consist, may conform more or less completely to the law of easy apprehension. Of course with these as with the larger members, the succession should be from the abstract to the concrete.

Now however we must notice a further condition to be fulfilled in the proper combination of the elements of a sentence; but still a condition dictated by the same general principle with the other; the condition, namely, that the words and expressions most nearly related in thought shall be brought the closest together. Evidently the single words, the minor clauses, and the leading divisions of every proposition, severally qualify each other. The longer the time that elapses between the mention of any qualifying member and the member qualified, the longer must the mind be exerted in carrying forward the qualifying member ready for use. And the more numerous the qualifications to be simultaneously remembered and rightly applied, the greater will be the mental power expended and the smaller the effect produced. Hence, other things equal, force will be gained by so arranging the members of a sentence that these suspensions shall at any moment be the fewest in number, and shall also be of the shortest duration. The following is an instance of defective combination.

—A modern newspaper-statement, though probably true, would be laughed at, if quoted in a book as testimony; but the letter of a court-gossip is thought good historical evidence, if written some centuries ago.

A re-arrangement of this, in accordance with the principle indicated above, will be found to increase the effect. Thus:

—Though probably true, a modern newspaper-statement quoted in a book as testimony, would be laughed at; but the letter of a court-gossip, if written some centuries ago, is thought good historical evidence.

By making this change some of the suspensions are avoided and others shortened; whilst there is less liability to produce premature conceptions. The passage quoted below from "Paradise Lost" affords a fine instance of sentences well arranged, alike in the priority of the subordinate members, in the avoidance of long and numerous suspensions, and in the correspondence between the order of the clauses and the sequence of the phenomena described, which by the way is a further prerequisite to easy comprehension, and therefore to effect.

> "As when a prowling wolf,
> Whom hunger drives to seek new haunt for prey,
> Watching where shepherds pen their flocks at eve
> In hurdled cotes amid the field secure,
> Leaps o'er the fence wth ease into the fold:
> Or as a thief bent to unhoard the cash
> Of some rich burgher, whose substantial doors,
> Cross-barr'd, and bolted fast, fear no assault,
> In at the window climbs, or o'er the tiles:
> So clomb the first grand thief into God's fold:
> So since into his church lewd hirelings climb."

The habitual use of sentences in which all or most of the descriptive and limiting elements precede those described and limited, gives rise to what is called the inverted style; a title, which is, however, by no means confined to this structure, but is often used where the order of the words is simply unusual. A more appropriate title would be the *direct style*, as contrasted with the other, or *indirect style*–the peculiarity of the one being that it conveys each thought into the mind step by step with little liability to error, and of the other that it gets the right thought conceived by a series of approximations.

The superiority of the direct over the indirect form of sentence, implied by the several conclusions that have been drawn, must not, however, be affirmed without limitation. Though up to a certain point it is well for all the qualifying clauses of a period to precede those qualified, yet, as carrying forward each qualifying clause costs some mental effort, it follows that when the number of them and the time they are carried become great, we reach a limit beyond which more is lost than is gained. Other things equal, the arrangement should be such that no concrete image shall be suggested until the materials out of which it is to be made have been presented. And yet, as lately pointed out, other things equal, the fewer the materials to be held at once, and the shorter the distance they have to be borne, the better. Hence in some cases it becomes a question whether most mental effort will be entailed by the many and long suspensions, or by the correction of successive misconceptions.

This question may sometimes be decided by considering the capacity of the persons addressed. A greater grasp of mind is required for the ready comprehension of thoughts expressed in the direct manner, where the sentences are anywise intricate. To recollect a number of preliminaries stated in elucidation of a coming image, and to apply them all to the formation of it when suggested, demands a considerable power of concentration and a tolerably vigorous imagination. To one possessing these, the direct method will mostly seem the best; whilst to one deficient in them it will seem the worst. Just as it may cost a strong man less effort to carry a hundred-weight from place to place at once, than by a stone at a time; so to an active mind it may be easier to bear along all the qualifications of an idea and at once rightly form it when named, than to first imperfectly conceive such an idea, and then carry back to it, one by one, the details and limitations afterwards mentioned. Whilst, conversely, as for a boy the only possible mode of transferring a hundred-weight, is that of taking it in portions; so for a weak mind the only possible mode of forming a compound conception may be that of building it up by carrying separately its several parts.

That the indirect method–the method of conveying the meaning by a series of approximations–is best fitted for the uncultivated, may indeed be inferred from their habitual use of it. The form of expression adopted by the savage as in "Water–give me," is the simplest type of the approximative arrangement. In pleonasms, which are comparatively prevalent among the uneducated, the same essential structure is seen; as, for instance in–"The men, they were there." Again, the old possessive case–"The king, his crown," conforms to the like order of thought. Moreover, the fact that the indirect mode is called the natural one, implies that it is the one spontaneously employed by the common people–that is, the one easiest for undisciplined minds.

Before dismissing this branch of our subject, it should be remarked that even when addressing the most vigorous intellects, the direct style is unfit for communicating thoughts of a complex or abstract character. So long as the mind has not much to do, it may be well able to grasp all the preparatory clauses of a sentence, and to use them effectively; but if some subtlety in the argument absorb the attention–if every faculty be strained in endeavoring to catch the speaker's or writer's drift, it may happen that the mind, unable to carry on both processes at once, will break down, and allow all its ideas to lapse into confusion.

Turning now to consider figures of speech, we may equally discern the same general law of effect. Underlying all the rules that may be given for the choice and right use of them, we shall find the same fundamental requirement–economy of attention. It is indeed chiefly because of their great ability to subserve this requirement, that figures of speech are employed. To bring the mind more easily to the desired conception, is in many cases solely, and in all cases mainly, their object.

Let us begin with the figure called Synechdoche. The advantage sometimes gained by putting a part for the whole is due to the more convenient, or more accurate, presentation of the idea thus secured. If, instead of saying "a fleet of ten ships," we say "a fleet of ten *sail*," the picture of a group of vessels at sea is more readily suggested; and is so because the sails constitute the most conspicuous part of vessels so circumstanced: whereas the word *ships* would very likely remind us of vessels in dock. Again, to say "All *hands* to the pumps" is better than to say, "All *men* to the pumps;" as it suggests the men in the special attitude intended, and so saves effort. Bringing "*grey hairs* with sorrow to the grave," is another expression, the effect of which has the same cause.

The occasional increase of force produced by Metonymy may be similarly accounted for. "The low morality of *the bar*" is a phrase both briefer and more significant than the literal one it stands for. A belief in the ultimate supremacy of intelligence over brute force, is conveyed in a more concrete, and therefore more realizable form, if we substitute *the pen* and *the sword* for the two abstract terms. To say, "Beware of drinking!" is less effective than to say, "Beware *the bottle!*" and is so, clearly because it calls up a less specific image.

The Simile, though in many cases employed chiefly with a view to ornament, yet whenever it increases the *force* of a passage, does so by being an economy. Here is an instance.

—The illusion that great men and great events came oftener in early times than now, is partly due to historical perspective. As in a range of equidistant columns, the furthest off look the closest, so the conspicuous objects of the past seem more thickly clustered the more remote they are.

To construct, by a process of literal explanation the thought thus conveyed, would take many sentences; and the first elements of the picture would become faint whilst the imagination was busy in adding the others. But by the help of a comparison all effort is saved; the picture is instantly realized, and its full effect produced.

Of the position of the Simile,[1] it needs only to remark, that what has been said respecting the order of the adjective and substantive, predicate and subject, principal and subordinate propositions, &c., is applicable here. As whatever qualifies should precede whatever is qualified, force will generally be gained by placing the simile before the object to which it is applied. That this arrangement is the best, may be seen in the following passage from the "Lady of the Lake":–

"As wreath of snow, on mountain breast,
Slides from the rock that gave it rest,
Poor Ellen glided from her stay,
And at the monarch's feet she lay."

Inverting these couplets will be found to diminish the effect considerably. There are cases, however, even where the simile is a simple one, in which it may with advantage be placed last; as in these lines from Alexander Smith's "Life Drama":–

"I see the future stretch
All dark and barren as a rainy sea."

The reason for this seems to be, that so abstract an idea as that attaching to the word "future," does not present itself to the mind in any definite form, and hence the subsequent arrival at the simile entails no reconstruction of the thought.

Nor are such the only cases in which this order is the most forcible. As the advantage of putting the simile before the object depends on its being carried forward in the mind to assist in forming an image of the object, it must happen that if, from length or complexity, it cannot so be carried forward, the advantage is not gained. The annexed sonnet, by Coleridge, is defective from this cause.

"As when a child, on some long winter's night,
Affrighted, clinging to its grandam's knees,
With eager wond'ring and perturb'd delight
Listens strange tales of fearful dark decrees,
Mutter'd to wretch by necromantic spell;
Or of those hags who at the witching time
Of murky midnight, ride the air sublime
And mingle foul embrace with fiends of hell;
Cold horror drinks its blood! Anon the tear
More gentle starts, to hear the beldame tell
Of pretty babes, that loved each other dear,
Murder'd by cruel uncle's mandate fell:
Ev'n such the shiv'ring joys thy tones impart,
Ev'n so, thou, Siddons, meltest my sad heart."

Here, from the lapse of time and accumulation of circumstances, the first part of the comparison becomes more or less dim before its application is reached, and requires re-reading. Had the main idea been first mentioned, less effort would have been required to retain it, and to modify the conception of it in conformity with the comparison, than to retain the comparison, and refer back to the recollection of its successive features for help in forming the final image.

The superiority of the Metaphor to the Simile is ascribed by Dr. Whately to the fact that "all men are more gratified at catching the resemblance for themselves, than in having it pointed out to them." But after what has been said, the great economy it achieves will seem the more probable cause. If, drawing an analogy between mental and physical phenomena, we say,

—As, in passing through the crystal, beams of white light are decomposed into the colours of the rainbow; so, in traversing the soul of the poet, the colourless rays of truth are transformed into brightly-tinted poetry;—

it is clear that in receiving the double set of words expressing the two portions of the comparison, and in carrying the one portion to the other, a considerable amount of attention is absorbed. Most of this is saved, however, by putting the comparison in a metaphorical form, thus:

—The white light of truth, in traversing the many-sided transparent soul of the poet, is refracted into iris-hued poetry.

How much is conveyed in a few words by the help of the Metaphor, and how vivid the effect consequently produced, may be abundantly exemplified. From "A Life Drama" may be quoted the phrase

"I spear'd him with a jest,"

as a fine instance among the many which that poem contains. A passage in the "Prometheus Unbound," of Shelley, displays the power of the Metaphor to great advantage:

"Methought among the lawns together
We wandered, underneath the young grey dawn,
And multitudes of dense white fleecy clouds
Were wandering in thick flocks along the mountains
Shepherded by the slow unwilling wind."

This last expression is remarkable for the distinctness with which it realizes the features of the scene; bringing the mind as it were, by a bound to the desired conception.

But a limit is put to the advantageous use of the Metaphor, by the condition that it must be sufficiently simple to be understood from a hint. Evidently, if there be any obscurity in the meaning or application of it, no economy of attention will be gained; but rather the reverse. Hence, when the comparison is complex, it is usual to have recourse to the Simile. There is, however, a species of figure, sometimes classed under Allegory, but which might perhaps, be better called Compound Metaphor, that enable us to retain the brevity of the metaphorical form even where the analogy is intricate. This is done by indicating the application of the figure at the outset, and then leaving the mind to continue the parallel itself. Emerson has employed it with great effect in the first of his "Lectures on the Times":–

> "The main interest which any aspects of the Times can have for us, is the great spirit which gazes through them, the light which they can shed on the wonderful questions, What we are? and Whither do we tend? We do not wish to be deceived. Here we drift, like white sail across the wild ocean, now bright on the wave, now darkling in the trough of the sea; but from what port did we sail? Who knows? Or to what port are we bound? Who knows? There is no one to tell us but such poor weather-tossed mariners as ourselves, whom we speak as we pass, or who have hoisted some signal, or floated to us some letter in a bottle from afar. But what know they more than we? They also found themselves on this wondrous sea. No; from the older sailors nothing. Over all their speaking-trumpets the gray sea and the loud winds answer–Not in us; not in Time."

The division of the Simile from the Metaphor is by no means a definite one. Between the one extreme in which the two elements of the comparison are detailed at full length and the analogy pointed out, and the other extreme in which the comparison is implied instead of stated, come intermediate forms, in which the comparison is partly stated and partly implied. For instance:

—Astonished at the performances of the English plough, the Hindoos paint it, set it up, and worship it; thus turning a tool into an idol: linguists do the same with language.

There is an evident advantage in leaving the reader or hearer to complete the figure. And

generally these intermediate forms are good in proportion as they do this; provided the mode of completing it be obvious.

Passing over much that may be said of like purport upon Hyperbole, Personification, Apostrophe, &c., let us close our remarks upon construction by a typical example. The general principle that has been enunciated is, that the force of all verbal forms and arrangements is great in proportion as the time and mental effort they demand from the recipient is small. The special applications of this general principle have been severally illustrated; and it has been shown that the relative goodness of any two modes of expressing an idea may be determined by observing which requires the shortest process of thought for its comprehension. But though conformity in particular points has been exemplified, no cases of complete conformity have yet been quoted. It is indeed difficult to find them; for the English idiom scarcely permits the order which theory dictates. A few, however, occur in Ossian. Here is one:–

> "As autumn's dark storms pour from two echoing hills, so towards each other approached the heroes. As two dark streams from high rocks meet and mix, and roar on the plain: loud, rough, and dark in battle meet Lochlin and Inisfail. * * * As the troubled noise of the ocean when rolls the waves on high; as the last peal of the thunder of heaven; such is the noise of the battle."

Except in the position of the verb in the first two similes, the theoretically best arrangement is fully carried out in each of these sentences. The simile comes before the qualified image, the adjectives before the substantives, the predicate and copula before the subject, and their respective complements before them. That the passage is more or less open to the charge of being bombastic proves nothing; or rather proves our case. For what is bombast but a force of expression too great for the magnitude of the ideas embodied? All that may rightly be inferred, is, that only in very rare cases, and then only to produce a climax, should *all* the conditions of effective expression be fulfilled.

Passing on to a more complex application of the doctrine with which we set out, it must now be remarked, that not only in the structure of sentences, and the use of figures of speech, may economy of the recipient's mental energy be assigned as the cause of force, but that in the choice and arrangement of the minor images, out of which some large thought is to be built, we may trace the same condition of effect. To select from the sentiment, scene, or event described, those typical elements which carry many others along with them, and so by saying a few things but suggesting many, to abridge the description, is the secret of producing a vivid impression. Thus if we say:— Real nobility is "not transferable"; besides the one idea expressed several are implied; and as these can be thought much sooner than they can be put in words, there is gain in omitting them. How the mind may be led to construct a complete picture by the presentation of a few parts, an extract from Tennyson's "Mariana" will well show.

> "All day within the dreamy house,
> The door upon the hinges creaked,
> The fly sung i' the pane; the mouse
> Behind the mouldering wainscot shrieked,
> Or from the crevice peered about."

The several circumstances here specified bring with them hosts of appropriate associations. Our attention is rarely drawn by the buzzing of a fly in the window, save when everything is still. Whilst the inmates are moving about the house, mice usually keep silence; and it is only when extreme quietness reigns that they peep from their retreats. Hence, each of the facts mentioned presupposing numerous others, calls up these with more or less distinctness, and revives the feeling of dull solitude with which they are connected in our experience. Were all these facts detailed instead of suggested, the attention would be so frittered away, that little impression of dreariness would be produced. And here, without further explanation, it will be seen that, be the nature of the sentiment conveyed what it may, this skilful selection of a few particulars which imply the rest, is the key to success. In the choice of component ideas, as in the choice of expressions, the aim must be to convey the greatest quantity of thoughts with the smallest quantity of words.

Before inquiring whether the law of effect, thus far traced, will account for the superiority of poetry to prose, it will be needful to notice some supplementary causes of force in expression that have not yet been mentioned. These are not, properly speaking, additional causes, but rather secondary ones, originating from those already specified—reflex manifestations of them. In the first place, then, we may remark that mental

excitement spontaneously prompts the use of those forms of speech which have been pointed out as the most effective. "Out with him!" "Away with him!" are the natural utterances of angry citizens at a disturbed meeting. A voyager, describing a terrible storm he had witnessed, would rise to some such climax as "Crack went the ropes, and down came the mast." Astonishment may be heard expressed in the phrase, "Never was there such a sight!" All which sentences are, it will be observed, constructed after the direct type. Again, every one will recognise the fact that excited persons are given to figures of speech. The vituperation of the vulgar abounds with them; often, indeed, consists of little else. "Beast," "brute," "gallows rogue," "cut-throat villain," these, and other like metaphors and metaphorical epithets, at once call to mind a street quarrel. Further, it may be remarked that extreme brevity is one of the characteristics of passionate language. The sentences are generally incomplete; the particles are omitted, and frequently important words are left to be gathered from the context. Great admiration does not vent itself in a precise proposition, as "It is beautiful," but in a simple exclamation, "Beautiful!" He who, when reading a lawyer's letter, should say, "Vile rascal!" would be thought angry; whilst "He is a vile rascal," would imply comparative coolness. Thus we see that alike in the order of the words, in the frequent use of figures, and in extreme conciseness, the natural utterances of excitement conform to the theoretical conditions of forcible expression.

Hence, then, the higher forms of speech acquire a secondary strength from association. Having, in actual life, habitually found them in connexion with vivid mental impressions; and having been accustomed to meet with them in the most powerful writing; they come to have in themselves a species of force. The emotions that have from time to time been produced by the strong thoughts wrapped up in these forms, are partially aroused by the forms themselves. They create a certain degree of animation; they induce a preparatory sympathy; and when the striking ideas looked for are reached, they are the more vividly realized.

The continuous use of these modes of expression that are alike forcible in themselves and forcible from their associations, produces the peculiarly impressive species of composition which we call poetry. Poetry, we shall find, habitually adopts those symbols of thought, and those methods of using them, which instinct and analysis agree in choosing as most effective, and becomes poetry by virtue of doing this. On turning back to the various specimens that have been quoted, it will be seen that the direct or inverted form of sentence predominates in them, and that to a degree quite inadmissible in prose. And not only in the frequency, but in what is termed the violence of the inversions will this distinction be remarked. In the abundant use of figures, again, we may recognise the same truth. Metaphors, similes, hyperboles, and personifications, are the poet's colours, which he has liberty to employ almost without limit. We characterize as "poetical" the prose which repeats these appliances of language with any frequency; and condemn it as "over florid" or "affected" long before they occur with the profusion allowed in verse. Further, let it be remarked that in brevity–the other requisite of forcible expression which theory points out, and emotion spontaneously fulfils–poetical phraseology similarly differs from ordinary phraseology. Imperfect periods are frequent, elisions are perpetual, and many of the minor words which would be deemed essential in prose are dispensed with.

Thus poetry, regarded as a vehicle of thought, is especially impressive partly because it obeys all the laws of effective speech, and partly because in so doing it imitates the natural utterances of excitement. Whilst the matter embodied is idealized emotion, the vehicle is the idealized language of emotion. As the musical composer catches the cadences in which our feelings of joy and sympathy, grief and despair, vent themselves, and out of these germs evolves melodies suggesting higher phases of these feelings; so the poet developes from the typical expressions in which men utter passion and sentiment, those choice forms of verbal combination in which concentrated passion and sentiment may be fitly presented.

There is one peculiarity of poetry conducing much to its effect–the peculiarity which is indeed usually thought to be its characteristic one–still remaining to be considered: we mean its rhythmical structure. This, unexpected as it may be, will be found to come under the same generalization with the others. Like each of them, it is an idealization of the natural language of emotion, which is known to be more or less metrical if the emotion be not violent; and like each of them it is an economy of the reader's or hearer's attention. In the peculiar tone and manner we adopt in uttering versified language may be discerned

its relationship to the feelings; and the pleasure which its measured movement gives us is ascribable to the comparative ease with which words metrically arranged can be recognised. This last position will scarcely be at once admitted; but a little explanation will show its reasonableness. For if, as we have seen, there is an expenditure of mental energy in the mere act of listening to verbal articulations, or in that silent repetition of them which goes on in reading–if the perceptive faculties must be in active exercise to identify every syllable–then any mode of combining words so as to present a regular recurrence of certain traits which the mind can anticipate, will diminish that strain upon the attention required by the total irregularity of prose. In the same manner that the body, in receiving a series of varying concussions, must keep the muscles ready to meet the most violent of them, as not knowing when such may come; so the mind in receiving unarranged articulations must keep its perceptives active enough to recognise the least easily caught sounds. And as, if the concussions recur in a definite order, the body may husband its forces by adjusting the resistance needful for each concussion; so, if the syllables be rhythmically arranged, the mind may economize its energies by anticipating the attention required for each syllable. Far-fetched as this idea will perhaps be thought, a little introspection will countenance it. That we *do* take advantage of metrical language to adjust our perceptive faculties to the force of the expected articulations, is clear from the fact that we are balked by halting versification. Much as at the bottom of a flight of stairs, a step more or less than we counted upon gives us a shock, so, too, does a misplaced accent or a supernumerary syllable. In the one case, we know that there is an erroneous preadjustment; and we can scarcely doubt that there is one in the other. But if we habitually preadjust our perceptions to the measured movement of verse, the physical analogy lately given renders it probable that by so doing we economize attention; and hence that metrical language is more effective than prose, simply because it enables us to do this.

Were there space, it might be worth while to inquire whether the pleasure we take in rhyme, and also that which we take in euphony, are not partly ascribable to the same general cause.

A few paragraphs only can be devoted to a second division of our subject that here presents itself. To pursue in detail the laws of effect, as seen in the larger features of composition, would exceed both our limits and our purpose. But we may fitly indicate some further aspect of the general principle hitherto traced out, and hint a few of its wider applications.

Thus far, then, we have considered only those causes of force in language which depend upon economy of the mental *energies:* we have now briefly to glance at those which depend upon economy of mental *sensibilities.* Indefensible though this division may be as a psychological one, it will yet serve roughly to indicate the remaining field of investigation. It will suggest that besides considering the extent to which any faculty or group of faculties is tasked in receiving a form of words and realizing its contained idea, we have to consider the state in which this faculty or group of faculties is left; and how the reception of subsequent sentences and images will be influenced by that state. Without going at length into so wide a topic as the exercise of faculties and its reactive effects, it will be sufficient here to call to mind that every faculty (when in a state of normal activity) is most capable at the outset; and that the change in its condition, which end in what we term exhaustion, begins simultaneously with its exercise. This generalization, with which we are all familiar in our bodily experiences, and which our daily language recognizes as true of the mind as a whole, is equally true of each mental power, from the simplest of the senses to the most complex of the sentiments. If we hold a flower to the nose for long, we become insensible to its scent. We say of a very brilliant flash of lightning that it blinds us; which means that our eyes have for a time lost their ability to appreciate light. After eating a quantity of honey, we are apt to think our tea is without sugar. The phrase, "a deafening roar," implies that men find a very loud sound temporarily incapacitates them for hearing faint ones. Now, the truth which we at once recognise in these, its extreme manifestations, may be traced throughout; and it may be shown that alike in the reflective faculties, in the imagination, in the perceptions of the beautiful, the ludicrous, the sublime, in the sentiments, the instincts, in all the mental powers, however, we may classify them—action exhausts; and that in proportion as the action is violent, the subsequent prostration is great.

Equally, throughout the whole nature, may be traced the law that exercised faculties are ever tending to resume their original state. Not only, after continued rest, do they regain their full power—not only do brief cessations partially rein-

vigorate them—but even whilst they are in action, the resulting exhaustion is ever being neutralized. The two processes of waste and repair go on together. Hence, with faculties habitually exercised as the senses in all, or the muscles in a labourer, it happens that, during moderate activity, the repair is so nearly equal to the waste, that the diminution of power is scarcely appreciable; and it is only when the activity has been long continued, or has been very violent, that the repair becomes so far in arrear of the waste as to produce a perceptible prostration. In all cases, however, when, by the action of a faculty, waste has been incurred, *some* lapse of time must take place before full efficiency can be re-acquired; and this time must be long in proportion as the waste has been great.

Keeping in mind these general truths, we shall be in a condition to understand certain causes of effect in composition now to be considered. Every perception received, and every conception realized, entailing some amount of waste—or, as Liebeg would say, some change of matter in the brain—and the efficiency of the faculties subject to this waste being thereby temporarily, though often but momentarily, diminished—the resulting partial inability must affect the acts of perception and conception that immediately succeed. And hence we may expect that the vividness with which images are realized will, in many cases, depend on the order of their presentation; even when one order is as convenient to the understanding as the other. We shall find sundry facts which alike illustrate this, and are explained by it. Climax is one of them. The marked effect obtained by placing last the most striking of any series of images, and the weakness—produced by reversing this arrangement, depends on the general law indicated. As immediately after looking at the sun we cannot perceive the light of a fire, whilst by looking at the fire first and the sun afterwards we can perceive both; so, after receiving a brilliant, or weighty, or terrible thought, we cannot appreciate a less brilliant, less weighty, or less terrible one, whilst, by reversing the order, we can appreciate each. In Antithesis, again, we may recognise the same general truth. The opposition of two thoughts that are the reverse of each other in some prominent trait insures an impressive effect; and does this by giving a momentary relaxation to the faculties addressed. If, after a series of images of an ordinary character, appealing in a moderate degree to the sentiment of reverence, or approbation, or beauty, the mind has presented to it a very insignificant, a very unworthy, or a very ugly image–the faculty of reverence, or approbation, or beauty, as the case may be, having for the time nothing to do, tends to resume its full power; and will immediately afterwards appreciate a vast, admirable, or beautiful image better than it would otherwise do. Improbable as these momentary variations in susceptibility will seem to many, we cannot doubt their occurrence when we contemplate the analogous variations in the susceptibility of the senses. Referring once more to phenomena of vision, every one knows that a patch of black on a white ground looks blacker, and a patch of white on a black ground looks whiter, than elsewhere. As the blackness and the whiteness must really be the same, the only assignable cause for this is a difference in their action upon us, dependent on the different states of our faculties. It is simply a visual antithesis.

But this extension of the general principle of economy–this further condition of effect in composition, that the power of the faculties must be continuously husbanded–includes much more than has been yet hinted. It implies not only that certain arrangements and certain juxtapositions of connected ideas are best; but that some modes of dividing and presenting the subject will be more effective than others; and that, too, irrespective of its local cohesion. It shows why we must progress from the less interesting to the more interesting; and why not only the composition as a whole, but each of its successive portions, should tend towards a climax. At the same time, it forbids long continuity of the same species of thought, or repeated production of the same effects. It warns us against the error committed both by Pope in his poems and by Bacon in his essays–the error, namely, of constantly employing the most effective forms of expression; and it points out that as the easiest posture by and by becomes fatiguing, and is with pleasure exchanged for one less easy; so the most perfectly constructed sentences will soon weary, and relief will be given by using those of an inferior kind. Further, it involves that not only should we avoid generally combining our words in one manner, however good, or working out our figures and illustrations in one way, however telling, but we should avoid anything like uniform adherence, even to the wider conditions of effect. We should not make every section of our subject progress in interest: we should not always rise to a climax. As we saw that, in single sentences, it is but rarely allow-

able to fulfil all the conditions of strength; so in the larger portions of composition we must not often conform entirely to the law indicated. We must subordinate the component effects to the total effect.

In deciding how practically to carry out the principles of artistic composition, we may derive help by bearing in mind a fact already pointed out–the fitness of certain verbal arrangements for certain kinds of thought. The constant variety in the mode of presenting ideas which the theory demands will in a great degree result from a skilful adaptation of the form to the matter. We saw how the direct or inverted sentence is spontaneously used by excited people; and how their language is also characterized by figures of speech and by extreme brevity. Hence these may with advantage predominate in emotional passages, and may increase as the emotion rises. On the other hand, for complex ideas, the indirect sentence seems the best vehicle. In conversation, the excitement produced by the near approach to a desired conclusion will often show itself in a series of short, sharp sentences; whilst, in impressing a view already enunciated, we generally make our periods voluminous by piling thought upon thought. These natural modes of procedure may serve as guides in writing. Keen observation and skilful analysis would, in like manner, detect many other peculiarities of expression produced by other attitudes of mind; and by paying due attention to all such traits, a writer possessed of sufficient versatility might make some approach to a completely organized work.

This species of composition which the law of effect points out as the perfect one, is the one which high genius tends naturally to produce. As we found that the kinds of sentence which are theoretically best are those generally employed by superior minds, and by inferior minds when excitement has raised them; so we shall find that the ideal form for a poem, essay, or fiction, is that which the ideal writer would evolve spontaneously. One in whom the powers of expression fully responded to the state of mind would unconsciously use that variety in the mode of presenting his thoughts which Art demands. This constant employment of one species of phraseology, which all have now to strive against, implies an undeveloped faculty of language. To have a specific style is to be poor in speech. If we glance back at the past, and remember that men had once only nouns and verbs to convey their ideas with, and that from then to now the growth has been towards a greater number of implements of thought, and consequently towards a greater complexity and variety in their combinations, we may infer that we are now, in our use of sentences, much what the primitive man was in his use of words, and that a continuance of the process that has hitherto gone on must produce increasing heterogeneity in our modes of expression. As now in a fine nature the play of the features, the tones of the voice and its cadences, vary in harmony with every thought uttered; so in one possessed of a fully developed power of speech, the mould in which each combination of words is cast will similarly vary with, and be appropriate to, the sentiment. That a perfectly endowed man must unconsciously write in all styles, we may infer from considering how styles originate. Why is Addison diffuse, Johnson pompous, Goldsmith simple? Why is one author abrupt, another rhythmical, another concise? Evidently in each case the habitual mode of utterance must depend upon the habitual balance of the nature. The predominant feelings have by use trained the intellect to represent them. But whilst long, though unconscious, discipline has made it do this efficiently, it remains, from lack of practice, incapable of doing the same for the less powerful feelings; and when these are excited, the usual modes of expression undergo but a slight modification. Let the powers of speech be fully developed, however—let the ability of the intellect to convey the emotions be complete—and this fixity of style will disappear. The perfect writer will express himself as Junius, when in the Junius frame of mind; when

he feels as Lamb felt, will use a like familiar speech; and will fall into the ruggedness of Carlyle when in a Carlylean mood. Now he will be rhymetical and now irregular; here his language will be plain and there ornate; sometimes his sentences will be balanced and at other times unsymmetrical; for a while there will be considerable sameness, and then again great variety. From his mode of expression naturally responding to his state of feeling, there will flow from his pen a composition changing to the same degree that the aspects of his subject change. He will thus without effort conform to what we have seen to be the laws of effect. And whilst his work presents to the reader that variety needful to prevent continuous exertion of the same faculties, it will also answer to the description of all highly organized products both of man and of nature; it will be, not a series of like parts simply placed in juxtaposition, but one whole made up of unlike parts that are mutually dependent.

---

1. Properly the term "simile" is applicable only to the entire figure, inclusive of the two things compared and the comparison drawn between them. But as there exists no name for the illustrative member of the figure, there seems no alternative but to employ "simile" to express this also. The context will in each case show in which sense the word is used.

Reprinted from *Westminster Review* (American edition), 58 (October 1852).

Cockburn Thomson

From "Modern Style" (1857)

Unlike most Victorians who theorized about style, Cockburn Thomson (1834-1860) was a professional philologist or student of language. Educated at Oxford, Bonn, and Munich, he was already, in his early twenties, an internationally known scholar of Sanskrit, who had translated the Bhagavad-Gita *(1855). In addition, he wrote with his mother, under the pseudonym Philip Warton, two successful volumes of anecdotes about high society. His essay on modern style, first published in the February 1857 issue of the* North British Review, *is significant for the breadth of issues it discusses; it was presented as a review of two books on the history of English words by the philologist Richard Chenevix Trench, but it takes up in broad polemic fashion the question of stylistic degeneracy, the role of prose style in making social discriminations in an anti-aristocratic age, the influence on stylistic developments of philosophy, of women writers, and of the rise of newspapers, and the emergence of nineteenth-century England's characteristic prose genre, the long, polemic periodical review-essay. Thomson refers in passing to a stunning variety of different prose stylists, from different modes, periods, and countries, but the broad lines of his argument, that the developments of prose style must be analyzed in their social context, come across clearly even for readers who are not familiar with all the authors to whom he refers.*—Ed.

. . .1. *English, Past and Present.* Five lectures by Richard Chenevix Trench, B.D., &c.&c. London, 1856.

. . .2. *On the Study of Words.* By Richard Chenevix Trench, B.D. &c. Sixth Edition. London, 1855.

When Will Shakspere and Ben Jonson fought in loving rivalry the battle of the Classic and Romantic Schools, the world, looking on delighted, said, "It is the age of the Drama." When Swift hurled unclean satires at those who refused him fat benefices; and Voltaire taught that Holy Writ was a meet study for Judæus Apella, they said, "It is the age of Humour." When stalwart grey-whiskered men sauntered along "untrodden ways," by the Cumberland Lakes, and wrote such balderdash as this:–

"She lived *unknown,* and few could *know*
  When Lucy ceased to be;
But she is in her grave, and *oh,*
  The difference to me,"–

the astonished world muttered, "It is the age of Poesy."

And now, when we have no Drama but the French–no Poetry but a Laureate's–no Humour but the shilling wit of Egyptian Hall,–What is the world to say?

The plea on which Sydney Smith excused the *Edinburgh* for being quarterly, was, that time was wanted to allow a sufficient number of books to be published from which to choose; but today we saw two whole pages of the *Times* filled with advertisements of forthcoming volumes. Is it not the age of books? Let Routledge and Mudie answer.

It is the old story of supply and demand. The Brahman caste exists no more in England. Walpole's valet might have his own copy of St. Simon now. We have educated all classes more or less, and the population has doubled itself. Cheap literature, however it be deplored, is a necessity of the times, like cheap flour, and to fill the hungry minds of masses, most write and many publish. Nor is this an accident of the Anglo-Saxon genius. France, too, has its railway libraries– its thousand novelists, and million vaudevillists; in Germany, each youth entering the battle of life trenches himself behind a neat octavo, of much learning and more theory. And wherever there is not a *Catalogus Expurgatus,* and a few adventurous Sosii may be found, the majority of those who write publish also.

It is the age of books. But is it the Augustan age? Sir Archibald Alison considers the period "immediately succeeding the fall of Napoleon," as the Augustan (or as he calls it, the *Augustine*[1]) age, in France and England, and extends it to the present day. Now, strictly speaking, a literary age ends when the stars which brightened it have set. No one will call this the age of Scott and the Lake Poets. The reign of Tennyson is not the reign of Byron; and forty years have sufficed to supplant the morbid sentimentalism of the one, with the healthier philosophy of the other.

That the Augustan age did not precede this century is easily shown. Neither one nor two swallows make a spring; and, in justice to the productions of the last three centuries, we cannot yield the palm even to the bright days of the two great dramatists. Still less do Queen Anne's deserve it, when we feel that Prior and Gay are dead among us; while Swift, Addison, Steele, and Pope are fast following in their wake.

There remain the last half of the eighteenth century, and the first of the present. Now, an Augustan age is the climax after which literature declines, and that, too, rapidly. We can mark this epoch clearly in the cases of Greece, Rome, Italy, and Spain. But not so with the tetrarchy of modern Europe. We feel that we are all progressing, and, if we have satisfied a single want in literature, it is that the countries of Racine and Shakspere have passed that early epoch in which the drama is brought to perfection. But Greece still wanted Thucydides, Plato, Demosthenes, when Æschylus flourished, and we cannot deny to our children all hope of excelling in so many other branches.

Perhaps no better proof could be offered of this, than that no history of English literature has yet been written. The time is not come for it. But another work, with which we cannot so easily dispense, is an Essay on Style. For this we must look to some critic of this age of critics. Doubtless it is felt that before justice can be done to this subject, we must be able to handle our language discreetly, and we know how little we know of our own tongue as yet. The very fact that the two admirable little works, which head this article, have first appeared since 1850, is a proof of the ignorance which Englishmen begin to feel of their own language.

Philology is yet in its cradle. Grimm, Bopp, Rask, Pictet, Latham, and now Dean Trench, have done, or are doing, their best to wean the baby science;[2] but, with all its value in connexion with Ethnology, Archæology, and History, and in spite of the new lights it sheds upon the mind of man, it is still confined to the student, nor will it be thrown open to the general reader, until its results are sufficiently ascertained to form an accompaniment to the history of literature.

Language is the escutcheon of to-day. We may indeed have an aristocracy of wealth superseding the old one that these levelling times have hunted down, but we have learnt with rude teaching the real worth of money without morality, and are not afraid that we are degenerating so far yet. We certainly have a Republic of Literature, and an aristocracy whose letters-patent are Letters indeed. But in such a republic, it may be asked, how is the aristocracy created? Public opinion dubs them, and is guided in its choice by their *Style*. For as acts are the test of moral, words are that of mental character,–the test, first of genius, next of education; and, in the world's annals, it will be said of this age, that in it language began to be the lawgiver of caste.

We are convinced that this same "Style," of which thousands of readers and not a few writers think so little, is of the greatest importance in the present day. We are certain that next to the matter of a book, the gravest consideration is the manner of treating it. It is this which, with the masses, no less than with men of education and taste, really, though without their knowing it, decides the merits of the book, and certifies its popularity; and it is simply on account of this that many a praiseworthy thinker becomes the nightmare of his publisher, and many a trashy scribbler, with nothing but his style to recommend him, achieves a fleeting reputation. If, then, we offer a few of the ideas on this subject which have flitted through our mind from time to time, it is because we feel that its importance will cover a multitude of their deficiencies.

What is style? Every idea may be expressed in two or three manners. We may select particular words, and arrange them in each of the admissible orders, still expressing the same thought. Style is the manner in which we do this, and in this its largest sense, may be applied to every kind of writing. But it is evident that in some of these the manner to be used is under certain rules, as, for instance, in metrical composition of every kind; and we may therefore take a narrower view of style as applying only to prose; and that not to all classes of prose. For in some the matter is so important, that the author cannot attend to the manner. Strict accuracy of minor details, for instance, is an excuse for awkwardness of expression; and there are works of science and even philosophy, (at least if it be purely speculative, and demand a clear string of syllogisms throughout,) in which it would be no more fair to expect the graces of style than in a grammar, a dictionary, or a catalogue. Again, in theological works we cannot complain if the manner be somewhat debased, since the matter is so lofty. The man who carries his head in Heaven may not be called down to the worldly consideration whether a Saxon or a Latin derivative should be used as an epithet of what he sees there.

Again, style is limited to the prose that is written. It may be doubted if oratory be prose at all, any more than conversation or dialectic argument. At any rate, it is clear that we cannot guide the orator by the rules which apply to the calm thinker at his desk; nor can we expect the same neatness in speech which is indispensable in writing. Indeed, it seems to be acknowledged that the best speeches and sermons are those which read worst, and the school-boy wonders why Demosthenes and Cicero should have acquired a distinctive reputation among the full-mouthed orators, born of the genius of Thucydides and Livy. On the other hand, not even the most devoted among a high-church congregation can maintain, that the extempore does not far surpass the written sermon in the pulpit. Yet the priests of St. Barnabas may publish and sell; Mr. Spurgeon can scarcely hope to be read as well as heard. And if this be true, we may say that, although a good style is such as not only to bear reading aloud, but even to profit by it, it will be spoiled, and sound ridiculous if *recited.*

Style, then, is the rhythm of prose, and it is confined to that kind of writing in which the matter is not too great to make the author forgetful of the manner; in short, to history, the essay, descriptive writing generally, and fiction. Now, rhythm is "measured movement," and in poetry is guided by definite rules. But as the good poet uses his ear and taste rather than any set canons, so in prose, if there be any laws of taste, it is they which must direct us in the criticism of style. It is these laws, vague as they are, which we propose to examine with reference to our modern literature.

Bacon says, in one of his essays, "Some books are to be tasted, others to be swallowed, and some few to be chewed and digested"; which means, from one point of view, that the manner may differ in proportion to the matter; that you must allow ten times the licence, and thirty times the length of tether to the railway novelist, who knows that his pages will light chibouks and meerschaums, when once read through, than you concede to Mr. Macaulay and Sir Archibald Alison, who naturally expect their ponderous tomes to be bound in rich-scented Russian, and set in the nooks of honour in the library book-case.

Not that these four styles are not often mingled in the same work. Macaulay, in spite of all his genius, and that course of self-education to which he has devoted his life, has, to our mind,

never risen–if it be a rise–from the essayist to the historian. Each chapter of his reads like an essay on political science, where the facts appear rather to be illustrations of the arguments, than the reflections to rise naturally from the facts. That dear old Herodotus, too, well knew he was writing a book of travellers' fiction, when he dignified his nine books with the name of History. On the other side we have often, to our bitterness, had to wade through a discursive novel–"Perversion" is a recent instance–and the novelists of the last century seemed to think that to insert, wherever possible, an essay on morals or religion, was the sole aim of their writing at all. That they were grossly mistaken, and that such is not the way to make novels instructive–if it be proved that they ought to be so–is shown by the skill with which every child will learn to avoid the reflections in Robinson Crusoe, to say nothing of the distaste for so-called religious novels, demonstrated by the majority.

This mixture of styles is not proper, though it scarcely requires censure, for it is so obvious that "there is a time to laugh, and a time to weep," that anomalies of this kind bring their own reward, and soon deter readers from going on.

These, however, are the differentiæ of style, and we have more to say under each head, but we cannot do so, until we have plainly pointed out the two genera, which consist of formed style, and style not formed. These, again, are subdivided. Under the head of style formed, we have that formed after a model, and that built on an original plan. Under the other head we have the purely original and the imitative. Again, styles may be formed on a good or bad model, and, to be brief, the following table best explains the divisions:

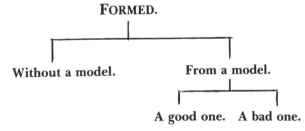

FORMED.

Without a model.   **From a model.**

A good one.   A bad one.

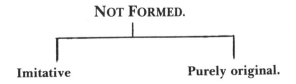

NOT FORMED.

Imitative   **Purely original.**

Is it lawful to form a style at all?–Yes. Is it necessary–Yes. But for whom is it lawful–for whom necessary?–For the man who is deficient in ear and taste. To form a style is an acknowledgment of inferiority. But if a man feels that inferiority, it is right and proper that he should do so. The first faults of style are sins against taste, as prolixity, repetition, long periods, alliterations, playing on words, and others. But there are faults which depend entirely on the writer's kind of mind. And these he is not likely to see–no, not if a "forty-parson power" bellowed them for ever into his ears. Such are affectation, coarseness, sneering, adulation, egotism, bombast and the use of trite phrases. Style is a test of genius. . . .

Well, then, if all these styles have so much that is bad in them, can we lay down a rule for good writing? Let every man, when he sits down, consider his genius with respect to his subject-matter. If you are not imbued with the spirit of history, eschew it. If you have no penetration for character, avoid biography. If you have no courage, no confidence, no spark of satire in your soul, eschew the critical, and measure your powers for the serious essay. Above all, if you want somewhat of all these, and passion into the bargain, know that you are not fit to write a good novel. Let each man write as he thinks, and as he would speak. Let not the pen and the ink-bottle frighten him into more solemnity than his topic demands. He is in company of the world, but really he will address individuals only. The world is not a Brobdignagian, it is a compound of lilliputian minds. The absolute requirements of a good style are few–clearness, easy flow, sustained interest, good taste; but if you have none of these in you, it is of no use to form your style, you must educate your mind. Then, when you have written a little, look over it carefully, or better still, get a friend of good judgment to look over it for you, and correct what is poor or bad. The next time you will avoid these errors intuitively.

In English there is one great advantage in writing conversationally. No language is richer in synonymes, but nothing but natural taste can direct us how to select. The man who writes as he thinks will choose the Saxon element naturally, in preference to the classical, wherever it is feasible. He will choose the commonest and best-known words, and his style will be stronger, broader, and strike more home. It is only when we attempt to *talk fine*, that we bring in the classical preponderance. Not that we would proscribe it altogether. We have a wardrobe of all kinds. It is as much an affectation to clothe ourselves only in the russet, sombre, and old-fashioned suit of the Quaker, as to deck our poor limbs in all the purple and gold of the dictionary.

But the style must differ in proportion to the subject, and when this requires it, there are beauties which must be brought in. Venus must not be slovenly and unkempt. These adornments, like the blemishes which we have pointed out, are some derived from genius, some from education. The former must not be striven after, but their absence in a writer of celebrity is justly censured. Such are power, warmth, enthusiasm, and lofty flights. Yet the excess of these virtues constitutes some of the vices mentioned. Mr. G. P. R. James is a signal instance of too much power, (whether natural or not, we leave the reader to decide,)– becoming bombastic, unnatural, and even ridiculous; and Mr. Dickens, whose forte lies in character, not in description, has often gone to the most absurd lengths in his attempts to divest a necessary picturing of its tedium. Again, all these beauties must be used sparingly, and in the right time and quantity. If you cry wolf too often, your neighbours become deaf. Mr. Macaulay might profit not a little by allowing his lofty style, beautiful as it is, to subside from time to time into quiet narrative, and take a lesson from Gibbon, or, (as he is an essayist and not a historian,) still better from Emerson, who, with all his originality, is not ashamed at times to kick away the stilts and speak like a common man, when the subject itself is commonplace. Other beauties to which one must be born are, terseness, in which the French far surpass us, and of which we need not say, the most remarkable instances in the whole literature of the world are Tacitus, Voltaire, Gibbon, Lamartine, and Emerson, though the terseness of Voltaire and Emerson is very different from that of the rest, for it is not the terseness of narrative, so rare, so admirable, so essential to the good historian; antithesis, well handled in Gibbon, and rarely found now-a-days; the close union of cause and effect, which is another beauty in the same writer, and metaphor. As to this last, it is evident that it best befits the essay and the novel, for in the former it serves in places of instances which become tedious if multiplied; and in the latter it gives a sweet poesy to the style, that enwraps the reader, and lifts him cloudwards with the romance of the story. Indeed, so great a beauty is this same metaphor, that it is admissible even in history, and the entire want of it, as in the case of Hume, is like the absence of water in a large garden, where you have every beauty, but no refreshment for the eye. The young England school is full of it; and Carlyle and Emerson have as much poetry in their likenings as any old divine of Queen Bess's Court. Who does not remember how sweetly Bacon speaks of truth in metaphor, "This same truth is a naked and open day-light, that doth not show the masks and mummeries and triumphs of the world, half so stately and daintily as candlelights." But he who uses it must beware that it be applicable in every particular, and simple, fetched from home, and a ground known to all, not from abroad, nor from the realm of science or learning, which savours of pedantry. To notice all the beauties that genius may bring to deck the simplicity of prose, but which must be used with the utmost care, would be far beyond our limits. If we point to Emerson, Wilson, and Bulwer, as quite modern writers, who may be called the Poets of Prose, we yield them no extravagant praise, because we are speaking solely of style and will not assert or deny that they are or might have been Poets of Poetry. . . .

But it is with the so-called "natural" style of to-day that we have to deal. There are three circumstances which account for the peculiarities of our present national style,–Practical Philosophy, Lady-writers, and the Newspapers.

"Philosophy," says Jeffrey (Essay i. p. 107,) "which has led to the investigation of causes, has robbed the world of much of its sublimity, and by preventing us from believing much, and from wondering at anything, has taken away half our enthusiasm, and more than half our admiration." This is but half true, and mostly for the vulgar. "Nil admirari" [Nothing is to be admired] is the gentility of puny minds. Philosophy is a stream, which near this huge city–the world–washes down the refuse of its sewers, its strong-smelling beliefs, and rotten superstitions; but mount the rivulet a little higher, a little beyond the world, and you will find it pure and refreshing, fit for Naiades to sport in. To wonder at nothing is the companion of being roused at nothing; and when the late war brought the first blush of enthusiasm into the faces of our newspapers, the world of London quaked, and readers were quite uncomfortable. It is true that "nil admirari" is the disgusting coxcombry of conceited Englishmen, and this spirit of listlessness has found its way into our press, and thence among those who are weak enough to imitate the style of the press; but, thank Heaven! there are yet a few authors who can and will write warmly and enthusiastically–

ay, and even admiringly on many things.

The ladies have had a very different effect on our literature. It is to them that we owe the foundation, or rather restoration, of the romantic school in England; and Mrs. Radcliffe, Mrs. Barbauld, and Mrs. Charlotte Smith, may be said to have paved the way for Scott to march in. Madame de Staël, herself among the earliest of European female writers of distinction, had already marked the influence of their softer feelings on the stiff orthodoxy of the Georges. . . . There is no doubt that this new element not only poured warmth and freshness into the rigid purity of last century's style, but also supplied that originality which it seems to have lacked. It is the absence of erudition in women, and the courage which their very weakness gives them, that support this originality. They think for themselves fearlessly, because they cannot clash with our stronger minds upon the same ground. They have no fear of the imputation of ignorance or want of learning, which has often deterred the greatest geniuses from putting forth the full powers of their original thought. It was the severity of Queen Anne's school which first forced Lady Mary Wortley Montague and others to match their minds with men's; and the ice once broken by the fair correspondents, it was natural that their daughters and granddaughters should come forward and assert their position in print.

But half a century has completely altered the state of things; and when we find our wives and sisters bringing their prejudice and their strong affections into works which require coolness and impartiality, and history sinking to the level of fiction, we are naturally anxious lest the masculine nerve pass wholly from our letters. Even in fiction we must needs look askance at the maudlin effeminacy that is stealing in, and sigh when we compare Fielding or Scott, or even Bulwer, with the young-ladyisms of Miss Yonge. Yet, on the other hand, we cannot wholly sympathize with the unfeminine strides of a Mrs. Shelley or a Mrs. Clive, and we must content ourselves with grumbling at cheap and railway literature, which, with all its advantages, is destroying the purity alike of our style and our tone of feeling.

But if we have to thank the fair sex for the originality of the age, we must blame the press for our want of courage. This is no place to discuss whether newspapers in a free country do really represent the opinions of the masses. It may be doubted whether the "masses" have any opinion of their own, and whether they be not always guided more or less by the small class of independent educated men. But it is certain that, putting politics on one side, there is a large number of social topics, which we may call "things in general," in which all newspapers mainly agree, and concerning which their decision is taken to be that of the people. We regret this oligarchy of common sense, which subjects all that is beautiful and chivalrous to the judgment of the useful and £ *s. d.* We believe that much-lauded judge to be sometimes very "common" indeed, and that conscience is a higher and a less worldly guide; yet who dare assert it, in the face of those unknown tyrants who issue their daily ukases from a dirty printing-office? What author, what essayist, but must subscribe to the articles of opinion which they authorize? We are convinced that this community of opinion, this tacit agreement with the apparent majority, this electioneering principle of decision, is opposed to the attainment of truth; and we look forward to a reaction against the newspaper monopoly of opinion with no less joy than we do to one against the young-ladyism of our literature. . . .

No class of literature belongs more peculiarly to modern ages and our Northern Islands than the essay–nay, if we examine the matter very closely we may say that it is indigenous to England and Scotland only; and that the Irish, like the French and Germans, have followed us in adopting it, but have never succeeded. The fact is, that the English and Lowland Scotch have an essentially Saxon characteristic, which not another people under the sun–except, perhaps, their American grandsons, possess–the love of individual opinion. It is a part of their love of general independence. In France a man's opinions are those of his party, or, if he is utterly indifferent to politics, those of his class. In Germany a man frames his whole mind according to the popular theory he espouses. England is the only country where men of the same church, the same party, and the same predilections can afford or dare to think differently on the most important points. The opinion of the Englishman is dearer to him than his wife or friend. It is sacred. It is his religion, in fact, and we regret to say, with too many of us, his only religion. It is this which makes him one-sided, even in ancient history, where party-spirit could have little influence on him; this which fills even our lightest literature with trite religious reflections, which makes us sarcastic, but seldom abusive; bilious, but rarely furious.

We, Lowlanders, outdo even Englishmen in

this peculiarity. Foreigners tell us that our conversation on any serious topic seems to be a succession of downright challenges. We are never satisfied that our neighbour does agree with us, we are always confident that he must entertain a different opinion, and "we'll just trouble him to speak out."

The end of it all is, that we must have an outlet. This we have sought and found in many different quarters. We never heard, for instance, of a debating society in any foreign university, even under the most liberal governments; and, during a long residence in France, we never knew a single dinner-table in ordinary society, at which criticism of the new books formed the staple conversation, as it so often does in England. It is true that the stage, and the new actors and actresses, appear to take the place of literature with the French in this respect; but it has always struck us that their remarks on this subject were less a criticism of the piece or the art, than a conversation on the talents and character of the artist.

But the path in which the English most delight to vent their opinions is evidently the critical essay. We do not, of course, speak of all essays. The mere form of an essay is the most convenient for several subjects, and for none more than for philosophy; so much so that the works of many ancient and most modern philosophers may be said to have been written in essays, or rather treatises, which, taken together, exhaust the whole subject, but have little consecutive connexion with one another. If these be called essays, the long essay may be said to have been in vogue much longer than is generally admitted. On the other hand, the short essay, in which the method was simply to propound and answer a hypothesis, and proceed to illustrate the solution by instances, or explanation, was used many centuries back by clever or learned men as a vehicle for their undeveloped opinions on various topics, whether high or low, as Bacon discoursed on gardens, buildings, and plantations, with the same tone and genius with which he treated truth, honour, and ambition, a few pages back.

But we do not mean in using the term *critical* essay to limit its theme to literature. On the contrary, it may be taken to embrace every essay which is critical, whatever its subject be–books, politics, social ethics, national characteristics, or, in fact, any such topic of the day; provided only the essayist sits on the judge's bench, and not in the chair of the teacher merely. With this view of the critical essay, we may include the writers of

Queen Anne's and the early Georges' reigns in the same list that holds Jeffrey, Smith, Cockburn, Brougham, Wilson, and Carlyle. But the mission of the one differed from that of the other, in the ratio of their times. The practical extravagancies of 1710 were theoretical in 1810. A hundred years had sufficed to take the baton of influence from fashion and rank, and place it in the hands of intellect. The humour that Addison justly whetted against the absurdities of opera, club, rout, and so forth, was replaced by the satire which Jeffrey levelled at the trivialities of petty poets. Again, the task of those was far easier than the labour of these. If Addison ridiculed fashionable vices, he was certain that he was in the right. The laws of social ethics are definite and acknowledged; but those of literary tastes still want a general council to decide them, and the reviewer of to-day is as much open to review, and the critic to criticism, as the author they handle.

It was not until the establishment of Sydney Smith's "Edinburgh," in the beginning of this century, that the reviewer's position began to be understood, for the criticism of the last was directed not by taste, education, and a long literary experience, so much as by those pretended laws of criticism which everybody disputed, and none but professional critics could defend. It was quite natural then—indeed it could not be otherwise—that the short should extend into a long essay, for the reviewer, while passing his examination had, and still has, to defend his own views, and his method of bringing them forward. But it was long before this necessity was felt, and Smith himself clung for at least the first two years to the old school of short brilliant condemnation. In the first number, for instance, he wrote no less than seven critiques, besides editing the whole, five in the third number, and so on.

The principle by which our first and best Reviewers were guided, *judex damnatur si nocens absolvitur* [the judge is condemned if the guilty is absolved], is a right one only when the *judex* is taken in the English sense of a judge with a jury. The critic has no right to condemn, because he has no power to punish. When the *Quarterly* extols what the *Edinburgh* runs down, or *vice versâ*, all criticism sinks into nothing more than party-spirit, and becomes not only useless, but absurd. But the highest ambition of the critic can only be to establish a precedent by which future critics and a future public may be guided; all that he is at present concerned to do, is to sum up the evidence, to point out the law, to guide the taste of

the public, and to leave it to their common sense to give the verdict. That verdict has been given and still is given in every case with or without the aid of a reviewer, and though no jury is infallible, the common-sense judgment of the public will scarcely err once in a thousand times. Nor can all the charging, and blustering, and bullying of the reviewer divert that judgment from its proper channel. Neither Keats, Byron, nor Barry Cornwall have suffered as *writers* from the blows of their critics. As men they may have suffered either in health or temper, but that was their own fault. But though public opinion always decides well sooner or later, its verdict is generally a long time in the finding, where there is anything to be said in extenuation of the prisoner. The public must be locked up for years before it becomes unanimous. But time gives the conquest to the majority. There can be only one opinion now about the merits of Shakspere, Marlowe, Vanbrugh, or Massinger, though there are two and more about those of Wordsworth, Southey, and—Hannah More. So, then, in this age of books, when a rapid decision is absolutely necessary, it is the critic's office to take the *onus* off the public shoulders, and point out the decision which they *ought* to come to.

It is this necessity for rapid critiques that has completely altered the character of our three-monthly reviews within the last fifteen years. No longer able to aid or guide the public in their judgment, as the new books are read and thrown aside before the quarterlies are even in print, they have left that office to the weekly and even daily papers, and exchanged the critique for the essay. The ponderous volumes which once rejoiced in fifteen or twenty brilliant, short and pithy articles, now groan beneath the burden of some seven or eight heavy and laboured treatises; critiques on single works are supplanted by reviews on a whole class of literature, headed by a list of volumes, fit to throw a nervous reader into hysterics, and the volume in the blue or the white cover, which was so anxiously awaited towards the end of December, March, June, or September, that was discussed in every club, drawing-room, and railway-carriage in the kingdom, now lies upon the table uncut for days, and producing a feeling of terrible nausea in the man of the world, who knows that etiquette obliges him to wade through its contents *in case* the talk should take that turn.

We regret the change, because the very position of a critic is lowered by it. It is impossible for a weekly paper to do justice to any book within the time and its own limits, and the weekly papers tacitly confess this by often continuing a critique from Saturday to Saturday. Again, a premium is thus placed on bad writing. The anonymous, which had so many advantages when the quarterlies were really reviews, is now only a shield for indifferent performance. Your well-known man, who has something to say, and will not take the trouble to say it in a proper style, writes it off in a few nights, and "gets" it into a three-monthly review. . . .

---

1. This is either a misprint or an intended amendment on the received form. If the latter, it cannot be supported. Johnson and Richardson have neither *Augustan* nor *Augustine*, Webster and Ogilvie have the former only. As to its derivation, Scheller and Forcellini give *Augustanus, Augustianus,* and *Augustinus;* but the first is found in Tacitus, with the meaning, "*ad Augustum pertinens*" [pertaining to Augustus]; the second and third only in Suetonius. The town of Berytus, too, was called Colonia Augus*tana,* not Augus*tina.* We believe that *Augustine* can only be used in speaking of the order of Monks, and that the eminent historian has been misled by no better an authority than Ainsworth's Latin Dictionary.

2. Among the little helps contributed to the study of English, is a list of the Greek roots, which have found their way into our language, by Mr. W. Hall. This valuable little book has reached a third edition, and is in constant use at King's College, London. It contains alphabetical lists of Greek roots, ranged according to their parts of speech, with an English translation, and the English words derived from each. To this Mr. Hall has added notes which do him great credit for labour and research, and are full of interesting and often surprising information. If the book has a fault, it is that of all philologists, who compare a mixed language to a single one. In his zeal for his hobby, we cannot but think Mr. Hall has sometimes overstepped the bounds of probability—*e.g,* lamb from αμνος. Lamb is a Moeso-Gothic word found in Ulphilas, and, if there be any connexion between the two, it could only be through the Sanskrit *urna,* which, however, is probably our *ram*–the Greek αρνος.

Reprinted from *North British Review,* 26 (February 1857): 339-375.

William Forsyth

From "Literary Style"[1] (1857)

William Forsyth (1818-1879) was a Scottish journalist, political writer, and minor poet from Aberdeen. In addition to his newspaper work he contributed extensively to such London-based reviews as Fraser's Magazine *and the* Cornhill. *His long, two-part essay on style first appeared in the March and April 1857 issues of* Fraser's *and was presented there as a review of the 1851 edition of Richard Whately's* Elements of Rhetoric *and an 1855 book on the history of the English language,* English, Past and Present, *by Richard Chenevix Trench, one of the founders of the great Oxford English Dictionary. Forsyth's essay is notable for its emphasis on style as something deliberate and acquired, rather than merely innate, and for its awareness of the influence on prose style of changing social and publishing conditions.*–Ed.

Although we have placed Archbishop Whately's work on Rhetoric at the head of this article, and we propose to say something on the subject of literary style which occupies a considerable portion of his book, it is not our intention to analyse or discuss the rules of composition, so much as to exhibit some peculiarities of it amongst the writers of the present day, and call attention to some faults which, if allowed to pass unnoticed, are likely to produce mischievous effects on the future literature of England. And as the best kind of instruction is that which teaches by examples, we think we shall be doing good service to the republic of letters if we devote a few pages to the task of pointing out specimens of good, and exposing what we believe to be false and vicious, modes of style.

It cannot be said that this is either inopportune or unnecessary. We live in an age of bookmaking, and authors multiply so fast that it is almost a distinction not to have published. Men and women rush now-a-days into print with an alacrity which has become alarming. Nobody of the slightest note dies without entailing upon the public a dull biography of half-a-dozen volumes; and every tourist to Switzerland or the Rhine considers himself entitled *laisser trotter sa plume* [to let his pen fly] and send an account of his travels to the publishers. Few, however, ask themselves whether they have anything to communicate which, as regards either matter or manner, is worth imparting to the world; and our shelves groan under the weight of books which will soon be as utterly forgotten as if they had never existed. But in the meantime, some wretched varieties of style are springing up which threaten to infect our whole literature, and unless the growth is vigorously checked, posterity may suffer from the prevalence of a corrupt task in composition, and permanent injury may be done to the noble inheritance of language we have received from our ancestors. We propose therefore to deal with the question as its importance deserves, and we shall endeavour to write with perfect fairness, although it may be in some cases with severity.

To use a homely illustration, style is to the subject matter very much what cookery is to food; and the parallel might be carried into considerable detail without ceasing to be appropriate. Thus, raw meat will support life, and the culinary art is not for that purpose absolutely necessary. So mental nutriment may be extracted from heaps of undigested facts, however repulsive the manner in which they are flung together. Again, good cookery will render palatable the most uninviting food. Excellent soup is made from bones; and we believe that M. Soyer can, at the cost of a farthing, produce a capital dish out of almost nothing. And an attractive style will throw a charm over the most unpromising subject and rivet the attention of the reader when, without that attraction, he would turn away in weariness or disgust. But there are bad as well as good cooks; not only cooks that give a piquant relish to ordinary food, but, as we all know to our cost, cooks who can and do spoil the choicest viands. Need we say that the best story may be spoiled in the telling, and that there are writers who possess a fatal facility for rendering whatever subject they discuss both tiresome and repulsive?

Or, to vary the metaphor, we may compare literary to architectural style, and as the same stones in the hands of the builder will form the most beautiful or the most unsightly edifice–the Parthenon of the Acropolis or the National Gallery of Trafalgar-square—so from the same subject-matter the pen may produce the dullest or the most interesting book.

So great is the success and so brilliant the reward of an attractive style, that it is to us a matter of astonishment that more earnest endeavours to acquire it are not made by those who aspire to the dignity of authorship. A good style will secure to a work a favourable reception with the public, much more than in proportion to what its merits in other respects deserve. There are some books—few indeed in number, we admit—which have been kept afloat on the stream of time, almost solely by the buoyancy of their style. And by this we do not mean merely the grammatical and proper arrangement of words in each sentence, but the due relation of sentences to each other. A rhythmical structure ought to exist, not only in the separate but in the collective periods; and the warp and woof of the entire texture should be so woven as to preserve continuity of pattern, and produce the effect of an harmonious whole. It is the charm of his easy, natural, unaffected manner, which still maintains Hume at the head of English historians, nor do we think he is likely to be displaced. We may accuse him of unfairness and partiality, and convict him of inaccuracy, but the verdict will be, as the French say, guilty under extenuating circumstances, and the extenuating circumstance in the case of Hume is his style. The shallow morality of Paley may be, and we hope is, exploded as the philosophy which is to train up the youth of England in the ways of virtue and truth; but his works are models of composition, and will be read with delight by those who disapprove his doctrines but are fascinated by the clear transparency of his style. In his *Aids to Reflection,* Coleridge expresses in enthusiastic terms his admiration of the manner, while dissenting from the matter, of Paley. 'How gladly,' he says, 'would I surrender all hope of contemporary praise, could I even approach to the incomparable grace, propriety, and persuasive facility of his writings.' Cobbett, again, is an author whose style will always secure for him a distinguished place amongst English writers. Those who dissent most from his political views, and care nothing for the opinions of the arch-radical, may read with delight, and derive instruction from, the works of one who was perhaps the most vigorous writer of Saxon English that can be found in the whole range of our literature. He knew how to put forth the utmost strength of his native tongue, and whatever he wrote is distinguished by a racy, sinewy, and idiomatic style. But it has one conspicuous blemish. It is defaced by an immoderate use of italics. This is a great and frequent fault. They are intended to supply the place of emphasis in speaking, but the whole force is lost when they are employed too constantly and without necessity.

Men doubt because they stand so thick i' the sky,
If they be stars that paint the galaxy.

In Cobbett's pages they are as thickly strewn as leaves in Vallombrosa, and appear like ugly fingerposts telling the reader what path he must pursue and to what objects he must pay attention. A writer ought to trust the collocation of his words to mark the emphatic parts of his statement, and not perpetually put up notices to point out his meaning: and it is curious that Archbishop Whately should so often fall into the same mistake; for no author with whom we are acquainted less requires such factitious aid. His style is pellucid to a remarkable degree, and none but those who are wilfully blind or hopelessly stupid can misunderstand what he says. He has a wonderful power of apt and happy illustration, drawn chiefly from images of external nature. And this gives a liveliness and force to his style which make every subject which he discusses not only interesting but clear to the dullest comprehension.

We may instance also the Letters of Cowper, and the works of Southey and Washington Irving, as examples of what may be effected by charm of manner. And as we have mentioned the best of American writers, we are tempted to quote a single passage as a specimen of his style. It is, we think, exquisitely beautiful, and we know not where we can find a more affecting image of that most sorrowful of all sorrowful things, a Broken Heart:—

She is like some tender tree, the pride and beauty of the grove, graceful in its form, bright in its foliage, but with the worm preying at its heart. We find it suddenly withering when it should be most fresh and luxuriant. We see it drooping its branches to the earth, and shedding leaf by leaf until, wasted and perished away, it falls, even in the stillness of the forest; and as we muse over the beautiful ruin, we strive in vain to recollect the blast or the thunderbolt that could have smitten it with decay.

Style, in fact, is an alchemy which can transmute the basest metal into gold. It is to the writer what manner is to the individual–that by which we are at once either attracted or repelled; and the most interesting subject may be so handled as to inspire the reader with nothing but disgust.

We may illustrate this by an example on a large scale. No one who is at all competent to form a judgment on the question, can doubt that in point of *calibre*–and as destined to influence the speculations and opinions of men on the most important subjects that can occupy the human mind–the prose literature of Germany is superior to that of France. But its momentum is impeded, and the number of its readers sensibly narrowed, by the astounding heaviness and desperate clumsiness of its style. And herein, we may remark in passing, there seems to be almost a providential safeguard, if we consider the nature and tendency of much that is published in that vast hive of busy thinkers and laborious writers. Mr. De Quincey, in one of his delightful Essays, which have within the last few years been collected and published in America, and are now *at last* in the course of publication in England, thus speaks of German composition:–

> Whatever is bad in our own ideal of prose style, whatever is repulsive in our own practice, we see there carried to the most outrageous excess. Herod is out-Heroded, Sternhold is out-Sternholded, with a zealotry of extravagance that really seems like wilful burlesque.

Its chief characteristics are involution and prolixity. The sentences are of suffocating length, and they are coiled together, parenthesis within parenthesis, like the folds of a monstrous snake, so as to bewilder and confound the reader. Instead of breaking up his matter into small and manageable pieces, in the shape of short and readable paragraphs, a German writer thinks it enough to quarry it out in an unwieldy mass, and gives himself no trouble about its form, structure, or polish. Indeed, we doubt if he ever bestows a thought upon the manner of saying anything that comes uppermost in his mind. But what man of woman born, not a German, can digest a book made up of passages, each varying in length from twelve to twenty or thirty lines (we have counted so many)–unrelieved by a single break, even so much as a semicolon–so that long before the end of the paragraph is reached,

the memory has forgotten the introductory part, which can alone render the meaning intelligible? Of Kant it is said, that his sentences have been measured by a carpenter, and some of them run two feet eight by six inches. A chief cause of this frightful cumbrousness is the attempt to embrace in one grasp as it were, and present to the reader at one view all the qualifications, limitations, and exceptions of a subject, before he has time to form an idea of it, which, without those qualifications, limitations, and exceptions, would, in the writer's judgment, be erroneous. Hence follows that discompounding of words–that tearing asunder of prepositions from their verbs, and that aggregation of subsidiary sentences, which make a Chinese puzzle of a large part of the prose literature of Germany.

It is this careless disregard, or rather positive contempt, of composition, which renders it so repulsive to foreigners, and deters even those who are accurately acquainted with the language from reading works which would otherwise invite, and in many instances well repay, perusal.

In direct opposition and contrast to the heavy lumber-waggon of German, is the light, quick post-chariot of French style. This corresponds also with, and is partly the effect of, certain well-known traits of the national character. No people have carried the art of conversation to such perfection as the French, and with none is it felt to be so much a social necessity. Conversation, as distinct from monologue, is more practised and better understood in France than in any other country in Europe. But this, of itself, requires and produces brevity of expression. It rests on the give-and-take principle, and is absolutely opposed to long-winded monopoly of talk. And that happy faculty of dexterous arrangement which distinguishes the nation, and which is so remarkably exhibited by French soldiers in a campaign, appears also in the neatness and accuracy of French style.[2] We will not go so far as Mr. De Quincey, who asserts that 'such a thing as a long or an involved sentence could not be produced from French literature, though a Sultan were to offer his daughter in marriage to the man who should find it;' but certainly the occurrence is so rare as almost to justify the reward proposed for the discovery.

In English literature, on the contrary, there would be no difficulty in finding such sentences in abundance. Carelessness about style has been a national failing of a very old date; and it has its origin in one of the most marked features of our character. We pride ourselves upon being a practical people; and, provided that a given end of utility is attained, we are too apt to disregard the means by which it is accomplished. This is strikingly shown in the architecture which prevailed in England until the last few years, when happily we may date the commencement of a better taste. The main object of houses is to provide shelter and comfort, and of churches to furnish accommodation. And what could be more miserable than the style of the houses and churches which were built during the last two hundred years? To say that they were ugly, but faintly expresses the utter ignorance or contempt of all the laws of architecture which they ostentatiously displayed. Beauty and grace, and harmony and proportion, were things almost unknown to our builders; and the consequence has been such an array of unsightly structures as gives positive pain to the eye that has been instructed in a better school. . . .

Nor indeed was it until a comparatively late period that some of the commonest and most elementary rules of grammar, as now observed, found general acceptance with even the best authors. For instance, far down into the last century, the auxiliary verb was joined to the preterite, instead of the past participle; and in fact the distinction between the two was almost disregarded.

It is, however, folly to imagine that excellence in literary composition can be attained without care and labour. Cobbett indeed has laid down the rule–'Never think of mending what you write: let it go: no patching. As your pen moves, bear constantly in mind that it is making strokes which are to remain for ever.' But independently of the fact that the latter part of this advice seems to nullify the former–for surely nothing that is destined for immortality can be produced by man without the *improbus labor* [persistent effort] which is one of the conditions of human excellence–what Cobbett here says must be taken with an important qualification. It is quite true that when a good style is *once formed,* it may be best to write without thinking much about it, lest the rule that *ars est celare artem* [it is art to conceal art] should be violated; but until that is the case, too much attention can hardly be paid to the choice of words and collocation of sentences. An expert swimmer enjoys the exercise without bestowing a thought upon the mechanical action of his limbs; but he who plunges into deep water without having first learnt how to swim, makes a few awkward struggles, and then

finds his way to the mud at the bottom. Nor do we think that in any case it is safe to dismiss altogether care about the manner of composition. And the example of great writers proves the truth of what we assert. It is said that the beginning of Plato's *Republic* was found written in his tablets in a great variety of ways; and yet Plato is an author who has never been surpassed in the beauty and transparency of his style. Nicole tells us that Pascal frequently spent twenty days in the composition of a single Provincial Letter, and sometimes commenced the same letter seven or eight times before he satisfied himself with the result. And Voltaire used to keep before him on his table, when engaged in the task of writing, the *Petit Carême* of Massillon and the tragedies of Racine.

We wish, therefore, that more pains were taken than has been the custom in our schools and colleges to teach habits of correct and graceful English composition. It is indeed wonderful how much this has been neglected, and to what a disproportionate extent the time and attention of the young have been devoted to the acquisition of a minute and critical knowledge of two dead languages, without help or instruction in the study of their own. Not that we mean for a moment to undervalue the advantages of accuracy in classical scholarship, which is nothing unless it is accurate; but we may say to those charged with the responsible office of education, 'This ought ye to have done, and not to have left the other undone.' And indeed the two are not only not opposed, but the one is perhaps the best mode of acquiring the other. Translations from the classic authors are of admirable use in forming habits of correct composition, if what ought to be considered good translation is properly understood. By this term we do not mean a bald, stiff rendering of the original–literally 'upsetting it' (*übersetzung*), as the Germans call it–but choosing always the most appropriate and equivalent word, giving idiom for idiom, and clothing the sentences in an English, and not in a Greek or Latin dress. Another useful method is to require students to write letters or narratives on easy familiar subjects–not themes or formal essays on Virtue or Happiness, or the *Summum Bonum,* which invariably produce a weak, stilted, and inflated style. They should always bear in mind the well-known answer said to have been given by an eminent prelate to a young clergyman who asked him for advice as to the composition of a sermon–'Read over what you have written, and whenever you come to any passage which you think particularly fine–strike it out.'

It is owing to the want of proper training in the laws of composition, that so few persons in England can write even a common letter correctly. We will give a familiar instance of a very frequent solecism which occurs in one of the most common acts of every-day life–the 'answer' to a dinner invitation; and it is one in which we are sorry to say that well-educated ladies are too often caught tripping. When 'Mr. A. and Mrs. A. request the pleasure of Mr. and Mrs. B.'s company at dinner,' the reply usually is, 'Mr. and Mrs. B. *will have* the pleasure of accepting' the invitation. But the acceptance is already *un fait accompli* by the very act of writing it; it is a present, not a future event; and the answer of course ought to be either 'Mr. and Mrs. B. *have* the pleasure of accepting,' or 'Mr. and Mrs. B. *will have* the pleasure of *dining*.'

Nor need there be any apprehension lest attention to rules and imitation of good models in learning the art of composition, should produce a monotonous uniformity of style. Characteristic differences will insensibly arise, having their origin in the separate constitution of each writer's mind, the individuality of which will be preserved in the expression of his thoughts, just as differences in handwriting exist amongst those who have been taught by the same master.

Indeed, every author who has any originality of thought, and whose works are worth reading or remembering, has a mode of expression peculiar to himself. He paints, so to speak, after his own manner. The style of Isaiah is not the style of Ezekial or Jeremiah: and St. Paul differs in the character of his writings from the other apostles, as much as–to use his own beautiful simile–one star differeth from another star in glory. His abrupt transitions, his long parentheses, his vehement adjurations, have no counterpart in the Epistles of St. Peter or St. John. Those two magnificent chapters, the fifteenth of the 1st Corinthians, and the eleventh of Hebrews, the one on the Resurrection and the other on Faith, could only have been written by the great Apostle of the Gentiles.

It has been so in all ages of the world. . . .

* * *

In conclusion, we venture to offer a few words of advice and warning to those who medi-

tate authorship. Those who have already adopted a vicious style are, we fear, incorrigible; but there are writers in embryo to whom our suggestions may not be addressed in vain. The first object of every author ought to be to write correctly; the second, to write naturally and unaffectedly; and the third, if indeed it is not combined in the other two, to write gracefully and attractively. We entirely agree with Dugald Stewart, that

> the works which continue to please from age to age are written with perfect simplicity, while those which captivate the multitude by a display of meretricious ornaments, if by chance they should survive the fashions to which they are accommodated, remain only to furnish a subject of ridicule to posterity.

And this explains the remark of Pascal, that *les meilleurs livres sont ceux que chaque lecteur croit qu'il auroit pu faire* [the best books are those that the reader believes he could have written himself]. Let every writer bear in mind, that the foundation and basis of the English language is Anglo-Saxon. Dean Trench, who is himself the master of an excellent style, in his *English, Past and Present*, says, as in fact had been substantially said by Sir Thomas Browne more than a century and a half ago:–

> All its joints, its whole *articulation,* its sinews and its ligaments, the great body of articles, pronouns, conjunctions, prepositions, numerals, auxiliary verbs, all smaller words which serve to knit together and bind the larger into sentences; these, not to speak of the grammatical structure of the language, are exclusively Saxon. The Latin may contribute its tale of bricks, yea, of goodly and polished hewn stones, to the spiritual building; but the mortar, with all that holds and binds the different parts of it together, and constitutes them into a house, is Saxon throughout.

And we may add that its most forcible and expressive words are also Saxon. So completely does that element pervade it, that it would be almost impossible to compose a sentence of moderate length consisting solely of works of Latin derivation. But there are many which can be rendered wholly in Anglo-Saxon. It would be easy to make the Lord's Prayer entirely, as it is in present use almost entirely, Anglo-Saxon. It consists of sixty words, and six of these only have a Latin root. But for each of them, except one, we have an exact Saxon equivalent. For 'trespasses,' we may substitute 'sins;' for 'temptation,' 'trials;' for 'deliver,' 'free;' and for 'power,' 'might.' Dr. Trench proposes for 'glory,' 'brightness;' but this we think is not a good substitute, although we are unable to suggest a better. No writer was fonder of Latinized forms of words than Sir Thomas Browne, and yet he could construct paragraphs wholly out of Anglo-Saxon, as, for instance, the following, quoted by Dean Trench out of several which the knight of Norwich has given as examples:–

> The first and foremost step to all good works is the dread and fear of the Lord of heaven and earth, which, through the Holy Ghost, enlighteneth the blindness of our simple hearts to tread the ways of wisdom, and lead our feet into the land of blessing.

The great lesson to be drawn from the fact that Anglo-Saxon underlies, like original granite, all the strata of the English language, is, that to write in it is to write for the hearts of the people. It is *their* mother-tongue, strong, sinewy, and expressive; and they cling to it with a fondness which no change of usage can uproot, and no caprice of fashion can destroy. Just compare, in point of force and significance, a 'sanguinary action,' with a 'bloody deed;' 'eternal felicity,' with 'everlasting happiness;' and 'the exemplar of the celestials,' in the Rhemish version of the Scriptures, with 'the pattern of things in the heavens,' in our own; and you will feel at once how the language is emasculated by such attempted equivalents.

It would, however, be a ridiculous kind of pedantry to insist that all words of Greek or Latin origin should be avoided. This would indeed be as impossible as the converse case. The necessities of science, philosophy, and the arts, and the wants of an advanced civilization, absolutely require the admixture of these elements, which contribute so much to the wealth and beauty of the language. Sir James Mackintosh has pointed out, in his *History of England,* that if you wished to express 'the penetrability of matter' in Anglo-Saxon, you would be compelled to say 'the thoroughfaresomeness of stuff.' But there is a rule which applies to the selection of all words, whether Greek, Latin, or Anglo-Saxon; and it is that which is laid down by the authors of *Guesses at Truth,* and is supposed to be addressed to a lady:–

> When you doubt between two words, choose the plainest, the commonest, the most idiomatic. Eschew fine words as you would rouge; love simple ones as you would native roses on your cheeks.

Above all things, avoid the habit of going out of your way to introduce long words or periphrastic expressions, to show off either your learning or your wit. In one of his early letters, Coleridge playfully asks a friend to look out for him a maid-servant 'scientific in vaccimulgence,' and says, 'That last word is a new one, but soft in sound and full of expression. Vaccimulgence! I am pleased with the word.' But this was only in joke. Chaucer says, in praise of his Virginia, that

> No contrefeted termes hadde she
> To semen wise;

and if you wish to write well, your English must be genuine, and not counterfeit. Do not, either, on the one hand, with Colonel Mundy, speak of the sea-breeze as 'a puff of the briny;' nor, on the other, call cow-milking 'vaccimulgence.' The simplest style is generally the safest. Not that we intend to proscribe the use of metaphor or image when it is appropriate to the subject; and we should be sorry to act as sternly as Coleridge's schoolmaster, the Rev. James Bowyer, who thus addressed his trembling pupil:–'Muse, boy, muse? Your nurse's daughter you mean! Pierian spring? Oh, ay! the cloister-pump, I suppose!'

Do not pollute the pure well of English undefiled, with the rubbish of affectation and conceit; nor imagine for a moment that liveliness of style consists in a running fire of jokes, nor that the want of wit can be redeemed by vulgarity. Remember what a noble heritage you possess in the English language, and strive to be, in the words of Dean Trench, 'guardians of its purity, and not corruptors of it.' He cites, in proof of the estimation in which it is held by those who are competent to appreciate it, one of the greatest philologers of modern times, Jacob Grimm, who ascribes to it 'a veritable power of expression, such as perhaps never stood at the command of any other language of men,' and says–

> In truth, the English language, which by no mere accident has produced and upborne the greatest and most predominant poet of modern times, as distinguished from the ancient classical poetry (I can of

course only mean Shakespeare), may with all right be called a world-language, and, like the English people, appears destined hereafter to prevail with a sway, more extensive even than its present, over all the portions of the globe, for in wealth, good sense, and closeness of structure, no other of the languages at this day spoken deserves to be compared with it—not even our German, which is torn even as we are torn, and must first rid itself of many defects before it can enter boldly into the lists as a competitor with the English.

Surely this is a language which is worth preserving in its purity, which is worth weaving into textures of beauty, and which ought not to be employed in the manufacture of literary slang.

---

1. *Elements of Rhetoric.* By Richard Whately, D.D., Archbishop of Dublin. London: John W. Parker and Son. 1851.

English, Past and Present. By Richard Chenevix Trench, B.D. London: John W. Parker and Son. 1855.

2. We remember visiting the citadel of Antwerp shortly after its siege and capture by the French in 1832, and we were struck by the tasteful way in which a little wicker gate had been arranged at the extremity of a covered sap through which the storming party was to have rushed, if the place had not surrendered immediately before the intended assault.

Reprinted from *Fraser's Magazine,* 55 (March 1857): 249-264; (April 1857): 424-439.

Wilkie Collins

From "The Unknown Public" (1858)

Wilkie Collins (1824-1889) is now best known as a pro-lific novelist, and as the virtual inventor of the English detective novel with such books as The Woman in White *(1860) and* The Moonstone *(1868). A friend of Charles Dickens, Collins was also a regular contribu-tor to the weekly magazines Dickens edited, and Collins's essay on "The Unknown Public," an analysis of the cheap penny papers for the new, vast urban reader-ship, first appeared in the 21 August 1858 issue of Dickens's* Household Words. *Collins's discussion is sig-nificant in showing the awareness among Victorian middle-class writers of shifting audiences for their work and of the certainty of further change as expanded educa-tional provision increased urban literacy rates.–Ed.*

Do the subscribers to this journal, the custom-ers at the eminent publishing-houses, the mem-bers of book-clubs and circulating libraries, and the purchasers and borrowers of newspapers and reviews, compose altogether the great bulk of the reading public of England? There was a time when, if anybody had put this question to me, I, for one, should certainly have answered, Yes.

I know better now. I know that the public just now mentioned, viewed as an audience for lit-erature, is nothing more than a minority.

This discovery (which I venture to consider equally new and surprising) dawned upon me gradually. I made my first approaches towards it, in walking about London, more especially in the second and third rate neighborhoods. At such times, whenever I passed a small stationer's or small tobacconist's shop, I became conscious, me-chanically as it were, of certain publications which invariably occupied the windows. These publications all appeared to be of the same small quarto size; they seemed to consist merely of a few unbound pages; each one of them had a pic-ture on the upper half of the front leaf, and a quantity of small print on the under. I noticed just as much as this, for some time, and no more. None of the gentlemen who are so good as to guide my taste in literary matters, had ever di-rected my attention towards these mysterious pub-lications. My favourite Review is, as I firmly be-lieve, at this very day, unconscious of their exis-

tence. My enterprising librarian who forces all sorts of books on my attention that I don't want to read, because he has bought whole editions of them a great bargain, has never yet tried me with the limp unbound picture quarto of the small shops. Day after day and week after week, the mys-terious publications haunted my walks, go where I might; and, still, I was too inconceivably care-less to stop and notice them in detail. I left Lon-don and travelled about England. The neglected publications followed me. There they were in every town, large or small. I saw them in fruit-shops, in oyster-shops, in lollypop-shops. Villages even–picturesque, strong-smelling villages–were not free from them. Wherever the speculative dar-ing of one man could open a shop, and the human appetites and necessities of his fellow mor-tals could keep it from shutting up again, there, as it appeared to me, the unbound picture quarto instantly entered, set itself up obtrusively in the window, and insisted on being looked at by everybody. "Buy me, borrow me, stare at me, steal me–do anything, O inattentive stranger, ex-cept contemptuously pass me by."

Under this sort of compulsion, it was not long before I began to stop at shop-windows and look attentively at these all-pervading specimens of what was to me a new species of literary pro-duction. I made acquaintance with one of them among the deserts of West Cornwall, with an-other in a populous thoroughfare of White-chapel, with a third in a dreary little lost town at the north of Scotland. I went into a lovely county of South Wales; the modest railway had not pene-trated to it, but the audacious picture quarto had found it out. Who could resist this perpetual, this inevitable, this magnificently unlimited appeal to notice and patronage? From looking in at the win-dows of the shops, I got on to entering the shops themselves, to buying specimens of this locust-flight of small publications, to making strict exami-nation of them from the first page to the last, and finally, to instituting inquiries about them in all sorts of well-informed quarters. The result–the astonishing result–has been the discovery of an Unknown Public; a public to be counted by millions; the mysterious, the unfathomable, the universal public of the penny-novel Journals.[1]

I have five of these journals now before me, represented by one sample copy, bought haphazard, of each. There are many more; but these five represent the successful and well-established members of the literary family. The eldest of them is a stout lad of fifteen years standing. The youngest is an infant of three months old. All five are sold at the same price of one penny; all five are published regularly once a week; all five contain about the same quantity of matter.

The weekly circulation of the most successful of the five, is now publicly advertised (and, as I am informed, without exaggeration) at half a Million. Taking the other four as attaining altogether to a circulation of another half million (which is probably much under the right estimate) we have a sales of a Million weekly for five penny journals. Reckoning only three readers to each copy sold, the result is a *public of three millions*—a public unknown to the literary world; unknown, as disciples, to the whole body of professed critics; unknown, as customers, at the great libraries and the great publishing-houses; unknown, as an audience, to the distinguished English writers of our own time. A reading public of three millions which lies right out of the pale of literary civilisation, is a phenomenon worth examining—a mystery which the sharpest man among us may not find it easy to solve.

In the first place, who are the three million—the Unknown Public—as I have ventured to call them? The known reading public—the minority already referred to—are easily discovered and classified. There is the religious public, with booksellers and literature of its own, which includes reviews and newspapers as well as books. There is the public which reads for information, and devotes itself to Histories, Biographies, Essays, Treatises, Voyages and Travels. There is the public which reads for amusement, and patronises the Circulating Library and the railway book-stalls. There is, lastly, the public which reads nothing but newspapers. We all know where to lay our hands on the people who represent these various classes. We see the books they like on their tables. We meet them out at dinner, and hear them talk of their favourite authors. We know, if we are at all conversant with literary matters, even the very districts of London in which certain classes of people live who are to be depended upon beforehand as the picked readers for certain kinds of books. But what do we know of the enormous out-

lawed majority—of the lost literary tribes—of the prodigious, the overwhelming three millions! Absolutely nothing. . . .

The Unknown Public is, in a literary sense, hardly beginning, as yet, to learn to read. The members of it are evidently, in the mass, from no fault of theirs, still ignorant of almost everything which is generally known and understood among readers whom circumstances have placed, socially and intellectually, in the rank above them. The mere references in Monte Cristo, The Mysteries of Paris, and White Lies (the scene of this last English fiction having been laid on French ground), to foreign names, titles, manners and customs, puzzled the Unknown Public on the threshold. Look back at the answers to correspondents, and then say, out of fifty subscribers to a penny journal, how many are likely to know, for example, that Mademoiselle means Miss? Besides the difficulty in appealing to the penny audience caused at the beginning by such simple obstacles as this, there was the great additional difficulty, in the case of all three of the fictions just mentioned, of accustoming untried readers to the delicacies and subtleties of literary art. An immense public has been discovered: the next thing to be done is, in a literary sense, to teach that public how to read. . . .

Meanwhile, it is perhaps hardly too much to say, that the future of English fiction may rest with this Unknown Public, which is now waiting to be taught the difference between a good book and a bad. It is probably a question of time only. The largest audience for periodical literature, in this age of periodicals, must obey the universal law of progress, and must, sooner or later, learn to discriminate. When that period comes, the readers who rank by millions, will be the readers who give the widest reputations, who return the richest rewards, and who will, therefore, command the service of the best writers of their time. A great, an unparalleled prospect awaits, perhaps, the coming generation of English novelists. To the penny journals of the present time belongs, the credit of having discovered a new public. When that public shall discover its need of a great writer, the great writer will have such an audience as has never yet been known.

---

1. It may be well to explain that I use this awkward compound word in order to mark the distinction between a penny journal and a penny newspaper. The "journal" is what I am now writing about. The "newspaper" is an entirely different subject, with which this article has no connection.

Reprinted from *Household Words,* 18 (21 August 1858).

Alexander Smith

"On the Writing of Essays" (1862)

One of the submerged prose genres of the early Victorian period was the familiar essay, because of the dominance of full-length review articles in the most prominent quarterly periodicals. Alexander Smith (1830-1867), a Scottish textile designer from Glasgow, developed a distinctive reputation for his informal essays, collected under the title Dreamthorp *(1863); "Dreamthorp" is the name he gave to a fictional suburban village retreat, where in imagination he could escape from contemporary city problems and controversies into a dreamlike world of books. Smith's "On the Writing of Essays," first published in the June 1862 issue of* Good Words, *discusses the tradition of the informal, familiar essay from its origins in Montaigne to its culmination in the essays that Charles Lamb wrote under the pseudonym Elia. Smith's turning from polemic and controversy to a more personal and familiar tone was influential with many later Victorian prose stylists, including Robert Louis Stevenson.—Ed.*

I have already described my environments and my mode of life, and out of both I contrive to extract a very tolerable amount of satisfaction. Love in a cottage, with a broken window to let in the rain, is not my idea of comfort; no more is Dignity, walking forth richly clad, to whom every head uncovers, every knee grows supple. Bruin in wintertime fondly suckling his own paws, loses flesh; and love, feeding upon itself, dies of inanition. Take the candle of death in your hand, and walk through the stately galleries of the world, and their splendid furniture and array are as the tinsel armour and pasteboard goblets of a penny theatre; fame is but an inscription on a grave, and glory the melancholy blazon on a coffin lid. We argue fiercely about happiness. One insists that she is found in the cottage which the hawthorn shades. Another that she is a lady of fashion, and treads on a cloth of gold. Wisdom, listening to both, shakes a white head, and considers that "a good deal may be said on both sides."

There is a wise saying to the effect that "a man can eat no more than he can hold." Every man gets about the same satisfaction out of life. Mr. Suddlechops, the barber of Seven Dials, is as happy as Alexander at the head of his legions. The business of the one is to depopulate kingdoms, the business of the other to reap beards seven days old; but their relative positions do not affect the question. The one works with razors and soap-lather, the other with battle-cries and well-greaved Greeks. The one of a Saturday night counts up his shabby gains and grumbles; the other on *his* Saturday night sits down and weeps for other worlds to conquer. The pence to Mr. Suddlechops are as important as are the worlds to Alexander. Every condition of life has its peculiar advantages, and wisdom points these out and is contented with them. The varlet who sang—

> "A king cannot swagger
> Or get drunk like a beggar,
> Nor be half so happy as I"—

had the soul of a philosopher in him. The harshness of the parlour is revenged at night in the servants' hall. The coarse rich man rates his domestic, but there is a thought in the domestic's brain, docile and respectful as he looks, which makes the matter equal, which would madden the rich man if he knew it—make him wince as with a shrewdest twinge of hereditary gout. For insult and degradation are not without their peculiar solaces. You may spit upon Shylock's gaberdine, but the day comes when he demands his pound of flesh; every blow, every insult, not without a certain satisfaction, he adds to the account running up against you in the day-book and ledger of his hate—which at the proper time he will ask you to discharge. Every way we look we see even-handed nature administering her laws of compensation. Grandeur has a heavy tax to pay. The usurper rolls along like a god, surrounded by his guards. He dazzles the crowd—all very fine; but look beneath his splendid trappings and you see a shirt of mail, and beneath *that* a heart cowering in terror of an air-drawn dagger. Whom did the memory of Austerlitz most keenly sting? The beaten emperors? or the mighty Napoleon, dying like an untended watch-fire on St Helena?

Giddy people may think the life I lead here

428

staid and humdrum, but they are mistaken. It is true, I hear no concerts, save those in which the thrushes are performers in the spring mornings. I see no pictures, save those painted on the wide sky-canvas with the colours of sunrise and sunset. I attend neither rout nor ball; I have no deeper dissipation than the tea table; I hear no more exciting scandal than quiet village gossip. Yet I enjoy my concerts more than I would the great London ones. I like the pictures I see and think them better painted, too, than those which adorn the walls of the Royal Academy; and the village gossip is more after my turn of mind than the scandals that convulse the clubs. It is wonderful how the whole world reflects itself in the simple village life. The people around me are full of their own affairs and interests; were they of imperial magnitude, they could not be excited more strongly. Farmer Worthy is anxious about the next market; the likelihood of a fall in the price of butter and eggs hardly allows him to sleep o' nights. The village doctor–happily we have only one–skirrs hither and thither in his gig, as if man could neither die nor be born without his assistance. He is continually standing on the confines of existence, welcoming the newcomer, bidding farewell to the goer-away. And the robustious fellow who sits at the head of the table when the Jolly Swillers meet at the Blue Lion on Wednesday evenings is a great politician, sound of lung metal, and wields the village in the taproom, as my Lord Palmerston wields the nation in the House. His listeners think him a wiser personage than the Premier, and he is inclined to lean to that opinion himself. I find everything here that other men find in the big world. London is but a magnified Dreamthorp.

And just as the Rev. Mr White took note of the ongoings of the seasons in and around Hampshire Selborne, watched the colonies of the rooks in the tall elms, looked after the swallows in the cottage and rectory eaves, played the affectionate spy on the private lives of chaffinch and hedgesparrow, was eavesdropper to the solitary cuckoo; so here I keep eye and ear open; take note of man, woman, and child; find many a pregnant text imbedded in the commonplace of village life; and, out of what I see and hear, weave in my own room my essays as solitarily as the spider weaves his web in the darkened corner. The essay, as a literary form, resembles the lyric, in so far as it is moulded by some central mood– whimsical, serious, or satirical. Give the mood, and the essay, from the first sentence to the last,

grows around it as the cocoon grows around the silkworm. The essay-writer is a chartered libertine, and a law unto himself. A quick ear and eye, an ability to discern the infinite suggestiveness of common things, a brooding meditative spirit, are all that the essayist requires to start business with. Jacques, in "As You Like It," had the makings of a charming essayist. It is not the essayist's duty to inform, to build pathways through metaphysical morasses, to cancel abuses, any more than it is the duty of the poet to do these things. Incidentally he may do something in that way, just as the poet may, but it is not his duty, and should not be expected of him. Skylarks are primarily created to sing, although a whole choir of them may be baked in pies and brought to table; they were born to make music, although they may incidentally stay the pangs of vulgar hunger. The essayist is a kind of poet in prose, and if questioned harshly as to his uses, he might be unable to render a better apology for his existence than a flower might. The essay should be pure literature as the poem is pure literature. The essayist wears a lance, but he cares more for the sharpness of its point than for the pennon that flutters on it, than for the banner of the captain under whom he serves. He plays with death as Hamlet plays with Yorick's skull, and he reads the morals– strangely stern, often, for such fragrant lodging– which are folded up in the bosoms of roses. He has no pride, and is deficient in a sense of the congruity and fitness of things. He lifts a pebble from the ground, and puts it aside more carefully than any gem; and on a nail in a cottage-door he will hang the mantle of his thought, heavily brocaded with the gold of rhetoric. He finds his way into the Elysian fields through portals the most shabby and commonplace.

The essayist plays with his subject, now in whimsical, now in grave, now in melancholy mood. He lies upon the idle grassy bank, like Jacques, letting the world flow past him, and from this thing and the other he extracts his mirth and his moralities. His main gift is an eye to discover the suggestiveness of common things; to find a sermon in the most uncompromising texts. Beyond the vital hint, the first step, his discourses are not beholden to their titles. Let him take up the most trivial subject, and it will lead him away to the great questions over which the serious imagination loves to brood,–fortune, mutability, death,–just as inevitably as the runnel, trickling among the summer hills, on which sheep are bleating, leads you to the sea; or as, turning down the first street you come to in the city, you are led finally, albeit by many an intricacy, out into the open country, with its waste places and its woods, where you are lost in a sense of strangeness and solitariness. The world is to the meditative man what the mulberry plant is to the silkworm. The essay-writer has no lack of subject-matter. He has the day that is passing over his head; and, if unsatisfied with that, he has the world's six thousand years to depasture his day or serious humour upon. I idle away my time here, and I am finding new subjects every hour. Everything I see or hear is an essay in bud. The world is everywhere whispering essays, and one need only be the world's amanuensis. The proverbial expression which last evening the clown dropped as he trudged homeward to supper, the light of the setting sun on his face, expands before me to a dozen pages. The coffin of the pauper, which to-day I saw carried carelessly along, is as good a subject as the funeral procession of an emperor. Craped drum and banner add nothing to death; penury and disrespect take nothing away. Incontinently my thought moves like a slow-paced hearse with sable nodding plumes. Two rustic lovers, whispering between the darkening hedges, is as potent to project my mind into the tender passion as if I had seen Romeo touch the cheek of Juliet in the moonlight garden. Seeing a curly-headed child asleep in the sunshine before a cottage door is sufficient excuse for a discourse on childhood; quite as good as if I had seen infant Cain asleep in the lap of Eve with Adam looking on. A lark cannot rise to heaven without raising as many thoughts as there are notes in its song. Dawn cannot pour its white light on my village without starting from their dim lair a hundred reminiscences; nor can sunset burn above yonder trees in the west without attracting to itself the melancholy of a life-time. When spring unfolds her green leaves I would be provoked to indite an essay on hope and youth, were it not that it is already writ in the carols of the birds; and I might be tempted in autumn to improve the occasion, were it not for the rustle of the withered leaves as I walk through the woods. Compared with that simple music, the saddest-cadenced words have but a shallow meaning.

The essayist who feeds his thoughts upon the segment of the world which surrounds him cannot avoid being an egotist; but then his egotism is not unpleasing. If he be without taint of boastfulness, of self sufficiency, of hungry vanity, the world will not press the charge home. If a man discourses continually of his wines, his plate, his titled acquaintances, the number and quality of his horses, his men-servants and maid-servants, he must discourse very skilfully indeed if he escapes being called a coxcomb. If a man speaks of death—tells you that the idea of it continually haunts him, that he has the most insatiable curiosity as to death and dying, that his thought mines in churchyards like a "demon-mole"—no one is specially offended, and that this is a dull fellow is the hardest thing likely to be said of him. Only, the egotism that over-crows you is offensive, that exalts trifles and takes pleasure in them, that suggests superiority in matters of equipage and furniture; and the egotism is offensive, because it runs counter to and jostles your self-complacency. The egotism which rises no higher than the grave is of a solitary and a hermit kind—it crosses no man's path, it disturbs no man's *amour propre*. You may offend a man if you say you are as rich as he, as wise as he, as handsome as he. You offend no man if you tell him that, like him, you have to die. The king, in his crown and coronation robes, will allow the beggar to claim that relationship with him. To have to die is a distinction of which no man is proud. The speaking about one's self is not necessarily offensive. A modest, truthful man speaks better about himself than about anything else, and on that subject his speech is likely to be most profitable to his hearers. Certainly, there is no subject with which he is better acquainted, and on which he has better title to be heard. And it is this egotism, this perpetual reference to self, in which the charm of the essayist resides. If a man is worth knowing at all, he is worth knowing well. The essayist gives you his thoughts, and lets you know, in addition, how he came by them. He has nothing to conceal; he throws open his doors and windows, and lets him enter who will. You like to walk round peculiar or important men as you like to walk round a building, to view it from different points, and in different lights. Of the essayist, when his mood is communicative, you obtain a full picture. You are made his contemporary and familiar friend. You enter into his humours and his seriousness. You are made heir of his whims, prejudices, and playfulness. You walk through the whole nature of him, as you walk through the streets of Pompeii, looking into the interior of stately mansions, reading the satirical scribblings on the walls. And the essayist's habit of not only giving you his thoughts, but telling you how he came by them, is interesting, because it shows you by what alchemy the ruder world becomes transmuted into the finer. We like to know the lineage of great earls and swift race-horses. We like to know that the discovery of the law of gravitation was born of the fall of an apple in an English garden on a summer afternoon. Essays written after this fashion are racy of the soil in which they grow, as you taste the lava in the vines grown on the slopes of Etna, they say. There is a healthy Gascon flavour in Montaigne's Essays; and Charles Lamb's are scented with the primroses of Covent Garden.

The essayist does not usually appear early in the literary history of a country: he comes naturally after the poet and the chronicler. His habit of mind is leisurely; he does not write from any special stress of passionate impulse; he does not create material so much as he comments upon material already existing. It is essential for him that books should have been written, and that they should, at least to some extent, have been read and digested. He is usually full of allusions and references, and these his reader must be able to follow and understand. And in this literary walk, as in most others, the giants come first: Montaigne and Lord Bacon were our earliest essayists, and, as yet, they are our best. In point of style, these essays are different from anything that could now be produced. Not only is the thinking different—the manner of setting forth the thinking is different also. We despair of reaching the thought, we despair equally of reaching the language. We can no more bring back their turns of sentence than we can bring back their tournaments. Montaigne, in his serious moods, has a curiously rich and intricate eloquence; and Bacon's sentence bends beneath the weight of his thought, like a branch beneath the weight of its fruit. Bacon seems to have written his essays with Shakspeare's pen. There is a certain want of ease about the old writers which has an irresistible charm. The language flows like a stream over a pebbled bed, with propulsion, eddy, and sweet recoil—the pebbles, if retarding movement, giving ring and dimple to the surface, and breaking the whole into babbling music. There is a ceremoniousness in the mental habits of these ancients. Their intellectual garniture is picturesque, like the garniture of their bodies. Their thoughts are courtly and high mannered. A singular analogy exists between the personal attire of a period and its written style. The peaked beard, the starched collar, the quilted doublet, have their correspondences in the high sentence and elaborate orna-

ment (worked upon the thought like figures upon tapestry) of Sidney and Spencer. In Pope's day men wore rapiers, and their weapons they carried with them into literature, and frequently unsheathed them too. They knew how to stab to the heart with an epigram. Style went out with the men who wore knee-breeches and buckles in their shoes. We write more easily now; but in our easy writing there is ever a taint of flippancy: our writing is to theirs, what shooting-coat and wide-awake are to doublet and plumed hat.

Montaigne and Bacon are our earliest and greatest essayists, and likeness and unlikeness exist between the men. Bacon was constitutionally the graver nature. He writes like one on whom presses the weight of affairs, and he approaches a subject always on its serious side. He does not play with it fantastically. He lives amongst great ideas, as with great nobles, with whom he dare not be too familiar. In the tone of his mind there is ever something imperial. When he writes on building, he speaks of a palace with spacious entrances, and courts, and banqueting-halls; when he writes on gardens, he speaks of alleys and mounts, waste places and fountains, of a garden "which is indeed prince-like." To read over his table of contents, is like reading over a roll of peers' names. We have, taking them as they stand, essays treating *Of Great Place, Of Boldness, Of Goodness, and Goodness of Nature, Of Nobility, Of Seditions and Troubles, Of Atheism, Of Superstition, Of Travel, Of Empire, Of Counsel,*—a book plainly to lie in the closets of statesmen and princes, and designed to nurture the noblest natures. Bacon always seems to write with his ermine on. Montaigne was different from all this. His table of contents reads in comparison like a medley, or a catalogue of an auction. He was quite as wise as Bacon; he could look through men quite as clearly, and search them quite as narrowly; certain of his moods were quite as serious, and in one corner of his heart he kept a yet profounder melancholy; but he was volatile, a humorist and a gossip. He could be dignified enough on great occasions, but dignity and great occasions bored him. He could stand in the presence with propriety enough, but then he got out of the presence as rapidly as possible. When, in the thirty-eighth year of his age, he—somewhat world weary, and with more scars on his heart than he cared to discover—retired to his chateau, he placed his library "in the great tower overlooking the entrance to the court," and over the central rafter he inscribed in large letters the device—"I

DO NOT UNDERSTAND; I PAUSE; I EXAMINE."
When he began to write his Essays he had no
great desire to shine as an author; he wrote simply to relieve teeming heart and brain. The best
method to lay the spectres of the mind is to commit them to paper. Speaking of the Essays, he
says, "This book has a domestic and private object. It is intended for the use of my relations
and friends; so that, when they have lost me,
which they will soon do, they may find in it some
features of my condition and humours; and by
this means keep up more completely, and in a
more lively manner, the knowledge they have of
me." In his Essays he meant to portray himself,
his habits, his modes of thought, his opinions,
what fruit of wisdom he had gathered from experience sweet and bitter; and the task he has executed with wonderful fidelity. He does not make
himself a hero. Cromwell would have his warts
painted; and Montaigne paints his, and paints
them too with a certain fondness. He is perfectly
tolerant of himself and of everybody else. Whatever be the subject, the writing flows on easy, equable, self-satisfied, almost always with a personal anecdote floating on the surface. Each event of his
past life he considers a fact of nature; creditable
or the reverse, there it is; sometimes to be speculated upon, not in the least to be regretted. If it
is worth nothing else, it may be made the subject
of an essay or, at least, be useful as an illustration. We have not only his thoughts, we see also
how and from what they arose. When he presents you with a bouquet, you notice that the flowers have been plucked up by the roots, and to
the roots a portion of the soil still adheres. On
his daily life his Essays grew like lichens upon
rocks. If a thing is useful to him, he is not squeamish as to where he picks it up. In his eyes there is
nothing common or unclean; and he accepts a favour as willingly from a beggar as from a prince.
When it serves his purpose, he quotes a tavern
catch, or the smart saying of a kitchen wench,
with as much relish as the fine sentiment of a classical poet, or the gallant *bon mot* of a king. Everything is important which relates to himself. That
his moustache, if stroked with his perfumed
glove, or handkerchief, will retain the odour a
whole day, is related with as much gravity as the
loss of a battle, or the march of a desolating
plague. Montaigne, in his grave passages, reaches
an eloquence intricate and highly wrought; but
then his moods are Protean, and he is constantly
alternating his stateliness with familiarity, anecdote, humour, coarseness. His Essays are like a

mythological landscape—you hear the pipe of Pan
in the distance, the naked goddess moves past,
the satyr leers from the thicket. At the core of
him profoundly melancholy, and consumed by a
hunger for truth, he stands like Prospero in the enchanted island, and he has Ariel and Caliban to
do his behests and run his errands. Sudden alternations are very characteristic of him. Whatever
he says suggests its opposite. He laughs at himself and his reader. He builds his castle of cards
for the mere pleasure of knocking it down again.
He is ever unexpected and surprising. And with
this curious mental activity, this play and linked
dance of discordant elements, his page is alive
and restless, like the constant flicker of light and
shadow in a mass of foliage which the wind is
stirring.

Montaigne is avowedly an egotist; and by
those who are inclined to make this a matter of reproach, it should be remembered that the value
of egotism depends entirely on the egotist. If the
egotist is weak, his egotism is worthless. If the egotist is strong, acute, full of distinctive character,
his egotism is precious, and remains a possession
of the race. If Shakspeare had left personal revelations, how we should value them; if, indeed, he
has not in some sense left them—if the tragedies
and comedies are not personal revelations
altogether—the multiform nature of the man rushing toward the sun at once in Falstaff, Hamlet,
and Romeo. But calling Montaigne an egotist
does not go a great way to decipher him. No
writer takes the reader so much into his confidence. He tells us everything about himself, we
think; and when all is told, it is astonishing how little we really know. The esplanades of Montaigne's palace are thoroughfares, men from
every European country rub clothes there, but
somewhere in the building there is a secret room
in which the master sits, of which no one but himself wears the key. We read in the Essays about
his wife, his daughter, his daughter's governess,
of his cook, of his page, "who was never found
guilty of telling the truth," of his library, the Gascon harvest outside his chateau, his habits of composition, his favourite speculations; but somehow
the man himself is constantly eluding us. His
daughter's governess, his page, the ripening Gascon fields, are never introduced for their own
sakes; they are employed to illustrate and set off
the subject on which he happens to be writing. A
brawl in his own kitchen he does not consider worthy of being specially set down, but he has seen
and heard everything; it comes in his way when

travelling in some remote region, and accordingly it finds a place. He is the frankest, most outspoken of writers; and that very frankness and outspokenness puts the reader off his guard. If you wish to preserve your secret, wrap it up in frankness. The Essays are full of this trick. The frankness is as well simulated as the grape-branches of the Grecian artist which the birds flew towards and pecked. When Montaigne retreats, he does so like a skilful general, leaving his fires burning. In other ways, too, he is an adept in putting his reader out. He discourses with the utmost gravity, but you suspect mockery or banter in his tones. He is serious with the most trifling subjects, and he trifles with the most serious. "He broods eternally over his own thought," but who can tell what his thought may be for the nonce? He is of all writers the most vagrant, surprising, and, to many minds, illogical. His sequences are not the sequences of other men. His writings are as full of transformations as a pantomime or a fairy tale. His arid wastes lead up to glittering palaces, his banqueting-halls end in a dog-hutch. He begins an essay about trivialities, and the conclusion is in the otherworld. And the peculiar character of his writing which is worth anything, arises from constitutional turn of mind. He is constantly playing at fast and loose with himself and his reader. He mocks and scorns his deeper nature; and, like Shakspeare in Hamlet, says his deepest things in a jesting way. When he is gayest, be sure there is a serious design in his gaiety. Singularly shrewd and penetrating–sad, not only from sensibility of exquisite nerve and tissue, but from meditation, and an eye that pierced the surfaces of things–fond of pleasure, yet strangely fascinated by death–sceptical, yet clinging to what the Church taught and believed–lazily possessed by a high ideal of life, yet unable to reach it, careless perhaps often to strive after it, and with no very high opinion of his own goodness, or of the goodness of his fellows–and with all these serious elements, an element of humour mobile as flame, which assumed a variety of forms, now pure fun, now mischievous banter, now blistering scorn–humour in all its shapes, carelessly exercised on himself and his readers–with all this variety, complexity, riot, and contradiction almost of intellectual forces within, Montaigne wrote his bewildering Essays–with the exception of Rabelais, the greatest modern Frenchman–the creator of a distinct literary form, and to whom, down even to our own day, even in point of subject-matter, every essayist has been more or less indebted.

Bacon is the greatest of the serious and stately essayists,–Montaigne the greatest of the garrulous and communicative. The one gives you his thoughts on Death, Travel, Government, and the like, and lets you make the best of them; the other gives you his on the same subjects, but he wraps them up in personal gossip and reminiscence. With the last it is never Death or Travel alone; it is always Death one-fourth, and Montaigne three-fourths; or Travel one-fourth, and Montaigne three-fourths. He pours his thought into the water of gossip, and gives you to drink. He gilds his pill always, and he always gilds it with himself. The general characteristics of his Essays have been indicated, and it is worth while inquiring what they teach, what positive good they have done, and why for three centuries they have charmed, and still continue to charm.

The Essays contain a philosophy of life, which is not specially high, yet which is certain to find acceptance more or less with men who have passed out beyond the glow of youth, and who have made trial of the actual world. The essence of his philosophy is a kind of cynical common sense. He will risk nothing in life; he will keep to the beaten track; he will not let passion blind or enslave him; he will gather around him what good he can, and will therewith endeavor to be content. He will be, as far as possible, self-sustained; he will not risk his happiness in the hands of man, or of woman either. He is shy of friendship, he fears love, for he knows that both are dangerous. He knows that life is full of bitters, and he holds it wisdom that a man should console himself, as far as possible, with its sweets, the principal of which are peace, travel, leisure, and the writing of essays. He values obtainable Gascon bread and cheese more than the unobtainable stars. He thinks crying for the moon the foolishest thing in the world. He will remain where he is. He will not deny that a new world may exist beyond the sunset, but he knows that to reach the new world there is a troublesome Atlantic to cross; and he is not in the least certain that, putting aside the chance of being drowned on the way, he will be one whit happier in the new world than he is in the old. For his part he will embark with no Columbus. He feels that life is but a sad thing at best; but as he has little hope of making it better, he accepts it, and will not make it worse by murmuring. When the chain galls him, he can at least revenge himself by making jests on it. He will temper the despotism of nature by epigrams. He has read Aesop's fable, and is the last man in the world to relinquish the shabbiest substance to grasp at the finest shadow.

Of nothing under the sun was Montaigne quite certain, except that every man–whatever his station–might travel farther and fare worse; and that the playing with his own thoughts, in the shape of essay-writing, was the most harmless of amusements. His practical acquiescence in things does not promise much fruit, save to himself; yet in virtue of it he became one of the forces of the world–a very visible agent in bringing about the Europe which surrounds us to-day. He lived in the midst of the French religious wars. The rulers of his country were execrable Christians, but most orthodox Catholics. The burning of heretics was a public amusement, and the court ladies sat out the play. On the queen-mother and on her miserable son lay all the blood of the St Bartholomew. The country was torn asunder; everywhere was battle, murder, pillage, and such woful partings as Mr Millais has represented in his incomparable picture. To the solitary humorous essayist this state of things was hateful. He was a good Catholic in his easy way; he attended divine service regularly; he crossed himself when he yawned. He conformed in practice to every rule of the church; but if orthodox in these matters, he was daring in speculation. There was nothing he was not bold enough to question. He waged war after his peculiar fashion with every form of superstition. He worked under the foundations of priestcraft. But while serving the Reformed cause, he had no sympathy with Reformers. If they would but remain quiet, but keep their peculiar notions to themselves, France would rest! That a man should go to the stake for an opinion, was as incomprehensible to him as that a priest or king should send him there for an opinion. He thought the persecuted and the persecutors fools about equally matched. He was easy-tempered and humane–in the hunting-field, he could not bear the cry of a dying hare with composure–martyr-burning had consequently no attraction for such a man. His scepticism came into play, his melancholy humour, his sense of the illimitable which surrounds man's life, and which mocks, defeats, flings back his thought upon himself. Man is here, he said, with bounded powers, with limited knowledge, with an unknown behind, an unknown in front, assured of nothing but that he was born, and that he must die; why, then, in Heaven's name should he burn his fellow for a difference of opinion in the matter of surplices, or as to the proper fash-

ion of conducting devotion? Out of his scepticism and his merciful disposition grew, in that fiercely intolerant age, the idea of toleration, of which he was the apostle. Widely read, charming every one by his wit and wisdom, his influence spread from mind to mind, and assisted in bringing about the change which has taken place in European thought. His ideas, perhaps, did not spring from the highest sources. He was no ascetic, he loved pleasure, he was tolerant of everything except cruelty; but on that account we should not grudge him his meed. It is in this indirect way that great writers take their place among the forces of the world. In the long run, genius and wit side with the right cause. And the man fighting against wrong to-day is assisted, in a greater degree than perhaps he is himself aware, by the sarcasm of this writer, the metaphor of that, the song of the other, although the writers themselves professed indifference, or were even counted as belonging to the enemy.

Montaigne's hold on his readers arises from many causes. There is his frank and curious self-delineation; *that* interests, because it is the revelation of a very peculiar nature. Then there is the positive value of separate thoughts imbedded in his strange whimsicality and humour. Lastly, there is the perennial charm of style, which is never a separate quality, but rather the amalgam and issue of all the mental and moral qualities in a man's possession, and which bears the same relation to these that light bears to the mingled elements that make up the orb of the sun. And style, after all, rather than thought, is the immortal thing in literature. In literature, the charm of style is indefinable, yet all-subduing, just as fine manners are in social life. In reality, it is not of so much consequence what you say, as how you say it. Memorable sentences are memorable on account of some single irradiating word. "But Shadwell never *deviates* into sense, for instance." Young Roscius, in his provincial barn, will repeat you the great soliloquy of Hamlet, and although every word may be given with tolerable correctness, you find it just as commonplace as himself; the great actor speaks it, and you "read Shakspeare as by a flash of lightning." And it is in Montaigne's style, in the strange freaks and turnings of his thought, his constant surprises, his curious alternations of humour and melancholy, his careless, familiar form of address, and the grace with which everything is done, that his charm lies, and which makes the hundredth perusal of him as pleasant as the first.

And on style depends the success of the essayist. Montaigne said the most familiar things in the finest way. Goldsmith could not be termed a thinker; but everything he touched he brightened, as after a month of dry weather, the shower brightens the dusty shrubbery of a suburban villa. The world is not so much in need of new thoughts as that when thought grows old and worn with usage it should, like current coin, be called in, and, from the mint of genius, reissued fresh and new. Love is an old story enough, but in every generation it is re-born, in the downcast eyes and blushes of young maidens. And so, although he fluttered in Eden, Cupid is young today. If Montaigne had lived in Dreamthorp, as I am now living, had he written essays as I am now writing them, his English Essays would have been as good as his Gascon ones. Looking on, the country cart would not for nothing have passed him on the road to market, the setting sun would be arrested in its splendid colours, the idle chimes of the church would be translated into a thoughtful music. As it is, the village life goes on, and there is no result. My sentences are not much more brilliant than the speeches of the clowns; in my book there is little more life than there is in the market-place on the days when there is no market.

Reprinted from *Dreamthorp: A Book of Essays Written in the Country* (London: Strahan, 1863).

George Henry Lewes

From *The Principles of Success in Literature* (1865)

George Henry Lewes (1817-1878) made his career as a serious journalist, with a steady output of essays and books on literary and dramatic criticism, philosophy, psychology, and popular science; he was a regular contributor to the Westminster Review *and the* British and Foreign Quarterly, *and other periodicals, the literary editor of the* Leader *in the 1850s, and the founding editor of the liberal* Fortnightly Review *in 1865-1866. It was for the* Fortnightly *that Lewes wrote his series of articles on literary careers and the underlying principles of literary success. The advice and analysis that he offered show an interesting attempt to bring together the mid-Victorian scientific attitudes of his mentor Herbert Spencer with the idealist aesthetic tradition that would increasingly dominate discussion of prose. The first extract is from the opening article in the series, first published in the 15 May 1865 issue of the* Fortnightly, *and the second is the fifth article, on the principle of beauty, first published in the 15 September 1865 issue of the* Fortnightly. *They are reprinted here from the first British book edition, edited by T. Sharper Knowlson (1898).*—Ed.

CHAPTER I: CAUSES OF SUCCESS AND FAILURE IN LITERATURE, AND DIVISION OF THE SUBJECT

1. Object of the Treatise

In the development of the great series of animal organisms, the Nervous System assumes more and more of an imperial character. The rank held by any animal is determined by this character, and not at all by its bulk, its strength, or even its utility. In like manner, in the development of the social organism, as the life of nations becomes more complex, Thought assumes a more imperial character; and Literature, in its widest sense, becomes a delicate index of social evolution. Barbarous societies show only the germs of literary life. But advancing civilisation, bringing with it increased conquest over material agencies, disengages the mind from the pressure of immediate wants, and the loosened energy finds in leisure both the demand and the means of a new activity: the demand, because long unoccupied hours have to be rescued from the weariness of in-

action; the means, because this call upon the energies nourishes a greater ambition and furnishes a wider arena.

Literature is at once the cause and the effect of social progress. It deepens our natural sensibilities, and strengthens by exercise our intellectual capacities. It stores up the accumulated experience of the race, connecting Past and Present into a conscious unity; and with this store it feeds successive generations, to be fed in turn by them. As its importance emerges into more general recognition, it necessarily draws after it a larger crowd of servitors, filling noble minds with a noble ambition.

There is no need in our day to be dithyrambic on the glory of Literature. Books have become our dearest companions, yielding exquisite delights and inspiring lofty aims. They are our silent instructors, our solace in sorrow, our relief in weariness. With what enjoyment we linger over the pages of some well-loved author! With what gratitude we regard every honest book! Friendships, profound and generous, are formed with men long dead, and with men whom we may never see. The lives of these men have a quite personal interest for us, like the little ways and phrases of our wives and children.

It is natural that numbers who have once been thrilled with this delight should in turn aspire to the privilege of exciting it. Success in Literature has thus become not only the ambition of the highest minds, it has also become the ambition of minds intensely occupied with other means of influencing their fellows—with statesmen, warriors, and rulers. Prime ministers and emperors have striven for distinction as poets, scholars, critics, and historians. Unsatisfied with the powers and privileges of rank, wealth, and their conspicuous position in the eyes of men, they have longed also for the nobler privilege of exercising a generous sway over the minds and hearts of readers. To gain this they have stolen hours from the pressure of affairs, and disregarded the allurements of luxurious ease, labouring steadfastly, hoping eagerly. Nor have they mistaken the value of the reward. Success in Literature is, in truth, the blue ribbon of nobility.

There is another aspect presented by Literature. It has become a profession: to many a serious and elevating profession; to many more a mere trade, having miserable trade-aims and trade-tricks. As in every other profession, the ranks are thronged with incompetent aspirants, without seriousness of aim, without the faculties demanded by their work. They are led to waste powers which in other directions might have done honest service, because they have failed to discriminate between aspiration and inspiration, between the desire for greatness and the consciousness of power. Still lower in the ranks are those who follow Literature simply because they see no other opening for their incompetence; just as forlorn widows and ignorant old maids thrown suddenly on their own resources open a school—no other means of livelihood seeming to be within their reach. Lowest of all are those whose esurient vanity, acting on a frivolous levity of mind, urges them to make Literature a plaything for display. To write for a livelihood, even on a complete misapprehension of our powers, is at least a respectable impulse. To play at Literature is altogether inexcusable: the motive is vanity, the object notoriety, the end contempt.

I propose to treat of the Principles of Success in Literature, in the belief that if a clear recognition of the principles which underlie *all* successful writing could once be gained, it would be no inconsiderable help to many a young and thoughtful mind. Is it necessary to guard against a misconception of my object, and to explain that I hope to furnish nothing more than help and encouragement? There is help to be gained from a clear understanding of the conditions of success; and encouragement to be gained from a reliance on the ultimate victory of true principles. More than this can hardly be expected from me, even on the supposition that I have ascertained the real conditions. No one, it is to be presumed, will imagine that I can have any pretension of giving recipes for Literature, or of furnishing power and talent where nature has withheld them. I must assume the presence of the talent, and then assign the conditions under which that talent can alone achieve real success. No man is made a discoverer by learning the principles of scientific Method; but only by those principles can discoveries be made; and if he has consciously mastered them, he will find them directing his researches and saving him from an immensity of fruitless labour. It is something in the nature of the

Method of Literature that I propose to expound. Success is not an accident. All Literature is founded upon psychological laws, and involves principles which are true for all peoples and for all times. These principles we are to consider here. . . .

* * *

CHAPTER 5: THE PRINCIPLE OF BEAUTY

1. The Secret of Style.

It is not enough that a man has clearness of Vision, and reliance on Sincerity, he must also have the art of Expression, or he will remain obscure. Many have had

"The visionary eye, the faculty to see
The thing that hath been as the thing which is,"

but either from native defect, or the mistaken bias of education, have been frustrated in the attempt to give their visions beautiful or intelligible shape. The art which could give them shape is doubtless intimately dependent on clearness of eye and sincerity of purpose, but it is also something over and above these, and comes from an organic aptitude not less special, when possessed with fullness, than the aptitude for music or drawing. Any instructed person can write, as any one can learn to draw; but to write well, to express ideas with felicity and force, is not an accomplishment but a talent. The power of seizing unapparent relations of things is not always conjoined with the power of selecting the fittest verbal symbols by which they can be made apparent to others: the one is the power of the thinker, the other the power of the writer.

"Style," says De Quincey, "has two separate functions—first, to brighten the *intelligibility* of a subject which is obscure to the understanding; secondly, to regenerate the normal *power* and impressiveness of a subject which has become dormant to the sensibilities. . . . Decaying lineaments are to be retraced, and faded colouring to be refreshed." To effect these purposes we require a rich verbal memory from which to select the symbols best fitted to call up images in the reader's mind, and we also require the delicate selective instinct to guide us in the choice and arrangement of those symbols, so that the rhythm and cadence may agreeably attune the mind, rendering it receptive to the impressions meant to be communicated. A copious verbal memory, like a copious memory of facts, is only one source of power, and without the high controlling faculty of the artist may lead to diffusive indecision. Just as one man, gifted with keen insight, will from a small stock of facts extricate unapparent relations to which others, rich in knowledge, have been blind; so will a writer, gifted with a fine instinct, select from a narrow range of phrases symbols of beauty and of power utterly beyond the reach of commonplace minds. It is often considered, both by writers and readers, that fine language makes fine writers; yet no one supposes that fine colours make a fine painter. The *copia verborum* [fullness of words] is often a weakness and a snare. As Arthur Helps says, men use several epithets in the hope that one of them may fit. But the artist knows which epithet does fit, uses that, and rejects the rest. The characteristic weakness of bad writers is inaccuracy: their symbols do not adequately express their ideas. Pause but for a moment over their sentences, and you perceive that they are using language at random, the choice being guided rather by some indistinct association of phrases, or some broken echoes of familiar sounds, than by any selection of words to represent ideas. I read the other day of the truck system being "rampant" in a certain district; and every day we may meet with similar echoes of familiar words which betray the flaccid condition of the writer's mind drooping under the labour of expression.

Except in the rare cases of great dynamic thinkers whose thoughts are as turning-points in the history of our race, it is by Style that writers gain distinction, by Style they secure their immortality. In a lower sphere many are remarked as writers although they may lay no claim to distinction as thinkers, if they have the faculty of felicitously expressing the ideas of others; and many who are really remarkable as thinkers gain but slight recognition from the public, simply because in them the faculty of expression is feeble. In proportion as the work passes from the sphere of passionless intelligence to that of impassioned intelligence, from the region of demonstration to the region of emotion, the art of Style becomes more complex, its necessity more imperious. But even in Philosophy and Science the art is both subtle and necessary; the choice and arrangement of the fitting symbols, though less difficult than in Art, is quite indispensable to success. If the distinction which I formerly drew between the Scientific and the Artistic tendencies be ac-

cepted, it will disclose a corresponding difference in the Style which suits a ratiocinative exposition fixing attention on abstract relations, and an emotive exposition fixing attention on objects as related to the feelings. We do not expect the scientific writer to stir our emotions, otherwise than by the secondary influences which arise from our awe and delight at the unveiling of new truths. In his own researches he should extricate himself from the perturbing influences of emotion, and consequently he should protect us from such suggestions in his exposition. Feeling too often smites intellect with blindness, and intellect too often paralyses the free play of emotion, not to call for a decisive separation of the two. But this separation is no ground for the disregard of Style in works of pure demonstration–as we shall see by-and-by.

The Principle of Beauty is only another name for Style, which is an art, incommunicable as are all other arts, but like them subordinated to laws founded on psychological conditions. The laws constitute the Philosophy of Criticism; and I shall have to ask the reader's indulgence if for the first time I attempt to expound them scientifically in the chapter to which the present is only an introduction. A knowledge of these laws, even presuming them to be accurately expounded, will no more give a writer the power of felicitous expression than a knowledge of the laws of colour, perspective, and proportion will enable a critic to paint a picture. But all good writing must conform to these laws; all bad writing will be found to violate them. And the utility of the knowledge will be that of a constant monitor, warning the artist of the errors into which he has slipped, or into which he may slip if unwarned.

How is it that while every one acknowledges the importance of Style, and numerous critics from Quintilian and Longinus down to Quarterly Reviewers have written upon it, very little has been done towards a satisfactory establishment of principles? Is it not partly because the critics have seldom held the true purpose of Style steadily before their eyes, and still seldomer justified their canons by deducing them from psychological conditions? To my apprehension they seem to have mistaken the real sources of influence, and have fastened attention upon some accidental or collateral details, instead of tracing the direct connection between effects and causes. Misled by the splendour of some great renown, they have concluded that to write like Cicero or to paint like Titian must be the pathway to success;

which is true in one sense, and profoundly false as they understand it. One pestilent contagious error issued from this misconception, namely, that all maxims confirmed by the practice of the great artists must be maxims for the art; although a close examination might reveal that the practice of these artists may have been the result of their peculiar individualities or of the state of culture at their epoch. A true Philosophy of Criticism would exhibit in how far such maxims were universal, as founded on laws of human nature, and in how far adaptations to particular individualities. A great talent will discover new methods. A great success ought to put us on the track of new principles. But the fundamental laws of Style, resting on the truths of human nature, may be illustrated, they cannot be guaranteed by any individual success. Moreover, the strong individuality of the artist will create special modifications of the laws to suit himself, making that excellent or endurable which in other hands would be intolerable. If the purpose of Literature be the sincere expression of the individual's own ideas and feelings, it is obvious that the cant about the "best models" tends to pervert and obstruct that expression. Unless a man thinks and feels precisely after the manner of Cicero and Titian it is manifestly wrong for him to express himself in their way. He may study in them the principles of effect, and try to surprise some of their secrets, but he should resolutely shun all imitation of them. They ought to be illustrations not authorities, studies not models.

2. Imitation of the Classics

The fallacy about models is seen at once if we ask this simple question: Will the practice of a great writer justify a solecism in grammar or a confusion in logic? No. Then why should it justify any other detail not to be reconciled with universal truth? If we are forced to invoke the arbitration of reason in the one case, we must do so in the other. Unless we set aside the individual practice whenever it is irreconcilable with general principles, we shall be unable to discriminate in a successful work those merits which *secured* from those demerits which *accompanied* success. Now this is precisely the condition in which Criticism has always been. It has been formal instead of being psychological: it has drawn its maxims from the works of successful artists, instead of ascertaining the psychological principles involved in the effects of those works. When the per-

plexed dramatist called down curses on the man who invented fifth acts, he never thought of escaping from his tribulation by writing a play in four acts; the formal canon which made five acts indispensable to a tragedy was drawn from the practice of great dramatists, but there was no demonstration of any psychological demand on the part of the audience for precisely five acts.[1]

Although no instructed mind will for a moment doubt the immense advantage of the stimulus and culture derived from a reverent familiarity with the works of our great predecessors and contemporaries, there is a pernicious error which has been fostered by many instructed minds, rising out of their reverence for greatness and their forgetfulness of the ends of Literature. This error is the notion of "models," and of fixed canons drawn from the practice of great artists. It substitutes Imitation for Invention; reproduction of old types instead of the creation of new. There is more bad than good work produced in consequence of the assiduous following of models. And we shall seldom be very wide of the mark if in our estimation of youthful productions we place more reliance on their departures from what has been already done, than on their resemblances to the best artists. An energetic crudity, even a riotous absurdity, has more promise in it than a clever and elegant mediocrity, because it shows that the young man is speaking out of his own heart, and struggling to express himself in his own way rather than in the way he finds in other men's books. The early works of original writers are usually very bad; then succeeds a short interval of imitation in which the influence of some favourite author is distinctly traceable; but this does not last long, the native independence of the mind reasserts itself, and although perhaps academic and critical demands are somewhat disregarded, so that the original writer on account of his very originality receives but slight recognition from the authorities, nevertheless if there is any real power in the voice it soon makes itself felt in the world. There is one word of counsel I would give to young authors, which is that they should be humbly obedient to the truth proclaimed by their own souls, and haughtily indifferent to the remonstrances of critics founded solely on any departure from the truths expressed by others. It by no means follows that because a work is unlike works that have gone before it, therefore it is excellent or even tolerable; it may be original in error or in ugliness; but one thing is certain, that in proportion to its close fidelity to the matter and manner of existing works will be its intrinsic worthlessness. And one of the severest assaults on the fortitude of an unacknowledged writer comes from the knowledge that his critics, with rare exceptions, will judge his work in reference to preexisting models, and not in reference to the ends of Literature and the laws of human nature. He knows that he will be compared with artists whom he ought not to resemble if his work have truth and originality; and finds himself teased with disparaging remarks which are really compliments in their objections. He can comfort himself by his trust in truth and the sincerity of his own work. He may also draw strength from the reflection that the public and posterity may cordially appreciate the work in which constituted authorities see nothing but failure. The history of Literature abounds in examples of critics being entirely at fault–missing the old familiar landmarks, these guides at once set up a shout of warning that the path has been missed.

Very noticeable is the fact that of the thousands who have devoted years to the study of the classics, especially to the "niceties of phrase" and "chastity of composition," so much prized in these classics, very few have learned to write with felicity, and not many with accuracy. Native incompetence has doubtless largely influenced this result in men who are insensible to the nicer shades of distinction in terms, and want the subtle sense of congruity; but the false plan of studying "models" without clearly understanding the psychological conditions which the effects involve, without seeing why great writing is effective and where it is merely individual expression, has injured even vigorous minds and paralysed the weak. From a similar mistake hundreds have deceived themselves in trying to catch the trick of phrase peculiar to some distinguished contemporary. In vain do they imitate the Latinisms and antitheses of Johnson, the epigrammatic sentences of Macaulay, the colloquial ease of Thackeray, the cumulative pomp of Milton, the diffusive play of De Quincey: a few friendly or ignorant reviewers may applaud it as "brilliant writing," but the public remains unmoved. It is imitation, and as such it is lifeless.

We see at once the mistake directly we understand that a genuine style is the living body of thought, not a costume that can be put on and off; it is the expression of the writer's mind; it is not less the incarnation of his thoughts in verbal symbols than a picture is the painter's incarnation of his thoughts in symbols of form and colour. A man may, if it please him, dress his thoughts in the tawdry splendour of a masquerade. But this is no more Literature than the masquerade is Life.

No Style can be good that is not sincere. It must be the expression of its author's mind. There are, of course, certain elements of composition which must be mastered as a dancer learns his steps, but the style of the writer, like the grace of the dancer, is only made effective by such mastery; it springs from a deeper source. Initiation into the rules of construction will save us from some gross errors of composition, but it will not make a style. Still less will imitation of another's manner make one. In our day there are so many who imitate Macaulay's short sentences, iterations, antitheses, geographical and historical illustrations, and eighteenth century diction, but who accepts them as Macaulay's? They cannot seize the secret of his charm, because that charm lies in the felicity of his talent, not in the structure of his sentences; in the fullness of his knowledge, not in the character of his illustrations. Other men aim at ease and vigour by discarding Latinisms, and admitting colloquialisms; but vigour and ease are not to be had on recipe. No study of models, no attention to rules, will give the easy turn, the graceful phrase, the simple word, the fervid movement, or the large clearness; a picturesque talent will express itself in concrete images; a genial nature will smile in pleasant turns and innuendoes; a rapid, unhesitating, imperious mind will deliver its quick incisive phrases; a full deliberating mind will overflow in ample paragraphs laden with the weight of parentheses and qualifying suggestions. The style which is good in one case would be vicious in another. The broken rhythm which increases the energy of one style would ruin the *largo* of another. Both are excellencies where both are natural.

We are always disagreeably impressed by an obvious imitation of the manner of another, because we feel it to be an insincerity, and also because it withdraws our attention from the thing said, to the way of saying it. And here lies the great lesson writers have to learn–namely, that they should think of the immediate purpose of their writing, which is to convey truths and emotions, in symbols and images, intelligible and suggestive. The racket-player keeps his eye on the ball he is to strike, not on the racket with which he strikes. If the writer sees vividly, and will say honestly what he sees, and how he sees it, he may want something of the grace and felicity of other men, but he will have all the strength and felicity with which nature has endowed him. More than that he cannot attain, and he will fall very short of it in snatching at the grace which is another's. Do what he will, he cannot escape from the infirmities of his own mind: the affectation, arrogance, ostentation, hesitation, native in the man will taint his style, no matter how closely he may copy the manner of another. For evil and for good, *le style est de l'homme même* [the style is of the man himself].

The French critics, who are singularly servile to all established reputations, and whose unreasoning idolatry of their own classics is one of the reasons why their Literature is not richer, are fond of declaring with magisterial emphasis that the rules of good taste and the canons of style were fixed once and for ever by their great writers in the seventeenth century. The true ambition of every modern is said to be by careful study of these models to approach (though with no hope of equalling) their chastity and elegance. That a writer of the nineteenth century should express himself in the manner which was admirable in the seventeenth is an absurdity which needs only to be stated. It is not worth refuting. But it never presents itself thus to the French. In their minds it is a lingering remnant of that older superstition which believed the Ancients to have discovered all wisdom, so that if we could only surprise the secret of Aristotle's thoughts and clearly comprehend the drift of Plato's theories (which unhappily was not clear) we should compass all knowledge. How long this superstition lasted cannot accurately be settled; perhaps it is not quite extinct even yet; but we know how little the most earnest students succeeded in surprising the secrets of the universe by reading Greek treatises, and how much by studying the universe itself. Advancing Science daily discredits the superstition; yet the advance of Criticism has not yet wholly discredited the parallel superstition in Art. The earliest thinkers are no longer considered the wisest, but the earliest artists are still proclaimed the finest. Even those who do not believe in this superiority are, for the most part, overawed by tradition and dare not openly question the supremacy of works which in their private convictions hold a very subordinate rank. And this reserve is encouraged by the intemperate scorn of those who question the supremacy without having the knowledge or the sympathy which could fairly appreciate the earlier artists. Attacks on the classics by men ignorant of the classical languages tend to perpetuate the superstition.

But be the merit of the classics, ancient and modern, what it may, no writer can become a classic by imitating them. The principle of Sincerity here ministers to the principle of Beauty by forbidding imitation and enforcing rivalry. Write what you can, and if you have the grace of felicitous expression or the power of energetic expression your style will be admirable and admired. At any rate see that it be your own, and not another's; on no other terms will the world listen to it. You cannot be eloquent by borrowing from the opulence of another; you cannot be humorous by mimicking the whims of another; what was a pleasant smile dimpling his features becomes a grimace on yours.

It will not be supposed that I would have the great writers disregarded, as if nothing were to be learned from them; but the study of great writers should be the study of general principles as illustrated or revealed in these writers; and if properly pursued it will of itself lead to a condemnation of the notion of models. What we may learn from them is a nice discrimination of the symbols which intelligibly express the shades of meaning and kindle emotion. The writer wishes to give his thoughts a literary form. This is for others, not for himself; consequently he must, before all things, desire to be intelligible, and to be so he must adapt his expressions to the mental condition of his audience. If he employs arbitrary symbols, such as old words in new and unexpected senses, he may be clear as daylight to himself, but to others, dark as fog. And the difficulty of original writing lies in this, that what is new and individual must find expression in old symbols. This difficulty can only be mastered by a peculiar talent, strengthened and rendered nimble by practice, and the commerce with original minds. Great writers should be our companions if we would learn to write greatly; but no familiarity with their manner will supply the place of native endowment. Writers are born, no less than poets, and like poets, they learn to make their native gifts effective. Practice, aiding their vigilant sensibility, teaches them, perhaps unconsciously, certain methods of effective presentation, how one arrangement of words carries with it more power than another, how familiar and concrete expressions are demanded in one place, and in another place abstract expressions unclogged with disturbing suggestions. Every author thus silently amasses a store of empirical rules, furnished by his own practice, and confirmed by the practice of others. A true Philosophy of Criticism would reduce these empirical rules to science by ranging them under psychological laws, thus demonstrating the validity of the rules, not in virtue of their having been employed by Cicero or Addison, by Burke or Sydney Smith, but in virtue of their conformity with the constancies of human nature.

3. Style in Philosophical and Scientific Literature

The importance of Style is generally unsuspected by philosophers and men of science, who are quite aware of its advantage in all departments of *belles lettres;* and if you allude in their presence to the deplorably defective presentation of the ideas in some work distinguished for its learning, its profundity or its novelty, it is probable that you will be despised as a frivolous setter up of manner over matter, a light-minded *dilettante,* unfitted for the simple austerities of science. But this is itself a light-minded contempt; a deeper insight would change the tone, and help to remove the disgraceful slovenliness and feebleness of composition which deface the majority of grave works, except those written by Frenchmen, who have been taught that composition is an art, and that no writer may neglect it. In England and Germany, men who will spare no labour in research, grudge all labour in style; a morning is cheerfully devoted to verifying a quotation, by one who will not spare ten minutes to reconstruct a clumsy sentence; a reference is sought with ardour, an appropriate expression in lieu of the inexact phrase which first suggests itself does not seem worth seeking. What are we to say to a man who spends a quarter's income on a diamond pin which he sticks in a greasy cravat? a man who calls public attention on him, and appears in a slovenly undress? Am I to bestow applause on some insignificant parade of erudition, and withhold blame from the stupidities of style which surround it?

Had there been a clear understanding of Style as the living body of thought, and not its "dress," which might be more or less ornamental, the error I am noticing would not have spread so widely. But, naturally, when men regarded the grace of style as mere grace of manner, and not as the delicate precision giving form and relief to matter—as mere ornament, stuck on to arrest incurious eyes, and not as effective expression—their sense of the deeper value of matter made them despise such aid. A clearer conception would have rectified this error. The matter is confluent with the manner; and only *through* the style can thought reach the readers' mind. If the manner is involved, awkward, abrupt, obscure, the reader will either be oppressed with a confused sense of cumbrous material which awaits an artist to give it shape, or he will have the labour thrown upon him of extricating the material and reshaping it in his own mind.

How entirely men misconceive the relation of style to thought may be seen in the replies they make when their writing is objected to, or in the ludicrous attempts of clumsy playfulness and tawdry eloquence when they wish to be regarded as writers.

> "Le style le moins noble a pourtant sa noblesse" [The least noble style, however, has its nobility],

and the principle of Sincerity, not less than the suggestions of taste, will preserve the integrity of each style. A philosopher, an investigator, an historian, or a moralist so far from being required to present the graces of a wit, an essayist, a pamphleteer, or a novelist, would be warned off such ground by the necessity of expressing himself sincerely. Pascal, Biot, Buffon, or Laplace are examples of the clearness and beauty with which ideas may be presented wearing all the graces of fine literature, and losing none of the severity of science. Bacon, also having an opulent and active intellect, spontaneously expressed himself in forms of various excellence. But what a pitiable contrast is presented by Kant! It is true that Kant having a much narrower range of sensibility could have no such ample resource of expression, and he was wise in not attempting to rival the splendour of the *Novum Organum;* but he was not simply unwise, he was extremely culpable in sending forth his thoughts as so much raw material which the public was invited to put into shape as it could. Had he been aware that much of his bad writing was imperfect thinking, and always imperfect adaptation of means to ends, he might have been induced to recast it into more logical and more intelligible sentences, which would have stimulated the reader's mind as much as they now oppress it. Nor had Kant the excuse of a subject too abstruse for clear presentation. The examples of Descartes, Spinoza, Hobbes, and Hume are enough to show how such subjects can be mastered, and the very implication of writing a book is that the writer has mastered his material and can give it intelligible form.

A grave treatise, dealing with a narrow range of subjects or moving amid severe abstractions, demands a gravity and severity of style which is dissimilar to that demanded by subjects of a wider scope or more impassioned impulse; but abstract philosophy has its appropriate elegance no less than mathematics. I do not mean that each subject should necessarily be confined to one special mode of treatment, in the sense which was understood when people spoke of the "dignity of history," and so forth. The style must express the writer's mind; and as variously constituted minds will treat one and the same subject, there will be varieties in their styles. If a severe thinker be also a man of wit, like Bacon, Hobbes, Pascal, or Galileo, the wit will flash its sudden illuminations on the argument; but if he be not a man of wit, and condescends to jest under the impression that by jesting he is giving an airy grace to his argument, we resent it as an impertinence.

4. Style in the Sense of Treatment

I have throughout used Style in the narrower sense of expression rather than in the wider sense of "treatment" which is sometimes affixed to it. The mode of treating a subject is also no doubt the writer's or the artist's way of expressing what is in his mind, but this is Style in the more general sense, and does not admit of being reduced to laws apart from those of Vision and Sincerity. A man necessarily sees a subject in a particular light–ideal or grotesque, familiar or fanciful, tragic or humorous. He may wander into fairyland, or move amid representative abstractions; he may follow his wayward fancy in its grotesque combinations, or he may settle down amid the homeliest details of daily life. But having chosen he must be true to his choice. He is not allowed to represent fairy-land as if it resembled Walworth, nor to paint Walworth in the colours of Venice. The truth of consistency must be preserved in his treatment, truth in art meaning of course only truth within the limits of the art, thus the painter may produce the utmost relief he can by means of light and shade, but it is peremptorily forbidden to use actual solidities on a plane surface. He must represent gold by colour, not by sticking gold on his figures[2]. Our applause is greatly determined by our sense of difficulty overcome, and to stick gold on a picture is an avoidance of the difficulty of painting it.

Truth of presentation has an inexplicable charm for us, and throws a halo around even ignoble objects. A policeman idly standing at the corner of the street, or a sow lazily sleeping against the sun, are not in nature objects to excite a thrill of delight, but a painter may, by the cunning of his art, represent them so as to delight every spectator. The same objects represented by an inferior painter will move only a languid interest; by a still more inferior painter they may be represented so as to please none but the most uncultivated eye. Each spectator is charmed in proportion to his recognition of a triumph over difficulty which is measured by the degree of verisimilitude. The degrees are many. In the lowest the pictured object is so remote from the reality that we simply recognise what the artist meant to represent. In like manner we recognise in poor novels and dramas what the authors mean to be characters, rather than what our experience of life suggests as characteristic.

Not only do we apportion our applause according to the degree of verisimilitude attained, but also according to the difficulty each involves. It is a higher difficulty, and implies a nobler art to represent the movement and complexity of life and emotion than to catch the fixed lineaments of outward aspect. To paint a policeman idly lounging at the street corner with such verisimilitude that we are pleased with the representation, admiring the solidity of the figure, the texture of the clothes, and the human aspect of the features, is so difficult that we loudly applaud the skill which enables an artist to imitate what in itself is uninteresting; and if the imitation be carried to a certain degree of verisimilitude the picture may be of immense value. But no excellence of representation can make this high art. To carry it into the region of high art, another and far greater difficulty must be overcome; the man must be represented under the strain of great emotion, and we must recognise an equal truthfulness in the subtle indications of great mental agitation, the fleeting characters of which are far less easy to observe and to reproduce than the stationary characters of form and costume. We may often observe how the novelist or dramatist has tolerable success so long as his personages are quiet, or moved only by the vulgar motives of ordinary life, and how fatally uninteresting, because unreal, these very personages become as soon as they are exhibited under the stress of emotion: their language ceases at once to be truthful, and becomes stagey; their conduct is no longer recognisable as that of human beings such as we have known. Here we note a defect of treatment, a mingling of styles, arising partly from defect of vision, and partly from an imperfect sincerity; and success in art will always be found dependent on integrity of style. The Dutch painters, so admirable in their own style, would become pitiable on quitting it for a higher.

But I need not enter at any length upon this subject of treatment. Obviously a work must have charm or it cannot succeed; and the charm will depend on very complex conditions in the artist's mind. What treatment is in Art, composition is in Philosophy. The general conception of the point of view, and the skilful distribution of the masses, so as to secure the due preparation, development, and culmination, without wasteful prodigality or confusing want of symmetry, constitute Composition, which is to the structure of a treatise what Style–in the narrower sense–is to the structure of sentences. How far Style is reducible to law will be examined in the next chapter.

1. English critics are much less pedantic in adherence to "rules" than the French, yet when, many years ago, there appeared a tragedy in three acts, and without a death, these innovations were considered inadmissible; and if the success of the work had been such as to elicit critical discussion, the necessity of five acts and a death would doubtless have been generally insisted on.

2. This was done with *naiveté* by the early painters, and is really very effective in the pictures of the Gentile de Fabriano– that Paul Veronese of the fifteenth century–as the reader will confess it he has seen the "Adoration of the Magi," in the Florence Academy; but it could not be tolerated now.

Reprinted from *The Principles of Success in Literature,* edited by T. Sharper Knowlson (London: Walter Scott, 1898).

Alexander Bain

From *English Composition and Rhetoric (1866)*

Alexander Bain (1818-1903) was Professor of Logic and English in the University of Aberdeen from 1860 onward. By background, he was a philosopher in the Utilitarian tradition of John Stuart Mill and Herbert Spencer, and in the ideas he developed for his Aberdeen lectures on English composition, he emphasized the functional expository uses of prose needed in science, technology, and the new competitive civil-service examinations many of his students would take. The book based on his Aberdeen lectures, from which the following extracts come, became an immediate success, and was especially influential in the development of later nineteenth-century American ideas of prose composition; for another hundred years, most American college composition textbooks drew on Bain's classification of the four modes of composition (narration, description, exposition, and argumentation), and his formulation of patterns for the expository paragraph is still remarkably influential. The first of the extracts illustrates Bain's mid-Victorian awareness of the variability of taste in judging literary style, though it also asserts that some more absolute judgments can be based, as Spencer had based them, on psychological theory. The second extract presents Bain's classic discussion of the expository paragraph and expository style.—Ed.

131. The word Taste, employed with reference to Fine Art, means, in the first instance, the susceptibility to pleasure from works of art. A person devoid of this enjoyment is said to have no taste.

There is a further use of the word, to denote the kind of artistic excellence that gives the greatest amount of pleasure to cultivated minds. Such minds are said to have taste, and others to want it. The words "elegance," "polish," "refinement," designate nearly the same thing. The distinction is sometimes expressed by the epithet *"good* taste," implying that taste may be *bad*, or enjoyment misplaced, in the judgment of those that claim to arbitrate between the two.

It being the end of Rhetoric, as a whole, to consider the various points of excellence in composition, the attention to these must be synonymous with good taste.

In regard to Taste, there is a permanent element and a variable element.

I. The *permanent* element comprises all the rules of composition, grounded on the admitted laws of our sensibility, and generally followed by the best speakers and writers. To avoid discords, to use bold figures sparingly, to set bounds to exaggeration, to admit painful effects only so far as they can be redeemed,—are rules of Taste, as being rules of Rhetoric.

Refinement in Taste consists partly in enhancing the pleasure of works of art, by the removal of what pains, and the addition of what pleases, the proper artistic sensibility; and partly in avoiding the tendencies of art compositions to infringe on truth, usefulness, humane sentiment, and morality.

II. The *variable* element includes the points on which men do not feel alike. Ages, countries, and individuals, differ in their sense of what is excellent in composition.

Thus, as regards age and country:—The taste of the Greeks, reverentially accepted in many things by after ages, allowed to orators and poets a license of personal vituperation that would now be condemned. Again, nothing has varied so much in different times as the mode of representing the passion of love; allusions forbidden by the taste of our day were permitted in former times. . . .

Taste is also a matter of personal peculiarity; varying with the emotional constitution, the intellectual tendencies, and the education of each individual. A person of strong tender feelings is not easily offended by the iteration of pathetic images; the sense of the ludicrous and of humor is in many cases entirely wanting; and the strength of humane and moral sentiment may be such as to recoil from inflicting ludicrous degradation. A mind bent on the pursuit of truth views with distaste the exaggerations of the poetic art. Each person is by education more attached to one school or class of writers than to another. . . .

* * *

73. The Expository Paragraph has certain peculiarities growing out of the nature of science. In the ordinary form of composition, there are no means of indicating successive degrees of subordination; and we have to consider the best modes of overcoming the defect.

In a sentence, there may be apparent a principal and subordinate clauses; but, in a paragraph, all the sentences are, to the eye, of equal or co-ordinate value.

In a technical scientific work, subordination is indicated, (1) by indenting the letter-press, (2) by the forms of the numerical characters employed,–I., II., 1, 2, (1), (2), *a, b,* &c., and (3) by difference of type.

When such devices are not resorted to, we have to trust, in a great measure, to the sense of the passage for deciding what is co-ordinate and what subordinate. Further assistance may be obtained, by attention to the following points:–

(1.) The theme of the paragraph, to which all the rest is ministerial, should be found at the beginning, at the end, or in both.

(2.) Iteration gives prominence, and therefore superiority. The circumstance that a thing is stated many times over, leads us to infer that it is more important and probably more comprehensive than the things stated only once.

(3.) When facts are plainly made known as examples or illustrations of a theme, they are thereby declared to be in subordination to that theme.

(4.) Statements of the second degree of subordination should, if possible, be included in the same sentence as their immediate principal; it being inexpedient to constitute distinct sentences of three different grades in the paragraph.

(5.) After descending to a second, or to a still lower, degree of subordination, we should avoid returning to the higher grade in the same paragraph.

(6.) A separate paragraph may be devoted to a series of examples or statements of a low, but uniform, degree of subordination. This is much better than mixing up the different degrees without change of paragraph.

(7.) It is possible to intimate by our phraseology when we pass from one degree of generality to another:–"The following facts come under this principle;" "We give examples, or cases, of the rule;" "The subordinate laws are these," &c.

A subordinate statement may happen to be difficult of understanding, but we are not at liberty to expand it by iteration or otherwise, so as to raise it out of its rank. To study clearness in the expression, or to append some brief example or illustration, is all that the case allows.

Mr. Herbert Spencer has introduced a division intermediate between the Sentence and the Paragraph, marked by a blank of about half an inch between two sentences.

The arts of relief are essential to Exposition throughout. Monotony can neither keep up attention nor impress the memory. Even when the subject is made up naturally of monotonous or co-ordinate particulars, means must be used to raise some of them into relief. Thus in the details of Anatomy–the muscles, blood-vessels, &c.–certain leading functions are indicated, as, in reference to the muscles, the two great facts of the erecting and the bending of the body.

74. The leading form of the Expository Paragraph (and of Exposition generally) is the statement of a principle, followed by such a choice of iterations, obverse statements, examples, illustrations, proofs, and applications, as the case may require.

Other forms of Paragraph are the Inductive (§ 61) and the Argumentative.

The simplest form of Argument is the adducing of a general principle in support of a particular allegation. The fact is affirmed that the freezing of water in a close tube will make it burst; the principle adduced in proof is that water in freezing expands with great force. There is in this nothing different from the ordinary type of Exposition, except an inversion,–the fact being stated first, and the principle afterwards.

An Argument may contain a succession of steps, called a chain of reasoning, and is then more difficult to follow. The precautions to be observed in this case are to reduce the number of steps to the fewest possible, and to give an adequate expression to each, yet so as to allow the whole to be grasped together. It is in such complicated reasonings that the rules of the Sentence and the Paragraph justify their importance. . . .

75. One cause of the difficulty of understanding science is the novelty of many of the terms employed.

Apart from the abstruseness of the notions, the mind is oppressed by the introduction of unfamiliar terms, sometimes in great numbers and in close succession. This should, as far as possible, be considered in the exposition; a certain time being allowed for one strange word to become familiar before bringing forward others.

It is scarcely necessary to remark that new language is in itself an evil. . . .

Reprinted from *English Composition and Rhetoric* (New York: Appleton, 1866).

T. H. Wright

From "Style" (1877)

Wright's essay on style, originally published in Macmillan's Magazine, *is important as a theoretically based answer to Herbert Spencer's "The Philosophy of Style," with its psychological arguments for the evolution of ideal prose style. Wright argues instead for a refurbished expressive theory of style, in which an unconscious individuality is given primacy over Spencer's principle of readability. Though the article was signed T. H. Wright on first publication, Wright's identity has not been established with certainty. He was surely not the well-known Thomas Wright the antiquary, but he may have been Thomas Howard Wright, an Oxford graduate and fellow of Merton College in the 1870s, who subsequently became a barrister.*–Ed.

A recent historian of Rome[1], towards the close of his famous attempt to undeceive the world at large with respect to the genius of Cicero, sums up his argument in the following words:– "Ciceronianism is a problem which, in fact, cannot be properly solved, but can only be resolved into that greater mystery of human nature–language, and the effect of language on the mind."

These words are suggestive–suggestive, too, of a wider question than at first sight appears. That men are influenced by language at least as much as by ideas; that power of expression is intimately associated with mental grasp generally; even that a fascination is exercised by style to which nothing equivalent is found in the accompanying thought–these are acknowledged truths, readily granted. But it is a most singular thing that they are so readily granted: it is singular that the question is not oftener asked–Why is this so?

How is it that language, which is but the vehicle of thought, comes to have a force which is not the mere weight of that which it carries? Even where this is not the case, where there is an equivalence of value in both style and ideas, great conceptions being nobly expressed, how is it that the matter and the form seem to have independent claims upon the attention? In a word, what is that in language which is not mere *expres-siveness* of the obvious intentions of the writer, but is yet a merit?

At first sight there appears to be a simple answer to the question. Any of the numerous treatises on style or rhetoric abound with rules for the embellishment of discourse: the reader learns the importance of a choice of fitting words, of the judicious use of figures of speech, of the effect of melodious sentences and suitable cadences: he is instructed in the manipulation of complex constructions, and discovers the force of the gradation, the antithesis and the climax: in short, he is easily led to the conclusion that, besides *expressiveness*, language may have the merit of *beauty*.

That this distinction is a superficial one has been shown with great ability in an article by Mr. Herbert Spencer on the "Philosophy of Style."[2] He there traces all excellence of composition to two principles–Economy of Attention, and Economy of the Sensibility of the recipient. Assuming that a reader can have at his command only a definite amount of power of attention, it is clear that whatever part of this is employed on the form of a composition must be subtracted, and leave so much the less to be occupied in the matter. . . .

Any one who has attentively read the article . . . will have seen that the theory furnishes a canon for determining, with some degree of certainty, which of two styles is the better. To quote again: "The relative goodness of any two modes of expressing an idea may be determined by observing which requires the shortest process of thought for its comprehension."[3]

Clearly, then, there must, in every case, be some form of expression which is absolutely the best; in other words, there is such a thing as an ideal style. Mr. Spencer accepts the conclusion, but at the same time reminds us that style must vary with its subject-matter.

"The perfect writer will express himself as Junius, when in the Junius frame of mind; when he feels as Lamb felt, will use a like familiar speech; and will fall into the ruggedness of Carlyle when in a Carlylean mood."[4]

The reservation is a proper one, and with it

the argument seems unimpeachable. Yet when Mr. Spencer throws the conclusion into the form of an epigram, and tells us that "to have a specific style is to be poor in speech,"[5] he makes the utmost possible demand upon our loyalty to exact reasoning. Like Adeimantus in the Republic, we are "confounded by this novel kind of draughtsplaying, played with words for counters."

But if the foregoing theory be carefully reviewed, it will be seen that throughout it the treatment is what may be described as objective rather than subjective. Or, to avoid words in which there is a degree of ambiguity, the definite product language is more or less isolated from the agency using it, and viewed more in relation to the reader's than the writer's mind. But there is another aspect of the relation, which cannot be left out without producing a result which must be onesided and may be inaccurate. The following pages will be an attempt to supply this omission by a consideration of the nature of the various devices of language, regarded as the outcome of the mind that employs them.

That "to have a specific style is to be poor in speech" has not been implied in the judgments which the world has from time to time passed upon its greatest writers. Perhaps it would be nearer the truth to say that much in proportion as an author has reached a high eminence in his art there has been found in his productions a corresponding tendency to an individuality of expression. Is it not a common complaint against inferior artists, whether in prose or verse, in painting or music, that their compositions lack character and originality? Uniformity is the distinguishing feature of mediocrity, while the work of genius is at once recognised and attributed to the origin whose impress it bears. And a little reflection will show that this is exactly what is meant by "style." Various tricks of voice, gesture, and dress are associated by every one with his friends, glimpses of the hidden self being granted in such half-unnoticed revelations. The chief value, indeed, of such peculiarities rests in the fact that they are commonly unknown to the man himself. For all of us, even the most sincere, are to a certain extent actors in our intercourse with others, and play a part that has been self-assigned, often without due pondering of the player's power. Nature, however, peeps out in countless little traits of character, which find their expression in language, habit, and even in movements. By what subtle union such tricks of manner are linked with what Dr. Johnson has called "the anfractuosities

of the human mind," is a curious and intricate question, but no one will doubt the fact of the connection. "That's father!" cries the child as she hears the well-known footfall in the hall; "How like the man!" we exclaim when some characteristic remark is reported to us. Spite of the progress in complexity from a sound to a sentiment, each obeys the same law; and the connection between the footfall and the foot, between the speech and the mind that conceived it, is one and the same.

Let us follow out the thought a little further. Not only, to put the fact in its popular aspect, has every one his peculiarities; but there are degrees of peculiarity accompanying degrees of individuality; as a man deviates in *character* from the type ordinarily met with, so are his *habits* singular to himself, till a point is reached where the personality is remarkable, and the behavior eccentric. Where such manners are perfectly unaffected they are a reflection of a self that stands alone among many, so that the common dictum, that genius is eccentric, has a philosophical foundation. There is no need to linger on the numerous and tolerably obvious reservations which make it impossible to convert the proposition, in other words, to infer unusual power from singularity; the broad fact remains that where there is that marked originality called genius, it is an originality not of thought, emotion, or pursuits, but of the man.

The application of this to literary style is easy, and will be found to lead to some interesting results.

In its power of direct expression, language is tolerably efficient, and were there nothing but facts, considered objectively, to be conveyed, even a simpler vehicle would suffice. Swift, in one of the most humorous passages of *Gulliver's Travels*, describes a set of philosophers, who, disdaining language as the ordinary means of expressing their thoughts, preferred to carry with them a pack of the things most commonly referred to in everyday parlance, by the dexterous manipulation of which they contrived to carry on long conversations. Now this represents, with the necessary freedom of caricature, a real truth with regard to a certain class of discourse. In any written composition, the less the author's personality is involved in the matter treated, the simpler the language which suffices. The extreme form of this truth is found in the case of Algebra, where the discourse is, so to speak, perfectly dispassionate, and the symbolism perfectly adequate. Similarly, the language employed in mathematical proof is found adequate in proportion as the statements are purely objective. As we ascend in the scale of literary composition the author's personality creeps in, and brings with it a corresponding complexity of language, not merely the complexity of structure of sentences, but of choice of words, use of figures of speech, and all the refinements of elaborate writing. It is true that much more than this has to be taken into consideration; the subjects themselves are infinitely more complex as the scale is ascended, the distinctions are more delicate, the contrasts present more sides to view, the gradations are subtler. But is not this a corollary from the main principle? Is it not because we are then dealing either with facts of our own or the general consciousness; with ideas, emotions, desires, and so forth; or at any rate with external facts looked at from the point of view of an interested and questioning observer, that there is this increase in complexity, or, in other words, decrease in adequacy of language?

But this idea admits of yet further development. The facts perfectly expressed in algebraical symbols receive a nearly perfect expression in mathematical language. The terminology of science is found very tolerably sufficient, if strictly adhered to, and mostly where expository and descriptive. In history and biography what we may call the subjective element is strong, and there we find all the refinements of composition. These express, not only facts and aspects of facts, not only are there delicate implications of expression, embodied in all the recognised figures of rhetoric, the trope, the simile, and the metaphor; but there are the glimpses at the very self of the author which lurks in unconscious tricks of diction and turns of thought, and emerges in epithets, in repetitions, and in phrases. In poetry the author reigns supreme, and there too the imperfection of language is most manifest. In a very fine passage every word is charged with meaning and riveted to its place, in fact the vehicle is strained to its utmost to bear the load imposed upon it. Hence Coleridge's well-known definition of poetry as "the best words in the best order." Meanwhile the personality of the Poet pervades every line of every poem, a hardly recognised but unfailing presence. He colours each picture, and is a spectator at every scene; he is beside Ulysses in the island of Calypso; with him he witnesses the death of Argus and the insolence of the suitors; he shares the recognition of Penelope and the welcome to home; and when dire retribution seizes the usurpers he looks upon their fall. . . .

Now this . . . would be hypercriticism if it were meant that all these points were before the mind of the poet, forming part of an intentional study of effect. On the contrary, the implication is the direct reverse. It is because Homer was such or such a man, because he had been in the habit of regarding what he saw after a certain fashion of his own, that when he set himself to compose poetry he composed it as he did. Hence there is a deep meaning in the saying of Milton, that he who would write good poetry must make his life a poem. It is by virtue of a thousand minute traits of character, the gradual deposit of life's experiences, that any one speaks, writes, even walks and moves, as we see him do. For there must be some reason why, if two men set about describing a scene, or giving even a plain, unvarnished account of some event, the mode of their narration differs, differs, too, in such a way that each can be ascribed to its author, as we say, by internal evidence, that is, by its style. While, then, no better explanation appears, that theory of style may perhaps be provisionally accepted which identifies it with character–with unconscious revelations of the hidden self.

This conclusion needs a little further elaboration before it is compared with that view of what is called the philosophy of style, which resolves all the devices of composition into schemes for economising the reader's attention. It is necessary to point out, and this may be done briefly, how not only is style generally the impress of the author's self, but there is a correspondence between the distinctive features of any particular passage and the points at which, in the manner just indicated, the writer's personality glides into the discourse. This is not difficult, if what has been already said be accepted. What indeed is meant by saying that an author is best where his writing is most natural?

Is it not implied that the happiest touches are those which are original–that those phrases and expressions are most welcome to the reader which set the matter they convey in a new light– and that the light in which the writer himself sees it? If the foregoing passage from the *Odyssey* be reviewed it will be found that its beauties are coincident with the parts where the presence of the poet seems to be hinted, and this is equally true, though not equally discernible in all writing that is at all elaborate.

Now, how does all this square with the dictum that "to have a specific style is to be poor in speech?" It will not at first sight appear so very incompatible. In a certain sense, style at all owes its existence to the imperfection of the vehicle of thought. Were language a perfectly adequate means of embodying ideas, what is now to be looked for in the *mode* of statement would be found directly declared in the statement itself. For the countless devices of language, the gestures and tones of discourse, the thousand rhetorical figures of written composition, are really one and all simple propositions not capable of exact expression in the body of the narrative. They are the lights and shades of the picture, or perhaps rather the finer touches, which are to tickle the imagination of the reader with suggested beauties. And it is exactly in these refinements of expression that the deepest meaning of any author, in other words, his *self* resides. There is something pathetic in the reflection that we walk this world half hidden from one another, a constant struggle going on to make known the thoughts, beliefs, and aspirations of the real but partly imprisoned being, which never can be known exactly as they are to any but the mind that conceives them. Like savages, we speak mostly by signs, which serve us well enough, but leave much uncommunicated. It is well, however, that this imperfection is an imperfection that produces beauty, that the grating of the machine is not harsh, but musical. Mr. Herbert Spencer is successful in showing that the various devices of language do serve to the economy of the reader's attention, and that beauties of style are beauties partly because they effect this end. But he has not raised a question which seems closely akin to the subject. Why is it needful to have recourse to these expedients at all, and why is there an infinite variety in every man's use of them? The answer to these questions seems to give an insight into a higher law, to which Mr. Spencer's principle stands rather as an empirical generalization. It is this:—that each man's inmost nature is a secret to all but himself—and that a secret which in no two cases is the same. Every attempt to communicate it partly fails, and so language is full of compromises and expedients; each nature to be revealed is different, and so there is a countless variety of styles. This then is not due to poverty of speech, rather it is due to multiplicity of individualities, each speaking its own language and telling its own tale.

The ideal style, then, is for an ideal being, but for an ideal being who is to be without personality. The perfect writer may write, now like Jun-

ius, now like Lamb, now like Carlyle, but like himself he can never write. He cannot, as we say, *express himself.* A significant phrase, for after all it is when a man, as far as he can, expresses *himself,* that his communication is most worth having. It is the one thing of which he certainly knows something, where he can indeed speak with authority. It is not so much what a man knows, as how he knows it, not so much the extent as the quality of his information, that gains him a right to be heard. Originality is far oftener originality of expression than idea, a fresh aspect of something old, not a discovery of something new. And so there starts up here an answer to the difficulties encountered at the outset, "Why men are influenced by language at least as much as by ideas;" and "Why power of expression is intimately associated with mental grasp generally." Partly, no doubt, because in language resides the personality of the speaker or writer, and men are influenced by personality—but far more for another reason. The highest form of ability is something which pervades the whole being; it is not restricted to an intellect preternaturally acute, to vividness of imagination, or fineness of feeling; but it is the manifestation of a nature—of a *self,* which is really great. And it has been seen that it is in expression, or style, that the self of the author is to be sought. That, then, is a true instinct which so intimately associates power of expression with power of character generally. Of this power, too, the distinguishing feature is its individuality. Just as in animal life the ascent of the scale of creation is a process of differentiation of functions; just as a higher form of life is marked off from a lower form by greater specialty of shape, by powers more accurately defined, by habits more peculiarly its own; so in the comparison of man with man, something similar to this law is traceable, pointing out that the superiority of genius in degree is mainly a consequence of its difference in kind.

Thus nature seems to speak in a continued protest against uniformity, by a thousand analogies insisting upon the supreme importance of the individual. And the critical verdict which pronounces that writing best which is the most natural can be affiliated to as wide a law as this. Whether or no it be thought that each man is put into the world the possessor of some particular truth, which his acts or words can set before his fellow-creatures, it is at any rate clear that the inevitable specialty of each man's experiences must present things to him in an aspect which can be exactly the same for no other. There are no real *doubles* in the world, no such thing as identity in constitution and circumstances. While, then, this is so, there is a significance in style, a value in the unconscious self-revelations of traits of personality. However a man may fail of the object he sets before him in what he does or says, yet if there has been in him that conscientious fidelity to his purpose, which is but an attempt to express *himself*, his work will not have been wasted, though its direct worth be unimportant.

1. The "recent historian" is probably Theodor Mommsen, whose *History of Rome* (1854-1856) was first published in English translation in 1862.–*Ed.*

2. *Essays: Scientific, Political, and Speculative.* Vol. ii. Essay I.

3. *Ibid.*, p. 33.

4. *Ibid.*, p. 47.

5. *Ibid.*, p. 46.

Reprinted from *Macmillan's Magazine*, 37 (November 1877): 78-84.

George Saintsbury
"Modern English Prose" (1876)

George Saintsbury (1845-1933) was a prolific reviewer and literary journalist for nearly twenty years before his appointment in 1895 as Regius Professor of Rhetoric and English Literature at Edinburgh University. He had an encyclopaedic knowledge of both English and European literature, and as a lifelong devotee of Carlyle, he developed a special interest in the description and appreciation of prose style; his more than fifty books and 450 editions included Specimens of English Prose Style *(1885), a three-volume* History of Criticism and Literary Taste in Europe *(1900-1904), and his innovative* History of English Prose Rhythm *(1912), where he applied to prose ideas about patterned stress from his previous studies of poetic meter. The early essay reprinted here first appeared in the February 1876 issue of* Fortnightly Review; *it is remarkable not only for its balanced discussion of the influence of journalism on prose style but also for the appreciative discussion it gives of the prose style of many of the Victorians that are still read—Ruskin, Swinburne, Froude, and Pater—and Saintsbury's central argument, that prose style is as much an art form as verse, fits well with the broader late Victorian movement to aestheticize discussion of prose.—Ed.*

In comparing for purposes of study the two great Histories of Greece which England produced in the last generation, a thought, which has most probably often presented itself to other students, has frequently occurred to me. Much as the two works differ in plan, in views, and in manner of execution, their difference has never struck me so much as in the point of style. And the remarkable feature of this difference is, that it is not by any means the natural variation which we allow for, and indeed expect, in the productions of any two men of decided and distinct literary ability. It is not as the difference between Hume and Gibbon, and the difference between Clarendon and Taylor. In the styles of these great writers, and in those of many others, there is the utmost conceivable diversity; but at the same time they are all styles. We can see (see it, indeed, so clearly that we hardly take the trouble to think about it) that each of them made a distinct effort to arrange his words into their clause, his clauses into their sentence, and his sentences into their paragraph according to certain forms, and that though these forms varied in the subtle and indescribable measure of the taste and idiosyncrasy of each writer, the effort was always present, and was only accidentally if inseparably connected with the intention to express certain thoughts, to describe certain facts, or to present certain characters. But when we come to compare Thirlwall with Grote, we find not a variation of the kind just mentioned, but the full opposition of the presence of style on the one hand and the absence of it on the other. The late Bishop of St. David's will probably never be cited among the greatest masters of English prose-style, but still we can see without difficulty that he has inherited its traditions. It would be difficult, on the other hand, to persuade a careful critic that Grote ever thought of such things as the cadence of a sentence or the composition of a paragraph. That he took so much trouble as might suffice to make his meaning clear and his language energetic is obvious; that in no case did he think of looking beyond this is I think certain.

But the difference between these two great historians is very far from being a mere isolated fact, of little more interest or significance than a parallel between Macedon and Monmouth. It marks with extraordinary precision the date and nature of a change which has affected English literature to a degree and in a manner worthy of the most serious consideration. What this change is, and whether it amounts to an actual decay or to a mere temporary neglect of style in English prose writing, are questions which are certainly of importance, and the answers to which should not, as it seems to me, lack interest.

If, then, we take up almost any book of the last century, we shall find that within varying limits the effort of which I have just spoken is distinctly present. The model upon which the writer frames his style may be and probably is faulty in itself, and still more probably is faultily copied;

453

there may be too much Addison in the mixture, or too much Johnson; but still we shall see that an honest attempt at style, an honest endeavour at manner as apart from matter, has been made, however clumsy the attempt may be, and however short of success it may fall. But if we take up any book of the last forty or fifty years, save a very few, the first thing that will strike us is the total absence of any attempt or endeavour of the kind. The matter will, as a rule, have been more or less carefully attended to, and will be presented to the reader with varying degrees of clearness and precision. But the manner, except in so far as certain peculiarities of manner may be conducive or prejudicial to clearness and precision of statement–sometimes perhaps to apparent precision with any sacrifice of clearness–will in most cases be found to have been totally neglected, if a thing may be said to be neglected which does not appear to have even presented itself within the circumference of the field of view. In other words, and to adopt a convenient distinction, though there may be a difference of manner, there is usually no difference of style, for there is no style at all.

Before going any further, it may be well to adopt a commendable, if antiquated and scholastic practice, and to set down accurately what is here meant by style, and of what it consists. Style is the choice and arrangement of language with only a subordinate regard to the meaning to be conveyed. Its parts are the choice of the actual words to be used, the further selection and juxtaposition of these words, the structure of the clauses into which they are wrought, the arrangement of the clauses into sentences, and the composition of the sentences into paragraphs. Beyond the paragraph style can hardly be said to go, but within that limit it is supreme. The faults incident to these parts (if I may be allowed still to be scholastic) are perhaps also worthy of notice. Every one can see, though everyone is by no means careful to put his knowledge into practice, that certain words are bad of themselves, and certain others to be avoided wherever possible. The mere grammar of style teaches us not to say "commence" where we can say "begin," or "reliable" where we can say "trustworthy." The next stage introduces difficulties of a higher order, though these also are more or less elementary. Most people can see the faults in the following sentences:–

"Had he always written upon the level we behold here there could be little question that the author would have taken his place amongst the front rank of dramatists." Here "writing upon the level we behold here" is a combination of the most obviously incongruous notions. Again, "They did reject him *of course*, but his speech remains as a model for all true men to follow, as a warning to all who may adopt another *course*," &c. Here the unintentional repetition of the word "course" in an entirely different sense within the compass of a couple of lines is unpardonable. But these are mere rudiments; it is in the breach or neglect of the rules that govern the structure of clauses, of sentences, and of paragraphs that the real secret of style consists, and to illustrate this breach or observation is less easy. The task will be perhaps made easier if we consider first in the rough how the prevalent English style of the present day differs from that of past times.

Some five-and-thirty years ago De Quincey had already noticed and deplored the deterioration of which we speak. In his Essay on Style (reprinted in the sixth volume of his collected works) he undertakes to discuss at some length the symptoms and causes of the disease. De Quincey, as any one who is at all acquainted with his works is aware, gave considerable attention to the subject of style, and professed to be no mean authority thereon. There were, indeed, two peculiarities about him which prevented him from deserving a very high place as a referee on such matters. The first was his mistaken idea that extremely ornate prose–the prose which his ally John Wilson called "numerous," and which others have called Asiatic–was the highest form attainable, and that any writer who did not aim at this fell naturally into a lower class. The other was his singular crotchetiness, which made him frequently refuse to see any good in the style of writers to whom, for some reason or for no reason, he had taken a dislike. It will probably be allowed, not merely by persons who hold traditional opinions, but by all independent students of literature, that we must look with considerable distrust on the dicta of a critic who finds fault with the styles of Plato and of Conyers Middleton. The Essay on Style, however (at least its first part, for the latter portions go off into endless digressions of no pertinence whatever), is much more carefully written and much more carefully reasoned than most of De Quincey's work. The purport of it is, that the decay of style is to be attributed partly to the influence of German literature, but chiefly to the prevalence of journalism. No one will deny that the influence of newspaper writing is in many ways bad, and that to it is due much of the decadence in style of which complaint is made. But either the prevalent manner of journalism has undergone a remarkable change during the past generation, or else the particular influence which De Quincey supposes it to have had was mistaken by him. I do not myself pretend to a very intimate acquaintance with the periodical literature of thirty or forty years ago, and I am afraid that not even in the pursuit of knowledge could I be tempted to plunge into such a dreary and unbuoyant *mare mortuum*. With respect to the papers of to-day it is certainly not difficult to discern a peculiarity in their styles, or in what does duty for style in them. A large volume, for instance, might be profitably written, if, perhaps, not so profitably read, on the various stylistic peculiarities of the *Times*. There used to be the famous and memorable affectation of peculiar spelling, or what one might perhaps, after the story of King Sigismund, call the *super-orthographicam* style. Then, some ten years ago, there came the great "Queen of Sheba" style, which consisted in opening an article with some fact or allusion which had the remotest (or not the remotest) connection with the subject. Of late, perhaps, there has been less unity; but one style has never been lacking–a style which might be called the magisterial, but which I (having been once informed by a great master thereof, with whom I presumed to differ, that "all persons of common sense and morality" thought as he did) prefer to call the common-sense-and-morality style. This style is convenient for reproof, for correction, and for instruction in righteousness. If you approve, you can point out not too enthusiastically that the view or proceeding in question is the only one which common sense and morality allow; if (which is possible) you do not understand, common sense, by not understanding also, will help you out of the difficulty; and if you disapprove, morality will be as violently outraged as you like. Of the weekly papers, it is impossible not to admire the free-and-easy doctrinaire-ism of the *Spectator*, which is almost entirely an affair of style depending on a sedulous avoidance of ornate language, and plentiful use of colloquial words and phrases about the least colloquial matters. Then there is the style of the *Saturday Review* in its political articles, a style which appears to be framed on the principle that thoughts and words economise weight by being meted out in small doses, and that a pound of buckshot will go farther than a pound of bullets.

Lastly, the inquirer into such things will not neglect the peculiar aridity of certain of the older *Quarterlies,* which seem to have retained the ponderous clauses of other days, while neglecting the form which saved those clauses from being cumbrous. But in most of all this we shall find little to bear out De Quincey's verdict. Long and involved sentences, unduly stuffed with fact and meaning, are what he complains of; and though there is no doubt that we should not have to go far in order to find such at the present day, yet it does not appear, to me at least, that the main fault of contemporary English style is of this kind. On the contrary, the sin of which I should chiefly complain is the sin of over-short sentences, of mere gasps instead of balanced periods. Such a paragraph as the following will illustrate what I mean: "That request was obeyed by the massacre of six out of the surviving princes of the imperial family. Two alone escaped. With such a mingling of light and darkness did Constantine close his career." I think that any one who considers this combination of two mutilated clauses with an interjectional copula, and who perceives with what ease its hideous cacaphony might have been softened into a complete and harmonious sentence, must feel certain that its present form is to some extent intentional. The writer might very well have written: "That request was obeyed by the massacre of six out of the eight surviving princes of the imperial family, and the career of Constantine was closed in a mixture of light and darkness." Why did he not?

Again, let us take a book of recent date, whose style has received considerable praise both in England and abroad–Mr. Greene's Short History of the English People. The character of Elizabeth is perhaps the most carefully written, certainly the most striking, passage in the book, and contains a most elaborate statement of that view of the great queen which many historical students now take. It enforces this view with the greatest energy, and sets it before us in every detail and difference of light and shade. But how inartistic it is! how thoroughly bad in conception, composition, and style! In the first place it occupies some seven printed pages of unusual extent and closeness, each of which is at least equal to two of the ordinary octavo pages of an English classic author. Let any one, if he can, imagine one of the great masters who could both draw and compose, Hume or Middleton, Clarendon or Swift, giving us a character of fourteen pages. A portrait on the scale of Brobdingnag, with all features and all defects unnaturally emphasized and enlarged, could hardly be more disgusting. .

It is not necessary to multiply examples, which if all the defects of contemporary style were to be noticed and illustrated, would occupy a space longer than the present article. In all but a very few writers we shall observe with certain variations the same defects—inordinate copiousness of treatment combined with an utter inability, or at best an extreme unwillingness to frame a sentence of due proportion and careful structure. It should certainly be possible to trace the origin and examine the nature of a phenomenon so striking and so universal.

The secret of the manner will not long escape us if we notice or can disengage the intention with which, willingly or unwillingly, this manner has been adopted. Nor is this intention very hard to discover. It is, as it appears to me, a desire to present the subject, whatever it may be, to the reader in the most striking and arresting fashion. The attention of the reading public generally has, from causes to be presently noticed, become gradually concentrated almost wholly upon subject-matter. Among what may be called, intellectually speaking, the lower classes, this concentration shows itself not in the preference but in the exclusive study of novels, newspapers, and sometimes of so-called books of information. A book must be as they say "about something," or it fails altogether to arrest their attention. To such persons a page with (as it has been quaintly put) no "resting-places," no proper names and capital letters to fix the eye, is an intolerable weariness, and to them it is evident that style can be only a name. Somewhat above them come the (intellectually) middle classes. They are not absolutely confined to personal adventure, real or fictitious, or to interesting facts. They can probably enjoy the better class of magazine articles, superior biographies, travels, and the other books that everybody reads and nobody buys. This class will even read poetry if the poet's name be known, and would consider it a grave affront if it were hinted to them that their appreciation of style is but dull and faulty. A certain amount of labour if therefore required on work which is to please these readers: labour, however, which is generally bestowed in a wrong direction, on ornament and trick rather than on really artistic construction and finish. Lastly there is the highest class of all, consisting of those who really possess, or might possess, taste, culture, and intellect. Of these the great majority are now somewhat alien-

ated from pure literature, and devoted rather to social matters, to science, or to the more fashionable and profitable arts of design. Their demand for style in literature is confined chiefly to poetry. They also are interested more by their favourite subjects treated anyhow, than by subjects for which they care little treated well, so that even by them little encouragement is given to the cultivation and little hinderance to the decay of prose style.

Intimately connected with the influences that arise from this attitude and temper of the general reader, are certain influences which spring from such prevalent forms and subjects of literature as present themselves to the general writer. The first of these forms, and unquestionably the most constant and pervading in its influence, is now, as it was in De Quincey's days, journalism. No one with the slightest knowledge of the subject will pretend that the influence of journalism upon writing is wholly bad. Whatever may have been the case formerly, a standard of excellence which is in some respects really high is usually aimed at, and not seldom reached, in the better class of newspapers. Some appropriateness in the use of words, a rigid avoidance of the more glaring grammatical errors, and a respectable degree of clearness in statement, are expected by the reader and usually observed by the writer. In these respects, therefore, there is no falling off to be complained of, but rather a marked improvement upon past times to be perceived. Yet, as regards the higher excellences of style, it is not possible that the influence of journalism should be good. For it must at any cost be rapid, and rapidity is absolutely incompatible with style. The journalist has as a rule one of two things to do; he has either to give a rapid account of certain facts, or to present a rapid discussion of certain arguments. In either case it becomes a matter of necessity for him to adopt stereotyped phrases and forms of speech which, being ready cut and dried, may abbreviate his labour and leave him as little as possible to invent in his limited time. Now there is nothing more fatal to the attainment of a good style than the habit of using such stereotyped phrases and forms. With the imperiousness natural to all art, style absolutely refuses to avail itself of, or to be found in company with, anything that is ready made. The rule must be a leaden one, the mould made for the occasion, and broken after it has passed. Every one who has ever seriously tried to write must be conscious how sorely he has been beset, and how often he has been overcome, by the almost insensible temptation to adopt the current phrases of the day. Bad, however, as the influence of journalism is in this respect, it is perhaps worse in its tendency to sacrifice everything to mere picturesqueness of style (for the word must be thus misused because there is no other). The journalist is bound to be picturesque by the law of his being. The old phrase, *segnius irritant*, is infinitely truer of pseudo-picturesque style as compared with literature which holds to its proper means of appeal, than it is of literal spectacle as compared with narrative. And the journalist is obliged at any cost *irritare animos*, and that in the least possible time.

This tendency of journalism is assisted and intensified by that of another current form of literature, novel-writing. A very little thought will show that if the novel-writer attains to style it is almost a marvel. Of the four constituent elements of the novel, plot, character, description, and dialogue, none lend themselves in any great degree to the cultivation of the higher forms of style, and some are distinctly opposed to it. The most cunning plot may be developed equally in the style of Plato and in the style of a penny dreadful. Character drawing, as the novelist understands or should understand it, is almost equally unconnected with style. On the other hand description and dialogue, unless managed with consummate skill, distinctly tend to develop and strengthen the crying faults of contemporary style, its picturesqueness at any cost, its gasping and ungraceful periods, its neglect of purely literary effect.

Lastly, there must be noticed the enormous influence necessarily exerted by the growth of what is called scientific study (to use the term in its largest and widest sense), and by the displacement in its favour of many, if not most, of the departments of literature which were most favourable to the cultivation of style. In whatever quarter we look, we shall see that the primary effort of the writer and the primary desire of the reader are both directed to what are called scientific or positive results, in other words to matter instead of manner. In using the word science here, I have not the slightest intention of limiting its meaning, as it is too often limited, to physical science, I extend it to every subject which is capable of being treated in a scientific way, And I think we shall find that all subjects and all kinds of prose literature which are not capable of this sort of treatment, or do not readily lend themselves to it, are yearly occupying less and less the atten-

tion of both artists and audiences. Parliamentary oratory, which furnished a vigorous if a somewhat dangerous stimulant to the cultivation of style, is dead utterly. Pulpit eloquence, which at its worst maintained stylistic traditions, and at its best furnished some of the noblest examples of style, is dying, partly owing to the persistent refusal of the men of best culture and abilities to enter the clerical profession, partly to the absence of the serene security of a settled doctrine and position, but most of all to the demands upon the time of the clergy which modern notions enforce, and which make it utterly impossible for the greater number to devote a proper time to study. Philosophy, another great nurse of style, has now turned stepmother, and turns out her nurselings to wander in "thorniest queaches" of terminology and jargon, instead of the ordered gardens wherein Plato and Berkeley walked. History even, the last or almost the last refuge of a decent and comely prose, is more busy about records and manuscripts than about periods and paragraphs. Only criticism, the youngest and most hopeful birth of time as far as prose style is concerned, has not yet openly apostatized. It is true that even here signs of danger are not wanting, and that already we are told that criticism must be scientific, that its reading must not be desultory, and so forth. But on the whole there is little fear of relapse. The man who would cut himself a coat from another's cloth must bring to the task the knowledge and genius, the care and labour, of a skilled fashioner if he is to make good his claim of ownership. The man who has good work in perpetual contemplation is not likely to be satisfied with the complacent production of what is bad.

There is, moreover, one influence, or rather one set of influences, hostile to the attainment of style in the present day which I have as yet left unnoticed, and the approach to which is guarded by ground somewhat dangerous to the tread. It will, I think, appear to any one who contemplates the subject fully and impartially that style is essentially an aristocratic thing; and it is already a commonplace to say that the spirit of today, or perhaps the spirit of the times immediately behind us, is essentially democratic. It is democratic not in any mere political sense, but in the intolerance with which it regards anything out of the reach of, or incomprehensible to, the ordinary Philistine, working by the methods of Philistia. Intellectual and artistic pre-eminence, except in so far as it ministers to the fancies of the vulgar (great or small), is perhaps especially the object of this intolerance. Every one has witnessed or shared the angry impatience with which the ordinary Briton resents anything esoteric, fastidious, or fine. And the charms of prose style especially merit these epithets, and are not to be read by any one who runs, or tasted by any one who swallows in haste. Gaudy ornament is intelligible, graphic drawing is intelligible; but the finer cadences of the period, the more intricate strokes of composition, fall unregarded on the common ear and pass unnoticed by the common eye. To be tickled, to be dazzled, to be harrowed, are impressions of which the uncultured man is capable; they require little intellectual effort, and scarcely any judgment or taste in the direction of that little. But the music of the spheres would form but a sorry attraction in a music-hall programme, and Christopher Sly is not willing to accept nectar in exchange for a pot of even the smallest ale. And if the angry resentment of not a few readers gives the votary of style but little chance of an audience, it must be admitted that the lack of what I have called an aristocratic spirit gives the audience little chance of a performer. The conditions of modern life are unfavourable to the attainment of the peculiar mood of somewhat arrogant indifference which is the characteristic of the scholar. Every one knows Dean Gaisford's three reasons for the cultivation of the Greek language; and I for my part have no doubt the tone of them most accurately describes an important feature of the *Wesen des Gelehrten* [the essence of the learned man]. It may not be necessary for him "to read the words of Christ in the original;" it may not be of absolute importance that he should "have situations of affluence opened to him." But it certainly is essential that he should "look down on his fellow-creatures from a proper elevation;" and this is what the tendency of modern social progress is making more and more difficult, at any rate in appearance. You cannot raise the level of the valleys without diminishing the relative height of the hills; and you cannot scatter education and elementary cultivation broadcast without diminishing the value of the privileges which appertain to superior culture. The old republic of letters was, like other old republics, a democracy only in name, but in reality a more or less close oligarchy, looking down on metics and slaves whose degradations and disabilities heightened its courage and gave a zest to its freedom. In letters, as in politics, we are doing our best to change all this; and the possible re-

sult may be, that every one will soon be able to write a *Daily Telegraph* article, and that no one will aspire to anything beyond.

The general characteristics of style which the influence, combined or partial, of these forces has produced have been already indicated, but may perhaps now be summed up. Diffuseness; sacrifice of the graces of literary proportion to real or apparent clearness of statement; indulgence in cut-and-dried phrases; undue aiming at pictorial effect; gaudiness of unnatural ornament; preference of gross and glaring effects *en bloc* to careful composition. Certain authors who are either free from these defects or have vigour enough to excuse or transform them must now be noticed.

For reasons obvious, though various, it is not my intention to discuss in any way at the present time the style of the author of Sartor Resartus. Mr. Carlyle being thus removed, there can be little question who must take the foremost place in a discussion as to the merits and demerits of modern English prose style. And yet, audacious or paradoxical as the assertion may seem, it is at least doubtful whether in strictness we can assign to Mr. Ruskin a position in the very highest rank of writers if we are to adopt style as a criterion. The objection to his manner of writing is an obvious one, and one which he might very likely take as a compliment: it is too spontaneous in the first place, and too entirely subordinate to the subject in the second. I hope that it may be very clearly understood that I can see passages in Modern Painters and in the Stones of Venice (for I must be permitted to neglect the legions of little books with parody-provoking titles which have appeared in the last three lustres) which, for splendour of imaginative effect, for appropriateness of diction, for novelty and grandeur of conception, stand beyond all chance of successful rivalry, almost beyond all hope of decent parallel among the writings of ancient and modern masters. But in every case this marvellous effect will, when carefully examined, be found to depend on something wholly or partially extrinsic to the style. Mr. Ruskin writes beautifully because he thinks beautifully, because his thoughts spring, like Pallas, ready armed, and the fashion of the armour costs him nothing. Everybody has heard of the unlucky critic whose comment on Scott's fertility was that "the invention was not to be counted, for that came to him of its own accord." So it is with Mr. Ruskin. His beauties of style "come to him of their own accord," and then he writes as the very gods might dream of writing. But in the moments when he is off the tripod, or is upon some casual and un-Delphic tripod of his own construction or selection, how is his style altered! The strange touches of unforeseen colour become splashed and gaudy, the sonorous roll of the prophetic sentence-paragraphs drags and wriggles like a wounded snake, the cunning interweaving of scriptural or poetic phrase is patched and seamy. A Balaam on the Lord's side, he cannot curse or bless but as it is revealed to him, whereas the possessor of a great style can use it at will. He can shine on the just and on the unjust; can clothe his argument for tyranny or for liberty, for virtue or for vice, with the same splendour of diction, and the same unperturbed perfection of manner; can convince us, carry us with him, or leave us unconvinced but admiring, with the same unquestioned supremacy and the same unruffled calm. Swift can write a *jeu d'esprit* and a libel on the human race, a political pamphlet and a personal lampoon, with the same felicity and the same vigour. Berkeley can present tar-water and the Trinity, the theory of vision and the follies of contemporary free-thinking, with the same perfect lucidity and the same colourless fairness. But with Mr. Ruskin all depends on the subject, and the manner in which the subject is to be treated. He cannot even blame as he can praise; and there must be many who are ready to accept everything he can say of Tintoret or of Turner, and who feel no call to object to any of his strictures on Canaletto or on Claude, who yet perceive painfully the difference of style in the panegyrist and the detractor, and who would demand the stricter if less obvious justice, and the more artistic if apparently perverted sensitiveness, of the thorough master of style.

But if we have to quarrel with Mr. Ruskin because he has not sufficient command of the unquestioned beauties of his style, because he is not in Carew's words—

"A king who rules as he thinks fit
The universal monarchy of wit,"

but is rather a slave to his own thoughts and fancies, a very opposite fault must be found with the next writer who falls to be mentioned. "We do not," says an author with whom I am surprised to find myself in even partial and temporary agreement, "we do not get angry so much with what Mr. Matthew Arnold says as with his insufferable manner of saying it." In other words, there is no fear of omitting to notice a deliberate command and peculiarity of manner in Mr. Arnold, whether that manner be considered "insufferable" or no. For myself I must confess, that though I have very rarely felt the least inclination to get angry with anything which the author of Culture and Anarchy may have chosen to say, and though I have in common with all the youth of Zion an immense debt to acknowledge to his vindication of our faith and freedom from the chains of Philistia, yet I could very frequently find it in my heart to wish that Mr. Arnold had chosen any other style than that which appears to afford him such extreme delight. Irony is an admirable thing, but it should not be affected. To have a manner of one's own is an admirable thing, but to have a mannerism of one's own is perhaps not quite so admirable. It is curious that his unfortunately successful pursuit of this latter possession should have led Mr. Arnold to adopt a style which has more than any other the fault he justly censured twenty years ago as the special vice of modern art—the fault of the *fantastic*. No doubt the great masters of style have each a *cachet* which is easily decipherable by a competent student; no doubt, in spite of Lord Macaulay, Arbuthnot is to be distinguished from Swift, and the cunningest imitators of Voltaire from Voltaire himself. But to simulate this distinction by the deliberate adoption of mere tricks and manners is what no true master of style ever yet attempted, because for no true master of style was it ever yet necessary. Mr. Ruskin, to use the old Platonic simile, has not his horses sufficiently well in hand; at times the heavenly steed, with a strong and sudden flight, will lift the car amid the empyrean, at times the earth-born yoke-fellow will drag it down, with scarcely the assistance and scarcely the impediment of the charioteer. But even this is better than the driving of one who has broken his horses, indeed, but has broken them to little but the mincing graces of the Lady's Mile.

It is not possible to speak with equal definiteness of the style of a third master of English prose, who ranks in point of age and of reputation with Mr. Ruskin and Mr. Arnold. It would certainly be an over-hasty or an ill-qualified critic who should assert that Mr. Froude's style is always faultless; but, on the other hand, it may be asserted, without any fear whatever of contradiction carrying weight, that at its best it is surpassed by no style of the present day, and by few of any other, and that at its worst its faults are, not of a venial character, for no fault in art is venial, but at any rate of a kind which may meet with more ready excuse than those of the writers previously noticed. These faults are perhaps two only–undue diffuseness and undue aiming at the picturesque. We have seen that these are the two most glaring faults of the age, and by his indulgence in them, and the splendid effects which he has produced by that indulgence, Mr. Froude has undoubtedly earned his place, if not as a *Säcularsicher Mensch* [Worldly Man], at any rate as a representative man. No one, perhaps, who has read can fail to count among the triumphs of English prose the descriptions of the Pilgrimage of Grace in the History, of Sir Richard Grenvil's last fight in the Short Stories, of the wreckers at Ballyhige in the English in Ireland. There are also many shorter passages which exhibit almost every excellence that the most exacting critic could demand. But it is not to be denied that Mr. Froude has very frequently bowed the knee before the altar of Baal. It is unlawful to occupy twelve mighty volumes with the history of one nation during little more than half a century: it is unlawful for the sound critical reason of St. John, that if such a practice obtained universally, the world could not contain the books that should be written; and also for the reason that in such writing it is almost impossible to observe the reticence and compression which are among the lamps of style. It is unlawful to imagine and set down, except very sparingly, the colour of which the trees probably were at the time when kings and queens made their entrance into such and such a city, the buildings which they may or may not have looked upon, the thoughts which may or may not have occurred to them. Such sacrificings at the shrine of Effect, such trespassings on the domains and conveying of the methods of other arts and alien muses, are not to be commended or condoned. But one must, at the same time, allow with the utmost thankfulness that there are whole paragraphs, if not whole pages, of Mr. Froude's, which, for practised skill of composition and for legitimate beauty of effect, may take their place among the proudest efforts of English art.

It will probably be agreed that the three writers whom I have noticed stand at the head of contemporary English prose authors in point of age and authority; but there are other and younger authors who must necessarily be noticed in any account of the subject which aims at completeness. Mr. Swinburne's progress as a prose writer can

hardly have failed to be a subject of interest, almost equally with his career as a poet, to every lover of our tongue. His earliest appearance, the Essay on Byron, is even now in many respects characteristic of his work; but it does not contain–and it is a matter of sincere congratulation for all lovers of English prose that it does not contain–any passage at all equal to the magnificent descant on Marlowe, which closes its ten years younger brother, the Essay on Chapman. In the work which has occupied this interval, the merits and defects of Mr. Swinburne as a prose writer may be read by whoso wills. At times it has seemed as if the weeds would grow up with the good seed and choke it. Mr. Swinburne has fallen into the error, not unnatural for a poet, of forgetting that the figures and the language allowable in poetry are not also allowable in prose. The dangerous luxury of alliteration has attracted him only too often, and the still more dangerous license of the figure called chiasmus has been to him even as a siren, from whose clutches he has been hardly saved. But the noticeable thing is that the excellences of his prose speech have grown even stronger and its weaknesses weaker since he began. In the Essay on Blake, admirable as was much thereof, a wilful waste of language, not unfrequently verging on a woful want of sense, was too frequently apparent. In the Notes on his Poems, and in Under the Microscope, just as was most of the counter-criticism, it was impossible not to notice a tendency to verbiage and a proneness, I will not say to prefer sound to sense, but unnecessarily to reinforce sense with sound. But at the same time, in the Essays and Studies, and the Essay on Chapman, no competent critic could fail to notice, notwithstanding occasional outbreaks, the growing reticence and severity of form, as well as the increasing weight and dignity of meaning. Mr. Swinburne, as a prose writer, is in need of nothing but the pruning-hook. Most of his fellows are in want chiefly of something which might be worth pruning.

It is obviously impossible in the present article to notice minutely all even of the more prominent names in contemporary prose. Some there are among the older of our writers who yet retain the traditions of the theological school of writing, to which style owes so much. A good deal might be said of Cardinal Manning's earlier style (for his progress in this hierarchy has hardly corresponded with his promotion in the other), as well as of Dr. Newman's admirable clearness and form, joined as it is, perhaps unavoidably, to a certain hardness of temper. Mr. Disraeli's stylistic peculiarities would almost demand an essay to themselves. They have never perhaps had altogether fair play; for novel-writing and politics are scarcely friends to style. But Mr. Disraeli has the root of the matter in him, and has never been guilty of the degradation of the sentence, which is the crying sin of modern prose; while his unequalled felicity in the selection of single epithets (witness the famous "Batavian graces" and a thousand others) gives him a supply of legitimate ornament which few writers have ever had at command. Tastes, I suppose, will always differ as to the question whether his ornamentation is not sometimes illegitimate. The parrot-cry of upholstery is easily raised. But I think we have at last come to see that rococo work is good and beautiful in its way, and he must be an ungrateful critic who objects to the somewhat lavish emeralds and rubies of the Arabian Nights. Of younger writers, there are not many whose merits it would be proper to specify in this place; while the prevailing defects of current style have been already fully noticed. But there is one book of recent appearance which sets the possibilities of modern English prose in the most favourable light, and gives the liveliest hope as to what may await us, if writers, duly heeding the temptations to which they are exposed, and duly availing themselves of the opportunities for study and imitation which are at their disposal, should set themselves seriously to work to develop *pro virili* [to the best] the prose resources of the English tongue. Of the merely picturesque beauty of Mr. Pater's Studies in the History of the Renaissance, there can be no necessity for me to say anything here. In the first place it cannot escape the notice of any one who reads the book, and in the second, if there be any truth in what has been already said, the present age by no means needs to be urged to cultivate or to appreciate this particular excellence. The important point for us is the purely formal or regular merit of this style, and this is to be viewed with other eyes and tested by other methods than those which are generally brought to bear by critics of the present day. The main point which I shall notice is the subordinate and yet independent beauty of the sentences when taken separately from the paragraph. This is a matter of the very greatest importance. In too much of our present prose the individual sentence is unceremoniously robbed of all proper form and comeliness. If it adds its straw to the heap, its duty is supposed to be done. Mr. Pater

has not fallen in this error, nor has he followed the multitude to do evil in the means which he has adopted for the production of the singular "sweet attractive kind of grace" which distinguishes these Studies. A bungler would have depended, after the fashion of the day, upon strongly coloured epithets, upon complicated and quasi-poetic cadences of phrase, at least upon an obtrusively volumptuous softness of thought and a cumbrous protraction of sentence. Not so Mr. Pater. There is not to be discovered in his work the least sacrifice of the phrase to the word, of the clause to the phrase, of the sentence to the clause, of the paragraph to the sentence. Each holds its own proper place and dignity while contributing duly to the dignity and place of its superior in the hierarchy. Let any reader turn to pp. 15, 16, or pp. 118, 119, of the book, and see, as he cannot fail to see, the extraordinary mastery with which this complicated success is attained. Often the cadence of the sentence considered separately will seem to be—and will in truth be—quite different from that of the paragraph, because its separate completeness demands this difference. Yet the total effect, so far from being marred, is enhanced. There is no surer mark of the highest style than this separate and yet subordinate finish. In the words of Mr. Ruskin, it is "so modulated that every square inch is a perfect composition."

It is this perfection of modulation to which we must look for the excellence that we require and do not meet with in most of the work of the present day, and it is exactly this modulation with which all the faults that I have had to comment upon in the preceding pages are inconsistent. To an artist who should set before him such a model as either of the passages which I have quoted, lapses into such faults would be impossible. He will not succumb to the easy diffuseness which may obliterate the just proportionate and equilibrium of his periods. He will not avail himself of the ready assistance of stereotyped phraseology to spare himself the trouble of casting new moulds and devising new patterns. He will not imagine that he is a scene painter instead of a prose writer, a decorator instead of an architect, a caterer for the desires of the many instead of a priest to the worship of the few. He will not indulge in a style which requires the maximum of ornament in order to disguise and render palatable the minimum of art and of thought. He will not consider it his duty to provide, at the least possible cost of intellectual effort on the part of the reader, something which may delude him into the idea that he is exercising his judgment and his taste. And, above all, he will be careful that his sentences have an independent completeness and harmony, no matter what purpose they may be designed to fulfil. For the sentence is the unit of style; and by the cadence and music, as well as by the purport and bearing, of his sentences, the master of style must stand or fall. For years, almost for centuries, French prose has been held up as a model to English prose writers, and for the most part justly. Only of late has the example come to have something of the Helot about it. The influence of Victor Hugo–an influence almost omnipotent among the younger generation of French literary men–has been exercised in prose with a result almost as entirely bad as its effect in verse has been good. The rules of verse had stiffened and cramped French poetry unnaturally, and violent exercise was the very thing required to recover suppleness and strength; but French prose required no such surgery, and it has consequently lost its ordered beauty without acquiring compensatory charms. The proportions of the sentence have been wilfully disregarded, and the result is that French prose is probably now at a lower point of average merit than at any time for two centuries.

That an art should be fully recognised as an art, with strict rules and requirements, is necessary to attainment of excellence in it; and in England this recognition, which poetry has long enjoyed, has hardly yet been granted to prose. No such verses as we find by scores in such books as Marston's Satires would now suggest themselves as possible or tolerable to any writer of Marston's powers; but in prose many a sentence quite as intolerable as any of these verses is constantly written by persons of presumably sound education and competent wits. The necessities of the prose writer are, an ear in the first place: this is indispensable and perhaps not too common. In the second place, due study of the best authors, as well to know what to avoid as what to imitate. Lastly, care, which perhaps is not too much to demand of any artist, so soon as he has recognised and has secured recognition of the fact that he is an artist. Care is indeed the one thrice-to-be-repeated and indispensable property of the prose writer. It is pre-eminently necessary to him for the very reason that it is so easy to dispense with it, and to write prose without knowing what one does. Verse, at least verse which is to stand, as Johnson says, "the test of the finger if not of the ear," can-

not be written without conscious effort and observation. But something which may be mistaken for prose can unfortunately be produced without either taste, or knowledge, or care. With these three requisites there should be no limit to the beauty and to the variety of the results obtained. The fitness of English for prose composition will hardly be questioned, though it may be contended with justice that perhaps in no other language has the average merit of its prose been so far below the excellence of its most perfect specimens. But the resources which in the very beginning of the practice of original composition in fully organised English could produce the splendid and thoughtful, if quaint and cumbrous, embroideries of Euphues and the linked sweetness of the Arcadia, which could give utterance to the symphonies of Browne and Milton, which could furnish and suffice for the matchless simplicity of Bunyan, the splendid strength of Swift, the transparent clearness of Middleton and Berkeley, the stately architecture of Gibbon are assuredly equal to the demands of any genius that may arise to employ them.

It is therefore the plain duty of every critic to assist at least in impressing upon the mass of readers that they do not receive what they ought to receive from the mass of writers, and in suggesting a multiplication and tightening of the requirements which a prosaist must fulfil. There are some difficulties in the way of such impression and suggestion in the matter of style. It is not easy for the critic to escape being bidden, in the words of Nicholas Breton, "not to talk too much of it, having so little of it," or to avoid the obvious jest of Diderot on Beccaria, that he had written an "ouvrage sur le style où il n'y a point de style." For, unluckily, fault-finding is an ungracious business, and in criticising prose as prose the criticism has to be mostly fault-finding, the pleasanter if even harder task of discriminating appreciation being as a rule withheld from the critic. But I can see no reason why this state of things should continue, and I know no Utopia which ought to be more speedily rendered *topic*, than that in which at least the same censure which is now incurred by a halting verse, a discordant rhyme, or a clumsy stanza, should be accorded to a faultily-arranged clause, to a sentence of inharmonious cadence, to a paragraph of irregular and ungraceful architecture.

Reprinted from *Fortnightly Review,* new series, 19 (February 1876):243-259.

Robert Louis Stevenson

"On Style in Literature: Its Technical Elements" (1885)

Robert Louis Stevenson (1850-1894), the Scottish novel-
ist and poet, was also an outstanding essayist, contribut-
ing to such periodicals as Temple Bar, *the* Cornhill
Magazine, *and W. E. Henley's* Magazine of Art; *his*
essays were published in collected volumes, including
Virginibus Puerisque *(1881),* Familiar Studies
(1882), and Memoirs and Portraits *(1887). He was,*
therefore, at the height of his fame as an essayist when
this study was published in the Contemporary Review. *While Stevenson echoes the general late-*
nineteenth-century emphasis on the formal qualities of
prose over matters of content, he is original in the de-
tailed analyses he provides of rhythmic and other aural
prose elements, especially in section three (on prose
meter) and in section four (on sound patterning).—Ed.

There is nothing more disenchanting to
man than to be shown the springs and mechanism of any art. All our arts and occupations lie
wholly on the surface; it is on the surface that we
perceive their beauty, fitness, and significance;
and to pry below is to be appalled by their emptiness and shocked by the coarseness of the strings
and pulleys. In a similar way, psychology itself,
when pushed to any nicety, discovers an abhorrent baldness, but rather from the fault of our
analysis than from any poverty native to the
mind. And perhaps in aesthetics the reason is the
same: those disclosures which seem fatal to the dignity of art, seem so perhaps only in the proportion of our ignorance; and those conscious and unconscious artifices which it seems unworthy of
the serious artist to employ, were yet, if we had
the power to trace them to their springs, indications of a delicacy of the sense finer than we conceive, and hints of ancient harmonies in nature.
This ignorance at least is largely irremediable.
We shall never learn the affinities of beauty, for
they lie too deep in nature and too far back in
the mysterious history of man. The amateur, in
consequence, will always grudgingly receive details of method, which can be stated but can
never wholly be explained; nay, on the principle
laid down in Hudibras, that

"still the less they understand,
The more they admire the sleight-of-hand,"

many are conscious at each new disclosure of a
diminution in the ardour of their pleasure. I
must therefore warn that well-known character,
the general reader, that I am here embarked
upon a most distasteful business: taking down
the picture from the wall and looking on the
back; and like the inquiring child, pulling the musical cart to pieces.

I. *Choice of Words.*—The art of literature
stands apart from among its sisters, because the
material in which the literary artist works is the dialect of life; hence, on the one hand, a strange
freshness and immediacy of address to the public
mind, which is ready prepared to understand it;
but hence, on the other, a singular limitation.
The sister arts enjoy the use of a plastic and duc-
tile material, like the modeller's clay; literature
alone is condemned to work in mosaic with finite
and quite rigid words. You have seen these
blocks, dear to the nursery; this one a pillar, that
a pediment, a third a window or a vase. It is with
blocks of just such arbitrary size and figure that
the literary architect is condemned to design the
palace of his art. Nor is this all; for since these
blocks, or words, are the acknowledged currency
of our daily affairs, there are here possible none
of those suppressions by which other arts obtain
relief, continuity and vigour; no hieroglyphic
touch, no smoothed impasto, no inscrutable
shadow, as in painting; no blank wall, as in architecture; but every word, phrase, sentence, and
paragraph must move in a logical progression,
and convey a definite conventional import.

Now the first merit which attracts in the
pages of a good writer, or the talk of a brilliant
conversationalist, is the apt choice and contrast of
the words employed. It is, indeed, a strange art
to take these blocks, rudely conceived for the purpose of the market or the bar, and by tact of application touch them to the finest meanings and distinctions, restore to them their primal energy, wit-
tily shift them to another issue, or make of them
a drum to rouse the passions. But though this

form of merit is without doubt the most sensible and seizing, it is far from being equally present in all writers. The effect of words in Shakespeare, their singular justice, significance, and poetic charm, is different, indeed, from the effect of words in Addison or Fielding. Or, to take an example nearer home, the words in Carlyle seem electrified into an energy of lineament, like the faces of men furiously moved; whilst the words in Macaulay, apt enough to convey his meaning, harmonious enough in sound, yet glide from the memory like undistinguished elements in a general effect. But the first class of writers have no monopoly of literary merit. There is a sense in which Addison is superior to Carlyle; a sense in which Cicero is better than Tacitus, in which Voltaire excels Montaigne; it certainly lies not in the choice of words; it lies not in the interest or value of the matter; it lies not in force of intellect, of poetry, or of humour. The three first are but infants to the three second, and yet each, in a particular point of literary art, excels his superior in the whole. What is that point?

2. *The Web.*–Literature, although it stands apart by reason of the great destiny and general use of its medium in the affairs of men, is yet an art like other arts. Of these we may distinguish two great classes; those arts, like sculpture, painting, acting, which are representative, or, as used to be said very clumsily, imitative; and those like architecture, music, and the dance, which are self-sufficient, and merely presentative.[1] Each class, in right of this distinction, obeys principles apart; yet both may claim a common ground of existence, and it may be said with sufficient justice that the motive and end of any art whatever is to make a pattern; a pattern, it may be, of colours, of sounds, of changing attitudes, geometrical figures, or imitative lines; but still a pattern. That is the plane on which these sisters meet; it is by this that they are arts; and if it be well they should at times forget their childish origin, addressing their intelligence to virile tasks, and performing unconsciously that necessary function of their life, to make a pattern, it is still imperative that the pattern shall be made.

Music and literature, the two temporal arts, contrive their patterns of sounds in time; or, in other words, of sounds and pauses. Communication may be made in broken words, the business of life be carried on with substantives alone; but that is not what we call literature; and the true business of the literary artist is to plait or weave his meaning, involving it around itself; so that

each sentence, by successive phrases, shall first come into a kind of knot, and then, after a moment of suspended meaning, solve and clear itself. In every properly constructed sentence there should be observed this knot or hitch; so that (however delicately) we are led to foresee, to expect, and then to welcome the successive phrases. The pleasure may be heightened by an element of surprise, as, very grossly, in the common figure of the antithesis, or, with much greater subtlety, where an antithesis is first suggested and then deftly evaded. Each phrase, besides, is to be comely in itself; and between the implication and the evolution of the sentence there should be a satisfying equipoise of sound; for nothing more often disappoints the ear than a sentence solemnly and sonorously prepared, and hastily and weakly finished. Nor should the balance be too striking and exact, for the one rule is to be infinitely various; to interest, to disappoint, to surprise, and yet still to gratify; to be ever changing, as it were, the stitch, and yet still to give the effect of an ingenious neatness.

The conjurer juggles with two oranges, and our pleasure in beholding him springs from this, that neither is for an instant overlooked or sacrificed. So with the writer. His pattern, which is to please the supersensual ear, is yet addressed, throughout and first of all, to the demands of logic. Whatever be the obscurities, whatever the intricacies of the argument, the neatness of the fabric must not suffer, or the artist has been proved unequal to his design. And, on the other hand, no form of words must be selected, no knot must be tied among the phrases, unless knot and word be precisely what is wanted to forward and illuminate the argument; for to fail in this is to swindle in the game. The genius of prose rejects the *cheville* no less emphatically than the laws of verse; and the *cheville*, I should perhaps explain to some of my readers, is any meaningless or very watered phrase employed to strike a balance in the sound. Pattern and argument live in each other; and it is by the brevity, clearness, charm, or emphasis of the second, that we judge the strength and fitness of the first.

Style is synthetic; and the artist, seeking, so to speak, a peg to plait about, takes up at once two or more elements or two or more views of the subject in hand; combines, implicates, and contrasts them; and while, in one sense, he was merely seeking an occasion for the necessary knot, he will be found, in the other, to have greatly enriched the meaning, or to have transacted the work of two sentences in the space of one. In the change from the successive shallow statements of the old chronicler to the dense and luminous flow of highly synthetic narrative, there is implied a vast amount of both philosophy and wit. The philosophy we clearly see, recognizing in the synthetic writer a far more deep and stimulating view of life, and a far keener sense of the generation and affinity of events. The wit we might imagine to be lost; but it is not so, for it is just that wit, these perpetual nice contrivances, these difficulties overcome, this double purpose attained, these two oranges kept simultaneously dancing in the air, that, consciously or not, afford the reader his delight. Nay and this wit, so little recognised, is the necessary organ of that philosophy which we so much admire. That style is therefore the most perfect, not, as fools say, which is the most natural, for the most natural is the disjointed babble of the chronicler; but which attains the highest degree of elegant and pregnant implication unobtrusively; or if obtrusively, then with the greatest gain to sense and vigour. Even the derangement of the phrases from their (so-called) natural order is luminous for the mind; and it is by the means of such designed reversal that the elements of a judgment may be most pertinently marshalled, or the stages of a complicated action most perspicuously bound into one.

The web, then, or the pattern: a web at once sensuous and logical, an elegant and pregnant texture: that is style, that is the foundation of the art of literature. Books indeed continue to be read, for the interest of the fact or fable, in which this quality is poorly represented, but still it will be there. And, on the other hand, how many do we continue to peruse and reperuse with pleasure whose only merit is the elegance of texture? I am tempted to mention Cicero; and since Mr. Anthony Trollope is dead, I will. It is a poor diet for the mind, a very colourless and toothless "criticism of life"; but we enjoy the pleasure of a most intricate and dexterous pattern, every stitch a model at once of elegance and of good sense; and the two oranges, even if one of them be rotten, kept dancing with inimitable grace.

Up to this moment I have had my eye mainly upon prose; for though in verse also the implication of the logical texture is a crowning beauty, yet in verse it may be dispensed with. You would think that here was a death-blow to all I have been saying; and far from that, it is but a new illustration of the principle involved. For if the versifier is not bound to weave a pattern of his own, it is because another pattern has been formally imposed upon him by the laws of verse. For that is the essence of a prosody. Verse may be rhythmical; it may be merely alliterative; it may, like the French, depend wholly on the (quasi) regular recurrence of the rhyme; or, like the Hebrew, it may consist in the strangely fanciful device of repeating the same idea. It does not matter on what principle the law is based, so it be a law. It may be pure convention; it may have no inherent beauty; all that we have a right to ask of any prosody is, that it shall lay down a pattern for the writer, and that what it lays down shall be neither too easy nor too hard. Hence it comes that it is much easier for men of equal facility to write fairly pleasing verse than reasonably interesting prose; for in prose the pattern itself has to be invented, and the difficulties first created before they can be solved. Hence, again, there follows the peculiar greatness of the true versifier: such as Shakespeare, Milton, and Victor Hugo, whom I place beside them as versifier merely, not as poet. These not only knit and knot the logical texture of the style with all the dexterity and strength of prose; they not only fill up the pattern of the verse with infinite variety and sober wit; but they give us, besides, a rare and special pleasure, by the art, comparable to that of counterpoint, with which they follow at the same time, and now contrast, and now combine, the double pattern of the texture and the verse. Here the sounding line concludes; a little further on, the well-knit sentence; and yet a little further, and both will reach their solution on the same ringing syllable. The best that can be offered by the best writer of prose is to show us the development of the idea and the stylistic pattern proceed hand in hand, sometimes by an obvious and triumphant effort, sometimes with a great air of ease and nature. The writer of verse, by virtue of conquering another difficulty, delights us with a new series of triumphs. He follows three purposes where his rival followed only two; and the change is of precisely the same nature as that from melody to harmony. Or if you prefer to return to the juggler, behold him now, to the vastly increased enthusiasm of the spectators, juggling with three oranges instead of two. Thus it is: added difficulty, added beauty; and the pattern, with every fresh element, becoming more interesting in itself.

Yet it must not be thought that verse is simply an addition; something is lost as well as something gained; and there remains plainly traceable, in comparing the best prose with the best verse, a certain broad distinction of method in the web. Tight as the versifier may draw the knot of logic, yet for the ear he still leaves the tissue of the sentence floating somewhat loose. In prose, the sentence turns upon a pivot, nicely balanced, and fits into itself with an obstrusive neatness like a puzzle. The ear remarks and is singly gratified by this return and balance; while in verse it is all diverted to the measure. To find comparable passages is hard; for either the versifier is hugely the superior of the rival, or if he be not, and still persist in his more delicate enterprise, he falls to be as widely his inferior. But let us select them from the pages of the same writer, one who was ambidexter; let us take, for instance, Rumour's Prologue to the Second Part of Henry IV., a fine flourish of eloquence in Shakespeare's second manner, and set it side by side with Falstaff's praise of sherris, act IV. scene i; or let us compare the beautiful prose spoken throughout by Rosalind and Orlando, compare, for example, the first speech of all, Orlando's speech to Adam, with what passage it shall please you to select–the Seven Ages from the same play, or even such a stave of nobility as Othello's farewell to war: and still you will be able to perceive, if you have an ear for that class of music, a certain superior degree of organization in the prose; a compacter fitting of the parts; a balance in the swing and the return as of a throbbing pendulum. We must not, in things temporal, take from those who have little, the little that they have; the merits of prose are inferior, but they are not the same; it is a little kingdom, but an independent.

3. *Rhythm of the Phrase.*–Some way back, I used a word which still awaits an application. Each phrase, I said, was to be comely; but what is a comely phrase? In all ideal and material points, literature, being a representative art, must look for analogies to painting and the like; but in what is technical and executive, being a temporal art, it must seek for them in music. Each phrase of each sentence, like an air or a recitative in music, should be so artfully compounded out of long and short, out of accented and unaccented, as to gratify the sensual ear. And of this the ear is the sole judge. It is impossible to lay down laws. Even in our accentual and rhythmic language no analysis can find the secret of the beauty of a verse; how much less, then, of those phrases, such as prose is built of, which obey no

law but to be lawless and yet to please! The little that we know of verse (and for my part I owe it all to my friend Professor Fleeming Jenkin) is, however, particularly interesting in the present connection. We have been accustomed to describe the heroic line as five iambic feet, and to be filled with pain and confusion whenever, as by the conscientious schoolboy, we have heard our own description put in practice.

All nìght/the dreàd/less àn/gel ùn/pursùed[2]

goes the schoolboy; but though we close our ears, we cling to our definition, in spite of its proved and naked insufficiency. Mr. Jenkin was not so easily pleased, and readily discovered that the heroic line consists of four groups, or if you prefer the phrase, contains four pauses:

All night/the dreadless/angel/unpursued.

Four groups, each practically uttered as one word: the first, in this case, an iamb; the second, an amphibrachys; the third, a trochee; and the fourth an amphimacer; and yet our schoolboy, with no other liberty but that of inflicting pain, had triumphantly scanned it as five iambs. Perceive, now, this fresh richness of intricacy in the web; this fourth orange, hitherto unremarked, but still kept flying with the others. What had seemed to be one thing it now appears is two; and, like some puzzle in arithmetic, the verse is made at the same time to read in fives and to read in fours.

But again, four is not necessary. We do not, indeed, find verses in six groups, because there is not room for six in the ten syllables; and we do not find verses of two, because one of the main distinctions of verse from prose resides in the comparative shortness of the group; but it is even common to find verses of three. Five is the one forbidden number; because five is the number of the feet; and if five were chosen, the two patterns would coincide, and that opposition which is the life of verse would instantly be lost. We have here a clue to the effect of polysyllables, above all in Latin, where they are so common and make so brave an architecture in the verse; for the polysyllable is a group of Nature's making. If but some Roman would return from Hades (Martial, for choice), and tell me by what conduct of the voice these thundering verses should be uttered–"*Aut Lacedæmonium Tarentum,*" for a case in point–I feel as if I should enter at last into the full enjoyment of the best of human verses.

But, again, the five feet are all iambic, or supposed to be; by the mere account of syllables the four groups cannot be all iambic; as a question of elegance, I doubt if any one of them requires to be so; and I am certain that for choice no two of them should scan the same. The singular beauty of the verse analysed above is due, so far as analysis can carry us, part, indeed, to the clever repetition of L, D and N, but part to this variety of scansion in the groups. The groups which, like the bar in music, break up the verse for utterance, fall uniambically; and in declaiming a so-called iambic verse, it may so happen that we never utter one iambic foot. And yet to this neglect of the original beat there is a limit.

"Athens, the eye of Greece, mother of Arts," [3]

is, with all its eccentricities, a good heroic line; for though it scarcely can be said to imitate the beat of the iamb, it certainly suggests no other measure to the ear. But begin

"Mother Athens, eye of Greece,"

or merely "Mother Athens," and the game is up, for the trochaic beat has been suggested. The eccentric scansion of the groups is an adornment; but as soon as the original beat has been forgotten, they cease implicitly to be eccentric. Variety is what is sought; but if we destroy the original mould, one of the terms of this variety is lost, and we fall back on sameness. Thus, both as to the arithmetical measure of the verse and the degree of regularity in scansion, we see the laws of prosody to have one common purpose; to keep alive the opposition of two schemes simultaneously followed; to keep them notably apart, though still coincident; and to balance them with such judicial nicety before the reader, that neither shall be unperceived and neither signally prevail.

The rule of rhythm in prose is not so intricate. Here, too, we write in groups, or phrases, as I prefer to call them, for the prose phrase is greatly longer and is much more nonchalantly uttered than the group in verse: so that not only is there a greater interval of continuous sound between the pauses, but, for that very reason, word is linked more readily to word by a more summary enunciation. Still, the phrase is the strict analogue of the group, and successive phrases, like successive groups, must differ openly in length and rhythm. The rule of scansion in verse is to suggest no measure but the one in hand; in prose, to suggest no measure at all. Prose must be rhythmical, and it may be as much so as you will; but it must not be metrical. It may be anything, but it must not be verse. A single heroic line may very well pass and not disturb the somewhat larger stride of the prose style; but one following another will produce an instant impression of poverty, flatness, and disenchantment. The same lines delivered with the measured utterance of verse would perhaps seem rich in variety. By the more summary enunciation proper to prose, as to a more distinct vision, these niceties of difference are lost. A whole verse is uttered as one phrase; and the ear is soon wearied by a succession of groups identical in length. The prose writer, in fact, since he is allowed to be so much less harmonious, is condemned to a perpetually fresh variety of movement on a larger scale, and must never disappoint the ear by the trot of an accepted metre. And this obligation is the third orange with which he has to juggle, the third quality which the prose writer must work into his pattern of words. It may be thought perhaps that this is a quality of ease rather than a fresh difficulty; but such is the inherently rhythmical strain of the English language, that the bad writer—and must I take for example that admired friend of my boyhood, Captain Reid?—the inexperienced writer, as Dickens in his earlier attempts to be impressive, and the jaded writer, as any one may see for himself, all tend to fall at once into production of bad blank verse. And here it might be pertinently asked, Why bad? And I suppose it might be enough to answer that no man ever made good verse by accident, and that no verse can ever sound otherwise than as trivial, when uttered with the delivery of prose. But we can go beyond such answers. The weak side of verse is the regularity of the beat, which in itself is decidedly less impressive than the movement of the nobler prose; and it is just into this weak side, and this alone, that the careless writer falls. A peculiar density and mass, consequent on the nearness of the pauses, is one of the chief good qualities of verse; but this our accidental versifier, still following after the swift gait and large gestures of prose, does not so much as aspire to imitate. Lastly, since he remains unconscious that he is making verse at all, it can never occur to him to extract those effects of counterpoint and opposition which I have referred to as the final grace and justification of verse, and, I may add, of blank verse in particular.

4. *Contents of the Phrase.*–Here is a great deal of talk about rhythm–and naturally; for in our canorous language rhythm is always at the door. But it must not be forgotten that in some languages this element is almost, if not quite extinct, and that in our own it is probably decaying. The even speech of many educated Americans sounds the note of danger. I should see it go with something as bitter as despair, but I should not be desperate. As in verse no element, not even rhythm, is necessary; so, in prose also, other sorts of beauty will arise and take the place and play the part of those that we outlive. The beauty of the expected beat in verse, the beauty in prose of its larger and more lawless melody, patent as they are to English hearing, are always silent in the ears of our next neighbours; for in France the oratorical accent and the pattern of the web have almost or altogether succeeded to their places; and the French prose writer would be astounded at the labours of his brother across the Channel, and how a good quarter of his toil, above all *invita Minerva* [without the help of Minerva, goddess of wisdom], is to avoid writing verse. So wonderfully far apart have races wandered in spirit, and so hard it is to understand the literature next door!

Yet French prose is distinctly better than English; and French verse, above all while Hugo lives, it will not do to place upon one side. What is more to our purpose, a phrase or a verse in French is easily distinguishable as comely and uncomely. There is then another element of comeliness hitherto overlooked in this analysis: the contents of the phrase. Each phrase in literature is built of sounds, as each phrase in music consists of notes. One sound suggests, echoes, demands, and harmonizes with another; and the art of rightly using these concordances is the final art in literature. It used to be a piece of good advice to all young writers to avoid alliteration; and the advice was sound, in so far as it prevented daubing. None the less for that, was it abominable nonsense, and the mere raving of those blindest of the blind who will not see. The beauty of the contents of a phrase, or of a sentence, depends implicity upon alliteration and upon assonance. The vowel demands to be repeated; the consonant demands to be repeated; and both cry aloud to be perpetually varied. You may follow the adventures of a letter through any passage that has particularly pleased you; find it, perhaps, denied awhile, to tantalize the ear; find it fired again at you in a whole broadside; or find it pass into congenerous sounds, one liquid or labial melting away into another. And you will find another and much stranger circumstance. Literature is written by and for two senses: a sort of internal ear, quick to perceive "unheard melodies;" and the eye, which directs the pen and deciphers the printed phrase. Well, even as there are rhymes for the eye, so you will find that there are assonances and alliterations; that where an author is running the open A, deceived by the eye and our strange English spelling, he will often show a tenderness for the flat A; and that where he is running a particular consonant, he will not improbably rejoice to write it down even when it is mute or bears a different value.

Here, then, we have a fresh pattern–a pattern, to speak grossly, of letters–which makes the fourth preoccupation of the prose writer, and the fifth of the versifier. At times it is very delicate and hard to perceive, and then perhaps most excellent and winning (I say perhaps); but at times again the elements of this literal melody stand more boldly forward and usurp the ear. It becomes, therefore, somewhat a matter of conscience to select examples; and as I cannot very well ask the reader to help me, I shall do the next best by giving him the reason or the history of each selection. The two first, one in prose, one in verse, I chose without previous analysis, simply as engaging passages that had long re-echoed in my ear.

"I cannot praise a fugitive and cloistered virtue, unexercised and unbreathed, that never sallies out and sees her adversary, but slinks out of the race where that immortal garland is to be run for, not without dust and heat."[4] Down to "virtue," the current S and R are both announced and repeated unobtrusively, and by way of a gracenote that almost inseparable group PVF is given entire.[5] The next phrase is a period of repose, almost ugly in itself, both S and R still audible, and B given as the last fulfilment of PVF. In the next four phrases, from "that never" down to "run for," the mask is thrown off, and but for a slight repetition of the F and V, the whole matter turns, almost too obtrusively, on S and R; first S coming to the front, and then R. In the concluding phrase all these favourite letters, and even the flat A, a timid preference for which is just perceptible, are discarded at a blow and in a bundle; and to make the break more obvious, every word ends with a dental, and all but one with T, for which we have been cautiously prepared since the beginning. The singular dignity of the first clause, and this hammer-stroke of the last, go far to make the charm of this exquisite sentence. But it is fair to own that S and R are used a little coarsely.

"In Xanadu did Kubla Khan	(KANDL)
A stately pleasure dome decree,	(KDLSR)
Where Alph the sacred river ran,	(KANDLSR)
Through caverns measureless to man,	(KANLSR)
Down to a sunless sea."	(NDLS)

Here I have put the analysis of the main group alongside the lines; and the more it is looked at, the more interesting it will seem. But there are further niceties. In lines two and four, the current S is most delicately varied with Z. In line three, the current flat A is twice varied with the open A, already suggested in line two, and both times ("where" and "sacred") in conjunction with the current R. In the same line F and V (a harmony in themselves, even when shorn of their comrade P) are admirably contrasted. And in line four there is a marked subsidiary M, which again was announced in line two. I stop from weariness, for more might yet be said.

My next example was recently quoted from Shakespeare as an example of the poet's colour sense. Now, I do not think literature has anything to do with colour, or poets anyway the better of such a sense; and I instantly attacked this passage, since "purple" was the word that had so pleased the writer of the article, to see if there might not be some literary reason for its use. It will be seen that I succeeded amply; and I am bound to say I think the passage exceptional in Shakespeare—exceptional, indeed, in literature; but it was not I who chose it.

The BaRge she sat iN, like a BuRNished throNe
BuRNt ON the water: the PooP was BeateN gold,
PuRPle the sails and so PuR[per]Fumèd that
The wiNds were lovesick with them,[7]

It may be asked why I have put the F of perfumèd in capitals; and I reply, because this change from P to F is the completion of that from B to P, already so adroitly carried out. Indeed, the whole passage is a monument of curious ingenuity; and it seems scarce worth while to indicate the subsidiary S, L and W. In the same article, a second passage from Shakespeare was quoted, once again as an example of his colour sense:

"A mole cinque-spotted like the crimson drops
I' the bottom of a cowslip."[8]

It is very curious, very artificial, and not worth while to analyse at length: I leave it to the reader. But before I turn my back on Shakespeare, I should like to quote a passage, for my own pleasure, and for a very model of every technical art:

But in the wind and tempest of her frown,
   W. P. V. F. (st)(ow)[9]
Distinction with a loud and powerful fan,
   W.P.F.(st)(ow) L
Puffing at all, winnowes the light away;
   W. P. F. L.
And what hath mass and matter by itself
   W. F. L. M. A.
Lies rich in virtue and unmingled.[10]
   V. L. M.

From these delicate and choice writers I turned with some curiosity to a player of the big drum–Macaulay. I had in hand the two-volume edition, and I opened at the beginning of the second volume. Here was what I read: "The violence of revolutions is generally proportioned to the degree of the maladministration which has produced them. It is therefore not strange that the government of Scotland, having been during many years greatly more corrupt than the government of England, should have fallen with a far heavier ruin. The movement against the last king of the house of Stuart was in England conservative, in Scotland destructive. The English complained not of the law, but of the violation of the law." This was plain sailing enough; it was our old friend PVF floated by the liquids in a body; but as I read on, and turned the page, and still found PVF with his attendant liquids, I confess my mind misgave me utterly. This could be no trick of Macaulay's; it must be the nature of the English tongue. In a kind of despair, I turned half-way through the volume; and coming upon his lordship dealing with General Cannon, and fresh from Claverhouse and Killiekrankie, here, with elucidative spelling, was my reward:

"Meanwhile the disorders of kannon's kamp went on inkreasing. He kalled a kouncil of war to konsider what kourse it would be advisable to take. But as soon as the kouncil had met a preliminary kuestion was raised. The army was almost Eksklusively a Highland army. The recent viktory had been won eksklusively by Highland

469

warriors. Great chie*f*s who had brought si*k*s or se*v*en hundred *f*ighting men into the *f*ield, did not think it *f*air that they should be out*v*oted by the gentlemen *f*rom Ireland and *f*rom the Low Kountries, who bore indeed King James's Kommission, and were Kalled Kolonels and Kaptains, but who were Kolonels without regiments and Kaptains without Kompanies."

A moment of FV in all this world of K's! It was not the English language, then, that was an instrument of one string, but Macaulay that was an incomparable dauber.

It was probably from this barbaric love of repeating the same sound, rather than from any design of clearness, that he acquired his irritating habit of repeating words; I say the one rather than the other, because such a trick of the ear is deeper-seated and more original in man than any logical consideration. Few writers, indeed, are probably conscious of the length to which they push this melody of letters. One, writing very diligently, and only concerned about the meaning of his words and rhythm of his phrases, was struck into amazement by the eager triumph with which he cancelled one expression to substitute another. Neither changed the sense; both being monosyllables, neither could affect the scansion; and it was only by looking back on what he had already written that the mystery was solved: the second word contained an Open A, and for nearly half a page he had been riding that vowel to death.

In practice, I should add, the ear is not always so exacting; and ordinary writers, in ordinary moments, content themselves with avoiding what is harsh, and here and there, upon a rare occasion, buttressing a phrase, or linking two together, with a patch of assonance or a momentary jingle of alliteration. To understand how constant is this pre-occupation of good writers, even where its results are least obtrusive, it is only necessary to turn to the bad. There, indeed, you will find cacophony supreme, the rattle of incongruous consonants only relieved by the jaw-breaking hiatus, and whole phrases not to be articulated by the powers of man.

Conclusion.—We may now briefly enumerate the elements of style. We have, peculiar to the prose writer, the task of keeping his phrases large, rhythmical and pleasing to the ear, without ever allowing them to fall into the strictly metrical: peculiar to the versifier, the task of combining and contrasting his double, treble, and quadruple pattern, feet and groups, logic and metre—

harmonious in diversity: common to both, the task of artfully combining the prime elements of language into phrases that shall be musical in the mouth; the task of weaving their argument into a texture of committed phrases and of rounded periods—but this particularly binding in the case of prose: and again common to both, the task of choosing apt, explicit, and communicative words. We begin to see now what an intricate affair is any perfect passage; how many faculties, whether of taste or pure reason, must be held upon the stretch to make it; and why, when it is made, it should afford us so complete a pleasure. From the arrangement of according letters, which is altogether arabesque and sensual, up to the architecture of the elegant and pregnant sentence, which is a vigorous act of the pure intellect, there is scarce a faculty in man but has been exercised. We need not wonder, then, if perfect sentences are rare, and perfect pages rarer.

---

1. The division of the arts may best be shown in a tabular form, thus:—

	In time.	In space.	In time and space
Presentative	Music	Painting, Sculpture, &c.	Dance
Representative	Literature	Architecture,	Acting

2. Milton.

3. Milton.

4. Milton.

5. As PVF will continue to haunt us through our English examples, take, by way of comparison, this Latin verse, of which it forms a chief adornment, and do not hold me answerable for the all too Roman freedom of the sense: "Hanc volo, quæ facilis, quæ palliolata vagatur."–*R.L.S.* Stevenson quotes Martial: "I like this kind of girl, the one who is easy [in both manner and appearance] and who wears a short Greek stole."–*Ed.*

6. Coleridge.

7. *Antony and Cleopatra.*

8. *Cymbeline.*

9. The *v* is in "of."

10. *Troilus and Cressida.*

Reprinted from *Contemporary Review*, 47 (April 1885): 548-561.

Walter Pater

"Style" (1888)

Walter Horatio Pater (1839-1894) was a fellow of Brasenose College, Oxford, and a major figure in the later nineteenth-century revaluation of Renaissance art and in the development of aesthetic criticism. His well-known essay on style, with its assertion that prose can be understood by the kind of aesthetic criteria normally reserved for poetry, first appeared in the December 1888 issue of the Fortnightly Review *and was included in Pater's volume* Appreciations *the following year.–Ed.*

Since all progress of mind consists for the most part in differentiation, in the severance of an obscure complex into its parts or phases, it is surely the stupidest of losses to wear off the edge of achieved distinctions, and confuse things which right reason has put asunder–poetry and prose, for instance; or, to speak more exactly, the characteristic laws and excellences of prose and verse composition. On the other hand, those who have dwelt most emphatically on the distinction between prose and verse, prose and poetry, may sometimes have been tempted to limit the proper functions of prose too narrowly; which again is at least false economy, as being, in effect, the renunciation of a certain means or faculty, in a world where after all we must needs make the most of things. Critical efforts to limit art *à priori*, by anticipations regarding the natural incapacity of the material with which this or that artist works, as the sculptor with solid form, or the prose-writer with the ordinary language of men, are always liable to be annulled by the facts of artistic production; and while prose is actually found to be a coloured thing with Bacon, picturesque with Livy and Carlyle, musical with Cicero and Newman, mystical and intimate with Plato and Michelet and Sir Thomas Browne, exalted or florid it may be with Milton and Taylor, it will be useless to protest that it can be nothing at all, except something very tamely and narrowly confined to mainly practical ends–a kind of "good round-hand;" as useless as the protest that poetry might not touch prosaic subjects as with Wordsworth, or an abstruse matter as with Browning, or treat contemporary life nobly as with Tennyson. In subordination to one essential beauty in all good literary style, in all literature as a fine art, as there are many beauties of poetry so the beauties of prose are many, and it is the business of criticism to estimate them as such; as it is good in the criticism of verse to look for those hard, logical, and quasi-prosaic excellences which that too has or needs. To find in the poem, amid the flowers, the allusions, the mixed perspectives, of Lycidas for instance, the thought, the logical structure: how wholesome! how delightful!–as to identify in prose what we call the poetry, the imaginative power, not treating it as out of place and a kind of gipsy intruder, but by way of an estimate of its rights, that is, of its achieved powers, there.

Dryden, with the characteristic instinct of his age, loved to emphasise the distinction between poetry and prose, the protest against their confusion with each other, coming with somewhat diminished effect from one whose poetry was so prosaic. In truth, his sense of prosaic excellence limited his verse rather than his prose, which is not only fervid, richly figured, poetic, as we say, but vitiated, all unconsciously, by many a scanning line. Setting up correctness, that humble merit of prose, as the central literary excellence, he is really a less correct writer than he may seem, still with an imperfect mastery of the relative pronoun. It might have been foreseen that, in the rotation of minds, the province of poetry in prose would find its assertor; and, a century after Dryden, amid very different intellectual needs, and with the need therefore of great modifications in literary form, the range of the poetic force in literature was effectively enlarged by Wordsworth. The true distinction between prose and poetry he regarded as the almost technical or accidental one of the absence or presence of metrical beauty, or say metrical restraint; and for him the opposition came to be between verse and prose of course (you can't scan Wordsworth's prose), but, as the essential dichotomy in this matter, between imaginative and unimaginative writing, parallel to De Quincey's distinction between "the literature of power and the literature of knowledge," in the former of which the composer gives us not fact, but his peculiar sense of fact, whether past or present, or prospective, it may be, as often in oratory.

Dismissing then, under sanction of Wordsworth, that harsher opposition of poetry to prose as savouring in fact of the arbitrary psychology of the last century, and with it the prejudice that there can be but one only beauty of prose style, I propose in this paper to point out certain qualities of all literature as a fine art, which, if they apply to the literature of fact, apply still more to the literature of the imaginative sense of fact, while they apply indifferently to verse and prose, so far as either is really imaginative–certain conditions of true art in both alike, which conditions may also contain in them the secret of the proper discrimination and guardianship of the peculiar excellences of either.

The line between fact and something quite different from external fact is, indeed, hard to draw. In Pascal, for instance, in the persuasive writers generally, how difficult to define the point where, from time to time, argument which, if it is to be worth anything at all must consist of facts or groups of facts, becomes a pleading–a theorem no longer, but essentially an appeal to the reader to catch the writer's spirit, to think with him, if one can or will–an expression no longer of fact but of his sense of it, his peculiar intuition of a world, prospective, or discerned below the faulty conditions of the present, in either case changed somewhat from the actual one. In science, on the other hand, in history so far as it conforms to scientific rule, we have a literary domain in which imagination may be thought to be always an intruder. And as in all science the functions of literature reduce themselves eventually to the transcript of fact, so the literary excellences of its form are reducible to various kinds of painstaking; this good quality being involved in all "skilled work" whatever, in the drafting of an act of parliament, as in sewing. Yet here again, the writer's sense of fact, in history especially, and all those complex subjects which do but lie on the borders of science, will still take the place of fact, in various degrees. Your historian, for instance, with absolutely truthful intention, amid the multitude of facts presented to him must needs select, and in selecting assert something of his own humour, something that comes not of the world without but of a vision within. So Gibbon moulds his unwieldy material to a preconceived view. Livy, Tacitus, Michelet

moving amid the records of the past full of poignant sensibility, each after his own sense modifies, who can tell how and where? and becomes something else than a transcriber; each, as he thus modifies, passing into the domain of art proper. For just in proportion as the writer's aim, consciously or unconsciously, comes to be a transcript, not of the world, not of mere fact, but of his sense of it, he becomes an artist, his work *fine* art; and good art (as I hope ultimately to show) in proportion to the truth of his presentment of that sense; as in those humbler or plainer functions of literature also, truth–truth to bare fact there–is the essence of such artistic quality as they may have. Truth! there can be no merit, no craft at all, without that. And further, all beauty is in the long run only fineness of truth–expression–the finer accommodation of speech to that vision within.

The transcript of his sense of fact rather than the fact, as being preferable, pleasanter, more beautiful to him. In literature, as in every other product of human skill, in the moulding of a bell or a platter, for instance, wherever this sense asserts itself, wherever the producer so modifies his work as, over and above its primary use or intention, to make it pleasing (to himself, of course, in the first instance) there, "fine" as opposed to merely serviceable art, exists. Literary art, that is, like all art which is in any way imitative or reproductive of fact–form, or colour, or incident, is the representation of such fact as connected with soul, of a specific personality, in its preferences, its volition and power.

Such is the matter of imaginative or artistic literature–this transcript, not of mere fact, but of fact in its infinite variety, as modified by human preference, in all its infinitely varied forms. It will be good literary art not because it is brilliant or sober, or rich, or impulsive, or severe; but just in proportion as its representation of that sense–that soul-fact–is true, verse being only one department of such literature, and imaginative prose, it may be thought, being the special art of the modern world. That imaginative prose should be the special and opportune art of the modern world results from two important facts about the latter: first, the chaotic variety and complexity of its interests, making the intellectual issue, the really master currents of the present time incalculable–a condition of mind little susceptible of the restraint proper to verse form, so that the most characteristic verse of the nineteenth century has been lawless verse; and secondly, an all-pervading naturalism, a curiosity about everything whatever as it really is—involving a certain humility of attitude cognate to what must, after all, be the less ambitious form of literature. And prose thus asserting itself as the special and privileged artistic faculty of the present day, will be, however critics may try to narrow its scope, as varied in its excellence as humanity itself reflecting on the facts of its latest experience—an instrument of many stops, meditative, observant, descriptive, eloquent, analytic, severe, fervid. Its beauties will be not exclusively "pedestrian:" it will exert, in due measure, all the varied charms of poetry, down to the rhythm which, as in Cicero, or Michelet, or Newman, at their best, gives its musical value to every syllable.

The literary artist is of necessity a scholar, and in what he proposes to do will have in mind, first of all, the scholar and the scholarly conscience—the male conscience in this matter, as we must think it, under a system of education which still to so large an extent limits real scholarship to men. In his self-criticism, he supposes always that sort of reader who will go (all over eyes) warily, considerately, though without consideration for him, over the ground which the female conscience traverses so lightly, so amiably. For the material in which he works is no more a creation of his own than the sculptor's marble. Product of a myriad various minds and contending tongues, compact of obscure and minute association, a language has its own abundant and often recondite laws, in the habitual and summary recognition of which scholarship consists. A writer, full of a matter he is before all things anxious to express, may think of those laws, the limitations of vocabulary, structure, and the like, as a restriction, but if a real artist will find in them an opportunity. His punctilious observance of the proprieties of his medium will diffuse through all he writes a general air of sensibility, of refined usage. *Exclusiones debitæ naturæ*—the exclusions, or rejections, which nature demands—we know how large a part these play, according to Bacon, in the science of nature. In a somewhat changed sense, we might say that the art of the scholar is summed up in the observance of those rejections demanded by the nature of his medium, the material he must use. Alive to the value of an atmosphere in which every term finds its utmost degree of expression, and with all the jealousy of a lover of words, he will resist a constant tendency on the part of the majority of those who use them to efface the distinctions of language, the facility of writers often reinforcing in this respect

the work of the vulgar. He will feel the obligation not of the laws only but of those affinities, avoidances, those mere preferences of his language, which through the associations of literary history have become a part of its nature, prescribing the rejection of many a neology, many a license, many a gipsy phrase which might present itself as actually expressive. His appeal, again, is to the scholar, who has great experience in literature, and will show no favour for short-cuts, or hackneyed illustration, or an affectation of learning designed for the unlearned. Hence a contention, a sense of self-restraint and renunciation, having for the susceptible reader the effect of a challenge for minute consideration; the attention of the writer, in every minutest detail, being a pledge that it is worth the reader's while to be attentive too, that the writer is dealing scrupulously with his instrument, and therefore, indirectly, with the reader himself, that he has the science of the instrument he plays on, perhaps, after all, with a freedom which in such case will be the freedom of a master.

For meanwhile, braced only by those restraints, he is really vindicating his liberty in the making of a vocabulary, an entire system of composition, for himself, his own true manner; and when we speak of the manner of a true master we mean what is essential in his art. Pedantry being only the scholarship of *le cuistre* (we have no English equivalent) he is no pedant, and does but show his intelligence of the rules of language in his freedoms with it, addition or expansion, which like the spontaneities of manner in a well-bred person will still further illustrate good taste.— The right vocabulary! Translators have not invariably seen how all-important that is in the work of translation, driving for the most part at idiom or construction; whereas, if the original be first-rate, one's first care should be with its elementary particles; Plato, for instance, being often reproducible by an exact following, with no variation in structure, of word after word, as the pencil follows a drawing under tracing paper, so only each word or syllable be not of false colour, to change my figure a little.

Well! that is because any writer worth translating at all has winnowed and searched through his vocabulary, is conscious of the words he would select if he read a dictionary, and still more of the words he would reject were the dictionary other than Johnson's; and doing this with his peculiar sense of the world ever in view, in search of an instrument for the adequate expression of that, begets a vocabulary faithful to the colouring of his own spirit, and in the strictest sense original. That living authority which language needs lies, in truth, in its scholars, who recognising always that every language possesses a genius, a very fastidious genius, of its own, expand at once and purify its very elements, which must needs change along with the changing thoughts of living people. Ninety years ago, for instance, great mental force, certainly, was needed by Wordsworth, to break through the consecrated poetic associations of a century, and speak the language that was his, and was to become in a measure the language of the next generation. But he did it with the tact of a scholar also. English, for a quarter of a century past, has been assimilating the phraseology of pictorial art; for half a century, the phraseology of the great German metaphysical movement of eighty years ago; in part also the language of mystical theology: and none but pedants will regret a great consequent increase of its resources. For many years to come its enterprise may well lie in the naturalisation of the vocabulary of science, so only it be under the eye of a sensitive scholarship: in a liberal naturalisation of the ideas of science too, for after all the chief stimulus of good style is to possess a full, rich, complex matter to grapple with. The literary artist therefore will be well aware of physical science; science too attaining, in its turn, its true literary ideal. And then, as the scholar is nothing without the historic sense, he will be apt to restore not really obsolete or really worn-out words, but the finer edge of words still in use:—ascertain, communicate, discover—words like these it has been part of our "business" to misuse. And still as language was made for man, he will be no authority for correctnesses which, limiting freedom of utterance, were yet but accidents in their origin; as if one vowed not to say "its," which ought to have been in Shakespere; "his" and "hers," for inanimate things, being but a barbarous and really inexpressive survivor. Yet we have known many things like that. Racy Saxon monosyllables, close to us as touch and sight, he will intermix readily with those long, savoursome, Latin words, rich in "second intention." In this late day certainly, no critical process can be conducted reasonably without eclecticism. Of such eclecticism we have a justifying example in one of the first poets of our time. How illustrative of monosyllabic effect, of sonorous Latin, of the phraseology of science, of metaphysic, of colloquialism even, are the writings of Tennyson; yet with what a fine, fastidious scholarship throughout!

A scholar writing for the scholarly, he will of course leave something to the willing intelligence of his reader. "To go preach to the first passer-by," says Montaigne, "to become tutor to the ignorance of the first I meet, is a thing I abhor;" a thing, in fact, naturally distressing to the scholar, who will therefore ever be shy of offering uncomplimentary assistance to the reader's wit. To really strenuous minds there is a pleasurable stimulus in the challenge for a continuous effort on their part, to be rewarded by securer and more intimate grasp of the author's sense. Self-restraint, a skilful economy of means—ascêsis—that too has a beauty of its own; and for the reader supposed there will be an æsthetic satisfaction in that frugal closeness of style which makes the most of a word, in the exaction from every sentence of a precise relief, in the just spacing out of word to thought—the logically filled space—connected always with the delightful sense of difficulty overcome.

Different classes of persons, at different times, make, of course, very various demands upon literature. Still, scholars, I suppose, and not only scholars but all disinterested lovers of books, will always look to it, as in all other fine art, for a refuge, a sort of cloistral refuge, from a certain vulgarity in the actual world. A perfect poem like *Lycidas*, a perfect fiction like *Transformation*, the perfect handling of a theory like Newman's *Idea of a University*, has for them something of the uses of a religious "retreat." Here, then, with a view to the central need of a select few, those "men of a finer thread," who have formed and maintain the literary ideal—everything, every component element, will have undergone exact trial, and, above all, there will be no uncharacteristic or tarnished or vulgar decoration, permissible ornament being for the most part structural or necessary. As the painter in his picture, so the artist in his book, aims at the production by honourable artifice of a peculiar atmosphere. "The artist," says Schiller, "may be known rather by what he *omits*;" and in literature, too, the true artist may be best recognised by his tact of omission. For to the grave reader words too are grave; and the ornamental word, the figure, the accessory form or colour or reference is rarely content to die to thought precisely at the right moment, but will inevitably linger awhile, stirring a long "brain-wave" behind it of perhaps quite alien associations.

Just there, it may be, is the detrimental tendency of the sort of scholarly attentiveness I am recommending. But the true artist allows for it. He will remember that, as the very word ornament indicates what is in itself non-essential, so the "one beauty" of all literary style is of its very essence, and independent, in prose and verse alike, of all removable decoration; that it may exist in its fullest lustre, as in Flaubert's *Madame Bovary,* for instance, or in Stendhal's *Rouge et Noir,* in a composition utterly unadorned, with hardly a single suggestion of visibly beautiful things. Parallel, allusion, the allusive way generally, the flowers in the garden,–he knows the narcotic force of these upon the negligent intelligence to which any diversion (literally) is welcome, any vagrant intruder, because one can go wandering away with him from the immediate subject. Jealous, if he have a really quickening motive within, of all that does not hold directly to that, of the facile, the otiose, he will never depart from the strictly pedestrian process, unless he gains a ponderable something thereby. Even assured of its congruity, he will still question its serviceableness:–is it worth while, can we afford, to attend to just that, to just that figure, or literary reference, just then?–Surplusage! he will dread that, as the runner on his muscles. For in truth all art does but consist in the removal of surplusage, from the last finish of the gem-engraver blowing away the last particle of invisible dust, back to the earliest divination of the finished work to be, lying somewhere, according to Michelangelo's fancy, in the rough-hewn block of stone.

And what applies to figure or flower must be understood of all other accidental or removable ornaments of writing whatever; and not of specific ornament only, but of all that latent colour and imagery which language as such carries in it. A lover of words for their own sake, to whom nothing about them is unimportant, a minute and constant observer of their physiognomy, he will be on the alert not only for obviously mixed metaphors, as we know, but of the metaphor that is mixed in all our speech, though a rapid use may involve no cognition of it. Currently recognising the incident, the colour, the physical elements or particles in words like absorb, consider, extract, to take the first that occur, he will avail himself of them, as further adding to the resources of expression. The elementary particles of language will be turned into colour and light and shade by his scholarly living in the sense of them. Still opposing the constant deg-

radation of language by those who use it carelessly, he will not treat coloured glass as if it were clear, and while half the world is using figure unconsciously, will be fully aware not only of all that latent figurative texture in speech, but of the vague, lazy, half-formed personification–a rhetoric, depressing, and worse than nothing, because it has no really rhetorical motive–which plays so large a part there, and, as with more ostentatious ornament, scrupulously exact of it, from syllable to syllable, its precise value.

So far I have been speaking of certain conditions of the literary art arising out of the medium or material in or upon which it works, the essential qualities of language and its aptitudes for contingent ornamentation, matters which define scholarship as science and good taste respectively. They are both subservient to a more intimate quality of good style; more intimate, as coming nearer to the artist himself. The otiose, the facile, surplusage:–why are these abhorrent to the true literary artist, except because, in literary as in all other art, structure is all-important, felt or painfully missed everywhere?–that architectural conception of work, which foresees the end in the beginning and never loses sight of it, and in every part is conscious of all the rest, till the last sentence does but, with undiminished vigour, unfold and justify the first–a condition of literary art, which, in contradistinction to another quality of the artist himself, to be spoken of later, I shall call the necessity of *mind* in style.

An acute philosophical writer, the late Dean Mansel–a writer whose works illustrate the literary beauty there may be in closeness, and with obvious repression or economy of a fine rhetorical gift–wrote a book, of fascinating precision on a very obscure subject, to show that all the technical laws of logic are but means of securing, in each and all its apprehensions, the unity, the strict identity with itself, of the apprehending mind. All the laws of good writing aim at a similar unity or identity of the mind in all the processes by which the word is associated to its import. The term is right, and has its essential beauty, when it becomes, in a manner, what it signifies, as with the names of simple sensations. To give the phrase, the sentence, the structural member, the entire composition, a song, or an essay, a similar unity with its subject and with itself:–style is in the right way when it tends towards that. All depends upon the original unity, the vital wholeness and identity, of the initiatory apprehension or view. So much is true of all art, which therefore requires always its logic, its comprehensive reason–insight, foresight, retrospect, in simultaneous action–true, most of all, of the literary art, as being of all the arts most closely cognate to the abstract intelligence. Such logical coherency may be evidenced not merely in the lines of composition as a whole, but in the choice of a single word, while it by no means interferes with, but may even prescribe, much variety, in the building of the sentence for instance, or in the manner, argumentative, descriptive, discursive, of this or that part or member of the entire design. The blithe, crisp sentence, decisive as a child's expression of its needs, may alternate with the long, contending, victoriously intricate sentence; the sentence, born with the integrity of a single word, relieving the sort of sentence in which, if you look closely, you can see much contrivance, much adjustment, to bring a highly qualified matter into compass at one view. For the literary architecture, if it is to be rich and expressive, involves not only foresight of the end in the beginning, but also development or growth of design, in the process of execution, with many irregularities, surprises, and afterthoughts; the contingent as well as the necessary being subsumed under the unity of the whole. As truly, to the lack of such architectural design, of a single, almost visual, image, vigorously informing an entire, perhaps complex composition, which shall be austere, ornate, argumentative, fanciful, yet true from first to last to that vision within, may be attributed those weaknesses of conscious or unconscious repetition of word, phrase, word, motive, or member of the whole matter, indicating, as Flaubert was aware, an original structure in thought not organically complete. With such foresight the actual conclusion will most often get itself written, out of hand, before, in the more obvious sense, the work is finished. With some strong and leading sense of the world, the tight hold of which secures composition and not mere loose accretion, the literary artist, I suppose, goes on considerately, setting joint to joint, sustained by yet restraining the productive ardour, retracing the negligences of his first sketch, repeating his steps only that he may give the reader a sense of secure and restful progress, readjusting mere assonances even that they may soothe the reader, or at least not interrupt him on his way; and then, somewhere before the end comes, is burdened, inspired, with his conclusion, and betimes delivered of it, leaving off, not in weariness and because he finds himself at an end, but in all the freshness of volition. His

work, now structurally complete, with all the accumulating effect of secondary shades of meaning, he finishes the whole up to the just proportion of that ante-penultimate conclusion, and all becomes expressive. The house he has built is rather a body he has informed. And so it happens, to its greater credit, that the better interest even of a narrative to be recounted will often be in its second reading. And though there are instances of great writers who have been no artists, an unconscious tact sometimes directing work in which we may detect, very pleasurably, many of the effects of conscious art, yet one of the greatest pleasures of really good prose literature is in the critical tracing out of that conscious artistic structure, and the pervading sense of it as we read. Yet of poetic literature too; for, in truth, the kind of constructive intelligence here supposed is one of the forms of the imagination.

That is the special function of mind, in style. Mind and soul:–hard to ascertain philosophically, the distinction is real enough practically, for they often interfere, are sometimes in conflict, with each other. Blake, in the last century, is an instance of preponderating soul, embarrassed, at a loss, in an era of preponderating mind. As a quality of style, at all events, soul is a fact, in certain writers–the way they have of absorbing language, of attracting it into the peculiar spirit they are of, with a subtlety which makes the actual result seem like some inexplicable inspiration. By mind, the literary artist reaches people, through static and objective indications of design in his work, legible to all. By soul he reaches them, somewhat capriciously perhaps, one and not another, through vagrant sympathy and a kind of immediate contact. Mind we cannot choose but approve where we recognise it; soul may repel us, not because we misunderstand it. The way in which theological interests sometimes avail themselves of language is perhaps the best illustration of the force I mean generally in literature. Ardent religious persuasion may exist, may make its way, without finding any equivalent heat in language: or, again, it may enkindle words to various degrees, and when it really takes hold on them doubles its force. Religious history presents many remarkable instances in which, through no mere phrase-worship, an unconscious literary tact has, for the sensitive, laid open a privileged pathway from soul to soul. "The altar-fire," people say, "has touched those lips!" The Vulgate, the English Bible, the English Prayer-book, the writings of Swedenborg, the Tracts for the Times:–there, we have instances of widely different and largely diffused phases of religious feeling in operation as soul in style. But something of the same kind acts with similar power in some writers of quite other than theological literature, on behalf of some wholly personal and peculiar sense of theirs. Most easily illustrated by theological literature, this quality lends to profane writers a kind of religious influence. At their best, these writers become, as people say, "prophets;" such character depending on the effect not merely of their matter, but of their matter as allied to, in "electric affinity" with, peculiar form, and working in all cases by an immediate sympathetic contact, on which account it is that it may be called soul, as opposed to mind, in style. And this too is a faculty of choosing and rejecting what is congruous or otherwise, with a drift towards unity–unity of atmosphere here, as there of design–soul-securing colour (or perfume, might we say?) as mind secures form, the latter being essentially finite, the former vague or infinite, as the influence of a living person is practically infinite. There are some to whom nothing has any real interest, or real meaning, except as operative in a given person; and it is they who best appreciate the quality of soul in literary art. They seem to know a *person*, in a book, and make way by intuition: yet, although they thus enjoy the completeness of a personal information, it is still a characteristic of soul, in this sense of the word, that it does but suggest what can never be uttered, not as being different from, or more obscure than, what actually gets said, but as containing that plenary substance of which there is only one phase or facet in what is there expressed.

If all high things have their martyrs, Gustave Flaubert might perhaps rank as the martyr of literary style. In his printed correspondence, a curious series of letters, written in his twenty-fifth year, records what seems to have been his one other passion–a series of letters which, with its fine casuistries, its firmly repressed anguish, its tone of harmonious grey, and the sense of disillusion in which the whole matter ends, might have been, a few slight changes supposed, one of his own fictions. Writing to Madame X. certainly he does display, by "taking thought" mainly, by constant and delicate pondering, as in his love for literature, a heart really moved, but still more, and as the pledge of that emotion, a loyalty to his work. Madame X., too, is a literary artist, and the best gifts he can send her are precepts of perfection in art, coun-

sels for the effectual pursuit of that better love. In his love-letters it is the pains and pleasures of art he insists on, its solaces: he communicates secrets, reproves, encourages, with a view to that. Whether the lady was dissatisfied with such divided or indirect service, the reader is not enabled to see; but sees that on Flaubert's part, at least, a living person could be no rival of what was, from first to last, his leading passion, a somewhat solitary and exclusive one.

"I must scold you," he writes, "for one thing, which shocks, scandalises me, the small concern, namely, you show for art just now. As regards glory be it so: there, I approve. But for art!–the one thing in life that is good and real,–can you compare with it an earthly love?–prefer the adoration of a relative beauty to the cultus of the true beauty? Well! I tell you the truth. That is the one thing good in me; the one thing I have, to me estimable. For yourself, you blend with the beautiful a heap of alien things, the useful, the agreeable, what not?–

"The only way not to be unhappy is to shut yourself up in art, and count everything else as nothing. Pride takes the place of all beside when it is established on a large basis. Work! God wills it. That, it seems to me, is clear.–

"I am reading over again the *Æneid*, certain verses of which I repeat to myself to satiety. There are phrases there which stay in one's head, by which I find myself beset, as with those musical airs which are for ever returning, and cause you pain, you love them so much. I observe that I no longer laugh much, and am no longer depressed. I am ripe. You talk of my serenity, and envy me. It may well surprise you. Sick, irritated, the prey a thousand times a day of cruel pain, I continue my labour like a good working-man, who, with sleeves turned up, in the sweat of his brow beats away at his anvil, never troubling himself whether it rains or blows, for hail or thunder. I was not like that formerly. The change has taken place naturally, though my will has counted for something in the matter.–

"Those who write in good style are sometimes accused of a neglect of ideas, and of the moral end, as if the end of the physician were something else than healing, of the painter than painting–as if the end of art were not, before all else, the beautiful."

What, then, did Flaubert understand by beauty, in the art he pursued with so much fervour, with so much self-command? Let us hear a sympathetic commentator:–

> "Possessed of an absolute belief that there exists but one way of expressing one thing, one word to call it by, one adjective to qualify, one verb to animate it, he gave himself to superhuman labour for the discovery in every phrase of that word, that verb, that epithet. In this way he believed in some mysterious harmony in expression, and when a true word seemed to him to lack euphony still went on seeking another, with invincible patience, certain that he had not yet got hold of the *unique* word.... A thousand preoccupations would beset him at the same moment, always with this desperate certitude fixed in his spirit: Among all the expressions in the world, all forms and turns of expression, there is but one–one form, one mode–to express what I want to say."

The one word for the one thing, the one thought, amid the multitude of words, terms, that might just do: there, was the problem of style! –the unique word, phrase, sentence, paragraph, essay, or song, absolutely proper to the single mental presentation or vision within. In that perfect justice, over and above the many contingent and removable beauties with which beautiful style may charm us, but which it can exist without, independent of them yet dexterously availing itself of them, omnipresent in good work, in function at every point, from single epithets to the rhythm of a whole book, lay the specific, indispensable, very intellectual beauty of literature, the possibility of which constitutes it a fine art.

One seems to detect the influence of a philosophic idea there–the idea of a natural economy, of some pre-existent adaptation, between a relative somewhere in the world of thought, and its correlative somewhere in the world of language–both alike, rather, somewhere in the mind of the artist, desiderative, expectant, inventive, meeting each other with the readiness of "soul and body reunited," in Blake's rapturous design; and, in fact, Flaubert was fond of giving his theory philosophical expression.

> "There are no beautiful thoughts," he says, "without beautiful forms, and conversely. As it is impossible to extract from a physical body the qualities which really

constitute it–colour, extension, and the like– without reducing it to a hollow abstraction, in a word, without destroying it; just so it is impossible to detach the form from the idea, for the idea only exists by virtue of the form."

All the recognised flowers, the removable ornaments of literature (including harmony and ease in reading aloud, very carefully considered by him) counted, certainly; for these too are part of the actual value of what one says. But still, after all, with Flaubert the search, the unwearied research, was not for the smooth, or winsome, or forcible word, as such, as with false Ciceronians, but quite simply and honestly, for the word's adjustment to its meaning. The first condition of this must be, of course, to know yourself, to have ascertained your own sense exactly. Then, if we suppose an artist, he says to the reader, I want you to see precisely what I see. Into the mind sensitive to "form," a flood of random sounds, colours, incidents, is ever penetrating from the world without, to become, by sympathetic selection, a part of its very structure, and, in turn, the visible vesture and expression of that other world it sees so steadily within, nay, already with a partial conformity thereto, to be refined, enlarged, corrected, at a hundred points; and it is just there, just at those doubtful points that the function of style, as tact or taste, intervenes. The unique term will come more quickly to one than another, at one time than another, according also to the kind of matter in question. Quickness and slowness, ease and closeness alike, have nothing to do with the artistic character of the true word found at last. As there is a charm of ease, so also a special charm in the signs of discovery, of effort and contention towards a due end, as so often with Flaubert himself–in the style which has been pliant, as only obstinate, durable, metal can be, to the inherent perplexities and recusancy of a certain difficult thought.

If Flaubert had not told us, perhaps we should never have guessed how tardy and painful his own procedure really was, and after reading his confession may think that his almost endless hesitation had much to do with diseased nerves. Often, perhaps, the felicity supposed will be the product of a happier, a more exuberant, nature than Flaubert's. Aggravated, certainly, by a morbid physical condition, that anxiety in "seeking the phrase," which gathered all the other small *ennuis* of a really quiet existence into a kind of battle, was connected with his life-long contention against facile poetry, facile art–art, facile and flimsy; and what constitutes the true artist is not the slowness or quickness of the process, but the absolute success of the result. As with those labourers in the parable, the prize is independent of the mere length of the actual day's work.

"You talk," he writes–odd, trying, lover–to Madame X.–"You talk of the exclusiveness of my literary tastes. That might have enabled you to divine what kind of a person I am in the matter of love. I grow so hard to please as a literary artist, that I am driven to despair. I shall end by not writing another line. Happy," he cries, in a moment of discouragement at that patient labour, which for him, certainly, was the condition of a great success–"happy those who have no doubts of themselves! who lengthen out, as the pen runs on, all that flows forth from their brains. As for me, I hesitate, I disappoint myself, turn round upon myself in despite; my taste is augmented in proportion as my natural vigour decreases, and I afflict my soul over some dubious word out of all proportion to the pleasure I get from a whole page of good writing. One would have to live two centuries to attain a true idea of any matter whatever. What Buffon said is a big blasphemy: genius is not long-continued patience. Still there is some truth in the statement, and more than people think, especially as regards our own day. Art! art! art! bitter deception! phantom that glows with light, only to lead one on to destruction."

Again–

"I am growing so peevish about my writing. I am like a man whose ear is true but who plays falsely on the violin: his fingers refuse to reproduce precisely those sounds of which he has the inward sense. Then the tears come rolling down from the poor scraper's eyes and the bow falls from his hand."

Coming slowly or quickly, when it comes, as it came with so much labour of mind, but also with so much lustre, to Gustave Flaubert, this discovery of the word will be, like all artistic success and felicity, incapable of strict analysis: effect of an intuitive condition of mind, it must be recognised by like intuition on the part of the reader, and a kind of immediate sense. In every one of those masterly sentences of Flaubert there was, below all, mere contrivance, shaping, and afterthought, by some happy instantaneous con-

course of the various faculties of the mind with each other, the exact apprehension of what was *needed* to carry the meaning. And that it fits with absolute justice will be a judgment of immediate sense in the appreciative reader. We all feel this in what may be called inspired translation. Well! all language involves translation from inward to outward. In literature, as in all forms of art, there are the absolute and the merely relative or accessory beauties; and precisely in that exact proportion of the term to its purpose is the absolute beauty of style, prose or verse. All the good qualities, the beauties, of verse also, are such only as precise expression.

In the highest as in the lowliest literature, then, the one indispensable beauty, is, after all, truth:–truth to bare fact here, as to a sense of fact there, diverted somewhat from men's ordinary sense of it; truth here as accuracy, truth there as expression, that finest and most intimate form of truth, the *vraie vérité*. And what an eclectic principle this really is! employing for its one sole purpose–that absolute accordance of expression to idea–all other literary beauties and excellences whatever: how many kinds of style it covers, explains, justifies, and at the same time safeguards! Scott's facility, Flaubert's deeply pondered evocation of "the phrase," are equally good art. Say what you have to say, what you have a will to say, in the simplest, the most direct and exact manner possible, with no surplusage:–there, is the justification of the sentence so fortunately born, "entire, smooth, and round," that it needs no punctuation, and also (there, is the point!) of the most elaborate period, if it be right in its elaboration. That is the office of ornament: it is also the purpose of restraint in ornament. As the exponent of truth, that austerity (the beauty, the function, of which in literature Flaubert understood so well) becomes not the correctness or purism of the mere scholar, but a security against the otiose, a jealous exclusion of what does not really tell, in the pursuit of relief, of life and vigour, in the portraiture of one's sense. License again, the making free with rule, if it be indeed, as people fancy, a habit of genius, flinging aside or transforming all that opposes the liberty of beautiful production, will be but faith to one's own meaning. The seeming baldness of *Le Rouge et le Noir* is nothing in itself; the wild ornament of *Les Misérables* is nothing in itself; and the restraint of Flaubert, amid a real natural opulence, only redoubled beauty,–the phrase so colourable and so precise at the same time, hard as bronze, in service to the more perfect adaptation of words to their matter. Afterthoughts, retouchings, finish, will be of profit only so far as they too really serve to bring out the original, initiative, germinating sense in them.

In this way, according to the well-known saying, "The style is the man," complex or simple, in his individuality, his plenary sense of what he really has to say, his sense of the world; all cautions regarding style arising out of so many natural scruples as to the medium through which alone he can expose that inward sense of things, its purity, its laws or tricks of refraction. Nothing is to be left there which might give conveyance to any matter save that. Style in all its varieties, reserved or opulent, terse, abundant, musical, stimulant, academic, so long as each is really characteristic or expressive, finds thus its justification, the sumptuous good taste of Cicero being as truly the man himself, and not another, justified, yet insured inalienably to him thereby, as would have been his portrait by Raffaelle, in full consular splendour, on his ivory chair.

A relegation, you say, perhaps—a relegation of style to the subjectivity, the mere caprice of the individual, which must soon transform it into mannerism. Not so! since there is, under the conditions supposed, for those elements of the man, for every lineament of the vision within, the one word, the one acceptable word, recognisable by the sensitive, by those "who have intelligence" in the matter, as absolutely as ever anything can be in the evanescent and delicate region of human language. The style, the manner, would be the man, not in his unreasoned and really uncharacteristic caprices, involuntary or affected, but in absolutely sincere apprehension of what is most real to him. But let us hear our French guide again:—

> "Styles," says Flaubert's commentator, "*Styles*" as so many peculiar moulds, each of which bears the mark of a particular writer, who is to pour into it the whole content of his ideas, were no part of his theory. What he believed in was *Style*: that is to say, a certain absolute and unique manner of expressing a thing, in all its intensity and colour. For him the *form* was the work itself. As in living creatures, the blood, nourishing the body, determines its very contour and external aspect, just so, to his mind, the *matter*, the basis, in a work of art, imposed, necessarily, the unique, the just expression, the measure, the rhythm—the *form* in all its characteristics."

If the style be the man in all the colour and intensity of a veritable apprehension, it will be in a real sense "impersonal."

I said, looking at books like Victor Hugo's *Les Misérables,* that prose literature was the characteristic art of the nineteenth century, as others, thinking of its triumphs since the youth of Bach, have placed music just there. Music and prose literature are, in one sense, the opposite terms of art; the art of literature presenting to the imagination, through the intelligence, a range of interests, as free and various as those which music presents to it through sense. And certainly the tendency of what has been here said is to bring literature too under those conditions, by conformity to which music takes rank as the typically perfect art. If music be the ideal of all art whatever, precisely because in it it is impossible to distinguish the form from the substance or matter, the subject from the expression, then, literature, by finding its specific excellence in the absolute correspondence of the term to its import, will be but fulfilling the condition of all artistic quality in things everywhere, of all good art.

Good art, but not necessarily great art; the distinction between great art and good art depending immediately, as regards literature at all events, not on its form, but on the matter. Thackeray's *Esmond,* surely, is greater art than *Vanity Fair,* by the greater dignity of its interests. It is on the quality of the matter it informs or controls, its compass, its variety, its alliance to great ends, or the depth of the note of revolt, or the largeness of hope in it, that the greatness of literary art depends, as *The Divine Comedy, Paradise Lost, Les Misérables, The English Bible,* are great art. Given the conditions I have tried to explain as constituting good art;—then, if it be devoted further to the increase of men's happiness, to the redemption of the oppressed, or the enlargement of our sympathies with each other, or to such presentment of new or old truth about ourselves and our relation to the world as may ennoble and fortify us in our sojourn here, or immediately, as with Dante, to the glory of God, it will be also great art—if, over and above those qualities I summed up as mind and soul—that colour and mystic perfume, and that reasonable structure—it has something of the soul of humanity in it, and finds its logical, its architectural place, in the great structure of human life.

Reprinted from *Fortnightly Review,* 50 (December 1888): 728-743.

Oscar Wilde

"The Critic as Artist" (1891)

Oscar Wilde (1854-1900), poet, dramatist, and critic, was the best-known exponent of Aestheticism, or the theory of art for art's sake. Though he was himself well known as an exquisite, epigrammatic stylist, his critical theories embrace the arts as a whole. He put forward his ideas in many forms, including fiction and dialogues as well as essays, but he left very little that focuses closely on prose style alone, instead ranging widely and allusively through analogies between the visual arts and literature. Nonetheless, his general critical position has great historical importance in its liberating reversals of many Victorian assumptions about prose and prose criticism. His writings have been widely anthologized, and the extracts given here are simply a sampling of the more direct comments Wilde made about the relatively new prose form of aesthetic criticism. The work from which they are taken first appeared in two parts in the Nineteenth Century *(July and September 1890) under the title "The True Function and Value of Criticism" and was subsequently revised under the title "The Critic as Artist" for republication in Wilde's volume* Intentions *(1891). Wilde presents his argument as a dialogue between two young men, the inquiring Ernest and his aesthetic mentor Gilbert, in the library of a fashionable London house. Gilbert's (and Wilde's) repeated theme is that prose criticism is itself creative because it is limited to no single artistic vision.*–Ed.

From Part I

Ernest. You have been talking of criticism as an essential part of the creative spirit, and I now fully accept your theory. But what of criticism outside creation? I have a foolish habit of reading periodicals, and it seems to me that most modern criticism is perfectly valueless.

Gilbert. So is most modern creative work also. Mediocrity weighing mediocrity in the balance, and incompetence applauding its brother– that is the spectacle which the artistic activity of England affords us from time to time. And yet, I feel I am a little unfair in this matter. As a rule, the critics–I speak, of course, of the higher class, of those in fact who write for the sixpenny papers– are far more cultured than the people whose work they are called upon to review. This is, indeed, only what one would expect, for criticism demands infinitely more cultivation than creation does.

Ernest. Really?

Gilbert. Certainly. Anybody can write a three-volumed novel. It merely requires a complete ignorance of both life and literature. The difficulty that I should fancy the reviewer feels is the difficulty of sustaining any standard. Where there is no style a standard must be impossible. The poor reviewers are apparently reduced to be the reporters of the police-court of literature, the chroniclers of the doings of the habitual criminals of art. It is sometimes said of them that they do not read all through the works they are called upon to criticise. They do not. Or at least they should not. If they did so, they would become confirmed misanthropes, or if I may borrow a phrase from one of the pretty Newnham graduates, confirmed womanthropes for the rest of their lives. Nor is it necessary. To know the vintage and quality of a wine one need not drink the whole cask. It must be perfectly easy in half an hour to say whether a book is worth anything or worth nothing. Ten minutes are really sufficient, if one has the instinct for form. Who wants to wade through a dull volume? One tastes it, and that is quite enough–more than enough, I should imagine. I am aware that there are many honest workers in painting as well as in literature who object to criticism entirely. They are quite right. Their work stands in no intellectual relation to their age. It bring us no new element of pleasure. It suggests no fresh departure of thought, or passion, or beauty. It should not be spoken of. It should be left to the oblivion that it deserves.

Ernest. But, my dear fellow–excuse me for interrupting you–you seem to me to be allowing your passion for criticism to lead you a great deal too far. For, after all, even you must admit that it is much more difficult to do a thing than to talk about it.

Gilbert. More difficult to do a thing than to talk about it? Not at all. That is a gross popular error. It is very much more difficult to talk about a thing than to do it. In the sphere of actual life that is of course obvious. Anybody can make history. Only a great man can write it. There is no mode of action, no form of emotion, that we do not share with the lower animals. It is only by language that we rise above them, or above each other—by language, which is the parent, and not the child, of thought. Action, indeed, is always easy, and when presented to us in its most aggravated, because most continuous form, which I take to be that of real industry, becomes simply the refuge of people who have nothing whatsoever to do. No, Ernest, don't talk about action. It is a blind thing dependent on external influences, and moved by an impulse of whose nature it is unconscious. It is a thing incomplete in its essence, because limited by accident, and ignorant of its direction, being always at variance with its aim. Its basis is the lack of imagination. It is the last resource of those who know not how to dream.

Ernest. Gilbert, you treat the world as if it were a crystal ball. You hold it in your hand, and reverse it to please a wilful fancy. You do nothing but rewrite history.

Gilbert. The one duty we owe to history is to rewrite it. That is not the least of the tasks in store for the critical spirit . . . .

Ernest. But is Criticism really a creative art?

Gilbert. Why should it not be? It works with materials, and puts them into a form that is at once new and delightful. What more can one say of poetry? Indeed, I would call criticism a creation within a creation. For just as the great artists, from Homer and Æschylus, down to Shakespeare and Keats, did not go directly to life for their subject-matter, but sought for it in myth, and legend and ancient tale, so the critic deals with materials that others have, as it were, purified for him, and to which imaginative form and colour have been already added. Nay, more, I would say that the highest Criticism, being the purest form of personal impression, is in its way more creative than creation, as it has least reference to any standard external to itself, and is, in fact, its own reason for existing, and, as the Greeks would put it, in itself, and to itself, an end. Certainly, it is never trammelled by any shackles of verisimilitude. No ignoble considerations of probability, that cowardly concession to the tedious repetitions of domestic or public life, affect it ever. One may appeal from fiction unto fact. But from the soul there is no appeal.

Ernest. From the soul?

Gilbert. Yes, from the soul. That is what the highest criticism really is, the record of one's own soul. It is more fascinating than history, as it is concerned simply with oneself. It is more delightful than philosophy, as its subject is concrete and not abstract, real and not vague. It is the only civilized form of autobiography, as it deals not with the events, but with the thoughts of one's life; not with life's physical accidents of deed or circumstance, but with the spiritual moods and imaginative passions of the mind. I am always amused by the silly vanity of those writers and artists of our day who seem to imagine that the primary function of the critic is to chatter about their second-rate work. The best that one can say of most modern creative art is that it is just a little less vulgar than reality, and so the critic, with his fine sense of distinction and sure instinct of delicate refinement, will prefer to look into the silver mirror or through the woven veil, and will turn his eyes away from the chaos and clamour of actual existence, though the mirror be tarnished and the veil be torn. His sole aim is to chronicle his own impressions. It is for him that pictures are painted, books written, and marble hewn into form.

Ernest. I seem to have heard another theory of Criticism.

Gilbert. Yes: it has been said by one whose gracious memory we all revere, and the music of whose pipe once lured Proserpina from her Sicilian fields, and made those white feet stir, and not in vain, the Cumnor cowslips, that the proper aim of Criticism is to see the object as in itself it really is.[1] But this is a very serious error, and takes no cognizance of Criticism's most perfect form, which is in its essence purely subjective, and seeks to reveal its own secret and not the secret of another. For the highest Criticism deals with art not as expressive but as impressive purely.

Ernest. But is that really so?

Gilbert. Of course it is. Who cares whether Mr. Ruskin's views on Turner are sound or not? What does it matter? That mighty and majestic prose of his, so fervid and so fiery-coloured in its noble eloquence, so rich in its elaborate symphonic music, so sure and certain, at its best, in subtle choice of word and epithet, is at least as great a work of art as any of those wonderful sunsets that bleach or rot on their corrupted canvases in England's Gallery; greater indeed, one is apt to think at times, not merely because its equal beauty is more enduring, but on account of the fuller variety of its appeal, soul speaking to soul in those long-cadenced lines, not through form and colour alone, though through these, indeed, completely and without loss, but with intellectual and emotional utterance, with lofty passion and with loftier thought, with imaginative insight, and with poetic aim; greater, I always think, even as Literature is the greater art. Who, again, cares whether Mr. Pater has put into the portrait of Monna Lisa something that Lionardo never dreamed of? The painter may have been merely the slave of an archaic smile, as some have fancied, but whenever I pass into the cool galleries of the Palace of the Louvre, and stand before that strange figure "set in its marble chair in that cirque of fantastic rocks, as in some faint light under sea," I murmur to myself, "She is older than the rocks among which she sits; like the vampire, she has been dead many times, and learned the secrets of the grave; and has been a diver in deep seas, and keeps their fallen day about her; and trafficked for strange webs with Eastern merchants; and, as Leda, was the mother of Helen of Troy, and, as St. Anne, the mother of Mary; and all this has been to her but as the sound of lyres and flutes, and lives only in the delicacy with which it has moulded the changing lineaments, and tinged the eyelids and the hands." And I say to my friend, "The presence that thus so strangely rose beside the waters is expressive of what in the ways of a thousand years man had come to desire;" and he answers me, "Hers is the head upon which all 'the ends of the world are come,' and the eyelids are a little weary."

And so the picture becomes more wonderful to us than it really is, and reveals to us a secret of which, in truth, it knows nothing, and the music of the mystical prose is as sweet in our ears as was that flute-player's music that lent to the lips of La Gioconda those subtle and poisonous curves. . . .

Ernest. But is such work as you have talked about really criticism?

Gilbert. It is the highest Criticism, for it criticises not merely the individual work of art, but Beauty itself, and fills with wonder a form which the artist may have left void, or not understood, or understood incompletely.

Ernest. The highest Criticism, then, is more creative than creation, and the primary aim of the critic is to see the object as in itself it really is not; that is your theory, I believe?

Gilbert. Yes, that is my theory. To the critic the work of art is simply a suggestion for a new work of his own, that need not necessarily bear any obvious resemblance to the thing it criticises. The one characteristic of a beautiful form is that one can put into it whatever one wishes, and see in it whatever one chooses to see; and the Beauty, that gives to creation its universal and æsthetic element, makes the critic a creator in his turn, and whispers of a thousand different things which were not present in the mind of him who carved the statue or painted the panel or graved the gem. . . .

From Part II

Ernest. . . . I will put another question. You have explained to me that criticism is a creative art. What future has it?

Gilbert. It is to criticism that the future belongs. The subject-matter at the disposal of creation becomes every day more limited in extent and variety. Providence and Mr. Walter Besant have exhausted the obvious. If creation is to last at all, it can only do so on the condition of becoming far more critical that it is at present. The old roads and dusty highways have been traversed too often. Their charm has been worn away by plodding feet, and they have lost that element of novelty or surprise which is so essential for romance. He who would stir us now by fiction must either give us an entirely new background, or reveal to us the soul of man in its innermost workings. The first is for the moment being done for us by Mr. Rudyard Kipling. As one turns over the pages of his *Plain Tales from the Hills*, one feels as if one were seated under a palm-tree reading life by superb flashes of vulgarity. The bright colours of the bazaars dazzle one's eyes. The jaded, second-rate Anglo-Indians are in exquisite incongruity with their surroundings. The mere lack of style in the story-teller gives an odd journalistic realism to what he tells us. From the point of view of literature Mr. Kipling is a genius who drops his aspirates. From the point of view of life, he is a reporter who knows vulgarity better than any one has ever known it. Dickens knew its clothes and its comedy. Mr. Kipling knows its essence and its seriousness. He is our first authority on the second-rate, and has seen marvellous things through keyholes, and his backgrounds are real works of art. As for the second condition, we have had Browning, and Meredith is with us. But there is still much to be done in the sphere of introspection. People sometimes say that fiction is getting too morbid. As far as psychology is concerned, it has never been morbid enough. We have merely touched the surface of the soul that is all. In one single ivory cell of the brain there are stored away things more marvellous and more terrible than even they have dreamed of, who, like the author of *Le Rouge et le Noir,* have sought to track the soul into its most secret places, and to make life confess its dearest sins. Still, there is a limit even to the number of untried backgrounds, and it is possible that a further development of the habit of introspection may prove fatal to that creative faculty to which it seeks to supply fresh material. I myself am inclined to think that creation is doomed. It springs from too primitive, too natural an impulse. However this may be, it is certain that the subject-matter at the disposal of creation is always diminishing, while the subject-matter of criticism increases daily. There are always new attitudes for the mind, and new points of view. The duty of imposing form upon chaos does not grow less as the world advances. There was never a time when Criticism was more needed than it is now. It is only by its means that Humanity can become conscious of the point at which it has arrived.

Hours ago, Ernest, you asked me the use of Criticism. You might just as well have asked me the use of thought. It is Criticism, as Arnold points out, that creates the intellectual atmosphere of the age. It is Criticism, as I hope to point out myself some day, that makes the mind a fine instrument. We, in our educational system, have burdened the memory with a load of unconnected facts, and laboriously striven to impart our laboriously-acquired knowledge. We teach people how to remember, we never teach them how to grow. It has never occurred to us to try and develop in the mind a more subtle quality of apprehension and discernment. The Greeks did this, and when we come in contact with the Greek critical intellect, we cannot but be conscious that, while our subject-matter is in every respect larger and more varied than theirs, theirs is the only method by which this subject-matter can be interpreted. England has done one thing; it has invented and established Public Opinion, which is an attempt to organize the ignorance of the community, and to elevate it to the dignity of physical force. But Wisdom has always been hidden from it. Considered as an instrument of thought, the English mind is coarse and undeveloped. The only thing that can purify it is the growth of the critical instinct.

It is Criticism, again, that, by concentration, makes culture possible. It takes the cumbersome mass of creative work, and distils it into a finer essence. Who that desires to retain any sense of form could struggle through the monstrous multitudinous books that the world has produced, books in which thought stammers or ignorance brawls? The thread that is to guide us across the wearisome labyrinth is in the hands of Criticism. Nay more, where there is no record, and history is either lost or was never written, Criticism can recreate the past for us from the very smallest fragment of language or art, just as surely as the man of science can from some tiny bone, or the mere impress of a foot upon a rock, recreate for us the winged dragon or Titan lizard that once made the earth shake beneath its tread, can call Behemoth out of his cave, and make Leviathan swim once more across the startled sea. Prehistoric history belongs to the philological and archæological critic. It is to him that the origins of things are revealed. The self-conscious deposits of an age are nearly always misleading. Through philological criticism alone we know more of the centuries of which no actual record has been preserved, than we do of the centuries that have left us their scrolls. It can do for us what can be done neither by physics nor metaphysics. It can give us the exact science of mind in the process of becoming. It can do for us what History cannot do. It can tell us what man thought before he learned how to write. You have asked me about the influence of Criticism. I think I have answered that question already; but there is this also to be said. It is Criticism that makes us cosmopolitan. The Manchester school tried to make men realize the brotherhood of humanity, by pointing out the commercial advantages of peace. It sought to degrade the wonderful world into a common market-place for the buyer and the seller. It addressed itself to the lowest instincts, and it failed. War followed upon war, and the tradesman's creed did not prevent France and Germany from clashing together in blood-stained battle. There are others of our own day who seek to appeal to mere emotional sympathies, or to the shallow dogmas of some vague system of abstract ethics. They have their Peace Societies, so dear to the sentimentalists, and their proposals for unarmed International Arbitration, so popular among those who have never read history. But mere emotional sympathy will not do. It is too variable, and too closely connected with the passions; and a board of arbitrators who, for the general welfare of the race, are to be deprived of the power of putting their decisions into execution, will not be of much avail. There is only one thing worse than Injustice, and that is Justice without her sword in her hand. When Right is not Might, it is Evil.

No: the emotions will not make us cosmopolitan, any more than the greed for gain could do so. It is only by the cultivation of the habit of intellectual criticism that we shall be able to rise superior to race prejudices. Goethe—you will not misunderstand what I say—was a German of the Germans. He loved his country—no man more so. Its people were dear to him; and he led them. Yet, when the iron hoof of Napoleon trampled upon vineyard and cornfield, his lips were silent. "How can one write songs of hatred without hating?" he said to Eckerman, "and how could I, to whom culture and barbarism are alone of importance, hate a nation which is among the most cultivated of the earth, and to which I owe so great a part of my own cultivation?" This note, sounded in the modern world by Goethe first, will become, I think, the starting point for the cosmopolitanism of the future. Criticism will annihilate race-prejudices, by insisting upon the unity of the human mind in the variety of its forms. If we are tempted to make war upon another nation, we shall remember that we are seeking to destroy an element of our own culture, and possibly its most important element. As long as war is regarded as wicked, it will always have its fascination. When it is looked upon as vulgar, it will cease to be popular. The change will, of course, be slow, and people will not be conscious of it. They will not say "We will not war against France because her prose is perfect," but because the prose of France is perfect, they will not hate the land. Intellectual criticism will bind Europe together in bonds far closer than those that can be forged by shopman or sentimentalist. It will give us the peace that springs from understanding.

Nor is this all. It is Criticism that, recognizing no position as final, and refusing to bind itself by the shallow shibboleths of any sect or school, creates that serene philosophic temper which loves truth for its own sake, and loves it not the less because it knows it to be unattainable. How little we have of this temper in England, and how much we need it! The English mind is always in a rage. The intellect of the race is wasted in the sordid and stupid quarrels of second-rate politicians or third-rate theologians.

It was reserved for a man of science to show us the supreme example of that "sweet reasonableness" of which Arnold spoke so wisely, and, alas! to so little effect. The author of the *Origin of Species* had, at any rate, the philosophic temper. If one contemplates the ordinary pulpits and platforms of England, one can but feel the contempt of Julian, or the indifference of Montaigne. We are dominated by the fanatic, whose worst vice is his sincerity. Anything approaching to the free play of the mind is practically unknown amongst us. People cry out against the sinner, yet it is not the sinful, but the stupid, who are our shame. There is no sin except stupidity.

Ernest. Ah! what an antinomian you are!

Gilbert. The artistic critic, like the mystic, is an antinomian always. To be good, according to the vulgar standard of goodness, is obviously quite easy. It merely requires a certain amount of sordid terror, a certain lack of imaginative thought, and a certain low passion for middle-class respectability. Æsthetics are higher than ethics. They belong to a more spiritual sphere. To discern the beauty of a thing is the finest point to which we can arrive. Even a colour-sense is more important, in the development of the individual, than a sense of right and wrong. Æsthetics, in fact, are to Ethics in the sphere of conscious civilization, what, in the sphere of the external world, sexual is to natural selection. Ethics, like natural selection, make existence possible. Æsthetics, like sexual selection, make life lovely and wonderful, fill it with new forms, and give it progress, and variety and change. And when we reach the true culture that is our aim, we attain to that perfection of which the saints have dreamed, the perfection of those to whom sin is impossible, not because they make the renunciations of the ascetic, but because they can do everything they wish without hurt to the soul, and can wish for nothing that can do the soul harm, the soul being an entity so divine that it is able to transform into elements of a richer experience, or a finer susceptibility, or a newer mode of thought, acts or passions that with the common would be commonplace, or with the uneducated ignoble, or with the shameful vile. Is this dangerous? Yes; it is dangerous—all ideas, as I told you, are so. But the night wearies, and the light flickers in the lamp. One more thing I cannot help saying to you. You have spoken against Criticism as being a sterile thing. The nineteenth century is a turning point in history simply on account of the work of two men, Darwin and Renan, the one the critic of the Book of

Nature, the other the critic of the books of God. Not to recognize this is to miss the meaning of one of the most important eras in the progress of the world. Creation is always behind the age. It is Criticism that leads us. The Critical Spirit and the World-Spirit are one.

Ernest. And he who is in possession of this spirit or whom this spirit possesses, will, I suppose, do nothing?

Gilbert. Like the Persephone of whom Landor tells us, the sweet pensive Persephone around whose white feet the asphodel and amaranth are blooming, he will sit contented "in that deep, motionless, quiet which mortals pity, and which the gods enjoy." He will look out upon the world and know its secret. By contact with divine things, he will become divine. His will be the perfect life, and his only.

Ernest. You have told me many strange things tonight, Gilbert. You have told me that it is more difficult to talk about a thing than to do it, and that to do nothing at all is the most difficult thing in the world; you have told me that all Art is immoral, and all thought dangerous; that criticism is more creative than creation, and that the highest criticism is that which reveals in the work of Art what the artist had not put there; that it is exactly because a man cannot do a thing that he is the proper judge of it; and that the true critic is unfair, insincere, and not rational. My friend, you are a dreamer.

Gilbert. Yes: I am a dreamer. For a dreamer is one who can only find his way by moonlight, and his punishment is that he sees the dawn before the rest of the world.

Ernest. His punishment?

Gilbert. And his reward. But see, it is dawn already. Draw back the curtains and open the windows wide. How cool the morning air is! Piccadilly lies at our feet like a long riband of silver. A faint purple mist hangs over the Park, and the shadows of the white houses are purple. It is too late to sleep. Let us go down to Covent Garden and look at the roses. Come! I am tired of thought.

---

1. Wilde here refers to Matthew Arnold.–*Ed.*

Reprinted from *Intentions* (London: Osgood, McIlvaine, 1891).

John Addington Symonds

"Personal Style" (1890)

John Addington Symonds (1840-1893) achieved a substantial reputation in the late-Victorian period as a critic of art and poetry, especially of the Italian Renaissance. His set of four essays on style, written in 1889, one year after Walter Pater's "Style," was published in his two-volume work Essays Speculative and Suggestive *(1890). The third essay, reprinted here, had pride of place as the opening item of volume two, and it is characteristic both of Symonds and of many late-Victorian prose critics in turning away from the social aspects of national and period styles to emphasize a mystical individuality. Symonds seems most modern when he follows his longstanding interest in psychological "temperaments" and suggests that prose style may be a clue to a writer's psyche.*—Ed.

I.

A survey of language, however superficial, makes it evident that when we speak of style, we have to take into account those qualities of national character which are embodied in national speech. If two men could be born of precisely the same physical, mental, and moral nature, at precisely the same moment of history, and under precisely the same social conditions; and if these men learned different languages in the cradle, and used those languages in after life, they would be unable to deliver exactly the same message to the world through literature. The dominant qualities of each mother-tongue would impose definite limitations on their power of expressing thoughts, however similar or identical those thoughts might be.

We cannot conceive two men born with the same physical, mental, and moral nature, at the same moment, under precisely the same conditions, and using the same language. They would be identical; and everything they uttered would be clothed with exactly the same words. The absurdity of this conception brings home to us the second aspect of style. Style is not merely a sign of those national qualities which are generic to es-

tablished languages, and which constitute the so-called genius of a race. It is also the sign of personal qualities, specific to individuals, which constitute the genius of a man. Whatever a man utters from his heart and head is the index of his character. The more remarkable a person is, the more strongly he is differentiated from the average of human beings, the more salient will be the characteristic notes of his expression. But even the commonest people have, each of them, a specific style. The marks of difference become microscopical as we descend from Dante or Shakespeare to the drudges of the clerk's desk in one of our great cities. Yet these marks exist, and are no less significant of individuality than the variations between leaf and leaf upon the lime-trees of an avenue.

It may be asked whether the manner of expression peculiar to any person is a complete index to his character—whether, in other words, there is "an art to find the mind's construction" in the style. Not altogether and exhaustively. Not all the actions and the utterances of an individual betray the secret of his personality. You may live with men and women through years, by day, by night, yet you will never know the whole about them. No human being knows the whole about himself.

The deliberate attitude adopted by a literary writer implies circumspection; invites suppression, reservation, selection; is compatible with affectation, dissimulation, hypocrisy. So much cannot be claimed for critical analysis as that we should pretend to reproduce a man's soul after close examination of his work. What we may assert with confidence is that the qualities of style are intimately connected with the qualities and limitations of the writer, and teach us much about him. He wrote thus and thus, because he was this or this. In the exercise of style it is impossible for any one to transcend his inborn and acquired faculties of ideation, imagination, sense-perception, verbal expression—just as it is impossible in the exercise of strength for an athlete to transcend the limits of his physical structure, powers of innervation, dexterity and courage.[1] The work of art produced by a writer is therefore, of necessity, complexioned and determined by the inborn and acquired faculties of the individual. This is what we mean by the hackneyed epigram: "Le style c'est l'homme."

II.

Certain broad distinctions of moral and emotional temperament may undoubtedly be detected in literary style. A tendency toward exaggeration, toward self-revelation, toward emphasis upon the one side; a tendency to reserve, to diminished tone in colouring, to parsimony of rhetorical resource upon the other; these indicate expansiveness or reticence in the writer. Victor Hugo differs by the breadth of the whole heavens from Leopardi. One man is ironical by nature, another sentimental. Sterne and Heine have a common gift of humour; but the quality of humour in each case is conditioned by sympathetic or by caustic under-currents of emotion. Sincerity and affectation, gaiety and melancholy, piety and scepticism, austerity and sensuality penetrate style so subtly and unmistakably that a candid person cannot pose as the mere slave of convention, a boon companion cannot pass muster for an anchorite, the founder of a religious sect cannot play the part of an agnostic. In dramatic work the artist creates characters alien from his own personality, and exhibits people widely different from himself acting and talking as they ought to do. This he achieves by sympathy and intuition. Yet all except the very greatest fail to render adequately what they have not felt and been. In playwrights of the second order, like our Fletcher, or of the third order, like our Byron, the individual who writes the tragedy and shapes the characters is always apparent under every mask he chooses to assume. And even the style of the greatest, their manner of presenting the varieties of human nature, betrays individual peculiarities. Æschylus sees men and women differently from Sophocles, Corneille from Racine, Shakespeare from Goethe.

In like manner the broad distinctions of mental temperament may be traced in style. The abstract thinker differs from the concrete thinker in his choice of terms; the analytical from the synthetic; the ratiocinative from the intuitive; the logical from the imaginative; the scientific from the poetical. One man thinks in images, another in for-

mal propositions. One is diffuse, and gets his thought out by reiterated statement. Another makes epigrams, and finds some difficulty in expanding their sense or throwing light upon them by illustrations. One arrives at conclusions by the way of argument. Another clothes assertion with the tropes and metaphors of rhetoric.

The same is true of physical and aesthetical qualities. They are felt inevitably in style. The sedentary student does not use the same figures of speech as come naturally to the muscular and active lover of field sports. According as the sense for colour, or for sound, or for light, or for form shall preponderate in a writer's constitution, his language will abound in references to the world, viewed under conditions of colour, sound, light, or form. He will insensibly dwell upon those aspects of things which stimulate his sensibility and haunt his memory. Thus, too, predilections for sea or mountains, for city-life or rural occupations, for flowers, precious stones, scents, birds, animals, insects, different kinds of food, torrid or temperate climates, leave their mark on literary style.

Acquired faculties and habits find their expression in style no less than inborn qualities. Education, based upon humanism or scientific studies; contact with powerful personalities at an impressible period of youth; enthusiasm aroused for this or that great masterpiece of literature; social environment; high or low birth; professional training for the bar, the church, medicine, or commerce; life in the army, at sea, upon a farm, and so forth, tinge the mind and give a more or less perceptible colour of language.

The use of words itself yields, upon analysis, valuable results illustrative of the various temperaments of authors. A man's vocabulary marks him out as of this sort or that sort—his preference for certain syntactical forms, for short sentences or for periods, for direct or inverted propositions, for plain or figurative statement, for brief or amplified illustrations. Some compose sentences, but do not build paragraphs—like Emerson; some write chapters, but cannot construct a book. Nor is punctuation to be disregarded, inasmuch as stops enable us to measure a writer's sense of time-values, and the importance he attaches to several degrees of rest and pause.

III.

It is impossible to do more than indicate some of the leading points which illustrate the meaning of the saying that style is the man; any one can test them and apply them for himself. We not only feel that Walter Scott *did not* write like Thackeray, but we also know that he *could not* write like Thackeray, and *vice versa*. This impossibility of one man producing work in exactly the same manner as another makes all deliberate attempts at imitation assume the form of parody or caricature. The sacrifice of individuality involved in scrupulous addiction to one great master of Latin prose, Cicero, condemned the best stylists of the Renaissance–men like Muretus–to lifeless and eventually worthless production. Meanwhile the exact psychology is wanting which would render our intuitions regarding the indissoluble link between style and personal character irrefutable.[2]

Literary style is more a matter of sentiment, emotion, involuntary habits of feeling and observing, constitutional sympathy with the world and men, tendencies of curiosity and liking, than of the pure intellect. The style of scientific works, affording little scope for the exercise of these psychological elements, throws less light upon their authors' temperament than does the style of poems, novels, essays, books of travel, descriptive criticism. In the former case all that need be aimed at is lucid exposition of fact and vigorous reasoning. In the latter, the fact to be stated, the truth to be arrived at, being of a more complex nature, involves a process akin to that of the figurative arts. The stylist has here to produce the desired effect by suggestions of infinite subtlety, and to present impressions made upon his sensibility.

Autobiographies, epistolary correspondence, notes of table-talk, are of the highest value in determining the correlation between a writer's self and his style. We not only derive a mass of information about Goethe's life from Eckermann, but we also discover from those conversations in how true a sense the style of Goethe's works grew out of his temperament and experience. Gibbon and Rousseau, Alfieri and Goldoni, Samuel Johnson in his "Life" by Boswell, John Stuart Mill in his autobiographical essay, Petrarch in his "Secretum" and fragment of personal confessions, have placed similar keys within our reach for unlocking the secret of their several manners.

The rare cases in which men of genius have excelled in more than one branch of art are no less instructive. Michel Angelo the sonnet-writer helps us to understand Michel Angelo the sculptor. Rossetti the painter throws light on Rossetti the poet; William Blake the lyricist upon William Blake the draughtsman. We find, on comparing the double series of work offered by such eminent and exceptionally gifted individuals, that their styles in literature and plastic art possess common qualities, which mark the men and issue from their personalities. Michel Angelo in the sonnets is as abstract, as ideal, as form-loving, as indifferent to the charm of brilliant colour, as neglectful of external nature as Michel Angelo in his statues and the frescoes of the Sistine Chapel. Rossetti's pictures, with their wealth of colour, their sharp incisive vision, their deep imaginative mysticism and powerful perfume of intellectual sensuousness, present a close analogue to his ballads, sonnets, and descriptive poems. With these and similar instances in our mind, we are prepared to hear that Victor Hugo designed pictures in the style of Gustave Doré; nor would it surprise us to discover that Gustave Doré had left odes or fiction in the manner of Victor Hugo.

The problems suggested by style as a sign and index of personality may be approached from many points of view. I have not aimed at exhaustiveness even of suggestion in my treatment of the topic; and while saying much which will appear perhaps trivial and obvious, have omitted some of the subtler and more interesting aspects of the matter. A systematic criticism of personal style would require a volume and would demand physiological and psychological knowledge which is rarely found in combination with an extensive study of literatures and arts.

---

1.   See Émile Hennequin, *La Critique Scientifique*, pp. 64-67, for a full and luminous exposition of these points.

2.   While I was engaged in writing this essay, a young French author, now, alas! dead, sent me a book which may be considered as an important contribution to the psychology of style. It is entitled *La Critique Scientifique*, par Émile Hennequin. Paris: Perrin et Cie., 1888.

Reprinted from *Essays Speculative and Suggestive*, volume 2 (London: Chapman & Hall, 1890).

W. H. Mallock

"Le Style c'est l'homme" (1892)

William Hurrell Mallock (1849-1923), a student at Oxford of the great Platonic translator Benjamin Jowett, achieved an early reputation for brilliance with his satiric dialogues on Victorian religion and philosophy, The New Republic *(1877, 1879). For over forty years afterward, he contributed to a wide variety of journals. This essay, first published in the* New Review *in April 1892, takes up the widely held idea that "the style is the man," only to refute it by examining prose style from the reader's as well as the writer's perspective and by distinguishing between style as expression and stylistic skill or style as effect.—Ed.*

Criticism is apt to be more literary than literature. It may easily be shown, I think, that it ought properly to be less so. What I mean can be put thus. We may say, without pushing the analogy too far, that literature is to the civilised life of the mind what food and drink of some sort are to the life of the body; and just as the aim of delicacy in wines and cookery is not principally the pleasure of cooks and wine-tasters, but the pleasure generally of a certain fastidious public, so the first and principal appeal of literature is not to those who are specially or technically interested in it, but to a certain general public whose thoughts and sympathies it affects. It is important from the way in which it enters not into libraries, but into lives.

We must, however—to go back to eating and drinking—recollect that, to enjoy fine wines and cookery properly, much more is wanted than the mere power to pay for them. The palate must be made self-conscious; it must learn to discriminate and expect. And precisely the same thing is true with regard to literature. In all literature which the general reader appreciates, there are qualities and flavours which are sure to escape his appreciation until they have been shown him or he has learned to discriminate and expect them. To show him these and teach him their value, this is the function of criticism.

If literature itself, then, is, as it is, important, because of its effect not on the literary world, but on the world, the same thing holds good of criticism in a yet greater degree. An original work of art, though it appeals to the world ultimately, may at first be understood by a limited circle only: but the function of the critic is to admit the world into this circle, and he must speak to the world immediately, or else he need speak to no one. He is an interpreter, knowing two languages—that of letters, and that of ordinary life. He has learnt through the medium of the first; but he must teach through the medium of the second. An ideal critic, in fact, is not an ideal writer; he is essentially the ideal general reader. He should look on general readers as if they were his brothers and his sisters, and treat them as if they could share with him every perception he possessed. He should never forget that they are his first and his legitimate audience.

But this is what critics far too often forget. They forget to whom they are writing, just as if a person in conversation were to forget to what company he was speaking. Thus, though what they say may be admirable when it is understood, it is not understood by those most concerned in understanding it. It does not touch their sympathies; it does not address them in terms of their own habitual experiences, their interests, tastes, prejudices, and ways of thought. In other words, there is a failure, not in their matter, but in their style.

And now let me give an instance which at first will seem to many to refute my allegation, but for that reason will the better illustrate and support it. The instance is Mr. Matthew Arnold. Now if one quality in Mr. Arnold's writings has been praised more than another, it has been the great beauty of their style; and in many, and most important ways, the praise is completely just. But, underlying all its merits, this style has one great defect. The audience to whom Mr. Arnold always conceives himself to be speaking is not the world but a clique; and his style is consequently full of peculiarities, specially suited, no doubt, to this peculiar people, but specially, on that very account, unsuited to anybody else. He has favourite words and phrases which in ordinary society are meaningless, or else odd and irritating, like some Bohemianism in dress. He al-

490

ludes to opinions, facts, and persons, as being of admitted importance, or familiarly known to everybody, which are so perhaps to a clique, but which to the outside world are not known at all, or at least are of no interest. What many of his admirers used to call his "Olympian air" was by nobody outside a clique ever suspected to be "Olympian"; but it either escaped notice altogether, or was merely wondered at as some curious solecism. If the subjects Mr. Arnold discussed had been the subjects of a clique merely, and if he had meant to address only such persons as belonged to it, what has been spoken of as a defect might have possibly been a signal merit. But the very reverse was the case. His subjects were of general interest, and he wanted to address the world. But the world unluckily was represented for him by an extremely narrow and unrepresentative section of it, and his style was narrow in consequence, as compared with the interest of his subjects.

I mention this defect of Mr. Arnold's for two distinct reasons. I am going myself to criticise a subject which is of general interest–namely, not Mr. Arnold's style, but style in general; and the fault I have attributed to this distinguished critic is the special fault I wish myself to avoid. Style has been written about by critics without number; but Mr. Arnold's defect has been usually theirs also. They have usually considered their subject from the point of view of the writer. My wish is to do so from the point of view of the reader.

But I have alluded to Mr. Arnold for another reason also, and a much more important one. The quality in his style which I have just spoken of as a defect, may also be considered merely as a strongly marked characteristic; and as such it happens to illustrate that element, which is at the bottom of all style whether for bad or good–which readers most generally feel, and least generally recognise, and which, for every reason, we ought to begin with examining.

We all feel, then, that, apart from the mere matter conveyed by it, one man's writing affects us differently from another's and we are accustomed to say, according as we are pleased by it or otherwise, that the style is good or bad. But though we all feel what we mean when we say this, most people do not know what they mean, or know it very imperfectly. Style is supposed popularly to be mere technical skill in writing–some felicity in the turning of phrases, or in the adroit conduct of sentences; and whenever a book exhibits

these characteristics the ordinary reader says indifferently with regard to it, that "the style is good," or that, "it is well written."

Such language, however, betrays a complete misconception of facts; and indeed often puzzles the very people who use it; for it is the commonest thing in the world to hear the complaint made that a book has a good style, and yet that it is difficult to read. The explanation is simple, and may be indicated in what seems a paradox, but is in reality a literal and fundamental truth. A book may be very ill-written, and yet have a charming style; it may be very well-written, and yet its style may be absolutely insufferable. The foundation of style, its essence, its colouring principle, is not the writer's skill as a writer, but his character as a man; and this shows itself in ways with which technical skill, or even technical genius, has not essentially anything at all to do. For style, if we go to the bottom of it and examine the secret of its effect on us, is merely a means by which one personality impresses itself on others; and the pleasure, the indifference, or the distaste, with which we read a writer is produced in just the same way as the corresponding feeling is produced in us by the company of a man.

There, is here, it must be remembered, no question of matter, or what is said; there is only a question of manner, or of how it is said. We may listen to a man with interest if he tells us important news, and yet all the while we may be conscious that the very fact of his presence is an offence to us. Another man may tell us a mere succession of trifles, and he yet may fascinate us, and we shall think his company charming. The same is the case with style, and for the same reasons. What primarily attracts or repels us in it– what is, as I say, its foundation–consists of those personal qualities in the writer which by its means he impresses on us.

How this is will explain itself very easily, if we will but think for a moment of the kind of qualities in question. They are qualities of temperament, of morals, of tastes, of sympathies, of experience, of social associations and prejudices, and of personal breeding and deportment–of deference or familiarity, of ease or stiffness, towards the reader. And these may show themselves clearly and strongly in ways with which technical skill in writing has nothing whatever to do.

Let us begin by considering the simplest way of all, and we shall at once see that this is so. Let us consider the selection and use of single words, in cases where there are numerous familiar synonyms to select from. We will take, for example, some occasion when the thing–a man–has to be mentioned. Now, for *man*, as a word, there are synonyms in great abundance, and of many writers each might select a different one–a human being, a gentleman, an old boy, a chap, an immortal soul, or even a bloke. All are known to anyone who ever put pen to paper, so the selection is not dependent on the writer's command of language, but on his feelings, his mood, his good or his bad breeding; and the selection affects us like the tone of a voice in speaking. It reveals to us something about the writer personally which attracts, which strikes, or which repels us.

Let us now go a step further, and advance from words to phrases. The following passage is from the *Vanity Fair* of Thackeray: "Love was Miss Amelia Sedley's last tutoress, and it was amazing what progress our young lady made under that popular teacher. In the course of fifteen or eighteen months' daily attention to this eminent finishing governess, what a deal of secrets Amelia learned!" Now with regard to the quality of Thackeray's mere writing, it is agreed generally that his English was singularly pure. But with regard to his style there is no such agreement. To some it is delightful and captivating; others, as the late Lord Lytton was, are repelled and affronted by it. The sentences just quoted are full of Thackeray's style; but this has nothing to do with any purity in their English. Their mere English might be the English of any man, woman, or child. Their style shows itself in the use of certain very common phrases, as equivalents for certain nouns or names. These last are "Love" and "Miss Amelia Sedley." Love is a word that we all use alike. No personal character is betrayed in doing so; but when love is described as "that popular teacher," and a moment after as "this eminent finishing governess," a piece of the writer's character at once pointedly shows itself. He gives us an indication of his mood and manners as a man. Again, if a girl is named Miss Amelia Sedley, no character is betrayed in calling her by her formal name; but the moment a person speaks of her as "our young lady," character shows itself by an act of personal familiarity. The writer seems, in our presence, to be patting the young lady on the back, and his behaviour excites a feeling in us either of coldness or cordiality towards him.

Thackeray, perhaps, gives us readier illustrations than anyone of what, in this way, style is. The above refer only to a writer's character as exhibited in his attitude towards the thing or person he is dealing with. What is equally important, and what colours his style equally, is his attitude towards the reader. Nobody shows us this also more clearly than Thackeray. Thackeray is a man always by deliberate choice in contact with company which he thinks a little too good for him; and he assumes that his reader is a person in the same position. He assumes that between them there is an identity of ideas and circumstances, and consequently a familiar understanding. He attracts attention by taking the reader's arm, and emphasises his observations by a nudge. Now whether this behavior is ingratiating, or whether it is the reverse, is nothing to the point here. It may or may not have given a charm to Thackeray's style; the point here is simply that it gave a marked quality to his style. And every style, to a greater or less degree, is affected by a similar cause. It implies some personal attitude on the part of the writer towards the reader, some assumption with regard either to the reader's position or his capacities; and betrays the consequent temper in which the writer accosts and addresses him. We all know when a man speaks to us how much the pleasure with which we listen to him depends on these very causes–on the opinion which his manner leads us to form of him, and still more on the opinion which it indicates he has formed of us. And with the style of a writer the case is just the same.

In a word, the primary thing by which style affects us, by which it pleases or displeases us, or in which one style differs from another, is not its literary quality, but its human quality.

And the application of this remark is considerably wider than it may seem to be. As has been said before, the interest of a writer's matter is obviously a distinct thing from the interest of his style or manner; but in the popular mind there is apt to be some confusion as to where the one ends and where the other begins. Many things are considered as part of a writer's matter which do in reality belong to his style or manner. It is no doubt true that the one runs into the other, and it is difficult sometimes to decide as to which is which. But day differs from night, in spite of the ambiguities of twilight; and between matter and manner the difference is practically as distinct. Matter is that which the writer intends primarily to convey; manner includes everything in the way of allusion or illustration which is subsidiary to the matter, and which he uses to help him in conveying it.

Let us take, for instance, Sam Weller's description of his place at Mr. Pickwick's: "Plenty to get, as the soldier said, when they ordered him three hundred lashes." The first clause of this sentence belongs to the speaker's matter, the second to his style or manner. Let us go from Sam Weller to Macaulay, and we shall be able to discriminate similarly between the two elements. I take Macaulay's case because there are few writers the charm of whose manner is so liable to be confused with the interest of the matter, and few in which they are so readily separable. Most people fancy that the charm of Macaulay's style lies in the prompt and athletic movement of his sentences; but this is no more than the varnish is to the picture, though, perhaps, without it the picture might be hardly seen. His real charm lies in the immense range of his knowledge, and the shrewd and caustic sense which enables him to be so constantly applying it. He is the Ulysses of literature, with a parallel, with an illustration for everything. As he proceeds with his main subject he prepares our minds for appreciating it. He adds to our knowledge or he revives it; we are electrified as we listen; and the result is primarily due, as it might have been in the case of Ulysses, not to the fact that his illustrations are neatly given, but the fact that they are so apposite, and that he has so many to give. We are charmed because we are listening to an impressive and delightful person, not because we are listening to a practised and adroit writer.

And now to sum up what we have seen thus far, a very few illustrations have been quite sufficient to show us that many of the most distinguishing qualities of style—by which one style differs from another, and pleases or displeases us—are qualities which express themselves independently of any literary skill beyond that belonging to the most ordinary educated man. Let a writer merely have this much command over language, that he can write it as unaffectively as he can speak it when entirely at his ease, and he will write a style which, according to his own character, will laugh or frown, show knowledge of the world or want of it, be diffident or self-possessed, well or ill bred, attractive or distasteful, or vapid. If the man has not much character, the style will have not much either; but whatever the style is, the sort of effect it has on us will be found to depend ultimately on the sort of character which it introduces to us. Style, in fact, is the vehicle of character.

And now let us pass to another part of the subject—the part which many readers are accustomed to think of as the whole. We are coming at last to that—I mean the question of literary skill. It may seem to some, perhaps, as if, according to the above analysis, literary skill went for nothing—as if there were no room for it. Such, however, is the very reverse of the case. Character is capable of various degrees of self-revelation in style as it is in conversation. Put a man amongst company to which he is unaccustomed, or whose language he talks imperfectly, and we know what little justice he will most likely do himself, and how much of his character will be hidden under the veil of shyness. Put a man on the ice who is unaccustomed to skating, and though every movement of his body may be naturally instinct with grace, yet, till he has learnt to skate, his grace will appear to nobody. The same thing holds good, though with one point of difference, as to writing. The point of difference is this. Every educated man can write with some facility. He is more at ease, he is more himself, in writing than in company which makes him shy, or on skates if he has not learnt skating; and therefore without anything that can be called literary skill—without any special gift except that of being unaffected—he will exhibit, as he writes, certain points of his character; in fact he will write a style, though probably without knowing it, as M. Jourdain talked prose. But though the writing of the ordinary man not only can, but inevitably will, reveal his character up to a certain point, and will so far possess a distinctive style, it will do this and possess this up to a certain point only, and to rise beyond that point exceptional skill is needed.

Let me pause here and go back to what I set out with urging. I urged that the colouring principle of style was not skill but character—was a human quality, not a literary accomplishment; and in order to prove this I adduced certain examples which showed how a writer's character was constantly revealing itself in ways with which literary skill had obviously nothing to do. But I did all this with the limited intention only of showing that style and skill were distinct things in essence, not of showing that the first had no need of the second. It has need of the second, and for the following reason. Just as style is the vehicle of character, so beyond a certain point must skill be the vehicle of style. The richer the character of the writer, the more delicate his power of perception; the deeper, the more composite, the more various the qualities he desires to convey, the more does his style need skill to show itself, to embody itself, one may almost say to exist. But none the less does this skill, no matter how great, depend for its charm—for its effects on us—not in itself, but on that which is conveyed to us through its medium. It is to the writer's personality what the telescope is to the heavens. It brings into view what would otherwise be unseen; but it is valuable not for what it is, but for what it reveals. The "watcher of the skies"—"When some new planet swims into his ken—"the thing which impresses him is not the object glass but a star.

And now let us descend from generalities to particulars, and inquire what the main constituents of literary skill are. First, then, we will deal with the broad and general question of the relation which written language bears to spoken language, and of how the first differs from the second, and why.

The simplest and most universal difference is this. It relates not to phraseology, or the quality of individual passages, but to the general arrangement and general management of the subject. When a man is describing or explaining anything to others in conversation, he sees the effect of what he says as he proceeds, and anything which his hearers either fail to understand or object to he can, as the occasion arises, explain more fully or defend. But if he is describing or explaining the same thing in writing, he has no hearer who will question him or state objections, and constantly force him to be at once lucid and convincing. He is therefore obliged to imagine one; and his writing, unlike his conversation, has to do duty for speaker and hearer both. In conversation he is asked questions: in writing he has to anticipate them. The ability to do this—to be two persons at the same time, and to adapt what the one desires to say to the imagined capacity of the other who is assumed to be anxious to understand it—the ability to do this is a distinctly literary gift. It is not a gift either of knowledge or of intellect; it is merely the power of conveying these through a certain peculiar medium.

Nor must it be thought that it has to do only with the anticipation of argumentative difficulties, or the disposition of the points of an argument. Anyone who carefully compares writing with intelligent talking, will be struck by the fact that, in the most forcible writing, statements are occurring constantly which, if made in conversation, would be platitudes. Let us take, for instance, the following from George Eliot's introduction to *Romola*. She is speaking of sunrise four hundred years ago. "As the faint light of its course," she says, "pierced into the dwellings of men, it

fell then as now on the rosy warmth of nestling children; on the haggard waking of sorrow and sickness; on the tardy uprising of hard-handed labour," and so on. Now, no one in conversation would think it worth his while to insist on, or even to mention, such obvious truths as these. But they have a use in writing of a peculiar and important kind. The writer has recourse to them not to inform the reader of what the reader does not know, or impress upon him anything he neglects, but merely, for the moment, to call his attention gently to some one of the many things familiar to him, as to which reader and writer are both in complete agreement; and thus to create or renew the sensation of their standing on common ground. This is one of the chief artifices by which a writer keeps in touch with his reader. It is not required in conversation, or only to a small degree, for in conversation the effect is produced by other means and circumstances. It is therefore an artifice which belongs to writing specially; and skill in using it is distinctly literary skill.

I have spoken of the way in which a writer should anticipate the objections of a reader: and I myself anticipate that many readers will think I have not even yet reached the real heart of the subject, that I have said nothing about what they are accustomed to call "good writing." I am going to do so now. I am going to consider the question of words, phrases, and sentences—the choice of the one, the construction and movement of the other; and ask how, in these respects, writing differs from speaking, and what room they consequently offer for special literary skill.

What I have just been saying will assist us in understanding this. I have been saying that a writer must do duty for two persons—himself and his reader also. In the same way his language must do duty for two things—or, indeed, for more than two. When a man speaks he conveys his meaning not by words alone, but by manner, by look, by tone, and by many other means. But in writing he can use words, and nothing else besides; and his writing, therefore, will either be inferior to his speaking; or, if it is not, he must somehow use language so as to give it the qualities not of speech only, but of the various circumstances and accompaniments which complete its effect when spoken. For this reason, in order to produce the effect of spoken language, it must, in its management, differ from spoken language. For instance, most of the effect of a speaker's words depends on the slowness or rapidity, the softness or the loudness of his utterances, which are regulated by, and which express, his passion or his feeling at the moment. But in writing these qualities must be transferred from the voice to the very structure of the sentences. Emphasis, which is given by the voice in speaking, must be given by a repetition or inversion, or some other artifice, in writing. Haste or slowness must be expressed in the same way, by so collocating the words that clause after clause, sentence after sentence, shall of necessity either hurry or move sedately; and more important still, by means of rhythm and modulation, the language must be made to contain in its own structure all those variations of feeling which tone imparts to it when it is spoken. When two lovers are parting, is either of them likely to care for the literary construction of the sentences in which each says good-bye to happiness? But to reproduce the effect of these words in writing, they would have to be changed, or rearranged, or reinforced by others; and skill would be required to incorporate into language alone what naturally expresses itself when language is united with life.

I am inclined to say myself that, of what may be called mere writing, construction and modulation form the most important part; but certainly not far from these, and as some may think before them, comes skill as exhibited in the choice of words and phrases. The reader will remember that I instanced words and phrases as the subject of a kind of choice which, though an element of style, exhibited no skill whatever. But, as I have said already, mere ordinary choice, ordinary command of language, and ordinary sensitiveness to the power of it, will exhibit character up to a certain point only. It will result, as it were, in a pencil sketch, in which lights and shades are given very imperfectly, and in which colour is not given at all. These elements, which mere ordinary choice of words fails to capture and express, are capable of expression by means of literary skill, in proportion to the degree in which a writer possesses it. Let us take, for instance, a writer like Mr. William Morris, who writes both prose and verse in a quasi-archaic dialect. We need not admire the dialect; we may, perhaps, think it ridiculous; but it exhibits a way of looking at things on the writer's part beyond the reach of language as commanded by the ordinary man. Again, another instance, of a kind equally marked, but far more genuine and legitimate, was recently put before the readers of this REVIEW, in Mr. Carlyle's novel. Things and events familiar to the kind of society he is describ-

ing are described by him in a strange and remote phraseology. A charming and distinguished hostess in a country house is, with him, "a woman of the stateliest yet humanest aspect, who presides over her company with the graceful dignity of a queen." A fisherman comes home with "some wonder-worthy fishes"; the younger men of the party are "brave young gallants"; and the ladies are "dames," who, when they sing after dinner in a summer-house, "heighten and, as it were, vivify with music the other charms of a scene and evening so lovely." This peculiar choice of words fills the reader with the sense that the writer is a recluse, viewing what he describes as a stranger, and watching it with that attention, and appreciating it with that freshness, which strangeness alone can give.

The highest skill, however, in this way, and the strongest and most delicate results, are to be found not in wording that strikes the ear as peculiar, but in that which seems as we read it to differ from ordinary language in one respect alone—that of being more expressive: which is, one may say, ordinary language bewitched, and which sets us wondering not at itself but at its effects.

How the power of language is capable of being thus heightened is to be explained as follows. Language is made of two sets of units—words and idioms, or phrases. Of these, some express nothing but what they express avowedly. Others carry with them some special set of associations. If I say "James struck John," I am conveying a simple fact. If I say "James hit John a crack," I am conveying something more. But, to begin with single words, let us take any set of synonyms, and some will be found scentless, others saturated with suggestion—the suggestions of no two being exactly similar. The French speak of a voice with tears in it; in the same way we may say that certain words have tears in them. And of phrases the same holds good. The ordinary man feels this to some degree; indeed the associations and secondary powers of language are derived from its ordinary use: and a certain effect, as I have pointed out already, becomes producible thus without any literary skill. Literary skill in this respect is merely the development of a common and universal faculty; but the difference between the faculty as developed, and as undeveloped, is great. Words and phrases of the kind alluded to are like colours on a painter's palette, the effect of which in the picture will depend on the colours near them. Again, to change the comparison, some words and phrases which will be scentless under some conditions, like night-smelling flowers, will become scented under others. Every chapter, every paragraph, of a book has some prevailing tone, and separate words and phrases, if they coincide with this tone, will support it; or, according as they differ from it, will bring themselves, as it were, into relief, and will attract attention by their special light or colour: and in this way the whole surface of the style will be alive. To push style to such perfection as this, a sensitiveness to language and a skill in writing are needed, which are gifts or accomplishments of just as special a kind as a painter's command over his colours, or a musician's over his instrument.

The fact, however, remains which I set out with asserting–that a style is pleasing or displeasing to us not because its writing is technically good or bad, but because it brings us in contact with a pleasing or displeasing, with a weak or a powerful, personality: and the most exquisite skill of a purely literary kind is valuable only for the completeness with which it fulfills this function.

There are certain special exceptions to what I have just said which may be mentioned here, but need not be dwelt upon. I refer to such writing as that of unsigned articles in papers, where the writer is writing, not on behalf of himself, but of an institution–as, for instance, *The Times*–having a position and, consequently, a style of its own, which the writer adopts, like the intonation which a priest adopts as Mass.

Putting aside, then, such cases as these, the quality of a style depends on the writer's character; and skill is only a condition–not always indispensable–of that quality showing itself. Such being the case, the question naturally is suggested–is there such a thing as a good style, in any more absolute sense than we can say that there is an attractive manner? In one respect, which I will speak of presently, I maintain that there is; but in every other respect there is not. A manner which is attractive to one set of people, or to one class of society, will to others be unattractive, or will not be understood; and with style it is the same. In times when readers were few, and when literature, like everything else, depended for its success on its power of pleasing aristocracies, style was good in proportion as it represented good breeding in manner. But as education has extended, and the reading public has increased, new schools of literature have naturally been developed, which address themselves directly to en-

tirely different patrons–to a public whose manner and ways of thinking are different, and who demand in style an equivalent to the breeding which prevails amongst themselves. It is no doubt true that with regard to certain subjects, and under certain circumstances, good breeding in style, as in manner, consists merely in complete simplicity; but, putting the cases aside to which this statement applies, we must admit that in these days of different reading publics, a style which seems good to one may seem very bad to another. Compare, for instance, Greene's style with that of Gibbon. Gibbon writes like a man who is conscious not only of the dignity of his subject but of a certain stateliness and social dignity in himself. He bows to his company, and begs permission to speak to them. But Mr. Greene seems to enter with a nod, and to say to them, "Here we are." Gibbon enters as if he were at some Court ceremony; Mr. Greene as if he were jumping into a third-class railway carriage. For each style there is no doubt much to be said, and it may fairly be argued that neither is the best absolutely. But with equal fairness we may argue in the same way about breeding. If high breeding is no better than low breeding, we need not dispute about their relative excellence. But if about manner or manners we may say absolutely that those of the higher classes have–or have had–a grace, a delicacy, and a finish, not to be found in other sections of the community; if we may say absolutely of the manners of the old French Court that they were superior to those of Mrs. Todgers' boarding-house; then we may say of style precisely the same thing–that the best style is the style which shows highest breeding, that corresponds most closely to the manners of the finished gentleman.

This point, however, is one which may perhaps be open to debate. The other, which I have still to mention, may be treated with decision and certainty. Whether or no a good style should be equivalent to the manners of the great world, it ought, at all events, to be equivalent to the manners of the world. I mean by this that it should affect us like the voice and the behaviour of a man who is giving us his own thoughts and his own experience, and who presumes to address us not because he has read more deeply than we have, but because he has lived more deeply. Every word and phrase he uses, which has any special quality, should derive this from having been dipped in his own life, dyed in his own blood, perfumed with his own memories–whether these be of courts or solitudes. He should use no word, phrase, or rhythm, acquired at second-hand, and dyed with the blood and perfumed with the memories of others, unless his own life has given them a second baptism, and made their qualities his own. His language as it comes to the reader should come straight, and should be felt to come straight, from life and not from books. A phraseology which suggests books before it suggests life is like a coloured window-pane intervening between ourselves and a view; or else like a dusty windowpane, which hides what it should reveal.

In other words, so far as form goes, the most perfect literary style is the style which, whilst conveying most, seems to be least literary. Written language should produce the effect on the reader not of language which no one would have used in life, but which everyone would have used under the circumstances, had they only been able to command it. This need not be always, or principally, the language of general society. It may be the language of the private interview, or the silent language of meditation or of day-dream; but it should be distinguishable as literary for this reason only, that it has more life, not less, in it than language as employed ordinarily; that it is not language only, but also voice and gesture: and the test of the highest art is the result that appears most natural, and which shows the writer most perfectly, not as a writer, but as a man. The style is the man; but it ought not to be the man of letters.

Reprinted from *New Review*, 6 (April 1892): 441-454.

W. H. Mallock

From *Memoirs of Life and Literature* (1920)

This brief extract from Mallock's autobiography is of interest for two reasons: first, because it shows in practice what Mallock meant by the stylistic skill and revision he had discussed theoretically in his 1892 essay "Le Style c'est l'homme" and second, because it is one of the few accounts by a Victorian prose writer of the actual process of composition.–Ed.

Let me begin with prose, which, merely as a pleasurable art, instinct has urged me, from my earliest days, to cultivate. Of what good prose is I have always had clear notions; and, whether I have been successful in my efforts to achieve it or not, my personal experience of the process may not be without some interest. My own experience is that the composition of good prose–prose that seems good to myself–is a process which requires a very great deal of leisure. True excellence in prose, so I have always felt, involves many subtle qualities which are appreciable by the reader through their final effects alone, which leave no trace of the efforts spent in producing them, but which without such effort could rarely be produced at all.

As examples of these qualities I may mention a melody not too often resonant, which captivates the reader's attention, and is always producing a mood in him conducive to a favourable reception of what the writer is anxious to convey. Next to such melody I should put a logical adaptation of stress, or of emphasis in the construction of sentences, which corresponds in detail to the movements of the reader's mind–a halt in the words occurring where the mind halts, a new rapidity in the words when the mind, satisfied thus far, is prepared to resume its progress. To these qualities, as essential to perfection in prose, I might easily add others; but these are so complex and comprehensive that they practically imply the rest.

With regard, then, to these essentials, the practice which I have had to adopt in my own efforts to produce them has been more or less as follows. The general substance of what I proposed to say I have written out first in the loosest language possible, without any regard to melody, to accuracy, or even to correct grammar. I have then re-written this matter, with a view, not to any verbal improvement, but merely to the re-arrangement of ideas, descriptions or arguments, so that this may accord with the sequence of questions, expectations or emotions, which are likely, by a natural logic, to arise in the reader's mind–nothing being said too soon, nothing being said too late, and nothing (except for the sake of deliberate emphasis) being said twice over. The different paragraphs would now be like so many stone blocks which had been placed in their proper positions so as to form a polylithic frieze, but each of which still remained to be carved, as though by a sculptor or lapidary, so as to be part of a continuous pattern, or a series of connected figures. My next task would be to work at them one by one, till each was sculptured into an image of my own minute intentions. The task of thus carving each and fitting it to its next-door neighbours, has always been, merely for its own sake, exceedingly fascinating to myself, but it has generally been long and slow. Most of my own books, when their general substance had been roughly got into order by means of several tentative versions, were, paragraph by paragraph, written again five or six times more, the corrections each time growing more and more minute, and finally the clauses and wording of each individual sentence were transposed, or re-balanced or re-worded, whenever such processes should be necessary, in order to capture some nuance of meaning, which had previously eluded me as a bird eludes a fowler.

As an example of this process I may mention a single sentence which occurs in my little book on Cyprus. It is a sentence belonging to a description of certain morning scenes–of dewy plains, with peasants moving across them, and here and there a smoke-wreath arising from burning weeds. The effect of these scenes in some poignant way was primitive, and I was able at once to reproduce it by saying that the peasants were moving like figures out of the Book of Genesis. I felt, however, that this effect was not produced by the groups of peasants only. I felt that somehow–I could not at first tell how–some part in producing it was played by the smoke-wreaths also. At last I managed to capture the suggestion, at first subconscious only, which had so far been eluding me. I finished my original description by adding the following words: "The smoke-wreaths were going up like the smoke of the first sacrifice."

It may be objected that prose, built up in this elaborate way, loses as much as it gains, because it is bound to lose the charm and the convincing force of spontaneity. This may be so in some cases, but it is not so in all. I have found myself that, so far as my own works are concerned, the passages which are easiest to read are precisely those which it has been most laborious to write. And for this, it seems to me, there is a very intelligible reason. Half of the interests and emotions which make up the substance of life are more or less subconscious, and are, for most men, difficult to identify. One of the functions of pure literature is to make the subconscious reveal itself. It is to make men know what they *are*, in addition to what spontaneously they *feel* themselves to be, but feel only, without clear comprehension of it. As soon as a writer, at the cost of whatever la-bour, manages to make these spontaneities, otherwise subconscious, intelligible, the spontaneity of the processes described by him adds itself at last to his description.

A signal example of this fact may be found, not in prose, but in love-poems. Most people can fall in love. It takes no trouble to do so, whatever trouble it may bring them. If any human processes are spontaneous, falling in love is one of them. Most lovers feel more than they know until great love-poetry explains it to them what they are; but great love-poems are great, not because they are composed spontaneously, but because they express spontaneities which are essentially external to themselves. In other words, the achievement of perfection, whether in prose or poetry, is comparable to the task of a piano-tuner, who may spend a whole morning in tightening or relaxing the strings, but who knows at once, when he gets them, the minutely precise tones which the laws of music demand.

Reprinted from *Memoirs of Life and Literature* (London: Chapman & Hall, 1920), pp. 260-263.

Walter Raleigh

From *Style* (1897)

Sir Walter Raleigh (1861-1922) was professor of English literature successively at the universities of Liverpool, Glasgow, and Oxford. Though he produced a number of appreciative critical studies on such figures as Shakespeare, Milton, and Wordsworth, he was not a typical literary scholar, and during his years at Liverpool in the 1890s, he was contributing to modern literary periodicals such as the New Review *and the aesthetic* Yellow Book. *His short book* Style *(1897) covers an enormous range of issues with enthusiasm. The extract here on how words have different histories for each user is typical of his summarily stated insights, though it is his bold conclusion that "Style cannot be taught" which has attracted most notice and disagreement.*–Ed.

It is not to be denied that there is a native force of temperament which can make itself felt even through illiterate carelessness. "Literary gentlemen, editors, and critics," says Thoreau, himself by no means a careless writer, "think that they know how to write, because they have studied grammar and rhetoric; but they are egregiously mistaken. The *art* of composition is as simple as the discharge of a bullet from a rifle, and its masterpieces imply an infinitely greater force behind them." This true saying introduces us to the hardest problem of criticism, the paradox of literature, the stumbling-block of rhetoricians. To analyse the precise method whereby a great personality can make itself felt in words, even while it neglects and contemns the study of words, would be to lay bare the secrets of religion and life–it is beyond human competence. Nevertheless a brief and diffident consideration of the matter may bring thus much comfort, that the seeming contradiction is no discredit cast on letters, but takes its origin rather from too narrow and pedantic a view of the scope of letters.

Words are things: it is useless to try to set them in a world apart. They exist in books only by accident, and for one written there are a thousand, infinitely more powerful, spoken. They are deeds: the man who brings word of a lost battle can work no comparable effect with the muscles of his arm; Iago's breath is as truly laden with poison and murder as the fangs of the cobra and the drugs of the assassin. Hence the sternest education in the use of words is least of all to be gained in the schools, which cultivate verbiage in a highly artificial state of seclusion. A soldier cares little for poetry, because it is the exercise of power that he loves, and he is accustomed to do more with his words than give pleasure. To keep language in immediate touch with reality, to lade it with action and passion, to utter it hot from the heart of determination, is to exhibit it in the plentitude of power. All this may be achieved without the smallest study of literary models, and is consistent with a perfect neglect of literary canons. It is not the logical content of the word, but the whole mesh of its conditions, including the character, circumstances, and attitude of the speaker, that is its true strength. "Damn" is often the feeblest of expletives, and "as you please" may be the dirge of an empire. Hence it is useless to look to the grammarian, or the critic, for a lesson in strength of style; the laws that he has framed, good enough in themselves, are current only in his own abstract world. A breath of hesitancy will sometimes make trash of a powerful piece of eloquence; and even in writing, a thing three times said, and each time said badly, may be of more effect than that terse, full, and final expression which the doctors rightly commend. The art of language, regarded as a question of pattern and cadence, or even as a question of logic and thought-sequence, is a highly abstract study; for although, as has been said, you can do almost anything with words, with words alone you can do next to nothing. . . .

When all has been said, there remains a residue capable of no formal explanation. Language, this array of conventional symbols loosely strung together, and blown about by every wandering breath, is miraculously vital and expressive, justifying not a few of the myriad superstitions that have always attached to its use. The same words are free to all, yet no wealth or distinction of vocabulary is needed for a group of words to take the stamp of an individual mind and character. "As a quality of style," says Mr. Pater, "soul is a fact." To resolve how words, like bodies, become transparent when they are inhabited by that luminous reality, is a higher pitch than metaphysic wit can fly. Ardent persuasion and deep feeling enkindle words, so that the weakest take on glory. The humblest and most despised of common phrases may be the chosen vessel for the next avatar of the spirit. It is the old problem, to be met only by the old solution of the Platonist, that

> Soul is the form, and doth the body make.

The soul is able to inform language by some strange means other than the choice and arrangement of words and phrases. Real novelty of vocabulary is impossible; in the matter of language we lead a parasitical existence, and are always quoting. . . .

Single words too we plagiarise, when we use them without realisation and mastery of their meaning. The best argument for a succinct style is this, that if you use words you do not need, or do not understand, you cannot use them well. It is not what a word means, but what it means to you, that is of the deepest import. Let it be a weak word, with a poor history behind it, if you have done good thinking with it, you may yet use it to surprising advantage. But if, on the other hand, it be a strong word that has never aroused more than a misty idea and a flickering emotion in your mind, here lies your danger. You may use it, for there is none to hinder; and it will betray you. The commonest Saxon words prove explosive machines in the hands of rash impotence. It is perhaps a certain uneasy consciousness of danger, a suspicion that weakness of soul cannot wield these strong words, that makes debility avoid them, committing itself rather, as if by some pre-established affinity, to the vaguer Latinised vocabulary. Yet they are not all to be avoided, and their quality in practice will depend on some occult ability in their employer. For every living person, if the material were obtainable, a separate historical dictionary might be compiled, recording where each word was first heard or seen, where and how it was first used. The references are utterly beyond recovery; but such a register would throw a strange light on individual styles. The eloquent trifler, whose stock of words has been accumulated by a pair of light fingers, would stand denuded of his plausible pretences as soon as it were seen how roguishly he came by his eloquence. There may be literary quality, it is well to remember, in the words of a parrot, if only its cage has been happily placed; mean-

ing and soul there cannot be. Yet the voice will sometimes be mistaken, by the carelessness of chance listeners, for a genuine utterance of humanity; and the like is true in literature. But writing cannot be luminous and great save in the hands of those whose words are their own by inheritance, or by conquest. Life is spent in learning the meaning of great words. . . .

Here, among words, our lot is cast, to make or mar. It is in this obscure thicket, overgrown with weeds, set with thorns, and haunted by shadows, this World of Words, as the Elizabethans finely called it, that we wander, eternal pioneers, during the course of our mortal lives. To be overtaken by a master, one who comes along with the gaiety of assured skill and courage, with the gravity of unflinching purpose, to make the crooked ways straight and the rough places plain, is to gain fresh confidence from despair. He twines wreaths of the entangling ivy, and builds ramparts of the thorns. He blazes his mark upon the secular oaks, as a guidance to later travellers, and coaxes flame from heaps of mouldering rubbish. There is no sense of cheer like this. Sincerity, clarity, candour, power, seem real once more, real and easy. In the light of great literary achievement, straight and wonderful, like the roads of the ancient Romans, barbarism torments the mind like a riddle. Yet there are the dusky barbarians!–fleeing from the harmonious tread of the ordered legions, running to hide themselves in the morass of vulgar sentiment, to ambush their nakedness in the sand-pits of low thought.

It is a venerable custom to knit up the speculative consideration of any subject with the counsels of practical wisdom. The words of this essay have been vain indeed if the idea that style may be imparted by tuition has eluded them, and survived. There is a useful art of Grammar, which takes for its province the right and the wrong in speech. Style deals only with what is permissible to all, and even revokes, on occasion, the rigid laws of Grammar or countenances offences against them. Yet no one is a better judge of equity for ignorance of the law, and grammatical practice offers a fair field wherein to acquire ease, accuracy, and versatility. The formation of sentences, the sequence of verbs, the marshalling of the ranks of auxiliaries are all, in a sense, to be learned. There is a kind of inarticulate disorder to which writers are liable, quite distinct from a bad style, and caused chiefly by lack of exercise. An unpractised writer will sometimes send a beautiful and powerful phrase jostling along in the midst of a clumsy sentence–like a crowned king escorted by a mob.

But Style cannot be taught. Imitation of the masters, or of some one chosen master, and the constant purging of language by a severe criticism, have their uses, not to be belittled; they have also their dangers. The greater part of what is called the teaching of style must always be negative, bad habits may be broken down, old malpractices prohibited. The pillory and the stocks are hardly educational agents, but they make it easier for honest men to enjoy their own. If style could really be taught, it is a question whether its teachers should not be regarded as mischief-makers and enemies of mankind. The Rosicrucians professed to have found the philosopher's stone, and the shadowy sages of modern Thibet are said, by those who speak for them, to have compassed the instantaneous transference of bodies from place to place. In either case, the holders of these secrets have laudably refused to publish them, lest avarice and malice should run amuck in human society. A similar fear might well visit the conscience of one who should dream that he had divulged to the world at large what can be done with language. Of this there is no danger; rhetoric, it is true, does put fluency, emphasis, and other warlike equipments at the disposal of evil forces, but style, like the Christian religion, is one of those open secrets which are most easily and most effectively kept by the initiate from age to age. Divination is the only means of access to these mysteries. The formal attempt to impart a good style is like the melancholy task of the teacher of gesture and oratory; some palpable faults are soon corrected; and, for the rest, a few conspicuous mannerisms, a few theatrical postures, not truly expressive, and a high tragical strut, are all that can be imparted. The truth of the old Roman teachers of rhetoric is here witnessed afresh, to be a good orator it is first of all necessary to be a good man. Good style is the greatest of revealers–it lays bare the soul. The soul of the cheat shuns nothing so much. "Always be ready to speak your mind," said Blake, "and a base man will avoid you." But to insist that he also shall speak his mind is to go a step further, it is to take from the impostor his wooden leg, to prohibit his lucrative whine, his mumping and his canting, to force the poor silly soul to stand erect among its fellows and declare itself. His occupation is gone, and he does not love the censor who deprives him of the weapons of his mendicity.

All style is gesture, the gesture of the mind and of the soul. Mind we have in common, inasmuch as the laws of right reason are not different for different minds. Therefore clearness and arrangement can be taught, sheer incompetence in the art of expression can be partly remedied. But who shall impose laws upon the soul? It is thus of common note that one may dislike or even hate a particular style while admiring its facility, its strength, its skilful adaptation to the matter set forth. Milton, a chaste. and more unerring master of the art than Shakespeare, reveals no such lovable personality. While persons count for much, style, the index to persons, can never count for little. "Speak," it has been said, "that I may know you"–voice-gesture is more than feature. Write, and after you have attained to some control over the instrument, you write yourself down whether you will or no. There is no vice, however unconscious, no virtue, however shy, no touch of meanness or of generosity in your character, that will not pass on to the paper. You anticipate the Day of Judgment and furnish the recording angel with material. The Art of Criticism in literature, so often decried and given a subordinate place among the arts, is none other than the art of reading and interpreting these written evidences. Criticism has been popularly opposed to creation, perhaps because the kind of creation that it attempts is rarely achieved, and so the world forgets that the main business of Criticism, after all, is not to legislate, nor to classify, but to raise the dead. Graves, at its command, have waked their sleepers, oped, and let them forth. It is by the creative power of this art that the living man is reconstructed from the litter or blurred and fragmentary paper documents that he has left to posterity.

Reprinted from *Style* (London & New York: Arnold, 1897), pp. 107-129.

Frederic Harrison

"On Style in English Prose" (1898)

Frederic Harrison (1831-1923) was a barrister, political reformer, and religious positivist. He wrote widely on both literary and social topics in the late-Victorian period, and his volumes of collected essays, such as On the Choice of Books *(1886), went through multiple printings. This essay on style was originally written as a talk and delivered to Oxford's Bodley Literary Society, an undergraduate group of which Harrison's son was president. Even in its printed form in the* Nineteenth Century, *the talk retains an informal, fatherly tone. Its importance lies in showing one of the most distinguished practitioners of Victorian prose as he grapples with new questions raised in recent literary and aesthetic criticism. The comments in the sixth paragraph on "an ingenious professor" were aimed at Walter Raleigh, whose book* Style *had appeared the previous year. Harrison's own instructions are rather simple and old-fashioned (write clearly, read good models). The intellectual, progressive Harrison's concluding advice that his audience read the King James Version of the Bible encapsulates many of the paradoxes of Victorian cultural attitudes.–Ed.*

Fili mi dilectissime [O dearest son of mine] (if, sir, I may borrow the words of the late Lord Derby when, as Chancellor of the University, he conferred the degree of D.C.L. on Lord Stanley, his son)–I fear that I am about to do an unwise thing. When, in an hour of paternal weakness, I accepted your invitation to address the Bodley Society on *Style*, it escaped me that it was a subject to which I had hardly given a thought, one with which undergraduates have but small concern. And now I find myself talking on a matter whereof I know nothing, and could do you little good if I did, in presence of an illustrious historian, to say nothing of your own Head, who was an acknowledged master of English, when my own literary style aspired to nothing more elegant than the dry forms of pleadings and deeds.

Everyone knows how futile for any actual result are those elaborate disquisitions on Style which some of the most consummate masters have amused themselves in compiling, but which serve at best to show how quite hackneyed truisms can be graced by an almost miraculous neatness of phrase. It is in vain to enjoin on us 'propriety,' 'justness of expression,' 'suitability of our language to the subject we treat,' and all the commonplaces which the schools of Addison and of Johnson in the last century promulgated as canons of good style. 'Proper words in proper places,' says Swift, 'make the true definition of a style.' 'Each phrase in its right place,' says Voltaire. Well! Swift and Voltaire knew how to do this with supreme skill; but it does not help us, if they cannot teach their art. *How* are we to know what is the *proper* word? *How* are we to find the *right* place? And even a greater than Swift or Voltaire is not much more practical as a teacher. 'Suit the action to the word, and the word to the action,' says Hamlet. 'Be not too tame neither. Let your own discretion be your tutor.' Can you trust your own discretion? Have undergraduates this discretion? And how could I, in presence of your College authority, suggest that you should have no tutor but your own discretion?

All this is as if a music master were to say to a pupil, Sing always in tune and with the *right* intonation, and whatever you do, produce your voice in the *proper* way! Or, to make myself more intelligible to you here, it is as if W. G. Grace were to tell you, Play a 'yorker' in the *right* way, and place the ball in the *proper* spot with reference to the field! We know that neither the art of acting, nor of singing, nor of cricket can be taught by general commonplaces of this sort. And good prose is so far like cricket that the W. G.'s of literature, after ten or twenty 'centuries,' can tell you nothing more than this–to place your words in the right spot, and to choose the proper word, according to the 'field' that you have before you.

The most famous essay on Style, I suppose, is that by one of the greatest wizards who ever used language–I mean the *Ars Poetica* of Horace, almost every line of which has become a household word in the educated world. But what avail his inimitable epigrams in practice? Who is helped by being told not to draw a man's head on a horse's neck, or a beautiful woman with the tail end of a fish? 'Do not let brevity become obscurity; do not let your mountain in labour bring forth a mouse; turn over your Greek models night and day; your compositions must be not only correct, but must give delight, touch the heart,' and so forth, and so forth. All these imperishable maxims—as clean cut as a sardonyx gem—these 'chestnuts' as you call them, in the slang of the day—serve as hard nuts for a translator to crack, and as handy mottoes at the head of an essay; but they are barren of any solid food as the shell of a cocoa-nut.

Then Voltaire, perhaps the greatest master of prose in any modern language, wrote an essay on *Style,* in the same vein of epigrammatic platitude. No declamation, says he, in a work on physics. No jesting in a treatise on mathematics. Well! but did Douglas Jerrold himself ever try to compose a Comic Trigonometry; and could another Charles Lamb find any fun in Spencer's First Principles? A fine style, says Voltaire, makes anything delightful; but it is exceedingly difficult to acquire, and very rarely found. And all he has to say is, 'Avoid grandiloquence, confusion, vulgarity, cheap wit, and colloquial slang in a tragedy.' He might as well say, Take care to be as strong as Sandow, and as active as Prince Ranjitsinhji, and whatever you do, take care not to grow a nose like Cyrano de Bergerac in the new play!

An ingenious professor of literature has lately ventured to commit himself to an entire treatise on Style, wherein he has propounded everything that can usefully be said about this art, in a style which illustrates everything that you should avoid. At the end of his book he declares that style cannot be taught. This is true enough: but if this had been the first, instead of the last, sentence of his piece, the book would not have been written at all. I remember that, when I stood for the Hertford Scholarship, we had to write a Latin epigram on the thesis:—

Omnia liberius nullo poscente—

—fatemur, (I replied—)

Carmina cur poscas, carmine si sit opus? [1]

And so I say now. Style cannot be taught. And this perhaps puts out of court the Professor's essay, and no doubt my own also. Nothing practical can be said about style. And no good can come to a young student by being anxious about Style. None of you by taking thought can add one cubit to his stature—no! nor one gem to his English prose, unless nature has endowed him with that rare gift—a subtle ear for the melody of words, a fastidious instinct for the connotations of phrase.

You will, of course, understand that I am speaking of Style in that higher sense as it was used by Horace, Swift, Voltaire, and great writers, that is, Style as an element of permanent literature. It is no doubt very easy by practice and good advice to gain a moderate facility in writing current language, and even to get the trick of turning out lively articles and smart reviews. ' 'Tis as easy as lying; govern these ventages with your finger and thumb, give it breath with your mouth, and it will discourse most eloquent music'—quite up to the pitch of the journals and the magazines of our day, of which we are all proud. But this is a poor trade: and it would be a pity to waste your precious years of young study by learning to play on the literary 'recorders.' You may be taught to fret them. You will not learn to make them speak!

There are a few negative precepts, quite familiar common form, easy to remember, and not difficult to observe. These are all that any manual can lay down. The trouble comes in when we seek to apply them. What is it that is artificial, incongruous, obscure? How are we to be simple? Whence comes the music of language? What is the magic that can charm into life the apt and inevitable word that lies hidden somewhere at hand—so near and yet so far—so willing and yet so coy—did we only know the talisman which can awaken it? This is what no teaching can give us—what skilful tuition and assiduous practice can but improve in part—and even that only for the chosen few.

About Style, in the higher sense of the term, I think the young student should trouble himself as little as possible. When he does, it too often becomes the art of clothing thin ideas in well-made garments. To gain skill in expression before he has got thoughts or knowledge to express, is somewhat premature: and to waste in the study of form those irrevocable years which should be absorbed in the study of things, is mere decadence and fraud. The young student—*ex hypothesi*—has to learn, not to teach. His duty is to digest knowledge, not to popularise it and carry it abroad. It is a grave mental defect to parade an external polish far more mature than the essential matter within. Where the learner is called on to express his thoughts in formal compositions—and the less he does this the better—it is enough that he put his ideas or his knowledge (if he has any) in clear and natural terms. But the less he labours the flow of his periods the more truly is he the honest learner, the less is his risk of being the smug purveyor of the crudities with which he has been crammed, the farther is he from becoming one of those voluble charlatans whom the idle study of language so often breeds.

I look with sorrow on the habit which has grown up in the University since my day (in the far-off fifties)–the habit of making a considerable part of the education of the place to turn on the art of serving up gobbets of prepared information in essays more or less smooth and correct–more or less successful imitations of the viands that are cooked for us daily in the press. I have heard that a student has been known to write as many as seven essays in a week, a task which would exhaust the fertility of a Swift. The bare art of writing readable paragraphs in passable English is easy enough to master; one that steady practice and good coaching can teach the average man. But it is a poor art, which readily lends itself to harm. It leads the shallow ones to suppose themselves to be deep, the raw ones to fancy they are cultured, and it burdens the world with a deluge of facile commonplace. It is the business of a university to train the mind to think and to impart solid knowledge, not to turn out nimble penmen who may earn a living as the clerks and salesmen of literature.

Almost all that can be laid down as law about Style is contained in a sentence of Madame de Sévigné in her twentieth letter to her daughter. 'Ne quittez jamais le naturel,' she says; 'votre tour s'y est formé, et cela compose un style parfait.' I suppose I must translate this; for Madame de Sévigné is no subject for modern Research, and our *Alma Mater* is concerned only with dead languages and remote epochs. 'Never forsake what is natural,' she writes; 'you have moulded yourself in that vein, and this produces a perfect style.' There is nothing more to be said. Be natural, be simple, be yourself; shun artifices, tricks, fashions. Gain the tone of ease, plainness, self-respect. To thine own self be true. Speak out frankly that which you have thought out in your own brain and have felt within your own soul. This, and this alone, creates a perfect style, as she says who wrote the most exquisite letters the world has known.

And so Molière, a consummate master of language and one of the soundest critics of any age, in that immortal scene of his *Misanthrope*, declares the euphuistic sonnets of the Court to be mere play of words, pure affectation, not worth a

snatch from a peasant's song. That is not the way in which Nature speaks, cries Alceste–*J'aime mieux ma mie*–that is how the heart gives utterance, without *colifichets*, with no quips and cranks of speech, very dear to fancy, and of very liberal conceit. And Sainte-Beuve cites an admirable saying: 'All peasants have style.' They speak as Nature prompts. They have never learned to play with words; they have picked up no tricks, mannerisms, and affectation like Osric and Oronte in the plays. They were not trained to write essays, and never got veterans to discourse to them on Style. Yet, as Sainte-Beuve says, they have style, because they have human nature, and they have never tried to get outside the natural, the simple, the homely. It is the secret of Wordsworth, as it was of Goldsmith, as it was of Homer.

Those masters of style of whom I have spoken were almost all French–Molière, Madame de Sévigné, Voltaire, Sainte-Beuve. Style, in truth, is a French art; there is hardly any other style in prose. I doubt if any English prose, when judged by the canons of perfect style, can be matched with the highest triumphs of French prose. The note of the purest French is a serene harmony of tone, an infallible nicety of keeping; a brightness and point never spasmodic, never careless, never ruffled, like the unvarying manner of a gentleman who is a thorough man of the world. Even our best English will sometimes grow impetuous, impatient, or slack, as if it were too much trouble to maintain an imperturbable air of quite inviolable good-breeding. In real life no people on earth, or perhaps we ought to say in Europe, in this surpass the English gentleman. In prose literature it is a French gift, and seems given as yet to the French alone. Italians, Spaniards, and Russians have an uncertain, casual, and fitful style, and Germans since Heine have no style at all.

Whilst we have hundreds of men and women to-day who write good English, and one or two who have a style of their own, our French critics will hardly admit that we show any example of the purest style when judged by their own standard of perfection. They require a combination of simplicity, ease, charm, precision, and serenity of tone, together with the memorable phrase and inimitable felicity which stamp the individual writer, and yet are obvious and delightful to every reader. Renan had this; Pierre Loti has it; Anatole France has it. But it is seldom that we read a piece of current English and feel it to be exquisite in form apart from its substance, refreshing as a work of art, and yet hall-marked from the mint of the one particular author. We have hall-marks enough, it is true, only too noisily conspicuous on the plate; but are they refreshing and inspiring? are they works of art? How is it that our poetry, even our minor poetry of the day, has its own felicitous harmony of tone, whilst our prose is notoriously wanting in that mellow refinement of form which the French call style?

If I hazard a few words about some famous masters of language, I must warn you that judgments of this kind amount to little more than the likes and dislikes of the critic himself. There are no settled canons, and no accepted arbiter of the elegances of prose. It is more or less a matter of personal taste, even more than it is in verse. I never doubt that the greatest master of prose in recorded history is Plato. He alone (like Homer in poetry) is perfect. He has every mood, and all are faultless. He is easy, lucid, graceful, witty, pathetic, imaginative by turns; but in all kinds he is natural and inimitably sweet. He is never obscure, never abrupt, never tedious, never affected. He shows us as it were his own Athene, wisdom incarnate in immortal radiance of form.

Plato alone is faultless. I will not allow any Roman to be perfect. Cicero even in his letters is wordy, rhetorical, academic. Livy is too consciously painting in words, too sonorous and diffuse for perfection; as Tacitus carries conciseness into obscurity and epigram into paradox. Of Latin prose, for my own part, I value most the soldierly simplicity of Caesar, though we can hardly tell if he could be witty, graceful, pathetic, and fantastic as we see these gifts in Plato.

One of the most suggestive points in the history of prose is Boccaccio's *Decameron*, where a style of strange fascination suddenly starts into life with hardly any earlier models, nay, two or three centuries earlier than organic prose in any of the tongues of Europe. For many generations the exquisite ease and melody of Boccaccio's language found no rival in any modern nation, nor had it any rival in Italy, and we have no evidence that anything in Italy had prepared the way for it. It is far from a perfect style, for it is often too fluid, loose, and voluminous for mature prose; but as a first effort towards an orderly array of lucid narrative it is an amazing triumph of the Italian genius for art.

Prose, as you all know, is always and everywhere a plant of much later growth than poetry. Plato came four or five centuries after Homer; Tacitus came two centuries later than Lucretius;

Machiavelli came two centuries after Dante; Voltaire a century after Corneille; Addison a century after Shakespeare. And while the prose of Boccaccio, with all its native charm, can hardly be called an organic, mature, and mellow style; in poetry, for nearly a century before Boccaccio, Dante and the minor lyrists of Italy had reached absolute perfection of rhythmical form.

Although fairly good prose is much more common than fairly good verse, yet I hold that truly fine prose is more rare than truly fine poetry. I trust that it will be counted neither a whim nor a paradox if I give it as a reason that mastery in prose is an art more difficult than mastery in verse. The very freedom of prose, its want of conventions, of settled prosody, of musical inspiration, give wider scope for failure and afford no beaten paths. Poetry glides swiftly down the stream of a flowing and familiar river, where the banks are always the helmsman's guide. Prose puts forth its lonely skiff upon a boundless sea, where a multitude of strange and different crafts are cutting about in contrary directions. At any rate, the higher triumphs of prose come later and come to fewer than do the great triumphs of verse.

When I lately had to study a body of despatches and State papers of the latter half of the sixteenth century, written in six modern languages of Europe, I observed that the Italian alone in that age was a formed and literary language, at the command of all educated men and women, possessed of organic canons and a perfectly mature type. The French, German, Dutch, English, and Spanish of that age, as used for practical ends, were still in the state of a language held in solution before it assumes a crystallised form. Even the men who wrote correct Latin could not write their own language with any real command. At the death of Tennyson, we may remember, it was said that no less than sixty poets were thought worthy of the wreath of bay. Were there six writers of prose whom even a logrolling confederate would venture to hail as a possible claimant of the crown? Assiduous practice in composing neat essays has turned out of late ten thousand men and women who can put together very pleasant prose. It has not turned out one living master in prose as Tennyson was master in verse.

I have spoken of Voltaire as perhaps the greatest master of prose in any modern language, but this does not mean that he is perfect, and without qualification or want. His limpid clearness, ease, sparkle, and inexhaustible self-possession have no rival in modern tongues, and are almost those of Plato himself. But he is no Plato; he never rises into the pathos, imagination, upper air of the empyrean, to which the mighty Athenian can soar at will. Voltaire is never tedious, wordy, rhetorical, or obscure; and this can be said of hardly any other modern but Heine and Swift. My edition of Voltaire is in sixty volumes, of which some forty are prose; and in all those twenty thousand pages of prose not one is dull or laboured. We could not say this of the verse. But I take *Candide* or *Zadig* to be the highwater mark of easy French prose, wanting no doubt in the finer elements of pathos, dignity, and power. And for this reason many have preferred the prose of Rousseau, of George Sand, of Renan, though all of these are apt at times to degenerate into garrulity and gush. There was no French prose, says Voltaire, before Pascal; and there has been none of the highest flight since Renan. In the rest of Europe perfect prose has long been as rare as the egg of the great auk.

In spite of the splendour of Bacon and of Milton, of Jeremy Taylor and of Hooker, and whatever be the virility of Bunyan and Dryden, I cannot hold that the age of mature English prose had been reached until we come to Defoe, Swift, Addison, Berkeley and Goldsmith. These are the highest types we have attained. Many good judges hold Swift to be our Voltaire, without defect or equal. I should certainly advise the ambitious essayist to study Swift for instruction, by reason of the unfailing clearness, simplicity, and directness of his style. But when we come to weigh him by the highest standard of all, we find Swift too uniformly pedestrian, too dry; wanting in variety, in charm, in melody, in thunder, and in flash. The grandest prose must be like the vault of Heaven itself, passing from the freshness of dawn to the warmth of a serene noon, and anon breaking forth into a crashing storm. Swift sees the sun in one uniform radiance of cool light, but it never fills the air with warmth, nor does it ever light the welkin with fire.

Addison, with all his mastery of tone, seems afraid to give his spirit rein. *Il s'écoute quand il parle* [He listens to himself when he talks]: and this, by the way, is the favourite sin of our best moderns. We see him pause at the end of each felicitous sentence to ask himself if he has satisfied all the canons as to propriety of diction. Even in the *Spectator* we never altogether forget the author of *Cato*. Now we perceive no canons of good

taste, no tragic buskin, no laborious modulations in the *Vicar of Wakefield*, which in its own vein is the most perfect type of eighteenth century prose. Dear old Goldie! There is ease, pellucid simplicity, wit, pathos. I doubt if English prose has ever gone further, or will go further or higher.

After all I have said I need not labour the grounds on which I feel Johnson, Burke, Gibbon, Macaulay, and Carlyle to be far from perfect as writers and positively fatal if taken as models. Old Samuel's Ciceronian pomp has actually dimmed our respect for his good sense and innate robustness of soul. Burke was too great an orator to be a consummate writer, as he was too profound a writer to be a perfect orator. Gibbon's imperial eagles pass on in one unending triumph, with the resounding blare of brazen trumpets, till we weary of the serried legions and grow dizzy with the show. And as to Macaulay and Carlyle, they carry emphasis to the point of exhaustion; for the peer bangs down his fist to clinch every sentence, and 'Sartor' never ceases his uncouth gesticulations and grimace.

In our own century Charles Lamb and Thackeray, I think, come nearest to Voltaire and Madame de Sévigné in purity of diction, in clearness, ease, grace, and wit. But a living writer—now long silent and awaiting his summons to the eternal silence—had powers which, had he cared to train them before he set about to reform the world, would have made him the noblest master who ever used the tongue of Milton. Need I name the versatile genius who laboured here in Oxford so long and with such success? In the mass of his writings John Ruskin has struck the lyre of prose in every one of its infinite notes. He has been lucid, distinct, natural, fanciful, humorous, satiric, majestic, mystical, and prophetic by turns as the spirit moved within him. No Englishman—hardly Milton himself—has ever so completely mastered the tonic resources of English prose, its majesty and wealth of rhythm, the flexibility, mystery, and infinitude of its mighty diapason.

Alas! the pity of it. These incomparable descants are but moments and interludes, and are too often 'chanted forth in mere wantonness of emotion. Too often they lead us on to formless verbosity and a passionate rhetoric, such as blind even temperate critics to the fact, that it is possible to pick out of the books of John Ruskin whole pages which in harmony, power, and glow have no match in the whole range of our prose.

And now I know I must not end without hazarding a few practical hints–what betting men and undergraduates call 'tips'–for general remarks upon literature have little interest for those whose mind runs on sports, and perhaps even less for those whose mind is absorbed in the Schools. But, as there are always some who dream of a life of 'letters,' an occupation already too crowded and far from inviting at the best, they will expect me to tell them how I think they may acquire a command of Style. I know no reason why they should, and I know no way they could set about it. But, supposing one has something to say–something that it concerns the world to know–and this, for a young student, is a considerable claim, 'a large order,' I think he calls it in the current dialect, all I have to tell him is this. Think it out quite clearly in your own mind, and then put it down in the simplest words that offer, just as if you were telling it to a friend, but dropping the tags of the day with which your spoken discourse would naturally be garnished. Be familiar but by no means vulgar. At any rate, be easy, colloquial if you like, but shun those vocables which come to us across the Atlantic, or from Newmarket and Whitechapel, with which the gilded youth and journalists 'up-to-date' love to salt their language. Do not make us 'sit up' too much, or always 'take a back seat;' do not ask us to 'ride for a fall,' to 'hurry up,' or 'boom it all we know.' Nothing is more irritating in print than the iteration of slang, and those stale phrases with which 'the half-baked' seek to convince us that they are 'in the swim' and 'going strong'–if I may borrow the language of the day–that Volapük of the smart and knowing world. It offends me like the reek of last night's tobacco.

It is a good rule for a young writer to avoid more than twenty or thirty words without a full stop, and not to put more than two commas in each sentence, so that its clauses should not exceed three. This, of course, only in practice. There is no positive law. A fine writer can easily place in a sentence one hundred words, and five or six minor clauses with their proper commas and colons. Ruskin was wont to toss off two or three hundred words and five-and-twenty commas without a pause. But, even in the hand of such a magician this ends in failure, and is really grotesque in effect, for no such sentence can be spoken aloud. A beginner can seldom manage more than twenty-five words in one sentence with perfect ease. Nearly all young writers, just as men did in the early ages of prose composition, drift into ragged, preposterous, inorganic

sentences, without beginning, middle, or end, which they ought to break into two or three.

And then they hunt up terms that are fit for science, poetry, or devotion. They affect 'evolution' and 'factors,' 'the inter-action of forces,' 'the co-ordination of organs'; or else everything is 'weird,' or 'opalescent,' 'debonair' and 'enamelled,' so that they will not call a spade a spade. I do not say, stick to Saxon words and avoid Latin words as a law of language, because English now consists of both: good and plain English prose needs both. We seldom get the highest poetry without a large use of Saxon, and we hardly reach precise and elaborate explanation without Latin terms. Try to turn *precise* and *elaborate explanation* into strict Saxon; and then try to turn 'Our Father which art in Heaven' into pure Latin words. No! current English prose–not the language of poetry or of prayer–must be of both kinds, Saxon and Latin. But, wherever a Saxon word is enough, use it: because if it have all the fulness and the precision you need, it is the more simple, the more direct, the more homely.

Never quote anything that is not apt and new. Those stale citations of well-worn lines give us a cold shudder, as does a pun at a dinner party. A familiar phrase from poetry or Scripture may pass when imbedded in your sentence. But to show it round as a nugget which you have just picked up is the innocent freshman's snare. Never imitate any writer, however good. All imitation in literature is a mischief, as it is in art. A great and popular writer ruins his followers and mimics, as did Raffaelle and Michel Angelo; and when he founds a school of style, he impoverishes literature more than he enriches it. Johnson, Macaulay, Carlyle, Dickens, Ruskin have been the cause of flooding us with cheap copies of their special manner. And even now Meredith, Stevenson, Swinburne, and Pater lead the weak to ape their airs and graces. All imitation in literature is an evil. I say to you, as Mat Arnold said to me (who surely needed no such warning), 'Flee Carlylese as the very devil!' Yes! flee Carlylese, Ruskinese, Meredithese, and every other *ese*, past, present, and to come. A writer whose style invites imitation so far falls short of being a true master. He becomes the parent of caricature, and frequently he gives lessons in caricature himself.

Though you must never imitate any writer you may study the best writers with care. And for study choose those who have founded no school, who have no special and imitable style. Read Pascal and Voltaire in French; Swift,

Hume, and Goldsmith in English; and of the moderns, I think, Thackeray and Froude. Ruskin is often too rhapsodical for a student; Meredith too whimsical; Stevenson too 'precious,' as they love to call it; George Eliot too laboriously enamelled and erudite. When you cannot quietly enjoy a picture for the curiosity aroused by its so-called 'brushwork,' the painting may be a surprising sleight-of-hand, but is not a masterpiece.

Read Voltaire, Defoe, Swift, Goldsmith, and you will come to understand how the highest charm of words is reached without your being able to trace any special element of charm. The moment you begin to pick out this or that felicity of phrase, this or that sound of music in the words, and directly it strikes you as eloquent, lyrical, pictorial–then the charm is snapped. The style may be fascinating, brilliant, impressive: but it is not perfect.

Of melody in style I have said nothing; nor indeed can anything practical be said. It is a thing infinitely subtle, inexplicable, and rare. If your ear does not hear the false note, the tautophony or the cacophony in the written sentence, as you read it or frame it silently to yourself, and hear it thus inaudibly long before your eye can pick it forth out of the written words, nay, even when the eye fails to localise it by analysis at all–then you have no inborn sense of the melody of words, and be quite sure that you can never acquire it. One living Englishman has it in the highest form; for the melody of Ruskin's prose may be matched with that of Milton and Shelley. I hardly know any other English prose which retains the ring of that ethereal music–echoes of which are more often heard in our poetry than in our prose. Nay, since it is beyond our reach, wholly incommunicable, defiant of analysis and rule, it may be more wise to say no more.

Read Swift, Defoe, Goldsmith, if you care to know what is pure English. I need hardly tell you to read another and a greater Book. The Book which begot English prose still remains its supreme type. The English Bible is the true school of English Literature. It possesses every quality of our language in its highest form–except for scientific precision, practical affairs, and philosophic analysis. It would be ridiculous to write an essay on Metaphysics, a political article, or a novel in the language of the Bible. Indeed, it would be ridiculous to write anything at all in the language of the Bible. But if you care to know the best that our literature can give in simple noble prose–mark, learn, and inwardly digest the Holy Scriptures in the English tongue.

---

1. The "thesis" (adapted from Virgil, *Georgics*, 1:128) asserts that "All things come more liberally when nothing is being demanded–we confess," and Harrison's response is "Why are you *demanding* songs, if it is a song that is needed?"–*Ed.*

Reprinted from *Nineteenth Century*, 43 (June 1898): 932-942.

Books for Further Reading

Altick, Richard D. *The English Common Reader: A Social History of the Mass Reading Public, 1800-1900.* Chicago: University of Chicago Press, 1957.

Altick. *Victorian People and Ideas.* New York: Norton, 1973.

Baldick, Chris. *The Social Mission of English Criticism 1848-1932.* Oxford: Clarendon Press, 1983.

Brantlinger, Patrick. *Bread & Circuses: Theories of Mass Culture as Social Decay.* Ithaca: Cornell University Press, 1983.

Briggs, Asa. *The Age of Improvement.* London & New York: Longmans, Green, 1959.

Brinton, Crane. *English Political Thought in the Nineteenth Century.* Cambridge: Harvard University Press, 1949.

Brown, Christopher C., and William B. Thesing. *English Prose and Criticism, 1900-1950: A Guide to Information Sources.* Detroit: Gale Research Company, 1983.

Brown, Lucy. *Victorian News and Newspapers.* Oxford: Clarendon Press, 1985.

Buckley, Jerome Hamilton. *The Turning Key: Autobiography and the Subjective Impulse Since 1800.* Cambridge: Harvard University Press, 1984.

Buckley. *Victorian Poets and Prose Writers.* New York: Appleton-Century-Crofts, 1977.

Buckley. *The Victorian Temper: a Study in Literary Culture.* Cambridge: Harvard University Press, 1951.

Cockshut, A. O. J. *The Art of Autobiography in 19th and 20th Century England.* New Haven: Yale University Press, 1984.

Cockshut. *Truth to Life: The Art of Biography in the Nineteenth Century.* New York: Harcourt Brace Jovanovich, 1974.

Cross, Nigel. *The Common Writer: Life in Nineteenth-Century Grub Street.* Cambridge: Cambridge University Press, 1985.

Culler, A. Dwight. *The Victorian Mirror of History.* New Haven: Yale University Press, 1985.

Dale, Peter Allan. *The Victorian Critic and the Idea of History: Carlyle, Arnold, Pater.* Cambridge: Harvard University Press, 1977.

DeLaura, David J. *Hebrew and Hellene in Victorian England: Newman, Arnold, and Pater.* Austin: University of Texas Press, 1969.

DeLaura, ed. *Victorian Prose: A Guide to Research.* New York: Modern Language Association of America, 1973.

Eagleton, Terry. *The Function of Criticism: From 'The Spectator' to Post-Structuralism.* London: Verso, 1984.

Fleishman, Avrom. *Figures of Autobiography: The Language of Self-Writing in Victorian and Modern England.* Berkeley: University of California Press, 1983.

Gibbons, Tom. *Rooms in the Darwin Hotel: Studies in English Literary Criticism and Ideas, 1880-1920.* Nedlands: University of Western Australia Press, 1973.

Gross, John. *The Rise and Fall of the Man of Letters: A Study of the Idiosyncratic and the Humane in Modern Literature. Literary Life Since 1800.* London: Weidenfeld & Nicolson, 1969.

Harris, Wendell V. *The Omnipresent Debate: Empiricism and Transcendentalism in Nineteenth Century English Prose.* DeKalb: Northern Illinois University Press, 1981.

Himmelfarb, Gertrude. *Victorian Minds.* New York: Knopf, 1968.

Holloway, John. *The Victorian Sage.* London: Macmillan, 1953.

Hough, Graham. *The Last Romantics.* London: Duckworth, 1949.

Houghton, Walter E. *The Victorian Frame of Mind, 1830-1870.* New Haven & London: Yale University Press, 1957.

Jann, Rosemary. *The Art and Science of Victorian History.* Columbus: Ohio State University Press, 1985.

Johnson, Lesley. *The Cultural Critics: From Matthew Arnold to Raymond Williams.* London & Boston: Routledge & Kegan Paul, 1979.

Knights, Ben. *The Idea of the Clerisy in the Nineteenth Century.* Cambridge: Cambridge University Press, 1978.

Levine, George, and William A. Madden, eds. *The Art of Victorian Prose.* New York: Oxford University Press, 1968.

Levine, Richard A., ed. *The Victorian Experience: the Prose Writers.* Athens: Ohio University Press, 1982.

Lucas, John. *Romantic to Modern Literature: Essays and Ideas of Culture, 1750-1900.* Brighton: Harvester, 1982.

Lucas, ed. *Literature and Politics in the Nineteenth Century.* London: Methuen, 1971.

Mulvey, Christopher. *Anglo-American Landscapes: Romantic Values in Nineteenth-Century Anglo-American Travel Literature.* Cambridge: Cambridge University Press, 1983.

Nadel, Ira Bruce. *Biography: Fiction, Fact and Form.* London: Macmillan / New York: St. Martin's, 1984.

Orel, Harold. *Victorian Literary Critics: George Henry Lewes, Walter Bagehot, Richard Holt Hutton, Leslie Stephen, Andrew Lang, George Saintsbury, and Edmund Gosse.* London: Macmillan / New York: St. Martin's, 1984.

Orel, and George Worth, eds. *The Nineteenth-Century Writer and His Audience: Selected Problems in Theory, Form, and Content.* Lawrence: University of Kansas Publications, 1969.

Paradis, James, and Thomas Postelwait, eds. *Victorian Science and Victorian Values: Literary Perspectives.* New York: New York Academy of Sciences, 1981.

Peckham, Morse. *Victorian Revolutionaries: Speculations on Some Heroes of a Culture Crisis.* New York: Braziller, 1970.

Peterson, Linda H. *Victorian Autobiography: The Tradition of Self-Interpretation*. New Haven & London: Yale University Press, 1986.

Siebenschuh, William R. *Fictional Techniques and Factual Works*. Athens: University of Georgia Press, 1983.

Smart, Ninian, John Clayton, Steven Katz, and Patrick Sherry, eds. *Nineteenth Century Religious Thought in the West (II & III)*. Cambridge & New York: Cambridge University Press, 1985.

Thornton, R. K. R. *The Decadent Dilemma*. London: Arnold, 1983.

Tillotson, Geoffrey. *Criticism and the Nineteenth Century*. London: Athlone, 1951.

White, Robert B., Jr. *The English Literary Journal to 1900*. Detroit: Gale Research, 1977.

Williams, Raymond. *Culture and Society, 1780-1950*. New York: Columbia University Press, 1958.

Wilson, Harris W., and Diane Long Hoeveler. *English Prose and Criticism in the Nineteenth Century: A Guide to Information Sources*. Detroit: Gale Research, 1977.

Wolff, Michael, ed. *The Victorian Periodical Press: Samplings and Soundings*. Leicester: Leicester University Press, 1982.

Contributors

Karl Beckson..........................*Brooklyn College of the City University of New York*
John W. Bicknell ....*Drew University*
Ronald J. Black ....*McKendree College*
Charles Blinderman...*Clark University*
Richard A. Boyle .... *Whiting, Indiana*
Patrick Brantlinger...*Indiana University*
Hans-Peter Breuer ....*University of Delaware*
Monika Brown..*Pembroke State University*
David L. Chapman .... *Los Angeles, California*
Joan Corwin .... *Evanston, Illinois*
Marc Demarest ....*University of South Carolina*
Philip Dodd...*University of Leicester*
Debra Edelstein .... *Medford, Massachusetts*
Suzanne O. Edwards ....*The Citadel*
Philip L. Elliott ....*Furman University*
Timothy J. Evans.............. *Richard Bland College of the College of William and Mary*
Barry Faulk ....*University of South Carolina*
Sandy Feinstein..*Southwestern College*
John Ferns ....*McMaster University*
William J. Gracie, Jr.. *Miami University*
Donald Gray ....*Indiana University*
John Greenfield ....*McKendree College*
James Hipp ....*University of South Carolina*
James G. Kennedy ....*Northern Illinois University*
Frederick Kirchhoff.................*Indiana University-Purdue University at Fort Wayne*
Donald Lawler..*East Carolina University*
Robert O'Kell ....*University of Manitoba*
Richard W. Oram ....*University of Toledo*
Jerold J. Savory..*Columbia College*
Patrick Scott..*University of South Carolina*
John Stasny ....*West Virginia University*
Harry R. Sullivan...*University of South Carolina*
Hayden Ward...*West Virginia University*

Cumulative Index

Dictionary of Literary Biography, Volumes 1-57
Dictionary of Literary Biography Yearbook, 1980-1986
Dictionary of Literary Biography Documentary Series, Volumes 1-4

Cumulative Index

DLB before number: *Dictionary of Literary Biography*, Volumes 1-57
Y before number: *Dictionary of Literary Biography Yearbook*, 1980-1986
DS before number: *Dictionary of Literary Biography Documentary Series*, Volumes 1-4

C

D

E

F

G

I

J

L

M

Osborne, John 1929- DLB-13

Osgood, Herbert L. 1855-1918 ....DLB-47

Osgood, James R., and Company............DLB-49

O'Shaughnessy, Arthur 1844-1881 ....DLB-35

O'Shea, Patrick [publishing house] DLB-49

Oswald, Eleazer 1755-1795 ....DLB-43

Otis, James (see Kaler, James Otis)

Otis, James, Jr. 1725-1783....................DLB-31

Otis, Broaders and Company..................DLB-49

Ottendorfer, Oswald 1826-1900 ....DLB-23

Ouida 1839-1908 ....DLB-18

Outing Publishing Company...................DLB-46

Outlaw Days, by Joyce Johnson...............DLB-16

The Overlook Press DLB-46

Overview of U.S. Book Publishing, 1910-1945...DLB-9

Owen, Guy 1925- DLB-5

Owen, John [publishing house]...............DLB-49

Owen, Wilfred 1893-1918 ....DLB-20

Owsley, Frank L. 1890-1956...................DLB-17

Ozick, Cynthia 1928- DLB-28; Y-82

P

Pack, Robert 1929- DLB-5

Packaging Papa: *The Garden of Eden* Y-86

Padell Publishing Company....................DLB-46

Padgett, Ron 1942- DLB-5

Page, L. C., and Company.....................DLB-49

Page, Thomas Nelson 1853-1922..............DLB-12

Paget, Violet (see Lee, Vernon)

Pain, Philip ?-circa 1666 ....DLB-24

Paine, Robert Treat, Jr. 1773-1811............DLB-37

Paine, Thomas 1737-1809 ....DLB-31, 43

Paley, Grace 1922- DLB-28

Palfrey, John Gorham 1796-1881.........DLB-1, 30

Palgrave, Francis Turner 1824-1897...........DLB-35

Paltock, Robert 1697-1767.....................DLB-39

Panama, Norman 1914- and
    Frank, Melvin 1913- DLB-26

Pangborn, Edgar 1909-1976...................DLB-8

"Panic Among the Philistines": A Postscript,
    An Interview with Bryan Griffin.............Y-81

Panshin, Alexei 1940- DLB-8

Pansy (see Alden, Isabella)

Pantheon Books DLB-46

Paperback Library...........................DLB-46

Paperback Science Fiction DLB-8

Paradis, Suzanne 1936- DLB-53

Parents' Magazine Press DLB-46

Parisian Theater, Fall 1984: Toward
    A New Baroque..............................Y-85

Parke, John 1754-1789 ....DLB-31

Parker, Dorothy 1893-1967.................DLB-11, 45

Parker, James 1714-1770 ....DLB-43

Parker, Theodore 1810-1860...................DLB-1

Parkman, Francis, Jr. 1823-1893 ....DLB-1, 30

Parks, Gordon 1912- DLB-33

Parks, William 1698-1750.....................DLB-43

Parks, William [publishing house] DLB-49

Parley, Peter (see Goodrich, Samuel Griswold)

Parrington, Vernon L. 1871-1929 ....DLB-17

Parton, James 1822-1891 ....DLB-30

Parton, Sara Payson Willis 1811-1872 ....DLB-43

Pastan, Linda 1932- DLB-5

Pastorius, Francis Daniel 1651-circa 1720......DLB-24

Patchen, Kenneth 1911-1972...............DLB-16, 48

Pater, Walter 1839-1894.......................DLB-57

Paterson, Katherine 1932- DLB-52

Patmore, Coventry 1823-1896 ....DLB-35

Paton, Joseph Noel 1821-1901.................DLB-35

Patrick, John 1906- DLB-7

Patterson, Eleanor Medill 1881-1948 ....DLB-29

Patterson, Joseph Medill 1879-1946 ....DLB-29

Pattillo, Henry 1726-1801 ....DLB-37

Paul, Elliot 1891-1958 ....DLB-4

Paul, Peter, Book Company DLB-49

Paulding, James Kirke 1778-1860 ....DLB-3

Paulin, Tom 1949- DLB-40

Pauper, Peter, Press DLB-46

Paxton, John 1911-1985 ....DLB-44

Payn, James 1830-1898 ....DLB-18

Q

R

Y

Z